CALIFORNIA

ELIZABETH LINHART VENEMAN

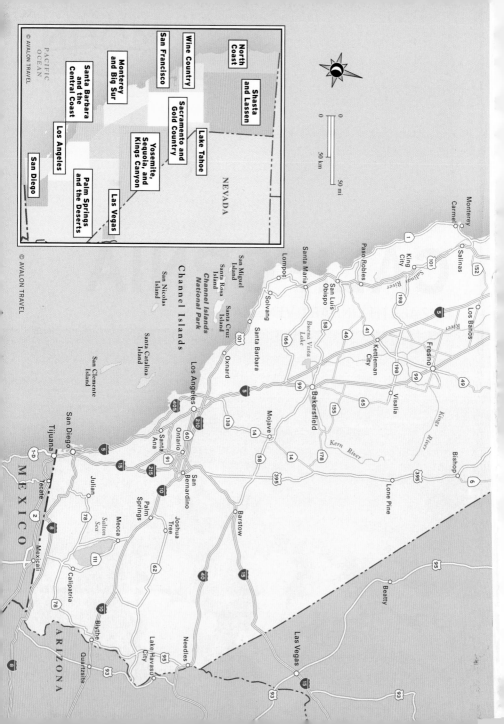

Contents

Discover California **6**
   Best of California in One Week 24
   Best of Northern California 27
   Best of Southern California 28
   Planning Your Trip 29

San Francisco **33**
   Sights 37
   Entertainment and Events........... 56
   Shopping 61
   Sports and Recreation............. 64
   Food 66
   Accommodations 73
   Transportation and Services 78
   North Bay 80
   East Bay........................ 98
   The Peninsula 104
   Silicon Valley 110

Wine Country **115**
   Napa Valley 120
   Sonoma Valley.................. 140
   Russian River Valley 148

North Coast **162**
   Sonoma Coast................... 166
   Mendocino Coast 171
   The Redwood Coast 179

Shasta and Lassen **192**
   Redding and Vicinity.............. 195
   Shasta Lake 200
   Lassen Volcanic National Park....... 205
   Mount Shasta and Vicinity......... 214

Lake Tahoe **227**
   South Shore 231
   North and West Shores 244
   Truckee-Donner 250
   Transportation and Services 255

Sacramento and
Gold Country **257**
   Sacramento and Vicinity 261
   Northern Gold Country........... 268
   Shenandoah Valley 278
   Southern Gold Country........... 283

Yosemite, Sequoia,
and Kings Canyon **291**
   Yosemite National Park 296
   Sequoia and Kings Canyon 320
   The Eastern Sierra 337

Monterey and Big Sur......... **350**
   Santa Cruz..................... 353
   Monterey...................... 363
   Carmel........................ 376

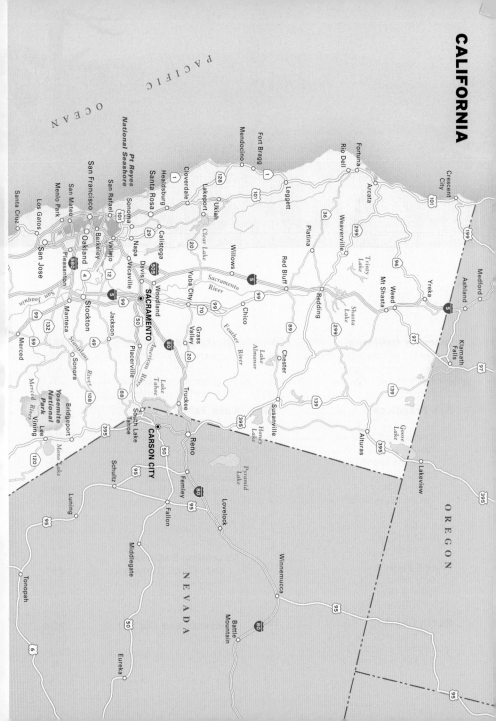

Big Sur 380
Cambria and San Simeon 391

**Santa Barbara and
the Central Coast** **395**
Santa Barbara 398
Ventura 411
San Luis Obispo and Vicinity 416

Los Angeles **422**
Sights 426
Entertainment and Events 441
Shopping 445
Sports and Recreation 447
Food 449
Accommodations 454
Transportation and Services 458
Disneyland and Orange County 460

San Diego **473**
Sights 478
Entertainment and Events 490
Shopping 497
Sports and Recreation 500
Food 507
Accommodations 517
Transportation and Services 523

**Palm Springs and
the Deserts** **526**
Palm Springs 530
Joshua Tree 542
Death Valley 548

Las Vegas **557**
Sights 560
Casinos 565
Entertainment 582
Food 583
Accommodations 586
Transportation and Services 588

Background **590**
The Landscape 591
Plants and Animals 593
History 597

Essentials **600**
Transportation 601
Visas and Officialdom 605
Travel Tips 605
Health and Safety 608
Internet Resources 610

Index **612**

List of Maps **623**

Diverse, wacky, and unforgettable, California is larger than life. The boisterous cities seem bigger, redwood forests and snow-capped mountains loom taller, and sandy coastlines stretch longer than anywhere else.

If you love the outdoors, remote backpacking spots, or extreme sports, you could spend a month exploring California and never once enter the city limits of San Francisco or Los Angeles. If high art, nightlife, and gourmet restaurants top your list, you can stay entirely inside those cities, soaking in their infinitely variable culture. Hot-spot clubbing, award-winning plays, splashy art openings, and some of the best cuisine in the country often coexist within the same six-block street.

There's no one true way to describe California, just as there's no one true way to experience it. Southern California isn't all surfers and movie stars, while Northern California is more than just expensive real estate and radical politics. Tiny coastal towns, sweeping farmlands, and forested mountain ranges all defy stereotypes—from oases of swimming pools in the desert to remote wineries nestled within rural mountains.

Clockwise from top left: rolling vineyards in Napa; giant sequoia tree in the Mariposa Grove, Yosemite National Park; Mission San Diego; Old Sacramento; Kings Canyon National Park; Julia Pfeiffer Burns State Park.

The pace of life is as diverse as everything else in the state. Fast moving and fast living are hallmarks of the Los Angeles basin, yet the quiet frenzy of the San Francisco Bay Area sometimes seems just as fast. Outside the major urban areas, the hectic speed diminishes. California's numerous wine regions invite visitors to relax and slow that pace even further. Beyond the farms and vineyards, an even more venerable and variable pace emerges—that of nature. The gushing water-falls of Yosemite, towering redwoods of Humboldt, bone-dry deserts of Death Valley, delicate native wildflowers along the coast… even the imperceptible crawl and occasional sudden jolt of the land itself all make up the unique rhythm of California.

To best discover what California has to offer, choose something that you want to fall in love with and pursue it here—whether your passion is organic wine, Gold Country ghost towns, Hollywood movie stars, or just lying on the beach. No matter who you are or what you're into, you can make this place your own.

Clockwise from top left: San Francisco cable car; Sonoma Coast; Asilomar Beach in Pacific Grove; Anderson Valley wine country.

20 TOP
EXPERIENCES

1 **Golden Gate Bridge:** Nothing beats the view from **San Francisco**'s famous and fascinating bridge (page 50).

2 **Point Reyes National Seashore:** Acres of unspoiled grassland, forest, and beaches make this one of the most diverse parks in the **San Francisco Bay Area** (page 93).

3 **California Cuisine:** California's farm-to-table ethos is celebrated throughout the state, from **destination restaurants** to **organic farmers markets** (page 68).

4 **Wine Tasting:** California's beautiful vineyards are renowned worldwide. Oenophiles will hit the **Napa Valley** and **Sonoma Valley** wine regions, but **Santa Barbara** and the **Gold Country** host plenty of less-crowded options (page 133).

5 **Redwoods:** No visit to California is complete without craning your neck along the **Avenue of the Giants** (page 180), in the **Redwood National and State Parks** (page 187), throughout **Sequoia National Park** (page 328), and in **Muir Woods** (page 88).

6 **Mount Shasta:** This dazzling glacier-topped **mountain peak** beckons from every angle for miles around (page 214).

7 **Lake Tahoe:** Tahoe's sparkling blue waters are best viewed from **Emerald Bay** (page 233).

8 **Yosemite Valley:** The famous valley is filled with iconic monuments like **El Capitan** and **Bridalveil Fall**. Scale **Half Dome** or hike the **Mist Trail** for the best perspective of this natural playground (page 297).

9 **The Great Outdoors:** With gushing waterfalls, snow-capped peaks, and everything in-between, California compels you to get outside—go **hiking, biking, climbing,** or **skiing** (page 303).

10 **Monterey:** Gorgeous Monterey Bay is famous for its sealife, best experienced at its world-renowned **aquarium** (page 363).

11 Big Sur Coast Highway: With jutting cliffs, crashing surf, and epic views, this twisty **coastal drive** is iconic Big Sur (page 380).

12 **Surfing:** California's coast lures surfers to legendary surf breaks in **Santa Cruz** (page 358), **Santa Barbara** (page 404), **Malibu** (page 448), and **San Diego** (page 501).

13 **Santa Barbara:** Sunny **beaches** are back-dropped by a dramatic mountain range, a burgeoning **wine valley** lures oenophiles, and the stunning Spanish Colonial Revival architecture is exemplified in the **"Queen of the Missions"** (page 398).

14 **Channel Islands:** Hop aboard a scenic **boat tour** of these undeveloped islands with stellar coastal views and epic wildlife watching (page 413).

15 **Hollywood:** From the **Walk of Fame** to the **Chinese Theatre**, Hollywood is ground zero for cinema buffs (page 431).

16 **Santa Monica Pier and the Venice Boardwalk:** For the ultimate in beachy kitsch and colorful characters, wander the **coastal path** of L.A.'s most free-spirited community to this **amusement park** by the sea (page 438).

17 **Theme Parks:** California may be the "Happiest Place on Earth," home to **Disneyland** (page 460), **Universal Studios Hollywood, Six Flags Magic Mountain,** and numerous other theme parks (page 465).

18 **Balboa Park:** These 1,200 acres are home to some of the city's best museums and gardens, as well as the famous **San Diego Zoo** (page 479).

19 **Palm Springs:** California's vacation haven is filled with mid-century architecture, rat pack-era lounges, and serious poolside lounging. View it all from above on the **Palm Springs Aerial Tramway** (page 530).

20 **Death Valley:** With monikers like **Furnace Creek,** the **Devil's Golf Course**, and **Badwater Basin**, Death Valley's forbidding landscape and uncompromising heat only add to its remote beauty (page 548).

Best of California in One Week

In just **five days,** you can experience California's two most famous cities and its biggest natural attraction (but you'll be doing a lot of driving). Make it a full **seven days** and you'll have enough time for a coastal drive along Big Sur.

Day 1
SAN FRANCISCO

Fly into San Francisco and rent a car. Spend your San Francisco day in **Golden Gate Park.** Indulge your artistic side at the **de Young Museum** or learn more about our world at the nearby **California Academy of Sciences.** Unwind with a walk through the park's **Japanese Tea Garden.** Then make your way to the **Golden Gate Bridge,** one of the world's most famous photo-ops. End your day with a meal at one of the city's culinary stars—or grab an authentic burrito at a local taqueria, which may be just as tasty.

For more suggestions on how to spend your time in San Francisco, see page 37.

IF YOU HAVE MORE TIME
Extend the love affair with a side trip to wander the redwoods in Marin. **Muir Woods National Monument,** just north of San Francisco, is home to acres of staggeringly beautiful redwoods accessible via the paved **Redwood Trail.** Afterwards, fill up on British comfort food at **The Pelican Inn.** It's just a short walk from the restaurant to lovely **Muir Beach,** perfect for wildlife-watching and beachcombing. End the day at the Farley Bar at **Cavallo Point Lodge** to watch the fog roll in over the Golden Gate Bridge.

To plan a day trip to the **Wine Country** instead, see page 120.

MOST ROMANTIC GETAWAYS

WINE COUNTRY
A weekend in the wine country means spas, pampering, and, of course, wine (page 120).

MENDOCINO
Windswept beaches, secret coves, and cozy cottages lure weekenders to this charming seaside town (page 174).

BIG SUR
Hole up with your honey in a rustic cabin or a deluxe spa and soak up the rugged coast (page 380).

SANTA BARBARA
Enjoy sunny beaches and excellent wines at this picturesque city by the sea (page 398).

PALM SPRINGS
For all the comforts of home in the remote desert, plan your getaway to this retro favorite (page 530).

Day 2
SAN FRANCISCO TO YOSEMITE
200 MILES / 4 HOURS

Leave San Francisco at 8am to reach Yosemite by noon. The drive to the **Big Oak Flat entrance** takes at least four hours; however, traffic, especially in summer and on weekends, can make it much longer.

Day 3
YOSEMITE VALLEY

Spend a day touring around **Yosemite Valley,** seeing **Half Dome, El Capitan,** and **Yosemite Falls.** If you want to break a sweat, hike the 5.4-mile round-trip **Mist Trail.** Spend a night under the stars at one of the park's campgrounds or enjoy a night indoors at the classic **Majestic Yosemite Hotel** (just be sure to make reservations well in advance).

For more suggestions on how to spend your time in Yosemite, see page 296.

IF YOU HAVE MORE TIME
In summer, combine a trip to Yosemite National Park with **Lake Tahoe** by crossing through

Napa Valley

Yosemite via Tioga Pass Road (Hwy. 120). On the **Eastern Sierra,** scenic U.S. 395 leads north almost to the Nevada border, and road-trippers can take forested Highway 89 west to its junction with U.S. 50 to continue to South Lake Tahoe.

For more suggestions on how to spend your time in Tahoe or the Eastern Sierra, see pages 231 and 337.

Day 4
YOSEMITE TO LOS ANGELES
300 MILES / 5 HOURS
Exit the park via its southern entrance and drive south on **Highway 41.** The majority of the trip will be spent on **Highway 99 south** before using **I-5 south, Highway 170 south,** and **U.S. 101 south** as you get closer to the city.

IF YOU HAVE MORE TIME
Cross Highway 120 into the Eastern Sierra and head south on **U.S. 395** for a side trip to **Death Valley** (page 548). From the Wild West town of Lone Pine, turn east onto **Highway 190** for the one-hour drive to **Panamint Springs,** where a rustic resort has serviced hungry travelers since 1937. From Panamint Springs, it's another hour east along Highway 190 to the aptly named park hub of **Furnace Creek.**

Day 5
LOS ANGELES
You've been to the mountains, you've seen the desert; now it's time for the beach! Experience the best of Southern California beach culture at the chaotic but entertaining **Venice Boardwalk** or the **Santa Monica Pier.** If time allows, head inland a few miles to stroll the **Hollywood Walk of Fame** and snap a pic at **TCL Chinese Theatre.** Of course, some people would give all of that up for a day at **Disneyland** (you know who you are).

For more suggestions on how to spend your time in Los Angeles, see page 428.

IF YOU HAVE MORE TIME
Plan a day trip to **Palm Springs** (page 530), a 2-4 hour drive east on I-10, or follow I-5 south to explore **San Diego** (page 479). Stop for a surf or a swim in one of the **beach towns,** wander through lush **Balboa Park,** and dine in the **Gaslamp Quarter.**

Carmel Beach

the Big Sur Coast

Days 6-7
BIG SUR COAST
500 MILES / 9-10 HOURS

You can make this drive in one long day if you make only a few stops (such as getting lunch midway in San Luis Obispo), but it's better to break it up over two days and enjoy the coast. On the first day, stop in **Santa Barbara** for lunch at one of the great restaurants off **State Street.** Continue on to **San Luis Obispo** to spend the night.

On the second day, plan on stopping for a tour of **Hearst Castle** in **San Simeon,** then driving up PCH through **Big Sur** on the way back to San Francisco. (If you really need to get from Los Angeles to San Francisco in one day, it's quicker to take **I-5,** which takes around six hours.)

For more suggestions on how to spend your time in Big Sur, see page 353.

IF YOU HAVE MORE TIME

Plan a boat trip from Santa Barbara or Ventura to the **Channel Islands,** or add an overnight stop in **Monterey** (page 363) and spend some time exploring the world-class **aquarium.**

BEST BEACH SPOTS

TRINIDAD STATE BEACH
This scenic stretch of shore on the North Coast is ideal for a picnic (page 185).

STINSON BEACH
In summer, surfers, kayakers, and paddleboarders test their skills in the San Francisco Bay Area surf (page 92).

SANTA CRUZ BEACH BOARDWALK
This beachy boardwalk in Santa Cruz entertains with rides, games, and sunbathers (page 353).

CARMEL BEACH
With its pale sand and contrasting blue-green ocean water, Carmel Beach is a jewel of the Monterey Bay (page 377).

PFEIFFER BEACH
Big Sur's windswept Pfeiffer Beach features picture-perfect rock formations offshore (page 384).

MOONSTONE BEACH
Pockets of sand are interspersed with jumbles of rocks on this gem of a beach in Cambria (page 392).

LEADBETTER BEACH
For a day of sunning, swimming, and lounging head to this wide beach in Santa Barbara (page 403).

REFUGIO STATE BEACH
On the Gaviota Coast, this postcard-perfect finger of sand is on a scenic cove shaded by towering palm trees (page 406).

SANTA MONICA STATE BEACH
Santa Monica State Beach is a people-watcher's paradise, with the nearby Venice Boardwalk filled with weightlifters, skateboarders, musicians, dancers, and vendors hawking their wares (page 448).

LA JOLLA COVE
This pocket beach sits nestled between two cliffs shelters, snorkelers, and kayakers north of San Diego (page 487).

Best of Northern California

Day 1

Start your trip San Francisco, where you can fly into **San Francisco International Airport** and **rent a car.** For suggestions on how to spend your time in the city, see page 37.

Day 2

Your journey north begins with a drive on U.S. 101 over San Francisco's iconic **Golden Gate Bridge**. After five miles, turn off U.S. 101 to Highway 1 at **Mill Valley.** On the slow, four-hour drive up the coast (around 160 miles), make time to stop at **Fort Ross State Historic Park** to explore the re-constructed Russian settlement.

End the day in the community of **Mendocino** with a view of the sunset at **Mendocino Headlands State Park** or a pint at the lively **Patterson's Pub.** At night, dine at the historic **MacCallum House Restaurant.**

Day 3

Follow Highway 1 north to **Fort Bragg** then continue inland to connect with U.S. 101 (about one hour). Take the **Avenue of the Giants,** a breathtaking drive through **Humboldt Redwoods State Park.** Even though it's only 31 miles, the trip could take a few hours if you get out of your car to ponder the big trees.

Get back on U.S. 101 and head an hour north (60 miles) to **Eureka.** Stop to wander the **Blue Ox Millworks and Historic Park** before continuing north another 10 minutes or so to charming **Arcata.** Wander through Arcata Plaza, then grab a dink at **The Alibi.** Afterward, dine at one of several restaurants surrounding the lively plaza.

Day 4

Start your morning with a tasty crepe from

Arcata's **Renata's Creperie** before hitting U.S. 101 north on your final day. About 20 minutes (15 miles) north of Arcata, exit to the scenic coastal city of **Trinidad.** Walk down to the beach at **College Cove** or explore the rugged coast by **kayak.**

After another half hour north on U.S. 101 (26 miles), turn onto Newton B. Drury Scenic Drive to explore **Prairie Creek Redwoods State Park.** If you have the energy, drive out Davison Road to **Gold Bluffs Beach,** where Roosevelt elk roam the sands. Continue on the dirt drive to hike the one-mile round-trip up **Fern Canyon,** which passes through a steep canyon draped in bright green ferns.

Head back out to U.S. 101 to drive the 45 minutes (38 miles) to **Crescent City,** where you can get a hotel room and a full night's sleep.

Best of Southern California

Day 1

Fly into LAX and rent a car for your Southern California road trip. Walk down the star-studded **Hollywood Walk of Fame** and a stop at the historic **TCL Chinese Theatre,** where you can find the handprints of your favorite movie stars. Or, for aesthetic stimulation, tour the **Los Angeles County Museum of Art.** End the day with a cocktail at Sunset Boulevard's **Rainbow Bar & Grill.**

Day 2

Grab breakfast **The Griddle Café** before heading to the coast for a day of culture. Jump on U.S. 101 to I-405 south to visit the world-famous **Getty Center.** Admire Richard Meier's soaring architecture before gazing at the magnificent works inside. Continue south on I-405 exiting towards **Santa Monica.** Enjoy the amusement park rides of the **Santa Monica Pier** or just take a break on Santa Monica Beach. Stroll along the **Venice Boardwalk** to take in the bodybuilders, street performers, and alternative-culture types of **Venice Beach.** After a day gazing at the sea, dine on seafood at **Salt Air.**

IF YOU HAVE MORE TIME

Kids (and kids at heart) might prefer to skip the L.A. beaches and spend a full day and night at **Disneyland** (page 460) instead.

Day 3

Follow I-405 south, stopping off in **Long Beach** for a tour on The **Queen Mary,** an ocean liner now home to restaurants, a hotel, and a museum. From Long Beach, head south on Highway 1 through the North County beach towns of **Encinitas, Carlsbad,** and **Oceanside.** Stop off for a surf or a swim, or soldier on to **La Jolla Cove** to go kayaking or snorkeling. Then satiate that appetite with lobster tacos from **Puesto.**

Day 4

Easygoing **San Diego** is a great place to end any vacation. Visit **Balboa Park,** where you'll spend most of your time at the **San Diego Zoo.** Follow a day in the park with a meal in the **Gaslamp Quarter,** then end your day with a craft beer at one of San Diego's many breweries, like the giant **Stone World Bistro & Gardens Liberty Station.**

Planning Your Trip

Where to Go

San Francisco Bay Area

The politics, the culture, the food—these are what make San Francisco world famous. Dine on **cutting-edge cuisine** at high-end restaurants and offbeat food trucks, tour classical and avant-garde **museums**, bike through **Golden Gate Park** and explore its hidden treasures, and stroll along **Fisherman's Wharf,** where barking sea lions and frenetic street performers compete for attention.

Surrounding San Francisco is a region as **diverse** as the city itself. To the north, **Marin** offers **wilderness** seekers a quick reprieve from the city, while ethnic diversity and intellectual curiosity give the **East Bay** a **hip, urban edge.** On the southern **Peninsula, beaches** and **farmland** are within quick driving distance of the entrepreneurial culture of Silicon Valley and **San Jose.**

Wine Country

Northern California's Wine Country is famous for a reason. This is the place to **pamper yourself** with excellent wines, fantastic food, and **luxurious spas. Napa** offers all of the above in spades, while **Sonoma** is the place to catch a bit of history and to enjoy a **mellow atmosphere.** The **Russian River** adds **redwoods** and a bit of river rafting to the mix.

North Coast

For deserted beaches, towering redwoods, and scenic coastal towns, cruise north along **The Redwood Coast.** Explore Russian history at Fort Ross on the **grassy bluffs** of the **Sonoma Coast,** be romanced by **Mendocino's** small-town charm and nearby wineries, and discover the quirky, **hippie charm** of towns like **Arcata** and **Trinidad.**

Yosemite National Park

Shasta and Lassen

At the southern end of the volcanic Cascade Range are **geologic wonders** alongside plentiful outdoor recreation. Rent a houseboat on **Shasta Lake** or spend a few days climbing or skiing dramatic **Mount Shasta.** You can traverse nearby **lava tunnels** or travel south to hike through **boiling mud pots** and fumaroles at **Lassen Volcanic National Park.**

Lake Tahoe

Bright blue skies, **granite mountains,** and **evergreen forests** surround jewel-like **Lake Tahoe.** Glossy hotels and casinos line the **South Shore,** while the low-key **North and West Shores** beckon with **quiet beaches** and miles of hiking, biking, and ski trails. Nevada's **East Shore** specializes in **uninhibited** good times, while the **Truckee-Donner** area adds a bit of **Old West flavor** to the outdoor scene.

Sacramento and Gold Country

The political epicenter of California is the Gold Rush-era town of **Sacramento.** More history awaits on the **winding scenic highways** that crisscross **Northern Gold Country.** Tour abandoned mines, raft some **high-octane white water,** go wine-tasting in the **Shenandoah Valley,** or explore the caves, caverns, and big trees of **Southern Gold Country.**

Yosemite, Sequoia, and Kings Canyon

The work of Ansel Adams and John Muir has made Yosemite a **worldwide icon.** Thousands crowd into **Yosemite Valley** to view the much-photographed **Half Dome, Bridalveil Fall,** and **El Capitan.** On the eastern side of the Sierras, **Mono Lake** and **Mammoth Lakes** provide more **scenic wilderness** to explore.

Aside from the dramatic **rugged terrain,** the real draws to this central Sierra region are the **giant sequoias** in the **General Grant Grove** and the **General Sherman Tree.** Visit the **Giant Forest Museum,** take an invigorating hike up to **Moro Rock,** and duck into glittering **Crystal Cave,** which is as beautiful as its name suggests.

Monterey and Big Sur

Some of the most beautiful and most

Hollywood Boulevard at sunset

adventurous coastline in the world is along Highway 1—the **Pacific Coast Highway.** Go surfing in **Santa Cruz.** Witness **gray whales** and sea lions off the rugged **Monterey Bay,** and then explore their environment at the **Monterey Bay Aquarium.** Camp and hike the unspoiled wilderness of **Big Sur,** and then tour **grandiose Hearst Castle** in San Simeon.

Santa Barbara and the Central Coast

Take in the picturesque **Santa Barbara Mission** and then stroll down the city's State Street, which is lined with shops, restaurants, and bars. Enjoy the lonely **Gaviota coastline** or, to truly get away from it all, take a boat ride out to **Channel Islands National Park.**

Los Angeles

Los Angeles is a massive mix of Southern California beach town, Hollywood dream factory, and 21st-century metropolis. Unmissable attractions include **world-class art,** a beach scene that begs for some time in the **sand and surf,** and an **amusement park** devoted to a cartoon mouse.

San Diego

For the sun-drenched, soft-sand California beach experience portrayed in endless films and TV shows, come to San Diego. Maritime museums ring the **downtown harbor,** while across the bay in **Coronado,** vibrant and historic Hotel del Coronado creates a centerpiece for visitors to the city. Gorgeous beaches stretch from **Point Loma** north to **La Jolla** and the **North County** coast, begging surfers, swimmers, strollers, and sun-bathers to ply their sands.

Palm Springs and the Deserts

A different kind of beauty makes the deserts of California legendary and popular attractions. **Palm Springs** takes the cake as the biggest and coolest desert city. **Joshua Tree**—named for its funky namesake plant--straddles two major desert ecosystems. **Death Valley** boasts the lowest and hottest spot in the Western Hemisphere. Far south, **Anza-Borrego** is California's biggest state park and one of its most intriguing regions.

Las Vegas

Rising out of the desert like a high-tech oasis, Las Vegas is an adult playground of **casinos, bars, buffets, over-the-top shows,** and **plush hotels.** Dig a little deeper to find fine food, a flourishing arts scene, and local hangouts in the shadows of **The Strip.**

Know Before You Go

Passports and Visas

Foreign travelers must have a valid **passport** and a **visa** to enter the United States, but holders of Canadian passports don't need visas or visa waivers.

Transportation

The easiest places to **fly** into are **San Francisco, Los Angeles,** and **San Diego.** If you're flying into San Francisco, you can avoid some of the hassle of San Francisco International Airport (SFO) by flying into nearby **Oakland** or **San Jose.** Similarly, Los Angeles offers several suburban airports, including **Burbank, Long Beach,** and **Ontario,** which are typically less congested than Los Angeles International Airport (LAX). For excursions outside major cities, you'll want to **rent a car.**

High and Low Seasons
SPRING

California's best feature is its all-season appeal. **Yosemite's waterfalls** are at their peak in spring, when the crowds are fewer. This is also a great time to visit **Big Sur**—lodging rates drop, as do the number of visitors, while blooming wildflowers make for colorful road trips.

SUMMER

Unsuspecting visitors are frequently surprised by the **wind and fog** that blow through San Francisco **June-August.** Regardless, **summer** remains California's travel season; expect crowds at popular attractions, wineries, national parks, and campgrounds. More visitors will not only add to the crowds, but also add to the traffic on the highways. Plan a little extra time to get from place to place.

FALL

Fall is a wonderful time to visit, as the summer crowds have left, but winter rain and snow have not yet closed **Yosemite, Shasta,** or **Tahoe. September** in particular is San Francisco's "summer," with **warm sunny days** and little summer fog.

WINTER

In **winter,** Tahoe draws crowds for **skiing and snowboarding.** Unfortunately, it also draws **heavy traffic** along **I-80,** which can close because of snow and related accidents. **Yosemite's roads are closed** in winter, including **Highway 120** and the **Tioga Pass,** which links the Eastern Sierra to the west entrance of the park. **Heavy rains** can also flood Wine Country roads, leaving travelers stranded.

Reservations

Book **hotels** and **rental cars** in advance for the best rates and availability, especially in the summer, which is high season for travel. If you plan to rent a car in one city and return it in another (for example, rent the car in San Francisco and return it in Los Angeles), you should expect to pay an additional fee, which can be quite high.

High-season travelers should also plan ahead for the **big-name attractions.** If you have your heart set on visiting **Alcatraz** in San Francisco or the **Hearst Castle** in San Simeon, purchase tickets at least two weeks in advance. You'll save money buying advance tickets for **Disneyland** online as well. Reservations are essential at **campgrounds** in Yosemite and Big Sur.

San Francisco

Sights 37

Entertainment and Events 56

Shopping........................ .61

Sports and Recreation 64

Food 66

Accommodations............... 73

Transportation and Services 78

North Bay 80

East Bay 98

The Peninsula 104

Silicon Valley 110

Look for ★ to find recommended sights, activities, dining, and lodging.

Highlights

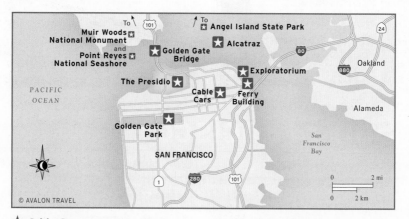

★ **Cable Cars:** Nothing is more iconic than climbing San Francisco's steep hills on a historic cable car (page 37).

★ **Ferry Building:** The 1898 Ferry Building has been renovated and reimagined as the foodie mecca of San Francisco (page 38).

★ **Exploratorium:** Kids and adults love to explore San Francisco's innovative and interactive science museum (page 44).

★ **Alcatraz:** Spend the day in prison at the historically famous former maximum-security penitentiary in the middle of the bay (page 44).

★ **The Presidio:** The original 1776 El Presidio de San Francisco is now a national park (page 49).

★ **Golden Gate Bridge:** Nothing beats the view from one of the most famous and fascinating bridges in the country (page 50).

★ **Golden Gate Park:** Home to stunning museums, botanical gardens, and outdoor festivals, the park is the place to be any day of the week (page 52).

★ **Angel Island State Park:** A visit to the largest island in the bay packs a lot into a short amount of time (page 85).

★ **Muir Woods National Monument:** Stand among trees nearly 1,000 years old and 200 feet tall in one of the nation's earliest national monuments (page 88).

★ **Point Reyes National Seashore:** Point Reyes is home to tule elk, desolate beaches, dairy and oyster farms, lighthouses, and remote wilderness trails (page 93).

The regular grid pattern found on maps of San Francisco leaves visitors unprepared for the precipitous inclines and stunning water views in this town built on 43 hills.

Geographically and culturally, San Francisco is anything but flat, and what level ground exists might at any moment give way. While earthquakes remake the land, social upheavals play a similar role, reminding locals that the only constant here is change. In the 1950s, the Beats challenged postwar conformity and left a legacy of incantatory poems and independent bookstores. The late 1960s saw a years-long Summer of Love, which shifted consciousness as surely as quakes shift tectonic plates. Gay and lesbian liberation movements sprung forth in the 1970s, as did a renewed push for women's rights. Since then, a vibrant culture of technological innovation has taken root and continues to rapidly evolve as groundbreaking companies and tech visionaries choose to make the city their home.

Although San Francisco is one of the most visited cities in the United States, it often seems like a provincial village, or a series of villages that share a downtown and a roster of world-class icons. Drive over the Golden Gate or the Bay Bridge as the fog is lifting and your heart will catch at the ever-changing beauty of the scene. Stand at the base of the Transamerica Pyramid, hang off the side of a cable car, or just walk through the neighborhoods that make the city more than the sum of its parts. Despite the hills, San Francisco is a city that cries out to be explored on foot.

PLANNING YOUR TIME

Try to spend at least **one weekend** in San Francisco, and focus your time downtown. Union Square makes a great home base, thanks to its plethora of hotels, shops, and easy access to public transportation, but it can be fairly dead at night. With a full **week,** you can explore Golden Gate Park's excellent museums—the de Young and the California Academy of Sciences. You can easily spend another full day exploring the Presidio and taking a scenic, foggy stroll across the Golden Gate Bridge.

Previous: the Golden Gate Bridge; lanterns in Chinatown. **Above:** Transamerica Pyramid.

San Francisco Bay Area

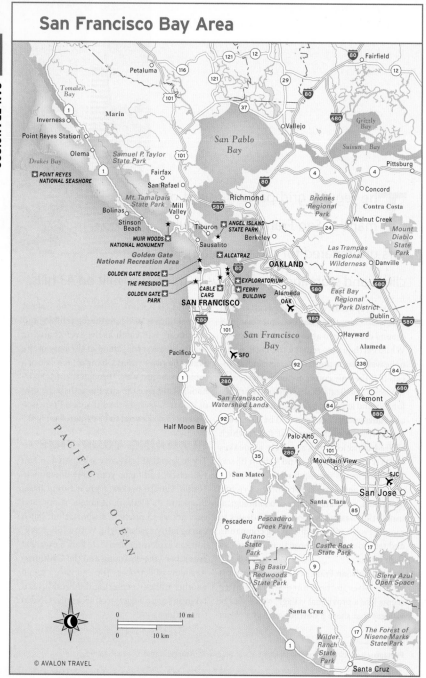

© AVALON TRAVEL

Two Days in San Francisco

San Francisco may only be roughly seven miles long and seven miles wide, but it packs in historic neighborhoods, one of the West Coast's most iconic landmarks, and dozens of stomach-dropping inclines within its small area. Exploring all its hills and valleys takes some planning.

DAY 1

Start your day at the **Ferry Building**. Graze from the many vendors, including **Blue Bottle Café, Cowgirl Creamery,** and **Acme Bread Company.**

After touring the gourmet shops, catch the Muni F line (Steuart St. and Market St., $2) to Jefferson Street and take a stroll along **Fisherman's Wharf**. Stop into the **Musée Mécanique** to play a few coin-operated antique arcade games. Near Pier 39, catch the ferry to **Alcatraz**—be sure to buy your tickets well in advance. Alcatraz will fill your mind with amazing stories from the legendary island prison.

After you escape from Alcatraz, take the N Judah line to 9th Avenue and Irving Street, then follow 9th Avenue north into **Golden Gate Park**, where you can delve into art at the fabulous **de Young Museum** or science at the **California Academy of Sciences**. Stroll the scenic **Japanese Tea Gardens** and get a snack at their Tea House.

Catch a cab to North Beach and **Tony's Pizza Napoletana** to get some real sustenance directly from one of its seven pizza ovens. Now you are ready to enjoy the talented performers, silly jokes, and gravity-defying hats of the long-running theater production *Beach Blanket Babylon*. If theater is not your thing, see some live music; choose a show at the **Great American Music Hall**.

DAY 2

Fortify yourself for a day of sightseeing with a hearty breakfast at **Brenda's French Soul Food,** then drive or take a cab out to the **Lands End Trail**, where you can investigate the ruins of the former Sutro Baths and get views of the city's rocky coastline. Then head back to **Crissy Field** for views of the **Golden Gate Bridge**.

Venture back downtown to wander the streets of **Chinatown** and adjacent North Beach with a browse through **City Lights**, the legendary Beat Generation bookstore. Wind down with a cocktail at **Vesuvio**, a colorful bar and former Beat writer hangout located next to City Lights.

For dinner, head to the bustling Mission District, where new eateries are always popping up. Opt for Mexican cuisine at **La Taqueria**, raw fish at **Anchor Oyster Bar** or cocktails and snacks at **Beretta**.

Sights

UNION SQUARE AND DOWNTOWN
★ Cable Cars

Perhaps the most recognizable symbol of San Francisco is the **cable car** (www.sfcablecar.com), originally conceived by Andrew Smith Hallidie as a safer alternative for traveling the steep, often slick hills of San Francisco. The cable cars ran as regular mass transit from 1873 into the 1940s, when buses and electric streetcars began to dominate the landscape. Dedicated citizens, especially "Cable Car Lady" Friedel Klussmann, saved the cable car system from extinction, and the cable cars have become a rolling national landmark.

Today you can ride the cable cars from one tourist destination to another for $6 per ride. A full day "passport" ticket ($15, also grants access to streetcars and buses) is totally worth it if you want to run around the city all day. Cable car routes can take you up Nob Hill from the Financial District, or from Union Square along Powell Street, through Chinatown, and out to Fisherman's Wharf. Take a seat, or grab one of the exterior poles and hang on! Cable cars have open-air seating only, making for a chilly ride on foggy days.

The cars get stuffed to capacity with tourists on weekends and with local commuters at rush hours. Expect to wait an hour or more for a ride from any of the turnaround points on a weekend or holiday. But a ride on a cable car from Union Square down to the Wharf is more than worth the wait. The views from the hills down to the bay inspire wonder even in lifetime residents. To learn a bit more, make a stop at the **Cable Car Museum** (1201 Mason St., 415/474-1887, www.cablecarmuseum.org, 10am-6pm daily Apr.-Sept., 10am-5pm daily Oct.-Mar., free), the home and nerve center of the entire fleet. Here a sweet little museum depicts the life and times of the cable cars while an elevated platform overlooks the engines, winding wheels, and thick steel cable that keeps the cars humming. You can even glimpse the 1873 tunnels that snake beneath the city.

Grace Cathedral

Local icon **Grace Cathedral** (1100 California St., 415/749-6300, www.gracecathedral.org, 7am-6pm Mon.-Fri., 8am-6pm Sat., 8am-7pm Sun.) is many things to many people. The French Gothic-style edifice, completed in 1964, attracts architecture and Beaux-Arts lovers by the thousands with its facade, stained glass, and furnishings. The labyrinths—replicas of the Chartres Cathedral labyrinth in France—appeal to meditative walkers seeking spiritual solace. Concerts featuring world music, sacred music, and modern classical ensembles draw audiences from around the bay and farther afield.

To view some of the church's lesser-seen areas, sign up for the 1.5-hour **Grace Cathedral Grand Tour** (800/979-3370, $25).

★ Ferry Building

Restored to its former glory, the 1898 **San Francisco Ferry Building** (1 Ferry Bldg., 415/983-8030, www.ferrybuildingmarketplace.com, 10am-6pm Mon.-Fri., 9am-6pm Sat., 11am-5pm Sun., check with businesses for individual hours) stands at the end of the Financial District at the edge of the water. Learn about the history of the edifice just inside the main lobby, where photos and

the Ferry Building

cable car

interpretive plaques describe the life of the Ferry Building.

On the water side of the Ferry Building, you can actually catch a ferry with the **Blue and Gold Fleet** (www.blueandgoldfleet.com), **Golden Gate Ferry** (www.goldengateferry.org), and **Bay Link Ferries** (www.baylinkferry.com).

Today, the building is home to the famous **Farmers Market** (10am-2pm Tues. and Thurs., 8am-2pm Sat.). Permanent shops provide top-tier artisanal food and drink, from wine and cheese to high-end kitchenware, while fresh produce and organic meats are on display outside. Local favorites Cowgirl Creamery and Acme Bread Company maintain storefronts here. For immediate gratification, a few incongruous quick-and-easy restaurants offer reasonable eats.

San Francisco Museum of Modern Art

SFMOMA (151 3rd St., 415/357-4000, www.sfmoma.org), as it's fondly called, is a local favorite. For nearly three years the museum was out of commission, getting a complete renovation. The makeover turned it into the neighborhood's newest architectural wonder while doubling the gallery space for the special exhibitions installed each year and for its growing permanent collection, which includes notable work from Henri Matisse, Shiro Kuramata, Wayne Thiebaud, Richard Diebenkorn, and Chuck Close.

NORTH BEACH AND FISHERMAN'S WHARF

North Beach has long served as the Little Italy of San Francisco, a fact still reflected in the restaurants in the neighborhood. North Beach truly made its mark in the 1950s when it was, for a brief time, home to many writers in the Beat Generation, including Jack Kerouac, Gary Snyder, and Allen Ginsburg.

Chinatown

The massive Chinese migration to California began almost as soon as the news of easy gold in the mountain streams made it to East Asia. And despite rampant prejudice, the Chinese not only stayed, but persevered and eventually prospered. Many never made it to the gold fields, preferring instead to remain in bustling San Francisco to open shops and begin the business of commerce in their new home. They carved out a thriving community at the border of **Portsmouth Square,** then center of the young city, which became known as Chinatown. Along with much of San Francisco, the neighborhood was destroyed in the 1906 earthquake and fire.

Today visitors see the post-1906 visitor-friendly Chinatown that was built after the quake, particularly if they enter through the **Chinatown Gate** (Grant Ave. and Bush St.) at the edge of Union Square. In this historic neighborhood, beautiful Asian architecture mixes with more mundane blocky city buildings to create a unique skyline. Small alleyways wend between the touristy commercial corridors, creating an intimate atmosphere.

San Francisco

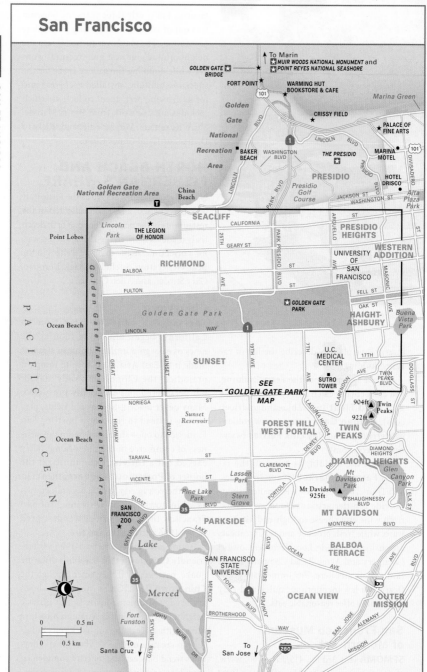

To Marin
MUIR WOODS NATIONAL MONUMENT and
POINT REYES NATIONAL SEASHORE

GOLDEN GATE
BRIDGE

FORT POINT

WARMING HUT
BOOKSTORE & CAFE

Golden
Gate
National
Recreation
Area

CRISSY FIELD

Marina Green

PALACE OF
FINE ARTS

BAKER
BEACH

WASHINGTON
BLVD

THE PRESIDIO

MARINA
MOTEL

PRESIDIO

Golden Gate
National Recreation Area

China
Beach

Presidio
Golf
Course

HOTEL
DRISCO

Alta
Plaza
Park

Point Lobos

Lincoln
Park

SEACLIFF

THE LEGION
OF HONOR

CALIFORNIA

GEARY ST

PRESIDIO
HEIGHTS

WESTERN
ADDITION

RICHMOND

BALBOA

FULTON

UNIVERSITY
OF
SAN
FRANCISCO

Golden Gate Park

GOLDEN GATE
PARK

HAIGHT-
ASHBURY

Buena
Vista
Park

Ocean Beach

LINCOLN

WAY

SUNSET

U.C.
MEDICAL
CENTER

SUTRO
TOWER

SEE
"GOLDEN GATE PARK"
MAP

904ft
922ft

Twin
Peaks

NORIEGA

Sunset
Reservoir

FOREST HILL/
WEST PORTAL

TWIN
PEAKS

DIAMOND
HEIGHTS

Ocean Beach

TARAVAL

CLAREMONT
BLVD

Lassen
Park

DIAMOND HEIGHTS

Mt
Davidson
Park

Glen
Canyon
Park

VICENTE

Pine Lake
Park

Stern
Grove

Mt Davidson
925ft

O'SHAUGHNESSY
BLVD

MT DAVIDSON

SAN
FRANCISCO
ZOO

PARKSIDE

MONTEREY

BALBOA
TERRACE

Lake

SAN FRANCISCO
STATE
UNIVERSITY

Merced

OCEAN VIEW

OUTER
MISSION

Fort
Funston

To
Santa Cruz

BROTHERHOOD

WAY

To
San Jose

PACIFIC

OCEAN

0   0.5 mi
0   0.5 km

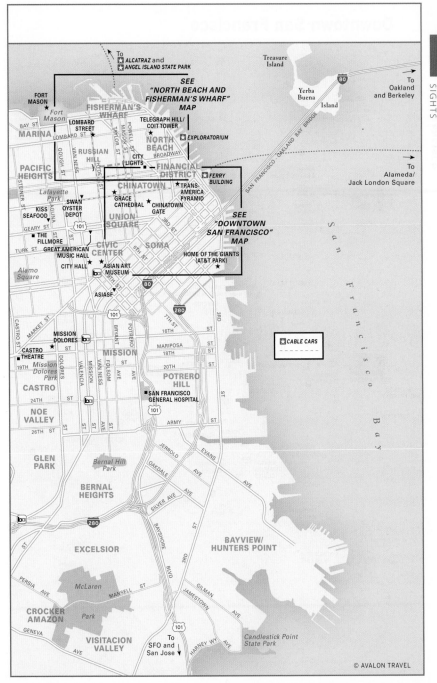

To
ALCATRAZ and
ANGEL ISLAND STATE PARK

Treasure
Island

To
Oakland
and Berkeley

FORT
MASON

Fort
Mason

FISHERMAN'S
WHARF

SEE
"NORTH BEACH AND
FISHERMAN'S WHARF"
MAP

Yerba
Buena
Island

80

LOMBARD
STREET

TELEGRAPH HILL/
COIT TOWER

MARINA

LOMBARD ST

BAY ST

NORTH
BEACH

EXPLORATORIUM

To
Alameda/
Jack London Square

PACIFIC
HEIGHTS

RUSSIAN
HILL

BROADWAY

CITY
LIGHTS

FINANCIAL
DISTRICT

FERRY
BUILDING

GOUGH ST

POWELL ST

TAYLOR ST

MASON ST

HYDE

VAN NESS

CHINATOWN

TRANS-
AMERICA
PYRAMID

Lafayette
Park

STEINER ST

LAGUNA

SWAN
OYSTER
DEPOT

GRACE
CATHEDRAL

CHINATOWN
GATE

KISS
SEAFOOD

101

UNION
SQUARE

SEE
"DOWNTOWN
SAN FRANCISCO"
MAP

GEARY ST

3RD ST

THE
FILLMORE

SOMA

TURK ST

GREAT AMERICAN
MUSIC HALL

6TH ST

CIVIC
CENTER

HOME OF THE GIANTS
(AT&T PARK)

Alamo
Square

CITY HALL

ASIAN ART
MUSEUM

8TH ST

80

ASIASF

San

CABLE CARS

F
r
a
n
c
i
s
c
o

101

280

7TH ST

16TH

ST

MISSION
DOLORES

BRYANT

POTRERO

MARIPOSA

ST

CASTRO ST

MARKET ST

CASTRO

ST

DOLORES

VALENCIA

MISSION

VAN NESS

FOLSOM

AVE

18TH

20TH

ST

ST

B
a
y

CASTRO
THEATRE

19TH

Mission
Dolores
Park

MISSION

POTRERO
HILL

CASTRO

24TH

ST

ST

ST

SAN FRANCISCO
GENERAL HOSPITAL

ST

NOE
VALLEY

26TH ST

ST

101

ARMY

GLEN
PARK

Bernal Hill
Park

JERROLD

EVANS

BERNAL
HEIGHTS

OAKDALE

AVE

AVE

SILVER AVE

AVE

280

BAYVIEW/
HUNTERS POINT

ST

EXCELSIOR

BAYSHORE

3RD

ST

GILMAN

BLVD

PERSIA

AVE

McLaren

MANSELL

ST

JAMESTOWN

AVE

CROCKER
AMAZON

Park

GENEVA

VISITACION
VALLEY

AVE

To
SFO and
San Jose ▼

HARNEY WY

AVE

Candlestick Point
State Park

© AVALON TRAVEL

Downtown San Francisco

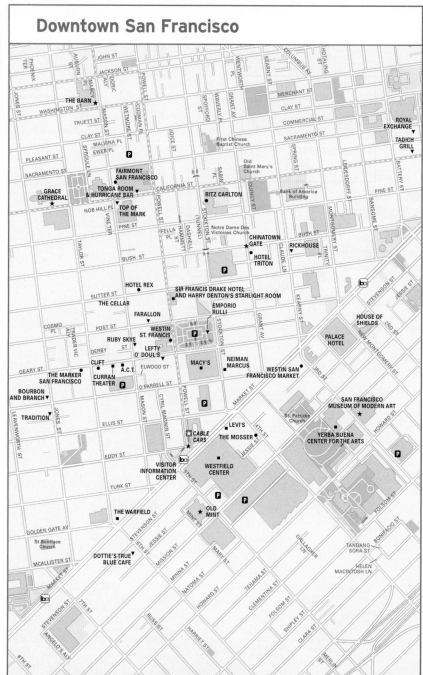

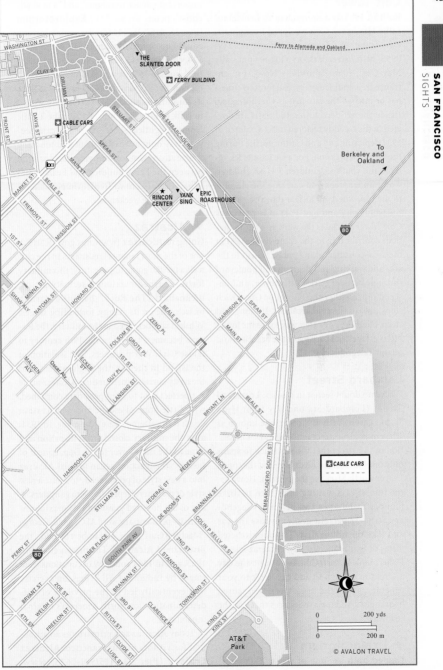

Coit Tower

Built in 1933 as a monument to benefactor Lillie Hitchcock Coit's beloved firefighters, **Coit Tower** (1 Telegraph Hill Blvd., 415/249-0995, http://sfrecpark.org, 10am-6pm daily May-Oct., 10am-5pm daily Nov.-Apr., entrance free, tour fees vary, call for tour times) has beautified the city just as Coit intended. Inside the art deco tower, the walls are covered in the recently restored frescos painted in 1934 depicting city and California life during the Great Depression. For a fee (adults $8, seniors and youth $5, children 5-11 $2, children 4 and under free), you can ride the elevator to the top, where on a clear day, you can see the whole city and bay. Part of what makes Coit Tower special is the walk up to it. Rather than contributing to the acute congestion in the area, consider taking public transit to the area and walking up Telegraph Hill Boulevard through Pioneer Park to the tower, and descend down either the Filbert or Greenwich steps toward the Embarcadero. It's long and steep, but there's no other way to see the lovely little cottages and gardens of the beautiful and quaint Telegraph Hill.

Lombard Street

You've no doubt seen it in movies: **Lombard Street** (Lombard St., one way from Hyde St. to Leavenworth St.), otherwise known as "the crookedest street in the world." The section of the street that visitors flock to spans only one block, from Hyde Street at the top to Leavenworth Street at the bottom. However, the line of cars waiting their turn to drive bumper-to-bumper can be just as legendary as its 27 percent grade. Bypass the car and take the hill by foot. The unobstructed vistas of San Francisco Bay, Alcatraz Island, Fisherman's Wharf, Coit Tower, and the city are reason enough to add this walk to your itinerary, as are the brick steps, manicured hydrangeas, and tony residences that line the roadway.

★ Exploratorium

Lauded both as "one of the world's most important science museums" and "a mad scientist's penny arcade," the **Exploratorium** (Pier 15, 415/528-4444, www.exploratorium.edu, 10am-5pm daily, adults $29, youth 13-17 $24, children 4-12 $19, children 3 and under free) houses 150 playful exhibits on physics, motion, perception, and the senses that utilize its stunning location. Make a reservation ($15) to walk blindly (and bravely) into the Tactile Dome, a lightless space where you can "see" your way only by reaching out and touching the environment around you. The location between the Ferry Building and Fisherman's Wharf makes a crowd-free trip impossible, especially on the weekends.

★ Alcatraz

Going to **Alcatraz** (www.nps.gov/alcatraz), one of the most famous landmarks in the city, feels a bit like going to purgatory; this military fortress-turned-maximum-security prison, nicknamed "The Rock," has little warmth or welcome on its craggy, forbidding shores. While it still belonged to the military, the fortress became a prison in the 19th century to house Civil War prisoners. The isolation of the island in the bay, the frigid waters, and the nasty currents surrounding Alcatraz made it a perfect spot to keep prisoners contained, with little hope of escape and near-certain death if the attempt were ever made. In 1934, after the military closed down its prison and handed the island over to the Department of Justice, construction began to turn Alcatraz into a new style of prison ready to house a new style of prisoner: Depression-era gangsters. A few of the honored guests of this maximum-security penitentiary were Al Capone, George "Machine Gun" Kelly, and Robert Stroud, "the Birdman of Alcatraz." The prison closed in 1963, and in 1964 and 1969 occupations were staged by Indians of All Tribes, an exercise that eventually led to the privilege of self-determination for North America's original inhabitants.

Today Alcatraz acts primarily as an attraction for visitors to San Francisco. **Alcatraz Cruises** (Pier 33, 415/981-7625, www.

alcatrazcruises.com, 9:10am-3:50pm, 5:55pm, 6:30pm, 9:30pm, 9:40pm daily, adults $30-37, children 5-11 $18.25-21.75, 4 and under free) offers ferry rides out to Alcatraz and tours of the island and the prison. Tours depart from Pier 33, and prices are steep, but family tickets are available for $90 and include passage for two adults and two kids of any age. Buy tickets at least a week in advance, especially if you'll be in town in the summer and want to visit Alcatraz on a weekend. Tours often sell out, especially in the evening, which has been voted one of the best tours in the Bay Area.

Pier 39

One of the most visited spots in San Francisco, **Pier 39** (www.pier39.com) hosts a wealth of restaurants and shops. If you've come down to the pier to see the sea life, start with the unusual **Aquarium of the Bay** (415/623-5300, www.aquariumofthebay.com, 9am-8pm daily summer, adults $20, seniors and children $12). This 300-foot, clear-walled tunnel lets visitors see thousands of species native to the San Francisco Bay, including sharks, rays, and plenty of fish. For a special treat, take the Behind the Scenes or Feed the Sharks tour. Farther down the pier, get close (but not *too* close) to the local colony of **sea lions.** These big, loud mammals tend to congregate at K-Dock in the West Marina. The best time to see the sea lions is winter, when the population grows into the hundreds. To learn more about the sea lions, visit the interpretive center on Level 2 of the **Marine Mammal Center** (415/289-7325, www.marinemammalcenter.org, 10am-5pm daily, free).

A perennial family favorite, the **San Francisco Carousel** (10am-7pm Sun.-Thurs., 10am-8pm Fri.-Sat., $3 per ride) is painted with beautiful scenes of San Francisco. Riders on the moving horses, carriages, and seats can look at the paintings or out onto the pier. Kids also love the daily shows by local street performers. Depending on when you're on the pier, you might see jugglers, magicians, or stand-up comedians on the **Alpine Spring Water Center Stage** (showtimes vary, free).

Fisherman's Wharf

Welcome to the tourist mecca of San Francisco! While warehouses, stacks of crab pots, and a fleet of fishing vessels let you know this is still a working wharf, it is also *the* spot where visitors to San Francisco come and snap photos. **Fisherman's Wharf** (Beach St. from Powell St. to Van Ness Ave., backs onto Bay St., www.fishermanswharf.org), reachable

Alcatraz

North Beach and Fisherman's Wharf

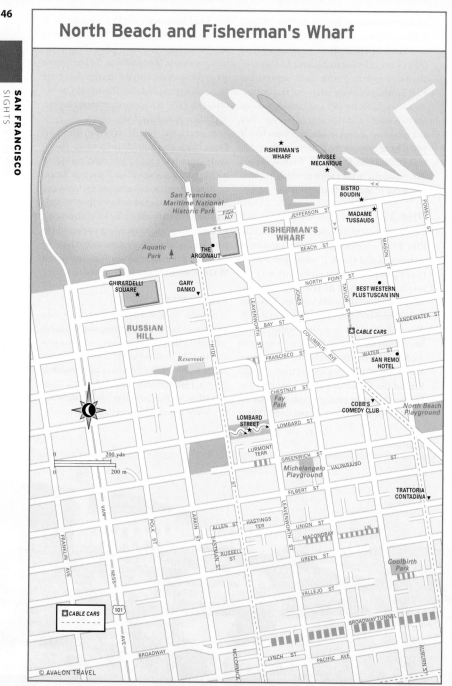

FISHERMAN'S
WHARF ★

MUSEE
MECANIQUE ★

BISTRO
BOUDIN ★

POWELL ST

MADAME
TUSSAUDS ★

JEFFERSON ST

San Francisco
Maritime National
Historic Park

FISH
ALY

FISHERMAN'S
WHARF

BEACH ST

MASON ST

Aquatic
Park

THE
ARGONAUT ●

NORTH POINT ST

BEST WESTERN
PLUS TUSCAN INN ●

GHIRARDELLI
SQUARE ★

GARY
DANKO ▼

JONES ST

TAYLOR ST

VANDEWATER ST

RUSSIAN
HILL

LEAVENWORTH ST

BAY ST

COLUMBUS AVE

★ CABLE CARS

WATER ST

HYDE ST

Reservoir

FRANCISCO ST

SAN REMO
HOTEL ●

CHESTNUT ST
Fay
Park

North Beach
Playground

COBB'S
COMEDY CLUB ▼

LOMBARD
STREET ★

LOMBARD ST

LURMONT
TERR

GREENWICH ST

Michelangelo
Playground

VALPARAISO

ST

TRATTORIA
CONTADINA ▼

FILBERT ST

ST

VAN

POLK ST

LARKIN ST

ALLEN ST

EASTMAN ST

HASTINGS
TER

LEAVENWORTH ST

UNION ST

MACONDRAY

LN

FRANKLIN
AVE

NESS

RUSSELL
ST

GREEN ST

Coolbirth
Park

VALLEJO ST

101

BROADWAY TUNNEL

★ CABLE CARS

BROADWAY

MCCORMICK

LYNCH ST

PACIFIC AVE

AUBURN ST

0   200 yds
0   200 m

© AVALON TRAVEL

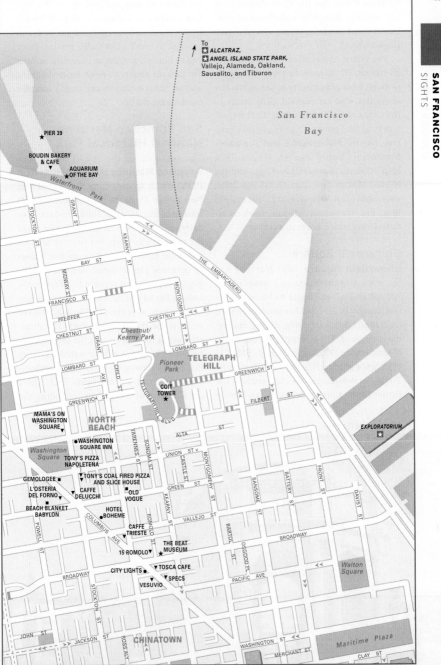

To
⊕ **ALCATRAZ,**
⊕ **ANGEL ISLAND STATE PARK,**
Vallejo, Alameda, Oakland,
Sausalito, and Tiburon

San Francisco
Bay

★ **PIER 39**

BOUDIN BAKERY
& CAFE ▼
★ **AQUARIUM**
OF THE BAY

Waterfront Park

STOCKTON ST

GRANT ST

KEARNY ST

MIDWAY ST

BAY ST

MONTGOMERY ST

THE EMBARCADERO

FRANCISCO ST

PFEIFFER

CHESTNUT ST

GRANT AVE

Chestnut/
Kearny Park

CHILD ST

CHESTNUT ST

LOMBARD ST

LOMBARD ST

Pioneer
Park

TELEGRAPH
HILL

GREENWICH ST

TELEGRAPH HILL BLVD

COIT
TOWER
★

GREENWICH ST

FILBERT ST

MAMA'S ON
WASHINGTON
SQUARE ▼

NORTH
BEACH

ALTA ST

EXPLORATORIUM
⊕

● **WASHINGTON**
SQUARE INN

VARENNES ST

SONOMA ST

UNION ST

CASTLE ST

MONTGOMERY ST

SANSOME ST

BATTERY ST

FRONT ST

DAVIS ST

Washington
Square

TONY'S PIZZA
NAPOLETENA

GEMOLOGEE ■

L'OSTERIA
DEL FORNO ▼

▼**TONY'S COAL FIRED PIZZA**
AND SLICE HOUSE

CAFFE
DELUCCHI

GREEN ST

■ **OLD**
VOGUE

KEARNY ST

BARTOL ST

BEACH BLANKET
BABYLON

COLUMBUS AVE

● **HOTEL**
BOHEME

ROMOLO ST

VALLEJO ST

BROADWAY

POWELL ST

CAFFE
TRIESTE

OSGOOD PL

Walton
Square

ST

15 ROMOLO ▼

THE BEAT
MUSEUM
★

BROADWAY

CITY LIGHTS ■

STOCKTON ST

▼**TOSCA CAFE**

★ **SPECS**

PACIFIC AVE

VESUVIO ▼

JOHN ST

JACKSON ST

ROSS ALY

CHINATOWN

WASHINGTON ST

MERCHANT ST

Maritime Plaza

CLAY ST

by Muni F line and the Hyde-Powell cable car, sprawls along the waterfront and inland several blocks, creating a large tourist neighborhood.

The Wharf, as it's called by locals, features all crowds, all the time. Be prepared to push through a sea of humanity to see sights, buy souvenirs, and eat seafood. Still, many of the sights of Fisherman's Wharf are important (and fun) pieces of San Francisco's heritage, like the **Fisherman's and Seaman's Memorial Chapel** (Pier 45, 415/674-7503, http://fishermanswharfchapel.org) and the **Musée Mécanique** (Pier 45, 415/346-2000, www.museemechanique.org, 10am-7pm Mon.-Fri., 10am-8pm Sat.-Sun., free), an arcade dating back more than a century.

Ghirardelli Square

Ghirardelli Square (900 North Point St., www.ghirardellisq.com), pronounced "GEAR-ah-DEL-ee," began its life as a chocolate factory in 1852, but has since reinvented itself as an upscale shopping, dining, and living compound. The **Ghirardelli Chocolate Manufactory** (900 North Point St., 415/474-3938, www.ghirardelli.com, 9am-11pm Sun.-Thurs., 9am-midnight Fri.-Sat.) anchors the corner of the square. Here you can browse

the rambling shop and pick up truffles, wafers, candies, and sauces for all your friends back home. Finally, get in line at the ice cream counter to order a hot fudge sundae. Once you've finished gorging on chocolate, wander out into the square to enjoy more shopping and an unbelievably swank condo complex overlooking the bay.

San Francisco Maritime National Historical Park

The real gem of the Wharf is the **San Francisco Maritime National Historical Park,** which spreads from the base of Van Ness to Pier 45. At the **visitors center** (499 Jefferson St., 415/447-5000, 9:30am-5pm daily), not only will rangers help you make the most of your visit, but you can also get lost in the labyrinthine museum that houses an immense Fresnel lighthouse lens and engaging displays that recount San Francisco's history. For $5 you can climb aboard the historical ships at permanent dock across the street at the **Hyde Street Pier.** The shiniest jewel of the collection is the 1886 square-rigged *Balclutha,* a three-masted schooner that recalls times gone by, complete with excellent historical exhibits below deck. There are also several steamboats, including the

the Palace of Fine Arts

workhorse ferry paddle-wheel *Eureka* and a cool old steam tugboat called the *Eppleton Hall.* Farther down at Pier 45, World War II buffs can feel the claustrophobia of the submarine **USS Pampanito** (415/775-1943, www.maritime.org, 9am-close daily, adults $12, children 6-12 $6, under 6 free) or the expansiveness of the Liberty ship **SS Jeremiah O'Brien** (415/544-0100, www.ssjeremiahobrien.org, adults $12, children 5-12 $6, children under 5 free).

The 1939 art deco **Aquatic Bathhouse Building** (900 Beach St., 415/561-7100, www.nps.gov/safr, 10am-4pm daily, adults $5, children free), built in 1939, houses the Maritime Museum, where you can see a number of rotating exhibits alongside its brilliant WPA murals.

MARINA AND PACIFIC HEIGHTS

The Marina and Pacific Heights are wealthy neighborhoods, with a couple of yacht harbors, plenty of open space, great dining, and shopping that only gets better as you go up the hill.

Palace of Fine Arts

The **Palace of Fine Arts** (3301 Lyon St.) was originally meant to be nothing but a temporary structure—part of the Panama-Pacific International Exposition in 1915. But the lovely building designed by Bernard Maybeck won the hearts of San Franciscans, and a fund was started to preserve the palace beyond the exposition. Through the first half of the 20th century, efforts could not keep it from crumbling, but in the 1960s and 1970s, serious rebuilding work took place, and today the Palace of Fine Arts stands proud, strong, and beautiful. It houses the **Palace of Fine Arts Theatre** (415/567-6642, www.palaceoffinearts.org), which hosts events nearly every day, from beauty pageants to conferences to children's musical theater performances.

★ The Presidio

A visit to the **Presidio** (Bldg. 105, Montgomery St. and Lincoln Blvd., 415/561-4323, www.nps.gov/prsf, visitors center 10am-4pm Thurs.-Sun., free) will remind visitors that this used to be an army town. Capping the northwestern part of the city, the Presidio has been a military installation since 1776. When defense budgets shrank at the end of the Cold War, the military turned it over to the National Park Service, making it a historical park in 1994.

The Presidio

While there is plenty of history and architecture here to thrill any military buff, the Presidio's nearly three square miles are also filled with hiking trails, restored wetlands, forests, and foreboding cliffs that offer spectacular views of the Golden Gate and the Marin Headlands.

To orient yourself among the more than 800 buildings that make up the Presidio, start at the visitors center in the beautiful Main Post. You'll also find the **Walt Disney Family Museum** (104 Montgomery St., 415/345-6800, www.waltdisney.org, 10am-6pm Wed.-Mon., adults $20, children 6-17 $15) and George Lucas's **Letterman Digital Arts Center** (Chestnut St. and Lyon St., www.lucasfilm. com), where you can snap a photo with a life-size Yoda statue. More history can be found at **Crissy Field,** which runs along the bay and includes the World War II grass airfield, and Civil War-era fortifications at the breathtaking **Fort Point** (end of Marine Dr., 415/556-1693, www.nps.gov/fopo, 10am-5pm Fri.-Mon.).

TOP EXPERIENCE

★ Golden Gate Bridge

People come from the world over to see and walk the **Golden Gate Bridge** (U.S. 101/Hwy. 1 at Lincoln Blvd., 415/921-5858, http://goldengatebridge.org, southbound cars $7, pedestrians free). A marvel of human engineering constructed in 1936 and 1937, the suspension bridge spans the narrow "gate" from which the Pacific Ocean enters the San Francisco Bay. Pedestrians are allowed on the **east sidewalk** (5am-6:30pm daily Nov.-Apr., 5am-9pm daily Apr.-Oct.). On a clear day, the whole bay, Marin Headlands, and city skyline are visible. Cyclists are allowed on both sidewalks (check the website for times), but as the scenery is stunning, be aware of pedestrians and cyclists not keeping their eyes on where they are going.

CIVIC CENTER AND HAYES VALLEY

The Civic Center functions as the heart of San Francisco. Not only is the seat of government here, but so are venerable high-culture institutions: the War Memorial Opera House and Davies Symphony Hall, home of the world-famous San Francisco Symphony. As the Civic Center melts into Hayes Valley, you'll find fabulous hotels and restaurants serving both the city's politicos and the well-heeled.

the Golden Gate Bridge

City Hall

Look at San Francisco's **City Hall** (1 Dr. Carlton B. Goodlett Pl., 415/554-6079, www.sfgov.org, 8am-8pm Mon.-Fri., free) and you'll think you've somehow been transported to Europe. The stately Beaux-Arts building with the gilded dome is the pride of the city and houses the mayor's office and much of the city's government. Enjoy walking through the parklike square in front of City Hall (though this area can get a bit sketchy after dark). Inside you'll find a combination of historical grandeur and modern accessibility and convenience as you tour the Arthur Brown Jr.-designed edifice.

Asian Art Museum

Across from City Hall is the **Asian Art Museum** (200 Larkin St., 415/581-3500, www.asianart.org, 10am-5pm Tues.-Wed. and Fri.-Sun., 10am-9pm Thurs., adults $15, seniors $10, ages 13-17 $10, children under age 13 free), with enormous Ionic columns. Inside you'll have an amazing window into the Asian cultures that have shaped and defined San Francisco and the Bay Area. The second and third floors of this intense museum are packed with great art from all across Asia, including a Chinese gilded Buddha dating from AD 338. The breadth and diversity of Asian culture may stagger you; the museum's displays come from Japan and Vietnam, Buddhist Tibet, and ancient China. Special exhibitions cost extra—check the website to see what will be displayed on the ground floor galleries when you're in town. The curators regularly rotate items from the permanent collection, so you'll probably encounter new beauty every time you visit.

Alamo Square

At this area's far western edge sits **Alamo Square** (Hayes St. and Steiner St.), possibly the most photographed neighborhood in San Francisco. Among its stately Victorians are the famous **"painted ladies,"** a row of brilliantly painted and immaculately maintained homes. From the lovely Alamo Square Park (Hayes St. and Steiner St.), the ladies provide a picturesque foreground to the perfect view of the Civic Center and the rest of downtown.

MISSION AND CASTRO

Castro is the heart of gay San Francisco, complete with nightlife, festivals, and LGBT community activism. With its mix of Latino immigrants, working artists, and hipsters, the Mission is a neighborhood bursting at the seams with idiosyncratic energy. Changing from block to block, the zone manages to be blue-collar, edgy, and gentrified all at once. While the heart of the neighborhood is still Latin American, with delicious burritos and *pupusas* around every corner, it is also the go-to neighborhood for the new tech economy with luxury condos, pricey boutiques, and international restaurants in a city famous for its food.

Mission Dolores

Mission Dolores (3321 16th St., 415/621-8203, www.missiondolores.org, 9am-4:30pm daily May-Oct., 9am-4pm daily Nov.-Apr., donation adults $5, children $3), formally named Mission San Francisco de Asís, was founded in 1776. Today the mission is the oldest intact building in the city, having survived the 1906 earthquake and fire, the 1989 Loma Prieta quake, and more than 200 years of use. You can attend Roman Catholic services here each Saturday, or you can visit the Old Mission Museum and the Basilica, which house artifacts from the Native Americans and Spanish of the 18th century. The beauty and grandeur of the mission recall the heyday of the Spanish empire in California, so important to the history of the state as it is today.

GOLDEN GATE PARK AND THE HAIGHT

The neighborhood surrounding the intersection of Haight and Ashbury Streets (known locally as "the Haight") is best known for the wave of countercultural energy that broke out in the 1960s. Haight Street terminates at the entrance to San Francisco's gem—Golden Gate Park.

★ Golden Gate Park

Dominating the western half of San Francisco, **Golden Gate Park** (main entrance at Stanyan St. at Fell St., McLaren Lodge Visitors Center at John F. Kennedy Dr., 415/831-2700, www.golden-gate-park.com) is one of the city's most enduring treasures. Its 1,000-plus acres include lakes, forests, formal gardens, windmills, museums, a buffalo pasture, and plenty of activities. Enjoy free concerts in the summer, hike in near solitude in the winter, or spend a day wandering and exploring scores of sights.

DE YOUNG MUSEUM

The **de Young Museum** (50 Hagiwara Tea Garden Dr., 415/750-3600, http://deyoung. famsf.org; 9:30am-5:15pm Tues.-Thurs. and Sat.-Sun., 9:30am-8:45pm Fri., Apr.-Nov.; 9:30am-5:15pm Tues.-Sun., Dec.-Mar.; adults $10, seniors $7, children 13-17 $6, children 12 and under free) is staggering in its size and breadth: You'll see everything from pre-Columbian art to 17th-century ladies' gowns. View paintings, sculpture, textiles, ceramics, "contemporary crafts" from all over the

world, and rotating exhibits that range from King Tut to the exquisite Jean Paul Gaultier collection. Competing with all of that is the building itself.

The museum's modern exterior is wrapped in perforated copper, while the interior incorporates pockets of manicured gardens. Poking out of the park's canopy is a twisted tower that offers a spectacular 360-degree view of the city and the bay. Entrance to the tower, lily pond, and art garden is free. Surrounded by sphinxes and draping wisteria, you can enjoy an art-filled picnic lunch.

CALIFORNIA ACADEMY OF SCIENCES

A triumph of the sustainable scientific principles it exhibits, the **California Academy of Sciences** (55 Music Concourse Dr., 415/379-8000, www.calacademy.org; 9:30am-5pm Mon.-Sat., 11am-5pm Sun.; adults $35; students, seniors, and children 12-17 $30; children 4-11 $25; children 3 and under free) drips with ecological perfection. From the grass-covered roof to the underground **aquarium,** visitors can explore every part of the universe. Wander through a steamy endangered **rainforest** contained inside a giant glass bubble, or travel through an all-digital

Mission Dolores, the oldest intact structure in San Francisco

outer space in the high-tech **planetarium.** More studious nature lovers can spend days examining every inch of the **Natural History Museum,** including favorite exhibits like the 87-foot-long blue whale skeleton. The Academy of Sciences takes pains to make itself kid-friendly, with interactive exhibits, thousands of live animals, and endless opportunities for learning. On **Thursday nights** (6pm-10pm, $12), the academy is an adults-only zone, where DJs play music and the café serves cocktails by some of the city's most renowned mixologists.

JAPANESE TEA GARDEN

The **Japanese Tea Garden** (75 Hagiwara Tea Garden Dr., 415/752-4227, http://japaneseteagardensf.com, 9am-6pm daily Mar.-Oct., 9am-4:45pm daily Nov.-Feb., adults $7, seniors $5, children 5-11 $2, children 4 and under free) is a haven of peace and tranquility that's a local favorite within the park, particularly in the spring. The planting and design of the garden began in 1894 for the California Exposition. Today the flourishing garden displays a wealth of beautiful flora, including stunning examples of rare Chinese and Japanese plants, some quite old. As you stroll along the paths, you'll come upon sculptures, bridges, ponds, and even traditional *tsukubai* (a tea ceremony sink). Take one of the docent-led tours and conclude your visit with tea and a fortune cookie at the tea house.

SAN FRANCISCO BOTANICAL GARDEN

Take a bucolic walk in the middle of Golden Gate Park by visiting the **San Francisco Botanical Garden** (1199 9th Ave. at Lincoln Way, 415/661-1316, www.sfbotanicalgarden.org, 7:30am-6pm daily early Mar.-Sept., 10am-5pm daily Oct.-early Mar., adults $7, students and seniors $5, ages 5-11 $2, families $15, under age 5 and city residents with ID free). The 55-acre gardens play home to more than 8,000 species of plants from around the world, including a California Natives garden and a shady redwood forest. Fountains, ponds, meadows, and lawns are interwoven with the flowers and trees to create a peaceful, serene setting in the middle of the crowded city.

CONSERVATORY OF FLOWERS

For a trip to San Francisco's Victorian past, step inside the steamy **Conservatory of Flowers** (100 John F. Kennedy Dr., 415/831-2090, www.conservatoryofflowers.org, 10am-4:30pm Tues.-Sun., adults $8, students

the de Young Museum

Golden Gate Park

and seniors $5, ages 5-11 $2, children under 5 free). Built in 1878, the striking wood and glass greenhouse is home to more than 1,700 plant species that spill out of containers, twine around rainforest trees, climb trellises reaching the roof, and rim deep ponds where eight-foot lily pads float serenely on still waters. Surrounded by the exotic flora illuminated only by natural light, it's easy to transport yourself to the heyday of colonialism when the study of botany was in its first bloom. Plus, it's one of the best places to explore on a rainy day.

Strollers are not permitted inside; wheelchairs and power chairs are allowed.

The Legion of Honor

A beautiful museum in a town filled with beauty, **The Legion of Honor** (100 34th Ave. at Clement St., 415/750-3600, http://legionofhonor.famsf.org, 9:30am-5:15pm Tues.-Sun., adults $10, seniors $7, students and ages 13-17 $6, 12 and under free) sits on its lonely promontory in Lincoln Park, overlooking the Golden Gate. A gift to the city from

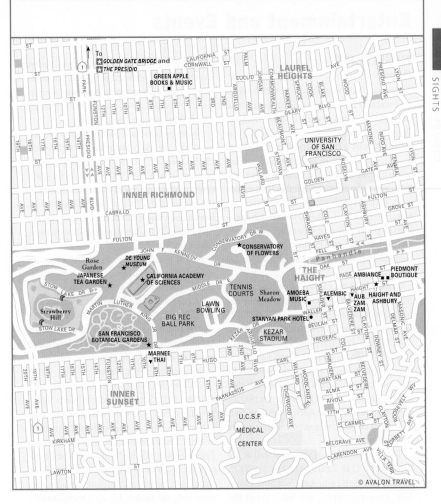

philanthropist Alma Spreckels in 1924, this French Beaux-Arts-style building was built to honor the memory of California soldiers who died in World War I. From its beginning, the Legion of Honor was a museum dedicated to bringing European art to the population of San Francisco. Today visitors can view gorgeous collections of European paintings, sculpture, decorative arts, ancient artifacts from around the Mediterranean, thousands of paper drawings by great artists, and much more. Special exhibitions come from the Legion's own collections and museums of the world.

Entertainment and Events

NIGHTLIFE

Bars

The ritzy Union Square and Nob Hill neighborhoods are better known for shopping than for nightlife, but a few upscale bars hang in there. Some inhabit major hotels, like the **Tonga Room & Hurricane Bar** (950 Mason St., 415/772-5278, www.tongaroom.com, 6pm-10pm Sun. and Wed.-Thurs., 6pm-11pm Fri.-Sat.), where an over-the-top tiki theme adds a whimsical touch to the stately Fairmont Hotel on Nob Hill. The 1940s-era lounge—with its fruity rum drinks served in coconuts, its "rainstorms," and its floating stage—is so beloved that it was designated a historical landmark.

Since World War II, the views and drinks from the **Top of the Mark** (InterContinental Mark Hopkins, 999 California St., 415/392-3434, www.intercontinentalmarkhopkins.com, 4:30pm-11:30pm Mon.-Thurs., 4:30pm-12:30am Fri.-Sat., 5pm-11:30pm Sun.) have drawn visitors from around the world. The cocktail lounge doubles as a restaurant that serves light dinners, while live bands play almost every night of the week. The dress code is business casual and is enforced, so leave the jeans at home.

The cocktail craze is alive and well at the **Rickhouse** (246 Kearny St., 415/398-2827, www.rickhousesf.com, 5pm-2am Mon., 3pm-2am Tues.-Fri., 6pm-2am Sat.). What Rickhouse truly specializes in are cocktails made from long-forgotten spirits and fresh ingredients. Grab a seat upstairs or down in the all-wood bar, and sample a Rye Maple Fizz or go in on a massive rum punch, served in a hollow clamshell. Get here before the after-work crowd or you may not get in at all.

The **House of Shields** (39 New Montgomery St., 415/284-9958, www.thehouseofshields.com, 2pm-2am Mon.-Fri., 3pm-2am Sat.-Sun.) has been in the city since 1908. The original incarnation was an illegal speakeasy during the Prohibition era. Today, the House of Shields serves upscale cocktails (with upscale prices) in its gorgeous interior. Expect a huge crowd during happy hour, which thins out after 8pm or so.

Secret passwords, a hidden library, and an art deco vibe make **Bourbon and Branch** (505 Jones St., 415/346-1735, www.bourbonandbranch.com, 6pm-2am Mon.-Sat., reservations suggested) a must for lovers of the brown stuff. Tucked behind a nameless brown door, this resurrected 1920s-era speakeasy evokes its Prohibition-era past with passwords and secret passages.

North Beach is famous for its watering holes, but perhaps its most iconic is **Vesuvio** (255 Columbus Ave., 415/362-3370, www.vesuvio.com, 6am-2am daily) for the simple reason that Jack Kerouac loved it. Not much has changed since then, except its jukebox, which has only gotten better. This cozy bi-level hideout is an easy place to spend the afternoon with a pint of Anchor Steam.

Walking into **Tosca** (242 Columbus Ave., 415/986-9651, http://toscacafesf.com, 5pm-2am Tues.-Sun., $16-42) is a step back in time to North Beach at its most romantic. Founded in 1919, Tosca spent much of its life as a bar. Take a seat at the bar and order the house cappuccino, a decadent concoction made of Armagnac, bourbon, chocolate ganache, and absolutely no coffee. It's also a restaurant, which *Bon Appétit* rated as the fourth-best new restaurant in 2014.

Comstock Saloon (155 Columbus Ave., 415/617-0071, www.comstocksaloon.com, noon-2am Mon.-Fri., 4pm-2am Sat., 4pm-midnight Sun.) salutes San Francisco's retro-fresh craze, with a cocktail menu that works to recall the city's early days. The heavy, ornate bar and a meat-and-potatoes menu conjure the 1860s, somehow making it feel modern and relevant.

Hayes Valley bleeds into Lower Haight

(Haight St. between Divisadero St. and Octavia Blvd.) and supplies most of the neighborhood bars. For proof that the independent spirit of the Haight lives on, have a drink at the **Toronado** (547 Haight St., 415/863-2276, www.toronado.com, 11:30am-2am daily). This dimly lit haven maintains one of the finest beer selections in the nation, with a changing roster of several dozen microbrews on tap, including many hard-to-find Belgian ales.

Channeling a shipwreck in the middle of the Caribbean, the hipster **Smuggler's Cove** (650 Gough St., 415/869-1900, http://smugglerscovesf.com, 5pm-1:15am daily) has been named one of America's best bars by *Esquire, Times of London, Food & Wine* magazine, and *Playboy*. The cocktail menu reads like an index of rum drinks from the heyday of tiki bars, many using fire as a key ingredient.

Dalva (3121 16th St., 415/252-7740, http://dalvasf.com, 4pm-2am daily) is a small but sophisticated oasis in an ocean of overcrowded Mission hipster hangouts. You'll find dramatic high ceilings, modern paintings, and a jukebox stuffed with indie rock and electronica. Way back in the depths of the club, the Hideaway bar serves up a delectable array of cocktails poured by a rotating staff of local celebrity mixologists.

Excellent draft beers, tasty barbecue plates, and a motorcycle-inclined crowd give **Zeitgeist** (199 Valencia St., 415/255-7505, http://zeitgeistsf.com, 9am-2am daily) a punk-rock edge. This Mission favorite endears itself to all sorts, thanks to its spacious outdoor beer garden and Friday barbecues.

Blackbird (2124 Market St., 415/503-0630, www.blackbirdbar.com, 3pm-2am Mon.-Fri., 2pm-2am Sat.-Sun.) draws a mixed crowd to its location on upper Market Street. The specialty here is cocktails that are mixed and then aged in either oak or bourbon barrels for up to two months. There are also carbonated cocktails on tap and an utterly unusual list of drinks utilizing herbs found in kitchen gardens a hundred years ago.

Haight Street crowds head out in droves to the **Alembic** (1725 Haight St., 415/666-0822, www.alembicbar.com, 4pm-2am Mon.-Fri., noon-2am Sat.-Sun.) for artisanal cocktails laced with American spirits. On par with the whiskey and bourbon menu is the cuisine: Wash down beef-tongue sliders with a Sazerac.

Club Deluxe (1511 Haight St., 415/552-6949, www.clubdeluxe.co, 4pm-2am Tues.-Sun.) is the perfect place to discover your inner Sinatra. Pull up a stool at this dark retro-style bar and order something classic while listening to live jazz or watching burlesque. A pizza menu gives patrons something to buffer those strong drinks.

Clubs

Ruby Skye (420 Mason St., 415/693-0777, www.rubyskye.com, 9pm-2am Thurs.-Sat., cover $15-60, dress code enforced) books top DJs and occasional live acts into a large, packed dance club. Crowds can get big on weekends, and the patrons tend to be young and pretty and looking for action. The sound system rocks, so conversation isn't happening, and the drinks tend toward overpriced vodka and Red Bull.

Harry Denton's Starlight Room (450 Powell St., 21st Fl., 415/395-8595, www.harrydenton.com, 6pm-2am Tues.-Sat., cover up to $15) brings the flamboyant side of San Francisco downtown. Enjoy a cocktail in the early evening or a nightcap and a bite of dessert after the theater in this truly old-school nightclub.

111 Minna Street Gallery (111 Minna St., 415/974-1719, www.111minnagallery.com, club hours and cover charge vary) really is an art gallery, but it's also one of the hottest dance clubs. After 5pm on event nights, the gallery transforms into a nightclub, opening the full bar and bringing in DJs who spin late into the weekend nights.

It's dark, it's dank, and it's very, very Goth. The **Cat Club** (1190 Folsom St., 415/703-8965, www.sfcatclub.com, 9pm-3am Tues.-Sun., cover $6-10) gets pretty energetic on '80s dance nights. You'll find a friendly crowd, decent bartenders, strong drinks, and easy access to smoking areas. Each of the two rooms has its own DJ, which somehow works perfectly even though they're only a wall apart from each other.

Looking for *the* DJs and dance parties? Head to the **DNA Lounge** (375 11th St., 415/626-1409, www.dnalounge.com, 9pm-5am daily, cover varies), with Bootie twice a month, '80s parties, and live music, and a 24-7 pizza joint next door. It's also one of the few clubs that's open after hours.

The **Rickshaw Stop** (155 Fell St., 415/861-2011, www.rickshawstop.com, hours vary, cover $7-25) in the Hayes Valley neighborhood welcomes one and all with a cavernous lower bar, stage area and dance floor, and a quirky balcony area complete with comfy old sofas.

Gay and Lesbian

Since 1973, **The EndUp** (401 6th St., 415/646-0999, www.theendup.com, 11pm-8am Fri., 10pm-8am Sat., 1pm-2am Sun., cover varies) has been where late-night revelers have, well, ended up. The mixed crowd dances to hip-hop and house music and parties until dawn. The venue also hosts Sundaze, an outdoor hip-hop party starting at 1pm.

The **Lookout** (3600 16th St., 415/431-0306, www.lookoutsf.com, 3:30pm-2am Mon.-Fri., 12:30pm-2am Sat.-Sun., cover up to $10) gets its name and much of its rep from its balcony overlooking the iconic Castro neighborhood. Get up there for some primo people-watching as you sip your industrial-strength alcoholic concoctions and nibble on surprisingly edible bar snacks and pizza.

Live Music

Opened in the late 1960s, **The Fillmore** (1805 Geary Blvd., 415/346-3000, www.thefillmore.com) ignited the careers of such legends as Santana and the Grateful Dead. Major acts still pass through here, and the Fillmore remains a local favorite of music lovers for its balcony seating, comfortable bar, and intimate stage setting.

The **Great American Music Hall** (859 O'Farrell St., 415/885-0750, www.slimspresents.com) is the other top small venue in San Francisco. It too has great acts, casual balcony seating, a small stage, ample bars, and ornate architectural detailing. In fact, the Great American is the oldest nightclub in the city and, like the Fillmore, located in a dodgy neighborhood, but is well worth the effort.

Started by rock veteran Boz Scaggs in 1988, **Slim's** (333 11th St., 415/255-0333, www.slims-sf.com) has filled the alternative pop niche in the city. Dinner tickets are the only way to score an actual seat, and when it's crowded, it can be difficult to see the small stage.

The beautiful and ornate **Warfield** (982 Market St., 415/345-0900, http://thewarfield-theatre.com) books all sorts of acts, from Bill Maher to alternative rock. Choose from limited table seating on the lowest level (mostly by reservation), reserved seats in the balconies, or open standing in the orchestra below the stage.

Bimbo's 365 Club (1025 Columbus Ave., 415/474-0365, www.bimbos365club.com) retains its reputation as a favorite venue for locals. Today major accessible acts such as Chris Isaak and the Brian Setzer Orchestra play here. The club itself, with its slightly tarnished midcentury vibe, remains a beloved elder statesman with a heavy following.

The **Boom Boom Room** (1601 Fillmore St., 415/673-8040, www.boomboomblues.com, 7pm-2am Mon., 4pm-2am Tues.-Sun.) has kept it real in the Fillmore for more than two decades. Today you'll find the latest in a legacy of live blues, boogie, groove, soul, and funk music in this fun, divvy joint.

On the other side of town, **Biscuits and Blues** (401 Mason St., 415/292-2583, www.biscuitsandblues.com, hours and days vary) is a local musicians' favorite. Headliners have included Joe Louis Walker, Jimmy Thackery, and Jim Kimo. Dinner is served nightly and features a surprisingly varied and upscale menu.

Bringing jazz to the high culture of Hayes Valley is **SFJazz Center** (201 Franklin St.,

866/920-5299, http://sfjazz.org, hours vary Tues.-Sun.), a stunning 35,000-square-foot space with state-of-the-art acoustics. It's designed to feel like a small club, thanks to steep seating that brings the large audience close to the performers, and has drawn major acts such as Herbie Hancock and the Afro-Cuban All Stars.

Comedy

San Francisco's oldest comedy club, the **Punch Line** (444 Battery St., 415/397-7573, www.punchlinecomedyclub.com, shows 8pm and 10pm Tues.-Sun., cover varies) is an elegant and intimate venue that earned its top-notch reputation with stellar headliners such as Robin Williams, Ellen DeGeneres, and Dave Chappelle. An on-site bar keeps the audience primed.

Cobb's Comedy Club (915 Columbus Ave., 415/928-4320, www.cobbscomedy.com, shows 8pm and 10:15pm Thurs.-Sun., cover varies, two-drink minimum) has played host to star comedians such as Louis CK, Sarah Silverman, and Margaret Cho since 1982. The 425-seat venue offers a full dinner menu and a bar to slake your thirst. Be sure to check your show's start time—some comics don't follow the usual Cobb's schedule.

THE ARTS
Theater

San Francisco may not be known as a big theater town, but it does boast a number of small and large theaters. A great way to grab last-minute theater tickets (or for music or dance shows) is to walk right up to **Union Square TIX** (Union Square, 415/433-7827, www.tix-bayarea.com, 10am-6pm daily) for same-day, half-price, no-refund tickets to all kinds of shows across the city. TIX also sells half-price tickets to same-day shows online—check the website at 11am daily for up-to-date deals. If you really, really need to see a major musical while you're in San Francisco, check out the three venues where big Broadway productions land when they come to town: the Orpheum and Golden Gate Theatres (www.

shnsf.com), and the Curran Theatre (www.sfcurran.com).

Just up from Union Square, the traditional San Francisco theater district continues to entertain crowds. The **American Conservatory Theater** (A.C.T., 415 Geary St., 415/749-2228, www.act-sf.org, shows Tues.-Sun., $22-82) puts on a season filled with big-name, big-budget productions, such as high-production-value musicals, American classics by the likes of Sam Shepard and Somerset Maugham, and intriguing new works. Discount parking is available with a ticket stub from A.C.T. at the Mason-O'Farrell garage around the corner.

The **Curran Theatre** (445 Geary St., 888/746-1799, www.sfcurran.com, $105-250), next door to A.C.T., has a state-of-the-art stage for classic, high-budget musicals, such as *Les Misérables, Phantom of the Opera,* and *Chicago.* Expect to pay a premium for tickets to these productions, which can sometimes run for months or even years. Check the schedule for current shows.

There's one live show that's always different, yet it's been running continuously since 1974. It's *Beach Blanket Babylon* (678 Green St., 415/421-4222, www.beachblanketbabylon.com, shows Wed.-Sun., $25-100), which mocks pop culture and continuously evolves to take advantage of tabloid treasures. Although minors are welcome at the Sunday matinees, evening shows are restricted to attendees 21 and over.

Located in seedy Mid-Market area, both the **Orpheum Theatre** (1192 Market St., 888/746-1799, www.shnsf.com, $50-200) and the **Golden Gate Theatre** (1 Taylor St., 888/746-1799, www.shnsf.com, $50-200) run touring productions of popular Broadway musicals.

Classical Music and Opera

Right around the Civic Center, culture takes a turn for the upscale. This is the neighborhood where the ultrarich and not-so-rich classics lovers come to enjoy a night out. Acoustically renovated in 1992, **Davies Symphony Hall**

(201 Van Ness Ave., 415/864-6000, www.sf-symphony.org) is home to Michael Tilson Thomas's world-renowned San Francisco Symphony. Loyal patrons flock to performances that range from the classic to the avant-garde. Whether you want to hear Mozart and Mahler or classic rock blended with major symphony orchestra, the San Francisco Symphony does it.

The **War Memorial Opera House** (301 Van Ness Ave., 415/621-6600, www.sfwmpac.org), a Beaux-Arts-style building designed by Coit Tower and City Hall architect Arthur Brown Jr., houses the **San Francisco Opera** (415/864-3330, http://sfopera.com) and **San Francisco Ballet** (415/861-5600, www.sf-ballet.org). Tours are available (415/552-8338, 10am-2pm Mon., $5-7).

Cinema

The **Castro Theatre** (429 Castro St., 415/621-6120, www.castrotheatre.com, $8.50-11) is a grand movie palace from the 1920s that has enchanted San Francisco audiences for almost a century. The Castro Theatre hosts everything from revival double features (from black-and-white through 1980s classics) to musical movie sing-alongs, live shows, and even the occasional book signing. The Castro also screens current releases and documentaries about queer life in San Francisco and beyond. Once inside, be sure to admire the lavish interior decor. If you get to your seat early, you're likely to be rewarded with a performance of the Mighty Wurlitzer pipe organ before the show.

For a more modern and upscale moviegoing experience, go to the **Sundance Kabuki** (1881 Post St., www.sundancecinemas.com/kabuki.html, $9.75-15.50). The "amenity fee" pays for reserved seating, film shorts rather than commercials, and bamboo decor. The Kabuki has eight screens, all of which show mostly big blockbuster Hollywood films, plus a smattering of independents and the occasional filmed opera performance. The Over 21 shows are in the two theaters connected to full bars.

the ornate Castro Theatre

FESTIVALS AND EVENTS

San Francisco is host to numerous events year-round. Following are some of the biggest that are worth planning a trip around.

During the **Chinese New Year Parade** (Chinatown, www.chineseparade.com, Feb.), Chinatown celebrates the lunar new year with a parade of costumed dancers, floats, and firecrackers.

Join rowdy, costumed revelers for **Bay to Breakers** (Embarcadero to Great Highway, www.baytobreakers.com, May), a 12K run/walk/stumble across the city through Golden Gate Park to a massive street party at Ocean Beach.

One of the year's biggest parades is the **San Francisco LGBT Pride Parade and Celebration** (Market St., www.sfpride.org, June). Hundreds of thousands of people of all orientations take to the streets for this quintessentially San Franciscan party-cum-social justice movement.

Golden Gate Park is host to two wildly

popular summer music festivals. **Outside Lands** (www.sfoutsidelands.com, Aug.) is a three-day music festival that floods the park with revelers, food trucks, and hundreds of bands. Headliners have included Radiohead, LCD Soundsystem, Kanye West, Metallica, Neil Young, and Elton John. The park barely recovers in time for **Hardly Strictly Bluegrass** (www.hardlystrictlybluegrass. com, late Sept. or early Oct.), a free music festival celebrating a wide variety of bluegrass sounds, from Lucinda Williams and Emmylou Harris to Ryan Adams and Yo La Tengo.

Shopping

UNION SQUARE

For the biggest variety of department stores and high-end international designers, plus a few select boutiques, locals and visitors alike flock to **Union Square** (bounded by Geary St., Stockton St., Post St., and Powell St.). The shopping area includes more than just the square proper: More designer and brand-name stores cluster for several blocks in all directions.

The big guys anchor Union Square. **Macy's** (170 O'Farrell St., 415/397-3333, www.macys.com, 10am-9pm Mon.-Sat., 11am-8pm Sun.) has two immense locations, one for women's clothing and another for the men's store and housewares. **Neiman Marcus** (150 Stockton St., 415/362-3900, www.neimanmarcus.com, 10am-7pm Mon.-Wed. and Fri.-Sat., 10am-8pm Thurs., noon-6pm Sun.) is a favorite among high-budget shoppers, and **Saks Fifth Avenue** (384 Post St., 415/986-4300, www.saksfifthavenue.com, 10am-7pm Mon.-Sat., 11am-7pm Sun.) adds a touch of New York style to funky-but-wealthy San Francisco.

Levi's (815 Market St., 415/501-0100, www.levi.com, 9am-9pm Mon.-Sat., 10am-8pm Sun.) may be a household name, but this three-floor fashion emporium offers incredible customization services while featuring new music and emerging art. Levi's got its start outfitting gold miners in 1849, so it's literally a San Francisco tradition.

The bones of fashion can be found at **Britex Fabrics** (146 Geary St., 415/392-2910, www.britexfabrics.com, 10am-6pm Mon.-Sat.), which draws designers, quilters, DIYers, and costume geeks from all over the Bay Area to its legendary monument to fabric. If you're into any sort of textile crafting, a visit to Britex has the qualities of a religious experience. All four floors are crammed floor to ceiling with bolts of fabric, swaths of lace, and rolls of ribbon. From $1-per-yard grosgrain ribbons to $95-per-yard French silk jacquard and $125-per-yard Italian wool coating, Britex has it all.

NORTH BEACH

One of the most famous independent bookshops in a city known for its literary bent is **City Lights** (261 Columbus Ave., 415/362-8193, www.citylights.com, 10am-midnight daily). It opened in 1953 as an all-paperback bookstore with a decidedly Beat aesthetic, focused on selling modern literary fiction and progressive political tomes. As the Beats flocked to San Francisco and to City Lights, the shop put on another hat—that of publisher. Allen Ginsberg's *Howl* was published by the erstwhile independent, which never looked back. Today City Lights continues to sell and publish the best of cutting-edge fiction and nonfiction. The store is still in its original location on the point of Columbus Avenue, though it's expanded somewhat since the '50s. Expect to find your favorite genre paperbacks along with the latest intriguing new works. The nonfiction selections can really make you take a step back and think about your world in a new way, which is just what founder Lawrence Ferlinghetti wanted.

MARINA AND PACIFIC HEIGHTS

The shopping is good in the tony Marina and its elegant neighbor Pacific Heights. **Chestnut and Union Streets** cater to the Marina's young and affluent residents with plenty of clothing boutiques and makeup outlets. Make a stop at **Books Inc.** (2251 Chestnut St., 415/931-3633, www.booksinc. net, 9am-10pm Mon.-Sat., 9am-9pm Sun.), one of the best bookstores in the city. You'll find everything from fiction to travel, as well as a great selection of magazines.

Fillmore Street is the other major shopping corridor. It's funkier than its younger neighbors in the Marina, probably because of its proximity to Japantown and the Fillmore. You'll still find fancy threads and accessories at places like **Marc by Marc Jacobs** (2141 Fillmore St., 415/447-9322, www.marcjacobs. com, 11am-7pm daily) and plenty to brighten up your home at the pricey **Jonathan Adler** (2133 Fillmore St., 415/563-9500, www.jonathanadler.com, 10am-7pm Mon.-Sat., 11am-5pm Sun.).

HAYES VALLEY

In Hayes Valley, adjacent to the Civic Center, shopping goes uptown, but the unique scent of counterculture creativity still permeates. This is a fun neighborhood to get your stroll on, checking out the art galleries and peeking into the boutiques for clothing and upscale housewares, and then stopping at one of the lovely cafés for a restorative bite to eat.

Ver Unica (437B Hayes St. and 526 Hayes St., 415/431-0688, www.verunicasf.com, 11am-7pm Mon.-Sat., noon-6pm Sun.) is a vintage boutique that attracts locals and celebrities with high-quality men's and women's clothing and accessories dating from the 1920s to the 1980s, along with a small selection of new apparel by up-and-coming designers.

Paolo Iantorno's boutique **Paolo Shoes** (524 Hayes St., 415/552-4580, http://paoloshoes.com, 11am-7pm Mon.-Sat., 11am-6pm Sun.) showcases his collection of handcrafted shoes, for which all leather and textiles are conscientiously selected and then inspected to ensure top quality.

You can hardly walk 10 feet without passing a sweet shop selling macarons. The original is **Miette** (449 Octavia St., 415/626-6221, www.miette.com, 11am-7pm daily), a cheery European-inspired candy shop, sister store to the Ferry Plaza bakery (415/837-0300). From double-salted licorice to handmade English

City Lights

toffee, the quality confections include imports from England, Italy, and France.

MISSION

In a city known for its quirky style, the Mission was the last neighborhood with a funky, easy-on-the-wallet shopping district. Sadly, the days are gone when you could buy cool vintage clothes by the pound, but **Valencia Street** is still the most vibrant and diverse neighborhood for shoppers in the city.

The **Bell Jar** (3187 16th St., 415/626-1749, https://belljarsf.com, noon-7pm Mon.-Sat., noon-6pm Sun.) has everything you need to make you and your home into stylish trend-setters of the 21st century, from dresses and jewelry to art books and soaps. A bit more extreme is **Five and Diamond** (510 Valencia St., 415/255-9747, www.fiveanddiamond.com, noon-8pm Mon.-Thurs., 11am-9pm Fri.-Sat., 11am-7pm Sun.). Inside this unique space, you'll find off-the-wall art, unusual clothing, and downright scary jewelry. Those who make an appointment in advance can also get a tattoo here, or purchase some keen body jewelry. A trip inside Five and Diamond can be an exciting adventure for the bold, but might be a bit much for the faint of heart. Decide for yourself whether you dare to take the plunge.

Author Dave Eggers's tongue-in-cheek storefront at **826 Valencia** (826 Valencia St., 415/642-5905, www.826valencia.org, noon-6pm daily) doubles as a pirate supply shop and youth literacy center. While you'll find plenty of pirate booty, you'll also find a good stock of literary magazines and books. Almost next door, **Paxton Gate** (824 Valencia St., 415/824-1872, www.paxtongate.com, 11am-7pm Sun.-Wed., 11am-8pm Thurs.-Sat.) takes the typical gift shop to a new level with taxidermy. This quirky spot is surprisingly cheery, with garden supplies, books, and candles filling the cases in addition to the fossilized creatures.

HAIGHT-ASHBURY

The **Haight-Ashbury shopping district** isn't what it used to be, but if you're willing to poke around a bit, you can still find a few bargains in the remaining thrift shops. One relic of the 1960s counterculture still thrives on the Haight: head shops. However, all pipes, water pipes, and other paraphernalia are strictly for use in smoking tobacco.

Music has always been a part of the Haight. To this day you'll find homeless folks pounding out rhythms on *doumbeks* and congas on the sidewalks and on Hippy Hill in the park.

colorful Victorian architecture in Haight-Ashbury

Located in an old bowling alley, **Amoeba** (1855 Haight St., 415/831-1200, www.amoeba. com, 11am-8pm daily) is a larger-than-life record store that promotes every type of music imaginable. Amoeba's staff, many of whom are musicians themselves, are among the most knowledgeable in the business.

The award-winning **Booksmith** (1644 Haight St., 800/493-7323, www.booksmith. com, 10am-10pm Mon.-Sat., 10am-8pm Sun.) boasts a helpful and informed staff, a fabulous magazine collection, and Northern California's preeminent calendar of readings by internationally renowned authors.

Originally a vaudeville theater, the capacious **Wasteland** (1660 Haight St., 415/863-3150, www.shopwasteland.com, 11am-8pm Mon.-Sat., noon-7pm Sun.) has a traffic-stopping art nouveau facade, a distinctive assortment of vintage hippie and rock-star threads, and a glamour-punk staff.

Make for the glam at **Piedmont Boutique** (1452 Haight St., 415/864-8075, www.piedmontsf.com, 11am-7pm daily). The narrow store is a riot of color, filled with feather boas, sequined shorts, fantastic wigs—and those who wear them. This is where San Francisco's drag queens shop.

Sports and Recreation

BEACHES
Ocean Beach

San Francisco boasts of being a city that has everything, and it certainly comes close. This massive urban wonderland even claims several genuine sand beaches within its city limits. No doubt the biggest and most famous of these is **Ocean Beach** (Great Hwy., parking at Sloat Blvd., Golden Gate Park, and the Cliff House, www.parksconservancy.org). This four-mile stretch of sand forms the breakwater for the Pacific Ocean along the whole west side of the city. Because it's so large, you're likely to find a spot to sit down and maybe even a parking place along the beach, except perhaps on that rarest of occasions in San Francisco—a sunny, warm day. Don't go out for an ocean swim at Ocean Beach: Extremely dangerous rip currents cause fatalities every year.

Aquatic Park

The beach at **Aquatic Park** (Beach St. and Hyde St., www.nps.gov/safr) sits at the west end of the Fisherman's Wharf tourist area. This makes Aquatic Park incredibly convenient for visitors who want to grab a picnic on the wharf to enjoy down on the beach. It was built in the late 1930s as a bathhouse catering to wealthy San Franciscans, and today, swimming remains one of Aquatic Park's main attractions: Triathletes and hard-core swimmers brave the frigid waters to swim for miles in the protected cove. More sedate visitors can find a seat and enjoy a cup of coffee, a newspaper, and some people-watching.

Baker Beach

Baker Beach (Golden Gate Point and the Presidio, www.parksconservancy.org) is best known for its scenery, and that doesn't just mean the lovely views of the Golden Gate Bridge. Baker is San Francisco's own clothing-optional (that is, nude) beach. But don't worry, plenty of the denizens of Baker Beach wear clothes while flying kites, playing volleyball and Frisbee, and even just strolling on the beach. Because Baker is much smaller than Ocean Beach, it gets crowded in the summer. Whether you choose to sunbathe nude or not, don't try to swim here. The currents get seriously strong and dangerous because it's so close to the Golden Gate.

PARKS
Golden Gate Park

The largest park in San Francisco is **Golden Gate Park** (main entrance at Stanyan St.

and Fell St., McLaren Lodge Visitors Center at John F. Kennedy Dr., 415/831-2700, www. golden-gate-park.com). In addition to housing popular sights like the **Academy of Sciences,** the **de Young,** and the **Japanese Tea Garden,** Golden Gate Park is San Francisco's unofficial playground. There are three botanical gardens, a **children's playground** (Martin Luther King Jr. Dr. and Bowling Green Dr.), tennis courts, and a golf course. **Stow Lake** (415/386-2531, http:// stowlakeboathouse.com, 10am-5pm Mon.- Thurs., 10am-6pm Fri.-Sun., $20-34 per hour) offers paddleboats for rent, and the park even has its own bison paddock. Weekends find the park filled with locals inline skating, biking, hiking, and even Lindy Hopping. John F. Kennedy Drive east of Transverse Drive is closed to motorists every Saturday from April through September and Sunday year-round for pedestrian-friendly fun.

Crissy Field

Crissy Field (Marina Blvd. and Baker St., 415/561-4700, www.parksconservancy.org), with its beaches, restored wetlands, and wide promenade, is the playground of the **Presidio** (415/561-4323, www.nps.gov/prsf, free). It's part of the Golden Gate National Recreation Area and is dedicated to environmental education. At the **Crissy Field Center** (1199 E. Beach, 415/561-7690, 9am-5pm daily), you'll find a list of classes, seminars, and fun hands-on activities for all ages. Many of these include walks out into the marsh and the Presidio.

Lands End

The **Lands End Trail** (Merrie Way, 415/561-4700, www.nps.gov/goga) is part of the Golden Gate National Recreation Area. Rising above rugged cliffs and beaches, Lands End feels wild, but the three-mile trail, which runs from El Camino Del Mar near the Legion of Honor to the ruins of the Sutro Baths, is perfect for any hiking enthusiast. For a longer adventure, there are plenty of auxiliary trails to explore that lead down to little beaches. Be sure to look out for the remains of three shipwrecks on the rocks of Point Lobos at low tide. Grab a cup of hot chocolate at the stunning **Lands End Lookout visitor center** (680 Point Lobos Ave., 415/426-5240, www. parksconservancy.org, 9am-5pm daily) when your hike is finished.

Mission Dolores Park

If you're looking for a park where the most strenuous activity is people-watching, then head to **Mission Dolores Park** (Dolores St. and 19th St., 415/554-9521, http://sfrecpark. org). Usually called Dolores Park, it's a favorite of Castro and Mission District denizens. Bring a beach blanket to sprawl on the lawn and a picnic lunch supplied by one of the excellent nearby eateries. On weekends, music festivals and cultural events often spring up at Dolores Park.

BIKING

In other places, bicycling is a sport or a mode of transportation. In San Francisco, bicycling is a religion. Some might say that the high church of this religion is the **San Francisco Bike Coalition** (415/431-2453, www.sfbike. org). In addition to providing workshops and hosting events, the Bike Coalition is an excellent resource for anyone who wants to cycle through the city. Check out its website for tips, maps, and rules of the road.

As a newcomer to biking in the city, it may be wise to start off gently, perhaps with a guided tour that avoids areas with dangerous traffic. **Blazing Saddles** (2715 Hyde St., 415/202-8888, www.blazingsaddles.com, $8-15/hour) rents bikes and offers tips on where to go. If you prefer the safety of a group, take the guided tour (10am daily, three hours, adult $55, child $35, reservations required) through San Francisco and across the Golden Gate Bridge into Marin County. With five locations, most in the Fisherman's Wharf area, it's easy to find yourself a cruiser. One of the most popular treks is the easy and flat nine-mile ride across the **Golden Gate Bridge** and back. This is a great way to see the bridge and the bay for the first time, and it takes only an hour or two to complete. Another option is to ride across the bridge and into the town of Sausalito (8 miles) or Tiburon (16 miles), enjoy an afternoon and dinner, and then ride the ferry back into the city (bikes are allowed on board).

Another easy and low-stress option is the paved paths of **Golden Gate Park** (main entrance at Stanyan St. and Fell St., McLaren Lodge Visitors Center at John F. Kennedy Dr., 415/831-2700, www.golden-gate-park.com) and the **Presidio** (Montgomery St. and Lincoln Blvd., 415/561-4323, www.nps.gov/prsf). A bike makes a perfect mode of transportation to explore the various museums and attractions of these two large parks, and you can spend all day and never have to worry about finding parking. At the entrance of Golden Gate Park, **Golden Gate Tours & Bike Rentals** (1816 Haight St., 415/922-4537, www.goldengateparkbikerental.com, 9:30am-6:30pm daily, $7-9/hour, $30-36/day) has a kiosk. Another choice is **Golden Gate Park Bike and Skate** (3038 Fulton St., 415/668-1117, http://goldengateparkbikeandskate.com; 10am-6pm Mon.-Fri., 10am-7pm Sat.-Sun., summer; 10am-5pm Mon.-Fri., 10am-6pm Sat.-Sun., winter; bike rental $5/hour, $25/day) located just north of the park on Fulton near the de Young Museum.

WHALE-WATCHING

With day-trip access to the marine sanctuary off the Farallon Islands, whale-watching is a year-round activity in San Francisco. **San Francisco Whale Tours** (Pier 39, Dock B, 888/235-6450 or 415/448/7570, www.sanfranciscowhaletours.com, tours daily, $60-89, advance purchase required) offers six-hour trips out to the Farallons almost every Saturday and Sunday, with almost-guaranteed whale sightings on each trip. Shorter whale-watching trips along the coastline run on weekdays, and 90-minute quickie trips out to see slightly smaller local wildlife, including elephant seals and sea lions, also go out daily. Children ages 3-15 are welcome on boat tours (for reduced rates), and kids often love the chance to spot whales, sea lions, and pelicans. Children under age three are not permitted for safety reasons.

SPECTATOR SPORTS

Since 2000, baseball's **San Francisco Giants** have called the beautiful **AT&T Park** (24 Willie Mays Plaza, 3rd St. and King St., 415/972-2000) home, where the food and the views woo even non-baseball fans. Giants games take place March-September. As the Giants continue to win championships, tickets have gotten harder to come by, not to mention more expensive. Still, it's not impossible to snag last-minute tickets to a regular season game.

The NFL's **San Francisco 49ers** have moved into a shiny new stadium in Santa Clara, an hour away from the city where they dominated the NFL through the 1980s and 1990s.

Food

UNION SQUARE AND DOWNTOWN
Bakeries and Cafés
Blue Bottle Café (66 Mint Plaza, 415/495-3394, www.bluebottlecoffee.net, daily 7am-7pm, $5-10) is a popular local chain with multiple locations around the city. The Mint Plaza location is Blue Bottle's only café with a full food menu. Other locations include the Ferry Building (1 Ferry Bldg., Ste. 7), the Heath Ceramics Factory (2900 18th St.), and a Hayes Valley kiosk (315 Linden St.). Expect a line.

Café de la Presse (352 Grant Ave., 415/398-2680, www.cafedelapresse.com, 7:30am-9:30pm Mon.-Thurs., 7:30am-10pm

Best Restaurants

★ **Brenda's French Soul Food:** Start the day with a hearty New Orleans-style breakfast, like crawfish beignets, at this Tenderloin eatery (page 67).

★ **Café Claude:** This authentic brasserie feels like it's been transported from Paris (page 68).

★ **Michael Mina:** The celebrity chef dishes out upscale cuisine, including a Maine lobster pot pie, at his namesake restaurant (page 68).

★ **Tadich Grill:** After 160 years, the Tadich Grill is still serving an extensive menu that includes sensational Italian seafood stew (page 69).

★ **Tony's Pizza Napoletana:** This North Beach pizzeria employs seven different kinds of ovens to cook its unique pies (page 70).

★ **Commissary:** Chef Traci Des Jardins combines Spanish and California dining elements in this upscale restaurant (page 71).

★ **Tartine Bakery:** Lines snake out the door all day long, but the fresh baked goods and sandwiches are worth the wait (page 71).

Fri., 8am-10pm Sat.-Sun., $10) is a 1930s-style French bistro serving breakfast, lunch, and dinner. Those in need of a relaxing espresso or glass of wine are welcome to take a table and drink in the atmosphere.

Breakfast

Even on a weekday morning, there will be a line out the door of ★ **Brenda's French Soul Food** (652 Polk St., 415/345-8100, http://frenchsoulfood.com, 8am-3pm Mon.-Tues., 8am-10pm Wed.-Sat., 8am-8pm Sun., $12-17). People come in droves to this Tenderloin eatery for its delectable and filling New Orleans-style breakfasts. Unique offerings include crawfish beignets, an Andouille sausage omelet, and beef cutlet and grits.

At **Dottie's True Blue Café** (28 6th St., 415/885-2767, 7:30am-3pm Mon. and Thurs.-Fri., 7:30am-4pm Sat.-Sun., $9-14), the menu is simple: classic egg dishes, light fruit plates, and an honest-to-goodness blue-plate special for breakfast as well as salads, burgers, and sandwiches for lunch. The service is friendly and the portions are huge. Everyone in San Francisco knows that there's a great breakfast

to be had at Dottie's. Expect lines up to an hour long for a table at this locals' mecca, especially on weekend mornings.

Asian

Le Colonial (20 Cosmo Pl., 415/931-3600, www.lecolonialsf.com, 5:30pm-10pm Sun.-Wed., 5:30pm-11pm Thurs.-Sat., $25-37), tucked away in an alley in Nob Hill, invokes 1950s Saigon, with a tin-tiled ceiling, heavy Victorian woodwork, and Vietnamese dishes like sea bass steamed in banana leaves and the crispy chili-glazed Brussels sprouts.

At ★ **The Slanted Door** (1 Ferry Plaza, Ste. 3, 415/861-8032, http://slanteddoor.com, 11am-2:30pm and 5:30pm-10pm Mon.-Sat., 11:30am-3pm and 5:30pm-10pm Sun., $19-45), owner Charles Phan utilizes organic local ingredients in both traditional and innovative Vietnamese cuisine, creating a unique dining experience. The light afternoon tea menu (2:30pm-4:30pm daily) can be the perfect pick-me-up for weary travelers.

California Cuisine

Everything about **Boulevard** (1 Mission St.,

California Cuisine

The San Francisco Bay Area may be considered the epicenter of California cuisine, but that culinary category has since expanded to include a wide variety of preparation methods, organic ingredients, ethnic influences, and locavore specialties. Come hungry.

California cuisine was defined by **The French Laundry** (page 128) and **Chez Panisse** (page 100). To learn their preparation secrets, sign up for a class at the **Culinary Institute of America** (page 134).

Peruse the **farmers markets** in **San Francisco** (page 39), **San Luis Obispo** (page 416), and **Los Angeles** (page 436) for the best in seasonal, organic produce.

With so many miles of coastline, seafood options are plentiful. Try a bowl of cioppino at **Tadich Grill** (page 69) or sample the catch of the day **at El Pesacdor Fish Market** (page 515) in La Jolla.

For authentic Mexican food, it doesn't get any better than **La Super-Rica Taqueria** (page 409) in Santa Barbara and **Yuca's** (page 450) in L.A....unless it's **fish tacos** in San Diego (page 514).

Food trucks are the hottest trend to hit the state since sliced artisan bread. **San Francisco** (page 71) and **Los Angeles** (page 453) have a fleet of tasty options.

San Francisco and LA are filled with destination dining spots, but don't overlook these hidden gems outside the big cities:

Cruise the orchards of **Apple Hill** (page 277) in Gold Country; brunch at **Deetjen's** (page 388) in Big Sur; tuck into heaping plates of lumberjack food at a **cookhouse** (page 184) on the North Coast; or sick a bowl of artichoke soup at **Duarte's** (page 109).

415/543-6084, www.boulevardrestaurant.com, 11:30am-2:15pm and 5:30pm-10pm Mon.-Thurs., 11:30am-2:15pm and 5:30pm-10:30pm Fri., 5:30pm-10:30pm Sat., 5:30pm-10pm Sun., $31-49), from its historical 1889 building to the Belle Epoque interior and rich contemporary cuisine, is beautiful. Plates of roasted quail and line-caught swordfish are ferried around the intimate dining room, where patrons sip velvety wines and flutes of champagne. In 2012, Boulevard was named Best Restaurant in America by the James Beard Foundation.

★ **Michael Mina** (252 California St., 415/397-9222, www.michaelmina.net, 11:30am-2pm and 5:30pm-9pm Mon.-Thurs., 11:30am-2pm and 5:30pm-10pm Fri., 5:30pm-10pm Sat., 5:30pm-9pm Sun., $44-52) finds the celebrity chef using Japanese ingredients and French influences to create bold California entrées. This sleek, upscale restaurant with attentive service is where Mina showcases his signature dishes. The nine-course chef's tasting menu is $99.

French

Hidden in a tiny alley that looks like it might have been transported from Saint-Michel in Paris, ★ **Café Claude** (7 Claude Ln., 415/392-3505, www.cafeclaude.com, 11:30am-10:30pm Mon.-Sat., 5:30pm-10:30pm Sun., $21-28) serves classic brasserie cuisine to French expatriates and Americans alike. Much French is spoken here, but the simple food tastes fantastic in any language. Café Claude is open for lunch through dinner.

Seafood

Make reservations in advance to dine at San Francisco legend ★ **Farallon** (450 Post St., 415/956-6969, www.farallonrestaurant.com, 5:30pm-9:30pm Mon., 11:30am-3pm and 5:30pm-9:30pm Tues.-Thurs., 11:30am-3pm and 5:30pm-10pm Fri.-Sat., 5pm-9:30pm Sun., $28-37). Dark, cave-like rooms are decorated in an underwater theme—complete with the unique Jellyfish Bar. Chef Mark Franz has made Farallon a 15-year icon that keeps gaining ground. Seafood dominates the pricey-but-worth-it menu.

One of the very first restaurants established in San Francisco during the Gold Rush in 1849, the ★ **Tadich Grill** (240 California St., 415/391-1849, www.tadichgrill.com, 11am-9:30pm Mon.-Fri., 11:30am-9:30pm Sat., $20-40) still serves fresh-caught fish and classic miner fare. The menu combines perfectly sautéed sand dabs, octopus salad, and the Hangtown Fry, an oyster and bacon frittata. Mix that with the business lunch crowd in suits, out-of-towners, and original dark wooden booths from the 1850s and you've got a fabulous San Francisco stew of a restaurant. Speaking of stew, the Tadich cioppino enjoys worldwide fame—and deserves it, even in a city that prides itself on the quality of its seafood concoctions.

Steak

How could you not love a steak house with a name like **Epic Roasthouse** (369 Embarcadero, 415/369-9955, www.epicroasthouse.com, 11:30am-9:30pm Mon.-Thurs., 11:30am-10pm Fri., 11am-10pm Sat., 11am-9:30pm Sun., $34-90)? Come for the wood-fired grass-fed beef; stay for the prime views over San Francisco Bay. The Epic Roasthouse sits almost underneath the Bay Bridge, where the lights sparkle and flash over the deep black water at night. On weekends, the steak house offers the hipster city crowd what it wants—an innovative prix fixe brunch menu complete with hair-of-the-dog cocktails.

NORTH BEACH AND FISHERMAN'S WHARF
Bakeries and Cafés

There is much talk about sourdough bread in San Francisco, but Boudin's, which was started in 1849 by French immigrants, is the original. Tourists at Boudin's **Bakers Hall** (160 Jefferson St., 415/928-1849, www.boudinbakery.com, 8am-9:30pm Sun.-Thurs., 8am-10pm Fri.-Sat., $8-12) can order a steaming bowl of clam chowder in a fresh bread bowl

and watch how the bread is made in its demonstration bakery. Upstairs, have a more formal dinner at **Bistro Boudin** (415/351-5561, 11:30am-9:30pm Sun.-Thurs., 11:30am-10pm Fri.-Sat., $16-38), which serves elegant American food and a whole host of oysters in its dark wood dining room overlooking the wharf. Boudin has another café location at Pier 39 (Space 5 Q, 8am-8pm Sun.-Thurs., 8am-9pm Fri.-Sat., $8-12).

Widely recognized as the first espresso coffeehouse on the West Coast, family-owned **Caffé Trieste** (601 Vallejo St., 415/392-6739, www.caffetrieste.com, 6:30am-10pm Sun.-Thurs., 6:30am-11pm Fri.-Sat., cash only) first opened its doors in 1956 and is rumored to be where Francis Ford Coppola penned the original *Godfather* screenplay. Sip a cappuccino and munch on Italian pastries at this treasured North Beach institution.

Breakfast

★ **Mama's on Washington Square** (1701 Stockton St., 415/362-6421, www.mamas-sf.com, 8am-3pm Tues.-Sun., $9-14) is legendary for breakfast—and so is the line. Starting from down the block, the line flows through the heart of the restaurant to the counter where you place your order, then wait for a table to open up. To minimize your wait, arrive at Mama's when it opens or go after noon.

California Cuisine

Gary Danko (800 North Point St., 415/749-2060, www.garydanko.com, 5:30pm-10pm daily, prix fixe $76-111) offers the best of San Francisco culinary celebrity Gary Danko's California cuisine, from the signature horseradish-crusted salmon medallions to an array of delectable fowl dishes. The herbs and veggies come from Danko's own farm in Napa. Make reservations in advance and be prepared to dress up a little.

Park Tavern (1652 Stockton St., 415/989-7300, http://parktavernsf.com, 5:30pm-10pm Mon.-Thurs., 11:30am-2:30pm and 5:30pm-11pm Fri., 10am-2:30pm and 5:30pm-11pm Sat., 10am-2:30pm and 5:30pm-10pm-Sun.,

$28-38) serves meat and fish dishes as well as exquisite appetizers in its elegant dining room. For a low-key meal at the bar, order off the "Jenn's Classics" menu.

Greek

At **Kokkari Estiatorio** (200 Jackson St., 415/981-0983, www.kokkari.com, 11:30am-2:30pm and 5:30pm-10pm Mon.-Thurs., 11:30am-2:30pm and 5:30pm-11pm Fri., 5pm-11pm Sat., 5pm-10pm Sun., $17-29), patrons enjoy Mediterranean delicacies made with fresh California ingredients amid rustic elegance, feasting on such classic dishes as zucchini cakes and grilled lamb chops.

Italian

North Beach is San Francisco's version of Little Italy. One of the last holdouts from North Beach's heyday is **Mario's Bohemian Cigar Store** (566 Columbus Ave., 415/362-0536, 10am-11pm daily, $10-15). Not much has changed has changed in this slender café since it opened in 1972, except that it no longer sells tobacco. There are just a few tables and stools at the bar, where the bartender/server/cook pulls espresso, pours beer and wine, and prepares personal pizzas and focaccia sandwiches baked in a tiny oven.

Nine-time World Pizza Champion Tony Gemignani runs ★ **Tony's Pizza Napoletana** (1570 Stockton St., 415/835-9888, www.tonyspizzanapoletana.com, noon-10pm Mon., noon-11pm Wed.-Sun., $15-30), where four different pizza ovens cook eight distinct styles of pizza. The chef's special Neapolitan-style pizza margherita is simple pizza made of perfection.

Quince (470 Pacific Ave., 415/775-8500, www.quincerestaurant.com, 5:30pm-10pm Mon.-Thurs., 5pm-9:30pm Fri.-Sat., $190) is a fine-dining Italian restaurant spotlighting chef-owner Michael Tusk's celebrated pastas. In the exposed-brick dining room, two tasting menus feature such delicacies as caviar, white truffle, and abalone with black garlic. Expect impeccable service and specialty cocktails made tableside. You can also book a table

crabs for sale at Fisherman's Wharf

at neighboring **Cotogna** (490 Pacific Ave., 415/775-8508, www.cotognasf.com, 11:30am-10:30pm Mon.-Thurs., 11:30am-11pm Fri.-Sat., 5pm-9:30pm Sun., $17-28), also owned by Tusk. Dressed down, with a chic farm-table look, Cotogna offers excellent pizzas, classic meat dishes, and Tusk's signature pastas.

Seafood

Dungeness crabs enjoy celebrity status in San Francisco. The season usually runs November-June, but the freshest crabs are caught and cooked from the start of the season through New Year's. Italian seafood restaurant **Alioto's** (8 Fisherman's Wharf, 415/673-0183, www.aliotos.com, 11am-11pm daily, $17-48) serves whole cracked Dungeness in the traditional style. They've also got crab soups, salads, sandwiches, and stews.

MARINA AND PACIFIC HEIGHTS
Bakeries and Cafés

Drop in at **The Chestnut Bakery** (2359

Chestnut St., 415/567-6777, www.chestnut-bakery.com, 7am-noon Mon., 7am-6pm Tues.-Sat., 8am-5pm Sun.) for a cookie, pastry, or one of the bakery's famous cupcakes. In the morning, you'll find scones, croissants, and other favorite breakfast pastries. **Le Marais Bistro and Bakery** (2066 Chestnut St., 415/359-9801, www.lemaraisbakery.com, 7am-7pm daily, $10) reflects the highly polished farm-to-table dining scene of the next generation. You'll find plenty of the buttery indulgences found in all good patisseries, plus soups, grilled sandwiches, and quiche.

Asian

If you're in Pacific Heights, give **Kiss Seafood** (1700 Laguna St., 415/474-2866, 5:30pm-9:30pm Tues.-Sat., $30-60) a try. This tiny restaurant (12 seats in total) boasts some of the freshest fish in town—no mean feat in San Francisco. The lone chef prepares all the fish himself, possibly because of the tiny size of the place. Reservations are a good idea.

California Cuisine

Famed chef Traci Des Jardins took over the 1895 mess hall in the Main Post and turned it into the ★ **Commissary** (Presidio, 101 Montgomery St., 415/561-3600, www.the-commissarysf.com, 11:30am-2pm and 5:30pm-9pm Mon.-Thurs., 11:30am-2pm and 5:30pm-9:30pm Fri., 5:30pm-9:30pm Sat., $19-30). The cuisine is a blend of San Francisco and Spanish influences and utilizes such ingredients as cod, anchovies, chorizo, and peppers.

Food Trucks

To get the very best food truck experience, plan a Sunday afternoon at the **Off the Grid Presidio Picnic** (Presidio, Main Post Lawn, 415/339-5888, http://offthegridsf.com, 11am-4pm Sun., Apr.-Nov., $5-15), where six trucks, 17 tents, and two carts roving through the crowds sell everything from Bloody Marys to Vietnamese soup. The Presidio Picnic is a party with live DJs and plenty of dogs, kids, hipsters, Frisbees, and picnic blankets.

CIVIC CENTER AND HAYES VALLEY
California Cuisine

Housed in a former bank, ★ **Nopa** (560 Divisadero St., 415/864-8643, http://nopasf.com, 5pm-1am Mon.-Fri., 11am-1am Sat.-Sun., $16-26) serves hip, farm-to-table food on long communal tables. Upscale comfort food is made with the best ingredients, a global sensibility, and excellent execution. But it's impossible to get a table without a reservation.

French

Absinthe (398 Hayes St., 415/551-1590, www.absinthe.com, 11:30am-midnight Mon.-Fri., 11am-midnight Sat., 11am-10pm Sun., $23-30) takes its name from the notorious "green fairy" drink made of liquor and wormwood. Absinthe does indeed serve absinthe—including locally made St. George Spirits Absinthe Verte. It also serves upscale French bistro fare, including what may be the best french fries in the city. The French theme carries on into the decor as well—expect the look of a Parisian brasserie or perhaps a café in Nice. The bar is open until 2am Thursday through Saturday.

German

★ **Suppenküche** (525 Laguna St., 415/252-9289, www.suppenkuche.com, 5pm-10pm Mon.-Sat., 10am-2:30pm and 5pm-10pm Sun., $11-20) brings a taste of Bavaria to the Bay Area. For dinner, expect German classics with a focus on Bavarian cuisine. Spaetzle, pork, sausage—you name it, they've got it, and it will harden your arteries right up. Suppenküche also has a **Biergarten** (424 Octavia St., http://biergartensf.com, 3pm-9pm Wed.-Sat., 1pm-7pm Sun.) two blocks away.

MISSION AND CASTRO
Bakeries and Cafés

Locals love the artful pastries and fresh breads at ★ **Tartine Bakery** (600 Guerrero St., 415/487-2600, www.tartinebakery.com, 8am-7pm Mon., 7:30am-7pm Tues.-Wed., 7:30am-8pm Thurs.-Fri., 8am-8pm Sat., 9am-8pm Sun., $4-13). Tartine's bakers use organic flour, sea salt, and locally sourced produce and cheeses to craft their culinary creations, and the French-Italian-California fusion pastries and panini have brought this bakery its word-of-mouth success.

Around the corner, satisfy your sweet tooth at **Bi-Rite Creamery & Bakeshop** (3692 18th St., 415/626-5600, http://biritecreamery. com, 11am-10pm Sun.-Thurs., 11am-11pm Fri.-Sat.), where the ice cream is made by hand with organic milk, cream, and eggs.

American

Range (842 Valencia St., 415/282-8283, 6pm-close Mon.-Thurs., 5:30pm-close Fri.-Sun., $23-28) is consistently rated one of the top Bay Area restaurants, serving up expertly crafted California cuisine. An inventive cocktail list doesn't hurt.

Café Flore (2298 Market St., 415/621-8579, www.cafeflore.com, 10am-midnight Mon.-Fri., 8am-midnight Sat.-Sun., $7-22) has been a Castro mainstay since 1973. Its food is good, unfussy, and very reasonably priced. Order the eggs Benedict for brunch or the Wagyu steak and frites for dinner. Part of the place's charm is the somewhat ramshackle wood building and lush outside garden patio.

French

Frances (3870 17th St., 415/621-3870, 5pm-10:30pm daily, $21-32) has been winning rave reviews ever since it opened its doors. The California-inspired French cuisine is locavore friendly, with an emphasis on sustainable ingredients and local farms. The short-but-sweet menu changes daily and includes such temptations as caramelized Atlantic scallops and bacon beignets. Reservations are strongly advised.

Italian

When the time is right for a plain ol' pizza, head for **Little Star Pizza** (400 Valencia St., 415/551-7827, www.littlestarpizza.com, noon-10pm Sun.-Thurs., noon-11pm Fri.-Sat., $20). A jewel of the Mission district, this pizzeria specializes in Chicago-style deep-dish pies.

★ **Delfina** (3621 18th St., 415/552-4055, www.delfinasf.com, 5pm-10pm Mon., 11:30am-10pm Tues.-Thurs., 11:30am-11pm Fri., noon-11pm Sat., 5pm-10pm Sun., $11-17) gives Italian cuisine a hearty California twist. From the antipasti to the entrées, the dishes speak of local farms and ranches, fresh seasonal produce, and the best Italian-American taste that money can buy.

The bar menu at **Beretta** (1199 Valencia St., 415/695-1199, www.berettasf.com, 5:30pm-1am Mon.-Fri., 11am-1am Sat.-Sun.) consistently wins rave reviews and is hard to pass up, particularly as the restaurant doesn't take reservations for parties under six and the only place to wait is at the bar. Order a Rattlesnake, then a pizza to suck up the venom of that bite.

Mexican

Much of the rich heritage of the Mission district is Hispanic, thus leading to the Mission being *the* place to find a good taco or burrito. It is generally agreed upon that **La Taqueria** (2889 Mission St., 415/285-7117, 11am-9pm Mon.-Sat., 11am-8pm Sun., $5-10) makes the best burrito in the city. Critics rave, as do locals grabbing dinner on their way home.

Seafood

For great seafood in a lower-key atmosphere, head for the ★ **Anchor Oyster Bar** (579 Castro St., 415/431-3990, www.anchoroysterbar.com, 11:30am-10pm Mon.-Sat., 4pm-9:30pm Sun., $19-28), an institution in the Castro since 1977. The raw bar features different varieties of oysters, while the dining room serves seafood, including local favorite Dungeness crab.

GOLDEN GATE PARK AND THE HAIGHT
California Cuisine

Adjacent to Golden Gate Park, **Park Chow** (1240 9th Ave., 415/665-9912, www.chowfoodbar.com, 8am-9:30pm Sun.-Thurs., 8am-10:30pm Fri.-Sat., $12-18) does a brisk business with locals and visitors alike. The cozy interior complements the organic comfort-food menu featuring everything from wood-fired pizzas to steak frites. Opt for the rooftop garden on the rare sunny day.

Magnolia (1398 Haight St., 415/864-7468, http://magnoliapub.com, 11am-midnight Mon.-Thurs., 11am-1am Fri., 10am-1am Sat., 10am-midnight Sun., $14-26) began its life channeling the spirit of the Grateful Dead into its strong beer and laid-back pub fare. When the gastropub craze hit, Magnolia jumped on board. To match its muscular beers, the excellent menu is meat-heavy, with a whole section of sausages. The aesthetic is dark and brooding, tapping into the neighborhood's Victorian past. Selections include oysters, bread pudding, flat iron steak, and, for dessert, a stout ice cream float.

The **Beach Chalet Brewery** (1000 Great Hwy., 415/386-8439, www.beachchalet.com, 9am-10pm Mon.-Thurs., 9am-11pm Fri., 8am-11pm Sat., 8am-10pm Sun., $20-30) is an attractive brewpub and restaurant directly across the street from Ocean Beach. Out back, sister restaurant **Park Chalet** (http://parkchalet.com, noon-9pm Mon.-Thurs., noon-10pm Fri., 11am-10pm Sat., 10am-9pm Sun., $15-20) offers a similar menu with outdoor seating and jumping live music on the weekends.

One of the most famous locations in San Francisco is the ★ **Cliff House.** The high-end eatery inhabiting the famed facade is **Sutro's** (1090 Point Lobos Ave., 415/386-3330, www.cliffhouse.com, 11:30am-3:30pm and 5pm-9:30pm Mon.-Sat., 11am-3:30pm and 5pm-9:30pm Sun., $26-46), where expensive plates of steak, lamb, and salmon are best with a glass of California wine. The more casual (and affordable) **Bistro** (9am-3:30pm and 4:15pm-9:30pm Mon.-Sat., 8:30am-3:30pm and 4:15pm-9:30pm Sun., $15-30) serves big bowls of cioppino at an ornately carved zinc bar. The **Lounge** (9am-11pm Sun.-Thurs., 9am-midnight Fri.-Sat.) is the best deal in the house, where you can sip coffee and drinks without all the fuss.

French

One of the best places in the Haight is in the pocket neighborhood of Cole Valley. Dripping with charm, ★ **Zazie** (941 Cole St., 415/564-5332, www.zaziesf.com, 8am-2pm and 5pm-9:30pm Mon.-Thurs., 8am-2pm and 5pm-10pm Fri.-Sat., $19-24), a tiny French bistro, is known mainly for brunch. Benedicts, croque monsieur, coq au vin, and boeuf Bourguignon go down perfectly with either a latte or Kir Royale.

Accommodations

Both the cheapest and most expensive places tend to be in Union Square and downtown. Consistently cheaper digs can be had in the neighborhoods surrounding Fisherman's Wharf. You'll find the most character in the smaller boutique hotels, but plenty of big chain hotels have at least one location in town if you prefer a known quantity. Valet parking and overnight garage parking can be excruciatingly expensive. Check with your hotel to see if they have a "parking package" that includes this expense.

UNION SQUARE AND DOWNTOWN

Union Square has the greatest concentration of hotels. Those closest to the top of Nob Hill or to Union Square proper are the most expensive. Lodging in the Financial District, Embarcadero, and SoMa run toward expensive big-name chains. Slightly farther away, you can get more personality and genuine San Francisco experience for less money and less prestige. Smaller boutique and indie accommodations won't tear your wallet to bits.

Best Hotels

★ **Golden Gate Hotel:** This bed-and-breakfast-like hotel has nice, moderate rooms in a narrow building right by Union Square (page 74).

★ **Hotel Monaco:** Explore downtown San Francisco from this comfortable hotel with a friendly staff and amenities, including a downstairs spa that is open to guests (page 74).

★ **Hotel Triton:** Hotel Triton reflects the city's independent spirit with vibrant rooms, including suites designed by pop culture figures like Jerry Garcia and Kathy Griffin (page 74).

★ **Mandarin Oriental San Francisco:** Every room in this luxury hotel has stunning views of the city (page 75).

★ **Marina Motel:** This moderately priced motel in the Marina district has something most accommodations in the city don't have: individual parking garages for guests (page 76).

Under $150

The ★ **Golden Gate Hotel** (775 Bush St., 415/392-3702 or 800/835-1118, $135-190) offers small, charming rooms with friendly, unpretentious hospitality. You'll find a continental breakfast every morning in the hotel lobby. There are only two rates: the higher rate ($190) gets you a room with a private bathroom, while the lower rate ($135) gets you a room with a bath down the hall.

The Mosser's (54 4th St., 415/986-4400, www.themosser.com, $129-289) inexpensive rooms have European-style shared baths in the hallway and bright modern decor that nicely complements the century-old building. Pricier options include bigger rooms with private baths. With a rep for cleanliness and pleasant amenities, including morning coffee and comfy bathrobes, this hotel provides visitors with a cheap crash space in a great location convenient to sights, shops, and public transportation.

$150-250

The **Hotel Bijou** (111 Mason St., 415/771-1200, www.hotelbijou.com, $140-220) is a fun spot. Whimsical decor mimics an old-fashioned movie theater, and a tiny "movie house" downstairs runs double features, free to guests, every night—with only movies shot in San Francisco. The rooms are small, clean, and nicely appointed.

The ★ **Hotel Monaco** (501 Geary St., 415/292-0100, www.monaco-sf.com, $179-389) shows the vibrant side of San Francisco. Big rooms are whimsically decorated with bright colors, while baths are luxurious and feature cushy animal-print bathrobes. Friendly service comes from purple-velour-coated staff, who know the hotel and the city and will cheerfully tell you all about both. Chair massage complements the free wine and cheese in the large, open guest lounge.

The ★ **Hotel Triton** (342 Grant Ave., 800/800-1299, www.hoteltriton.com, $179-389) adds a bit of whimsy and eco chic to the stately aesthetic of Union Square. Jerry Garcia decorated a room here, and Häagen-Dazs tailored its own suite, complete with an ice cream-stocked freezer case in the corner. You'll find the rooms tiny but comfortable and well stocked with ecofriendly amenities and bath products. The flat-panel TVs offer a 24-hour yoga channel, and complimentary yoga props can be delivered to your room on request.

Hotel Rex (562 Sutter St., 415/433-4434, www.jdvhotels.com, $195-300) channels San Francisco's literary side, evoking a hotel in the early 1900s when Bohemians such as Jack

London, Ambrose Bierce, and even Mark Twain roamed and ruminated about the city. Rooms are comfortable and spacious, decorated with the work of local artists and artisans. The dimly lit lobby bar is famous in the city for its literary bent—you may find yourself engaged in a fascinating conversation as you enjoy your evening glass of wine.

Over $250

A San Francisco legend, the **Clift** (495 Geary St., 415/775-4700, www.clifthotel.com, $269-400) has a lobby worth walking into. The high-ceilinged industrial space is devoted to modern art. Yes, you really are supposed to sit on the antler sofa and the metal chairs. By contrast, the rooms are almost Spartan in their simplicity, with colors meant to mimic the city skyline. Stop in for a drink at the Redwood Room, done in brown leather and popular with a younger crowd.

At the 1904-built **Westin St. Francis** (335 Powell St., 415/397-7000, www.westinstfrancis.com, $250-500), the hotel's robber-baron and Jazz-Age past is evident as soon as you walk into the immense lobby. The hotel's two wings are the original section, called the Landmark Building, and the 1972 renovation is The Tower. There are 1,200 rooms, making it the largest hotel in the city. Rooms in the historical section are loaded with lavish charms like ornate woodwork and chandeliers, while the modern rooms are large and sport fantastic views of the city and the bay.

The **Fairmont San Francisco** (950 Mason St., 415/772-5000, www.fairmont.com, $350-595) opened shortly after the 1906 earthquake, designed in the Beaux-Arts style of the time. The Fairmont has historical rooms and a Tower addition; large Tower rooms feature marble baths and even more spectacular views than the historical rooms.

Rooms at the ★ **Mandarin Oriental San Francisco** (222 Sansome St., 415/276-9888, www.mandarinoriental.com, $525-765) boast unparalleled views, top amenities, and Asian-inspired decor. In the swank corner rooms and suites, raised bathtubs let bathers enjoy stunning sights such as the Transamerica Pyramid, Alcatraz, and the Golden Gate Bridge.

The **Palace Hotel** (2 New Montgomery St., 415/512-1111, www.sfpalace.com, $425-600) enjoys its reputation as the grande dame of all San Francisco hotels. The Palace opened its doors in 1875 to be gutted by fires following the 1906 earthquake. It was rebuilt and reopened in 1909. In 1919 President Woodrow Wilson negotiated the terms of the Treaty of Versailles over lunch at the Garden Court. Today guests take pleasure in beautiful bedrooms, exercise and relax in the full-service spa and fitness center, and dine in the Palace's three restaurants. A meal in the exquisite Garden Court dining room is a must, though you may forget to eat as you gaze upward at the stained-glass domed ceiling.

NORTH BEACH AND FISHERMAN'S WHARF
Under $150

The **San Remo Hotel** (2237 Mason St., 415/776-8688 or 800/352-7366, www.san-remohotel.com, $119-159) is one of the best bargains in the city. The rooms boast the simplest of furnishings and decorations. None have telephones or TVs, and the bathrooms are located down the hall. Downstairs, Fior d'Italia is the oldest Italian restaurant in the country and has a generous happy hour seven days a week.

$150-250

The **Washington Square Inn** (1660 Stockton St., 800/388-0220, www.wsisf.com, $219-359) doesn't look like a typical California B&B, but more like a small, elegant hotel. The inn offers 16 rooms with queen or king beds, private baths, elegant appointments, and fine linens. Standard rooms are "cozy" in the European urban style, while some have spa bathtubs and others have views of Coit Tower and Saints Peter and Paul Church. A few of the amenities include a generous continental breakfast brought to your room daily, afternoon tea, a flat-screen TV in every room, and free Wi-Fi.

Over $250

In a district not known for its luxury, **The Argonaut** (495 Jefferson St., 415/563-0800 or 800/790-1415, www.argonauthotel.com, $249-579) in Fisherman's Wharf stands out. Housed in an exposed-brick 1907 warehouse, the hotel embraces its nautical connections to the nines. Many rooms have great views of the bay, and its location is ideal, only steps away from Aquatic Park, Pier 45, Ghirardelli Square, and the excellent Maritime Museum.

MARINA AND PACIFIC HEIGHTS
Under $150

For an unexpected, bucolic park hostel within walking and biking distance of frenetic downtown, stop for a night at the **Fisherman's Wharf Hostel** (Fort Mason Bldg. 240, 415/771-7277, www.sfhostels.com/fishermans-wharf, dorm $40-49, private room $90-120). The hostel sits on Golden Gate National Recreation Area land, pleasantly far from the problems that plague other SF hostels. The best amenities (aside from the free linens and breakfast, and no curfews or chores) are the views of the bay and Alcatraz and the sweeping lawns and mature trees all around the hostel.

$150-250

The rooms at the ★ **Marina Motel** (2576 Lombard St., 415/921-9406, www.marina-motel.com, $189-349) may be small, but the place is big on charm and character. This friendly little motel, decorated in French-country style, welcomes families with kids and dogs. Just ask for the room type that best suits your needs when you make your reservations. Rooms are pleasantly priced for budget travelers, and several vacation packages offer deep discounts on tours, spa treatments, and outdoor adventures.

The **Hotel del Sol** (3100 Webster St., 415/921-5520, www.thehoteldelsol.com, $209-449) embraces its origins as a 1950s motor lodge, with the rooms decorated in bright, bold colors with whimsical accents, a heated courtyard pool, and the ever-popular free parking. Family suites and larger rooms have kitchenettes. The Marina locale offers trendy cafés, restaurants, bars, and shopping within walking distance as well as access to major attractions.

The stately **Queen Anne Hotel** (1590 Sutter St., 415/441-2828, www.queenanne.com, $175-665) is Victorian through and through. Sumptuous fabrics, ornate antiques, and rich colors in the rooms and common areas add to the feeling of decadence and luxury in this boutique bed-and-breakfast. Small, moderate rooms offer attractive accommodations on a budget, while superior rooms and suites are more upscale. Continental breakfast is included, as are a number of high-end services.

A Pacific Heights jewel, the **Jackson Court** (2198 Jackson St., 415/929-7670, www.jacksoncourt.com, $229) presents a lovely brick facade in the exclusive neighborhood. The 10-room inn offers comfortable, uniquely decorated queen rooms and a luscious continental breakfast each morning.

Over $250

The **Inn at the Presidio** (42 Moraga Ave., 415/800-7356, www.innatthepresidio.com, $250-385) is inside historical Pershing Hall right in the center of the Presidio. Built in 1903, the large brick building was formerly home to single military officers. In the classic rooms and suites (some with fireplaces), subtle contemporary furnishings complement the framed photos and other Presidio memorabilia sprinkled throughout. On-site amenities include a breakfast buffet, wine and cheese reception, free Wi-Fi, a covered front porch with rocking chairs overlooking the Main Post, and an outdoor deck with fire pit. There is a $7 fee for self-parking, or take advantage of the PresidiGo shuttle.

Tucked in with the money-laden mansions of Pacific Heights, ★ **Hotel Drisco** (2901

Pacific Ave., 800/634-7277, www.hoteldrisco.com, $293-428) offers elegance to discerning visitors. You get quiet, comfy rooms that include a "pillow menu"; continental breakfast with a latte, smoked salmon, and brie; hors d'oeuvres and a glass of wine in the evening; and bicycles on loan.

CIVIC CENTER AND HAYES VALLEY
Under $150
At the **Chateau Tivoli** (1057 Steiner St., 415/776-5462 or 800/228-1647, www.chateautivoli.com, $130-300), the over-the-top colorful exterior matches the American Renaissance interior decor perfectly. Each unique room and suite showcases an exquisite style evocative of the Victorian era. Most rooms have private baths, though the two least expensive share a bath. Try to get a room for a weekend, so you can partake of the gourmet champagne brunch.

$150-250
Located in Hayes Valley a few blocks from the Opera House, the **Inn at the Opera** (333 Fulton St., 888/298-7198, www.shellhospitality.com, $229-329) promises to have guests ready for a swanky night of San Francisco culture. French interior styling in the rooms and suites once impressed visiting opera stars and now welcomes guests from all over the world.

The Parsonage (198 Haight St., 415/863-3699, www.theparsonage.com, $240-280) is a classy Victorian bed-and-breakfast whose elegance fits in with the Civic Center and Hayes Valley chic. Rooms are decorated with antiques, and baths have stunning marble showers. Enjoy pampering, multicourse breakfasts, and brandy and chocolates when you come "home" each night.

MISSION AND CASTRO
Under $150
At the **Inn on Castro** (321 Castro St., 415/861-0321, www.innoncastro.com, $135-275), you've got all kinds of choices. You can pick an economy room with a shared bath, a posh private suite, or a self-service apartment. Once ensconced, you can chill out on the cute patio, or go out into the Castro to take in the legendary entertainment and nightlife. The self-catering apartments can sleep up to four and have fully furnished and appointed kitchens and dining rooms. Amenities include LCD TVs with cable, DVD players, and colorful modern art.

GOLDEN GATE PARK AND THE HAIGHT
$150-250
The **Stanyan Park Hotel** (750 Stanyan St., 415/751-1000, www.stanyanpark.com, $179-299) graces the Upper Haight area across the street from Golden Gate Park. This renovated 1904-1905 building, listed on the National Register of Historic Places, shows off its Victorian heritage both inside and out. Rooms can be small but are elegantly decorated, and a number of multiple-room suites are available. All 36 rooms include free Wi-Fi and flat-screen TVs, but for a special treat, ask for a room overlooking the park.

Transportation and Services

AIR

San Francisco International Airport (SFO, 800/435-9736, www.flysfo.com) isn't within the City of San Francisco; it is actually about 13 miles south in the town of Millbrae, right on the bay. You can easily get a taxi ($35) or other ground transportation into the heart of the city from the airport. BART is available from SFO's international terminal, but Caltrain is only accessible via a BART connection from SFO. Some San Francisco hotels offer complimentary shuttles from the airport as well. You can also rent a car here.

As one of the 30 busiest airports in the world, SFO has long check-in and security lines much of the time and dreadful overcrowding on major travel holidays. Plan to arrive at the airport two hours prior to departure for domestic flights and three hours prior to an international flight.

TRAIN AND BUS

Amtrak does not run directly into San Francisco. You can ride into San Jose, Oakland, or Emeryville station, and then take a connecting bus into San Francisco.

Greyhound (200 Folsom St., 415/495-1569, www.greyhound.com, 5:30am-1am daily) offers bus service to San Francisco from all over the country.

CAR

The **Bay Bridge** (toll $6) links I-80 to San Francisco from the east, and the **Golden Gate Bridge** (toll $7) connects Highway 1 from the north. From the south, U.S. 101 and I-280 snake up the peninsula and into the city. Be sure to get a detailed map and good directions to drive into San Francisco—the freeway interchanges, especially surrounding the east side of the Bay Bridge, can be confusing, and the traffic congestion is legendary. For traffic updates and route planning, visit **511.org** (www.511.org).

If you have your car with you, try to get a room at a hotel with a parking lot and either free parking or a parking package for the length of your stay.

Car Rental

All the major car rental agencies have a presence at the **San Francisco Airport** (SFO, 800/435-9736, www.flysfo.com). In addition, most reputable hotels can offer or recommend a car rental. Rates tend to run $50-100 per day and $200-550 per week (including taxes and fees), with discounts for weekly and longer rentals.

Parking

Parking a car in San Francisco can easily cost $50 per day or more. Most downtown and Union Square hotels do not include free parking with your room. Expect to pay $35-65 per night for parking, which may not include in-and-out privileges.

Street parking meters cost up to $2 per hour, often go late into the night, and charge during the weekends. At least many now take credit cards. Unmetered street parking spots are as rare as unicorns and often require residential permits for stays longer than two hours during the day. Lots and garages fill up quickly, especially during special events.

MUNI

The **Muni** (www.sfmta.com, adults $2.25, youth and seniors $0.75, children under 4 free) transit system can get you where you want to go as long as time isn't a concern. Bus and train tickets can be purchased from any Muni driver; underground trains have ticket machines at the entrance. Exact change is required, except on the cable cars, where drivers can make change for up to $20. See the website for a route map, tickets, and schedules.

BART

Bay Area Rapid Transit, or **BART** (www.bart.gov, one-way $1.85-7.50), is the Bay Area's late-coming answer to major metropolitan underground railways like Chicago's L trains and New York's subway system. Sadly, there's only one arterial line through the city. However, service directly from San Francisco Airport into the city runs daily, as does service to Oakland Airport, the cities of Oakland and Berkeley, and many other East Bay destinations. BART connects to the Caltrain system and San Francisco Airport in Millbrae. See the website for route maps, schedules (BART usually runs on time), and fare information.

To buy tickets, use the vending machines found in every BART station. If you plan to ride more than once, you can add money to a single ticket and then keep that ticket and reuse it for each ride.

Caltrain

This traditional commuter rail line runs along the peninsula into Silicon Valley, from San Francisco to San Jose, with limited continuing service to Gilroy. **Caltrain** (www.caltrain. com, one-way $3-13) Baby Bullet trains can get you from San Jose to San Francisco in an hour during commuting hours. Extra trains are often added for San Francisco Giants, San Francisco 49ers, and San Jose Sharks games.

You must purchase a ticket in advance at the vending machines found in all stations. The main Caltrain station in San Francisco is at the corner of 4th and King Streets, within walking distance of AT&T Park and Moscone Center.

Taxis

You'll find some taxis scooting around all the major tourist areas of the city. If you have trouble hailing a cab, try **City Wide Dispatch** (415/920-0700).

SERVICES
Tourist Information

The main San Francisco **Visitor Information Center** (900 Market St., 415/391-2000, www. sanfrancisco.travel; 9am-5pm Mon.-Fri., 9am-3pm Sat.-Sun., May-Oct.; 9am-5pm Mon.-Fri., 9am-3pm Sat., Nov.-Apr.) can give you information about attractions and hotels, and discounted tickets for various museums and attractions. The Market Street location (just below Hallidie Plaza at Powell Street) has brochures in 14 different languages and a few useful coupons.

Medical Services

The **San Francisco Police Department** (766 Vallejo St., 415/315-2400, www.sf-police.org) is headquartered in Chinatown, on Vallejo Street between Powell and Stockton Streets.

San Francisco boasts a large number of full-service hospitals. The **UCSF Medical Center at Mount Zion** (1600 Divisadero St., 415/567-6600, www.ucsfhealth.org) is renowned for its research and advances in cancer treatments and other important medical breakthroughs. The main hospital is at the corner of Divisadero and Geary Streets. Right downtown, **St. Francis Memorial Hospital** (900 Hyde St., 415/353-6000, www.saintfrancismemorial.org), at the corner of Hyde and Bush Streets, has an emergency department.

North Bay

Marin County, in the North Bay, is San Francisco's backyard. Beginning with the Marin Headlands at the terminus of the Golden Gate Bridge, there is a nearly unbroken expanse of wildlands from San Francisco Bay to Tomales Bay. Here you'll find rugged cliffs plunging into the Pacific, towering redwoods, and verdant pastures.

MARIN HEADLANDS

The Marin Headlands lie north of San Francisco at the end of the Golden Gate Bridge. The land here encompasses a wide swath of virgin wilderness, former military structures, and a historical lighthouse. You can cross the Golden Gate Bridge and explore Marin County on a day trip, but you may spend more time in the car than strolling beaches and forests. To better enjoy the parks and hiking trails, plan an overnight stay.

Vista Point

At the north end of the Golden Gate Bridge, the aptly named **Vista Point** offers views from the Marin Headlands toward San Francisco. If you dream of walking across the **Golden Gate Bridge** (gates 5am-9pm daily Apr.-Oct., 5am-6:30pm daily Nov.-Mar.), be sure to bring a warm coat as the wind and fog can really whip through. The bridge is 1.7 miles long, so a round-trip walk will turn into a 3.4-mile hike. Bikes are allowed daily 24 hours on the west side. Bicycle riders may also use the east side, but must be careful to watch for pedestrians. Dogs are never allowed on either side.

To reach Vista Point, take U.S. 101 north across the Golden Gate Bridge. The first exit on the Marin County side is Vista Point; turn right into the parking lot. This small parking lot often fills early.

Marin Headlands Visitors Center

A great place to start your exploration of the headlands is at the **Marin Headlands Visitors Center** (Field Rd. and Bunker Rd., 415/331-1540, www.nps.gov/goga, 9:30am-4:30pm daily), located in the old chapel at Fort Barry. The park rangers can give you the current lowdown on the best trails, beaches, and campgrounds in the Headlands. Grab a complimentary coffee and peruse the displays highlighting the park's human and natural history, as well as the small but well-stocked bookstore.

Point Bonita Lighthouse

The **Point Bonita Lighthouse** (415/331-1540, www.nps.gov/goga, 12:30pm-3:30pm Sat.-Mon.) has been protecting the Headlands for more than 150 years. You'll need some dedication to visit Point Bonita, since it's only open a few days each week and there's no direct access by car. A 0.5-mile trail with steep sections leads from the trailhead on Field Road. Along the way, you'll pass through a hand-cut tunnel chiseled from the rock by the builders of the lighthouse, then over the bridge that leads to the building. Point Bonita was the third lighthouse built on the West Coast and is now the last staffed lighthouse in California. Today the squat hexagonal building shelters automatic lights, horns, and signals.

Marine Mammal Center

Inspired by the ocean's beauty and want to learn more about the animals that live in it? Visit the **Marine Mammal Center** (2000 Bunker Rd., 415/289-7325, www.marine-mammalcenter.org, 10am-5pm daily, free) at Fort Cronkhite in the Marin Headlands. The center is a hospital for sick and injured seals and sea lions. Visitors are free to wander around and look at the educational displays to learn more about what the center does, but the one-hour docent-led tours (daily, times vary by season, adults $9, seniors and ages 5-17

North Bay

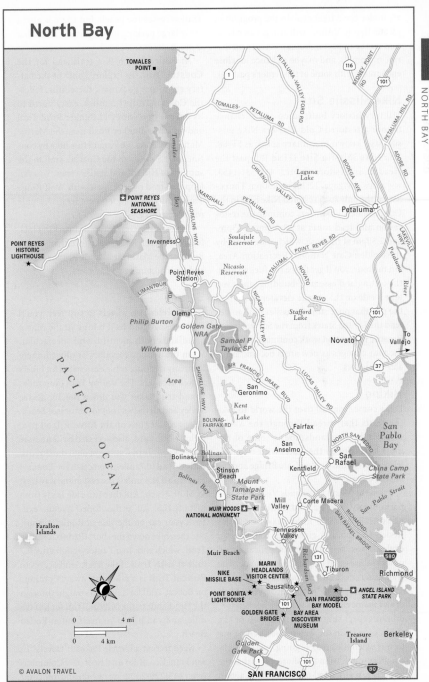

© AVALON TRAVEL

$5, under age 5 free) explain the program in greater depth. Visitors will also get an education on the impact of human activity on marine mammals, and maybe a chance for close encounters with some of the center's patients.

Nike Missile Site

Military history buffs jump at the chance to tour a restored Cold War-era Nike missile base, known in military speak as SF-88. The **Nike Missile Site** (Field Rd. past the Headlands Visitors Center, 415/331-1453, www.nps.gov/goga, 12:30pm-3:30pm Thurs.-Sat.) is the only such restored Nike base in the United States. Volunteers continue the restoration and lead tours at 12:45pm, 1:45pm, and 2:30pm at the base, which is overseen by the Golden Gate National Recreation Area. On the tour, you'll get to see the fueling area, the testing and assembly building, and even take a ride on the missile elevator down into the pits that once stored missiles built to defend the United States from the Soviet Union. Because restoration work continues endlessly, the tour changes as new areas become available to visitors.

Hiking

Folks come from all over the world to hike the trails that thread through the Marin Headlands. The landscape is some of the most beautiful in the state, with unparalleled views of the Golden Gate Bridge and the Pacific Ocean.

From the Marin Headlands Visitors Center parking lot (Field Rd. and Bunker Rd.), the **Lagoon Trail** (1.75 miles, easy) encircles Rodeo Lagoon and gives bird-watchers an eagle's-eye view of the egrets, pelicans, and other seabirds that call the lagoon home. The trailhead is near the restrooms.

An easy spot to get to, **Rodeo Beach** draws many visitors on summer weekends—do not expect solitude on the beach or the trails, or even in the water. Locals come out to surf when the break is going, while beach-combers watch from the shore. Note that the wind can really howl out here. The Lagoon Trail accesses the beach, but there is also a fairly large parking lot on Bunker Road that is much closer.

At Rodeo Beach is a trailhead for the **Coastal Trail.** To explore some of the battery ruins that pockmark these hills, follow the Coastal Trail (1.5 miles, easy) north to its intersection with Old Bunker Road Trail and return to Bunker Road near the Marine Mammal Center. Or extend this hike by continuing 2.3 miles up the Coastal Trail to the summit of **Hill 88** and stellar views. You can loop this trail by linking it with Wolf Ridge Trail to Miwok Trail for a moderate 3.8-mile round-trip hike.

To reach the trailheads and parking lots, follow Bunker Road west to either Rodeo Beach or the Marin Headlands Visitors Center and their adjoining parking lots.

Biking

If you prefer two wheels to two feet, you'll find the road and trail biking in the Marin Headlands both plentiful and spectacular. From the Tennessee Valley Trailhead, there are many multiuse trails designated for bikers as well as hikers. The **Valley Trail** (four miles round-trip) takes you down the Tennessee Valley and all the way out to Tennessee Beach. A longer ride runs up the **Miwok Trail** (two miles) northward, also accessed by Tennessee Valley Road. Turn southwest onto the **Coyote Ridge Trail** (0.7 mile); then catch the **Coastal Fire Road** (1.4 miles) the rest of the way west to Muir Beach. Another fun ride leads from just off U.S. 101 at the Rodeo Avenue exit. Park your car on the side of Rodeo Avenue, and then bike down the short **Rodeo Avenue Trail,** which ends in a T intersection after 0.7 mile at **Alta Trail.** Take a left, and access to **Bobcat Trail** is a few yards away. Continue on Bobcat Trail for 2.5 miles straight through the Headlands to the **Miwok Trail** for just 0.5 mile, and you'll find yourself out at Rodeo Beach.

Need to rent a bicycle for your travels? In San Francisco, **Bike and Roll** (899 Columbus Ave., 415/229-2000, www.bikeandroll.com/

sanfrancisco, 8am-6pm daily) offers road ($58-110/day), mountain ($39-58/day), and hybrid ($32-39/day) bikes and loads of helpful advice.

Camping and Hostel

Camping here requires some planning. You must book a site in advance (up to 30 days for primitive sites, and six months for full-service sites). Bring warm camping gear, even during summer.

The most popular campground is **Kirby Cove** (877/444-6777, www.recreation. gov, Apr.-Oct., reservations required, $25). Secluded and shaded campsites provide a beautiful respite complete with bay views and a private beach. Make reservations well in advance for summer weekends since this popular campground fills up fast.

The **Bicentennial Campground** (Battery Wallace parking lot, 415/331-1540, reservations required, free) boasts three campsites easily accessible from the parking lot. Each site can accommodate a maximum of three people in one tent, and there's no water available or fires allowed on-site. A nearby picnic area has barbecue grills that campers can use to cook.

Travelers who want budget accommodations indoors often choose the **Marin Headlands Hostel** (Bldg. 941, Fort Barry, 415/331-2777, www.norcalhostels.org/marin, dorm $28-35, private room $82-132). You'll find full kitchen facilities, Internet access, laundry rooms, and a rec room. Surprisingly cozy and romantic, the hostel is sheltered in the turn-of-the-20th-century buildings of Fort Barry, creating a unique atmosphere. With the headlands right outside your door, there is no lack of activities or exploration opportunities.

Transportation

Fort Baker and the Marin Headlands are located just north of the Golden Gate Bridge on Highway 1 and U.S. 101. Traffic can be heavy on beautiful weekend days, particularly in the headlands, so plan to get here early.

Once over the bridge, the Alexander Avenue exit offers two options for exploring the headlands. Follow Alexander Avenue to Fort Baker and the Bay Area Discovery Museum, or turn left onto Bunker Road for the Marin Headlands Visitors Center and Nike Missile Site. If the Bonita Lighthouse is your first stop, follow Alexander Avenue right and travel under the highway to Conzelman Road, which leads up the hill along the edge of the headlands. Keep in mind that many of the roads are very narrow and become one-way in places.

SAUSALITO

A former commercial fishing town, the now-affluent town of Sausalito still has a few old cannery buildings and plenty of docks, most of which are now lined with pleasure boats. Bridgeway, the main drag, runs along the shore, and the concrete boardwalk is perfect for strolling and biking. Farther north is the heart of working Sausalito, where the lovely waterfront Dunphy Park is rarely crowded. The main strip eventually leads to Fort Baker, with views of the city.

In town, the **San Francisco Bay Model** (2100 Bridgeway, 415/332-3871, www.spn. usace.army.mil, 9am-4pm Tues.-Fri., 10am-5pm Sat.-Sun., summer; 9am-4pm Tues.-Sat., winter; free) is a scale hydraulic model that demonstrates how the currents and tides of the bay and the Sacramento-San Joaquin River Delta affect the bay and estuary surrounding San Francisco.

Fort Baker

Fort Baker (435 Murray Cir., Sausalito, 415/331-1540, www.nps.gov/goga, sunrise-sunset daily) is a 335-acre former Army Post established in 1905. With the transfer of many of the Bay Area's military outposts to parkland and civilian use, Fort Baker was handed over to the Golden Gate National Recreation Area. The location, just east of the Golden Gate Bridge, secluded in a shallow valley, makes it a great destination to enjoy city views and a wind-free beach. The fort includes many elegant homes with large porches centered around the oval parade grounds. On-site is the Cavallo Point Lodge, the nonprofit Institute at the Golden Gate, and two restaurants.

Bay Area Discovery Museum

If you want to go someplace where kids will have fun, visit the **Bay Area Discovery Museum** (557 McReynolds Rd., Sausalito, 415/339-3900, www.baykidsmuseum.org, 9am-5pm Tues.-Sun., adults and children 1 and up $14, seniors and babies 6-12 months $13). The indoor-outdoor space is filled with the stuff that excites kids' imaginations—a train room, a tot room, an art studio, frequent story times, and a "construction site" where hard workers can don hard hats and dig to their heart's content. Most of the exhibits are directly related to the museum's location.

Food

Sausalito's main drag is full of places to eat. Most are expensive, reflecting the quality of the view, not necessarily the food. Fortunately, there are some standouts. A sidewalk café across the street from the waterfront, **Copita Tequileria y Comida** (739 Bridgeway, 415/331-7400, www.copitarestaurant.com, 11:30am-10pm Mon.-Thurs., 11:30am-11pm

Fri., 11am-11pm Sat., 11am-10pm Sun., $10-19) serves upscale Mexican food such as oyster tacos and slow-cooked carnitas alongside a variety of tangy ceviche. The noise level and long wait on sunny summer or weekend days may beat out the restaurant's other charms.

Fish (350 Harbor Dr., 415/331-3474, www.331fish.com, 11:30am-4:30pm and 5:30pm-8:30pm daily, $10-25, cash only) can hook you up with some of the best sustainable seafood in the North Bay, in a charming, unpretentious café overlooking the water. Fresh wild fish prepared using a California-style mix of international cooking techniques results in amazing dishes.

Continue down Bridgeway to **Cibo** (1201 Bridgeway, 415/331-2416, www.cibosausalito.com, 7am-5pm daily, $8-15), in the hip center of Sausalito. In crisp modern surroundings, this café serves a number of hot and cold panini, hearty salads with locally sourced ingredients, and a rich array of coffee drinks and boutique sodas.

Snag a blanket and a seat on the porch to watch the fog roll in over the Golden Gate Bridge at ★ **Farley Bar** (Cavallo Point Lodge, 601 Murray Cir., Fort Baker, Sausalito, 415/339-4750, www.cavallopoint.com, 11am-11pm Sun.-Thurs., 11am-midnight Fri.-Sat.,

Sausalito's promenade

$20). With cocktails, wine, and oysters, Farley is the perfect end to a day of hiking. Upstairs from Farley, **Murray Circle Restaurant** (415/339-4750, www.cavallopoint.com; 7am-11am, 11:30am-2pm, and 5:30pm-9pm Mon.-Thurs.; 7am-11am, 11:30am-2pm, and 5:30pm-10pm Fri.; 7am-11am, 11:30am-2:30pm, and 5:30pm-10pm Sat.; 11:30am-2:30pm and 5:30pm-9pm Sun.; $29-36) has a menu based on the best Marin produce, seafood, meat, and dairy, with touches from cuisines around the world.

Accommodations

The Gables Inn (62 Princess St., 415/289-1100, www.gablesinnsausalito.com, $199-495) opened in 1869 and is the oldest B&B in the area. Although this inn honors its long history, it has also kept up with the times, adding four rooms with panorama bay views and flat-screen televisions, Internet access, and luxurious baths to all 13 rooms. Genial innkeepers serve a buffet breakfast each morning and host a wine and cheese soiree each evening.

With a checkered history dating back to 1915, the **Hotel Sausalito** (16 El Portal, 888/442-0700, www.hotelsausalito.com, $180-225) was a speakeasy, a bordello, and a home for the writers and artists of the Beat generation. Today this tiny boutique hotel, with its yellow walls and wrought iron beds, evokes the Mediterranean coast.

For a taste of the Marin good life, stay at Sausalito's **Inn Above Tide** (30 El Portal, 800/893-8433, www.innabovetide.com, $345-645). The inn sits over the edge of the water looking out at the San Francisco skyline and most rooms have private decks that show off sublime views. Guests love the smart upscale furnishings, the stand-alone fireplaces, and the rooms with oversize bathtubs set by windows.

★ **Cavallo Point Lodge** (601 Murray Cir., Fort Baker, Sausalito, 415/339-4700, www.cavallopoint.com, $500) offers a stay in beautiful historical homes that feature early 20th-century woodwork and wraparound porches, but 21st-century amenities such as lush carpets, beds dressed in organic linens, flat-screen TVs, wireless Internet, gas fireplaces, and bathtubs so deep you can get lost. Cavallo Lodge also has eco-chic accommodations in its newer two-story buildings. You'll find floor-to-ceiling windows framing spectacular views, radiant floor heating, and private porches. The lodge has excellent environmental credentials and is dog friendly. The excellent Murray Circle Restaurant and Farley Bar are on-site.

Transportation

Sausalito is north of San Francisco just over the Golden Gate Bridge; it is easily accessible by bicycle on side roads or by car on U.S. 101. In town, the narrow oceanfront main road gets very crowded on weekends; park and walk around instead. Street parking is mostly metered.

A great way to get to Sausalito from San Francisco is by ferry. Two companies make the trip daily, which takes up to an hour. The **Blue and Gold Fleet** (415/705-8200, http://blueandgoldfleet.com, 11am-8:15pm Mon.-Fri., 9:45am-6pm Sat.-Sun., adults $11.50, children and seniors $6.75, under age 5 free) makes the trip from Pier 41. Largely serving commuters, the **Golden Gate Ferry** (415/455-2000, http://goldengate.org, 7:40am-7:20pm Mon.-Fri., 10:40am-6:50pm Sat.-Sun., adults $10.75, children and seniors $5.25, under age 5 free) leaves from the Ferry Building, closer to downtown San Francisco. The trip across the bay is cheaper and faster.

TIBURON

Tiburon's small downtown backs onto a popular marina. Aside from the views, one of the greatest draws to Tiburon is its proximity to Angel Island, the largest island in the bay and one of the most unique state parks around.

★ Angel Island State Park

Angel Island (415/435-5390, www.parks.ca.gov, 8am-sunset daily, rates vary by ferry company) has a long history, beginning with regular visits (though no permanent settlements) by the Coastal Miwok people. During the Civil War the U.S. Army created a fort on the island in anticipation of Confederate attacks from the Pacific. The attacks never came, but the Army maintained a base here. Today many of the 19th-century military buildings remain and can be seen on the hour-long **tram tour** (415/435-3392, http://angelislandsf.com, daily Apr.-Sept., $10-15), on foot, or on a docent-led two-hour **Segway tour** (days and times vary, $68). Later, the Army built a Nike missile base on the island to protect San Francisco from possible Soviet attacks. The missile base is not open to the public but can be seen from roads and trails.

Angel Island's history also has a sobering side. From 1910-1940, it served as an immigration station for inbound ships and as a concentration camp for Chinese emigrants attempting to escape turmoil in their homeland. Europeans were waved through, but Chinese were herded into barracks as government officials scrutinized their papers. After months and sometimes years of waiting, many were sent back to China. Poetry lines the walls of the barracks, expressing the despair of the immigrants who had hoped for a better life. The **Immigration Station** (11am-3pm daily, adults $5, children 6-17 $3, under 6 free) is open to visitors and do-cent-led tours are also available (11am and 12:30pm daily, $7).

Angel Island is a destination for both casual and serious hikers. Multiuse trails of varying difficulty crisscross the island. Adventurous trekkers can scale Mount Livermore via either the **North Ridge Trail** or the **Sunset Trail.** Each runs about 4.5 miles round-trip for a moderate, reasonably steep hike. At the top, enjoy gorgeous bay views. For the best experience, make a loop, taking one trail up the mountain and the other back down. If you're up for a long paved-road hike, take the **Perimeter Road** (five miles, moderate) all the way around the island.

Pick up a boxed lunch or take a table at the **Angel Island Café** (415/435-3392, www.angelisland.com, 11am-3pm Mon.-Fri., 11am-4pm Sat.-Sun., $9-14), which serves hot sandwiches, wraps, salad, soup, and ice cream. Open summer only, the nearby **Angel Island Cantina** (11:30am-4:30pm Fri.-Sun., $7-14) serves burgers, tacos, oysters, beer, wine, and pitchers of mimosas and sangria.

CAMPING

Camping is available at nine primitive **campsites** (800/444-7275 or www.reserveamerica.com, $30) that fill up quickly; successful campers reserve their campsites six months in advance. Each "environmental site" is equipped with food lockers (a must), sur-prisingly nice outhouses, running water, and a barbecue. You must bring your own charcoal, as wood fires are strictly prohibited. The three **Ridge Sites** sit on the southwest side of the island, known to be fairly windy; the six **East Bay** and **Sunrise Sites** face the East Bay. Despite the dramatic urban views, camping here is a little like backpacking; plan on walking up to 2.5 miles from the ferry to your campsite.

GETTING THERE

The harbor at Tiburon is the easiest place to access Angel Island, located in the middle of San Francisco Bay. The private **Angel Island-Tiburon Ferry** (21 Main St., Tiburon, 415/435-2131, www.angelislandferry.com, adults $15, seniors $14, ages 6-12 $13, ages 3-5 $5, bicycles $1) can get you out to the island in about 10 minutes and runs several times a day. You can also take the **Blue and Gold Fleet** (415/705-8200, www.blueandgoldfleet.com, one-way $8.50) to Angel Island from San Francisco's Pier 41. Blue and Gold ferries leave once in the morning (10am Mon.-Fri., 9:40am Sat.-Sun.) from San Francisco, and the last ferry back departs at 2:50pm Monday-Friday and 4:10pm Saturday-Sunday. Although the ferry out of Tiburon has more sailings during the day, the last ferry is still early (3pm-5pm daily), with very few sailings on weekdays during the winter.

Ferries have plenty of room for you to bring your own bicycle, or you can rent one at the **main visitors area** (415/435-3392, http://angelislandsf.com, Sat.-Sun. Mar.-Nov., daily Apr.-Oct., $13.50 per hour, $50 per day) near the ferry dock. Rentals must always be returned at 3pm.

Accommodations and Food

The lovely **Waters Edge Hotel** (25 Main St., 415/789-5999, www.marinhotels.com, $233-355) is a boutique lodge that lives up to its name. You can stumble right out of your room onto the dock and over to the Angel Island ferry. Inside, you'll love the feather beds, cushy robes, a fireplace, and breakfast delivered to your room each morning.

Wonderfully close to the water and attractions of downtown Tiburon, the **Lodge at Tiburon** (1651 Tiburon Blvd., 415/435-3133, www.thelodgeattiburon.com, $130-330) offers the comforts and conveniences of a larger hotel while providing the style and atmosphere of a boutique inn. For a special treat, book a table at the attached Tiburon Tavern, a favorite watering hole.

Anchor Café (27 Main St., 415/435-4527, www.samscafe.com, 11am-9:30pm Mon.-Fri., 9:30am-9:30pm Sat.-Sun., $14-28) sits on the water with a large glassed-in deck and specializes in seafood and wine. Catch some rays over oysters on the half shell, fish-and-chips, or a burger. At night, the place becomes a bit fancier, with white tablecloths and low lighting inside.

Transportation

Tiburon is located on a peninsula about eight miles north of the Golden Gate Bridge. From San Francisco, take U.S. 101 north to the Tiburon Boulevard (CA 131) exit. Stay to the right and follow the road along the water for nearly six miles until you reach the small downtown area.

Tiburon is very walkable and is a great destination via ferry from San Francisco. The **Blue and Gold Fleet** (415/705-8200, http://blueandgoldfleet.com) runs daily trips (30-45 minutes, 10:10am-8pm Mon.-Fri., 9:45am-6:30pm Sat.-Sun., adults $11, children and seniors $6.75, under age 5 free) to Tiburon from San Francisco's Pier 41 and from the Ferry Building (6am-7:30pm).

MILL VALLEY

Mill Valley is a gateway to Marin's most breathtaking parkland—from the bayside marshlands to the slopes of Mount Tamalpais. Continue past the turnoff to Highway 1 along Miller Avenue to reach the charming downtown, tucked in a redwood valley. The small square is filled with cute shops, galleries, and great food.

Tennessee Valley

After U.S. 101 enters Marin County, the Stinson Beach/Mill Valley exit leads through barely noticed and unincorporated Tamalpais Valley. One of the most popular—and crowded, especially on summer weekends—places to hike is the **Tennessee Valley Trailhead** (end of Tennessee Valley Rd.). A quick hike from the trailhead can take you out to the **Haypress Campground** (about one mile, moderate), which has picnic tables and pretty views. For a nice long hike, take the **Old Springs Trail** (1.3 miles) down to the **Miwok Trail.** Turn right, and after 0.3 mile, take another right at **Wolf Ridge Trail** (0.7 mile) to the **Coastal Trail.** Taking a right, you'll intersect the **Tennessee Valley Trail** after 1.3 miles, which, taking another right toward the east, leads you back to the trailhead (1.4 miles).

To reach the Tennessee Valley Trailhead, take the Stinson Beach/Highway 1 exit off U.S. 101 and drive 0.6 mile, passing under the freeway and continuing straight. Turn left on Tennessee Valley Road and continue two miles to the trailhead.

Accommodations and Food

The **Mill Valley Inn** (165 Throckmorton Ave., 415/389-6608, www.marinhotels.com, $246-340) is the only hotel in downtown Mill Valley. The inn offers 25 rooms, including private cottages. Rooms in the Creekhouse have a historical feel and overlook the creek, and all main building rooms have French doors that open onto private patios. Furnishings are classic yet contemporary, and some rooms have fireplaces.

★ **Mill Valley Beerworks** (173 Throckmorton Ave., 415/888-8218, http://millvalleybeerworks.com, 5:30pm-9:30pm Mon., 5:30pm-10:30pm Tues.-Fri., 11am-3pm and 5:30pm-10:30pm Sat., 11am-3pm and 5:30pm-9:30pm Sun., $17-26) tailors a local, seasonal menu to pair with its handcrafted beer. Eight beers are available, or try the flight of four ($12). Seating is at communal tables that allow for an intimate dinner. There is a bar in the back overlooking the stainless steel fermentation tanks.

Molina (17 Madrona St., 415/383-4200, http://molinarestaurant.com, 5:30pm-10pm Sun.-Thurs., 5:30pm-11pm Fri.-Sat., $20-34) exudes Mill Valley's woodland charm. With only 42 seats in a Craftsman house, the restaurant uses a wood-fire oven to fill its earthenware plates with game hen, rabbit rillettes, and Manila clams *cazuela*. The wine list is small but perfectly paired to the menu, as is the restaurant's playlist: a stack of records next to a turntable, manned by the chef himself.

Next door to Molina is the equally original and adored **Avatars Punjabi Burrito** (15 Madrona St., 415/381-8293, www.enjoyavatars.com, 11am-8pm daily, $7-10). Burritos are filled with garbanzo beans, basmati rice, herb salsa, fruit chutney, yogurt, and tamarind sauce, or opt for a more traditional rice plate. The small shop mostly caters to takeout orders, but there are a few tables with plastic chairs.

A nice 2.5-mile hike from the Tennessee Valley Trailhead leads to **Hawk Campground** (415/331-1540, reservations required, free) with three primitive sites. Your reward for the work of packing in all your gear and water is a near-solitary camping experience. Amenities include chemical toilets but no water, and fires are not allowed.

★ MUIR WOODS NATIONAL MONUMENT

Established in 1908 and named for naturalist and author John Muir, **Muir Woods National Monument** (1 Muir Woods Rd., 415/388-2596, www.nps.gov/muwo, 8am-sunset daily, adults $7, under 16 free) comprises acres of staggeringly beautiful redwood forest. More than six miles of trails wind through the redwoods and accompanying Mount Tamalpais area, crossing verdant creeks and the lush forest. These are some of the most stunning—and accessible—redwoods in the Bay Area.

The visitors center is a great place to begin your exploration. The **Muir Woods Visitors Center** (8am-sunset daily) abuts the main parking area and marks the entrance to Muir Woods. In addition to maps, information, and advice about hiking, you'll also find a few amenities. Inside the park, slightly past the visitors center, is a **café** (415/388-7059, www.muirwoodstradingcompany.com, 9am-5:30pm daily, closing hours vary) where you can purchase souvenirs and food.

Hiking

Many lovely trails crisscross the gorgeous redwood forest. First-time visitors should follow the wheelchair- and stroller-accessible **Redwood Creek Trail** (one mile, easy). Leading from the visitors center on an easy and flat walk through the beautiful redwoods, this trail has an interpretive brochure (pick one up at the visitors center) with numbers along the trail that describe the flora and fauna. Hikers can continue the loop on the **Hillside Trail** for an elevated view of the valley.

One of the first side trails off the Main Trail is the **Ocean View Trail** (3.4 miles, moderate). Some advice: Either bring water or pick up a bottle at the visitors center before starting up the trail. The trail climbs through the

Muir Woods National Monument

Muir Woods is accessed via the long and winding Muir Woods Road. From U.S. 101, take the Stinson Beach/Highway 1 exit. On Highway 1, also named the Shoreline Highway, follow the road under the freeway and proceed until the road splits in a T junction at the light. Turn left, continuing on Shoreline Highway for 2.5 miles. At the intersection with Panoramic Highway, make a sharp right turn and continue climbing uphill. At the junction of Panoramic Highway and Muir Woods Road, turn left and follow the road 1.5 twisty miles down to the Muir Woods parking lots on the right.

If you're visiting on a holiday or a summer weekend, get to the Muir Woods parking areas early—they fill fast, and afternoon hopefuls will not find a spot. Lighted signs on U.S. 101 will alert you to parking conditions at the main parking lot. To avoid the traffic hassle, the **Muir Woods Shuttle** (415/455-2000, http://www.marintransit.org/routes/66.html, Sat.-Sun. summer, $5 round-trip, under 16 free) leaves from various points in southern Marin County, including the Sausalito ferry terminal.

MUIR BEACH

Few coves on the California coast can boast as much beauty as **Muir Beach** (just south of the town of Muir Beach, www.nps.gov/goga, sunrise-sunset daily). From the overlook above Highway 1 to the edge of the ocean beyond the dunes, Muir Beach is a haven for both wildlife and beachcombers; many trails lead from the beach into the surrounding headlands. The south side of the beach houses the windswept picnic grounds, while the north cove attracts nudists.

Muir Beach is directly off Highway 1. The most direct route is to take U.S. 101 to the Stinson Beach/Highway 1 exit and follow Highway 1 (also called Shoreline Highway) for 6.5 miles to Pacific Way (look for the Pelican Inn). Turn left onto Pacific Way and continue straight to the Muir Beach parking lot. If arriving from Muir Woods, simply continue on

redwoods for 1.5 miles until its junction with **Lost Trail.** Turn right on Lost Trail and follow it downhill for 0.7 mile to **Fern Creek Trail.** Bear left onto the Fern Creek trail for a lush and verdant return to the Main Trail. Along the way you'll see the much-lauded Kent Tree, a 250-foot-tall Douglas fir.

It's easier to avoid the crowds by following the Main Trail to its terminus with the **Bootjack Trail** (6.4 miles, moderate). The Bootjack Trail climbs uphill for 1.3 miles before its junction with the **TCC Trail.** Bear left for the TCC Trail and meander through the quiet Douglas firs. At 1.4 miles, the trail meets up with the **Stapleveldt Trail;** turn left again to follow this trail for 0.5 mile to **Ben Johnson Trail,** which continues downhill for 1 more mile to meet up with the Main Trail.

You may notice signs in this area for the **Dipsea Trail,** an out-and-back hike to Stinson Beach. This is a strenuous, unshaded 7.1-mile hike, and the only way back is the way you came—but uphill.

Muir Woods Road down to the junction with Highway 1 and turn right onto Pacific Way.

Accommodations and Food

Inside the Tudor **Pelican Inn** (10 Pacific Way, Muir Beach, 415/383-6000, www.pelican-inn.com, $206-289), the historical ambience shines with big-beam construction, canopy beds, and lovely portrait prints. The seven mostly small rooms each come with private baths and full English-style breakfast, but no TVs or phones. You can also get hearty food at the inn's **restaurant** (11:30am-3pm and 5:30pm-9pm Mon.-Fri.; 8am-11am, 11:30am-3pm, and 5:30pm-9pm Sat.-Sun.; $15-34). The cuisine brings home the flavors of old England, with dishes like beef Wellington, shepherd's pie, and fish-and-chips.

MOUNT TAMALPAIS STATE PARK

Mount Tamalpais State Park (801 Panoramic Hwy., Mill Valley, 415/388-2070, www.parks.ca.gov, 7am-sunset daily, day-use parking $8) boasts stellar views of the San Francisco Bay Area—from Mount St. Helena in Napa down to San Francisco and across to the East Bay. The Pacific Ocean fills the western view, including a unique view of the distant Farallon Islands, while on a clear day you can just make out the foot-hills of the Sierra Nevada Mountains to the east. The **East Peak Visitors Center** (end of East Ridgecrest Blvd., 11am-4pm Sat.-Sun.), located at the top of Mount Tam, houses a small museum and gift shop as well as a picnic area with tables and restrooms. The **Pantoll Ranger Station** (3801 Panoramic Hwy. at Pantoll Rd., 415/388-2070, 9am-5pm Fri.-Mon.) anchors the western and larger edge of the park, and provides hikers with maps and camping information.

Enjoy the views without setting out on the trail at the **Bootjack Picnic Area** (Panoramic Hwy.), which has tables, grills, water, and re-strooms. The small parking lot northeast of the Pantoll Ranger Station fills quickly and early in the day.

Hiking

Mount Tam's hiking areas are divided into three major sections: the East Peak, the Pantoll area, and the Rock Springs area. Each of these regions offers a number of beautiful trails, so grab a map from the visitors center or online to get a sense of the hikes. For additional hikes, visit the **Friends of Mount Tam** (www.friendsofmttam.org).

the overlook from Mount Tamalpais

EAST PEAK

The charming, interpretive **Verna Dunshee Trail** (0.75 mile, easy) offers a short, mostly flat walk along a wheelchair-accessible trail. The views are fabulous, and you can get a leaflet at the visitors center that describes many of the things you'll see along the trail. Turn this into a loop hike by continuing on Verna Dunshee counterclockwise; once back at the visitors center, make the climb up to **Gardner Fire Lookout** for stellar views from the top of Mount Tam's East Peak (2,571 feet).

PANTOLL

The Pantoll Ranger Station is ground zero for some of the best and most challenging hikes in the park. The **Old Mine Trail** (0.5 miles, easy) is an accessible trail that leads to a lovely lookout bench and the Lone Tree Spring. Ambitious hikers can continue on the Dipsea Trail (1.4 miles, moderate), making it a loop by turning right on the **Steep Ravine Trail** (3.8 miles, moderate) as it ascends through lush Webb Creek and gorgeous redwoods back to the Pantoll parking lot.

The **Dipsea Trail** loop (7.3 miles round-trip, strenuous) is part of the famous Dipsea Race Course (second Sun. in June), a 7.4-mile course renowned for both its beauty and its challenging stairs. The trailhead that begins in Muir Woods, near the parking lot, leads through Mount Tam all the way to Stinson Beach. Hikers can pick up the Dipsea on the Old Mine Trail or at its intersection with the Steep Ravine Trail in Mount Tam, but a common loop is to take the **Matt Davis Trail** (across Panoramic Hwy. from the Pantoll parking area) west all the way to Stinson Beach and then return via the Dipsea Trail to Steep Ravine Trail. This is a long, challenging hike, especially on the way back, so bring water and endurance.

ROCK SPRINGS

A variety of trails lead off the historic venue **Mountain Theater** (E. Ridgecrest Blvd. at Pan Toll Rd., 415/383-1100, www.mountainplay.org, May-June, $30-40), an outdoor theater built in the 1930s that hosts plays. To get there, cross Ridgecrest Boulevard and take the **Mountain Theater Fire Trail** to Mountain Theater. Along the top row of the stone seats, admire the vistas while looking for **Rock Springs Trail** (it's a bit hidden). Once you find it, follow Rock Springs Trail all the way to historical West Point Inn. The views here are stunning, and you'll see numerous cyclists flying downhill on Old Stage Road below. Cross this road to pick up Nora Trail, following it until it intersects with **Matt Davis Trail.** Turn right to reach the Bootjack day-use area. Follow the **Bootjack Trail** right (north) to return to the Mountain Theater for a 4.6-mile loop.

Here's your chance to see waterfalls via the lovely **Cataract Trail** (three miles, easy-moderate). From the trailhead, follow Cataract Trail for a short bit before heading right on **Bernstein Trail.** Shortly, turn left onto **Simmons Trail** and continue to Barth's Retreat, site of a former camp that is now a small picnic area with restrooms. Turn left on **Mickey O'Brien Trail** (a map can be helpful here), returning to an intersection with the Cataract Trail. It's worth the short excursion to follow Cataract Trail to the right through the Laurel Dell picnic area and up to Cataract Falls. Enjoy a picnic at Laurel Dell before returning to Cataract Trail to follow it down to the Rock Springs trailhead.

Accommodations and Food

When the **West Point Inn** (100 Old Railroad Grade Rd., Mill Valley, 415/388-9955, www. westpointinn.com, Tues.-Sat., $50) was built in 1904, guests would take the old train to its doorstep. Today it's a two-mile hike on a dirt road. The inn has no electricity; instead, it's lit by gaslights and warmed by fires in the large fireplaces in the downstairs lounge and parlor. There are seven rooms upstairs and five rustic cabins nearby. Guests must bring their own linens, flashlights, and food, which can be prepared in the communal kitchen. May-October, the inn hosts a monthly Sunday pancake breakfast (9am-1pm, adults $10, children $8). The wait can be long, but it's a lot of fun.

Boasting terrific views, **Mountain Home Inn** (810 Panoramic Hwy., 415/381-9000, www.mtnhomeinn.com, $195-345) was built during the heyday of the railroad. With 10 rooms, many with jetted tubs, wood-burning fireplaces, and private decks, the inn specializes in relaxation. Slip downstairs for a complimentary breakfast, or dine in the cozy and warmly lit dining room (11:30am-7pm Mon.-Fri., 8am-11am and 11:30am-7pm Sat.-Sun., prix fixe 5:30pm-8:30pm Wed.-Sun., $9-26).

Camping

With spectacular views of the Pacific Ocean, it's no wonder that the rustic accommodations at ★ **Steep Ravine** (800/444-7275, www.reserveamerica.com, cabins $100, campsites $25) stay fully booked. On the namesake ravine are six primitive campsites and nine cabins. Each rustic cabin comes equipped with a small wood stove, a table, a sleeping platform, and a grill. The campsites have a table, a fire pit, and a food locker. Restrooms and drinking water are nearby. To reserve a cabin or campsite, you need to be on the phone at 8am six months before the date you intend to go.

If you want to camp within hiking distance of the top of the mountain, the **Pantoll Campground** (1393 Panoramic Hwy., 415/388-2070, www.parks.ca.gov, $25) has 16 sites with drinking water, firewood, and restrooms. Camping here is first-come, first-served, paid for at the ranger station, so get here early. The sites are removed from the parking lot, which means that you'll need to haul in all your gear; it also makes for a peaceful campground.

Transportation

Panoramic Highway is a long and winding two-lane road across the Mount Tamalpais area and extending all the way to Stinson Beach. Take Highway 1 to the Stinson Beach exit, and then follow the fairly good signs up the mountain. Turn right at Panoramic

Highway at the top of the hill. Follow the road for five winding miles until you reach the Pantoll Ranger Station. To get to the East Peak Visitors Center, take a right on Pantoll Road, and another right on East Ridgecrest Boulevard. To access the park from Stinson Beach, take a right on Panorama Highway at the T intersection with Highway 1 just south of town.

STINSON BEACH

The primary attraction at Stinson Beach is the tiny town's namesake: a broad 3.5-mile sandy stretch of coastline that's unusually congenial to visitors. Stinson Beach is the favorite destination for San Franciscans seeking some surf and sunshine.

To get out on the water, swing by **Stinson Beach Surf and Kayak** (3605 Hwy. 1, 415/868-2739, www.stinsonbeachsurfandkayak.com, weekdays by appointment, 9:30am-6pm Sat.-Sun., $20-40 per day). The owner will set you up with a surfboard, kayak, boogie board, or stand-up paddleboard, plus a wetsuit, which you will certainly need.

Accommodations and Food

The **Sandpiper Inn** (1 Marine Way, 415/868-1632, www.sandpiperstinsonbeach.com, $130-245) has six rooms and four cabins. Two of the rooms have kitchenettes and all have gas fireplaces and comfortable queen beds. The individual redwood cabins offer additional privacy, bed space for families, and full kitchens.

Stinson Beach Motel (3416 Shoreline Hwy. 1, 415/868-1712, www.stinsonbeachmotel.com, $130-150) features eight vintagey beach bungalow-style rooms that sleep 2-4 guests each. Some of the blue-themed rooms have substantial kitchenettes; all have private baths, garden views, and TVs.

A few small restaurants dot the town. The **Sand Dollar Restaurant** (3458 Hwy. 1, 415/868-0434, www.stinsonbeachrestaurant.com; 11am-9pm daily, summer; 3pm-9pm Mon.-Fri., 11am-9pm Sat.-Sun., winter; $13-25) serves more land-based dishes than seafood, as well as a popular Sunday brunch. The dining room is constructed out of three old barges.

With the vibe of a seaside hamburger joint, **Parkside Café** (43 Arenal Ave., 415/868-1272, www.parksidecafe.com, 7:30am-9pm daily, $12-28) is the perfect place to stop with your feet still sandy from the beach. Order the local rock cod tacos, the burger on a brioche bun, or a half dozen oysters on the half shell.

Getting There
Take the Stinson Beach exit off U.S. 101 and follow Shoreline Highway (Hwy. 1) until it descends into Stinson Beach. Most of the town is strung along the highway, and signs make it easy to navigate to the beach. Traffic can be a huge problem on weekend days, with backups that stretch for miles. Your best bet is to drive in on a weekday or in the evening.

TOP EXPERIENCE

★ POINT REYES NATIONAL SEASHORE
The Point Reyes area boasts acres of unspoiled grassland, forest, and beach. Cool weather presides even in the summer, but the result is lustrous green foliage and spectacular scenery. **Point Reyes National Seashore** (1 Bear Valley Rd., 415/464-5100, www.nps.gov/pore, dawn-midnight daily) stretches between Tomales Bay and the Pacific, north from Stinson Beach to the tip of the land at the end of the bay. Dedicated hikers can trek from the bay to the ocean, or from the beach to land's end. The protected lands shelter a range of wildlife. In the marshes and lagoons, a wide variety of birds—including three different species of pelicans—make their nests. The pine forests shade shy deer and larger elk. A few ranches and dairy farms operate inside the park. Grandfathered in at the time the park was created, these sustainable, generations-old family farms give added character and historical depth to Point Reyes.

The Point Reyes area includes the tiny towns of Olema, Point Reyes Station, and Inverness.

Visitors Centers
The **Bear Valley Visitors Center** (1 Bear Valley Rd., 415/464-5100; 10am-5pm Mon.-Fri., 9am-5pm Sat.-Sun., May-Nov.; 10am-4:30pm Mon.-Fri., 9am-4:30pm Sat.-Sun., Nov.-May) acts as the central visitors center for Point Reyes National Seashore. In addition to maps, fliers, and interpretive exhibits, the center houses a short video introducing the region. You can also talk to park rangers, either to ask advice or to obtain beach fire permits and backcountry camping permits.

The **Ken Patrick Visitors Center** (Drakes Beach, 415/669-1250, 9am-5pm daily summer; 9:30am-4:30pm Sat.-Sun. fall-spring) sits right on the beach in a building made of weathered redwood. Its small museum focuses on the maritime history of the region. It's also the location for the annual Sand Sculpture event.

Point Reyes Historic Lighthouse
The rocky shores of Point Reyes make for great sightseeing but incredibly dangerous maritime navigation. In 1870 the first lighthouse was constructed on the headlands. Its first-order Fresnel lens threw light far enough for ships to avoid the treacherous granite cliffs. Yet the danger remained, and soon after, a lifesaving station was constructed alongside the light station. It wasn't until the 20th century, when a ship-to-shore radio station and newer lifesaving station were put in place, that the Point Reyes shore truly became safer for ships.

The **Point Reyes Historic Lighthouse** (415/669-1534, www.nps.gov/pore, 10am-4:30pm Fri.-Mon.) still stands today on a point past the visitors center, accessed by descending a sometimes treacherous, cold, and windblown flight of 300 stairs, which often closes to visitors during bad weather. Still, it's worth a visit. The Fresnel lens and original machinery all remain in place, and the adjacent equipment building contains foghorns, air compressors, and other safety implements from decades past. Check the website for information about twice-monthly special events when the light is switched on.

Tomales Bay State Park

At the northeast edge of the Point Reyes Peninsula, pine forests shroud **Tomales Bay State Park** (1208 Pierce Point Rd., 415/669-1140, www.park.ca.gov, 8am-sunset daily, $8), home to four lovely beaches. Protected from the wind and waves by the Inverness Ridge to the west, the beaches are calm, gently sloping, and partially secluded. All require a walk from the parking lots, but the walks are scenic, taking you through meadows and forest.

There are also places to picnic or hike. An easy one-mile trail leads to the **Jepson Memorial Grove**, home to the last virgin groves of bishop pine trees in California. Access is via the Jepson Trail, which leads to **Heart's Desire Beach**, perhaps the most popular beach in the park.

Hiking

To list all the hikes in Point Reyes would require a book in itself. For just a taste of what the area has to offer, start at the **Bear Valley Visitors Center.** This is the trailhead for several simple hikes, and here you can obtain maps and trail information. Trails are accessed along four main roads (south to north): Mesa Road, Limantour Road, Sir Francis Drake Boulevard, and Pierce Point Road.

BOLINAS

At the very south end of Point Reyes, Olema-Bolinas Road leads to the Palomarin Trailhead. The trailhead provides access to the **Coastal Trail**, which offers both day hikes and overnight backpacking trips to **Wildcat Camp** (5.5 miles one-way, permit required). Day hikers can follow the trail out past Bass Lake, Pelican Lake, and Crystal Lake.

BEAR VALLEY

From the visitors center, the **Bear Valley Trail** runs south all the way to the ocean and the dramatic perch above **Kelham Beach** (8.2 miles round-trip, moderate). For a shorter hike, follow Bear Valley Trail to **Divide Meadow**, which makes a moderate 3.2-mile loop.

Bear Valley Trail also provides access to **Mount Wittenberg** (two miles, strenuous), though there is an easier trailhead off Limantour Road. This is the highest point in

the Point Reyes Historic Lighthouse

the park (1,407 feet), and you'll feel it on the climb up. From Bear Valley Trail, turn right at the intersection with Mount Wittenberg Trail and follow it to the top. Hikers can return via either the **Meadow Trail** (turn left on Sky Trail, then left again on Meadow Trail) or take **Z Ranch Trail** (left) to return via **Horse Trail** for a 5- or 6.1-mile loop.

LIMANTOUR ROAD

Limantour Road is north of the Bear Valley Visitors Center: Take Bear Valley Road north and turn west on Limantour Road. One of the first trailheads along this road is for the **Sky Trail** (moderate). The Sky Trail provides easier access to Mount Wittenberg with the bonus of passing by Sky Camp, one of the area's most popular hike-in campgrounds.

Limantour Road eventually passes Point Reyes Hostel, where you'll find the trailhead for the **Coast-Laguna Loop** (five miles, easy to moderate). Follow Coast Trail down to Drakes Bay, where it hugs the shoreline until reaching **Coast Camp**, another backpacking campsite. From Coast Camp, take **Fire Lane Trail** north to **Laguna Trail** and return to Limantour Road. You may have to walk along Limantour toward the hostel to reach your car. Birders will want to make a beeline for the **Limantour Spit Trail** (two miles, easy). From the parking lot at Limantour Beach, it's a quick hike to the beach; look for a spur trail headed west.

SIR FRANCIS DRAKE BOULEVARD

The Estero Trailhead is located off Sir France Drake Boulevard, shortly after the junction with Pierce Point Road. **Estero Trail** offers several options for hikers. For a short two-mile hike, follow the trail to Home Bay and turn around there. You can extend the hike to **Sunset Beach** (7.8 miles round-trip, moderate), which overlooks Drakes Estero; or continue farther to **Drakes Head** (9.4 miles round-trip), via Estero Trail and **Drakes Head Trail,** with views overlooking Estero de Limantour and Drakes Bay.

Sir Francis Drake Boulevard continues rolling through pastures south and west until it ends at the Point Reyes Lighthouse. From the parking area on Chimney Rock Road, just south of the Point Reyes Lighthouse, follow the **Chimney Rock Trail** (1.6 miles, easy) through grassy cliffs to a wooden bench at the tip of the peninsula. The views of the Pacific and the Point Reyes coast are stunning even though the wind tends to whip mercilessly here.

PIERCE POINT ROAD

Splitting off from Sir Francis Drake Boulevard at Tomales Bay State Park, Pierce Point Road extends to the northern end of the peninsula, where windswept sandy beaches, lagoons, and tule elk await. The trek to **Abbots Lagoon** (two miles round-trip) is an easy hike that will be a hit with bird lovers. From there, Pierce Point Road continues north to another hiking option at **Kehoe Beach** (one mile, easy), where a gravel trail descends to the beach. (Note that this is the only trail in Point Reyes where leashed dogs are permitted.)

Pierce Point Road runs almost to the tip of Tomales Point. From the trailhead at Pierce Point Ranch, there are two hiking options. For a short and easy hike to the beach, follow **McClures Beach Trail** (one mile, easy) to explore tide pools bordered by granite cliffs. A bit longer, **Tomales Point Trail** is a wide, smooth path through the middle of the Tule Elk Reserve to a viewpoint at Bird Rock. From Bird Rock, the "trail" to Tomales Point (9.5 miles round-trip, moderate) becomes trickier and less defined, but is worth it for the views.

Biking

For road biking, most paved roads in Point Reyes are open to both bicycles and cars. Ask at one of the local bike shops for information about this year's hot biking spots and any trail closures. You can find bike rentals at **Point Reyes Outdoors** (11401 Hwy. 1, Point Reyes Station, 415/663-8192, www.pointreyesoutdoors.com, 9am-5pm daily, half day $35, full day $42). The small shop rents mountain bikes, child trailers, and car racks. The staff will point you to the best roads and trails for your skill level and mood.

Kayaking

The calm water of Tomales Bay practically calls out to be explored by kayak. **Blue Waters** (12944 Sir Francis Drake Blvd., Inverness and 19225 Shoreline Hwy., Marshall, 415/669-2600, www.bwkayak.com) offers both kayak tours ($68-98) and rentals (full day $70-110) with two launch sites, one in Inverness and one in Marshall, on the east side of the bay. In addition to paddles around the bay, tours include exploring Drake's Estero in Point Reyes. If you want to go it alone, Blue Waters rents stand-up paddleboards and single and double kayaks. Rates include all the gear you need plus a paddle lesson.

Point Reyes Outdoors (415/663-8192, www.pointreyesoutdoors.com) also provides the widest variety of kayak tours ($75-110) in the area. Tours last 3-6 hours and include a picnic of gourmet goodies from local businesses.

Horseback Riding

Five Brook Ranch (8001 Hwy. 1, 415/663-1570, www.fivebrooks.com, $40-180 per hour) can get you saddled up to ride through Point Reyes's wide variety of ecosystems on tours that last 1-6 hours. The most popular tour is up to an ospreys' nest along Inverness Ridge, then dropping down for a peaceful amble along Olema Creek.

Food

Inside the soot-colored **Sir and Star at the Olema** (10000 Sir Francis Drake Blvd., Olema, 415/663-1034, http://sirandstar.com, 5pm-9pm Wed.-Sun., $20) are taxidermy animals, bouquets of dried kelp, and Shaker-esque furniture. The cuisine highlights the bounty of West Marin, from the cheese to the "faux gras," in style and execution.

The star of the Point Reyes Station restaurant scene is the ★ **Station House Café** (11180 Hwy. 1, Point Reyes Station, 415/663-1515, www.stationhousecafe.com, 8am-9pm Thurs.-Tues., $17-25), which is both casual and upscale. Since 1974, the Station House has been dedicated to serving comfort food with ingredients that reflect the area's agrarian culture.

For a drink and a bit of local color, slip through the swinging doors of the **Old Western Saloon** (11201 Hwy. 1, Point Reyes Station, 415/663-1661, 10am-2am daily), a crusty old West Marin haunt. Overlooking the bay in an expansive weathered redwood building, **Nick's Cove** (23240 Hwy. 1, Point Reyes Station, 415/663-1033, www.nickscove.com, 11am-9pm Mon.-Fri., 10am-9pm Sat.-Sun., $24-34) has a well-designed menu, from light nibbles to a high-end meal. Out back are a long deck and a boathouse, perfect to explore with the little ones.

There is no better place to stock a picnic basket than the **Bovine Bakery** (11315 Hwy. 1, Point Reyes Station, 415/663-9420, 6:30am-5pm Mon.-Fri., 7am-5pm Sat.-Sun.), where you can pick up a cup of coffee, loaves of bread, and cookies. **Cowgirl Creamery** (80 4th St., Point Reyes Station, 415/663-9335, www.cowgirlcreamery.com, 10am-6pm Wed.-Sun.), just around the corner, produces the best cheese in the Bay Area. Tours of the facility are available Friday mornings (by appointment only). The retail shop inside sells their Red Hawk and Mount Tam favorites, as well as other gourmet treats.

The oysters at **Hog Island** (20215 Hwy. 1, Point Reyes Station, 415/663-9218, www.hogislandoysters.com, 9am-5pm daily, $5 table fee) grace many upscale menus. At this open-air stand, you can buy and barbecue the excellent oysters. Hog Island gets busy on weekends and parking can be tricky; expect to wait to get a grill and picnic table.

The sundrenched **Saltwater Oyster Depot** (12781 Sir Francis Drake Blvd., Inverness, 415/669-1244, www.saltwateroysterdepot.com, 5pm-9pm Mon. and Thurs.-Fri., noon-9pm Sat.-Sun., $27) faces the bay and serves a variety of oysters prepared different ways. This charming seafood "shack," lit by skylights and warmed by long rustic wood tables, is the ideal spot after a day of hiking in Point Reyes.

Accommodations

The **Point Reyes Seashore Lodge** (10021 Hwy. 1, Olema, 415/663-9000 or 800/404-5634, www.pointreyesseashorelodge.com, $155-245) offers both budget and luxury lodging in its 22 rooms. All rooms have private baths, some with whirlpool tubs and fireplaces. Larger suites offer kitchens and private patios. There are two cottages, which sleep four people, with outdoor hot tubs that are a relative bargain ($305). The Farm House Restaurant, Bar, and Deli adjoin the hotel, providing plenty of food and drink options.

The five-room **Point Reyes Station Inn** (11591 Hwy. 1, Point Reyes Station, 415/663-9372, www.pointreyesstationinn.com, $125-225) drips with turn-of-the-20th-century charm. Rooms feature vaulted ceilings, large windows, and glass doors leading to private porches. All but one have fireplaces and private en-suite baths. A communal hot tub is in the garden, and the continental breakfast features eggs from the inn's own chickens.

Located just a few miles from the beach, **Point Reyes Hostel** (1390 Limantour Spit Rd., Point Reyes Station, 415/663-8811, www. norcalhostels.org/reyes, $26-130) is steps from fantastic hiking and lush natural scenery. Accommodations are spare but comfortable; pick from the affordable dorm rooms ($26) or a private room ($87-130). The hostel has a communal kitchen, three lounge areas, and a place to lock up bicycles.

★ **Manka's Inverness Lodge** (30 Callendar Way, Inverness, 415/669-1034, www.mankas.com, $215-615) is not so much a lodge as a compound dressed in an ethereal combination of hunting lodge and arts and crafts styles. Stay in the lodge or annex, where rooms are decked out with plush beds with tree-limb posts and antique fixtures. Additional cabins are scattered throughout; all feature large sitting rooms with stone fireplaces.

Constructed of natural wood with fanciful flourishes, **Motel Inverness** (12718 Sir Francis Drake Blvd., 415/236-1967, www.motelinverness.com, $99-195) is more like a classic lodge than a typical motel. The parking lot abuts the entrance to each room, but the rooms open onto the serene wetlands bordering the bay. Inside the main lodge is a grand lounge with an antique pool table and a great stone fireplace.

Camping

Although you would expect the Point Reyes area to abound in camping opportunities, finding a place to pitch a tent is a tall order. The only camping nearby is in the **Point Reyes National Seashore** (www.nps.gov/pore, 415/663-8522, reservations 877/444-6777 or www.recreation.gov, $20), and all are hike-in sites that require reservations months in advance. **Sky Camp** (11 sites, 1.4 miles) is the closest to the Bear Valley Visitors Center and is accessed via a trail on Limantour Road. Near the end of Limantour Road is the trailhead for **Coast Camp** (12 sites, 1.8-2.7 miles). **Wildcat Camp** (five sites, 5.5-6.3 miles) is set away from the beach along the Coastal Trail. The most secluded campground is **Glen Camp** (12 sites), a healthy 4.6 miles from the Bear Valley Trailhead. All campsites have a pit toilet, a water faucet, a picnic table, a charcoal grill, and a food locker.

Transportation and Services

Point Reyes is only about an hour north of San Francisco by car, but getting here can be quite a drive. From the Golden Gate Bridge, take U.S. 101 north to just south of San Rafael. Take the Sir Francis Drake Boulevard exit toward San Anselmo. Follow Sir Francis Drake Boulevard west for 20 miles to the small town of Olema and Highway 1. At the intersection with Highway 1, turn right (north) to Point Reyes Station and the Bear Valley Visitors Center.

A slower but more scenic route follows Highway 1 into Point Reyes National Seashore and provides access to the trails near Bolinas in the southern portion of the park. From the Golden Gate Bridge, take U.S. 101 north to the Mill Valley/Stinson Beach exit. Follow Shoreline Highway for almost 30 miles through Stinson Beach and past Bolinas Lagoon to the coast. From the lagoon, it's 11 miles north to Point Reyes Station. Expect twists, turns, and slow going as you approach Point Reyes.

You can get gas only in Point Reyes Station.

There are full-service grocery stores in Point Reyes Station at **Palace Market** (11300 Highway 1, 415/663-1016, www.palacemarket.com, 7am-9pm Mon.-Sat., 8am-8pm Sun.) and in Inverness at **Inverness Store** (12784 Sir Francis Drake Blvd., 415/669-1041, 9am-7pm daily). The closest hospital is **Novato Community Hospital** (180 Rowland Way, Novato, 415/209-1300, www.novatocommunity.sutterhealth.org).

East Bay

Across the bay, the cities of Berkeley and Oakland rival San Francisco in cultural diversity, radical thinking, and cutting-edge gastronomy. Built around the university and the war effort of the 1940s, the East Bay has grown to become as cosmopolitan as its neighbor to the west.

Note that the East Bay is spread out and is often clogged by commuter traffic in the afternoon. Oakland and Berkeley offer easier access via the BART commuter rail system and have concentrated sights in their downtown areas.

BERKELEY

Berkeley has long been known for its radical, liberal, progressive activism. The youthful urban culture tends to revolve around the University of California, Berkeley, yet the spirit of the 1960s is alive and well on the slightly grungy Telegraph Avenue, where students, street kids, and tourists browse eclectic shops, independent bookstores, and record stores.

University of California, Berkeley

Berkeley is a college town and, fittingly, the **University of California, Berkeley** (www.berkeley.edu) offers the most interesting places to go and things to see. As an introduction to the school, take a guided **campus tour** (510/642-5215, www.berkeley.

edu, 10am Mon.-Sat., 1pm Sun., by reservation only, free). To get a great view of the campus from above, take an elevator ride up the **Campanile** (10am-3:45pm Mon.-Fri., 10am-4:45pm Sat., 10am-1:30pm and 3pm-4:45pm Sun., adults $3, seniors and ages 4-17 $2, under age 4 free), formally called Sather Tower. Stop in at the **Lawrence Hall of Science** (1 Centennial Dr., 510/642-5132, www.lawrencehallofscience.org, 10am-5pm daily, adults $12, seniors and students $10, under age 3 free) for a look at the latest exhibits and interactive displays. Also on campus is the **University of California Botanical Garden** (200 Centennial Dr., 510/643-2755, http://botanicalgarden.berkeley.edu, 9am-5pm daily, adults $10, seniors $8, ages 13-17 $5, ages 5-12 $2, free under age 5), an immense space with an astounding array of wild plants from around the world.

Entertainment and Events

There's a reasonable variety of evening entertainment to be had in Berkeley. The major regional theater is the **Berkeley Repertory Theatre** (2025 Addison St., 510/647-2949, www.berkeleyrep.org, Tues.-Sun., $25-87), which puts on several unusual shows, from world premieres of edgy new works to totally different takes on old favorites.

The big-name acts come to the **Greek Theater** (2001 Gayley Rd., 510/548-3010, www.apeconcerts.com), an outdoor

the Campanile on the UC Berkeley campus

amphitheater constructed in the classic Greek style on the UC Berkeley campus. The **Starry Plough** (3101 Shattuck Ave., 510/841-0188, www.starryploughpub.com, 4pm-2am daily) is an Irish pub with a smallish stage setup. Fabulous Celtic rock groups, folk musicians, and indie bands play here almost every day of the week.

For a slightly less formal outing, **Jupiter** (2181 Shattuck Ave., 510/843-8277, www.jupiterbeer.com, 11:30am-1am Mon.-Thurs., 11:30am-1:30am Fri., noon-1:30am Sat., noon-midnight Sun.) serves excellent wood-fired pizzas and a wide selection of locally brewed beer in their outdoor beer garden as jazz ensembles play or DJs spin the night away.

Sports and Recreation

Tilden Regional Park (Grizzly Peak Blvd., 888/327-2757, www.ebparks.org, 5am-10pm daily) covers the ridge directly above Berkeley. Within its more than 2,000 acres, the park has a celebrated botanical garden, the swimmable Lake Anza and its sandy beaches, an antique carousel, and miniature steam trains, perfect to thrill the little ones. Tilden also offers scores of hiking and mountain biking trails that almost convince you that you are in absolute wilderness, except for the breathtaking views of the Bay Area. Taking a trail map is advisable, as multiple trails crisscross one another, allowing for more adventure but also potential confusion. For a simple stroll, take the **Jewel Lake Nature Trail** (one mile, easy), located in the Nature Area of the park. From the parking lot, the trail heads north along Wildcat Creek and out to Jewel Lake. For a more rigorous climb, the **Wildcat Peak Loop** (3.5 miles, moderate) leaves from the same trailhead behind the Environmental Education Center. Spend some time on the **Bay Area Ridge Trail** (3.5 miles, moderate), a pleasant loop that starts at the Quarry Trailhead off Wildcat Canyon Road. Take **Wildcat Canyon Trail** to **Seaview Trail** and turn right. After some time, the trail changes names to **East Bay Skyline National Trail** and **Bay Area Ridge Trail.** At **Upper Big Springs Trail,** take a right back down the mountain. After nearly one mile, take a left on **Quarry Trail;** it will take you back to the parking lot.

Tilden offers many roads and trails for cyclists. The paved roads snaking through the park (Wildcat Canyon Rd., Grizzly Peak Blvd., and South Park Dr.) twist and turn while gaining and losing enough elevation to keep any cyclist busy.

North of Tilden, the equally large **Wildcat Canyon Regional Park** (5755 McBryde Ave., Richmond, 510/544-3092, www.ebparks.org, sunrise-sunset daily) is filled with wide fire roads, all of which are open to cyclists. Wildcat Canyon has fewer trails than Tilden, but it's quieter, and the trails traverse a more challenging topography and allow for longer treks. A healthy loop (seven miles, moderate-strenuous) that allows you to see most of the park and some ridge-top views begins at the Alvarado Trailhead at the north end of the park.

Food

The very best fine-dining venue is ★ **Chez Panisse** (1517 Shattuck Ave., 510/548-5525, www.chezpanisse.com, $65-100), where founder Alice Waters and her successors create French-California dishes at the cutting edge of current trends. Every dinner is prix fixe, and there are two seatings per evening (5:30pm-6pm and 8pm-8:45pm Mon.-Thurs., 6pm-6:30pm and 8:30pm-9:15pm Fri.-Sat.). You'll need to make reservations up to one month in advance (28 days when booked online) and pay a deposit ($25 pp). Eating at the upstairs **café** (510/548-5049, 11:30am-2:45pm and 5pm-10:30pm Mon.-Thurs., 11:30am-3pm and 5pm-11:30pm Fri.-Sat., $19-25) is a bit more relaxed. The food is just as good and the casual atmosphere is less intimidating.

A worker-owned co-op since 1971, ★ **Cheese Board Collective** (1504 Shattuck Ave., 510/549-3183, http://cheeseboardcollective.coop, 7am-1pm Mon., 7am-6pm Tues.-Fri., 8am-5pm Sat., under $10) is filled with fresh bread, pastries, and cheese. At the counter are up to 400 different cheeses, which the clerks encourage customers to taste. Step next door to the Cheese Board's **pizzeria** (1512 Shattuck Ave., 11:30am-3pm and 4:30pm-8pm daily, $2.50-20), where one type of pizza is made each day with organic and vegetarian toppings.

The food is all locally sourced at **Gather** (2200 Oxford St., 510/809-0400, www.gatherrestaurant.com, 11:30am-2pm and 5pm-9:30pm Mon.-Fri., 10am-2:30pm and 5pm-9:30pm Sat.-Sun., $16-29). The thick menu details each ingredient's former life in a field, out in the bay, or on a ranch. Vegetarians and vegans will find many choices here, including vegetarian charcuterie, lentil ragout, and hearty pizzas.

At **Triple Rock Brewery** (1920 Shattuck Ave., 510/843-2739, http://triplerock.com, 11:30am-1am Mon.-Wed., 11:30am-2am Thurs.-Sat., 11:30am-midnight Sun., $9-14), an ever-evolving menu of beer includes seasonal specialties and favorites, ranging from the Pinnacle Pale Ale to the Stonehenge Stout. The food is exceptional, made from local and organic ingredients. Triple Rock boasts a well-worn wood bar, large windows, and a rooftop beer garden.

Accommodations

Offering great value is the **Golden Bear Inn** (1620 San Pablo Ave., 510/525-6770, www.goldenbearinn.com, $80-99). At this family-friendly place, parents can rent an inexpensive room with two twin beds in a separate bedroom.

Spend a weekend in the charming Claremont district by booking a room at **Mary's Bed and Breakfast** (47 Alvarado Rd., 510/848-1431, http://marysbedandbreakfast.com, weekend two-day minimum, $175). The Craftsman-style home has been meticulously maintained and is elegantly decorated with antiques from the period. Three rooms with private baths are available, as is an apartment for longer stays. A deluxe continental breakfast is served daily in the dining room. Mary's is within walking distance of the Claremont Hotel's spa and restaurant.

The **Hotel Durant** (2600 Durant St., 510/845-8981, www.hoteldurant.com, $189-220) has it all: location and views. Get a room on the upper floors for a view of Oakland, San Francisco, or the bay. Inside, you'll enjoy the high thread-count sheets, pet-friendly options, and the pillow menu. From here, you can walk to the university, Telegraph Avenue, and the Elmwood shopping district.

Since 1915, the **Claremont Resort and Spa** (41 Tunnel Rd., 510/843-3000, www.claremontresort.com, $180-280) has catered to the rich and famous. No two of the 279 elegantly furnished rooms look quite the same, so you'll have a unique experience even in this large resort hotel. The real focus at the Claremont is fitness and pampering. A full-fledged health club, complete with yoga, Pilates, and spinning classes, takes up part of the huge complex. And the full-service spa, which offers popular body treatments plus aesthetic services, finds favor with visitors and locals alike.

Transportation and Services

Berkeley is north of Oakland, along the east side of the San Francisco Bay. To drive into Berkeley, take the Bay Bridge from San Francisco, then merge onto I-80 East. Major roads in town include San Pablo, Ashby, Shattuck, Telegraph, and University Avenues. Parking in Berkeley can be frustrating. If you're visiting for the day or for an evening show, consider taking BART to avoid the parking hassle.

BART (www.bart.gov, one-way $1.85-7.50) is a major form of transit in the Bay Area. The Downtown Berkeley station is located underneath Shattuck Avenue. Other stations in the city include North Berkeley and Ashby. **AC Transit** (510/891-4706, www.actransit.org, adults $2.10, children and seniors $1.05) is the local bus service, offering routes that connect the East Bay and San Francisco (adults $4.20, children and seniors $2.10).

The closest airport is **Oakland International Airport** (OAK, 1 Airport Dr., Oakland, 510/563-3300, www.flyoakland.com). From the Oakland airport, you can rent a car, catch a cab, or take BART ($8-10) from the terminals to the BART Coliseum/Airport station. If you fly into San Francisco, you can take BART from SFO to Berkeley.

OAKLAND

Oakland is the biggest city in the East Bay. Although its reputation hasn't always been perfect, today a great deal of downtown urban renewal has made it a visitor-friendly place with plenty of attractions, accommodations, and exceptional food.

Oakland Museum of California

The **Oakland Museum of California** (1000 Oak St., 510/318-8400, www.museumca.org, 11am-5pm Wed.-Thurs., 11am-9pm Fri., 10am-6pm Sat.-Sun., adults $15, students and seniors $10, children 9-17 $6, parking $1 per hour) has launched itself into the stratosphere of must-see museums. Its multidisciplinary approach tells California's story through art, history, and science. Within its modernist concrete walls you'll be able to see Thiebaud's and Diebenkorn's take on the urban California landscape, a rare and authentic Ohlone basket, and a casting of a once-endemic mastodon. The museum also hosts special themed exhibits that complement its three-pronged approach. The museum has a café, the Blue Oak, which serves wine, espresso, and a selection of salads and sandwiches.

the Oakland Museum of California

Chabot Space and Science Center

One of the most spectacular sights in the East Bay, **Chabot Space and Science Center** (10000 Skyline Blvd., 510/336-7300, www. chabotspace.org, 10am-5pm Tues.-Thurs. and Sun., 10am-10pm Fri.-Sat., adults $16, students and seniors $13, youths 3-12 $12) makes science and space super cool. Up in the Oakland Hills, the Chabot complex includes observatories, a planetarium, a museum, and the Megadome theater, all open to the public (most Bay Area observatory telescopes are private). If your visit runs long, grab a bite to eat and a cup of coffee at the on-site café.

Entertainment and Events

Yoshi's (510 Embarcadero W., 510/238-9200, www.yoshis.com, 5:30pm-9pm Mon.-Wed., 5:30pm-10pm Fri.-Sat., 5pm-9pm Sun., shows 8pm and 10pm daily) has a sushi restaurant in one room and the legendary jazz club next door, so it's possible to enjoy the sushi without attending the concert, or vice versa.

The renovated **Fox Theater** (1807 Telegraph Ave., 510/302-2250, www. thefoxoakland.com) attracts big names to this city landmark. Originally opened in 1928 and designed in the Moorish style, the theater is now in league with some of the more venerated venues across the bay. Past acts in this intimate venue have included Sufjan Stevens, the Pixies, and 2 Chainz. It also has a bar and café where you can get champagne with your fish tacos.

Luka's Taproom & Lounge (2221 Broadway, 510/451-4677, www.lukasoakland. com, 11:30am-midnight Mon.-Wed., 11:30am-2am Thurs.-Fri., 10:30am-2am Sat., 10:30am-midnight Sun.) is a restaurant during the day, then a lounge and dance club at night. With a separate room for DJs and dancing; another space reserved just for pool and a 45-playing jukebox; and the Taproom, with its brasserie-style food, 16 beers on tap, and full bar, almost everyone can find something to enjoy at Luka's.

Plank (98 Broadway, 510/817-0980, http://plankoakland.com, 11am-midnight Sun.-Thurs., 11am-midnight Fri.-Sat.) in Jack London Square has an indoor bowling alley, arcade, and pool tables. Outside, bocce ball courts and a beer garden overlook the Oakland harbor. There is a full bar and the menu is affordable and eclectic.

Era Art Bar (19 Grand Ave., 510/832-4400, www.oaklandera.com, 4:30pm-1:30am Mon.-Sat., noon-1:30am Sun.) is carefully crafted with modern and antique furnishings, blown-glass chandeliers, and rotating art shows. Its cocktails employ unique spirits and fresh ingredients. Evenings are usually booked with DJs, live music, and unusual acts.

Sports and Recreation

The jewel of Oakland is **Lake Merritt** (650 Bellevue Ave., 510/238-7275), where you can take a walk around the lake, play a few holes of golf, rent a kayak for a peaceful paddle, or even get in a set of tennis. For families, **Children's Fairyland** (699 Bellevue Ave., 510/452-2259, www.fairyland.org; 10am-4pm Mon.-Fri., 10am-5pm Sat.-Sun., summer; 10am-4pm Wed.-Sun., spring-fall; 10am-4pm Fri.-Sun., winter; $10) provides hours of entertainment and diversion on 10 acres at the edge of the lake.

Oakland is also home to several professional sports teams. The best consistent players are the Major League Baseball **Oakland A's** (510/538-5600, http://oakland.athletics. mlb.com). Unstoppable action can always be found at a **Golden State Warriors** (888/479-4007, www.nba.com/warriors) game. In 2015, the NBA team won its first championship since 1975, igniting basketball fever throughout the Bay Area. The most notorious team in pro football, the **Oakland Raiders** (510/864-5020, www.raiders.com) call the East Bay home. All three teams play at the **Oracle Arena and O.co Coliseum** (7000 Coliseum Way, Oakland, 510/569-2121, www.coliseum. com). The Oakland Coliseum is a complex with both a covered basketball arena and an open-air stadium that hosts both the A's and the Raiders.

Food

In Jack London Square, you can't walk 10 yards without running into a restaurant, from the old-school and new-style seafood spots to wood-fired pizza joints and Korean barbecues. Perhaps the king is **Bocanova** (55 Webster St., 510/444-1233, www.bocanova. com, 11:30am-9:30pm Mon.-Wed., 11:30am-10:30pm Thurs.-Fri., 11am-10:30pm Sat., 11am-9:30pm Sun., $19-35), which boasts meat, fish, and vegetable dishes made with the spice and zest of the Americas. The full bar has a dizzying selection of spirits, perfect for the 1960s bossa nova vibe.

There's no place more Oakland than the ★ **Home of Chicken and Waffles** (444 Embarcadero W., 510/836-4446, http://homeofchickenandwaffles.com, 10am-midnight Mon.-Thurs., 10am-4am Fri.-Sat., 9am-midnight Sun., $7-17), which serves up good ol' Southern comfort food late into the night. Specialties of the house include the gooey mac and cheese, true Southern sides (lots of grits), and chicken and waffles.

Many believe that the best pizza in the Bay Area can be found in Temescal at ★ **Pizzaiolo** (5008 Telegraph Ave., Oakland, 510/652-4888, www.pizzaiolooakland.com, 8am-noon and 5:30pm-10pm Mon.-Thurs., 8am-noon and 5:30pm-10:30pm Fri.-Sat., $12-28) where the pies are always fire-roasted, thin-crusted, and topped with ingredients both traditional and inventive. Despite the fanfare, Pizzaiolo retains a casual vibe with simple wood tables, an open kitchen, and a cool patio.

Hogs Apothecary (375 40th Ave., Oakland, 510/338-3847, www.hogsapothecary.com, 5pm-11pm Mon.-Thurs., 5pm-midnight Fri., 10am-2:30pm and 5pm-midnight Sat., 10am-2:30pm and 5pm-11pm Sun., $14-25) is Temescal's version of a German beer hall. Here you'll find lots of beer and lots of pork, as well as more than 30 California microbrews.

In Rockridge, the place to go is **Wood Tavern** (6317 College Ave., Oakland, 510/654-4607, www.woodtavern.net, 11:30am-10pm Mon.-Thurs., 11:30am-10:30pm Fri.-Sat., $26-32). The restaurant serves sophisticated California fare in its cool, classy interior. Come with enough room to start with either a cheese or charcuterie plate and one of the restaurant's famous cocktails.

Southie (6311 College Ave., Oakland, 510/654-0100, 9am-9pm Mon.-Sat., 9am-3pm Sun., $13-18) is a sandwich joint with an epicurean twist. Sandwiches of seared ahi, crab, and beef-pork meatballs are served on the white marble counter alongside poached egg and bacon salad and a coffee toffee ice cream sandwich. In the evening, the red-walled restaurant turns more upscale. The beer and wine lists are small but very carefully selected.

Accommodations

Located in the thick of Jack London Square, the **Inn at Jack London Square** (233 Broadway, 510/452-4565, www.innatthesquare.com, $129-159) offers comfortable digs for reasonable rates. In addition to its clean and modestly stylish decor, the hotel has standard amenities such as complimentary Wi-Fi plus an exercise room and an outdoor pool perfect for relaxing during summer days. The hotel is within easy walking distance of Oakland's waterfront.

Compact, but packed with character and bright colors, **Waterfront Hotel** (Jack London Square, 10 Washington St., 510/836-3800, www.jdvhotels.com, $210-330) boasts stellar views, an outdoor pool, and complimentary wine in the afternoons. Some of the more luxurious rooms have private balconies where you can sip your coffee in the morning.

★ **The Washington Inn** (495 10th St., Oakland, 510/452-1776, www.thewashingtoninn.com, $114-139) brings a hint of European elegance to Oakland. Rooms are smartly decorated in a refined style that highlights the 1913 landmark building while giving it a boutique hotel vibe. Downstairs, the white tablecloth Seison restaurant serves classic California fare and serious cocktails. Located in the heart of downtown, the inn offers a hip and convenient Oakland experience.

With all the amenities of a higher-priced chain motel, the **Bay Breeze Inn** (4919 Coliseum Way, 510/536-5972, www.baybreezeinnoakland.com, $56-150) offers both comfort and convenience. Located just down the street from the Oakland Coliseum and only a few miles from Oakland Airport, this is the perfect place to stay if you're into football, baseball, basketball, or live concerts, or just need to be near the airport.

Transportation and Services

Oakland is across the bay from San Francisco and slightly south of Berkeley. It's accessible by car from San Francisco via I-80 over the Bay Bridge. From I-80, I-580 borders Oakland to the east and north, and I-880 runs along the bay on the west. Try to avoid driving I-80, I-880, or I-580 during the commuting hours (7am-10am and 4pm-7pm).

The **Oakland International Airport** (OAK, 1 Airport Dr., Oakland, 510/563-3300, www.flyoakland.com) sees less traffic than San Francisco's airport and has shorter security lines and fewer delays. Major airlines include Alaska, Delta, JetBlue, Southwest, and Spirit.

BART (Bay Area Rapid Transit, www.bart. gov) is a good means of public transportation. The 12th Street/Oakland City Center station is convenient to downtown Oakland, but there are also trains out to 19th Street, Lake Merritt, Rockridge, and the Oakland Airport (via AirBART shuttle bus, $3). BART fares (most East Bay destinations $1.85-7.50 one-way) are based on distance, and ticket machines that accept cash and debit or credit cards are in every station.

Bus service in Oakland is run by **AC Transit** (510/891-4706, www.actransit.org, adults $2.10, children and seniors $1.05). Transbay routes connect the East Bay and San Francisco (adults $4.20, children and seniors $2.10).

The Peninsula

The San Francisco peninsula encompasses the coastal area from Pacifica down to Año Nuevo State Reserve and inland to Palo Alto. Many Bay Area locals enjoy the small-town atmosphere in Half Moon Bay and Pescadero along with the unspoiled beauty of the dozens of miles of undeveloped coastline. Peak seasons include October's pumpkin season and winter, when elephant seals return to Año Nuevo.

The San Andreas Fault splits the coastal and inland peninsula, with dramatic views and curves from aptly named Skyline Boulevard (Hwy. 35). On the bay side, Palo Alto and Stanford University form the intellectual and financial epicenter of Silicon Valley.

MOSS BEACH

Between San Francisco and Half Moon Bay on Highway 1, Moss Beach is one of several residential towns that line the coast south of the imposing Devil's Slide. There is little here besides stunning scenery, a few small businesses, and the Fitzgerald Marine Reserve. North of Moss Beach is the lovely Montara, and south is the Half Moon Bay Airport, El Granada, Princeton, and then Half Moon Bay.

Fitzgerald Marine Reserve

The 32-acre **Fitzgerald Marine Reserve** (200 Nevada Ave., Moss Beach, 650/728-3584, http://parks.smcgov.org, 8am-sunset daily) is considered one of the most diverse intertidal zones in the Bay Area. On its rocky reefs, you can hunt for sea anemones, starfish, eels, and crabs—there's even a small species of red octopus. The reserve is also home to egrets, herons, an endangered species of butterfly, and a slew of sea lions and harbor seals that enjoy sunning themselves on the beach's outer rocks. Rangers are available to answer any questions and, if need be, to remind you of tide pool etiquette (including a strict no-dog policy). For the best viewing, come at low tide (www.protides.com). For a more leisurely and drier experience, numerous trails crisscross the windswept bluffs and through sheltering groves of cypress and eucalyptus trees.

Montara State Beach

Just north of Moss Beach is **Montara State Beach** (2nd St. and Hwy. 1, Montara, www.parks.ca.gov, 650/726-8819, 8am-sunset daily), one of the most beautiful beaches in this area. It is as popular with tidepool visitors, surfers, and anglers as it is with picnickers and beachcombers. For those who want a heart-pounding hike instead of a stroll on the beach, cross Highway 1 to the trailhead at **McNee Ranch.** Fire roads crisscross this eastern section of the state park, but the big hike is eight miles up **Montara Mountain** (1,900 feet), through California chaparral. Parking is in a small and poorly marked dirt lot directly across Highway 1 from the parking lot at Montara Beach. McNee Ranch is also a popular mountain biking area, and dogs are welcome on leash.

Accommodations and Food

Tucked away in the cypress and pine forest of Moss Beach, **Seal Cove Inn** (221 Cypress Ave., Moss Beach, 800/995-9987, www.sealcoveinn.com, $235-350) is a highly regarded 10-room B&B. Outside, the gabled roof, climbing ivy, and expansive gardens let guests know they have entered the inn's rarified world, as do the interior's warm colors, creamy soft linens, private decks and fireplaces, pre-breakfast coffee-and-newspaper room service, and complimentary wine stocked in the mini fridge.

The **Point Montara Lighthouse Hostel** (16th St. and Hwy. 1, Montara, 650/728-7177, www.norcalhostels.org, dorm $27, private room $78, nonmembers add $3 per night) offers great views in the shared dorm rooms (either coed or gender-specific), each with 3-6 beds. Enjoy use of the shared kitchen,

common areas with wood-burning fireplaces, the eclectic garden perched on the cliff, and the private cove beach. Other amenities include Wi-Fi, laundry facilities, an espresso bar, and complimentary linens.

The **Moss Beach Distillery** (140 Beach Way, Moss Beach, 650/728-5595, www.mossbeachdistillery.com, noon-8:30pm Mon.-Thurs., noon-9pm Fri.-Sat., 11am-8:30pm Sun., $13-38) is famous for its hearty portions of comfort food, friendly (though sometimes slow) service, and for the spine-tingling stories of the Blue Lady, the Distillery's legendary ghost. But the real draw is the terrace overlooking the ocean.

Swing by **Gherkin's Sandwich Shop** (171 8th St., Montara, 650/728-2211, 7am-7pm daily, $10) for a picnic lunch. You'll find oddities like the Ooey Gooey, with peanut butter, Nutella, and marshmallows, and hallowed favorites like the BLT, burgers, and pastrami and swiss. Sides include garlic fries and macaroni salad.

Poised above Montara Beach, **La Costanera** (8150 Cabrillo Hwy., Montara, 888/294-0679, www.lacostanerarestaurant.com, 5pm-9pm Tues.-Thurs. and Sun., 5pm-10pm Fri.-Sat., $21-39) is a sophisticated Peruvian restaurant and the only eatery on this part of the coast to earn a Michelin star three years in a row. There are a variety of ceviche options to choose from and the bar menu offers hearty plates that could serve as a light dinner.

HALF MOON BAY

Half Moon Bay retains its character as an "ag" (agricultural) town. Strawberries, artichokes, and Brussels sprouts are the biggest crops, along with flowers, pumpkins, and Christmas trees, making the coast a destination for holiday festivities. Four miles north are Pillar Point Harbor and the neighboring blue-collar town of **Princeton-by-the-Sea**, where hardworking anglers haul in crab, salmon, and herring, and local businesses cater to their needs.

A Festival of Pumpkins

The biggest annual event in this small agricultural town is the **Half Moon Bay Art & Pumpkin Festival** (www.miramarevents.com). Every October, nearly 250,000 people trek to Half Moon Bay to pay homage to the big orange squash. The festival includes live music, food, artists' booths, contests, activities for kids, an adults' lounge area, and a parade. Perhaps the best-publicized event is the pumpkin weigh-off, which takes place before the festivities begin. Farmers bring their tremendous squash in on flatbed trucks from all over the country to determine which is the biggest of all. The winner gets paid per pound, a significant prize when the biggest pumpkins weigh more than 1,000 pounds.

Beaches

The beaches of Half Moon Bay draw visitors from over the hill and farther afield all year long. **Half Moon Bay State Beach** (www.parks.ca.gov, 650/726-8819, parking $10 per day) encompasses three discrete beaches stretching four miles down the coast, each with its own access point and parking lot. **Francis Beach** (95 Kelly Ave.) has the most developed amenities, including a good-size campground with grassy areas to pitch tents and enjoy picnics, a visitors center, and indoor hot showers. **Venice Beach** (Venice Blvd., off Hwy. 1) offers outdoor showers and flush toilets. **Dunes Beach** (Young Ave., off Hwy. 1) is the northernmost major beach in the chain and the least developed.

Sports and Recreation
SURFING

It's hard to miss the surfers while driving down Highway 1. The most popular surfing spot is appropriately named **Surfers Beach**, just south of Princeton. The break is long and small, perfect for beginners. In the summer you're likely to see "surf camps" (the coast's answer to kids' summer camp) as kids of all ages practice paddling, standing up on their board, and taking a wave. More experienced surfers tend to pick **Kelly, Montara,** and **Dunes Beaches,** where the waves are bigger and more unpredictable and the currents challenging. Of course, nothing can touch **Mavericks Break,** west of Pillar Point Harbor. Formed by unique underwater topography, the giant waves are the site of the legendary **Mavericks Surf Contest**, for which the top surfers in the world are given 48 hours' notice to compete on the peak of the winter swells. The deadly break is a half mile offshore, keeping it a safe distance from anyone not seasoned enough to survive it.

If the waves prove too tempting to resist, **Cowboy Surf Shop** (2830 N. Cabrillo Hwy., Half Moon Bay, 650/726-6968, www.cowboy-surfshop.com, 10am-6pm daily, surfboard $20/day, wetsuit $10/day) can rent you what you need while providing advice.

KAYAKING AND WHALE-WATCHING

Depending on the time of year, you can book whale-watching (Jan.-Apr., $40), deep-sea salmon fishing (Apr.-Nov., $98), shallow-water rock fishing (May-Dec., $68-82), Farallon Island rock fishing (call for season, $95), and deep-sea albacore fishing (July-Oct., call for rates) trips aboard the **Queen of Hearts** (Pillar Point Harbor, 510/581-2628, www.fishingboat.com).

One of the coolest ways to see the coast is from the deck of a sea kayak. Many kayak tours with the **Half Moon Bay Kayaking Company** (2 Johnson Pier, 650/773-6101, www.hmbkayak.com, $75-80) require no previous kayaking experience; all tours are roughly three hours. Rental kayaks are also available ($25-60 per hour), as are stand-up paddleboards ($25 per hour). The price of the rental includes a wetsuit, life jacket, and some basic instruction.

Food

★ **Pasta Moon** (315 Main St., 650/726-5125, www.pastamoon.com, 11:30am-2pm and 5:30pm-9pm Mon.-Thurs., 11:30am-2pm and 5:30pm-9:30pm Fri., noon-3pm and 5:30pm-9:30pm Sat., noon-3pm and 5:30pm-9pm Sun., $17-26) is the godmother of fine dining, serving updated Italian cuisine with an emphasis on fresh, light dishes. The wood-fired pizzas are particularly good and affordable, as are any of the pasta dishes, created with house-made noodles. The bar and lounge hums with live jazz, offering an urbane evening out.

The brightly painted **Chez Shea** (408 Main St., 650/726-6868, www.chez-shea. com, lunch 11am-3pm Mon.-Fri., dinner 5pm-8:30pm daily, brunch 10am-4:30pm Sat.-Sun., $18) serves an eclectic mix of comfort food from Spain, Mexico, Lebanon, Italy, and South Africa. Don't miss the Mezza Platter, with its wonderful array of dipping sauces, or the Shwarma Platter, with lean strips of seasoned beef and lamb.

The virtual parking lot out front on Highway 1 speaks to the golden touch of **Sam's Chowder House** (4210 N. Cabrillo Hwy., Pillar Point Harbor, 650/712-0245, www.samschowderhouse.com, 11:30am-9pm Mon.-Thurs., 11:30am-9:30pm Fri., 11-9:30am Sat., 11am-9pm Sun., $12-35). This is the place to get seafood and soak in the surf and sun. Facing the water you'll find ample views and plentiful decks with Adirondack chairs and fire pits, where you can sip cocktails, slurp down oysters, and indulge in steaming plates of whole lobster, seafood paella, and seared tuna.

Stop into the **Moonside Bakery & Café** (604 Main St., 650/726-9070, www.moonsidebakery.com, 7am-5pm daily) for breakfast pastries and espresso or opt for a casual lunch.

Accommodations

Half Moon Bay offers several lovely bed-and-breakfasts and one luxury resort hotel.

The **Ritz-Carlton Half Moon Bay** (1 Miramontes Point Rd., 650/712-7000, www. ritzcarlton.com, $500) has a top-tier restaurant, Navio; a world-class day spa; and posh rooms that are worth the rates. If you can, get a room facing the ocean. While you're here, enjoy free access to the spa's bathing rooms, an outdoor hot tub overlooking the ocean, tennis courts, and the basketball court.

For a personal lodging experience, try the ★ **Old Thyme Inn** (779 Main St., 650/726-1616, www.oldthymeinn.com, $159-349)

beach at Half Moon Bay

downtown. Each uniquely decorated room has its own garden theme and luxurious amenities. Guests can enjoy the common sitting rooms, gorgeous garden, and sumptuous breakfast.

Built out of weathered redwood, the **Cypress Inn** (407 Mirada Rd., 650/726-6002, www.cypressinn.com, $229-459) is a neat compound where most of the rooms come with fireplaces, private decks, jetted tubs, and fridges. A full-service breakfast and a cocktail hour are offered in the Main House. The inn is an easy bike ride to downtown Half Moon Bay.

Transportation

Half Moon Bay is on Highway 1 about 45 minutes south of San Francisco. From San Francisco, take I-280 south to Highway 92 west to Half Moon Bay and Highway 1. You can also take the scenic route by following Highway 1 directly south from San Francisco. Parking in downtown Half Moon Bay is usually easy—except if you're in town during the Pumpkin Festival. Your best bet is to stay in town with your car safely stowed in a hotel parking lot before the festival.

PESCADERO AND VICINITY

Pescadero is a tiny dot on the coastline, south of Half Moon Bay and well north of Santa Cruz, with one main street, one side street, several smallish farms—and the legendary Duarte's Tavern.

Sights

San Gregorio is a tiny picturesque town of rolling rangeland, neat patches of colorful crops, and century-old homes, including a one-room schoolhouse and an old brothel. Its beating heart is the **San Gregorio General Store** (Hwy. 84 and Stage Rd., 650/726-0565, www.sangregoriostore.com, 10:30am-6pm Mon.-Thurs., 10:30am-7pm Fri., 10am-7pm Sat., 10am-6pm Sun.), open since 1889. Like at any good country store, you'll find a collection of books, a variety of cast-iron cookery, oil lamps, work pants, and raccoon traps. On weekends the store is packed with out-of-towners, and live music keeps things moving.

South of Pescadero is **Pigeon Point Lighthouse** (210 Pigeon Point Rd., at Hwy. 1, 650/879-2120, www.parks.ca.gov, 8am-sunset daily). First lit in 1872, Pigeon Point is one of the most photographed lighthouses in the United States. Its hostel still shelters travelers, and visitors can marvel at the incomparable views from the point. In winter, look for migrating whales from the rocks beyond the tower.

Beaches

Pescadero State Beach (Hwy. 1, north of Pescadero Rd., 650/879-2170, www.parks.ca.gov, 8am-sunset daily) is the closest beach to the town of Pescadero. It's a great spot to walk in the sand and stare out at the Pacific, but near-constant winds make it less than ideal for picnics or sunbathing. Bird lovers flock to **Pescadero Marsh Natural Preserve** (Hwy. 1, www.smcnha.org), located on Highway 1 right across the highway from Pescadero State Beach. This protected wetland, part of Pescadero State Beach, is home to a variety of avian species, including great blue herons, snowy egrets, and northern harriers.

North of Pescadero, at the intersection of Highway 84 and Highway 1, **San Gregorio State Beach** (650/726-8819, www.parks.ca.gov, 8am-sunset daily, $10) stretches out beyond the cliffs to create a beach perfect for contemplative strolling. San Gregorio is clothing-optional at the far north end and a local favorite in the summer, despite the regular appearance of fog. Brave beachgoers can swim and bodysurf, though you'll need a wetsuit. Picnic tables and restrooms cluster near the parking lot, but can be hampered by the wind.

Año Nuevo State Park

Año Nuevo State Park (Hwy. 1, south of Pescadero, 650/879-2025, reservations 800/444-4445, www.parks.ca.gov, 8am-sunset daily, $10 per car) is world-famous as the winter home and breeding ground of once-endangered elephant seals. The reserve also has extensive dunes, marshland, and excellent bird habitat. The beaches and wilderness are open year-round. The elephant seals start showing up in late November and stay to breed, birth pups, and loll on the beach until early March. Visitors are not allowed down to the elephant seal habitats on their own and must sign up for a guided walking tour. Once you see two giant males crashing into one another in a fight for dominance, you won't want to get too close. Book your tour at least a day or two in advance since the seals are popular with both locals and travelers.

Food

★ **Duarte's Tavern** (202 Stage Rd., Pescadero, 650/879-0464, www.duartestavern.com, 7am-8pm daily, $15-28) is famous for its artichoke soup and olallieberry pie. For the best experience, sit in the bar, where locals of all stripes sit shoulder to shoulder with travelers, sharing conversation and a bite to eat. Pick out a selection from the outdated jukebox and order a Bloody Mary, garnished with a pickled green bean.

Inside the gas station across the street,

Mercado & Taqueria De Amigos (1999 Pescadero Creek Rd., 650/879-0232, 9am-9pm daily, $7-12 cash only) has been written up by the *New York Times* and is rumored to be the best taqueria between San Francisco and Santa Cruz. Squeezed in next to coolers of beer and energy drinks, the open kitchen prepares excellent shrimp burritos, *al pastor* tacos, and not-too sweet *horchata*. You'll find mainly locals here, most speaking Spanish, and the wait can be long.

Accommodations and Camping

Pigeon Point Hostel (210 Pigeon Point Rd., at Hwy. 1, 650/879-0633, http://norcalhostels.org/pigeon, dorm $26-28, private room $76) is a Hostelling International spot with simple but comfortable accommodations, both private and dorm-style. Amenities include three kitchens, free Wi-Fi, and beach access.

At **Costanoa Lodge and Campground** (2001 Rossi Rd., at Hwy. 1, 650/879-1100, www.costanoa.com, campsite $31-45, rooms $80-245), lodging options include pitching a tent in the campground, staying in a tent or log-style cabins, or renting a whirlpool suite. A small general store offers s'mores fixings and souvenirs while "comfort stations" provide

elephant seal at Año Nuevo State Park

outdoor fireplaces, private indoor-outdoor showers, baths with heated floors, and saunas that are open 24 hours to all guests.

★ **Butano State Park** (1500 Cloverdale Rd., Pescadero, 650/879-2040, reservations 800/444-7275, www.parks.ca.gov, Apr.-Nov., $35) offers 21 drive-in and 18 walk-in campsites. Although there are no showers and few amenities, there are clean restrooms, fire pits, and drinking water. The walk-ins sites are particularly beautiful nestled in a glen of redwoods. You can choose quiet strolls through the canopy of redwoods or more athletic treks up dusty ridgelines.

Farther inland, past the tiny town of Loma Mar, is **Memorial Park** (9500 Pescadero Creek Rd., 650/879-0238, www.co.sanmateo.ca.us, year-round, $30), with 158 campsites.

Each site accommodates up to eight people and has a fire pit, picnic tables, and a metal locker to store food and sundries. Drinking water, baths with coin-operated showers, and a general store can also be found within the park. Memorial boasts an amphitheater and swimming holes.

Transportation

Pescadero is 17 miles south of Half Moon Bay. At Pescadero State Beach, Highway 1 intersects Pescadero Road. Turn east on Pescadero Road and drive two miles to the stop sign (the only one in town). Turn left onto Stage Road to find the main drag. Parking is free and generally easy to find on Stage Road or in the Duarte's parking lot. On weekends, you might need to park down the road a ways.

Silicon Valley

Palo Alto, San Jose, and the Santa Clara valley form the trifecta known as Silicon Valley, home to tech-media giants and the wizards who run them. Palo Alto owes much of its prosperity and character to Stanford University, an incubator for some of Silicon Valley's great talents and entrepreneurs. Sprawled across the south end of Silicon Valley, San Jose proudly claims the title of biggest city in the Bay Area. It is the workhorse of the valley's high-tech industry and is home to eBay, Cisco, Adobe, IBM, and many others.

SIGHTS
Stanford University

Stanford University (University Ave., Palo Alto, 650/723-2560, www.stanford.edu) is one of the top universities in the world, and fewer than 10 percent of the high school students who apply each year are accepted. The **visitors center** (295 Galvez St., www.stanford.edu, 8:30am-5pm Mon.-Fri., 10am-5pm Sat.-Sun.) is in a handsome one-story brick building; inside, well-trained staff can help you with campus maps and tours. Definitely

download or procure a map of campus before getting started on your explorations, as Stanford is infamously hard for newcomers to navigate.

For a taste of the beauty that surrounds the students on a daily basis, begin your tour with **The Quad** (Oval at Palm Dr.) and **Memorial Church.** Located at the center of campus, these architectural gems are still in active use. Classes are held in the quad every day, and services take place in the church each Sunday. Almost next door to the Quad is **Hoover Tower** (650/723-2053, 10am-4pm daily, $2), the tall tower that's visible from up to 30 miles away. For great views of the Bay Area, head up to its observation platform.

On the other side of the Quad, just past the Oval, is the **Cantor Arts Center** (328 Lomita Dr. at Museum Way, 650/723-4177, www.museum.stanford.edu, 11am-5pm Wed. and Fri.-Sun., 11am-8pm Thurs.). This free art museum features both permanent collections of classic paintings and sculpture donated by the Cantors and other philanthropists, along with traveling exhibitions. One of the center's highlights is the **Rodin Sculpture Garden,** pieces cast in France from Rodin's originals that include *The Burghers of Calais* and *The Gates of Hell.* The most famous member of this collection, *The Thinker,* can be found in the Susan and John Diekman Gallery inside the museum.

San Jose Museum of Art

The highly regarded **San Jose Museum of Art** (110 S. Market St., San Jose, 408/271-6840, www.sjmusart.org, 11am-5pm Tues.-Sun., adults $8, students and seniors $5, under age 6 free) is right downtown. Housed in a historical sandstone building that was added in 1991, the beautiful light-filled museum features modern and contemporary art. Its permanent collection focuses largely on West Coast artists, but major retrospectives of works by the likes of Andy Warhol, Robert Mapplethorpe, and Alexander Calder come through often, giving the museum a broader scope. As a bonus, the Museum Store offers perhaps the best gift shopping in downtown San Jose. The café, with both an indoor lounge and outside sidewalk tables, is a great place to grab a quick bite.

Tech Museum of Innovation

The **Tech Museum of Innovation** (201 S. Market St., San Jose, 408/294-8324, www. thetech.org, 10am-5pm daily, adults $20, seniors and children 3-17 $15) brings technology of all kinds to kids, families, and science lovers. The interactive displays at the Tech invite touching and letting children explore and learn about medical technology, computers, biology, chemistry, physics, and more, using all their senses. The IMAX theater (additional $5) shows films dedicated to science, learning, technology, and adventure (and the occasional blockbuster).

Winchester Mystery House

For good old-fashioned haunted fun, stop in at the **Winchester Mystery House** (525 S. Winchester Blvd., San Jose, 408/247-2101, www.winchestermysteryhouse.com, 9am-5pm daily), a huge bizarre mansion built by famous eccentric Sarah Winchester. Kids love the doors that open onto brick walls, stairwells that go nowhere, and oddly shaped rooms, while adults enjoy the story of Sarah and the antiques displayed in many of the rooms. Sarah married into the gunmaking Winchester family and became disturbed later in life by the death wrought by her husband's products. She designed the house to both facilitate communication

Stanford University

with the spirits of the dead and to confound them and keep herself safe. Whether or not ghosts still haunt the mansion is a matter of debate and of faith—visit and make up your own mind. Admission to the grounds is free, but to get a peek inside the house, you must be on one of the many **tours** (adults $27-40, seniors $26-36, children 6-12 $24-30, 5 and under free). For an extra-spooky experience, take a Friday the 13th or Halloween flashlight tour (book early, as these tours fill up fast).

FOOD
San Jose
The center of San Jose's hip restaurant scene is San Pedro Square, the long narrow block of North San Pedro Street, east of West Santa Clara Street. Offerings include the **San Pablo Square Market** (87 N. San Pedro St., www.sanpedrosquaremarket.com, 7am-10pm daily); **71 Saint Peter** (71 N. San Pedro St., 408/971-8523, www.71saintpeter.com, 11am-1pm and 5pm-8:30pm Mon.-Fri., 5pm-8:30pm Sat., $16-27), serving solid Mediterranean classics; and **Firehouse No. 1 Gastropub** (69 N. San Pedro St., 408/287-6969, http://firehouse1.com, 11:30am-midnight Mon.-Wed., 11:30am-2am Thurs.-Fri., 4pm-2am Sat.,

11am-midnight Sun., $12-35), serving meat-heavy comfort food.

Mezcal (25 W. San Fernando St., 408/283-9595, http://mezcalrestaurantsj.com, 11:30am-9pm Mon., 11:30am-10pm Tues.-Thurs., 11:30am-11:30pm Fri., 4pm-11:30pm Sat., 4pm-9pm Sun., $10-19) specializes in food from the Oaxaca region of Mexico. The menu is full of mole, pork cracklings, and fresh fish, fruit, and vegetables.

Gombei (193 E. Jackson St., 408/279-4311, http://gombei.com, 11:30am-2:30pm and 5pm-9:30pm Mon.-Sat., $9), in Japantown, is known for traditional Japanese food at good prices. The menu is as minimal as the decor, with simple categories such as *udon,* tofu, and curry rice.

Little has changed at **Original Joe's** (301 S. 1st St., San Jose, 408/292-7030, www.originaljoes.com, 11am-11pm Sun.-Thurs., 11am-midnight Fri.-Sat., $18-40) since it opened in 1937. Veal parmigiana and pot roast share the menu with calf's liver served four different ways. There are a variety of pasta and steaks, as well as the midcentury bar, The Hideout.

About 10 miles southwest of San Jose, ★ **Manresa** (320 Village Ln., Los Gatos, 408/354-4330, www.manresarestaurant.com, 5:30pm-9pm Wed.-Sun., tasting menu $198)

the Winchester Mystery House

is the Michelin-starred darling of the South Bay. The menu features such delicate oddities as panna cotta topped with abalone "petals." Surprisingly, they do accept walk-ins, but if you're looking for a special Saturday night, reserve now.

Palo Alto

The **Rose and Crown** (457 Emerson Ave., Palo Alto, 650/327-7673, www.roseandcrownpa.com, kitchen 11:30am-2pm and 6pm-9pm Mon.-Fri., 11:30am-9pm Sat.-Sun., $8-14) is a pub with a serious selection of beer and a menu of British food (including the to-die-for Stilton burger). The kitschy decor at the **Palo Alto Creamery** (566 Emerson St., Palo Alto, 650/323-3131, www.paloaltocreamery.com, 7am-10pm Mon.-Wed., 7am-11pm Thurs., 7am-midnight Fri., 8am-midnight Sat., 8am-10pm Sun., $8-20) feels like a genuine 1950s soda shop. The food runs to American classics, but what patrons really come for is the house-made ice cream.

ACCOMMODATIONS

San Jose

The **Four Points Sheraton Downtown San Jose** (211 S. 1st St., 408/282-8800, www.fourpoints.com, $119-234) prides itself on its old-school elegance and hospitality. Rooms add a touch of comfort, with Egyptian cotton linens and cushy comforters on the beds. Amenities include a restaurant and bar, room service, and free Wi-Fi.

The **Sainte Claire Hotel** (302 S. Market St., 408/295-2000, www.thesainteclaire.com, $113-162) offers big city-style accommodations. Standard rooms are small but attractive, with carved wooden furniture and rich linens and draperies. Amenities include a flat-screen TV with a DVD player, a CD and MP3 player, free Wi-Fi, plush robes, and turndown service.

For a taste of Silicon Valley luxury, stay at **The Fairmont San Jose** (170 S. Market St., 408/998-1900, www.fairmont.com, $150-180), with a day spa and limousine service. Standard rooms feature elegant fabrics and appointments, and a marble-clad private bath.

The top-tier **Hotel Valencia Santana Row** (355 Santana Row, 408/551-0010, www.hotelvalencia-santanarow.com, $219-319) offers ultramodern elegance and convenience with an outdoor pool and hot tub, a slick lounge perched on the hotel's balcony, and the swank Citrus Restaurant. Inside the rooms are Egyptian cotton sheets and lavish baths with upscale toiletries.

Palo Alto

Cheap lodgings near Palo Alto can be found in the serene farm setting of **Hidden Villa Hostel** (26870 Moody Rd., Lost Altos, 650/949-8648, www.hiddenvilla.org, Sept.-May, $27-60). Sustainably constructed, the hostel provides access to hiking trails, the surrounding organic farm, and the small wealthy town of Los Altos Hills. Reservations are required on weekends and a good idea even on weekdays.

Down on El Camino Real, **Dinah's Garden Hotel** (4261 El Camino Real, 650/493-2844 or 800/227-8220, www.dinahshotel.com, $119-169) has basic rooms the size and shape of a motel, but the high-priced suites are something to behold. Attached to the hotel are both a casual poolside grill and an upscale seafood restaurant with a decidedly Japanese bent. The **Creekside Inn** (3400 El Camino Real, 650/493-2411, www.creekside-inn.com, $115-250) provides garden accommodations set back a bit from the noisy road. The rooms are more upscale than many motels, with stylish fabrics and up-to-date amenities. All rooms have free Wi-Fi, fully stocked private baths, refrigerators, coffee makers, in-room safes, and comfy bathrobes.

TRANSPORTATION AND SERVICES

Air

Travelers heading straight for Silicon Valley should fly into **Mineta San José International Airport** (SJC, 1701 Airport Blvd., 408/392-3600, www.flysanjose.com). This suburban commercial airport has shorter lines, has less parking and traffic congestion, and is convenient to downtown San Jose.

Train

Amtrak (800/872-7245, www.amtrak.com) trains come into San Jose, and you can catch either the once-daily Seattle-Los Angeles *Coast Starlight* or the commuter *Capitol Corridor* to Sacramento at the **San Jose-Diridon Station** (65 Cahill St.). **Caltrain** (95 University Ave., 800/660-4287, www.caltrain. com, $3.25-13.25) can get you here as well; the commuter rail line runs from Gilroy to San Francisco with a hub in San Jose.

Public Transit

At Caltrain's Diridon station you can catch the **VTA Light Rail** (408/321-2300, www.vta. org, $2-4), a streetcar network that serves San Jose and some of Silicon Valley as far north as Mountain View. The VTA also operates Silicon Valley **buses,** which can get you almost anywhere you need to go if you're patient enough.

Car

San Jose is 50 miles south of San Francisco via U.S. 101 or I-280 south; I-280 is much prettier but less convenient. Palo Alto lies about 20 miles north of San Jose and is accessed by U.S. 101, I-280, or Highway 82. Highway 87, sometimes called the Guadalupe Parkway, can provide convenient access to downtown San Jose and the airport. Avoid San Jose's freeways during **rush hour** (7am-9:30am and 4pm-7:30pm Mon.-Fri.).

Services

The nearest 24-hour emergency room is **Stanford University Hospital** (900 Quarry Rd., 650/723-5111, http://stanford-hospital.org), and for non-life-threatening emergencies, visit the **Palo Alto Medical Foundation Urgent Care Center** (795 El Camino Real, 650/321-4121, www.pamf. org, 7am-9pm daily). **Good Samaritan Hospital** (2425 Samaritan Dr., 408/559-2011, www.goodsamsj.org) has 24-hour emergency services.

Wine Country

Napa Valley.................... 120 Russian River Valley............ 148

Sonoma Valley................. 140

Look for ★ to find recommended sights, activities, dining, and lodging.

Highlights

★ **Domaine Chandon:** This Yountville winery offers a gorgeous setting in which to sample its premier California sparkling wine (page 127).

★ **Frog's Leap Winery:** Tour the organic and biodynamic vineyards at this down-to-earth winery known for its sense of fun—and excellent cabernets (page 130).

★ **Mumm:** This sophisticated yet easygoing winery excels in friendly service, sparkling wines, and generous pours (page 131).

★ **Culinary Institute of America:** Stop by for cooking classes and demonstrations, to peruse the museum, or to indulge in a meal at the exemplary restaurant (page 134).

★ **Gundlach Bundschu Winery:** Pack a picnic and relax at the beautiful grounds at this local favorite (page 140).

★ **Cline Cellars:** Rhone varietals, lush gardens, a museum, and a historical adobe make Cline a must-stop in Carneros (page 142).

★ **Mission San Francisco Solano de Sonoma:** The final Spanish mission built in California is the centerpiece of Sonoma State Historic Park (page 142).

★ **Russian River:** Rafting, canoeing, and kayaking make this area as much a destination for outdoors enthusiasts as for wine fans (page 154).

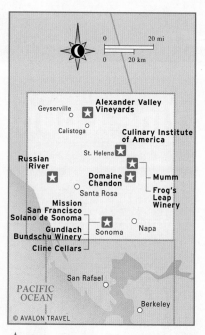

© AVALON TRAVEL

★ **Alexander Valley Vineyards:** Visit the grave of Cyrus Alexander, who planted the first vineyards here, then taste decadent zinfandels surrounded by beautiful scenery (page 157).

Entering California's Wine Country is an incomparable experience. From the crest of the last hill, sunlight paints golden streaks on endless rows of grapevines that stretch in every direction for as far as the eye can see.

Trellises run alongside every road, with unpicked weeds beneath the vines and rose bushes capping each row. A heady aroma of earth and grapes permeates the area. Welcome to the Napa and Sonoma Valleys.

The area's beautiful grapevines are renowned worldwide for producing top-quality vintages and economical table wines. Foodies also know the area as a center for stellar cuisine. Yountville, a tiny upscale town in the middle of Napa Valley, is the favorite of celebrity chef Thomas Keller. The food served at his French Laundry restaurant is legendary, as are the prices. Keller's influence helped to usher in a culinary renaissance, and today the lush flavors of local sustainable produce are available throughout the region.

Sonoma Valley has long played second fiddle to Napa in terms of prestige, but the wines coming out of the area are second to none. Russian River Valley wineries are often friendlier and less crowded, while the wineries in the southern Carneros region are few and far between. Each offers a more personal experience than Napa and the chance to sample unique varietals.

PLANNING YOUR TIME

Napa and Sonoma are the epicenter of Wine Country. Many visitors plan a weekend in Napa, with another weekend to explore Sonoma and the Russian River. During summer and fall, you'll find packed tasting rooms in the valley; even the smaller boutique labels do big business during the high season (May-Oct.).

Highway 29, which runs through the heart of Napa Valley, gets jammed up around St. Helena and can be very slow on weekends. U.S. 101 slows through Santa Rosa during the weekday rush hour and late in the day on sunny summer weekend afternoons. Downtown tasting rooms in Napa Valley and Sonoma can offer an alternative.

Previous: vintage truck in Sonoma; picturesque building at Napa Valley winery. **Above:** Most wineries provide tastings.

Wine Country

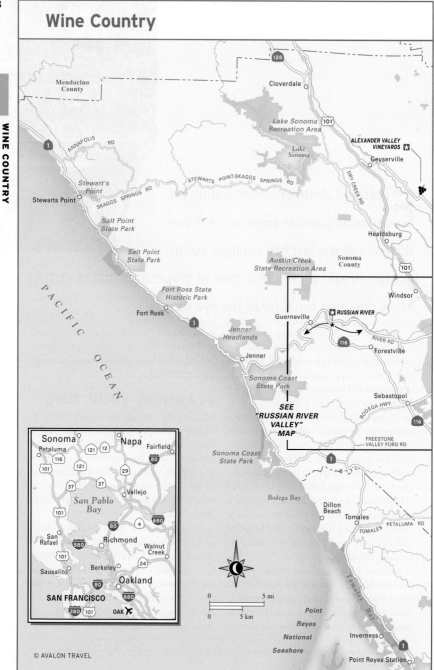

Mendocino County

Cloverdale

128

Lake Sonoma Recreation Area

101

Lake Sonoma

ALEXANDER VALLEY VINEYARDS ✈

Geyserville

1

ANNAPOLIS RD

STEWARTS POINT-SKAGGS SPRINGS RD

DRY CREEK RD

Stewart's Point

Stewarts Point

SKAGGS SPRINGS RD

Healdsburg

Salt Point State Park

Salt Point State Park

Austin Creek State Recreation Area

Sonoma County

101

Fort Ross State Historic Park

Windsor

P A C I F I C

Fort Ross

Jenner Headlands

Guerneville

RUSSIAN RIVER ✦

RIVER RD

116

Forestville

O C E A N

Jenner

Sonoma Coast State Park

Sebastopol

BODEGA HWY

116

SEE "RUSSIAN RIVER VALLEY" MAP

FREESTONE VALLEY FORD RD

Sonoma Coast State Park

1

Sonoma
Napa
Fairfield

Petaluma
121 12

101
121

29

37

37

Vallejo

San Pablo Bay

101

80

4

580

San Rafael

580

Richmond

Walnut Creek

24

Berkeley

Sausalito

101

Oakland

80

SAN FRANCISCO

880

280 101

OAK ✈

Bodega Bay

Dillon Beach

Tomales

TOMALES PETALUMA RD

Point Reyes National Seashore

Inverness

Point Reyes Station

0   5 mi

0   5 km

© AVALON TRAVEL

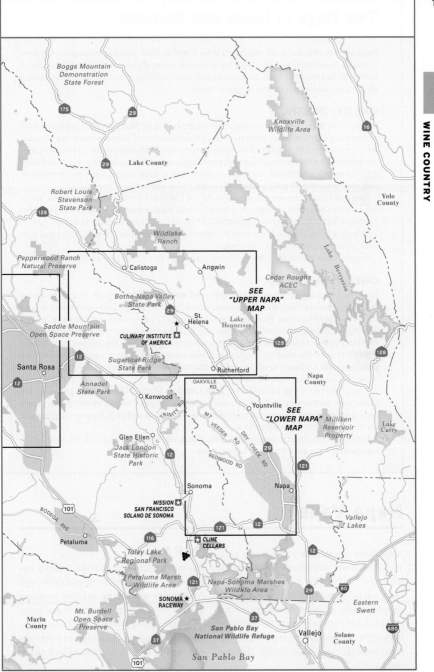

Two Days in Napa and Sonoma

Napa and Sonoma are about one hour's drive from San Francisco, and are popular day trips. Traffic on the winding, two-lane Wine Country roads can easily become clogged, especially on weekends. To avoid the crowds, try to get an early start or visit on a weekday. Most wineries close by 4pm, and some are open only by appointment.

ONE DAY IN NAPA

In downtown Napa, get your bearings at the **Oxbow Public Market.** Shop, nibble pastries, and sip a cup of coffee, or just pick up some picnic supplies before hopping over to the Silverado Trail. Drive north to **Rutherford** and enjoy some bubbly at **Mumm,** followed by some cabernet at **Frog's Leap,** a famously fun and relaxed Napa winery. Get back on Highway 29 and lunch in St. Helena at **Farmstead,** where the excellent farm-to-table cuisine, rustic chic atmosphere, plus wine- and olive oil-tasting make it the perfect all-in-one stop.

Give your taste buds a rest and stroll through the **Culinary Institute of America,** where the country's top chefs are trained, or soak in some steamy mud at **Dr. Wilkinson's Hot Springs Resort** in easygoing **Calistoga.** Afterward, you'll undoubtedly be hungry, so take a table next to the floating fireplace at the Michelin-starred **Solbar.** From Calistoga, the drive back to San Francisco will take two hours.

Stay the night at **Indian Springs** before spending a second day exploring Sonoma.

ONE DAY IN SONOMA

From Napa, Highway 121 winds west through the **Carneros wine region.** Stop off for a bit of bubbly at gorgeous **Domaine Carneros,** where the views and gardens are almost as impressive as the sparkling wines. From Highway 121, Highway 12 twists north into **Sonoma.** Stretch your legs in Sonoma Plaza and explore the charming downtown area. Stop in at the **Sonoma Mission** for a bit of history, and then grab lunch at **the girl & the fig,** housed in the historic Sonoma Hotel. If the sunshine is calling, you may want to get picnic supplies at the **Basque Boulangerie Cafe** and head over to **Gundlach Bundschu Winery,** which boasts some of the best picnic grounds in the valley.

Then it may be time for a short hike at **Jack London State Historic Park** in quaint Glen Ellen, north on Highway 12. Practically next door, **Benziger Family Winery** offers more tasting opportunities, plus tractor tours of its beautiful hilltop vineyards. Dine on farm-to-table comfort food at the **Glen Ellen Star.**

From Glen Ellen, head to downtown **Santa Rosa,** where you can catch U.S. 101 south to San Francisco, 52 miles and a little over an hour away.

Napa Valley

Napa Valley can feel like a wine theme park. Wineries cluster along Highway 29 and the Silverado Trail, tasting rooms are plentiful, tours sell out in advance, and special events draw hundreds. As the wine industry in Napa exploded, top-tier chefs rose to the challenge, flocking to the area and opening amazing restaurants in the tiny towns that line the wine trails.

NAPA

The blue-collar heart of Napa Valley is the city of Napa. The Napa River snakes through downtown, tempering the hot summer weather and providing recreation and natural beauty. Along the river, you'll find sparkling new structures with high-end clothiers and cutting-edge restaurants as well as the Oxbow Market.

Wineries

The base of the valley has few wineries that host visitors without appointment. The best place to casually taste in Napa is the **Vintner's Collective** (1245 Main St., 707/255-7150, www.vintnerscollective.com, 11am-6pm daily, $10-30) in the historical Pfeiffer Building. A house of ill repute during its Victorian youth, it is now the public face of 18 different wineries and winemakers. The standard tasting includes a flight of three everyday wines, and the premium tasting features six wines.

Entertainment and Events

The historical **Napa Valley Opera House** (1030 Main St., 707/226-7372, http://nvoh.org) hosts comedians, jazz ensembles, and musical acts—you can count on something going on nearly every night of the week. The building itself is also a treat, with antique tile floors, curving banisters, a café, and two lounges that make the 500-seat venue feel intimate.

The **Uptown Theatre** (1350 3rd St., Napa, 707/259-0123, www.uptowntheatrenapa.com) is another great place to see a show. Originally opened in 1937, this art deco theater hosts acts from Lindsey Buckingham to Hannibal Buress and Boz Scaggs.

The live music at **Silo's** (Napa Mill, 530 Main St., 707/251-5833, www.silosnapa.com, cover charge up to $25) is an eclectic mix that includes everything from jazz to standup comedy and Johnny Cash tribute bands. There is a decent wine list and a small food menu.

Shopping

The south end of Main Street has some flashy buildings with equally flashy clothiers, but the place to go is the **Historic Napa Mill** (Main St., www.historicnapamill.com), one block down. The former mill is now a shopping and dining center, decorated with rustic touches. The **Napa General Store** (540 Main St., 707/259-0762, www.napageneralstore.com, 8am-6pm daily) offers wine-related knick-knacks and local artwork, including leather crafts and fiber art.

Across the river from downtown Napa, the **Oxbow Public Market** (610-644 1st St., 707/226-6529, www.oxbowpublicmarket.com, 9am-7pm daily) has breathed life into this "across the tracks" section of Napa. Grab a cup of **Ritual Coffee** and browse through the epicurean wares. Pick through cooking- and kitchen-related knickknacks at the **Napastak.** Or get lost in the myriad spices and seasonings at the **Whole Spice Company.** There is also a chocolatier, an

downtown Napa

Upper Napa Valley

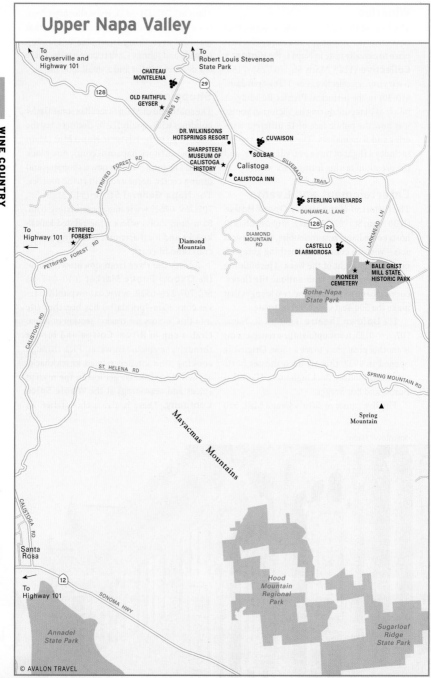

To Geyserville and Highway 101

To Robert Louis Stevenson State Park

CHATEAU MONTELENA

128

29

OLD FAITHFUL GEYSER

TUBBS LN

DR. WILKINSONS HOTSPRINGS RESORT

CUVAISON

SHARPSTEEN MUSEUM OF CALISTOGA HISTORY

SOLBAR

Calistoga

PETRIFIED FOREST RD

SILVERADO TRAIL

CALISTOGA INN

STERLING VINEYARDS

DUNAWEAL LANE

To Highway 101

PETRIFIED FOREST

PETRIFIED FOREST RD

Diamond Mountain

DIAMOND MOUNTAIN RD

128 29

LARKMEAD LN

CASTELLO DI ARMOROSA

BALE GRIST MILL STATE HISTORIC PARK

PIONEER CEMETERY

CALISTOGA RD

Bothe-Napa State Park

ST. HELENA RD

SPRING MOUNTAIN RD

Mayacmas Mountains

Spring Mountain

CALISTOGA RD

Santa Rosa

12

To Highway 101

SONOMA HWY

Hood Mountain Regional Park

Annadel State Park

Sugarloaf Ridge State Park

© AVALON TRAVEL

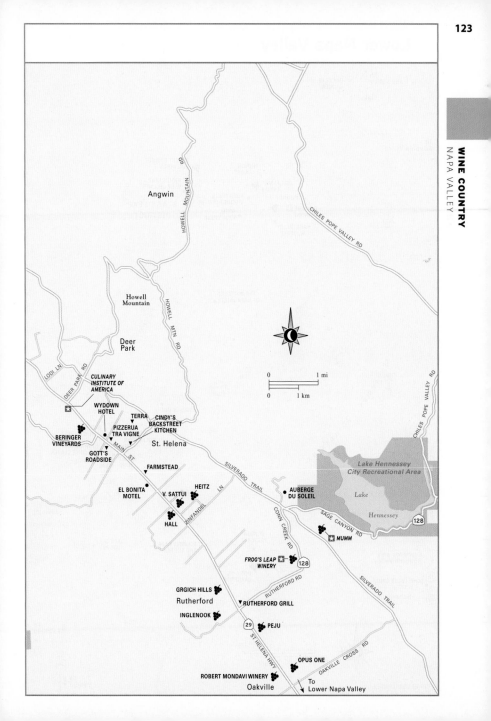

Lower Napa Valley

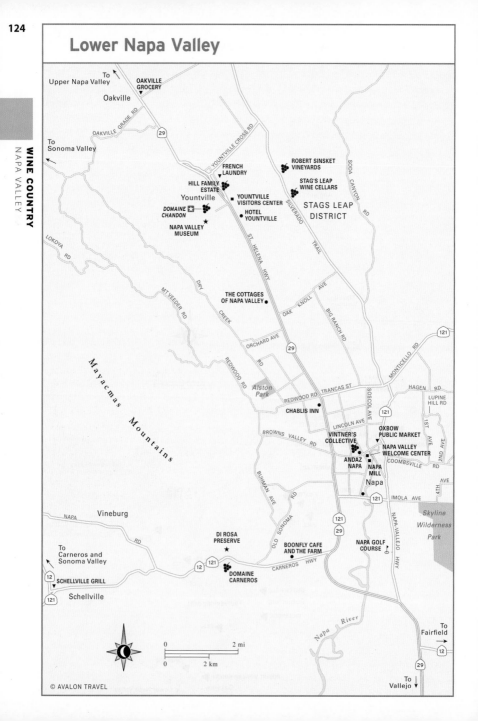

To Upper Napa Valley

OAKVILLE GROCERY

Oakville

OAKVILLE GRADE RD

29

To Sonoma Valley

YOUNTVILLE CROSS RD

ROBERT SINSKET VINEYARDS

FRENCH LAUNDRY

HILL FAMILY ESTATE

Yountville

STAG'S LEAP WINE CELLARS

YOUNTVILLE VISITORS CENTER

STAGS LEAP DISTRICT

SODA CANYON RD

DOMAINE CHANDON

HOTEL YOUNTVILLE

NAPA VALLEY MUSEUM

ST. HELENA HWY

SILVERADO TRAIL

LOKOVA RD

MT VEEDER RD

DRY CREEK

THE COTTAGES OF NAPA VALLEY

OAK KNOLL AVE

BIG RANCH RD

121

ORCHARD AVE

29

REDWOOD RD

Mayacmas Mountains

Alston Park

MONTICELLO RD

REDWOOD RD

TRANCAS ST

HAGEN RD

CHABLIS INN

LINCOLN AVE

LUPINE HILL RD

SOSCOL AVE

121

BROWNS VALLEY RD

VINTNER'S COLLECTIVE

OXBOW PUBLIC MARKET

NAPA VALLEY WELCOME CENTER

1ST AVE

2ND AVE

ANDAZ NAPA

NAPA MILL

COOMBSVILLE RD

BUHMAN AVE

OLD SONOMA RD

Napa

121

4TH AVE

IMOLA AVE

NAPA

Vineburg

RD

121
29

NAPA-VALLEJO HWY

Skyline Wilderness Park

To Carneros and Sonoma Valley

DI ROSA PRESERVE

BOONFLY CAFE AND THE FARM

NAPA GOLF COURSE

12
121

DOMAINE CARNEROS

CARNEROS HWY

SCHELLVILLE GRILL

Schellville

Napa River

To Fairfield

12

To Vallejo

29

0   2 mi
0   2 km

© AVALON TRAVEL

olive oil company, and the in-house **Oxbow Wine and Cheese Market.**

Sports and Recreation

Want to see Napa Valley without battling the crowds? **Balloons Above the Valley** (603 California Blvd., 707/253-2222 or 800/464-6824, www.balloonrides.com, $209) will guarantee a bird's-eye view of Napa without so much as a traffic light. You'll float serenely over the valley's vineyards before a gentle descent, followed by a champagne brunch. Be sure to make reservations in advance as trips can fill up quickly, especially during high season. Flights originate at the Napa Valley Marriott.

Food

Morimoto's (610 Main St., 707/252-1600, www.morimotonapa.com, 11:30am-2:30pm and 5pm-10pm Sun.-Thurs., 11:30am-2:30pm and 5pm-11pm Fri.-Sat., $14-65) is an esoteric and sleek Japanese eatery by celebrity chef Massaharu Morimoto. The food includes traditional Japanese dishes, each with a unique and modern twist. Michael and Christina Gyetvan, veterans of Tra Vigne in St. Helena, opened **Azzurro Pizzeria** (1260 Main St., 707/255-5552, www.azzurropizzeria.com, 11:30am-9:30pm Sun.-Thurs., 11:30am-10pm Fri.-Sat., $15) with the intention of bringing their wood-fired pizzas to downtown Napa. The menu includes classic Italian starters, a handful of pasta dishes, and pizzas. The wine list is dominated by Napa and Sonoma wines.

★ **Bounty Hunter Wine Bar and Smokin' BBQ** (975 1st St., 707/226-3976, www.bountyhunterwinebar.com, 11am-10pm Sun.-Thurs., 11am-midnight Fri.-Sat., $13-28) is a wine shop, tasting bar, and barbecue joint, housed in a historical brick-walled Victorian building with wine barrels for table bases. The menu includes gumbo, a beer-can chicken (a Cajun-spiced chicken impaled on a Tecate beer can), and big plates of barbecue pork, brisket, and ribs. There are 400 wines (40 by the glass) sold here or served as part of a tasting flight.

Across the Napa River is the ★ **Oxbow Public Market** (610-644 1st St., 707/226-6529, www.oxbowpublicmarket.com). Inside this large, open space, you can snack on oysters at the **Hog Island Oyster Company,** lunch on tacos from **C Casa,** or indulge at **Kara's Cupcakes.** Hamburgers are just out the side door at **Gott's Roadside,** and around the corner you can find some of the best charcuterie around in take-out sandwiches at the **Fatted Calf** or pizza by the slice at **The Model Bakery.** Head to the market's **Kitchen Door** (707/226-1560, www.kitchendoornapa.com, 11:30am-8pm Mon., 11:30am-9pm Tues.-Fri., 10am-9pm Sat., 10am-8pm Sun., $15-25) to escape the loud and congested interior, and order a big plate of global gourmet comfort food like wood-oven pizzas and roast chicken.

Accommodations

$150-250

At the **Chablis Inn** (3360 Solano Ave., 707/257-1944, www.chablisinn.com, $90-219), rooms include all the usual amenities: a wet bar with a mini fridge, an in-room coffee maker, and cable TV. Rooms are simply decorated, but the beds are comfortable and the address is central to both the attractions of downtown Napa and the famous Highway 29 wine road. Dogs are welcome.

Napa Inn (1137 Warren St., 707/257-1444 or 800/435-1144, www.napainn.com, $169-339) comprises two Victorian houses in historical downtown Napa. You can walk to downtown shops and restaurants, and the Wine Train depot is a very short drive away. There are eight rooms and seven suites, each with period antiques and a bathroom. Breakfast is an event, with multiple courses served by candlelight. Talk to the inn well in advance to get one of the two pet-friendly rooms.

OVER $250

Napa's first and still most unique boutique hotel, the ★ **Napa River Inn** (500 Main St., Napa, 707/251-8500 or 877/251-8500, www.

napariverinn.com, $209-359) has perhaps the best location in the city. Located at the historical red-brick Napa Mill, it sits next to the river surrounded by shops, restaurants, and entertainment. The 66 rooms are spread across three buildings. All rooms are furnished in an eclectic mix of contemporary, Victorian, and nautical styles. Many have fireplaces, balconies, or views (which vary from a parking lot to the river). Complimentary hot breakfast is brought to your room.

The 141-room **Andaz Napa** (1450 1st St., 707/687-1234, www.andaz.hyatt.com, $239-400) is the chic hipster brand from Hyatt whose cool urbane style is a breath of fresh air in Wine Country. The standard room, known as the Andaz King, is roughly the same size as any other hotel room (but with far plusher amenities). The Andaz restaurant, **Farmers Table,** serves simple farm-to-table food that is tasty and filling.

Transportation and Services

Napa does not have infrastructure designed for the number of visitors it receives. The best way to experience the valley is to avoid the ever-popular autumn crush and summer weekend afternoons. November and early spring are beautiful seasons to see the valley. But if a summer Saturday spent wine-tasting is impossible to resist, hit the wineries early and stay off the roads from midafternoon to early evening.

CAR

Napa is not all that easy to get to. Most of the highways in this region are two lanes and frequently go by colloquial names. They are also susceptible to gridlocked traffic, thanks to the numerous wine lovers and the races at nearby Sonoma Raceway.

Highway 29 is the central conduit that runs north into the valley from the city of Napa. It is also known as the Napa-Vallejo Highway between those two cities, and as the St. Helena Highway from Napa to Calistoga, where it becomes Foothill Boulevard. To reach Highway 29 from San Francisco, take U.S. 101 north across the Golden Gate Bridge to Novato. In Novato, take the exit for Highway 37 East to Highway 121. Take Highway 121 until you reach Napa. From San Francisco, the trip is a little over 50 miles, taking about an hour.

If you're coming from I-80, Highways 121, 29, and 37 connect around Vallejo, making a quick jump over to the Napa Valley. Coming from Highway 121 in Sonoma, Highway 12 East leads directly to Napa. Highway 121 then picks up again at West Imola Avenue and leads east to the Silverado Trail, an alternate north-south route in the Napa Valley.

BUS

The **VINE bus** (707/251-2600 or 800/696-6443, http://nctpa.net, adults $1.50-5.50, children $1-2.50) provides public transportation around Napa Valley, including Napa, Yountville, Oakville, Rutherford, St. Helena, and Calistoga. Route 10 makes stops along Highway 29 from Napa to Calistoga daily. If you don't want to drive at all, jump aboard the commuter VINE 29 Express (Mon.-Fri.). The Express travels from the El Cerrito BART station in the East Bay and from the Vallejo Ferry Terminal into Napa Valley. Fares are cash-only and require exact change.

NAPA VALLEY WINE TRAIN

The **Napa Valley Wine Train** (1275 McKinstry St., Napa, 800/427-4124, www.winetrain.com, $124-234) offers a relaxing sightseeing experience aboard vintage train cars, where you can sit back and enjoy the food, wine, and views. The train runs from Napa to St. Helena and back, a 36-mile, three-hour round-trip. Each package includes seating in a different historical railcar. Advance reservations are strongly suggested.

YOUNTVILLE

Yountville is the quintessential wine-loving town. Although there are some prestigious wineries and champagneries, it is really restaurateur Thomas Keller who put this town on the map with The French Laundry, then

Bouchon and the Bouchon Bakery, and eventually Ad Hoc.

Wineries

★ DOMAINE CHANDON

One of the premier champagneries in Napa Valley, **Domaine Chandon** (1 California Dr., 888/242-6366, www.chandon.com, 10am-5pm daily, $20-40) offers one of the best tours in Napa. Walk out into the vineyards to look at the grapes, head down to the tank- and barrel-filled cellars to learn about the champagne-making process, then proceed into the aging rooms to see the racked bottles, tilted and dusty, aging to the point of drinkability. Finally, you'll adjourn to the tasting room. Chandon also makes still wines, which you can also taste. Reservations are required for tours, and booking in advance is a good idea.

ROBERT SINSKEY VINEYARDS

Robert Sinskey Vineyards (6320 Silverado Tr., 707/944-9090, www.robertsinskey.com, 10am-4:30pm daily, $25-75) is best known for its pinot noir. Perched on a hill, the stone and redwood cathedral-like tasting area is surrounded by lavender and wisteria. The kitchen serves a menu of small bites made with ingredients from the vineyard's organic garden, served alongside their list of wines. The appointment-only tour ($75) includes a look in the cave and cellar, and discussions about the art of winemaking make a visit worthwhile.

STAG'S LEAP WINE CELLARS

Perhaps the most famous winery near Yountville is **Stag's Leap Wine Cellars** (5766 Silverado Tr., Napa, 866/422-7523, www.cask23.com, 10am-4:30pm daily, $25-40), which made the cabernet sauvignon that beat out the best French bordeaux in the now-famous 1976 blind tasting in Paris. It still makes outstanding single-vineyard cabernet. Such renowned wines command high prices, none more so than the Cask 23 cabernet, which retails at about $210. Although a magnet for serious wine enthusiasts, this family-run winery exudes an unassuming and friendly atmosphere, making it far less intimidating for the casual day-tripper than many of the valley's other big names.

Sights

More about the history of Napa and the entire valley can be found at the **Napa Valley Museum** (55 Presidents Cir., Yountville, 707/944-0500, www.napavalleymuseum.org, 11am-4pm Wed.-Sun., adults $7, seniors $3.50,

Domaine Chandon

17 and under $2.50). It has a fascinating mix of exhibits exploring the valley's natural and cultural heritage. You'll learn about the modern wine industry with an interactive high-tech exhibit on the science of winemaking, as well as the local Native American tribes. You'll even find kid-friendly exhibits.

Entertainment and Events

At the **Lincoln Theater** (100 California Dr., 707/944-9900, http://lincolntheater.com, $10-125), a packed year-round season brings top-end live entertainment of all kinds to Wine Country. See touring Broadway shows, locally produced plays, and stand-up comedy. Although this large theater seats hundreds, purchase tickets in advance, especially for one-night-only performances.

Shopping

You'll find plenty of shops lining Yountville's main drag, but most of the action is around the giant brick **V Marketplace** (6525 Washington St., Yountville, 707/944-2451, 10am-5:30pm daily). Built in 1870, the former winery and distillery building lends an air of sophistication to the little boutique stores selling everything from clothes and accessories to toys, art, and the usual Wine Country gifts. **V Wine Cellar** (797/531-7053, 10am-7pm daily) occupies 4,000 square feet selling fine boutique wines. It has a lounge and a tasting area within the shop.

Arts-and-crafts lovers should cross Washington Street to **Beard Plaza,** where some of the town's galleries can be found. Another gallery hub is farther down Washington Street at the little plaza at the corner of Mulberry Street.

Sports and Recreation

Biking is a popular way to see the vineyards, forests, and wineries of Napa. You can get away from the highways and the endless traffic of the wine roads on two wheels. If you don't know the area, the best way to bike it is to take a tour. **Napa Valley Bike Tours** (6500 Washington St., 707/251-8687, www.

napavalleybiketours.com, 8:30am-5pm daily, tours $99-159, bike rentals $45-90/day) offers guided and self-guided tours of the area in which you'll pedal through the vineyards, and a half-day or full-day tour that includes wine-tasting and meals. Bike rentals are also available if you want to explore on your own.

Food

The tiny town of Yountville boasts perhaps the biggest reputation for culinary excellence in California—a big deal when you consider the offerings of San Francisco and Los Angeles. The reason for this reputation is restaurateur Thomas Keller's indisputably amazing ★ **The French Laundry** (6640 Washington St., 707/944-2380, www. frenchlaundry.com, 5:30pm-9pm Mon.-Fri., 11am-1pm and 5:30pm-9pm Sat.-Sun., by reservation only, $310). The menu, which changes often, offers two main selections: the regular nine-course tasting menu and the vegetarian nine-course tasting menu. The sommelier is at your beck and call to assist with a wine list that weighs several pounds. From the start of your meal, waiters and footmen ply you with extras—an *amuse-bouche* here, an extra middle course there—and if you mention that someone else has something on their plate that you'd like to try, it appears in front of you as if by magic. Finally, the desserts come . . . and come and come. Altogether, a meal at The French Laundry can run up to 13 courses and take four hours to eat.

If you can't get to The French Laundry, try another Thomas Keller option, **Bouchon** (6534 Washington St., 707/944-8037, www. bouchonbistro.com, 11am-midnight Mon.-Fri., 10am-midnight Sat.-Sun., $34). Reservations are still strongly recommended, but you should be able to get one just a week in advance. Bouchon's atmosphere and food suggest a Parisian bistro. Order traditional favorites such as the *croque monsieur* or steak frites, or opt for a California-influenced specialty salad or entrée made with local sustainable ingredients. For a pastry or sandwich, walk next door to the **Bouchon Bakery** (6528 Washington St., 707/944-2253, www.bouchonbakery.com, 7am-7pm daily). Locals and visitors flock to the bakery at breakfast and lunchtime, so expect a line.

Ad Hoc (6476 Washington St., 707/944-2487, 5pm-10pm Mon. and Thurs.-Sat., 10am-1pm and 5pm-10pm Sun., prix fixe menu $52) is Thomas Keller's fourth adventure in Yountville. The four-course rustic menu changes nightly, and you'll get no choices, but considering the quality of the seasonal fare, that's not a bad thing. The wine list is endowed with moderately priced Californian and international wines. Reservations are not required, but don't expect to walk in and get a table.

A local favorite is **Bistro Jeanty** (6510 Washington St., 707/944-0103, www.bistro-jeanty.com, 11:30am-10:30pm daily, $15-39). The menu is a single page devoted to Parisian bistro classics. Tomato bisque served with a puff pastry shell, cassoulet, and coq au vin are all crafted with joy. Service is friendly and locals hang out at the bar, watching the TV tuned to a sports channel. Jeanty has two dining rooms, making walk-in dining easy on off-season weeknights. Make a dinner reservation on the weekend or in high season.

Accommodations

If you've come to Napa Valley for its high-wattage dining scene, you'll want to stay in Yountville if you can. Several inns are within stumbling distance of The French Laundry, which is convenient for gourmands who want to experience a range of wines with the meal.

$150-250

A French-style inn, the **Maison Fleurie** (6529 Yount St., 800/788-0369, www.foursisters.com, $160-265) offers the best of small-inn style for a reasonable nightly rate. It is in a perfect location for exploring Yountville by foot. The 13 rooms in this "house of flowers" have an attractive but not overwhelming floral theme. All guests enjoy a full breakfast each morning as well as an afternoon wine reception, fresh cookies, and complimentary access to the inn's bicycles.

The **Napa Valley Railway Inn** (6503 Washington St., 707/944-2000, www.napa-valleyrailwayinn.com, $125-260) is the only place in the valley where you can sleep on a train. The inn's nine railcars and cabooses took their last trip many decades ago and are fitted out with king or queen beds, air-conditioning, skylights, flat-screen TVs, and private bathrooms, making surprisingly comfortable accommodations right in the middle of Yountville. Some of the perks include the in-house Coffee Caboose and a Napa Valley Travel Packet ($20), which includes tasting vouchers, maps, bottled water, and Advil.

OVER $250

At **The Cottages of Napa Valley** (1012 Darms Lane, two miles south of Yountville, 707/252-7810, www.napacottages.com, $305-575), you'll pay a princely sum to gain a home away from home in the heart of Wine Country. Each cottage has its own king bed, private garden, outdoor fireplace, and kitchenette. Every morning the quiet staff drops off a basket of fresh pastries from Bouchon Bakery and a pot of great coffee for breakfast, and a free shuttle will deliver you to your Yountville restaurant of choice for dinner.

The **Hotel Yountville** (6462 Washington St., 707/867-7900 or 888/944-2885, www.hotelyountville.com, $341-545) has a distinctively French farmhouse appeal. The 80-room hotel has a cobblestone exterior, exposed beams, and tons of natural light. The rooms have vaulted ceilings, a four-poster bed, white Italian linens, a fireplace, a spa tub, and French doors opening onto a private patio. Suites are also available with all the same amenities. There is a full-service spa, pool, and high-end restaurant.

Transportation

Yountville is on Highway 29, nine miles north of Napa. Downtown Yountville is on the east side of Highway 29, and Washington Street is the main drag, connecting with Highway 29 at the south and north ends of town. To reach the heart of Yountville, exit on California Drive in the south and Madison Street in the north. The Yountville Cross Road will take you from the north end of town to the Silverado Trail.

To reach Yountville by bus, jump aboard the VINE (707/251-2600 or 800/696-6443, www.ridethevine.com, adults $1.50-5.50, children $1-2.50), which has routes running to Yountville daily. Around town, take the Yountville Trolley (www.ridethevine.com, 10am-11pm Mon.-Sat., 10am-7pm Sun., free). The trolley runs on a fixed track from Yountville Park along Washington Street to California Drive, near Domaine Chandon. The trolley also offers free pickup service (707/944-1234, after 7pm 707/312-1509).

OAKVILLE AND RUTHERFORD

Driving north along Highway 29, you might not even notice the tiny hamlets of Oakville and Rutherford. Neither town has much in the way of a commercial or residential district, and both have tiny populations.

Wineries

ROBERT MONDAVI WINERY

This sprawling mission-style complex, with its distinctive giant archway and bell tower, is considered the temple of modern Napa winemaking, with the late Robert Mondavi the high priest. The Robert Mondavi Winery (7801 Hwy. 29, Oakville, 888/766-6328, www.robertmondaviwinery.com, 10am-5pm daily, $20-45), started in the 1960s, has some very special wines (particularly the classic cabernet, chardonnay, and sauvignon blanc) that draw crowds. The impressive grounds and buildings are certainly highlights. Choose from a variety of tours ($20-50, reservations recommended), all of which include a tasting.

INGLENOOK WINERY

When a fabled Hollywood director buys a storied Napa Valley winery, it's inevitable that the result would be one of the most impressive in the valley. And so it is at Inglenook Winery (1991 St. Helena Hwy., Rutherford, 707/986-1100 or 800/782-4266, www.inglenook.com, 11am-5pm daily, reservations required, $50). The Inglenook Estate was established in 1871 and bought by Francis Ford Coppola in 1975. At the estate, a great effort is underway to recreate the style of wines made in the winery's heyday. To taste the wines, you must sign up for a tour and tasting, or a seated tasting paired with cheese or small bites. These generally last 1.5 hours and occur daily. Although the price is stiff, the tours are fascinating and the food pairings are significant enough to serve as lunch.

Another option is to stop by The Bistro (10am-5pm daily), a café space on the estate grounds. The menu offers French-inspired food that pairs perfectly with wine served by the bottle or glass. If you want a casual tasting at Inglenook, buying a glass at The Bistro is the only option.

GRGICH HILLS WINERY

When winemaker Mike Grgich (then working for Calistoga's Chateau Montelena) took his California chardonnay to the Paris Wine Tasting of 1976 and entered it in the white burgundy blind-tasting competition, it won. French winemakers were incensed. They demanded that the contest be held again; Grgich's chardonnay won for a second time. This event has gone down in the lore of American winemaking as the 1976 Judgment of Paris. Today, Grgich Hills Winery (1829 St. Helena Hwy., Rutherford, 707/963-2784, www.grgich.com, 9:30am-4:30pm daily, $20-50), an entirely biodynamic winemaking operation, is still making some of the best wines in the valley. The best might be the descendants of Mike's legendary chardonnay—arguably the best chardonnay made in Napa or anywhere else. But don't ignore the reds; Grgich offers some lovely zinfandels and cabernets.

★ FROG'S LEAP WINERY

Frog's Leap Winery (8815 Conn Creek Rd., Rutherford, 707/963-4704, www.frogsleap.

of wine—some of it high-end—and you get three pours per tasting. Nonalcoholic gourmet grape sodas and bottled water are complimentary for designated drivers. Dogs are welcome in the tasting room, too.

For the best of the winery, join a tour (10am, 11am, 1pm, 3pm daily, no reservation necessary, $30) of the sample vineyard and the production facility. The knowledgeable and articulate tour guides describe the process of making sparkling wine in detail. Tasting and a champagne flute are included in the price.

Accommodations and Food

Perched above the valley, off the Silverado Trail, ★ **Auberge du Soleil** (180 Rutherford Hill Rd., St. Helena, 707/963-1211 or 800/348-5406, www.aubergedusoleil.com, $700) is the ultimate in Wine Country luxury. The compound features dining options in addition to a pool, a fitness room, a store, and well-kept gardens accented by modern art. The rooms are appointed with Italian sheets, private patios, fireplaces, and TVs in both the living room and the bath. The main **restaurant** (7am-11am, 11:30am-2:30pm, 5:30pm-9:30pm daily, $110-150) offers a set menu of three-, four-, or six-course dinners with exquisitely prepared French-Californian food. Request a table on the terrace for the best views, especially at sunset. For a less indulgent affair, visit the adjacent **Bistro & Bar** (11am-11pm daily, $17-29). Choose from braised short ribs, a plate of charcuterie, or a light salad, accompanied by a rotating and wide selection of wines.

For down-to-earth dining, often without the need of a reservation, the **Rutherford Grill** (1180 Rutherford Rd., Rutherford, 707/963-1792, www.hillstone.com, 11:30am-9:30pm Mon.-Thurs., 11:30am-10:30pm Fri., 11am-10:30pm-Sat., 11am-9:30pm Sun., $15-40) offers traditional steakhouse fare in a slightly corporate setting. It has become one of the most popular steakhouses among Napa Valley residents and is a great place for a reliably cooked and aged steak paired with a Rutherford cabernet.

Frog's Leap Winery

com, 10am-4pm daily, $25) is known for environmental stewardship and organic wine production. This understated winery is housed in a historical red barn surrounded by vineyards and gardens. Tasting here is relaxing; sample a flight of four wines on the wraparound porch or inside the vineyard house, accompanied by cheese, crackers, and jam. The highly recommended tour (one hour, by appointment only, $25) also provides a tasting of four wines, and each pour is enjoyed in a different spot along the tour route.

★ MUMM

Even for genuine wine aficionados, it's worth spending an hour or two at **Mumm** (8445 Silverado Tr., Rutherford, 707/967-7700, http://mummnapa.com, 10am-6pm daily, $18-40), a friendly and surprisingly down-to-earth winery on the Silverado Trail. Tastings take place at tables, in restaurant fashion. The prices may look very Napa Valley, but you'll get more wine and service for your money at Mumm. Each pour is three ounces

For a picnic lunch or snacks for the road, stop by the **Oakville Grocery** (7856 St. Helena Hwy., Oakville, 707/944-8802, www.oakvillegrocery.com, 6:30am-5pm Mon.-Thurs., 6:30am-6pm Fri.-Sun., $12), a long-standing Napa Valley institution. Browse the tightly packed shelves or order a hot lunch at the center counter. To find the building from the northbound highway, look for the large Coca-Cola sign painted on the south side of the building.

Transportation

Oakville is four miles north of Yountville on Highway 29; Rutherford is another two miles north. Both can be easy to miss because of their loose organization and rural character. The Silverado Trail runs parallel to Highway 29 along this stretch. To reach it from Oakville, take Oakville Road east; in Rutherford, take Rutherford Road (Hwy. 128) east.

ST. HELENA

There are few Northern California towns as picturesque and well groomed as St. Helena. It is filled with fine eateries and quaint shops housed in historical buildings and surrounded by well-maintained craftsman homes. The Napa campus of the Culinary Institute of America is a major employer in the area, as is the St. Helena Hospital. Highway 29 runs north-south through the center of town, which can give you a quick peek at the sights, but it's not so nice when sitting in traffic on a sunny weekend.

Wineries
V. SATTUI

A big winery that doesn't distribute to retailers, **V. Sattui** (1111 White Ln., 707/963-7774, www.vsattui.com, 9am-5pm Sun.-Fri., 9am-5:30pm Sat., $15) has won several Best Winery awards at the California State Fair. V. Sattui produces a wide selection of varietals—everything from light-bodied whites to full-flavored cabernet sauvignons. The dessert madeira is particularly fine; if it's not on the tasting menu, ask your pourer at the bar if they've got a bottle open.

The big tasting room boasts three spacious bar areas, a separate register, and a full deli. The surrounding gardens include picnic tables, making V. Sattui a popular lunchtime stop for all-day tasters. The tasting room fills on weekends in high season.

vineyards at Mumm

Wine Tasting

Chardonnay: Most of the white wine made and sold in California is chardonnay. The grapes grow best in a slightly cooler climate, such as the vineyards closer to the coast. Most California chardonnays taste smooth and buttery and a bit like fruit, and they often take on the oak flavor of the barrels they sit in. Chardonnay doesn't keep (age), so most chards are sold the year after they're bottled and consumed within a few months of purchase.

- Best Place to Sample: **Grgich Hills Winery** (p. 130)

Sauvignon blanc: This pale-green grape is used to make both sauvignon blanc and fumé blanc wines. Sauvignon blanc grapes grow well in Napa, Sonoma, and other warm-hot parts of the state. The difference between a sauvignon blanc and a fumé blanc is in the winemaking more than in the grapes. Fumé blanc wines tend to have a strong odor and the taste of grapefruit; they pair well with fish dishes and spicy Asian cuisine. The California sauvignon blanc wine goes well with salads, fish, vegetarian cuisine, and even spicy international dishes.

- Best Place to Sample: **Hanna Winery** (p. 148).

Pinot noir: Pinot noir grapes do best in a cool coastal climate with limited exposure to high heat. The Anderson Valley and the Monterey coastal growing regions tend to specialize in pinot noir, though many Napa and Sonoma wineries buy grapes from the coast to make their own versions. California vintners make up single-varietal pinot noir wines that taste of cherries, strawberries, and smoke.

- Best Place to Sample: **Robert Sinskey Vineyards** (p. 127) and **Hop Kiln** (p. 153)

Zinfandel: These grapes grow best when tortured by their climate; a few grow near Napa, but most come from Dry Creek Valley, Gold Country, and the inland Central Coast. A true zinfandel is a hearty deep-red wine that boasts the flavors and smells of blackberry jam and the dusky hues of venous blood. Zinfandel often tastes wonderful on its own, but it's also good with beef, buffalo, and even venison.

- Best Place to Sample: **Ravenswood Winery** (p. 140)

Cabernet sauvignon: Cabernet sauvignon, a grape from the Bordeaux region of France, creates a deep, dark, strong red wine. The grapes that get intense summer heat make the best wine, which makes them a perfect fit for the scorching Napa Valley. In California, especially in Napa, winemakers use cabernet sauvignon on its own to brew some of the most intense single-grape wines in the world. A good dry cab might taste of leather, tobacco, and bing cherries. Cabs age well, often hitting their peak of flavor and smoothness more than a decade after bottling.

- Best Place to Sample: **Stag's Leap Wine Cellars** (p. 127)

HEITZ

One of the oldest wineries in the valley, **Heitz** (436 St. Helena Hwy., 707/963-3542, www.heitzcellar.com, 11am-4:30pm daily, free) brings sincere elegance to the glitz and glamour of Napa. The high-ceilinged tasting room is dominated by a stone fireplace with comfy chairs. Heitz's cabernets are well balanced and easy to drink, and though costly, they approach affordable by Napa standards. Most of the grapes used for these wines grow right in the Napa Valley.

HALL WINES

At **HALL Wines** (401 St. Helena Hwy. S., St. Helena, 707/967-2626, www.hallwines.com, 10am-5:30pm daily, $30) you'll notice two things. One is that the Halls are big fans of modern art and design; the other is that their winery is the first LEED Gold certified winery in California. The new "winery complex" and tasting room has an industrial chic that's different from the typical chateau aesthetic. HALL offers highly rated wines to taste, but to really experience the grounds, book a spot on the HALLmark **Tour and Tasting** (daily, $40) or Wine and Art Exploration (Sun., $40).

BERINGER VINEYARDS

The oldest continuously operating winery in Napa Valley, **Beringer Vineyards** (2000 Main St., 707/302-7592 or 866/708-9463, www.beringer.com, 10am-6pm daily June-late Oct., 10am-5pm daily late Oct.-May, $20-25) is a huge tourist attraction that often contributes to St. Helena's summer traffic jams. It is still worth a visit (ideally midweek, when it's a bit quieter) for its significance and for some outstanding reserve wines.

The winery was established in 1876 and the entire estate, including the lavish and ornate Rhine House, was placed on the National Register of Historic Places in 2001. It is an impressive location to taste some of Beringer's reserve wines. The regular tasting is in the old winery building up the hill and offers several themed flights for less money (and atmosphere). Stroll in the beautiful estate gardens that stretch for acres on prime land. **Tours** (daily, reservation only, $25-40) show off the highlights of the vast estate and its winemaking facilities.

Sights

Under the cool shade trees of the Napa hills, the gristmill at **Bale Grist Mill State Historic Park** (3369 N St. and Hwy. 29, three miles north of St. Helena, 707/942-2236, www. parks.ca.gov, 10am-5pm Fri.-Mon. summer, 10am-5pm Sat.-Sun. fall-spring) is quiet. The huge water wheel no longer turns, and the vast network of elevated and ground-level wooden pipes and ducts has dried out. Visitors can take a pleasant nature walk to the site of Dr. Edward Bale's old wheel and mill structures. Take a tour inside the flour mill with a docent who will tell the story of the gristmill and show off the facility built from local stone, redwood, and fir.

In St. Helena, the **Robert Louis Stevenson Museum** (1490 Library Ln., 707/963-3757, www.silveradomuseum.org,

noon-4pm Tues.-Sat., free) is a rich collection honoring the celebrated 19th-century author.

★ CULINARY INSTITUTE OF AMERICA

Napa Valley takes food very seriously, so it's fitting that the West Coast outpost of the **Culinary Institute of America** (CIA, 2555 Main St., 707/967-1100, www.ciachef. edu, 10am-6pm daily) is housed in the fortress-like former Greystone Winery, one of the grandest winery buildings in California. Just north of downtown St. Helena, hour-long cooking demonstrations are open to the public. You can also pop into the **Bakery Café** (10:30am-5pm daily), take a seat at the highly celebrated **Wine Spectator Restaurant** (707/967-1010, 5:30pm-8:30pm Tues.-Sat., $22-29), or visit the slightly more casual farm-to-table **Conservatory Restaurant** (707/967-2300, 5:30pm-9pm Fri.-Sat.). The **Spice Islands Marketplace** (707/967-2309, 10:30am-6pm daily) is considered one of the best kitchen stores in the valley.

Food

Run by the Rutherford-based Long Meadow Ranch, ★ **Farmstead** (738 Main St., 707/963-9181, 11:30am-9:30pm Mon.-Thurs., 11:30am-10pm Fri.-Sat., 11am-9:30pm Sun., $23-36) takes the idea of farm-fresh to a new level. The ranch supplies many of the vegetables, herbs, olive oil, eggs, and grass-fed beef served at the restaurant. The restaurant is housed in a former nursery, where farm equipment has found new life as fixtures, fittings, and furnishings. Even the booths are covered in leather sourced from the ranch's cattle. The food hits the right balance of sophistication and familiarity. To escape the noisy barn, ask for one of the tables on the tree-shaded patio. Visit the ranch's General Store (11am-6pm daily) to taste its estate wines and olive oils.

For Michelin-starred dining, make a reservation at romantic ★ **Terra** (1345 Railroad Ave., 707/963-8931, www.terrasrestaurant.

com, 6pm-9:30pm Thurs.-Mon., $78-105) located in the historical stone Hatchery Building. The menu is French and Californian with Asian flourishes. Diners create their own prix fixe by selecting four ($78), five ($93), or six ($105) courses from the 17 savory dishes on the menu. For something more casual but with the same fusion flair, dine at adjacent Bar Terra (5:30pm-9:30pm Thurs.-Mon., $15-29), with its full liquor license and à la carte menu. Nibble on any one of Terra's signature dishes for considerably less.

The Cindy of ★ Cindy's Backstreet Kitchen (1327 Railroad Ave., 707/963-1200, www.cindysbackstreetkitchen.com, 11:30am-9pm daily, $14-30) is Cindy Pawlcyn, who is credited with bringing casual-sophisticated dining to Napa Valley. Backstreet is a charming hole-in-the-wall with a side entrance that makes it feel like you're walking into someone's house. The menu goes for homey charm, with large plates including meatloaf, wood-oven duck, and steak frites. Lunch (small plates, sandwiches) can be ordered to go. The patio is a hive of activity at lunch and can require a wait.

Inside the relaxed Pizzeria Tra Vigne (1016 Main St., 707/967-9999, www.travignerestaurant.com, 11:30am-9pm Sun.-Thurs., 11:30am-9:30pm Fri.-Sat., $10-21), the famous thin-crust Italian pizzas lure locals on many weekend nights. Wash it all down with a pitcher of any number of beers on tap. If you're traveling with kids, Pizzeria Tra Vigne is a great place.

Gott's Roadside (933 Main St., 707/963-3486, http://gotts.com, 8am-9pm daily, $10-20) is a classic roadside diner that has been around since 1949, but the burgers, fries, and milk shakes have been updated with local, organic ingredients. There is also some California-eclectic comfort food like fish tacos and smoked chicken po'boys. Gott's has earned three James Beard awards.

Fortunately for locals, the quick stop for a morning cup of joe also happens to be one of the most celebrated bakeries in the valley. Known chiefly for its bread, the Model Bakery (1357 Main St., 707/963-8192, www.themodelbakery.com, 7am-7pm daily, $5-12) has been around since 1920. There are shelves of flour-dusted bread and display cases full of pastries, scones, and croissants. Sandwiches, wood-fired pizzas, and salads also make this an easy stop for lunch.

Accommodations

For the best rates, the El Bonita Motel (195 Main St. and Hwy. 29, 707/963-3216 or 800/541-3284, www.elbonita.com, $109-309) can't be beat. It's within walking distance of downtown and has a 1950s motel charm. The 42-room hotel wraps around a patio shaded by oak trees and filled with tables, chairs, and umbrellas. In the center are a pool, a hot tub, and a sauna. The rooms may not match the indulgence of other Napa inns, but they are clean, comfortable, and pet-friendly, with refrigerators and microwaves; some even boast kitchenettes.

The Hotel St. Helena (1309 Main St., 707/963-4388, www.hotelsthelena.net, $115-275) is as central as can be, down a little alley off Main Street, right in the middle of town. The old Victorian building is full of original features and stuffed with knickknacks. The 18 rooms get some limited modern touches like air-conditioning, but you'll have to tolerate temperamental plumbing and poor sound insulation. The four smallest and cheapest rooms share a bathroom. The best deals are the North Wing rooms, which are small but have private bathrooms.

In the thick of downtown St. Helena, the Wydown Hotel (1424 Main St., 707/963-5100, www.wydownhotel.com, $270-370) offers a break from Victorian excess. The 12 rooms are smartly decorated, while the lobby downstairs outdoes itself in urban chic. The small hotel has little in the way of luxury amenities, but it offers a convenient location and historical digs that are modern and stylish.

Transportation

St. Helena is on Highway 29 in the middle of Napa Valley, eight miles south of Calistoga. To reach the Silverado Trail from St. Helena, take Zinfandel Lane or Pope Street east.

To avoid the headache of driving, hop aboard the **VINE St. Helena Shuttle** (707/963-3007, http://nctpa.net, 7:45am-6pm Mon.-Thurs., 7:45am-11pm Fri., $0.50-1). During weekends, the shuttle runs on demand (10am-11pm Sat., noon-7pm Sun.). The price is the same; call to schedule a pickup.

CALISTOGA

Calistoga couldn't be more different from St. Helena, despite their proximity. Sporting a laid-back, mountain-town crunchiness, Calistoga is the land of great and affordable spas.

Wineries

CASTELLO DI AMOROSA

Driving up to **Castello di Amorosa** (4045 N. St. Helena Hwy., 707/967-6272, www. castellodiamorosa.com, 9:30am-6pm daily Mar.-Nov., 9:30am-5pm daily Dec.-Feb., general admission 21 and over $20, children 5-20 $10), it is difficult to remember that it's a winery. Everything from the parking attendant directing cars through the crowded parking lot to the admission prices (which include a tasting of five wines, and juice for the kids) screams "Disneyland." And then there is the castle itself, complete with 107 rooms and eight floors, and made from 8,000 tons of stone and 850,000 European bricks.

Admission includes access to the main floors of the castle. Tours (adults $35, children $25) include barrel tasting and take visitors to the armory and torture chamber.

STERLING VINEYARDS

Sterling Vineyards (1111 Dunaweal Ln., 800/726-6136, www.sterlingvineyards.com, 10:30am-4:30pm Mon.-Fri., 10am-5pm Sat.-Sun., general admission adults $29, under 21 $15, children 3 and under free) is more appealing for folks who are touring Wine Country for the first time than for serious wine aficionados. Once you've stood in line and bought your tickets, a gondola ride up the mountain

shows off Napa Valley at its best. Admire the stellar views of forested hills and endless vineyards. The wine doesn't match the effort or the high price tag, but the views and experience can be unforgettable.

CHATEAU MONTELENA

The beautiful French- and Chinese-inspired **Chateau Montelena** (1429 Tubbs Ln., 707/942-5105, www.montelena.com, 9:30am-4pm daily, $25) will forever be remembered for putting Napa Valley on the map when its 1973-vintage chardonnay trounced the best French white burgundies at the famous 1976 Paris tasting. But if the wines aren't enough, the grounds are worth a visit. The stone chateau was built in 1882; the ornamental Chinese garden was added in 1965. It is centered around the lush five-acre Jade Lake, crisscrossed with lacquered bridges. Several tours (reservations required, $40) are available. Check the website for times and to book a spot.

Sights and Events

No, you haven't accidentally driven to Yellowstone. The Napa Valley has its own **Old Faithful Geyser** (1299 Tubbs Ln., 707/942-6463, www.oldfaithfulgeyser.com, 8:30am-8pm Sun.-Thurs., 8:30am-9pm Fri.-Sat. Mar.-Oct., 8:30am-6pm daily Nov.-Feb., adults $14, seniors $12, children ages 4-11 $8, under age 4 free). Unlike its more famous counterpart, this geothermal geyser is artificial. In the 19th and early 20th centuries, more than 100 wells were drilled into the geothermal springs of the Calistoga area, and many created geysers. Old Faithful is one of the few that wasn't eventually capped, and it's the only one that erupts (60 feet) with clockwork regularity (roughly every 40 minutes). The cute petting zoo houses several fainting goats, plus a few sheep and llamas, making the wait with the kids easier.

The **Sharpsteen Museum of Calistoga History** (1311 Washington St., 707/942-5911, www.sharpsteen-museum.org, 11am-4pm daily, $3 donation) takes its name from its founder, Ben Sharpsteen, an Academy Award-winning animator for Disney who had a passion for dioramas. Go for the immense, exquisitely detailed dioramas depicting the 1860s Calistoga hot springs resort and life in 19th-century Calistoga. You'll also learn about the success and subsequent ruin of Sam Brannan, the Calistoga pioneer who was the first to build a hot-springs resort in the area.

The **Napa County Fair** (1435 North Oak St., 707/942-5111, www.napacountyfair.org, adults $12, ages 7-12 $7, under age 7 free) is held every July 4th weekend at the Napa County Fairgrounds and is open to all.

Spas

For an old-school Calistoga spa experience, head down the main drag to **Dr. Wilkinson's Hot Springs Resort** (1507 Lincoln Ave., 707/942-4102, www.drwilkinson.com, 8:30am-3:45pm daily, $89-179). The spa is part of the perfectly preserved midcentury compound rigorously dedicated to health and relaxation opened by "Doc" Wilkinson in 1952. Doc's proprietary blend of Calistoga mineral water and volcanic ash, Canadian peat, and lavender is still the gold standard for the Calistoga mud bath today. "The Works" includes the mud bath (complete with a soothing mud masque for your face), mineral bath, sauna, and a blanket wrap, and is finished with a massage. The men's and women's spa areas are separated, and the whole experience is very down-to-earth, as are the prices. If you're a guest of the hotel, be sure to take a swim or a soak in one of the three mineral-water pools (there are two outdoor pools and one huge spa inside).

At the **Calistoga Hot Springs Spa** (1006 Washington St., 707/942-6269, www.calistogaspa.com, 8:30am-4:30pm Tues.-Thurs., 8:30am-9pm Fri.-Mon.), indulge in a mud bath, a mineral bath, or other typical spa treatments. Also available to the public and guaranteed with a spa reservation is access to Calistoga Hot Springs's four outdoor mineral pools, each one catering to serious swimmers, families, and adults eager to relax and enjoy the serenity of spa country. **Indian Springs** (1712 Lincoln Ave., 707/942-4913, www.indianspringscalistoga.com, 9am-8pm daily, $85-125) also offers mud baths, spa services, and use of its pools, including the meditative Buddha pond.

If you want to get pampered without the muck, the **Lincoln Avenue Spa** (1339 Lincoln Ave., 707/942-2950, www.lincolnavenuespa.com, 10am-6pm Sun.-Thurs.,

Indian Springs

10am-7pm Fri.-Sat.) offers a wider array of spa and esthetic treatments, including a detoxifying body wrap.

Sports and Recreation

There are several great state parks where you can indulge in the beauty of the valley. **Bothe-Napa State Park** (3801 St. Helena Hwy., 707/942-4575, www.parks.ca.gov, 8am-sunset daily) is south of Calistoga on the west side of Highway 29. The park's 2,000-foot elevation provides fantastic views of the valley below and the craggy Vaca Mountains beyond. The nearly 2,000 acres include oak woodlands, coastal redwoods, and occasional open grassland. There are a number of great hikes in the park. **Coyote Peak Trail** climbs to 1,170 feet and forms a 6.5-mile loop with **Upper Ritchey Canyon Trail,** providing great scenery and a backcountry feel.

Robert Louis Stevenson State Park (Hwy. 29, seven miles north of Calistoga, 707/942-4575, www.parks.ca.gov, sunrise-sunset daily) is named for the author who spent his honeymoon in a tiny cabin here. The park offers few amenities, but it does have a strenuous 11.2-mile round-trip trail to the top of Mount St. Helena. All that huffing and puffing is rewarded at the 4,300-foot summit, where great views of the valley unfold. The park also has picnic tables for a lovely outdoor lunch.

Biking in Calistoga is a fun and scenic alternative to sitting in traffic. **Calistoga Bikeshop** (1318 Lincoln Ave., 707/942-9687, http://calistogabikeshop.com, 10am-6pm daily, $15-120 per day) offers guided tours, self-guided tours, and bike rentals. Hybrids run $39 per day, road bikes $60 per day, and mountain bikes $120 per day. On the self-guided Calistoga Cool Wine Tour ($90), the bike shop books your tastings, pays the fees, picks up any wine you buy, and provides roadside assistance.

Take in Calistoga's dramatic scenery from the air with **Calistoga Balloons** (1458 Lincoln Ave., 707/942-5758 or 888/995-7700, www.calistogaballoons.com, $199-239), the only company offering regular flights in the north end of Napa Valley. In addition to the vineyards, wineries, spas, and the charming town of Calistoga, you'll also see Mount St. Helena and lush forested hills. The company provides a variety of packages that include winery tours and tastings, bicycle tours, and a post-flight champagne breakfast.

Food

The beauty of Calistoga is how well the locals rub shoulders with the tourists. Just take a booth at the **Café Sarafornia** (1413 Lincoln Ave., 707/942-0555, http://cafesarafornia.com, 7am-2:30pm daily, $9-15) and see. Farmers and tradespeople sidle up next to out-of-towners for a down-home breakfast and bottomless cups of coffee. The huevos rancheros stand up to their claim of being the best and the Brannon Benedict is one-of-a-kind. Breakfast here may be the most expensive meal of the day in the otherwise quite affordable Calistoga.

Pacifico Mexican Restaurant (1237 Lincoln Ave., 707/942-4400, 11am-9pm Sun.-Thurs., 11am-10pm Fri., 10am-10pm Sat., $11-19), on the corner of Lincoln Avenue and Cedar Street, is just the place for a margarita. The food may not be hole-in-the-wall authentic, but it makes up for it in atmosphere, particularly at the sidewalk tables lining Cedar Street.

Perhaps the hottest restaurant is the trendy **Solbar** (755 Silverado Tr., 877/684-6146, www.solagecalistoga.com, 7am-3pm and 5:30pm-9pm Sun.-Thurs., 7am-3pm and 5:30pm-9:30pm Fri.-Sat., $26-33). Part of the luxurious Solage Calistoga resort at the eastern edge of town, the sleek dining room is a fine backdrop for the innovative cuisine that gives farm-fresh a modern twist. The result garnered the restaurant a Michelin star in 2009. The biggest draw in the summer and fall is the spacious patio with its floating fireplace.

Accommodations

A plethora of places to stay cluster at the north end of Napa Valley, where you'll find most of the hotel-and-spa combos plus plenty of mineral-water pools and hot tubs. Calistoga also has some of the best lodging rates around.

$100-150

The **Calistoga Inn** (1250 Lincoln Ave., 707/942-4101, www.calistogainn.com, $119-169) has been in operation since 1882, giving guests an old-school hotel experience complete with shared baths and showers. The inn provides some of the best bargain accommodations in Napa Valley. Each of the 17 rooms is a cozy haven with a queen bed, simple but charming furnishings, and a view of the town. Amenities include a daily continental breakfast and an English pub downstairs that serves lunch and dinner. Make reservations in advance, especially in high season. The pub has live music four nights a week and gets loud on weekends.

$150-250

Embracing its midcentury charm, ★ **Dr. Wilkinson's Hot Springs Resort** (1507 Lincoln Ave., 707/942-4102, www.drwilkinson.com, $165-270) feels as though it is frozen in the 1950s. Options range from the motel's main rooms to bungalows with kitchens and rooms in the adjacent restored Victorian. Guests are welcome to use the pools, including the indoor hot mineral pool with its Eichleresque touches. In addition to complimentary bathrobes, all rooms have coffee makers, refrigerators, and hypoallergenic bedding. Dr. Wilkinson's even has bathing suits on loan.

The old-school **Hideaway Cottages** (1412 Fair Way, 707/942-4108, www.hideawaycottages.com, $164-315) is a collection of 1940s-era bungalows that retain their original details. Most have sitting rooms, full kitchens, and patios, all of which face the outdoor mineral pool and hot tub. In the interest of quiet, no pets or children under 18 are allowed. In the main house, built in 1877, guests pick up their complimentary "tote" breakfast, filled with fruit and pastries.

OVER $250

One of the prettiest spa resorts in Calistoga is **Indian Springs** (1712 Lincoln Ave., Calistoga, 707/942-4913, www.indianspringscalistoga.com, $199-479). Located on the site of Sam Brannan's original Calistoga resort, Indian Springs is best known for its charming cottages, but rooms in the two-story mission-style lodge are far more affordable. Cottages and bungalows have kitchenettes and patios, but you're really paying for the pools. Both are spring-fed and kept 82-102°F. The Olympic-size pool is one of the biggest in California; the smaller pool is quieter and adults-only.

On Calistoga's charming main drag is the **Mount View Hotel and Spa** (1457 Lincoln Ave., 707/942-6877, www.mountviewhotel.com, $199-399). All 29 rooms and suites have an eclectic mix of modern furnishings with Victorian antique and art deco touches that harken back to the hotel's 1920s and 1930s heyday. The list of standard features includes espresso machines, breakfast in bed, and an outdoor pool.

Transportation

Calistoga is eight miles north of St. Helena on Highway 29. In Calistoga, Highway 29 turns east, becoming Lincoln Avenue. It intersects with the Silverado Trail at the east end of town.

Highway 128 also runs through Calistoga, connecting to U.S. 101 north near Healdsburg. To reach Calistoga from U.S. 101 in Santa Rosa, take exit 494 off U.S. 101 labeled River Rd./Guerneville. Turn right on Mark West Springs Road and continue up the mountain. The road name changes to Porter Creek Road in the process. At the T intersection with Petrified Forest Road, turn left and travel a few miles until Highway 128. Turn right and follow Highway 128 south for one mile to Lincoln Avenue, Calistoga's main drag.

Sonoma Valley

The Sonoma and Carneros wine regions are in the southeast part of Sonoma Valley. The scenery features oak forests, vineyard-covered open spaces, and pristine wetlands bordering San Pablo Bay. The terminus of El Camino Real is in the small city of Sonoma, which includes the famed Sonoma Mission, historical sights, and a charming town square with plenty of shopping and great places to grab a bite.

SONOMA AND CARNEROS
Sonoma Wineries
★ GUNDLACH BUNDSCHU WINERY

Not many wineries in California can boast that they won awards for their wines 100 years ago, but **Gundlach Bundschu Winery** (2000 Denmark St., 707/938-5277, www.gunbun.com, 11am-4:30pm daily, $10), or GunBun, as it's known, is one of them. The 19 Gundlach Bundschu wines entered into the 1915 Panama-Pacific International Exhibition all won medals.

Today the winery focuses on red bordeaux- and burgundy-style wines, and the cabernets and merlots tend to have plenty of tannic backbone. The tasting room is housed in one of the original stone winery buildings, and nearby is the hillside cave, which is often part of the winery tour. GunBun is most loved for its picnicking area that boasts one of the nicest outdoor winery spaces in the valley.

RAVENSWOOD WINERY

Ravenswood Winery (18701 Gehricke Rd., Sonoma, 707/933-2332 or 888/669-4679, www.ravenswood-wine.com, 10am-4:30pm daily, $18) prides itself on making "no wimpy wines." Zinfandel is Ravenswood's signature varietal and the winery strives to make tasters of all types feel at home. Tours and barrel tastings (10am daily, $25, reservations required) teach newcomers the process of winemaking, but "blend your own" seminars beckon to serious wine connoisseurs. Ravenswood wines range $15-60 per bottle.

Gundlach Bundschu picnic grounds

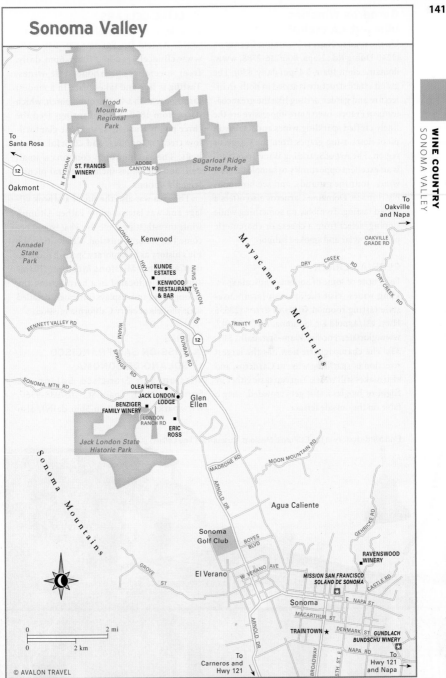

Sonoma Valley

Carneros Wineries
DOMAINE CARNEROS

On the road to Napa is **Domaine Carneros** (1240 Duhig Rd., Napa, 800/716-2788, www.domaine.com, 10am-5:45pm daily, $30). The grand estate structure is styled in both architecture and garden setting like the great châteaux of France. Even more impressive are the finely crafted sparkling wines and a few still pinot noirs using grapes from the Carneros region. The Art of Sparkling Wine Tour ($40) is an excellent opportunity to sample the best wines, tour the grounds, and see how bubbly is made. Domaine Carneros also offers a seated tasting. To nibble on something while sipping, select from a cheese or charcuterie plate or caviar and smoked salmon.

GLORIA FERRER

For a taste of some of Sonoma's upscale sparkling wines, visit the Spanish farmhouse-style tasting room at **Gloria Ferrer** (23555 Hwy. 121/Arnold Dr., Sonoma, 707/933-1917, www.gloriaferrer.com, 10am-5pm daily, $18-33). The champagnerie now has the largest selection of sparkling wine in Carneros, and also makes still wines. You can taste either by flight or by glass. If it gets crowded, snag a table on the outside terrace.

★ CLINE CELLARS

For a departure from bubbly, **Cline Cellars** (24737 Arnold Dr., Sonoma, 707/940-4030, www.clinecellars.com, 10am-6pm daily, free) specializes in rhone-style wines. Tasting is free and takes place in a modest farmhouse with a wraparound porch, which dates from 1850. Natural springs feed the three ponds and help sustain the giant willow trees, magnolias, and colorful flower beds. The tasting room contains a small deli, and the wines include several picnic-friendly options.

The area was also the site of a Miwok village and was later used by Father Altimira while investigating a site for what would become the Sonoma mission. Celebrating the site's history as a temporary Spanish mission, the **California Missions Museum** (10am-4pm daily) is located in a barn behind the tasting room and displays intricately detailed scale models of every California mission.

Sights
★ MISSION SAN FRANCISCO SOLANO DE SONOMA

Mission San Francisco Solano de Sonoma (114 E. Spain St., 707/938-9560, www.parks.ca.gov, 10am-5pm daily), also

Find a little history at the California Missions Museum at Cline Cellars.

simply called the Sonoma Mission, is the northernmost Spanish mission in California. It's at the corner of the historical plaza in downtown Sonoma. The Sonoma Mission isn't the prettiest or most elaborate of the missions, but it's the last mission established (in 1823) and one of the first restored as a historical landmark. Visitors can see exhibits depicting the life of the missionaries and indigenous people who lived here. Outdoors is the Native American mortuary monument and a cactus "wall" that has been growing on the property since the mission era.

The mission is a central piece of **Sonoma State Historic Park,** which consists of five other historical attractions. The majority of the sights were built in the heyday of General Mariano Vallejo, the Mexican army commander who became a key figure in California's transition from Mexican province to statehood. The sites include the two-story adobe **Sonoma Barracks**, the old **Toscano Hotel**, and Vallejo's opulent home, **Lachryma Montis.** Tours for both Lachryma Montis and the Toscano Hotel are free with the park's $3 admission fee and are available Saturday and Sunday.

TRAIN TOWN

Riding the only trains left in town requires a visit to the brightly painted station of **Train Town** (20264 Broadway, 707/938-3912, www.traintown.com, 10am-5pm daily June-Aug., 10am-5pm Fri.-Sun. Sept.-May, $2.75-6.25). The often-crowded amusement park, model railway, and petting zoo are a treat for little ones. Ride the 15-inch scale railroad that winds through 10 forested acres, take a spin on the roller coasters, or ride the vintage carousel and Ferris wheel. Rides are paid for with coupons, which add up quickly, so buy a Family Pack (six for $12.75).

DI ROSA PRESERVE

As Sonoma Valley yields to the open spaces of Carneros, history gives way to modern art. To visit the 217-acre **di Rosa Preserve** (5200 Sonoma Hwy., 707/226-5991, www.dirosapreserve.org, 10am-4pm Wed.-Sun., $5-15) is to enter an eclectic, artistic wonderland, where giant sculptures march up into the hills, a car hangs from a tree, and every indoor space is crammed with photographs, paintings, and video installations. Even nature seems to do its part to maintain the sense of whimsy as di Rosa's 85 peacocks (including two albinos)

WINE COUNTRY
SONOMA VALLEY

Mission San Francisco Solano de Sonoma

strut, screech, and occasionally crash-land around the galleries.

The preserve is on the north side of the Carneros Highway (Highway 121) almost opposite the Domaine Carneros winery. Look for the two-dimensional sheep on the hillside. A $5 donation will get you into the Gatehouse Gallery, which displays rotating exhibits along with some pieces from the permanent collection. To wander around the property or explore other indoor gallery space, you have to join one of the three or four daily tours (1.5-2 hours, $12-15). During the dry summer months, the Nature Hike takes visitors up Milliken Peak, a 2.5-mile round-trip to the highest peak in Carneros. Chances are you'll need a reservation for tours, especially on weekends.

CORNERSTONE SONOMA

Find outdoor art and design at **Cornerstone Sonoma** (23570 Hwy. 121, 707/933-3010, www.cornerstonegardens.com, 10am-5pm daily). This unique installation combines an art gallery with the work of the foremost landscape and garden designers in the world. Stroll the unusual gardens, which range from traditional plantings to postmodern multimedia installations, and then finish up your excursion by visiting the boutiques, upscale food shops, and wine bars that populate the garden complex.

Sports and Recreation

Just when you think Wine Country is a little too genteel, you'll hear the buzzing of the **Sonoma Raceway** (29355 Arnold Dr., Sonoma, 800/870-7223, www.racesonoma. com). This massive motorsports complex hosts every sort of vehicular race possible, with several NASCAR events each year, various American Motorcyclist Association motorcycle races, an Indy car race, and a National Hot Rod Association drag race. Ticket prices vary widely, so check the website for event prices. The turnoff to Sonoma Raceway is near the intersection of Highways 37 and 121, and wretched traffic jams can last for hours as people exit the racetrack into the non-signaled intersection. Check the race schedule online to avoid this area for at least four hours before or after a big race.

The area around downtown Sonoma is perfect for exploring by bike. The **Sonoma Valley Visitors Bureau** (453 1st St. E., 866/996-1090, www.sonomaplaza.com, 9am-5pm Mon.-Sat., 10am-5pm Sun.) has a helpful map that gives the best bike routes, including one that hits all the historical downtown sites as well as the Ravenswood and Gundlach Bundschu Wineries. The **Sonoma Valley Cyclery** (20091 Broadway, Sonoma, 707/935-3377, 10am-6pm Mon.-Sat., 10am-4pm Sun., $7-15/hour, $30-75/day) rents bikes, including mountain and tandem bikes, as well as bike trailers for kids. For an extra $25, you can have your bike delivered to and picked up from your hotel. Maps and advice come at no extra charge.

Food
SONOMA
★ **the girl & the fig** (110 W. Spain St., 707/938-3634, www.thegirlandthefig.com, 11:30am-11pm Fri.-Sat., 11:30am-10pm Sun.-Mon., $20-28), right on Sonoma Plaza, is a valley institution. The French country menu includes main courses like free-range chicken and duck confit, Sonoma rabbit, and steak frites. The wine list focuses on rhone varietals, with many from local Sonoma producers.

It's rare when locals and travelers agree on the best restaurant. Traditional Portuguese eatery ★ **LaSalette** (452 1st St. E., 707/938-1927, www.lasalette-restaurant.com, 11:30am-9pm daily, $19-28) has a simple, charming atmosphere with a wood-fired oven facing a bar and a large outdoor patio. The menu features fresh fish and hearty meat dishes plus some good meatless options, or make an easy choice with the Tasca Tasting Plates ($16-34).

For a cup of coffee or a quick pastry, swing by the **Basque Boulangerie Café** (460 1st St. E., 707/935-7687, http://basqueboulangerie. com, 6am-6pm daily, $5-12). The line often snakes out the door on weekend mornings, but it usually moves fast. The wide selection of soups, salads, and sandwiches can also be bought to go, handy since table space inside and out is scarce. Pay attention after ordering: Customer names are only called once when food is ready. If the Basque Boulangerie is too busy, cross the square to the **Sunflower Caffé** (421 1st St. W., 707/996-6645, www.sonomasunflower.com, 7am-4pm daily, $5-15), which has basic breakfast selections and upscale salads and sandwiches.

CARNEROS

For breakfast, make a trip to Carneros Inn's ★ **The Boon Fly Café** (707/299-4870, www.boonflycafe.com, 7am-9pm daily, $16-27). At this industrial chic spot, gourmet takes on hearty egg favorites fill the menu. Wash one down with the signature bacon Bloody Mary. Lunch and dinner are just as good, with decadent salads and fried chicken.

Book a table at Carneros Inn's **The FARM** (707/299-4880, www.thecarnerosinn.com, 5:30pm-10pm Wed.-Sun., $32-49). It serves upscale California cuisine, complete with a chef's tasting menu and big white plates topped with tiny artistic piles of food. Dress up a little—despite its name, The FARM has an upscale vibe. More casual, but still with a whiff of luxury, the bar (4pm-11pm daily) serves lighter fare like burgers, flatbreads, and lobster risotto.

The **Schellville Grill** (22900 Broadway, Sonoma, 707/996-5151, www.schellvillegrill.com, 8am-2pm Mon., 8am-3pm and 5:30pm-8:30pm Thurs.-Sat., 8am-3pm Sun., $12-25), at the intersection of Highways 12 and 121, is primarily a sandwich joint with plenty of burgers, pulled pork, and fish sandwiches. Hearty plates of comfort food are delivered by a crew of relaxed locals. If the weather is nice, take a table on the covered back patio.

Accommodations

SONOMA

In 1840, General Vallejo's brother built a home for his family on the town square. In the 1890s, it became a hotel, which would eventually become the **Swiss Hotel** (18 W. Spain St., 707/938-2884, www.swisshotel-sonoma.com, $110-240). The rooms have plenty of modern amenities, though the exterior and the public spaces retain the feel of the original adobe building. Enjoy a meal at the restaurant or have a drink at the historical bar.

For price and character, the **Sonoma Hotel** (110 W. Spain St., Sonoma, 707/996-2996 or 800/468-6016, www.sonomahotel.com, $150-210) can't be beat. Built in 1880, the hotel is one of Sonoma's landmark buildings. The rooms, all with private baths, are outfitted in trim Victorian fixtures, and many have sloped ceilings, creating a cozy, intimate atmosphere.

Located just a few blocks from the square, **El Pueblo Inn** (896 W. Napa St., 707/996-3651, www.elpuebloinn.com, $189-249) has rooms facing a lush central courtyard with a pool and hot tub. Some boast adobe brick walls or lounge areas with fireplaces, but many are standard hotel accommodations—clean and modestly decorated. For the location and amenities it's a good deal, especially if you're traveling with kids.

CARNEROS

South of Sonoma, **The Carneros Inn** (4048 Sonoma Hwy., 707/299-4900, www.thecarnerosinn.com, $350-600) is an expansive cottage resort. The immense property, which backs onto the countryside, has three restaurants, a spa, two pools, and even a small market. Unpretentious cottages spread out in small clusters for acres, each group surrounding its own garden paths and water features. Inside, the cozy cottages sparkle with white linens, tile floors, and windows overlooking sizeable private backyards with decks and comfy chaises.

Transportation

The town of Sonoma is over the mountains west of the Napa Valley. The main route through the valley is Highway 12, also called the Sonoma Highway. From the Bay Area, take U.S. 101 north to Highway 37 east. At the light near Sonoma Raceway, turn left on Highway 121, the central conduit through Carneros. To reach Sonoma, turn left on Highway 12 midway through Carneros.

For public transit, use the buses run by **Sonoma County Transit** (SCT, 707/576-7433, www.sctransit.com, $1.25-3.65). Several routes serve the Sonoma Valley daily. It's also possible to use SCT to get from Sonoma Valley to Santa Rosa, Guerneville, and other parts of the Russian River Valley.

GLEN ELLEN AND KENWOOD

North of the town of Sonoma, the valley becomes more rural. The next hamlet on Highway 12 is Glen Ellen (pop. 784), surrounded by a couple of regional parks and Jack London State Historic Park. Despite having some excellent wineries, downtown Glen Ellen has not caught the Wine Country bug; instead, it feels like a historical farm town.

Wineries
ERIC ROSS WINERY

You can almost imagine author Jack London relaxing with a book in the cozy tasting room of the **Eric Ross Winery** (14300 Arnold Dr., 707/939-8525, www.ericross.com, 11am-5pm daily, $10), across the street from the Jack London Village complex. The bright red rustic building is thronged with visitors on summer weekends, but during the week you'll likely have the comfy leather sofa inside to yourself. The metal-topped corner tasting bar almost seems like an afterthought. The pinots in particular are worth trying, and there are usually two or three available to taste, each featuring classic Russian River complexity and smoothness.

BENZIGER FAMILY WINERY

With vines poking out from the hillside grass, free-range cockerels crowing, and rustic wooden buildings hidden among the trees, the mountainside **Benziger Family Winery** (1883 London Ranch Rd., Glen Ellen, 707/935-3000, www.benziger.com, 10am-5pm daily, $10) feels like the family-run operation that it is. It's also the valley's only biodynamic winery.

To get a better understanding of biodynamic methods, hop aboard a 45-minute, tractor-drawn wine tram tour ($25, under 21 $10). You'll wind through the gorgeous and slightly wild-looking estate while learning about biodynamic principles, the natural environment, and winemaking in general. The tour concludes with stops at the winemaking facility and hillside storage cave, a special tasting of biodynamic wines, and a tasting back at the large commercial tasting room. It's the best tour in the valley for the money. Tours are offered every half hour 11am-3:30pm. Tram space is limited, so in the summer you should buy a ticket in advance. If you miss the tour, take the short (and free) Biodynamic Discovery Trail just off the parking lot.

KUNDE ESTATES

One of the largest wineries in the West, **Kunde Estates** (9825 Hwy. 12, Kenwood, 707/833-5501, www.kunde.com, 10:30am-5pm daily, $10) has wines that are well worth the price, and the variety of tours makes the most of the large estate. Free tours of the aging caves under the hillside occur almost daily (inquire with staff). Other tours, which are more like hikes, go up the mountain every Saturday (reservations required, $40) to explore the caves and vineyards and learn about the winery's sustainable practices, culminating with a tasting at the mountaintop tasting room 1,400 feet above the valley floor. To get to the mountaintop tasting room without the hike, jump aboard one of the winery's passenger vans ($10, two-day advance reservations required).

ST. FRANCIS WINERY

Named to honor the Franciscan monks who are widely credited with planting California's first wine grapes, **St. Francis Winery** (100 Pythian Rd., Kenwood, 707/538-9463 or 888/675-9463, www.stfranciswine.com,

10am-5pm daily, $15) is a place for red-wine lovers, particularly merlot, and fans of Spanish architecture. The spacious tasting room is one of the best-designed in the valley. Windows running the length of the room look out onto vineyards and mountains; escape into the garden if it gets too crowded.

Picnickers are welcome on the sun-drenched patio across from the tasting room, but the tables just outside the picture windows are reserved for indulging in the charcuterie and wine pairing ($35, 11am-4pm daily, no reservation required). Want to make it into a lunch? For $68, you can get five courses that highlight the diversity of the wine selection. Call or check the website for the current seating schedule and to make a reservation.

Jack London State Historic Park

Travelers come to Sonoma not just for the fine food and abundant wine, but also for the chance to visit **Jack London State Historic Park** (2400 London Ranch Rd., Glen Ellen, 707/938-5216, www.parks.ca.gov or http://jacklondonpark.com, 10am-5pm daily Mar.-Nov., 10am-5pm Thurs.-Mon. Dec.-Feb., $10). Author Jack London lived and wrote in rural Sonoma County at the beginning of the 20th century. Docents offer tours of the park, which include talks on London's life and history. Explore the surviving buildings on London's prized Beauty Ranch or hike up Sonoma Mountain and check out the artificial lake and bathhouse. The pretty stone House of Happy Walls, a creation of London's wife, houses a small museum. There's no camping at the park.

The **Triple Creek Horse Outfit** (707/887-8700, www.triplecreekhorseoutfit.com, $75-220) offers guided horseback rides at Jack London State Historic Park that last from one hour up to half a day. Tours take you through the writer's life in Sonoma County and the literary history of the region. At the conclusion of your ride, you'll be given complimentary tasting passes to Benziger and Imagery Estate wineries.

Food

Glen Ellen has a small but distinguished collection of eateries. One of the oldest is the **Glen Ellen Inn Restaurant** (13670 Arnold Dr., Glen Ellen, 707/996-6409, www.glenelleninn.com, 11:30am-9pm Thurs.-Tues., 5pm-9pm Wed., $13-26). This oyster grill and martini bar seats 80, but is broken up into various dining rooms, patios, and porches, giving it an intimate feel. In addition to the seafood-heavy gourmet menu, the restaurant boasts a full bar and a wine list worthy of its location.

★ **Glen Ellen Star** (13648 Arnold Dr., Glen Ellen, 707/343-1384, www.glenellenstar.com, 5:30pm-9pm Sun.-Thurs., 5:30pm-9:30pm Fri.-Sat., $14-32) represents the newest wave of California and Wine Country cuisine, serving locally sourced, wood-oven fare (pizzas, roasted meats and vegetables, iron-skillet quick breads) that lean toward comfort food with an urban sensibility. The wood and brushed metal interior is spare, with a gleaming, stainless steel kitchen. Reservations are encouraged, but patio and bar seating are open for walk-ins.

Eating outdoors right next to the vineyards is one of the attractions of the **Kenwood Restaurant and Bar** (9900 Sonoma Hwy., Kenwood, 707/833-6326, www.kenwoodrestaurant.com, 11:30am-8:30pm Wed.-Sun., $11-35). The small plates and main courses are simple, unpretentious combinations of local ingredients. The wine list includes selections from almost every Sonoma Valley winery, plus a few bottles from Napa, France, and Italy for good measure.

Accommodations

Attached to the red-brick Jack London Saloon and Wolf House Restaurant, the **Jack London Lodge** (13740 Arnold Dr., Glen Ellen, 707/938-8510, www.jacklondonlodge.com, $95-185) anchors central Glen Ellen. The 22-room lodge is modern, with a broad patio, a kidney-shaped pool, and groomed lawns. Vines draping the balcony add to the ambience, as do the hot tub and the creek running through the back of the property.

For historical lodgings, book a room, suite, or cottage at the ★ **Olea Hotel** (5131 Warm Springs Rd., Glen Ellen, 707/996-5131, www.oleahotel.com, $235-415), a B&B tucked away in Glen Ellen. Built at the turn of the 20th century, the property has since received a sleek update. Some rooms come with a stone fireplace, and others boast an expansive porch overlooking the well-maintained grounds. For more privacy, 300-square-foot cottages dot the property. Guests receive a hot two-course breakfast, and can soak in the outdoor hot tub or partake in the complimentary wine-tasting in the lobby.

If you're pinching pennies or just want to sleep beneath the stars, **Sugarloaf Ridge State Park** (2605 Adobe Canyon Rd., Kenwood, 707/833-5712, www.parks.ca.gov or www.sugarloafpark.org, reservations 800/274-7275 or www.reserveamerica.com, $35) has 47 campsites with showers and free Wi-Fi at the park's visitors center.

Transportation

Glen Ellen is located just off Highway 12, seven miles north of Sonoma. Arnold Drive is the main street through town, and it runs south to Sonoma. To reach Glen Ellen from Santa Rosa, take Highway 12 east through Kenwood for about 15 miles.

Kenwood is located about 10 miles east of downtown Santa Rosa on Highway 12, and about five miles north of Glen Ellen. To reach Kenwood from U.S. 101 in Santa Rosa, take the exit for Highway 12 east.

Russian River Valley

The Russian River Valley may be the prettiest part of Wine Country. The Russian River runs through it, providing ample water for forests and meadows as well as wide calm spots with sandy banks. Rafting, canoeing, and kayaking opportunities abound on the zippier stretches of the river. The area encompasses several prestigious American Viticultural Areas. Wineries are clustered along three main roads: the Gravenstein Highway (Hwy. 116), River Road, and Dry Creek Road.

To the west of the area's concentrated wine region, you'll reach the river in Guerneville, a noted gay and lesbian resort destination. A general sense of friendliness and fun permeates the area, including its kitschy downtown and the clothing-optional resorts.

SANTA ROSA

Santa Rosa functions as a gateway to Wine Country and a transportation hub. It's a convenient place to stay as you venture out to Napa and Sonoma, or as a stopover on your way.

Wineries

The specialty at **Hanna Winery** (5353 Occidental Rd., 707/575-3371, www.hannawinery.com, 10am-4pm daily, $10-25) is crisp, steel-fermented sauvignon blanc. A hit with critics, it's exactly what you want to drink while soaking in the sun, either on the winery's wraparound front porch or beneath the great live oak out front. Hanna offers a large tasting list, along with a reserve flight of the finest vintages.

Kendall-Jackson Wine Center (5007 Fulton Rd., Fulton, 707/576-3810 or 866/287-9828, www.kj.com, 10am-5pm daily, tours 1pm daily, tasting $15, tour $25) surprises even serious oenophiles with the quiet elegance of its tasting room and the extensive sustainable gardens and demonstration vineyards surrounding the buildings. Choose between moderately priced regular wine-tasting and the food-and-wine pairing, one of the best in Wine Country. In high season, make a reservation well in advance—KJ doesn't have many tables. Tour the gardens in spring and summer, and taste fresh wine grapes during the fall harvest.

Sights

In honor of former resident Charles Schulz and the *Peanuts* gang, the **Charles M. Schulz Museum** (2301 Hardies Ln., 707/579-4452, www.schulzmuseum.org; 11am-5pm Mon.-Fri., 10am-5pm Sat.-Sun. summer; 11am-5pm Mon. and Wed.-Fri., 10am-5pm Sat.-Sun. fall-spring; adults $10, seniors and ages 4-18 $5, under age 4 free) exhibits original *Peanuts* strips, a large collection of Schulz's personal possessions, and an astonishing array of tribute artwork from other comic-strip artists and urban installation designers.

The **Pacific Coast Air Museum** (1 Air Museum Way, 707/575-7900, www.pacificcoastairmuseum.org, 10am-4pm Tues., Thurs., and Sat.-Sun., adults $10, seniors $7, ages 6-17 $5, under age 6 free) is worth a visit. Learn about the history of aviation in the United States through interpretive and photographic exhibits. Many of the planes are examples of ones that can be found on aircraft carriers today. Check out the funky Pitts aerobatic plane, the likes of which you'll see doing impossible-looking tricks during the museum's annual **Wings Over Wine Country Air Show** (Sept.).

If you love gardening, don't miss the **Luther Burbank Home and Gardens** (204 Santa Rosa Ave., 707/524-5445, www.lutherburbank.org; gardens 8am-dusk daily year-round, free; museum and tours 10am-4pm Tues.-Sun. Apr.-Oct., $7). Using hybridization techniques, Luther Burbank personally created some of the most popular plants grown in California gardens and landscapes today. Burbank's own house, where he lived until 1906, is preserved along with a small greenhouse and the gardens as part of the 1.6-acre National and State Historic Landmark.

Sports and Recreation

A popular way to get a great view of the Russian River Valley is from the basket of a hot-air balloon. **Wine Country Balloons** (707/538-7359 or 800/759-5638, www.balloontours.com, adults $225, children $195) maintains a fleet of balloons that can carry 2-16 passengers. Expect the total time to be 3-4 hours, with 1-1.5 hours in the air. You'll end your flight with brunch and a handful of wine-tasting coupons. Groups meet at Kal's Kaffe Mocha (397 Aviation Blvd.).

Accommodations and Food

Santa Rosa has all the familiar chain motels. In the Historic Railroad Square, **Hotel la Rose** (308 Wilson St., 707/579-3200, www.hotellarose.com, $119-189) offers historical and modern accommodations for very reasonable prices. In the stone-clad main building, guests will enjoy antique furniture and floral wallpaper, but across the street, the carriage house offers modern decor and amenities.

Get in line for breakfast, brunch, or lunch at the ★ **Omelette Express** (112 4th St., 707/525-1690, http://omeletteexpress.com, 6:30am-3pm Mon.-Fri., 7am-4pm Sat.-Sun., $7-11), a spot favored by locals. The very casual dining rooms are decorated with the front ends of classic cars, and the menu involves lots of omelets. Portions are huge and come with a side of toast made with homemade bread, so consider splitting with a friend.

The cavernous ★ **La Rosa Tequileria & Grille** (500 4th St., 707/523-3663, http://larosasantarosa.com, 11:30am-9pm Sun.-Thurs., 11:30am-2am Fri.-Sat., $10-19) is the place to go for a casual lunch downtown or a late night out with friends. The large restaurant has multiple dining rooms and a large back patio, each done up in a Mexican Gothic style with deep booths, luscious murals of roses, and collections of crucifixes. The classic south-of-the-border cuisine is excellent and delivered with artistic panache.

Transportation

Santa Rosa is 50 miles north of San Francisco on U.S. 101. Traffic on this major corridor gets congested, particularly during the morning and evening commutes and sunny summer afternoons. The side roads that lead to various tasting rooms and recreation spots are seldom crowded.

From U.S. 101, take exit 489. West of the

Russian River Valley

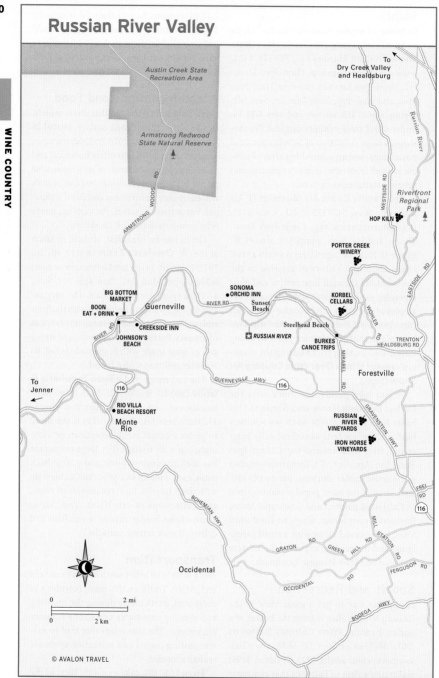

To
Dry Creek Valley
and Healdsburg

Russian River

Austin Creek State
Recreation Area

Armstrong Redwood
State Natural Reserve

ARMSTRONG WOODS RD

WESTSIDE RD

Riverfront
Regional
Park

HOP KILN

EASTSIDE RD

PORTER CREEK
WINERY

BIG BOTTOM
MARKET
BOON
EAT + DRINK

SONOMA
ORCHID INN

RIVER RD

Sunset
Beach

Guerneville

KORBEL
CELLARS

WOHLER RD

CREEKSIDE INN

RIVER RD

JOHNSON'S
BEACH

Steelhead Beach

RUSSIAN RIVER

BURKES
CANOE TRIPS

TRENTON
HEALDSBURG RD

MIRABEL RD

Forestville

To
Jenner

116

GUERNEVILLE HWY

116

RIO VILLA
BEACH RESORT

Monte
Rio

RUSSIAN
RIVER
VINEYARDS

GRAVENSTEIN HWY

IRON HORSE
VINEYARDS

FREI
RD

116

BOHEMIAN HWY

MILL STATION RD

GRATON RD

GREEN HILL RD

FERGUSON RD

Occidental

OCCIDENTAL RD

BODEGA HWY

0   2 mi

0   2 km

© AVALON TRAVEL

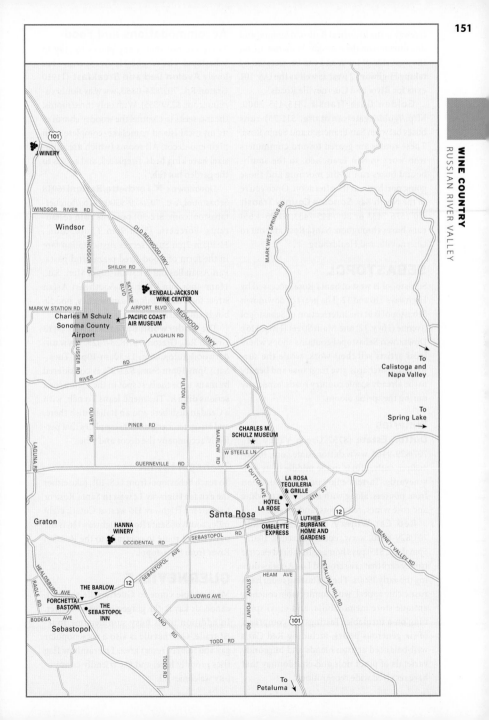

freeway is the historical Railroad Square, and downtown is on the east side. Wineries are on the west side of town and can be accessed by taking Highway 12 west as well as the U.S. 101 exits for River and Guerneville Roads.

Golden Gate Transit (415/455-2000, http://goldengatetransit.org, $11.75) runs buses between San Francisco and Santa Rosa. These routes are geared toward commuters who work in San Francisco, so the southbound buses run in the morning and those going north run in the afternoon. Once you're in the North Bay, **Sonoma County Transit** (707/576-7433 or 800/345-7433, $1.25-3.65) runs buses throughout Santa Rosa and out to Guerneville and Healdsburg.

SEBASTOPOL

Sebastopol is west of Santa Rosa, accessed by Highways 116 and 12. The heart of downtown Sebastopol is at the intersection of Sebastopol Avenue (Hwy. 12) and Main Street (Hwy. 116). Downtown Sebastopol contains shops where local artists sell their work, while the surrounding orchards give fragrance and beauty to the already scenic country roads, especially during the spring bloom.

Wineries

Dutton Estate (8757 Green Valley Rd., 707/829-9463, www.duttonestate.com, 10am-4:30pm daily, $10) is in the middle of its own vineyards. Tasters enjoy personal attention from pourers, along with a small list of white and rosé wines, red pinots, and syrahs.

Red Car Winery (8400 Graton Rd., 707/829-8500, www.redcarwine.com, 10am-5pm daily, $15) pays homage to the red electric trolley cars that crisscrossed Los Angeles during the early 1900s. The hip tasting room has a rustic chic appeal, with comfortable couches, antique store memorabilia, and vinyl spinning on a turntable. Tastings are comprised of six generous pours, including Red Car's well-balanced artisan blends and burgundy varietals of pinot noir and chardonnay that have received wide recognition.

Accommodations and Food

There are not that many places to stay in Sebastopol. The very best is the expensive but lovely **Avalon Bed and Breakfast** (11910 Graton Rd., 707/824-0880, www.avalonluxuryinn.com, $239-355). With only three rooms, the inn seeks to channel the woodsy charm of its mystical island namesake, complete with high-end decor. All rooms (which are suite-size) have king beds, fireplaces, and access to the garden hot tub.

Downtown's ★ **Forchetta/Bastoni** (6948 Sebastopol Ave., 707/829-9500, http://forchettabastoni.com, $12-30) presents twin restaurants. Forchetta (5pm-9pm Thurs.-Mon., 11:30am-2pm Sun.) serves rustic Italian fare in the form of wood-fired pizzas and pasta. Pan-Asian Bastoni (11:30am-10pm Mon.-Sat., 11am-4pm Sun.) features Southeast Asian street food like *bánh mì* sandwiches, noodle bowls, and curry plates.

The **Underwood Bar and Bistro** (9113 Graton Rd., Graton, 707/823-7023, www.underwoodgraton.com, 11:30am-10pm Tues.-Sat., 5pm-10pm Sun., $23-35) is considered by many to be the best spot in the region for a serious dinner. The menu leans French, with a Catalan dish here and an Italian dish there, and an oyster menu and cheese plates that perfectly accompany the decor and vibe.

Transportation

To reach Sebastopol from U.S. 101, take either the exit for Highway 12 west in Santa Rosa or the exit for Highway 116 west at Cotati, eight miles south of Santa Rosa. Highway 116 is the most direct route to continue to the Russian River from Sebastopol.

GUERNEVILLE

Most people come to Guerneville to float, canoe, or kayak the gorgeous Russian River. In addition to its busy summertime tourist trade, Guerneville is also a very popular gay and lesbian resort area. The rainbow flag flies proudly here, and the friendly community welcomes all.

Wineries

HOP KILN

Hop Kiln (6050 Westside Rd., Healdsburg, 707/433-6491, www.hopkilnwinery.com, 10am-5pm daily, $10), true to its name, is housed in an old hop kiln. The Russian River Valley once grew more beer-making ingredients than grapes, and this distinctively shaped kiln dried the valley's crop of hops each year. Inside the main kiln is an extensive wine-tasting bar with typical Wine Country varietals including Hop Kiln's award-winning pinot noir. Tastings are comprised of six wines.

J WINERY

J Winery (11447 Old Redwood Hwy., 888/594-6326, www.jwine.com, 11am-5pm daily, $20-75) loves the cutting edge of the California wine scene. J specializes in California-style sparkling wines, and its tasting room is a triumph of modern design. Make a reservation at the Bubble Lounge, where there are tables and waitstaff, to enjoy wines specially paired with small bites of high-end California cuisine prepared in J's kitchen by their team of gourmet chefs. Or just sidle up to the stylish tasting bar and enjoy a tasting flight ($20).

KORBEL CELLARS

Korbel Cellars (13250 River Rd., 707/824-7316, www.korbel.com, 10am-4:30pm daily, free) is the leading producer of California champagne-style sparkling wines. The large, lush estate welcomes visitors with elaborate landscaping and attractive buildings, including a small area serving as a visitors center. Tours of the estate are offered several times daily. Korbel makes and sells a wide variety of high-end California champagnes, plus a few boutique still wines and brandies. The facility also has a full-service gourmet deli and picnic grounds.

PORTER CREEK WINERY

Serious cork dorks recommend the tiny tasting room at **Porter Creek Winery** (8735 Westside Rd., Healdsburg, 707/433-6321, www.portercreekvineyards.com, 10:30am-4:30pm daily, $15), which casual tasters might otherwise miss. Turn onto the dirt driveway, pass the farm-style house (the owner's family home), and park in front of a small converted shed—the tasting room. Porter Creek's wines are almost all reds, made from grapes grown organically within sight of the tasting room.

downtown Guerneville

RUSSIAN RIVER VINEYARDS

At **Russian River Vineyards** (5700 Gravenstein Hwy., Forestville, 707/887-3344, www.russianrivervineyards.com, 11am-5pm daily, $10), the friendly staff create a classy small-winery experience, and the small list of wines reflects the locale. You'll enjoy full-bodied, fruity pinot noirs as well as pinot noir rosés and a couple of Sonoma Coast chardonnays. Stick around for lunch or dinner at the winery's **Cork Restaurant** (11:30am-4pm and 5pm-8pm Mon.-Fri., 10am-4pm and 5pm-8pm Sat.-Sun., $25), which serves earthy plates of locally sourced gourmet food in an 1890s farmhouse.

IRON HORSE VINEYARDS

Iron Horse Vineyards (9786 Ross Station Rd., 707/887-1507, www.ironhorsevineyards.com, 10am-4:30pm daily, $20) is down a one-lane road that winds through orchards, over a creek, and past some wild turkeys before climbing up the palm-lined driveway to the winery. The rustic simplicity of the barn-like building and its indoor-outdoor tasting bar belies the pedigree of the sparkling wines made here—they have been served to presidents and won accolades from wine critics since the 1970s. On Friday, tours (10am Mon.-Fri. by appointment only, $25) are led by the winemaker, David Muskgard.

★ Russian River

Guerneville and its surrounding forest are the center for fun on the river. In summer the water is usually warm and dotted with folks swimming, canoeing, or simply floating tubes serenely downriver amid forested riverbanks. **Burke's Canoe Trips** (8600 River Rd., Forestville, 707/887-1222, www.burkescanoetrips.com, Memorial Day-mid-Oct., $65) rents canoes and kayaks on the Russian River. The put-in is at Burke's beach in Forestville; paddlers then canoe downriver 10 miles to Guerneville, where a courtesy shuttle picks them up. Burke's also offers overnight campsites for tents, trailers, and RVs.

On the north bank, **Johnson's Beach & Resort** (16241 1st St., Guerneville, 707/869-2022, www.johnsonsbeach.com, 10am-6pm daily May-Oct., $35) rents canoes, kayaks, pedal boats, and inner tubes for floating on the river. There is a safe, kid-friendly section of the riverbank that's roped off for small children; parents and beachcombers can rent beach chairs and umbrellas for use on the small beach. The boathouse sells beer and snacks.

the Russian River

Fly fishers can cast their lines off **Wohler Bridge** (9765 Wohler Rd., Forestville) and **Steelhead Beach** (9000 River Rd., Forestville).

Armstrong Redwoods

Armstrong Redwoods (17000 Armstrong Woods Rd., 707/869-2015, www.parks.ca.gov, 8am-sunset daily, $8 per vehicle) is an easy five-minute drive from Guerneville. Take a fabulous hike—either a short stroll in the shade of the trees or a multiple-day backcountry adventure. The easiest walk to a big tree is the 0.1 mile from the visitors center to the tallest tree in the park, named the **Parson Jones Tree.** If you saunter another 0.5 mile, you'll reach the **Colonel Armstrong Tree;** another 0.25 mile more leads to the **Icicle Tree.**

Right next to Armstrong is the **Austin Creek State Recreation Area** (17000 Armstrong Woods Rd., Guerneville, 707/869-2015, www.parks.ca.gov, 8am-sunset daily, $8 per vehicle). It's rough going on 2.5 miles of steep, narrow, treacherous dirt road to get to the main entrance and parking area; no vehicles over 20 feet long and no trailers of any kind are permitted. But once you're in, some great—and very difficult—hiking awaits you. The eponymous **Austin Creek Trail** (4.7 miles one-way) leads down from the hot meadows into the cool forest fed by Austin Creek. To avoid monotony on this challenging route, create a loop by taking the turn onto **Gilliam Creek Trail** (four miles one-way).

Entertainment and Events

Guerneville wouldn't be a proper gay resort town without at least a couple of good gay bars that create proper nightlife for visitors and locals. The most visible and funky-looking of these is the **Rainbow Cattle Company** (16220 Main St., Guerneville, 707/869-0206, www.queersteer.com, noon-2am daily). The Rainbow has cold drinks and hot men with equal abandon. Think cocktails in Mason jars, wood paneling, and leather nights. This is just the kind of queer bar where you can bring your mom or your straight-but-not-narrow friends, and they'll have just as much fun as you will.

The **Stumptown Brewery** (15045 River Rd., 707/869-0705, www.stumptown.com, 11am-midnight Sun.-Thurs., 11am-2am Fri.-Sat.) is *the* place to hang out on the river. This atypical dive bar has a pool table, Naugahyde barstools, a worn wooden bar crowded with locals, plus a deck out back overlooking the river. The brewery only makes a few of the beers sold on tap, but they are all great and perfect to enjoy by the pitcher. Stumptown also serves a menu of burgers and grilled sandwiches; the food is a perfect excuse to stay put.

Held at Johnson's Beach in Guerneville, the **Russian River Jazz and Blues Festival** (www.omegaevents.com, 707/869-1595, $50-60 each day, Sept.) is a two-day affair with jazz one day and blues the next. Much more than just a music festival, this event is the last big bash of the summer season; it takes place at the end of September, just before the weather reliably turns cold. If you plan to stay both days, consider camping here. **Johnson's Beach** (707/869-2022, http://johnsonsbeach.com) has designated campsites available on a first-come, first-served basis.

Food

Pat's Restaurant (16236 Main St., 707/869-9905, www.pats-restaurant.com, 7am-3pm daily, $10) is a homey, casual diner where locals come to sit at the counter and have breakfast. At night Pat's is another restaurant entirely, home to **Dick Blomster's Korean Diner** (5pm-9pm Sun.-Thurs., 5pm-10pm Fri.-Sat., $15-25), where comfort food (short ribs, hamburgers, fried chicken) is served up Korean style with twists such as deep-fried pickles, kimchi aioli, sake ice cream, and hash browns with a seafood medley.

Big Bottom Market (16228 Main St., 707/604-7295, www.bigbottommarket.com, 8am-5pm Sun.-Mon. and Wed.-Thurs., 8am-6pm Fri.-Sat., $8-12) is a café that serves its coffee via French press and has a small but select local wine list. The food includes excellent cold and hot-pressed sandwiches, savory bread pudding, and a wide assortment of biscuits so dense and satisfying, they can be a meal on their own.

It was ★ **boon eat + drink** (16248 Main St., 707/869-0780, http://eatatboon.com, 11am-3pm and 5pm-9pm Sun.-Tues. and Thurs., 11am-3pm and 5pm-10pm Fri.-Sat., $16-26) that first put Guerneville on the culinary map. Light and airy with splashes of metal and bright colors, the bistro is related to the nearby boon hotel + spa, where some of the vegetables are grown. Lunch usually consists of panini, small plates, and the grass-fed Boon burger. For dinner, hearty mains combine lamb shank with mint pesto or flat iron steak with truffle fries.

Accommodations and Camping

You'll find a few dozen bed-and-breakfasts and cabin resorts in town. Many of these spots are gay friendly, some with clothing-optional hot tubs.

The **Creekside Inn & Lodge** (16180 Neeley Rd., 707/776-6586 or 800/776-6586, www.creeksideinn.com, $98-300) is right beside the Russian River and just a few minutes' stroll to Guerneville's main street. The several acres of grounds include a main house with the cheapest rooms, a pool, and eight cottages, from studios to two-bedrooms.

The experience at the ★ **Sonoma Orchid Inn** (12850 River Rd., 707/869-4466 or 888/877-4466, www.sonomaorchidinn.com, pets welcome, $149-249) is made by its amazing owners, who can not only recommend restaurants and spas, but can also make reservations for you. The best rooms have microwaves and small fridges, while the budget rooms are tiny but cute, with private baths and pretty decorations. The Orchid is dog and kid friendly, clothing mandatory in the communal hot tub, and welcoming.

On the road to Armstrong Redwoods, **boon hotel + spa** (14711 Armstrong Woods Rd., 707/869-2721, www.boonhotels.com, $155-265) is minimal in the extreme, with

a palette of white, slate, and chrome. Many of the 14 rooms have freestanding cast-iron fireplaces, private patios, and fridges, and all have large beds with fair trade organic cotton sheets. There is a pool and hot tub (both saltwater), and plenty of facial and massage options. In the morning, wake up to a pressed pot of locally roasted coffee; in the evening, chill out with a cocktail by the pool.

There are numerous resort campgrounds along the Russian River. Catering to summer crowds and RVs, they usually charge a premium price for the extensive services and facilities they offer. Reservations are essential during the busy summer months. One of the more reasonably priced is **Burke's Canoe Trips** (8600 River Rd., Forestville, 707/887-1222, www.burkescanoetrips.com, $10 pp/day), hidden in the redwoods right next to the river (and the road) just north of Forestville. The full-service campground, open May-October, has 60 sites for tents or RVs.

The more serene campgrounds are generally off the beaten track, as is the case for the primitive and scenic creekside campgrounds in the **Austin Creek State Recreation Area** (17000 Armstrong Woods Rd., Guerneville, 707/869-2015, www.parks.ca.gov, $25). The road into the park through Armstrong Redwoods State Reserve ends at the **Bullfrog Pond Campground,** with 23 sites, toilets, and drinking water. No vehicles over 20 feet long are allowed. Camping is first-come, first-served; to register for a campsite, stop by the Armstrong Redwoods park office (17000 Armstrong Woods Rd., Guerneville, 707/869-2958, 11am-3pm daily).

Transportation

Guerneville is on Highway 116, alternately named River Road. In downtown Guerneville, Highway 116 is briefly called Main Street. The most direct access is via U.S. 101 north of Santa Rosa; take the River Road/Guerneville exit and follow River Road west for 15 miles to downtown Guerneville.

Alternatively, a more scenic and often less crowded route is to take U.S. 101 to Highway

116 near Cotati, south of Santa Rosa. Also called the Gravenstein Highway, Highway 116 winds about 22 twisty miles through Sebastopol, Graton, and Forestville to emerge onto River Road in Guerneville.

HEALDSBURG

Healdsburg, a small city of 11,000, is so charming it's easy to forget that people live and work here. The **Healdsburg Plaza** is one of the town's most treasured features and anchors the downtown area, while the wide and slow Russian River creates the town's natural southern border. Boutiques, chic restaurants, and galleries dot the town. Fresh paint brightens the historical storefronts and planters are filled with flowers and trailing vines. Healdsburg is also the nexus of three American Viticulture Areas (AVAs): the Russian River AVA, best known for producing pinot noir and chardonnay; Dry Creek AVA, famous for its zinfandel and sauvignon blanc; and the Alexander Valley AVA, which produces predominantly cabernet sauvignon and merlot.

Wineries
DRY CREEK VINEYARD

The midsize **Dry Creek Vineyard** (3770 Lambert Bridge Rd., 800/864-9463, www.drycreekvineyard.com, 10:30am-4:30pm daily, $10-15) focuses much effort within its own AVA (Dry Creek), producing many single-vineyard wines from grapes grown within a few miles of the estate. It occasionally produces something unusual, like a chenin blanc or a sauterne-style dessert wine. Try as many as you can in the ivy-covered tasting room, styled after a French château.

PRESTON VINEYARDS

At Lou Preston's idiosyncratic establishment, **Preston Vineyards** (9282 W. Dry Creek Rd., Healdsburg, 707/433-3372, www.prestonvineyards.com, 11am-4:30pm daily, $10), homemade bread, organic vegetables, and olive oil get nearly equal attention as the wine. Inside the homespun tasting room, you'll taste some

organic wine from its small portfolio dominated by rhone varietals. The selection of locally produced foods makes this an ideal place to buy everything you need for an impromptu picnic next to the bocce courts.

FERRARI-CARANO

One of the best large wineries in Dry Creek Valley, **Ferrari-Carano** (8761 Dry Creek Rd., 707/433-6700 or 800/831-0381, www.ferrari-carano.com, 10am-5pm daily, $5-15) provides great standard and reserve wines in an upscale tasting room and winery facility. Upstairs you'll get to taste from Ferrari-Carano's extensive menu of large-production, moderately priced whites and reds. Downstairs, enjoy the elegant lounge area, which includes comfortable seating and a video describing the winemaking process, from grape to glass.

★ ALEXANDER VALLEY VINEYARDS

Alexander Valley Vineyards (8644 Hwy. 128, Healdsburg, 707/433-7209 or 800/888-7209, www.avvwine.com, 10am-5pm daily, free) shares a name with the historical valley for good reason. In the 1960s the founders of the winery bought a chunk of the homestead once owned by Cyrus Alexander, the man credited with planting the valley's first vineyards in 1846.

The winery's vineyards provide the grapes for two decadent blends, Temptation Zin and Redemption Zin, and the bordeaux-style Cyrus flagship wine. Historical sites pepper the estate, including a wooden schoolhouse built by Alexander in 1853 and the Alexander family gravesite, up the hill. Complimentary tours of the expansive wine caves are available daily at 11am and 2pm.

PORTALUPI

There are a number of tasting rooms in downtown Healdsburg, but if you go to one, make it **Portalupi** (107 North St., 707/395-0960, www.portalupiwine.com, 11am-7pm daily, $5-10). You'll find Russian River lush and inky pinot noirs and zinfandel, as well as Italian barbera, a port made from carignane, and the Vaso di Marina, a blend of pinot noir, zinfandel, and cabernet sauvignon. As a nod to Jane Portalupi's grandmother, who used to make wine in her native village in Italy, the wine comes in a liter ($28) or half-gallon glass jug ($48). The sole white is the bianco blend of sauvignon blanc, chardonnay, and muscat canelli. The sophisticated tasting room is filled with two large couches, perfect to relax and taste a flight, enjoy a glass, or nibble on cheese and charcuterie.

Entertainment and Events

The **Raven Players** (115 North St., 707/433-6335, www.ravenplayers.org, adults $15-26) ply their art in the boutique town of Healdsburg. This ambitious company stages five plays per year—primarily award-winning and established works. Past offerings have included Arthur Miller's *After the Fall* and Christopher Durang's *Beyond Therapy*. For the last show each season, the Ravens produce a dramatic musical.

The slim **Bergamot Alley** (328A Healdsburg Ave., 707/433-8720, www.bergamotalley.com, noon-1am Tues.-Sun.) is all exposed brick, cool lighting, and microbrews. European wines are sold by the glass and a turntable plays full albums from start to finish. Nibble on small offerings, like spiced popcorn and pickled eggs, or bring your own snacks.

Sports and Recreation

Wine Country Bikes (61 Front St., 707/473-0610, www.winecountrybikes.com, 9am-5pm daily, tours $139) is on the square in downtown Healdsburg. Its Classic Wine Tour pedals through the Dry Creek region, where you'll stop and taste wine, take walks in vineyards, and learn more about the history of wine. A gourmet picnic lunch is included with the tour. For independent souls who prefer to carve their own routes, Wine Country Bikes also rents road bikes, tandem bikes, and hybrids ($39-145 per day).

The Russian River provides water-related recreation opportunities. On the south side of town is **Memorial Beach** (13839 Old Redwood Hwy., 707/433-1625, http://parks.sonomacounty.ca.gov, sunrise-sunset daily, parking $7), a stretch of sandy and rocky shoreline along the river with a swimming area and a few concessions. There, **River's Edge Kayak & Canoe Trips** (13840 Healdsburg Ave., 707/433-7247, www.riversedgekayakandcanoe.com, trips $50-120)

Alexander Valley

offers two self-guided tours aboard stand-up paddleboards and single and double kayaks. After checking in between 8:30am and 11:30am, you'll be shuttled up the river and left to paddle downstream. River's Edge has lots of tips for the best beaches, swimming holes, and picnic spots along the way. If you are more interested in joining a guided tour, another local outfit, **Russian River Adventures** (20 Healdsburg Ave., Healdsburg, 707/433-5599, http://russianriveradventures.com, adults $45-60, children $25-30, dogs $10) offers guided paddles down a secluded section of the river in stable, sturdy inflatable canoes. Dogs, children, and even infants are welcome. Trips usually last 2-6 hours, with little whitewater and lots of serene shaded pools.

Food

The concrete, wood, and glass dining room of ★ **Spoonbar** (219 Healdsburg Ave., 707/433-7222, http://spoonbar.com, 5pm-9pm Sun.-Thurs., 5pm-9pm Fri.-Sat., $21-33) excels at minimalism. The warehouse-like space opens out to bustling Healdsburg Avenue. Servers carry out plates of slow-cooked pork belly, braised clams and mussels, and Cornish game hen roulade. Small plates of raw and cured fish, snacks such as chicken cracklings, a wine list that ranges from local to European, and an artisanal cocktail menu polish off the experience.

The large barn housing **Barndiva** (231 Center St., Healdsburg, 707/431-0100, www.barndiva.com, noon-3pm and 5:30pm-9pm Wed.-Thurs., noon-3pm and 5:30pm-10pm Fri.-Sat., 11am-1:45pm and 5:30pm-9pm Sun., $24-38) looks very Wine Country from the outside, but the inside is more Manhattan. The menu has 10 items (a $20 filet mignon burger is one), all French inspired and Sonoma County sourced, and an impressive, retro fresh cocktail menu.

At **Mateo's Cocina Latina** (214 Healdsburg Ave., 707/433-1520, www.mateoscocinalatina.com, 11:30am-9pm Wed.-Mon., $13-25), the flavors of the Yucatan are served surrounded by colorful textiles and wood furniture. Order several of the finger food *tacones* or the *cochinita pibil*, a slow-roasted suckling pig, the signature dish. There is a well-balanced drink menu of a dozen microbrews, local wines, and a host of tequila cocktails.

For an independent cup of coffee in Healdsburg, **Flying Goat Coffee** (324 Center St., 707/433-3599, www.flyinggoatcoffee.com, 7am-7pm daily) sits opposite the square. The place to go for picnic supplies is **Oakville Grocery** (124 Matheson St., 707/433-3200, www.oakvillegrocery.com, 9am-5pm daily, $7-12), a block away. It sells a great selection of cheeses, fresh local breads, and wine, plus fresh eats from its upscale deli counter.

The **Jimtown Store** (6706 Hwy. 128, 707/433-1212, www.jimtown.com; 7am-4pm Mon.-Thurs., 7am-5pm Fri.-Sun. May-Dec.; 7am-3pm Mon. and Wed.-Fri., 7:30am-5pm Sat., 7:30am-3pm Sun. Jan.-Apr.; $6-12), six miles out of town on a country road, has been in operation since 1895. At this old-fashioned country store with gourmet sensibility, you'll find house-made jams, condiments, penny toys, housewares, and, best of all, hot lunches. The chalkboard menu presents a tasty assortment of smoked-brisket sandwiches, chili, buttermilk coleslaw, and chorizo and provolone grilled-cheese sandwiches. Enjoy table service in the back, unwrap your sandwich on benches outside, or pick up one of their prepared box lunches to go.

Accommodations

None of the boutique inns and hotels in Healdsburg come cheap. The **Haydon Street Inn** (321 Haydon St., Healdsburg, 707/433-5228 or 800/528-3703, www.haydon.com, $195-450) is a small inn on a quiet residential street about a 10-minute walk from the plaza. The Queen Anne-style house was built in 1912 and is perfectly maintained with original detailing and period antiques. The six rooms in the main house all have private baths, with the exception of the Blue Room, which has a bathroom across the hall. Two additional deluxe rooms ($400 and up) are in a separate cottage on the manicured grounds. Expect a sumptuous three-course breakfast, and wonderful hors d'oeuvres at the inn's nightly wine hour.

On the town plaza, the **Hotel Healdsburg** (25 Matheson St., 707/431-2800, www.hotelhealdsburg.com, $309-509) is a local icon. The 55-room boutique hotel offers the most upscale amenities, including Frette towels and linens, soaking tubs, walk-in showers, and beautiful modern decor. Rooms include free Wi-Fi and a gourmet breakfast, and guests can enjoy the outdoor pool, fitness center, and full-service day spa. Downstairs, grab a cocktail at the chic **Spirit Bar** (5pm-11:30pm Mon.-Thurs., noon-11:30pm Fri.-Sun.) or a table on the leafy patio at the renowned **Dry Creek Kitchen** (707/431-0330, www.charliepalmer.com, 5:30pm-9:30pm Sun.-Thurs., 5:30pm-10pm Fri.-Sat., $27-39).

Transportation

Healdsburg is an easy destination, as it's about 15 miles north of Santa Rosa on U.S. 101. To reach downtown Healdsburg from U.S. 101, take exit 503 for Central Healdsburg. Healdsburg can also be accessed from Calistoga. Drive north of Calistoga on the beautiful Highway 128 for almost 20 miles. At Jimtown, Highway 128 intersects Alexander Valley Road. Continue straight on Alexander Valley Road as Highway 128 turns right, heading north to Geyserville. In about three miles, turn left onto Healdsburg Avenue, which runs to downtown Healdsburg.

GEYSERVILLE

Geyserville has a small mountain-town feel, with a tiny downtown, a few shops and restaurants, and a number of historic buildings.

Wineries

The first thing you'll notice at the Italianate **Trentadue** (19170 Geyserville Ave., 707/433-3104, www.trentadue.com, 10am-5pm daily, $5-10) is how the gardens sweep out toward the vineyards. Many of Trentadue's vintages are made from estate-grown grapes, including Italian varietals. Inside the narrow tasting room, pours include still wines and a couple of sparkling varieties. The stars of the show are the array of different ports. To take in the beautiful estate, book a seat on the gondola tour ($25) offered daily by appointment.

The little town of Geyserville boasts a fair share of tasting rooms, but the best is **Locals Tasting Room** (Geyserville Ave. at Hwy. 128, 707/857-4900, www.tastelocalwine.com, 11am-6pm daily, free). Tasting

Jimtown Store

is complimentary, with more than 40 wines available. Most of the wines hail from northern Sonoma's boutique wineries, but the overall mix is broad-ranging, from the Central Coast to Mendocino.

Accommodations and Food

The best bed-and-breakfast is the ★ **Hope-Merrill and Hope-Bosworth Houses** (21253 Geyserville Ave., 707/857-3356 or 800/825-4233, www.hope-inns.com, $153-309). This Victorian charmer comprises two historical houses across the street from one another. Aficionados of the Victorian style will love the flowers, lace, frills, and gewgaws that fill the rooms. Each room has its own private bath and amenities include a saltwater pool, two hot tubs, and a homemade breakfast each morning.

Catelli's (21047 Geyserville Ave., 707/857-3471, www.mycatellis.com, 11:30am-8pm Tues.-Thurs., 11:30am-9pm Fri., noon-9pm Sat., noon-8pm Sun., $15-21) is helmed by Domenica Catelli and her brother Nick. Honoring their family's roots, but with an added dedication to healthy local food, they have created an earthy, high-quality Italian eatery geared toward sophisticated comfort food.

Diavola Restaurant (21021 Geyserville Ave., 707/814-0111, www.diavolapizzeria.com, 11:30am-9pm daily, $15-26) is a great Italian joint in a historical brick building. Centered around a wood-burning oven, this small restaurant is all about pizzas and its housemade *salumi* and sausages. Diavola has a well-stocked deli case if you're eager to take some cured meats home with you.

Transportation

Geyserville is located about 10 miles north of Healdsburg at the junction of U.S. 101 and Highway 128. It's also 25 miles north of Calistoga via Highway 128.

North Coast

Sonoma Coast 166

Mendocino Coast 171

The Redwood Coast 179

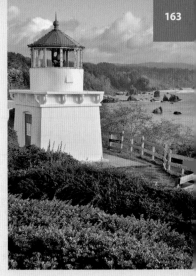

The rugged North Coast is a spectacular place. Its wild beauty is unspoiled and almost desolate. The cliffs are forbidding, the beaches are rocky and windswept, and the surf thunders in with formidable authority.

From Bodega Bay, Highway 1 twists and turns north along hairpin curves that will take your breath away. The Sonoma and Mendocino coasts offer lovely beaches and forests, top-notch cuisine, and a friendly, uncrowded wine region. Along the way, tiny coastal towns—Jenner, Gualala, Mendocino, Fort Bragg—dot the hills and valleys, beckoning travelers with bed-and-breakfasts, organic farms, and relaxing respites from the road. Inland, Mendocino's hidden wine region offers the rural and relaxed pace missing from that other famous wine district.

For most travelers, the North Coast means redwood country, and U.S. 101 marks the gateway to those redwoods beginning south of the small town of Willits. A plethora of state and national parks lure travelers: pitch a tent in Humboldt Redwoods State Park, cruise the Avenue of the Giants, and gaze in wonder at the primordial Founders Grove. The coastal seaside town of Crescent City marks the northern terminus of the North Coast.

PLANNING YOUR TIME

The outdoors is the primary attraction in this region. Driving is the way to get from place to place, unless you're a hard-core backpacker. Make time to explore the redwoods in the parks and spend time on the rugged beaches (in warm waterproof clothes) as well. Hiking is the one don't-miss activity. Close seconds are fishing, whale-watching, and watching the fog roll in as you sit in a cozy café.

Previous: the Mendocino coast; giant coastal redwoods at Jedediah Smith State Park. **Above:** Trinidad Memorial Lighthouse.

Look for ★ to find recommended sights, activities, dining, and lodging.

Highlights

★ **Whale-Watching:** Bodega Bay offers the perfect coastal setting for spying Pacific gray whales during their migration to Alaska (page 166).

★ **Fort Ross State Historic Park:** For a taste of California history, explore this fortified outpost that served as a waypoint for 19th-century traders (page 170).

★ **Mendocino:** This quaint and art-filled seaside community provides a romantic coastal getaway (page 174).

★ **Avenue of the Giants:** This aptly named scenic drive parallels U.S. 101 for 31 miles through Humboldt Redwoods State Park and stands of virgin redwoods (page 180).

★ **Blue Ox Millworks and Historic Park:** This working lumber mill, park, and school are filled with 19th-century tools used to customize historical homes (page 184).

★ **Redwood National and State Parks:** Northern California's legendary redwoods stretch along the coast from Garberville to Crescent City, offering unlimited photo ops of redwood giants (page 187).

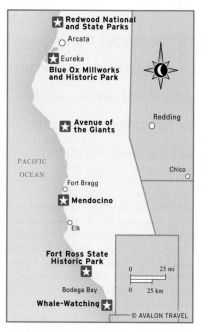

North Coast

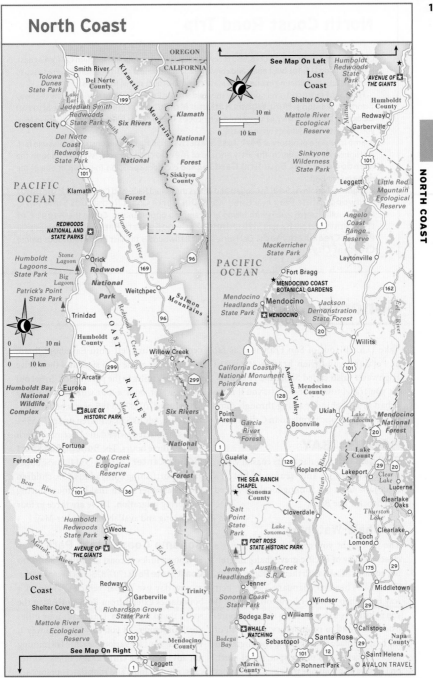

OREGON
CALIFORNIA

Smith River
Tolowa Dunes State Park
Del Norte County
Lake Earl
Jedediah Smith Redwoods State Park
199
Klamath Mountains
Klamath
Crescent City
Del Norte Coast Redwoods State Park
Smith River
Six Rivers
National
National Forest
Siskiyou County

PACIFIC OCEAN

101
Klamath
Forest

REDWOODS NATIONAL AND STATE PARKS

Humboldt Lagoons State Park
Stone Lagoon
Orick
Big Lagoon
Redwood National Park
Patrick's Point State Park
Weitchpec
96
169
Klamath River
Salmon Mountains

Trinidad
96

0   10 mi
0   10 km

Humboldt County
Coast Creek
Redwood Creek

Willow Creek

299
Arcata
299
Eureka
Humboldt Bay National Wildlife Complex
BLUE OX HISTORIC PARK
COAST RANGES
Mad River
Six Rivers

Fortuna
National

Ferndale
Bear River
101
36
Forest

Owl Creek Ecological Reserve

Humboldt Redwoods State Park
Weott
AVENUE OF THE GIANTS

Mattole River
Eel River

Lost Coast
Redway
Trinity
Shelter Cove
Garberville
Mattole River Ecological Reserve
Richardson Grove State Park
101
Mendocino County

See Map On Right

1   Leggett

See Map On Left

Humboldt Redwoods State Park
AVENUE OF THE GIANTS
Lost Coast

Shelter Cove
Mattole River Ecological Reserve
Mattole River
Humboldt County
Redway
Garberville

0   10 mi
0   10 km

Sinkyone Wilderness State Park
101

Leggett
Little Red Mountain Ecological Reserve

Angelo Coast Range Reserve

MacKerricher State Park
1
Laytonville

PACIFIC OCEAN

Fort Bragg
MENDOCINO COAST BOTANICAL GARDENS
162
Mendocino Headlands State Park
Mendocino
MENDOCINO
Jackson Demonstration State Forest
20
Eel River

Willits

1
California Coastal National Monument
Point Arena
Anderson Valley
Mendocino County
101

128
Ukiah
Lake Mendocino
Mendocino National Forest

Point Arena
Garcia River Forest
Boonville
20

1
Lake County

Gualala
128
Hopland
Lakeport
29
20
Clear Lake
Lucerne

THE SEA RANCH CHAPEL
Sonoma County
Russian River
Clearlake Oaks

Salt Point State Park
Cloverdale
Lake Sonoma
Thurston Lake
Clearlake
Loch Lomond

FORT ROSS STATE HISTORIC PARK
175
29
Middletown

Jenner Headlands
Austin Creek S.R.A.
Jenner
Sonoma Coast State Park
Windsor
29

Bodega Bay
Williams
Calistoga
Napa County

WHALE-WATCHING
Bodega Bay
Santa Rosa
Saint Helena

1
Sebastopol
101
12
Marin County
Rohnert Park

© AVALON TRAVEL

North Coast Road Trip

Crashing surf, towering redwoods, and rocky beaches typify the rugged Northern California coast. Highway 1 and U.S. 101 twist apart and converge again for almost 400 miles from San Francisco to Crescent City, culminating in one of the state's best and most scenic road trips.

From San Francisco, travel north over the Golden Gate Bridge and into Marin. Follow Highway 1 north with a stop at **Muir Woods National Monument.** Continue north past **Stinson Beach** to **Bodega Bay,** where Alfred Hitchcock's *The Birds* was filmed. From January to May, you may even spot whales off the coast.

Stop for a dose of history at **Fort Ross State Historic Park,** a reconstructed Russian fort. As Highway 1 winds north, the artsy enclave of **Mendocino** beckons. Wander through the **Mendocino Coast Botanical Gardens** and consider spending the night at one of the many quaint B&Bs.

Highway 1 rejoins U.S. 101 in Leggett and enters the famed Redwood Coast. From **Humboldt Redwoods State Park** near Garberville to **Del Norte Coast Redwoods State Park,** this 150-mile stretch is rich with hiking and camping opportunities. Cruise the **Avenue of the Giants** and pitch a tent in **Humboldt Redwoods State Park** or snag a campsite at **Prairie Creek Redwoods.** Del Norte Coast Redwoods is the last of the redwoods before Crescent City.

Sonoma Coast

Take U.S. 101 out of San Francisco as far as Petaluma, and then head west toward Highway 1 (also called Shoreline Highway). As you travel toward the coast, you'll leave urban areas behind, passing through some of the most bucolic farmland in California.

BODEGA BAY

Bodega Bay is popular for its coastal views, whale-watching, and seafood—but it's most famous as the filming locale of Alfred Hitchcock's *The Birds.*

★ Whale-Watching

The best sight you could hope to see is a close-up view of Pacific gray whales migrating home to Alaska with their newborn calves. The whales head past January-May on their way from their summer home off Mexico. If you're lucky, you can see them from the shore. **Bodega Head,** a promontory just north of the bay, is a place to get close to the migration route. To get to this prime spot, travel north on Highway 1 about one mile past the visitors

center and turn left onto Eastshore Road; make a right at the stop sign, and then drive three more miles to the parking lot. To get out on the water, book a tour with **Bodega Bay Charters** (707/875-3495, www.bodegacharters.com, adults $50, children under 13 $35). Tours are offered twice daily December-April and last three hours. The **Bodega Bay Sport Fishing Center** (707/875-3344, www.bodegabaysportfishing.com, adults $55, children $35) is another outfit that has tours during the spring migration. These are three to four hours long and available December-May.

Sonoma Coast State Park

Seventeen miles of coast are within **Sonoma Coast State Park** (707/875-3483, www.parks.ca.gov, day use $8 per vehicle). The park's boundaries extend from Bodega Head at the south up to the Vista Trailhead, four miles north of Jenner. As you drive up Highway 1, you'll see signs for various beaches (swimming not advised). The cliffs, crags, inlets, whitecaps, mini islands, and rock outcroppings are

Sonoma and Mendocino Coasts

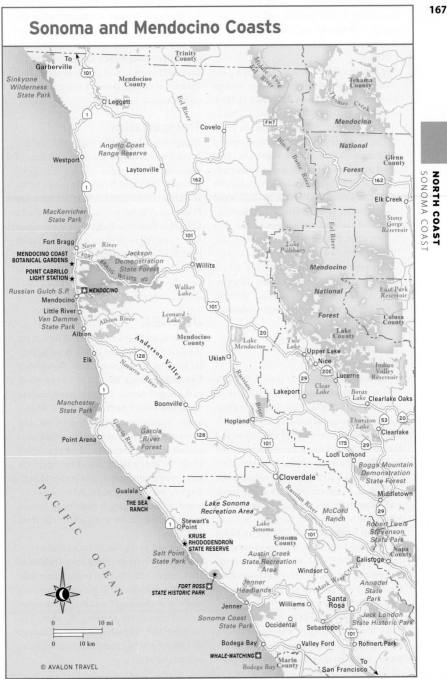

To
Garberville
101
Sinkyone
Wilderness
State Park

Trinity
County

Tehama
County

1
Leggett

Mendocino
County

Thomes Creek

Mendocino

Middle Fork Eel River

Covelo

FH7

National

Angelo Coast
Range Reserve

Black Butte River

Forest

Glenn
County

Westport

1

Laytonville

162

162

Elk Creek

MacKerricher
State Park

Eel River

Eel River

Stony
Gorge
Reservoir

Fort Bragg

MENDOCINO COAST
BOTANICAL GARDENS ★

POINT CABRILLO
LIGHT STATION ★

Noyo River

FORT
BRAGG-WILLITS RD

101

Jackson
Demonstration
State Forest

Lake
Pillsbury

Mendocino

Willits

Walker
Lake

National

East Park
Reservoir

Russian Gulch S.P.

Mendocino

Little River
Van Damme
State Park

Albion

Albion River

Leonard
Lake

Forest

Colusa
County

Mendocino

101

Elk

Anderson Valley

Mendocino
County

Ukiah

20

Lake
Mendocino

Tule
Lake

Lake
County

Upper Lake
Nice

128

Navarro River

29

20E

Lucerne

Indian
Valley
Reservoir

Manchester
State Park

Boonville

Russian River

Lakeport

Clear
Lake

Borax
Lake

Clearlake Oaks

1

Hopland

Garcia River

Garcia
River
Forest

128

Thurston
Lake

53

20

Clearlake

Point Arena

101

175

29

Loch Lomond

Boggs Mountain
Demonstration
State Forest

Cloverdale

Russian River

Middletown

Gualala

THE SEA
RANCH

Lake Sonoma
Recreation Area

McCord
Ranch

29

Robert Louis
Stevenson
State Park

1

Stewart's
Point

Lake
Sonoma

Sonoma
County

101

Napa
County

Calistoga

KRUSE
RHODODENDRON
STATE RESERVE ★

Austin Creek
State Recreation
Area

Windsor

PACIFIC OCEAN

Salt Point
State Park

FORT ROSS ★
STATE HISTORIC PARK

Jenner
Headlands

Mark West Creek

Annadel
State
Park

Jenner

Williams

Santa
Rosa

Jack London
State Historic Park

N

Sonoma Coast
State Park

Occidental

Sebastopol

101

0   10 mi

0   10 km

Bodega Bay

WHALE-WATCHING ★

Valley Ford

Rohnert Park

© AVALON TRAVEL

Bodega Bay

Marin
County

To
San Francisco

fascinating in any weather, and their looks change with the shifting tides and fog.

Food

Any fishing village worth its salt has a good place to get a basket of fish-and-chips. Bodega Bay's is named **The Birds Café** (1407 N. Hwy. 1, 707/875-2900, 11:30am-6pm Mon.-Thurs., 11:30am-7pm Fri.-Sat., $10). From its perch on the west side of Highway 1, the exposed patio overlooks the harbor as patrons chow down on oysters, fish tacos, and artichoke fritters while drinking Lagunitas IPA. Orders are taken and food is made in the no-frills stand where a couple of stools offer indoor seating.

One of the best restaurants in the area is **Terrapin Creek** (1580 Eastshore Dr., 707/875-2700, www.terrapincreekcafe.com, 4:30pm-9pm Thurs.-Sun., $23-32), which makes creative use of fresh seafood. Billing itself as a "casual neighborhood spot," Terrapin Creek serves elegant food in a refurbished old farmhouse.

Accommodations and Camping

The **Inn at the Tides** (800 Hwy. 1, 707/875-2751, www.innatthetides.com, $159-250) takes full advantage of its location. Settled on a hill, the inn's collection of redwood-shingle buildings provides lovely views of the harbor and the surrounding hills. A complimentary full breakfast and a bottle of wine upon arrival are included, as is access to the pool, fitness room, and sauna. Massages are extra as are lunch and dinner at the inn's two restaurants, one of which was a backdrop for the film *The Birds.*

Doran Regional Park (201 Doran Beach Rd., 707/875-3540, www.sonoma-county.org, reservations 707/565-2267 or http://sonoma-countycamping.org, $26-32, $9.50 reservation fee, $7 day use) has 130 campsites along the jetty separating the bay from the harbor.

Sonoma Coast State Park (707/875-3483, www.parks.ca.gov, $35) encompasses several campgrounds along its 17-mile expanse. Get a lovely sandy spot in the trees in **Bodega Dunes Campground** (98 sites, 2585 Hwy. 1), complete with hot showers and flush toilets. Another option is the smaller **Wrights Beach Campground** (27 sites, 7095 Hwy. 1). Campers may use the hot showers at Bodega Dunes a few miles south on Highway 1.

Transportation

Bodega Bay is located on Highway 1 north of Point Reyes National Seashore and west of Petaluma. It's a beautiful drive north, hugging the coast, but the cliffs and the road's twists and turns mean a slow 1.5-hour trek from San Francisco. A faster way to get here is to take U.S. 101 to Petaluma. Exit at East Washington Street and follow Bodega Avenue to Valley Ford Road, cutting across to the coast. You'll hit Bodega Bay just about two miles after you pass through Valley Ford. This route takes about 1.25 hours.

JENNER

Jenner is on Highway 1 at the mouth of the Russian River and one of the most beautiful spots on the Sonoma Coast. **Goat Rock Beach** (Goat Rock Rd., 707/875-3483, www.parks.ca.gov, day use $8) is the northernmost tip of **Sonoma Coast State Park**. With a lovely boardwalk, abundant wildlife, and an impressive hunk of serpentine rock, it is a lovely place to spend the afternoon. You'll likely see gray whales, sea otters, elephant seals, shorebirds and, if you arrive March-August, harbor seal pups. Pets are not allowed, and swimming is prohibited. Access to the beach is on the south side of the river, off Highway 1.

To get out on the water, rent a kayak or join a tour at **WaterTreks** (10438 Hwy. 1, 707/865-2249, rentals $30-70). Next to the Jenner boat ramp, the folks here will get you set up on a single or double kayak and suggested routes around the estuary or along the river. The company also offers shuttle drop-off farther up river for a longer paddle and guided tours around the estuary.

Accommodations and Food

Tiny Jenner is blessed with both great food and digs. The ★ **River's End** (11048 Hwy. 1, 707/865-2484, www.ilovesunsets.com, noon-3:30pm, 5pm-8:30pm Sun.-Tues. and Thurs., noon-3:30pm, 5pm-9pm Fri.-Sat. winter, noon-3:30pm, 5pm-8:30pm Sun.-Thurs., noon-3:30pm, 5pm-9pm Fri.-Sat. summer, $25-45) is perched above the spot where the Russian River flows into the Pacific, and it's a beautiful sight to behold. Prices are high, but if you get a window table at sunset, you may forget about them. If you can't get enough of the view, rent one of the five two-person cabins ($239-279) down the hill from the restaurant. The cabins have excellent views and a romantic atmosphere. Children under 12 are "not recommended."

The **Jenner Inn** (10400 Hwy. 1, 707/865-2377 or 800/732-2377, www.jennerinn.com, $118-268) offers a variety of options, including gingerbread cottages nestled in tea roses, charming economy rooms in the main lodge, and waterfront suites that make you feel like you are hovering just above the river. Luxurious perks such as hot tubs and private decks can be found in many of the rooms, and all feel like a great deal for the price.

Fourteen miles north of Jenner, Bene Bufano's "Peace Obelisk" rises 93 feet from its high rocky perch to survey the coast and send its message of transcendence out across the sea. This is the totem of the 1960s-era **Timber Cove Inn** (21780 N. Hwy. 1, 707/847-3231 or 800/987-8319, www.timbercoveinn.com, $195-310). Large and luxurious, the wood-framed lodge has a capacious bar and lounge, an oceanfront patio, rooms with spa tubs and fireplaces, and hiking trails nearby. The decor of the swinging sixties and seventies has been perfectly preserved, adding a bit of kitsch to the spectacular setting. At the lodge's **Alexander's Restaurant** (8am-11:30am, 5pm-9pm daily, $21-36) and the **Sequoia Lounge** (noon-5pm daily, $10-16) you can savor the vibe over a stiff drink and a plate of farm-to-fork food.

Transportation

Jenner is located on Highway 1, right along the ocean. The fastest route from San Francisco (about 1.75 hours) is to drive up U.S. 101, make a left onto Washington Street in Petaluma, and continue north on Highway 1. You can also reach Jenner by following the Russian River from the River Road exit off U.S. 101 in Santa Rosa, a little over 20 miles.

Fort Ross State Historic Park

★ FORT ROSS STATE HISTORIC PARK

The "Ross" in **Fort Ross State Park** (19005 Hwy. 1, Jenner, 707/847-3286, www.parks. ca.gov, grounds sunrise-sunset daily, fort and visitors center 10am-4:30pm Fri.-Tues., parking $8) is short for "Russian" and the park commemorates the history of Russian settlement on the North Coast. Stretching from Tomales Bay to Point Arena, the network of fortified settlements lasted less than 50 years. In addition to plundering the seas for seal fur, the Russians also grew food for the more lucrative Alaskan trade. Learn more at the park's large visitor center and museum.

You can also walk into the reconstructed fort buildings and see how the settlers lived. The only original building still standing is the captain's quarters—a large, luxurious house for the time. The other buildings, including the large bunkhouse, the chapel, and the two cannon-filled blockhouses, were rebuilt using much of the original lumber. A visit to the whole fort and the beach beyond takes some time as the park is fairly spread out. Wear comfortable shoes and bring a bottle of water.

Fort Ross is located almost eight miles north of Jenner on Highway 1.

SALT POINT STATE PARK

Stretching for miles along the Sonoma coastline, **Salt Point State Park** (25050 Hwy. 1, Jenner, 707/847-3221, www.parks.ca.gov, visitors center 10am-3pm Sat.-Sun., day use $8) provides easy access from U.S. 101 to more than a dozen sandy state beaches. You don't have to visit the visitors center to enjoy this park and its many beaches—just follow the signs along the highway to the turnoffs and parking lots.

If you're looking to scuba dive, head for **Gerstle Cove,** accessible from the visitors center just south of Salt Point proper. The cove was designated one of California's first underwater parks, and divers who can deal with the chilly water have a wonderful time exploring the diverse undersea wildlife.

Tucked above the northeast corner of Salt Point State Park, **Kruse Rhododendron State Reserve** (707/847-3221, www.parks. ca.gov, sunrise-sunset daily, free) offers a chance to meander along the **Chinese Gulch Trail** in the spring, admiring the profusion of pink rhododendron flowers blooming beneath the second-growth redwood forest.

Camping and Food

The park has plenty of camping options. **Gerstle Cove Campground** has 30 sites near the visitors center, and just across Highway 1 on the east side, **Woodside Campground** has a total of 79 sites. Both have flush toilets, but no showers, and must be reserved by phone (800/444-7275, $35). Near the Woodside Campground, 10 hike- or bike-in sites ($6) are available on a first-come, first-served basis.

Stewart's Point (six miles north on Hwy. 1) is home to a post office, a small store, and a restaurant—and that's it. **Stewart's Point Store** (32000 S. Hwy. 1, 707/785-2406, 8am-6pm daily, hours vary by season) sells groceries, wine, collectible dishes, and hand-knitted hats. They've also got a deli and a bakery on-site.

Mendocino Coast

The Mendocino coast is a popular retreat for Bay Area residents for its windswept beaches, secret coves, and luscious cuisine. Art is especially prominent and a number of small galleries display local artworks.

The most popular inns fill up fast many weekends year-round. To stay someplace specific, book your room at least a month in advance for weekday stays and six months or more in advance for the fall high season.

GUALALA

Located on Highway 1 between Bodega Bay and Mendocino, Gualala ("wa-LA-la") caters to The Sea Ranch and coastal tourists with the greatest variety of services between Jenner and Mendocino.

Accommodations and Food

The **Breakers Inn** (39300 Hwy. 1, 707/884-3200, www.breakersinn.com, $135-265) resembles a series of large seaside cottages, each with flower boxes in the windows and a private deck overlooking the ocean. All rooms are individually decorated with ocean views. Many have refrigerators and microwaves.

Try **Bones Roadhouse** (39080 Hwy. 1, 707/884-1188, www.bonesroadhouse.com, 8am-9pm daily, $15-25) for barbecue and pulled pork in giant portions, served in a casual atmosphere with ocean views.

The **Surf Market** (39250 Hwy. 1, 707/884-4184, http://surfsuper.com, 7:30am-8pm daily) has everything you need for a gourmet picnic, plus camping essentials like firewood and ice. You can get a cheap cup of Peet's coffee at the coffee station.

Located six miles south of Gualala, the **Sea Ranch Lodge** (60 Sea Walk Dr., Sea Ranch, 707/785-2371 or 800/732-7262, http://searanchlodge.com, $279-409) offers 19 rooms right along the bluffs, all sporting unobstructed ocean views, and many featuring 1970s Malm fireplaces. Food and drinks can be found in the surprisingly casual **Black Point Grill** (7am-9pm daily, $16-28). The lodge is dog friendly.

the rocky Mendocino coast

Side Trip to Anderson Valley

The Anderson Valley is the apex of Mendocino's wine region. The **Anderson Valley Wine Trail** (Hwy. 128) begins in Boonville and continues 27 scenic, twisty miles north toward the coast, with most wineries clustered between Boonville and Navarro.

WINERIES AND BREWERIES

- **Scharffenberger Cellars** (8501 Hwy. 128, Philo, 707/895-2957, www.scharffenbergercellars.com, 11am-5pm daily, $3) makes highly rated sparkling wine.

- **Roederer Estate**'s (4501 Hwy. 128, 707/895-2288, www.roedererestate.com, 11am-5pm daily, $6) sparkling wines are some of the best you'll taste.

- **Husch Vineyards** (4400 Hwy. 128, 800/554-8724, www.huschvineyards.com, 10am-6pm daily May-Oct., 10am-5pm daily Nov.-Apr., free) pours excellent sauvignon blanc in a rustic, flower-filled barn with a friendly atmosphere.

- **Goldeneye** (9200 Hwy. 128, Philo, 800/208-0438, www.goldeneyewinery.com, 10:30am-4:30pm daily, $15) is a must stop for any pinot lover.

- **Anderson Valley Brewing Company** (17700 Hwy. 253, Boonville, 707/895-2337 or 800/207-2337, www.avbc.com, 11am-6pm Sat.-Thurs., 11am-7pm Fri. spring-fall, 11am-6pm Thurs. and Sat.-Mon., 11am-7pm Fri. winter) serves an array of microbrews that change seasonally.

- **Brutocao Cellars** (7000 Hwy. 128, Philo, 800/661-2103, www.brutocaocellars.com, 10am-5pm daily, free), the star of the Hopland region, has a tasting room in the Anderson Valley.

REDWOODS

- **Hendy Redwoods State Park** (18599 Philo-Greenwood Rd., 707/895-3557 or 707/895-3141

Camping

Gualala Point Regional Park (42401 Hwy. 1, 707/785-2377, camping reservations 707/565-2267, www.sonoma-county.org, sunrise-sunset daily, day use $7 per vehicle), one mile south of the town of Gualala, has 19 campsites ($32 per night), as well as six bike-/hike-in sites ($5), right along the river, with flush toilets and showers. The private **Gualala River Redwood Park** (46001 Gualala Rd., 707/884-3533, www.gualalapark.com, May-Sept., day use $5 pp, camping $42-49 for 2 people) has 235 sites, most of which are on the river.

POINT ARENA

Point Arena is located 10 miles north of Gualala on Highway 1. Surrounded by bucolic dairy land, the town boasts one of the quaintest main streets on the Mendocino coast. The biggest draw is the **Point Arena Lighthouse** (45500 Lighthouse Rd., 707/882-2777 or 877/725-4448, www.pointarenalighthouse.com, 10am-4:30pm daily summer, 10am-3:30pm daily winter, adults $7.50, children $1), which offers stunning views of the windswept coast as well as a fantastic place to spot migrating whales. The extensive interpretive museum is housed in the fog station beyond the gift shop. Docent-led **tours** up to the top of the lighthouse are well worth the trip.

Accommodations and Food

The attractive yet plain **Coast Guard House** (695 Arena Cove, 707/882-2442, www.coastguardhouse.com, $145-265) was originally built in 1901 as housing for the U.S.

- in summer, www.parks.ca.gov, $8) offers several sedate forest walks as well as **campsites** (800/444-7275 and www.reserveamerica.gov, $35).

- **Navarro River Redwoods State Park** (Hwy. 128, 2 miles east of Hwy. 1, www.parks. ca.gov, 707/937-5804) snakes along the highway and the river, with picnic sites tucked in amid lush redwood groves.

HOT SPRINGS

- **Vichy Springs** (2605 Vichy Springs Rd., 707/462-9515, www.vichysprings.com, treatments $115-155 per hour, baths $50 per day) offers mineral-heavy and naturally carbonated baths, a hot pool, an Olympic-size swimming pool, and a day spa. Accommodations ($195-390) are in a genteel and rustic old inn and cottages.

- **Orr Hot Springs** (13201 Orr Springs Rd., Ukiah, 707/462-6277, 10am-10pm daily, $30) soaks are either in claw-foot tubs or carved into the rock hillside. Six primitive campsites ($60), six yurts ($180-190), and three cottages include access to the lodge, all pools, and the communal kitchen.

ACCOMMODATIONS AND FOOD

- **The Boonville Hotel** (14050 Hwy. 128, Boonville, 707/895-2210, www.boonvillehotel.com, $125-375) has 15 charming rooms; upstairs rooms facing the highway can be loud. Amenities include a bar and the on-site **Table 128** (by reservation only Thurs.-Mon. Apr.-Nov., Fri.-Sun. Dec.-Mar., $38-58).

- **Lauren's** (14211 Hwy. 128, Boonville, 707/895-3869, http://laurensgoodfood.com, 11:30am-2:30pm, 5pm-9pm Thurs.-Sun. May-Oct., 5pm-9pm Tues.-Sat. Nov.-Apr., $11-17) is a sweet little restaurant with an unpretentious menu filled with burgers, pot pies, and meat loaf.

Life-Saving Service, which later became part of the Coast Guard. It was decommissioned in 1957. Now it's an appealing bed-and-breakfast, with four rooms in the main building and two cottages. Some rooms have ocean views. Check online for last-minute specials—you may get a deal if it's not booked up.

The **Wharf Masters Inn** (785 Port Rd., 707/882-3171 or 800/932-4031, www.wharfmasters.com, $135-200) offers historical lodging at reasonable prices. The Victorian building retains its original charm, including elaborate porches to take in the views. Each of the 10 rooms is decorated in antiques, and many have a whirlpool tub, fireplace, and refrigerator.

The **Uneda Eat Café** (206 Main St., 707/882-3800, http://unedaeat.com, 5:30pm-8:30pm Wed.-Sun., $9-20) brings some hipster locavorism to tiny Point Arena. A family-run operation, this small restaurant serves a limited menu that changes daily. Expect to find house-made sausage, pork confit, rabbit, and oysters served up in a dining room lined in reclaimed wood.

Arena Market & Café (185 Main St., 707/882-3663, www.arenaorganics.org, 7am-7pm Mon.-Sat., 8am-6pm Sun.) is a co-op committed to a philosophy of local, sustainable, and organic food. At this medium-size grocery store, stock up on staples or sit at one of the tables in front and enjoy a bowl of homemade soup.

ELK

The town of **Elk** is about 20 miles north of Point Arena on Highway 1. From the mid-19th century until the 1920s, the stretch of shoreline that comprises Elk's **Greenwood State Beach** (Hwy. 1, Elk, 707/937-5804, www.parks.ca.gov, visitors center 11am-1pm Sat.-Sun. Memorial Day-Labor Day) was a stop for large ships carrying timber to San Francisco and China. The visitors center displays photographs and exhibits about Elk's past. Take a short walk (less than one mile) down to the cliffs to experience lush woods, sandy cliffs, and dramatic ocean overlooks.

Accommodations and Food

The ★ **Elk Cove Inn** (6300 S. Hwy. 1, 707/877-3321 or 800/275-2967, www.elkcoveinn.com, $100-305) is the perfect spot for a secluded getaway. Choose from antiques-furnished rooms in the historical main building or plush spa cabins overlooking the lawn. The tiny restaurant serves a sumptuous champagne breakfast.

For breakfast and lunch, join the locals at **Queenie's Roadhouse Café** (6061 Hwy. 1, 707/877-3285, http://queeniesroadhousecafe.com, 8am-3pm Thurs.-Mon., $8-15). A classic small-town diner, Queenie's serves excellent, inexpensive American food with a dash of the hippie ethos that pervades this part of the coast. Don't pass up the burger or Reuben sandwich. The only spot for dinner is **Bridget Dolan's Pub** (707/877-1820, 4:30pm-8pm daily, $12-22) where you'll find casual pub food and a pint or two.

VAN DAMME STATE PARK

At **Van Damme State Park** (Hwy. 1, 3 miles south of Mendocino, 707/937-5804 or 707/937-4016 summer only, www.parks.ca.gov, sunrise-sunset daily, free), take a walk to the park's centerpiece, the **Pygmy Forest.** Here you'll see a true biological rarity: mature yet tiny cypress and pine trees perpetually stunted by a combination of always-wet ground and poor soil-nutrient conditions. You can get to the Pygmy Forest from the **Fern Canyon Trail** (6 miles one-way, difficult), or drive Airport Road to the trail parking

lot (opposite the county airport) directly to a wheelchair-accessible loop trail (0.25 mile, easy).

Kayak Mendocino (707/813-7117, www.kayakmendocino.com) launches four Sea Cave Nature Tours (9am, 11:30am, 2pm, and sunset daily, $60 pp, $40 children 12 and under) from Van Damme State Park. No previous experience is necessary, as the expert guides provide all the equipment you need and teach you how to paddle your way through the sea caves and around the harbor seals.

Camping

Camping is available in **Van Damme State Park** (Hwy. 1, 3 miles south of Mendocino, 800/444-7275, www.parks.ca.gov, $35). There are 74 sites, in addition to a handful of hike-/bike-in sites. The campground offers picnic tables, fire rings, and food lockers, as well as restrooms and hot showers and a communal campfire. Reservations are strongly encouraged, especially during the summer and early fall.

Transportation

Van Damme State Park is along Highway 1 almost 35 miles north of Point Arena and about 3 miles south of Mendocino. From Santa Rosa, it's a two-hour drive along U.S. 101 north for about 30 miles to Highway 128 north before reaching Highway 1 after about 60 miles.

★ MENDOCINO

The town of Mendocino has long been an inspiration and a gathering place for artists of many varieties, and the **Mendocino Art Center** (45200 Little Lake St., 707/937-5818 or 800/653-3328, www.mendocinoartcenter.org, 10am-5pm daily, donation) is the main institution that gives these diverse artists a community, provides them with opportunities for teaching and learning, and displays their work. Founded in 1959, the center now has a flourishing schedule of events and classes, five galleries, and a sculpture garden. You can even drop in and make some art of your own. Supervised "open studios" in ceramics,

Mendocino

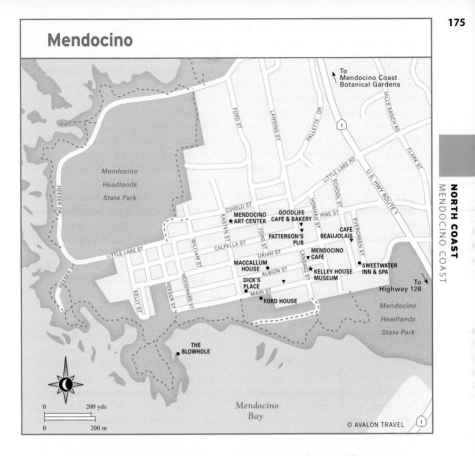

jewelry making, watercolor, sculpture, and drawing take place throughout the year (call for specific schedules, $5-20 per session).

Sights

Whether you're into scenery or history, you won't want to miss a visit to the **Point Cabrillo Light Station Historic Park** (12301 N. Hwy. 1, 707/937-6122, www.parks. ca.gov, sunrise-sunset daily, lighthouse 10am-4pm daily, $5), about five miles north of Mendocino. Built in 1908, this beautiful lighthouse has been functioning for more than 100 years. Take a tour to see the famous Fresnel lens, learn about the infamous *Frolic* shipwreck of 1850, and explore the tide pool aquarium.

Sports and Recreation

Some of the most popular hiking trails in coastal Mendocino wind through **Russian Gulch State Park** (Hwy. 1, 2 miles north of Mendocino, 707/937-5804, www.parks.ca.gov, $8). Russian Gulch has its own **Fern Canyon Trail** (3 miles round-trip), with the second-growth redwood forest filled with lush green ferns, and finishing at an ever-popular waterfall. To make the trek a loop, take a left at **Loop Falls Trail** (2 miles, moderate) to the top of the waterfall. The trail will continue and hook back up with Fern Trail. If you prefer the shore to the forest, hike west to take in the lovely wild headlands and see blowholes, grasses, and even trawlers out seeking the day's catch.

For a stroll along ocean bluffs, you don't need to go farther than Main Street. The **Mendocino Headlands State Park** (735 Main St., 707/937-5397, www.parks.ca.gov) anchors the southwest corner of town, protecting its picturesque beaches and bluffs. The visitors center, located in the **Historic Ford House** (11am-4pm daily), has a number of exhibits about the human and natural history of the area. Trails wend through the open space, many of which lead down **Big River Beach,** where you may find locals catching some rays.

Kayak and canoe trips are a popular summer activity on the coast. To explore the sedate waters of the Big River estuary, rent an outrigger or a sailing canoe from **Catch a Canoe & Bicycles Too** (Hwy. 1 and Comptche Ukiah Rd., 707/937-0273, www.catchacanoe.com, 9am-5pm daily, boat rentals adults $28-40, ages 6-17 $14-20, guided tours June-Sept. $65-85) at the Stanford Inn. For an adventurous day on the ocean, consider taking a sea-cave tour by kayak.

Food

The **Mendocino Café** (10451 Lansing St., 707/937-6141, www.mendocinocafe.com, 11am-4pm, 5pm-8:30pm daily, $14-33) has simple, well-prepared food, a small kids' menu, a wine list, and a beer list. Enjoy a Thai burrito, a fresh salmon fillet, or a steak in the warm, well-lit dining room. The café is in the gardens of Mendocino Village, and thanks to a heated patio, you can enjoy outdoor dining any time of day.

Café Beaujolais (961 Ukiah St., 707/937-5614, www.cafebeaujolais.com, 5:30pm-close Mon.-Tues., 11:30am-2:30pm, 5:30pm-close Wed.-Sun., $23-35) is a standout French-California restaurant. This charming out-of-the-way spot is a few blocks from the center of Mendocino Village in a quaint Victorian home. Despite the white tablecloths and fancy crystal, the atmosphere is casual at lunch and gets only slightly more formal at dinner.

The cozy dining room at the ★ **MacCallum House Restaurant** (45020 Albion St., 707/937-6759, www.maccallumhouse.com, 8am-10am, 5:30pm-close Mon.-Fri., 8am-11am, 5:30pm-close Sat.-Sun., $28-39) makes the most of the historical house's charm, with dark wood paneling, two huge fireplaces that roar on chilly evenings, and windows overlooking the garden. The food encapsulates Mendocino, from the Pacific Rim oysters to the venison with wild boar sausage. For a pre-dinner drink, stop by

Café Beaujolais

the friendly Grey Whale Bar located in the house parlor.

Grab coffee and pastries at the **GoodLife Café and Bakery** (10483 Lansing St., 707/937-0836, http://goodlifecafemendo. com, 8am-5pm Mon.-Sat., 8am-4pm Sun., $7). Snag a table in the café, or take your order to go and find a quiet perch in the Mendocino Headlands.

Patterson's Pub (10485 Lansing St., 707/937-4782, www.pattersonspub.com, bar 10am-midnight daily, restaurant 11am-11pm daily), a traditional Irish-style pub, is in the former rectory of a 19th-century Catholic church. Locals drink at **Dick's Place** (45080 Main St., 707/937-6010, 2am-close daily), where the slightly younger crowd is always having a good time.

Accommodations

★ **Sweetwater Inn and Spa** (44840 Main St., 800/300-4140, www.sweetwaterspa. com, $125-275) harks back to the days when Mendocino was a colony of starving artists. A redwood water tower was converted into a room, joined by cottages that guarantee privacy. Every room and cottage has its own style—you'll find a spiral staircase in the water tower, a two-person tub set in a windowed alcove in the Zen Room, and fireplaces in many of the cottages. Thick gardens surround the building complex, with a path leading back to the Garden Spa. The location is perfect for dining, shopping, and art walks.

For luxurious lodging at a great value, book a room at **MacCallum House** (45020 Albion St., 707/937-0289 or 800/609-0492, www.maccallumhouse.com, $145-275). The facility includes several properties in addition to the main 1882 inn building in Mendocino Village, and you can choose from private cottages with hot tubs, suites with jetted tubs, and regular rooms with opulent antiques. A two-night minimum is required on weekends, and a three-night minimum goes into effect for most holidays. Full breakfast at the Grey Whale Restaurant is included in the room rates.

The **Stanford Inn** (44850 Comptche Ukiah Rd., 707/937-5615 or 800/331-8884, www.stanfordinn.com, $211-335) is one of the largest accommodations in the Mendocino area. This resort hotel sits away from the beaches in a redwood forest and is surrounded by gardens. Accommodations range from economy rooms to larger suites, but all have a wood-burning fireplace and a TV. Also included in the price is access to the indoor pool, sauna, and hot tub, use of mountain bikes, and breakfast at Ravens (8am-10:30am, 5:30pm-9pm Mon.-Fri., 8am-11pm, 5:30pm-9pm Sat.-Sun., $23-27), the onsite vegan restaurant. The place prides itself on its exceptional cell phone service and its pro-environmental practices.

After you check in at the **Sea Rock Bed & Breakfast Inn** (11101 Lansing St., 707/937-0926 or 800/906-0926, www.searock.com, $185-395), sit outside on the Adirondack chairs to watch the sunset, or take it all in from the viewing platform across the street, right above the beach. This little village of cottages, junior suites, and suites sleeps 2-4 people each. Breakfast is included in the room rates.

Five miles south in Little River is the ★ **Heritage House Resort** (5200 N. Hwy. 1, Little River, 707/202-9000, http://heritage-houseresort.com, $200-310), one of the oldest resorts on the Mendocino Coast. This 37-acre compound is a collection of duplexes and triplexes, in which stylish rooms have private decks, fireplaces, giant soaking tubs, and excellent views. The **5200 Restaurant** (8am-10:30am, 5pm-9pm Mon.-Fri., 8am-11am, 5pm-9pm Sat.-Sun., $17-35) serves farm-to-fork fare, while the **5200 Lounge** (4pm-9pm daily) overlooks the water.

Transportation

To get to Mendocino from U.S. 101 near Cloverdale, take Highway 128 northwest for 60 miles. Highway 128 becomes Highway 1 on the coast; Mendocino is another 10 miles north. You can also jump over to the coast on Highway 20. In only 30 (albeit slow) miles it connects Fort Bragg with

Willits along U.S. 101, about 3 hours north of San Francisco. Mendocino is 10 miles south of Fort Bragg. A slower, more scenic alternative is to take Highway 1; from San Francisco to Mendocino via Highway 1 takes at least 4.5 hours. Mendocino has a fairly compact downtown area, Mendocino Village, with a concentration of restaurants, shops, and inns a block away from the beach. Turn off at Main Street, park the car, and explore by foot.

FORT BRAGG

This blue-collar town is home to lumber mills, fishing boats, and scores of working train tracks. It is rougher around the edges than its gentle cousin down the coast, but it has some great attractions, beautiful scenery, and tons of local color.

Sights

One of the famed attractions in Mendocino County is the California Western Railroad, popularly called the **Skunk Train** (depot at end of Laurel St., 707/964-6371, www.skunktrain.com, departure 10am daily, adults $54, children 2-12 $34), named for the pungent early locomotives. The restored steam locomotives pull trains from the coast at Fort Bragg 40 miles through the redwood forest to the town of Willits and back. The ride lets passengers see the majesty of the redwoods while giving insight into life in Northern California before the era of highways. The gaily painted trains appeal to children, and the historical aspects and scenery call to adults.

MENDOCINO COAST BOTANICAL GARDENS

Mendocino Coast Botanical Gardens (18220 N. Hwy. 1, Fort Bragg, 707/964-4352, www.gardenbythesea.org, 9am-5pm daily Mar.-Oct., 9am-4pm daily Nov.-Feb., adults $14, seniors $10, ages 6-17 $5) is an expanse of land with an astonishing variety of vegetation. Stretching 47 acres down to the sea, these gardens offer miles of paths through careful plantings and wild landscapes. The garden map is also a guide that shows visitors what's in season. Informative labels show plant names clearly. Children can pick up their own brochure and enjoy an exploratory adventure designed just for them.

Accommodations and Food

Fort Bragg may not boast the type of luxurious accommodations found in Mendocino, but many of the options are a quarter of the price.

★ **Weller House** (524 Stewart St., 707/964-4415, www.wellerhouse.com, $110-320) is a picture-perfect B&B with elegantly restored Victorian-style rooms, ocean views, and sumptuous home-cooked meals. There are even a few rooms in the old water tower, which is the highest point in the city. Weller House is one block west of Main Street, in view of the Skunk Train depot, and an easy walk to good restaurants and shopping. The stately **Grey Whale Inn** (615 N. Main St., 707/964-0640 or 800/382-7244, www.greywhaleinn.com, $135-195) prides itself on simplicity and friendliness. The 13 spacious and individually decorated rooms have water or city views, with a private bath and queen or king bed. The inn's location downtown makes for an easy walk to dinner.

The king of the culinary scene is ★ **Mendo Bistro** (301 N. Main St., 707/964-4974, www.mendobistro.com, 5pm-9pm daily, $15-28), located in the top floor of the old Company Store building looking over downtown. Everything at the casual and unassuming bistro is excellent and made in-house.

North Coast Brewing Company Taproom & Grill (444 N. Main St., 707/964-3400, www.northcoastbrewing.com, 2pm-9pm Sun.-Thurs., 2pm-10pm Fri.-Sat., $14-30) is one of the country's most respected microbreweries. Just across the street from the brewery, the taproom pours the beloved Red Seal Ale, Old Rasputin Russian Imperial Stout, and the resurrected Acme beer, first introduced in the 1860s. At 4pm, the kitchen opens, serving top-notch pub food, including half Dungeness crabs (in season).

Transportation

Fort Bragg is located on Highway 1, 10 miles north of Mendocino. Driving here from San Francisco or Sacramento takes about 4 hours; from Ukiah it's about 1.5 hours. There is no "fast" way to reach Fort Bragg. The most expeditious way from the Bay Area is up U.S. 101. At Willits, take Highway 20 (Fort Bragg-Willits Rd.) west for 30 miles.

MACKERRICHER STATE PARK

Located about six miles north of Fort Bragg, **MacKerricher State Park** (Hwy. 1,

707/964-9112, visitors center 707/964-8898, www.parks.ca.gov, sunrise-sunset daily, free) offers the small duck-filled Cleone Lake, six miles of sandy ocean beaches, four miles of cliffs and crags, and **camping** (800/444-7275, www.reserveamerica.com, $35). The main attraction is a gigantic, almost complete skeleton of a whale near the park entrance. The best hike is the **Ten Mile Beach Trail** (14 miles round-trip, moderate), starting at the Beachcomber Motel at the north end of Fort Bragg and running seven miles up to the Ten Mile River. Most of the path is fairly level and paved.

The Redwood Coast

Of all the natural wonders California has to offer, the one that seems to inspire the purest awe is the giant redwood. *Sequoia sempervirens,* also called coast redwood, grows along the California coast from around Big Sur in the south and into southern Oregon in the north. The two best places to experience extensive wild groves of these gargantuan treasures are **Humboldt Redwoods State Park,** in Humboldt County, and **Redwood National and State Parks,** near the north end of California, around Eureka and Crescent City.

Most of the major park areas along the Redwood Coast can be accessed via U.S. 101 and U.S. 199. To get to the redwood parks from the south, drive up U.S. 101 or the much slower but prettier Highway 1. The two roads merge at Leggett, north of Fort Bragg, and continue north as U.S. 101.

GARBERVILLE
Accommodations and Food

Luxurious and charming, the ★ **Benbow Inn** (445 Lake Benbow Dr., 707/923-2124 or 800/355-3301, www.benbowinn.com, $85-450) is a swank resort dating back to the 1920s. It has a gourmet **restaurant**

(7am-3pm, 5pm-9:30pm Sun.-Thurs., 7am-3pm, 5pm-10pm Fri.-Sat. $18-45) serving upscale California cuisine, an 18-hole golf course, and a woodsy atmosphere that blends perfectly with the surrounding ancient redwood forest. Rooms glow with dark polished woods and jewel-toned carpets; the historical rooms, though smaller, have the most charm, best views, and the best price.

Several small motels offer reasonable rooms, and many have outdoor pools. The best of these is the **Best Western Humboldt House Inn** (701 Redwood Dr., 707/923-2771 or 800/862-7756, www.humboldthouseinn. com, $140-200). Rooms are clean and comfortable, the pool is sparkling and cool, and the location is convenient to restaurants and shops in Garberville. Most rooms have two queen beds.

Garberville has several modest eateries that appeal to weary travelers and families with kids. The **Woodrose Café** (911 Redwood Dr., 707/923-3191, www.thewoodrosecafe. com, 8am-2pm daily, $9-14) is a small, independent spot serving a traditional American-style breakfast and lunch. A lot of the food is organic, local, and healthy, but it doesn't come cheap.

Camping

Richardson Grove State Park (1600 U.S. 101, 800/444-7275, www.parks.ca.gov, reservations www.reserveamerica.com, day-use $8, camping $35) has 169 campsites in three campground areas surrounded by redwoods and the Eel River. Oak Flat (mid-June-mid-Sept.), the largest campground, is across the river and farther away from the highway. The **visitors center** (May-Sept.) in the 1930s Richardson Grove Lodge has cool exhibits and a nature store. Richardson Grove State Park is seven miles south of Garberville.

Transportation and Services

Garberville is located 65 miles south of Eureka and 200 miles north of San Francisco on U.S. 101. The nearest hospital with an emergency room is **Redwood Memorial Hospital** (3300 Renner Dr., Fortuna, 707/725-3361, www.redwoodmemorial.org). There is a **Shell** (860 Redwood Dr.) and a **Chevron** (830 Redwood Dr.) on the main drag.

Benbow Inn

TOP EXPERIENCE

HUMBOLDT REDWOODS STATE PARK

The largest stand of unlogged redwood trees is here in Humboldt Redwoods State Park. Start your visit at the **Humboldt Redwoods State Park Visitors Center** (17119 Avenue of the Giants, Weott, 707/946-2409, www.parks.ca.gov or www.humboldtredwoods.org, 9am-5pm daily Apr.-Oct., 10am-4pm daily Nov.-Mar.), located along the Avenue of the Giants next to the Burlington Campground. The visitors center has plenty of information for hiking or camping, a theater, an interpretive museum, and a gift shop. There is no entrance fee for Humboldt Redwoods State Park, but there is for the Williams Grove Day Use Area ($8 per vehicle).

★ Avenue of the Giants

The most famous stretch of redwood trees is the **Avenue of the Giants** (Hwy. 254, between Weott and Myers Flat), which parallels U.S. 101 and the Eel River for 32 miles between Garberville and Scotia (look for signs on U.S. 101). Visitors come from all over the world to drive this two-lane road and gaze in wonder at the sky-high old-growth redwoods along the way. Campgrounds and hiking trails sprout among the trees off the road. Park your car at various points at any of the eight stops along the way to walk among the giants. If you're just looking for the big trees, jump on at Myers Flat and continue through Pepperwood.

Hiking

Many visitors start with the **Founder's Grove Nature Loop Trail** (0.6 mile, easy), at mile marker 20.5 on the Avenue of the Giants. This sedate, flat nature trail gives walkers a taste of the big old-growth trees in the park. The onetime tallest tree in the world, the Dyerville Giant, fell in 1991 at the age of about 1,600. But it's still doing its part in this astounding ecosystem, decomposing on the forest floor and feeding new life in the forest.

The Lost Coast

From Shelter Cove to Mattole, the **Lost Coast** is the remote rugged coastline accessible by few roads and miles of wilderness trails.

- **Mattole Road** is a narrow, mostly paved two-lane road that stretches 28 miles from Ferndale to Cape Mendocino, before heading inland through Humboldt Redwoods State Park, reaching U.S. 101 just north of Weott. It is one of the few drivable routes from which to view the Lost Coast.
- **Big Black Sands Beach** (King Range National Conservation Area, end of Beach Rd., Shelter Cove, 707/986-5400, www.blm.gov), just north of the town of Shelter Cove, serves as the south end of the Lost Coast Trail. Walk the dark sands to either Horse Creek or Gitchell Creek.
- **Cape Mendocino Lighthouse** (Mal Coombs Park, Shelter Cove) began life on Cape Mendocino in 1868. In 1951 the 43-foot tower was abandoned and then moved to Shelter Cove in 1998. The original Fresnel lens is on display in Ferndale.
- The **Lost Coast Trail** (26 miles, 3 days) is accessible at Usal Campground, Big Black Sands Beach, and Mattole Beach. Campsites are clustered along the trail. A backcountry permit (free) is required, available in **Whitethorn** (768 Shelter Cove Rd., 707/986-5400, www.blm.gov, 8am-4:30pm Mon.-Fri.) or **Arcata** (1695 Heindon Rd., 707/825-2300, www.blm.gov, 7:45am-4:30pm Mon.-Fri.). Bear canisters are mandatory, as is a current tide table.

ACCOMMODATIONS AND CAMPING

- **Shelter Cove Beachcomber Inn** (412 Machi Rd., Shelter Cove, 707/986-7551 or 800/718-4789, $75-115) has rooms with views of the coast or the woods.
- **The Tides Inn of Shelter Cove** (59 Surf Point, 707/986-7900 or 888/998-4337, www.sheltercovetidesinn.com, $150-205) has standard rooms and luxurious suites with fireplaces and full kitchens.
- **Inn of the Lost Coast** (205 Wave Dr., 707/986-7521 or 888/570-9676, www.innofthelostcoast.com, $160-275) has an array of large and airy rooms and suites with stellar views to suit even luxurious tastes.
- **Cliff House at Shelter Cove** (141 Wave Dr., 707/986-7344, www.cliffhousesheltercove.com, $180-200) has two suites; each has a full kitchen, living room, bedroom, gas fireplace, and satellite TV.
- **Sinkyone Wilderness State Park** (707/986-7711, www.parks.ca.gov) has the only drive-in campground at **Usal Beach** (Usal Rd., no reservations, year-round, $35).

FOOD

- **Chart Room** (210 Wave Dr., 707/986-9696, www.chartroom.cc, 5pm-8:30pm Mon.-Wed., 5pm-9pm Sat., $20-25). serves seafood, meat, and pasta dishes along with vegetarian fare.
- **The Cove Restaurant** (10 Seal Court, 707/986-1197, www.thesheltercoverestaurant.com, 5pm-9pm Thurs.-Sun., $15-32) has a hearty American menu, heavy on the seafood.
- The Inn of the Lost Coast is home to: **Delgada Pizzeria and Bakery** (205 Wave Dr., 707/986-7672, 1pm-9pm daily, $15-20) and the **Fish Tank Café** (707/986-7850, 7am-2pm Mon.-Thurs., 7am-2pm, 5pm-9pm Fri.-Sat.).

Access the Lost Coast via Highway 1 or U.S. 101. From the south, dirt Usal Road connects to Highway 1, just as the highway turns east toward Leggett. Usal Road eventually reaches the Sinkyone Wilderness State Park in less than 10 miles. Outside of Garberville, the Briceland Thorn-Shelter Cove Road takes 20 miles to reach the coast. Mattole Road out of Ferndale is a popular route from the north.

Right at the Humboldt Redwoods State Park Visitors Center, you can enjoy the **Gould Grove Nature Trail** (0.6 mile, easy)—a wheelchair-accessible interpretive nature walk with helpful signs describing the denizens of the forest.

For a longer walk in the woods, try the lovely **River Trail** (Mattole Rd., 1.1 miles west of Ave. of the Giants, 7 miles round-trip, moderate), which follows the South Fork Eel River. Check with the visitors center to be sure that the summer bridges have been installed before trying to hike this trail.

Camping

Few lodging options are close to the park. Fortunately, Humboldt Redwoods State Park has three developed **campgrounds** (800/444-7275, www.reserveamerica.com, $35) and primitive backcountry campsites ($5). Each developed campground has its own entrance station. Reservations are strongly recommended, as the park is quite popular with weekend campers.

Burlington Campground (707/946-1811, year-round) is adjacent to the visitors center and is a convenient starting point. It's dark and comfortable, engulfed in trees, and has ample restroom facilities and hot showers. **Albee Creek** (Mattole Rd., 5 miles west of Ave. of the Giants, 707/946-2472, May-mid-Oct.) offers some redwood-shaded sites and others in open meadows. ★ **Hidden Springs Campground** (Avenue of the Giants, 5 miles south of the visitors center, 707/943-3177, Memorial Day-Labor Day) is large and popular. Minimalist campers will enjoy the seclusion of hike-in trail camps at **Johnson** and **Grasshopper Peak.**

FERNDALE

Ferndale was built in the 19th century by Scandinavian immigrants who came to California to farm. Dairy pastures and farmland still surround the town today. The main sight in Ferndale is the town itself—it's a designated historical landmark. Ferndale is all Victorian, all the time—just ask about the

Humboldt Redwoods State Park

building you're in and you'll be told all about its specific architectural style, its construction date, and its original occupants. Main Street's shops, galleries, inns, and restaurants are all set into these scrupulously maintained and restored late-19th-century buildings, and make for an idyllic morning stroll.

The **Ferndale History Museum** (515 Shaw St., 707/786-4466, www.ferndale-museum.org, 11am-4pm Tues.-Sat., 1pm-4pm Sun. June-Sept., 11am-4pm Wed.-Sat., 1pm-4pm Sun. Oct.-Dec. and Feb.-May, $1) is a block off Main Street and tells the story of the town. Life-size dioramas depict period life in a Victorian home, and an array of antique artifacts brings history to life. Downstairs, the implements of rural coast history vividly display the reality that farmers and craftspeople faced in the preindustrial era.

Food

The restaurant and saloon at the **Hotel Ivanhoe** (315 Main St., 707/786-9000, http://hotel-ivanhoe.com, 5pm-9pm Wed.-Sun.,

$14-20) is a favorite for diners from as far away as Eureka for its hearty homemade Italian dishes and friendly personal service. **VI Restaurant** (400 Ocean Ave., 707/786-4950, http://virestaurant.com, 8am-9pm daily, $24-38), on the bottom floor of the Victorian Inn, aims to be high end and contemporary. Expect to find oysters, artisan mac 'n' cheese, steak, and lobster on the menu while the bar pours chic cocktails and a respectable wine list.

Stop in at the local favorite **Poppa Joe's** (409 Main St., 707/786-4180, 6am-2pm Mon.-Fri., 6am-noon Sat.-Sun., $6-12) for a hearty breakfast, or a hamburger at lunch. At ★ **Curley's Full Circle** (460 Main St., 707/876-9696, 11:30am-9pm Fri.-Tues., $14-30), find an eclectic, locally sourced menu in a charming, cozy atmosphere. On sunny days, opt to eat on the postage-size back patio. Standouts include the coconut prawn appetizer, the fish-and-chips, and the braised lamb shanks.

Accommodations

In Ferndale, lodgings tend to be Victorian-style inns, mostly bed-and-breakfasts. The queen of the B&Bs is **Shaw House Inn** (703 Main St., 707/786-9958, www.shawhouse.com, $125-275). Its eight rooms are festooned with lace, quilts, and floral wallpaper accenting the pop-out windows and Victorian woodwork of this historical home. A delightful continental breakfast is served in the morning. Out back, huge shade trees and perfectly positioned garden benches make a lovely spot to sit and read a book, hold a quiet conversation, or just enjoy the serene beauty.

The **Victorian Inn** (400 Ocean Ave., 707/786-4949 or 888/589-1808, www.victorianvillageinn.com, $135-255) is an imposing structure at the corner of Ocean Avenue and Main Street that also houses Silva's Jewelry. The inn comprises 13 rooms, all decorated with antique furnishings, luxurious linens, and pretty knickknacks. Package deals are available, and rates include a full breakfast downstairs.

An inexpensive non-inn lodging option in Ferndale is the **Redwood Suites** (332 Ocean Ave., 707/786-5000 or 888/589-1863, www.redwoodsuites.com, $115-145). Only a block off Main Street, the property has rooms that are simple but comfortable, complete with modern amenities like flat-screen TVs. Family suites with full kitchens are available, and rates include a full breakfast.

Transportation

Ferndale is not directly accessible from U.S.

Ferndale

101. Exit at Fernbridge and follow Highway 211 to Ferndale. Main Street will guide you into the center of town. Walking provides the best views and feel of the town.

EUREKA

Eureka sports an enjoyable waterfront boardwalk, shopping and dining in its charming downtown, and a Victorian lumber-baron history that pervades the town.

Sights

Established in 1853 to protect white settlers from the local Native Americans, **Fort Humboldt State Historic Park** (3431 Fort Ave., 707/445-6567, www.parks.ca.gov, 8am-5pm daily) gives visitors a glimpse into the lives of 19th-century soldiers and loggers. The **Clarke Historical Museum** (240 E St., 707/443-1947, www.clarkemuseum.org, 11am-4pm Wed.-Sat., by donation) showcases changing exhibits that illuminate the Native American history.

★ BLUE OX MILLWORKS AND HISTORIC PARK

The **Blue Ox Millworks and Historic Park** (1 X St., 707/444-3437 or 800/248-4259, www.blueoxmill.com, tours 9am-5pm Mon.-Fri., 9am-4pm Sat. Apr.-Oct., 9am-5pm Mon.-Fri. Nov.-Mar., adults $10, seniors $9, ages 6-12 $5, under 6 free) is a rambling complex of old buildings—there's a working lumber mill, upscale wood and cabinetry shop, ceramics studio, blacksmith forge, shipbuilding yard, and a historical park. All the tools date back to the 1800s and are still used to create ornate custom items for historical buildings nationwide. Arrive at least an hour before closing to give yourself plenty of time for the self-guided tour and an opportunity to peruse the gift shop—a converted lumberjack barracks—stocked with wares made by students of the Blue Ox.

Accommodations and Food

While there are plenty of chain motels, the historical inns are more interesting. The ★ **Carter House Inns** (301 L St., 800/404-1390, www.carterhouse.com, $179-595) is a compound of historical inns and cottages at the east end of Old Town. Accommodations range from charming cottages ($595/night) to suites with soaking tubs ($350/night) and the economical "really nice rooms" ($179). All are clean and stylish, with nods to the Victorian era. The best values are found in the standard rooms at the Hotel Carter, and at the Bell Cottage ($179-250), which also offers a full communal kitchen and sitting room. The rooms and suites of the stately Carter House ($312-412) are the most lovely.

The ★ **Samoa Cookhouse** (511 Vance Rd., Samoa, 707/442-1659, www.samoacookhouse.net, 7am-9pm daily summer, 7am-8pm daily winter, $14-17) has been around since 1890. Red-checked tablecloths cover long rough tables to recreate the atmosphere of the logging-camp dining hall it once was. The all-you-can-eat meals are served family-style from huge serving platters. Think big hunks of roast beef, mountains of mashed potatoes, and piles of vegetables.

Oenophiles flock to **Restaurant 301** (301 L St., 707/444-8062, www.carterhouse.com, 6pm-9pm daily, $22-29) for the 3,400-plus bottles on the wine list, as well as the food. The sophisticated menu relies heavily on local ingredients (including from its own kitchen garden), or opt for bites at the bar (4pm-11pm daily, $7-16).

Some of the best barbecue can be found at **Humboldt Smokehouse** (310 5th St., 707/497-6261, http://humboldtsmokehouse.com, 11am-9pm Mon.-Sat., $10-12), a no-frills joint with walk-up counter service, limited seating, and extremely reasonable prices.

For a quick breakfast or a quiet cup of coffee, **Ramone's Bakery & Café** (209 E St., 707/442-2923, www.ramonesbakery.com, 7am-6pm Mon.-Fri., 8am-5pm Sat., 8am-4pm Sun.) sells from-scratch baked goods, premade sandwiches, and a variety of coffee drinks. Another excellent option, **Los Bagels** (403 2nd St., 707/442-8525, http://losbagels.com, 6:30am-5pm Mon.-Fri., 7am-5pm Sat.,

Side Trip to Trinidad

Trinidad, 24 miles north of Eureka, juts out from the ragged coastline and is the place to go for **beaches** and **kayaking.** To reach downtown, take Exit 728 and follow signs pointing toward the coast. Main Street runs through the heart of town.

- **Clam Beach** (7.5 miles north of Arcata, 707/445-7651, http://co.humboldt.ca.us) is the largest beach, with a huge expanse of sand hugging the coastline. It is a popular spot for surfers, horseback riders, dog lovers, and the occasional drum circle. Nine campsites are situated close to the beach.

- **Moonstone Beach** (12.5 miles north of Arcata, 707/445-7651, http://co.humboldt.ca.us) is a county park cradled between Little River and the redwoods. Moonstone has tide pools, sea caves, and plenty of large rocks for bouldering.

- **Trinidad State Beach** (Stagecoach and State Park Rd., 707/677-3570, www.parks.ca.gov, sunrise-sunset daily) covers the coast on the north side of town.

- **College Cove** is one of its most popular beaches, with plenty of shelter from the wind. It's known as a clothing-optional spot. The park also offers picnic areas and easy to moderate hikes through the grassy bluffs and spruce forests.

- **Kayak Zak's** (115336 Hwy. 101, Trinidad, 707/498-1130, 2-hr tour $100) rents kayaks ($25-35/hour, $40-70/half day, and $65-100/24 hours) out of its main location at Stone Lagoon and seasonally at Big Lagoon. Both lagoons are a part of **Humboldt Lagoons State Park** (15336 Hwy. 101, Trinidad, 707/677-3570, sunrise-sunset daily), about 15 miles north of Trinidad proper.

- **Humboats Kayak Adventures** (Woodley Island Marina, 707/443-5157, www.humboats.com) offers a three-hour tour of Trinidad Bay ($75).

ACCOMMODATIONS AND FOOD

- **Trinidad Inn** (1170 Patrick's Point Dr., 707/677-3349, www.trinidadinn.com, $75-195) has clean, comfortable rooms at excellent prices.

- **Trinidad Bay Bed & Breakfast** (560 Edwards St., 707/677-0840, www.trinidadbaybnb.com, $200-350) has four rooms and serves a filling three-course breakfast.

- **Lost Whale Inn** (3452 Patrick's Point Dr., 707/677-3425 or 800/677-7859, http://lostwhaleinn.com, $199-325, 2-night min.) has eight rooms that overlook the ocean, a private beach, and a buffet-style breakfast.

- **The Larrupin' Café** (1658 Patrick's Point Dr., 707/677-0230, www.larrupin.com, 5pm-9pm daily, $23-36) is the most magical restaurant on the Redwood Coast. Guests dine on Cornish game hen, Creole prawns, and filet mignon. There's an excellent wine list and live jazz (Wed. and Sun.).

- **Seascapes Restaurant and Pier** (1 Bay St., 707/677-3762, 7am-8pm daily spring-fall, 7am-9:30pm daily summer, $15) serves burgers, seafood, hearty breakfasts, and no-frills desserts from its location at the pier.

7am-4pm Sun.) sells house-made bagels, spreads, and sandwiches at reasonable prices.

Transportation

Eureka is on U.S. 101, easily accessed by car from north or south. From San Francisco, Eureka is a five-hour drive north on U.S. 101, and it's 1.5 hours south of Crescent City. Driving is the only option if you're not staying downtown. The small commercial **Arcata-Eureka Airport** (3561 Boeing Ave., McKinleyville, 707/839-5401, http://

co.humboldt.ca.us/aviation) offers direct flights to Portland, Oregon, San Francisco, and Sacramento.

ARCATA

Located about 10 miles north of Eureka on U.S. 101, Arcata is a small college town largely populated by Humboldt State University students and alumni. The town's main plaza is filled with benches and surrounded by lovely places to eat and shop.

Food

Local favorite **Tomo** (708 9th St., 707/822-1414, www.tomoarcata.com, 11:30am-2pm, 4pm-9pm Mon.-Sat., 4pm-9pm Sun., $18-21) is a Japanese restaurant and sushi bar at the base of the Arcata Hotel.

At quiet **Folie Douce** (1551 G St., 707/822-1042, www.foliedoucearcata.com, 5:30pm-9pm Tues.-Thurs., 5:30pm-10pm Fri.-Sat., $16-30), the French-inspired food includes plenty of Humboldt twists, such as local oysters presented in a "Japanese" style. Most come for pizzas baked in the wood-fired oven, but the fish specials are expertly executed.

For breakfast, go to **Renata's Creperie** (1030 G St., 707/825-8783, 8am-3pm Tues.-Thurs. and Sun., 8am-3pm, 5pm-9pm Fri.-Sat., $8-14), which has plenty of sweet and savory crepes to choose from.

A number of bars cater to the college crowd, but the best by far is **The Alibi** (744 9th St., 707/822-3731, 8am-2am daily), a dive bar par excellence. The Alibi pours 42 different beers, mean martinis, and the best Bloody Mary on the Redwood Coast. A full kitchen serves breakfast, lunch, and dinner.

Accommodations

Arcata is an attractive place to stay, but the digs are extremely limited. On the outskirts of town are plenty of chain hotels that fill up on graduation weekend. This leaves the historical **Hotel Arcata** (708 9th St., 707/826-0217 or 800/344-1221, http://hotelarcata.com, $89-115) as the only game in town. Service is subpar and rooms are rather small and grungy

(and smokey), but it's cheap and perfectly located on the plaza.

One of the more stately Victorians, **Lady Anne Victorian Inn** (902 14th St., 707/822-2797, http://ladyanneinn.com, $115-220) has five rooms appointed in antiques, floral wallpaper, and handmade quilts. All rooms have private bathrooms and two have their own sitting rooms.

Transportation

Arcata is about 10 miles north of Eureka on U.S. 101. For an alternate scenic route, take Highway 255 at the north end of Eureka. It crosses the bay over Woodley Island and travels along the bay's northern peninsula through wetlands and farmland to downtown Arcata.

PATRICK'S POINT STATE PARK

Patrick's Point State Park (4150 Patrick's Point Dr., Trinidad, 707/677-3570, www.parks.ca.gov, $8) is a rambling coastal park 25 miles north of Eureka replete with campgrounds, trails, beaches, and landmarks. Get a map at the **visitors center** (707/677-1945, 9am-4:30pm daily), to the right of the entry gate.

Prominent among the local landmarks is **Patrick's Point,** which can be reached by a brief hike from a convenient parking lot. **Wedding Rock** is adjacent to Patrick's Point in a picturesque cove (people really do hike out to the rock to get married). Stop at the **Sumeg Village,** a re-creation of a native Yurok village, to peek through the perfectly round doors into semi-subterranean homes, meeting places, and storage buildings. (The local Yurok people still use Sumeg Village as a gathering place; please tread lightly.) Check out the native plant garden, a collection of local plants the Yurok people used for food, basketry, and medicine.

A steep trail leads down to **Agate Beach**, a wide stretch of coarse sand bordered by cliffs shot through with shining quartz veins. The semiprecious stones for which it is named do appear here. Six miles of trails thread through the park, including the **Rim Trail,** which will take you along the cliffs for a view of the sea and migrating whales (Sept.-Jan, Mar.-June). **Penn Creek** and **Ceremonial Rock Trails** both cut through the heart of the park.

Camping

Three **campgrounds** (707/677-3570, reservations 800/444-7275, www.reserveamerica.com, $35) have a total of 120 sites. Most campsites are pleasantly shaded by the groves of trees. All include a picnic table, a grill, and a food storage cupboard, and you'll find running water, restrooms, and showers nearby.

Transportation

Patrick's Point State Park is located on the coast 30 miles north of Eureka and 15 miles south of Orick on U.S. 101.

TOP EXPERIENCE

★ REDWOOD NATIONAL AND STATE PARKS

The lands of **Redwood National and State Parks** (www.nps.gov/redw) meander along the coast and include three state parks— **Prairie Creek Redwoods, Del Norte Coast Redwoods,** and **Jedediah Smith.** This complex of parkland encompasses most of California's northern redwood forests. The main landmass of Redwood National Park is just south of Prairie Creek State Park along U.S. 101, stretching east from the coast and the highway.

Redwood National Park

The **Thomas H. Kuchel Visitor Center** (U.S. 101, south of Orick, 707/465-7765, 9am-5pm daily spring-fall, 9am-4pm daily winter) is a large facility with a ranger station, clean restrooms, and a path to the shore. You can get maps, advice, permits for backcountry camping, and books. In the summer, rangers run patio talks and coast walks that provide a great introduction to the area. You can also have a picnic at one of the tables outside the visitors center, or walk a short distance to Redwood Creek.

HIKING

One of the easiest, most popular ways to get close to the trees is to walk the **Lady Bird Johnson Trail** (Bald Hills Rd., 1.4 miles, easy). This nearly level loop provides an intimate view of the redwood and fir forests that define this region. Another easy-access trail is

Patrick's Point State Park

Trillium Falls (Davison Rd. at Elk Meadow, 2.5 miles, easy-moderate). The redwood trees along this cool, dark trail are striking, and the small waterfall is a nice treasure in the woods. This little hike is lovely any time of year but best in spring, when the water volume over the falls is at its peak.

The **Lost Man Creek Trail** (east of Elk Meadow, 1 mile off U.S. 101, up to 22 miles, easy-difficult) has it all. The first 0.5 mile is perfect for wheelchair users and families with small children. But as the trail rolls along, the grades get steeper and more challenging. If you reach the Lost Man Creek picnic grounds, your total round-trip distance is 22 miles with more than 3,000 feet of elevation gain and several stream crossings. Bikes are permitted on this trail.

ACCOMMODATIONS AND CAMPING

If you want to sleep indoors but still stay close to the national park, your best bet is the **Palm Café & Motel** (121130 U.S. 101, Orick, 707/488-3381, $60-90). It's a far cry from fancy, but it's a great location, and the food in the attached café (6am-8pm daily summer, $10-12) is good.

Redwood National Park has no designated campgrounds, but free backcountry camping is allowed; permits may be necessary in certain areas. **Elam Camp** and **44 Camp** are both hike-in primitive campgrounds along the Redwood Creek and Tall Trees Trails, respectively.

TRANSPORTATION

The Thomas H. Kuchel Visitor Center, at the south end of the park, is 40 miles (45-min. drive) north of Eureka on U.S. 101.

Prairie Creek Redwoods State Park

At the junction of the south end of the Newton B. Drury Scenic Parkway and U.S. 101, **Prairie Creek Redwoods State Park** (Newton B. Drury Scenic Pkwy., 25 miles south of Crescent City, 707/488-2039, www. parks.ca.gov, $8) offers 14,000 acres of lush and shady hiking trails through redwoods as well as several large campgrounds.

The **Prairie Creek Visitor Center** (Newton B. Drury Scenic Pkwy., 707/488-2171, 9am-5pm daily summer, 9am-4pm Thurs.-Mon. fall-spring) includes a small interpretive museum describing the history of the California redwood forests. A tiny bookshop adjoins the museum, well stocked with books describing the history, nature, and culture of the area.

One of the things that make a drive to Prairie Creek worth the effort is the herd of **Roosevelt elk.** These big guys hang out at the Elk Prairie, a stretch of open grassland along the highway. To find the viewing platform, watch for the road signs. The best times to see the elk out grazing in the field are early morning and around sunset.

NEWTON B. DRURY SCENIC PARKWAY

A gorgeous scenic road through the redwoods, **Newton B. Drury Scenic Parkway,** off U.S. 101 about halfway between Orick and Klamath, features old-growth trees lining the roads, a close-up view of the redwood forest ecosystem, and a grove or trailhead every hundred yards or so. A great place to turn off is at the **Big Tree Wayside.** The eponymous tree is only a short walk from the parking area, and several trails radiate from the little grove.

HIKING

Fern Canyon (1 mile, Davison Rd.), near Gold Bluffs Beach, runs through a narrow canyon carved by Home Creek. Ferns, mosses, and other water-loving plants grow thick up the sides of the canyon, creating a beautiful vertical carpet of greenery (scenes from both *Jurassic Park 2* and *Return of the Jedi* were filmed here). This area is home to the very large and relatively rare Roosevelt elk; look for them around Gold Bluffs Beach. You can extend this hike into a longer (6.2 miles, moderate) loop. To get to the Fern Canyon trailhead, take U.S. 101 three miles north of Orick, and then at Elk Meadow, turn west onto Davison

Road (no trailers allowed) and travel two more miles. This rough dirt road takes you through the campground and ends at the trailhead in 1.5 miles.

The **Miners' Ridge** and **James Irvine Loop** (12 miles, moderate) starts from the visitors center and reaches the beach. From the trailhead, start out on **James Irvine Trail** and bear right when you can, following the trail all the way until it joins Fern Canyon Trail. Turn left when you get to the coast and walk along Gold Bluffs Beach for 1.5 miles. Then make a left onto the **Clintonia Trail** and head back toward the visitors center.

The **California Coastal Trail** (www.californiacoastaltrail.info) runs along the entire coast of this park and can be accessed by taking Davison Road to the coast in the south and by Newton B. Drury Scenic Parkway in the north, via the one-mile, moderate **Ossagon Creek Trail.**

CAMPING

The **Elk Prairie Campground** (127011 Newton B. Drury Scenic Pkwy., campground 707/488-2171, reservations 800/444-7275, www.reserveamerica.com, vehicles $35, hikers and cyclists $5) has 75 sites for tents (and some RVs) and a full range of comfortable camping amenities, including showers and firewood. Several campsites are wheelchair-accessible (request at reservation). A big campfire area is an easy walk north of the campground, with evening programs put on by rangers and volunteers.

For beach camping, head out to **Gold Bluffs Beach Campground** (Davison Rd., www.parks.ca.gov, no reservations, $35). There are about 26 sites for tents or RVs. Amenities include flush toilets, water, solar showers, and wide ocean views. The surf can be quite dangerous here, so be extremely careful if you go in the water.

TRANSPORTATION

Prairie Creek Redwoods is located 50 miles north of Eureka and 25 miles south of Crescent City on U.S. 101. Newton B. Drury

Scenic Parkway traverses the park and can be accessed from U.S. 101 north or south.

Del Norte Coast Redwoods State Park

South of Crescent City, **Del Norte Coast Redwoods State Park** (Mill Creek Campground Rd., off U.S. 101, 707/465-5128, www.parks.ca.gov, $8) encompasses a variety of ecosystems, including eight miles of wild coastline, second-growth redwood forest, and virgin old-growth forests. One of the largest in this system of parks, Del Norte is a great place to get lost in the backcountry with just your knapsack.

Del Norte State Park has no visitors center, but you can get information from the **Crescent City Information Center** (1111 2nd St., Crescent City, 707/465-7335, 9am-5pm daily spring-fall, 9am-4pm daily winter).

HIKING

Several rewarding yet gentle and short excursions start and end in the Mill Creek Campground. Dress in layers to hike as it can get down into the 40s even in summer. The **Trestle Loop Trail** (1 mile, easy) begins across from the campfire center in the campground. Notice the trestles and other artifacts along the way; the loop follows the route of a defunct railroad from the logging era. Another easy stroll is the nearby **Nature Loop Trail** (1 mile, easy), which begins near the campground entrance gate.

The northern section of the great **California Coastal Trail** (CCT, www.californiacoastaltrail.info) runs right through Del Norte Coast Redwoods State Park. The Coastal Trail is reasonably well marked; look for signs with the CCT logo. The "last chance" section of the California Coastal Trail (Enderts Beach-Damnation Creek, 14 miles, strenuous) makes a challenging day hike. To reach the trailhead, turn west from U.S. 101 onto Enderts Beach Road, three miles south of Crescent City. The 14-miles trail (round-trip) begins at the end of the road.

CAMPING

The **Mill Creek Campground** (U.S. 101, 800/444-7275, www.reserveamerica.com, mid-May-Oct., vehicles $35, hikers and cyclists $5) has 145 sites for RVs and tents. Facilities include restrooms and fire pits. (Online, the campsite is referred to as the Del Norte Coast Redwoods SP, not Mill Creek.)

TRANSPORTATION

Del Norte Coast Redwoods is located seven miles south of Crescent City on U.S. 101. The park entrance is on Hamilton Road and at the Mill Creek Campground, both east of U.S. 101.

Jedediah Smith Redwoods State Park

The best redwood grove in the old growth of **Jedediah Smith Redwoods State Park** (U.S. 199, 9 miles east of Crescent City, 707/465-7335, www.parks.ca.gov) is **Stout Memorial Grove.** These are some of the biggest and oldest trees on the North Coast and were somehow spared the loggers' saws. This grove is very quiet and less populated than others, since its far-north latitude makes it harder to reach than some of the other big redwood groves in California.

Jedediah Smith has two visitors centers, each about five minutes apart: the **Jedediah Smith Visitor Center** (U.S. 101, Hiouchi, 707/458-3496, noon-8pm daily summer) and the **Hiouchi Information Center** (U.S. 199, Hiouchi, 707/458-3294, 9am-5pm daily summer).

HIKING

The shaded trails make for cool summer hiking. Many trails run along the river and the creeks, offering beach access and lush scenery to enjoy. The **Simpson Reed Trail** (1 mile, easy) takes you from U.S. 199 down to the banks of the Smith River.

To get a good view of the Smith River, hike the **Hiouchi Trail** (2 miles, moderate). From the Hiouchi Information Center and campgrounds on U.S. 199, cross the Summer

Footbridge and then follow the river north. The Hiouchi Trail then meets the Hatton Loop Trail and leads away from the river and into the forest.

For a longer and more aggressive trek, try the **Mill Creek Trail** (7.5 miles round-trip, difficult). A good place to start is at the Summer Footbridge. The trail then follows the creek down to the unpaved Howland Hill Road.

The **Boy Scout Tree Trail** (5.2 miles, moderate) is usually quiet, with few hikers, and the gargantuan forest will make you feel truly tiny. Check at the visitors center first to make sure the road to the trailhead is open.

CAMPING

The ★ **Jedediah Smith Campground** (U.S. 199, Hiouchi, 800/444-7275, www.reserveamerica.com, open year-round) is beautifully situated on the banks of Smith River, with most sites near the River Beach Trail. There are 86 RV and tent sites (vehicles $35, hike/bike in primitive sites $5). Facilities include restrooms, fire pits, and coin-operated showers. Reservations (accepted Memorial Day-Labor Day) are advised, especially for summer and holiday weekends.

TRANSPORTION

Jedediah Smith Redwoods State Park is north of Crescent City along the Smith River, next to the immense Smith River National Recreation Area.

CRESCENT CITY

The northernmost city on the coast of California perches on the bay whose shape gave the town its name. **Crescent City** is a tough town and sees little of the boom brought by tourist dollars. Still, its proximity to state and national parks, deep-sea fishing, and beaches make it a good destination.

Accommodations and Food

The aptly named **Curly Redwood Lodge** (701 U.S. 101 S., 707/464-2137, www.curlyredwoodlodge.com, $56-98) is constructed of a single rare curly redwood tree. A 1950s feel pervades this friendly unpretentious motel, conveniently located right on U.S. 101 near the area's restaurants. At the **Lighthouse Inn** (681 U.S. 101 S., 707/464-3993 or 877/464-3993, www.lighthouse101.com, $89-145), every room has a refrigerator, a microwave, and a coffeemaker. Corner suites come with oversize whirlpool tubs and fireplaces, but standard double rooms are downright cheap and comfortable.

The Chart Room (130 Anchor Way, 707/464-5993, www.chartroomcrescentcity.com, 11am-4pm Tues., 7am-8pm Wed.-Sun., $10-28) is right on the bay, so you can watch sea lions cavort on the pier while you eat. **The Good Harvest Café** (575 U.S. 101 S., 707/465-6028, 7:30am-9pm Mon.-Sat., 8am-9pm Sun., $10-27) offers plenty of hearty breakfast, lunch, and dinner options. Everything is made from scratch with wholesome ingredients.

Transportation and Services

The main routes through Crescent City are U.S. 101 and U.S. 199. Both are well maintained but are twisty in spots, so take care at night. It is 85 miles (under 2 hours) from Eureka north to Crescent City on U.S. 101. Parking is free and easy to find throughout town. **Jack McNamara Field** (CEC, 707/464-7311http://flycrescentcity.com) has daily nonstop flights to San Francisco and Sacramento.

Any aches and pains can be attended to at the emergency room of **Sutter Coast Hospital** (800 E. Washington Blvd., 707/464-8511, www.suttercoast.org).

Shasta and Lassen

Redding and Vicinity 195

Shasta Lake. 200

Lassen Volcanic National Park. . 205

Mount Shasta and Vicinity 214

The mountains in the far northern reaches of California are some of the most unspoiled areas in the state, protected by a wealth of national and state parks and forestlands.

The most prominent features of this region are two iconic mountains: Shasta and Lassen. The stunning snowcapped peak of Mount Shasta may look familiar—it often graces calendars, postcards, and photography books. Shasta is a dormant volcano, which means it's not extinct—it will erupt again—but unlike an active volcano, it probably won't do so soon. Mount Shasta, and the town and lake that share its name, are easy to get to. The mountain itself, though, is daunting to climb and should be attempted only by experienced climbers. South of Mount Shasta is the major resort area of Shasta Lake, which attracts boaters and water enthusiasts from far and wide.

Mount Lassen, about 150 miles southeast of Shasta, is classified as an active volcano, and the national park that surrounds it includes many volcanic features—boiling mud pots, steam vents, and sulfur springs. Both mountains make great vacation destinations,

beautiful to behold and surrounded by recreation opportunities. Not quite as many visitors flock to Lassen as they do to Shasta, yet scaling Mount Lassen's peak is only a moderate day hike, accessible to almost anyone who is fit and game to try it.

As you drive up into this remote area, you'll discover a number of quirky places worth a visit of their own. Go underground at Lava Beds National Monument, scale the cliffs at Castle Crags, feel the spray of waterfalls at McArthur-Burney Falls, and discover the sad and shameful history of a World War II Japanese "segregation center" at Tule Lake.

PLANNING YOUR TIME

Either Shasta or Lassen makes for a fabulous weekend getaway—particularly if you've got a three-day weekend. Mount Shasta offers fairly easy and reliable year-round access along I-5, with both winter and summer outdoor recreation. The weather on and near

Previous: Mount Shasta; Bumpass Hell. **Above:** Lassen Volcanic National Park.

Look for ★ to find recommended sights, activities, dining, and lodging.

Highlights

★ **Lake Shasta Caverns:** These wondrous caverns are filled with natural limestone, marble, and crystal-studded stalactites and stalagmites (page 201).

★ **Lassen Peak:** This 10,462-foot volcano offers a rewarding hike to the top and a dramatic view below (page 208).

★ **Loomis Museum and Manzanita Lake:** This small but lovely museum offers a history of Lassen's volcanic eruptions through a series of startling and revealing photographs (page 208).

★ **Bumpass Hell:** This two-mile hike leads through a hotbed of geothermal activity (page 209).

★ **Mount Shasta:** This dazzling glacier-topped mountain peak is truly one of the greatest visions the state has to offer (page 214).

★ **Castle Crags State Park:** A longtime favorite of rock climbers, this park offers great hiking, camping, and scenic views (page 222).

★ **McArthur-Burney Falls Memorial State Park:** This park is home to 129-foot Burney Falls, touted as California's most beautiful waterfall (page 223).

★ **Lava Beds National Monument:** With

more than 700 natural caves, ancient rock art, and 14 species of bats, this strange place amazes (224).

Shasta can get extreme; expect winter storms half the year and, occasionally, brutally high temperatures in the summer months. Check the weather reports so you can pack the right clothes for your trip. If you're planning to climb even part of Mount Shasta, be aware that it's high enough to create its own weather.

The best time to visit Mount Lassen is mid- to late-summer. Lassen is in the remote eastern part of the state, where the weather gets extreme; it can still be snowy on Lassen as late as June, so keep that in mind when you make your camping plans. During winter the main road through the park closes, making a visit to the region far less interesting—unless you've brought snowshoes or skis to explore the backcountry.

Redding and Vicinity

The biggest city in the region, Redding has all the amenities you might need on your journey. The town has a lot of turnover, so establishments that were here last time might have moved or been replaced. If you just want to get off I-5 for some quick food, skip the Market Street exit; the largest concentration of food and shops is west of the Lake Boulevard exit.

SIGHTS

The best-known sight in the Redding region is the **Sundial Bridge** (800/887-8532, daily 24 hours, free). This beautiful bit of architecture was designed by Santiago Calatrava and features a single large pylon structure that anchors suspension cables that fan out over the bridge. Most people get to the bridge from Turtle Bay Exploration Park and walk north across its 200 tons of green glass, strips of granite, and ceramic tiles from Spain.

Shasta State Historic Park

The Shasta region was once crowded with 19th-century gold miners and the people providing goods and services to them. Today **Shasta State Historic Park** (Hwy. 299, 5 miles west of I-5, 530/243-8194, www.parks. ca.gov, 10am-5pm Thurs.-Sun.) honors that regional history with two on-site museums: the **Litsch Store Museum** (530/244-1848, 11am-2pm Sat., hours vary Sun.-Fri., free) and the **Courthouse Museum** (530/243-8194, 10am-5pm Thurs.-Sun., adults $3, ages 6-17 $2). See everything from an extensive collection of California landscape paintings to the area's original gallows. Outside, wander through the brick ruins of the former Gold Rush town.

Whiskeytown National Recreation Area

Whiskeytown National Recreation Area comprises 39,000 acres of wilderness for hiking, biking, and water sports just 10 miles west of Redding. Exhibits at the **Whiskeytown Visitors Center** (Hwy. 299 and John F. Kennedy Memorial Dr., 530/246-1225, www. nps.gov/whis, 9am-5pm daily Memorial Day-Labor Day, 10am-4pm daily Labor Day-Memorial Day, $5 day-use fee per vehicle for recreation area) illuminate the area's history as a gold-mining destination. It's also a good place to get maps, advice, and information about camping, hiking, and tours in the park.

Whiskeytown Lake is the centerpiece of this delightfully uncrowded outdoor playground, with 30 miles of shoreline and plenty of room to fish. Personal watercraft are prohibited on the lake, but kayaking, canoeing, and swimming are permitted. In season, sign up for 2.5-hour ranger-led **kayak tours** (reservations 530/242-3462, 9:30am Mon.-Sun. spring-fall, 5:30pm Thurs.-Sun. summer) or a moonlight kayak tour (1 hour, 1:30pm Mon. and Thurs. in summer).

On Whiskeytown Lake, **Oak Bottom Marina** (12485 Hwy. 299 W., Whiskeytown, 530/359-2671, www.whiskeytownmarinas.

Shasta and Lassen

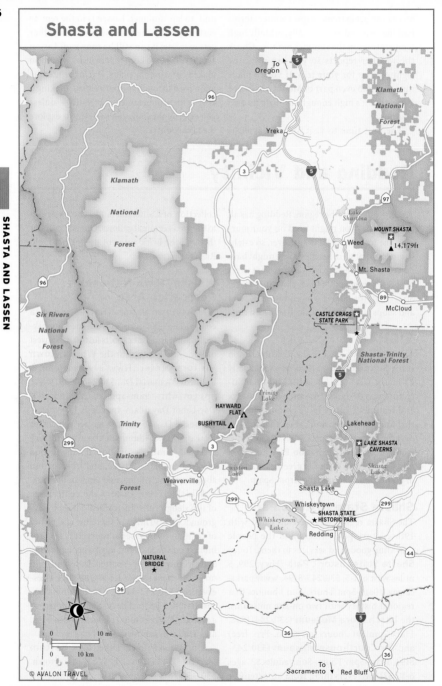

To Oregon

96

Klamath National Forest

Yreka

3

5

97

Klamath National Forest

Lake Shastina

MOUNT SHASTA ✦
▲ 14,179ft

Weed

Mt. Shasta

89

McCloud

CASTLE CRAGS ✦
STATE PARK
★

Shasta-Trinity
National Forest

96

Six Rivers National Forest

5

Trinity Lake

HAYWARD
FLAT ⋀

BUSHYTAIL ⋀

Lakehead

✦ LAKE SHASTA
CAVERNS
★

Shasta Lake

Trinity

3

National

Lewiston Lake

299

Forest

Weaverville

299

Shasta Lake

Whiskeytown

SHASTA STATE
★ HISTORIC PARK

Whiskeytown Lake

Redding

299

44

NATURAL
BRIDGE
★

36

0   10 mi

0   10 km

36

36

5

To
Sacramento ↓ Red Bluff

© AVALON TRAVEL

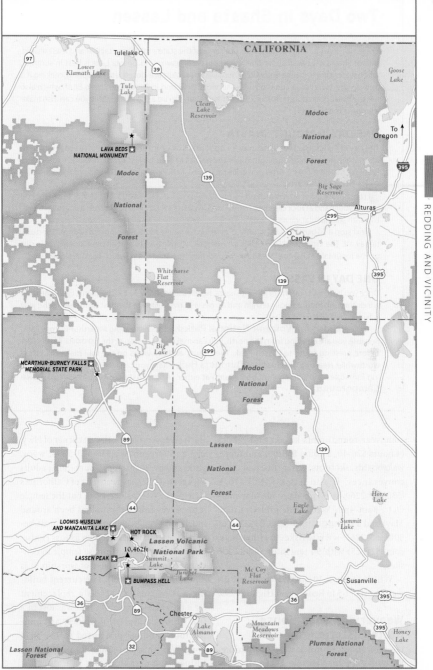

Two Days in Shasta and Lassen

These northern peaks and parklands are some of the state's most spectacular and least visited. Mount Shasta is a paradise for outdoor enthusiasts year-round. Shasta Lake is best in summer, when water sports can be enjoyed. Mount Lassen's roads are closed late fall-spring, making it a mid- to late-summer destination. Most services are found in Redding and Red Bluff, which also are the best access points from I-5. Each destination can be a trip in itself, but you can also make a loop via Highway 89.

ONE DAY IN MOUNT SHASTA

The city of Redding acts as a gateway for both **Shasta Lake** and **Mount Shasta.** From Redding, drive north on I-5 for eight miles to Shasta Lake. Turn west on Highway 151 to explore looming **Shasta Dam.** After marveling at its size, head over to the other side of I-5 to tour the **Lake Shasta Caverns.**

From Shasta Lake, drive north on I-5 for 40 miles to **Castle Crags State Park,** where you can try your hand at rock climbing or hike the **Crags Trail to Castle Dome,** a 5.5-mile round-trip with spectacular views.

Next stop is **Mount Shasta,** only 15 miles up I-5, where more climbing and hiking opportunities await. The **Gray Butte Trail** is a moderate 3.4-mile hike to a small peak. Spend the night on the mountain at Panther Meadows, or backtrack to Castle Crags, which has developed sites.

ONE DAY IN LASSEN

Once you have had your fill of Mount Shasta, head east on Highway 89. The scenic two-lane road winds through mountainous terrain and across wild rivers. One of the best sights along the way is **McArthur-Burney Falls.**

You'll enter **Lassen Volcanic National Park** shortly after leaving McArthur-Burney Falls. Because you are entering from the north, you can make a quick stop at the **Loomis Museum** before pressing south to Lassen Peak. The beauty and the views on the trail make the effort worthwhile. Nearby is another treat, **Bumpass Hell,** where you can hike surrounded by smoking fumaroles and boiling mud pots. Camp at either **Manzanita Lake** or **Summit Lake Campground.**

com, year-round) rents kayaks and canoes (4 hours $20-40, 8 hours $30-60) and tubes, wakeboards, ski boats, water skis, and other conveyances. It also has a **small store** (530/359-2269, 8am-7pm daily late May-mid-Oct., 8am-4pm Wed.-Sun. mid-Oct.-late May) and a **campground** (530/359-2269 or 800/365-2267, www.whiskeytownmarinas. com, $20-25) with 94 tent sites and 22 RV sites.

Whiskeytown is 10 miles (15 minutes) directly west of I-5 in Redding on Highway 299.

Weaverville Joss House State Historic Park

Located about 50 miles west of Redding, **Weaverville Joss House State Historic Park** (Weaverville, southwest corner of Hwy. 299 and Oregon St., 530/623-5284, www. parks.ca.gov, 10am-4pm Thurs.-Sun., adults $4, ages 6-17 $2) has been part of California's state park system since 1956, but the temple it preserves and celebrates has been around much longer. The Temple of the Forest beneath the Clouds, also known as Joss House, is California's oldest Chinese temple in continual use. A Taoist house of worship, it is now a museum as well. The current building was erected in 1874 as a replacement for a previous incarnation that was lost in a fire. Through displays of Chinese art, mining tools, and weapons used in the 1854 Tong War, this museum tells some of the Chinese immigrant history in California.

Admission includes a tour of the temple (hourly 10am-4pm).

Weaverville is due west of Shasta Lake. The drive from Redding west on Highway 299 takes about an hour.

FOOD

From the Hearth Artisan Bakery (1292 College View Dr., Redding, 530/245-0555, http://fromthehearth.wix.com, 7am-9pm Mon.-Sat., 7am-6pm Sun., $3.75-10) offers homemade sourdough bread, chocolate croissants, and other baked goods as well as smoothies and sandwiches.

A cute, friendly diner in a historical 1930s building, **Red House Coffee** (86 S. Miner St., Weaverville, 530/623-1635, 6:30am-6pm Mon.-Fri., 7:30am-6pm Sat. summer., 6:30am-5:30pm Mon.-Fri., 7:30am-6pm Sat. winter, $5-12) serves breakfast, lunch, and the gamut of coffee beverages.

Bartels Giant Burger (18509 Lake Blvd. E., Redding, 530/243-7313, www.bartelsgiantburger.com, 10am-9pm Mon.-Sat., 11:30am-9pm Sun. summer, 10am-8pm Mon.-Sat., 11:30am-8pm Sun. winter, $4-7.50) has plenty of raving fans. If you're extra hungry, ask for double or triple. Enjoy it with lots of onions and the highly recommended special sauce.

With slick decor and roomy booths, **Clearie's Restaurant and Lounge** (1325 Eureka Way, Redding, 530/241-4535, http://cleariesrestaurant.com, 11am-3pm, 5pm-9pm Mon.-Fri., 11am-3pm, 5pm-10pm Sat., $20-75) feels like a throwback to the swanky eateries of the 1950s and '60s. The menu has standard American fare, such as steaks and fresh fish, while the lounge stays open late on Friday and Saturday evenings.

For a hearty Italian meal, **Gironda's Restaurant** (1100 Center St., Redding, 530/244-7663, www.2girondas.com, 4:30pm-9pm Sun.-Thurs., 4:30pm-10pm Fri.-Sat., $16-30) serves ravioli and other pasta as well as big Italian-style dinner entrées. Dine in the casually elegant dining room or order takeout.

The plate-busting portions at **Beckett's Trail End Steakhouse** (1324 Nugget Ln., Weaverville, 530/623-2900, noon-3pm, 4:30pm-7pm Mon., 4:30pm-9pm Tues. and Thurs., 11am-3pm, 4:30pm-9pm Wed. and Fri.-Sat. summer, shorter winter hours, $10-30) come with two generous sides like the sweet potato fries or crunchy onion rings; a big hit is the Black and Blue Steak, which comes slathered in a Cajun rub and bleu cheese.

Whiskeytown Lake

ACCOMMODATIONS

For something more than a standard-issue motel, stay at the **Bridge House Bed and Breakfast** (1455 Riverside Dr., Redding, 530/247-7177, www.bridgehousebb.com, $119-189). The distinctive yellow house with a steeply pitched roof is along the Sacramento River just a few blocks from historical downtown Redding. Inside, you'll find a tranquil haven in one of four rooms. Each room is named after a bridge and is decorated with prints of its namesake and attractive furniture. All rooms have TVs, spa bathrobes, and lots of amenities—the two largest rooms boast upscale "massage tubs." Four additional (and just as comfy) rooms next door in The Puente are owned by the same innkeepers as the Bridge House.

TRANSPORTATION AND SERVICES

Redding is on I-5 about 160 miles (3 hours) north of Sacramento and acts as the gateway to the Shasta and Lassen region. Redding is easy to navigate by car and parking is plentiful and free. The **Redding Municipal Airport** (RDD, 6751 Woodrum Circle, 530/224-4320, http://ci.redding.ca.us) offers flights on United Express, which runs multiple daily nonstop trips to and from San Francisco. Flying in and out of the small airport isn't cheap, but ticketing and security lines are short.

Most visitors to the region will need a car to explore farther. Outside of the nearby airports, the best opportunities to rent a car are in Redding at **Hertz** (773 N. Market St., 530/241-2257; 6751 Woodrum Circle in the airport, 530/221-4620, www.hertz.com, $250-550 per week) and **Budget** (2945 Churn Creek Rd., 530/225-8652; 6751 Woodrum Circle, 530/722-9122, www.budget.com, $182-1,245 per week). **Avis** (6751 Woodrum Circle, 530/221-2855, www.avis.com, $204-1,235 per week) has an office at the airport. **Enterprise** (217 Cypress Ave., 530/223-0700, www.enterprise.com, $172-387 per week) has a full range of cars in stock.

Redding has the only major medical services available in the entire Shasta-Lassen region. **Mercy Medical Center Redding** (2175 Rosaline Ave., 530/225-6000, www.redding.mercy.org) has a 24-hour emergency room with a full trauma center for major medical problems.

Shasta Lake

Shasta Lake doesn't look like most lakes. Rather than a bowl shape, the lake is fed by three major rivers—the Sacramento, the Pit, and the McCloud—plus Squaw Creek, and each of these has an arm of the lake named after it. To create this sprawling artificial lake, five towns were drowned. The remains are still down there, most sunk so deep that even scuba divers cannot explore them. Altogether, the lake has 29,500 acres of surface area, and it's 517 feet deep when it's full. It also has 369 miles of shoreline, which means lots of great places for camping in a tent or an RV as well as hiking and wildlife viewing. The unusual layout of this lake makes it all the more interesting for houseboats, waterskiing, fishing, swimming, canoeing, and wakeboarding.

The lake's four main arms and its many inlets all have their own characters, shapes, and surprises. Surrounding many fingers of the lake and some of the bigger pools are marinas, campgrounds, resorts, cabins, and restaurants for lakeside vacations. Marinas dot the shores of the lake's fingers, offering boat rentals, gas, snacks, water, ice, and more. For those few who don't want to spend all day every day on the water, hiking trails and 4WD roads thread through the forested wilderness areas surrounding the lake.

There are several very small towns close to Shasta Lake and Shasta Dam. At the south side of the lake is the tiny City of Shasta Lake. You won't find much besides a couple of motels and a pizza parlor. At the north side of the lake is Lakehead, right on I-5 midway between Redding to the south and the city of Mount Shasta to the north.

SIGHTS
★ Lake Shasta Caverns

Summer lake visitors can find themselves longing for cool air—hard to come by at Shasta in August. The best natural air-conditioning in the region is inside the **Lake Shasta Caverns** (20359 Shasta Caverns Rd., Lakehead, 530/238-2752 or 800/795-2283, www.lakeshastacaverns.com, 9am-4pm daily Memorial Day-Labor Day, 9am-3pm daily Apr.-May and Sept., tours 10am, noon, 2pm daily Oct.-Mar., adults $24, ages 3-15 $14). Tours begin across the lake from the caverns at the Caverns Park and gift shop. In summer, tours leave every 30 minutes 9am-4pm. When your tour is called, you walk down to the boat launch and board a broad flat-bottomed ferry with plenty of bench seats and a canopy. On the quick ride across a narrow section of the lake, the pilot regales you with tales of the caverns. At the dock, where boaters can meet their tour groups, if they prefer, you board a bus and take a staggeringly steep drive 800 feet up to the cavern entrance. The road has some fabulous views out over the lake and all the way to Mount Shasta.

Your cavern tour guide meets you at the entrance and leads you into an artificial tunnel. You'll head up a bunch of stairs and into a series of natural limestone and marble caverns. The guide describes the amazing formations that spring from the walls, the ceiling, and the floor. The cathedral size of most of the cavern areas and the railed walkways help to remind visitors not to touch the delicate stalactites, drapes, pancakes, and ribbons of "cave bacon" that decorate each space. You're welcome to bring a camera to record the marvels here, but memories may provide better lighting.

Both kids and adults enjoy the tour of the Lake Shasta Caverns, but you'll want to keep an eye on younger children throughout the trip for their safety. No matter how hot it is outside, bring a jacket or sweater for your tour; the caverns remain cold year-round. The tour isn't extremely strenuous, but you need to be able to walk and to climb 100 stairs at a time. To get to Shasta Caverns, take the exit for O'Brien Road on I-5 north of Redding.

Shasta Caverns also offers a **Lake Shasta Dinner Cruise** (530/238-2752 or

Shasta Lake

800/795-2283, www.lakeshastadinnercruises.com, 6pm-8pm Fri.-Sat. Memorial Day-Labor Day, adults $65, under age 12 $33). The cruises depart from the Lake Shasta Caverns Gift Store, the same location as the regular cavern boat trips, 17 miles north of Redding, near I-5 exit 695. Dinner cruises may also be available at a slightly earlier time for a few weeks after Labor Day; call for reservations.

Shasta Dam

Completed in 1945 and operated by the U.S. Bureau of Reclamation, **Shasta Dam** is a massive concrete dam that is second in size only to Hoover Dam. At 60 stories high and weighing 30 billion pounds, it is an impressive sight, and the water it stores is one of the reasons California has such fertile farmland.

Even if you're not fascinated by engineering statistics and superlatives, the **one-hour tour** (9am, 10:15am, 11:30am, 1pm, 2:15pm, and 3:30pm daily Memorial Day-Labor Day, 9am, 11am, 1pm, and 3pm daily Labor Day-Memorial Day, free) is a great experience, and it offers one of the best ways to get a broad view of Shasta Lake. Tours are limited to 40 people; it's recommended to arrive 45 minutes before start time. The tours begin at the **visitors center** (530/275-4463, 8am-5pm daily). It's a bit of a walk from the parking lot. To explore the area yourself, you can walk across Shasta Dam daily 6am-10pm to take in the views of the lake and Mount Shasta. This is a beautiful walk, especially at sunset, and one of many wonderful vantage points to see and photograph the mountain.

Shasta Dam is officially located at 16349 Shasta Dam Boulevard. To get here, take I-5 exit 685 onto Shasta Dam Boulevard. Drive west six miles on Highway 151 to the Shasta Dam visitors center.

Marinas

Most of the marinas along the shores of Shasta Lake provide all the rentals and services you'll need. One of the nearest marinas to the Shasta Caverns gift shop and loading dock is the **Shasta Marina Resort** (18390 O'Brien Inlet Rd., Lakehead, 800/959-3359, www.shastalake.net, Apr.-Oct.). Easily accessed from I-5 toward the south end of the lake, this marina offers midsize houseboats and SeaSwirl BowRider ski boats with wakeboard towers. Marina facilities include a gas dock, a convenience store with ice and swimsuits, and a boat launch (free with moorage or houseboat rental).

The **Packers Bay Marina** (16814 Packers

Lake Shasta Caverns

Bay Rd., Lakehead, 530/275-5570 or 800/331-3137, www.packersbay.com, 8am-6pm Mon.-Sat., weekly houseboat rentals $1,365-7,135) is located in Packers Bay, a couple of miles west of I-5 near the big bridge. Getting to the marina from Redding is tricky; you must get off northbound I-5 at the exit for Shasta Caverns and O'Brien Road, then get back on I-5 southbound to reach the Packers Bay Road exit. A small independent operator, this marina offers some of the rare honest-to-goodness modest houseboats on Shasta Lake. No pets are allowed on any boats.

Bridge Bay Resort Marina (10300 Bridge Bay Rd., Redding, 530/275-3021 or 800/752-9669, www.bridgebayhouseboats.com, patio boat $110-840, ski boat $190-1,250, houseboat $1,050-3,500) is the largest on the lake, part of a full-scale resort with a large rental fleet that includes small-medium houseboats, closed-bow speedboats, patio boats, and ski boats. Three docks are available for various kinds of services. The Courtesy Dock, located next to the launch ramp, is open to the public.

Jones Valley Marina (22300 Jones Valley Marina Dr., Redding, 530/275-7950 or 877/468-7326, www.houseboats.com, $3,533-15,965, open year-round) is situated on the secluded Pit River Arm, away from the higher-traffic areas near the bridge, but still accessible from Redding and I-5. The McCloud Arm and the Squaw Creek Arm adjoin this marina (one of the few that sells gas in this part of the lake). Jones Valley Marina has a floating recreation area, wheelchair-accessible docks and houseboat, modest houseboats, plus the usual array of patio party boats and smaller craft.

FOOD

The **Bridge Bay Resort** (10300 Bridge Bay Rd., Redding, 530/275-3021, www.bridgebay-houseboats.com, 8am-3pm Mon.-Wed., 8am-9pm Thurs.-Sun., $8-20) has a casual dining room that's perfect for lakeside vacationers. The lengthy menu has plenty of American favorites. Seating is on the porch or inside with views of Shasta Lake through the large windows. Upstairs is a **lounge** (4pm-10pm Fri.-Sat., 11am-9pm Sun.), with its own share of views.

On the east side of the lake, the Silverthorn Resort has the best (and only) pizza at the **Silverthorn Pizza and Pub** (16250 Silverthorn Rd., Redding, 530/275-1571 or 800/332-3044, www.silverthornresort.com, 4pm-9pm Thurs., 2pm-midnight Fri., noon-midnight Sat., noon-9pm Sun. late May-early

Shasta Dam

Sept., $6-29). This casual eatery offers ice-cold beer and piping-hot pizzas. A huge deck overlooking the lake lures people out for cocktails.

In the little town of Shasta Lake, you'll find fast food as well as one local place with a little character, the **Old Mill Eatery** (4132 Shasta Dam Blvd., Shasta Lake, 530/275-0515, 7am-3pm Wed. and Fri.-Sun., 8am-2pm Thurs. $11-16), noted for its large portions of basic fare such as hamburgers, omelets, and pancakes, its low prices, and its friendly hometown atmosphere.

The **Lakeshore Villa Market** (20750 Lakeshore Dr., Lakehead, 530/238-8615, 7am-8pm daily winter, 7am-9pm Sun.-Thurs., 7am-10pm Fri.-Sat. Memorial Day-Oct.) has plenty of food plus basic camping, fishing, and outdoor recreation supplies for visitors staying at the north end of the lake. The market often stays open until 10pm during the summer if business permits.

ACCOMMODATIONS

If your main purpose is to visit Shasta Dam, a good place to stay is the **Shasta Dam Motel** (1529 Cascade Blvd., Shasta Lake, 530/275-1065, www.shastadammotel.com, $50-75). Just four miles from the dam, this is a simple little motel without many amenities, but it does have an outdoor pool. Free Internet access is also on the menu, though management does not guarantee that it's always working.

In the woods one mile south of the lakeshore, the **Fawndale Lodge & RV Park** (15215 Fawndale Rd., 530/275-8000 or 800/38-0941, www.fawndale.com, $73-123) offers comfortable lodge rooms and cabins at bargain prices. You can't see the lake from the lodge, but the surrounding forest has charm, and the garden and pool offer beauty. Rooms include a fridge, a microwave, and a private bath. Suites have full kitchens, sleeping space for six, and air-conditioning. The decor is rustic wood walls and furniture. Tent campers are welcome at Fawndale ($18-21); full-hookup RV spots ($30) are available, though you may need a reservation to guarantee a spot.

Toward the north end of the lake, the **Shasta Lake Motel** (20714 Lakeshore Dr., Lakehead, 530/238-2545 or 886/355-8189, www.shastalakemotel.com, $80-140) is a favorite for regular visitors. For low rates you'll get air-conditioning, cable TV, and microwaves. Each room glows softly with wood-paneled walls and furniture, and the decor is rustic prints and artifacts. All the twin and double beds are extra long, making them a treat for people over six feet tall. Enjoy the motel pool or walk down to the shores of the lake. The motel is only a few minutes off I-5, close enough for convenience but not so near that you'll be listening to the trucks all night.

The ★ **Bridge Bay Resort** (10300 Bridge Bay Rd., Redding, 800/752-9669, www.sevencrown.com, $115-190) has one of the best locations of any resort here, right where the big I-5 bridge crosses the lake. It's close to the center of the lake's arms, making its full-service marina a perfect spot from which to launch a boat. Bridge Bay also includes a restaurant and a store with groceries, souvenirs, and bait and tackle. The lodgings aren't terribly stylish; rooms are decorated with particle-board furniture and generic prints. But this is a cheerful, family-friendly place—many of the rooms sleep 4-6, and some have full kitchens.

Well east of I-5, on the tip of a small peninsula in the Pit River Arm, the **Silverthorn Resort** (16250 Silverthorn Rd., Redding, 530/275-1571, www.silverthornresort.com, $594-1,194 per week, houseboats $4,990-8,490 for 7 nights) has the advantage of a location right on the water. The views from the common areas and guest cabins are phenomenal, and the resort has its own full-service marina with houseboats for rent. Cabins rent only by the week in summer and require a three-day minimum the rest of the year. Each cabin sleeps 4-6 people (the large family cabin can handle 8). Inside, you'll find wood-paneled interior walls and simple but attractive lodge-style decor. All cabins include a full kitchen with a full-size fridge. Bedrooms are small but cute, and the atmosphere is woodsy and restful. Book your boat rentals with the marina at the same time you book your cabin to ensure that you get what you want. A small grocery store and a "Pizza and Pub" room offer easy shopping and dining on-site.

CAMPING

For a nominal fee, the U.S. Forest Service rents ★ **Hirz Mountain Lookout Tower** (information 530/275-8113, reservations 877/444-6777, www.recreation.gov, late Apr.-mid-Oct., up to 4 people $75). Located in the Shasta-Trinity National Forest, this 20-foot tower is on top of a 3,540-foot peak, so the views are phenomenal. In addition to the vast overview of the McCloud Arm, you can see both Mount Lassen and Mount Shasta. Getting here is a little tricky. Drive 5 miles down a dirt road (Forest Rd. 35N04) in a high-clearance 4WD vehicle, then walk the last 0.25 mile, and climb a couple of flights of metal steps to the tower.

For more traditional camping in the vicinity of Shasta Lake, one of the best places around is the **Hirz Bay Campground** (Gilman Rd., 20 miles northeast of Redding, 530/275-1589, www.fs.usda.gov, reservations 877/444-6777, www.recreation.gov, reservations accepted mid-May-mid-September, walk-ups only mid-Sept.-mid-May, $20-35). This 42-site U.S. Forest Service family campground has nice amenities, such as flush toilets, picnic tables, and paved parking. It also offers easy access to the lake via the Hirz Bay boat ramp.

TRANSPORTATION AND SERVICES

Most people come to Shasta Lake by car via I-5, which runs over the lake in two different places. Bridge Bay is one of the more popular spots on the lake because of its proximity and easy access to I-5. The Sacramento Arm to the north is also easily accessible from I-5.

The **Shasta Lake Ranger Station** (530/275-1587, www.fs.usda.gov, 8am-4:30pm Mon.-Fri. year-round) sells campfire permits and permits to enter the Trinity Alps Wilderness. For the Shasta Wilderness, go to the **Mount Shasta Ranger Station** (204 W. Alma St., Mount Shasta, 530/926-4511, 8am-4:30pm Mon.-Sat. Memorial Day-Labor Day, 8am-4:30pm Mon.-Fri. Labor Day-Memorial Day). The nearest major medical facilities are in Redding.

Lassen Volcanic National Park

Lassen Volcanic National Park (www.nps.gov/lavo, 530/595-4480, 9am-5pm daily, visitors center 530/595-4480, 9am-5pm daily Apr.-Oct., 9am-5pm Wed.-Sun. Nov.-Mar., $20 per vehicle, $10-15 pp for visitors on bike, motorcycle, foot, or visiting as part of a large group) resulted from the merger of two National Monuments—**Cinder Cone** and **Lassen Peak**—in 1916. As such, it is one of the oldest national parks in the United States; it is also one of the remotest and most primitive. A paved road runs through the middle of the park, making it easy in summer for visitors to enjoy many of the major attractions—including the park's active volcanic features. The rugged weather and isolated location mean that a visit to Lassen Volcanic National Park is a trip to a largely unspoiled wilderness rather than an overdeveloped amusement park with rocks. A good half of the park has only minimal dirt-road access and offers its rugged beauty only to those travelers willing to hike for miles into the backcountry. Even the trails and campgrounds accessible by the paved main road maintain a kind of charm that's hard to find in the more popular California parks.

Mount Lassen itself is an active volcano with a long recorded history of eruptions, the last of which took place in 1914-1917. The mountain is a beautiful sight, and it's only accessible to most people during the short summer months when the temperatures rise and the snow melts.

SIGHTS

Lassen Volcanic National Park has ample hiking trails, lovely little ponds scattered throughout, and many campsites that let visitors settle in and really enjoy the amazing panoramas of Mount Lassen. A wonderful loop drive through the park takes you from the stark slopes and jagged rocks of the most recent eruption around the back to an enormous ancient crater, the remains of a long-gone volcano as big as or bigger than Mount Shasta. Beyond the bounds of the national park, national forest lands allow for additional exploration.

Although it is officially open year-round, snow chokes the area from as early as October until as late as June, closing the main road through the park and making even the lower-altitude campground snowy and cold. The only time to visit Lassen is the height of summer; most visitors pick August and early September. Call 530/595-4480 for updates on road conditions before planning a trip.

Kohm Yah-mah-nee Visitors Center

Lassen's first permanent year-round visitors center, **Kohm Yah-mah-nee Visitors Center** (530/595-4480, www.nps.gov/lavo, 9am-5pm daily Apr.-Oct., 9am-5pm daily Wed.-Sun. Nov.-Mar.), opened in 2008, which was 92 years after the park was created. The name Kohm Yah-mah-nee is from the language of the local Maidu people and means "snow mountain," which was their name for Lassen Peak.

Awarded the highest level of Leadership in Energy and Environmental Design (LEED) certification, this modern, comfortable, state-of-the-art facility was worth the wait. It's got an auditorium showing films about the park, interactive exhibits illuminating local geology and ecology, an unusually well-stocked snack bar and grill, a souvenir-and-sundries shop, an attractive amphitheater, a first-aid center, and large modern restrooms. Outside, strategically placed benches make great spots to enjoy lunch or a snack while you take a load off and enjoy gorgeous views of the mountains. One of the best features for a group with mixed ages and abilities is the very short interpretive trail just outside, with paved walkways and informative signage.

the crater of Cinder Cone

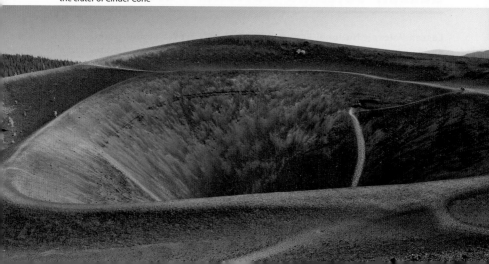

Lassen Volcanic National Park

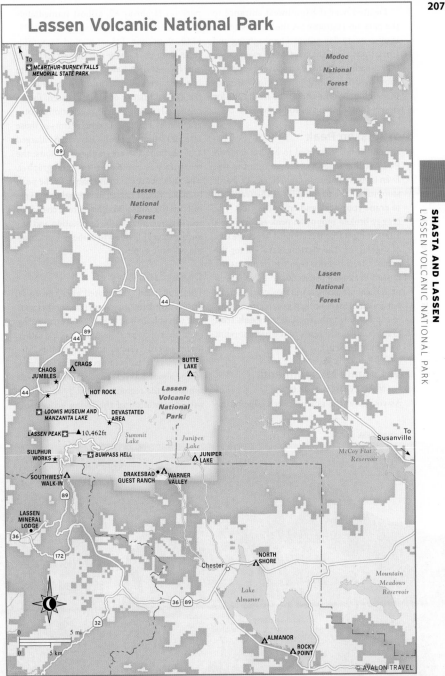

To
★ McARTHUR-BURNEY FALLS
MEMORIAL STATE PARK

Modoc
National
Forest

89

Lassen
National
Forest

44

Lassen
National
Forest

44 89

BUTTE
LAKE

CHAOS
JUMBLES ★ CRAGS

HOT ROCK

Lassen
Volcanic
National
Park

44 ★

★ LOOMIS MUSEUM AND
MANZANITA LAKE

DEVASTATED
AREA

LASSEN PEAK ★ ▲10,462ft

Summit
Lake

Juniper
Lake

To
Susanville

SULPHUR
WORKS ★ ★ BUMPASS HELL

JUNIPER
LAKE

McCoy Flat
Reservoir

SOUTHWEST
WALK-IN

DRAKESBAD ●
GUEST RANCH

WARNER
VALLEY

89

LASSEN
MINERAL
LODGE

36

172

NORTH
SHORE

Chester

Mountain
Meadows
Reservoir

Lake
Almanor

36 89

32

0   5 mi

0   5 km

ALMANOR

ROCKY
POINT

© AVALON TRAVEL

Located near the southwest entrance to the park on Highway 89, the visitors center is open every day except Thanksgiving and Christmas, and it's accessible even when other roads in the park are closed because of snow (which is common). It's convenient to the Sulphur Works and to the trailheads for Brokeoff Mountain and Ridge Lakes.

★ Lassen Peak

It's not as tall as it used to be, but **Lassen Peak** still reaches 10,457 feet into the sky. Even if you're not up to climbing it, it's worth stopping at the parking lot at the trailhead to crane your neck and enjoy the view. The craggy broken mountain peak is what's left after the most recent eruption—hence the lack of vegetation. The starting elevation for the summit trail is 8,000 feet, which means the Lassen Peak trailhead tends to be cool even in the heat of summer. You may need to break out a windbreaker or light sweater if you plan to explore at length. The **Lassen Peak Trail** (5 miles, difficult) leads to the highest point on Mount Lassen.

★ Loomis Museum and Manzanita Lake

As you enter the northwestern edge of the park on Highway 89, almost immediately you'll find **Loomis Museum** (530/595-6140, 9am-5pm Fri.-Sun. mid-May-mid-June, 9am-5pm daily mid-June-Oct., free) and **Manzanita Lake.** Inside the museum is a wonderful opportunity to learn about the known history of Mount Lassen, focusing heavily on the 1914-1915 eruptions photographed by Mr. B. F. Loomis. Prints of those rare and stunning photos have been enlarged and captioned to create these exhibits; the museum was named for the photographer, who later became a major player in the push to make Mount Lassen a national park. This interpretive museum offers a rare chance to see, through photos, the devastation and following stages of regrowth of the ecosystem on the volcanic slopes.

Chaos Jumbles

The broken and decimated area known as **Chaos Jumbles** may seem like another spot that was splashed with rocks and lava during the 1915 eruption of Mount Lassen, but rather than a volcanic eruption, this interesting formation was actually caused by a massive avalanche about 300 years ago. The results look similar to the regions affected by volcanoes, with devastation of the living ecosystem,

Lassen Peak

displacement of massive rocks, and the general disorder of the landscape. The avalanche that occurred here was so big and came down so fast that it actually trapped a pocket of air underneath it, adding to the destruction. Now visitors can enjoy a wealth of new life, including a broader-than-average variety of coniferous trees. The newness of the living landscape has allowed a greater variety of competing types of plants to get a foothold.

Hot Rock

No, it's not hot anymore, but this huge boulder, called **Hot Rock,** was untouchable back when the Loomises explored the eruption zone soon after the 1915 blast. Frankly, the site isn't all that amazing now, except when you think that that big rock remained warm to the touch for months. The Hot Rock turnout also offers more great views of the Devastated Area.

Devastated Area

It seems like an odd name for a point of interest, but in fact the **Devastated Area** is one of the most fascinating geological and ecological sites in California. When Mount Lassen blew its top in 1915, after nearly a year of sporadic eruptions, a tremendous part of the mountain and all the life on its slopes was destroyed. Boiling mud and exploding gases tore off the side of Lassen's peak and killed all the vegetation in the area. A hail of lava rained down, creating brand-new rocks, in sizes from gravel to boulders, across the north side of the mountain.

Today visitors can easily see how a volcano's surface ecosystem recovers after an eruption. First, park at the Devastated Area lot and take the interpretive walk through a small part of the recently disrupted mountainside. You'll see everything from some of the world's youngest rocks to grasses and shrubs to tall pine trees. Be sure to check out the photos in the Loomis Museum that depict the area during and immediately after the eruption for a great comparison to the spot as it looks now.

The Devastated Area offers ample parking, and the interpretive walk is flat and wheelchair accessible. Don't pick up any of the red and black volcanic rocks; they are part of the redeveloping ecosystem and necessary to the area's recovery.

Summit Lake

Lassen National Park is dotted with tiny lakes, though many might better be called ponds or puddles. One of the most popular and most easily accessible of these is **Summit Lake,** along the main road. The bright and shiny small lake attracts many campers to its two forest-shaded campgrounds. There's an easy walk around the lake that lets you see its waters and the plants that proliferate nearby. You can also follow one of the small trails down to the edge of the water to eke out a spot on the miniscule beach with all the other visitors who come to escape the heat. You can swim and fish in Summit Lake, and even take rafts and canoes out to paddle around. No power boats are permitted on any lake in Lassen Volcanic National Park.

★ Bumpass Hell

The best and most varied area of volcanic geothermal activity on Lassen is at a location called **Bumpass Hell** (6 miles from the southwest entrance). The region was named for Kendall Vanhook Bumpass, who, during his explorations, stepped through a thin crust over a boiling mud pot and severely burned his leg, ultimately losing the limb. In fact, the tale of the unfortunate Bumpass illustrates a good point for travelers visiting the mud pots and fumaroles: Stay on the paths! The dangers at Bumpass Hell are real, and if you step off the boardwalks or let your children run wild, you are risking serious injury.

Still, a hike down to Bumpass Hell on the Bumpass Nature Trail is fun. As long as you're careful, it's worth the risk. You'll need to walk about two miles from the parking lot and trailhead out to the interesting stuff—boiling mud pots, fumaroles, steaming springs, and pools of steaming boiling water cluster here. Prepare for the strong smell of sulfur, more evidence that this volcano is anything but extinct. Boardwalks are strategically placed through the area, creating safe walking paths for visitors.

The spacious parking lot at Bumpass offers stunning views to the east and south, giving you a hint at the scope of the ancient volcano that once stood here. Right at the parking lot you can see a famous "glacial erratic," a boulder carried along by a glacier; this one is about 10 feet high, demonstrating the colossal forces of nature that have been at work in this park over the millennia. There are also primitive toilet facilities in the parking lot.

Sulphur Works

For visitors who can't quite manage the trek out to Bumpass Hell, the **Sulphur Works** offers a peek at the geothermal features of Lassen from the main road. A boardwalk runs along the road, and a parking area is nearby, making it easy for visitors to get out of the car and examine the loud boiling mud pots and small steaming stream. The mud pots both look and sound like a washing machine, sending up steam and occasional bursts of boiling water. Keep hold of your children.

Starting from the Sulphur Works is a two-mile round-trip trail to Ridge Lakes. It's a fairly steep climb, but the payoff at the top is a view of two alpine lakes between Brokeoff Mountain and Mount Diller. Along the way, you'll walk through beautiful green meadows dotted with bright yellow wildflowers and then into a forest before reaching the lakes.

HIKING

Most of the easy interpretive walks and short day hikes run out to the sights of Mount Lassen Volcanic National Park. For hikers who want to get out and away from the more heavily visited areas but still make it back to the car before dark, several moderate-difficult hiking trails offer adventure, challenge, and maybe even a touch of solitude.

Be aware that the lower elevations of Mount Lassen's trails are still more than 7,000 feet above sea level. If you're planning to do serious hiking, it's good to come a day early, if you can, to acclimate to the elevation.

Lassen Peak Trail

The must-do hike for any serious hiker is **Lassen Peak Trail** (5 miles, difficult, 3-5 hours round-trip). A large parking lot with chemical-toilet facilities is at the trailhead, and you're likely to see a lot of other cars here. This path not only takes you to the highest point on Mount Lassen, it's also a starkly beautiful, unusual trail that offers long views of the rest of the park and beyond.

The climb to the top is dramatic, challenging, and worth it. It's not actually a long hike—only 5 miles round-trip—but the trail gains more than 2,000 vertical feet in only 2.5 miles on the way up. The trail is well graded and has many switchbacks, which help manage the steepness. And some good news: Exhibits along the way explain some of the fascinating views of volcanic remains, lakes, wildlife, and rock formations.

The recent (by geologic standards) eruption and prevailing weather conditions leave this peak without much plant life, which means nothing blocks your views downward and outward, and the rocky terrain is visually interesting. Only the last 0.25 mile or so actually involves any scrambling over large rocks; most of the trail is just a steady upward walk. When you get to the top, ooh la la! Be sure to turn all the way around to get 360-degree views back down to the newest volcanic landscape, across to the remains of the giant caldera of a huge extinct volcano, and then out north toward the Cascade Range, where you'll see Mount Shasta shining in the distance.

Kings Creek Falls Trail

The **Kings Creek Falls Trail** (Hwy. 89, road marker 32, 3 miles round-trip, moderate) starts out easy. The initial walk begins downhill to the falls. Be sure to stop to admire the small cascade and pool and maybe sit down and have a snack as you prepare for the 700-foot climb back up to the trailhead. This is a good hike for fit day hikers who've already been on the mountain for a few hours.

Summit Lake to Echo and Twin Lakes

It's the length of the trail that runs from **Summit Lake to Echo and Twin Lakes** (east side of Summit Lake, 8 miles round-trip, moderate-difficult) that makes it challenging. But you can choose how many little lakes you really want to see if you run short of breath. The elevation gain over the course of this long trail is only 500 feet in total—a gentle slope in these mountainous reaches. A pleasant and sedate four-mile walk is out to Echo Lake. It's another two miles to get to Upper Twin Lake and back, and two more miles to reach Lower Twin Lake. You might want to wear a swimsuit under your hiking clothes on hot summer days to cool off in one of the lakes before trekking back to base.

Brokeoff Mountain

For a good solid all-day hike with some invigorating uphill stretches, climb **Brokeoff Mountain** (Hwy. 89, road marker 2, 7.5 miles round-trip, difficult). Brokeoff makes a good second- or third-day Lassen hike, after you've seen the sights and climbed Mount Lassen. It's near the Kohm Yah-mah-nee Visitors Center and the southern entrance to the park along Highway 89, so it can serve as a last big adventure before you head back to the Bay Area or points south. Brokeoff involves a 2,600-foot ascent from a mile-high starting point, so the thin air and rigorous climb can be quite difficult for hikers who are unused to altitude or are out of shape. On the other hand, if you're ready for it, this is one of the prettiest and most serene hikes in the more visited section of the park. Enjoy the pretty mountain streams and stellar views out over the mountains and valleys of Northern California.

ACCOMMODATIONS AND FOOD

Accommodations near Lassen Volcanic National Park are few and far between. Plan to camp in the park, or stay near Redding or Chester and take day trips into the park. The nearest lodgings are about nine miles south in Mineral.

Lassen Mineral Lodge (Hwy. 36, Mineral, 530/595-4422, www.minerallodge. com, May-early Nov., $85-115) is on Highway 36 near the southwest entrance to the park. The lodge offers 20 small motel-style rooms with private baths and few frills; pets are not

Brokeoff Mountain

allowed. The lack of TVs and telephones encourages visitors to get out and enjoy the park and its surrounding landscape. Hiking and fishing are favorite pastimes of lodge guests. The on-site **Mineral Lodge Restaurant** (8am-8pm daily summer, 8am-7pm Sat. and 8am-6pm Sun. winter, $12-21) has a bar and is open to nonguests.

Located near the southern entrance station is the ★ **Drakesbad Guest Ranch** (end of Warner Valley Rd., Chester, 866/999-0914, www.drakesbad.com, June-mid-Oct., $189-209, $119 and up spring and fall). This all-inclusive ranch includes three meals per day, though the national park entrance fee is not included. Spend anywhere from a couple of hours to a full day taking guided trail rides through the national park ($75-190) on one of the ranch's horses. Guests can board their own horses ($37.50 per day, includes feed). You're also within easy reach of hiking trails. Bring your tackle along on a walk or a ride to take advantage of the fishing available in the local lakes and streams; the ranch can also connect you with local guides from the **Lake Almanor Fly-Fishing Company** (530/258-3944, http://almanorflyfishing.com). The ranch even has a wonderful pool that's fed by the water from a local hot spring.

Mount Lassen offers little in the way of dining options. If you're camping, shop in Redding and bring in lots of food. Don't expect to get to a restaurant during your stay unless you're willing to drive a long way. The best food available in the park is at **Kohm Yah-mah-nee Visitors Center** (Hwy. 89, 530/595-4480, www.nps.gov/lavo, 9am-5pm daily Apr.-Oct., 9am-5pm Wed.-Sun. Nov.-Mar.), where the snack bar sells burgers, slices of pizza, hot coffee, and ice cream. Hours can vary during the winter.

Part of the year, a small **camp store** (9am-5pm daily late spring and early fall, 8am-8pm daily summer) opens near Manzanita Lake. The store sells gifts, camping supplies, hot food, snacks (including s'more ingredients for campfires), and ice cream. The park's only gas

station is located right behind the camp store and is available 24 hours per day.

CAMPING

Lassen has eight campgrounds, four of which are accessible via the paved park road. The remaining four campgrounds offer primitive facilities or are accessible via a short hike.

Inside the Park

Closest to the park entrance along Highway 89 is the pleasant and serene **Manzanita Lake Campground** (179 sites, 877/444-6777, www.recreation.gov, May-Oct. or first snowfall, $18). By far the largest campground in Lassen, Manzanita Lake has a full slate of amenities, including flush toilets, potable running water, fire rings or pits, picnic tables in all campsites, and an RV dump station, and it's the only place in the park where showers are available, in the nearby camp store (quarters required). Trailers and campers up to 35 feet are allowed. Advance reservations are recommended at this popular campground.

Farther south along Highway 89 at Summit Lake, ★ **Summit Lake North** (46 sites, 877/444-6777, www.recreation.gov, late June-Sept., $18) and ★ **Summit Lake South** (48 sites, 877/444-6777, www.recreation.gov, late June-late Sept., $16) campgrounds are some of the most popular spots in the park, so reservations are recommended. Visitors can swim in Summit Lake, easily accessing its banks from trails and campsites. These two developed campgrounds have flush toilets, fire pits, and tables, but to be safe bring enough potable water for the length of your trip for drinking and washing. At 6,650 feet elevation, the Summit Lake campgrounds are among the highest in the park. Be sure to take it easy setting up camp on your first day so that you can get used to the thin air.

Out in the backcountry, well away from the main road, the **Butte Lake Campground** (101 sites, 877/444-6777, www.recreation.gov, June-Oct., $16) shows off the beauty of Lassen to its best advantage. Despite its remote location at the northeast corner of the park, you'll find this to be a fairly well-developed campground, with pit toilets and running water. Check with the National Park Service to be sure the water at this campground is drinkable. Each site has a fire pit and a table. Trailers and RVs up to 35 feet that can negotiate the road can camp at Butte Lake. To reach the campground, take Highway 44 to the dirt road, and then drive six miles to the campground. Reservations are recommended.

The **Juniper Lake Campground** (18 sites, June-Oct., $10) takes campers farther off the beaten path. Since the campground is located on the east side of the park, at the end of a rough dirt road near Chester, you'll do much better if you're a tent camper rather than if you have an RV or trailer. This small campground beside beautiful Juniper Lake has pit toilets, fire pits, and tables, but the water isn't drinkable. Either bring purifying agents or your own drinking water in containers. Because the campground is at almost 7,000 feet elevation, definitely take it easy during your first day.

Warner Valley (18 sites, June-Sept., $14) is along the south edge of the park. Another small gem of a semi-developed campground, Warner Valley has pit toilets and drinking water as well as tables and fire pits at each site. Trailers are not allowed: Although the dirt road is only one mile long, it's too rough for large campers and RVs to navigate.

The only campground open year-round is the **Southwest Walk-In Campground** (21 sites, tents only, first-come, first-served, $14). Plumbing is turned off in this campground when the snows come, so don't expect flush toilets and drinking water unless it's summer. However, you won't be far from the Kohm Yah-mah-nee Visitors Center, so you can use the facilities and get water there. The restrooms are located outside the main building, so they're accessible all night. "Walk-in," by the way, doesn't mean this is for backpackers only. The parking lot for this campground is quite close to the campsites; you just can't park right beside your tent.

Outside the Park

The tiny town of Chester is 25 miles east of the southwest entrance to Lassen Volcanic National Park on Highway 89/36. From Red Bluff, the 70-mile drive takes about 1.5 hours. The primary interest is Chester's proximity to the southwest entrance station of the national park and activities on nearby Lake Almanor.

Drakesbad Guest Ranch (Chester Warner Valley Rd., 866/999-0914, www.drakesbad.com, June-mid-Oct., $189-209 summer) offers the closest lodging to Lassen Volcanic National Park. The all-inclusive rates include meals, and stables, hiking trails, and fishing opportunities are nearby. Drakesbad is 17 miles north of Chester on Chester Warner Valley Road.

North Shore Campground (Hwy. 36/89, 530/258-3376, www.northshorecampground.com, Apr.-Oct., tents $26-36, RVs $40-56) is two miles east of Chester with 130 sites for tents and RVs. Facilities include picnic tables, fire rings, drinking water, restrooms with flush toilets and showers, and a small store.

Rocky Point Campground (916/386-5164 or 530/284-1785, www.pge.com, May-Oct., $23-46) is at the southwest end of Lake Almanor, with 131 sites for tents and RVs. Facilities include picnic tables, fire rings, drinking water, and vault toilets. You can reserve most of those sites online starting in early March; 24 sites are first-come, first-served only.

Almanor North and South Campgrounds (877/444-6777, www.recreation.gov, May-Sept., $15-100) are operated by the Almanor Ranger District (530/258-2141, www.fs.fed.us). Situated directly on the lake, the 104 campsites offer great views of Lassen as well as biking, hiking, and fishing. Facilities include picnic tables, fire rings, drinking water, vault toilets, and a boat ramp. To reach the campgrounds, turn right on Highway 89 two miles west of Chester and drive six miles to County Road 310; turn left for the campground.

TRANSPORTATION

Lassen Volcanic National Park is about three hours north of Sacramento on I-5. At the town of Red Bluff, exit I-5 onto Highway 36 and head east for about 43 miles before making a left onto Highway 89, which leads into the park.

On Mount Lassen, **winter** usually begins in November and continues through May. Highway 89 through the park closes from about October until May, June, or July depending on the weather and snowfall in any given year. Highway 89 serves as the main road through the park, and the visitors center, campgrounds, trailheads, and lakes cluster along it. You can get a good feel for Lassen by taking a day trip along Highway 89.

South of Lassen, roads run from the tiny town of Chester to the park. Warner Valley Road is paved, but other roads from the town to the park are good old-fashioned dirt. On the northeast side of the park, Highway 44 leads from the remote town of Susanville. Dirt roads lead from Highway 44 into the park.

However you get to Lassen, be sure to bring a good map and possibly a GPS device as well. The only **gas** station in the park is located by the Manzanita Lake Campground store. It's available 24 hours per day and accepts credit cards. Gas up in Red Bluff, Chester, or Susanville before driving up to Mount Lassen.

Mount Shasta and Vicinity

One of the most iconic natural formations in the United States, Mount Shasta is stunning from every angle at any time of day. Like Utah's Delicate Arch or the Grand Canyon, Shasta is immediately recognizable from calendars, book covers, and photographs on the walls of hotels and restaurants—but you need to see it with your own eyes. Once you experience it in person, you'll never forget it, and you'll find yourself longing to see it again.

The gorgeous sunny village known as the "City of Mount Shasta" is a shining jewel of Northern California. A visit is a must for hikers, boaters, skiers, anglers, and others who revel in the outdoors.

TOP EXPERIENCE

★ MOUNT SHASTA

Mount Shasta is a tremendous dormant volcano that last erupted in 1786. Although it may someday erupt again, for now it's a delightful playground and a magnetic attraction. At 14,162 feet, Mount Shasta is the 49th highest peak in the country, the fifth highest in California, and the second tallest volcano in the Cascade Range. It has a 17-mile perimeter

and stands pretty much alone, with no close neighbors of anywhere near similar stature. In winter, snow covers much of the mountain; in summer a series of glaciers make the mountain appear white and glistening.

Mount Shasta is an appealing, if not always accessible, destination for skiers of all kinds. Some people like to go to the back side of the mountain (the "bowl"), climb as high as they can with skis strapped to their backpacks, and then ski down. Families with children can bring plastic sleds, hike a little less far up the mountain, and then let everyone sled down. The **Bunny Flat Trailhead** (6,900 feet) is recommended for this kind of activity.

Hiking

Some of the best hiking in California can be found on and around Mount Shasta. This beautiful region abounds with waterfalls, pine forests, rivers, streams, and fascinating geology. Informal camping and backpacking (wilderness permits required) can create a wonderful multiday hiking trip. Day hikes offer everything from easy strolls great for kids to strenuous miles that can take you up to minor mountain peaks for tremendous views of the whole southern Cascade mountain region.

GRAY BUTTE

If you want to hike on Mount Shasta but don't have the time or the training to go all the way to the top, try a nice day hike to **Gray Butte** (3.4 miles, moderate), an intermediate peak on the south slope of the mountain. The trail runs east across Panther Meadow, which is quite beautiful and full of heather and other wildflowers, and into the nearby forest. At the first fork in the trail (just past 0.5 miles), choose the fork to the right. In 1.5 miles, you'll come to a saddle—a good place for views, but there are more to come. From the saddle, bear right again to reach the peak of Gray Butte in less than 0.25 mile. Not only can you see the peak of Mount Shasta, but on a clear day you can see all the way to Castle Crags, Mount Eddy, and even Lassen Peak. Return the same way. To reach the trailhead, take I-5 to the Central Mount Shasta exit. Turn east onto Lake Street, which becomes Everitt Memorial Highway. In 13.5 miles, you'll reach Panther Meadows Campground, which has extensive trail signage and plenty of information about the ecology and wildlife of the area.

SIMS FLAT HISTORIC TRAIL

The name of the **Sims Flat Historic Trail** (Sims Rd., south of the river, 1 mile, easy) refers to the name of a former logging town, but the trail itself is flat too. Sims Flat was once a bustling town with the railroad running through it to carry products from the busy sawmill to the big cities that needed lumber. Nearly a century later, a few signs tell the history of this diverse former town. Take in the up-close views of Mount Shasta, which looms over Sims Flat.

LAKE SISKIYOU TRAIL

If you like hikes that are big on views and not so much about climbing, the place for you is the **Lake Siskiyou Trail.** This mostly flat seven-mile loop circumnavigates the spectacular lake and offers changing perspectives on the nearby mountains, bridges, and shorelines. You can start from any one of several well-marked parking areas and enjoy four rest stops with pit toilets and helpful signage along the way. This gently undulating, easy-to-follow trail is also a great place for a run. To get to one of the main trailheads, start from the town of Mount Shasta and head west on W. A. Barr Road until you see signs for Lake Siskiyou Trail.

Mount Shasta

MOUNT EDDY

For a lovely long hike that takes you up to views of the whole of the Far North mountain region and into Oregon, trek up **Mount Eddy** (Forest Rd. 17, Mount Shasta Ranger Station 530/926-4511, 10 miles round-trip, difficult). This steep trail reaches a 9,000-foot peak, where you can turn around and check out the various highlights of the Cascade Range: Mount Shasta, Mount Lassen, the Trinity Alps, and even Mount McLoughlin in Oregon. Bring plenty of water as there's none at the Deadfall Lake trailhead, where the hike starts. Along the way, Deadfall Lake and Deadfall Creek both offer what appears to be very clear, clean water, but, as always, it's best to treat it before you drink it. The early part of the trail is mostly mild climbing, and there's some shade to keep you cool as you do it. The last 0.8 mile is the hard part: It's a series of steep exposed switchbacks, guaranteed to give you a workout no matter how fit you are. The reward is worth it, though: You'll soon be on a truly exceptional mountaintop with views you'll remember for a long time. If you're not up for such a long day hike, consider an overnight camping trip; the lake makes a great informal primitive campground.

Climbing

Climbers from all over the world come to tackle Shasta's majestic 14,162-foot peak. Be sure to pack your sturdiest hiking boots and your strongest leg muscles; fewer than one-third of the 15,000 intrepid mountaineers who try to conquer Mount Shasta each year actually make it to the top. Shasta's steep and rocky slopes, its long-lasting snowfields, and the icy glaciers that persist year-round all contribute to making this one of the most difficult climbs in the country. On top of all that, the thin air at this altitude makes breathing a challenge. If you're serious about doing the climb, though, you can get plenty of help from the locals.

Bagging this peak is not for everyone, but for healthy, well-trained, and well-equipped climbers, this can be the adventure of a lifetime; you'll see Mount Shasta up close in ways that most casual visitors could never imagine. The main climbing season is June-August, but do not expect sunny weather and easy footing even then. Casual visitors should exercise care accessing even the trailheads that lead to Shasta's peak. Some of the dirt roads around the base of the mountain require a 4WD vehicle, and weather conditions can have severe impacts on the roads. Contact the **Mount Shasta Climbing Advisory** (530/926-4511, www.shastaavalanche.org) before your trip for current weather and climbing conditions.

Mountaineering and glacier classes are available, and several guides and outfitters can provide equipment and even lead you up the mountain. Private mountain guide **Robin Kohn** (530/926-3250, www.mountshastaguide.com) maintains a comprehensive website with up-to-date information and helpful advice. Contact her for help hiring a guide or arranging trip plans. **Shasta Mountain Guides** (Mount Shasta, 530/926-3117, www.shastaguides.com, $550-750 pp) has been taking climbers to the top for decades. Join one of its scheduled group trips along various routes up the mountain, or call to arrange a custom expedition. Snowboard and backcountry ski tours ($129-650 pp, minimum 2 people) are also available. **Sierra Wilderness Seminars** (210 E. Lake St., 888/797-6867, www.swsmtns.com, Jan.-Sept., $525-695 pp) leads groups of up to eight people up Mount Shasta. If you want to learn as well as climb, check out the Ice & Snow Expedition Course (June-Sept., 5 days $995). The rigorous training on the use of ice axes and crampons, and what to do if someone falls into a crevasse, may come in handy during the climb to Shasta's summit along a "glaciated north-side route." If you're new to this, start with one of the company's one-day courses, such as the Ice Ax Clinic (Jan.-Aug., $135), which teaches basic snow-climbing techniques. Or make a weekend of it by combining this with the Basic Mountaineering Clinic (1 day $150). All clinics and climbs take place on Mount Shasta.

Alpine Skills International (530/582-9170, www.alpineskills.com, $495-980 pp) provides training and guides for climbers of various skill levels. The founder, Bela Vadasz, has earned a lifetime achievement award from the American Mountain Guides Association and was instrumental in establishing certification programs for mountain guides in the United States.

Fishing

Almost all the major rivers and feeder streams running through the Mount Shasta region are open for fishing. You can tie your fly on and cast into the McCloud, Sacramento, and Trinity Rivers, among many others. These rivers carry salmon, steelhead, and trout. If you want a guide to help you navigate these waters, contact one of the many services that can take you out to the perfect fishing holes. For fly-fishing or scenic rafting tours, call **Jack Trout International Fly Fishing Guide Service** (530/926-4540, www.jacktrout.com, year-round, $325-400 for 2 people, gear rentals $25). Jack will take you out on the McCloud, Klamath, Upper and Lower Sacramento, Pit, or Trinity Rivers, or to Hat Creek. Jack supplies all the gear and brings a gourmet lunch complete with wine and homemade strawberry shortcake for you to enjoy by the side of the river. It you're an expert fly-fisher who wants to improve your technique, Jack can help you. If you've never been fly-fishing before but think you might like to try, give him a call—he loves beginners and says they always catch something. You have to bring a California fishing license, available online at www.dfg.ca.gov.

Outdoor Adventures Sport Fishing (530/221-6151 or 800/670-4448, www.sac-riverguide.com, year-round by appointment only, $175-600 pp/day) takes anglers on fly-fishing drift trips on the Sacramento and Trinity Rivers, where guides specialize in fishing for salmon, trout, and steelhead; they'll also take you on a jet-boat trip on Shasta Lake, where you can catch salmon and trout.

Rafting and Kayaking

In the Cascades, the best white-water rafting is definitely on the Trinity River. A good guide service to take you out onto this river is **Trinity River Rafting** (530/623-3033 or 800/307-4837, www.trinityriverrafting.com, guided trips $65-180 per day, kayak rental $40 per day). In addition to its flagship runs on the Trinity, this major rafting company runs on the Klamath, Salmon, and Upper Fork Sacramento Rivers as well as Canyon Creek. Depending on where you're staying and what level of rafting you can handle, you can choose the river to paddle. Half-day to three-day trips ($65-375) are available. Select from a placid Class I-II float suitable for the whole family to a Class IV-V run for fit, experienced rafters only. Trinity Rafting also rents rafts and 1-2-person inflatable kayaks for paddlers who want to go off on their own.

Another major player in the northern mountains rafting scene is the **Bigfoot Rafting Company** (530/629-2263, www.bigfootrafting.com, $69-410). With day trips on the Trinity and Salmon Rivers and multiday rafting campouts on the Trinity and Klamath Rivers, Bigfoot presents a depth of knowledge of the rivers it runs. Your guide will know a great deal about the history and natural surroundings of your chosen river and, as a bonus, can cook you up fabulous meals on the full-day and multiday trips. Bigfoot also rents equipment.

Skiing and Snowboarding

The snowpack on Mount Shasta each winter creates a haven for downhill skiers, cross-country skiers, snowboarders, and snowshoers. The place to go for all this is the **Mount Shasta Ski Park** (Ski Park Hwy., off Hwy. 89 between McCloud and Mount Shasta, 530/926-8600 or 530/926-8619, www.skipark.com, 9am-4pm daily mid-Dec.-mid-Apr., night skiing 3pm-8pm Thurs.-Sat., adults $20-55, ages 8-12 and seniors $12-33, under age 8 $7-13). This small but exciting downhill park has 425 skiable acres, three chairlifts, and two carpet lifts. Nearly half the runs are open for night skiing (if there's enough snow) and the Marmot lift in the beginner area makes a perfect spot for new skiers of all ages to gain their snow legs (at a fraction of the cost of the resorts at Lake Tahoe). Half-day discount lift tickets and night-skiing-only lift tickets make skiing here even more attractive for snow-loving bargain hunters. Call ahead if you're interested in night skiing (adults $20, youth and seniors $12, children $7); the park offers extended night skiing until 9pm on some holiday weekends, but sometimes doesn't offer night skiing at all if snow conditions aren't favorable.

Cross-country skiers can also get their fix at the **Mount Shasta Nordic Center** (Ski Park Hwy., 1 mile before downhill park, 530/925-3495, www.mtshastanordic.org, 9am-4pm daily winter, adults $15, youth and seniors $8). Since 2006 this lovely ski center has been a not-for-profit organization dedicated to the promulgation of physical and mental health through cross-country skiing. It's open for the winter season, as determined by when the snow comes, usually in late December, and closes in mid-April; the center is closed Tuesdays after Jan. 1. The center has about 16 miles of groomed trails for cross-country skiing, and there's ample backcountry where you're welcome to explore off-trail. Snowshoers are allowed on the groomed trails as long as they stay to the side. Call the hotline (530/925-3495) for conditions and grooming updates. Memberships and other donations are tax deductible. The organization sponsors clinics, demos, races, and other events. Ski and snowshoe rentals and lessons are available.

Horseback Riding

The wilderness around Mount Shasta beckons to anyone with a penchant for trail rides. One good outfit that serves the area is the **Rockin Maddy Ranch** (11921 Cram Gulch Rd., Yreka, 530/340-2100, www.rockinmaddyranch.com, year-round, by reservation only, 1-2 hours $55-75 pp, full day $175 pp). Choose from rides like the popular 90-minute Shasta

View ride, featuring grand vistas of the mountain, or a full-day excursion into the Marble Mountains. Rockin Maddy allows smaller children to ride double on the same horse.

Camping

The **Shasta-Trinity National Forest** (Shasta Ranger District, 530/926-4511, www.fs.usda.gov, 8am-4:30pm Mon.-Fri.) manages three campgrounds on Mount Shasta. All are popular and fill quickly on summer weekends. Reservations are not accepted; weekdays are when it's easiest to find space. **McBride Springs** (12 sites, first-come, first-served, late May-Oct., $10) is conveniently located on the mountain at 5,000 feet, just four miles from Mount Shasta city. Facilities include drinking water, vault toilets, and picnic tables. ★ **Panther Meadows** (Everitt Memorial Hwy., 1.7 miles past Bunny Flat, 15 sites, first-come, first-served, mid-July-Nov., free) is 14 miles northeast of Mount Shasta city at an elevation of 7,500 feet on the slopes of Mount Shasta. Because of the high elevation, it can be cold at night and snowed in well into summer. Although this is a walk-in campground, it is only 100-500 feet from the parking lot to the campsites. Facilities include picnic tables, fire rings, and vault toilets; bring your own water. Because this is the most popular campground on Mount Shasta, the maximum stay is three nights. The third campground is **Red Fir Flat** (530/926-4511, $12), a group site (8-75 people) available by reservation. Facilities include picnic tables, fire rings, and vault toilets, but not drinking water.

Dispersed camping is allowed throughout the Shasta-Trinity National Forest. A wilderness permit is required on Mount Shasta itself. Otherwise, anywhere you want to sleep is fair game, though you do need a campfire permit, available for free at any ranger station. For permits and information, contact the **Mount Shasta Ranger Station** (204 W. Alma St., 530/926-4511, www.fs.usda.gov, 8am-4:30pm Mon.-Fri. fall-spring, 8am-4:30pm Mon.-Sat. summer).

The main street of Mount Shasta city is Mount Shasta Boulevard, and nearly every business in town includes "Shasta" in its name. A plaque outside the **Mount Shasta Police Department** (303 N. Mt. Shasta Blvd.) proclaims "Mount Shasta—Where Heaven and Earth Meet," and in the town center, near a coin-operated telescope aimed at the mountain, is an inscription of a quote from Joaquin Miller that reads "Lonely as God and white as a winter moon."

Food

Mountain Song Natural Foods (314 N. Mt. Shasta Blvd., 530/926-3391, www.mountain-song.biz, 10am-5pm Mon.-Sat., noon-4pm Sun.) offers health-food groceries, including a large selection of trail mix, homemade bread from the Oven Bakery, and local beans from Northbound Coffee Roasters, along with the best dried mango. The regular Monday **farmers market** (N. Mt. Shasta Blvd. between E. Castle and E. Alma Sts., 530/436-2532, www.mtshastafarmersmarket.com, 3:30pm-6pm Mon. early June-mid-Oct.) is a treat.

Seven Suns Coffee and Café (1011 S. Mt. Shasta Blvd., 530/926-9701 or 530/926-9700, 6am-4pm daily, $7-12) is very pleasant. Breakfast and lunch are available in the form of local baked goods, burritos, wraps, and salads. The café makes all sorts of coffee and espresso drinks and sells beans by the pound. There's a spacious porch on the south side with umbrella-shaded tables, but the prime spot is the front sidewalk, with two small tables. During the summer, visit the small coffee outpost across the street with drive-through and walk-up windows.

The best baked goods in town come from the ★ **Oven Bakery** (214 N. Mt. Shasta Blvd., 530/926-0960, www.theoven-bakery.com, 7:30am-noon Mon. and Wed., 7:30am-5pm Tues. and Thurs., 7:30am-noon, 5pm-7pm Fri., 2pm-5pm Sun.), which not only supplies the local coffee shops and grocery stores but also has its own storefront, where you can come in, sit down, and enjoy a hot scone and a cup of coffee while you smell the bread baking in the background. The bakery also serves mouthwatering pizzas every Friday night ($24).

At the south end of town is the ★ **Wayside Grill** (2217 S. Mt. Shasta Blvd., 530/918-9234, www.waysidegrill.com, 4pm-10pm daily summer, 4:30pm-9pm Wed.-Sun. winter, $10-30), a big casual place that's so popular there's sometimes a wait in spite of its size. Reservations at busy times of year are a good idea. It has lots of brick-oven pizza plus burgers, sandwiches, pasta, steak, tacos, 12 beers on tap, and wine. All menu items are also available to take out and there's an outdoor patio with mountain views and live music on weekends.

At the north edge of the town center is the retro **Burger Express Frosty & Grill** (415 N. Mt. Shasta Blvd., 530/926-3950, 11am-6pm Mon.-Fri., 11am-5pm Sat., $5-22). With great 1950s-style red stools and tables, a cheerful red-and-white counter, and a checkerboard floor, the place feels up-to-the-minute and delightfully old-fashioned at the same time. It serves basic burgers and hot dogs, shakes, sundaes, and soft-serve ice cream in cones. Eat in or take your food out to the small patio and enjoy the sun and the community. Either way, the eating and the nostalgia are good.

Casa Ramos (1136 S. Mt. Shasta Blvd., 530/926-0250, www.casaramos.net, 11am-9pm daily, $8-15) is a small chain of 11 authentic Mexican family restaurants in Northern California. The local incarnation is particularly cheerful and welcoming. "It's Taco Time!" says the sign out front, and when you see the place, you'll probably agree. Prices are reasonable, portions are ample, and the whole family is welcome. It has specials for kids and lots of choices, including steak, chicken, and cheeseburgers, to satisfy anyone who isn't in the mood for Mexican.

At the white-tablecloth end of the dining spectrum in Mount Shasta is **Lily's** (1013 S. Mt. Shasta Blvd., 530/962-3372, www.lilys-restaurant.com, 8am-2pm, 5pm-9pm daily,

$12-24), a lovely, spacious place with a white picket fence. Breakfast is a full selection of omelets, pancakes, and other American favorites, plus huevos rancheros, biscuits and gravy, and healthier choices like tofu and fruit. Lunch is usually burgers, salads, and choices like the eggplant hoagie and the walnut dal burger. Dinner entrées might include a tofu vegetable curry or char-grilled filet mignon au poivre flambéed with brandy, finished in a green peppercorn sauce, and wrapped in bacon.

Accommodations

One of the first lodgings you'll come across as you arrive from the south is the **Finlandia Hotel and Lodge** (1621 S. Mt. Shasta Blvd., 530/926-5596, www.finlandiamotelandlodge. com, $65-125), offering comfortable, pet-friendly rooms, from a single with a queen bed at the low end to a suite with king bed and a kitchen at the top. The lodge ($200-250) can sleep up to eight people; amenities include three bedrooms, a fully equipped kitchen, a sauna, an outdoor spa, and wood-burning fireplace crafted out of lava rock.

One of the most pleasant inexpensive lodging options is the ★ **Mount Shasta Ranch Bed & Breakfast** (1008 W. A. Barr Rd., 530/926-3870 or 877/926-3870, www. stayinshasta.com, $45-125), offering homey luxury just slightly out of town. The budget-friendly rooms in the Carriage House offer small spaces, queen beds, and shared baths. The separate Cottage ($150-180) is the largest option, with two bedrooms that can comfortably sleep up to six. The four rooms in the Ranch House are spacious and furnished with country-Victorian antiques and tchotchkes, and each has its own big private bath. All rooms include a full country breakfast.

The cute **Dream Inn** (326 Chestnut St., 530/926-1536 or 877/375-4744, www.dream-innmtshastacity.com, $80-160) offers bed-and-breakfast accommodations at the base of the magnificent mountain. The four small inexpensive upstairs rooms have shared hall-way baths. Downstairs, a bigger white antique

bedroom has its own private bath and a view of Mount Eddy out the lace-curtained window. Next door, two large suites share space in a Spanish adobe-style home; each has its own living space, bath, and truly homelike cluttered decor. Rooms at the Dream Inn include a daily full breakfast.

If you drive north through the center of town to the other side, you'll find the **Cold Creek Inn** (724 N. Mt. Shasta Blvd., 530/926-9851 or 800/292-9421, www.coldcreekinn. com, $92-155 summer), a small motel with 19 simple but comfortable rooms and suites, some with mountain views. Amenities include free wireless Internet access, a continental breakfast with organic coffee, and a sundeck for those who want to get out of the room for a while. The inn prides itself on using environmentally friendly cleaning products. All rooms are nonsmoking, and pets are welcome. Cold Creek offers discounts for travelers who stay more than four nights.

To get a sense of life in this region, book one of the rooms at the ★ **Shasta Mountlnn Retreat & Spa** (203 Birch St., 530/926-1810, www.shastamountinn.com, $150-175). The white farmhouse exterior fits perfectly into its semi-alpine setting, while the rooms ooze country charm and modern comforts. Each of the four rooms has its own private bath and memory-foam mattress. In the morning, head downstairs for a healthy continental breakfast and a cup of organic coffee. There are also on-site massage services and a barrel-shaped redwood sauna. The retreat's hosts can guide you to the sacred spots that dot this area.

In a location and a class by itself is the **Tree House** (111 Morgan Way, 530/926-3101, www. bestwesterncalifornia.com, $162-230), a Best Western Plus hotel. It is slightly off the main drag, near the Mount Shasta Shopping Center. Best Western hotels are individually owned and operated, but most of them tend to be at the upper-middle end of the chain hotel spectrum, and the ones designated "Plus" are a little nicer than average. The Mount Shasta version is a large, full-service hotel with an indoor pool, a hot tub, and a fitness center; full hot breakfast included; microwaves, fridges, and blow-dryers in the rooms; wireless Internet access; and a computer station in the lobby. The on-site **Tree House Restaurant** (6:30am-10:30am and 5pm-9pm daily, $13-24) serves breakfast and dinner, and **Cooper's Bar and Grill** (11am-10pm Mon.-Thurs., 11am-11pm Fri.-Sun., $6-10) serves tacos, burgers, pasta, cocktails, wine, and beer.

Off the boulevard are a few more elegant and more pricey places to stay, often with spacious grounds and lots of beautiful scenery. One of the nicest of these is **Mount Shasta Resort** (1000 Siskiyou Lake Blvd., 530/926-3030, reservations 800/958-3363, www.mt-shastaresort.com, summer $159-339, winter $169-289). If you're looking for a spa treatment or a golf course (530/926-3030, 18 holes $30-75) in addition to a beautiful suite to sleep in, this is the place for you. The staff from **Sacred Mountain Spa** (530/926-2331, http://sacredmountainresortspa.com, by appointment 10am-5pm daily, 1-hour massage $90) offers massages, facials, waxing, and hair and nail care on the resort premises. Every room is special at the Mount Shasta Resort. If you want a lakeside deck, a fireplace, a jetted tub, two TVs, or a kitchenette or full kitchen, just ask, and the resort can probably accommodate you. All rooms come with free wireless Internet access, ironing boards and irons, blow-dryers, and all the other amenities expected from upscale lodgings.

Camping

If the campgrounds on Mount Shasta are full, there are several options on the west side of I-5. The McCloud area also has developed camping.

Lake Siskiyou Beach and Camp (4239 W. A. Barr Rd., 530/926-2618 or 888/926-2618, www.lakesiskiyouresort.com, Apr.-Oct.) is located on the shore of glacier-fed Lake Siskiyou, just three miles west of Mount Shasta city. It has hundreds of tent sites ($20) and RV sites ($26-29) with partial and full hookups as well as cabins ($65-250). Plentiful amenities include a beach, boat and equipment rentals,

a **Splash Zone** water park for kids ($8 per hour, $15 per 4 hours), a **Snack Shack** (10am-6pm daily Memorial Day-Labor Day), and the on-site **Lake Sis Grille & Brew** (530/926-1865, 8am-9pm Sun.-Thurs., 8am-10pm Fri.-Sat. Memorial Day-Labor Day, $10-15).

Castle Lake Campground (Castle Lake Rd., 6 sites, first-come, first-served, May-Nov., free) is about nine miles southwest of Mount Shasta city on beautiful Castle Lake. Facilities include picnic tables, fire rings, and vault toilets, but not drinking water. A stay at this campground has a three-night limit.

Chateau Shasta Mobile Home & RV Park (704 S. Old Stage Rd., 530/926-3279, year-round, $25) offers a great location to park your vehicle and enjoy the area. Some of the spots are a bit crowded and exposed, but they all have great views.

Gumboot Lake (Forest Rd. 26, 6 sites, first-come, first-served, June-Oct., free) is an undeveloped campground located on Gumboot Lake about 12 miles west of Mount Shasta city. Facilities include fire rings and a vault toilet but no picnic tables or drinking water. A campfire permit is required.

Transportation and Services

Mount Shasta is on I-5; from Sacramento it's 220 miles (3.5 hours). From San Francisco, the trip is 275 miles and takes 4.75 hours. Parking in the town is usually easy, except during local events that draw numerous visitors. The nearest commercial airport is 60 miles (1 hour) away. **Redding Municipal Airport** (RDD, 6751 Woodrum Circle, 530/224-4320, http://ci.redding.ca.us) is served by United Express.

For wilderness permits and trail advice, head for one of the local ranger stations. The **Mount Shasta Ranger Station** (204 W. Alma St., 530/926-4511, www.fs.usda.gov, 8am-4:30pm Mon.-Fri. fall-spring, 8am-4:30pm Mon.-Sat. summer) can supply wilderness and summit passes, plus park maps and information about current mountain conditions. A summit pass ($20 for three days, $30 for all year) is required when hiking above 10,000 feet on Mount Shasta, and it allows you to climb to the summit; you can buy one at the ranger station during business hours. A free wilderness pass is also necessary. You have the option of self-registering at the trailhead and leaving payment in an envelope as long as you have a check or cash. In person at the ranger station you can use a credit card as well. California campfire permits are free, but you must get them in person, so plan to come to the ranger station during business hours. The Shasta Wilderness requires you to have a permit just to enter, even if you're not spending the night. Those permits are also available at the ranger station or from a self-service station out front.

The town of Mount Shasta has a full-service hospital, **Mercy Medical Center Mount Shasta** (914 Pine St., 530/926-6111, www.mercymtshasta.org), with a 24-hour emergency room.

VICINITY OF MOUNT SHASTA
★ Castle Crags State Park

Castle Crags State Park (20022 Castle Creek Rd., Castella, 530/235-2684, www.parks.ca.gov, $8 per vehicle) is one of the greats in California's extensive network of state parks. With 4,350 acres of land, 28 miles of hiking trails, and some very dramatic granite peaks and cliffs, it is a wonderful destination or a convenient place to camp while you enjoy Mount Shasta to the north or Shasta Lake to the south. You can fish and swim in the Sacramento River, rock-climb the spectacular 6,000-foot crags, take a variety of hikes, or just enjoy stunning views of Shasta and other nearby mountains and ranges.

If you don't have much time, you can still have a nice little walk and a great Castle Crags experience. After you enter at the gate, drive through the park, following the signs for "Vista Point." A paved walk of no more than 0.25 mile from the Vista Point parking lot leads to a spectacular overlook with views all around. Bring your binoculars and your camera.

If you can stay longer, use the Vista Point parking lot to access the Crags Trailhead. The **Crags Trail to Castle Dome** (5.5 miles round-trip) is strenuous but worth every step. If you're a strong hiker with a brisk pace, it will take about 2 hours on the way up and 1-1.5 hours on the way down. Feel free to go slower, though—it's a steep climb with memorable views all along the way. Pull out your camera for an excuse to take lots of

Castle Crags State Park

breaks. About 2 miles up the trail is a sign for Indian Springs, a 0.25-mile jaunt off the main trail.

Castle Crags has more than 40 established **rock climbing** routes plus plenty of wide, open formations for explorers who prefer to make their own paths. You'll get to tackle domes, spires, and walls of granite that reach 6,000 feet into the sky. The crags first thrust upward and then broke off and were scrubbed by glaciers into the fascinating climbable formations visible today. Some favorite climbs at Castle Crags are the Cosmic Wall on Mount Hubris, Castle Dome, and Six Toe Crack.

The park also has a **campground** (www.reserveamerica.com, reservations May-Sept., first-come, first-served Oct.-Apr., $25) with 64 sites as well as 12 environmental sites ($15) available year-round on a first-come, first-served basis. Some sites are close to the freeway and can be loud, but others are tucked deep enough in the pines to feel miles away from civilization.

Castle Crags is easy to find. Take I-5 north toward the city of Mount Shasta and follow signs for the park. From San Francisco, it's a 260-mile trip on I-5 north to exit 724 at Castella. Turn left onto Castle Creek Road, and the park is less than 0.5 mile. If you're coming from the north, the park is just 6 miles south of Dunsmuir and about 13 miles (15 minutes) south of the city of Mount Shasta.

McCloud

A wonderful waterfall to visit is **McCloud Falls** (McCloud Ranger Station, 530/964-2184, www.shastacascade.com) on the McCloud River. At Lower McCloud Falls you'll see roiling white water pouring over a 30-foot rock wall into an aerated river pool below. Middle McCloud Falls resembles a tiny Niagara, a level fall of water that's wider than it is tall. Upper McCloud Falls cascades powerfully but briefly down into a chilly pool that can double as a swimming hole if you're feeling brave. The loop trail that takes you past all three is about 3.5 miles long. To get here, take the McCloud exit from I-5 onto Highway 89

east. After about five miles, look for a sign on the left directing you to Fowlers Camp and Lower McCloud Falls. After another mile is the Lower Falls picnic area, where you can park.

The McCloud area has several campgrounds with access to the McCloud River as well as to nearby Mount Shasta. Popular **Fowlers Camp** (39 sites, first-come, first-served, Apr.-Nov., $15) is at 3,400 feet elevation on the Upper McCloud River. Facilities include picnic tables, fire rings, vault toilets, and drinking water. Fowlers Camp is five miles east of McCloud on Highway 89.

At 3,700 feet elevation, **Cattle Camp** (27 sites, first-come, first-served, Apr.-Nov., $15) is the second campground on the Upper McCloud River. Facilities include picnic tables, fire rings, vault toilets, and drinking water. Cattle Camp is 10 miles east of McCloud on Highway 89.

Ah-Di-Na (16 sites, first-come, first-served, Apr.-Nov., $10) is a remote campground located at 2,300 feet elevation on the Lower McCloud River. Facilities include picnic tables, flush toilets, and drinking water. The campground is located 10 miles south of McCloud. Access is via a rough dirt road.

★ McArthur-Burney Falls Memorial State Park

Often billed as the most beautiful waterfall in California, even by regular visitors to Yosemite, Burney Falls in **McArthur-Burney Falls Memorial State Park** (24898 Hwy. 89, Burney, 530/335-2777, www.parks.ca.gov, $8) has been thrilling viewers for generations. No less a naturalist than Theodore Roosevelt declared these falls one of the wonders of the world. The park is the second oldest in the California State Parks system and is about halfway between Mount Lassen and Mount Shasta.

Burney Falls flows strong and true year-round and is just as beautiful in September as in April. More good news: You don't have to hike to reach the falls; they're right by the parking lot. Still, it's more than worth your time to get out of your car and take a walk around the wide sheets of water that almost look like a miniature Niagara; it's only a quick walk to the pool at the base of the falls. For the best views, take the one-mile hike around the 129-foot waterfall.

The McArthur-Burney Falls campground (Hwy. 89, 530/335-2777, reservations May-Sept. 800/444-7275, www.reserveamerica.com, year-round, $35) has 102 reservable campsites and three primitive hike-in/bike-in sites. It also has 24 cabins ($105) with heaters and platform beds. Facilities include restrooms with flush toilets, showers, picnic tables, and fire rings.

McArthur-Burney Falls Memorial State Park is on Highway 89 near Burney; from Redding, take Highway 299 east to Burney, and then head north on Highway 89 for six miles.

★ Lava Beds National Monument

spectacular Burney Falls

One of the best places to see the results of volcanic activity is at **Lava Beds National Monument** (Hill Rd., 530/667-8113, www.nps.gov/labe, sunrise-sunset daily, visitors center 8am-6pm daily late May-early Sept., 8:30am-5pm daily early Sept.-late May, $10). This fascinating 47,000-acre park is delightfully under visited, no doubt owing to its remote location. With ancient Native American petroglyphs, an unrivalled series of deep and twisting "tube" caves, primordial piles of lava, and an abundance of desert wildlife, it is a mother lode of history, nature, and awe-inspiring sights.

Over the course of about 500,000 years, Medicine Lake Volcano has created an amazing landscape. Among the hiking trails, Modoc battle sites, and scrubby high-desert wilderness are more than 700 caves created by underground lava flows. Some of the caves have been developed for fairly easy access—outfitted with ladders, walkways, and lights—but others remain in their original condition. All are home to whole ecosystems that thrive in the damp darkness.

In summer about 200,000 bats live in the park; 2 of the 14 species represented here live in trees, and the other 12 live in caves. Park officials monitor where and when bats are likely to be concentrated, and they'll steer you away from those places, mainly for the safety of the bats.

HIKING AND CAVING

The **visitors center** (530/667-8113, 8am-6pm daily late May-early Sept., 8:30am-5pm daily early Sept.-late May) recommends bringing up to three flashlights per person to explore the caves, as well as caving or bicycle helmets (it's easy to hit your head on the low ceilings of the caves). The visitors center will lend you a large flashlight and sells a simple helmet ($8.15). For the more challenging caves, gloves, knee pads, a cave map, and a compass are also recommended.

However, you don't necessarily need a lot of equipment to visit the caves here. The short, paved **Cave Loop Trail** (2.25 miles) outside the visitors center leads past 16 different caves—their cool rocky entrances are fascinating in themselves. Three more caves are accessible via a short hiker-only trail beside the visitors center. The park recommends **Mushpot Cave** (770 feet) as an introductory cave; it's well lit and easy to get into.

In addition to the numerous caves are 12 hiking trails. One of the best-known trails is **Captain Jack's Stronghold** (1.5 miles, moderate); the interpretive signage will help you understand the contentious history of this area. Start at the visitors center and take the park's main road seven miles north.

The wide, easy **Schonchin Butte Trail** (1.4 miles round-trip, moderate) leads to a working fire tower, along with the trail built by the Civilian Conservation Corps (CCC) between 1939 and 1941. If a ranger is present when you get to the top, you may be able to go up to the fire tower's lookout deck. To get to the Schonchin Butte Trail from the visitors center, turn left onto the main park road and drive 3.2 miles to the trail sign on the right. From here, it's a 0.5-mile drive on a gravel road to the parking area.

CAMPING

Lava Beds National Monument (Hill Rd., 530/667-8113, www.nps.gov/labe) features one campground, **Indian Well** (43 sites, first-come, first-served, $10), close to the visitors center. The campground has ample potable water, modern restrooms with flush toilets (no showers), and an amphitheater; don't expect much shade at the campsites, however. One of the best features for history buffs are the picnic tables, built by hand out of local lava stone by the CCC in the 1930s.

TRANSPORTATION

Lava Beds National Monument is in the remote northeastern corner of the state, about 70 miles from Mount Shasta city. To get here from I-5, take U.S. 97 north at Weed. Drive 50 miles north, and at the state line just north of Dorris, turn east onto Highway 161. Continue 16 miles east on Highway 161 to Hill Road, then turn right (south), and drive 9 miles to the park entrance. Plan at least two hours for the drive from Weed, and note that U.S. 97 gets snow at high elevations.

a cave in Lava Beds National Monument

Tule Lake

Tule Lake

Near the very tip of California, north of Lava Beds National Monument, is large and lovely Tule Lake, visible from a long distance across the high-desert landscape. Although the lake you see today is still beautiful, blue, and deep, it is much smaller than it used to be. One of the early projects of the U.S. Bureau of Reclamation was to "reclaim" the land beneath Tule Lake and Lower Klamath Lake and make it available for homesteading. What was once underwater, and later homestead land, is now mostly farmland.

You can still see some striking evidence of the lake's original size from **Petroglyph Point,** a section of Lava Beds National Monument located east of the lake and separate from the main lava beds area. Along **Petroglyph Point Trail,** you may wonder how the ancient markings on the rock walls high above got up there. Tule Lake was much bigger 5,000-6,000 years ago, and what is now hot, dry land was all underwater. The Modoc artists simply steered their boats to the edge of the lake and worked on the lakeshore rock face—now far out of reach.

From 1942 to 1946 Tule Lake was the name of one of the 10 internment camps where Japanese Americans were held during World War II. In commemoration of the events that went on here and in the other camps, in December 2008 a total of nine sites were made into one national monument, collectively called the **Tule Lake Unit, World War II Valor in the Pacific National Monument** (530/260-0537, www.nps.gov/tule). This is the site of the largest and most controversial of the internment locations, where a "segregation center" stayed open even after the war, incarcerating Japanese Americans who had given unsatisfactory answers to the infamous loyalty questionnaire.

The temporary **visitors center** (800 Main St., 530/260-0537, 8:30am-5pm daily late May-early Sept.) is in the Tulelake-Butte Valley Fairgrounds Museum (530/667-5312, 9:30am-4:30pm Mon.-Fri.). Take a tour (530/260-0537, 1pm Sat. late May-early Sept., hours vary early Sept.-late May) of the very interesting **Tule Lake Segregation Center**'s jail and **Camp Tulelake.** The visitors center at Lava Beds National Monument (530/667-8113) can arrange tours during the off-season.

Lake Tahoe

South Shore 231

North and West Shores 244

Truckee-Donner 250

Transportation and Services ... 255

Highlights

★ **Heavenly Gondola:** Winter or summer, a ride up the gondola at Heavenly ski resort rewards with views from 9,163 feet (page 231).

★ **Emerald Bay:** The most beautiful section of the "Most Beautiful Drive in America," Emerald Bay sparkles year-round (page 233).

★ **Ed Z'berg Sugar Pine Point State Park:** Visit one of the state's best parks and ski on trails from the 1960 Olympics (page 244).

★ **The Village at Squaw Valley:** This adorable mountainside village is the perfect place to while away a winter day amid boutiques, galleries, and restaurants (page 244).

★ **Donner Memorial State Park:** Donner offers a lake that's perfect for recreation, along with interpretive trails and monuments illuminating one of the most compelling stories about the settlement of the West (page 250).

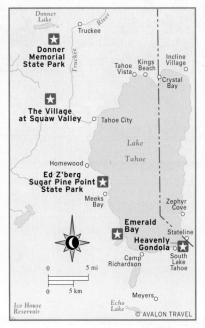

S parkling blue Lake Tahoe and its surrounding mountains, lakes, ski resorts, hiking trails, hot springs, charming mountain towns, casinos, and varied wilderness areas say "vacation" to just about anyone.

The Tahoe area has an international reputation as a skiing paradise, with some of the finest ski resorts in the nation and many opportunities for skiers, snowboarders, cross-country skiers, and snowshoers. Tahoe is slightly less crowded in the summer months than during ski season, and the weather is gorgeous every day. Between the pristine lake and the unspoiled wilderness areas, it is a delight for wakeboarders, water-skiers, campers, hikers, and families to swim, sun, play in the sand, rent kayaks, or just be in a beautiful place.

Californians often refer to Lake Tahoe simply as Tahoe, but the locals get more specific— it's all about the North Shore, with ski resorts, the South Shore, with its sprawling town, and East Shore, with glittering casinos just across the state line in Nevada.

It's possible to drive all the way around the lake, stopping at both the South and North Shores and enjoying the eastern and western perspectives as well as the attractions and natural beauty of both California and Nevada. Whether you're looking for radical recreation or traditional relaxation of the more restful kind, you can find it at Tahoe year-round.

PLANNING YOUR TIME

Lake Tahoe is usually accessible year-round. Weekend jaunts are popular, but one- to two-week vacations also are common because there's so much to see and do. The number-one reason people come to Tahoe is for the snow. The North Shore boasts the most downhill ski resorts, many of them clustered near Truckee. However, it's not unheard of to run into a snowstorm on Memorial Day, so keep snow chains in the car.

Summers (June-Aug.) are usually sunny and clear, but thanks to the elevation around the lake (5,000-7,000 feet), the temperature never gets too high, with average highs around 80°F and nights getting down to the 40s.

Previous: Emerald Bay; Lake Tahoe's unique boulders. **Above:** Heavenly Gondola.

Lake Tahoe

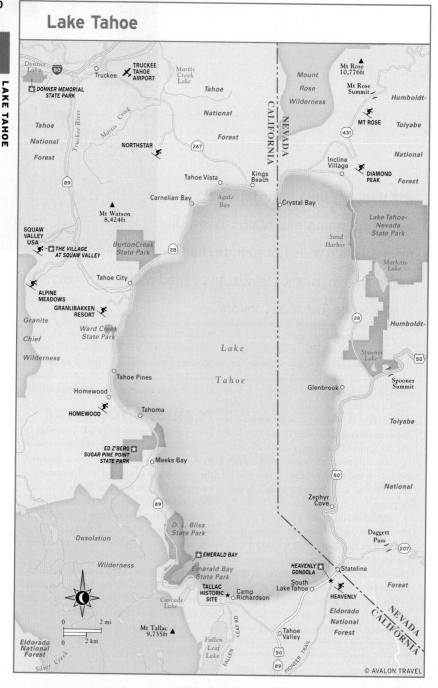

© AVALON TRAVEL

One Day in Tahoe

U.S. 50 enters the Tahoe region on the popular **South Shore** of Lake Tahoe. Stop at one of the casinos across the **Nevada** state line, or take in the lay of the land on the **Heavenly** gondola. Highway 89 heads west to glittering **Emerald Bay,** where you can hike the **Rubicon Trail** to **Vikingsholm Castle.** Continue north on Highway 89 to reach the **North and West Shores,** which hold Tahoe's legendary appeal. The lively center of **Tahoe City** has plenty of restaurants, hotels, and campgrounds. Spend the night at the **Pepper Tree Inn** in Tahoe City, or camp at General Creek Campground in **Sugar Pine Point State Park.**

In the morning, take Highway 89 east toward Truckee. Along the way, you'll pass Squaw Valley, which may merit a detour through **The Village at Squaw Valley.** On your way home, stop by **Donner Memorial State Park.** Although the park history tells a grim tale, the hiking trails around the lake are quite beautiful.

WINTER OPTION

Nothing says winter like sliding down the slopes at Tahoe. Numerous ski resorts line the lake and mountains. **Heavenly** rules the roost on the South Shore, while **Squaw Valley** draws in snowboarders and skiers on the North and West Shores. Cross-country skiers should head to **Royal Gorge** in the Truckee-Donner area.

Highway 89 and U.S. 50 are the main arteries to the Tahoe area, and they can become congested and blocked by snow into spring. Bring tire chains and plenty of patience—in inclement weather, it can take up to eight hours to drive here from San Francisco.

South Shore

Approaching Tahoe from the Bay Area or Sacramento, the **South Shore** will likely be your point of entry on U.S. 50 to the town of South Lake Tahoe. If you're looking for basic services such as supermarkets, banks, and drugstores before heading elsewhere, this is the place to stop. You'll find lively restaurants and bars, upscale lodging options, and lovely lake views and beaches. Just west of the California-Nevada border is the ski resort of Heavenly Village, jam-packed summer and winter. Heading east on U.S. 50, the town of South Lake Tahoe becomes Stateline, Nevada, with barely a sign announcing the transition.

SIGHTS

★ Heavenly Gondola

The ride up the **Heavenly Gondola** (1001 Heavenly Village Way, South Lake Tahoe, 775/586-7000 or www.skiheavenly.com, 9am-4pm Mon.-Fri., 8:30am-4pm Fri.-Sun. and holidays in winter; 10am-5pm daily in summer; adults $52, seniors and ages 13-18 $37, ages 5-12 $27) is a must in any season. The gondola travels 2.4 miles up the mountain to an elevation of 9,123 feet, stopping at an observation deck along the way. From here, you can view the whole of Lake Tahoe, the surrounding Desolation Wilderness, and more. Season passes (adults $70, children, youth, and seniors $50) allow multiple rides June-October.

Tallac Historic Site

The **Tallac Historic Site** (Hwy. 89, 3.1 miles north of U.S. 50, South Lake Tahoe, 530/541-5227, www.fs.usda.gov, Sat.-Sun. late May-mid-June, daily mid-June-mid-Sept., free) was originally called "The Grandest Resort in the World." Most of the complex's 33 buildings, including three mansions, exude wealth and privilege. The centerpiece of the 74-acre

South Shore

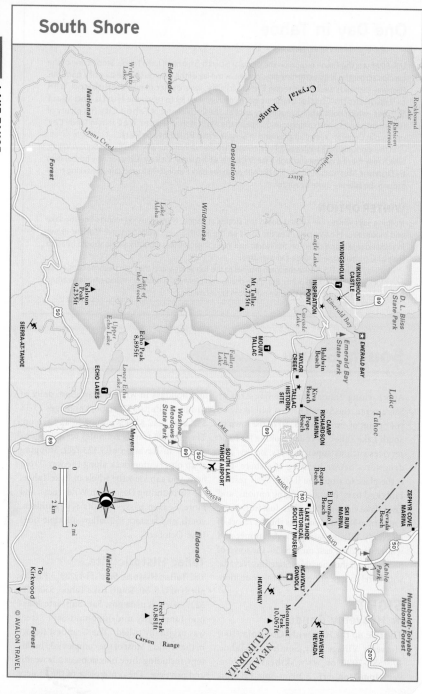

complex is the **Baldwin Museum** (10am-4:30pm daily June-late Sept., free), located in the Baldwin Estate. The museum features exhibits about the local Washoe people and the importance of Lucky Baldwin to the history of California.

You can tour the interior of the 1894 **Pope Mansion** (1pm, 2:30pm Thurs.-Tues. late-May-late June, 11am, 1pm, 2:30pm daily late June-early Sept., reservations recommended, adults $8, children under 13 $3) and sign up for children's activities, like the "Kitchen Kids" workshop (age 6-12, Wed. and Fri. early July-late Aug., $10), where kids learn to cook using old-fashioned recipes in the Pope Estate kitchen.

The **Heller Estate** (530/541-4975, www.valhallatahoe.com) was called Valhalla by its original owners. It is not open for tours but is set aside to showcase the art and music of the Tahoe region. The Heller boathouse has been converted into a 164-seat theater where concerts and plays are presented in summer. Smaller cabins on the grounds serve as summer galleries for photographers and local artists.

The **Pope-Baldwin Recreation Area** includes easy nature trails, a picnic ground, and a beach for swimming and kayaking (rentals are available). In winter, the Tallac buildings are closed, but the grounds are a great spot for cross-country skiing and snowshoeing.

TOP EXPERIENCE

★ Emerald Bay

Driving north from South Lake Tahoe, Highway 89 passes through Emerald Bay State Park. Even if you don't have plans to visit the park, pull over at one of the several scenic overlooks, such as **Inspiration Point** (Hwy. 89, 8 miles north of South Lake Tahoe). Emerald Bay offers views you won't want to miss.

Emerald Bay State Park (Hwy. 89, 10 miles north of South Lake Tahoe, 530/541-3030 or 530/525-3345, www.parks.ca.gov, $10) was designated an "underwater" state park in 1994. It now encompasses the historical Vikingsholm mansion; Fannette Island (mid-June-Feb.), the only island in Lake Tahoe; the Eagle Point Campground; and a boat-in campground on the north side of the bay. In addition, there are miles of hiking trails, including the **Rubicon Trail,** from Emerald Bay State Park to nearby D. L. Bliss State Park.

The elegant Scandinavian-style mansion **Vikingsholm Castle** (Emerald Bay State Park, Hwy. 89, 530/525-9530, www.vikingsholm.org or www.parks.ca.gov, tours 10:30am-3:30pm daily late May-late Sept., grounds free, tours adults $10, ages 7-17 $8, cash or check only) is an architectural gem. Built by a Swedish architect in 1929, the castle-like structure is composed of granite boulders and includes towers, hand-cut timbers, and sod roofs green with growing grass. The interior is furnished with authentic Scandinavian period reproductions. Visitors can enjoy the beach, the grounds, and the exterior at no charge; the mansion is only accessible on the tours. Access is via a steep one-mile trail from the Harvey West parking lot at the **Emerald Bay Overlook** (Hwy. 89, $10).

D. L. Bliss State Park (Hwy. 89, 2 miles north of Emerald Bay, 530/525-3345 or 530/525-7277, www.parks.ca.gov, spring-fall, $10), directly north of Emerald Bay State Park, has some of the best views in Tahoe. Hiking is a popular activity; trails include the **Rubicon-Lighthouse Trail** to Rubicon Point's lighthouse. Swimming is great at the Lester and Calawee Cove Beaches, and trout and salmon fishing are also popular. Three campgrounds are within the park.

SPORTS AND RECREATION
Downhill Skiing and Snowboarding
HEAVENLY

On the less skied South Shore, the queen bee of the few resorts is undoubtedly **Heavenly** (Wildwood Rd. and Saddle Rd., South Lake Tahoe, 775/586-7000, www.skiheavenly.com,

9am-4pm Mon.-Fri., 8:30am-4pm Sat.-Sun. Dec.-Apr., adults $98-125, youth $90-103, children $58-69, seniors $90-103). At 10,067 feet, Heavenly offers the highest elevation of any mountain at Tahoe, along with the longest tubing hill on the West Coast and one ski run that's five miles long.

Parking is a challenge and crowds and lift lines can get bad on weekends and holidays. The **BlueGo Shuttle** (530/541-7149, www.bluego.org, free) picks up at all the major lodging areas around town and drops skiers off at any of Heavenly's four lodges.

KIRKWOOD

The South Shore's mid-tier resort is **Kirkwood** (1501 Kirkwood Meadows Dr., off Hwy. 88, Kirkwood, 209/258-6000, www.kirkwood.com, 9am-4pm daily Dec.-Apr., adults $86-102, seniors $77-92, ages 13-18 $77-92, ages 6-12 $63-74). Kirkwood offers dozens of downhill runs, plus everything from pipes to a cross-country space. Lift-ticket prices change seasonally, and the pricing scheme is complex, with special rates for military personnel and college students, multiday packages, and more. If you prefer to stay where you ski, look into Kirkwood's array of lodges and vacation rentals.

Heavenly ski resort

Sierra-at-Tahoe

For a smaller and less crowded ski experience, **Sierra-at-Tahoe** (1111 Sierra-at-Tahoe Rd., Twin Bridges, 530/659-7453, www.sierraattahoe.com, 9am-4pm Mon.-Fri., 8:30am-4pm Sat.-Sun. late Nov.-Apr., rates vary) has plenty of long, sweeping advanced runs as well as many good intermediate tracks. Eight different eateries are also on the mountain. Sierra-at-Tahoe prides itself on being "the most affordable mountain in Lake Tahoe," so check the website for rates and discounts.

Cross-Country Skiing and Snowshoeing

A **Sno-Park** parking pass (recording 916/324-1222, information 916/324-4442, www.ohv.parks.ca.gov, $5 per day, all-season $25) is required for many forest ski trailheads November-May. You can pick up the pass at the **Placerville Ranger Station** (4260 Eight Mile Rd., Camino, 530/644-2324, 8am-4:30pm Mon.-Fri.), the **Kyburz Silverfork Store** (13200 U.S. 50, Kyburz, 530/293-3172), and the **Tahoe Roadrunner** gas station (2933 U.S. 50, South Lake Tahoe, 530/577-6946). The website lists additional vendors, and you can buy Sno-Park passes online (www.ohv.parks.ca.gov).

There's also **Adventure Mountain** (21200 U.S. 50, Echo Summit, 530/577-4352 or 530/659-7217, http://adventuremountaintahoe.com, 10am-4:30pm Mon.-Fri., 9am-4:30pm Sat.-Sun., $25 per vehicle), a privately operated sno-park on Echo Summit, with snowshoe trails, six groomed sledding runs, and a lodge with a fireplace and café. Equipment rentals include two-person sleds ($10 per day), inner tubes ($20 for 2 hours, $25 all day), and snowshoes with poles ($18 per day). Cash only at the entrance gate, but the lodge does take credit cards.

Sections of the beautiful **Tahoe Rim Trail** (775/298-4485, www.tahoerimtrail.org) can be ideal for snowshoeing, depending on conditions, which are never predictable. The west side of the lake gets a lot more snow than the east. The Rim Trail office suggests calling close to your planned trip dates for an updated report on conditions and specific advice on where to go. In the heart of winter (Jan.-Mar.), the Tahoe Rim Trail Association (775/298-4485, www.tahoerimtrail.org) offers guided snowshoe hikes on Saturday.

Beginner cross-country explorers can have the safest backcountry fun at **Taylor Creek** (Hwy. 89, just west of Camp Richardson, 530/543-2600, www.fs.usda.gov or www.parks.ca.gov), an uncongested but reasonably populous area with many flat marked trails to help newcomers get a feel for the forest. Lots of trails for skiers of all levels run along the South and West Shores of Lake Tahoe.

Water Sports

The vast clear waters of Lake Tahoe are irresistible to water-skiers, wakeboarders, Jet Skiers, and powerboaters. Full-service **Tahoe Keys Marina** (2435 Venice Dr. E., South Lake Tahoe, 530/541-2155, www.tahoekeysmarina.net) is one of the largest marinas, selling gas, providing launch access, and renting slips as well as offering boat rentals and charter fishing trips. **Tahoe Keys Boat & Charter Rentals** (2435 Venice Dr. E., South Lake Tahoe, 530/544-8888, www.tahoesports.com) operates out of the Tahoe Keys Marina and offers boat rentals of various kinds: a 49-passenger 52-foot yacht, pontoon boats, powerboats, kayaks, and Yamaha Jet Skis. Powerboats rent for $145-234 per hour, $435-702 per four hours, and $870-1,404 for eight hours.

The marina at **Camp Richardson** (1900 Jameson Beach Rd., South Lake Tahoe, 530/542-6570, www.camprichardson.com, 9am-5pm daily late May-late June and mid-Sept.-mid-Oct., 8am-8pm daily

boat anchored on Lake Tahoe

mid-June-mid-Sept.) rents kayaks ($20-30 per hour), pontoon boats ($180 per hour, $1,080 per day), paddleboards ($30 per hour), Sea-Doos ($125 per hour), and more. You can also take the 1.5-hour **Rum Runner Emerald Bay Cruise** (530/542-6570, 1pm, 3:30pm daily, late May-mid-Oct., adults $49, children $19).

For a guided kayak tour of Emerald Bay, contact **Kayak Tahoe** (Timber Cove Marina, 3411 Lake Tahoe Blvd., South Lake Tahoe, 530/544-2011, www.kayaktahoe.com, 9am-2:30pm daily, by reservation only, $70-95 pp, minimum 6 people). You'll paddle the entire perimeter of the bay with a knowledgeable guide, stopping at Vikingsholm and Fannette Island. The company also rents kayaks ($20-32 per hour, $30-50 per 2 hours, $65-85 per day) and stand-up paddleboards ($20 per hour, $30 per 2 hours, $65 per day) at Timber Cove Marina.

Fishing

Several companies offer charter trips on Lake Tahoe for anglers looking to score mackinaw, rainbow, and brown trout or kokanee salmon. Operating out of the Ski Run Marina (900 Ski Run Blvd., South Lake Tahoe, 530/541-5448, www.skirunmarina.com) and the Zephyr Cove Marina (760 U.S. 50, Zephyr Cove, NV, 775/586-9338, www.zephyrcove.com), **Tahoe Sport Fishing** (530/541-5448 or 800/696-7797, www.tahoesportfishing.com, $110-120) offers half-day and full-day fishing trips tailored to suit all styles of lake fishing. The fishing boats have heated cabins and modest restroom facilities, and trips include all the trimmings: bait and tackle, cleaning and bagging services, cold beer and soda on board, and a choice of morning or afternoon half-day trips.

With the proliferation of rivers and streams surrounding Lake Tahoe, it's easy to find a good place to cast if you prefer fly-fishing to lake fishing. **Tahoe Fly Fishing Outfitters** (2705 Lake Tahoe Blvd., South Lake Tahoe, 530/541-8208, www.tahoeflyfishing.com, $225-400) can take you on an expert-guided fly-fishing or spin-fishing trip on one of the smaller lakes, Walker River, Carson River, Truckee and Little Truckee Rivers, or the Pleasant Valley Fly Fishing Preserve.

Boat Tours and Cruises

To get out on the water in a big boat, book a cruise with **Lake Tahoe Cruises** (800/238-2463, www.laketahoecruises.com or www.zephyrcove.com). Two honest-to-goodness paddle-wheel riverboats cruise Lake Tahoe on a near-daily basis—even in winter. The first boat, *Tahoe Queen,* sails from Ski Run Marina (900 Ski Run Blvd., South Lake Tahoe, 530/543-6191) and offers a 2.5-hour sightseeing cruise (adults $51, children $15) around Emerald Bay. If you're lucky, Mark Twain may even be your narrator. This is a beautiful way to see the lake, with photo opportunities that never end. If you really want to luxuriate, try the *Tahoe Queen's* sunset cruise (6:30pm daily Sat. May-Oct., adults $83, children $35), which lasts 2.5 hours. It includes a gourmet dinner onboard followed by dancing to live music.

The other boat is the *MS Dixie II,* a rear paddle wheeler that was imported from the Mississippi River. It sails from the **Zephyr Cove Marina** (760 U.S. 50, Zephyr Cove, NV, 775/589-4907, www.zephyrcove.com) and offers a 2.5-hour-long morning or afternoon cruise (adults $51, ages 3-11 $15). The Dinner Dance Cruise (adults $83, children $35) includes an on-board narrator, a live band, and a four-course meal. As with most things in Tahoe, weather can affect the cruise schedules, so be sure to check in advance.

Hiking and Biking
TALLAC HISTORIC SITE

Along the South Shore, hikes range from easy walks along the shore at the **Tallac Historic Site** to hard-core treks up the **Mount Tallac Trail** (Hwy. 89 at Baldwin Beach, South Lake Tahoe, 10 miles round-trip, difficult, wilderness permit required, $5 for overnight hiking). This long hike starts out easy, taking casual strollers past the Floating Island

and Cathedral Lakes, and then gets steeper and harsher as it ascends the front face of the mountain. To access the trail, turn off Highway 89 away from the beach toward a dirt road to the trailhead parking lot. For a more moderate but equally beautiful hike, choose the **Echo Lakes Trail** (Johnson Pass Rd. at Lower Echo Lake, 5-12 miles, moderate-strenuous, wilderness permit required). You can pick your distance on this route, depending on how many small alpine lakes you want to see. Start with a short walk to Upper Echo Lake, where you have the option to catch a water taxi rather than continuing on the trail along the lake. If you keep going, you'll see Tamarack Lake, Lucille and Margery Lakes, Lake in the Woods, and maybe even Aloha Lake.

EMERALD BAY STATE PARK

Emerald Bay State Park is a treasure trove of easy-moderate hiking trails. Near campsite 28 in Eagle Point Campground is the beginning of the **Overlook Trail,** a short (0.5 mile) walking trail to a camera-ready spot. Near campsite 34 and the campfire center amphitheater you can park in a lot and take one of two trails. The first is another short walk to an overlook. The second is the **Rubicon Trail**

(1.7 miles), which takes you to Vikingsholm. The well-marked trail features undulating terrain, shade, and gorgeous views. If it's been a wet year, some sections may be muddy, so wear boots. From the bridge, take a brief (0.2-mile) detour to your left to visit Lower Eagle Falls, or turn right to reach the visitors center in less than a mile. At the visitors center, you can buy tickets for a Vikingsholm tour or just walk another 0.2 mile to explore the Vikingsholm grounds on your own. Bring food, water, money for the tour, and a bathing suit to take a dip in the very cold water near the sandy beach beside Vikingsholm. Altogether, the Rubicon Trail runs 4.5 miles along the shoreline of Emerald Bay. Hikers who complete it will see osprey nests and an old wooden lighthouse in addition to the many other highlights.

D.L. BLISS STATE PARK

Hiking trails within **D. L. Bliss State Park** include the **Rubicon-Lighthouse Trail** (complete trail 4.5 miles one-way, easy) to Rubicon Point's lighthouse, which was built in 1919 and restored and stabilized in 2001. You can take a short portion of this trail, from Calawee Cove Beach to the lookout at Rubicon Point, or walk a little farther to see

Tahoe Queen

the lighthouse. For a longer adventure, follow the Rubicon Trail all the way down around the bay, past Vikingsholm, and on to its end point at Upper Eagle Point Campground in Emerald Bay State Park.

On the west side of D. L. Bliss is a short (0.5-mile) self-guided **nature trail** to Balancing Rock that nearly anyone can enjoy. Nineteen numbered signs along the way illuminate the history and geology of the area.

TAHOE RIM TRAIL

If you're in good shape and like a challenge, you will definitely want to experience the 165-mile **Tahoe Rim Trail** (775/298-4485, www.tahoerimtrail.org). This beautiful and varied trail, built between 1984 and 2001, encircles the entire lake through six counties in California and Nevada, one state park, three national forests, and three wilderness areas. About one-third of it overlaps the Pacific Crest Trail. You can hike the trail in segments, or if you're up for a little planning, do it in a multiday loop. Casual day hikers can pick one portion of the trail and tackle it, either doing an out-and-back or using a shuttle service to get back at the end of the day.

Much of the **Tahoe Rim Trail** on the California side is not open to bicycles, but the one segment that is accessible is the five miles from Big Meadow to Echo Summit and Echo Lake. To reach the trailhead from South Lake Tahoe, drive south on U.S. 50 to Highway 89. Continue south on Highway 89 for about five miles, until the Tahoe Rim Trail crosses the road at Big Meadow, where you can park. The trail starts out heading south but soon turns northwest up to Echo Summit and then Echo Lake. When you near the lake, you'll see a sign warning that the trail is about to join the Pacific Crest Trail and cyclists must turn around. This round-trip is a scenic and invigorating 10-mile ride.

KIRKWOOD

A great place to get out and cycle in summer is **Kirkwood** (1501 Kirkwood Meadows Dr., off Hwy. 88, Kirkwood, www.kirkwood.com, 209/258-7277, early July-early Sept.). When there's no snow, the slopes of this ski resort become great mountain-biking tracks. Two lifts run on weekends in the summer (10am-4pm Sat., 10am-3pm Sun., adults $36), and a third lift operates occasionally on holidays. At the Red Cliffs Lodge base area (9am-4pm Sat.-Sun. summer) at Kirkwood, you can rent high-end mountain bikes (adults $45-80, children $19-25, includes helmets, gloves, and protective gear). Kirkwood also offers several mountain-bike clinics through the season to help hone your skills.

Horseback Riding

For travelers who prefer to explore the forests and trails on horseback, a few stables offer guided rides. On the west side of the South Shore, find the **Camp Richardson Corral** (Emerald Bay Rd. between Fallen Leaf Rd. and Valhalla Rd., 530/541-3113 or 877/541-3113, www.camprichardsoncorral.com, $43-83). Choose a one- or two-hour trail ride to explore the meadows and the forest or a ride with a meal included. Camp Richardson offers an early morning ride that culminates in a hearty, hot cowboy-style breakfast and a two-hour evening ride with a steak barbecue. Riders must be at least six years old and weigh 225 pounds or less.

To get out and see the Sierra foothills and mountains from the back of a horse, check **Kirkwood Corrals** (51965 Hwy. 88, 775/315-1932 or 775/315-6222, 30-90-minute rides $35-95). Kids will especially love the **Little Buckaroo Day Camp** (9am-noon Tues.-Wed. early July, ages 7-12, $160) available during the middle of summer. If you're more advanced and want a gorgeous guided trail ride out into the Mokelumne Wilderness, join **Kirkwood Sierra Outfitters** (209/258-7433, www.kirkwoodsierraoutfitters.com) for a ride of half a day or more.

ENTERTAINMENT AND EVENTS
Nightlife

The casinos over the Nevada border in

Stateline are nearby, but the South Shore has its own entertainment. The **Brewery at Lake Tahoe** (3542 Lake Tahoe Blvd., South Lake Tahoe, 530/544-2739, www.breweryla-ketahoe.com, 11am-9pm daily, $12-28) is a casual, comfortable bar with a menu of local microbrews, including the signature Bad Ass Ale and the popular Washoe Wheat Ale, as well as a selection of seasonal brews. The food includes pizza, pasta, salads, salmon, steaks, and barbecued ribs. The Brewery is across the street from the lake; the outdoor picnic tables are a great place to watch the scenery.

A happening place is **Whiskey Dick's Saloon** (2660 Lake Tahoe Blvd., South Lake Tahoe, 530/544-3425, 1pm-2am daily), with a full bar and live bands several times a week. Cover charges range from free to $20, depending on the band.

Casinos

On the South Shore, just over the Nevada state line, various casinos attract a young crowd looking for a lively, hip night out. Note that the casinos sometimes call the town Lake Tahoe, Nevada, though it's legally Stateline.

The gaming floor of the **MontBleu Resort Casino and Spa** (55 U.S. 50, Stateline, NV, 775/588-3515 or 800/648-3353, www.montbleuresort.com) is great fun on weekend evenings, with youthful gamblers enjoying free drinks as they hammer the slots. You'll find full-fledged table games of the Vegas variety: craps, roulette, blackjack, and Texas hold 'em, among others. For late-night entertainment, **The Opal Ultralounge** (10pm-dawn Thurs.-Sat., cover $10-20) includes expert mash-up DJs, resident body painters (midnight Thurs.-Sat.), and go-go dancers (11:30pm Thurs.-Sat.).

Gambling fans should definitely bring their frequent-player cards to the casino floor at **Harrah's Lake Tahoe** (15 U.S. 50, Stateline, NV, 775/588-6611 or 800/427-7247, www.caesars.com/harrahs-tahoe), which has all the Vegas gaming favorites—classic craps, rapid roulette, and Keno pads and monitors scattered all over the place. The atmosphere is a bit more classic casino, with dim lights in the evening and a warren of slot machines that make it easy to get lost. A favorite night-club for many locals is **PEEK at Harrah's** (10:30pm-4am Fri.-Sat., $5-20 cover), a late-night watering hole featuring in-house and guest DJs.

For an evening of laughter, get tickets to **The Improv at Harveys** (18 U.S. 50, Stateline, NV, 775/588-6611, www.caesars.com/harveys-tahoe, from 9pm Wed.-Sun., $25-30). This is the place where many of to-day's major comedy stars honed their acts—come see who'll be famous next.

Smaller and less flashy, **Lakeside Inn and Casino** (168 U.S. 50, Stateline, NV, 775/588-7777 or 800/624-7980, www.lakesideinn.com) looks more like a mountain lodge than a high-rise gaming emporium, but it has won the most votes for Best Casino, Loosest Slots, and Friendliest Casino Employees. The casino offers all the usual games and machines, and it is particularly welcoming for beginners.

SHOPPING

South Lake Tahoe is a good place to stock up on batteries and basic foodstuffs before heading out. For athletic equipment and apparel, check out the **Tahoe Sports Limited** (4000 Lake Tahoe Blvd., South Lake Tahoe, 530/542-4000, www.tahoesportsltd.com, 9am-7pm Mon.-Thurs., 8am-8pm Fri.-Sun. winter, 9am-7pm daily summer). You can rent or buy a wide array of winter equipment at **Powder House Ski & Snowboard** (4045 Lake Tahoe Blvd., 530/542-6222, www.tahoepowderhouse.com, 7am-8pm Mon.-Fri., 7am-9pm Sat.-Sun.), with eight locations in South Lake Tahoe.

At the upscale **Shops at Heavenly Village** (1001 Heavenly Village Way, www.theshopsatheavenly.com) you'll find a **Patagonia** (530/542-3385, www.patagonia.com, 8:30am-7pm Mon.-Thurs., 8:30am-8pm Fri., 8am-8pm Sat., 8am-7pm Sun. winter, 8:30am-8pm Mon.-Thurs., 8:30am-9pm Fri., 8am-9pm Sat., 8am-8pm Sun. summer) and a **Quiksilver** (530/542-4857, www.quiksilver.

com, 10am-6pm Mon.-Fri., 9:30am-7pm Sat.-Sun.).

At **Heavenly Mountain Village, North Face** (4118 Lake Tahoe Blvd., 530/544-9062, www.skiheavenly.com, 8am-8pm daily) is where you can rent recreational gear as well as buy it.

FOOD
South Lake Tahoe

For a classic American breakfast, it's tough to do better than the ★ **Original Red Hut Café** (2723 Lake Tahoe Blvd., 530/541-9024, www.redhutcafe.com, 6am-2pm daily, $6-10). This down-home waffle spot serves classic crispy-thin waffles, plus biscuits and gravy, omelets, and plenty more. Locals recommend the waffle sandwich, a complete breakfast in a single dish. Expect to wait for a table or a seat at the counter on weekend mornings, as this spot is very popular with visitors and locals. If you can't get in, try the **New Red Hut Café** (3660 Lake Tahoe Blvd., 530/544-1595, 6am-8pm daily).

Rude Brothers Bagel & Coffee (3117 Harrison Ave., Suite B, www.rudebrothersbagels.com, 530/541-8195) looks and feels just right for an indie coffee shop and sandwich bar. It has a big open room for hanging out, outstanding breakfast burritos, and plenty of lunch goodies. All the usual espresso drinks are available at the counter.

For a great combination of delicious healthy food and budget dining, check out ★ **Sprouts Café** (3123 Harrison Ave., 530/541-6969, 8am-9pm daily, $8-10). This cute, casual walk-up eatery offers ultra-healthy dishes made with fresh, mostly organic ingredients. Breakfast is served all day, and the lunch and dinner menus run to several pages. Choose among salads, burritos, rice bowls, and tasty vegetarian and vegan desserts.

An unassuming local joint with great food and veggie options is **Freshies Restaurant & Bar** (3330 Lake Tahoe Blvd., http://freshiestahoe.com, 530/542-3630, www.freshiestahoe.com, 11:30am-9pm daily, $10-22). This

small, popular Hawaiian-themed restaurant has been voted the "Best Place for Dinner" and "Best Place for Lunch" by the *Tahoe Daily Tribune*. The main dining room is accessed through a mall, but the best way to experience Freshies is to go to the side entrance and add your name to the list for a rooftop table, where you can see the lake.

Blue Angel Café (1132 Ski Run Blvd., South Lake Tahoe, 530/544-6544, www.blueangelcafe.com, 11am-9pm daily summer, 11am-9pm Tues.-Sun. winter, $14-18) has a globetrotting menu with a distinct West Coast flavor. The pizzas are amazing; try the Thai chili chicken with goat cheese and gluten-free dough. If you're thinking of chowing down on something lighter for dinner, try the salmon with smoked paprika, mango coulis, quinoa, and veggies.

Boasting a *Wine Spectator* Award of Excellence and a creative California cuisine menu that includes wild boar chops, Asian chicken mandarin orange stir-fry, and summer *ragu* bolognese, **Nepheles** (1169 Ski Run Blvd., 530/544-8130, www.nepheles.com, daily by reservation, $26-38) is the perfect place for a romantic dinner or a celebration of any kind. Another is **Café Fiore** (1169 Ski Run Blvd., 530/541-2908, www.cafefiore.com, 5:30pm-10pm daily, $18-35), a tiny bistro serving upscale Italian fare with a fabulous wine list. The exterior charms with its alpine-chalet look while the interior is the definition of a romantic restaurant.

Serious sushi aficionados might be concerned about eating raw ocean fish so far from the Pacific, but **Off the Hook** (2660 Lake Tahoe Blvd., 530/544-5599, www.offthehooksushi.com, 4:30pm-9:30pm Mon.-Fri., 5pm-9:30pm Sat.-Sun fall-spring, 4:30pm-9pm Mon.-Thurs., 4:30pm-9:30pm Fri., 5pm-9:30pm Sat., 5pm-9pm Sun. summer, $6-23) offers good rolls and fresh *nigiri* at reasonable prices.

For an all-around fine dining experience and some of the best fish ever, try **Kalani's** (1001 Heavenly Village Way, South Lake Tahoe, 530/544-6100, www.kalanis.com, noon-close daily, $18-65). Serving Pacific Rim fusion cuisine, Kalani's offers subtly spiced salmon, mahimahi, sushi, barbecued ribs, and house specialties like the *kalua* smoked pork quesadilla and Portuguese bean soup. The sushi bar is open all day, as is Kalani's Puka Lounge, which serves wine, sake, and cocktails. Kalani's is located in the Shops at Heavenly Village complex.

One of the area's best restaurants, the ★ **Beacon Bar & Grill** (1900 Jameson Beach Rd., South Lake Tahoe, 530/541-0630, www.camprichardson.com, brunch, lunch, and dinner daily, $19-40) is located inside Camp Richardson, just a few miles north of South Lake Tahoe on Highway 89. If you're driving Highway 89 from the north, look for the entrance on the left, seven miles south of Emerald Bay State Park. In addition to excellent food (filet mignon, fresh seafood, and a great spinach salad), the Beacon offers a beachfront patio and live music (Wed.-Sun. summer, Fri.-Sat. winter).

Stateline

The **Ciera Steak + Chophouse at the MontBleu** (55 U.S. 50, Stateline, NV, 775/588-3515 or 800/648-3353, www.montbleuresort.com, 5:30pm-10pm Wed.-Sun., $28-56) provides plenty of steak and non-steak options, with preparations designed to appeal to visitors from around the country. At the end of your meal, you'll be presented with a complimentary dish of chocolate-covered strawberries resting atop a frothing container of dry ice, and a selection of delicious flavored whipped creams accompany your coffee.

With decor as cute as its name, **Thai One On** (292 Kingsbury Grade, Suite 33, Stateline, NV, 775/586-8424, www.thaioneontahoe.com, 11am-9pm Mon.-Fri., 2pm-9:45pm Sat.-Sun., $11-15) serves delicious food at reasonable prices. The menu is eclectic: French toast, tacos, egg rolls, and curry in addition to traditional Thai favorites such as pad thai. Most of the food is prepared on the premises with fresh ingredients, and the results are tantalizing.

One of the best dining experiences is at ★ **Edgewood Tahoe Restaurant** (100 Lake Pkwy., Stateline, NV, 775/588-2787, www.edgewoodtahoe.com, 5:30pm-9pm daily summer, 5:30pm-9pm Wed.-Sun. winter, $28-40). Located on the world-famous Edgewood golf course, the restaurant features elk chops, sea bass, and rack of spring lamb. The prices are reasonable considering the quality of the food. For dessert, try the nightly crème brûlée.

ACCOMMODATIONS
$100-150

South Lake Tahoe has quite a few basic motels that offer a room for the night without breaking the bank. Midsummer rates, however, can rival resort prices. One of the nicer ones is the **Matterhorn Motel** (2187 Lake Tahoe Blvd., South Lake Tahoe, 530/541-0367, $69-199). The rooms are clean and adequate, with free Internet access, and it has a small outdoor pool. It's family owned, and the proprietors are warm and helpful beyond expectations.

For inexpensive rooms year-round, check into the **Ambassador Motor Lodge** (4130 Manzanita Ave., South Lake Tahoe, 530/544-6461, www.laketahoeambassador.com, $50-157, under age 16 free with adult), with private beach access and water-recreation options. Rooms have a basic motel feel, but a few soft touches make them prettier than the average bargain chain. The Ambassador is right on the lake and only a short walk to the Heavenly Gondola.

The **Apex Inn** (1171 Emerald Bay Rd., South Lake Tahoe, 530/541-2940, reservations 800/755-8246, www.apexinntahoe.com, $65-249) offers the winning combination of a good location and rates almost on par with camping. It has a small outdoor hot tub and free Internet access. Breakfast is included.

The small rustic **Lazy S Lodge** (609 Emerald Bay Rd., South Lake Tahoe, 530/600-3721, www.lazyslodge.com, $59-263) is in a great location away from the center of town and has some of the most reasonable rates in the region. The 21 rooms all have microwaves, wet bars, and private baths. The two-room cabins have room for several people, along with a kitchenette and fireplace. Facilities include a year-round hot tub, a summer-only swimming pool, barbecue grills and picnic tables, and easy access to hiking and biking trails, swimming, and Heavenly.

★ **Camp Richardson** (1900 Jameson Beach Rd., South Lake Tahoe, 530/541-1801 or 800/544-1801, www.camprichardson.com, $95-262) is a full-spectrum resort with 33 rooms and suites featuring rustic furnishings and luxurious fabrics. Rooms in the hotel are comfortable and quaint, with private baths and upscale amenities. The 38 individual cabins offer full kitchens and linens but no TVs or phones. It also has an RV Village (late May-Oct., $40-45) with 100 sites. Accommodations include use of the beach, the lounge, and the marina. Facilities include the excellent **Beacon Bar & Grill,** the **Mountain Sports Center,** and a coffee shop. Cross-country ski and snowshoe rentals are available in winter, and paddleboats in summer.

Over $150

The **Pine Cone Acre Motel** (735 Emerald Bay Rd., South Lake Tahoe, 530/541-0375, www.pineconeacremotel.com, rooms $150-175, cabin $300) has a great location on Highway 89 (Emerald Bay Rd.), just north of where Highway 89 crosses U.S. 50—which means the motel is very close to the center of South Lake Tahoe, but it's also out of the traffic in the attractive rustic vicinity of Emerald Bay. Rooms have microwaves and fridges, and a pool and picnic tables are on the grounds.

On the road to Heavenly, the lovely, large ★ **Black Bear Inn** (1202 Ski Run Blvd., South Lake Tahoe, 530/544-4451 or 877/232-7466, www.tahoeblackbear.com, $235-315) features lodgepole pine and river rock, which blend in with the surrounding nature. A giant fireplace dominates the great room, and smaller but equally cozy river-rock fireplaces are in each of the upstairs lodge rooms. The 10 rooms feature king beds, plush private baths, free Internet access, and an energy-building full breakfast.

Cabin and Condo Rentals

South Lake Tahoe's **Marriott Grand Residence** (1001 Heavenly Village Way) has about 40 condos available for rent through **Condos at Tahoe** (775/586-1587 or 888/666-0773, www.condosattahoe.com). All units here have full kitchens and provide easy access to the Heavenly Gondola. Studios run $260-525, and three-bedroom units—which are huge and sleep up to 14 people—are $400-675 a night.

Spruce Grove Cabins (3599-3605 Spruce Ave., South Lake Tahoe, 530/802-2343, www.sprucegrovetahoe.com, $99-235) offers a gay-friendly and dog-friendly Tahoe vacation experience. With only seven cabins, you're guaranteed peace and privacy. The one- and two-bedroom cabins all have full kitchens, dining rooms, and living rooms. Each cabin has its own wilderness-based theme, including Snowshoe, Steamboat, and Washoe Native American. As one of the closest resorts to the Heavenly ski resort, Spruce Grove gets its heaviest traffic in the winter. **The Lodge at Lake Tahoe** (3840 Pioneer Trail, South Lake Tahoe, 530/541-6226 or 800/469-8222, www.lodgeatlaketahoe.com, $120-230) rooms have the elegant look of proper vacation condos, with colorful furnishings and tasteful prints on the walls. The smallest studios have only kitchenettes, but the larger condos offer fully equipped kitchens as well as a nice table and chairs. Complex amenities include a summertime pool and spa, a swing set, a horseshoe pit, and outdoor barbecues near the pool area. Skiers will have easy access to Heavenly, and gamblers can get to the Stateline casinos in Nevada in a few minutes.

Casino Hotels

Tahoe's **casino hotels** are some of the spiffiest places to stay on the Nevada side, offering upscale attractive hotel rooms often at lower than expected rates. You'll also find the occasional non-casino lakeshore resort that focuses more on recreation than the slots.

The most popular casino resort is **Harrah's** (15 U.S. 50, Stateline, NV, 775/588-2411 or

800/427-7247, www.caesars.com/harrahs-tahoe, $99-589), with upscale accommodations and easy access to Heavenly and other South Shore ski resorts in winter and the lakeshore in summer. The high-rise hotel has more than 500 upscale rooms; even the lower-end rooms have ample space, a California king or two double beds, two baths, Wi-Fi, cable TV, and minibars. Premium rooms provide excellent views of the lake and the mountains.

With 437 rooms, **MontBleu Casino** (55 U.S. 50, Stateline, NV, 775/588-3515 or 800/648-3353, www.montbleuresort.com, $115-335 summer) is prepared to offer a range of affordable choices. For luxury, try a spa room, which includes a pink-marble bath, walk-in shower, and two-person hot tub in the bedroom. MontBleu used to be a Caesar's, and though it's been renovated beautifully, the walls remain paper thin—bring earplugs. Free wireless Internet access is also available.

CAMPING

Camping at Lake Tahoe in the summer is so easy and gorgeous that you almost wonder why anyone would sleep indoors. June-August, the weather is usually perfect and the prices are reasonable, with campsites just minutes from mountain-bike trails or beaches.

The two great state parks of the South Shore both have gorgeous campgrounds. **Emerald Bay State Park** (Hwy. 89, north of South Lake Tahoe, 800/444-7275, www.reserveamerica.com, $35) has the 100-site Eagle Point Campground and a Boat-in Campground (July-Sept.) on the north side of the bay. Campsites include fire rings, and restrooms and showers are available in the park.

★ **D. L. Bliss State Park** (Hwy. 89, 800/444-7275, www.parks.ca.gov, May-Sept., $35-45) has some of the best campsites around. Of the 150 sites, beachfront campsites have a premium price of $45, and they're worth it. All campsites have picnic tables, bear-proof food lockers, and grills. Hot showers, flush toilets, and potable water are available in the park. **Camp Richardson Resort** (530/541-1801 or 800/544-1801, www.camprichardson.com, $35-45) offers sites for tents, campers, and RVs. Amenities include a beach, a group recreation area, and a marina. On-site facilities include the Beacon Bar & Grill and the Mountain Sports Center.

The U.S. Forest Service runs 206 sites at **Fallen Leaf Lake Campground** (Fallen Leaf Lake Rd., off Hwy. 89, 3 miles north of U.S. 50, 530/543-2600 or 877/444-6777, www.recreation.gov, mid-May-mid-Oct., $32-34). RVs up to 40 feet are welcome, though there are no hookups or dump stations. Each campsite has a barbecue grill, a picnic table, and a fire ring. And not only are there modern baths with flush toilets, but some restrooms even have free showers. The campground is just 0.25-mile north of Fallen Leaf Lake.

The **Tahoe Valley RV Resort** (1175 Melba Dr., South Lake Tahoe, 530/541-2222 or 877/570-2267, www.rvonthego.com, May-Sept. $41-74; Oct.-Apr. $29) has 439 sites that can accommodate everything from small tents to big-rig RVs with water, electric, and cable TV hookups. Tall pine trees give each site some shade and privacy. Amenities include tennis courts, a swimming pool, an ice-cream parlor serving Tahoe Creamery products, activities for children and families, a dog run, and free wireless Internet access.

North and West Shores

The **North and West Shores** are often considered the most desirable areas of Lake Tahoe, filled with ski resorts, beachfront property, and tall pines. One of the larger towns on the West Shore is Tahoe City, a lively, happening place with good restaurants, bars, and entertainment and a sparkling waterfront. The smaller communities of Lake Forest, Sunnyside, Tahoe Pines, Homewood, and Tahoma are close by and easy to access.

SIGHTS

★ Ed Z'berg Sugar Pine Point State Park

The Tahoe area has more than its share of outstanding state parks, and **Ed Z'berg Sugar Pine Point State Park** (7360 Hwy. 89, Tahoma, 530/525-7982, www.parks. ca.gov, $10) is one of the greats. Located on the West Shore, north of Emerald Bay and a few miles south of the town of Homewood, ski trails from the 1960 Winter Olympics, and great camping, among other attractions. The 1903 **Ehrman Mansion** is located within the day-use area of Sugar Pine Point State Park. Tours (530/583-9911, www. sierrastateparks.org, 10:30am-3:30pm daily late May-late Sept., adults $10, ages 7-17 $8, under age 7 free) of this beautifully preserved 12,000-square-foot house are available in summer.

Tahoe Maritime Museum

The **Tahoe Maritime Museum** (5205 W. Lake Blvd., Homewood, 530/525-9253, www. tahoemaritimemuseum.org, 10am-4:30pm Thurs.-Tues. late May-Oct., 10am-4:30pm Fri.-Sun. Oct.-late May, adults $5, children under 13 free) seeks to illuminate the significant marine history of Lake Tahoe. Located on the West Shore, the museum resembles a big old boathouse and has a great collection of historical boats, photos, and artifacts related to the lake's history.

Gatekeeper's Museum and Marion Steinbach Indian Basket Museum

Together, the **Gatekeeper's Museum and Marion Steinbach Indian Basket Museum** (130 West Lake Blvd., Tahoe City, 530/583-1762, www.northtahoemuseums.org, 10am-5pm daily early June-Sept., noon-4pm Wed.-Sun. Oct.-late May, adults $5, seniors $4, under age 13 free accompanied by an adult) offer an in-depth history of society around the lake. You'll find transcribed oral histories, photographs, dolls, costumes, and many other artifacts displayed in attractive and unusual pine-and-glass cases that match the wooden floors of the galleries. The authentic Native American artifacts include a large collection of baskets and caps made of willow, tule, and pine needles, among other things.

★ The Village at Squaw Valley

You might think of **The Village at Squaw Valley** (1750 Village East Rd., Olympic Valley, 530/584-1000, www.squawalpine.com) as a ski area, but it's actually a small upscale town designed to mimic a European Alpine village. There's no need to hit the slopes to enjoy what the village has to offer. Spend hours rambling around the colorfully painted clusters of buildings or strolling the cute exclusive boutiques and galleries.

More than half a dozen restaurants, snack bars, and coffee shops offer sushi, pizza, high-end wine, and more. Entertainment options include skiing and ice-skating in the winter, hiking in summer, and riding the **Aerial Tram** (hours vary, daily winter and summer, Sat.-Sun. spring and fall, adults $39, youth and seniors $25, children under 13 $10) up to **High Camp** (1960 Squaw Valley Rd., Olympic Valley, 530/584-1000, www.squawalpine.com) at 8,200 feet elevation. At High Camp, you can play tennis or paintball, roller-skate, soak in a hot tub, browse the **Olympic Museum**

North and West Shores

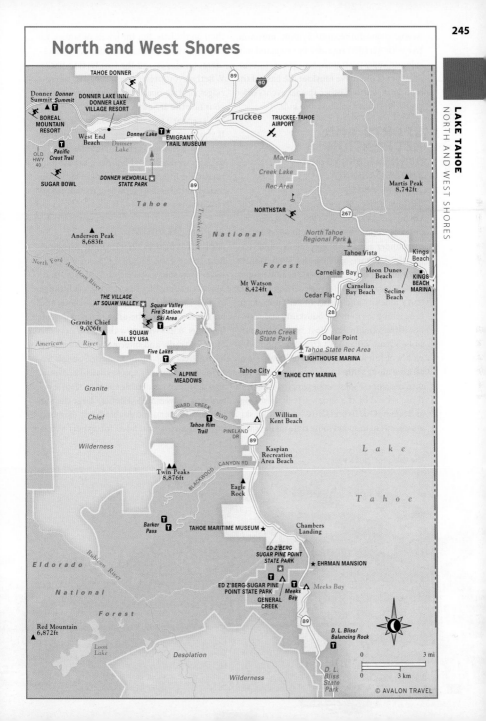

TAHOE DONNER

Donner *Donner*
Summit *Summit*
BOREAL
MOUNTAIN
RESORT

DONNER LAKE INN/
DONNER LAKE
VILLAGE RESORT

West End
Beach

Donner Lake

EMIGRANT
TRAIL MUSEUM

Truckee

TRUCKEE-TAHOE
AIRPORT

Martis

Creek Lake

Rec Area

Martis Peak
8,742ft

OLD
HWY
40

*Pacific
Crest Trail*

SUGAR BOWL

*Donner
Lake*

DONNER MEMORIAL
STATE PARK

Tahoe

NORTHSTAR

North Tahoe
Regional Park

Tahoe Vista

Kings
Beach

Anderson Peak
8,683ft

National

Forest

Carnelian Bay

Moon Dunes
Beach

KINGS
BEACH
MARINA

North Fork American River

Mt Watson
8,424ft

Cedar Flat

Carnelian
Bay Beach

Secline
Beach

THE VILLAGE
AT SQUAW VALLEY

Granite Chief
9,006ft

American

River

Squaw Valley
Fire Station/
Ski Area

SQUAW
VALLEY USA

Five Lakes

*Burton Creek
State Park*

Dollar Point

Tahoe State Rec Area
LIGHTHOUSE MARINA

Tahoe City

TAHOE CITY MARINA

Granite

Chief

ALPINE
MEADOWS

WARD CREEK

BLVD

William
Kent Beach

Wilderness

*Tahoe Rim
Trail*

PINELAND
DR

89

Kaspian
Recreation
Area Beach

Lake

Twin Peaks
8,876ft

CANYON RD

BLACKWOOD

Eagle
Rock

Tahoe

*Barker
Pass*

TAHOE MARITIME MUSEUM

Chambers
Landing

Rubicon River

ED Z'BERG
SUGAR PINE
STATE PARK

EHRMAN MANSION

Eldorado

National

Forest

ED Z'BERG-SUGAR PINE
POINT STATE PARK

GENERAL
CREEK

*Meeks
Bay*

Meeks Bay

Red Mountain
6,872ft

*Loon
Lake*

Desolation

89

D. L. Bliss/
Balancing Rock

Wilderness

*D. L.
Bliss
State
Park*

0 --- 3 mi

0 --- 3 km

© AVALON TRAVEL

(www.squawalpine.com/olympic-museum, free with Aerial Tram ride), or just stand outside and enjoy the tremendous views. In summer there's often live music at the base of the mountain; various other special events offer year-round fun for adults and kids.

SPORTS AND RECREATION
DOWNHILL SKIING AND SNOWBOARDING
Squaw Valley

Squaw Valley (1960 Squaw Valley Rd., Olympic Valley, 530/583-6985, www.squawalpine.com, adults $95-119, youth $82-98, children under 12 $55-68) was the headquarters for alpine sports during the 1960 Winter Olympics. Today it is perhaps the most popular ski resort in California, with practically every amenity and plenty of activities, from geocaching to ziplining, but skiing and snowboarding remain the most important pursuits. Squaw Valley has a great ski school with plenty of fun for new skiers and boarders of all ages along with a wide selection of intermediate slopes. Some slopes are long, such as those served by the Squaw Creek, Red Dog, and Squaw One Express lifts—perfect for skiers who want to spend more time on the snow

than on the lifts. But the jewels of Squaw are the many black-diamond and double-black-diamond slopes and the two terrain parks. Whether you prefer trees, moguls, narrow ridges, or wide-open vertical bowls, you'll find your favorite at Squaw. The slopes off KT-22 are legendary with skiers around the world. If you want to try freestyle for the first time, head for Belmont Park. During the day, especially weekends and holidays, expect long lines at the lifts, crowds in the nice, big locker rooms, and still more crowds at the numerous restaurants and cafés.

ALPINE MEADOWS
Alpine Meadows (2600 Alpine Meadows Rd., Tahoe City, 530/583-4232 or 800/441-4423, www.squawalpine.com, mid-Nov.-mid-May) is a sprawling resort with a full range of trails, an all-day every-day ski school, and brand-new state-of-the-art rental equipment. Beginner skiers will enjoy the scenic network of green trails, and intermediate skiers will have a great time coming off the Summit Six or the Roundhouse Express chairlifts. Alpine also devotes considerable space to what it refers to as "Adventure Ski Zones," large clusters of black-diamond and double-black-diamond bowls and runs intended for expert skiers

The Village at Squaw Valley

only. Thirteen lifts serve the mountains, including three high-speed chairs.

GRANLIBAKKEN

Granlibakken (725 Granlibakken Rd., Tahoe City, 530/583-4242 or 800/543-3221, www. granlibakken.com, lift tickets $16-30, lodging $165-665) is a lovely historical resort that dates back to the turn of the 20th century. Granlibakken offers some downhill skiing, but those who crave the excitement of bigger mountains should sleep here and take advantage of the package deals at other resorts, which include discount lift tickets and shuttle transportation to one of seven other ski areas. With a large outdoor pool and hot tub, an on-site spa, hiking, cross-country ski trails, and one of the best-groomed sledding hills anywhere, this is an ideal spot for family vacations. Most of the 84 condos on the site are available for rent year-round.

Cross-Country Skiing and Snowshoeing

One of the best cross-country ski trails for beginners is the **General Creek Trail**, also known as the 1960 Winter Olympiad X-C Ski Trail. A lot of the Olympic facilities in the area were neglected or forgotten for many years, but some of the ski trails were rediscovered and restored in connection with the 50th anniversary celebration in 2010. The trailhead is located inside Sugar Pine Point State Park (Hwy. 89, Tahoma, 530/525-7982, www. parks.ca.gov, $10), just a few miles south of the town of Tahoma. On entering the park, drive through the campground to campsite 148. Signs and a trail map are posted and explain a little about the trail's Olympic history. The trail is largely flat, so it's not too challenging for skiers at most levels—it's also amazingly beautiful. It's an out-and-back trip, so you can glide silently through the woods for as long as you like then turn around before you get too tired. Snowshoers are welcome but must stay out of the ski tracks.

Snowshoeing enthusiasts will be happy to hear that rangers in Sugar Pine Point State Park (Hwy. 89, Tahoma, 530/525-7982, www. parks.ca.gov, $10) lead **full-moon snowshoe tours** (West Shore Sports, reservations 530/525-9920, $25, under age 12 free, includes snowshoe rental) on specific dates in winter; call for details.

Hiking

Sugar Pine Point State Park (Hwy. 89, Tahoma, 530/525-7982, www.parks.ca.gov, $10) offers trails suitable for all levels of hikers. One simple and pleasant hike is the **Edward F. Dolder Nature Trail** (1.5 miles, easy). To reach the trailhead, enter the northeast section of the park—the Edwin L. Z'Berg Natural Preserve—and begin hiking the paved Rod Beaudry trail. The Dolder Trail circles the Z'berg Preserve, with views of the subalpine meadow and wildlife habitats. Along the way you'll pass through trees, a sandy beach, and the world's highest-elevation operating navigational lighthouse, the Sugar Pine Point Lighthouse.

A good hike in the southwestern section of Sugar Pine Point State Park is along the 1960 Olympic Ski Trails out to **Lily Pond** (3-6 miles, easy-moderate). Start in General Creek Campground, near site 148, and take the **General Creek Trail**, also known as the 1960 Winter Olympiad X-C Ski Trail. This sunny wooded path is wide enough that it almost feels like an unpaved forest road. After about 1.5 miles, you'll come to a wooden bridge curving off to the left across General Creek. If you're ready to turn around, take the bridge to complete the loop back to the trailhead for a total of three miles.

If you're up for a few more miles, bear right; at this point, the path becomes more trail-like, narrow and winding through the woods. In 0.5 mile you'll come to a trail marker directing you to Lily Pond on the right. The next 0.75 mile is a bit of climbing, but then you're at Lily Pond, a small lake that actually has lily pads. You can walk around the pond or just turn around and head back, rejoining the General Creek Trail for a total of 5-6 miles.

If you like easy terrain and great views,

the **Lakeside Trail,** a kind of paved boardwalk, is a great place for a stroll or a hike. The 1-mile boardwalk is actually part of a larger 19-mile trail network that links the North Shore, West Shore, Truckee River, and Squaw Valley. Access the trail from Heritage Plaza in the center of Tahoe City.

The 165-mile **Tahoe Rim Trail** (775/298-4485, www.tahoerimtrail.org) runs above the entire lake. The northern trailhead is at Brockway Summit. To get to the Brockway trailhead, start in Kings Beach, at the junction of Highways 28 and 267. Travel north on Highway 267 for four miles. Look for a "Tahoe Rim Trail" sign on the right, and then park on the nearby dirt road or on the roadside pullout. This trailhead has no restrooms, water, or other services.

The southern trailhead is Barker Pass. To get to the Barker Pass trailhead from Tahoe City, travel about 4.25 miles south on Highway 89. Make a right (west) onto Blackwood Canyon Road. When the road splits, take the left fork. Drive 7 miles to the crest of the hill and then another 0.2 mile on a dirt road. Park at the pullout to the right. Pit toilets are available at this trailhead, but there's no water. The famous **Pacific Crest Trail** (916/285-1846, www.pcta.org) joins the Tahoe Rim Trail here at Barker Pass and runs concurrent with it for the next 50 miles into the Desolation Wilderness.

ACCOMMODATIONS AND FOOD
Tahoma and Homewood

For homey cabin living on the West Shore, you can't beat **The Tahoma Lodge** (7018 Westlake Blvd., Tahoma, 866/819-2226, www.tahomalodge.com, $170-240), a series of 11 distinctive cabins, including studios and one- and two-bedroom units. Each cabin has a modern kitchen, and the picnic tables, barbecues, and heated swimming pool outside help you enjoy your stay in summer. In winter, you'll appreciate the fireplace in each unit and the year-round outdoor hot tub.

At the ★ **West Shore Café & Inn** (5160 West Lake Blvd., Homewood, 530/525-5200, www.skihomewood.com, 11am-9pm daily winter, 11am-3pm, 5pm-9pm daily summer, 5pm-9pm daily spring and fall, $16-34), the atmosphere is classy, with white tablecloths and well-dressed patrons. On the back patio, you can watch the sun go down over the lake, or grab a table out on the pier, illuminated by strings of lights. The West Shore Burger ($16) is the dish you'll be talking about when you get home, and the service is both professional and friendly. Try one of the signature cocktails, such as the West Shore Margarita or the Mango Zombie.

Tahoe City

Mother Nature's Inn (551 N. Lake Blvd., Tahoe City, 530/581-4278 or 800/558-4278, www.mothernaturesinn.com, $65-145) brings the Tahoe camping experience inside while still providing creature comforts. Rooms are themed based on a distinct wild creature, and you can expect plenty of decorative tchotchkes in keeping with your room's animal totem. You'll also find lodge-style furnishings in cozy if somewhat cluttered arrangements. All rooms have private baths, fridges, and coffeemakers. Pets are welcome for a small additional fee. The inn is only a few steps from the lakeshore and downtown Tahoe City.

The exclusive and beautiful ★ **Stanford Alpine Chalet** (1980 Chalet Rd., Tahoe City, 530/583-1550, www.stanfordalpinechalet.com, $120-309) is situated at the base of Alpine Meadow's mountain. With only 14 rooms, each is special enough to make you feel like a rock star during your stay. Rooms are decorated in a simple yet elegant style, with wood, private baths, and striking mountain views. Meals are served family style at communal tables. In summer the chalet offers a heated swimming pool, sports courts, and horseshoe pits. Winter guests enjoy a private ski shuttle and a giant great-room fireplace. An outdoor hot tub lures guests with its bubbling year-round warmth.

To fuel up for a day out on the lake or in the mountains, head over to the **Fire Sign Café**

(1785 W. Lake Blvd., Tahoe City, 530/583-0871, 7am-3pm daily, $8-12). This breakfast-and-lunch spot is a favorite with locals, serving up an enormous menu of hearty fare. Choose whole-grain waffles with fruit, a kielbasa omelet, crepes, or blueberry coffee cake. Expect a wait for a table on weekend mornings.

If you want to relax with some fine caffeine and really soak in the vacation vibe, you'll revel in **Syd's Bagelry & Espresso** (550 N. Lake Blvd., Tahoe City, 7am-5pm daily). Syd's offers free wireless Internet access, and one of its best features is the location next door to Heritage Plaza, so you can take your latte outdoors while you watch the sunrise over the water.

A good choice for casual, inexpensive dining and drinking in Tahoe City is **Fat Cat Café** (599 N. Lake Blvd., Tahoe City, 530/583-3355, www.fatcattahoe.com, 11am-9pm Mon.-Thurs., 9am-10pm Fri.-Sat., 9am-9pm Sun., $9-14), especially if you like entertainment with your food. Thursday is karaoke night, and Friday and Saturday have live music starting around 10pm. The food includes decent sandwiches, salads, and burgers. The café also has free wireless Internet access.

The Blue Agave (425 N. Lake Blvd., Sunnyside-Tahoe City, 530/583-8113, www.tahoeblueagave.com, 11:30am-9pm daily, $10-30) is the place to go for Mexican food on the West Shore. It's located in the Tahoe Inn, built circa 1934, which has a long history involving gold miners, bootleggers, and film stars. The ample and delicious food is absolutely current and draws loyal patrons from all over.

An ideal spot for a delicious dinner and some lake-watching is ★ **Christy Hill Lakeside Bistro** (115 Grove St., Tahoe City, 530/583-8551, www.christyhill.com, 5pm-9:30pm daily summer, 5pm-9pm daily winter, $21-33) and its outdoor Sand Bar (beer and wine only) on the back deck. Entrées range from fresh cannelloni with homemade lemon ricotta to Moroccan spiced lamb loin.

The **River Grill** (55 West Lake Blvd. Tahoe City, 530/581-2644, www.rivergrilltahoe.com,

5pm-close daily, $19-45) is located where the Truckee River meets Tahoe City. Eat outside on the rustic heated wooden porch, enjoying the river view while listening to live music, or sit indoors in the casually elegant dining room, complete with a fireplace. Happy hour (5pm-6:30pm daily) features discounted drinks and food in the bar and at the outdoor fire pit.

Olympic Valley

For the ultimate convenience in ski vacations, get a condo at **The Village at Squaw Valley** (1750 Village East Rd., Olympic Valley, 866/818-6963, www.squawalpine.com, 1-bedroom condo $99-700, 3-bedroom $299-1,300) and never leave the vicinity of the lifts. Elegant, modern condos range from compact studios perfect for singles or couples to three-bedroom homes that sleep up to eight. Condos have full kitchens—some with granite countertops—as well as a living room with a TV and maybe a fireplace, and a dining table. The skiers' favorite condo has heated tile floors in the kitchen and bath. Included in the price is use of the Village's eight outdoor hot tubs, five saunas, five fitness rooms, and heated underground parking garage. Stay in Building 5; it has the clearest view of the mountain and the most comfortable amenities.

There are more than half a dozen restaurants, snack bars, and coffee shops offering sushi, pizza, expensive wine, and more, including **Mamasake Sushi** (1850 Village South Rd., 530/584-0110, www.mamasake.com, 11:30am-9pm Mon.-Thurs., 11:30am-10pm Fri.-Sun., $6-76) and **Fireside Pizza Co.** (1985 Squaw Valley Rd., 530/584-6150, www.firesidepizza.com, $13-26).

CAMPING

Sugar Pine Point State Park's ★ **General Creek Campground** (Hwy. 89, Tahoma, 800/444-7275, www.reserveamerica.com, mid-May-mid-Sept., $25-35) is a great place to stay on a family vacation or an overnight trip while exploring West Shore attractions. Every campsite has a picnic table, a charcoal grill, and ample space for a tent or camper. Some sites are ADA compliant. There are clean showers, and you can get a hot five-minute shower for $0.50 (bring quarters). The campground can get crowded in midsummer, so make reservations. The campground offers 16 sites for off-season camping on a first-come, first-served basis.

Not far from Sugar Pine Point State Park, the Washoe Tribe runs the **Meeks Bay Resort** (7941 Hwy. 89, Tahoma, 530/525-6946 or 877/326-3357, www.meeksbayresort.com, May-Oct., tent sites $20-30, RV sites $30-50). The 14 tent sites and 23 RV sites all have a two-night minimum; pets are not allowed. The resort features a sandy beach and a marina (530/525-5588), where you can rent single kayaks and paddleboats ($20 per hour) and double kayaks, canoes, and stand-up paddleboards ($30 per hour). You can also launch your own boat ($15 one-way, $25 round-trip) or rent a slip ($60 per night, weekly $360).

For great tree-lined campsites with easy beach access, the **William Kent Beach and Campground** (Hwy. 89, 2 miles south of Tahoe City, 877/444-6777, www.recreation.gov, mid-May-mid-Oct., $27-29) is a good choice. The 95 sites are suitable for tents or campers, but have no showers or electrical hookups. There are restrooms with flush toilets and bear lockers for your food.

If you don't mind giving up a woodsy camping experience, the **Tahoe State Recreation Area** (Hwy. 28, east of Tahoe City, 530/583-3074 or 800/444-7275, www.reserveamerica.com, late May-early Sept., $35) is a good choice, with 23 sites and coin-operated showers, and you can walk to the lake or to the shops of Tahoe City. A utilitarian place to sleep is the **Lake Forest Campground** (Lake Forest Rd., 1.5 miles east of Tahoe City on Hwy. 28, 530/583-3796, www.tahoecity-pud.com, mid-May-early Oct., $20), run by the Tahoe City Public Utilities District. The 20 sites are first-come, first-served; RVs up to 25 feet are welcome, though there are no hookups. Facilities include drinking water, flush toilets, picnic tables, and a boat ramp.

Truckee-Donner

Gateway to the Tahoe ski world, Truckee is a historical Old West town that really has no off-season. Storefronts line the main street, Donner Pass Road, offering ski rentals, a bite to eat, and places to stay. Parking is hard to find and expensive, and both the prices and the lines at restaurants can resemble those in San Francisco. But this bustling small mountain town has its charms.

★ DONNER MEMORIAL STATE PARK

In April 1846, 25 members of the Donner party, who had left Springfield, Illinois, on their way to new lives in California, stopped to repair their wagons in the fall after being slowed down by an ill-fated shortcut through Hastings Cutoff. It was only October when they got here, but a blizzard hit hard. Some of the party ended up staying the whole winter, and some, as you may know, never left.

Donner Memorial State Park (12593 Donner Pass Rd., off I-80, 530/582-7892, www.parks.ca.gov, daily year-round, $8) offers a much easier way to experience the lush beauty that the Donner party was heading to California to find. Near the entrance to the park is the **Pioneer Monument,** a massive structure celebrating the courage and spirit of the Donners and others who made their way west in harder times.

The visitors center (10am-5pm daily year-round) offers uplifting information about the human and natural history of the area. The 0.5-mile **Nature Trail** at the visitors center is an easy self-guided trek through a forest of Jeffrey and lodgepole pines past the site of the cabin built by the Murphy family during the Donner

Truckee-Donner

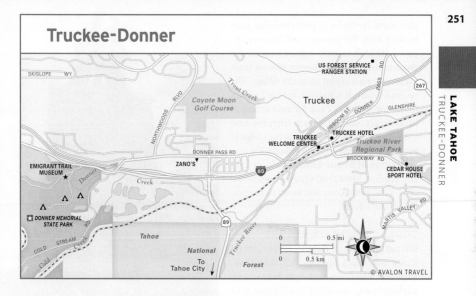

party's layover here in the winter of 1846-1847. A moving plaque at the cabin site lists those who perished and those who survived. The trail continues over a creek and through the **campground** (152 sites, reservations 800/444-7275, www.reserveamerica.com, Memorial Day-mid-Sept., sites first-come, first-served rest of the year, $35). Guided nature **hikes** are offered from the museum starting daily at 10am during summer. Donner Lake is a paradise for children and adults alike, offering swimming, boating, fishing, and hiking. Walking the **Lakeside Interpretive Trail** along the shore is a great way to enjoy close-up views of the lake.

Just west of Truckee, **Donner Summit** (I-80, 530/587-3558, www.exploredonnersummit. com or www.donnersummithistoricalsociety. org) offers a stunning view of Donner Lake and the surrounding area from the Donner Summit Bridge on Donner Pass Road.

SPORTS AND RECREATION
Downhill Skiing and Snowboarding
NORTHSTAR CALIFORNIA
Northstar California Resort (100 Northstar Dr., Truckee, 800/466-6784, www.

northstarattahoe.com, lifts 8:30am-4pm daily winter, adults $102-120, youth $93-98, children $61-70) is often a bit less crowded than the big resorts. Beginners can head up the mountain on the fast Vista Express quad chair and still find slopes heading gently all the way back to the village. Slow Zones provides good spots for young children fresh out of ski school and wobbly adults who haven't spent their whole lives on the slopes. Intermediate runs crisscross the front of the mountain, and the backside is reserved for black-diamond skiers, although adventurous intermediates can test their ski legs here.

SUGAR BOWL
A great mid-tier ski area is **Sugar Bowl** (629 Sugar Bowl Rd., Norden, 530/426-9000, www.sugarbowl.com, lifts 9am-4pm daily Nov.-May, adults $80-95, seniors $63-78, ages 13-22 $63-78, ages 6-12 $40-55, under age 5 free). With lots of skiable snow spread across a wide area and plenty of vertical drop, Sugar Bowl can satisfy skiers and boarders of all abilities. Blue and black-diamond runs toward the top of the peaks offer intense variety, with a smattering of double-black-diamond runs out toward the edges and down

the ridges. At the base, green and blue runs make it easy for younger and less experienced athletes to have a good time in the mountains. A gondola ferries visitors from the remote parking lot up to the village. The resort's Summit Chairlift brings visitors to the top of Judah Peak for easy access to backcountry trails. The resort offers two base lodges: a day lodge at Judah and the Lodge at Sugar Bowl, located in the village. The on-site **Lodge at Sugar Bowl** (750 Mule Ears Dr., Truckee, 530/426-6742, www.sugarbowl. com, $210-698) allows you to ski right up to your room's door.

BOREAL MOUNTAIN RESORT

Boreal Mountain Resort (19749 Boreal Ridge Rd., Soda Springs, 530/426-3666, www.rideboreal.com, 9am-9pm daily winter, adults $34-64, ages 13-18 $34-54, ages 5-12 $24-34) may not feel as fabulous as Squaw or Alpine, but many Californians find their snow legs here. The Accelerator Chair serves Boreal's Superpipe, its Core terrain park, and a night-skiing area; the 49er Chair serves the intermediate and advanced terrain. Even on weekends, the lines at Boreal seem pleasingly short compared to the bigger resorts. Boreal is very family friendly, with ski and snowboard lessons for beginners and a lodge where parents can relax with a cup of coffee or a drink at the Upper Deck bar and watch their children ski; the cafeteria (8am-7pm daily) offers limited service after 4pm.

SODA SPRINGS

Small **Soda Springs** (10244 Soda Springs Rd., Soda Springs, 530/426-3901, www.ski-sodasprings.com, 10am-4pm Thurs.-Mon., adults $44, under age 18 $34) is a great family resort. Its claim to fame is tubing, included with every lift ticket, or you can buy a $34 tubing-only package. The Planet Kids area for young athletes (under age 9, $34) offers a safe place for the little ones to practice tubing, skiing, and snowboarding. Rentals and instruction are included in the price, and there are even two tubing carousels to add to the thrills.

Pioneer Monument in Donner Memorial State Park

Soda Springs has no on-site lodging but does have an adequate cafeteria.

TAHOE DONNER SKI AREA

Tahoe Donner Ski Area (11603 Snowpeak Way, Truckee, 530/587-9444, www.tahoedonner.com/downhill-ski, hours vary Dec.-May, adults $39-47, youth $34-42, children $16-22) prides itself on being "a great place to begin." With only five lifts, including two conveyor belts and one carpet, 15 runs, and 120 skiable acres, Donner will seem miniscule to skiers used to the big resorts. It's a great spot to bring your family, however, to get a feel for snowboarding or skiing, take lessons, and enjoy the snow in the beautiful Tahoe forest. To be truly family friendly, Tahoe Donner offers lessons for children as young as age three, interchangeable lift tickets for parents, and even kid-friendly items on the snack-bar menu.

Cross-Country Skiing and Snowshoeing

The granddaddy of Tahoe cross-country ski

areas, the **Royal Gorge Cross Country Ski Resort** (Summit Station, Soda Springs, 530/426-3871 or 800/500-3871, www.royalgorge.com, 8:30am-4pm daily winter, adults $27-35, ages 13-22 $21-30, up to age 12 free) has a truly tremendous chunk of the Sierra—6,000 acres—within its boundaries. Striving to provide a luxurious ski experience comparable to what downhillers expect, the Royal Gorge offers lodging, food, drink, a ski school, equipment rentals, equipment care facilities and services, and much more. With the most miles of groomed trails anywhere in the Tahoe area, Royal Gorge offers two stride tracks and a skate track on every trail to allow easy passing. It even has a surface lift for skiers who want to practice downhill technique or try telemarking.

Tahoe Donner Cross Country (15275 Alder Creek Rd., Truckee, 530/587-9484, www.tahoedonner.com/cross-country, hours vary, adults $19-29, ages 60-69 $14-21, ages 7-12 $11, under age 7 free) offers some of the better cross-country ski action in the area. Tahoe Donner has almost 3,500 acres crisscrossed with trails ranging from easy greens all the way up through double-black-diamond trails, and has four trails set aside just for snowshoers. A cross-country ski school introduces newcomers to the sport and helps more experienced skiers expand their skills. A separate day lodge just for cross-country skiers and a snack bar are halfway up the mountain in Euer Valley.

FOOD

For a cool, crisp salad or a relaxing espresso, you can't beat the simply named ★ **CoffeeBar** (10120 Jibboom St., Truckee, 530/587-2000, www.coffeebartruckee.com, 6am-7pm daily, $5-9). Expect lots of space, free wireless Internet access, and good food—homemade baked goods, crepes, panini, salads, and breakfast calzones.

Jax at the Tracks (10144 W. River St., Truckee, 530/550-7450, www.jaxtruckee.com, 7am-10pm daily, $10-19) looks authentic inside and out. Housed in an actual 1940s diner, it has been thoroughly fixed up to be clean, fresh, and original. Jax has a creative California-style chef who puts his own stamp on comfort food.

Zano's Pizza (11401 Donner Pass Rd., Truckee, 530/587-7411, www.zanos.net, 4pm-9pm Mon.-Wed., 11:30am-9pm Thurs.-Sun., $14-24) serves huge pizzas and tremendous salads in a big casual dining room with sports playing on TV. The full menu includes pastas and Italian entrées, but it's the thin-crust pizzas that rule here.

The best restaurant in Truckee is ★ **Moody's Bistro and Lounge** (10007 Bridge St., Truckee, 530/587-8688, www.moodysbistro.com, 11:30am-9pm daily, $16-40), a casual yet elegant eatery adjoining the historical Truckee Hotel, just off the main drag. A wooden bar and booths give the main lounge an old-time feel, but the white-tablecloth dining room in the back feels more classically elegant. The chef promises ingredients that are "fresh, local, seasonal, and simple" and then jazzes them up with creative preparations. For weekend evenings, make a reservation.

The menu at **Bar of America** (10040 Donner Pass Rd., Truckee, 530/587-2626, www.barofamerica.com, 11:30am-9:30pm Mon.-Thurs., 11:30am-10:30pm Fri., 10:30am-10:30pm Sat., 10:30am-9:30pm Sun., $11-42) offers fresh organic ingredients and daily specials, as well as local beers and creative cocktails with professional service; the wood-fired pizzas are especially a hit. Reservations are recommended.

ACCOMMODATIONS

The **Truckee Hotel** (10007 Bridge St., at Donner Pass Rd., Truckee, 530/587-4444, www.truckeehotel.com, $79-229) offers fabulous period ambience at reasonable rates. The hotel has welcomed guests to the North Shore since 1873. Rooms show their age, with high ceilings, claw-foot tubs, and little Victorian touches. Part of the historical charm includes third- and fourth-floor rooms without an elevator. Most of the 36 rooms have shared baths in the hall that are clean and comfortable, with either a shower or a bathtub and a privacy lock. Breakfast is included, and the hotel also houses Moody's, the best restaurant in town.

Low-priced accommodations around Truckee are not easy to come by, especially in ski season. A decent basic hotel with affordable rates is the **Inn at Truckee** (11506 Deerfield Dr., Truckee, 530/587-8888 or 888/773-6888, www.innattruckee.com, $90-195). It's pet friendly ($25 per night) and offers a spa and sauna, included continental breakfast, and free wireless Internet access. The rooms are nothing special, but the convenience to major ski areas and other attractions makes it a good buy.

If you prefer a longer stay, call the **Donner Lake Village Resort** (15695 Donner Pass Rd., Truckee, 855/979-0402 or 530/587-6081, www.donnerlakevillage.com, $110-297), on the shores of Donner Lake. Choose from regular motel rooms without kitchens or studio, one-bedroom, and two-bedroom condos with full kitchen facilities. Guest rooms include all the amenities of a nicer motel. Donner Lake Village has its own marina with rental ski boats, fishing boats, and slips if you've brought your own watercraft; a bait and tackle shop is across the street. The nearby North Shore ski resorts are an easy drive. A two-night minimum is sometimes required in summer.

The ★ **Cedar House Sport Hotel** (10918 Brockway Rd., Truckee, 866/582-5655, www.cedarhousesporthotel.com, $170-270) sports an exposed wood exterior and is landscaped with trees, fallen stumps, and a rusty steel girder. Rooms are all about luxury, with wood platform beds, designer leather chairs and sofas, and shiny stainless-steel fixtures in the private baths. Choose comfortable rooms with queen or king beds or fancy suites with flat-screen TVs and every possible amenity. The expert staff can put together guided hikes, bike rides, and rafting or kayaking trips.

CAMPING

Donner Memorial State Park (12593 Donner Pass Rd., off I-80 west of downtown Truckee, 800/444-7275, www.reserveamerica.com, reservations late May-mid-Sept., first-come, first-served early Sept.-late May, $35) offers a spacious tree-filled campground with easy access to the lake, the new visitors center, and the trails in the park. It has 152 sites spread across three campgrounds: Ridge Campground (May-Oct.), Creek Campground (June-Sept.), and Splitrock (June-Sept.). Sites include fire rings and picnic tables, and there are restrooms with showers.

The Forest Service (877/444-6777, www.fs.usda.gov or www.recreation.gov) maintains three campgrounds along Highway 89 between Truckee and Tahoe City: **Granite Flat** (74 sites, Hwy. 89, 1.5 miles south of Truckee, mid-May-mid-Oct., $22-44) and **Goose Meadow** (24 sites, Hwy. 89, 4 miles south of Truckee, mid-May-Sept., $20) offer potable water and vault toilets; **Silver Creek** (27 sites, Hwy. 89, 6 miles south of Truckee, mid-May-Sept., $20) offers potable water and both flush and vault toilets. All three campgrounds get noise from the highway as well as the gentler sounds of the nearby Truckee River.

Tahoe's East Side

Lake Tahoe straddles California and Nevada, and so do visitors to the area. I-80 and U.S. 50 are the main roads to the Nevada side of Lake Tahoe from points west. On the North Shore, just west of the intersection of Highways 28 and 267, Crystal Bay marks the California-Nevada border crossing. The drive along the Nevada side of Lake Tahoe is beautiful, woodsy, and quiet, with stopping points along the way.

SKI RESORTS

- **Mt. Rose** (22222 Mt. Rose Hwy., Reno, NV, 775/849-0704 or 800/754-7673, www.mtrose.com, lift 9am-4pm daily winter, adults $79-89, seniors $69, ages 13-17 $69, ages 6-12 $47, ages under 6 $15) offers the most choices in terms of both variety and beginner routes.

- **Diamond Peak** (1210 Ski Way, Incline Village, NV, 775/832-1177, www.diamondpeak.com, lift 9am-4pm daily winter, adults $59-69, seniors and youth $44-59, ages 7-12 $22-33, children under 7 free) is easy to access from Incline Village and has two green runs at the bottom of the hill.

BEACHES AND WATER SPORTS

- **Sand Harbor Beach** (Hwy. 28, 3 miles south of Incline Village, NV, 775/831-0494, www.parks.nv.gov, 8am-7pm daily May and Sept., 8am-9pm daily June-Aug., 8am-5pm daily Oct.-Apr., $7-12 per vehicle) is one of the most popular places to swim at Lake Tahoe. There's a large picnic area, and the on-site restaurant-snack bar **Char-Pit Sand Harbor** (530/546-3171, www.charpit.com, 11am-9pm daily, $4-23).

- **Sand Harbor Rentals** (530/581-4336, www.sandharborrentals.com, $25-40 per hour, $75-95 per day, reservations recommended) is right on the beach, next to the boat ramp, and also offers kayak tours ($65-95).

- **Zephyr Cove Marina** (750 U.S. 50, Zephyr Cove, NV, 775/589-4901, www.zephyrcove.com) offers a full complement of services and watercraft rentals ($110-189), as well as lodge rooms and individual cabins ($179-339 summer, $119-219 winter).

CAMPING

- **Nevada Beach Campground** (Elks Point Rd., 3 miles north of Stateline, NV, 877/444-6777, www.recreation.gov, mid-May-mid-Oct., $32-34) offers 54 lakefront sites on the Nevada side of Lake Tahoe.

Transportation and Services

AIR

The nearest airports are **Reno-Tahoe International Airport** (RNO, 2001 E. Plumb Lane, Reno, NV, 775/328-6400, www.renoairport.com) and **Sacramento International Airport** (SMF, 6900 Airport Blvd., Sacramento, 916/929-5411, www.sacramento.aero). Both are served by several major airlines.

CAR

U.S. 50 provides the quickest access to **South Lake Tahoe.** From South Lake Tahoe, following U.S. 50 east brings you into **Stateline, Nevada,** in about three miles. From the San Francisco Bay Area, the drive via U.S. 50 takes about five hours in good weather (without traffic); from Sacramento it's only about two hours. However, heavy weekend traffic can significantly slow down the route. Check traffic reports before you hit the road.

U.S. 89 runs along the **West Shore** from the south. From U.S. 50 in South Lake Tahoe, take Highway 89 north for 25 miles along the West Shore, passing Meeks Bay, Tahoma, and Tahoe Pines on the way to Tahoe City on the North Shore. **I-80** leads toward the **North Shore** from Sacramento or the San Francisco Bay Area. From I-80, take Highway 89 south for 14 miles to Tahoe City.

Truckee is located on I-80. From San Francisco to Truckee is 185 miles, a 3.5-hour drive in good weather. From Sacramento, the trip is about 105 miles and 1.75 hours.

Winter Travel

In winter, carry **snow chains** that fit your vehicle (unless you have a 4WD vehicle and you know how to navigate in snow). Chains are often required near and around Tahoe in winter. You can pull off the road to attach your chains at many spots on I-80 and U.S. 50. You can also buy chains on the road, but the closer you get to Tahoe, the more expensive they are.

In winter, highways can close during major storms, and smaller roads surrounding the lake can shut down for weeks at a time. Traffic reports both on the radio and online offer information about road closures and alternate routes. If you're planning a winter trip, be aware of the weather and plan for some uncertainty.

Car Rentals

Avis (4130 Lake Tahoe Blvd., South Lake Tahoe, 530/544-5289, www.avis.com, 8am-5pm Mon.-Fri., 8am-3pm Sat.-Sun.) and **Budget** (4130 Lake Tahoe Blvd., 530/544-3439, www.budget.com, 8am-5pm Mon.-Fri., 8am-3pm Sat.-Sun.) are next door to the Stateline Transit Center bus station. You can also try **Enterprise** (2281 Lake Tahoe Blvd., 530/544-8844, www.enterprise.com, 9am-5pm Mon.-Fri., 9am-noon

Sat.), which has a full range of cars and small-midsize SUVs.

TRAIN AND BUS

The **Amtrak *California Zephyr*** (800/872-7245, www.amtrak.com, reservations required, $41-44 one-way) services Truckee at least once from the San Francisco Bay Area and Sacramento. However, this is a long-distance route covering a lot of ground, so delays are common.

In a few places, a free **Night Rider bus service** (866/216-5222, http://northlaketahoeexpress.com, 7pm-midnight daily, free) is provided by North Lake Tahoe Express. The winter service goes to Squaw Valley, Tahoe City, Northstar, and the Biltmore in Crystal Bay, Nevada. In summer, the West Shore Night Rider offers service from the Tahoe City Y to Granlibakken, Sunnyside, Homewood, and Tahoma.

Truckee Transit (530/550-7451, www.townoftruckee.com or www.laketahoetransit.com, adults $2.50 one-way, day pass $5, seniors $1, under age 12 $1.50) handles routes between the Truckee Tahoe Airport, downtown Truckee, and the Donner Memorial State Park and Donner Lake.

SERVICES

For medical attention in South Lake Tahoe, go to **Barton Memorial Hospital** (2170 South Ave., South Lake Tahoe, 530/541-3420, www.bartonhealth.org) or the **Tahoe Urgent Care Center** (2130 Lake Tahoe Blvd., South Lake Tahoe, 530/541-3277, www.tahoeurgentcare.com, 8am-5:30pm daily). If you need medical attention on the North Shore, the **Tahoe Forest Hospital** (10121 Pine Ave., Truckee, 530/587-6011, www.tfhd.com) has a full-service emergency room, among other services. **Incline Village Community Hospital** (880 Alder Ave., Incline Village, NV, 775/833-4100 or 800/419-2627, www.tfhd.com) is the place to go for help on the Nevada side. The hospital has a 24-hour emergency room.

Sacramento and Gold Country

Sacramento and Vicinity 261

Northern Gold Country 268

Shenandoah Valley 278

Southern Gold Country 283

Look for ★ to find recommended
sights, activities, dining, and lodging.

Highlights

★ **Capitol Building:** This building is the epicenter for the city's political history, past and present (page 261).

★ **Old Sacramento:** Stroll the wooden side-walk and cobblestone streets to get a sense of the state's origins (page 262).

★ **Empire Mine State Historic Park:** The best example of Gold Country mining is this living history museum and park (page 269).

★ **Marshall Gold Discovery State Historic Park:** This is the place that started it all—the spot where gold was discovered in 1848. The rest is literally history (page 275).

★ **Apple Hill:** This 20-mile swath of grower heaven includes dozens of orchards, vineyards, and pit stops for dining and relaxing along the way (page 275).

★ **Rafting the American River:** Both rookie and expert rafters will find opportunities to hit the water on the American River (page 276).

★ **Daffodil Hill:** This private ranch is carpeted in golden color every March, when visitors can explore the more than 300 species of daffodils on display (page 282).

★ **Columbia State Historic Park:** This

former Gold Rush town is now an indoor-outdoor museum, with exhibits, shops, and even a saloon (page 287).

The capital of California, Sacramento is a cosmopolitan city with a friendly vibe and a newly energized entertainment scene. The city grew along the Sacramento and American Rivers during the Gold Rush era.

In the city's midtown, downtown, and East Sacramento neighborhoods, an urban renaissance has remade this storied city into a vibrant, multicultural metropolis with cutting-edge art museums and packed bistros. More than ever, Sacramento is a place of brilliant contrasts, a town always caught in the crucible of compelling styles and personalities.

The fun continues in the Gold Country, a gorgeous 130-mile-long belt of award-winning wineries and rugged outdoor scenery deep in the Sierra Nevada foothills. After prospectors first discovered precious metal here in 1848, California was forever changed by the Gold Rush and the pioneers who poured into the new state searching for riches. These days, modern-day Gold Country prospectors search for antiques, explore caves, find hole-in-the-wall eateries, try river rafting, and discover luxurious inns in renovated farmhouses.

PLANNING YOUR TIME

Sacramento makes a nice day trip or weekend getaway from the Bay Area, or a fun one- to two-day start to a longer Gold Country and Sierra adventure. Winters are mild, but summers get blisteringly hot.

The Gold Country is too large to experience in one day; plan a weekend. Highway 49 runs more than 100 miles through the rugged Sierra foothills, with many side trips to smaller towns and specific caverns, mines, and museums along the way. If you've got one day, pick a specific Gold Country town as your destination, and one or two of the major parks and attractions nearby. In a weekend, you can get an overview of either the northern or southern Gold Country, driving from town to town and making short stops. The weather is best late spring to late fall. Winter brings snow, which draws skiers and winter-sports enthusiasts.

Previous: the covered bridge at Bridgeport; Gold Country is also horse country. **Above:** the town of Auburn.

Sacramento and Gold County

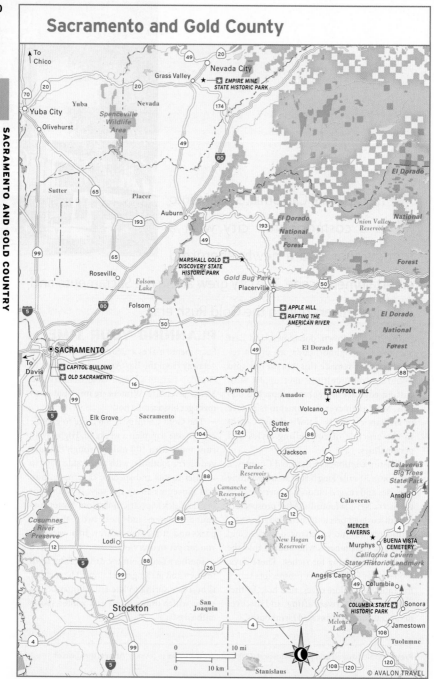

To Chico

49

20

Nevada City

Grass Valley

★ EMPIRE MINE STATE HISTORIC PARK

70

20

174

Yuba

Nevada

Yuba City

Olivehurst

Spenceville Wildlife Area

49

80

El Dorado

Sutter

65

Placer

Union Valley Reservoir

National

Auburn

El Dorado National Forest

193

193

99

65

49

Forest

Roseville

MARSHALL GOLD DISCOVERY STATE HISTORIC PARK ★

Gold Bug Park

Placerville

50

El Dorado

Folsom Lake

80

Folsom

APPLE HILL RAFTING THE AMERICAN RIVER

National

5

50

Forest

★ SACRAMENTO

49

El Dorado

To Davis

CAPITOL BUILDING OLD SACRAMENTO

88

16

Plymouth

Amador

DAFFODIL HILL ★

99

Elk Grove

Sacramento

Volcano

104

124

Sutter Creek

88

5

Jackson

26

Calaveras Big Trees State Park

88

Pardee Reservoir

Camanche Reservoir

26

Calaveras

Arnold

Cosumnes River Preserve

88

12

New Hogan Reservoir

49

MERCER CAVERNS ★

4

12

Lodi

Murphys

BUENA VISTA CEMETERY

5

88

California Cavern State Historic Landmark

99

26

Angels Camp

49

Columbia

Sonora

Stockton

San Joaquin

COLUMBIA STATE HISTORIC PARK

4

99

New Melones Lake

Jamestown

108

Tuolumne

0   10 mi

0   10 km

Stanislaus

108   120

120

© AVALON TRAVEL

Gold Country Road Trip

A tour through Gold Country is a road trip rich in history, beautiful scenery, outdoor adventure, and even wine-tasting. Highway 49 runs for 127 miles through the heart of Gold Country from Nevada City to Jamestown. Sacramento is near the northern Gold Country and is a great place to start a historical tour.

In **Sacramento,** start your day early with a tour of the **Capitol Building** and see where all the big decisions are made. Walk over to **Old Sacramento,** where you'll find the Gold Rush-era part of this town lovingly preserved. To really drink in the atmosphere, step into **Fat City Bar and Café** to enjoy comfort food served in a 19th-century dining room.

Take I-80 east for 32 miles until you reach Auburn in **Northern Gold Country,** then detour north on Highway 49 for 23 miles to **Grass Valley.** Stop at the **Empire Mine State Historic Park** and get a feel for the toil, hardship, and occasional wild luck that shaped the Gold Country. Charming Grass Valley offers food and shopping, or go straight to **Nevada City,** only three miles away, and spend the afternoon strolling its narrow streets. The **Outside Inn** offers unique rooms that border the creek.

Head back south on Highway 49 for one hour to reach **Placerville.** Take a thrilling white-water rafting trip on the American River near Coloma, or tour **Marshall Gold Discovery State Historic Park,** the site where James Marshall discovered gold in 1848. Next, hit the wineries and orchards around **Apple Hill** and taste the Gold Country's best vintages. Consider staying nearby at the **Historic Cary House Hotel.**

It is 60 winding miles from Placerville down Highway 49 to Angels Camp, the heart of **Southern Gold Country.** Visit the **Angels Camp Museum and Carriage House,** which beautifully showcases 30 carriages and wagons from the Gold Rush era. Venture east for eight miles on Highway 4 to **Murphys** and descend 162 feet below the ground into **Mercer Caverns.**

Continue south to **Columbia,** where most of downtown is part of the **Columbia State Historic Park.** Stroll the preserved streets of this Gold Rush boomtown to get a feel for what life was like when the mines operated. Stick around for dinner at the **Columbia City Hotel Restaurant,** where fine dining meets Old West elegance.

Accommodations await a short jog west on Highway 108 in **Jamestown,** where the **National Hotel** has been in operation since 1859. In the morning, make the return trip to Sacramento (two hours, 114 miles).

Sacramento and Vicinity

California's state capital has blossomed into a hip, thriving metropolis with renowned museums, an evolving nightlife scene, and an exploding lineup of innovative eateries.

SIGHTS
★ Capitol Building

The **California State Capitol Building** (10th St. and L St., 916/324-0333, http://capitolmuseum.ca.gov, 8am-5pm Mon.-Fri., 9am-5pm Sat.-Sun., free) displays a grandeur befitting the great state of California. On the ground floor, the museum's magnificent art collection includes California art and artifacts, oil portraits of the state's governors, two murals, and a collection of antiques. You can take a free tour that highlights the neoclassical architecture of the building, or watch from the galleries as members of the California State Legislature debate new laws.

Once you've finished absorbing the history of California from inside the museum, go outside and take a stroll around the grounds. At the rear of the building is an unusual treat—the **Arbor Tour.** Trees from around the world are planted in the sweeping space, an amazing array that's perfect for exploring or sitting and relaxing in the shade. The Arbor Tour is self-guided during the winter months. Docents offer guided tours in spring and fall.

★ Old Sacramento

Sacramento became an important town as the Gold Rush progressed and supplies were sent up the Sacramento River from San Francisco. The most important part of the early town was the embarcadero along the river, and that's still where **Old Sacramento** (visitors center, 1002 2nd St., 916/442-7644, www. discovergold.org, 10am-5pm daily) is today. The charming cobblestone streets and clattery wooden sidewalks pass old-time shops, restaurants, and attractions. You can take a carriage ride through the streets or walk the wharf along the river and wander the decks of the *Delta King* steamboat. Check out the tiny **Wells Fargo History Museum** (1000 2nd St., 916/440-4263, www.wellsfargohistory. com, 10am-5pm daily) and **Old Sacramento Schoolhouse Museum** (1200 Front St., 916/483-8818, www.oldsacschoolhouse.org), or lighten your wallet in the shops and boutiques. To really get into the spirit, join a

guided walk (Sat.-Sun. June-Aug., www. historicoldsac.org, $5 general admission) to hear tales of Gold Rush history or learn more about the capital's architecture. The fun continues beneath the city's bustling streets with **Old Sacramento Underground Tours** (916/808-7059, www.historicoldsac.org, hours vary Apr.-Dec., adults $15, youth $10, children not recommended), which reveal the hidden corridors and passageways that were buried when the city was elevated.

California State Railroad Museum

Inside the **California State Railroad Museum** (125 I St., 916/323-9280, www. csrmf.org, 10am-5pm daily, adults $10, youth $5, children free), artifacts and models illustrate the building of the railroads to the West, especially the all-important Transcontinental Railroad. The main floor plays host to the museum's fabulous collection of rolling stock—locomotives, freight and passenger cars, and cabooses.

You can look in on the stylish appointments of the private rail cars of the wealthy and stand next to the immense wheels of mighty steam locomotives. Along the edges of the room are memorabilia from the heyday

the California State Capitol Building

Downtown Sacramento

of the railroads, including timetables and fine china. A gift shop offers souvenirs for visitors of all ages.

Cross the plaza to board the steam-powered **Excursion Train** (916/445-6645, 11am-5pm Sat.-Sun. Apr.-Sept., adults $10, youth $5, children free) for a 40-minute ride along the riverfront.

Sutter's Fort State Historic Park

Sutter's Fort State Historic Park (2701 L St., 916/445-4422, www.parks.ca.gov, 10am-5pm daily, adults $5, youth $3, children free), situated in the middle of downtown Sacramento, was originally the center of John Sutter's "New Helvetia" settlement. A tour of the park begins with the mazelike museum at the entrance. Inside the fort structure, the story of John Sutter is told in photos, artifacts, and placards. After perusing the interpretive area, wander outside into the sunlight and into the fort's inner courtyard to see how the early settlers lived. Denizens of the park, dressed in 19th-century costumes, engage in the activities that filled the days of California's settlers. With their help, you can try your hand at making rope, baking bread, and doing all sorts of pioneer activities. Admission prices increase (adults $7, youth $5) on special interpretive days that occur occasionally Monday-Friday.

Leland Stanford Mansion

Railroad baron, former California governor, and Stanford University founder Leland Stanford and his family spent a number of years living in the capital city at what is now the **Leland Stanford Mansion State Historic Park** (800 N St., 916/324-9266, www.parks.ca.gov, 10am-5pm Wed.-Sun., free). Tours begin in the visitors center, next to the museum store outside the mansion. From here you'll journey inside the lavish main building, where you can admire the lovingly restored furnishings, carpets, walls, and antiques. You must be part of a tour to explore the mansion; the last tour each day starts at 4pm.

Crocker Art Museum

The **Crocker Art Museum** (216 O St., 916/808-7000, www.crockerartmuseum.org, 10am-5pm Tues.-Wed. and Fri.-Sun., 10am-9pm Thurs., adults $10, seniors and students $8, youth $5, children free) hosts centuries of fine art and historical exhibits. Notable California artists include Thomas Hill, Joan Brown, Guy Rose, and Wayne Thiebaud.

American River Parkway

A trip to Sacramento wouldn't be complete without a hike along the **American River Parkway** (www.regionalparks.saccounty.net, 23 miles, easy-moderate). The parkway is actually a series of paved trails that run through wetlands, oak woodlands, and several regional parks along the American River. The trails start at **Discovery Park,** a grassy 302-acre park at the confluence of the Sacramento and American Rivers, and end 23 miles away in the city of Folsom. Along the way, you'll pass cyclists pedaling by river levees, families pushing strollers by the water, and plenty of dog owners taking their pets for a walk.

ENTERTAINMENT AND EVENTS

The sleek, urbane interior of **Harlow's** (2708 J St., 916/441-4693, www.harlows.com, tickets $10-70, shows age 21 and over) has a big-city feel and a moneyed vibe; make sure to spiff up before rubbing elbows with the swanky crowd. The live acts range from local favorites like Tainted Love and Irish rockers Young Dubliners to up-and-coming local DJs.

the *Delta King* steamboat

Harlow's often has a line to get in, especially if there's a show.

Mix (1525 L St., 916/442-8899, www.mix-downtown.net, hours vary Tues.-Sun.) is the destination for Sacramento's elite. It's also a great spot to meet friends for a night on the town. Polished wooden ceilings and wall panels give a minimalist European feel with California flair. A rooftop patio with fire pits and comfy chairs invites relaxing with a glass of wine or a beer. Mix is popular on weekends and will have a line later in the evening.

De Vere's Irish Pub (1521 L St., 916/231-9947, http://deverespub.com, 11am-2am Mon.-Fri., 9am-2am Sat., 9am-midnight Sun.) oozes Irish history. All of the furniture and fixtures were designed and imported from Ireland, including the towering wooden bar that spans two rooms. The 20-ounce pints of Guinness are popular, but you can also order from a sizeable cocktail list. The pub also has a full menu of Irish and British cuisine.

There's no secret password, but the **Shady Lady Saloon** (1409 R St., 916/231-9121, http://shadyladybar.com, 11am-2am Mon.-Fri., 9am-2am Sat.-Sun.) feels like a speakeasy with a Gold Rush vibe in the heart of Midtown's up-and-coming R Street Historic Corridor. Bartenders don vintage vests and wear garters on their sleeves, all while serving up libations like the White Linen or the Horse Neck. The bar decor is stylish and decadent, and you can catch a variety of live acts nightly. The bar also serves dinner and weekend brunch with a Southern-inspired menu.

58 Degrees and Holding (1217 18th St., 916/442-5858, www.58degrees.com, 11am-10pm Sun.-Thurs., 11am-11pm Fri., 10am-11pm Sat.) is a wine bar and upscale eatery in Midtown's Handle District. The wine list is stacked with European and Californian wines, including a few from Amador County, and the waitstaff is knowledgeable about the vino.

Capitol Garage (1500 K St., 916/444-3633, www.capitolgarage.com, 6am-midnight Mon.-Thurs., 6am-2am Fri., 8am-2am Sat.-Sun.) is an espresso bar-nightclub serving coffee and cocktails all day long. Stop by for karaoke every Thursday and Sunday.

FOOD

Sacramento is experiencing a foodie revolution. The city recently became the Farm-to-Fork Capital of America, which means local restaurants are serving fresh produce harvested the very same day from farms just a short drive from town. Sacramento's culinary

the Tower Bridge over the Sacramento River

boom is even attracting top chefs from nearby San Francisco and the Napa Valley who dig the city's location and hip, urban vibe. Make sure to check out the hugely popular **Farm-to-Fork Festival** (September, 916/808-7777, www.farmtofork.com), which throws a month-long party in downtown; events have included a cattle drive to the California State Capitol, a tractor parade, a gourmet dinner for 700 guests on the Tower Bridge over the Sacramento River, a sprawling farmers market on Capital Avenue, and plenty of smaller events around town.

Bakeries and Cafés

One of the city's caffeine pioneers is **Naked Lounge** (1500 Q St., 916/442-0174, www.nakedcoffee.net, 6am-11pm daily, $4). This café has a neo-grungy vibe that's manifested in edgy artwork on the wall and overstuffed couches where folks sip drinks like the Bowl of Soul (chamomile tea steamed with condensed milk and honey). The best of the best may just be ★ **Old Soul** (1716 L St., 916/443-7685, www.oldsoulco.com, 6am-9pm daily, $2-5), perhaps the purest Seattle-style coffeehouse in town. Choices are simple here: just tea, house coffee, basic lattes and mochas, and great breakfasts.

Breakfast

★ **Fox and Goose Pub and Restaurant** (1001 R St., 916/443-8825, www.foxandgoose.com, 6:30am-9:30pm Mon.-Sat., 6:30am-3pm Sun., $10) might just dish up Sacramento's best breakfast. Whether you're jonesing for fresh pastries, delicious pancakes, or killer omelets, make sure to come here. Show up early: A line starts forming around 9am on weekends.

American

At Old Sacramento's **Fat City Bar and Café** (1001 Front St., 916/446-6768, www.fatsrestaurants.com, 11:30am-9pm Mon.-Fri., 10:30am-10pm Sat.-Sun., $11-29), you'll imagine you've walked into an Old West saloon from the gold-mining heyday. Except you can get chow mein, tacos, meatloaf, pot pie, or an enormous cheeseburger (the bourbon barbecue burger is the best of these). On weekends, enjoy a mixed brunch menu that includes the best of the lunch menu, plus breakfast specialties.

The hottest restaurant is **Mother** (1023 K St., 916/594-9812, http://mothersacramento.com, 11am-2:30pm Mon., 11am-4pm and 5pm-9pm Tues.-Thurs., 11am-4pm and 5pm-10pm Fri.-Sat., $12). The menu is Southern-themed but vegetarian, the decor hip yet friendly. Mother's menu changes seasonally, but a few standbys include the mouthwatering nut burger and the fried green tomato sandwich. Check the restaurant's live web feed to see the line before arriving.

★ **Mulvaney's Building & Loan** (1215 19th St., 916/441-6022, www.mulvaneysbl.com, 11:30am-2:30pm and 5pm-10pm Tues.-Fri., 5pm-10pm Sat., $14-38) is a product of Midtown's renaissance, an upscale eatery showcasing the best of California cuisine. The menu changes often to take advantage of local seasonal produce. Go for a standard appetizer and main dish, or order small plates. The wine list offers a reasonable number of tastings and interesting vintages.

★ **Ella Dining Room and Bar** (1131 K St., 916/443-3772, www.elladiningroomandbar.com, 11:30am-9pm Mon.-Thurs., 11:30am-10pm Fri., 5:30pm-10pm Sun., $10-40) is downtown Sacramento's culinary superstar. This swanky eatery dishes up local, sustainably farmed fare. Typical plates might be Scottish salmon with succotash, juniper-braised oxtail, or naturally raised trout from a nearby fish farm. Call ahead on weekends to secure a table.

Asian

For American-style sushi and an upbeat atmosphere, try **Mikuni Japanese Restaurant and Sushi Bar** (1530 J St., 916/447-2112, www.mikunisushi.com, 11:30am-10pm Mon.-Thurs., 11:30am-midnight Fri., noon-midnight Sat., noon-9pm Sun., $5-17). The crowd skews young on weekends as bar-hoppers start their evenings. Expect to wait on busier nights unless you have a reservation.

Frank Fat's (806 L St., 916/442-7092, www.fatsrestaurants.com, 11am-10pm Mon.-Fri., 5pm-10pm Sat.-Sun., $9-27) is a legendary Sacramento institution, opened by Frank Fat in 1939, serving authentic upscale Chinese food. For years, Frank's has been a favorite among local politicos for power lunches. The interior has a hip, cosmopolitan vibe with classy leather booths, a long shiny bar, and modern furniture.

Mexican

Both the atmosphere and the mole are authentic at ★ **Tres Hermanas** (2416 K St., 916/443-6919, www.treshermanasonk.com, 11am-9pm Mon.-Thurs., 11am-10pm Fri., 7am-10pm Sat., 7am-8pm Sun., $10-14). The food is influenced by northern Mexican cuisine, so expect quesadillas, tacos, and enchiladas heavy on herbs and veggies; lots of pork and fish; and enchiladas smothered in one of three amazing sauces. This Midtown spot gets busy. Between 7pm and 9pm, figure on waiting 30 minutes for a table.

ACCOMMODATIONS

Sacramento tends to be a working town. The best bets for cheap-and-easy rooms are the various Holiday Inns, Quality Inns, and Sheratons. Most Sacramento hotels don't provide airport shuttles, so you'll have to take a taxi or make other plans for transportation.

Under $150

For budget accommodations, you can't beat the **Sacramento Hostel** (925 H St., 916/443-1691, www.norcalhostels.org/sac, $30-99), in a grand old Victorian home in downtown. Lodgings include coed and single-sex dorms, plus a few private rooms. Only one private room includes a private bath. The hostel has free wireless Internet access, laundry, on-site parking, a large shared kitchen, 24-hour guest access, but no linens, so bring your own.

The **Inn off Capitol Park** (1530 N St., 916/447-8100, www.innoffcapitolpark.com, $100-179) offers luxury at moderate prices. The inn is within easy walking distance of the Capitol and the Sacramento Convention Center. The furniture and lighting feel more like home than a motel. Amenities include free Wi-Fi and a continental breakfast. With only 36 rooms, this friendly boutique hotel can fill up fast during conventions. The Inn off Capitol Park does not allow smoking.

$150-250

An integral part of the Old Town neighborhood, the riverboat *Delta King* (1000 Front St., 916/444-5464, www.deltaking.com, $150-230) is a hotel, restaurant, theater, and gathering space. Of the modern, elegant staterooms, the less expensive ones can be quite small, but all have private bathrooms.

The best B&B in Sacramento has long been the 10-room ★ **Amber House** (1315 22nd St., 916/444-8085, www.amberhouse.com, $180-280), located on a quiet residential street in Midtown within walking distance of shopping, restaurants, and nightlife. Every room at the inn has either a jetted tub or a deep-soaking bathtub, a very comfortable bed, and top-end amenities. The stellar comfort and service extend to the food as well.

The majestic art deco brownstone ★ **Citizen Hotel** (926 J St., 916/447-2700, www.jdvhotels.com, $127-250) is one of downtown's most recognizable landmarks. Inside, the retro decor has a 1960s vibe, with a marble foyer and rooms with vintage pinstriped wallpaper and upholstered headboards. Amenities include a minibar, flat-screen TV, and Italian linens. Other services include same-day laundry, a fitness center, and valet parking ($25 per day).

TRANSPORTATION AND SERVICES
Air

Major carriers fly into **Sacramento International Airport** (SMF, 6900 Airport Blvd., 916/929-5411, www.sacairports.org), a great starting point for trips into the Gold Country.

Train

If you're coming into Sacramento from the San Francisco Bay Area, one of the best ways is on the *Capitol Corridor* train run by **Amtrak** (800/872-7245, www.amtrak.com). Serving the centrally located Amtrak station (401 I St.), this train runs from Sacramento to Oakland and on to San Jose and back several times each day. The Oakland-Sacramento trip takes two hours, and San Jose-Sacramento is just over three hours.

Bus

Sacramento has a busy and reasonably extensive public transit system that includes both buses and a light-rail train system, **Sacramento Regional Transit** (SACRT, www.sacrt.com, single ride $2.50, day pass $6). Including the downtown trolley and the light-rail lines, SACRT has nearly 100 routes; check the website for schedules and maps.

Greyhound (420 Richards Blvd., 916/444-6858 or 800/231-2222, www.greyhound.com, $7.50-48) sells cheap tickets from San Francisco ($7.50-13), Modesto ($7-13), Redding ($30-46.50), and Los Angeles ($24-48).

Car

I-80 runs through Sacramento roughly east-west, and the I-80 Business adjunct goes into downtown on a slightly different route. I-5 splits the city on its north-south route. U.S. 50 runs east to Lake Tahoe, and Highway 99 runs south to Los Angeles and north to Chico.

Parking in town can get difficult during major events, but otherwise spots aren't hard to come by. Near the Capitol Building, bring change to feed the meters; some meters also take credit cards. In Old Sacramento, spots right in the middle of the action can be at a premium during high season—you may have to walk a few blocks to get to Front Street, but there are pay lots at the north and south ends of Old Sacramento. The theaters and arenas tend to have ample parking lots, though you'll pay at many of those. Most hotels offer parking free with your room.

Services

Sutter General Hospital (2801 L St., 916/454-2222, http://suttermedicalcenter.org) is right in downtown and has an emergency room, or go to the emergency center run by **UC Davis Medical Center** (2315 Stockton Blvd., 916/734-5010).

Northern Gold Country

California's Gold Country is a great sprawling network of small towns and roads crisscrossing the Sierra Nevada foothills where much of California's modern history began. The northern Gold Country extends from Nevada City down into the Shenandoah Valley; it's easiest to traverse from north to south. Interstate 80 can take you from Sacramento or the Bay Area to the northern Gold Country town of Auburn. Here you can pick up Highway 49 north to Grass Valley and Nevada City. On Highway 49 south of Auburn, head east to Placerville, Coloma, and Fair Play, and south into the Shenandoah Valley, where small highways and roads lead to other tiny dots on the map.

NEVADA CITY AND GRASS VALLEY

Both Nevada City and Grass Valley are chock-full of tiny boutiques, art galleries, and quirky gift stores. In Nevada City, most shopping is on Broad and Commercial Streets; in Grass Valley, head for Main and Mill Streets. Parking in either town can be a challenge and is mostly on the street, so be patient and check side streets for empty spaces. In Grass Valley, **Booktown Books** (107 Bank St., 530/272-4655, http://booktownbooks.com,

Side Trip to Davis

Davis is home to the region's agricultural brainpower—the University of California, Davis, home of the "Aggies." The town is among rice fields and orchards in the fertile valley between Sacramento and California's coastal mountains. Most of the region's organic and community-supported farms are just northwest of Davis, and much of this bounty can be found twice a week at the town's renowned farmers market.

Known for its progressive vibe and left-leaning politics, Davis also consistently earns national recognition as a top-notch cycling town with some of the country's most prolific and well-maintained bike paths. Downtown, you'll find plenty of arty boutiques and antiques stores scattered throughout the town's shady streets, a perfect place for avoiding the hot valley sun.

UNIVERSITY OF CALIFORNIA, DAVIS

One of the country's most esteemed educational institutions is the **University of California, Davis** (1 Shields Ave., 530/752-1011, www.ucdavis.edu). Students at UC Davis are known as Aggies, a nod to the school's storied agricultural background. First opened in 1905 as a farm school, the expansive campus, California's largest at 5,300 acres, has an on-site dairy and a working farm. Today UC Davis is renowned for its biological and political science programs, along with one of the nation's biggest engineering schools. Sports are also an important part of Aggie life, and the UC Davis athletic program has rivalries with other NCAA Division I schools like Stanford, UC Berkeley, and nearby Sacramento State. If you visit Davis, make sure to stop by the beautiful campus for a stroll or to catch an Aggies game.

At the **Robert Mondavi Institute for Wine and Food Science** (392 Old Davis Rd., 530/754-6349, http://robertmondaviinstitute.ucdavis.edu, tours $5), the on-campus brewery is just one of the world-class research facilities dedicated to food and beverage-making at UC Davis. Completed in 2008, the sprawling agricultural complex also boasts a green-certified winery and an organic vegetable garden. Stop by for a student-led tour or pay a little more for a faculty member to guide you around the institute. Tours are available Monday-Friday.

With more than seven million insects, the **Bohart Museum of Entomology** (1124 Academic Surge, 530/752-0493, http://bohart.ucdavis.edu, 9am-noon and 1pm-5pm Mon.-Thurs., free, parking $9) has one of the largest collections in North America, and 50,000 new specimens are added every year.

GETTING THERE

Davis is 14 miles west of Sacramento on I-80. The Richards Boulevard exit provides easy access to downtown. **Amtrak** (840 2nd St., 530/758-4220 or 800/872-7245, www.amtrak.com) stops several times daily in downtown Davis on the way to Oakland, San Jose, and Sacramento. **Unitrans** (1 Shields Ave., Davis, 530/752-2877, http://unitrans.ucdavis.edu, $1) provides student-run public transit around Davis and the university campus.

10am-6pm Mon.-Sat., 11am-5pm Sun.) is truly the mother lode for rare and used tomes.

★ Empire Mine State Historic Park

Arguably the best mining museum in the Gold Country is the **Empire Mine State Historic Park** (10791 E. Empire St., Grass Valley, 530/273-8522, www.empiremine.org, 10am-5pm daily, adults $7, children $3, tour

included). Walking into the yard, you can see and feel the life of the 19th- and 20th-century miners who extracted tons of gold from the earth below your feet. The showpiece of the museum collection is the scale model of the Empire Mine and the various nearby interconnected tunnels. Turn on the lights surrounding the mammoth glass case to highlight and hear the stories of the different

Northern Gold Country

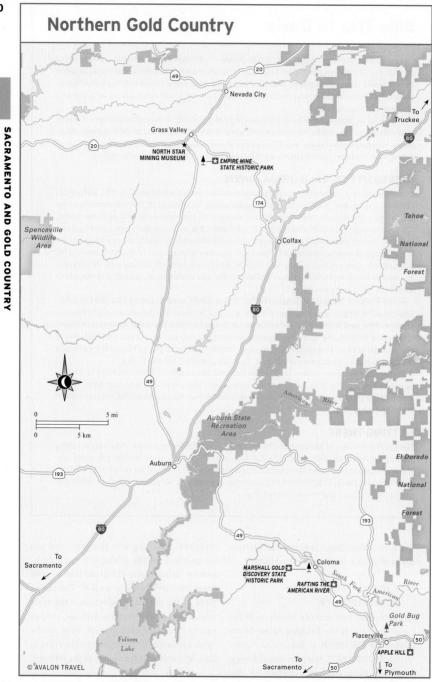

© AVALON TRAVEL

parts of the overwhelmingly vast and complex underground maze.

In addition to the fabulous museum, there are 14 miles of hiking trails. The **Hardrock Trail** (1-3.5 miles) loops from the visitors center to the remains of the Pennsylvania, WYOD, and Orleans Mines before heading out to the Osborn Hill Loop or back to the parking lot. Along the trail you'll see the remains of the major hard-rock mines that once produced gold.

North Star Mining Museum

The **North Star Mining Museum** (10933 Allison Ranch Rd., Grass Valley, 530/273-4255, http://nevadacountyhistory.org, 10am-4pm Wed.-Sat., noon-4pm Sun., May-Oct., donation requested) is a tribute to the industrial machinery that once powered the North Star Mine, one of California's most successful mines during the Gold Rush. The museum has plenty of mining relics, such as the largest Pelton wheel in the world, and a working stamp mill. The museum is closed in winter, so plan your visit accordingly.

South Yuba River State Park

The **South Yuba River State Park** (17660 Pleasant Valley Rd., Penn Valley, 530/273-3884, sunrise-sunset daily, visitors center 11am-4pm Thurs.-Sun., free) stretches 20 miles along the Yuba River, from Malakoff Diggins State Historic Park to the covered bridge at Bridgeport. There are plenty of Gold Rush ruins on the river, including an old mining camp and several sections of the Virginia Turnpike, a 14-mile-long toll road. A short nature walk leads through oak woodlands and wildflowers. In summer, enjoy a small gravel beach just a short hike east of the covered bridge. Parking is provided in a fenced lot ($5); street parking on Pleasant Valley Road is not allowed.

Malakoff Diggins State Historic Park

Malakoff Diggins State Historic Park (Tyler Foote Rd., 26 miles north of Nevada City, 530/265-2740, www.parks.ca.gov, sunrise-sunset daily, $8 per vehicle) was once the site of California's largest hydraulic mine. The best way to explore the park is by hiking the **Diggins Loop Trail** (three miles round-trip). The park includes the ghost town of **North Bloomfield,** which has several notable structures, including a one-room schoolhouse, an old cemetery, St. Columncille's Church, and a small museum. Malakoff Diggins is about

Empire Mine State Historic Park

25 miles north of Nevada City, but it can take almost an hour to drive. To reach the park from Nevada City, take Highway 49 north for about 10 miles toward the small town of Downieville. Turn right onto Tyler Foote Road and follow the road into the park.

Food

The ★ **Flour Garden Café and Bakery** (999 Sutton Way, Grass Valley, 530/272-2043, www.flourgarden.com, 6am-6pm Mon.-Sat., 6am-5pm Sun., $5) serves homemade pastries, soups, sandwiches, and cakes using local, natural ingredients. For lunch, pick up any number of prepared items, have a sandwich made, or order the fresh homemade soup of the day. The Flour Garden has two other locations, in downtown Grass Valley (109 Neal St., Grass Valley) and Auburn (340C Elm Ave., Auburn).

Tofanelli's (302 W. Main St., Grass Valley, 530/272-1468, www.tofanellis.com, 8am-9pm daily, $13-28), an "Italian-inspired" restaurant, serves lamb shanks, different cuts of beef, seared ahi, meatloaf, and lots of pasta dishes. The claim to fame is the omelet menu, which features 101 variations.

The last thing you might expect in Nevada City is high-quality sushi. But before opening **Sushi in the Raw** (315 Spring St., Nevada City, 530/478-9503, 5:30pm-9pm Tues.-Sat., $6-15) in 2002, owner Ru Suzuki already had a dedicated following as one of Gold Country's premier sushi chefs, and he's topped himself with this cozy authentic location. Call several days ahead for a reservation; the restaurant is small and very popular.

Lefty's Grill (101 Broad St., Nevada City, 530/265-5838, www.leftysgrill.com, 11:30am-9:30pm daily, $15-28) serves upscale bar food in a handsome brick building, a historical landmark that was once a bank. For starters, order a side of sweet-potato fries slathered in apricot chipotle sauce. Leave room for the Napa pizza.

★ **South Pine Café** (110 S. Pine St., Nevada City, 530/265-0260, http://southpinecafe.com, 8am-3pm daily, $8-12) is a homey little breakfast spot serving healthy grub made from local produce. Some dishes favor a Southwestern theme and others are more international. South Pine also boasts a fantastic lunch menu with a similar international theme as breakfast.

Accommodations

Built in 1862, the **Holbrooke Hotel** (212 W. Main St., 530/273-1353, www.holbrooke.com, $75-239) in downtown Grass Valley is one of the oldest lodgings in California. A host of famous 19th-century figures stayed here, including U.S. presidents Ulysses S. Grant and Grover Cleveland, writer Mark Twain, and entertainers Lotta Crabtree and Lola Montez. Expect updated amenities in all 28 rooms, which are fully stocked with modern conveniences like a private bath with antique claw-foot tub, cable TV, and free Wi-Fi; some rooms also have balconies or fireplaces.

History permeates **Emma Nevada House** (528 E. Broad St., Nevada City, 530/265-4415, www.emmanevadahouse.com, $170-250), a large Victorian house that once belonged to the family of noted opera singer Emma Nevada. You'll see real antiques in the front rooms and charming collectibles in the six uniquely styled rooms, all with comfortable beds and plush baths, some with claw-foot tubs. A multicourse gourmet breakfast is served each morning.

A short stroll from downtown Nevada City is the **Outside Inn** (575 E. Broad St., Nevada City, 530/265-2233, www.outsideinn.com, $85-165). Converted from a 1930s motel, each room has a different outdoor theme, including the Single Track Room and the romantic Creekside Hideaway cabin. A natural creek runs through the laid-back patio area, which includes a pool and a brick fire pit. The inn is pet-friendly.

Just minutes from downtown Grass Valley, the charming motel-style accommodations at **Sierra Mountain Inn** (816 W. Main St., Grass Valley, 530/273-8133, www.sierramountaininn.com, $110-185) offer a romantic and relaxing option to get away from it all. The rooms combine rustic decor with luxurious touches like marble baths and vaulted ceilings for a quirky farmhouse feel. The inn usually requires a two-night minimum; call for single-night stays. Dogs are at least $25 extra, depending on the room.

Transportation and Services

Grass Valley and Nevada City are on Highway 49, north of I-80 and Auburn. To reach the area by car, take I-80 to Auburn and follow Highway 49 (Golden Chain Hwy.) northwest. Grass Valley is 25 miles from Auburn, and Nevada City is four miles farther north. Weekend traffic on I-80 between San Francisco and Lake Tahoe can be quite congested, and the area can receive heavy snowfall in winter. Check on the weather, road conditions, and traffic reports with **Caltrans** (http://dot.ca.gov) before heading out.

The closest airport is **Sacramento International Airport** (SMF, 6900 Airport Blvd., Sacramento, 916/929-5411, www.sacairports.org), 60 miles south. **Gold Country Stage** (www.mynevadacounty.com, adults $1.50, day pass $4.50, under age 5 free) runs buses and minibuses through Nevada City, Grass Valley, Auburn, and points north of the Gold Country.

The major hospital with an emergency room is **Sierra Nevada Memorial Hospital** (155 Glasson Way, Grass Valley, 530/274-6000, www.snmh.org).

AUBURN
Sights

Located on the first floor of the historical Placer County courthouse, the **Placer County Museum** (101 Maple St., 530/889-6500, www.placer.ca.gov, 10am-4pm daily, free) offers a glimpse into the town's rustic past. The exhibits span different themes and time periods in Placer County history, such as the women's jail, a recreated sheriff's office, and the stagecoach that ran from Auburn up into the mountains. Outside the museum, views from the courthouse are photo-worthy. Free guided tours of Old Town are offered Saturday at 10am.

Auburn was one of California's first mining settlements, built after gold was discovered in 1848. Learn more about the area's history at the **Gold Country Museum** (601 Lincoln Way, 530/889-6500, www.placer.ca.gov, 10:30am-4pm Tues.-Sun., free). Many standard Gold Country exhibits are on display, including a reconstructed mine, a stamp mill, and a miner's tent.

Emma Nevada House

Auburn State Recreation Area

At **Auburn State Recreation Area** (www.parks.ca.gov, 7am-sunset daily, $10), more than 100 miles of trails wind through leafy oak woodlands and past seasonal waterfalls like Codfish Falls. The area is used by hikers, joggers, mountain bikers, dirt bikers, and horseback riders. Parking is easiest at the confluence of the American River's North and Middle Forks, and it's also where most of the trails begin. This area is arguably one of the best local places for water sports: Rafting, kayaking, and boating are all available along various stretches of the river. Pack a swimsuit in summer and enjoy the cooling waters of the river confluence, which has plenty of swimming holes and jumping rocks.

Accommodations and Food

The **Best Western Golden Key** (13450 Lincoln Way, 530/885-8611, www.bestwesterngoldenkey.com, $78-150) has tidy and comfortable accommodations in a location perfect for exploring nearby Gold Country attractions. Wi-Fi is included, and a hearty continental breakfast with hubcap-size waffles is another perk. The slightly more upscale **Auburn Holiday Inn** (120 Grass Valley Hwy., 530/887-8787, www.auburnhi.com, $139-179) has an outdoor pool and large, well-equipped rooms with flat-screen TVs and king beds. The convenient location is less than a mile from the historical town center and offers a decent view of the courthouse.

Located in Old Town Auburn, ★ **Carpe Vino** (1568 Lincoln Way, 530/823-0320, www.carpevinoauburn.com, 5pm-10pm Tues.-Sun., $10-31) serves sustainably grown ingredients from local farms and vendors. The red-wine braised beef, Muscovy duck breast, and roasted Angus strip loin are all standout dishes. Carpe Vino opens at noon Tuesday through Sunday for wine-tasting.

Ikeda's California Country Market (13500 Lincoln Way, 530/885-4243, www.ikedas.com, 11am-7pm Mon.-Thurs., 10am-8pm Fri.-Sun., $10; fruit stand 8am-7pm Mon.-Thurs., 8am-8pm Fri.-Sun.) is a roadside burger joint and fruit stand that has become a de facto rest stop for travelers headed to Lake Tahoe. The food is a culinary mash-up of traditional diner fare and Japanese cuisine. Lunch and dinner hours can bring a crowd, so expect a short wait for your food.

Katrina's Cafe (456 Grass Valley Highway, 530/888-1166, www.katrinas-cafe.com, 7am-2:30pm Wed.-Sat., 7am-2pm Sun., $6-11 cash only) serves a delicious home-cooked breakfast. Famous for their awesome pancakes and mouthwatering eggs Benedict, this place is legendary for whipping up belt-busting meals.

Auburn Alehouse Brewery and Restaurant (289 Washington St., 530/885-2537, http://auburnalehouse.com, 11am-9pm Mon.-Tues., 11am-10pm Wed.-Thurs., 11am-11pm Fri., 10am-11pm Sat., 10am-9pm Sun., $9-22) is a local microbrewery and bustling sports bar, where every pint is brewed in the gleaming silver tanks in the back. The cuisine is typical bar food, with burgers, sandwiches, and sides like sweet potato fries.

Transportation and Services

Auburn is located on I-80 and provides access to Highway 49 north and south. As such, it experiences heavy weekend traffic as well as snow in winter. Check weather, road conditions, and traffic reports before traveling in winter.

The closest major airport is **Sacramento International Airport** (SMF, 6900 Airport Blvd., Sacramento, 916/929-5411, www.sacairports.org), 30 miles south. The **Amtrak** *Capitol Corridor* train (www.amtrak.com, 800/872-7245) departs several times a day on its way to Sacramento, Oakland, and San Jose at Auburn Station (277 Nevada St.), but there are no ticket services. The **Gold Country Stage** (www.mynevadacounty.com, adults $1.50, day pass $3, under age 5 free) runs buses and minibuses through Nevada City, Grass Valley, Auburn, and to points north of the Gold Country.

For medical assistance, **Sutter Auburn Faith Hospital** (11815 Education St., 530/888-4500, www.sutterauburnfaith.org)

offers an emergency room and a full range of hospital services.

PLACERVILLE AND VICINITY
★ Marshall Gold Discovery State Historic Park

One day in 1848, a carpenter named James W. Marshall took a fateful stroll by the sawmill he was building for John Sutter on the American River and found gold specks shining in the water. Marshall's discovery sparked the California Gold Rush and one of the greatest migrations in history. See where it all began at **Marshall Gold Discovery State Historic Park** (310 Back St., Coloma, 530/622-3470, www.parks.ca.gov, 8am-7pm daily summer, 8am-5pm daily fall-spring, $8 per vehicle). Start inside the visitors center (10am-5pm daily Mar.-Nov., 10am-4pm daily Nov.-Mar.) for a quick lesson on the park's storied past, complete with artifacts from the indigenous Nisenan and Miwok people who lived in the area before the Gold Rush. Outside the visitors center, history buffs will love the park's interactive exhibits—catch a live pioneer cooking demonstration or help load a real wagon with mining supplies like a true forty-niner.

Feel like recreating Marshall's discovery for yourself? Take a gold-panning lesson at the park's Eureka Experience Center, and then try your luck by the river. Kids will especially love getting elbow-deep in the mud for a chance to strike it rich. The park also provides nature walks and hikes through the scenic American River canyon; the **Gold Discovery Loop Trail** (3.6 miles) takes you to the very spot where Marshall made his discovery. Surrounded by beautiful wildflowers in spring, a full-size replica of **Sutter's Mill** stands near several immaculately restored historical buildings, like the tiny one-bedroom Mormon cabin, the Chinese-operated Wah Hop and Man Lee stores, the old blacksmith shop, and the Price-Thomas home. The park is undergoing renovations but is open during the construction.

Gold Bug Park

If you're traveling with kids and want them to experience a gold-mining museum, don't miss **Gold Bug Park** (Bedford Ave., 530/642-5207, www.goldbugpark.org, 10am-4pm daily Apr.-Oct., noon-4pm Sat.-Sun. Nov.-Mar., adults $6, youth $4, children $3). This smaller mine, originally called the Hattie, dates from the 1850s. Today the museum offers lessons in history, including tours of the mine, an interpretive museum, and a gift shop. For a small fee, you can pan for gold in a manufactured sluice. Many of the tour features and exhibits are designed for children, combining education and entertainment as kids don their hard hats, check out the mine shaft, and learn the function of a stamp mill.

★ Apple Hill

The farms of **Apple Hill** (Apple Hill Dr./Carson Rd., north of U.S. 50, between Placerville and Pollack Pines, 530/644-7692, www.applehill.com), east of Placerville, produce many of the apples grown in California. You'll find dozens of family-owned orchards, vineyards, and Christmas tree farms clustered near the quaint community of Camino. For a scenic tour, download a map from the website or visit in person by taking exit 48 or 54 from U.S. 50 onto Apple Hill Drive (also known as Carson Road). Charming country roads and cute farm buildings fronted by orchards fill the landscape. At some orchards you can pick your own apples in season. At others you'll find a large shop stuffed with homemade pies frozen and ready to be baked, as well as preserves, cookbooks, and every type of apple product you can imagine. Come in the middle of summer to enjoy the raspberry, blackberry, and blueberry crops, and in summer or fall for the dozens of apples varieties grown in the region. Check the website for information about events and festivals that draw crowds out to Apple Hill, including country fair-style activities, arts and crafts shows, food and drink tastings, and more.

★ Rafting the American River

For guided river trips, Placerville is the white-water capital of the Gold Country. From here, outfitters can take you to all three forks of the American River, including the rugged Class IV-V rapids of the North Fork and the more moderate Class III-IV white water of the Middle Fork. Rafting trips are designed for all experience levels, and you can even book overnight excursions; if you're a rookie rafter, try a more leisurely half-day trip down the lower section of the South Fork. The season usually runs April-October, except for trips on the North Fork, which usually run April-May or June, depending on weather and water levels. Check online for specific dates.

All-Outdoors Whitewater Rafting (925/932-8993, www.aorafting.com, $100-495) offers half-day, full-day, and multi-day trips on the North, Middle, and South Forks of the American River. If you have time, take a two- to three-day jaunt and camp deep in the stunningly beautiful river canyons. Guides prepare all your meals, and it's an excellent way to experience a different side of the Gold Country. You can also book full-day trips on any of the three forks if a multi-day expedition isn't feasible. If you have small kids or just want to calmly drift down the river, consider the full-day Tom Sawyer Float Trips along the rapids-free section of the South Fork.

Beyond Limits Adventures (530/622-0553, www.rivertrip.com, $100-300) offers mostly half-day and one-day excursions to the North, Middle, and South Forks; you can also take two-day trips on the South Fork with complimentary wine and beer served at dinner. Two-day trips also include a stop at a riverside resort where you can fish, play basketball, and try your hand at panning gold.

American Whitewater Expeditions (800/825-3205, www.americanwhitewater.com, $50-288) offers half-day, full-day, and multi-day trips to all three forks of the American River. All expeditions come with delicious meals, friendly guides, and jaw-dropping Sierra Nevada scenery.

O.A.R.S. (800/346-6277, www.oars.com, $110-320) offers trips to all three forks of the American River. This is one of the most experienced rafting companies in the West, and the guides are extremely knowledgeable. O.A.R.S. offers full-day trips with a picnic on the Middle and North Forks; you can also take half-day, full-day, and two-day trips on the South Fork with meals included. Or enjoy a two-day wine-and-raft tour that includes side trips to several El Dorado County wineries.

Whitewater Connection (530/622-6446, www.whitewaterconnection.com, $95-421) offers the standard full-day trips to the North, Middle, and South Forks, along with multi-day expeditions. You can also book half-day trips on the South Fork if time is an issue. Whitewater Connection also offers two-day trips combining one day on the North Fork with another day on either the Middle or South Fork.

Food

The Shoestring (1320 Broadway, 530/622-7125, 11am-8pm daily summer, 11am-7pm daily fall, 11am-6pm daily winter, $10) is a roadside hole-in-the-wall serving burgers, hot dogs, and chili cheese fries. The restaurant is conveniently located near the northern tip of downtown Placerville, but doesn't have restrooms.

★ **The Heyday Café** (325 Main St., 530/626-9700, www.heydaycafe.com, 11am-3pm Mon., 11am-9pm Tues.-Thurs., 11am-10pm Fri.-Sat., 11am-8pm Sun., $12-26) is one of the best eateries in Placerville. The California bistro-style food is fused with Asian, Italian, and Mediterranean influences. Try the bacon-artichoke-pesto pizza or the lemon salsa skewers; pair with a crisp riesling from Apple Hill to sample the extensive wine list.

For upscale Mexican food in the heart of Gold Country, grab a table at **Cascada** (384 Main St., 530/344-7757, 11am-8pm Sun.-Thurs., 11am-9pm Fri.-Sat., $12-18) in downtown Placerville. Cascada is Mexican with a California-bistro twist, but you'll find familiar favorites like burritos, tacos, and

Apple Hill Eateries

There's plenty of good, healthy food to be had in the Apple Hill region. But what if you need more than a nice fresh apple to keep hunger away? Stop at one of the orchard-based restaurants along the meandering trails, where the food ranges from sandwiches to hot handmade apple pies. The area maps available at almost every orchard point out which establishments offer a restaurant.

For a fresh slice of pie, some of the best is sold at the **Apple Pantry Farm** (2310 Hidden Valley Lane, Camino, 530/318-2834, www.applepantryfarm.com, 9am-4pm Thurs.-Sun., Sept.-Nov., pies $16-18). The farm's attractive small store sells apples and an array of frozen uncooked pies ready to be baked in your home oven. To the right of the main store, a small trailer exudes aromas that draw visitors as if by magic. You can buy just a slice or a whole apple, apple-blackberry, or other seasonal fruit pie. Every from-scratch Apple Pantry pie is sold hot out of the industrial ovens in the trailer. The frozen ready-bake pies in the shop are made by the same team. The farm also sells other goodies like turnovers, crisps, and apple butter.

For more filling grub, try the **Forester Pub and Grill** (4110 Carson Rd., Camino, 530/644-1818, www.foresterpubandgrill.com, 11:30am-9pm daily, $8-19). This English-style pub serves German-themed food like stroganoff and schnitzel, along with good ol' American comfort food such as meatloaf. Sides include red cabbage kraut and spätzle, which is a pile of pea-sized dumplings with gravy. **Apple Blossom Coffee House** (4077 Carson Rd., 530/644-0284, http://appleblossomcoffeehouse.com, 7am-2pm Mon.-Sat., $2-10) serves espresso and pastries for breakfast. At lunch, power up for a busy day of hayrides and pumpkin patches with an order of soup, salad, or one of this joint's famous empanadas.

Once you've picked out pumpkins, scarfed some pie, and braved Apple Hill's crowds, head to **Jack Russell Brewery** (2380 Larsen Dr., Camino, 530/647-9420, 11am-6pm Mon.-Thurs., 11am-7pm Fri., 10am-6pm Sat.-Sun.) for a pint of English-style beer. Located behind an apple orchard, Jack Russell has handicraft vendors and live music on weekends. But the best things about this place are the beer and the cider. The sampler comes with taster cups filled with every Jack Russell brew. The brewery sometimes stays open right up until sunset during the summer.

enchiladas. The restaurant is elegant-casual and reservations are a good idea.

The ★ **Café Mahjaic** (1006 Lotus Rd., Coloma, 530/622-9587, www.cafemahjaic.com, 5pm-8pm Wed.-Sun., $17-26), housed inside a historical brick building, offers fine dining near the banks of the American River. The New American fare, made with natural and organic ingredients, includes subtle Mediterranean touches. The white tablecloths and cosmopolitan interior will make you want to spiff up before dinner. The last reservation is at 8pm; make sure to reserve a table, as this restaurant is very popular.

The ★ **Argonaut** (331 Hwy. 49, Coloma, 530/626-7345, http://argonautcafe.com, 8am-4pm daily, $8) is a tiny shack steps from where James Marshall discovered gold in 1848. The homemade sandwiches, soups, chili, and pie are made nearby in Apple Hill and are reasonably priced. The Argonaut is conveniently located across Highway 49 from the visitors center at the Marshall Gold Discovery State Park.

Accommodations

More safari resort than bed-and-breakfast, the renovated hay barn of **Eden Vale Inn** (1780 Springvale Rd., 530/621-0901, http://edenvaleinn.com, $170-400) combines a rustic foothill vibe with Napa-style luxury. Inside are seven rooms with gas fireplaces and lavish amenities; five rooms have private hot tubs and enclosed patios. Don't miss the homemade breakfast buffet made from locally grown ingredients and herbs from the inn's garden. The inn is only a 10-minute drive from Coloma.

The 1857 **Historic Cary House Hotel** (300 Main St., 530/622-4271, www.caryhouse.

com, $109-169) is an imposing brick building in downtown Placerville. The rooms are small but bristle with character, with period antiques and old tintype photographs on the walls. From the elaborately decorated lobby, a 1920s-style elevator lifts visitors to the rooms. Amenities include Wi-Fi, continental breakfast, and cable TV. Guests frequently report ghost sightings and other strange activity—the second floor is supposedly the most haunted. Live bands play most weekends, so noise may be a factor.

Step back into the Gilded Age at the **Albert Shafsky House** (2942 Coloma St., 530/642-2776, www.shafsky.com, $135-185), a cozy Victorian bed-and-breakfast built in 1902. Three rooms boast luxurious antiques from the late 19th century. The mouthwatering breakfasts are fixed with local gourmet ingredients. Guests are treated to a complimentary bottle of El Dorado wine and an artisanal cheese plate. The house was originally built for a wealthy Placerville man whose friendly ghost supposedly still haunts the rooms.

The **Mother Lode Motel** (1940 Broadway, 530/622-0895, www. placervillemotherlodemotel.com, $60-80) has clean and reasonably priced accommodations halfway between Placerville and Apple Hill. You'll find modern amenities like included Wi-Fi, microwaves, mini fridges, and private hot tubs, as well as a decent-size pool and lounge area.

Transportation and Services

Placerville is 45 miles east of Sacramento at the intersection of U.S. 50 and Highway 49. Stoplights on U.S. 50 can cause traffic to back up on weekends; winter snows can close the roads in the winter. To reach Apple Hill, take U.S. 50 two exits east of Placerville. Coloma is almost nine miles north of Placerville on Highway 49; the Marshall Gold Discovery State Historic Park is the easiest landmark. It snows in Coloma from November to April, and sometimes even into May, so check road conditions (http://dot.ca.gov) before driving.

For medical assistance, **Marshall Hospital** (1100 Marshall Way, 530/622-1441, www.marshallmedical.org) offers an emergency room and a full range of hospital services in Placerville.

Shenandoah Valley

The best-known wine region in the Gold Country is the Shenandoah Valley. Dozens of wineries are near the towns of Plymouth, Amador City, Sutter Creek, Jackson, and even tiny Volcano, and most use locally grown grapes that show the best of what the Sierra foothills can produce.

PLYMOUTH
Wineries

To visit local wineries, a good place to start is the **Amador Vintner's Association visitor center** (9310 Pacific St., 209/245-6992, 10am-2pm Mon.-Fri., 10:30am-2:30pm Sat.-Sun.) for brochures and directions. The **Amador 360 Wine Collective** (18590 Hwy. 49, 209/245-6600, www.amador360.com, 11am-6pm daily)

offers tastings and advice about smaller boutique wineries that can be hard to find.

Arguably the best of the small-medium Shenandoah wineries is **Story Winery** (10525 Bell Rd., 800/713-6390, www.zin.com, noon-4pm Mon.-Thurs., 11am-5pm Fri.-Sun. winter, 11am-5pm daily summer, free), where you can taste the true history of Amador County wines. Some of the Story vineyards have been around for nearly 100 years and still produce grapes for wines made today. The specialty of the house is zinfandel—check out the amazing selection of old-vine single-vineyard zins. Tastings takes place in a charming, casual environment where you'll feel at home even if you're new to high-end wine.

With only the barest of nods to California

Shenandoah Valley wineries

some flavored sparklers, but reds are unquestionably the mainstay. At the tasting bar you can sip a range of intense layered zins and syrahs, or get bold with a carignan or a barbera.

Wilderotter Vineyard (19890 Shenandoah School Rd., 209/245-6016, www.wilderottervineyards.com, 10:30am-5pm daily, $5) started as a vineyard that sold all its grapes to various winemakers and only transformed into a winery in 2002. Zinfandel, grenache, viognier, and barbera are what's planted in the vineyards, so that's what's available in the bottles.

Accommodations and Food

The exterior of the ★ **Amador Harvest Inn** (12455 Steiner Rd., 800/217-2304, www.amadorharvestinn.com, $164-186) is a simple farmhouse set on a green lawn surrounded by trees and water. Inside are four rooms decorated in a charming country style. The dining room continues the farmhouse charm, with kitchen-style tables and chairs and a home-cooked breakfast each morning.

For a Californian experience, book a cabin at **Rancho Cicada Retreat** (10001 Bell Rd., 209/245-4841, www.ranchocicadaretreat.com, $85-159) in the backwoods of the foothills. The retreat offers both tent cabins and wood-sided cabins, most of which share gender-divided restrooms. The main attraction is the Cosumnes River, where you can go swimming, inner-tubing, and fishing. Bring your own sleeping bags or bedding, pillows, towels, and food to cook, plus ice chests for drinks.

Set in a modest building off Plymouth's main drag, ★ **Taste Restaurant** (9402 Main St., 209/245-3463, http://restaurant-taste.com, 5pm-9pm Mon. and Thurs.-Fri., 11:30am-2pm and 4:30pm-9pm Sat.-Sun., $21-44) is stocked with gourmet food made from seasonal healthy ingredients, and the entrées are meat-heavy fare done to perfection.

If you're craving burgers, pop into **Marlene and Glen's Diner** (18726 Hwy. 49, 209/245-5778, 7am-2:30pm Wed.-Sun., $4-14), a quirky roadside stop that has polished chrome and red leather seats at the counter,

favorite varietals, the friendly folks at **Bray Vineyards** (10590 Shenandoah Rd., 209/245-6023, www.brayvineyards.com, 10am-5pm Wed.-Mon., $5) go their own way, pouring wines made from grapes even savvy wine lovers won't find familiar. Taste a wine made from verdelho, tempranillo, alicante bouschet, or an intriguing blend of Portuguese grapes.

One of the biggest names in the Shenandoah Valley, **Montevina** (20680 Shenandoah School Rd., 209/245-6942, www.montevina.com, 10am-4:30pm daily, free) prides itself on its zinfandels, boasting that it makes "the best in the world." That's a bold claim in Amador County, which is the zinfandel heartland, but Montevina doesn't box itself in—you can taste white wines, light red wines, medium red wines, blends, and more at this fun tasting room.

For a small winery experience, stop by the charming barn at **Deaver Vineyards** (12455 Steiner Rd., 209/245-4099, www.deavervineyard.com, 10:30am-5pm daily, $5). Deaver produces a couple of white and rosé wines and homey curios on the wall, and heaping portions of American diner food. The service can slow down considerably on weekends.

Transportation

Plymouth is just off Highway 49, north of Jackson and Sutter Creek. If you're driving from the north, follow Highway 49 south from Placerville for about 20 miles. From Sacramento, take Highway 16 southeast to Highway 49 and then head northeast. These highways are all two-lane roads and can become packed on weekends, so adjust your travel time accordingly.

Amador Transit (209/267-9395, http://amadortransit.com, $2) runs buses between Plymouth and Sutter Creek, where you can catch connections to Jackson and other towns in the region.

SUTTER CREEK

Miners, their wives, and everybody else who came to live in the bustling boomtowns of Gold Country needed supplies: food, cloth, tools, and medicines. In 19th-century California, many of those supplies were sold at the general store. The **Monteverde Store Museum** (11A Randolph St., 209/267-1344, www.suttercreek.org, by appointment) sold staples to Sutter Creek residents for 75 years. After its last shopkeepers, Mary and Rose Monteverde, died, the city took over the building. The sisters had stipulated that it was to become a museum, and so it has—a look into the hub of town life in the 19th century.

To shop Sutter Creek, simply take a stroll down historic **Main Street.** You'll find cluttered antiques shops filled with treasures great and small.

Food

Pizza Plus (20 Eureka St., Sutter Creek, 209/267-1900, 11am-9pm daily, $16) serves the best pizza in Amador in one of the best settings. The pizza is great, but the cheese-covered breadsticks are just as famous. An old Wells Fargo bank vault is even available for banquets.

★ **Andrae's Bakery** (14141 Hwy. 49, Amador City, 209/267-1352, www.andraes-bakery.com, 7:30am-4pm Thurs.-Sun., $8) feels like eating at grandmother's house. Locals order the gourmet sandwiches; for dessert, have one of the pastries. The cookies are dangerously good, but the seasonal scones (strawberry and peach in summer, cranberry in winter) are worth the trip.

Locals swear that **Susan's Place** (15

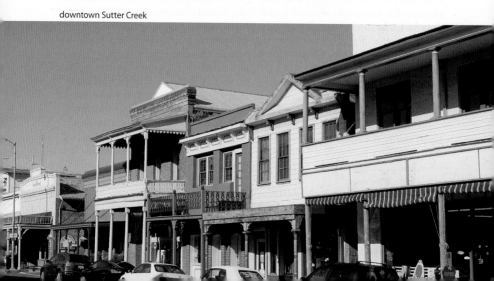
downtown Sutter Creek

Eureka St., 209/267-0945, www.susansplace.com, 11:30am-2:30pm and 5pm-8pm Thurs.-Sun., $14-28) is the best restaurant in town, with its relaxing patio shaded by wisteria. The menu advertises itself as Mediterranean fare, but most dishes are mainstream California cuisine. Susan's is the only fine dining option in Sutter's Creek.

Accommodations

The **Hanford House** (61 Hanford St., 209/267-0747, www.hanfordhouse.com, $135-295) is a brick manor house with nine rooms, each decorated in a floral country style with unique furnishings and textiles. Beds are large and comfy, and baths squeak with cleanliness. Enjoy the hearty breakfast and spend the morning reading the walls and ceiling of the inn, where guests have signed and commented over the years.

The **Imperial Hotel** (14202 Hwy. 49, Amador City, 209/267-9172, www.imperial-amador.com, $105-195) shows off the brick facade and narrow-column architecture of a classic Old West hotel. You'll get a true mining town experience in one of six rooms on the second floor, or in one of three rooms in the cottage out back, which include private baths. Each room is a haven of peace and quiet, without a TV or phone. Take your meals downstairs, including the full hot breakfast included in the room rate.

Transportation

Sutter Creek is 10 miles south of Plymouth and roughly 5 miles north of Jackson on Highway 49. From Placerville, head south on Highway 49 for about 30 miles to reach Sutter Creek. From the Central Valley, take Highway 88 northeast from Stockton and drive 42 miles to Highway 49; turn north for 2.5 miles to Sutter Creek.

If you're interested in exploring the mines, drive along the **Sutter Creek Gold Mine Trail** (209/267-1344, www.suttercreek.org). Highways 49 and 88 are the main thoroughfares through the Amador County gold-mining district; a commercial map of the area makes a good companion to the hand-drawn map in the official brochure.

Amador Transit (115 Valley View Way, 209/267-9395, http://amadortransit.com, $2 most routes, $1 to Jackson) runs several bus routes all over Amador County and to Sacramento from its station.

JACKSON

Historic Kennedy Gold Mine

The **Historic Kennedy Gold Mine** (12594 Kennedy Mine Rd., 209/223-9542, www.kennedygoldmine.com, guided tours 10am-3pm Sat.-Sun., Mar.-Oct., adults $10, children $6) is a great place to learn about life in a California gold mine. The Kennedy Mine was one of the deepest hard-rock gold mines in the state, extending more than a mile into the earth. Tour the stately Mine House, marvel at the size of the head frame, and learn how a stamp mill worked to free the gold from the rocks. For the best experience, take a guided tour and learn the true stories of the mine.

Accommodations and Food

El Campo Casa (12548 Kennedy Flat Rd., Jackson, 209/223-0100, http://elcampocasa.com, $50-110) is a throwback motel with Old World character. The 15 simple rooms evoke a midcentury motel feel, and have ceiling fans, air-conditioning, and TVs. There's also an outdoor pool and a shady patio area. It makes a perfect base for excursions to the Shenandoah Valley. The rooms are somewhat Spartan, and the baths are a little too cozy. All rooms are nonsmoking.

The **Mother Lode Market and Deli** (36 Main St., 209/223-0652, 8am-3pm Mon.-Sat., $5) is a local institution in downtown Jackson that serves down-home meals and some local history. The menu is filled with standard sandwiches, deli items, salads, and soups, and everything is prepared from scratch.

Thomi's Café (627 S. Hwy. 49, 209/257-0800, www.thomiscafe.com, 8am-9pm Mon.-Sat., 8am-8pm Sun., $10-25) is an old-fashioned family restaurant with a meat-heavy surf-and-turf menu. Locals like the breakfasts here, especially the California Benedict. To say the portions are hearty is an understatement.

Transportation and Services

Jackson is near the intersection of Highways 49 and 88, and is fairly easy to reach by car. From the north or south, take Highway 49; from the Bay Area or the Central Valley, Highway 88 is the best bet. Both highways are two-lane roads that become congested during summer and on weekends. Jackson can also receive snowfall; check weather and traffic reports (http://dot.ca.gov) before traveling.

Public transit options are limited in the area, but **Amador Transit** (209/267-9395, http://amadortransit.com, Mon.-Fri., $1-2) runs several bus routes between Sutter Creek and Jackson. For medical emergencies and health needs, visit **Sutter Amador Hospital** (200 Mission Blvd., 209/223-7500, www.sutteramador.org).

VOLCANO
Black Chasm Caverns

For an underground experience in nature, take an easy one-hour tour of the **Black Chasm Caverns** (Volcano-Pioneer Rd., 866/762-2837, www.caverntours.com, 9am-5pm daily Apr.-Aug., 10am-4pm daily Sept.-Mar., adults $15, children $8). Enjoy a sedate stroll into the immense chasm filled with amazing calcite formations. In the Landmark Room, you'll get a chance to check out the rare helictite formations (a crystalline cave formation) that made Black Chasm famous. Tour schedules can fluctuate during holidays. Tours aren't accessible to strollers or wheelchairs.

★ Daffodil Hill

Spring is the time to visit the famed **Daffodil Hill** (18310 Rams Horn Grade, 209/296-7048, http://suttercreek.org, daily mid-Mar.-mid-Apr., free). Perfect for travelers who love the greenery aboveground as much as the minerals beneath it, Daffodil Hill explodes each March into a profusion of sunny yellow that lasts for about a month. Daffodil Hill

is actually the private working ranch of the McLaughlin family, who have been planting daffodil bulbs on their property since they first acquired the land in 1887. Today you'll see more than 300,000 flowers blooming, and more are planted each year. In addition to the more than 300 different species of daffodils, other bulb flowers and plants help create carpets of color across the meadows and hills. Even among the many fabulous landscapes and gardens of California, Daffodil Hill is special; out here, you can't help but feel the joy and promise of spring.

Daffodil Hill opens to the public only during daffodil season. Exact opening and closing dates vary each year; call ahead to get the latest information. Parking can be scarce during busier times, so prepare to park a distance from the farm.

Indian Grinding Rock State Historic Park

Indian Grinding Rock State Historic Park (14881 Pine Grove-Volcano Rd., 209/296-7488, www.parks.ca.gov, sunrise-sunset daily, $8 per vehicle) focuses on the history of the state before the European influx. This park, 12 miles east of Jackson, celebrates the life and culture of the Miwok people, specifically the Northern Sierra Miwok who inhabited the foothills for centuries. One of the central aspects of Miwok life was grinding acorns, their principal food. Women came to the grinding rock to grind and then soak their acorns for the day's meals. The park's focal point is a huge grinding rock, one used by all the women of the group who lived in the adjacent meadow and forest. The dozens of divots in the rock, plus the fading petroglyphs drawn over generations, attest to the lengthy use of this chunk of marble. The grinding rock's marble is frail, so don't walk on it.

Follow the pathways past the grinding rock to the reconstructed roundhouse, a sacred space in current use by local Miwoks, implying that visitors should be respectful. Walk farther toward the **Miwok village,** where you can enter the dwellings to see how these native

Californians once lived. If you're up for a longer hike, the **North Trail** winds around most of the park. For a deeper look into Miwok history, spend some time in the visitors center and museum (11am-2:30pm Fri.-Mon.).

Accommodations and Food

The **Union Inn and Pub** (21375 Consolation St., 209/296-7711, www.volcanounion.com, $85-140) has only four rooms, but each is decorated with a different luxurious theme. Modern amenities include flat-screen TVs and radios with iPod docks; some rooms have sunken porcelain tubs. A gourmet breakfast is served each day. Children and pets are not allowed. Some of the best food is served in the hotel's **restaurant** (5pm-8pm Mon. and Thurs., 5pm-9pm Fri., noon-9pm Sat., noon-8pm Sun., $11-24).

The venerable **St. George Hotel** (16104 Main St., Volcano, 209/296-4458, www.stgeorgevolcano.com, $55-200) has affordable rooms with vintage Gold Country charm. This attractive, plain building houses a hodgepodge of 14 second- and third-floor rooms, some that peer out onto Volcano's main drag,

and a bungalow in the back. Only two of the rooms in the main building and the bungalow have private baths. Rooms have polished wood floors and antique-styled bedsteads. The hotel has a **restaurant** (5pm-9pm Thurs.-Fri., noon-9pm Sat., 9am-8pm Sun., $15-30), but the food is uninspiring.

Transportation and Services

Volcano is on the eastern edge of Gold Country, where the elevation starts to climb among towering pine trees that blanket the hillsides. By car, take Highway 88 northeast from Jackson for about nine miles; turn left on Pine Grove-Volcano Road. Volcano will appear in about three miles. Because of the higher elevation, Volcano often has heavy snowfall in winter, and chains may be required. Check weather and traffic reports with Caltrans (http://dot.ca.gov) before planning your trip.

In Volcano you won't find much in the way of services. The closest bank branches and gas stations are located four miles southwest in Pine Grove or eight miles east in Pioneer, both on Highway 88.

Southern Gold Country

Southern Gold Country runs south from Jackson and includes the towns of Angels Camp, Murphys, Sonora, Columbia, Jamestown, and Arnold. Highway 49 can take you north-south through the region. Highway 4 runs northeast-southwest, intersecting Highway 49 at Angels Camp and running east to Murphys. Highway 4 also runs south from Vallecito to Columbia and then south to Sonora. You can also drive Highway 49 all the way to Jamestown and pick up Highway 108 east to Sonora.

ANGELS CAMP
California Caverns

California Caverns (9565 Cave City Rd., Mountain Ranch, 866/762-2837, www.

caverntours.com, 9am-5pm daily Apr.-Aug., 10am-4pm Sat.-Sun. Sept.-Mar., adults $15, children $8) has been welcoming underground explorers for more than 150 years. The basic tour is geared toward families and lasts just over an hour; a knowledgeable guide leads you through a wonderland of subterranean chambers while describing the cavern's history and geology. Kids will love gazing at the numerous forms of stalactites, especially the vine-like formations in the **Jungle Room** cavern. If you're not claustrophobic, you can also do some serious spelunking on the **Middle Earth Expedition** (4 hours, $130) or the **Mammoth Expedition** (2-3 hours, $99). Make sure to bring hiking shoes or boots, since the underground paths can

Southern Gold Country

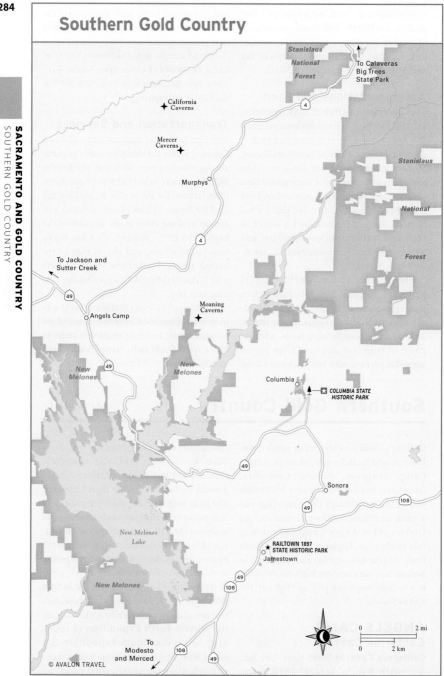

Stanislaus National Forest

To Calaveras Big Trees State Park

California Caverns

Mercer Caverns

Murphys

To Jackson and Sutter Creek

Angels Camp

Moaning Caverns

New Melones

New Melones

New Melones Lake

New Melones

Columbia

COLUMBIA STATE HISTORIC PARK

Sonora

RAILTOWN 1897 STATE HISTORIC PARK

Jamestown

To Modesto and Merced

© AVALON TRAVEL

0   2 mi
0   2 km

be quite slippery, and wear clothes you won't mind getting muddy. Many of the tours can't be accessed in certain seasons, so call the visitors center or check the website for more information.

Moaning Cavern

The haunting sounds of **Moaning Cavern** (5350 Moaning Cave Rd., 209/736-2708, www.caverntours.com, 9am-6pm daily summer, 10am-4pm Mon.-Fri. and 9am-5pm Sat.-Sun. winter, adults $15, youth $8) can still be heard in this enchanting cave, the largest public chamber in California. Spring is the best time to hear Moaning Cavern's "chamber" orchestra, when rainy weather guarantees plenty of underground dripping. The cavern has other attractions besides the "moaning." Visitors can rappel 165 feet into the main chamber's yawning expanse, a trip that takes 45 minutes ($72), or sign up for the three-hour Adventure Tour ($130 with rappel, $76 without rappel).

Angels Camp Museum and Carriage House

Inside the **Angels Camp Museum and Carriage House** (753 S. Main St., 209/736-2963, www.angelscamp.gov, 10am-4pm Thurs.-Mon., adults $5, children $2.50), you'll see meticulously preserved artifacts of the mining era. Outside is old mining equipment. (The huge waterwheel sits in its original position in Angels Camp.) The Carriage House shelters more than 30 horse-powered vehicles of the 19th and early 20th centuries. Better restored than many similar displays, the carriages and wagons here show off the elegance and function of true horse-powered transportation.

Calaveras County Fair and Jumping Frog Jubilee

Each May in Angels Camp, the **Calaveras County Fair and Jumping Frog Jubilee** (209/736-2561, www.frogtown.org, third weekend in May, adults $8-15, youth $5-10, frog jumping $5, parking $6) comes to town. During the fair, frogs jump on command

in the contest that honors the famous Mark Twain story. You'll also find all sorts of other classic fair activities, such as livestock shows, baking contests, auctions, historical readings, and exhibits. During the frog-jumping contest, you'll see literally thousands of frogs leaping toward victory. The top 50 from all heats compete in a final contest; all hope to beat the world record, a feat that carries a $5,000 prize. Find lots of food at the concessionary, places to camp, and ample restroom facilities. Children under 13 usually get into the fair for free on the first day of the event.

Sports and Recreation

Angels Camp is within a short shuttle ride of churning white water. Here you can take guided tours on the South Fork of the American River with local outfitters, but the North Fork of the Stanislaus River is closer to Angels Camp and offers more intermediate-advanced trips through roaring Class III-IV rapids. The season is shorter on the Stanislaus and runs mid-April-May, weather and river conditions permitting; be sure to call ahead.

All-Outdoors (925/932-8993, www.aorafting.com, mid-Apr.-late May, $164-184) runs full-day trips to the North Fork of the Stanislaus. You can plunge through Class IV rapids with hair-raising names like Beginner's Luck, Rattlesnake, and Maycheck's Mayhem; the last rapid is a partial Class V drop. You can also take full-day and two-day trips on the calmer South Fork of the American River if the Stanislaus is beyond your experience level.

O.A.R.S. (209/736-4677, www.oars.com, Apr.-June, $144-170) also offers trips to the mighty North Fork of the Stanislaus River, where it churns through Calaveras Big Trees State Park. The guides are knowledgeable and friendly, and lunch is provided. If you'd rather raft the South Fork of the American River, O.A.R.S. offers half-day, full-day, and two-day excursions.

Accommodations and Food

The **Cooper House Inn** (1184 Church St., 888/330-3764, www.cooperhouseinn.com,

$190-260) is a renovated Victorian-era country home with three rooms featuring queen or double beds, private showers (no en suite baths), free Wi-Fi, and flat-panel TVs. Breakfast is made with organic and local ingredients.

Mike's Pizza (294 S. Main St., 209/736-9246, www.mikespizzaangelscamp.com, 11am-9pm Sun.-Thurs., 11am-10 pm Fri.-Sat., $6-40) whips up the finest pies in town. The interior oozes an old-fashioned pizza parlor vibe with dark-paneled walls, arcade games, and glowing neon signs. There's plenty of other pub grub like burgers, pasta, and ribs, as well as a salad bar.

Crusco's (1240 S. Main St., 209/736-1440, www.cruscos.com, 11:30am-3pm and 5pm-9pm Thurs.-Mon., $18-27) serves hearty homemade Italian food with a Californian flair. The best part about this restaurant is the Old World hospitality and attentive service from the owner, who is usually on hand to greet customers.

Transportation

Angels Camp is in the heart of Gold Country, on Highway 49 about 28 miles south of Jackson. From Stockton, take Highway 4 east for 50 miles and turn south on Highway 49; Angels Camp is another 2 miles. Sacramento is 75 miles away, and Placerville is 60 miles north.

There's isn't much public transportation in Angels Camp, but **Calaveras Transit** (209/754-4450, www.calaverastransit.com, $2) runs three bus routes to the surrounding area Monday-Friday, including trips to Arnold and Murphys.

MURPHYS AND VICINITY

The bustling shopping district in the heart of this old mining town has antiques shops, small boutiques, and a few surprises. Most shops are between the parallel Church and Main Streets, with a few stores farther out along Highway 4. On weekends, parking can be a frustrating challenge, so arrive earlier in the day if you can.

Mercer Cavern

One of the fascinating caverns that pock the Sierra foothills, **Mercer Cavern** (1665 Sheep Ranch Rd., 209/728-2101, www.mercercaverns.com, 10am-4:30pm daily early Sept.-late May, 9am-5pm daily late May-early Sept., adults $15, children $8.50) winds into the mountains just outside of Murphys. Visitors descend 172 steps into the narrow cavern, crowding the numerous walkways that run 162 feet down from the surface entrance. The 45-minute standard tour is a fun family activity, provided that everyone is reasonably fit and mobile.

Wineries

Downtown Murphys has a number of tasting rooms. Out in the countryside, a few vineyards boast major estates. The largest estate belongs to **Ironstone Vineyards** (1894 Six Mile Rd., 209/728-1251, www.ironstonevineyards.com, 10am-5pm daily, $5). This huge complex of vineyards, winery buildings, a museum, an amphitheater, and gardens can draw hundreds of visitors in a single day. Inside the vast tasting room are three bars and a pleasant surprise. The complimentary regular tasting includes any number of wines, most priced at $10 per bottle.

The tiny but elegant tasting room of **Black Sheep Winery** (221 Main St., 209/728-2157, www.blacksheepwinery.com, 11am-5pm daily, free) offers higher-end red wines at a bar that could fit maybe six people—if they're friendly. Black Sheep's specialty is zinfandel made from Calaveras County and Amador County grapes, but they also make cabernet sauvignon, cabernet franc, and more unusual varietals like cinsault.

With a focus on Spanish and Rhône varietals and an unlikely rubber-chicken mascot, **Twisted Oak Winery** (363 Main St., 209/736-9080, www.twistedoak.com, 11:30am-5:30pm Mon.-Fri., 10:30am-5:30pm Sat.-Sun., $5) makes award-winning wines. The tasting fee buys the option to try 15 different wines.

Food

Grounds (402 Main St., 209/728-8663, www.groundsrestaurant.com, 7am-3pm Mon.-Tues., 7am-3pm and 5pm-8pm Wed.-Thurs., 7am-3pm and 5pm-9pm Fri.-Sat., 8am-3pm and 5pm-9pm Sun., $16-29) is one of the best places to eat in Murphys. The California cuisine features standard dishes like a grilled eggplant sandwich and seared swordfish steak over linguini. For breakfast, make your own omelet from fresh ingredients. This restaurant is one of the busiest in town, so reservations are recommended.

At **Firewood** (420 Main St., 209/728-3248, www.firewoodeats.com, 11am-9pm Sun.-Thurs., 11am-9:30pm Fri.-Sat., $12), housed in a former fire station, everything has a fiery theme—from wood-fired pizzas to the ax handles that grace the front doors. You can't go wrong with the chicken pesto pizza; or try the gorgonzola burger or the fish tacos.

For fancy steak dinners, go to **V Restaurant** (402 Main St., 209/728-0107, http://vrestaurantandbar-murphys.com, bistro 11am-8pm Mon.-Thurs., 11am-9pm Fri.-Sun.; dining room 11am-8pm Wed.-Thurs., 11am-9pm Fri.-Sun., $18-32). This small but elegant dining room dishes upscale American fare with plates like bacon-wrapped filet mignon and lamb T-bone. Call ahead on busy weekends to nab a table.

Accommodations

From the outside, the blocky **Dunbar House 1880** (271 Jones St., 209/728-2897, www.dunbarhouse.com, $190-280) evokes a Dickensian air. Inside are modern comforts and Victorian decor. For breakfast, feast on homemade baked goods, a delicious hot entrée, coffee, tea, and specially blended hot chocolate. **Murphys Inn Motel** (76 Main St., 888/796-1800, www.murphysinnmotel.com, $130-180), centrally located downtown, has 37 rooms, most with two queen beds furnished and decorated in traditional motel style.

Transportation and Services

Reach Murphys by taking Highway 4 northeast from Angels Camp for 10 miles. It is a fair drive from any major city; you'll have to drive about 80 miles from Sacramento and about 60 miles from Modesto. If you need public transportation, **Calaveras Transit** (209/754-4450, www.calaverastransit.com, $2) runs round-trip bus routes between Murphys and Angels Camp Monday-Friday.

SONORA AND COLUMBIA

★ Columbia State Historic Park

A stroll down Main Street in **Columbia State Historic Park** (11255 Jackson St., Columbia, 209/588-9128, www.parks.ca.gov, daily year-round, free; most businesses 10am-5pm daily) is a stroll into California's boomtown past. Start with the **Columbia Museum** (Main St. and State St., 209/532-3184, 10am-4pm daily, free) to discover the history of this fascinating place, one of the early California mining towns. Gold was discovered here in the spring of 1850, and the town sprang up as miners flowed in, growing to become one of California's largest cities for a short time. It inevitably declined as the gold ran out, and in 1945 the state took it over and created the State Historic Park. In the museum, you'll see artifacts of the mining period, from miners' equipment and clothing to the household objects used by women who lived in the bustling city. After the museum, walk the streets, poking your head into the exhibits and shops selling an array of period and modern items. Examine the contents of the Dry Goods Store, imagine the multiculturalism of another age in the Chinese Store Exhibit, or grab a bite to eat in the City Hotel Saloon.

This large indoor-outdoor museum experience is an easy, flat walk, with plenty of wheelchair-accessible areas. The horses, carriages, and staff in pioneer costumes delight children. It can get hot in the summer and cold in winter, and you'll be on your feet a lot, so dress accordingly and wear sensible shoes. Docent-led tours happen at 11am Saturday-Sunday.

Food

The ★ **Diamondback Grill** (93 S. Washington St., Sonora, 209/532-6661, www. thediamondbackgrill.com, 11am-9pm Mon.-Thurs., 11am-9:30pm Fri.-Sat., 11am-8pm Sun., $10) serves good grill food at extremely reasonable prices. Everyone loves the burgers and the sweet potato fries, and the garlic fries are a treat. Fresh salads feed lighter appetites, and you can enjoy a glass of wine with your meal. Expect a wait, especially on weekends.

Talulah's (13 S. Washington St., Sonora, 209/532-7278, www.talulahs.com, 11:30am-2:30pm and 5:30pm-8pm Tues.- Thurs., 11:30am-2:30pm and 5pm-9pm Friday, noon-3pm and 5pm-9pm Sat., $14-20) serves up piping-hot pastas and homemade veggie lasagna with local, organic ingredients.

Columbia Kate's (22727 Columbia St., Columbia, 209/532-1885, www.columbiakates. com, bakery 8am-4pm daily, teahouse 11am-4pm daily, $12-16) is a cozy English-style tea house with plenty of country hospitality. You can eat lunch here or stop by for a full afternoon tea.

Legends (131 S. Washington St., Sonora, 209/532-8120, 11am-5pm daily) is a bookstore, coffee bar, and old-fashioned soda fountain. Grab some ice cream or a hot dog while browsing the rare books and antiques, or settle onto a comfy barstool for a sandwich.

Accommodations

For history in your hotel room, you can't beat the **Gunn House Hotel** (286 S. Washington St., Sonora, 209/532-3421, http://gunnhouse-hotel.com, $84-125). A dozen rooms are done up in elegant jewel tones and rich fabrics, each with a king or queen bed with a teddy bear to welcome you. The Gunn House offers cable TV in every room, plus full heating and air-conditioning. Each morning, partake in the included sumptuous Innkeeper's Breakfast.

The **Bradford Place Inn** (56 W. Bradford St., Sonora, 209/536-6075, www.bradfordplaceinn.com, $145-265) has been a bed-and-breakfast since the 1980s. Four rooms are decorated with Victorian-style floral wallpaper, plush furniture, and vintage wooden headboards. Each room has private heating and air-conditioning, a flat-screen TV, Wi-Fi, and a phone. Breakfast is included.

The two authentic Wild West hotels in town have been restored in similar fashion. The **Columbia City Hotel** (22768 Main St., Columbia, 209/532-1479, http://reserveamerica.com, $75-126) is located near the north end of the state park. The **Fallon Hotel** (11175

Columbia State Historic Park

Calaveras Big Trees State Park

Highlights of **Calaveras Big Trees State Park** (Hwy. 4, three miles east of Arnold, 209/795-2334, www.bigtrees.org, sunrise-sunset daily, $10) include the North and South Groves of rare giant sequoia trees; be sure to take a walk in both groves to check out the landmark trees and stumps. Beyond the sequoias, you can hike and bike in 6,000 acres of pine forest crisscrossed with trails and pretty groves set up for picnicking. Take a dip in the cool, refreshing Stanislaus River running through the trees, or cast a line out to try to catch a rainbow trout. The **visitors center** (209/795-3840, 10am-4pm daily) has trail maps, exhibits, and artifacts depicting different periods in California history. In winter, many of the roads through the park are closed.

There are two seasonal **campgrounds** (800/444-7275, www.parks.ca.gov or www.reserveamerica.com, reservations Memorial Day-Labor Day, reservation fee $8, sites $35) for tents and RVs. The North Grove Campground (Apr.-Nov.) lies closest to the park entrance on Highway 4 and has 74 sites. Oak Hollow Campground (May-Oct.) is four miles inside the park and two miles from the Stanislaus River. The 55 sites are set on a hill and are a bit quieter. All campsites include a fire ring, a picnic table, and parking. Flush toilets, coin-operated showers, and drinking water are available in the campgrounds. Reservations are accepted up to seven months in advance and are strongly recommended in summer. Off-season, campsites are first-come, first-served.

Washington St., Columbia, 209/532-1470, http://reserveamerica.com, $75-126) is near the park's southern boundary on the county road. The cozy rooms in each hotel have been faithfully restored with Victorian-style wallpaper, handmade furniture, Gold Rush-era photos, and double beds. Both hotels have a strict no-pets policy. Cottages ($126-170) with complete kitchens and bathrooms are also available near the Columbia City Hotel.

Transportation and Services

Sonora is at the tip of the southern Gold Country. By car, it's about 15 miles south of Angels Camp on Highway 49. South of Sonora, it's 55 miles to Mariposa. From the Central Valley, take Highway 108 from Modesto for 48 miles and then head north on Highway 49 for another 2 miles to reach Sonora. If you need to rent a car, **Enterprise** (14860 Mono Way, Sonora, 209/533-0500) and **Hertz** (13413 Mono Way, Sonora, 209/588-1575) have rentals available.

Sonora has several public transit options. Don't miss a ride on the **Historic 49 Trolley** (209/532-0404, www.tuolumnecountytransit.com, Sat.-Sun. early Apr.-Labor Day, adults $1.50, day pass $4, under age 13 free), an old-fashioned (but air-conditioned) way

to see local sights in Sonora, Columbia, and Jamestown. For bus rides during the week, **Tuolumne County Transit** (209/532-0404, www.tuolumnecountytransit.com, Mon.-Fri., adults $1.50, day pass $4, under age 13 free) runs six bus routes in Sonora and the immediate vicinity.

JAMESTOWN
Railtown 1897 State Historic Park

Start your tour of **Railtown 1897** (Hwy. 108, 209/984-3953, www.railtown1897.org, 9:30am-4:30pm daily Apr.-Oct., 10am-3pm daily Nov.-Mar., adults $5, youth $3) inside the old depot waiting room, which includes artifacts, a video describing the filmography of the Railtown trains, and locomotives used in films and TV shows. Prize locomotives sit in the century-old roundhouse. Train fans, history lovers, film buffs, and children all love this unusual indoor-outdoor museum. Behind the roundhouse you can check out the functioning turntable, then wander out to the rolling stock (some of it in fairly decrepit condition) and poke around a little. You can take a six-mile, 40-minute ride in a car of a steam locomotive into the Sierra foothills. Trains depart on the hour (11am-3pm Sat.-Sun.

Apr.-Oct., adults $15, youth $8, fares include admission to the park).

Accommodations and Food

The at-times infamous ★ **National Hotel** (18183 Main St., 209/984-3446, www.national-hotel.com, $140) has operated almost continuously since 1859—either as a hotel, a brothel, a small casino, or a Prohibition-era bar. Each of the nine rooms features antique furniture and comfy linens and comforters on the one queen bed. All rooms have their own baths with a shower and access to the soaking room, which the hotel describes as its "1800s Jacuzzi." A restaurant is downstairs, and the Gold Rush Saloon serves up signature cocktails and wines.

The **Victorian Gold B&B** (10382 Willow St., 888/551-1851, www.victoriangoldbb. com, $115-185) is a stunningly renovated Gilded Age mansion built in the 1890s. The eight rooms are charmingly decorated with modern amenities and include a private bath with either a shower or a claw-foot tub; some rooms have both. The inn is fully air-conditioned, with Wi-Fi in every room. Don't miss the homemade breakfast with fresh fruit and made-to-order omelets.

At Jamestown's ★ **Willow Steakhouse and Saloon** (Willow St. and Main St., 209/984-3998, www.willowsteakjamestown. com, 11am-9pm daily, $11-41), the steaks are good rather than great, but the baked potatoes and the bucket of fixings make up for it. For an after-dinner cocktail, head into the saloon and have a drink with the locals.

Transportation and Services

By car, Jamestown is less than four miles south of Sonora on Highway 49. If you're driving from Modesto, take Highway 108 northeast for 43 miles and then head north on Highway 49 for three more miles to reach Jamestown.

Railtown 1897 State Historic Park

Yosemite, Sequoia, and Kings Canyon

Yosemite National Park 296

Sequoia and Kings Canyon..... 320

The Eastern Sierra 337

Highlights

★ **Bridalveil Fall:** It's the most monumental—and the most accessible—of Yosemite's marvelous collection of waterfalls (page 297).

★ **Half Dome:** Whether you come to scale its peak or just to see the real-life model for all those wonderful photographs, Half Dome lives up to the hype (page 300).

★ **Mist Trail:** A hike along the Mist Trail to the top of Vernal Fall brings the valley views alive (page 302).

★ **Tuolumne Meadows:** Explore the wonders of the park's high elevations at this rare alpine meadow, where numerous hiking trails thread through Yosemite's backcountry (page 310).

★ **General Grant Grove:** A paved walkway leads to the General Grant Tree, the world's second-largest tree and the country's only living war memorial (page 322).

★ **General Sherman Tree:** The biggest tree on the face of the earth is here in Sequoia National Park (page 330).

★ **Giant Forest Museum:** It's great to wander outside and see all the big trees, but if you want to learn more about what you're seeing, this is the place to be (page 331).

★ **Crystal Cave:** Well-lit tunnels lead into the grand chambers of this cavern, filled with dramatic calcite formations and polished marble (page 331).

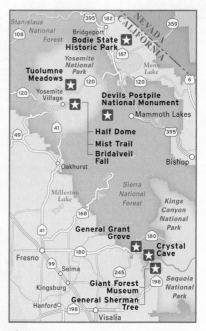

★ **Bodie State Historic Park:** A state of "arrested decay" has preserved this 1877 gold-mining ghost town (page 341).

★ **Devils Postpile National Monument:** A mix of volcanic heat and pressure created these near-perfect straight-sided hexagonal posts that have to be seen to be believed (page 343).

O f all the natural wonders that California has to offer, few are more iconic than the national parks nestled within the Sierra Nevada.

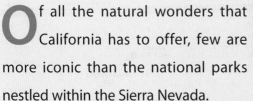

Yosemite National Park is a natural playground that has been immortalized in the photographs of Ansel Adams. The naturalist John Muir called it "the grandest of all the special temples of Nature I was ever permitted to enter," and it was Muir who introduced Yosemite to President Theodore Roosevelt. That event eventually resulted in Yosemite's national park designation in 1890. If this is your first visit, prepare to be overwhelmed.

South of Yosemite, Sequoia and Kings Canyon National Parks offer some of the tallest and oldest trees on earth, numerous hiking trails, thriving wildlife, and far smaller crowds than their famous neighbor.

East of Yosemite, the Eastern Sierras offer deep snows in winter and dry heat in summer. The eerie stillness of Mono Lake and the ghost town of Bodie give visitors a taste of the high desert. South of Mono Lake, the picturesque town of Mammoth Lakes supports the Mammoth Mountain ski area. Hiking, mountain biking, fishing, backpacking, and sightseeing are a great part of the Eastern Sierra.

PLANNING YOUR TIME

Plan at least **2-3 days** just in **Yosemite Valley,** with an excursion to Glacier Point. With a week, add Tuolumne Meadows (summer only) or Wawona. To explore the **Eastern Sierra**, visit in summer and plan a **full weekend** to explore Mono Lake and Bodie State Historic Park. Mammoth Lakes makes a great ski getaway in winter, but you'll need a three-day weekend here.

Sequoia and Kings Canyon National Parks are large and spread out—to explore the parks in any depth, plan at least **three days** for the scenic drives past towering redwoods, plus time to hike or visit Crystal Cave.

Summer is high season; traffic jams and parking problems plague both parks, but Yosemite Valley provides free shuttles to popular sights and trailheads. Tuolumne Meadows and the Eastern Sierra are less congested, making them good summer options. **Spring** is best for waterfalls and wildflowers, and there are fewer crowds, as in **fall**. In **winter,** roads close and crowds are minimal.

Previous: Half Dome; the ghost town of Bodie **Above:** Nevada Fall from John Muir Trail.

Yosemite National Park

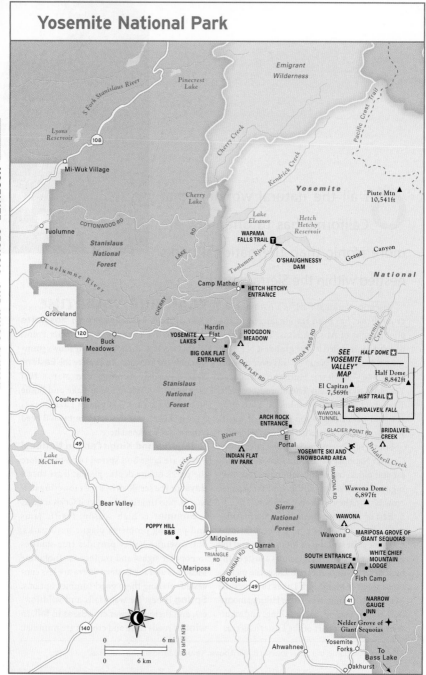

S Fork Stanislaus River

Emigrant
Wilderness

Pinecrest
Lake

Pacific Crest Trail

Lyons
Reservoir

108

Cherry Creek

Kendrick Creek

Mi-Wuk Village

Cherry
Lake

Yosemite

Piute Mtn
10,541ft

Tuolumne

COTTONWOOD RD

Lake
Eleanor

Hetch
Hetchy
Reservoir

Stanislaus
National
Forest

LAKE RD

WAPAMA
FALLS TRAIL

Tuolumne River

Grand   Canyon

National

Tuolumne River

O'SHAUGHNESSY
DAM

Camp Mather

HETCH HETCHY
ENTRANCE

CHERRY

Yosemite Creek

Groveland

120

Hardin
Flat

YOSEMITE
LAKES

HODGDON
MEADOW

TIOGA PASS RD

SEE
"YOSEMITE
VALLEY"
MAP

HALF DOME

Buck
Meadows

BIG OAK FLAT
ENTRANCE

BIG OAK FLAT RD

El Capitan
7,569ft

Half Dome
8,842ft

Coulterville

Stanislaus
National
Forest

WAWONA
TUNNEL

MIST TRAIL

BRIDALVEIL FALL

49

River

ARCH ROCK
ENTRANCE

GLACIER POINT RD

BRIDALVEIL
CREEK

Lake
McClure

Merced

El
Portal

YOSEMITE SKI AND
SNOWBOARD AREA

Bridalveil Creek

INDIAN FLAT
RV PARK

WAWONA RD

Wawona Dome
6,897ft

Bear Valley

140

Sierra
National
Forest

WAWONA

POPPY HILL
B&B

Midpines

Darrah

Wawona

MARIPOSA GROVE OF
GIANT SEQUOIAS

TRIANGLE
RD

DARRAH RD

SOUTH ENTRANCE

WHITE CHIEF
MOUNTAIN
LODGE

Mariposa

Bootjack

49

SUMMERDALE

Fish Camp

BEN HUR RD

41

NARROW
GAUGE
INN

0   6 mi

Nelder Grove of
Giant Sequoias

0   6 km

140

Ahwahnee

Yosemite
Forks

To
Bass Lake

Oakhurst

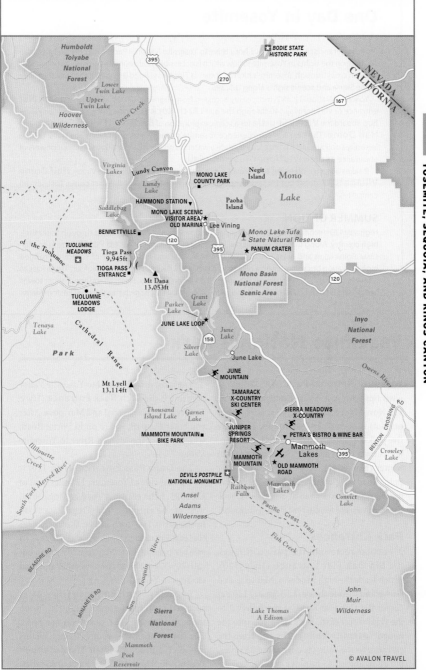

© AVALON TRAVEL

One Day in Yosemite

From San Francisco, it's just a four-hour drive to Yosemite National Park. With only one day, concentrate on the sights in Yosemite Valley, which is accessible year-round. A summer option means you can cross through Yosemite's high country via Tioga Pass Road (Hwy. 120) to the eastern side of the Sierra and scenic sights along U.S. 395.

Yosemite National Park is most easily accessed from Highway 120 through the **Big Oak Flat** entrance or via Highway 140 through the main **Arch Rock** entrance. Once in Yosemite Valley, hop aboard the **Valley Shuttle** for a scenic exploration of **Bridalveil Fall, El Capitan,** and **Half Dome.** The best way to experience Yosemite's beauty is on one of its many trails. Enjoy a leisurely stroll around **Mirror Lake,** scale a waterfall on the **Mist Trail,** or test your powers of endurance on the way to **Upper Yosemite Fall.**

It takes advance planning to score an overnight reservation in Yosemite Valley. **Half Dome Village** is your best bet for last-minute tent cabins or try one of the first-come, first-served campsites.

SUMMER OPTION

Highway 120 becomes **Tioga Road** (open in summer only) as it heads east through Yosemite's high country. Along the way, gape at jaw-dropping vistas from **Olmsted Point,** gaze at crystal-clear alpine lakes and grassy **Tuolumne Meadows,** and explore some of Yosemite's rugged high-elevation backcountry on a hike to **Cathedral Lakes.** Tioga Road peaks at Tioga Pass as it leaves the park, descending to the arid desert along U.S. 395. Here, abandoned ghost towns like **Bodie State Historic Park** and saline **Mono Lake** characterize the drier Eastern Sierra.

Yosemite National Park

Yosemite National Park (209/372-0200, www.nps.gove/yose, $30 per vehicle Apr.-Oct., $25 Nov.-Mar.; $20 motorcycles, $15 bikes or on foot) is open daily year-round. There are five park entrances, two of which close in winter; entrance fees are valid for seven days. In winter (Nov.-May), Tioga Road and Glacier Point Road are closed, and chains may be required on any park road at any time. Check the park website for current road conditions.

Park Entrances

A popular route into the park is through the **Big Oak Flat Entrance** (Hwy. 120), which leads through Modesto, Manteca, and Groveland. Inside the park, Highway 120 becomes Big Oak Flat Road; if you follow it to the right (southeast), it will lead you into the famed **Yosemite Valley.** The trip from the entrance to the valley is only about 25 miles, but allow at least 45 minutes.

The most direct route into Yosemite Valley is through the **Arch Rock Entrance** (Hwy. 140), reached via Merced and Mariposa. After you enter the park you're on El Portal Road, which follows the Merced River to Yosemite Valley.

The **Tioga Pass Entrance** (Hwy. 120) is on the east side of Yosemite, 12 miles west of U.S. 395. (The entrance road is Tioga Road west of the entrance and Tioga Pass Road to the east.) The town of Lee Vining is near the east entrance. Tioga Pass is **closed in winter** (usually Oct.-May or early June), but call (209/372-0200) to check weather and road closings in Yosemite.

Yosemite's **South Entrance** (Hwy. 41) is accessed from Fresno and Oakhurst. Inside the park, Highway 41 becomes Wawona Road. The road is open year-round, though chains may be required in winter. The drive from Wawona to Yosemite Valley is about 35 miles,

Yosemite Name Changes

As of 2016, several names of the park's historic facilities have changed:

- Half Dome Village (formerly Curry Village)
- Yosemite Valley Lodge (formerly Yosemite Lodge)
- The Majestic Yosemite Hotel (formerly The Ahwahnee)
- Big Trees Lodge (formerly Wawona Hotel)
- Yosemite Ski & Snowboard Area (formerly Badger Pass Ski Area)
- Yosemite Conservation Heritage Center (formerly LeConte Memorial Lodge)

For more information, visit www.nps.gov/yose.

---

or 1.25 hours. Along the way, you can make a turn onto Glacier Point Road (closed in winter) to reach Glacier Point.

The northern **Hetch Hetchy Entrance** (off Hwy. 120) accesses Hetch Hetchy Reservoir and the vast backcountry in the less developed section of the park. To get here from Highway 120, make a left (north) onto Evergreen Road before the Big Oak Flat Entrance. After about seven miles, Evergreen Road becomes Hetch Hetchy Road, which leads right through the entrance and on to O'Shaughnessy Dam. This entrance and Hetch Hetchy Road are open sunrise-sunset year-round.

TOP EXPERIENCE

YOSEMITE VALLEY

The first place most people go is Yosemite Valley (Hwy. 140, Arch Rock Entrance), the most visited region in the park, filled with sights, hikes, and services. Park in the Yosemite Village day-use lot and use the **park shuttle** (7am-10pm daily year-round, free) to get around.

Sights

Your first stop in Yosemite Valley should be the **Valley Visitors Center** (shuttle stops 5 and 9, in Yosemite Village off Northside Dr., 209/372-0299, www.nps.gov/yose, 9am-5pm daily year-round), where you'll find an interpretive museum describing the geological and human history of Yosemite in addition to information, books, maps, and assistance from park rangers. The complex of buildings includes the **Yosemite Museum** (daily 9am-5pm, free) and store, the **Yosemite Theater LIVE** ($8), the **Ansel Adams Gallery** (209/372-4413, www.anseladams.com, 10am-5pm daily winter, 9am-6pm daily summer), and the all-important public restrooms.

A short, flat walk from the visitors center takes you down to the re-created **Miwok Native American Village.** The village includes many different types of structures, including some made by the later Miwoks, who incorporated European architecture into their building techniques.

The **Yosemite Valley Auditorium** and **Yosemite Theater** (Northside Dr.) share a building behind the visitors center in the heart of Yosemite Village. Programs and films include the **John Muir Performances** (209/372-0731, 7pm Sun.-Thurs. May-Sept., adults $8, children $4), starring Yosemite's resident actor Lee Stetson.

★ BRIDALVEIL FALL

Bridalveil Fall (Southside Dr., past the Hwy. 41 turnoff) is many visitors' first introduction to Yosemite's famed collection

Yosemite Valley

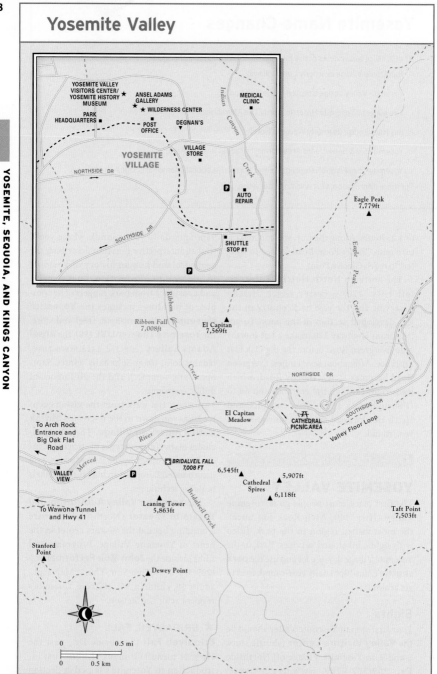

YOSEMITE VALLEY
VISITORS CENTER/
YOSEMITE HISTORY
MUSEUM ★

★ ANSEL ADAMS
GALLERY

★ WILDERNESS CENTER

PARK
HEADQUARTERS ■

POST
OFFICE

DEGNAN'S ▾

MEDICAL
CLINIC

YOSEMITE
VILLAGE

VILLAGE
STORE ■

NORTHSIDE DR

P

AUTO
REPAIR ■

SOUTHSIDE DR

P

SHUTTLE
STOP #1

P

Indian
Canyon

Creek

Eagle Peak
7,779ft ▲

Eagle
Peak
Creek

Ribbon
Fall

Ribbon Fall
7,008ft

El Capitan
7,569ft ▲

Creek

NORTHSIDE DR

SOUTHSIDE DR

El Capitan
Meadow

⛺ CATHEDRAL
PICNIC AREA

Valley Floor Loop

To Arch Rock
Entrance and
Big Oak Flat
Road

River

Merced

P

VALLEY
VIEW

⭐ BRIDALVEIL FALL
7,008 FT

6,545ft ▲

5,907ft ▲

Cathedral
Spires ▲
6,118ft

To Wawona Tunnel
and Hwy 41

Leaning Tower
5,863ft ▲

Bridalveil Creek

Taft Point
7,503ft ▲

Stanford
Point ▲

Dewey Point ▲

0   0.5 mi
0   0.5 km

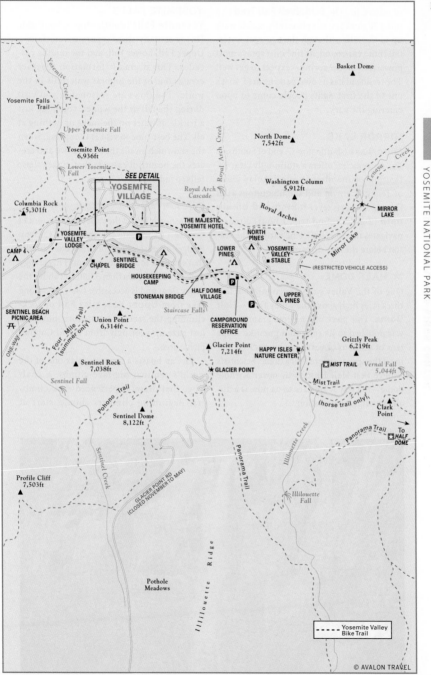

Basket Dome

Yosemite Falls Trail

Upper Yosemite Fall

Yosemite Point 6,936ft

Lower Yosemite Fall

North Dome 7,542ft

SEE DETAIL

YOSEMITE VILLAGE

Royal Arch Cascade

Washington Column 5,912ft

Columbia Rock 5,301ft

THE MAJESTIC YOSEMITE HOTEL

Royal Arches

MIRROR LAKE

YOSEMITE VALLEY LODGE

NORTH PINES

LOWER PINES

YOSEMITE VALLEY STABLE

CAMP 4

CHAPEL

SENTINEL BRIDGE

HOUSEKEEPING CAMP

STONEMAN BRIDGE

HALF DOME VILLAGE

Staircase Falls

UPPER PINES

(RESTRICTED VEHICLE ACCESS)

SENTINEL BEACH PICNIC AREA

Union Point 6,314ft

Four-Mile Trail (summer only)

CAMPGROUND RESERVATION OFFICE

Glacier Point 7,214ft

HAPPY ISLES NATURE CENTER

Grizzly Peak 6,219ft

ONE-WAY

Sentinel Rock 7,038ft

GLACIER POINT

MIST TRAIL

Vernal Fall 5,044ft

Sentinel Fall

Mist Trail

Pohono Trail

(horse trail only)

Clark Point

Sentinel Dome 8,122ft

Panorama Trail

To HALF DOME

Profile Cliff 7,503ft

Sentinel Creek

GLACIER POINT RD (CLOSED NOVEMBER TO MAY)

Illilouette Creek

Illilouette Fall

Pothole Meadows

Illilouette Ridge

- - - - Yosemite Valley Bike Trail

© AVALON TRAVEL

of waterfalls. The **Bridalveil Fall Trail** (0.5 mile, 20 minutes) is a pleasantly sedate walk up to the fall. Although the 620-foot waterfall runs year-round, its fine mist sprays most powerfully in the spring—expect to get wet! The trailhead has its own parking area, so it's one of the first sights people come to upon entering the park.

MIRROR LAKE

Mirror Lake (shuttle stop 17, end of Southside Dr., no vehicles) offers a stunningly clear reflection of the already spectacular views of Tenaya Canyon and the ubiquitous Half Dome. A short, level **hiking and biking path** (2 miles round-trip, 1 hour) circumnavigates the lake, but come early in the season before the lake dries out.

★ HALF DOME

One of the Valley's most recognizable features rises high above the valley floor—**Half Dome**. This piece of a narrow granite ridge was polished to its smooth dome-like shape tens of millions of years ago by glaciers, giving it the appearance of half a dome. Scientists believe that Half Dome was never a whole dome—the way it appears to us now is actually its original formation.

YOSEMITE FALLS

Yosemite Falls (shuttle stop 6, Southside Dr.) is actually three separate waterfalls—Upper Fall, Lower Fall, and the middle cascades. This dramatic formation together creates one of the highest waterfalls in the world. The flows are seasonal; if you visit during the fall or the winter, you'll see just a trickle of water on the rocks or nothing at all. The best time to visit is the spring, when the snowmelt swells the river above and creates the beautiful cascade that makes these falls so famous.

EL CAPITAN

On the north side of the valley is 7,569-foot **El Capitan** (Northside Dr., west of El Capitan Bridge), a massive hunk of Cretaceous granite that's named for this formation. This craggy rock face rises more than 3,000 feet above the valley floor and is accessible two ways: a long hike from **Upper Yosemite Fall** or rock-climbing the face. Most visitors, however, just gaze up adoringly from the El Capitan picnic area.

El Cap boasts a reputation as one of the world's seminal big-face climbs, a challenge that draws experienced rock climbers. Beginning climbers should start at

Bridalveil Fall

the **Yosemite Mountaineering School** (209/372-1000, www.travelyosemite.com, 8:30am daily Mar.-Nov., $148-173), where you'll find beginner, intermediate, and advanced classes for adults and children over age 10. Guided hikes and backpacking trips are also available.

Hiking

Talk to the rangers about trail conditions and be sure to bring your map—and water—on the trail with you. Valley hiking maps are available at the Valley Visitors Center (Yosemite Valley at Valley Village, Northside Dr.). Be aware that many people love the valley trails, so you likely won't be alone.

COOK'S MEADOW

Soak in quintessential Yosemite Valley views from the easy **Cook's Meadow Loop** (1 mile, 30 minutes, shuttle stop 5 or 9). From the trailhead at the visitors center, you'll observe Ansel Adams's famous view of Half Dome from Sentinel Bridge and also the Royal Arches and Glacier Point. You can extend this hike into a loop (2.25 miles) by circling both Cook's and Sentinel Meadows. Trail signs, and the plethora of other hikers, make it easy to find the turns.

VALLEY LOOP TRAIL

The **Valley Loop Trail** (paved path beside Northside Dr. and Southside Dr.) traverses the El Capitan Bridge, following the path of many old wagon roads and historical trails. From the Lower Yosemite Falls trailhead (shuttle stop 6), the **half loop** (6.5 miles, 3 hours) offers a moderate half-day hike, while the **full loop** (13 miles, 6 hours) spends a full day wandering the valley. Though paved, the route can be hard to follow; pick up a map at the visitors center.

LOWER YOSEMITE FALL

The **Lower Yosemite Fall** (1.1 miles round-trip, 30 min., shuttle stop 6) trail enjoys the wondrous views of both Upper and Lower Yosemite Falls, complete with lots of cooling spray. This easy trail works well for families with children; hike in the spring or early summer, when the flow of the falls is at its peak.

YOSEMITE FALLS TRAIL

One of the most strenuous, yet most rewarding, treks is the **Yosemite Falls Trail** (7.2 miles round-trip, 6-8 hours, shuttle stop 7). From the trailhead at Camp 4, the climb starts getting steep right away—2,700 vertical feet in just 3 miles. In one mile (and 1,000 feet),

Lower Yosemite Fall

you'll reach **Columbia Rock,** with astonishing views of the valley below. Turn back here for a two-mile (2-3 hours) round-trip hike. The trail to the top of the falls is made passable with stone steps, switchbacks, and occasional railings, but much of the trail tends to be wet and slippery. Plan all day for this hike, and bring plenty of water and snacks to replenish your energy for the potentially tricky climb down.

★ MIST TRAIL

Starting at the Happy Isles Nature Center (shuttle stop 16), the moderately strenuous **Mist Trail** leads over steep, slick granite—including more than 600 stairs—up to the top of **Vernal Fall** (2.4 miles round-trip, 3 hours). Your reward is the stellar view of the valley below from flat granite boulders that abut the Merced River. Hardier souls can continue another steep and strenuous 1.5-2 miles of switchbacks to the top of **Nevada Fall** (5.4 miles round-trip, 5-6 hours) and return via the John Muir Trail. Plan six hours for this hike, with a 2,000-foot elevation gain, and bring a lightweight rain jacket. This popular trail is **closed in winter** due to ice and snow and can be dangerous in the spring months, when the river is at its peak; hikers have been lost in the waters here. Exercise caution in extreme conditions, and obey all trail signage.

HALF DOME

The most famous climb in Yosemite Valley takes you to the top of monumental **Half Dome** (14-16 miles round-trip, 10-12 hours, May-Oct. only, shuttle stop 16). The trail follows the Mist Trail to Nevada Fall (5.4 miles) and then is signed for Half Dome. The final 400-foot ascent is via metal cables. Once you stagger to the top, you'll find a restful expanse of stone on which to enjoy the scenery.

All hikers must have a **permit** (877/444-6777, www.recreation.gov, $12.50-14.50 pp) to climb Half Dome. There are 300 permits issued per day; 225 permits are allotted for day hikers, and the rest are for backpackers. The park distributes permits through an online lottery starting in March. A daily permit lottery awards up to 50 permits; applications must be received two days prior to the hike day. The park's public information office (209/372-0826) can answer questions about the lottery process.

Do not attempt this trail lightly—it is not suitable for small children or anyone out of shape. Potential issues include altitude sickness, unsafe weather conditions, and physical

El Capitan

The Great Outdoors

Yosemite may be synonymous with the "great outdoors," but all of California is rich with opportunities for getting outside. While the Sierras are rife for adventure, don't miss these other picks across the state.

Backpack the **Lost Coast** (page 181), the **Pacific Crest Trail** or the **John Muir Trail** (page 345).

Cyclists love **Point Reyes National Seashore** (page 95), while mountain bikers head for Tahoe's **Rim Trail** (page 238).

Day-hikers can take their pick of trails in Yosemite, Sequoia, and Kings Canyon, amble paths in the **Redwood State and National Parks** (page 187), or watch waterfalls plummet to the sea in **Big Sur** (page 385).

Kayak the saline waters of **Mono Lake** (page 341), explore sea caves at **Channel Islands** (page 413) or glide along the **Russian River** in Guerneville (page 154).

Mountain climbers dream of summiting the toothy peaks of **Mount Whitney** (page 329) and **Mount Shasta** (page 216).

Rock climbers ascend the face of **El Capitan** in Yosemite Valley, scramble around boulders in **Joshua Tree** (page 545), or scale the volcanic spires of **Pinnacles** (page 374).

Skiers and snowboarders hit the slopes at **Tahoe's ski resorts** (page 246) or at **Mammoth Mountain** (page 344), while the ski parks in Yosemite and **Mount Shasta** (page 217) give beginners a leg up.

injuries. Hikers must begin the trail *before sunrise* and turn around by 3:30pm or whenever the trail is closed. Continuing on when conditions deem otherwise risks your life and the lives of others.

Food

For casual food options, head to Yosemite Village for **Degnan's Loft Pizza** (hours vary seasonally May-Sept., $10-20) for pizza, soups, and appetizers. **Degnan's Deli** (7am-5pm daily year-round, $10) offers an array of sandwiches, salads, and other take-out munchies, and **Degnan's Café** (hours vary seasonally May-Sept.) has coffee and baked goods. The **Village Grill Deck** (11am-6pm daily Apr.-Oct., $10-15) offers standard burgers and grilled food.

Half Dome Village is where to go for relatively cheap fast food. The **Village Pavilion** (7am-10am, 5:30pm-8pm daily, $10-12) serves breakfast and dinner. There is also **Coffee Corner** (7am-11am daily Mar.-Nov.), the **Village Bar** (noon-10pm daily summer), **Pizza Deck** (noon-9pm daily Jan.-Nov.),

and the **Meadow Grill** (11am-5pm daily summer).

Enjoy a spectacular view of Yosemite Falls at the **Mountain Room Restaurant** (5pm-8pm daily, $22-40) at the Yosemite Valley Lodge. The glass atrium lets every table take in the view. The menu runs to American food, and there is a full bar. The **Yosemite Valley Lodge Food Court** (6:30am-8pm daily, $8-15) offers basic meals in a cafeteria-style setting. A casual bar menu is available at the **Mountain Room Lounge** (4:30pm-10pm Mon.-Fri., noon-10pm Sat.-Sun., $8-21), across from the Mountain Room Restaurant.

The dining room at ★ **The Majestic Yosemite Lodge** (7am-10:30am, 11:30am-2:30pm, 5:30pm-9pm Mon.-Sat., 7am-3pm and 5:30pm-9pm Sun., $35-60) enjoys a reputation for fine cuisine that stretches back to 1927. The grand dining room features expansive ceilings, wrought-iron chandeliers, and a stellar valley view. Reservations are recommended. For dinner, "resort casual" attire (semiformal) is requested.

Accommodations

All lodgings, including campsites, book quickly—up to one year in advance. **Reservations** (888/413-8869, www.travelyosemite.com) for overnight accommodations are essential. All rates vary seasonally.

HALF DOME VILLAGE

Half Dome Village (shuttle stop 13, daily Mar.-Nov. and Dec.-Jan.; Sat.-Sun. only Jan.-Mar.) is a sprawling array of wood and tent cabins (with or without heat, and with or without a private bath), originally created in 1899. There are 403 **Canvas Tent Cabins** (from $90), small, wood-frame, canvas-covered structures that sleep 2-4 in a combination of single and double cot beds. A small dresser, sheets, blankets, and pillows are provided, but there is no electricity or heat. Bear-proof lockers and shared showers and restrooms are available. A few **heated tent cabins** (from $115) are also available.

The 46 **Yosemite Cabins** (from $150) are wood structures with private baths and 1-2 double beds that sleep up to five. There are also 14 cabins (without bath) that share a central bathhouse. The 18 **Stoneman Standard Motel Rooms** (from $235) sleep 2-6 and have heat, private baths, and daily maid service. An extra charge of $10-12 applies for each person beyond the first two. There are no TVs or telephones in any of the lodgings.

HOUSEKEEPING CAMP

Want to camp, but don't want to schlep all the gear? The three-sided tent cabins at **Housekeeping Camp** (mid-Apr.-mid-Oct., from $100) have cement walls, white canvas roofs, and a white canvas curtain separating the bedroom from a covered patio. Each cabin has a double bed, a bunk bed (with room for two additional cots), electrical outlets, a bear-proof food container, and an outdoor fire ring. Bring your own linens, or rent a "bed pack" (no towels, $3). Central bathrooms are available.

YOSEMITE VALLEY LODGE

★ **Yosemite Valley Lodge** (shuttle stop 8, open year-round, from $235) has a location perfect for touring the park. The motel-style rooms are light and pretty, with polished wood furniture, bright bed linens, and Native American design details. Lodge rooms with king beds offer romantic escapes for couples, complete with balconies overlooking the valley. Enjoy the heated pool in the summer and free shuttle transportation up to the Glacier

Yosemite Valley Lodge

Point ski area in winter. The lodge has a post office, an ATM, the on-site **Mountain Room Restaurant** (5pm-8pm daily), the **Mountain Room Lounge** (4:30pm-10pm Mon.-Fri., noon-10pm Sat.-Sun.), and a food court (6:30am-8pm daily).

THE MAJESTIC YOSEMITE HOTEL

Built as a luxury hotel in the early 1900s, the ★ **The Majestic Yosemite Hotel** (shuttle stop 3, open year-round, from $500) boasts a gorgeous stone facade, striking stone fireplaces, and soaring ceilings in the common areas. The hotel includes 24 cottages and 99 hotel rooms in the main building. The rooms drip with sumptuous appointments and Native American decor; hotel rooms come with either one king bed or two double beds; cottages come with small stone patios as well as TVs, telephones, small refrigerators, and private baths. A bonus is the stunningly elegant on-site **Dining Room** (7am-10:30am, 11:30am-2:30pm, 5:30pm-9pm Mon.-Sat., 7am-3pm and 5:30pm-9pm Sun.).

Camping

There are four campgrounds in Yosemite Valley, and they are deservedly popular. **Reservations** (877/444-6777, www.

recreation.gov, $9 fee) for Upper Pines, Lower Pines, and North Pines are very competitive. At 7am (Eastern time) on the 15th of each month, campsites become available for a period up to five months in advance. A few minutes after 7am, choice sites and dates—maybe even all of them—will be gone. If you need a reservation for a specific day, get up early and call or check online diligently starting at 7am.

If you're in the valley and don't have a campsite reservation, call the **campground status line** (209/372-0266) for a recording of what's available that day. Or try one of the first-come, first-served campgrounds (but get there early).

LOWER PINES

Sites at the **Lower Pines campground** (60 sites, Mar.-Oct., $26) accommodate tents and RVs up to 40 feet and include fire rings, picnic tables, a bear-proof food locker, water, flush toilets—and very little privacy. Supplies and showers ($5) are available nearby. Reservations are required and can be made up to five months in advance.

UPPER PINES

Upper Pines campground (238 sites, year-round, $26) is the largest campground

The Majestic Yosemite Hotel

in the valley. It lies immediately southwest of Lower Pines and is encircled by the park road. Sites accommodate tents and RVs up to 35 feet and include fire rings, picnic tables, a bear-proof food locker, water, and flush toilets. Supplies and showers ($5) are available nearby. Reservations are required February-November and can be made up to five months in advance. Sites are first-come, first-served December-January.

NORTH PINES

Set along the Merced River and Tenaya Creek, **North Pines** (81 sites, Apr.-Nov., $26) offers slightly more privacy than its Upper and Lower Pines siblings. Sites accommodate tents and RVs up to 40 feet and include fire rings, picnic tables, a bear-proof food locker, water, and flush toilets. Supplies and showers ($5) are available nearby. Reservations are required and can be made up to five months in advance.

CAMP 4

Camp 4 (35 sites, $6) stays open year-round. Bring a tent—no RVs or trailers are allowed. Sites include fire pits, picnic tables, and a shared bear-proof food locker. You'll find showers, food and groceries, and restrooms with water and flush toilets nearby. Pets are not permitted.

Reservations are not accepted. Spring-fall, hopeful campers must register with a park ranger. Plan to wait in line at the campground kiosk well before the ranger arrives at 8:30am. Sites are available **first-come, first-served** and hold six people each, so you may end up sharing with another party.

Transportation and Services

Yosemite Valley is about 195 miles from the San Francisco Bay Area, a drive of about 4.5 hours. From the Bay Area, take I-580 east to I-205 to I-5 to Highway 120, and enter through Groveland and the **Big Oak Flat Entrance** on the west side of the park. After you enter the park, it's 25 miles (45 min.) to the valley.

In summer—especially on weekends—traffic and parking can be slow and stressful. Park your car at the Yosemite Village day-use lot during those busy times and use the free shuttle buses to get around. The **Yosemite Valley shuttle** (7am-10pm daily year-round, free) runs every 10-20 minutes, stopping at Yosemite Valley Lodge, the Valley Visitors Center, Half Dome Village, all campgrounds, and the Happy Isles trailhead.

Twelve miles of mostly flat biking trails wind across the valley floor (but mountain biking is not permitted). **Bicycle rentals** (10am-4pm daily spring-fall, $12/hour, $34/day) are available from **Yosemite Valley Lodge** (shuttle stop 8) and **Half Dome Village** (shuttle stops 13 and 21). Wheelchairs and stroller rentals are also available

The **Yosemite Area Regional Transportation System** (YARTS, 877/989-2787, www.yarts.com) runs daily buses from Mariposa ($8-12 round-trip, $4-6 one-way) and Merced ($18-25 round-trip, $9-13 one-way) to Yosemite Valley. You can buy tickets on the bus and no reservations are necessary; children under 12 ride free. Buses run more frequently in summer. Check the YARTS website for current schedules.

If your car breaks down, you can take it to the **Yosemite Village Garage** (9002 Village Dr., off Northside Dr., Yosemite Village, 209/372-8320, 8am-5pm daily, towing 24 hours daily), but expect to pay a high premium for towing and repairs. The nearest **gas stations** are in El Portal and at Crane Flat. **ATMs** are available in Yosemite Village, as are gift shops and limited **groceries.** Emergencies should be brought to **Yosemite Medical Clinic** (9000 Ahwahnee Dr., 209/372-4637).

GLACIER POINT

The drive up Glacier Point Road (16 miles from Chinquapin junction) to **Glacier Point** is an easy one, but the vistas down into Yosemite Valley are anything but common. The first five miles of Glacier Point

Road stays open all year, except when storms make it temporarily impassable, to allow access to the ski area, but chains may be required.

Yosemite Ski & Snowboard Area

Downhill skiing at **Yosemite Ski & Snowboard Area** (www.travelyosemite.com, Glacier Point Rd., 5 miles from Chinquapin junction, 9am-4pm daily mid-Dec.-early Apr.) is a favorite winter activity at Yosemite. This was the first downhill ski area created in California, and it's still the perfect resort for moderate skiing. With plenty of beginner runs and classes, Yosemite has helped thousands learn to ski and snowboard, but has enough intermediate runs to make it interesting for mid-level skiers as well. The **Cross-Country Ski School** (www.travelyosemite.com, 8:30am-4pm daily in winter) offers classes, rentals, and guided cross-country ski tours, including an overnight trip to **Glacier Point Ski Hut.**

Ski and snowboard lessons ($80-95), cross-country lessons ($35-46), and season passes are available ($229-461, rates vary). Lift tickets run $30-50 for a full day ($40 for a half day). Equipment rentals are also available.

Hiking

SENTINEL DOME AND TAFT POINT

The trail to **Sentinel Dome** (2.2 miles round-trip, 2-3 hours) is a surprisingly easy walk; the only steep part is climbing the dome at the end of the trail. From the trailhead (1-2 miles south of Glacier Point on Glacier Point Rd.), turn right and follow an old road through the forest to the top of the dome where you can see all the way from the High Sierras to Mount Diablo in the Bay Area.

At the same trailhead turn left instead to reach **Taft Point and the Fissures** (2 miles round-trip), which takes you along unusual rock formations called the Fissures, through the always lovely woods, and out to precarious vistas at Taft Point, 2,000 feet above the valley.

PANORAMA TRAIL

The very difficult **Panorama Trail** runs all the way from Glacier Point to Yosemite Valley, with 3,000-4,000 feet of elevation change each way, and can be impassable in winter when snows are heavy. The trailhead is located at Glacier Point (road usually open late May-Oct.), but if that sounds like a bit much, park a car in the valley and take the **Glacier Point Tour shuttle** (209/372-1240, www.travelyosemite.com, 8:30am, 10am, and

Taft Point and the Fissures

1:30pm daily May-Nov., $25 one-way) from Yosemite Valley Lodge to Glacier Point and hike 8.5 miles (6-8 hours) down. Along the way, you'll see Illilouette Fall and Panorama Point, with views of Half Dome, Upper and Lower Yosemite Falls, and a sweeping vista of Yosemite Valley.

FOUR MILE TRAIL

For a challenging, mid-level hike, take the **Glacier Point Tour shuttle** (209/372-1240, www.travelyosemite.com, 8:30am, 10am, and 1:30pm daily May-Nov., $25 one-way) from Yosemite Valley Lodge to Glacier Point and hike the **Four Mile Trail** (4.8 miles one-way, 3-4 hours) to Southside Drive in Yosemite Valley. The climb down into the valley affords an ascending series of views of Yosemite Falls and Yosemite Valley that grow more spectacular with each switchback.

Camping

Bridalveil Creek (110 sites, first-come, first-served, mid-July-early Sept., $18) is halfway up Glacier Point Road, eight miles from Chinquapin junction and 45 minutes south of the valley. Its season is fairly short because of the snow that blankets this area, but its location along Bridalveil Creek makes it an appealing spot. Sites permit tents and RVs up to 35 feet and include fire pits, picnic tables, a shared bear-proof food locker, and a bathroom with water and flush toilets nearby.

Transportation

Glacier Point is about an hour's drive from Yosemite Valley. From the Valley Visitors Center, drive 14 miles south to Chinquapin junction and turn left onto Glacier Point Road (closed Nov.-May). In winter (Dec.-Mar.), the first five miles of the road are plowed; however, chains may be required.

The **Glacier Point Tours shuttle** (209/372-1240, www.travelyosemite.com, 8:30am, 10am, and 1:30pm daily May-Nov.) meets at Yosemite Valley Lodge to travel to Glacier Point Road when the road is open.

Tickets are available one-way ($15-25) or round-trip ($25-41).

WAWONA

The small town of **Wawona**, four miles from the South Entrance of Yosemite, is home to a lovely historical district, complete with a hotel and restaurant, outdoor exhibits, and even a golf course.

Sights

The **Wawona Visitors Center at Hill's Studio** (209/375-9531, 8:30am-5pm daily mid-May-mid-Oct.) is located in the former studio and gallery of Thomas Hill, a famous landscape painter from the 1800s. The visitors center is perfect for gathering information, getting free wilderness permits, and renting bear-proof canisters.

The **Pioneer Yosemite History Center** (open daily year-round) is a rambling outdoor display area housing an array of historic vehicles and many of the original structures built in the park. Pass through the covered bridge to an uncrowded stretch of land where informative placards describe the history of Yosemite National Park through its structures. In summer, take a 10-minute tour by **horse-drawn carriage** (adults $5, ages 3-12 $4), or check the *Yosemite Guide* for listings of living history programs and live demonstrations.

MARIPOSA GROVE OF GIANT SEQUOIAS

At time of publication, the Mariposa Grove area remained closed due to a restoration project expected to complete in spring 2017.

The **Mariposa Grove** (Wawona Rd./ Hwy. 41) offers a rare view of giant sequoia redwoods in the park. Several trails wind throughout the grove, allowing you to see some of the most impressive trees in a mile or less. Within the grove, the **Mariposa Grove Museum** (Upper Mariposa Grove) is a replica of the cabin of Galen Clark, a former guardian of Yosemite National Park who is credited as the first nonnative to see Mariposa Grove.

Hiking

In addition to the trails that weave throughout the Mariposa Grove of Giant Sequoias, there are easy walks along the **Swinging Bridge Loop** (4.8 miles, 2 hours) from the trailhead at the Pioneer Gift & Grocery.

WAWONA MEADOW LOOP

From the trailhead at the Pioneer Yosemite History Center, start with the easy **Wawona Meadow Loop** (3.5 miles, 2 hours), a flat and uncrowded sweep around the lovely Wawona meadow and a somewhat incongruous nine-hole golf course. This wide trail can be traversed by bike, but the pavement has eroded and there is much dirt and tree detritus.

CHILNUALNA FALLS

If you're up for a hard-core hike and a waterfall experience, take the strenuous trail to **Chilnualna Falls** (8.2 miles, 5 hours), with a 2,300-foot elevation gain. From the trailhead at the Chilnualna Falls parking area, the trail switchbacks all the way up to the top of the falls (avoid entering the stream during spring and summer high flow), with stunning views of Wawona below.

Horseback Riding

You'll find horses at **Big Trees Lodge Stable** (Pioneer Yosemite History Center, Wawona Rd., 209/375-6502, www.travelyosemite.com, 7am-5pm daily June-Sept., $65-88.50), and many travelers too—reservations are strongly recommended. From Wawona you can take a sedate two-hour ride around the historical wagon trail or the more strenuous half-day trip into the mountains.

Accommodations and Food

The charming **Big Trees Lodge** (888/413-8869, www.travelyosemite.com, Mar.-Nov. and mid-Dec.-early Jan., $150-220) opened in 1879 and has been a Yosemite institution ever since. The black-and-white hotel complex includes a wraparound porch and on-site dining. Rooms (with bath and without) come complete with Victorian wallpaper, antique furniture, and a lack of in-room TVs and telephones.

The ★ **dining room at the Big Trees Lodge** (209/375-1425, 7:30am-10am, 11am-1:30pm, 5pm-9pm daily Mar.-Nov. and mid-Dec.-early Jan., $25-30) serves upscale California cuisine in a large white dining room. Reservations are not accepted, so you'll

Pioneer Yosemite History Center

probably have to wait for a table on high-season weekends, but the large common area offers seating, drinks, and live piano music (Tues.-Sat.).

Camping

Lovely and forested **Wawona Campground** (877/444-6777, www.recreation.gov, 93 sites, reservations required Apr.-Oct., $26; first-come, first-served Oct.-mid-Apr., $18), one mile north of Wawona, welcomes tent campers, RVs (no hookups), and even has two equestrian sites. Amenities include drinking water, fire rings, picnic tables, and food lockers; there are no showers.

Transportation

Enter the park at the **South Entrance** (year-round) and continue four miles up Highway 41 (Wawona Rd.) to Wawona. From Wawona, it's another 1.5 hours to Yosemite Valley.

TIOGA PASS AND TUOLUMNE MEADOWS

Tioga Road (Hwy. 120, summer only), Yosemite's own "road less traveled," crosses Yosemite from west to east, leading from the more visited west edge of the park east to the Eastern Sierra. Along the road, you'll find several campgrounds, plus a few natural wonders.

Sights

From Crane Flat, at the junction with Big Oak Flat, Tioga Road (summer only) climbs 39 miles east into Yosemite's High Sierra. Take in the vista at **Olmsted Point,** stroll along the sandy beach at **Tenaya Lake,** and scramble atop **Pothole Dome** to gaze at **Tuolumne Meadows.**

The **Tuolumne Meadows Visitors Center** (9am-6pm daily June-Sept.) is in a rustic building near the campground and the Tuolumne Meadows Store. Frequent ranger talks are held in the parking lot throughout the summer; details on upcoming programs are available in the *Yosemite Guide.* Wilderness permits are available year-round, and a separate structure across the parking lot houses large wheelchair-accessible restrooms.

★ TUOLUMNE MEADOWS

In tones of brilliant green, the waving grasses of **Tuolumne Meadows** offer a rare peak at a fragile alpine meadow that supports a variety of wildlife. Park at the visitors center and get out for a quiet,

Tuolumne Meadows

contemplative view of the meadows along the short, easy trail to **Soda Springs and Parsons Lodge** (1.5 miles, 1 hour). From the trailhead at Lembert Dome, the trail leads past a carbonated spring to the historical **Parsons Lodge** (10am-4pm daily in season) before ending at the Tuolumne Meadows Visitors Center.

Hiking

For smaller crowds along the trails, take one or more of the many scenic hikes along Tioga Road. Remember to take the elevation into account when deciding which trails to explore (they don't call it "high country" for nothing). Trailheads are listed west to east along Tioga Road.

TUOLUMNE GROVE OF GIANT SEQUOIAS

If you're aching to see some giant trees, try the **Tuolumne Grove of Giant Sequoias** (2.5 miles round-trip). The trailhead and parking are at the junction of Tioga Road and Old Big Oak Flat Road. This hike takes you down 400 vertical feet into the grove, which contains more than 20 mature giant sequoias. (You do have to climb back up the hill to get to your car.)

OLMSTED POINT

For a short walk to an amazing view, **Olmsted Point** (0.5 mile round-trip, shuttle stop 12) may be the perfect destination. The trip from the parking lot exists to show off Clouds Rest in all its grandeur. Half Dome peeks out behind Clouds Rest, and right at the trail parking lot, a number of large glacial erratic boulders draw almost as many visitors as the point itself.

TENAYA LAKE

The loop trail to **Tenaya Lake** (2.5 miles round-trip, shuttle stop 9) offers an easy walk, sunny beaches, and possibly the most picturesque views in all of Yosemite. The only difficult part around the lake is fording the outlet stream at the west end (the water gets chilly and can be high).

MAY LAKE AND MOUNT HOFFMAN

May Lake (2 miles round-trip, shuttle stop 11) sits peacefully at the base of the sloping granite of Mount Hoffman. Although the hike is short, the elevation gain up to the lake is a steady, steep 500 feet. For more energetic hikers, a difficult trail leads another two miles and 2,000 vertical feet higher to the top of Mount Hoffman. Much of this walk is along

Tenaya Lake

granite slabs and rocky trails, and some of it is cross-country, but you'll have clear views of Cathedral Peak, Mount Clark, Half Dome, and Clouds Rest along the way.

ELIZABETH LAKE

The trail to **Elizabeth Lake** (4.8 miles round-trip, 4-5 hours, shuttle stop 5) begins at Tuolumne Campground (Loop B) and climbs almost 1,000 vertical feet up to the lake, with most of the climb during the first mile. Evergreens ring the lake, and the steep granite Unicorn Peak rises high above.

NORTH DOME

For an unusual look at a Yosemite classic, take the strenuous **North Dome Trail** (9 miles, 4-5 hours) from the trailhead at Porcupine Creek through the woods out to the dome. Getting to stare right at the face of Half Dome and Clouds Rest just beyond at what feels like eye-level makes the effort worth it.

CATHEDRAL LAKES

If you can't get enough of Yosemite's granite-framed alpine lakes, take the moderately strenuous walk out to the **Cathedral Lakes** (7 miles round-trip, 4-6 hours, shuttle stop 7) from the trailhead west of Tuolumne Meadows Visitors Center. You'll climb about 800 vertical feet over 3.5 miles to picture-perfect lakes that show off the dramatic alpine peaks, surrounding lodgepole pines, and crystalline waters of Yosemite to their best advantage.

GAYLOR LAKES

From the trailhead at the Tioga Pass entrance station, **Gaylor Lakes Trail** (2 miles, 2 hours) starts at almost 10,000 feet and climbs a steep 600 vertical feet up the pass to the Gaylor Lakes valley. Once in the valley, you can wander around five lovely lakes, stopping to admire the views out to the mountains surrounding Tuolumne Meadows or visiting the abandoned 1870s mine site above Upper Gaylor Lake.

Accommodations and Food

Located 15 miles up Tioga Road, **White Wolf Lodge** (801/559-5000, www.yosemite-park.com, mid-June-Sept., $124-156) rents 24 heated canvas-tent cabins and four wood cabins. The wood cabins include a private bath, limited electricity, and daily maid service, while the tent cabins share a central restroom and shower facility; all cabins include linens and towels. Amenities are few, but the scenery is breathtaking.

Tuolumne Meadows Lodge (801/559-5000, www.yosemitepark.com, early June-mid-Sept., $125) offers rustic lodgings in a gorgeous subalpine meadow setting. Expect no electricity, no private baths, and no other amenities. What you will find are small, charming wood-frame tent cabins that sleep up to four, with wood stoves for heat and candles for light. Central facilities include restrooms, hot showers, and a **dining room** (209/372-8413, breakfast and dinner daily early June-mid-Sept., $11-30); dinner reservations are required.

Camping

Yosemite visitors who favor the high country tend to prefer camping. Accordingly, most of Yosemite's campgrounds are north of the valley. **Reservations** (877/444-6777, www.recreation.gov) are accepted or required for Crane Flat, Hodgdon Meadow, and Tuolumne Meadows and usually book far in advance April-September. The remaining campgrounds are first-come, first-served with limited amenities.

HODGDON MEADOW

Hodgdon Meadow (Hwy. 120, 105 sites, reservations required Apr.-Oct., $26; first-come, first-served Oct.-Apr., $18) can be an excellent choice for people who arrive Friday night, since you can set up camp right after entering through Big Oak Flat. At 4,900 feet, the campground accommodates tents or RVs (no hookups) with fire rings, picnic tables, bear-proof food lockers, drinking water, and flush toilets. Supplies are available at Crane Flat; the closest showers are in Yosemite Valley. Pets are permitted.

CRANE FLAT

Crane Flat (Big Oak Flat and Tioga Rds., 166 sites, reservations required, mid-July-Sept., $26) is 17 miles from Yosemite Valley at 6,200 feet elevation. The campground allows RVs up to 35 feet (no hookups) as well as tents, with fire rings, picnic tables, bear-proof food lockers, drinking water, and flush toilets. Supplies are available at Crane Flat; the closest showers are in Yosemite Valley. Pets are permitted.

TAMARACK FLAT

Along Tioga Road, **Tamarack Flat** (Tioga Rd., 52 sites, first-come, first-served, late June-early Oct., $12) is a primitive tent-only campground at 6,300 feet elevation. Sites include picnic tables and bear-proof food lockers, but there is no drinking water. Restroom facilities are restricted to pit toilets.

WHITE WOLF

White Wolf (Tioga Rd., 74 sites, first-come, first-served, July-early Sept., $18) is at 8,000 feet elevation on Tioga Road. The turnoff is on the left, down a narrow side road. Sites accommodate tents and RVs up to 27 feet and include fire pits and picnic tables; there are bear-proof food lockers, water, and flush toilets. Crane Flat is the closest place for supplies. Pets are permitted.

YOSEMITE CREEK AND PORCUPINE FLAT

Yosemite Creek (Tioga Rd., 75 sites, first-come, first-served, late July-mid-Sept., $12) is a primitive tent-only campground with few amenities—fire pits, picnic tables, and bear-proof food lockers. There is no drinking water, and only vault toilets. In the same vicinity is **Porcupine Flat** (52 sites, first-come, first-served, July-Oct. 15, $12), at 8,100 feet, with some limited RV sites but no water.

TUOLUMNE MEADOWS

★ **Tuolumne Meadows** (Tioga Rd. at Tuolumne Meadows, 304 sites, July-Sept., $26) is one of the largest campgrounds in the park and it can fill every night. Half of the sites are available by reservation; the remaining half are first-come, first-served. Sites with fire rings and picnic tables accommodate tents and RVs up to 35 feet (no hookups), and there are bear-proof food lockers, water, and flush toilets. Tuolumne Meadows is at about 8,600 feet elevation, so it can get quite chilly even in midsummer. Leashed pets are permitted.

HIGH SIERRA CAMPS

For backpackers, the ★ **High Sierra Camps** (www.travelyosemite.com, July-Sept., adults $180, ages 7-12 $109) offer tent cabins with amenities, breakfast and dinner in camp, and a sack lunch. Choose from Merced Lake, Vogelsang, Glen Aulin, May Lake, and Sunrise Camp—or hike 6-10 miles from one to another. Reservations are by lottery; applications are accepted September-October for the following summer. You must submit an application to join the lottery; even if you get a spot, there's no guarantee you'll get your preferred dates.

Transportation

Tuolumne Meadows is located along Tioga Road (Hwy. 120), from Crane Flat to Tioga Pass, the east entrance, where it becomes Tioga Pass Road. **The road is open only in summer.** To check weather conditions and road closures, call 209/372-0200.

From the west, Highway 120 becomes Big Oak Flat Road at the Big Oak Flat park entrance. In nine miles, at Crane Flat junction, the left fork becomes Tioga Road. The Tuolumne Meadows Visitors Center is 38 miles from the west entrance. To get to Tioga Road from Yosemite Valley, take Northside Road to Big Oak Flat Road. At the Tioga Road junction, turn east.

In summer, the free **Tuolumne Meadows Hikers Bus** (209/372-1172, www.nps.gov/yose, hours vary May-Sept.) runs along Tioga Road between Olmsted Point and the Tuolumne Meadows Lodge. Service varies

Tioga Pass and Tuolumne Meadows

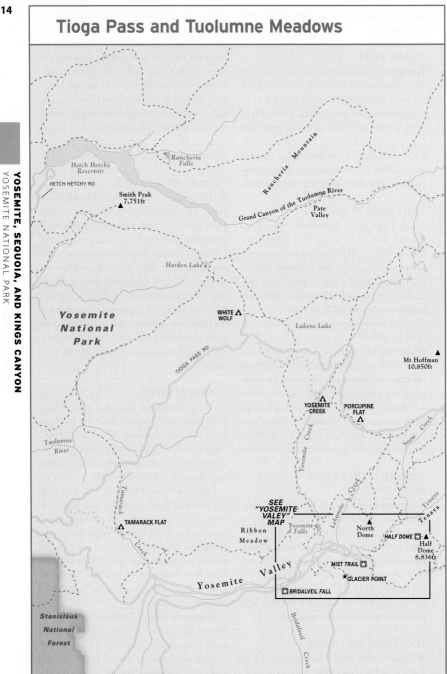

Hetch Hetchy
Reservoir

HETCH HETCHY RD

Rancheria
Falls

Rancheria Mountain

Grand Canyon of the Tuolumne River

Pate
Valley

Smith Peak
▲ 7,751ft

Harden Lake

Yosemite
National
Park

WHITE △
WOLF

Lukens Lake

TIOGA PASS RD

Mt Hoffman
▲ 10,850ft

YOSEMITE △
CREEK

PORCUPINE
FLAT △

Snow Creek

Tuolumne
River

Yosemite Creek

Tamarack

SEE
"YOSEMITE
VALEY"
MAP

Tenaya

TAMARACK FLAT △

Ribbon
Meadow

Yosemite
Falls

Lehamite Creek

North
Dome ▲

HALF DOME ✪ ▲
Half
Dome
8,836ft

Tamarack Creek

Yosemite Valley

MIST TRAIL ✪

★ GLACIER POINT

✪ BRIDALVEIL FALL

Stanislaus
National
Forest

Bridalveil Creek

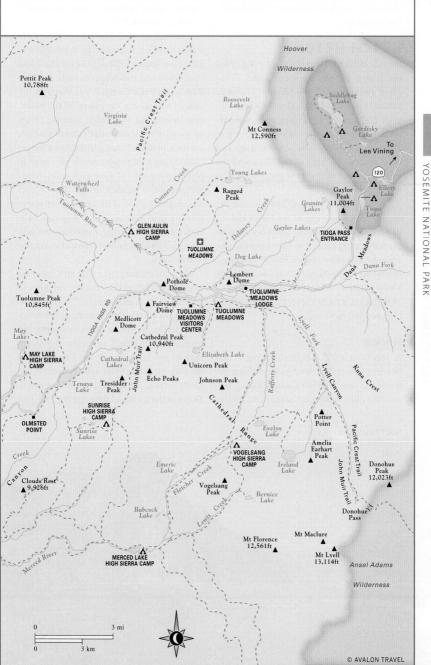

Hoover

Wilderness

Saddlebag
Lake

Pettit Peak
10,788ft

Roosevelt
Lake

Virginia
Lake

Pacific Crest Trail

Gardisky
Lake

Mt Conness
12,590ft

To
Lee Vining

120

Ellery
Lake

Waterwheel
Falls

Conness Creek

Young Lakes

Gaylor
Peak
11,004ft

Tioga
Lake

Tuolumne River

Ragged
Peak

Creek

Granite
Lakes

Delaney

Gaylor Lakes

TIOGA PASS
ENTRANCE

GLEN AULIN
HIGH SIERRA
CAMP

Creek

Dog Lake

TUOLUMNE
MEADOWS

Dana Meadows

Dana Fork

Tuolumne Peak
10,845ft

Pothole
Dome

Lembert
Dome

TUOLUMNE
MEADOWS
LODGE

Lyell Fork

May
Lake

TIOGA PASS RD

Medlicott
Dome

Fairview
Dome

TUOLUMNE
MEADOWS
VISITORS
CENTER

TUOLUMNE
MEADOWS

Elizabeth Lake

Lyell Fork

Kuna Crest

MAY LAKE
HIGH SIERRA
CAMP

Cathedral
Lakes

Cathedral Peak
10,940ft

Unicorn Peak

Rafferty Creek

Lyell Canyon

John Muir Trail

Tenaya
Lake

Tresidder
Peak

Echo Peaks

Johnson Peak

Cathedral

Pacific Crest Trail

OLMSTED
POINT

SUNRISE
HIGH SIERRA
CAMP

Sunrise
Lakes

Range

Evelyn
Lake

Potter
Point

Amelia
Earhart
Peak

Creek

Canyon

Clouds Rest
9,926ft

Emeric
Lake

VOGELSANG
HIGH SIERRA
CAMP

Ireland
Lake

John Muir Trail

Donohue
Peak
12,023ft

Fletcher

Creek

Vogelsang
Peak

Bernice
Lake

Donohue
Pass

Babcock
Lake

Lewis Creek

Merced River

MERCED LAKE
HIGH SIERRA CAMP

Mt Florence
12,561ft

Mt Maclure

Mt Lyell
13,114ft

Ansel Adams

Wilderness

0   3 mi

0   3 km

© AVALON TRAVEL

seasonally; check the *Yosemite Guide* for current schedules.

HETCH HETCHY

Hetch Hetchy (Hetch Hetchy Rd. past the Hetch Hetchy park entrance) is located about 30 minutes north of Highway 120. It is home to Hetch Hetchy Reservoir, with 1,972 acres of surface area, a maximum depth of 312 feet, and a capacity of 117 billion gallons. The water is deep and blue, and the gushing waterfalls along the sides are some of the most gorgeous in the whole park.

Named for Michael M. O'Shaughnessy, the original chief engineer of the Hetch Hetchy Project, **O'Shaughnessy Dam** is a massive curved gravity dam that turns part of the Tuolumne River into Hetch Hetchy Reservoir. It originally opened in 1923 at 344 feet high; a later phase of construction, completed in 1938, raised it to its current size of 426 feet high and 900 feet long.

Hiking

At less than 4,000 feet in elevation, Hetch Hetchy is one of the lowest parts of Yosemite; it gets less snow and has a longer hiking season than many other areas of the park. It's also warmer here in summer, so you may want to plan a spring or fall visit.

The easy-to-moderate hike to **Wapama Fall** (5 miles round-trip, 2 hours) begins by crossing O'Shaughnessy Dam and then following the Wapama Falls Trail (or Rancheria Falls Camp Trail) through the tunnel and along the shore of the reservoir. Along the way, you'll also see close-up views of the spectacular **Tueeulala Fall,** set back in the hillside a little. For a longer hike, bring a large poncho or rain gear to protect yourself and your pack before stepping onto the wooden bridge that crosses under these falls. The amount of water flowing over Tueeulala and Wapama Falls varies greatly; in spring, it can be especially powerful and the falls can be quite dangerous at times.

For a short, easy hike that still includes a nice waterfall at the end, try the hike to **Carlon Falls** (4 miles, easy). The trail actually begins outside the Yosemite park boundaries, in the Stanislaus National Forest, but soon enters the park to follow the South Fork of the Tuolumne River. The payoff at the end, after one brief uphill climb, is the lovely Carlon Falls, a year-round waterfall. To get to the trailhead from the Big Oak Flat

Hetch Hetchy

Entrance, drive north on Highway 120 for one mile. Bear right onto Evergreen Road, toward Mather and Hetch Hetchy, and continue another mile. Just past the Carlon Day Use Area is a pullout on the right with room for a few cars.

Accommodations and Camping

Just one mile from the Hetch Hetchy park entrance, the **Evergreen Lodge** (33160 Evergreen Rd., Groveland, 209/379-2606, www.evergreenlodge.com, $180-415) rents 88 cabins in a variety of styles and sizes. Most visitors are here for the easy access to Yosemite, but the lodge is almost a destination in itself with a summer camp atmosphere and organized activities.

There are no developed campgrounds in the Hetch Hetchy region of the park. The **Hetch Hetchy Backpackers Campground** is next to the overnight parking lot at the end of Hetch Hetchy Road. To backpack overnight in the Hetch Hetchy area, you need a bear canister ($5) for your food and a wilderness permit (free) from the Hetch Hetchy entrance station (209/372-0200, 7am-9pm daily May-Labor Day, 8am-7pm daily Apr. and Labor Day-Oct., 8am-5pm daily Nov.-Mar.).

Transportation

Hetch Hetchy is in the northwest corner of Yosemite National Park. The Hetch Hetchy Entrance is about 10 miles north of the Big Oak Flat Entrance on Highway 120. From Highway 120, take the Hetch Hetchy turn-off onto Evergreen Road, and then follow Evergreen Road north for 7.2 miles. At the town of Mather, turn onto Hetch Hetchy Road and proceed another 16 miles through the gate and to the parking lot near O'Shaughnessy Dam.

If you're already in the park, you have to leave through the Big Oak Flat Entrance and onto Highway 120 before reentering at the Hetch Hetchy Entrance. It takes about 1.25-1.5 hours to get to Hetch Hetchy from Yosemite Valley, a distance of about 40 miles.

GATEWAYS TO YOSEMITE
Groveland (Hwy. 120)

Groveland, 26 miles outside the north entrance to Yosemite National Park on Highway 120, is the perfect place to stop for gas, food, coffee, and a place to sleep. The most elegant option is the historical ★ **Groveland Hotel** (18767 Main St., 800/273-3314, www.groveland.com, $131-257), built in 1849 and

Wapama Fall

located in the center of town. The hotel's 17 rooms are furnished with down comforters, feather beds, and large flat-screen HDTVs. Amenities include fresh coffee beans, chocolate chip cookies, and an open-door policy for dogs and cats.

Yosemite Riverside Inn (11399 Cherry Lake Rd., 209/962-7408 or 800/626-7408, www.yosemiteriversideinn.com, $69-295) is located just 11 miles west of the Big Oak Flat Entrance. Rooms include kitchenettes with river or courtyard views. Cabins with full kitchens are also available. The **Yosemite Westgate Lodge** (7633 Hwy. 120, 800/253-9673 or 209/962-5281, www.yosemitewestgate.com, $185-235) is 13 miles from the Big Oak Flat Entrance, with 45 nonsmoking and pet-free rooms, a heated pool, spa, and a playground.

Yosemite Lakes (31191 Harden Flat Rd., 800/533-1001, ranger station 209/962-0103, www.thousandtrails.com, RVs $58, tents $41) is a sprawling wooded campground beside the Tuolumne River with more than 250 RV sites with full hookups, 130 tent sites, a few dozen cabins, tent cabins, yurts, and a 12-bed hostel.

The **Cellar Door** (18767 Main St., 800/273-3314, www.groveland.com, 8am-10am, 5:30pm-9:30pm daily spring-fall, 8am-10am, 5:30pm-9:30pm Thurs.-Mon. winter, $19-27, reservations suggested in summer) is the excellent restaurant at the Groveland Hotel. The **Priest Station Café** (16756 Old Priest Grade, Big Oak Flat, 209/962-1888, http://prieststation.com, 8am-8pm daily summer, 8am-3pm Mon.-Thurs., 8am-8pm Fri.-Sun. fall and spring, $13-22) is a tiny roadside eatery serving up hearty dishes like jambalaya, ribs, and roasted turkey.

The **Iron Door Saloon** (18761 Main St., 209/962-6244, www.iron-door-saloon.com, bar 11am-2am daily year-round, grill 7am-9pm daily summer, 7am-9pm Thurs.-Sat., 7am-3pm Sun.-Mon. and Wed. winter, $9-25) is the center of nightlife for miles around.

Mariposa (Hwy. 140)

Mariposa lies about 30 miles from the Arch Rock Entrance and about 40 miles from Yosemite Valley. You can't miss the **River Rock Inn and Deli Garden Café** (4993 7th St., 209/966-5793, www.riverrockmariposa.com, $135-149), a quirky, whimsical motel with unusually decorated rooms a 45-minute drive from the west entrance to Yosemite.

Several campgrounds surround the Arch Rock Entrance near Mariposa. The **Yosemite Bug Rustic Mountain Resort** (6979 Hwy.

The Iron Door Saloon is California's oldest drinking establishment.

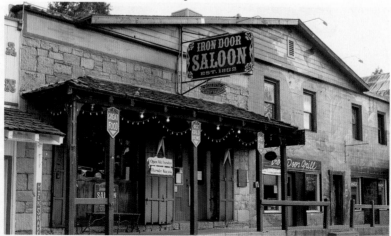

140, Midpines, 209/966-6666 or 866/826-7108, www.yosemitebug.com, dorm $23-30, tent cabin $30-70, private room $50-95, private cabin $65-155) is part hostel, part rustic lodge with five hostel dormitories, attractively appointed tent cabins with real beds (bring your own sleeping bag), and a few cabins with private rooms, some with private baths.

El Portal (Hwy. 140)

El Portal is less than 4 miles from the Arch Rock Entrance and just 15 miles from Yosemite Valley, making it one of the closest places for a final overnight on the way to the park. RVers flock to the **Indian Flat RV Park** (9988 Hwy. 140, 209/379-2339, www.indianflatrvpark.com, tents $20-30, RVs $42-48, tent cabins $79, cottages $129, pet fee $5), a full-service low-end resort with everything from RV sites (some hookups) to tent cabins and full-fledged cottages. Showers are available ($3), and the lodge next door allows campers to use its outdoor pool. Indian Flat is relatively small (25 RV sites, 25 tent sites), so reservations are strongly recommended May-September.

Oakhurst (Hwy. 41)

Oakhurst lies less than 15 miles from the South Entrance of Yosemite National Park. The **Best Western Plus Yosemite Gateway Inn** (40530 Hwy. 41, www.yosemitegateway-inn.com, 559/683-2378 or 888/256-8042, www.yosemitegatewayinn.com, $149-159) offers both indoor and outdoor pools and spas, free wireless Internet, better-than-your-average-chain rooms, and an on-site restaurant (6:30am-11am, 5pm-9pm Mon.-Sat., 6:30am-1pm, 5pm-9pm Sun., $8-20). The **Oakhurst Lodge** (40302 Hwy. 41, 559/683-4417 or 800/655-6343, www.theoakhurstlodge.com, $155-165) is within walking distance of the shops and restaurants of Oakhurst.

The best restaurant in the Oakhurst area is **Erna's Elderberry House** (48688 Victoria Ln., Oakhurst, 559/683-6800, www.elderberryhouse.com, 5:30pm-8:30pm Mon.-Sat., 11am-1pm, 5:30pm-8:30pm Sun., $45-108) on the grounds of the **Chateau du Sureau** (www.chateausureau.com, $385-585), a breathtakingly beautiful lodge with just 10 rooms.

Fish Camp (Hwy. 41)

Fish Camp is 40 miles from Yosemite Valley via the South Entrance, a little over an hour's drive. The **Narrow Gauge Inn** (48571 Hwy. 41, 559/683-7720 or 888/644-9050, www.narrowgaugeinn.com, $149-248) is a charming 26-room mountain inn offering one- and two-bed nonsmoking rooms, outdoor tables and chairs, and an on-site restaurant. East of Fish Camp, check in to the **White Chief Mountain Lodge** (7776 White Chief Mountain Rd., 559/683-5444, www.whitechiefmountainlodge.com, Apr.-Dec., $159-179), with basic rooms, small TVs, and wireless Internet.

The **Tenaya Lodge** (1122 Hwy. 41, 559/683-6555 or 888/514-2167, www.tenayalodge.com, $305-540) offers plush lodge-style accommodations: choose from rooms in the lodge or one of the three dozen cottages. Tenaya Lodge focuses on guest care, offering five dining venues on-site, a full-service spa, and daily guided nature walks.

A mile south of the South Entrance is the small **Summerdale Campground** (Hwy. 41, northeast of Fish Camp, 877/444-6777, www.recreation.gov, May-Sept., $28-30). This lovely spot has a two-night minimum on weekends and a three-night minimum on holiday weekends, only 26 campsites, and a strict limit on RV size (24 feet). You'll have a fire ring and a grill at your site, plenty of room under mature shade trees, and maybe even a water spigot (boiling the water is recommended).

Sequoia and Kings Canyon

Sequoia and Kings Canyon National Park (559/565-3341, www.nps.gov/seki, open year-round, $30 per vehicle, $20 motorcycles, $15 bike or on foot) actually encompasses two distinct parks, a forest, and a monument: **Kings Canyon National Park** to the north, **Sequoia National Park** to the south, Sequoia National Forest surrounding much of the parkland, and Giant Sequoia National Monument, a subset of the national forest to the south and west of the parks. Sequoia and Kings Canyon are jointly administered by the National Park Service, and together they encompass more than 864,000 acres.

Generals Highway is the main road running north-south through the two parks; it connects Highway 180 (Kings Canyon National Park) in the north to Highway 198 (Sequoia National Park) in the south. The steep, narrow, twisting mountain road can be treacherous in bad weather and road construction may also create delays. The maximum allowed RV length on Generals Highway is 22 feet, and trailers are not permitted. Neither RVs nor trailers are permitted on Mineral King Road or Moro Rock-Crescent Meadow Road.

Park Entrances

There are three entrances to Sequoia and Kings Canyon National Parks.

The **Big Stump Entrance** (Hwy. 180) is the most direct route to either park from the west or north. When leaving the pay station, turn left to return to Highway 180 heading north into the park. If your goal is Kings Canyon National Park, continue straight 3.5 miles to Grant Grove Village. To reach Sequoia National Park, turn right onto Generals Highway at the next junction and head south.

The **Ash Mountain Entrance** (Hwy. 198) enters Sequoia National Park from the south. Once inside the park, Highway 198 becomes Generals Highway heading north. This road can be slow going thanks to a combination of heavy traffic (especially in summer) and ongoing road construction. In winter, the Ash Mountain Entrance is probably the better choice as it is plowed sooner. Call (559/565-3341 or 800/427-7623) to check road conditions.

Located on Mineral King Road, east of the Ash Mountain Entrance, the **Lookout Point Entrance** is only used by travelers headed for the Mineral King area of Sequoia National Park. Mineral King Road is narrow, winding, and closed in winter (Nov.-May) and cannot be used by RVs or trailers.

Sequoia National Park provides free **shuttle service** (559/565-3341, www.nps.gov/seki, 9am-6pm daily late May-Sept.) in summer, stopping at Giant Forest Museum, the Lodgepole Visitor Center, and Moro Rock.

GRANT GROVE

The Grant Grove area of Kings Canyon National Park is located near the Big Stump Entrance, accessed via Highway 180. It is home to three campgrounds, lodging, a visitors center, and several hikes.

Grant Grove Village (year-round) is one of the busiest visitor areas in Kings Canyon and one of the best places to come if you need services. It has a large visitors center, a restaurant, a gift shop (9am-6pm Sun.-Thurs., 9am-7pm Fri.-Sat.), a market, public showers, a lodge, and cabins. Three of the park's nicest campgrounds are close by, as is the gargantuan General Grant Tree. Grant Grove is on the west side of the park, 3.5 miles from the Big Stump park entrance.

The large **Kings Canyon Visitor Center** (83918 Hwy. 180 E., 559/565-4307, 8am-5pm daily May-Nov., 9am-4:30pm daily Nov.-May) is three miles from the Highway 180 entrance and is the place to get maps, information about

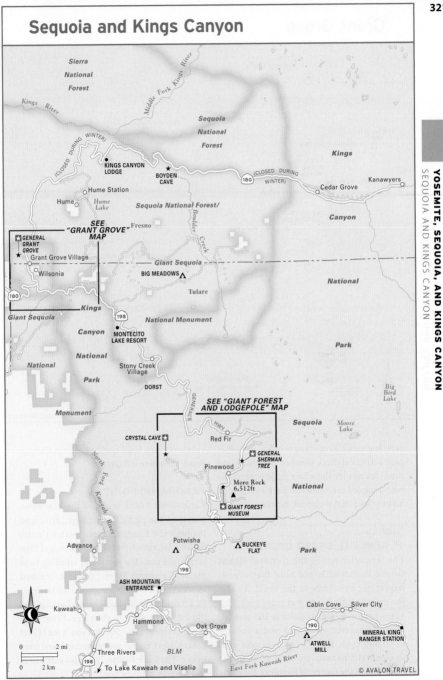

Sequoia and Kings Canyon

Sierra National Forest

Kings River

Middle Fork Kings River

Sequoia National Forest

Kings

KINGS CANYON LODGE

BOYDEN CAVE

180 (CLOSED DURING WINTER)

Cedar Grove

Kanawyers

(CLOSED DURING WINTER)

Hume Station

Hume

Hume Lake

Sequoia National Forest/

Canyon

SEE "GRANT GROVE" MAP

Fresno

Boulder Creek

GENERAL GRANT GROVE

Grant Grove Village

Giant Sequoia

National

Wilsonia

BIG MEADOWS

180

Tulare

Giant Sequoia

198

National Monument

Park

Kings

Canyon

MONTECITO LAKE RESORT

National

Park

Stony Creek Village

Big Bird Lake

Monument

DORST

GENERAL'S HWY

SEE "GIANT FOREST AND LODGEPOLE" MAP

Sequoia

Moose Lake

CRYSTAL CAVE

Red Fir

Pinewood

GENERAL SHERMAN TREE

North Fork Kaweah River

Moro Rock 6,512ft

National

GIANT FOREST MUSEUM

Advance

Potwisha

BUCKEYE FLAT

Park

198

ASH MOUNTAIN ENTRANCE

Kaweah

Cabin Cove

Silver City

Hammond

Oak Grove

190

MINERAL KING RANGER STATION

0   2 mi

0   2 km

Three Rivers

198

To Lake Kaweah and Visalia

BLM

ATWELL MILL

East Fork Kaweah River

© AVALON TRAVEL

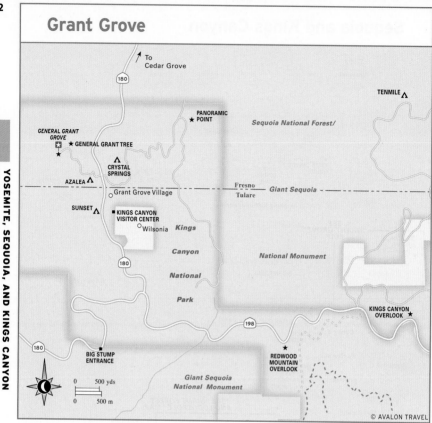

Grant Grove

camping and hiking, ranger talks, and other park activities; check weather conditions and road closures for the whole park; explore the well-designed exhibits about park ecology and history; and chat with park rangers.

Sights

★ GENERAL GRANT GROVE

The tree after which the **General Grant Grove** is named is not only the second-largest tree by volume in the world, it's also the nation's only living war memorial. This 1,700-year-old giant sequoia is 268 feet tall with a diameter of 40 feet and a volume of 46,608 cubic feet. Grant is second only to General Sherman, its compatriot at the other end of the Generals Highway. From the

visitors center, head north on Kings Canyon Road, then turn left (signed).

PANORAMIC POINT

Panoramic Point is one of the best viewpoints in the parks. To get here, drive east through the Kings Canyon Visitor Center parking lot, turn left at the meadow, and then turn right onto the steep and winding road marked Panoramic Point. (This route is closed in winter and is not appropriate for trailers.) In 2.3 miles you'll reach the parking lot and the 0.25-mile walk to the ridge. From your perch at more than 7,500 feet you'll see Hume Lake, Kings Canyon, and mountains and trees galore. The **Park Ridge Trail** also starts here and leads to a fire lookout.

General Grant Grove

General Grant Tree, which truly lives up to its hype. The **General Grant Tree Trail** (0.3 mile, easy) leads past many other stunning sights on the way to and from its namesake tree in just a short distance. Along this trail is the **Fallen Monarch,** an immense tree lying on its side and hollowed out in the middle, the 1872 **Gamlin Cabin,** used as the living quarters for the first ranger stationed here, and the **Centennial Stump,** so large that whole Sunday school classes have stood on top of it.

The General Grant Tree Trail is a paved, short, and easy walk and is accessible for wheelchairs. Trail guides ($1.50) are available at the trailhead, which has a large parking lot, with restrooms. From the visitors center, head north on Kings Canyon Road, then turn left (signed).

After visiting the General Grant Tree, take the **North Grove Loop Trail** (1.5 miles), which starts from the same parking lot. Most of the loop is along an old park road through the grove.

REDWOOD MOUNTAIN OVERLOOK

From Grant Grove, travel south on Generals Highway for six miles and look for the signed **Redwood Mountain Overlook.** Park your car to look out over one of the world's largest groves of giant sequoias. The trailhead for the **Redwood Mountain Grove** is two miles farther down a dirt road.

KINGS CANYON OVERLOOK

Kings Canyon Overlook is very close to Redwood Mountain Overlook and about six miles southeast of Grant Grove. Watch for signs (they're large and easy to spot) along Generals Highway and pull over into the ample roadside parking area. Descriptive signs help identify the peaks and groves surrounding you. Break out the binoculars if you've got a pair.

Hiking
GENERAL GRANT GROVE

General Grant Grove is home to dozens of giant sequoias. The largest of these is the

PARK RIDGE TRAIL

Enjoy the vistas from the **Park Ridge Trail** (Panoramic Point Rd. parking area, 2.5 miles east of Grant Grove Village, closed in winter, 4.7 miles, easy). There's little elevation change on this walk, and much of it is on a wide, easy-to-follow fire road, but the altitude can make it a little challenging. To reach the trailhead, drive east through the Kings Canyon Visitor Center parking lot; turn left at the meadow and then turn right onto the steep and winding road marked Panoramic Point.

SEQUOIA LAKE OVERLOOK-DEAD GIANT LOOP

The **Sequoia Lake Overlook-Dead Giant Loop** (lower end of General Grant Tree parking area, 2.2 miles, easy) takes you to the Dead Giant, a first-growth giant sequoia that was mostly likely killed by loggers who tried, and failed, to cut it for lumber. The trail continues to an overlook of Sequoia Lake, actually an old mill pond from the logging days.

SUNSET TRAIL

For a longer, more demanding day hike, check out the **Sunset Trail** (across the street from Kings Canyon Visitor Center, 6 miles, strenuous). From the visitors center, cross Kings Canyon Road, entering the Sunset Campground (the trail leaves the campground at site 118). After 1.25 miles, follow the South Boundary Trail for 0.25 mile to Voila Falls. Then, on the Sunset Trail, hike downhill to Ella Falls. Altogether, you'll climb about 1,400 vertical feet round-trip through magnificent mixed forests. To return to the trailhead, either head back the way you came or follow the fire road north to the General Grant Tree trailhead.

BIG STUMP TRAIL

Immediately outside the Big Stump Entrance (three miles south of Grant Grove Village), take the **Big Stump Trail** (2 miles round-trip) through a grove that was heavily logged in the late 19th century but is now reclaiming its true nature as a sequoia grove. One of the sights along here is the Mark Twain stump, the remains of a 26-foot-wide tree that was cut in 1891.

REDWOOD MOUNTAIN SEQUOIA GROVE

Redwood Canyon is home to the largest grove of giant sequoias in the world. The 16 miles of trails within the canyon make it a good place to wander around and see the trees up close. At the trailhead, turn left to begin the **Hart Tree and Fallen Goliath Loop.** This easy 6.5-mile trek leads across Redwood Creek and past the former logging site of Barton's Post Camp. About halfway around the loop, you'll come to a short spur trail that takes you to the Hart Tree, the largest in the grove and the 25th largest known in the world. Fallen Goliath, a little farther along, is another impressive sight, even lying down.

To get here, take Generals Highway seven miles south of Grant Grove Village. When you see the sign for Redwood Canyon, turn right onto the dirt road and travel another two miles along Quail Flat. At the end of this road, you'll find ample room for parking.

BUENA VISTA PEAK

Buena Vista Peak is an ideal spot for gazing out at the Western Divide, Mineral King, and Farewell Gap and pondering the regrowth of a sequoia forest after a fire. (This area had a prescribed burn in 2004.) The hike to reach the peak is a fairly easy two miles. Park at the Buena Vista trailhead, which is near the Kings Canyon Overlook, three miles north of Montecito Sequoia Lodge on Generals Highway and six miles south of Grant Grove.

BIG BALDY TRAIL

The **Big Baldy Trail** (4 miles, easy-moderate) is a popular out-and-back hike with only 600 feet of elevation gain. It's one of the most rewarding hikes in the park, considering the relatively small effort you have to expend for the major views. From the granite summit of Big Baldy, you'll be able to see far into Redwood Canyon. The trailhead and parking area are along the Generals Highway, eight miles south of Grant Grove.

Food

Grant Grove Restaurant (Hwy. 180 at Generals Hwy., 559/335-5500, 7am-10am, 11:30am-4pm, 5pm-9pm daily summer, 7:30am-10:30am, 11:30am-3pm, 5pm-8pm daily winter, $13-25) serves three meals each day. The food is nothing special, but it's a good place for a decent meal and a glass of wine or beer.

You'll find a minimart at **Grant Grove Village** (86728 Hwy. 180, 8am-8pm Sun.-Thurs., 8am-9pm Fri.-Sat. summer, 9am-6pm Sun.-Thurs., 9am-7pm Fri.-Sat. fall and spring, 9am-5:30pm Fri.-Sun. winter) selling a few staples. You can also get some non-food supplies like batteries, flashlights, and moleskin.

Accommodations

Reservations at Grant Grove can fill up 4-6 months in advance. The **Grant Grove**

Cabins (877/436-9615 or 866/807-3598, www. visitsequoia.com) offer an array of lodging styles at a variety of prices. The economy option is the **tent cabins** (17 cabins, May-Sept., $62), which are short on amenities, with no electricity or heat and with shared central baths. The so-called **camp cabins** (May-Nov., $89-103) are at the low end of the fully enclosed cabins. They have solid walls and 2-3 double beds, plus electricity, a propane heater, and daily maid service, but no private baths. **Rustic cabins** (May-Nov., $99) come with at least two double beds and have carpets and insulation. The **bath cabins** (8 duplex cabins, 1 single, year-round, $129-140) have all of the amenities of the other cabins, plus private baths with a tub and shower.

The attractive, simple, and sturdy **John Muir Lodge** (866/565-6343, www.jmlodge. com, 36 rooms, year-round, summer $201-211, winter as low as $101) is both a comfortable motel and a classic woodsy lodge. Rooms are simply decorated in an alpine theme, with comfortable beds, private baths, and good views out into the forest. Since you're at the edge of Grant Grove Village, you'll find plenty of nearby food and services, and convenient access to hiking and the Generals Highway. John Muir Lodge is two stories with no elevator; if anyone in your party has a problem with stairs, be sure to mention that when you book.

Montecito Sequoia Lodge (63410 Generals Hwy., 559/565-3388 or 800/227-9900, www.mslodge.com, mid-Aug.-mid-June, $99-318, meals included) is a rustic full-service resort located on Generals Highway nine miles southeast of Grant Grove Village. The main lodge has 22 rooms; four smaller lodges sleep up to five people each and eight heated cabins sleep up to eight people each. The cabins do not have private baths, but bathhouses with free showers are nearby. Four deluxe two-story cabins each accommodate up to five people; all four cabins have full baths. In summer, Montecito operates primarily as a family camp, but it is available to non-campers (Sat. only, $100-400). The **restaurant** (7:30am-9am, noon-1:30pm, 5:30pm-7pm daily mid-June-mid-Aug., 8am-9am, noon-1pm, 6pm-7pm daily mid-Aug.-mid-June, $9-30) is open to nonguests year-round.

Camping

The **Sunset** (159 sites, summer only, $18-40) and ★ **Azalea** (110 sites, year-round, summer $18) campgrounds are both located 3.5 miles from the Kings Canyon park entrance and are close to the visitors center and Grant Grove Village. Only slightly farther, on the east side of Highway 180, is **Crystal Springs** (49 sites, summer only, $18-35). All campgrounds are supplied with picnic tables, fire rings, bear lockers, drinking water, and restrooms with flush toilets; they are all beautifully decorated in top-of-the-line national park scenery, with towering trees, artistically jumbled boulders, and winding paths. Showers are available at Grant Grove Village. Campgrounds are first-come, first-served and fill up on weekends in July-August. To confirm campground opening and closing dates, call 559/565-3341 prior to your visit.

Other campgrounds are managed by the Hume Lake Ranger District of the Sequoia National Forest/Giant Sequoia National Monument (559/338-2251, www.fs.fed.us/ r5/sequoia). **Princess Campground** (Hwy. 180, 877/444-6777, www.recreation.gov, June-Sept., $18) is 6 miles north of Grant Grove Village, with 88 sites and vault toilets. **Hume Lake** (Generals Hwy., 877/444-6777, www.recreation.gov, May-Sept., $20) is 10 miles northeast of Grant Grove, with 74 sites and flush toilets. **Tenmile** (Generals Hwy., May-Sept., $16) is 5 miles northeast of Grant Grove, with 13 first-come, first-served sites; it allows RVs up to 22 feet long but has no drinking water and has vault toilets. **Landslide** (Generals Hwy., summer only, $16) is 13 miles northeast of Grant Grove with 9 first-come, first-served sites and vault toilets. **Convict Flat** (Hwy. 180, summer only, free) is 19 miles northeast of Grant Grove with 5 first-come, first-served sites. To verify all campground availability, call 559/565-3341.

Transportation and Services

Grant Grove is located in Kings Canyon National Park, four miles east of the Big Stump Entrance on Highway 180. **ATMs** and **showers** are available at Grant Grove Village.

CEDAR GROVE

Cedar Grove Village (May-Oct., weather permitting) is located within Kings Canyon National Park, 30 miles northeast of Grant Grove on Highway 180. In mid- to late October, the eastern part of Highway 180 closes past the junction of Highway 180 with Generals Highway, near the Princess Campground in Sequoia National Forest. If you visit when the road is open, the drive out to Cedar Grove is a treat in itself. *There is no way to cross the Sierra through Kings Canyon by car.*

The centerpiece of **Cedar Grove Village** (8am-9pm daily summer, 8am-8pm daily spring and fall) is the **Cedar Grove Lodge** (559/565-0100, May-Oct.). Other services in the village include a snack bar (7:30am-10:30am, 11:30am-2:30pm, 5pm-8pm daily), gift shop, small market, laundry, showers, and an ATM. Located next to the Sentinel Campground near Cedar Grove Village, the **Cedar Grove Visitor Center** (559/565-3793, 9am-5pm daily mid-May-late Sept.) has books, maps, first aid, and park rangers.

Kings Canyon Scenic Byway

The section of Highway 180 through Cedar Grove is known as the **Kings Canyon Scenic Byway,** and it offers tremendous views of the vast canyons that give the park its name. The drive starts at 6,600 feet at Grant Grove, weaving down as far as 3,000 feet around Convict Flat before climbing back up to 5,000 feet before its terminus at Road's End. Though curvy, the road is not treacherous; most vehicles maintain a reasonable-to-slow speed. Ample roadside pullouts are available on both sides of the highway, so you'll find it easy to stop for photos along the way.

On Kings Canyon Road, approximately one mile east of Cedar Grove Village, pull off the road and really take in the shape of this stunning canyon at **Canyon View.** The U-shaped canyon was carved through these soaring peaks by glaciers; the Kings River now flows through its dramatic descent.

Small but picturesque **Knapp's Cabin** was built in the 1920s by George Knapp, a Santa Barbara businessman who stored the extensive gear he used on fishing expeditions here. To get there, take the Kings Canyon Scenic Byway and pull over two miles east of the Cedar Grove Village turnoff. The cabin is just a short walk from the road.

Roads End really is the end of Highway 180 (E. Kings Canyon Rd.). Roads End is located deep in the middle of Kings Canyon, a few miles past Cedar Grove Village and about 35 miles from Grant Grove. Beyond Roads End, the park is trails, canyons, forests, and lakes.

What you will find at the end of the road is the **Roads End Permit Station** (7am-3:45pm daily late May-late Sept.). This small wooden building is the place to get your wilderness permit ($15) and to talk to the rangers about trail conditions, recommended routes, and food storage and bear management regulations before you begin any backcountry adventure.

Sights

Boyden Cave (74101 E. Kings Canyon Rd., 888/965-8243, www.caverntours.com, tours 10am-5pm daily May-Sept., adults $14.50, under age 12 $8.75) contains plenty of draperies, pancakes, stalactites, and other calcite structures. Boyden Cave is operated on national forest land by Boyden Cavern Adventures and Tours, a private company. Due to its location along Highway 180 (Kings Canyon Scenic Byway/E. Kings Canyon Rd.), visitors must first enter Kings Canyon National Park and pay the park entry fee ($30) before driving to the cavern. However, the cavern is not in the park, so you must also pay a fee for the tour.

SHEEP CREEK CASCADE

Moderate hikes abound in this area. A good place to bring a picnic is Sheep Creek Cascade. The hike to **Sheep Creek** (2 miles, 1.5 hours) ascends 600 vertical feet to a picturesque shaded glen that's perfect for taking a load off your feet and enjoying the serene surroundings.

DON CECIL-LOOKOUT PEAK

One of the more challenging day hikes in the Cedar Grove area is **Don Cecil Trail to Lookout Peak** (13 miles round-trip, strenuous). As you climb 4,000 feet to the top, you'll see long distances into the wild parts of Sequoia. The Don Cecil trailhead is well marked with a large sign along Highway 180 near Sheep Creek, 0.2 mile east of Cedar Grove Village.

HOTEL CREEK-LEWIS CREEK LOOP

The **Hotel Creek-Lewis Creek Loop** (8 miles, moderate) has only 1,200 feet of elevation gain and offers a variety of forest and mountain scenery in addition to two creeks. Expect to pop in and out of the woods along the way and be prepared for sun, as significant portions of the trail are exposed. Enjoy long views of the canyon, and look for Monarch Divide in the distance. The hike starts from the Lewis Creek trailhead on the north side of Kings Canyon Scenic Byway, just before you get to Cedar Grove.

ROARING RIVER FALLS

Even if you're not really a hiker, you'll want to get out of the car and stroll the negligible distance (less than 0.25 mile) from the parking area three miles east of Cedar Grove Village to the **Roaring River Falls.** The whole tiny trail is under a canopy of trees, making it cool even in the hottest parts of summer, and just looking at the falls feels refreshing after driving the Generals Highway.

ZUMWALT MEADOW TRAIL

The **Zumwalt Meadow Trail** (1.5 miles, easy) leads through the meadow for optimal viewing and continues through a grove of heavenly smelling incense cedar and pine trees along the Kings River. The trailhead parking lot is one mile west of Roads End.

MIST FALLS

The **Mist Falls Trail** (park at the Roads End trailhead) is a popular jumping-off point for backpackers destined for the Kings Canyon

Mist Falls

backcountry. You can hike to Mist Falls (8 miles round-trip, moderate-strenuous) or keep going all the way to Paradise Valley (14 miles, strenuous). Plan for dust and heat on the first couple of miles of the trail, and then steep switchbacks that take you up 1,500 vertical feet to the falls.

Horseback Riding

Cedar Grove Pack Station (1 mile east of Cedar Grove Village, summer 559/565-3464, www.nps.gov/seki, May-Oct., weather permitting) offers customized backcountry horseback riding trips for up to two weeks. Guides will provide the food and do the cooking, bring all the gear (except your sleeping bag), and will take care of the horses along the way. The minimum for backcountry pack trips ($250 per day for each person) is three days for four people. Short trips in the Cedar Grove area are also possible, provided horses are still available after the pack trips have left. Day trips (first-come, first-served) include one-hour ($40) and two-hour ($70) excursions along the Kings River, a half-day ride to Mist Falls or the Kings Canyon Overlook ($100), and an all-day trip ($150). Reservations are required for multiday trips.

Accommodations and Food

Cedar Grove Lodge (559/565-0100, reservations 866/522-6966, May-Oct., $119-135) has 21 rooms in the main building, each with two queen beds, private baths, telephones, and air-conditioning. It also offers three patio rooms, each with one queen bed, a private bath, a phone, and a patio looking directly on the Kings River. The snack bar at Cedar Grove (559/565-0100, 7:30am-10:30am, 11:30am-2:30pm, 5pm-8pm daily in season, $10-20) is a no-frills place serving simple hamburgers and other items.

Camping

Several attractive campgrounds are available within a short distance of Cedar Grove Village. In order, the campgrounds are **Sheep Creek** (111 sites, May-Nov., $18), **Sentinel** (82 sites, Apr.-Sept., $18), **Canyon View** (12 group sites, no RVs or trailers, May-Sept., $35-40), and **Moraine** (120 sites, May-Sept., $18). Campgrounds are first-come, first-served and have drinking water, flush toilets, and food lockers. Most are open in summer only, as this section of the park is inaccessible once the snows come. To confirm seasonal opening and closing dates, call 559/565-3341 prior to visiting.

Transportation and Services

Cedar Grove is 30 miles northeast of Grant Grove on Highway 180, less than 35 miles from the Big Stump Entrance to Kings Canyon. Only the first six miles of the road are open in winter, so this section of the park is unreachable October-April. Exact opening and closing dates depend on snowfall, and chains can be required at any time. Call the park (559/565-3341) to confirm road conditions and seasonal status.

ATMs and **showers** are available in Cedar Grove.

TOP EXPERIENCE

GIANT FOREST AND LODGEPOLE

If you have limited time to spend in Sequoia National Park, visit the **Lodgepole** and **Giant Forest** area. Here you can see and learn about some of the most impressive living things on earth, all within a fairly small geographical area. The Giant Forest contains some of the best natural attractions, and the Lodgepole complex provides support services and human comforts to help you enjoy and appreciate it all.

Sights

WUKSACHI VILLAGE

Wuksachi Village (year-round, weather permitting) is located near Generals Highway, about two miles north of Lodgepole. Of all the accommodations and restaurants in the parks, those at Wuksachi Village are the most upscale and elegant, and the drive here (1 hour

Mount Whitney

One of the most famous climbing or backpacking trips in Northern California is **Mount Whitney** (www.nps.gov/seki). At 14,500 feet, Whitney is the highest peak in the continental United States, and this must-do trek draws intrepid hikers and climbers from around the world. Whitney also marks the southern end of the **John Muir Trail** and makes for a dramatic end or beginning for through-hikers doing the whole trail.

Mount Whitney is located at the far eastern edge of Sequoia National Park, just west of the town of Lone Pine. You can see the impressive peak from a few places in the backcountry of Sequoia and Kings Canyon, but you can't get there from within the parks. There is no road that crosses the parks all the way from west to east. If you're coming from the west, you have to circle around the parks and enter from the eastern side.

Although Mount Whitney is a very challenging climb, it need not be a technical one. You can climb all the way to the top of Mount Whitney and back in one day if you're in good shape and prepared properly for the journey. Very fit hikers can walk the trail to the top, even without ropes and carabiners. The climbs up the steep East Face of the mountain or up the Needles are not beginners' journeys, but the East Face isn't out of reach for intermediate climbers. Most of the East Face is rated a Class 3, with the toughest bits rated 5.4. It's important to plan ahead, start early, bring all the right safety gear, and prepare for extreme weather.

Permits are required for anyone entering the Mount Whitney Zone—even day hikers. May-October, there's a quota for hikers; those who want to hike must enter the February lottery in order to have a good chance of getting a permit for the following summer. For more information about the lottery, and to download an application, visit www.fs.fed.us/r5/inyo or call the wilderness permit information and reservation line for Inyo National Forest (760/873-2483, recreation. gov). November-April, hikers still need a permit, but there are no quotas in place. Pick up a permit in person at the **Mount Whitney Ranger Station** within the **Interagency Visitors Center** (U.S. 395 and Hwy. 136, 1 mile south of Lone Pine, 760/876-6200, www.fs.fed.us/r5/inyo, 8am-6pm daily Apr.-Oct., 8am-5pm daily Nov.-Apr.). During the off-season, you can self-register for a permit if the visitors center is closed.

Hikers should plan to stay nearby and get an early start in the morning—very early if you're planning to summit. The nearest campground is **Whitney Portal** (end of Whitney Portal Rd., 6 miles west of Lone Pine, 877/444-6777, www.recreation.gov, 47 sites, late Apr.-late Oct., $21) in the Inyo National Forest; it's seven miles from the trailhead. If you're planning to climb the summit, you'll want to stay even closer to wake up in the wee hours and start your ascent. Twenty-five walk-in sites are located near the **Mount Whitney trailhead** (first-come, first-served, one-night limit, $12).

from Grant Grove) may well be worth it for at least one really nice meal. Other services at Wuksachi include a luxurious lodge, a gift shop (8am-8pm daily), wireless Internet access, and an ATM.

LODGEPOLE VILLAGE

Lodgepole Village (559/565-3301) contains the major visitor services for Sequoia National Park, including a large visitors center, a market, the Watchtower Deli (9am-6pm daily early Mar.-early May, 8am-8pm daily early May-late Oct.), a gift shop, coin laundry, ATM,

shuttle services, and a post office. The market, gift shop, and laundry stay open spring-fall (8am-9pm daily early May-late Oct., 9am-6pm daily late Mar.-early May). Showers are also available (9am-1pm, 3pm-5pm daily Apr.-May, 8am-1pm, 3pm-8pm daily early May-late Oct., $1 for 3 minutes). Many of the facilities here are closed in winter, so check the website before you come.

LODGEPOLE VISITOR CENTER

The **Lodgepole Visitor Center** (Lodgepole Rd., 559/565-4436, 7am-7pm daily May-Oct.,

Giant Forest and Lodgepole

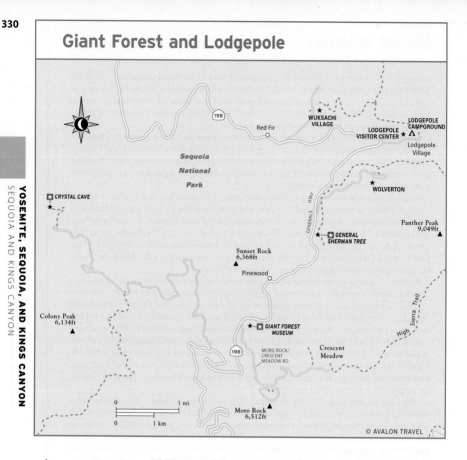

hours vary in spring and fall) is one of the major information centers run by the National Park Service. Visitors can get books, maps, and souvenirs and join a ranger talk or walk. Wilderness permits (summer $15, off-season free) are available inside the visitors center when it's open. Self-register outside when it's closed. Crystal Cave tour tickets are sold here (daily mid-May-late Oct.) until the visitors center closes for the winter. It's about an hour's drive to Lodgepole from either park entrance.

WOLVERTON

Wolverton is a picnic area two miles north of the General Sherman Tree. It's a wide-open space with plenty of room for sledding in winter and barbecue and dinner theater events in summer (tickets sold at Lodgepole or Wuksachi Lodge).

★ GENERAL SHERMAN TREE

The **General Sherman Tree** (Wolverton Rd., off Generals Hwy., 4 miles north of the Giant Forest Museum) is, by sheer volume of wood, the largest tree known on earth. It's an easy 0.5-mile walk down from the parking lot or from the shuttle stop at Wolverton Road. When you get to the viewing area, you'll find masses of people paying their respects. This enormous attraction can get crowded on summer weekends, so if you're able to visit on a weekday, or early in the morning, you may enjoy the experience even more.

General Sherman Tree

★ GIANT FOREST MUSEUM

The **Giant Forest Museum** (Generals Hwy., 16 miles from the Ash Mountain Entrance, 559/565-4480, 9am-4:30pm daily) is a lively place full of giant sequoias and touchable exhibits that provide context to all the facts and figures about these trees. You'll learn how the park used to look and why many of the buildings have been removed to make way for more trees. Numerous hikes branch out into the Giant Forest Sequoia Grove. Crystal Cave tour tickets are also sold here (daily 9am-90 minutes before day's last tour) in November after the Lodgepole Visitor Center closes for the winter.

★ CRYSTAL CAVE

Magical **Crystal Cave** (Generals Hwy., 3 miles south of the General Sherman Tree) is one of the most beautiful of the 200 or so caves that occur naturally in the park. Its immense underground rooms are filled with sparkling stalagmites and stalactites made of limestone that has metamorphosed into marble

over time. The **Sequoia Natural History Association** (559/565-3759, www.sequoia-history.org) offers 45-minute guided tours of the cave (daily mid-May-late Oct., adults $16, ages 5-12 $8). A more challenging two-hour tour takes you deeper into the caverns and gives you a much more detailed lesson on the cave's history and geology. Best of all, serious spelunkers can sign up for the Adventure Tour (559/565-4222, $135), a 4-6-hour crawl off the well-lit trails and into the depths of Crystal Cave. You must be at least 16 years old and in good physical condition to join this expedition. Caving gear is provided.

Tickets are only available at either the **Foothills Visitor Center** (one mile north of the Ash Mountain Entrance, 559/565-4212, ticket sales 8am daily May-late Oct.), the **Lodgepole Visitor Center** (Lodgepole Rd., 559/565-4436, ticket sales 8am daily May-late Oct.), or the **Giant Forest Museum** (ticket sales 9am daily Nov.). You must stop here in advance to purchase tickets. The long, winding dirt road to the cave parking lot can take more than an hour from either visitors center (no trailers or RVs over 22 feet). Tours fill up quickly, so get your tickets early in the morning or even a day in advance. Ticket sales close daily at the visitors centers and museum about 90 minutes before each day's final tour.

MORO ROCK

The granite dome of **Moro Rock** stands starkly alone in the middle of the landscape, providing an amazing vantage point for much of the park. For maximum impact, park in the lot at the base of the rock and climb the 400 steps to the top, a distance of about 0.25 mile. The stairs are solid, and there are handrails all along the way. You'll want to take it slow, in any case; the entire route is filled with photo ops as you look down on the canyons of the Great Western Divide and across the peaks of the Sierra Nevada.

To reach the parking area from Generals Highway, take Moro Rock/Crescent Meadow Road south. There are restrooms and interpretive signage in the large parking lot. A free shuttle is available in summer (9am-6pm). The road is closed to vehicles weekends and holidays.

CRESCENT MEADOW

A sort of oasis beside the Giant Forest, **Crescent Meadow** is a bright-green and yellow plain, thick with grasses and teeming with wildlife. You can walk around the whole meadow in about an hour, watching for all manner of birds, squirrels, chipmunks, marmots, and even black bears. To reach the parking area from Generals Highway, take Moro Rock/Crescent Meadow Road south, past Moro Rock to the road's terminus. A free shuttle is available in summer (9am-6pm). The road is closed to vehicles weekends and holidays.

Hiking

Numerous trails characterize this region, offering options for hikers of all levels and abilities. The following are just a sample; pick up trail maps ($1.50-3.50) at the visitors centers for even more hikes.

LITTLE BALDY

How can you resist a hike to a granite formation called **Little Baldy** (9 miles north of the General Sherman Tree, 3.4 miles round-trip)? This moderate climb takes you up about 700 feet to the top of the granite dome. Look down from the peak, which tops out at over 8,000 feet, into the Giant Forest and snap a few photos.

TOKOPAH FALLS

To cool off, head for **Tokopah Falls** (trailhead near Marble Fork Bridge in Lodgepole Campground, 3.4 miles round-trip, easy). Early summer, when the flow is at its peak, is the best time to trek out the almost two miles along the Marble Fork of the Kaweah River to this fantastic 1,200-foot waterfall.

CONGRESS TRAIL

One of the best short trails in the whole area is the **Congress Trail** (trailhead at General Sherman Tree, 2 miles, easy), which begins from the parking lot for the General Sherman Tree off Wolverton Road. Pick up a pamphlet and map to get the best experience on this trail, which includes many of the park's most famous giant sequoias—Chief Sequoyah, General Lee, and President McKinley—as well as the House and Senate Groups. This round-trip trail is paved, making it wheelchair accessible and

Crystal Cave

an easy walk even for people who usually aren't big hikers.

BIG TREES TRAIL

A level loop hike, **Big Trees Trail** (trailhead at Giant Forest Museum, 1.2 miles, easy) travels around Round Meadow near the Giant Forest Museum. Interpretive panels make this a fun walk for kids, and the paved boardwalk is wheelchair accessible. Accessible parking is available at the Big Trees trailhead. Otherwise, park at the Giant Forest Museum and follow the hike from the Trail Center trailhead.

HAZELWOOD NATURE TRAIL

For a charming interpretive walk, head down the **Hazelwood Nature Trail** (trailhead at Giant Forest Museum, 1 mile, easy). Signs along this flat stroll detail the history of humans' relationship with the giant sequoia trees—both beneficial and destructive. This walk works well for families with children. From the Giant Forest Museum, take the Alta Trail to the Hazelwood Loop. In the same vicinity, you can putter along the 0.25-mile **Trail for All People.** This interpretive nature walk is best in spring, when the wildflowers bloom.

CRESCENT MEADOW-LOG MEADOW LOOP TRAIL

The **Crescent Meadow-Log Meadow Loop Trail** (1.6 miles, easy) starts at the Crescent Meadow parking lot and picnic area. This short loop lets you experience more wildflowers and forest. It also takes you past Tharp's Log, the park's oldest cabin. Start by following the High Sierra Trail a short distance to its intersection with the Crescent Meadow Loop (you'll see signs for Tharp's Log). Take the Tharp's Log Trail north to the namesake cabin along Log Meadow. Explore the "cabin," then turn west to visit the Chimney Tree at the northern edge of Crescent Meadow. Follow the Crescent Meadow Loop south to return to the parking area.

Food

The closest thing to an upscale restaurant is the ★ **Peaks Restaurant** (Wuksachi Lodge, 64740 Wuksachi Way, off Generals Hwy., 2 miles north of Lodgepole, 559/565-4070 or 866/807-3598, www.visitsequoia.com, 7am-10am, 11:30am-3pm, 5pm-9:30pm daily summer, 7:30am-9:30am, 11:30am-2:30pm, 5pm-8:30pm daily winter, $13-34). The elegant dining room features sweeping forest views outside picture windows. The Wuksachi

Crescent Meadow

restaurant offers three meals daily and non-guests are welcome. Make a reservation if you plan to dine here on a summer weekend.

You'll find basic groceries and other necessary camping supplies at the **Lodgepole Market** (Generals Hwy., Lodgepole, 559/565-3301, 8am-9pm daily early May-late Oct., 9am-6pm daily late Mar.-early May). The **Watchtower Deli** (559/565-3301, 9am-6pm daily early Mar.-early May, 8am-8pm daily early May-late Oct.) at Lodgepole Village serves pizza, premade sandwiches, and other light snacks.

Accommodations

Built in 1999, the ★ **Wuksachi Lodge** (64740 Wuksachi Way, off Generals Hwy. west of Lodgepole, 866/807-3598, www.visit-sequoia.com, $215-276) offers the most luxurious accommodations inside the parks, with 102 rooms of various sizes. Rooms have a woodsy-motel decor, with colorful Native American-print bedspreads and mission-style wooden furniture, a private bath, a TV, a phone, a coffeemaker, a fridge, ski racks, daily maid service, and Internet access. An on-site restaurant, a Native American-themed gift shop, and close proximity to the Lodgepole visitors complex round out the attractions of this popular lodge.

Stony Creek Village (May-Sept. or Oct.) is located in the Sequoia National Forest on Generals Highway, just north of the boundary of Sequoia National Park. Facilities here are operated by the Sequoia-Kings Canyon Park Services Company (877/828-1440) and include the **Stony Creek Lodge** (559/565-3909, www.sequoia-kingscanyon.com, $159-179) and **restaurant** (11am-6pm daily, $10-25), a market and gift shop (7am-8pm daily), a coin laundry (9am-6pm daily), showers (9am-6pm daily, $4), an ATM, and a gas station (with credit card 24 hours daily).

Camping

Lodgepole Campground (214 sites, year-round, reservations summer only 877/444-6777, www.recreation.gov, May-Sept., $22) is located along the Kaweah River, 21 miles from the Ash Mountain park entrance. The campground has flush toilets, picnic tables, and bear-proof containers, and it's less than 0.25 mile from Lodgepole Village, where you'll find showers, laundry, and groceries. Off-season, only 16 first-come, first-served walk-in tent sites are available.

Dorst Creek Campground (222 sites, reservations 877/444-6777, www.recreation. gov, late June-Labor Day, $22-60) is located along Generals Highway, six miles north of Wuksachi Village. This is one of only two campgrounds (the other is Lodgepole) in the parks that accept reservations; and they are definitely recommended; Dorst fills up fast in summer. The campground has flush toilets, drinking water, picnic tables, fire rings, bear-proof containers, and a dump station.

The U.S. Forest Service maintains two campgrounds near Stony Creek Village. **Stony Creek Campground** (Generals Hwy., 14 miles southeast of Grant Grove, 49 sites, 877/444-6777, www.recreation.gov, May-Oct., $20) has tent and RV sites with fire rings, flush toilets, water, and food storage. **Upper Stony Creek Campground** (Generals Hwy., 14 miles southeast of Grant Grove, 18 sites, first-come, first-served, $16) has fire rings, picnic tables, water, and pit toilets.

Transportation and Services

Lodgepole is located on Generals Highway 22 miles north of the Ash Mountain (south) Entrance and 27 miles south of the Big Stump (northwest) Entrance. It takes about an hour to drive to Lodgepole from either entrance. Wuksachi Village is just two miles northwest of Lodgepole, and the General Sherman Tree parking lot is 2.5 miles south of Lodgepole, off Wolverton Road.

Gas is available at **Stony Creek Village** (Generals Hwy., 559/565-3909, 24 hours daily with credit card, summer only), as are showers and laundry facilities. **Lodgepole Village** has ATMs, showers, and laundry.

FOOTHILLS

The **Foothills** area of Sequoia National Park is in the southern part of the park, with lower elevations and drier snow-free weather. It is accessed from the Ash Mountain Entrance on Highway 123, east of Three Rivers.

The **Foothills Visitor Center** (559/565-4212, 8am-4:30pm daily), one mile north of the Ash Mountain Entrance, serves as the park headquarters. It includes a bookstore and exhibits about the nearby area, and ranger talks and walks begin here. You can also buy Crystal Cave tickets (ticket sales 8am daily May-late Oct.) or get a wilderness permit (late May-late Sept., $15 for up to 15 people).

Hiking

MARBLE FORK TRAIL

For a vigorous adventure with a big payoff, take the **Marble Fork Trail** (upper end of Potwisha Campground, 7.4 miles, moderate-strenuous) to Marble Falls. This hike starts in the Potwisha Campground near site 14. Start out on a forest road, and you'll soon see a sign directing you to keep left; the way becomes more trail-like, winding upward through the woods. After 2.5 miles, you'll emerge from the trees for sweeping views of the canyons around you and the water below. In four miles or less you'll come to Marble Falls. The falls are beautiful, noisy, and dramatic, and you'll see why they got their name—the viewpoint actually looks like a very large slab of white marble.

PARADISE CREEK

A nice short nature walk in the Foothills area starts in Buckeye Flat Campground and leads alongside **Paradise Creek** (Buckeye Flat Campground, 3 miles, easy). Start by crossing the footbridge near campsite 28 and then bear right to follow the trail beside the creek. The Middle Fork of the Kaweah River heads off to the left. In about 1.5 miles the trail will start to peter out. At that point, turn around and return the same way. No day parking is allowed at Buckeye Flat; park at Hospital Rock Picnic Area and walk about a mile on a paved road to Buckeye Flat.

Camping

Potwisha (42 sites, year-round, $22) is on the Kaweah River, about four miles north of the Ash Mountain Entrance. Amenities at this first-come, first-served campground include flush toilets, drinking water, a dump station, and bear-proof containers.

Just a few miles farther north along Generals Highway, and on a little spur to the east, you'll find **Buckeye Flat** (28 sites, May-Sept., $22) in a lovely spot along the Kaweah River. This tent-only campground is first-come, first-served and has flush toilets; it does not accommodate RVs or trailers.

The **South Fork** (10 sites, year-round, May-Oct., $12, Oct.-May. free) is a tent-only campground 13 miles off Highway 198 on South Fork Drive near Three Rivers. The campground is first-come, first-served with pit toilets and bear-proof containers, but no drinking water.

Transportation

The Foothills area is easily accessed from the south via Highway 198; it's the first part of the park you encounter after the Ash Mountain Entrance.

MINERAL KING

The **Mineral King** area (Mineral King Rd., 25 miles east of Hwy. 198) of Sequoia National Park includes just a few examples of human intervention: the Mineral King Ranger Station, the Silver City Mountain Resort, a few private cabins, and two campgrounds (Atwell Mill and Cold Springs). The nearest food and gas are in the town of Three Rivers, and the 22-mile road to get there takes at least 1.5 hours to drive in good weather. The one-lane road is open to two-way traffic, so expect to pull over and wait now and then.

The **Mineral King Ranger Station** (Mineral King Rd., 559/565-3768, 8am-4pm daily May-Sept.) is located near the end of Mineral King Road, beyond the

Silver City Resort and close to Cold Springs Campground. You can get information and wilderness permits here, and there is a self-service wilderness permit box ($15 summer, free winter).

Hiking

Many hikes begin in Mineral King Valley, and you can visit a number of charming alpine lakes if you're up for a hike of 7-12 miles. However, at 7,500 feet elevation, hikes in the Mineral King area are demanding and strenuous. Bring lots of water and honestly gauge the fitness level of yourself and others before hitting the trail.

A good place to start walking in Mineral King is the **Cold Springs Nature Trail** (1 mile). This easy interpretive walk describes and displays the natural wonders and the formation of the valley.

TIMBER GAP

The **Timber Gap Trail** (4 miles round-trip) follows an old mining road through a forest of red fir trees. You'll enjoy pretty views out to Alta Peak and the Middle Fork of the Kaweah River. Remember that you're at over 7,500 feet elevation, so you may feel you're getting a workout even on this short hike.

MONARCH LAKES

Upper and Lower Monarch Lakes (8.5 miles round-trip) sit nestled beneath majestic Sawtooth Peak. The trek is mostly flat and easy walking through forest and meadows, with views of the Great Divide. Bring a picnic to enjoy beside the lakes.

EAGLE AND MOSQUITO LAKES

Plan to spend all day on the hike out to **Eagle and Mosquito Lakes** (7 miles round-trip), which lies in the backcountry beyond the Mineral Creek Ranger Station. The Eagle and Mosquito Lakes trailhead is at the end of Mineral King Road. From the trailhead, climb two miles up Mineral King Valley to Eagle Basin. Where the trail splits, head left to Eagle Lake (3.4 miles from trailhead) or right to Mosquito Lake (3.6 miles from trailhead).

WHITE CHIEF TRAIL

The **White Chief Trail** (5.8 miles round-trip) begins at the Eagle and Mosquito Lakes trailhead at the end of Mineral King Road. The trail leads to the abandoned mine site at White Chief Bowl. It's a fairly steep climb at times, but the rewards include scenic views of the Mineral King Valley and a look at some remnants from the area's mining history,

Eagle and Mosquito Lakes

including the Crabtree Cabin, which dates to the 1870s.

Accommodations and Food

Silver City Mountain Resort (559/561-3223, www.silvercityresort.com, May-mid-Oct.) is a privately owned resort on national park land. The resort has 13 different cabins; the most economical are the three small "historical cabins" built in the 1930s ($100-150). A step up in comfort are the three "family cabins" that sleep up to five people ($195). Five luxurious modern "chalets" ($250-395) are outfitted with decks, fireplaces, showers, phones, and outstanding mountain views. Wi-Fi is included in the rates.

The **Silver City Restaurant** (8am-8pm Thurs.-Mon., $10-17.50) is the only place to get food…and pie (9am-5pm Tues.-Wed.), but most cabins come with a kitchen. The on-site souvenir shop (8am-8pm Thurs.-Mon., 9am-5pm Tues.-Wed.) usually only has energy bars and sodas.

Camping

There are two campgrounds in the Mineral King area: **Atwell Mill** (21 sites, May-Oct., $12) and **Cold Springs** (40 sites, May-Oct., $12). Both are first-come, first-served and have vault toilets. If you want showers or food, you can drive to Silver City, 0.5 mile east of Atwell Mill and 2.5 miles west of Cold Springs. Both campgrounds have drinking water available May-mid-October. The water is turned off the rest of the year. The Mineral King Ranger Station is located beside the Cold Springs campground.

Transportation

To get to Mineral King, approach Sequoia National Park from the south on Highway 198. Instead of entering the park, make a right turn onto Mineral King Road, two miles before the Ash Mountain Entrance, and drive 25 miles east. It will take about 30 minutes to come to the end of this narrow, winding road; trailers and RVs are not allowed. Along the way, you will enter the boundaries of Sequoia National Park through the small Lookout Point entrance (May-Oct., $30) and pay the entrance fee at a self-serve station. November-April, the gate is locked for the season.

The Eastern Sierra

LEE VINING AND VICINITY

The town of Lee Vining sits on the eastern edge of Yosemite National Park. Although it's not large (pop. 222) and some of its services close down in the winter months, Lee Vining is convenient to Mono Lake, Bodie, and June Lake, and is a good stopover for travelers heading south to Mammoth Lakes and Bishop, with restaurants, lodging, and two visitors centers.

Lee Vining has ATMs at the gas stations, the Mono Lake visitors center, and the grocery-minimart. The **Mono Lake Committee Information Center & Bookstore** (U.S. 395, 760/647-6595, 8am-9pm daily summer, 9am-5pm daily winter) has a big selection of free maps and brochures and a helpful staff.

Food

Tioga Pass Resort's simple diner-restaurant, the **Tioga Pass Resort Café** (85 Hwy. 120 W., Lee Vining, www.tiogapassresort.com, 8am-8pm Mon.-Fri., 7am-9pm Sat.-Sun. summer, $20), offers breakfast, lunch, and dinner, served with plenty of good cheer.

The best way to kick off any vacation in the Eastern Sierra is with a memorable meal (and a tank of gas) at the ★ **Whoa Nellie Deli** (Hwy. 120 and U.S. 395, 760/647-1088, www.whoanelliedeli.com, 6:45am-9pm daily late Apr.-Oct., $8-14) at the Tioga Gas Mart. The deli is right at the east entrance to Yosemite, so

The Eastern Sierra

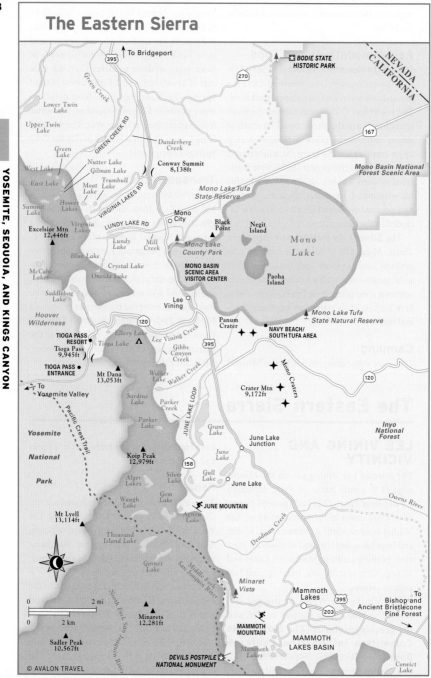

To Bridgeport

395

270

★ BODIE STATE HISTORIC PARK

NEVADA
CALIFORNIA

167

Lower Twin Lake

Upper Twin Lake

Green Creek

GREEN CREEK RD

Dunderberg Creek

Conway Summit 8,138ft

Green Lake

West Lake

East Lake

Nutter Lake
Gilman Lake
Trumbull Lake
Moat Lake

Summit Lake

Hoover Lakes

VIRGINIA LAKES RD

Mono Lake Tufa State Reserve

Mono Basin National Forest Scenic Area

Excelsior Mtn 12,446ft

Virginia Lakes

LUNDY LAKE RD

Mono City

Black Point

Negit Island

Mono Lake

Blue Lake

McCabe Lakes

Lundy Lake

Mill Creek

Mono Lake County Park

MONO BASIN SCENIC AREA VISITOR CENTER

Paoha Island

Saddlebag Lake

Crystal Lake

Oneida Lake

Hoover Wilderness

Lee Vining

120

TIOGA PASS RESORT
Tioga Pass 9,945ft

TIOGA PASS ENTRANCE

Ellery Lake

Tioga Lake

Lee Vining Creek

Gibbs Canyon Creek

395

Panum Crater

NAVY BEACH/ SOUTH TUFA AREA

Mono Lake Tufa State Natural Reserve

To Yosemite Valley

Pacific Crest Trail

Mt Dana 13,053ft

Walker Lake

Walker Creek

Mono Craters

Crater Mtn 9,172ft

120

Sardine Lake

Parker Creek

JUNE LAKE LOOP

Inyo National Forest

Yosemite

National

Park

Koip Peak 12,979ft

Parker Lake

Grant Lake

June Lake Junction

Owens River

158

June Lake

Gull Lake

June Lake

Mt Lyell 13,114ft

Alger Lakes

Silver Lake

Gem Lake

Waugh Lake

JUNE MOUNTAIN

Agnew Lake

Deadman Creek

Thousand Island Lake

Minaret Vista

0   2 mi

0   2 km

Garnet Lake

San Joaquin River

Middle Fork

Mammoth Lakes

395

To Bishop and Ancient Bristlecone Pine Forest

203

North Fork San Joaquin River

Minarets 12,281ft

MAMMOTH LAKES BASIN

Sadler Peak 10,567ft

DEVILS POSTPILE NATIONAL MONUMENT

MAMMOTH MOUNTAIN

Mammoth Lakes

Convict Lake

© AVALON TRAVEL

it's the perfect place to stop when leaving the park or heading in. You'll get a hearty meal of fish tacos, buffalo meat loaf, or pizza; a pleasant place to eat it all; and a friendly, festive atmosphere. Expect to wait in line at the counter to order, as Whoa Nellie is popular. Seating is available both inside and out, so there are usually enough tables to go around. There's a fairly large grocery store and souvenir shop, and the restrooms are large and clean. The place is closed in winter, since Tioga Pass tends to be closed.

Lee Vining has several charming independent coffee shops. The **Latte Da Coffee Café** (1 3rd St. at U.S. 395, 760/647-6310, 7am-8pm daily summer) uses organic coffee and local fresh water to create delicious coffee drinks at the El Mono Motel. Over at the Lake View Lodge, enjoy a cup of joe at the **Garden House Coffee Shop** (51285 U.S. 395, 760/647-6543, www.bwlakeviewlodge.com, 7am-11am daily June-Sept.). To get a great start to your day, you can pick up a smoothie or a fresh pastry in addition to your favorite espresso drinks.

A classic American diner, **Nicely's** (U.S. 395 and 4th St., Lee Vining, 760/647-6477, 7am-9pm daily summer, 7am-8pm Thurs.-Mon. winter, $15-25) offers friendly service and familiar food. Inside, you'll find a large dining room with half-circle booths upholstered in cheerful red vinyl. The cuisine includes eggs and pancakes in the morning; salads and sandwiches for lunch; and steak, trout, and salmon in the evening. Portions are more than generous. Nicely's has longer hours and a longer season than most places in the area. This is a good place for comfort foods like burgers, fries, and macaroni and cheese.

If you're looking for a Wild West atmosphere and a good spicy sauce, have lunch or dinner at **Bodie Mike's Barbecue** (51357 U.S. 395 at 4th St., Lee Vining, 760/647-6432, 11:30am-10pm daily June-Sept.). Use your fingers to dig into barbecued ribs, chicken, beef, brisket, and more. A rustic atmosphere with rough-looking wood, red-checked tablecloths, and local patrons in cowboy boots completes your dining experience. Don't expect the fastest service in the world. At the back of the dining room is the entrance to a small, dark bar populated by locals.

Pop into **Mono Cone** (51508 Highway 395, 760/647-6606, 11am-8pm daily summer, $5, cash only), where you can get mouthwatering burgers, fries, and soft-serve ice cream, but figure on waiting in line at this popular little roadside shack. Indoor and outdoor seating is available.

The **Hammond Station Restaurant** (54411 U.S. 395, Lee Vining, reservations 619/320-8868, 760/647-6423, www.tioga-lodgeatmonolake.com, 7:30am-10am, 5pm-9:30pm daily mid-June-early Oct., $10-24), at the Tioga Lodge, offers an excellent variety of good food. Choose from the health-conscious menu, which includes vegan, gluten-free, and dairy-free options; the California Casual menu; or the Drinks & Desserts menu. The small dining room has attractive wrought-iron furniture plus an ample outdoor seating area perfect for warm summer evenings. The food is tasty, and the service makes you feel like a local even if you're from out of town.

A great place to get a to-go breakfast or lunch is the **Mono Market** (51303 U.S. 395, 760/647-1010, 7am-9pm daily summer, 7:30am-6pm Thurs., 7:30am-8pm Fri.-Wed. winter). Breakfast sandwiches and pastries are made fresh daily, as are the sandwiches, wraps, and larger entrées you can carry out for lunch or dinner.

Accommodations

Soon after exiting the Tioga Pass Entrance on the east side of Yosemite, you'll come to the rustic ★ **Tioga Pass Resort** (85 Hwy. 120 W., Lee Vining, www.tiogapassresort.com or tiogapassresortllc@gmail.com, summer only, $195-520, cash or check only), which offers both charm and convenience. The resort rents 10 cabins and four rooms; the rooms don't have kitchens or showers but do have access to shared showers. The cabins require a two-night minimum stay. The resort doesn't have reliable telephone and Internet access, which means it cannot accept credit cards, but you can book online.

For clean, comfortable, affordable lodgings, try **Murphey's Motel** (51493 U.S. 395, 760/647-6316 or 800/334-6316, www.murpheysyosemite.com, $63-143). Open all year, this motel provides double-queen and king beds with cozy comforters, TVs, tables and chairs, and everything you need for a pleasant stay in the Mono Lake area. Its central location in downtown Lee Vining makes dining and shopping convenient.

El Mono Motel (1 3rd St. at U.S. 395, 760/647-6310, www.elmonomotel.com, late May-Oct., depending on weather, $69-95 shared bath, $89-99 private bath) offers comfy beds and clean rooms at very reasonable prices. Enjoy the location in downtown Lee Vining, and start each morning with a fresh cup of organic coffee from the on-site café (7am-8pm daily summer).

At the junction of Highway 120 and U.S. 395, stay at the comfortable and affordable **Lake View Lodge** (51285 U.S. 395, 760/647-6543 or 800/990-6614, www.bwlakeviewlodge.com, $59-269). This aptly named lodge offers cottages, which can be rented in summer only, and motel rooms available year-round. Whether you choose a basic room for a night or two or a larger option with a kitchen for more than three days, you'll enjoy the simple country-style decor, the outdoor porches, and the views of Mono Lake. All rooms have TVs with cable, and Internet access is available in the motel rooms but is spotty in the cottages.

Named for its main claim to fame—its proximity to the park, only 14 miles from Yosemite's east gate—the **Yosemite Gateway Motel** (51340 U.S. 395, 760/647-6467, www.yosemitegatewaymotel.com, $89-259) offers a charming rustic experience for travelers to the Eastern Sierra. The red-and-white exterior is echoed in the decoration of the rooms, which are supplemented with gleaming wood, new furnishings, and clean baths. TVs and Internet access provide entertainment on chilly evenings, and the wonderful outdoor recreation opportunities of the Eastern Sierra are just outside the door.

Just across the freeway from Mono Lake, the **Tioga Lodge at Mono Lake** (54411 U.S. 395, Lee Vining, reservations 619/320-8868, 760/647-6423, www.tiogalodgeatmonolake.com, late May-mid-Oct., $99-159) offers a view of the lake from every room. This old lodge offers the perfect location for sightseeing and outdoor adventures, plus heated rooms and comfortable beds. Rooms are simple and appealingly decorated, each with tile floors and a full private bath. Some rooms sleep two, and others have room for up to four. The two-bedroom suites are perfect for families. Don't expect to find TVs or other digital entertainment, though.

Camping

There are campgrounds in the Inyo National Forest on the east side of Yosemite, near U.S. 395 and Tioga Pass. You can stay at **Ellery Lake Campground** (Hwy. 120, Upper Lee Vining Canyon, ranger station 760/873-2400, www.fs.fed.us/r5/inyo, $21), which has 12 campsites at an elevation of 9,500 feet, with drinking water, pit toilets, and garbage cans. It's not possible to reserve these sites, so get here at dawn if you want a site on a weekend. Another option is **Sawmill Walk-In** (Saddlebag Rd., on Forest Rd. 04, 1.6 miles north of Hwy. 120, ranger station 760/873-2400, www.fs.fed.us/r5/inyo, June-Oct., $16). This primitive hike-in campground, at an elevation of 9,800 feet, has 12 sites and no water, so walk in slowly. It's not possible to reserve these sites.

Transportation

Lee Vining is located just north of the junction of Highway 120 (also known as Tioga Pass Rd.) and U.S. 395. In summer the drive is quite beautiful, if not always fast. Traffic near and through Yosemite can be intense—especially on summer weekends—and many of the other travelers are enjoying the scenery. In winter, Tioga Pass Road is closed.

The nearest airport to Lee Vining is the

Mono Lake

Mono Lake

Unusual and beautiful, Mono Lake is 2.5 times as salty as the ocean and is 1,000 times more alkaline. Over time, the lake has collected huge stores of calcium carbonate, which solidifies into strange-looking tufa towers. The lake surrounds two large islands: **Negit Island,** a volcanic cinder cone and nesting area for California gulls, and **Paoha Island,** which was created when volcanic activity pushed sediment from the bottom of the lake up above the surface.

The **South Tufa area** (off Hwy. 120, 11 miles east of Lee Vining, $3 pp) is one of the best places to view the spectacular tufa towers. A one-mile **interpretive trail** (southeast of the visitors center, adjacent to Navy Beach) winds through the South Tufa area; panels describe the natural history of the area and the formations. In summer, naturalists lead a one-mile, one-hour **walking tour** (10am, 1pm, and 6pm daily summer, free) around South Tufa.

The **Old Marina** (1 mile north of Lee Vining, off U.S. 395, www.monolake.org, $3 per car) is another good spot for a short stroll down to the edge of the lake. A 1.5-mile trail leads from the Mono Basin Scenic Area Visitors Center to the Old Marina, and an even shorter boardwalk trail is wheelchair accessible.

To learn more, visit the **Mono Basin National Forest Scenic Area Visitor Center** (U.S. 395, 0.5 mile north of Lee Vining, 760/647-3044, www.monolake.org, 8am-5pm daily summer, 9am-4:30pm Thurs.-Mon. spring-fall) and the **Mono Lake Tufa State Natural Reserve** (U.S. 395, just north of Lee Vining, 760/647-6331, www.parks.ca.gov, 24 hours daily, free), which offers free tours in summer.

Mammoth Yosemite Airport (MMH, 1200 Airport Rd., Mammoth Lakes, 760/934-3813, www.ci.mammoth-lakes.ca.us). For more options at a major hub, book a flight to **Reno-Tahoe International Airport** (RNO, 2001 E. Plumb Lane, Reno, NV, 775/328-6400, www.renoairport.com), then drive 137 miles (3 hours) south on U.S. 395 to Lee Vining.

★ BODIE STATE HISTORIC PARK

Bodie State Historic Park (end of Hwy. 270, 13 miles east of U.S. 395, 760/647-6445, www.parks.ca.gov, 9am-6pm daily Apr. 15-Oct, 9am-4pm daily Nov.-Apr. 14, adults $5, ages 1-17 $3) is the largest ghost town in California and possibly the best-preserved in the whole country. Its preservation in a state of "arrested decay" means you get to see each house and public building just as it was when it was abandoned. What you see is not a bright, shiny museum display; you get the real thing: dust and broken furniture and trash and all. It would take all day to explore the town on foot, and even then you might not see it all. If you take a tour, you can go into the abandoned mine and gain a deeper understanding of the history of the buildings and the town.

The town of Bodie sprang up around a gold mine in 1877. It was never a nice place to live at all. The weather, the work, the scenery, and, some say, the people all tended toward the bleak or the foul. By the 1940s mining had dried up, and the remote location and lack of other viable industry in the area led to Bodie's desertion.

A visit to Bodie takes you back in time to a harsh lifestyle in an extreme climate, miles from the middle of nowhere. As you stroll down the dusty streets, imagine the whole town blanketed in 20 feet of snow in winter and scorched by 100°F temperatures in summer, with precious few trees around to provide shade. In a town filled with rough men working the mines, you'd hear the funeral bells tolling at the church every single day—the

only honor bestowed on the many murder victims Bodie saw during its existence. Few families came to Bodie (though a few hardy souls did raise children in the hellish town), and most of Bodie's women earned their keep the old-fashioned way: The prostitution business boomed as mining did.

To reach Bodie, take U.S. 395 to Highway 270 and turn east. Drive 10 miles to the end of the paved road and then continue another 3 miles on a rough dirt-and-gravel road to the ghost town.

JUNE LAKE

The small community of **June Lake** lies east of Yosemite, just 15 minutes south of Mono Lake and Lee Vining. June Lake is a popular ski destination, thanks to June Mountain, which offers everything you need in a ski resort, yet manages to hold onto the feeling of an unspoiled outdoor wonderland. Even though the town is named for just one of the alpine lakes nearby, there are actually three others—Gull Lake, Silver Lake, and Grant Lake—enjoyed by driving the 15-mile scenic **June Lake Loop** (Hwy. 158), accessible from U.S. 395 south of Lee Vining.

A popular place to hit the slopes is the **June Mountain Ski Resort** (3819 Hwy. 158,

Bodie State Historic Park

760/648-7733, www.junemountain.com, lifts 8:30am-4pm daily Dec.-Apr., adults $72, seniors $48, ages 13-18 $48, up to age 12 free). About 20 miles north of Mammoth Lakes, June Mountain offers seven lifts (two quads, four doubles, and a carpet) and more than 2,500 feet of vertical drop on 1,400 skiable acres. The resort caters to beginners and intermediate skiers, and 80 percent of its trails are green or blue.

Accommodations and Food

The **Double Eagle Resort and Spa** (5587 Hwy. 158, June Lake, 760/648-7004, www.doubleeagle.com, year-round, $169-649) has 15 two-bedroom cabins ($249-349) that sleep six; all come complete with decks and fully equipped kitchens. The 16 luxurious lodge rooms ($169-229) come with coffee service, free Internet access, a refrigerator, and whirlpool tubs. There's also a sprawling guest house ($599-649) that sleeps 12. The on-site Creekside Spa includes an indoor pool and a fitness center, and the resort's **Eagle's Landing Restaurant** (7:30am-9pm daily, $16-36).

A little more rustic but also very pleasant is **The Four Seasons** (24 Venice St., 760/648-7476, www.junelakesfourseasons.com, late Apr.-Oct., $135-195), which, ironically, is only open in summer. The five A-frame cabins each sleeps up to six, with a master bedroom and a sleeping loft as well as a full kitchen, a living room, and a large deck. The resort is just two miles from the town of June Lake.

Camping

The U.S. Forest Service maintains several campgrounds near June Lake in the Inyo National Forest. A particularly good one is **Silver Lake Campground** (Hwy. 158, 7 miles west of U.S. 395, reservations www.recreation.gov, mid-Apr.-mid-Nov., $22, $5 for each additional vehicle). Each of the 39 sites has a bear-proof food locker, a picnic table, and a fire ring; the campground has flush toilets, drinking water, and even a small store. The campground is right on the shore of lovely Silver Lake, which is a good place to fish, watch for wildlife, or just sit and enjoy the view.

Transportation

June Lake is located east of Yosemite, west of U.S. 395, south of Lee Vining, and north of Mammoth Lakes. To get to June Lake, take U.S. 395 and turn west onto Highway 158 at the June Lake Loop. June Mountain Ski Resort is about four miles west of U.S. 395.

MAMMOTH LAKES

The town of **Mammoth Lakes,** located south of Tioga Pass, is a prime tourist destination for outdoor sports—skiing in particular. In winter, the roads are subject to the whims of weather, though they rarely close. It's best to carry chains and to check weather reports before starting out. **The Village at Mammoth** (www.villageatmammoth.com) offers lodging, dining, and shopping—all organized around a central pedestrian plaza. In summer, the plaza is sprinkled with outdoor benches and tables with umbrellas.

In winter, the **Village Gondola** (7:45am-5pm, free) takes you from The Village at Mammoth to Canyon Lodge, while the **Panorama Gondola** (8:30am-4pm, last ride to top at 3:30pm, summer and winter) runs from the Main Lodge at Mammoth to McCoy Station and the top of the mountain. In winter, the gondola is extremely popular with skiers; in **summer** (9am-4:30pm daily June-Sept., adults $21, ages 13-18 $17, under age 13 free with an adult), it serves anyone who wants to get to the top of the 11,053-foot mountain where you can see as far as 400 miles. The ride to the top takes about 20 minutes. Stop for a meal or a snack at the **Top of the Sierra Café** (9:30am-4pm daily summer, 11am-2pm daily winter, $8-20), open when the gondola is running.

★ Devils Postpile National Monument

Devils Postpile National Monument (Minaret Vista Rd., 760/934-2289, www.

nps.gov/depo, mid-June-mid-Oct., ranger station 9am-5pm daily late June-Labor Day, adults $7, ages 3-15 $4) is small, but what you'll see is worth a visit. The park is named for the strange natural rock formation called the Devils Postpile—straight-sided hexagonal posts created by volcanic heat and pressure. Devils Postpile has hikes to serene meadows and unspoiled streams; free guided ranger walks are held at 11am most days throughout the summer, starting from the ranger station.

Part of the monument, the beautiful crystalline **Rainbow Falls** cascades 101 feet down to a pool, throwing up stunning rainbows of mist. For the best rainbows at the waterfall, hike the three miles (round-trip) from Red Meadow near the middle of the day when the sun is high in the sky.

The $7 park entry fee includes the Red Meadow-Devils Postpile Shuttle. During summer, visitors must access the park via **shuttle** (hourly 7am-10pm daily from the Village at Mammoth Lakes; every 15-30 minutes 7am-7pm daily mid-June-early September from the Mammoth Mountain Adventure Center). When the shuttle isn't running, visitors may drive their cars into the park ($10 vehicle fee).

Skiing

The premier downhill ski and snowboard mountain is, aptly, **Mammoth Mountain** (1 Minaret Rd., information 760/934-2571, lodging and lift tickets 800/626-6684, snow report 888/766-9979, www.mammothmountain.com, lifts 8:30am-4pm daily, adults $95, seniors $89, ages 13-18 $82, ages 5-12 $35). Whether you're completely new to downhill thrills or a seasoned expert looking for different terrain, you'll find something great on Mammoth Mountain. More than two dozen lifts, including three gondolas and 10 express quads, take you up 3,100 vertical feet to the 3,500 acres of skiable and snowboardable terrain; there are also three pipes.

Tamarack Cross-Country Ski Center (163 Twin Lakes Rd., 760/934-2442, www.tamaracklodge.com, 8:30am-5pm daily mid-Nov.-Apr., adults $16-28, youths and seniors $13-22, children $5) offers 19 miles of groomed cross-country ski tracks, some with groomed skating lanes, for all abilities and levels. This lovely resort also has a restaurant, a lounge, and a bar where you can enjoy a nice cup of hot chocolate and a good book if you get tired of skiing. And getting here from Mammoth Lakes is free: Just take the Orange shuttle line from Mammoth Village hourly

Devils Postpile National Monument

on the half hour (8:30am-5:15pm daily late Jan.-mid-Apr.).

The **Blue Diamond Trails** (www.mammothlakes.us) system starts just behind the **Mammoth Lakes Welcome Center** (Hwy. 203, 3 miles west of U.S. 395, 760/924-5500, www.visitmammoth.com, 8am-5pm daily), at the entrance to Mammoth Lakes, and winds through 25 miles of Inyo National Forest, marked by signs bearing a blue diamond on the trees. Pick up a free trail map in the Welcome Center before you set out. The **Shady Rest Trails** (Hwy. 203, just before the Welcome Center) is a group of beginner loops with plenty of shade trees to keep skiers cool through their exertions. The **Knolls Trail** (Mammoth Scenic Loop, 1.5 miles north of Hwy. 203) makes a good intermediate day out. Beginners beware of the deceptively named **Scenic Loop Trail** (Mammoth Scenic Loop, across from Knolls Trail), a reasonably short trail (4 miles) with steep descents and some difficult terrain.

Hiking

Mammoth Lakes also acts as a jumping-off point for adventurers who want to take on the **John Muir Wilderness** (south of Mammoth Lakes to Mount Whitney, www.sierrawild.gov). John Muir pioneered the preservation of the Sierra Nevada, and more than 500,000 acres in the area have been designated national wilderness areas in his honor. The main attractions are the **John Muir Trail** (JMT, 215 miles Yosemite-Mount Whitney, www.johnmuirtrail.org) and the **Pacific Crest National Scenic Trail** (PCT, 2,650 miles, www.pcta.org), both among the holiest of grails for backpacking enthusiasts from around the world. For backcountry exploration and wilderness permits, contact the **High Sierra Ranger District Office** (29688 Auberry Rd., Prather, 559/297-0706 or 559/855-5355, www.fs.usda.gov/sierra, 8am-4:30pm daily Apr.-Nov., 8am-4:30pm Mon.-Fri. Nov.-Apr.) or the **Mammoth Lakes Welcome Center** (Hwy. 203, 3 miles west of U.S. 395, 760/924-5500, www.visitmammoth.com, 8am-5pm daily).

Biking

The **Mammoth Mountain Bike Park** (1 Minaret Rd., 800/626-6684, www.mammothmountain.com, 8am-6pm daily in summer, $16 for trail access, $49 for trail, gondola, and shuttle access) has almost 90 miles of trails that suit all levels. The park headquarters is at the **Mammoth Adventure Center** (Main Lodge, 1 Minaret Rd., 760/934-0706 or 800/626-6684, 8am-6pm daily June-Sept.), at the Main Lodge at Mammoth Mountain. You can also buy bike park tickets at the Mountain Center at the Village (760/924-7057). Both the Mammoth Adventure Center and **Mammoth Sports at Mountain Center** (6201 Minaret Rd., inside the Village, 760/934-2571, ext. 2078) offer new high-end rental bikes for adults and kids, and can help with parts and repairs.

Horseback Riding

Perhaps the most traditional way to explore the Eastern Sierra is on the back of a horse or mule. From the **McGee Creek Pack Station** (2990 McGee Creek Rd., Crowley Lake, June-Sept. 760/935-4324, Oct.-May 760/878-2207, www.mcgeecreekpackstation.com, $40 per hour, $140 full day), 10 miles south of Mammoth Lakes on U.S. 395, you can ride into McGee Canyon, a little-visited wilderness area. Other day-trip destinations include Baldwin Canyon and Hilton Lakes. Standard rides range from one hour to a full day, but McGee's specialty is multiday and pack trips.

Food

Petra's Bistro and Wine Bar (6080 Minaret Rd., 760/934-3500, www.petrasbistro.com, 5:30pm-close Tues.-Sun.) offers a seasonal menu that's designed to please the palate and a wine list that's worth a visit itself. Two dining rooms and a wine bar divide the seating, and the atmosphere feels romantic without being too dark. Reservations are a good idea during ski season.

Skadi (587 Old Mammoth Rd., 760/934-3902, www.skadirestaurant.com, 5:30pm-9:30pm Wed.-Sun., $24-32) describes its menu as "alpine cuisine," offering a creative menu of fresh local goods to their best advantage.

Roberto's Mexican Café (271 Old Mammoth Rd., 760/934-3667, www.robertoscafe.com, 11am-close daily, $7-15) serves classic California-Mexican food in great quantities but includes specialty items like lobster burritos and duck tacos. It's perfect for skiers and boarders famished after a long day on the slopes.

Hopheads will love the **Eatery By Bleu at Mammoth Brewing Company** (18 Lake Mary Rd., 760/934-7141, www.mammothbrewingco.com, 10am-10:30pm Wed.-Sun., hours vary in summer, $8-24). Standard pub grub gets a new twist with dishes like flatbread pizzas, lobster corn dogs, and Irish Caesar salad. Order a pitcher of suds, like the crisp and malty Golden Trout Pilsner, or go for the hoppy Epic IPA.

Look for the best steaks in town at **The Mogul Restaurant** (1528 Tavern Rd., 760/934-3039, www.themogul.com, 5:30pm-close daily, $20-40), where the menu is chock-full of standard surf-and-turf entrées like crab legs, pork tenderloin, rack of lamb, and ribs. Stop by for the happy hour (5:30pm-6:30pm), when bottled beer starts at only $2.50.

For drinks, the **Clocktower Cellar Pub** (Alpenhof Lodge, 6080 Minaret Rd., 760/934-2725, www.clocktowercellar.com, 4pm-11pm daily winter, 5pm-11pm daily summer) has a full bar with more than 160 whiskeys, 26 brews on tap, and 50 different bottled beers. For a French-style wine bar, try the vintages at the **Side Door Bistro** (100 Canyon Blvd., 760/934-5200, www.sidedoormammoth.com, 11am-9pm Mon.-Thurs., 9am-11pm Fri.-Sat., 9am-9pm Sun. winter, 11am-9pm daily summer). The **Lakanuki Tiki Bar** (6201 Minaret Rd., 760/934-7447, www.lakanuki.

net, noon-2am Tues.-Sun., 3pm-2am Mon. winter, 3pm-2am daily summer) is a popular tiki bar, especially on weekends.

Accommodations

Want to ski the slopes of Mammoth, but can't afford the hoity-toity condo resorts? Stay at the **Innsbruck Lodge** (Forest Trail, between Hwy. 203 and Sierra Blvd., 760/934-3035, www.innsbrucklodge.com, $85-295). Economy rooms offer twin beds, a table and chairs, and access to the motel whirlpool tub and lobby with a stone fireplace at very reasonable nightly rates. The quiet North Village location is on the ski area shuttle route for easy access to the local slopes. It's also an easy walk to most restaurants and other Village attractions. The inexpensive **Boulder Lodge** (2282 Hwy. 158, 760/648-7533 or 800/458-6355, www.boulderlodgejunelake.com, $88-375) provides an array of options, from simple motel rooms to multiple-bedroom apartments and even a five-bedroom lake house.

The **Sierra Lodge** (3540 Main St., 760/934-8881 or 800/356-5711, www.sierralodge.com, $109-199) offers reasonably priced nonsmoking rooms right on the ski shuttle line, and only 1.5 miles from the Juniper Ridge chair lift. Rooms have either a king or two double beds, a kitchenette, and plenty of space for gear. Breakfast, cable TV, and Internet access are included.

One of the best things about the **Tamarack Lodge & Resort** (163 Twin Lakes Rd., Mammoth Lakes, 760/934-2442, www.tamaracklodge.com) is that you can cross-country ski right up to your door. The 11 lodge rooms ($100-269) and 35 cabins ($179-749) range from studios to three-bedroom units that sleep up to nine. Tamarack prides itself on its rustic atmosphere, so accommodations have fireplaces or wood stoves, but no televisions.

Inside the ornate, carved-wood **Austria Hof** (924 Canyon Blvd., 760/934-2764 or 866/662-6668, www.austriahof.com, $150-188) are motel rooms with stylish American appointments. Austria Hof's location adjacent to the Canyon Lodge and the free gondola to the Village make it a great base camp for winter skiing or summer mountain biking.

Right beside the Panorama Gondola is the **Mammoth Mountain Inn** (10400 Minaret Rd., Mammoth Lakes, 760/934-2581 or 800/626-6684, www.themammothmountain-inn.com), with standard hotel rooms ($169-299) and condos ($249-329). All rooms and condos have flat-screen TVs in addition to other ski lodge amenities.

It's not cheap, but the ★ **Juniper Springs Resort** (4000 Meridian Blvd., reservations 760/924-1102 or 800/626-6684, www.juniper-springsmammoth.com, $249-1,100) has absolutely every luxury amenity to make your ski vacation complete. Condos and townhouses have stunning appointments and deep soaking tubs, with heated pools and six outdoor heated spas. On-site eateries include **Talons Diner** (760/934-0797 or 760/934-2571, ext. 3797, 7:30am-4:30pm daily Nov.-Apr., hours vary) and the **Daily Grind** (7am-1pm daily summer, 7am-11pm daily winter).

Transportation

U.S. 395 is the main access road to the Mammoth Lakes area. To reach the town of Mammoth Lakes from U.S. 395, turn onto Highway 203, which will take you right into town. In winter, it snows at Mammoth Lakes—carry tire chains. For the latest traffic information, including chain control areas and weather conditions, call Caltrans (800/427-7623).

Parking in Mammoth Lakes is a breeze in the off-season, but in the winter, it can get a bit more complicated. Most of the major resorts and hotels offer heated parking structures, and many of the restaurants, bars, and ski resorts have plenty of covered parking.

The **Eastern Sierra Transit Authority** (ESTA, 760/920-3359 or 760/914-1315, www.estransit.com) operates local bus routes around Mammoth Lakes, including the **June Mountain Shuttle** ($14.50 round-trip), which takes skiers from Mammoth Lakes to the June Lake ski area. Some routes

only run on certain days of the week, so check the schedule ahead of time for updated info. The **Mammoth Transit System** (www.visitmammoth.com, Nov.-May, free) offers complimentary rides all over town in the winter; download a copy of the transit map from the website.

The nearest airport is the **Mammoth Yosemite Airport** (MMH, 1200 Airport Rd., 760/934-3813, www.ci.mammoth-lakes.ca.us).

BISHOP

Bishop is a great jumping-off point for travelers to explore the natural wonders of this area. Bishop is the largest city in Inyo County, and its main street offers some low-key hotels and restaurants and ample places to rent equipment. With an elevation of just over 4,000 feet, Bishop doesn't get as cold or snowy as nearby Mammoth Lakes. Still, be prepared for emergencies: carry chains, food, and water in your car, and fill the gas tank in town.

The **Laws Railroad Museum and Historic Site** (Silver Canyon Rd., off U.S. 6, 760/873-5950, www.lawsmuseum.org, 10am-4pm daily, donation), 4.5 miles north of Bishop, is a historical village with artifacts from the area's history. Come and see the self-propelled Death Valley Car from 1927, a caboose from 1883, model railroad displays, and more.

Ancient Bristlecone Pine Forest

Directly to the east of Bishop near the Nevada border is the little-visited **Ancient Bristlecone Pine Forest,** a section of the Inyo National Forest in the White Mountains where the world's oldest trees reside. The most famous bristlecone pine, **Methuselah,** at the ripe age of about 4,750, is believed to be 1,000 years older than any other tree in the world. To protect the tree, the Forest Service has chosen not to mark it or produce maps directing people to it, but almost all the trees around here are beautiful to behold.

There are two main groves of trees. The **Schulman Grove** is where you'll find the **Ancient Bristlecone Pine Forest Visitors Center** (Hwy. 168, 23 miles east of Big Pine, 760/873-2500, www.fs.usda.gov/inyo, 10am-4pm Fri.-Mon. mid-May-early Nov., $3 pp or $6 per car).

The second notable grove, 12 miles north of Schulman on a dirt road, is the **Patriarch Grove,** home of the Patriarch Tree—the world's largest bristlecone pine. A self-guided nature trail enables you to get out among the trees. Note that the road from the visitors center to the Patriarch Grove isn't paved and can be treacherous for light passenger vehicles. At 11,000 feet, the grove's elevation can also be difficult for visitors with health issues.

You can get to the Ancient Bristlecone Pine Forest by car from the town of Bishop in about an hour. Take U.S. 395 south to Big Pine and turn left (east) onto Highway 168. Take Highway 168 for 13 miles to White Mountain Road. Turn left (north) and drive 10 miles to the visitors center in Schulman Grove.

Ancient Bristlecone Pine Forest

Food

Bishop has a couple of eateries that will satisfy the mightiest of hunger pangs. **Holy Smoke Texas Style BBQ** (772 N. Main St., 760/872-4227, www.holysmoketexasstylebbq.com, 11am-9pm Wed.-Mon., $10-15) grills meats that might rival the Lone Star State's itself. **Bishop Burger Barn** (2675 W. Line St, 760/920-6567, www.bishopburgerbarn.com, 10:30am-8pm Mon., Wed.-Fri., 10:30am-3pm Tues., 10am-9pm Sat.-Sun. winter, 10am-9pm daily summer, hours can vary by season, $5-10) serves mouthwatering local grass-fed beef burgers, as well as breakfast burritos, coffee, smoothies, and ice cream.

Camping

A nice place to stay near Bishop is **Keough's Hot Springs** (800 Keough Hot Springs Rd., 760/872-4670, www.keoughshotsprings.com, open year-round, adults $10-75, children $7-55). The 100- by 30-foot swimming pool is

heated by natural hot springs. Lodging options include "dry" tent or RV sites ($23), campsites with water and electricity ($28), four tent cabins ($85-100), and a mobile home ($125-135). To get to Keough's, travel six miles south of Bishop on U.S. 395. When you see the big blue sign on your left, turn right. You'll be there in less than 10 minutes.

Campgrounds are also available in the Inyo National Forest near Bishop. **Bishop Park** (Hwy. 168, 12 miles west of Bishop, 760/873-2400, www.fs.usda.gov, 21 sites, first-come, first-served, Apr.-Oct., $23) is right on the banks of Bishop Creek, with flush toilets and space for RVs. **Intake Two** (Hwy. 168, 16 miles west of Bishop, 8 sites, first-come, first-served, Apr.-Oct., $23) is located near Intake Two Lake. **Sabrina Campground** (Hwy. 168, 18 miles west of Bishop, 18 sites, first-come, first-served, late May-Sept., $23) is at 9,300 feet elevation, making it low on oxygen but high on views; Lake Sabrina is nearby. Showers are not available, but you can buy a shower at

Bishop Creek Lodge (2100 S. Lake Rd., 760/873-4484, www.bishopcreekresort.com, Apr.-Oct., $6) and **Parchers Resort** (5001 S. Lake Dr., 760/873-4177, www.parchersresort. net, showers year-round, $6).

Transportation

Bishop is located at the junction of U.S. 395 and U.S. 6, west of Sequoia National Forest and east of the Inyo National Forest's Ancient Bristlecone Pine Forest.

Monterey and Big Sur

Santa Cruz................... 353

Monterey.................... 363

Carmel 376

Big Sur 380

Cambria and San Simeon 391

H ere begins the California coast that movies and literature have made legendary. Soaring cliffs drop straight down into the sea in some areas, making the white-sand beaches that occasionally appear all the more inviting.

The coastal city of Santa Cruz, with its ultraliberal culture, redwood-clad university, and general sense of funky fun, prides itself on keeping things weird. The beach and Boardwalk are prime attractions for surfing and enjoying the sun.

Gorgeous Monterey Bay is famous for its sea life. Sea otters dive and play at the world-renowned aquarium while sea lions sun themselves on offshore rocks. The historic Cannery Row was immortalized by John Steinbeck in his novel of the same name, but the tourist district now bears only a superficial resemblance to its fishing past. Carmel basks in the beauty of the Central Coast, with lovely beaches, storybook cottages, and a history of art, literature, and theater. Its allure has drawn not only bohemians, but millionaires.

South of Carmel, Highway 1 begins its scenic tour down the stunning Big Sur coast. The rugged cliffs and protected forests have little development to mar their natural charms. Waterfalls and redwoods beckon hikers and campers, while cliff-side resorts pamper guests. Nearing San Simeon and Cambria, the coast becomes less rugged, though no less beautiful. Seaside Cambria makes a good base from which to visit the grand Hearst Castle, an homage to excess.

PLANNING YOUR TIME

Monterey and Big Sur are favorite destinations of many California residents for romantic weekend getaways. If you're coming for a weekend, pick an area and explore it in depth. Don't try to get everywhere in only two days—this is a big region and driving from one spot to another can take hours. Plan ahead: Reservations at hotels, campgrounds, and some must-eat restaurants fill up fast.

Previous: Bixby Bridge in Big Sur; sea otter. **Above:** Big Basin State Park.

Look for ★ to find recommended sights, activities, dining, and lodging.

Highlights

★ **Santa Cruz Beach Boardwalk:** This is the best beach boardwalk in the state (page 353).

★ **Big Basin Redwoods State Park:** California's first state park still awes with some of the tallest redwoods in the world (page 362).

★ **Monterey Bay Aquarium:** This mammoth aquarium astonishes with a vast array of sea life and exhibits (page 363).

★ **Pinnacles National Park:** Climbers, hikers, and campers can't get enough of the huge rock formations, deep caves, and amazing topography found in this tucked-away treasure (page 374).

★ **Carmel Mission:** Father Junípero Serra's favorite California mission is still a working parish, with an informative museum and stunning gilded altar (page 376).

★ **Big Sur Coast Highway:** This twisty coastal drive is iconic Big Sur, with jutting cliffs, crashing surf, and epic views (page 380).

★ **Hearst Castle:** This grand mansion on a hill was conceived and built by publishing magnate William Randolph Hearst (page 391).

Highway 1 Road Trip

Attractions in Santa Cruz and Monterey, plus charming Carmel, can easily fill your itinerary. Add a road trip down the Big Sur Coast Highway to get the most of the breathtaking vistas and the area's ethereal charm.

ONE DAY IN MONTEREY

From San Francisco, take U.S. 101 south to Highway 17 through the redwoods to the laid-back town of Santa Cruz. Ride the rides on the **Santa Cruz Beach Boardwalk,** then soak up some rays on the beach. Once you've had your fill of sunshine, continue an hour south to Monterey and the **Monterey Bay Aquarium.** Jump over to charming **Carmel-by-the-Sea** and dig your toes into the white sand at **Carmel Beach** as the sun goes down. Splurge on dinner at **Casanova,** and overnight at the delightful **La Playa Hotel,** which provides a quick launch to the coastal wonders of Big Sur the next day.

ONE DAY IN BIG SUR

Much of Big Sur's appeal is the drive along the Pacific Coast Highway, lined with historic bridges, pastures of grazing sheep, and breathtaking cliffs. From Carmel, head south on Highway 1 to the **Bixby Bridge,** which marks the official entrance to Big Sur. Stop at **Pfeiffer Big Sur State Park** to hike through the redwoods to Pfeiffer Falls. Thumb through the books at **Henry Miller Memorial Library,** then make your way south and walk the short trail to **McWay Falls** in **Julia Pfeiffer Burns State Park.** Spend the night with high-end camping at **Treebones Resort** or score a quirky room at **Deetjens,** a rustic charmer with a breakfast that should not be missed.

Santa Cruz

Nowhere else can you find another town that has embraced the radical fringe of the nation and made it into a municipal-cultural statement like Santa Cruz. Most visitors come to hit the Boardwalk and the beaches, while locals tend to hang out on Pacific Avenue and stroll on West Cliff. The sizable town is broken up into neighborhoods such as Seabright and the West Side. Beyond the city limits there is a ton to explore, from the rocky northern coast and the redwood backcountry inland, to the beach town of Capitola, east of the city.

SIGHTS

★ Santa Cruz Beach Boardwalk

Since 1907, the **Santa Cruz Beach Boardwalk** (400 Beach St., 831/423-5590, www.beachboardwalk.com, 11am-close daily June-Aug., hours vary Sept.-May, parking $6-15) has beckoned to young children, too-cool teenagers, and adults of all ages.

The amusement park rambles along the Boardwalk. Entry is free, but you must buy either ride tickets ($3-6 per ride) or an unlimited ride wristband ($24-34). The 34 rides keep the whole family entertained. In summer, a log ride cools down guests hot from hours of tromping around. Ten rides are geared toward toddlers and young kids, while avid gamers choose between the lure of prizes from the traditional midway games and the large arcade. At the 1911 carousel, reach for the brass ring.

Across the beach, food, shopping, and parking can be found along the **Santa Cruz Municipal Wharf** (831/420-6025, www.cityofsantacruz.com, parking $1-3/hour or $12-24/day). The wharf was built in 1914 to accommodate steamships and eventually became a home for warehouses and a cannery.

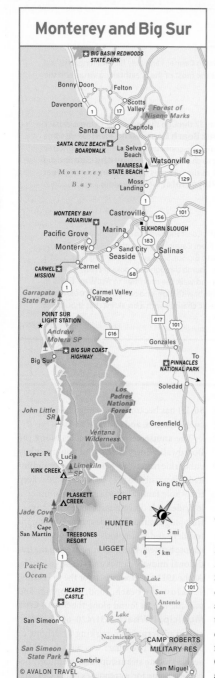

Monterey and Big Sur

BIG BASIN REDWOODS STATE PARK
Bonny Doon
Felton
Davenport
Scotts Valley
Forest of Nisene Marks
Santa Cruz
Capitola
SANTA CRUZ BEACH BOARDWALK
La Selva Beach
Watsonville
MANRESA STATE BEACH
Monterey Bay
Moss Landing
MONTEREY BAY AQUARIUM
Castroville
ELKHORN SLOUGH
Pacific Grove
Marina
Monterey
Sand City
Seaside
Salinas
CARMEL MISSION
Carmel
Garrapata State Park
Carmel Valley Village
POINT SUR LIGHT STATION
Andrew Molera SP
BIG SUR COAST HIGHWAY
Big Sur
Gonzales
To PINNACLES NATIONAL PARK
Los Padres National Forest
Soledad
John Little SR
Greenfield
Ventana Wilderness
Lopez Pt
Lucia
Limekiln SP
KIRK CREEK
King City
PLASKETT CREEK
FORT
Jade Cove RA
Cape San Martin
TREEBONES RESORT
HUNTER
LIGGET
0   5 mi
0   5 km
Pacific Ocean
Lake
HEARST CASTLE
San Antonio
San Simeon
Lake
Nacimiento
CAMP ROBERTS MILITARY RES
San Simeon State Park
Cambria
San Miguel
© AVALON TRAVEL

Today, it has given way to tourism, offering caramel apples, seashell tchotchkes, Santa Cruz apparel, and views of the Monterey Bay.

For a little fun-filled education to go with your hot dog and kettle corn, stop by the **Monterey Bay Aquarium's Sanctuary Exploration Center** (35 Pacific Ave., 831/421-9993, http://montereybay.noaa.gov, 10am-5pm Wed.-Sun., free). Designed for kids and adults, this free museum is filled with interactive exhibits that illuminate not only the wonders of the undersea canyon just off the coast, but also humans' impact, positive and negative, on the ocean.

Santa Cruz Surfing Museum

It's fitting that the original "Surf City" has its own museum dedicated to the sport. Perched above the famous Steamers Lane break and housed inside the small but handsome Mark Abbott Memorial Lighthouse, the **Santa Cruz Surfing Museum** (701 W. Cliff Dr., 831/420-6289, www.santacruzsurfingmuseum.org, 10am-5pm Wed.-Mon. July-Aug., noon-4pm Thurs.-Mon. Sept.-June, free) showcases vintage surfboards, nostalgia-inducing photos, and a motley collection of memorabilia from the 1930s through the 1990s. Learn about the early origins of surfing in Hawaii and how three Hawaiian princes surfed the mouth of the San Lorenzo River on plank boards in 1885, forever embedding surfing into Santa Cruz culture.

Seymour Marine Discovery Center

Take a tour of the **Seymour Marine Discovery Center** (100 Shaffer Rd., 831/459-3800, http://seymourcenter.ucsc.edu, 10am-5pm daily July-Aug., 10am-5pm Tues.-Sun. Sept.-June, adults $8, seniors, students, and children 3-16 $6, children 2 and under free) at Long Marine Laboratory. Sitting right on the edge of the cliff overlooking the ocean, the center is a research facility for students and faculty of the University of California, Santa Cruz (UCSC). Sign up an hour in advance for a 45-minute tour (1pm, 2pm, and 3pm daily).

Santa Cruz

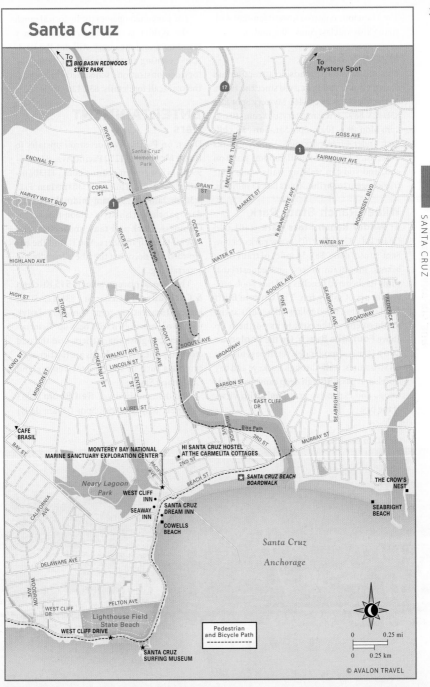

To BIG BASIN REDWOODS STATE PARK

To Mystery Spot

17

GOSS AVE

ENCINAL ST

Santa Cruz Memorial Park

FAIRMOUNT AVE

EMELINE AVE TUNNEL

CORAL ST

GRANT ST

MARKET ST

N BRANCIFORTE AVE

MORRISSEY BLVD

HARVEY WEST BLVD

RIVER ST

OCEAN ST

WATER ST

HIGHLAND AVE

RIVER ST

Bike Path

WATER ST

SOQUEL AVE

HIGH ST

STOREY ST

PINE ST

SEABRIGHT AVE

BROADWAY

FREDERICK ST

KING ST

MISSION ST

CHESTNUT ST

FRONT ST

PACIFIC AVE

WALNUT AVE

LINCOLN ST

CENTER ST

SOQUEL AVE

BROADWAY

LAUREL ST

BARSON ST

EAST CLIFF DR

SEABRIGHT AVE

RIVERSIDE AVE

Bike Path

3RD ST

MURRAY ST

CAFE BRASIL

BAY ST

MONTEREY BAY NATIONAL MARINE SANCTUARY EXPLORATION CENTER

PACIFIC AVE

2ND ST

BEACH ST

HI SANTA CRUZ HOSTEL AT THE CARMELITA COTTAGES

SANTA CRUZ BEACH BOARDWALK

THE CROW'S NEST

CALIFORNIA AVE

Neary Lagoon Park

WEST CLIFF INN

SEAWAY INN

SANTA CRUZ DREAM INN

COWELLS BEACH

SEABRIGHT BEACH

Santa Cruz

Anchorage

DELAWARE AVE

WOODROW AVE

WEST CLIFF DR

PELTON AVE

Lighthouse Field State Beach

WEST CLIFF DRIVE

SANTA CRUZ SURFING MUSEUM

Pedestrian and Bicycle Path
- - - - - - -

0   0.25 mi

0   0.25 km

© AVALON TRAVEL

The 11am tour is geared toward families with young kids and lasts only 30 minutes.

Mystery Spot

This old-fashioned roadside attraction has drawn visitors young and old since the 1940s. At the **Mystery Spot** (465 Mystery Spot Rd., 831/423-8897, www.mysteryspot.com, 10am-4pm Mon.-Fri., 10am-5pm Sat.-Sun., $6, children under 4 free, parking $5), gravity works differently: balls roll uphill, brooms stand on end, and you can walk up walls while your friends seem to shrink. Tours last 45 minutes.

Wilder Ranch State Park

At **Wilder Ranch State Park** (1401 Old Coast Rd., 831/423-9703, www.parks.ca.gov, 8am-sunset daily, $8), 34 miles of trails draw hikers, mountain bikers, and equestrians, while its sheltered beaches and tide pools provide hours of sandy fun. The **Ohlone Bluff Trail** (4 miles, easy) follows the bluffs at the southern end of the park to its northern tip above **Four Mile Beach.** On the **Engleman Loop** (4 miles, moderate), you'll pass historical structures, walk through buckeye and bay laurel, and pass through deep canyons of redwoods and expansive grasslands with views of the bay.

The park encompasses the historical ranch of the Wilder family. Their 19th-century farmhouse and creamery still dot the landscape, coming alive in tours and living-history demonstrations scheduled throughout the year (call for details; 831/426-0505).

ENTERTAINMENT

Bars

Down on Pacific Avenue, stroll upstairs to **Rosie McCann's** (1220 Pacific Ave., 831/426-9930, www.rosiemccanns.com, 11:30am-midnight Mon.-Thurs., 11:30am-1am Fri., 9:30am-2am Sat., 9:30am-midnight Sun.), a dark-paneled, Irish-style saloon that serves Guinness, black and tans, snakebites, and several tasty draft beers. You'll find the bar crowded and noisy, but the vibe is friendly and entertaining.

The hippest place in town is **515 Kitchen & Cocktails** (515 Cedar St., 831/425-5051, http://515santacruz.com, 4pm-2am daily), with two levels strewn with beat-up Victorian couches, cut-glass chandeliers, and the odd crooked print. The cocktails are top tier, with originals such as the Violent Femme and Cinder and Smoke.

The deliciously divey **Red Room** (1003 Cedar St., 831/426-2994, 3pm-1:30am daily)

Santa Cruz Beach Boardwalk

is illuminated mainly by the red lights above the bar. This spot is all black and red vinyl, a great juke box, whiskey, and cigarette smoke. On weekend nights, the crowd can make getting a table or booth nearly impossible.

Brewpubs

Beer lovers will be in heaven at **99 Bottles of Beer on the Wall** (110 Walnut Ave., 831/459-9999, 11:30am-1:30am Mon.-Thurs., 11:30am-2am Fri.-Sat., 11:30am-midnight Sun.). Yes, the bar does have 99 different varieties of beer, many of which are local microbrews. Hearty pub food is served until midnight on Friday and Saturday nights.

Another beer lover's paradise is **Santa Cruz Mountain Brewing** (402 Ingalls St., 831/425-4900, www.scmbrew.com, 11:30am-10pm daily). Located in the laid-back West Side in a hip commercial hub, the organic brewery is a dog-friendly, kid-friendly spot with an eclectic tasting room and a friendly beer garden. Nibble on food made at the scrumptious **Kelly's French Bakery** around the corner and order a flight of the seven flagship ales. You can also opt for a pint of one of the brewery's seasonal beers.

Live Music and Clubs

The Catalyst (1011 Pacific Ave., 831/423-1338, advance tickets 866/384-3060, www.catalystclub.com, $12-35), right downtown on Pacific Avenue, is *the* Santa Cruz nightclub. This live-rock venue hosts all sorts of big-name national acts and DJ dance nights. Be sure to check the calendar when you buy tickets—some shows are 21 and over. The main concert hall is standing room only, while the balconies offer seating. The vibe at The Catalyst tends to be low-key. Some of the more retro acts draw an older crowd, while the techno-DJ dance parties cater to the UCSC set.

South of downtown, the small, clubby **Moe's Alley** (1535 Commercial Way, 831/479-1854, www.moesalley.com, $5-45) hosts live acts six nights a week. You'll get your pick of ska, hip-hop, salsa, and legends like Los Lobos

and the English Beat. The full bar and small stage give it the vibe of a cozy dive joint, while the patio outside provides a great respite, where you can grab a taco or a smoke.

SPORTS AND RECREATION
Beaches

At **Main Beach** (108 Beach St., 831/420-5270, www.cityofsantacruz.com), everyone comes to stroll, surf, and sunbathe. Just below the Boardwalk, the beach stretches from the mouth of the San Lorenzo River to the wharf. There are year-round volleyball courts, and the waves are perfect for body-boarding. Beyond the wharf is **Cowell Beach** (101 Beach St.), a good surf spot for beginners. There are free outdoor showers to rinse off the sand and salt. Lifeguards stand watch to keep everyone safe.

NATURAL BRIDGES STATE PARK
Natural Bridges State Park (2531 W. Cliff Dr., 831/423-4609, www.parks.ca.gov, 8am-sunset daily, $10) is a wonderful state park offering fantastic wildlife viewing, from butterflies to whales. The unique rock formations create an inconsistent break, making surfing at Natural Bridges fun on occasion, and it's a diverse habitat where seals, sea otters, and porpoises frolic. From atop the cliffs, it's possible to see migrating whales farther out. Tide pools are found on the west side of the beach, and are accessed by a somewhat scrambling short hike (0.25-0.5 mile) on the rocky cliffs.

Monarch butterflies migrate here year after year. The best time to see them is October-February, when nearly 100,000 monarchs come to winter in the park's Eucalyptus Grove. Rangers offer guided tours of the **monarch reserve** (11am, 2pm Sat.-Sun. Oct.-Feb.) and the tide pools (year-round) at low tide.

SEABRIGHT BEACH
Residents flock to **Seabright Beach** (E. Cliff Dr. at Seabright Ave., 831/685-6500, www.thatsmypark.org, 6am-10pm daily, free) all

summer long. This miles-long stretch of sand, protected by the cliffs from the worst of the winds, is a favorite retreat for sunbathers and loungers. While there's little in the way of facilities, you can still have a great time at Seabright. There's no surfing here—Seabright has a shore break that delights skim-boarders, but makes wave-riding impossible.

NEW BRIGHTON STATE BEACH

Six miles east of Santa Cruz, Capitola is the quintessential beach town. Capitola life centers around the beautiful **New Brighton State Beach** (1500 Park Ave., Capitola, 831/464-6330, www.parks.ca.gov, 8am-sunset daily, $10). This forest-backed beach has everything: a strip of sand that's perfect for lounging, calm water for cold-water swimming, two miles of hiking trails, and ranger-led nature programs. The forest-shaded **campground** ($35) has 111 sites for both tent and RV campers, plus hot showers. New Brighton can get crowded on sunny summer days.

TOP EXPERIENCE

Surfing

The coastline of Santa Cruz has more than its share of great surf breaks. The water is cold, demanding full wetsuits year-round, and the shoreline is rough and rocky.

At **Cowell Beach** (stairs at W. Cliff Dr. and Cowell Beach), it is all about surfing. If you're a beginner, this is the best place to start surfing in Santa Cruz. The waves are low and long, making for fun longboard rides perfect for surfers just getting their balance. Because the Cowell's break is acknowledged as the newbie spot, the often sizable crowd tends to be polite to newcomers and tourists. Not far away, the most famous break in all of Santa Cruz can also be the most hostile to newcomers. **Steamer Lane** (W. Cliff Dr. btwn. Cowell's and the Lighthouse) has both a fiercely protective crew of locals and a dangerous break that actually kills someone about every other year.

Visitors who know their surfing lore will want to surf the more famous spots along the Santa Cruz shore. **Pleasure Point** (btwn. 32nd Ave. and 41st Ave., Soquel) encompasses a number of different breaks. You may have heard of **The Hook** (steps at 41st Ave.), a well-known experienced longboarder's paradise. But don't mistake The Hook for a beginner's break; the locals feel protective of the waves here and aren't always friendly toward inexperienced tourists. The break at **36th and East Cliff** (steps at 36th Ave.) can be a better place to go on weekdays—on the weekends, the crowd makes catching your own wave a challenge. Up at **30th and East Cliff** (steps at 36th Ave.), you'll find challenging sets and hot-dogging shortboarders.

The **Santa Cruz Surf School** (131 Center St., 831/426-7072, www.santacruzsurfschool. com, $45-120 per hour) and the **Richard Schmidt School of Surfing** (849 Almar Ave., 831/423-0928, www.richardschmidt. com, $45-150 per hour) offer private and semi-private lessons, as does **Club Ed** (2350 Paul Minnie Ave., 831/464-0177, http://club-ed.com, $38-120 per hour). You can also get stand-up paddleboarding lessons as well as surfing rentals, from boards to booties, at Ed's.

Kayaking

The semi-protected coves around Santa Cruz offer some great kayaking. At the tip of Monterey Bay, you'll enjoy rich marine life, fun swells, and plenty of company. The best places to launch are **Main Beach** (108 Beach St., 831/420-5270, www.cityofsantacruz.com) and the **Santa Cruz Harbor** (135 5th Ave., 831/475-6161, www.santacruzharbor.org). At Main Beach, you can enter the water near the Boardwalk and by Cowell's break. Paddling out from the Boardwalk will be a more relaxing ride, but if you want a thrill, chase the waves over at Cowell's.

Rentals are available at **Venture Quest Kayaking** (2 Santa Cruz Wharf, 831/425-8445, http://kayaksantacruz.com, 10am-7pm Mon.-Fri., 9am-7pm Sat.-Sun. May-Oct., by appointment Oct.-Apr.) on the wharf. You can pick open or closed kayaks, single ($35-60) or double ($55-100) for three hours or all day. If you're new to paddling in Santa Cruz, join a tour.

On the east side of the harbor, the launch ramp is close to parking, making getting in and out of the water easy. The harbor itself is fun to explore, as it is a haven for barking sea lions, and extends all the way to Woods Lagoon. For rentals at the harbor, **Kayak Connection** (413 Lake Ave. no. 3, 831/479-1121, 10am-5pm Mon.-Fri., 9am-5pm Sat.-Sun., 4 hours $35 single, $55 double) is the place to go. It also has the gear you'll need to keep warm, in addition to stand-up paddleboards. The company also offers whale-watching tours (3 hours, $60).

Fishing and Whale-Watching

With the Monterey Bay Sanctuary just offshore and teeming with life, it is no surprise that Santa Cruz has some excellent **fishing and whale-watching** trips. Many companies wear both hats: Taking folks fishing in the morning and taking others to look for porpoises, sea otters, and migrating whales later in the day. One such operation is **Stagnaro Sport Fishing** (1718 Brommer St., 831/427-0230, www.stagnaros.com). Throughout the year, the company leads fishing trips for salmon, albacore, cod, and sand dab. Trips cost $50-85 and do not include your license or rod and reel, which can be purchased or rented from Stagnaro. If just observing the ocean's bounty is more your thing, you can pick from a number of sea-life tours ($48 for 3-4 hours) or the one-hour scenic Bay Cruise ($20).

FOOD
Coffee and Tea

The perpetual influx of students, thinkers, and foodies means Santa Cruz has plenty of excellent places to pick up a cup of coffee. **Verve** (1540 Pacific Ave., 831/600-7784, www.vervecoffeeroasters.com, 6:30am-9pm daily), with its reclaimed wood, subway tile, and soot-colored walls, receives the most buzz. If the loud music and hipster vibe are too much for you, venture across the street to **Lulu Carpenter's** (1545 Pacific Ave., 831/439-9200, www.lulucarpenters.com, 6am-midnight daily). The exposed brick and beam interior speaks to the 1990s wave of cafés, while the small tables and lush outdoor patio create the perfect atmosphere to read or study.

Seabright expresses a laid-back beach vibe. For coffee, pastries, and sandwiches to go, stop by ★ **The Buttery** (702 Soquel Ave., 831/458-3020, www.butterybakery.com, 7am-7pm daily, $3-10). At the corner of Soquel and Branciforte in a large Victorian building, The Buttery bustles with locals. Grab a number before you peruse the rich assortment in the pastry cases. For a hot meal, the counter on the other side is the place to be, while the outside patio is the place to dig in.

American

For an all-American meal, head over to **Jack's** (202 Lincoln St., 831/423-4421, 10am-7pm Mon.-Thurs., 10am-8pm Fri.-Sat., $5-10). While hipster burger joints have started to infiltrate the Santa Cruz scene, Jack's still has the best cheeseburger in town. The walk-up window, outside seating, and simple selection of burgers, fries, dogs, and shakes can't help but charm.

Undoubtedly the most romantic restaurant in the region is Capitola's ★ **Shadowbrook** (1750 Wharf Rd., 831/475-1511, www.shadowbrook-capitola.com, 5pm-8:45pm Mon.-Fri., 4pm-9:45pm Sat., 4pm-8:45pm Sun., $23-45). The restaurant is down a steep and lush ravine along Soquel Creek. To get there, diners take a trip aboard the antique cable car or by foot along the winding illuminated path through thick flora. The restaurant is inviting, with roses, candlelight, and robust plates of lobster and black truffle gnocchi, followed by fine chocolate desserts. The adjacent **Rock Room Lounge** (4pm-10pm Mon.-Fri., 3:30pm-10pm Sat., 2:30pm-10pm Sun., $13-27) offers a more casual atmosphere and menu. The Rock Room does not take reservations, unlike Shadowbrook, where they are a must.

Brazilian

The West Side neighborhood draws locals with a love of good food. Opened in 1991, **Cafe Brasil** (1410 Mission St., 831/429-1855, www.cafebrasil.us, 8am-3pm daily, $7-10) has been serving up Brazilian fare since well before there was a foodie craze, and it is still packed every weekend morning. At the brightly painted café, the breakfast fare runs to omelets, while lunch includes pressed sandwiches, meat and tofu dishes, and Brazilian house specials. A juice bar provides rich but healthy meal accompaniments that can act as light meals on their own.

Japanese

A couple blocks away, **Shogun Sushi** (1123 Pacific Ave., 831/469-4477, noon-2:30pm, 5pm-9pm Mon.-Wed., noon-2:30pm, 5pm-10pm Thurs.-Fri., 3pm-10pm Sat., $12-30) is the place locals go when they need their sushi fix. The *nigiri* arrives at your table in big, fresh slabs, and you'll have an interesting collection of rolls to choose from. The restaurant is relatively small, so expect a wait for a table in the evenings and on weekends.

Mexican

One of the favorites on Pacific Avenue is ★ **El Palomar** (1336 Pacific Ave., 831/425-7575, 11am-3pm, 5pm-10pm Mon.-Fri., 10am-3pm, 5pm-10pm Sat.-Sun., $8-15). This family-owned Mexican joint has been serving family recipes since 1983. The salsa and tortillas are handmade, and the flavors are fresh and comforting, with the appropriate amount of spice. Don't pass up a margarita—the bar has scores of tequilas and the drinks have scored critical attention.

Seafood

Since 1937, **Stagnaro Bros. Restaurant** (59 Municipal Wharf, 831/423-2180, http://stagnarobros.com, 11am-9pm daily, $11-27) has been selling fish to the people of Santa Cruz. Come and check out the outdoor fish market or go upstairs to the nautically themed restaurant. Pick from over 50 seafood dishes, ranging from crab melt sandwiches to blackened ahi. Many items have an Italian bent, and the must-try is the cioppino.

Perched above the harbor in a handsome building, ★ **Johnny's Harborside** (493 Lake Ave., 831/479-3430, www.johnnysharborside.com, 11:30am-8:30pm Mon.-Thurs., 11:30am-9:30pm Fri.-Sat., 10am-8:30pm Sun., $12-32) delivers plates of fish-and-chips, blackened New York steak, and tempura ahi. The dining room is spare, and the menu is eclectic, revolving mainly around seafood. Johnny's offers an extensive gluten-free menu as well as happy hour drink specials.

ACCOMMODATIONS
Under $150

The **Santa Cruz Youth Hostel Carmelita Cottages** (321 Main St., 831/423-8304, www.hi-santacruz.org, $23-26 dorm, $55-90 private room) offers a great local atmosphere, and it's clean, cheap, friendly, and close to the beach. You'll even find a spot to store your surfboard or bike. The big, homey kitchen is open for guest use, and might even be housing some free food in its cupboards. Expect all the usual hostel amenities, a nice garden out back, free linens, laundry facilities, and a free Internet kiosk.

Cheap digs can also be found across the street from the Boardwalk at the **Aqua Breeze Inn** (204 2nd St., 831/426-7878, http://aquabreezeinn.com, $55-80). While this classic beach motel may not be the most charming accommodation in town, you will get a mini-fridge, microwave, use of the heated pool, and a place for Fido to lay his head at night.

$150-250

Conveniently located on Highway 1, the Spanish-style **Mission Inn** (2250 Mission St., 831/425-5455 or 800/895-5455, http://mission-inn.com, $150) is an easy jog to downtown, the beach, and points north. Other perks include the outdoor hot tub and sauna, and the complimentary continental breakfast.

Hidden in a hillside residential neighborhood perched above downtown, the four-room bed-and-breakfast ★ **Adobe on Green Street** (103 Green St., 831/469-9866, www.adobeongreen.com, $129-219) lets you soak in the local atmosphere. Each room has a queen bed, a private bathroom (most with tubs and colorful tile work), a small TV with DVD player, and lots of other comforting amenities. Visit the dining room for an expanded continental spread each morning 8am-10:30am. Expect local pastries, organic and soy yogurts, and eggs laid by a neighbor's flock of chickens. Adobe runs on solar power.

For a room overlooking the ocean, stay at the **Sea & Sand Inn** (201 W. Cliff Dr., 831/427-3400, www.santacruzmotels.com, $129-319). Thanks to its unbeatable location on the ocean side of West Cliff in a quiet neighborhood, you'll be close enough to downtown and the Boardwalk to enjoy the action of Santa Cruz. Other than the complimentary breakfast and wine and cheese hour in the afternoon, you won't find fancy amenities.

Sophisticated urban chic can be found at the 162-room **Hotel Paradox** (611 Ocean St., 831/425-7100, www.thehotelparadox.com, $219-349). At the higher end of the price range, expect plenty of designer touches that incorporate Santa Cruz's woodland environs, as well as plush beds, flat screen TVs, and mini-fridges. Completing the posh accommodations are an outdoor pool and hot tub with rentable cabanas and poolside service from the hotel's bar and restaurant.

Over $250

You won't get closer to the beach than the **Santa Cruz Dream Inn** (175 W. Cliff Dr., 831/426-4330, http://jdvhotels.com, $240-480), which channels a classic throwback kitsch. Take your morning coffee out on your private deck or lounge poolside beneath bright umbrellas. Since it's across from the Boardwalk and close to downtown, you'll never have to change out of your flip-flops.

TRANSPORTATION AND SERVICES

Car

From San Francisco, Santa Cruz is 75 miles south, about 1.5 hours away. Take either **U.S. 101** or I-280 south (101 can be slightly faster, but less scenic and more prone to traffic) to **Highway 17** toward Santa Cruz. Most locals take this 50-mile-per-hour corridor fast—probably faster than they should. Each year, several people die in accidents on Highway 17, so keep to the right and take it slow, no matter what the traffic to the left of you is doing. Check traffic reports before you head out; Highway 17 is known as one of the worst commuting roads in the Bay Area, and weekend beach traffic in the summer jams up fast in both directions.

For a more leisurely drive, opt for two-lane **Highway 1.** Once in town, Highway 1 becomes Mission Street on the West Side and acts as the main artery through Santa Cruz and down to Capitola, Soquel, Aptos, and coastal points farther south.

Parking in Santa Cruz can be challenging. Downtown, head straight for the parking structures one block away from Pacific Avenue on either side. They're much easier to deal with than trying to find street parking. The same goes for the beach and Boardwalk areas. At the Boardwalk, just pay the fee to park in the big parking lot adjacent to the attractions. You'll save an hour and a possible car break-in or theft trying to find street parking in the sketchy neighborhoods that surround the Boardwalk.

Public Transit

Santa Cruz METRO (831/425-8600, www.scmtd.com, $2/single ride, passes available) runs 42 bus routes in Santa Cruz County, helping you get nearly anywhere you'd want to go. In the summer, take advantage of the **Santa Cruz Trolley** (831/420-5150, http://santacruztrolley.com, 11am-9pm daily May-Sept., $0.25). The vintage trolley car connects the Boardwalk and downtown via a three-stop route running every 15-20 minutes. And it only costs $0.25.

Services

Despite its reputation as a funky bohemian beach town, Santa Cruz's dense population dictates at least one full-fledged hospital of its own. You can get medical treatment and emergency care at **Dominican Hospital** (1555 Soquel Ave., 831/426-7700, www.do-minicanhospital.org). For less life-threatening issues, the Palo Alto Medical Foundation (www.pamf.org) has two urgent care clinics in Santa Cruz: the **Main Clinic** (2025 Soquel Ave., 831/458-5537, 8am-9pm daily) and the **Westside Clinic** (1301 Mission St., 831/458-6310, 9am-9pm Mon.-Thurs., 9am-6pm Fri.-Sun.).

SANTA CRUZ MOUNTAINS

Highway 9, the main road snaking through the redwood-dense mountains, is lined with the towns of **Felton, Ben Lomond,** and **Boulder Creek,** in addition to the stellar state parks of **Henry Cowell Redwoods** and **Big Basin.** Less than 20 minutes from downtown Santa Cruz, residents commute for work and school, but tucked into the forest, these mountain towns still feel worlds away.

Henry Cowell Redwoods State Park

Before entering the town of Felton, Highway 9 slows to wind through the bottom of a steep river gorge. This is the beginning of the 4,600-acre **Henry Cowell Redwoods State Park** (101 N. Big Trees Park Rd., Felton, 831/335-4598, www.parks.ca.gov, $10). Encompassing old-growth redwoods, waterfalls, and, high in the hills, views of Monterey Bay, the park offers 20 miles of trails as well as campsites. There is also swimming at the sandy **Frisbee** and **Cable Car Beaches** along the San Lorenzo River.

The park is broken up into two large swaths. The main section is in the heart of Felton and has a ranger kiosk, a **Nature** Center with displays and interactive exhibits, and the accessible **Redwood Grove Loop,** an interpretive trail winding through giant trees. Trails crisscross this entire section of park, making any number of moderate loops possible. Longer, backcountry trails can be found in the northern **Fall Creek** section of the park. Trailheads line the Felton-Empire Grade Road, including for the **Fall Creek Trail,** a 3.2-mile loop via the **Ridge Trail.** To make this into a full-day adventure, take **Fall Creek Trail,** then turn left onto **Big Ben Trail,** followed by another left onto **Lost Empire Trail,** and back to **Fall Creek** via the **Cape Horn** and **South Fork Trails.** On this strenuous nine-mile loop, you'll pass the famous giant Big Ben redwood tree and the old lime kilns along South Fall Creek.

Camping ($35) is available at Henry Cowell April-October. Sites are near the creek, nestled in the redwoods, and come with fire rings, lockers, and picnic tables, with flush toilets and hot showers close by.

Roaring Camp Railroads

If the river and the redwoods aren't enough, walk over to **Roaring Camp Railroads** (5401 Graham Hill Rd., Felton, 831/335-4484, www.roaringcamp.com, 9am-5pm daily, 13 and over $27-29, children 2-12 $20-23, parking $8). Running out of a re-created 1880s logging town, antique steam engines wind through the Santa Cruz Mountains, over trestles and beneath towering redwoods, on hour-long tours. You can jump aboard a three-hour round-trip down to the Boardwalk for a whole day of fun. Picnicking is encouraged at the camp, as is exploring the myriad of activities, from gold panning and blacksmithing to volleyball.

★ Big Basin Redwoods State Park

Big Basin Redwoods State Park (21600 Big Basin Way, Boulder Creek, 831/338-8860, www.parks.ca.gov, $10) is home to the largest continuous stand of old-growth coast redwoods south of San Francisco and owes this distinction to becoming California's first state park in 1902, at the height of the logging frenzy. Today this means an area rich in biodiversity.

Big Basin has 80 miles of trails to explore, stretching from the crown of the Santa Cruz Mountains down to the mouth of Waddell Creek just south of Año Nuevo. One of the most popular hikes is to **Berry Creek Falls** (12 miles, strenuous), a series of four waterfalls cascading through old-growth redwoods. Usually done as a one-way trek, **Skyline to the Sea** to **Waddell Creek Beach** (12.5 miles, strenuous) is a rite of passage for many local outdoor enthusiasts. There are plenty of shorter and more moderate hikes, like the **Shadowbrook Trail** (4.7 miles, moderate) and **Sequoia Trail** (4 miles, easy), which both lead to Sempervirens Falls.

At the main entrance, 146 traditional **campsites** (800/444-7275, www. reserveamerica.com, $35) are divided into four areas. These all have access to bathroom facilities, showers, and a group amphitheater, where campers are often entertained by music or ghost stories. Tent cabins ($75) are also available. Backpacking sites must be reserved in advance by phone (831/338-8861). The park is big, but all the visitor services are clustered together. You'll find a general store, a gift shop, and a museum near the visitors center, where you can pay fees, buy a trail map, and query a happy-to-oblige ranger. Docent-led hikes leave from here and generally occur every Saturday morning.

Big Basin is located 25 miles northeast of Santa Cruz, smack in the middle of the mountains, near the intersections of Highways 35 and 9. The park's main entrance is seven miles down Highway 236 (also known as Big Basin Highway). Boulder Creek is the closest town, nine miles south on Highway 9.

Monterey

The Monterey Peninsula juts out from the California coast to create the wide and magnificent Monterey Bay. The creation of the Monterey Bay National Marine Sanctuary in 1992 protected the bay's astounding biological diversity, including its kelp forests and the Monterey Submarine Canyon, one of the deepest in the world.

Monterey is the commercial hub of the Monterey Peninsula, filled with offices, malls, and parks; it's also the launch point to the protected waters just off the coast. Pacific Grove (PG to locals) is sandwiched between Monterey and Pebble Beach. David Avenue is the border between Monterey and PG.

TOP EXPERIENCE

SIGHTS
★ Monterey Bay Aquarium
At the **Monterey Bay Aquarium** (886 Cannery Row, 831/648-4800, www. montereybayaquarium.org, 9:30am-6pm daily Sept.-June, 9:30am-6pm Mon.-Fri., 9:30am-8pm Sat.-Sun. July-Aug., adults $40, seniors and students 13-17 $35, children 3-12 $25, under 3 free), you'll get to explore the ocean beyond the beach, where sharks roam the deep, sardines circle forests of kelp, and sea otters relax over a lunch of abalone. All the exhibits you'll see in this mammoth complex contain only local sea life and convey a message of sustainability. The exhibits and shows put on by the residents of Monterey Bay delight children and adults alike, especially the playful sea otters, the intelligent and stealthy giant octopus, and the bat rays, who love a good petting.

The aquarium is one of the best places to eat on Cannery Row. Try for a table at the full-service restaurant and bar, complete with white tablecloths and a view of the bay. A self-service café offers sandwiches, salads, and international dishes for decent prices and with equally excellent views. Everything served is sustainable.

Cannery Row and Fisherman's Wharf

Cannery Row (www.canneryrow.com) and **Fisherman's Wharf** (www.montereywharf.com) are Monterey's manufactured tourist meccas. These are the places that most locals avoid. Filled with boutique hotels, big seafood restaurants, and cheesy souvenir stores, this stretch of coastline, extending past the lower tip of the Presidio to Fisherman's Wharf, is hard to imagine as being the center of Monterey's booming fishing industry in the early 20th century. Here, thousands of tons of sardines were hauled in, processed, and canned by low-wage workers at the 16 canning plants and 14 reduction plants lining Cannery Row. In the 1950s the industry collapsed.

If you look close enough, you can still see traces of Steinbeck's Cannery Row. Ed Rickett's lab still looks as it did, complete with the concrete specimen tanks out back, and the city has maintained several of the one-room cottages that housed Filipino and Japanese workers. Inside the aquarium, itself once an old cannery, you can check out old steam boilers.

Monterey State Historic Park

For history that is beautifully preserved, uncrowded, and still an active part of the city, visit **Monterey State Historic Park** (20 Custom House Plaza, 831/649-7118, www.parks.ca.gov, 10am-5pm daily, free). Usually called Old Monterey by locals, "the park" is a collection of 55 historical sites along a 2.5-mile trail that weaves through downtown Monterey.

To find all the historic sites, follow the yellow medallions embedded in the sidewalks. Organized walking **tours** (10:30am, 12:30pm Fri.-Sun., $5) meet at the Pacific House Museum and last 45 minutes. Tours of several of the brick and adobe buildings are also available. Although many of the structures are not (or at least are rarely) open to the public, you

are encouraged to spend time in the splendid gardens, which are open daily.

The best place to start is the **Custom House Plaza** at the base of Fisherman's Wharf. Here, the **Custom House** (10am-4pm Fri.-Sun., adults $3, children 12 and under free) is California State Historic Landmark Number 1, and the oldest bureaucratic building to still stand in the state. Nearby are **California's First Theater** (Pacific St. and Scott St.); the **Old Whaling Station** (391 Decatur St.), with its whalebone sidewalk out front; and the **Casa del Oro** (210 Oliver St., 11am-3pm Thurs.-Sun.), a two-story adobe building home to the quaint Boston Store and the Picket Fence garden shop.

Downtown, another great starting point is **Colton Hall** (351 Pacific St., 831/646-5640, www.monterey.org, 10am-4pm daily). Though technically not part of the Monterey State Historic Park, Colton Hall is a city museum honoring the drafting of California's first constitution in 1849.

Museum of Monterey

More history can be found at the **Museum of Monterey** (5 Custom House Plaza, 831/372-2608, http://museumofmonterey.org, 11am-5pm Wed.-Sat., noon-5pm Sun., free). The large modern facility in the middle of Custom House Plaza provides plenty of space for art and historic artifacts collected over the decades. You can explore the history of the native Rumisen and Ohlone people, going through the Spanish exploration and conquistador era, and on into the American military and fishing presence on the Central Coast. The original Fresnel lens from the Point Sur light station sits in here, as does an array of sardine fishing equipment.

Pacific Grove Monarch Sanctuary

From November to February, the best place to see the nearly 10,000 monarch butterflies that travel thousands of miles to winter in the eucalyptus and pine forests of Pacific Grove is in the **Monarch Sanctuary** (250

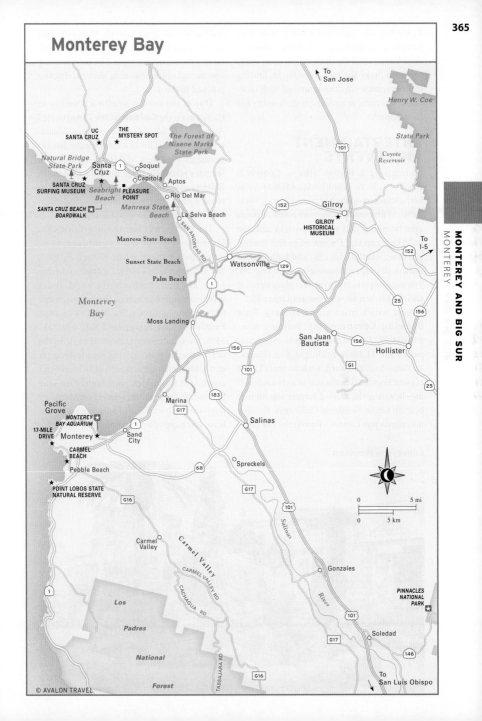

Monterey Bay

To San Jose

Henry W. Coe

State Park

Coyote Reservoir

UC SANTA CRUZ

THE MYSTERY SPOT

The Forest of Nisene Marks State Park

Natural Bridge State Park

Santa Cruz

Soquel

Capitola

Aptos

Rio Del Mar

La Selva Beach

SANTA CRUZ SURFING MUSEUM

Seabright Beach

PLEASURE POINT

SANTA CRUZ BEACH BOARDWALK

Manresa State Beach

Gilroy

GILROY HISTORICAL MUSEUM

To I-5

Manresa State Beach

Sunset State Beach

Palm Beach

Watsonville

Monterey Bay

Moss Landing

San Juan Bautista

Hollister

Marina

Salinas

Pacific Grove

MONTEREY BAY AQUARIUM

17-MILE DRIVE

Monterey

Sand City

Spreckels

CARMEL BEACH

Pebble Beach

POINT LOBOS STATE NATURAL RESERVE

0   5 mi

0   5 km

Carmel Valley

Carmel Valley

CARMEL VALLEY RD

CACHAGUA RD

Gonzales

PINNACLES NATIONAL PARK

Los

Padres

Salinas River

Soledad

National

TASSAJARA RD

Forest

To San Luis Obispo

SAN ANDREAS RD

© AVALON TRAVEL

Ridge Rd., off Lighthouse Ave.). Here they hang in great clusters, resembling clumps of dead leaves, until the fluttering of their wings seems to make the trees take flight. During this time, museum docents armed with viewing scopes come to answer questions every day (noon-3pm).

ENTERTAINMENT AND EVENTS

Channeling a British vibe is **Crown & Anchor** (150 W. Franklin St., 831/649-6496, http://crownandanchor.net, 11am-1:30am daily). With considerably more polish, it pours aged bourbons and vintage port, in addition to 20 beers on tap. Decorated in rich leather, gleaming nautical devices, and high-backed booths, the imperial atmosphere will impress. The outside patio is also a great place to relax, and the kitchen serves food until midnight.

You won't miss the **Cannery Row Brewing Company** (95 Prescott Ave., 831/643-2722, www.canneryrowbrewingcompany.com, 11:30am-midnight Sun.-Thurs., 11:30am-2am Fri.-Sat.), with its installation of giant kegs fixed to the side of its brick building. Boasting the second-largest selection of beer on tap in Northern California, this is a microbrew pub Cannery Row-style. The large,

industrial-chic space is loud, often crowded, and serves a large and tasty selection of pub food. Live music, multiple TVs broadcasting sports, and outdoor seating with roaring fire pits add to the mix.

One of the coolest small-rock venues in California is the **Golden State Theatre** (417 Alvarado St., 831/649-1070, www.goldenstatetheatre.com). This beautiful theater has retained its 1920s-era Middle Eastern chic. It features relatively large acts like Ozomatli, Robert Cray, and Kenny Wayne Shepard. On other nights, the theater hosts touring musicals and National Geographic talks.

The **Monterey County Fairgrounds** has hosted some of the most significant music events in American music history. In 1967, the Monterey Pop Festival introduced Janis Joplin and Jimi Hendrix to the world. Today it remains home to one of the biggest music festivals in California, the **Monterey Jazz Festival** (2004 Fairground Rd., 831/373-3366, www.montereyjazzfestival.org). As the site of the longest-running jazz festival on earth, Monterey attracts top performers from around the world. Held each September—the best month for beautiful weather on Monterey Bay—this long weekend of amazing music can leave you happy for the whole year.

Cannery Row Monument

SPORTS AND RECREATION

Beaches

Much of the coastline between Cannery Row and Fisherman's Wharf is rocky, but a couple of postage-stamp-size beaches are perfect places to get your toes wet or build a sand castle. **San Carlos Beach** (Cannery Row at Reese Ave.) is a protected little cove, with both sand and a grassy area upon which to throw down your picnic blanket. Even smaller is **McAbee Beach** (Cannery Row and Hoffman Ave.). Here you'll find tide pools as well as offshore kelp forests, where you may spy sea otters if you keep your eyes peeled.

The widest, flattest beach in Monterey can be found on the other side of the municipal pier at **Monterey State Beach** (Del Monte Ave. and Park Ave., 831/649-2836, www.parks.ca.gov), a 21-mile-long network of beaches stretching from Monterey to north of Moss Landing. The two-mile stretch between Monterey and Seaside is a favorite with families and beachcombers.

The beach, particularly the section known as **Del Monte Beach** (just east of the pier), is also a draw for surfers who favor the long rollers, ideal for beginners. More seasoned surfers may want to continue north to **Marina State Beach** (off Reservation Rd.), also within the Monterey State Beach system. Here, the crowds are thinner and the steady winds, strong riptides, and heavy currents create a moderate-to-challenging ride. Gear, rentals, and advice can be found at **On the Beach** (693 Lighthouse Ave., 831/646-9283, 10am-6pm Sun.-Thurs., 10am-7pm Fri.-Sat., surfboards $20 half day or $30 full day, bodyboards $5 half day or $10 full day, wetsuits $10 half day or $15 full day), a local surf shop since 1986.

In Pacific Grove, **Asilomar State Beach** (Sunset Dr. near Asilomar Ave., www.parks.ca.gov, 831/646-6440, sunrise-sunset daily) is a beautiful stretch of sand. Rocky, with tons of tide pools and plenty of wind, Asilomar is the place to go to look for tiny sea creatures or fly a kite. Continuous breakers also draw lots of surfers. Aside from the maintained trail down to the beach, don't expect anything in the way of comforts, like bathrooms or picnic tables.

Scuba

The Monterey Bay Marine Sanctuary, with its underwater canyons, kelp forests, and rich biological diversity, is a world-class place to dive. Dozens of dive schools cluster in and around Monterey, and several companies lead trips from shore or by boat.

Aquarius Dive Shop (2040 Del Monte Ave., 831/375-1933, www.aquariusdivers.com, 9am-6pm Mon.-Fri., 7am-6pm Sat.-Sun.) sits across from Monterey State Beach and offers everything you need to go diving out in Monterey Bay, including air and nitrox fills, equipment rental, certification courses, guided shore tours, and help booking a trip on a local dive boat. Aquarius works with four boats to create great trips for divers of all interests and ability levels.

Near Cannery Row, **Bamboo Reef Enterprises** (614 Lighthouse Ave., 831/372-1685, http://bambooreef.com, 9am-6pm Mon.-Fri., 7am-6pm Sat.-Sun.) is a full dive shop and has equipment rentals, certification classes, and tours that leave from different points around the bay.

If you are an experienced diver, eager to explore the depths beyond the shore, the *Monterey Express* (831/915-0752, www.montereyexpress.com) will take you there. This popular dive boat knows all the great spots and has scheduled 3.5-hour trips (8am, 1:30pm Sat.-Sun., $90).

Kayaking

Sea **kayaking** is popular here. Whether you want to try paddling your first kayak, or you're an expert who needs to rent gear, you'll find a local outfit ready and willing to hook you up. Fisherman's Wharf is a great launch point with an easy paddle through the harbor. Once you're on the bay, passing over the kelp can slow the kayak, as paddles can become tangled. Dolphins in the distance and sea otters are the rewards: In spring, you are likely to spy otter mothers holding baby pups on their bellies.

Adventures by the Sea (299 Cannery Row, 831/372-1807, www.adventuresbythesea.com, 9am-6pm daily winter, 9am-8pm daily summer, tours $60/person, rentals $30/day) rents kayaks for full days to let you choose your own route around the magnificent Monterey Bay kelp forest. Adventures also offers tours from Cannery Row. The tours last about 2.5 hours, and the available tandem sit-on-top kayaks make it a great experience for school-age children. Adventures by the Sea also runs a tour of Stillwater Cove at Pebble Beach ($85). Reservations are recommended for all tours, but during the summer, the Cannery Row tour leaves regularly at 10am and 2pm.

Monterey Bay Kayaks (693 Del Monte Ave., 831/373-5357, www.montereybaykayaks.com, 8:30am-5pm daily winter, 8:30am-6:30pm daily summer, tours $55-85) specializes in tours of central Monterey and Elkhorn Slough. You can choose between open-deck and closed-deck tours, beginning tours (perfect for kids), romantic sunset or full moon paddles, or even long paddles designed for more experienced sea kayakers. If you prefer to rent a kayak and explore the bay or slough on your own, Monterey Bay Kayaks can help you out there, too.

Fishing and Whale-Watching

Whales pass quite near the shores of Monterey year-round. Although you can sometimes even see them from the beach, boats can take you out for a closer look. The area hosts many humpbacks, blue whales, and gray whales, plus the occasional killer whale, minke whale, and pod of dolphins. Bring your own binoculars for a better view, but the experienced boat captains will do all they can to get you as close as possible. Most tours last 2-3 hours and leave from Fisherman's Wharf, which is easy to get to and has ample parking.

Monterey Bay Whale Watch (84 Fisherman's Wharf, 831/375-4658, www.montereybaywhalewatch.com, half-day trips adults $41-49, children 4-12 $29-39, children 3 and under $15, full-day trips adults only $145) leaves right from an easy-to-find red building on Fisherman's Wharf and runs tours in every season. You must make a reservation in advance, even for regularly scheduled tours. Morning, afternoon, and all-day tours are available.

Princess Monterey **Whale-Watching** (96 Fisherman's Wharf, 831/372-2203, www.montereywhalewatching.com) prides itself on its knowledgeable guides and its comfortable, spacious vessels. The *Princess Monterey* offers morning and afternoon tours, and you can buy tickets online or by phone. Tours last 2.5 hours and cost $45.

Randy's Fishing and Whale-Watching Trips (66 Fisherman's Wharf, 800/251-7440 or 831/372-7440, www.randysfishingtrips.com, fishing trips $75-300, whale-watching adults $40, children 12 and under $20) can take you out whale-watching or fishing for salmon, halibut, albacore, mackerel, rock cod, flatfish, and even squid and Dungeness crab in season. Trips begin early in the morning and can last for several hours. You can bring your own food—catering is not provided—including a small cooler for your drinks. If you don't have a California fishing license, you can purchase a one-day license through Randy. Although you can try to walk up to the bright teal-painted shop at Fisherman's Wharf, it's best to get tickets for your trip in advance. Like his fishing trips, whale-watching excursions change with the seasons. Call or check the website for the current schedule.

Chris's Fishing Trips and Whale-Watching (48 Fisherman's Wharf, 831/372-5951, www.chrissfishing.com, fishing adults $75-80, children $50, whale-watching adults $37, children $22) offers both scheduled deep-sea trips for cod and salmon in addition to boats for charter. You can get your license, bait, and tackle here, but it will cost extra. Chris also offers whale-watching trips. Tours depart daily at 10am and 1:30pm and last three hours.

Biking

The **Monterey Bay Coastal Recreation Trail** (http://monterey.org) is a two-lane bike trail that stretches 18 miles from Castroville to Pacific Grove. Relatively flat and hugging the coast much of the way, it is an easy and safe way to see the sights around Monterey. If you have left your bike at home, there are many outfits happy to rent you one. Located on Cannery Row, **Bay Bike** (585 Cannery Row, 831/655-2453, www.baybikes.com, 9am-5pm Sun.-Thurs., 9am-5:30pm Fri., 9am-6pm Sat.) has a wide selection of bike rentals from cruisers ($8/hour, $32/day), road bikes ($12/hour, $48/day), and tandem bikes ($16/hour, $48/day), plus kids' bikes, and all sorts of gear. Another choice with several locations is **Adventures by the Sea** (299 Cannery Row, 831/372-1807, http://adventuresbythesea.com, 9am-5pm Mon.-Fri., 9am-6pm Sat.-Sun.). It has cruisers ($8/hour, $30/day) and tandem bikes ($16/hour, $60/day), plus large family surreys ($20-30/hour, $120-180/day).

FOOD

Cannery Row and Fisherman's Wharf

In Cannery Row, fill up for a day of sightseeing, kayaking, and whale-watching at **First Awakenings** (125 Ocean View Blvd., Pacific Grove, 831/372-1125, www.firstawakenings. net, 7am-2pm Mon.-Fri., 7am-2:30pm Sat.-Sun., $8-12). Technically in Pacific Grove, First Awakenings is on the other side of the aquarium, with great views, but away from the hubbub.

The Sardine Factory (701 Wave St., 831/373-3775, www.sardinefactory.com, 5pm-9:30pm Sun.-Thurs., 5pm-10pm Fri.-Sat., $27-44) is *the* Monterey restaurant. Opened in 1968 on what was the then rundown Cannery Row, The Sardine Factory saw the potential in this abandoned stretch of real estate. The restaurant has made an appearance in a Clint Eastwood movie, and its signature abalone dish was served at President Ronald Reagan's inaugural dinner. Still old school, the Factory serves steak and Italian-inspired seafood

dishes, and the wine list has won awards. The lounge offers a scaled-down menu with plenty of stiff drinks, live music, and a chance to soak in the ambience.

Steinbeck would be shocked if he saw all the high-dollar joints filling his poetically soiled Cannery Row, but the one locals swear by is ★ **Bistro Moulin** (867 Wave St., 831/333-1200, www.bistromoulin.com, 5pm-9:30pm daily, $19-29). Owned and operated by a veteran of Carmel's Casanova, Bistro Moulin serves authentic French and Belgian cuisine in a small, intimate setting. Expect bountiful local seafood, continental-style vegetables, and a wine list that is both Californian and European.

Downtown

In general, downtown is where you will find more casual spots that are less expensive and less anxious to show what they've got than those in Cannery Row. **Restaurant 1833** (500 Hartnell St., 831/643-1833, www.restaurant1833.com, 5:30pm-10pm Sun.-Thurs., 5:30pm-1am Fri.-Sat., $24-39) is the exception. Housed in the historical Stokes Adobe building built in 1833, it has had the foodie community buzzing since it opened in 2011. The food is original and amazing; however, Restaurant 1833 is really about the house. Maintaining the original rooms as dining rooms, the restaurant digs into history to create a romantic mood of Old Monterey. Cocktails are aged in barrels behind the bar, but some dining rooms verge on being *too* dark, and the music can be incongruously loud.

When locals crave seafood, they head to the **Monterey Fish House** (2114 Del Monte Ave., 831/373-4647, 11:30am-2:30pm, 5pm-9:30pm Mon.-Fri., 5pm-9:30pm Sat.-Sun., $15-30). The tiny dining room serves cioppino, fish-and-chips, grilled oysters, and seafood pastas and entrées at almost-reasonable prices.

"Real Good" is what the "R.G." stands for in **R. G. Burgers** (570 Munras Ave., 831/372-4930, www.rgburgers.com, 11am-9pm Sun.-Thurs., 11am-10pm Fri.-Sat., $8-11). And they're not kidding. The menu offers dozens of burgers, dogs, sandwiches, sides, and salads that are cooked to big, juicy, American standards. Then there are the shakes: With over 20 selections, it is almost enough to make your brain freeze.

Pacific Grove

The food in PG is unpretentious, reasonably affordable, and high quality. Undoubtedly, the best location is ★ **Beach House** (620 Ocean View Blvd., 831/375-2345, www.beach-housepg.com, 4pm-close daily, $13-34). At the only restaurant on Lovers Point, every seat is treated to fantastic views of the bay, and the French-inspired food is equally rave-worthy. Prices are extremely reasonable, especially if you come in time for the Sunset Supper Menu. If seated by 5:30pm, you'll pay only $10 for your entrée (including the beloved bacon-wrapped meatloaf) and only $3 for wine or beer. This is one of the best deals on the bay.

After visiting the aquarium, you will likely be picking your seafood selections carefully. At ★ **Passionfish** (701 Lighthouse Ave., 831/655-3311, www.passionfish.net, 5pm-close daily, $16-36) there is no need to worry. Since opening in 1997, Passionfish has been serving sustainable seafood. For those wanting something of the turf instead of the surf, grass-fed tenderloin and "spoonable" 12-hour lamb are both equally beloved.

ACCOMMODATIONS
Under $150

The **Monterey Hostel** (778 Hawthorne St., 831/649-0375, http://montereyhostel.com, dorm $26-37, room $79-199) offers inexpensive accommodations within walking distance of the major attractions of Monterey. The kitchen serves a free pancake breakfast every morning and linens are included. There's no laundry facility on-site, and the dorm rooms can be pretty crowded. But you can't beat the location for the prices.

A cute, small, budget motel, the **Monterey Bay Lodge** (55 Camino Aguajito, 831/372-8057 or 800/558-1900, www.monterey-baylodge.com, $119-199) has small rooms decorated in classic yellows and blues and a sparkling pool with a fountain in the shallow end. It is a perfect base for budget-minded families.

If all you're really looking for is a room with an ocean view, **Borg's Ocean Front Motel** (635 Ocean View Blvd., Pacific Grove, 831/375-2406, www.borgsoceanfrontmotel.com, $114-179) may be the place for you. This independently owned economy hotel sits directly across the street from Lovers Point and the Monterey Bay Coastal Recreation Trail. There is little in the way of amenities aside from a clean bed to lay your head, but with this location and the money you'll save, who needs them?

$150-250

The **Colton Inn** (707 Pacific St., 831/649-6500, www.coltoninn.com, $149-199) offers a touch of class above that of a standard beach-town motel. Located in the midst of downtown Monterey, the inn has queen and king bedrooms that boast pretty appointments. Although you'll find restaurants and historic adobe buildings adjacent to the Colton, expect to drive or take public transit to Cannery Row and the aquarium.

Down along bustling Alvarado Street, the **Monterey Hotel** (406 Alvarado St., 831/375-3184 or 800/966-6490, www.montereyhotel.com, $175-206) has welcomed guests since 1904. The 45 rooms reflect its Victorian heyday with carved details, antique furnishings, and floral prints. Continental breakfast is included in the room rates, and the convenient location makes it easy to explore Old Monterey on foot.

One of the better bargains can be found at the **Casa Munras Hotel and Spa** (700 Munras Ave., 831/375-2411, www.hotelcasa-munras.com, $150-240), a large, updated downtown hotel with historical roots. Part of the hotel's original structure was built in 1824. Although the original adobe walls can be seen in one part of the hotel, the rest of it is decorated with a contemporary chic that feels right at home in Monterey. Book a spa treatment or

Designed by Julia Morgan, Asilomar is feet away from one of the most beautiful beaches on the peninsula. With amenities like a heated pool, in-room massage, and an outdoor fire pit, where you can roast gourmet s'mores, Asilomar is spread out like a compound. To make the most of the location, book one of the Surf rooms, nestled in the dunes with a private deck. Be sure to enjoy Morgan's work by wandering around the grounds and poking your head in the chapel, Social Hall, and Merrill Hall.

Over $250

Monterey visitors looking for elegant accommodations love the ★ **Old Monterey Inn** (500 Martin St., 831/375-8284, www.oldmontereyinn.com, $199-379). The lovely old edifice stands in the midst of mature gardens that blossom all spring and summer. Inside the inn, the 10 rooms carry the garden motif, and all have private bathrooms and some have fireplaces. Additional amenities include a full breakfast (often served in the garden or brought to your room) and a menu of spa treatments that can be enjoyed downstairs in the serene treatment room.

With the arrival of the **InterContinental Clement Monterey** (750 Cannery Row, 831/375-4500 or 877/834-3613, www.intercontinental.com, $299-419), Cannery Row went from being a loud tourist attraction to the center of Monterey's new wave of luxury. The minimal, sleek interior provides a serene respite from the outside noise. There are 110 rooms that hover over the water, while 98 sit across the street, adjoined by a covered walkway bridge. The rooms have chic appointments, but what you are really paying for is the location. There is also convenient access to the stellar restaurant and lounge, spa services, in-room yoga, and child care.

TRANSPORTATION AND SERVICES
Car

Most visitors drive into Monterey via the scenic Highway 1. From San Francisco, the drive

Asilomar Conference Grounds

dine at the Estéban Restaurant, which serves daily breakfast, lunch, and dinner, leaning heavily on Spanish cuisine.

Call well in advance to get a room at ★ **The Jabberwock** (598 Laine St., 831/372-4777, www.jabberwockinn.com, $199-309), a favorite with frequent visitors to Monterey. This Alice in Wonderland-themed B&B is both whimsical and elegant. Expect to find a copy of the namesake novel in your tastefully appointed room. Join the owners at their daily wine-and-cheese reception in the afternoon. Though located up a steep hill, the Jabberwock is within walking distance of Cannery Row and all its adjacent attractions (it's worth the extra exercise to avoid the cost and hassle of parking in the tourist lots).

In Pacific Grove, the ★ **Asilomar Conference Grounds** (800 Asilomar Ave., 888/635-5310, www.visitasilomar.com, $120-284), originally built in 1913 as a YWCA Leadership Camp, is a part of Asilomar State Beach and makes it a mission to be accessible to nonprofit groups and individuals.

down the coast is 120 miles and takes a little less than 2.5 hours. Others opt for taking U.S. 101 south to Prunedale, jumping over to the coast on Highway 156. Highway 68 connects directly to U.S. 101 at Salinas for travelers coming from the south.

Air and Train

For a more leisurely ride, the *Coast Starlight* route of **Amtrak** (11 Station Pl., Salinas, 800/872-7245, www.amtrak.com) travels through Salinas daily. Amtrak provides a bus into downtown Monterey. Along Highway 68, you'll also find the **Monterey Peninsula Airport** (MRY, 200 Fred Kane Dr., 831/648-7000, www.montereyairport.com). The small but efficient airport has daily service by Alaska Airlines, American Airlines, Allegiant, and United. The airport has several national car rental agencies.

Public Transit

Once you're in Monterey, the **Monterey-Salinas Transit** (888/678-2871, http://mst. org, $1.50-2.50) runs routes all over the Monterey Peninsula and into Salinas, Carmel, and Big Sur. Many of the lines connect at the **Monterey Transit Plaza,** conveniently located in downtown Monterey at the intersection of Munras Avenue and Alvarado Street. The agency also operates the free **Monterey Trolley** (10am-7pm daily), which makes stops all around historic Monterey and Cannery Row every 10-15 minutes.

Services

For medical needs, the **Community Hospital of the Monterey Peninsula** (23625 Holman Hwy., 831/624-5311, www. chomp.org) provides emergency services to the area.

DETOURS INLAND
Mission San Juan Bautista

San Juan Bautista has one of the best historic parks in the state and a charming independent main street, and it's surrounded by the fertile fields and bucolic rolling hills that were once a part of San Justo Rancho, a 34,000-acre 1839 Mexican land grant.

Founded in 1797, the **Mission San Juan Bautista** (406 2nd St., San Juan Bautista, 831/623-4528, http://oldmissionsjb.org, 9:30am-4:30pm daily) was the 15th in the chain and one of California's richest missions. It also has the dubious distinction of having had one of the largest Native American populations, which at one point reached 1,200 people. Taken and held largely by force, this mix of Mutsun and Yokut people suffered under the yoke of hard labor and succumbed to many waves of disease. A mass graveyard beside the mission is where an estimated 4,000-5,000 souls are buried.

The mission holds **mass** (8am Mon.-Fri., 5pm Sat., 8:30am and 10am Sun.), and visitors are welcome to stroll the grounds and explore many of the buildings. There is a small museum and gift shop, as well as daily tours (adults $4, seniors $3, children 5 and over $2, under 5 free).

Adjoining the mission is the wonderful **San Juan Bautista State Historic Park** (2nd St. at Washington and Mariposa Sts., 831/623-4881, www.parks.ca.gov, 10am-4:30pm daily, $3). Centered around the large plaza, the park is home to many of the original 19th-century wood and adobe buildings that made up the once-largest town in Central California. Try to time your visit during one of the **Living History Days** (11am-4pm first Sat. of every month), when docents dress in period costumes, giving a taste of what life was like in this Californio (Spanish-Californian) town.

GETTING THERE

San Juan Bautista is located off Highway 156, three miles east of the intersection with U.S. 101. From Monterey, 33 miles away, it takes 40 minutes. Once you reach San Juan Bautista, turn left at the light onto the Alameda. It will take you directly to the historic downtown.

National Steinbeck Center

East of Eden, Steinbeck's 1952 novel, made

Pebble Beach

Polo grounds, manned gates, large estates shrouded in cypress and Spanish moss, and golf courses define Pebble Beach. The land inside the gates of Pebble Beach is some of the area's most beautiful, making the price of admission worth it, at least once.

- **17-Mile Drive** (20 min., $10/vehicle) can introduce you to some of the most beautiful and representative land- and seascapes on the Central Coast. Pay your toll at the gatehouse and you'll get a map of the drive that describes the parks and sights that you will pass as you make your way along the winding coastal road. These include the much-photographed Lone Cypress (now held up by cables), the beaches of Spanish Bay, Pebble Beach's golf courses, and some of the outsized mansions.

GOLF COURSES

Golf has been a major pastime on the peninsula since the late 19th century, and today avid golfers come from around the world to tee off in Pebble Beach. There are two highly exclusive private golf clubs and six public courses.

- **Pebble Beach Golf Links** (1700 17-Mile Dr., 800/877-0597, www.pebblebeach.com, 18-hole par 72, $495) is both the priciest in the region and the most acclaimed. In operation since 1919, it is home to the annual AT&T Pebble Beach National Pro-Am, and has hosted five U.S. Open Championships.

- **Spyglass Hill** (1700 17-Mile Dr., Pebble Beach, 800/654-9300, www.pebblebeach.com, 18-hole par 72, $385) boasts some of the most challenging play even in this golf course-laden region.

- **Links at Spanish Bay** (2700 17-Mile Dr., 800/877-0597, www.pebblebeach.com, 18-hole par 72, $270) evokes Scotland in its setting amid native grasses, waterways, and the never-ending prevailing wind.

- **Peter Hay Golf Course** (1700 17-Mile Dr., 831/622-8723, www.pebblebeach.com, adults $30, students 13-17 $10, children 12 and under free) offers the prestige of teeing off in Pebble Beach but at a fraction of the cost.

ACCOMMODATIONS AND FOOD

The only restaurants in Pebble Beach are attached to the high-priced hotels.

- **Inn at Spanish Bay** (2700 17-Mile Dr., 831/647-7500 or 800/877-0597, www.pebblebeach.com, $650-975) has 269 rooms and suites, each with its own fireplace and modern decor. On-site, you'll find **Peppoli at Pebble Beach** (831/647-7433, 6pm-10pm daily, $25-65); **Roy's at Pebble Beach** (831/647-7423, 5:30pm-10pm daily, $18-45); and **Sticks** (831/647-7470, 6:30am-4pm, 5pm-8pm daily, $10-25), the resort's version of a sports bar. Late-night bites can be found at **Traps** (831/647-7210, 5:30pm-midnight daily, $15-25).

- **Lodge at Pebble Beach** (1700 17-Mile Dr., www.pebblebeach.com, 831/647-7500 or 800/877-0597, $765-980) has 161 modern rooms with fireplaces and lovely views of the ocean and the golf course. Inside are four restaurants and one bar: **Gallery Café** (831/625-8577, 6am-2pm daily, $13-21); **The Bench** (800/877-0597, 11am-10pm daily, $11-31); and **Stillwater Bar & Grill** (831/625-8524, $39-68).

GETTING THERE

The main entry gates to Pebble Beach are: the **Highway 1 Gate** (Hwys. 1 and 68 West); the **Carmel Gate** (N. San Antonio Ave. and 2nd Ave.); and the **Sunset Gate** (Sunset Dr./Hwy. 68 and 17-Mile Dr.) in Pacific Grove. Once you're inside, stick to 17-Mile Drive ($10), as the roads in the forest wind randomly and are perfect for getting lost.

a star out of hard-scrabble Salinas. Over the years, there has been an effort to revitalize the city's historic downtown, but make no mistake about it: Salinas is still a tough town, just as it was in Steinbeck's day.

Standing at the entrance of Salinas's historic Main Street is the **National Steinbeck Center** (1 Main St., 831/775-4721, www.steinbeck.org, 10am-5pm daily, adults $15, seniors and students $9, students 13-17 $8, children 6-12 $6, children under 6 free). You'll learn through engaging, artistic, and interactive displays about the life of John Steinbeck; his body of work, which includes *Cannery Row, Of Mice and Men, East of Eden, Tortilla Flat,* and *The Grapes of Wrath*; and the impact his work had on American culture. The museum showcases Salinas Valley, as well as the lives of its workers, a cause that Steinbeck was passionate about.

GETTING THERE

Salinas sits on U.S. 101, 20 miles and nearly 30 minutes from Monterey via Highway 68, which runs through Salinas, just south of Oldtown. If you are coming south on Highway 1, but not going to the Monterey Peninsula, Highway 183 starts in Castroville, 11 miles north of Monterey, and cuts east through the valley's agricultural fields to Salinas.

★ Pinnacles National Park

East of the Salinas Valley, in the parched hills of the Galiban Mountains, **Pinnacles National Park** (5000 Hwy. 146, Paicines, 831/389-4486, www.nps.gov/pinn, $10) attracts hikers, rock climbers, cave explorers, and birders. True to its name, the 26,000-acre park is studded with huge rock formations jutting up into the sky. The park has two entrances and no road that connects them. Plenty of hiking trails can be found at both entrances. The park is generally warm and dry throughout the year and blazing hot in the summer. It is essential to bring plenty of water.

In western Pinnacles, the **Balconies Cliffs-Cave Loop** (2.4-miles round-trip, easy to moderate) passes through the famous caves and is a great introduction to the area. To see more of the park, make this trail into a loop by taking **High Peaks Trail to Balconies Cave Loop** (8.4 miles, strenuous). You'll get into the heart of the park, but be sure to start with the High Peaks Trail, as the elevation gain is significantly easier. Not only will you need to take a flashlight to navigate through the caves, but it is also important to check if they

San Juan Bautista State Historic Park

Pinnacles National Park

at the east end of the park, where there are beginner to advanced routes. For more information, visit **Friends of Pinnacles** (www.pinnacles.org), an organization dedicated to climbing at Pinnacles.

CAMPING

The **Pinnacles Campground** (831/389-4538, reservations 877/444-6777 or www.recreation.gov, open year-round, tents $23, RVs $36) is located at the east entrance and has 99 tent sites, 36 RV sites, and 14 group sites. Most are shaded by oaks and all come with a picnic table, fire ring, and bathrooms, with showers nearby. To accommodate RVs, there is a dump station, and all sites have electrical hookups. A general store helps with any forgotten food or necessities.

GETTING THERE

Pinnacles has two entrances, but no road that connects them, making the drive from one to the other a two-hour endeavor. To reach the **east entrance** from the north, take U.S. 101 to Highway 25 through the town of Hollister. After another 30 miles, turn right on Highway 146 to the park entrance, which is not much farther. From San Francisco, the trip is 130 miles and takes nearly 2.5 hours. From Monterey, it is 75 miles and 1.5 hours.

For the **west entrance,** continue south on U.S. 101, past Salinas to Highway 146 in Soledad. Take Highway 146 east for a very slow 14 miles. There are no services at this entrance. The trip from Monterey, via Highway 68, is 60 miles, taking a little over an hour.

are open. The caves can close because of high water from rain or when bat colonies are raising their young, generally mid-May-mid-July.

More trails can be found at the east end of the park. You'll get a bit of everything, including a reservoir, on the **Moses Spring to Rim Trail Loop** (2.2 miles, moderate). After climbing up the peaks, you'll enjoy the meadows and shade of sycamore, buckeye, and oak trees on the **High Peaks to Bear Gulch Loop** (6.7 miles, strenuous). Most of the park's best **rock climbing** can be found

Carmel

Carmel's landscape is divided into three distinct parts: Carmel-by-the-Sea, Carmel Valley, and the Carmel Highlands. The village of Carmel-by-the-Sea sits above white-sand beaches, nestled in a forest of pine and cypress. Carmel Valley is the long east-west valley carved by the Carmel River. About five miles south of town on the way to Big Sur, the Carmel Highlands stand perched above the rich Carmel Bay. The jewel of this area is the splendid Point Lobos State Natural Reserve.

SIGHTS

★ Carmel Mission

The **Carmel Mission** (3080 Rio Rd., 831/624-1271, www.carmelmission.org, 9:30am-7pm daily, adults $6.50, seniors $4, children 7-18 $2, children under 7 free), formally called the San Carlos Borromeo de Carmelo Mission, was Father Junípero Serra's personal favorite among his California mission churches. He lived, worked, and eventually died here, and visitors today can see a replica of his cell. A working Catholic parish remains part of the complex, so be respectful when taking the self-guided tour. The highlight of the complex is the church, with its gilded altar front, its shrine to the Virgin Mary, the grave of Father Serra, and an ancillary chapel dedicated to the memory of Father Serra. Round out your visit by walking out to the gardens to admire the flowers and fountains and to read the grave markers in the small cemetery.

Tor House

When poet Robinson Jeffers began hauling great granite boulders up from the beach to this spot in 1919, Carmel was young and Carmel Point was a barren and treeless out-cropping. Jeffers named the family home he built **Tor House** (26304 Ocean View Ave., 831/624-1813, www.torhouse.org, tours hourly 10am-3pm Fri.-Sat., adults $10, students 12 and over $5, children under 12 not permitted) for its rocky location. A year later he began construction on Hawk Tower, named for a hawk that he saw daily as he built the Irish-style stone structure. It was here where Jeffers wrote his most enduring work.

Two days a week, visitors can tour the stone

Carmel Mission

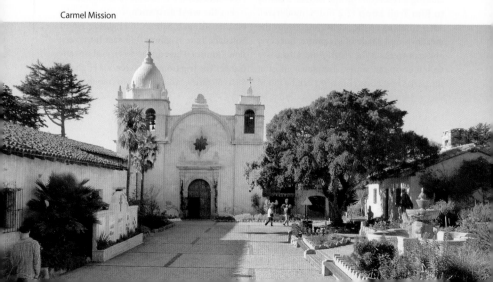

cottage and tower, stroll the lush English garden, and imagine what it was like to live here surrounded only by the forest and the pounding surf, before electricity (installed in 1949), during the innocent and dark romance of this poetic era.

Carmel Beach

The mile-long **Carmel Beach** (Ocean Ave. and Scenic Rd., 831/620-2000, 6am-10pm daily) lies at the foot of Ocean Avenue and is known for its sparkly white sand that squeaks beneath your feet. Its aqua-blue waters teem with life, including sea otters, dolphins, surfers, and bodyboarders. There is a price for the beauty, though, as the beach is often windy and rarely offers a goose-pimple-free day of sunbathing. Dogs and small bonfires are allowed on the beach south of 10th Avenue. You can park at a relatively large lot at the base of Ocean Avenue or along the one-way Scenic Road, which also has a pleasant footpath above the beach to catch the views without getting your shoes sandy.

Around the point from Carmel Beach is **Carmel River State Beach** (Scenic Rd. and Carmelo St., 831/649-2836, www.parks.ca.gov, sunrise-sunset daily, free). Sheltered from the wind and with stellar views of Point Lobos,

this is a favorite with families. The beach is less well-known than the popular Carmel Beach, making it the less crowded option on the rare hot and sunny day.

Point Lobos State Natural Reserve

Jutting out into the sea three miles south of Carmel, **Point Lobos State Natural Reserve** (Hwy. 1 and Point Lobos St., 831/624-4909, www.parks.ca.gov, 8am-sunset daily, $10) is filled with ragged cliffs, hidden coves, rich marine ecosystems, lovely meadows, and dense pine and cypress forests. Hiking trails crisscross the reserve, the most spectacular of which hug the coastline, including the **North Shore Trail** (0.75 mile), which rises dramatically above the crashing sea, and the **Cypress Grove Trail** (2.4 miles), a loop that passes through one of only two wild groves of Monterey cypress. **South Shore Trail** (1 mile) runs along the southern edge of the point. Take it to **Bird Island Trail** (0.8 mile), where you will get a view of not only a loud and messy bird colony, but also China Cove, one of the most splendid sites at Point Lobos. A popular stroll, particularly if you walk into the park, is the **Granite Point Trail** (0.5 mile, easy) along Whalers Cove. Not

Carmel River State Beach

Side Trip to Carmel Valley

This narrow valley, carved by the lazy Carmel River, stands on its own as a sublime destination. Several world-class golf courses blanket the valley floor, while vines of Syrah, merlot, and pinot noir climb the hills.

WINERIES

- **Chateau Julien** (8940 Carmel Valley Rd., 831/624-2600, www.chateaujulien.com, 8am-5pm Mon.-Fri., 11am-5pm Sat.-Sun., $15): Call ahead and reserve a spot on the twice-daily complimentary vineyard and winery tour, which concludes with a special tasting outside on the flagstone patio.

- **Joyce Vineyards** (19 E. Carmel Valley Rd., 831/659-2885, www.joycevineyards.com, 11:30am-5pm daily, $10): The tasting fee lets guests sample seven vintages, a great bargain for any winery.

- **Cowgirl Winery** (25 Pilot Rd., 831/298-7030, http://cowgirlwinery.com, 11:30am-5pm Sun.-Thurs., 11:30am-6pm Fri.-Sat., $13-20): Enjoy a bottle at one of the outside tables, surrounded by cowboy gear and scratching chickens (that you can feed for $0.25).

GOLF COURSES

- **Rancho Cañada Golf Club** (4860 Carmel Valley Rd., 800/536-9459, www.ranchocanada. com, $25-70): The two 18-hole courses, the East Course and the West Course, vary in difficulty and length and cross back and forth over the river.

- **Quail Lodge** (8205 Valley Greens Dr., 831/624-2888, www.quaillodge.com, $50-185): This par-71 championship course provides some challenges, but is comfortably walkable.

- **Carmel Valley Ranch** (1 Old Ranch Rd., 831/620-6406, $95-175): A championship 18-hole course, this is the only Northern California course designed by Pete Dye.

SPA

- **Refuge** (27300 Rancho San Carlos Rd., 831/620-7360, www.refuge.com, 10am-10pm daily, $44): At this outdoor, coed spa, the focus is on the hot/cold plunge, silence, and Adirondack chairs circling the fire pits. Book a massage ($109, includes price of soak) in advance.

From Carmel, the valley is due east along Carmel Valley Road, which intersects with Highway 1 at the south end of town. You may also reach Carmel Valley from Highway 68, which connects Salinas and U.S. 101 to Monterey. Simply take the Los Laureles Grade south and over the hill. Be sure you have good brakes, as it is a steep descent.

only will you get a taste of the diverse landscape and wildlife, but you can also visit the **Whalers Cabin Museum** (9am-5pm daily), which shows off the history of Point Lobos with artifacts from Native Americans and Chinese, Japanese, and Portuguese whalers and anglers.

If you're willing to don a wetsuit and plunge into the 55°F water, you'll see the other half of Point Lobos's protected areas. The Point Lobos State Marine Reserve is nearly six square miles and is home to 70-foot-high kelp forests, wolf eels, rockfish, crabs, abalone, and giant sunflower stars, along with seals, sea otters, and the occasional shark. Diving is permitted at **Whalers Cove** and **Blue Fish Cove,** but permits (831/624-8413, http://pointlobos.org) are required. These can be obtained at the front gate, but reservations are strongly recommended, as only a limited number of divers are allowed per day. It's best to call or make a reservation online.

Kayaking and boating are also allowed, and there is a boat launch at Whalers Cove, an easy entrance.

FOOD

You won't find Starbucks or Peet's in Carmel, but you will find the **Carmel Valley Roasting Company** (Ocean Ave. and Lincoln St., 831/626-2913, www.carmel-coffeeroasters.com, 6am-6pm Sun.-Thurs., 6am-7pm Fri.-Sat., $5). Coffee, espresso, and pastries are served, and a few tables fill the delightful shop.

If the weather is right, a picnic on the beach may win out over a bistro lunch. **Bruno's Market** (Junipero Ave. and 6th Ave., 831/624-3821, www.brunosmarket.com, 7am-8pm daily, $8) is the local pick for provisions, which include huge deli sandwiches, premade salads, and daily barbecue. The Italian **Salumeria Luca** (Dolores St. and 7th Ave., 831/625-0264, http://salumerialuca.com, 11am-6pm Sun.-Thurs., 11am-7pm Fri.-Sat., $8) has a deli case stocked with Italian cheese and house-made *salumi*, cold sandwiches, grilled panini, and pizza by the slice.

Serving breakfast in a cuter-than-cute Carmel cottage is the **Tuck Box** (Dolores St. and 7th Ave., 831/624-3396, www.tuckbox.com, 7:30am-2:30pm daily, $6-12). A Carmel institution, the Tuck Box has been around in some form since 1931. Today it serves straightforward and extremely affordable breakfast and lunch. You can also swing by for afternoon tea.

The local joint is **Katy's Place** (Mission St. and 6th Ave., 831/624-0199, www.katysplacecarmel.com, 7am-2pm daily, $10-23). Katy's serves only breakfast and lunch, but the menu is huge. Burgers, salads, quesadillas, crab cakes, omelets, and pancakes all come in a wide variety, but the true king is the eggs Benedict. Portions are hearty, as are the prices, but the food is excellent.

The king of Carmel dining is **Casanova** (5th Ave. and Mission St., 831/625-0501, 11:30am-3pm, 5pm-10pm Sun.-Thurs., 11:30am-3pm, 5pm-10:30pm Fri.-Sat.,

$22-49). The rebuilt old house is designed after a Belgian farmhouse, with low ceilings and intimate dining rooms. The cuisine is rustic French-Italian and is made in-house, including all the pasta and bread. Reservations, even for lunch, are strongly encouraged.

★ **La Bicyclette** (Dolores St. and 7th Ave., 831/622-9899, www.labicycletterestaurant.com, 8am-11am, 11:30am-3:30pm, 5pm-10pm daily, $14-26) is owned by the same folks as Casanova. The food is rustic Italian-French, with an emphasis on thin-crust, wood-fired pizza. The simple margherita and the butternut squash, speck, and Gruyère pizzas are standouts.

ACCOMMODATIONS

Pink **La Playa Hotel** (Camino Real and 8th Ave., 831/293-6100 or 800/582-8900, www.laplayahotel.com, $249-399) is considered by many to be the "Grande Dame of Carmel." Built in 1905, it's only blocks from the beach and boasts manicured gardens, a giant outdoor chess set, and a secluded pool. Splurge for an oceanview room to experience the best of the hotel. Indulge in the complimentary champagne breakfast, with a bounty of pastries, hot egg dishes, fruit, and an expansive waffle bar, out on the patio.

The **Cypress Inn** (Lincoln St. and 7th St., 831/624-3871 or 800/443-7443, www.cypressinn.com, $249-549) competes with La Playa for the most charm and luxury. Built in the Mediterranean style of the day, it also has a touch of old Hollywood thanks to Doris Day, its co-owner. Day is a well-known animal rights advocate, and her hotel is one of the most pet-friendly around.

Owned since 1986 by Clint Eastwood, ★ **Mission Ranch** (26270 Dolores St., 831/624-6436 or 800/538-8221, www.mission-ranchcarmel.com, $125-300) sits on 22 acres (some with grazing sheep) and has 31 rooms spread over 10 buildings, a well-respected restaurant, and spectacular views of Point Lobos and River Beach. There are plenty of rooms where you can spend a chunk of your rent payment, but the ranch also offers a number of "economy rooms" in the Main Barn and Farmhouse. Either way, your stay will be graced with historical charm, great views, and a quiet setting.

Despite its playful name, the cliff-top **Tickle Pink Inn** (155 Highlands Dr., 831/624-1244, www.ticklepinkinn.com, $314) offers tasteful luxury. Each room has a view of the ocean, an array of high-end furniture and linens, and all the top-end amenities you'd expect from a distinctive Carmel hostelry. For a special treat, shell out for the spa bath suite and watch the ocean while you soak in the tub with your sweetie.

TRANSPORTATION AND SERVICES

If you've made it to the Monterey Peninsula by car, getting to Carmel is a piece of cake. Simply take Highway 1 south and then turn right on Ocean Avenue into the middle of downtown Carmel. **Monterey-Salinas Transit** (MST, 888/678-2871, http://mst.org, $2.50) runs a bus daily from Monterey to downtown Carmel. For major or minor issues, head for the **Community Hospital of Monterey** (23625 Holman Hwy., Monterey, 831/622-2746, www.chomp.org).

Big Sur

Big Sur is the spectacular collision of land and sea between Carmel and Cambria, home to coastal redwoods, thermal hot springs, jade deposits, and, some would say, a spiritual energy vortex. This 90-mile stretch of road was completed in the 1930s and many of the inns and restaurants along it retain a midcentury hideaway atmosphere. There are plenty of places to jump off the road and explore the beaches and backcountry.

TOP EXPERIENCE

★ BIG SUR COAST HIGHWAY

The **Big Sur Coast Highway,** a 90-mile stretch of Highway 1, runs along jagged cliffs and rocky beaches, through dense redwood forest, over historical bridges, and past innumerable parks. Construction on this stretch of road was completed in the 1930s, connecting

Big Sur Coast Highway

Cambria to Carmel. You can start at either of these towns and spend a whole day making your way to the other end of the road. The road has plenty of wide turnouts set into picturesque cliffs, making it easy to stop and admire the glittering ocean and stunning wooded cliffs running right out to the water. Be sure to bring a camera—you'll find yourself wanting to take photos every mile for hours on end.

Garrapata State Park

Note: At time of publication, this park was closed due to the 2016 Soberanes Fire. Please visit the state park website for information before planning a trip.

Covering a long, thin line of coast and steep terrain to the east of Highway 1, **Garrapata State Park** (Hwy. 1, 6.7 miles south of Carmel, 831/624-4909, www.parks.ca.gov) is the first state park south of Point Lobos.. With few facilities, rely on numbered gates for orientation. To access the **Garrapata State Beach,** use gates 18 and 19.

The **Soberanes Point Trails** wind through the windswept area and offer wonderful views of the coastline and coastal inhabitants, including seals, sea otters, and sea lions, and migrating whales in the winter.

This area is accessible at gates 8, 9, and 10. For something more strenuous, cross the highway. Just north of Soberanes Point, **Soberanes Canyon Trail** and the **Rocky Ridge Trail** together form a strenuous 4.5-mile loop through a trickling creek, lush forest, fields of poppies, and unrelenting chaparral. If you're feeling up to it, take the 1.5-mile spur **Peak Trail** to Doud Peak. At 1,977 feet, it is a truly breathtaking hike.

Bixby Bridge

The picturesque **Bixby Bridge** (Hwy. 1) is one of the most photographed bridges in the state. The cement open-spandrel arched bridge was built in the early 1930s as part of a massive project that completed Highway 1 through Big Sur, connecting the road through California from north to south. Today you can pull out north or south of the bridge to take photos, or just admire the attractive span and Bixby Creek flowing into the Pacific far below.

Point Sur Lighthouse

Sitting lonely and isolated out on its 360-foot rock, the **Point Sur Lighthouse** (Hwy. 1 at milepost 54.1, 831/625-2006, www.pointsur. org, tours 10am Sat.-Sun., 1pm Wed. Nov.-Mar., 10am, 2pm Sat. and Wed., 10am Sun.

Garrapata State Park

MONTEREY AND BIG SUR
BIG SUR

Big Sur

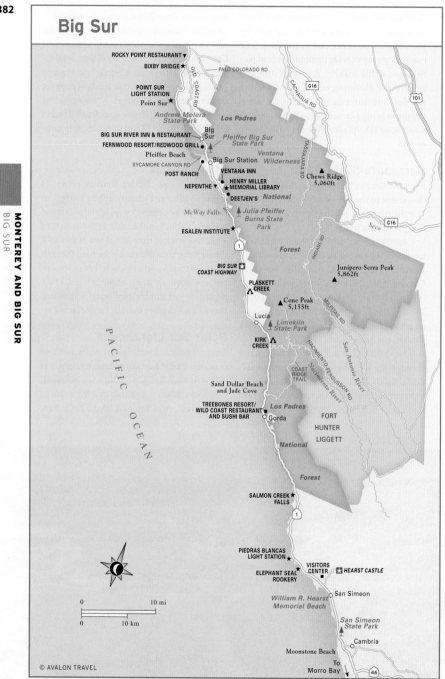

ROCKY POINT RESTAURANT ▼
BIXBY BRIDGE ★
PALO COLORADO RD
CACHAGUA RD
G16
101
POINT SUR
LIGHT STATION ★
Point Sur ★
Andrew Molera State Park
Los Padres
BIG SUR RIVER INN & RESTAURANT
FERNWOOD RESORT/REDWOOD GRILL
Big Sur
Pfeiffer Big Sur State Park
Pfeiffer Beach
Ventana Wilderness
SYCAMORE CANYON RD
Big Sur Station
POST RANCH
VENTANA INN
Chews Ridge 5,060ft
TASAJARA RD
HENRY MILLER MEMORIAL LIBRARY ★
NEPENTHE ▼
DEETJEN'S
National
McWay Falls
Julia Pfeiffer Burns State Park
ESALEN INSTITUTE ★
G16
Seco
1
Forest
Junipero Serra Peak 5,862ft
SAN ANTONIO RD
BIG SUR COAST HIGHWAY
PLASKETT CREEK ⛺
Cone Peak 5,155ft
MILPITAS RD
Lucia
Limekiln State Park
KIRK CREEK ⛺
NACIMIENTO FERGUSSON RD
San Antonio River
NACIMIENTO RD
San Antonio River
COAST RIDGE TRAIL
Nacimiento River
Sand Dollar Beach and Jade Cove
TREEBONES RESORT/ WILD COAST RESTAURANT AND SUSHI BAR
Los Padres
Gorda
FORT HUNTER LIGGETT
National
Forest
SALMON CREEK ★ FALLS
1
PACIFIC OCEAN
PIEDRAS BLANCAS LIGHT STATION ★
VISITORS CENTER ✚ HEARST CASTLE
ELEPHANT SEAL ROOKERY
San Simeon
William R. Hearst Memorial Beach
San Simeon State Park
Cambria
Moonstone Beach
To Morro Bay
46

0   10 mi
0   10 km

© AVALON TRAVEL

Apr.-June and Oct., 10am, 2pm Sat. and Wed., 10am Thurs. and Sun. July-Aug., adults $12, children 6-17 $5, under 6 free) has been keeping watch over ships near the rocky waters of Big Sur since 1889. It's the only complete 19th-century light station in California that you can visit, and even here, access is severely limited.

You can't make a reservation for a Point Sur tour (but calling ahead is encouraged), so you must park your car off Highway 1 on the west side by the farm gate and wait for the tour guide. **Tours** are filled on a first-come, first-served basis, so be on time and ready to go. You will be led to the base of the paved road and walk for 0.5 mile, then climb a number of stairs to the light station (wear comfortable shoes). The tour lasts three hours, and you'll get to explore the restored keepers' homes and service buildings and walk out to the cliff edge. Expect to see a great variety of wildlife, from brilliant wildflowers in the spring and gray whales in the winter to flocks of pelicans at any time of year. Be sure to dress in layers; it can be sunny and hot or foggy and cold (and sometimes both on the same tour!), no matter the time of year.

The farm gate is locked and there's no access to the light station without a tour group.

If you need special assistance for your tour or have questions about accessibility, call 831/667-0528 as far in advance as possible of your visit to make arrangements. No strollers, food, pets, or smoking are allowed on light station property. Moonlight tours are also available every full moon for a magical, if spooky, experience. Check the website for schedules.

Andrew Molera State Park

Note: At time of publication, this park was closed due to the 2016 Soberanes Fire. Please visit the state park website for information before planning a trip

The first "Big Sur" park you'll encounter south from Carmel is **Andrew Molera State Park** (Hwy. 1, 22 miles south of Carmel, 831/667-2315, www.parks.ca.gov, $8). Once home to small camps of Esselen Native Americans, this area eventually became the Molera Ranch. It was turned over to the California State Parks system in 1965. Today the **Molera Ranch House Museum** (11am-3pm Sat.-Sun. June-Aug.) displays stories of the life and times of Big Sur's pioneers and artists as well as the wildlife and plants of the region. Take the road toward the horse tours to get to the ranch house. To learn more

Andrew Molera State Park

about the natural history of the region, visit the **Big Sur Discovery Center** (831/624-1202, www.ventanaws.org, 10am-4pm Sat.-Sun. June-Aug.) nearby. Interactive exhibits and enthusiastic volunteers tell the story of the flora and fauna that call Big Sur home.

The park has numerous hiking trails that run down to the beach and up into the forest along the river—many are open to biking and horseback riding as well. The beach is a one-mile walk down the easy, multi-use **Trail Camp.** From there, climb out on the **Headlands Trail,** a 0.25-mile loop, for a beautiful view from the headlands. If you prefer to get a better look at the Big Sur River, take the flat, moderate **Bobcat Trail** (5.5 miles round-trip) and perhaps a few of its ancillary loops.

There are no services, so bring plenty of water and snacks.

Pfeiffer Big Sur State Park

Note: At time of publication, this park was closed due to the 2016 Soberanes Fire. Please visit the state park website for information before planning a trip

The most developed park in Big Sur is **Pfeiffer Big Sur State Park** (47225 Hwy. 1, 831/667-2315, www.parks.ca.gov, $8), which has the Big Sur Lodge, a restaurant and café, a shop, an amphitheater, a softball field, plenty of hiking trails, and lovely redwood-shaded campsites. The park is in a coastal redwood forest, with a network of roads through the trees and along the Big Sur River.

Pfeiffer Big Sur has the tiny **Ernest Ewoldsen Memorial Nature Center** (open seasonally, call for hours), which features taxidermy examples of local wildlife, and the **Homestead Cabin,** once the home to part of the Pfeiffer family—the first European immigrants to settle in Big Sur.

No bikes or horses are allowed on the trails in this park, which makes it quite peaceful for hikers. For a starter walk, take the easy, 0.7-mile **Nature Trail** in a loop from Day Use Parking Lot 2. For a longer stroll, head out on the popular **Pfeiffer Falls Trail** (1.5 miles round-trip, moderate). You'll find stairs on the steep sections and footbridges across the creek, then a lovely platform at the base of the 60-foot waterfall, where you can rest and relax midway through your hike.

Pfeiffer Beach

Certainly not the biggest beach, **Pfeiffer Beach** (Sycamore Canyon Rd., 805/434-1995, www.fs.usda.gov, 9am-8pm daily, $10) is

Pfeiffer Big Sur State Park

McWay Falls

visitors to browse, pour themselves a cup of coffee, and meditate on art and beauty. The library offers a glimpse into the "real" world of Big Sur as a spread-out artists' colony that has inspired countless works. Just look for the hand-painted sign on the east side of Highway 1.

Julia Pfeiffer Burns State Park

One of the best-known and easiest hikes in all of the Big Sur region sits in **Julia Pfeiffer Burns State Park** (Hwy. 1, 12 miles south of Pfeiffer Big Sur State Park, 831/667-2315, www.parks.ca.gov). The **Overlook Trail** runs less than 0.75 mile round-trip, along a level, wheelchair-accessible boardwalk. Stroll under Highway 1, past the Pelton wheelhouse, and out to the observation deck and the stunning view of **McWay Falls.** The waterfall cascades year-round off a cliff and onto the beach of a remote cove, where the water wets the sand and trickles out into the bright-blue sea. Adding to the beauty is the remaining terrace of the McWay Waterfall House, built in the 1920s. If the parking lot for the state park is full, there are plenty of pullouts along Highway 1, where the trail is accessible from the road. However, use caution.

Limekiln State Park

At the southern end of Big Sur, **Limekiln State Park** (63025 Hwy. 1, 805/434-1996, www.parks.ca.gov, $8), named for the lime-kilns that cured the mountain's limestone (used in San Francisco's earliest brick buildings), offers a couple easy strolls through this redwood-rich gulch. From the parking lot, the **Limekiln Trail** (1 mile round-trip, easy) ventures back into the canyon where the enormous furnaces still stand. Halfway there, **Falls Trail** is a short spur to a 100-foot waterfall. Also leaving from the parking lot, the **Hare Trail** follows the creek for a gentle 0.5-mile stroll.

Sand Dollar Beach

To surf Big Sur, the place to go is **Sand Dollar**

undoubtedly the best-known beach in Big Sur and certainly its most photographed. Located directly across Highway 1 from Big Sur Station, it sits at the end of a pretty, slightly residential coastal road, nestled in a cove. From the parking lot, you'll walk through a canopy of cypress, then out to the beach. Here, huge rock formations, with arches and caves, keep the brilliant blue waves foamy and alive while the white sand, flecked with red and black, changes color from every angle.

Henry Miller Memorial Library

It is quite possible that the coolest bookstore on the Central Coast (for avant-garde literary fiction, at least) is found tucked in the redwoods, near the edge of a cliff. The **Henry Miller Memorial Library** (Hwy. 1, 0.25 mile south of Nepenthe, 831/667-2574, www.henrymiller.org, 11am-6pm daily) is neither a memorial nor a library. It is not even the home where Miller lived and worked for the 18 years he was in Big Sur. Instead, the bookstore, sitting in a sun-dappled meadow, encourages

Beach (Hwy. 1, 60 miles south of Carmel and across from Plaskett Creek Campground, 805/434-1996, 9am-8pm daily, $10). For surfers, the waves break far enough from shore for a pleasant ride, and low tide exposes a cave to the north, for adventurous explorers. The longest stretch of sand in Big Sur, this beach is perfect for long walks, beachcombing, and sunbathing (weather permitting, of course).

Jade Cove

To add to the splendors of the Big Sur coast is the presence of jade along the shore. Jade Cove (Hwy. 1, 2 miles south of Sand Dollar Beach) has, over the years, attracted beachcombers and divers to its rocky shore in search of the semiprecious stone. You won't find any impressive pieces like in the art galleries of Big Sur, but searching may yield a few small treasures, and you can still reach out and touch a boulder shot through with jade. A road sign marks the area, but there's not much in the way of a formal parking lot or anything else to denote the treasures of this jagged stretch of Big Sur. Park in the dirt/gravel strip off the road and head past the fence and into the park. Once you get to the edge of the cliff, the short trail gets rough. It's only 0.25 mile, but it's almost straight down a rocky, slippery cliff. Good shoes are a must, and keep your hands free for support. Don't try to climb down if you're not in reasonably good condition. For mineral hunting that is a little less hair-raising, the rocky beach at Willow Creek (Hwy. 1, 62 miles south of Carmel) has jade scattered about. Better yet, the descent from the parking lot is an easy walk, doable in flip-flops.

RECREATION
Ventana Wilderness

Note: At time of publication, this area was subject to the 2016 Soberanes Fire. Please visit the forest service website for information before planning a trip

The vast Ventana Wilderness (831/385-5434 or 831/667-2315, www.fs.usda.gov) stretches nearly 250,000 acres from Palo Colorado Road, east of the Bixby Bridge, to the rangeland below Hearst Castle. There are 273 miles of trails that cross up, over, and through its steep hillsides, sharp ridges, and dramatic V-shaped valleys with waterfalls and thermal springs. You'll find abundant wildlife, including condors, black bears, and rattlesnakes, and 55 designated primitive campsites where you can recharge after a long day of hiking.

Trails are geared toward backpackers and offer few scenic loops. Still, there are plenty of opportunities for day hikers. From Bottchers Gap (end of Palo Colorado Rd., 831/667-2315, $5), the Skinner Ridge Trail is a popular option, traveling through redwood forests and rocky canyons and up to hilly, challenging terrain. A spur takes you to Mount Carmel (9.8-miles round-trip, strenuous). This is a tough hike, but the rewards are views of Monterey Bay.

Most of the trails in Ventana Wilderness are strenuous and exposed. Plan with care, and bring plenty of water, sunscreen, layers, and even a map. Getting lost out here is no joke. For help planning your adventure, call or visit the rangers at the multiagency Big Sur Station (just south of Pfeiffer Big Sur State Park, 831/667-2315, 9am-4pm daily).

Scuba

There's not much for beginner divers in Big Sur, but if you've got some underwater experience, you'll want to bring your gear when you visit. Expect cold water. Temperatures range in the mid-50s in the shallows, dipping into the 40s as you dive deeper down. Visibility is 20-30 feet, though rough conditions can diminish this significantly. The best season for clear water is September-November.

The biggest and most interesting dive locale here is the Julia Pfeiffer Burns State Park (Hwy. 1, 12 miles south of Pfeiffer Big Sur, 831/667-2315, www.parks.ca.gov, sunrise-sunset daily). You'll need to acquire a special permit at Big Sur Station and prove your experience to dive at this protected underwater park. The park, along with the rest of the Big Sur coast, is part of the Monterey Bay

National Marine Sanctuary. Enter the water at Partington Point, and check out the ecosystems as you go, beginning with the busy life of the beach sands and heading out to the rocky reefs, then into the lush green kelp forests.

Divers at access-hostile **Jade Cove** (Hwy. 1, 2 miles south of Sand Dollar Beach) aren't usually interested in cute, colorful nudibranchs or even majestic gray whales. Jade Cove divers come to stalk the wily jade pebbles and rocks that cluster in this special spot. The semiprecious stone striates the coastline right here, and storms tear clumps of jade out of the cliffs. Much of it settles just off the shore of the tiny cove, and divers hope to find jewelry-quality stones to sell for a huge profit.

If you're looking for a guided scuba dive of the Big Sur region, contact **Adventure Sports Unlimited** (303 Potrero St., no. 15, Santa Cruz, 831/458-3648, www.asudoit.com).

Spas

To sink into the spiritual vortex of Big Sur, book a massage at the **Esalen Institute** (55000 Hwy. 1, 888/837-2536, www.esalen. org). Founded in 1962, Esalen's mission is to delve into the human condition. Seekers and neophytes come from around the world to attend retreats and workshops at this spiritual and ecological think tank, also known as "The New Age Harvard." To dip your toes into Esalen's healing ways, visit the institute's mineral-fed hot tubs perched over the Pacific. To do so, you'll need to make an appointment for a **massage** (831/837-2536 or 831/667-3002, 11am or 4pm Mon.-Thurs and Sat., 11am Fri. and Sun., $165). You are granted access to the hot tubs for an hour before and an hour after your 75-minute treatment session. If you just want to sit in the mineral water, you'll need to stay up very late. Inexpensive access ($25) to the Esalen tubs begins on a first-come, first-served basis at 1am and ends at 3am daily (reservations 831/667-3047). Many locals consider the sleep deprivation well worth it to enjoy the mineral waters and the stunning astronomical shows. The tubs are clothing-optional.

Physical exertion is one side of the Big Sur experience; relaxation is the other. At **The Spa at Ventana** (48123 Hwy. 1, 831/667-4222, www.ventanainn.com, 10am-7pm daily, $140/50-minute massage), you can indulge in a soothing massage, purifying body treatment, or rejuvenating or beautifying facial. If you're a guest of Ventana, you can choose to have your spa treatment in the comfort of your own room or out on your private deck.

FOOD
Casual Dining

The first restaurant you'll find south of the Carmel Highlands is the isolated **Rocky Point Restaurant** (36700 Hwy. 1, 831/624-2933, www.rocky-point.com, 11:30am-8pm daily, $15-36). Built in 1947, it offers your standard American lunch and dinner, albeit in a world-class setting.

In the heart of Big Sur, you'll find a selection of ultracasual restaurants attached to hotels that offer good, reasonably priced food, frothy pints of beer, and shady creek-side tables. The **Redwood Grill** (Hwy. 1, 831/667-2129, www.fernwoodbigsur.com, 11am-9pm daily, $15-205) at Fernwood Resort looks and feels like a grill in the woods ought to: rustic, in need of some repair, and like a living room for locals. Burgers, fish-and-chips, pizza, and barbecue ribs go perfectly with a cold beer from the bar.

A locals' choice is the **Restaurant at the River Inn** (46840 Hwy. 1, 831/667-2700 or 800/548-3610, www.bigsurriverinn.com, 8am-9pm daily, $15-33), which serves big plates of standard American breakfast, lunch, and dinner fare. If you can, order the Roadhouse Ribs at the backyard barbecue and enjoy the sunshine on the creek-side porch. If you need something on the go, the inn's General Store has a **burrito bar** (11am-7pm daily) where you can build your own hearty lunch.

Serving three meals each day to lodge guests and passersby, the **Big Sur Lodge Café and Restaurant** (47225 Hwy. 1, 800/242-4787, www.bigsurlodge.com, 8am-9pm daily, $14-32) has a dining room as well as a cute espresso bar and deli out front. The dining room dishes up a full menu of American classics for every meal, or you can grab a quick sandwich and cappuccino to go.

The ★ **Big Sur Bakery** (47540 Hwy. 1, 831/667-0520, www.bigsurbakery.com, 9am-3:30pm Mon., 9am-3:30pm 5:30pm-close Tues.-Fri., 10:30am-2:30pm, 5:30pm-close Sat.-Sun., $17-32) might sound like a casual, walk-up spot, and, sure enough, you can get a homemade jelly donut or a flaky croissant sandwich along with a latte. But in the dining room, an elegant surprise awaits diners. Be sure to make reservations so you can experience the wood-fired pizza, pan-roasted halibut, and grilled octopus.

Since 1949, ★ **Nepenthe** (48510 Hwy. 1, 831/667-2345, www.nepenthebigsur.com, 11:30am-10pm daily, $15-45) has been entertaining guests in its cool midcentury modern building and out on the terraced patio warmed by the open fire pit, overlooking perhaps the most brilliant vista in Big Sur. The menu is short, but carefully selected, and the full bar pours a healthy variety of beer, wine, and cocktails. The downside of Nepenthe is the crowds. If you stop in on a sunny weekend or during the summer, expect a wait. Luckily, you can lounge on the patio with a drink from the bar. Should the wait be too excruciating, the seasonal **Café Kevah** (Mar.-Jan., $10-16) serves soup, salads, and sandwiches, along with coffee and pastries, from a walk-up window.

The best breakfast can be had at ★ **Deetjens** (48865 Hwy. 1, 831/667-2378, www.deetjens.com, 8am-noon, 6pm-9pm Mon.-Fri., 8am-12:30pm, 6pm-9pm Sat.-Sun., $24-42). The funky dining room, with its mismatched tables, dark wooden chairs, and cluttered wall decor, accentuates the high quality of the cuisine served. Dinner veers toward the epicurean, with plates of seared duck and filet mignon, but breakfast is more down-to-earth, filled with fresh eggs, bright berries, and maple syrup.

Past Deetjens, dining options get slimmer. With a perpetual wait for a table at Treebone's

Wild Coast Restaurant and Sushi Bar (71895 Hwy. 1, 805/927-2390, www.treebonesresort.com, noon-2pm, 6pm-8:30pm daily, sushi bar 5:30pm-8:30pm Wed.-Mon. Mar.-Dec., $25-33), this eco-lodge is doing something right. Utilizing the large garden, the restaurant serves a select menu of locally inspired dishes. The 12-seat sushi bar delivers a dizzying array of sashimi and sushi rolls. Can't get enough of the view? Take a table outside on the wraparound deck.

Two options on this remote part of the coast are **Lucia Lodge Restaurant** (62400 Hwy. 1, 831/667-2718 or 866/424-4787, www.lucialodge.com, 11am-4pm, 5pm-8pm daily, $15-32) and **Ragged Point Inn** (19019 Hwy. 1, 805/927-4502, http://raggedpointinn.com, 8am-11am, noon-4pm, 5pm-9pm daily, $22-40). Both boast spectacular views and French-inspired California cuisine. The fish-and-chips at the Lucia Lodge are rave-worthy, and the cozy dining room, built in the 1930s, is charming. At the Ragged Point Inn, lunch is the best deal, as the eclectic menu is the most affordable and appeals to more palates. In summer, the restaurant opens a sandwich stand, serving classic American fast food along with locally made ice cream, while live music keeps the mood festive.

Fine Dining

You don't need to be a guest at the Ventana to enjoy a refined dinner at the **Restaurant at Ventana** (Hwy. 1, 831/667-4242, www.ventanainn.com, 7:30am-4:30pm, 6pm-9pm daily, $28-38). The spacious dining room boasts a wood fire, open kitchen, and comfortable banquettes with throw pillows to lounge against. Request a table outside to take in the environs. The dining room also has great views, along with a forest of wood lining the walls, floors, and bars.

The **Sierra Mar** (47900 Hwy. 1, 831/667-2800, www.postranchinn.com, 12:15pm-3pm, 5:30pm-9pm daily, $125) restaurant at the Post Ranch Inn offers decadent prix fixe lunch and dinner in a stunning oceanview setting.

ACCOMMODATIONS
Under $150

It doesn't look like a spot where famous writers, artists, and Hollywood stars have laid their heads, but ★ **Deetjens Big Sur Inn** (48865 Hwy. 1, 831/667-2378, www.deetjens.com, $115-270) can indeed boast a guest register that many hostelries in Beverly Hills would kill for. Still very rustic, expect thin, weathered walls, funky cabin construction, and no outdoor locks on the doors. Many rooms have shared baths, but you can request a private bath when you make reservations. Deetjens asks that families with children under eight rent both rooms of a two-room building. Deetjens has no TVs or stereos, no phones in rooms, and no cell phone service. Two pay phones are available for emergencies.

In the town of Big Sur, you'll find a couple small motels. A popular one is the **Fernwood Resort** (47520 Hwy. 1, 831/667-2422, www.fernwoodbigsur.com, $135-165), which includes a 12-room motel, convenience store, restaurant, and tavern that passes for the local nighttime hot spot. Farther down the road are the resort's campgrounds, which include tent cabins as well as tent and RV sites. Rooms have queen beds and private bathrooms, but no TVs. Cabins accommodating six along with full kitchens are also available ($215). In the summer, book in advance, especially on weekends.

First opened in the 1930s by a member of the Pfeiffer family, the **Big Sur River Inn** (46840 Hwy. 1, 831/667-2700 or 800/548-3610, www.bigsurriverinn.com, $130-350) boasts 20 rooms, a restaurant, and a gift shop. Families and small groups can choose between standard rooms with two queen beds and two-room suites with multiple beds and attractive decks that look out over the Big Sur River. Enjoy the pool with its surrounding lawn that leads down to the river.

$150-250

If you want to stay in one of the parks but tents aren't your style, book a cabin at the **Big Sur Lodge** (47225 Hwy. 1, 831/667-3100 or 800/424-4787, www.bigsurlodge.com, $159-399) in Pfeiffer Big Sur State Park. Built by the Civilian Conservation Corps during the Great Depression, the Big Sur Lodge is set in the redwood forest along an array of paths and small roads. The cabins feature rustic furniture and simple but clean bathrooms, and many cabins have lots of beds, and some have fireplaces and kitchens. There is a swimming pool, but the real attraction is the access to the Pfeiffer Big Sur trails.

Ragged Point Inn (19019 Hwy. 1, 805/927-4502, http://raggedpointinn.com, $149-339) perches on one of Big Sur's famous cliffs, offering stellar views, even from the spacious budget rooms. To compensate for its remote location, the inn has a restaurant, snack bar, mini-mart, gas station, gift shop, and gallery, plus its own hiking trail, which travels past a waterfall to Ragged Point's private beach.

Over $250

At ★ **Ventana** (48123 Hwy. 1, 800/628-6500, www.ventanainn.com, $670), the morning begins with home-baked pastries, fresh yogurt, in-season fruit, and organic coffee delivered to your room. Enjoy that sumptuous breakfast outdoors on a private patio overlooking a wildflower-strewn meadow. Next, don a plush spa robe and rubber slippers and head for the Japanese bathhouse. Two swimming pools offer a cool respite: The lower pool is clothing-optional, and the upper pool perches on a high spot for enthralling views. Many other amenities are available, including daily complimentary yoga classes. Rooms range from the standard rooms, with king beds and exposed cedar walls, up to full-sized multi-bedroom houses.

Sleek, modern, and built into the landscape as is only possible in Big Sur, **Post Ranch** (47900 Hwy. 1, 831/667-2200 or 800/527-2200, www.postranchinn.com, $675-995) sits directly across Highway 1 from Ventana, rivaling its New Age luxury. Spa, yoga, hot and cold pools, and a unique yet rustic atmosphere are just a few of its perks.

CAMPING

Note: At time of publication, Andrew Molera State Park was closed due to the 2016 Soberanes Fire. Please visit the state park website for information before planning a trip.

Andrew Molera State Park (Hwy. 1, 22 miles south of Carmel, 831/667-2315, www.parks.ca.gov, $35/night) offers 24 walk-in, tent-only campsites located 0.25-0.5 mile from the parking lot via a level, well-maintained trail. Site include a picnic table and a fire ring. No reservations are taken, so come early in summer to get one of the prime spots under a tree. Bring your own water; there is no potable water available. Pit toilets sit a short walk from the camping area.

The **Fernwood Resort** (47520 Hwy. 1, 831/667-2422, www.fernwoodbigsur.com) maintains a large campground on both sides of the Big Sur River. You can choose between pitching your own tent, pulling in your RV, or renting a tent cabin. The resort has easy access to the river, where you can swim, inner tube, and hike, plus a restaurant, store, and tavern. Tent cabins ($90-120 for 2 people) sleep up to four. Hot showers and bathrooms are a short walk away. Tent campsites ($55-65) are scattered in great places—tucked down by the river under vast, shady redwood trees. You can even park your RV under a tree and then hook it up to water and electricity.

The biggest and most developed campground in Big Sur sits at **Pfeiffer Big Sur State Park** (47225 Hwy. 1, 800/444-7275 or www.reserveamerica.com, $35). Each of the 150 individual sites that sit along the Big Sur River can take two vehicles and eight people or an RV (32 feet or shorter, trailers 27 feet max, dump station on-site). During the summer, a grocery store and laundry facilities are available, while plenty of flush toilets and hot showers are scattered throughout the campground. In the evenings, walk down to the Campfire Center for entertaining and educational programs. If you prefer a quieter and less asphalt-oriented camping experience, check out the hike-in and bike-in campgrounds that make up part of the Pfeiffer Big

Sur complex. Advanced reservations, particularly in the summer and on weekends, are strongly encouraged.

The small but pretty campground at **Limekiln State Park** (63025 Hwy. 1, 800/444-7275 or www.reserveamerica.com, summer only, $35) offers 29 campsites with hot showers and flush toilets along an attractive creek and abutting the beach. RVs (up to 24 feet) and trailers (up to 15 feet) can stay anywhere but the Redwood Sites; hookups and dump stations aren't available. In summer, the park recommends making reservations early. In winter, no reservations are available and many sites are closed. Call for more information if you want to camp here in the off-season.

For the ultimate high-end California camping experience, book a yurt at the ★ **Treebones Resort** (71895 Hwy. 1, 877/424-4787, www.treebonesresort.com, $95-215). The resort got its name from the locals' description of this scrap of land, which was once a wood-recycling plant with sun-bleached logs lying about—in other words, "tree bones." Yurts ($215) at Treebones are spacious and charming, with polished wood floors, queen beds, seating areas, and outdoor decks for lounging. There are also walk-in campsites ($95 for two people), which include "Ocean View" sites—a round canvas tent on a wood platform ($130). In the central lodge, you'll find hot showers and clean restroom facilities, plus a heated pool and hot tub. Treebones offers a somewhat pricey casual dinner each night and basic linens. Check the website for a list of items to bring. Treebones does not recommend bringing kids under six years old.

TRANSPORTATION AND SERVICES

The heart of Big Sur lies about 22 miles south of Carmel, but for many locals, Big Sur starts once you exit the Carmel Highlands. The ride is slow, as Highway 1 hugs the plunging cliffs and crosses steep river gorges. The scenery competes with the road for your attention, but there are plenty of wide turnouts if you need to take a moment and catch the view.

Gas stations are rare. A couple of the resorts have their own filling stations, but you pay for that convenience. Best to fuel up before you leave Carmel or San Simeon. This is especially important to remember, as cell phones do not work on much of the coast. Call boxes are set at regular intervals along the highway in case of an emergency.

The ranger-led **Big Sur Station** (just south of Pfeiffer Big Sur State Park, 831/667-2315, 9am-4pm daily) is run by Caltrans, the Los Padres National Forest, and the California State Parks system. Inside the fairly large complex you'll find all sorts of maps and information about local flora and fauna and a staff that can help you with everything from getting a backcountry permit to deciding where to eat dinner.

Pfeiffer Big Sur State Park (47225 Hwy. 1, 831/667-2315, www.parks.ca.gov) offers some basic staples, as does **Fernwood Resort** (47200 Hwy. 1, 831/667-2422, www.fernwood-bigsur.com). There are no supermarkets anywhere on the 90-mile stretch of road.

Should a medical emergency arise, the **Big Sur Health Center** (46896 Hwy. 1, Big Sur, 831/667-2580, http://bigsurhealth-center.org, 10am-5pm Mon.-Fri.) can take care of minor medical needs and limited emergency care. The **Big Sur Volunteer Fire Brigade** (831/667-2113, http://bigsurf-ire.org) is the emergency responder for the area and has an ambulance and a 24-hour paramedic team.

Cambria and San Simeon

San Simeon and **Cambria** offer travelers a remarkable final stop at the end of a remarkable road. Hearst Castle draws thousands of visitors each year. Less than five miles south, Cambria is a picturesque small town with an artist colony pedigree and plenty of restaurants, accommodations, and shopping to round out a weekend away.

SIGHTS
★ Hearst Castle
There's nothing in California quite like **Hearst Castle** (Hwy. 1 and Hearst Castle Rd., 800/444-4445, www.hearstcastle.com, tours 9am-3:40pm daily, adults $25, children 5-12 $12, under 5 free). Newspaper magnate William Randolph Hearst conceived the idea of a grand mansion on the land where he and his parents had camped above the Pacific. He hired Julia Morgan, the first female civil engineering graduate from the University of California, Berkeley, to design and build the house for him. She did a brilliant job with every detail, despite the ever-changing wishes of her employer. Completed in 1947, the house was to be a museum, of sorts, for Hearst's vast holding of European medieval and Renaissance antiquities, from tiny tchotchkes to whole gilded ceilings. As most of these pieces were from the Mediterranean region, the castle was modeled after a Mediterranean village, complete with a plaza and grand church facade. Because Hearst adored exotic animals, he created one of the largest private zoos in the nation on his land. Though most of the zoo is gone now, you can still see the occasional zebra grazing peacefully along Highway 1, south of the castle.

Like the estate itself, visiting is no small affair. The castle sits five miles up the hill from the visitors center, along a steep and winding road. The only way there is aboard the shuttle bus run by the park, and the only way to board the bus is by purchasing a ticket to one of the four tours offered, each focusing on a different space and aspect of the castle. The **Grand Rooms Tour** is recommended for first-time visitors, and you can tack on other tours (the **Upstairs Suites Tour** and the **Cottages and Kitchen Tour**), if you have the time, interest, and money. For those who wish to get a glimpse of the glamour of Hearst Castle, the **Evening Tour** (adults $65, children 5-12 $18), offered in spring and fall, takes you through a wider swath of rooms populated by docents in 1930s attire.

Tours last 45 minutes, with the exception of the Evening Tour, which lasts 100 minutes. Expect to walk for at least an hour on whichever tour you choose and to climb up and down many stairs. Even the most jaded traveler can't help but be amazed by the beauty and opulence that drips from every room in the house. Afterward, you are free to explore the grounds until the last shuttle departs, around 5pm.

The park recommends that visitors buy tour tickets at least a few days in advance, and even farther ahead for the Evening Tour and on summer weekends. For visitors with limited mobility, a special wheelchair-accessible tour is available. Strollers, food, drink, and gum are not permitted. The visitors center is quite impressive, built to accommodate the large volume of guests that visit each day. Ticket windows have screens that illuminate up-to-the minute tour departure times. A theater plays the much-touted film *Hearst Castle—Building the Dream* (ticket included in the tour price). There is also a gift shop, a café selling wares from Hearst Ranch, and a bank of portable toilets lining the massive parking lot.

Piedras Blancas Lighthouse

Visible from Hearst Castle is the **Piedras Blancas Lighthouse** (15950 Cabrillo Hwy., 805/927-7361, www.piedrasblancas.org, tours 9:45am Tues., Thurs., and Sat., adult $12, children 6-17 $5, under 6 free). Six miles north of San Simeon, the handsomely restored lighthouse was established in 1875 and sits surrounded by protected coastal prairie. The immense white rock outcroppings just offshore not only gave the lighthouse its name, but also are home to a rich array of shorebirds and marine wildlife. To visit the lighthouse, you must be part of a tour. These occur three mornings a week, do not require reservations, and leave promptly from the old Piedras Blancas Motel, 1.5 miles north of the lighthouse.

Just south of the lighthouse is the popular **Northern Elephant Seal Rookery** (Hwy. 1, 805/924-1628, www.elephantseal.org), home to nearly 16,000 giant elephant seals. From the large parking lot off the highway, take the well-marked trails down to the bluffs overlooking the beach where this large colony breeds, births, and brawls from late November until February.

Hearst San Simeon State Park

Extending from the wetlands of San Simeon Creek, along the celebrated **Moonstone Beach,** to the lagoon filled by Santa Rosa Creek in Cambria, **Hearst San Simeon State Park** (500 San Simeon Creek Rd., Cambria, 805/927-2035, www.parks.ca.gov, sunrise-sunset daily, free) is perfect for a few hours' break from the road or an overnight stay. To get the most out of the coast, the mile-long **Moonstone Boardwalk** hugs the beach. It starts at the parking lot of **Leffingwell Landing,** where you will also find a boat launch and excellent opportunities for tide pooling. The boardwalk and the beach are both open to dogs.

FOOD

As with accommodations, the best food options in the area are found in Cambria. The one shining exception is the historical **Sebastian's Store** (442 Slo San Simeon Rd., San Simeon, 805/927-3307, 11am-4pm daily, $8-12). Built in 1852 and established as the town's general store in 1914, Sebastian's Store serves burgers, hot sandwiches, and sides from a walk-up counter.

The local favorite is ★ **Robin's** (4095 Burton Dr., Cambria, 805/927-5007, www.robinsrestaurant.com, $17-34). Inside the homey and quirky restaurant, decorated with eclectic paintings and charming knick-knacks, you'll find global comfort food. Order Malaysian yellow curry, wild prawn enchiladas, or a

Cambria and San Simeon

■ PIEDRAS BLANCAS LIGHT STATION

■ PIEDRAS BLANCAS ELEPHANT SEAL ROOKERY

HEARST CASTLE RD

San Simeon

✚ HEARST CASTLE

William Randolph Hearst Memorial State Beach

SEBASTIAN'S STORE

San Simeon State Beach

SAN SIMEON CREEK RD

1

Cambria

SANTA ROSA CREEK RD

0   3 mi
0   3 km

GREEN VALLEY RD

As suggested by the long line and crowded tables below its yellow awning, *the* place to go for coffee in Cambria is the **Cambria Coffee Roasting Company** (761 Main St., Cambria, 805/927-0670, http://cambriacoffeeroasting. com, 7am-5:30pm daily). Expect a perfect cup of joe, whether it's a fancy macchiato or a filtered drip.

ACCOMMODATIONS

A favorite among the many inns of Cambria, the charming **Olallieberry Inn** (2476 Main St., Cambria, 805/927-3222, www.olallieberry.com, $140-225) is walking distance from downtown. Each of the nine rooms features its own quaint Victorian-inspired decor, with comfortable beds and attractive appointments. Six rooms have private baths. A full daily breakfast (complete with olallieberry jam) rounds out the experience.

For a great selection of anything from economical standard rooms up to sizable cabins, pick the **Cambria Pines Lodge** (2905 Burton Dr., 805/927-4200 or 800/445-6490, www.cambriapineslodge.com, $129-259). All rooms have plenty of creature comforts, including TVs, kitchenettes, and, in some cases, fireplaces. The country kitsch may be a little over the top, but this resort does its best and is perfect for traveling families.

Many of Cambria's hotels sit along the small town's very own Hotel Row, aka Moonstone Beach Drive. One of these is **Moonstone Landing** (6240 Moonstone Beach Dr., Cambria, 805/927-0012 or 800/830-4540, www.moonstonelanding. com, $180-272), which provides inexpensive partial-view rooms with the decor and amenities of a mid-tier chain motel, as well as oceanfront luxury rooms featuring travertine marble bathrooms. **Moonstone Cottages** (6580 Moonstone Beach Dr., Cambria, 805/927-1366 or 800/222-9157, http://moonstonecottages.com, $250-369) offers peace and luxury along with proximity to the sea. Expect your cottage to include a fireplace, a marble bathroom with a whirlpool tub, a flat-screen TV with a DVD

Kansas City-style New York steak. The kids' menu is reasonably priced. Take a table outside on the patio, draped in flowering vines and adorned with wooden birdhouses.

If you can't get a table at Robin's, walk over to **Linn's Restaurant** (2277 Main St., Cambria, 805/927-0371, www.linnsfruitbin. com, 8am-9pm daily, $17-29). Part of an expansive, but still local, family business, Linn's serves tasty, unpretentious American favorites in a casual, family-friendly atmosphere. Order the famous olallieberry pie.

One of the best bargains in town is ★ **Wild Ginger** (2380 Main St., Cambria, 805/927-1001, www.wildgingercambria.com, 11am-2:30pm, 5pm-9pm Mon.-Wed. and Fri.-Sat., 5pm-9pm Sun., $14-19). This tiny pan-Asian café serves delicious, fresh food at its few tables and carries an array of takeout fare displayed in a glass case crammed into the back of the dining room. Come early for the best selection of dishes.

player, Internet access, and a view of the ocean.

TRANSPORTATION AND SERVICES

San Simeon sits roughly 140 miles south of Carmel on the slow and scenic Highway 1. Cambria is less than five miles south of that. From San Francisco, take U.S. 101 to the Paso Robles area and then turn west onto Highway 46, which brings you right to the town of Cambria. To get to downtown Cambria, exit Highway 1 at Windsor Boulevard, turning right onto Main Street. This route is 230 miles, which is a four-hour drive.

There is an ATM at **Bank of America** (734 Main St.) in downtown Cambria. For medical assistance, contact the **Cambria Community Health Center** (2515 Main St., Cambia, 805/927-5292, http://community-healthcenters.org, 8:30am-5:30pm Mon.-Fri.). The nearest emergency room to Cambria is the **Twin Cities Hospital** (1100 Las Tablas Rd., Templeton, 805/434-3500, www.twin-citieshospital.com), 25 miles east, near the junction of U.S. 101 and Highway 46.

Piedras Blancas Lighthouse

Santa Barbara and the Central Coast

Santa Barbara 398

Ventura 411

San Luis Obispo and Vicinity . . . 416

Highlights

★ **Santa Barbara Mission:** Graceful architecture, serene surroundings, and an informative museum make this the "Queen of the Missions" (page 398).

★ **Santa Barbara Beaches:** Superb meetings of sand and sea abound in Santa Barbara (page 403).

★ **Channel Islands National Park:** This series of islands has undeveloped beauty, stellar coastal views, and stunning sea caves that can be explored by kayak (page 413).

★ **Madonna Inn:** The rooms, restaurants, bars—and even the bathrooms—are worth a look at this monument to kitsch (page 416).

★ **Montaña de Oro State Park:** This underrated natural treasure comprises 8,000 mostly undeveloped acres of coves, peaks, and canyons (page 419).

One of California's most picturesque cities, Santa Barbara is where Southern California begins.

It's famous for its pleasant Mediterranean climate and Spanish colonial revival architecture in the style of the Santa Barbara Mission, arguably the most beautiful of the California missions. Along Highway 1 north of Santa Barbara are the popular state parks and beaches of the Gaviota Coast. Places like idyllic Refugio State Beach offer escape from suburban civilization.

South of Santa Barbara, the city of Ventura has a grittier, more urban feel than Santa Barbara. It's charming and walkable, with a historic downtown and popular beach boardwalk, but its biggest attraction is its reliable surf break. Offshore, the Channel Islands hover on the horizon. Commonly reached by boat, these isolated islands offer visitors a glimpse of the wild, undeveloped coastline, as well as amazing recreational opportunities and encounters with rare endemic animal species.

It's worth detouring north to visit college town San Luis Obispo, with its vibrant weekly farmers market, a California mission, and the kitschy but cool Madonna Inn, and nearby Paso Robles' thermal springs and up-and-coming wineries.

PLANNING YOUR TIME

It's possible to explore Santa Barbara in a **weekend,** or to use the city as a base of operations to enjoy the region, though accommodations can be quite pricey. Those wanting to travel out to more remote places like Channel Islands National Park should add a few days to their stay. Going to the Channel Islands involves getting a space on a boat or plane. In addition, boats travel to some islands only every few days. It's nice to secure a hotel in Ventura or Santa Barbara after a camping expedition on the islands to ease yourself back into civilization before heading on to your next destination.

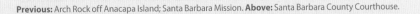

Previous: Arch Rock off Anacapa Island; Santa Barbara Mission. **Above:** Santa Barbara County Courthouse.

One Day in Santa Barbara

Begin your day with a hearty Southern-meets-California breakfast at the **Tupelo Junction Café,** located right on State Street. Take advantage of your hard-won parking space and strike out on foot, with your destination an easy 0.25 mile away: the **Santa Barbara County Courthouse,** one of the finest examples of the city's distinctive Mediterranean architecture. Be sure to climb up to the top of the 85-foot-high **Clock Tower** for views of the city laid out between the Santa Ynez Mountains and the Pacific Ocean. Wander back down **State Street,** strolling on its wide brick sidewalk and taking some time to enjoy the shops. Follow State Street until it ends at **Stearns Wharf,** the long wooden pier. If you're hungry, stop for a bite at **Eladio's.**

Now fueled up, head back up State Street, pick up your car, and drive to the stunning **Santa Barbara Mission.** Take a self-guided tour through the scenic courtyards and wander among the historic markers in the on-site cemetery. For dinner, climb Highway 154 to **Cold Spring Tavern** for brews, barbecues, and a sunset view from the ridge overlooking Santa Barbara.

Santa Barbara

Nestled between the Pacific Ocean and the mountains, Santa Barbara is where beach culture meets high culture. You'll find lots of museums, outdoor shopping areas, great restaurants, and four-star resorts. And a growing young wine region thrives here.

TOP EXPERIENCE

SIGHTS

Though **State Street** travels through different sections of Santa Barbara, the roadway that cuts through 12 blocks downtown is the heart of the city. Wide brick sidewalks on either side are shaded by palm trees and decorated with flowers, giving the city a tropical feel. Clothing stores, restaurants, and bars line the street along with popular attractions including the Santa Barbara Museum of Art and The Granada Theatre.

★ Santa Barbara Mission

It's easy to see why the **Santa Barbara Mission** (2201 Laguna St., 805/682-4713, http://santabarbaramission.org; self-guided tours 9am-5pm daily, adults $8, seniors $6, children $3, children 4 and under free; docent-guided tours 11am Thurs.-Fri., 10:30am Sat., adults $12, seniors and military $10, children $7) is referred to as the "Queen of the Missions." It is larger, more beautiful, and more impressive than many of the other missions. When you visit, you'll find the collection of buildings, artwork, and even the ruins of the water system in better shape than at many other missions in the state. The self-guided tour includes a walk through the mission's striking courtyard with its blooming flowers and towering palm trees and entrance to the mission museum, which has among other displays a collection of Chumash artifacts and a photo of the church after an earthquake in 1925 toppled its towers. The original purpose of the mission was to transform the native Chumash into Christians. The mission's cemetery is the final resting place of more than 4,000 of these Chumash people.

In late May the plaza in front of the mission is awash in color during the **I Madonnari Italian Street Painting Festival** (805/964-4710, ext. 4411, www.imadonnarifestival.com, late May, free), inspired by a similar event in Grazie di Curtatone, Italy. The festival benefits the nonprofit Children's Creative Project.

Santa Barbara Maritime Museum

The **Santa Barbara Maritime Museum** (113 Harbor Way, Ste. 190, 805/962-8404, www.sbmm.org, 10am-5pm Thurs.-Tues., until 6pm Memorial Day-Labor Day, adults $8, students and seniors $5, children 6-12 $4, free for military personnel in uniform) sits right on the working harbor. Exhibits tell the maritime history of California, beginning with the local Chumash Native Americans, running through the whaling and fur-hunting eras and up through the modern oil drilling and commercial fishing industries. The children's area features hands-on exhibits that make learning about the sea lots of fun for younger visitors.

Stearns Wharf

Stretching out into the harbor for 2,250 feet, **Stearns Wharf** (State St. and Cabrillo Blvd., www.stearnswharf.org, parking $2.50/hr., first 90 min. free with validation) was the longest deepwater pier between Los Angeles and San Francisco when it was constructed by John P. Stearns in 1872. A tourist favorite, the wooden wharf hosts candy stores, gift shops, and casual seafood eateries. It is also home to the **Ty Warner Sea Center** (211 Stearns Wharf, 805/962-2526, www.sbnature. org, 10am-5pm daily, adults $8, seniors and teens $7, children $5), which is operated by the Museum of Natural History.

Santa Barbara Museum of Natural History

The **Santa Barbara Museum of Natural History** (2559 Puesta del Sol, 805/682-4711, www.sbnature.org, 10am-5pm daily, adults $12, seniors and teens $8, children $7) has large galleries that display stories of the life and times of insects, mammals, birds, and dinosaurs. Of particular interest is a display showcasing the remains of a pygmy mammoth specimen that was found on the nearby Channel Islands. Head outdoors to circle the immense skeleton of a blue whale, and to hike the Mission Creek Nature Trail. The **Gladwin Planetarium** hosts shows portraying the moon and stars, plus monthly Star Parties and special events throughout the year.

Santa Barbara Botanic Gardens

The **Santa Barbara Botanic Gardens** (1212 Mission Canyon Rd., 805/682-4726, www.sbbg.org, 9am-6pm daily Mar.-Oct., 9am-5pm daily Nov.-Feb., adults $10, seniors and teens $8, children $6) focuses solely on

Santa Barbara Mission

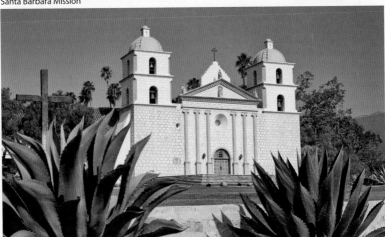

Santa Barbara and the Central Coast

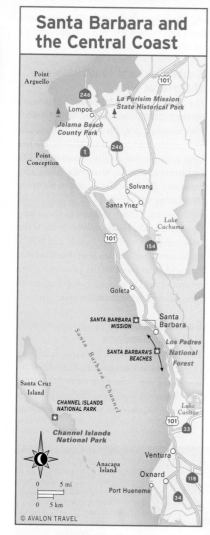

© AVALON TRAVEL

Santa Barbara Museum of Art

The two-floor **Santa Barbara Museum of Art** (1130 State St., 805/963-4364, www. sbma.net, 11am-5pm Tues.-Wed. and Fri.-Sun., 11am-8pm Thurs.; adults $10; seniors, students with ID, and children $6) has an impressive art collection that would make some larger cities envious. Wander the spacious, well-curated museum and take in some paintings from the museum's collection of Monets, which is the largest collection of the French impressionist's paintings on the West Coast. The museum also has ancient works like a bronze head of Alexander from Roman times and a collection of Asian artifacts including a 17th- or 18th-century Tibetan prayer wheel.

Santa Barbara County Courthouse

If only all government buildings could be as striking as the **Santa Barbara County Courthouse** (1100 Anacapa St., 805/962-6464, www.santabarbaracourthouse.org, 8am-5pm Mon.-Fri., 10am-4:30pm Sat.-Sun.; free docent-led tours 10:30am and 2pm Mon.-Fri., 2pm Sat.-Sun.). Constructed in 1929, the courthouse, which is actually four buildings comprising a whole city block, is one of the city's finest examples of Mediterranean-style architecture. The interior's high ceilings, tile floors, ornate chandeliers, and art-adorned walls give it the feel of a California mission. Visit El Mirador, the clock tower, where an open deck 85 feet off the ground provides great views of the towering Santa Ynez Mountains and the Pacific Ocean.

ENTERTAINMENT AND EVENTS
Bars and Clubs

The proximity of UCSB to downtown Santa Barbara guarantees a livelier nighttime scene. Bars cluster on State Street and beyond, and plenty of hip clubs dot the landscape.

The best place to start an evening out on the town is at **Joe's Café** (536 State St., 805/966-4638, www.joescafesb.com, 7:30am-10pm daily). This steak house and bar is known for the stiffest drinks in town. Just go

the indigenous plants of California, with plantings from the deserts, chaparral, arroyo, and more. The gardens spread out over many acres and cross several hiking trails. Guided tours are offered on Saturdays and Sundays at 11am and 2pm (included with admission ticket), or take a self-guided tour with a map and the advice of the docents. The shop offers books and garden-themed gifts, while the nursery sells native Californian plants.

Santa Barbara

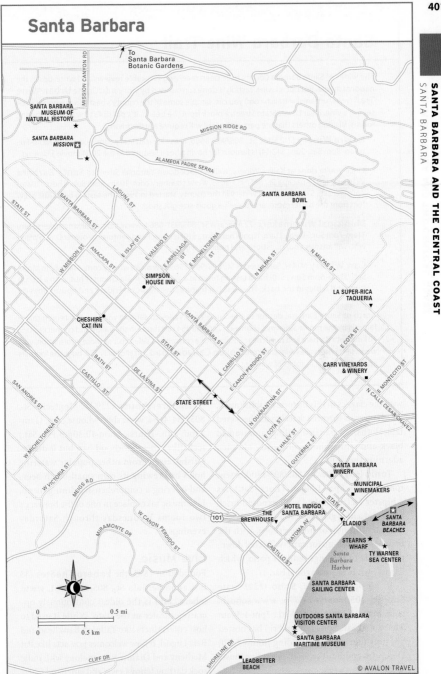

To Santa Barbara Botanic Gardens

MISSION CANYON RD

SANTA BARBARA MUSEUM OF NATURAL HISTORY

SANTA BARBARA MISSION

MISSION RIDGE RD

ALAMEDA PADRE SERRA

STATE ST

LAGUNA ST

SANTA BARBARA ST

W MISSION ST

ANACAPA ST

E ISLAY ST

E VALERIO ST

E ARRELLAGA ST

E MICHELTORENA ST

N MILPAS ST

N MILPAS ST

SANTA BARBARA BOWL

SIMPSON HOUSE INN

LA SUPER-RICA TAQUERIA

CHESHIRE CAT INN

SANTA BARBARA ST

E COTA ST

STATE ST

BATH ST

DE LA VINA ST

E CARRILLO ST

E CANON PERDIDO ST

N QUARANTINA ST

CARR VINEYARDS & WINERY

N CALLE CESAR CHAVEZ

N E MONTECITO ST

SAN ANDRES ST

CASTILLO ST

STATE STREET

E COTA ST

E HALEY ST

W MICHELTORENA ST

E GUTIERREZ ST

W VICTORIA ST

MEIGS RD

SANTA BARBARA WINERY

MUNICIPAL WINEMAKERS

MIRAMONTE DR

W CANON PERDIDO ST

101

THE BREWHOUSE

HOTEL INDIGO SANTA BARBARA

STATE ST

NATOMA AV

ELADIO'S

SANTA BARBARA BEACHES

CASTILLO ST

STEARNS WHARF

TY WARNER SEA CENTER

Santa Barbara Harbor

SANTA BARBARA SAILING CENTER

0   0.5 mi

0   0.5 km

OUTDOORS SANTA BARBARA VISITOR CENTER

SANTA BARBARA MARITIME MUSEUM

CLIFF DR

SHORELINE DR

LEADBETTER BEACH

© AVALON TRAVEL

Santa Barbara Wine Trail

The wines of Santa Barbara County have been receiving favorable reviews and write-ups in the national media. But not all wine-tasting is done surrounded by vineyards. On the **Urban Wine Trail** (www.urbanwinetrailsb.com) you can sample some of the county's best wines without even seeing a vine. Near Lower State Street, a block from the beach, it's possible to walk to six tasting rooms. Visiting others that are part of the trail will require a little driving.

- **Kalyra Winery** (212 State St., 805/965-8606, www.kalyrawinery.com, noon-7pm Mon.-Fri., noon-8pm Sat.-Sun., $12-14) is famous for having been featured in the 2004 movie *Sideways*.

- Once you're done at Kalyra Winery, walk a block down Yanonali Street to **Santa Barbara Winery** (202 Anacapa St., 805/963-3633, www.sbwinery.com, 10am-6pm Sun.-Thurs., 10am-7pm Fri.-Sat., $10), the oldest winery in the county, started in 1962. The tasting bar is just a few feet from the barrel room, and there's a good-size gift shop.

- **Municipal Winemakers** (22 Anacapa St., 805/931-6864, www.municipalwinemakers.com, 11am-7pm Sun.-Wed., 11am-11pm Thurs.-Sat., $10) is a weekend venture for owner Dave Potter, who will answer your questions and pour his wines.

- **Carr Winery** (414 N. Salsipuedes St., 805/965-7985, www.carrwinery.com, 11am-8pm Mon.-Sat., 11am-6pm Sun., $10) has a tasting room in a World War II-era Quonset hut, with a bar up front and tables in the back. The wine bar features live music on Fridays and house wines on tap.

North of Santa Barbara, detour to the Santa Ynez Valley to sample wines in the region made famous by the movie *Sideways*. Highways 246 and 154 run through the valley and connect to U.S. 101 in Santa Barbara and north near Solvang for a convenient side trip. For more information, visit www.santaynezvalleywinetrail.com. **Foxen Canyon Road,** off Highway 154, hugs the foothills and is home to a number of wineries.

with the classics in this historic establishment, which owes its throwback feel to its checkered tablecloths, tin-paneled ceiling, and framed black-and-white photos of mostly old men adorning the walls.

Tonic (634 State St., 805/897-1800, www.tonicsb.com, 8pm-1:30am Thurs.-Sat.) has a hipster feel, complete with exposed brick walls and a long glass bar. Top-flight DJs spin a mostly hip-hop or house groove, with the occasional mash-up for variety. To cool down, go outside to the huge outdoor patio, which has its own funky octagonal bar.

In an upstairs suite, **Soho** (1221 State St., Ste. 205, 805/962-7776, www.sohosb.com, 6pm-11:30pm Sun.-Wed., 7pm-1:30am Thurs. and Sat., 5pm-1:30am Fri.) has hosted big-time touring acts including Jimmy Cliff, Donovan, and Built to Spill. It has live music seven nights a week.

The Brewhouse (229 W. Montecito St., 805/884-4664, www.sbbrewhouse.com, 11am-10pm Sun.-Thurs., 11am-10:30pm Fri.-Sat.) feels like a neighborhood bar, but it distinguishes itself from other popular watering holes by brewing its own small-batch beers and offering a comprehensive dining menu. Live music takes place in one of the brewery's two rooms Wednesday through Saturday evenings.

Live Music

Founded in 1873, the **Lobero Theater** (33 E. Canon Perdido St., 805/963-0761, www.lobero.com) is the oldest continuously operating theater in the state. While it used to host entertainers like Tallulah Bankhead and Bela Lugosi, it now welcomes jazz acts like Pat Metheny and Dianne Reeves along with indie rock darling Jenny Lewis and jam band Chris

Robinson Brotherhood. The medium-size theater has only one level, and it's filled with cushy red-velvet seats—perfect for a music-filled night out on the town.

The **Santa Barbara Bowl** (1122 N. Milpas St., 805/962-7411, www.sbbowl.com) is a great place to take in a concert during the summer and fall. Built in 1936, it's the largest outdoor amphitheater in the county. In the past it has hosted concerts by Neil Young, Florence & The Machine, and Death Cab for Cutie.

SPORTS AND RECREATION
★ Beaches
EAST BEACH

Named because it is east of Stearns Wharf, **East Beach** (1400 Cabrillo Blvd., www.santabarbaraca.gov, sunrise-10pm daily) is all soft sand and wide beach, with a dozen volleyball nets in the sand close to the zoo (if you look closely, you can see the giraffes and lions). It has all the amenities a sun worshipper could hope for: a full beach house, a snack bar, a play area for children, and a path for biking and in-line skating. The beachfront has picnic facilities and a full-service restaurant at the East Beach Grill. The **Cabrillo Pavilion Bathhouse** (1119 East Cabrillo Blvd.), built

in 1927, offers showers, lockers, a weight room, a single rentable beach wheelchair, and volleyball rental.

WEST BEACH

On the west side of Stearns Wharf, **West Beach** (Cabrillo Blvd. and Chapala St., between Stearns Wharf and the harbor, sunrise-10pm daily) has 11 acres of picturesque sand for sunbathing, swimming, kayaking, windsurfing, and beach volleyball. There are also large palm trees, a wide walkway, and a bike path, making it a popular tourist spot. Outrigger canoes also launch from this beach.

LEADBETTER BEACH

Considered by many to be the best beach in Santa Barbara, **Leadbetter Beach** (Shoreline Dr. and Loma Alta Dr., sunrise-10pm daily) divides the area's south-facing beaches from the west-facing ones. It's a long, flat beach with a large grassy area. Sheer cliffs rise from the sand, and trees dot the point. The beach, which is also bounded by the harbor and the breakwater, is ideal for swimming because it's fairly protected, unlike the other flat beaches. The grassy picnic areas have barbecue sites that can be reserved for more privacy, but otherwise there is a lot of room. The beach and the

Joe's Café

park can get packed during the many races and sporting events held here. There are restrooms, a small restaurant, and outdoor showers.

ARROYO BURRO BEACH

To the north of town, **Arroyo Burro Beach** (Cliff Dr., 805/687-3714, www.sbparks.org, 8am-sunset daily), also known as Hendry's, is a favorite for locals and dog owners. To the right as you face the water, past Arroyo Burro Slough, dogs are allowed off-leash to dash across the packed sand and frolic and fetch out in the gentle surf. Arroyo Burro is rockier than the downtown beaches, making it less friendly to games and sunbathers. You'll find a snack bar, restrooms, outdoor showers, and a medium-size pay parking lot for your convenience. At peak times, when the parking lot is full, there's no other parking around.

GOLETA BEACH

At the base of the University of California, Santa Barbara campus, **Goleta Beach Park** (5986 Sandspit Rd., sunrise-10pm daily) is popular for its picnic tables, barbecue pits, horseshoes, multiple restrooms, and fishing opportunities. The grassy area is partially shaded by trees, and there's also a small jungle gym for the kids. The pier is popular for fishing, and the low breaks make it an easy entry for kayakers. On the mountain-facing side along the bike path are a few platforms for viewing birds in the slough behind the beach.

BUTTERFLY BEACH

Butterfly Beach (Channel Dr., across from the Four Seasons Hotel, Montecito, sunrise-10pm daily) is accessed by a handful of steps leading to the narrow beach. Butterfly is the most west-facing beach in Santa Barbara, meaning that you can actually see the sun set over the Pacific here. To find it, take U.S. 101 to Olive Mill Road in Montecito (a few minutes south of Santa Barbara). At the stop sign, turn toward the ocean (away from the mountains) and follow it 0.25 miles along the coast; Butterfly Beach is on the left. The beach is packed most weekends and often weekdays,

too, and parking is limited. Park on either side of the street along the beach, or drive up Butterfly Road and park in the nearby neighborhoods. Bring your lunch, water, and sunscreen; there are no public facilities at this beach. Dogs roam freely here.

CARPINTERIA STATE BEACH

Carpinteria State Beach (5361 6th St., Carpinteria, 805/968-1033, 7am-sunset daily, day use $10, camping $35-65) has designated itself the "world's safest beach." Whether that's true or not, this beautiful wide, flat beach is definitely a favorite for locals and visitors alike. With plenty of campgrounds, picnic tables, outdoor showers, RV hookups, telephones, and a short walk to Linden Avenue's restaurants, shops, and grocery store, you'll have everything you need within walking distance. Parts of the campgrounds are tree-lined but right next to the train tracks; passing trains might wake up light sleepers.

TOP EXPERIENCE

Surfing

During the summer months, the Channel Islands block the south swells that would otherwise hit the county. But, during fall and winter, the big north and northwest swells wrap around Point Conception and transform places like Rincon into legendary surf breaks.

Leadbetter Point (Shoreline Park, just north of the Santa Barbara Harbor) is a slow, mushy wave perfect for beginners and longboarders. The locals are reasonably welcoming, and the small right break makes for easy and fun rides.

For a bit more of a challenge, paddle out to the barrels at **Sandspit** (Santa Barbara Harbor). The harbor's breakwater creates hollow right breaks for adventurous surfers. Be careful though: Sandspit's backwash has been known to toss surfers onto the breakwater.

Known as the "Queen of the Coast," **Rincon** (U.S. 101 at Bates Rd. on the Ventura County/Santa Barbara County line) is considered California's best right point break. If you catch a wave outside, there's a chance you can score a memorable-for-life, 300-yard-long ride. But if it's firing, you'll also most likely be sharing the break with lots of other surfers. The time to investigate Rincon is during the winter.

Looking for surfing lessons? Check out the **Santa Barbara Surf School** (805/708-9878, www.santabarbarasurfschool.com, surf lessons $65-85, surf camp $395). The instructors have decades of surfing experience and pride themselves on being able to get beginners up and riding in a single lesson.

Kayaking and Stand-Up Paddleboarding

One of the best ways to see the Santa Barbara Harbor and Bay is under your own power in a kayak or stand-up paddleboard. A number of rental and touring companies offer lessons, guided paddles, and good advice for exploring the region. **Channel Islands Outfitters** (117B Harbor Way, 805/617-3425, www.channelislandso.com, 7am-7pm daily, kayaks $15/hr., SUPs $30/hr.) has everything you need to paddle the waters of Santa Barbara and Ventura. Rent a sea kayak or a stand-up paddleboard to take your own ride around the harbor or out into the bay. The company also leads adventurous sea-kayak tours around the nearby Channel Islands.

The **Santa Barbara Sailing Center** (133 Harbor Way, 805/350-9090, www.sbsail.com, kayaks $10-15/hr., SUPs $15-30/hr.) also provides kayak rentals and stand-up paddleboard rentals, as well as sea-kayaking tours.

Whale-Watching

Santa Barbara's prime location on the coast makes it a great spot for whale-watching. With its proximity to the feeding grounds of the blue and humpback whales, Santa Barbara is one of the state's best places to spot the marine mammals.

If you're looking for a whale-watching expedition, birding expedition, or dinner cruise, check out the **Condor Express** (301 W. Cabrillo Blvd., 805/882-0088, www.condorexpress.com; whale-watching trips: adults $45-99, children $30-50). In the summertime, cruise out to the Channel Islands to see the blue and humpback whales feed; in the winter, the captain sails into the path of migrating gray whales. The boat is an 88-foot vessel that can seat 68 people. Whale-watching cruises depart almost daily all year long; call to purchase tickets in advance.

Parks

Along a rural stretch of the U.S. 101 coastline are three state parks—El Capitan State Beach, Refugio State Beach, and Gaviota State Park. All are typically crowded during the summer months, but also provide a great place to camp for the night.

JALAMA BEACH COUNTY PARK

Jalama Beach County Park (9999 Jalama Rd., Lompoc, front gate 805/736-3504, weather and information 805/736-6316, www.sbparks.org, day use $10) draws families, surfers hoping to score uncrowded waves, anglers hoping to reel in a few fish, and beachgoers who like their beaches undeveloped. Jalama Road winds 14.5 miles toward the park, which includes a playground, a horseshoes pit, a basketball court, flush toilets, and the **Jalama Beach Store and Grill.** From Jalama it's a six-mile beach hike to the east to Point Conception, one of California's best-known maritime landmarks. Check to make sure it's low tide before heading out.

The park has 117 first-come, first-served **campsites** (tent sites $30-45, RV sites with hookups $40-45). There are 12 spots whose sites blend into the beach out front and a row of RV-friendly sites on a bluff with a view of the park below. The amenities here include clean bathrooms with flush toilets, fire pits, picnic tables, and an outdoor shower. The park also rents seven popular **cabins** (805/686-5050, $170-220).

GAVIOTA STATE PARK

Gaviota State Park (10 Refugio Beach Rd., Goleta, 805/968-1033, www.parks.ca.gov,

7am-sunset daily, $10) is the place for hiking. The park has multiple trails leading into its 2,000 acres of oak woodland and chaparral backcountry, including a strenuous three-mile one-way hike to **Gaviota Peak,** a 2,458-foot peak that offers one of the best views of the Gaviota Coast. Besides the hiking trails, Gaviota State Park has a nice little beach area under the shadow of an 811-foot-high train trestle.

There are 39 **campsites** (800/444-7275, www.reserveamerica.com, $45) in a small loop by Gaviota Creek just 100 yards from the beach. These sites are mostly open to the elements, including the wind that roars through Gaviota Pass and the heat.

REFUGIO STATE BEACH

Refugio State Beach (10 Refugio Beach Rd., Goleta, 805/968-1033, www.parks.ca.gov, $10) is the best place for a beach day. This thin but long finger of beach is lined with scenic palm trees and has a well-protected cove for sea kayaking or stand-up paddleboarding. There are also beginning and advanced kayak tours, which include kayak usage, provided by Refugio's park rangers.

There are 67 **campsites** (800/444-7275, www.reserveamerica.com, $45) for crashing out after a day at the nearby beach, which is just feet away from some sites. The sites are fairly close together, and in summer can feel a bit crowded, but this is still a scenic campground with plenty of trees providing shade.

EL CAPITAN STATE BEACH

El Capitan State Beach (10 Refugio Rd., Goleta, 805/986-1033, www.parks.ca.gov, dawn-dusk daily, $10) offers a narrow, rocky beach with tide pools and the largest campground of the three Gaviota Coast state parks. A stairway provides access from the bluffs to the beach area. Amenities include RV hook-ups, pay showers, restrooms, hiking and biking trails, a fabulous beach, a seasonal general store, and an outdoor arena.

Home to the largest state park **campground** (800/444-7275, www.

reserveamerica.com, $45) on the Gaviota Coast, the 123 campsites are strung along multiple loops in the shade or sun, and offer a little more privacy than Refugio or Gaviota.

El Capitan Canyon (11560 Calle Real, 866/352-2729, www.elcapitancanyon.com, canvas safari tents $170, cabins $245-795) offers 300 acres of land with private hiking trails and a spa. The accommodations here include canvas safari tents, yurts, and cedar cabins that are like small wooden studio apartments, complete with kitchenettes. In front of each is a picnic table and fire pit for communing with nature. The on-site **Canyon Market** serves a nice selection of breakfast, lunch, and dinner options.

FOOD
Breakfast and Cafés

The ★ **Tupelo Junction Café** (1218 State St., 805/899-3100, www.tupelojunction.com, 8am-2pm and 5pm-8pm Tues.-Sun., 8am-2pm Mon., dinner $14-22) serves breakfast, lunch, and dinner, but it is the breakfast that shouldn't be missed. The collision between cuisines takes place in morning menu items including a breakfast wrap with Southern elements like Andouille sausage mixed into what is basically a California Mexican-style breakfast burrito with a tasty avocado salsa. Don't miss the biscuit covered in a spicy red sausage gravy that is served as a breakfast side item.

Enjoy a sea breeze and views of Stearns Wharf on the fountain patio section at **Eladio's** (28 W. Cabrillo Blvd., 805/963-4466, www.eladiosrestaurantsb.com, 7am-9:30pm daily, $12-25), which is connected to the Harbor View Inn. These folks are known for their breakfasts, but they also do good work at brunch, lunch, dinner, and happy hour (3pm-7pm daily).

A long, narrow coffee shop right on State Street, **The French Press** (1101 State St., 805/963-2721, http://thefrenchpress.com, 6am-7pm Mon.-Fri., 7am-7pm Sat.-Sun.) is lined with hipsters and couples getting caffeinated and using the free Wi-Fi. The very popular café has a small seating area out

Side Trip to Solvang

Founded in 1911 as a Danish retreat, Solvang makes a fun side trip. It's ripe with Scandinavian heritage as well as a theme-park atmosphere not lacking in kitsch.

In the 1950s, far earlier than other themed communities, Solvang decided to promote itself via a focus on Danish architecture, food, and style, which still holds a certain charm more than 50 years later. You'll still hear the muted strains of Danish spoken on occasion, and you'll notice storks displayed above many of the stores in town as a traditional symbol of good luck.

Solvang draws nearly two million visitors each year. During peak summer season and holidays, people clog the brick sidewalks. Try to visit during off-season, when meandering the lovely shops can still be enjoyed. It's at its best in the fall and early spring when the hills are verdant green and the trees in town are beautiful.

The **Elverhøj Museum** (1624 Elverhøj Way, 805/686-1211, www.elverhoj.org, 11am-4pm Wed.-Sun., $5 suggested donation) features exhibits of traditional

Solvang

folk art from Denmark, including paper-cutting and lace-making, wood clogs, and the rustic tools used to create them. It also offers a comprehensive history of the area with nostalgic photos of the early settlers.

The small **Hans Christian Andersen Museum** (1680 Mission Dr., 805/688-2052, www.solvangca.com, 10am-5pm daily, free) chronicles the author's life, work, and impact on literature. Displays include first editions of his books from the 1830s in Danish and English.

Contact the **Solvang Visitor Information Center** (1639 Copenhagen Dr., 805/688-6144, www.solvangusa.com, 9am-5pm daily) for more advice on a Solvang visit.

GETTING THERE

If you're heading from Santa Barbara north to Solvang, you have two choices. You can drive the back route, Highway 154, also known as the San Marcos Pass Road, and arrive in Solvang in about 30 minutes. This is a two-lane road, with only a few places to pass slower drivers, but it has some stunning views of the coast as you climb into the hills. You pass Cachuma Lake, then turn west on Highway 246 to Solvang. The other option is to take U.S. 101, which affords plenty of coastal driving before you head north into the Gaviota Pass to reach Solvang. This route is longer, about 45 minutes' drive time. Highway 246 is known as Mission Drive in the town, and it connects both to U.S. 101 and Highway 154, which connects to Santa Barbara in the south and U.S. 101 farther north.

front on State Street and out back on Figueroa Street.

Sojourner Café (134 E. Canon Perdido St., 805/965-7922, www.sojournercafe.com, 11am-10pm Tues.-Sun., $9-16) features healthful dishes made with ingredients that showcase local organic and sustainable farms. Daily specials use ingredients that are fresh and in-season, including some seafood. Then again, Sojourner also serves a classic root beer

float and chocolate milk shakes as well as a big selection of house-baked confections to go along with their health food.

Barbecue

★ **Cold Spring Tavern** (5995 Stagecoach Rd., 805/967-0066, www.coldspringtavern.com; restaurant 11am-3pm and 5pm-9pm Mon.-Fri., 8am-3pm and 5pm-9pm Sat.-Sun.; tavern noon-9pm daily; $18-33) is a former stagecoach stop, built in 1886; it hasn't changed much since. The on-site restaurant, in a separate building from the bar, serves up wild game, rabbit, venison, boar, and very good chili. Summer weekends (11am-5pm Sat.-Sun.) feature tender tri-tip sandwiches ($10) grilled outdoors over an open flame. A visit to the tavern is as much about enjoying the charming space as it is about the food. The complex includes an old jail, a one-room wood building that used to hold unruly customers. Rustic and secluded, it hosts live music Friday-Sunday.

California Cuisine

Bouchon (9 W. Victoria St., 805/730-1160, www.bouchonsantabarbara.com, 5pm-9pm Sun.-Thurs., 5pm-10pm Fri.-Sat., $26-38) prides itself on both creative cuisine and top-notch service every night. The wine list consists entirely of wines from Santa Barbara County. The dining room features romantic low lighting, smallish tables, interesting artwork, and an outdoor patio that's perfect for balmy summer nights.

A bit less fancy, **Opal** (1325 State St., 805/966-9676, http://opalrestaurantandbar.com, 11:30am-2:30pm and 5pm-10pm Mon.-Thurs., 11:30am-2:30pm and 5pm-11pm Fri.-Sat., 5pm-10pm Sun., $14-37) is a favorite of Santa Barbara locals. In addition to its eclectic offerings, most with an Asian twist, the stylish eatery serves up gourmet pizzas from a wood-burning oven and fine cocktails from a small bar.

Creole

The Palace Grill (8 E. Cota St., 805/963-5000, www.palacegrill.com, 11:30am-3pm and 5:30pm-10pm Sun.-Thurs., 11:30am-3pm and 5:30pm-11pm Fri.-Sat., $17-32) boasts of being one of Santa Barbara's most popular restaurants and a little piece of old New Orleans in sunny California. The atmosphere gets lively in the evenings, so this isn't the place to come for a quiet meal. The food is pure Louisiana bayou; look for classically prepared étouffées, jambalaya, and gumbo ya-ya. While you dine, take a moment to appreciate the particularly fine service that is a staple of the Palace's reputation.

Italian

For a superb Italian meal and a sophisticated dining experience, ★ **Olio e Limone** (11 W. Victoria St., Ste. 17, 805/899-2699, www.olioelimone.com, 11:30am-2pm and 5pm-9pm Mon.-Thurs., 11:30am-2pm and 5pm-10pm

Cold Spring Tavern

Fri.-Sat., 5pm-9pm Sun., $18-37) is the place to go. Among the specialties of the house are its quail dishes, but the homemade duck ravioli with creamy porcini mushroom sauce is a rich, rave-worthy offering. There's an impressive wine list, or opt for a creative cocktail.

Mexican

Have you ever wanted to know what true, authentic Mexican food tastes like? ★ **La Super-Rica Taqueria** (622 N. Milpas St., 805/963-4940, 11am-9pm Sun.-Tues. and Thurs., 11am-9:30pm Fri.-Sat., $2.50-5) can hook you up. Of course, you must be prepared to stand in line with dozens of locals and even the occasional Hollywood celeb, all of whom think La Super-Rica's got some of the best down-home Mexican cuisine in all of SoCal.

Middle Eastern

For a Middle Eastern feast, go to **Zaytoon** (209 E. Canon Perdido St., 805/963-1293, www.zaytoon.com, noon-10pm Mon.-Thurs., noon-11pm Fri.-Sat., 5pm-10pm Sun., $18-32). This restaurant and hookah bar is popular with groups of friends eager to share a hookah and platters of baba ghanoush, shawarma, and kebabs as talented belly dancers shimmy among the tables. Try to get a table out on the garden patio, a large, softly lit space almost completely enveloped by a living green jungle.

Seafood

It takes something special to make Santa Barbara residents take notice of a seafood restaurant, and **Brophy Brothers** (119 Harbor Way, 805/966-4418, www.brophybros.com, 11am-10pm daily, $19-25) has it. With a prime location looking out over the masts of the sailboats in the harbor, it's no surprise that Brophy Brothers gets crowded at both lunch and dinnertime, especially on weekends in the summertime. There's also a location in Ventura Harbor.

Yes, they do mean *that* **Endless Summer** (113 Harbor Way, 805/564-4666, http://chuckswaterfrontgrill.com, 11:30am-9:30pm daily, $13-19); the restaurant is inspired by and named for the famous surfing film. The drinks here are strong, and the menu nods toward burgers and seafood. The sesame-crusted ahi on a warm spinach salad rides the perfect wave of healthy and tasty. Service is friendly, and the atmosphere tends toward casual local hangout.

In downtown Santa Barbara, ★ **The Hungry Cat** (1134 Chapala St., 805/884-4701, www.thehungrycat.com, 3pm-10pm Tues.-Thurs., 3pm-11pm Fri., 11am-3pm and 5pm-11pm Sat., 11am-3pm and 5pm-10pm Sun., $17-32) has the expected seafood options and more exotic offerings (sturgeon caviar, local sea urchin). Sit at the bar for happy hour (3pm-6pm Tues.-Fri.) to dine on a lobster roll or fried oysters while enjoying reduced-price cocktails and beers.

ACCOMMODATIONS
Under $150

Even the hostels in Santa Barbara are upscale, but you'd be hard pressed to find a better room in a better location than at **The Wayfarer** (12 E. Montecito St., 805/845-1000, www.pacifica-hotels.com/thewayfarer, dorm beds $60-99, private rooms $220-399). In the city's arty Funk Zone, The Wayfarer has unhostel-like features including a heated outdoor pool and a sleek, contemporary decor. Save money by cooking in the communal kitchen and partaking in the morning continental breakfast.

$150-250

★ **Hotel Indigo Santa Barbara** (121 State St., 805/966-6586, www.ihg.com, $239-314) offers sleek, compact rooms with hardwood floors and a European-style collapsible glass shower wall. Some rooms also have small outdoor patios. Upstairs is a vertical garden, two outdoor lounges, and a library with art-related books. The hotel is in a great location, one block from the beach and two blocks from Santa Barbara's downtown. It's also near the train station, so expect to hear a train roll by occasionally.

If you're in Santa Barbara to soak up the sun on the sandy beaches, book a room at the **Inn at East Beach** (1029 Orilla Del Mar, 805/965-0546, www.innateastbeach.com, $180-300). It's just a block from East Beach, and a nice walk along the waterfront boardwalk will take you to Stearns Wharf and downtown. The rooms are clean and stylish with modern furniture and plants, giving them a homey feel. The junior kitchen suites include a full kitchen with a large fridge, oven, and stovetop. The rooms circle a courtyard with a heated pool. Other amenities include a continental breakfast, free parking, flat-screen TVs with 146 channels, and a washer and dryer.

The **Cheshire Cat Inn** (36 W. Valerio St., 805/569-1610, www.cheshirecat.com, $199-400) can provide you with true luxury B&B accommodations. Each room has an *Alice in Wonderland* name, but is filled with comfortable Victorian elegance. Rooms are spread out through two Victorian homes, the coach house, and two private cottages. Relax in the evening in the spacious octagonal outdoor spa, or order a massage in the privacy of your own room. Each morning, come downstairs and enjoy a breakfast. In addition to the fine facilities, the Cheshire Cat's warm innkeepers will make you feel immediately at home.

Over $250

For a taste of Santa Barbara's posh side, stay at the **Inn of the Spanish Garden** (915 Garden St., 805/564-4700, www.spanishgardeninn. com, $320-580). This building in the historic Presidio neighborhood has the characteristic whitewashed adobe exterior with a red-tiled roof, arched doorways, and wooden balconies. Courtyards seem filled with lush greenery and tiled fountains, while the swimming pool promises relief from the heat. Inside, rooms and suites whisper luxury with fireplaces, deep soaking bathtubs, French press coffee makers, plush bathrobes, and honor bars. The complimentary continental breakfast can be delivered right to your door upon request. The Spanish Inn sits only three blocks from State Street, and within walking distance

of a number of theaters and historic Santa Barbara attractions.

The historic ★ **Simpson House Inn** (121 E. Arrellaga St., 805/963-7067, www.simpsonhouseinn.com, $255-610) is a historic landmark that was constructed in 1874. Stay inside one of the six ornately decorated rooms, one of the four rooms in the reconstructed carriage house, or one of the four garden cottages. The service here is first rate. In the morning, dine on a vegetarian breakfast in the main house's dining room or in your own room. The grounds include an acre of English gardens with fragrant flowers, gurgling fountains, fruit trees, and the oldest English oak tree in Southern California.

The ★ **Canary Hotel** (31 W. Carrillo St., 805/884-0300, www.canarysantabarbara.com, $300-665) offers elegant rooms with wooden floors, extremely comfortable canopied beds, and giant flat-screen TVs. While it may be difficult to leave such comforts, the hotel has a rooftop pool and lounge on its sixth floor that offers stunning views of the Santa Ynez Mountains and the red-tiled roofs of the beautiful coastal city. Downstairs, the hotel restaurant and bar **Finch & Fork** serves breakfast, lunch, dinner, and a recommended happy hour menu 4pm-7pm Monday-Friday.

TRANSPORTATION AND SERVICES

Santa Barbara is on U.S. 101, 325 miles and 5.5 hours south of San Francisco, and almost 2 hours and 95 miles north of Los Angeles. To head out to the Santa Ynez Valley and other local wine regions, take CA Highway 154 east. Highway 154 connects with U.S. 101 at Santa Barbara and north of Solvang, making it an alternate route to Santa Barbara from the north. Parking can be challenging at the beach on sunny summer weekends. Instead, take the local public streetcar from the downtown area to the beach and leave your car elsewhere.

To reach Santa Barbara by air, fly into the **Santa Barbara Municipal Airport** (500 Fowler Rd., 805/683-4011, www.santabarbaraca.gov). A number of major commercial airlines fly into Santa Barbara, including United, Alaska/Horizon, U.S. Airways, and American Airlines. A more beautiful and peaceful way to get to Santa Barbara is by train. The **Amtrak *Coast Starlight*** (www. amtrak.com) runs into town daily. It travels between Los Angeles and Seattle.

Santa Barbara has its own transit authority. The **MTD Santa Barbara** (805/963-3366, www.sbmtd.gov, regular fare: local service $1.75, waterfront service $0.50) runs both the local bus service and the Waterfront Shuttle and Downtown-Waterfront lines. Have exact change to pay your fare when boarding the bus or shuttle; if transferring buses, ask the driver for a free transfer pass.

The major hospital in town is **Santa Barbara Cottage Hospital** (400 W. Pueblo St., 805/682-7111, www.sbch.org), which includes a full-service emergency room.

Ventura

Downtown Ventura is compact and easy to walk around; it is three blocks from the beach with buildings that date to the 1800s (a long time by California standards). It's still a bit scruffier than nearby Santa Barbara, with a sizable homeless population for its relatively small area. Farther away, the Ventura Harbor has a cluster of restaurants, bars, and hotels around the harbor, which is the gateway to the nearby Channel Islands National Park.

MISSION SAN BUENAVENTURA

Referred to as the "mission by the sea," **Mission San Buenaventura** (211 E. Main St., 805/643-4318, www.sanbuenaventura-mission.org, self-guided tours 10am-5pm Sun.-Fri., 9am-5pm Sat., adults $4, seniors $3, children $1) sits right on Ventura's Main Street, just blocks from the beach. A one-room museum on the grounds displays the church's original doors and a collection of native Chumash artifacts. Between the museum and the church is a scenic garden with a tile fountain, an old olive press, and a shrine.

BEACHES
San Buenaventura State Beach

San Buenaventura State Beach (San Pedro St. off U.S. 101, 805/968-1033, www. parks.ca.gov, dawn-dusk daily, $10) has an impressive two miles of beach, dune, and ocean.

It also includes the 1,700-foot Ventura Pier, home to Eric Ericsson's Seafood Restaurant and Beach House Tacos. This is a safer place to swim than some area beaches, as it doesn't get the breakers that roll into the nearby point. Cyclists can take advantage of trails connecting with other nearby beaches, and sports enthusiasts converge on the beach for occasional triathlons and volleyball tournaments. Facilities include a snack bar, an equipment rental shop, and an essential for the 21st-century beach bum—Wi-Fi (although to pick up the signal, you need to be within about 200 feet of the lifeguard tower).

Emma Wood State Beach

Bordering the estuary north of the Ventura River, **Emma Wood State Beach** (W. Main St. and Park Access Rd., 805/968-1033, www. parks.ca.gov, dawn-dusk daily, $10) includes the remnants of a World War II artillery site. There are no facilities, but a few minutes' walk leads to the **campgrounds** (one for RVs and one group camp; first-come, first-served in winter, reservations required spring-fall). At the far eastern side of the parking lot is a small path leading out to the beach that goes under the train tracks. The beach itself has many rocks strewn about, some nearly the size of footballs.

Harbor Cove Beach

Families flock to **Harbor Cove Beach** (1900

Spinnaker Dr., http://venturaharbor.com, dawn-dusk daily), directly across from the Channel Islands Visitors Center at the end of Spinnaker Drive. The harbor's breakwaters provide children and less confident swimmers with relative safety from the ocean currents. The wind can kick up at times, but when it's calm it's practically perfect. There's plenty of free parking, lifeguards during peak seasons, restrooms, and foot showers. Food and other amenities can be found across the street at Ventura Harbor Village.

Faria Beach

Farther north, the Ventura County-run **Faria Beach** (4350 W. U.S. 101, at State Beach exit, 805/654-3951, www.ventura.org, 7am-sunset daily, $4) is available for tent camping and has 15 RV hookups. The **campground** (sites $35, reservation fee $10) has a playground, horseshoe pits, barbecues, and shower facilities, but is quite small. It's also very crowded with campers, trucks, and people during nice weather because of its proximity to the water.

WHALE-WATCHING

December-March is the ideal time to see Pacific gray whales pass through the channel off the coast of Ventura. Late June-late August is the narrow window for both blue and humpback whales as they feed offshore near the islands. **Island Packers Cruises** (1691 Spinnaker Dr., Ste. 105B, 805/642-1393, www.islandpackers.com, $25-75) has operated whale-watching cruises for years and is the most experienced. It also runs harbor cruises with a variety of options, including dinner cruises and group charters. Most whale-watching trips last about three hours.

ACCOMMODATIONS AND FOOD

If you are traveling to Channel Islands National Park out of Ventura Harbor, the **Four Points By Sheraton Ventura Harbor Resort** (1050 Schooner Dr., 805/658-1212, www.fourpoints.com, $145-175) is a great place to lay your head before an early morning boat ride or to relax after a few days camping on the islands. The rooms are clean and comfortable and have balconies and patios. A few hundred yards from the Ventura Pier and right by the beach, the **Crowne Plaza Ventura Beach** (450 E. Harbor Blvd., 800/842-0800, www.cpventura.com, $139-389) has rooms with ocean-view balconies if you get a room on the fifth floor or higher. It also offers pet-friendly rooms for $75 more.

Ventura Harbor

Anacapa Brewing Company (472 E. Main St., 805/643-2337, http://anacapabrewing.com, 11:30am-10pm Sun.-Wed., 11:30am-midnight Thurs.-Sat., $14) looks like a brewpub should. Regulars sit at a long bar drinking the brewery's Pierpoint IPA, while families eat burgers, salads, and pizzas at booths and tables.

In a prime spot on the Ventura Pier, **Beach House Tacos** (668 Harbor Blvd., 805/648-3177, 11am-8:30pm Mon.-Fri., 8:30am-8:30pm Sat.-Sun., $3-8) offers creative options like soy-ginger-lime cream sauce-soaked ahi and ground beef tacos with raisins. Order at the counter and dine at an enclosed seating section on the pier. Expect long lines on summer weekends.

Sleek **Lure Fish House** (60 California St., 805/567-4400, www.lurefishhouse.com, 11:30am-9pm Sun.-Thurs., 11:30am-10pm Fri.-Sat., $15-33) is a local favorite for seafood downtown. The menu focuses on charbroiled seafood including fresh and sustainable wild local halibut, wild mahi-mahi, and other tasty morsels from the sea.

TRANSPORTATION AND SERVICES

Ventura is 34 miles south of Santa Barbara on U.S. 101 and 65 miles north of Los Angeles on the highway. **Amtrak** (Harbor Blvd. and Figueroa St., 800/872-7245, www.amtrak.com) also comes to town.

Community Memorial Hospital (147 N. Brent St., 805/652-5011, www.cmhshealth.org) has the only emergency room in the area.

TOP EXPERIENCE

★ CHANNEL ISLANDS NATIONAL PARK

Only accessible by boat or plane, Channel Islands National Park (1901 Spinnaker Dr., Ventura, 805/658-5730, www.nps.gov, 8:30am-5pm daily) is home to uncrowded trails, isolated beaches, and an extensive marine sanctuary. The most frequented of the park's islands are **Santa Cruz Island,**

California's largest island at 24 miles long and up to six miles wide, and **Anacapa,** a dramatic five-mile spine jutting out from the sea. **Santa Rosa** is the second-largest island, but it takes nearly three hours to reach and the 20-foot steel-rung ladder to access the island is often a deterrent. **San Miguel** is currently closed to visitors. The southernmost **Santa Barbara Island** is one square mile, but teems with wildlife. Its size and distance, however, make it a rare stop except for experienced sea-kayakers and avid birders.

Santa Cruz, Anacapa, and, to a lesser degree, Santa Rosa can be visited as day trips. There can be tough weather conditions, and it's often very windy since there's little shelter. Ferries depart from the Ventura Harbor and take between 90 minutes and three hours, depending on the island sailing conditions. Only Santa Cruz and Anacapa can be visited year-round.

Santa Cruz Island

Santa Cruz is the largest of the islands, and by far the most popular island to visit. The environmental organization The Nature Conservancy owns 76 percent of Santa Cruz Island (accessed by special permit only, www.nature.org), while the National Park Service possesses and maintains the remaining 24 percent. This is the only place in the world to see endemic species such as the Channel Islands fox and island scrub-jay.

Santa Cruz Island hosted an extensive ranching operation from the mid-1800s up until the 1980s. The **Scorpion Ranch Complex** gives park visitors a glimpse into this isolated way of life with various farming equipment and wooden ranch structures in states of decay. The small visitors center has displays on threatened species, conservation, and the native Chumash people.

A quick introduction to Santa Cruz's cliff-top coastal views and, on clear days, views to the mainland can be found on the moderate two-mile-long **Cavern Point Loop.** If you have more time, the more strenuous 7.5-mile round-trip **Smugglers Cove Trail** is an old ranch road that cuts across the island's eastern interior to arrive at a south-facing beach. Even if you don't find the elusive island scrub-jay on the 4.5-mile **Scorpion Canyon Loop,** you'll be treated to a hike up one of the island's unique canyons followed by a series of stunning vistas.

The two primary points of entry onto Santa Cruz are **Scorpion Anchorage** and **Prisoners Harbor.** In addition to hiking, the island has two campgrounds and an abundance of amazing sea caves that can be explored by sea kayak. Travel time from Ventura is 90 minutes, and travelers offload onto a short pier directly connected to shore, though shore landings from a skiff are possible depending on conditions.

Anacapa Island

Anacapa is actually three islets that are five miles long and a quarter-mile wide. Visitors are able to access **East Anacapa,** a desert-like island with steep cliffs that is home to the stunning Inspiration Point, the **Anacapa Lighthouse,** a two-mile trail system, a small visitors center, a campground, and **Arch Rock,** a 40-foot-high rock window in the waters just east of the island. The easy, flat **Inspiration Point Loop** (1.5 miles

round-trip, easy) leads around the island. Even shorter is the walk slightly uphill on the **Lighthouse Trail** (0.5 mile round-trip, easy). The trail doesn't go right up to the lighthouse, but it comes close enough for a great picture and view.

Santa Rosa Island

Rugged and windy **Santa Rosa Island** is less visited than Anacapa and Santa Cruz. Its mountainous spine rises to 1,574 feet at Soledad Peak and spectacular views of neighboring Santa Cruz Island and the mainland coastline in the distance. The white-sand beaches and coastal lagoons seem virtually untouched, as is the Torrey pine forest, considered home to some of the rarest pines in the world.

Due to the frequent high winds, sea kayaking, snorkeling, diving, and swimming are only recommended for those with significant experience. But for those who want to explore dry land, Santa Rosa has a handful of trails for hikers who don't mind sweating. The strenuous 12-mile **East Point Trail** takes in the Torrey pine forest and some unrestricted beaches. The 13-mile **Lobo Canyon Trail** goes to a water-sculpted canyon that looks like it could be in the Southwest. There

Channel Islands National Park

are also easier outings, including exploring **Water Canyon Beach,** as long as it isn't too windy out.

Travel time is about three hours by boat; you'll need to climb a 20-foot steel-rung ladder to reach flat land.

Kayaking

Santa Cruz Island is pocked with some of the world's most incredible and largest sea caves, and the best way to explore them is by kayak. The easiest way to find some sea caves is to paddle northwest (left) out of **Scorpion Anchorage.**

Anacapa is ripe for exploration by sea kayak. Access to the water is only available from East Anacapa's Landing Cove due to the islands' rugged cliffs. Paddle out to **Arch Rock,** the 40-foot-high rock arch in the waters just east of the islet, or **Cathedral Cove.** This scenic section of coast has an arch known as **Cathedral Arch** as well as **Cathedral Cave,** which can be explored by kayak during higher tides. The cave has five entrances that lead into an impressive chamber.

To book a kayak or tour, contact the **Channel Islands Kayak Center** (3600 S. Harbor Blvd., Ste. 2-108, Ventura Harbor, 805/984-5995, www.cikayak.com, single kayaks $35, double kayaks $55, two-person tour with transportation $200). You must first secure a space for your kayak by calling Island Packers (805/642-1393), the concession that takes people out to the island.

Another option is to sign up for the multihour Caves and Coves Tour with **Channel Islands Outfitters** (805/899-4925, www.channelislandso.com, $140 pp). The knowledgeable guides will set you up onshore at Scorpion Anchorage and then take you on a tour of the area's caverns. This is a good option for first-timers to Santa Cruz Island. Tours don't include transportation.

Snorkeling and Scuba Diving

Santa Cruz Island offers some fine snorkeling and scuba diving right where the boat pulls in at Scorpion Harbor. The kelp east and west of the Scorpion Anchorage Pier are rich in sea life, while the wreck of the **USS Peacock** 50 yards off Scorpion Rocks in 40 to 60 feet of water captivates divers. The wreck is a fairly intact World War II minesweeper.

To dive the island's other spots, you'll have to have your own boat or be on a charter dive boat to access the sites. Diving trips need to be scheduled from Ventura Harbor. Options include the **Peace Dive Boat** (1691 Spinnaker Dr., G Dock, Ventura Harbor, 805/650-3483, www.peaceboat.com, $115-540 trips) and **Truth Aquatics** (301 W. Cabrillo Blvd., 805/962-1127, www.truthaquatics.com, $100-1,000).

Camping

Multi-day trips allow for extended **camping** (877/444-6777, www.recreation.gov, $15) into the islands' interiors and for visiting several of the islands. The most popular campground on Santa Cruz Island is the **Scorpion Ranch Campground,** a 0.5-1-mile walk in from the pier at Scorpion Anchorage. The lower campground has 22 sites in a eucalyptus-shaded canyon, while the upper loop has three regular sites and six group sites in a meadow. The upper loop is a nice spot but it's twice as far to lug your camping gear. The campgrounds have a picnic table and food storage box at every site. There are also pit toilets and water available.

There's also camping out of Prisoners Harbor if you hike the strenuous 3.5 miles to the **Del Norte Backcountry Campsite.** This remote spot in an oak grove at 700 feet elevation has picnic tables and a pit toilet.

The **Anacapa Campground** is reachable by a 0.5-mile hike on East Anacapa that includes 154 stairs. This primitive camping area has seven sites with flat spots and picnic tables. There are also some regularly serviced pit toilets. The Anacapa campsites are very exposed to the sun and the wind.

Camping on Santa Rosa can be done at the **Water Canyon Campground,** reached by a level 1.5-mile hike. There are 15 sites with picnic tables and pit toilets. You can do backcountry camping (805/658-5711, free) right on the beach mid-August-December.

Transportation

In preparation for a trip to the islands, visit the **Channel Islands National Park Visitors Center** (1901 Spinnaker Dr., 805/658-5730, www.nps.gov, 8:30am-5pm daily) in Ventura Harbor Village, where you'll find a bookstore, displays of marine life, exhibits, and a 25-minute introductory film on the islands.

The most popular way to get to Channel Islands National Park is by hopping onboard a boat run by **Island Packers Cruises** (1691 Spinnaker Dr., Ste. 105B, Ventura Harbor, 805/642-1393, www.islandpackers.com; day trips adults $59-82, seniors $54-74, children ages 3-12 $41-65; overnight trips adults $79-114, seniors $74-104, children 3-12 $57-90). The boat schedules change according to the seasons, so it's best to visit the website to find out what departing and returning boat times work best with your schedule. It's possible to have a full day on Anacapa Island or Santa Cruz Island by departing at 9am and returning at 4pm. Anacapa is the closest island and the trip there takes an average of 45 minutes. Santa Cruz has a crossing time of 90 minutes, while Santa Rosa and Santa Barbara islands take 2.5-3 hours to reach.

San Luis Obispo and Vicinity

Inland from the coast, San Luis Obispo, otherwise known as SLO (pronounced "slow"), is a worthy home base for exploring nearby Montaña de Oro State Park and Morro Bay. Higuera Street is a one-way, three-lane street lined with restaurants, clothing stores, and bars. A half-block away, restaurant decks are perched over the small San Luis Obispo Creek, a critical habitat for migrating steelhead.

SIGHTS
Mission San Luis Obispo de Tolosa

Founded by Junipero Serra way back in 1772, **Mission San Luis Obispo de Tolosa** (751 Palm St., 805/781-8220, www.missionsanluisobispo.org, 9am-5pm daily summer, 9am-4pm daily winter) was the fifth in the chain of 21 California missions. The church itself is narrow and long with exposed wooden beams on the ceiling. On the grounds, there is a small **museum** (805/543-6850, 9am-5pm daily summer, 9am-4pm daily winter, suggested donation $5) with artifacts from the Native Chumash people and exhibits on the mission and its missionaries. A nice garden and the Mission Plaza out front of the mission complex are pleasant places to spend the afternoon on a warm day.

★ Madonna Inn

A kitschy attraction worth seeing even if you aren't spending the evening, the **Madonna Inn** (10 Madonna Rd., 805/543-3000, www.madonnainn.com) is a sprawling complex right off U.S. 101 that includes a café, a steak house, a bar, a dance floor, a wine cellar, and a collection of 110 themed rooms like "The Caveman," a unit with a solid-rock wall and a waterfall shower.

Obviously, the rooms are for overnight guests, but there is still a lot to take in if you pull over for a peek. The **Copper Café & Pastry Shop** has copper-plated tables and a copper-plated circular bar, while the **Gold Rush Steak House** is a garish explosion of giant fake flowers and rose-colored furniture. It might remind you of a room in your grandmother's or great aunt's home—on steroids.

FOOD

The ★ **San Luis Obispo Farmers Market** (Higuera St. between Osos and Nipomo Sts., 805/544-9570, www.slocountyfarmers.org, http://downtownslo.com, Thurs.

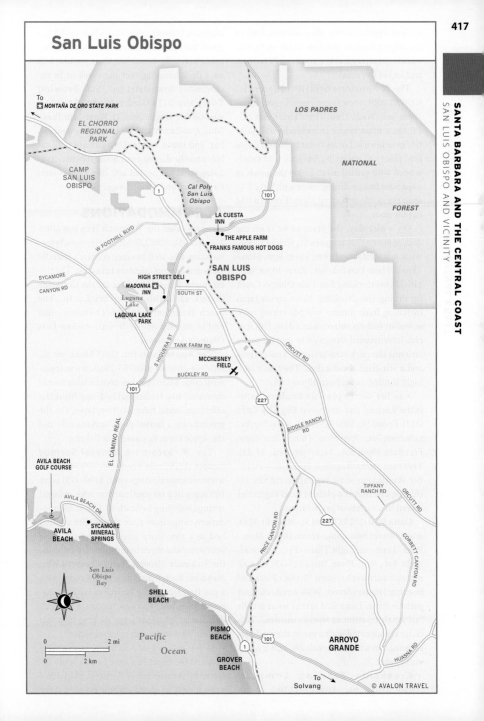

San Luis Obispo

6:10pm-9pm) is a true phenomenon. One of the largest farmers markets in the state, this weekly gathering has the goods of 70 farmers and lots of live music.

The ★ **Firestone Grill** (1001 Higuera St., 805/783-1001, www.firestonegrill.com, 11am-10pm Sun.-Wed., 11am-11pm Thurs.-Sat., $5-18) has a masterpiece in its tender and tasty tri-tip sandwich. Locals swear by it. You'll also find plenty of pork ribs, burgers, and salads topped with grilled meat. Enjoy the goods in a spacious indoor dining room with large TVs or in the outdoor seating plaza. Expect a line out the door.

On a nice day, the place to be is on the deck of **Novo** (726 Higuera St., 805/543-3986, www.novorestaurant.com, 11am-9pm Mon.-Thurs., 11am-1am Fri.-Sat., 10am-10pm Sun., $16-32) overlooking San Luis Obispo Creek for dining and drinking. Novo serves tapas including fresh shrimp avocado spring rolls, as well as full-on entrées like a daily fish special. International flavors creep into the menu on items like pork *carnitas sopes,* Thai curries, and a stir-fried noodle dish. They do a late-night limited menu from 10pm-1am.

Another worthy place for lunch or dinner is the Rachael Ray-approved **Big Sky Café** (1121 Broad St., 805/545-5401, www.bigsky-cafe.com, 7am-9pm Mon.-Thurs., 7am-10pm Fri., 8am-10pm Sat., 8am-9pm Sun., $9-22). There are plenty of options for carnivores, but Big Sky also has some vegetarian entrées, including one that is a plate of local vegetables served in a variety of preparations.

Luna Red (1023 Chorro St., 805/540-5243, www.lunaredslo.com, 11am-10pm Mon.-Wed., 11am-midnight Thurs.-Fri., 9am-midnight Sat., 9am-10pm Sun., $15-32) is in an enviable location between Mission Plaza and bustling Higuera Street. With ample outdoor patio seating, Luna Red serves what it calls "an amalgamation of world cuisines." This claim is supported with a menu that includes sashimi, ceviche, lamb kebabs, and a hummus platter.

Creekside Brewing Company (1040 Broad St., 805/439-4200, www. creeksidebrewing.com, 11am-1am daily) is a small brewpub that serves a menu of house-made beers. Sip brews like their popular IPA on a deck hanging over the creek or in the cavernous downstairs bar. **SLO Brewing Company** (1119 Garden St., 805/543-1843, www.slobrewingco.com, 11:30am-2am Tues.-Sun., 3pm-2am Mon.) is a brewery, restaurant, bar, and music venue. Upstairs are pool tables and the dining area, while downstairs is a stage that has hosted acts like The Strokes, Green Day, and Snoop Dogg.

ACCOMMODATIONS

A superb value, the ★ **Peach Tree Inn** (2001 Monterey St., 800/227-6396, http://peachtree-inn.com, $89-160) has nice rooms, a friendly staff, and a complimentary breakfast. The finest rooms at the Peach Tree are the Creekside Rooms, each with its own brick patio. The Peach Tree is on the Old SLO Trolley route and is an easy one-mile walk to San Luis Obispo's downtown.

The **Apple Farm Inn** (2015 Monterey St., 805/544-2040 or 800/255-2040, www.apple-farm.com, $129-269) has comfortable rooms decorated like traditional bed-and-breakfast offerings; some have gas fireplaces. On the grounds are a heated pool, soaking tub, and the Apple Farm Restaurant & Bakery.

The ★ **Sycamore Mineral Springs Resort** (1215 Avila Beach Dr., 805/595-7302, www.sycamoresprings.com, $199-479) is on 100 acres in a tranquil canyon with mineral springs bubbling beneath it. The accommodations range from cozy rooms with a queen bed to a two-story guesthouse with three bedrooms and three bathrooms. Up on stilts, the Sycamore Mineral Springs Resort's West Meadows Suites include a living room with a gas fireplace and a bedroom with a four-poster king bed. The best feature is the back decks, which include large soaking tubs that can be filled with fresh mineral water.

If you ever wanted to know how it feels to spend the night in a cave or in a room inspired by the country of Portugal, plop down some money to spend a whole evening at the

★ **Madonna Inn** (10 Madonna Rd., 805/543-3000, www.madonnainn.com, $199-469). An under-hyped asset on Madonna Inn's 2,200 acres is the pool deck, with a large heated pool, two hot tubs, a poolside bar, and a view of a cascade tumbling down the hillside.

The **Granada Hotel & Bistro** (1126 Morro St., www.granadahotelandbistro.com, $249-679) is a 17-room boutique hotel just a half block off Higuera Street. The 1920s-era hotel has been renovated and modernized, with exposed brick walls and hardwood floors. Most rooms also have fireplaces. Attached to the hotel is the **Granada Bistro,** which serves Spanish-inspired cuisine from paella to squash-potato tacos.

TRANSPORTATION AND SERVICES

San Luis Obispo sits squarely on U.S. 101/Highway 1. It is 230 miles and nearly four hours south of San Francisco, and 95 miles and two hours north of Santa Barbara. There's also an **Amtrak** station in San Luis Obispo (1011 Railroad Ave., www.amtrak.com) where the *Coast Starlight* train stops. Use **SLO Transit** (www.slocity.org, adults $1.25, seniors $0.60) to get around town.

In case of emergencies, San Luis Obispo is home to two hospitals: **Sierra Vista Regional Medical Center** (1010 Murray Ave., 805/546-7600, www.sierravistaregional.com) and **French Hospital Medical Center** (1911 Johnson Ave., 805/543-5353, www.dignityhealth.org).

MORRO BAY

The picturesque fishing village of Morro Bay is dominated by **Morro Rock,** a 576-foot-high volcanic plug. The rock was an island until the 1930s, when a road was built connecting it to the mainland. The area around the rock is accessible, but the rock itself is off-limits because it is home to a group of endangered peregrine falcons.

★ Montaña de Oro State Park

Montaña de Oro State Park (Pecho Rd., six miles south of Morro Bay, 805/528-0513, www.parks.ca.gov, 6am-10pm daily, free) is for those seeking a serious nature fix on the Central Coast. This sprawling 8,000-acre park with seven miles of coastline has coves, tide pools, sand dunes, and almost 50 miles of hiking trails. A great way to get a feel for the park's immense size is to hike up the two-mile **Valencia Peak Trail** (four miles round-trip). In springtime the sides of the trail are decorated with blooming wildflowers, and the 1,347-foot-high summit offers commanding views of Montaña de Oro's pocked coastline and Morro Rock jutting out in the distance. The hike is steep and exposed, so make sure to bring plenty of water on warm days.

For a feel of the coast, park right in front of **Spooner's Cove** and walk out on its wide, coarse-grained beach. On the cove's north end, Islay Creek drains into the ocean. There's also a picturesque arch across the creek in the rock face on the north side. The **Spooner Ranch House Museum** informs visitors about early inhabitants of the park's land, the Spooner family. The small facility also has displays about the area's plants, mountain lions, and raptors.

Getting There

From San Luis Obispo, Morro Bay is 13 miles west on Highway 1. Main Street is the main artery through downtown. Highway 41 stretches between Morro Bay and Atascadero, making it a good shortcut if you are coming from San Francisco. If you are coming south from Big Sur, Morro Bay is 30 miles south of Hearst Castle on Highway 1.

PISMO BEACH

Walking around Pismo Beach feels like you've stepped back in time to a Southern California beach town from 50 years ago. The town's one-way Pomeroy Avenue is lined with beachwear shops, candy stores, and fish-and-chips restaurants. The main attraction—besides the surf and sand—is the 1,200-foot-long Pismo Pier (end of Pomeroy Ave.). The first **Pismo Pier** was built for shipping back in 1881.

Paso Robles

Paso Robles has become a familiar destination and wine-growing appellation for state residents as well as a popular stop along U.S. 101 between Northern and Southern California. The densest concentration of wineries cluster along Highway 46 West and the little roads that spring off that main thoroughfare. Many intrepid wine-tasters never make it past this short and easy-to-travel stretch, which locals refer to as the Westside.

- **Rotta Winery** (250 Winery Rd., 805/237-0510, www.rottawinery.com, 10:30am-5:30pm daily, tasting fee $5) has been making wine in the region since 1908. It is best known for its estate zinfandel and black monukka dessert wine, which is sweet but not cloying.

- One of the best wineries in these parts is **Hunt Cellars** (2875 Oakdale Rd., 805/237-1600, www.huntcellars.com, 10am-5:30pm daily, tasting fee $5-10). The friendly and intensely knowledgeable staff members pour some of the finest wines in Paso at this midsize, informal tasting room.

- If you favor small wineries that only produce tiny runs of wine, **Dark Star Cellars** (2985 Anderson Rd., 805/237-2389, www.darkstarcellars.com, 10:30am-5pm Fri.-Sun., tasting fee $10) is perfect for you. Ask at the bar about the "synthetic gravity" that is so important to the slow fermentation process used at Dark Star.

- On the Eastside, **Eberle Winery** (3810 Hwy. 46 E., 3.5 miles east of U.S. 101, 805/238-9607, www.eberlewinery.com, 10am-6pm daily Apr.-Oct., 10am-5pm daily Nov.-Mar., free) is one of the pioneers of the Paso wine region. The free cave tour is a great way to escape the heat on a summer's day.

Even before Paso Robles was known for its wineries, the inland town was a destination for people who wanted to soak in its hot mineral waters. At the **Paso Robles Inn** (1103 Spring St., 800/676-1713, http://pasoroblesinn.com, $169-305), you can splurge on a room with a private mineral tub, or soak in the communal heated pool and spa that date back to 1891.

For a bite to eat, grab a taco or two at **Papi's** (840 13th St., 805/239-3720, 11am-9pm daily, $10) or a pint and some pub food at the **Firestone Taproom** (1400 Ramada Dr., 805/225-5911, www.firestonebeer.com, 11am-9pm daily).

Though that pier and another were destroyed by storms, the third version, built in 1985 and 1986, still stands today. Walking out on the pier is a great way to get an eyeful of the far-ranging Pismo Beach and the Oceano Dunes to the south. A small concession shack on the pier sells snacks and rents bodyboards and fishing rods.

Accommodations and Food

Every room at the moderately priced **Kon Tiki Inn** (1621 Price St., 805/773-4833, www.kontikiinn.com, $188-228) has a sweeping view of the ocean as well as a patio or balcony. In front of the large hotel are a heated pool, hot tubs, and a staircase to the beach below. One perk of staying at the Kon Tiki is that guests get full use of the adjacent Pismo Beach Athletic Club, which offers Zumba classes and has an indoor lap pool.

Giuseppe's Cucina Italiana (891 Price St., 805/773-2870, www.giuseppesrestaurant.com, 11:30am-10pm Sun.-Thurs., 11:30am-11pm Fri.-Sat., $12-32) began as the senior project of a Cal Poly student. Now, almost 25 years later, the restaurant is still highlighting the cuisine of the Pugliese region of Italy with pastas, meat dishes, and wood-fired pizzas, including one topped with clams.

For a more sophisticated menu and better views, dine at **Steamers of Pismo** (1601 Price St., 805/773-4711, www.steamerspismobeach.com, 11:30am-3pm and 4:30pm-9pm Mon.-Thurs., 11:30am-3pm and 4:30pm-10pm Fri.-Sat., 11:30am-3pm and 4pm-9pm Sun., $16-33). The menu has deep-fried seafood-and-chips platters along with shrimp jambalaya and chorizo and clam linguine. Happy hour (3pm-7pm Sun.-Thurs., 3pm-6pm Fri.-Sat.) offers a sampler of steamed clams, a fish taco, and a cocktail for the price of a dinner entrée.

It's not a good idea to wear your best clothes to the **Cracked Crab** (751 Price St., 805/773-2722, www.crackedcrab.com, 11am-9pm Sun.-Thurs., 11am-10pm Fri.-Sat., $12-53). The signature dish is a bucket for two that features three kinds of shellfish steamed with Cajun sausage, red potatoes, and corn. You are given a mallet, a crab cracker, and a bib. If that sounds like too much work, order a seafood sandwich or another entrée like grilled albacore.

Getting There

While there may be no must-see attractions in Pismo, the town makes a good stopover along U.S. 101. It is 12 miles south of San Luis Obispo, and 80 miles, 1.5 hours, north of Santa Barbara.

Los Angeles

Sights 426
Entertainment and Events 441
Shopping. 445
Sports and Recreation 447
Food 449
Accommodations. 454
Transportation and Services . . . 458
Disneyland and Orange County 460

Los Angeles is the California that the rest of the world envisions—palm trees line sunny boulevards, the Pacific Ocean warms to a swimmable temperature, and traffic is always a mess.

Yet celebrities don't crowd every sidewalk signing autographs and movies aren't filming on every corner. Instead, L.A. has the glitz, crowds, and speed of the big city with an easier, friendlier feel in its suburbs. A soft haze often envelops the warm beaches, which draw lightly clad crowds vying to see and be seen while children play in the water. Power shoppers pound the pavement lining the ultra-urban city streets. Tourists can catch a premiere at the Chinese Theatre, try their feet on a surfboard at Huntington Beach, and view the prehistoric relics at the La Brea Tar Pits.

For visitors who want a deeper look into the Los Angeles Basin, excellent museums dot the landscape, as do theaters, comedy clubs, and live-music venues. L.A. boasts the best nightlife in California, with options that appeal to star-watchers, hard-core dancers, and cutting-edge music lovers alike.

Out in the suburbs of Orange County lies the single most recognizable tourist attraction in California: Disneyland. Even the most jaded native residents tend to soften at the bright colors, cheerful music, sweet smells, and sense of fun that permeate the House of Mouse.

PLANNING YOUR TIME

When you get into Los Angeles, you'll understand quickly that you'll need to pick and choose your itinerary. The vast urban sprawl is just too big to take in unless you've got several weeks in the area. Your best bet is to follow your own heart to whatever types of activities are your favorites. If you're a first-timer to the Los Angeles area, a great initial tour is a drive down Wilshire Boulevard from end to end, stopping to check out all the various sights along the 15-mile way.

If you're planning a trip to Disneyland with your family or a group of friends, stick with the Mouse as your main plan. Many people spend several days exploring the parks, never

Previous: Hollywood Boulevard at sunset; Santa Monica Pier. **Above:** TCL Chinese Theatre.

Look for ★ to find recommended sights, activities, dining, and lodging.

Highlights

★ **California Science Center:** Learn about the daily life of an astronaut and then marvel at the space shuttle *Endeavour* at this museum (page 430).

★ **Griffith Park:** This large urban park in the Santa Monica Mountains is home to the iconic Hollywood Sign and the Griffith Observatory (page 431).

★ **Hollywood Walk of Fame:** Walk all over your favorite stars—they're embedded in the ground beneath your feet (page 431).

★ **TCL Chinese Theatre:** Take in a movie premiere, step into the footprints of movie stars, or grab a photo op in front of this Hollywood icon (page 433).

★ **Los Angeles County Museum of Art:** You can easily spend a full day taking in this diverse array of exhibits, showcasing art from the ancient to the ultramodern (page 436).

★ **The Getty Center:** The art collections, soaring architecture, beautiful grounds, and remarkable views of the skyline make this a must-see (page 437).

★ **Santa Monica Pier:** Ride the Scrambler, take in the view from the solar-powered Ferris wheel, or dine on a hot dog on a stick at this hundred-year-old amusement park by the sea (page 438).

★ **Venice Boardwalk:** L.A.'s most free-spirited beach community is crowded with street performers, bodybuilders, and self-identified freaks (page 438).

★ **The *Queen Mary:*** Tour this huge art deco ocean liner that's rumored to be haunted (page 440).

★ **Disney California Adventure Park:** Tour a Disneyfied version of the Golden State at the Disneyland Resort (page 463).

Los Angeles

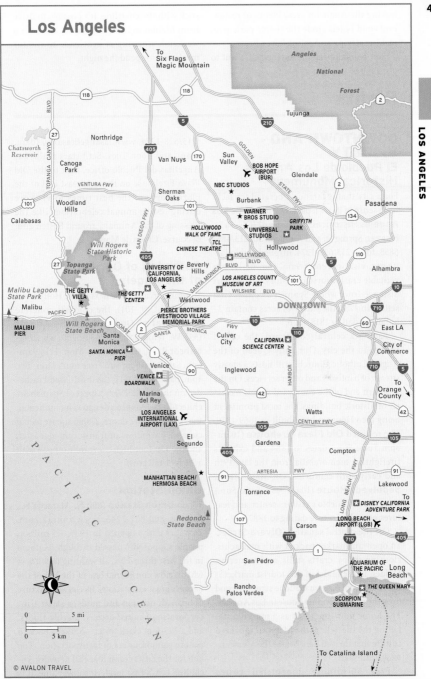

To Six Flags
Magic Mountain

Angeles

National

Forest

Tujunga

Northridge

Chatsworth
Reservoir

Canoga
Park

VENTURA FWY

Van Nuys

Sun
Valley

GOLDEN

BOB HOPE
AIRPORT
(BUR)

Glendale

Pasadena

STATE FWY

Woodland
Hills

Sherman
Oaks

Burbank

NBC STUDIOS ★

WARNER
★ BROS STUDIO

Calabasas

HOLLYWOOD
WALK OF FAME

★ UNIVERSAL
STUDIOS

GRIFFITH
PARK ★

Will Rogers
State Historic
Park

SAN DIEGO FWY

TCL
CHINESE THEATRE

Hollywood

Topanga
State Park

UNIVERSITY OF
CALIFORNIA,
LOS ANGELES

HOLLYWOOD
BLVD

Alhambra

Malibu Lagoon
State Park

THE GETTY
VILLA ★

THE GETTY
CENTER ★

Beverly
Hills

SANTA MONICA

LOS ANGELES COUNTY
MUSEUM OF ART ★

Malibu

PACIFIC

Will Rogers ★
State Beach

COAST

Westwood

WILSHIRE   BLVD

DOWNTOWN

MALIBU
PIER ★

PIERCE BROTHERS
WESTWOOD VILLAGE
MEMORIAL PARK

SANTA

MONICA

FWY

East LA

Santa
Monica

SANTA MONICA
PIER ★

Culver
City

CALIFORNIA
SCIENCE CENTER ★

HARBOR FWY

City of
Commerce

Venice

HWY

To
Orange
County

VENICE
BOARDWALK ★

Inglewood

Marina
del Rey

LOS ANGELES
INTERNATIONAL
AIRPORT (LAX) ✈

El
Segundo

Gardena

Watts

CENTURY FWY

Compton

MANHATTAN BEACH/
HERMOSA BEACH ★

ARTESIA   FWY

Torrance

Lakewood

PACIFIC

Redondo
State Beach

Carson

To
DISNEY CALIFORNIA
ADVENTURE PARK ★

LONG BEACH
AIRPORT (LGB) ✈

OCEAN

San Pedro

AQUARIUM OF
THE PACIFIC ★

Long
Beach

Rancho
Palos Verdes

★ THE QUEEN MARY

SCORPION
SUBMARINE ★

0   5 mi

0   5 km

To Catalina Island

© AVALON TRAVEL

118
118
5
210
2
27
170
405
101
101
134
2
27
405
2
110
101
5
2
110
10
710
1
2
10
110
60
1
90
42
710
5
105
42
105
405
91
107
91
710
405
110
1

leaving the Anaheim area. Plenty of restaurants and hotels circle the theme park area, making staying and eating here a breeze.

Sun-worshippers and surfers will want to stick with the coastline. It's possible to drive from Malibu to San Juan Capistrano over a weekend, stopping at beachside towns for meals and to spend the night.

Sights

DOWNTOWN AND VICINITY
El Pueblo de Los Angeles Historical Monument

For a city that is famously berated for lacking a sense of its own past, **El Pueblo de Los Angeles Historical Monument** (Olvera St. between Spring St. and Alameda St., 213/485-6855, tours 213/628-1274, http://elpueblo.lacity.org, visitors center 9am-4pm daily) is a veritable crash course in history. Just a short distance from where Spanish colonists first settled in 1781, the park's 44 acres contain 27 buildings dating 1818-1926.

Facing a central courtyard, the oldest church in the city, Our Lady Queen of the Angels Catholic Church, still hosts a steady stream of baptisms and other services. On the southern end of the courtyard stands a cluster of historic buildings, the most prominent being Pico House, a hotel built in 1869-1870. The restored **Old Plaza Firehouse** (10am-3pm Tues.-Sun.) dates to 1884 and exhibits firefighting memorabilia from the late 19th and early 20th centuries. On Main Street, **Sepulveda House** (10am-3pm Tues.-Sun.) serves as the Pueblo's visitors center and features period furniture dating to 1887.

Off the central square is **Olvera Street,** an open-air market packed with mariachis, clothing shops, crafts stalls, and taquerias. Hidden in the midst of this tourist market is the Avila Adobe, a squat adobe structure said to be the oldest standing house in Los Angeles. The home now functions as a museum detailing the lifestyle of the Mexican ranchero culture that thrived here before the Mexican-American War.

Free 50-minute docent-led **tours** (213/628-1274, www.lasangelitas.org, 10am, 11am, and noon Tues.-Sat.) start at the Las Angelitas del Pueblo office, next to the Old Plaza Firehouse on the southeast end of the plaza. Some of the best times to visit are during festive annual celebrations like the Blessing of the Animals, around Easter, and, of course, Cinco de Mayo.

Cathedral of Our Lady of the Angels

Standing on a hillside next to the Hollywood Freeway (U.S. 101), the colossal concrete **Cathedral of Our Lady of the Angels** (555 W. Temple St., 213/680-5200, www.olacathedral.org, 6:30am-6pm Mon.-Fri., 9am-6pm Sat., 7am-6pm Sun., free tours Mon.-Fri. 1pm, parking $4-18) is the third-largest cathedral in the world. Every aspect of Spanish architect Rafael Moneo's design is monumental: the 25-ton bronze doors, 27,000 square feet of clerestory windows of translucent alabaster, and the 156-foot-high campanile topped with a 25-foot-tall cross.

Union Station

When **Union Station** (800 N. Alameda St., Amtrak 800/872-7245, www.amtrak.com, 24 hours daily) opened in 1939, 1.5 million people supposedly passed through its doors in the first three days, all wanting to witness what is now considered one of the last of the nation's great rail stations. Its elegant mixture of Spanish mission and modern styles—incorporating vaulted arches, marble floors, and a 135-foot clock tower—harkens back to a more glamorous era of transportation. The hub for the city's commuter rail network, including L.A.'s first modern subway line, it is

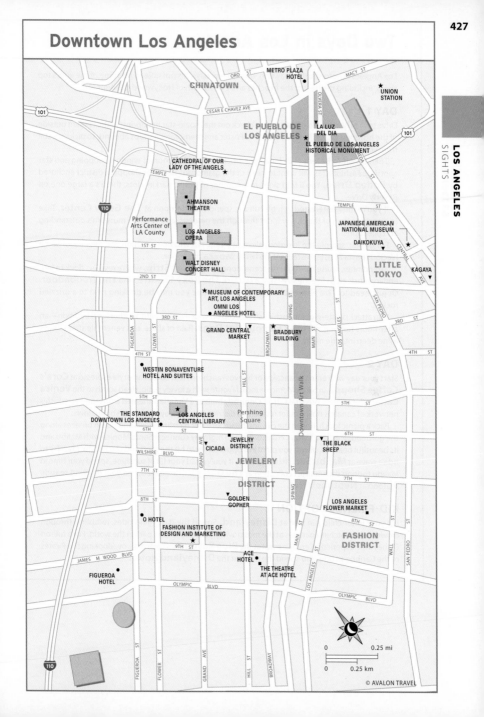

Two Days in Los Angeles

Los Angeles is notoriously sprawling, but in a few days, it's possible to hit some of the area's top spots, including the best of the beaches and even a dash of Hollywood glamour.

DAY 1

Drive to **Hollywood Boulevard** to check out the movie-star handprints in the cement outside of the historic **TCL Chinese Theatre.** Poster and memorabilia shops abound, so pick up a still from your favorite movie.

Then it's off to Beverly Hills for a light lunch and an afternoon of window shopping and star spotting. Fashionistas will want to head to the glamorous designer shopping district anchored by **Rodeo Drive.** You'll find signs to a number of public parking lots; there's a large one on Beverly Drive.

If you're more interested in high culture, spend the afternoon at **The Getty Center.** Take in dizzying views of the city, wander through the gardens, and tour the museum's outstanding art collections.

For dinner, sample the luxurious slices at **Pizzeria Mozza** on Highland Avenue, or some luscious pasta at sister restaurant **Osteria Mozza** next door.

After dinner, cruise the nightlife scene along the **Sunset Strip,** where revelers flock to legendary music clubs like the **Whisky a Go Go, The Roxy Theatre,** and **The Troubadour.** Or just head to **The Rainbow Bar & Grill,** where you may be drinking next to a grizzled rocker.

If an attack of late-night munchies strikes, cap off your evening with another local tradition—an after-hours hot dog at **Pink's Famous Hot Dogs.** Rain or shine, this venerable stand draws a line deep into the night.

DAY 2

Start your day with orange pancakes or huevos rancheros and European-style espresso at **Cora's Coffee Shoppe** in Santa Monica, a local favorite with a lovely patio. Head south to the **Venice Canals** for an after-breakfast stroll. Originally built as a Venetian-themed amusement park, this network of canals is now a quiet residential district of waterways lined with bungalows.

Pack a picnic lunch, hop in the car, and head north for dazzling views and ocean breezes along the gorgeous **Pacific Coast Highway.** The highway connects Santa Monica with Malibu and its beautiful beaches, giving you plenty of opportunity to hit the sand and catch some rays. Try to ride a wave at **Malibu Surfrider Beach.** If you've had your fill of sunshine, spend your time in Malibu touring the small art collection at **The Getty Villa** instead. End your day with seaside seafood at **Neptune's Net.**

KID-FRIENDLY OPTION

Let your inner child run free at **Disneyland.** Spend the day riding rides, rambling through crowds, and watching parades at the most lovingly crafted theme park in the world. For a full-on Disney-rific experience, enjoy a meal at the **Blue Bayou Restaurant** overlooking the Pirates of the Caribbean ride, and spend the night at the **Disneyland Hotel.**

also a vision of the future, as it's slated to be a major hub of the planned California High Speed Rail System.

MOCA

The **Museum of Contemporary Art, Los Angeles** (MOCA, 250 S. Grand Ave., 213/626-6222, www.moca.org, 11am-5pm Mon. and Fri., 11am-8pm Thurs., 11am-6pm Sat.-Sun., adults $12, students and seniors $7, under age 12 free) is where you'll see an array of artwork created between 1940 and yesterday afternoon. Highlights include pop art and abstract expressionism from Europe and the United States. Temporary exhibits have displayed the work of Andy Warhol and British artist-turned-Oscar-winning filmmaker Steve McQueen. MOCA has two other locations: The **Geffen Contemporary at MOCA** (152 N. Central Ave., www.moca.org, 11am-5pm Mon. and Fri., 11am-8pm Thurs., 11am-6pm Sat.-Sun.) and the **MOCA Pacific Design Center** (8687 Melrose Ave., West Hollywood, 11am-5pm Tues.-Fri., 11am-6pm Sat.-Sun.).

Downtown Art Walk

The dramatic sculptures and fountains adorning two blocks on **Hope Street** (300-500 Hope St.) include Alexander Calder's enormous *Four Arches* (1974) beside the Bank of America Plaza and Nancy Graves's whimsical *Sequi* (1986) near the Wells Fargo Center. A free, self-guided, public **Downtown Art Walk** (213/617-4929, http://downtownart-walk.org, hours vary but usually noon-10pm on the second Thursday of each month) centers predominantly on the galleries bounded by Spring, Main, 2nd, and 9th Streets, but also spreads out to the Calder and Graves pieces on Hope Street.

Bradbury Building

One of several historic L.A. structures featured in the movies *Chinatown* (1974), *Blade Runner* (1982), and *The Artist* (2011), the 1893 **Bradbury Building** (304 S. Broadway, lobby 9am-5pm daily) is an office building that wows filmmakers with its light-filled Victorian court that includes wrought-iron staircases, marble stairs, and open-cage elevators. On Saturday mornings, the 2.5-hour, docent-led **Historic Downtown Walking Tour** (213/623-2489, www.laconservancy. org, 10am Sat., reservations required, adults $10, under age 13 $5), run by the Los Angeles Conservancy, takes visitors through Downtown to sights including the Bradbury Building.

Japanese American National Museum

The **Japanese American National Museum** (100 N. Central Ave., 213/625-0414, www.janm.org, 11am-5pm Tues.-Wed. and Fri.-Sun., noon-8pm Thurs., adults $9, students and seniors $5, under age 5 free) focuses on the experiences of Japanese people coming to and living in the United States, particularly California. This museum shows the Japanese American experience in vivid detail, with photos and artifacts telling much of the story.

Fashion Institute of Design and Marketing

The **Fashion Institute of Design and Marketing Museum and Galleries** (FIDM, 919 S. Grand Ave., Ste. 250, 213/623-5821, http://fidmmuseum.org, 10am-5pm Tues.-Sat., free) are open to the public, giving costume buffs and clotheshorses a window into high fashion and Hollywood costume design. FIDM pulls from its collection of more than 10,000 costumes and textiles to create exhibits based on style, era, movie genre, and whatever else the curators dream up. Parking is available in the underground garage for a fee. When you enter the building, tell the folks at the security desk that you're headed for the museum. A small but fun museum shop offers student work, unique accessories, and more.

Also housed in the FIDM building is the **Annette Green Perfume Museum** (10am-5pm Mon.-Sat., free). This is the world's first museum dedicated to scent and the role of perfume in society.

Natural History Museum of Los Angeles County

If you'd like your kids to have some fun with an educational purpose, take them to the **Natural History Museum of Los Angeles County** (900 Exposition Blvd., 213/763-3466, www.nhm.org, 9:30am-5pm daily, adults $12, students and seniors $9, children $5, parking $10 cash only). This huge museum features many amazing galleries; some are transformed into examples of mammal habitats, while others display artifacts of various peoples indigenous to the Western Hemisphere. The Discovery Center welcomes children with a wide array of live animals and insects, plus hands-on displays that let kids learn by touching as well as looking.

★ California Science Center

The **California Science Center** (700 Exposition Park Dr., 323/724-3623, www.californiasciencecenter.org, 10am-5pm daily, admission free, parking $10) focuses on the notable achievements and gathered knowledge of humankind. There are many interactive exhibits here, including one that lets visitors "lift" a giant truck off the ground. The Ecosystems section showcases 11 different natural environments, such as a living kelp forest and a polar ice wall. Other galleries are dedicated to air and space technology, life as we know it, and human creativity.

One major reason people come to the California Science Center is to view the last of NASA's space shuttles, the *Endeavour*. The 132-foot-long shuttle hangs on display in a pavilion and eventually will be shown in its launch position. To see the shuttle exhibit, reserve a timed entry by calling (213/744-2019) or going online (www.californiasciencecenter.org).

Many people also come to the California Science Center for the **IMAX theater** (213/744-2019; adults $8.25; seniors, teens, and students $6; children $5), which shows educational films on its tremendous seven-story screen. Your IMAX tickets also get you onto the rideable attractions of the Science Court.

LOS FELIZ AND SILVER LAKE

East of Hollywood and northwest of Downtown, Los Feliz ("loss FEEL-is") is home to an eclectic mix of retired professionals, Armenian immigrants, and movie-industry hipsters lured by the bohemian vibe, midcentury modern architecture, and the neighborhood's proximity to Griffith Park.

California Science Center

★ Griffith Park

Griffith Park (Los Feliz Blvd., Zoo Dr., or Griffith Park Blvd., 323/913-4688, www. laparks.org, 5am-10:30pm daily, free) is the country's largest municipal park with an urban wilderness area. Griffith Park has also played host to many production companies over the years, with its land and buildings providing backdrops for many major films. Scenes from *Rebel Without a Cause* were filmed here, as were parts of the first two *Back to the Future* movies.

If you love the night skies, visit the **Griffith Observatory** (2800 E. Observatory Rd., 213/473-0800, www.griffithobservatory.org, noon-10pm Tues.-Fri., 10am-10pm Sat.-Sun., free), where free telescopes are available and experienced demonstrators help visitors gaze at the stars. Or take in a film about the earth or sky in the aluminum-domed **Samuel Oschin Planetarium** (www.griffithobservatory.org for showtimes, $3-7).

If you prefer a more structured park experience, try the **L.A. Zoo and Botanical Gardens** (5333 Zoo Dr., 323/644-4200, www.lazoo.org, 10am-5pm daily, adults $19, seniors $16, children $14, parking free), where you can view elephants, rhinos, and gorillas. If the weather is poor, step inside **The Autry National Center of the American West** (4700 Western Heritage Way, 323/667-2000, www.theautry.org, 10am-4pm Tues.-Fri., 10am-5pm Sat.-Sun., adults $10, students and seniors $6, children $4), which showcases artifacts of the American West.

Kids love riding the trains of the operating miniature railroad at both the **Travel Town Railroad** (5200 Zoo Dr., 323/662-9678, www. griffithparktrainrides.com, 10am-3:15pm Mon.-Fri., 10am-4:45pm Sat.-Sun. in summer; 10am-3:15pm Mon.-Fri., 10am-4:15pm Sat.-Sun. in winter; $2.75), which runs the perimeter of the **Travel Town Museum** (5200 Zoo Dr., 323/662-5874, http://traveltown.org, 10am-5pm Mon.-Fri., 10am-6pm Sat.-Sun. in summer; 10am-4pm Mon.-Fri., 10am-6pm Sat.-Sun. in winter, free), and the **Griffith Park & Southern Railroad** (4730 Crystal Springs Rd., www.griffithparktrainrides.com, 10am-4:45pm Mon.-Fri., 10am-5pm Sat.-Sun. in summer; 10am-4:15pm Mon.-Fri., 10am-4:30pm Sat.-Sun. in winter, adults $2.75, seniors $2.25), which takes riders on a one-mile track.

The **Hollywood Sign** sits on Mount Lee, which is part of the park and indelibly part of the mystique of Hollywood. A strenuous five-mile hike will lead you to an overlook just above and behind the sign. To get there, drive to the top of Beachwood Drive, park, and follow the Hollyridge Trail.

TOP EXPERIENCE

HOLLYWOOD

You won't find blocks of movie studios in Hollywood, and few stars walk its streets except on premiere evenings. But still, if you've ever had a soft spot for Hollywood glamour or American camp, come and check out the crowds and bustle of downtown Tinseltown (and be aware that no local would *ever* call it that). Hollywood is also famous for its street corners. While the most stuff sits at Hollywood and Highland, the best-known corner is certainly Hollywood and Vine.

★ Hollywood Walk of Fame

One of the most recognizable facets of Hollywood is its star-studded **Walk of Fame** (Hollywood Blvd. from La Brea Ave. to Vine St., 323/469-8311, www.walkoffame.com). This area, portrayed in countless movies, contains more than 2,500 five-pointed stars honoring both real people and fictional characters that have contributed significantly to the entertainment industry and the Hollywood legend. Each pink star is set in a charcoal-colored square and has its honoree's name in bronze. Eight stars were laid in August 1958 to demonstrate what the walk would look like. Legal battles delayed the actual construction until February 1960, and the walk was dedicated in November 1960. At each of the four corners of Hollywood and Vine is a moon that honors the three Apollo 11 astronauts: Neil

Hollywood

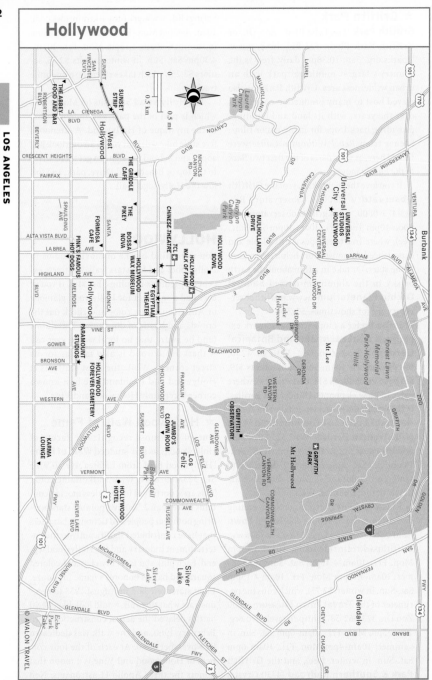

SAN VICENTE BLVD

SUNSET

West Hollywood

SUNSET STRIP

ROBERTSON BLVD

LA CIENEGA BLVD

BEVERLY BLVD

CRESCENT HEIGHTS BLVD

FAIRFAX AVE

THE ABBEY FOOD AND BAR

THE GRIDDLE CAFE

SPAULDING AVE

FORMOSA CAFE

ALTA VISTA BLVD

LA BREA AVE

PINK'S FAMOUS HOT DOGS

HIGHLAND BLVD

THE PIKEY

THE BOSSA NOVA

SANTA MONICA BLVD

Hollywood BLVD

MELROSE AVE

CHINESE THEATRE

TCL

HOLLYWOOD WAX MUSEUM

EGYPTIAN THEATER

HOLLYWOOD WALK OF FAME

VINE ST

GOWER ST

BRONSON AVE

PARAMOUNT STUDIOS

WESTERN AVE

HOLLYWOOD FOREVER CEMETERY

KARMA LOUNGE

SUNSET BLVD

FOUNTAIN AVE

VERMONT AVE

HOLLYWOOD BLVD

FRANKLIN AVE

JUMBO'S CLOWN ROOM

HOLLYWOOD HOTEL

Barnsdall Park

COMMONWEALTH AVE

RUSSELL AVE

SILVER LAKE BLVD

MICHELTORENA ST

Silver Lake

Los Feliz

LOS FELIZ BLVD

GLENDOWER AVE

GRIFFITH OBSERVATORY

CRYSTAL SPRINGS DR

GRIFFITH PARK DR

Mt Hollywood

WESTERN CANYON RD

VERMONT CANYON RD

COMMONWEALTH CANYON DR

GRIFFITH PARK

Mt Lee

Lake Hollywood

LAKE HOLLYWOOD DR

LEDGEWOOD DR

DERONDA DR

BEACHWOOD DR

Forest Lawn Memorial Park-Hollywood Hills

BARHAM BLVD

UNIVERSAL CENTER DR

Universal Studios Hollywood

UNIVERSAL STUDIOS HOLLYWOOD

Universal City

CAHUENGA BLVD

MULHOLLAND DR

Runyon Canyon Park

NICHOLS CANYON RD

LAUREL CANYON BLVD

Laurel Canyon Park

MULHOLLAND DR

MULHOLLAND DRIVE

HOLLYWOOD BOWL

101

170

LANKERSHIM BLVD

VENTURA BLVD

Burbank

134

ALAMEDA AVE

ZOO DR

GRIFFITH PARK DR

GOLDEN STATE FWY

5

SAN FERNANDO RD

Glendale

CHEVY CHASE DR

BRAND BLVD

134

GLENDALE BLVD

FLETCHER ST

GLENDALE FWY

2

Echo Park Lake

SUNSET BLVD

101

5

0   0.5 km
0   0.5 mi

© AVALON TRAVEL

Armstrong, Michael Collins, and Edwin E. "Buzz" Aldrin Jr. At the edges of the Walk of Fame, you'll find blank stars waiting to be filled by up-and-comers making their mark on Tinseltown.

The complete walk is about 3.5 miles. You'll be looking down at the stars, so watch out for other pedestrians crowding the sidewalks in this visitor-dense area. Careful reading of the information on the Walk of Fame website (www.walkoffame.com) should help you find every star you need to see.

Hollywood Wax Museum

It immortalizes your favorite stars, all right. If you want to see the Hollywood heavyweights all dressed up in costume and completely unable to run away, visit the **Hollywood Wax Museum** (6767 Hollywood Blvd., 323/462-5991, www.hollywoodwaxmuseum.com, 10am-midnight daily, adults $17, seniors $15, children $10). The exhibits are re-creations of the sets of all sorts of films, and as you pass through, you'll be right in the action (if staring at eerie, life-size wax likenesses of real people can be called action). You can even get a glimpse of stars on the red carpet at an awards show-style set. Save a dollar by purchasing a ticket online.

If you need yet another cotton-candy museum experience, right across the street is the **Ripley's Believe It or Not! Odditorium** (6780 Hollywood Blvd., 323/466-6335, www.ripleyattractions.com, 10am-midnight daily, adults $15, children $9). You'll find everything from duct tape art to a real shrunken head.

★ TCL Chinese Theatre

You can't miss the **TCL Chinese Theatre** (6925 Hollywood Blvd., 323/461-3331, www.tclchinesetheatres.com) on Hollywood Boulevard. With its elaborate 90-foot-tall Chinese temple gateway and unending crowd of visitors, the Chinese Theatre may be the most visited and recognizable movie theater in the world. Along with the throngs of tourists out front, there are usually elaborately costumed movie characters, from Captain Jack Sparrow to Spider-Man, shaking hands with fans and posing for pictures (for a fee). Inside the courtyard you'll find handprints and footprints of legendary Hollywood stars. Stop and admire the bells, dogs, and other Chinese artifacts in the courtyard; most are the genuine article, imported from China by special permit in the 1920s.

The studios hold premieres at the Chinese Theatre all the time. Check the website for

TCL Chinese Theatre

Film Festivals

Home of Hollywood and many of the world's most famous movie stars, Los Angeles is an ideal place to go to the movies. It's even better when you can attend a film festival.

There seems to be an endless array of film festivals in the Los Angeles area. Cofounded by actor Danny Glover, the **Pan African Film and Arts Festival** (310/337-4737, www.paff.org) takes place in February and highlights the works of people of African descent from all over the world.

Movies including Pixar's *Brave* have debuted at the **Los Angeles Film Festival** (866/345-6337, www.lafilmfest.com). The LAFF happens in June and includes the screening of 100 films.

Outfest (213/480-7088, www.outfest.org) is the oldest continuous film festival in Los Angeles, and it highlights LBGT-oriented movies in July.

The **Downtown Film Festival L.A.** (www.dffla.com), which also happens in July, is for filmgoers who enjoy under-the-radar indie cinema.

The **Sundance Next Fest** (www.sundance.org/next) is a new and worthy entry to the L.A. film festival scene. This unique summer fest in August includes movie premieres and concerts by musical acts.

The nonprofit American Film Institute plays some of the biggest pictures of the year at its November **AFI Fest** (866/234-3378, www.afi.com). Come to see what are sure to be some of the year's most talked-about movies.

showtimes and ticket information. The Chinese Theatre has only one screen, but seats over 1,000 people per showing. Daily 20-minute tours (323/463-9576 or tours@chinesetheatres.com for tickets, adults $13.50, seniors $11.50, children $6.50) featuring anecdotes about the fabled theater are available with a reservation. While you're welcome to crowd the sidewalk to try to catch a glimpse of the stars at a premiere, most of these are private events.

Egyptian Theater

Built under the auspices of the legendary Sid Grauman, the **Egyptian Theater** (6712 Hollywood Blvd., 323/466-3456, www.americancinematheque.com, adults $11, students and seniors $9) was the first of the grandiose movie houses in Hollywood proper and a follower of those in Downtown Los Angeles. King Tut's tomb had been discovered in 1922, and the glorified Egyptian styling of the theater followed the trend for all things Egyptian that came after. The massive courtyard and the stage both boast columns, sphinxes, and other Egyptian-esque decor. The first movie to premiere at the Egyptian was *Robin Hood*, in 1922.

Today, get tickets to an array of old-time films, film festivals, and double features, or take a morning tour to get a glimpse of the history of this magnificent theater. Expect to pay $5-20 for parking in one of the nearby lots.

Hollywood Forever Cemetery

The final resting place of such Hollywood legends as Rudolph Valentino, Marion Davies, Douglas Fairbanks, and Johnny Ramone, the **Hollywood Forever Cemetery** (6000 Santa Monica Blvd., 323/469-1181, www.hollywoodforever.com, 8am-5pm daily) has received a dramatic makeover and now offers live funeral webcasts. During the summer, the cemetery screens films and holds concerts by national touring acts on its Fairbanks Lawn and in its Masonic Lodge. Visit the website for a list of upcoming events.

Paramount Studios

Paramount Studios (5515 Melrose Ave., 323/956-1777, www.paramountstudiotour.com, tours $55-178) is the only major movie studio still operating in Hollywood proper. The wrought-iron gates that greet visitors were erected to deter adoring Rudolph Valentino fans in the 1920s. Tours ranging

2-4.5 hours are available. Visit the website or call the studio for tour information.

Mulholland Drive

As you drive north out of central Hollywood into the residential part of the neighborhood, you will find folks on street corners hawking maps of stars' homes on **Mulholland Drive** (entrance west of U.S. 101 via Barham Blvd. exit) and its surrounding neighborhoods. Whether you choose to pay up to $10 for a photocopied sheet of dubious information is up to you. What's certain is that you can drive the famed road yourself. When you reach the ridge, you'll see why so many of the wealthy make their homes here. From the ridgeline, on clear days you can see down into the Los Angeles Basin and the coast to the west, and the fertile land of the San Fernando Valley to the east. Whether you care about movie-star homes or not, the view itself is worth the trip, especially if it has rained recently and the smog is down.

Universal Studios Hollywood

The longtime Hollywood-centric alternative to Disneyland is the **Universal Studios Hollywood** (100 Universal City Plaza, Los Angeles, 800/864-8377, www.universalstudios.com, hours vary, adults $95, ages 3 to 9 $87, parking $16-22) theme park. (Save up to $10 by getting tickets online.) Kids adore this park, which puts them right into the action of their favorite movies. Flee the carnivorous dinosaurs of *Jurassic Park,* take a rafting adventure on the pseudo-set of *Waterworld,* quiver in terror of an ancient curse in *Revenge of the Mummy,* or race around in the new *Fast & Furious* ride. You can also experience the shape-shifting Transformers in a ride based on the movies and the Hasbro toy.

If you're more interested in how the movies are made than the rides made from them, take the Studio Tour with a recorded Jimmy Fallon as host. You'll get an extreme close-up of the sets of major blockbuster films like *War of the Worlds.* Better yet, get tickets at the Audiences Unlimited Ticket Booth and be part of the studio audience of TV shows currently taping. Serious movie buffs can get a VIP pass for $329; a six-hour tour takes you onto working sound stages and into the current prop warehouse.

LA BREA, FAIRFAX, AND MIRACLE MILE

Lined with fabric emporiums, antiques dealers, and contemporary furniture design shops, Beverly Boulevard and La Brea Avenue north of Wilshire Boulevard are increasingly trendy haunts for interior decorators. Along bustling and pedestrian-friendly Fairfax Avenue, kosher bakeries and signs in Hebrew announce the presence of the neighborhood's sizable Jewish population. Around the corner on 3rd Street, The Original Farmers Market is one of L.A.'s historic gathering places. And farther south, Wilshire Boulevard is home to some of the city's many museums, including the Los Angeles County Museum of Art.

La Brea Tar Pits and Museum

Nothing can stop the smell of the **La Brea Tar Pits,** where untold thousands of animals became trapped in the sticky tar and met their ancient fate. Paved paths lead around the most accessible pits, while others (mostly those that are in active excavation) are accessible by guided tour only. If what interests you most are the fossilized contents, head for the beautiful **La Brea Tar Pits Museum** (5801 Wilshire Blvd., 213/763-3499, www.tarpits.org, 9:30am-5pm daily, adults $12, students and seniors $9, children $5, parking $10). The museum's reasonably small size and easy-to-understand interpretive signs make it great for kids. Genuine mammoths died and were fossilized in the tar pits, as were the tiniest of mice and about a zillion dire wolves. For a closer look at how the fossils were buried, get tickets to one of the **Excavator Tours** (11am and 3pm Mon.-Fri.; noon, 1pm, 2pm, and 3pm Sat.-Sun.; free with museum ticket), which are available online.

★ Los Angeles County Museum of Art

Travelers who desperately need a break from the endless shiny and mindless entertainments of L.A. can find respite and solace in the **Los Angeles County Museum of Art** (5905 Wilshire Blvd., 323/857-6000, www.lacma.org, 11am-5pm Mon.-Tues. and Thurs., 11am-8pm Fri., 10am-7pm Sat.-Sun., adults $15, seniors and students with ID $10, under age 17 free), the largest art museum in the western United States. Better known to its friends as LACMA, this museum complex prides itself on a diverse array of collections and exhibitions of art from around the world, from ancient to modern. There are nine full-size buildings filled with galleries, so don't expect to get through the whole thing in an hour, or even a full day. Specialties of LACMA include Japanese art and artifacts in the beautifully designed Pavilion for Japanese Art and the costumes and textiles of the Doris Stein Research Center. Several galleries of LACMA West are dedicated to arts and crafts for children. Perhaps best of all, some of the world's most prestigious traveling exhibitions come to LACMA.

You'll do a lot of walking from gallery to gallery and building to building at LACMA. The layout resembles a Southern California shopping mall, with lots of space to take in the warm weather between buildings, and is equipped with four dining options, including the acclaimed farm-to-table restaurant Ray's.

The Original Farmers Market

Begun in 1934 as a tailgate co-op for a handful of fruit farmers, **The Original Farmers Market** (6333 W. 3rd St., 323/933-9211 or 866/993-9211, www.farmersmarketla.com, 9am-9pm Mon.-Fri., 9am-8pm Sat., 10am-7pm Sun.) remains a favorite locale for shopping and people-watching. Along with the adjacent shopping center, The Grove, there are now more than 30 restaurants and 50 shops hawking everything from hot sauce to stickers. Annual events include a vintage auto show in early June, free summer concerts every Friday, and a fall festival.

BEVERLY HILLS AND WEST HOLLYWOOD

Although the truly wealthy live above Hollywood on Mulholland Drive, in Bel Air, or on the beach in Malibu, there's still plenty of money floating around Beverly Hills. Some of the world's best and most expensive shops line its streets. You'll also find plenty

La Brea Tar Pits and Museum

of high-end culture in this area, which bleeds into West L.A.

Sunset Strip

The **Sunset Strip** really is part of Sunset Boulevard—specifically the part that runs 1.5 miles through West Hollywood from the edge of Hollywood to the Beverly Hills city limits. The Strip exemplifies all that's grandiose and tacky about the L.A. entertainment industry. You'll also find many of the Strip's legendary rock clubs, such as **The Roxy** and the **Whisky a Go Go** and the infamous after-hours hangout **The Rainbow Bar & Grill.** Over several decades, up-and-coming rock acts first made their names on the Strip and lived at the "Riot Hyatt."

WESTWOOD

Designed around the campus of UCLA and the Westwood Village commercial district, this community situated between Santa Monica and Beverly Hills won national recognition in the 1930s as a model of innovative suburban planning.

University of California, Los Angeles

From its original quad of 10 buildings, the campus of the **University of California, Los Angeles** (UCLA, bounded by Hilgard Ave., Sunset Blvd., Le Conte Ave., and Gayley Ave., tours 310/825-8764, www.ucla.edu) has become the largest in the University of California system, with more than 400 buildings set on and around 419 beautifully kept acres. Today its facilities include one of the top medical centers in the country, a library of more than eight million volumes, and renowned performance venues, including **Royce Hall** and **Schoenberg Hall.**

★ The Getty Center

The Getty Center (1200 Sepulveda Blvd., 310/440-7300, www.getty.edu; 10am-5:30pm Tues.-Thurs. and Sun., 10am-9pm Fri.-Sat., summer; 10am-5:30pm Tues.-Fri. and Sun., 10am-9pm Sat., winter; admission free; parking $15) is a famed institution of art and culture. Donated by the family of J. Paul Getty to the people of Los Angeles, this museum features European art, sculpture, manuscripts, and European and American photos. The magnificent works are set in fabulous modern buildings with Richard Meier's soaring architecture, and you're guaranteed to find something beautiful to catch your eye and feed your imagination. There are frequent temporary

The Getty Center

exhibitions on diverse subjects. On a clear day, the views from The Getty, which sweep from Downtown L.A. west to the Pacific, are remarkable. There is also a central garden to stroll through and a cactus garden perched on a south-facing promontory with a view of the city below.

Pierce Brothers Westwood Village Memorial Park

The **Pierce Brothers Westwood Village Memorial Park** (1218 Glendon Ave., 310/474-1579, www.dignitymemorial.com, 8am-sunset daily) is the final resting place of some of the world's most popular entertainers and musicians. Under the shadows of the towering high-rises of Wilshire Boulevard, this small cemetery is the home of **Marilyn Monroe's crypt** (frequently decorated with lipstick marks), as well as Rat Packer **Dean Martin,** author **Truman Capote,** eclectic musician **Frank Zappa,** and the stars of *The Odd Couple,* **Walter Matthau** and **Jack Lemmon**.

SANTA MONICA, VENICE, AND MALIBU

Some of the most famous and most expensive real estate in the world sits on this stretch of sand and earth. Of the communities that call the northern coast of L.A. County home, the focal points are Malibu to the north, Santa Monica, and Venice to the south.

★ Santa Monica Pier

For the ultimate in SoCal beach kitsch, you can't miss the **Santa Monica Pier** (Ocean Ave. at Colorado Ave., 310/458-8901, www.santamonicapier.org, hours vary). As you walk the rather long stretch of concrete out over the water, you'll see an amazing array of carnival-style food stands, an arcade, a small amusement park, a trapeze school, and restaurants leading out to the fishing area at the tip of the pier. There's even an aquarium under the pier. The main attraction is **Pacific Park** (310/260-8744, www.pacpark.com, hours vary, $3-5 per ride, all-ride pass $15-27, parking $6-12). This park features a roller coaster, a Scrambler, and the world's first solar-powered Ferris wheel. Several rides are geared for the younger set, and a 20-game midway offers fun for all ages.

★ Venice Boardwalk

If the Santa Monica Pier doesn't provide you

Santa Monica Pier

Santa Monica and Venice

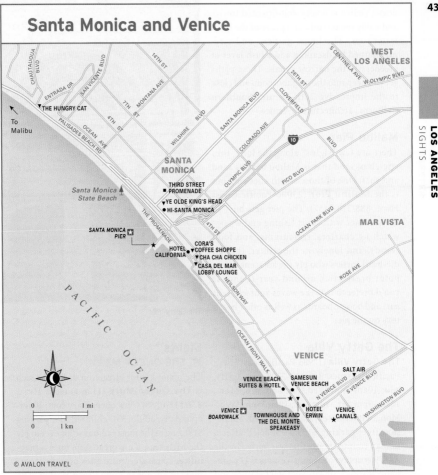

with enough chaos and kitsch, head on down to the **Venice Boardwalk** (Ocean Front Walk at Venice Blvd., 310/396-6764, www.venicebeach.com) for a nearly unlimited supply of both year-round. As you shamble down the tourist-laden path, you'll pass an astonishing array of tacky souvenir stores, tattoo and piercing parlors, walk-up food stands, and more. On the beach side of the path, dozens of artists create sculptures and hawk their wares. This area has more than its share of L.A.'s colorful characters, including some who perform for tips. The beach side includes the famous

Muscle Beach (two blocks north of Venice Blvd., www.musclebeach.net), an easily distinguishable chunk of sand filled with modern workout equipment and encircled by a barrier, and the **Venice Skate Park** (310/399-2775, www.laparks.org), where skaters get some serious air.

Venice Canals

Take a sedate walk along the paths of the **Venice Canals** (bounded by Washington Blvd., Strongs Dr., S. Venice Blvd., and Ocean Ave.), where locals take a stroll or walk their dogs (Venice is a very dog-oriented town), and enjoy the serenity and peace of the quiet waterways. The home gardens and city-maintained landscaping add a lush layer of greenery to the narrow canals. These paths get you deep into the neighborhood and close to the impressive 20th-century Southern California architecture of Venice.

Malibu Pier

There are few "sights" along the long, thin stretch of sand that is Malibu besides sand and surf. One of those worth checking out is the **Malibu Pier** (23000 Pacific Coast Hwy., 888/310-7437). The pier gets busy in the summer with sport fishing and whale-watching charters, restaurants, and food stands, and lonely in the winter, though die-hard surfers who ply the adjacent three-point break stick around year-round. If you'd prefer to ride the waves yourself, rent surf and boogie boards as well as other beach toys on the pier.

The Getty Villa

The Getty Villa

The Getty Villa (17985 Pacific Coast Hwy., Pacific Palisades, 310/440-7300, www.getty.edu; 10am-5pm Wed.-Fri. and Sun.-Mon., 10am-9pm Sat., summer; 10am-5pm Wed.-Mon., winter; reservations required; admission free; parking $15) is modeled after a Roman country house that was buried by the AD 79 eruption of Mount Vesuvius. The museum features amazingly intact statues and jewelry from the ancient Greeks, Romans, and Etruscans. Tickets are free, but you have to reserve them in advance if you want to enjoy this exclusive, intimate, and dazzling experience.

LONG BEACH

Long Beach has several worthy attractions befitting its size, including the historic and possibly haunted *Queen Mary* ocean liner and the Aquarium of the Pacific. Long Beach Harbor is also one of the best places to catch a boat ride out to Catalina Island, about 22 miles from shore.

Sights

★ THE *QUEEN MARY*

The major visitor attraction of Long Beach is **The *Queen Mary*** (1126 Queens Hwy., 877/342-0738, www.queenmary.com, 10am-6pm daily, adults $31, children $19, parking $15), one of the most famous ships ever to ply the high seas. This great ship, once a magnificent pleasure-cruise liner, now sits at permanent anchor in Long Beach Harbor. The *Queen Mary* acts as a **hotel** (877/342-0742, $99-389), a museum, and an entertainment center with several restaurants and bars. Book a stateroom and stay aboard, come for dinner, or just buy a regular ticket and take a self-guided tour. The museum exhibits describe the history of the ship, which took its maiden voyage in 1936, with special emphasis on its tour of duty as a troop transport during World War II.

It's not just the extensive museum and the attractive hotel that make the *Queen Mary* well known today. The ship is also one of the most famously haunted places in California. Over its decades of service, a number of people lost their lives aboard the *Queen Mary.* Rumors say several of these unfortunate souls have remained on the ship since their tragic deaths. If you're most interested in the ghost stories of the *Queen Mary,* book a spot on the **Paranormal Ship Walk** (877/342-0738, 8pm-10pm Sun.-Thurs., $39), which takes you to the hottest haunted spots; **Dining with the Spirits** (7pm Fri.-Sat., includes three-course dinner, $129), a combination dinner and two-hour haunted tour; or **Paranormal Investigation** (11pm Fri.-Sat., 10pm Sun., $75), for serious ghost hunters. During the day, the 35-minute **Ghosts and Legends Tour** (11am-6pm Mon.-Thurs., 11am-9pm Fri.-Sat., prices vary) includes a haunted experience complete with smoke machines and flashing lights.

The *Queen Mary* **Passport** (adults $27, children 4-11 $17.50) includes a self-guided audio tour, a look at the vessel's historic exhibits, a viewing of a film showing in the 4-D Theater, and admission to the Ghosts and Legends Tour. The **First Class Passport** (adults $34, children 4-11 $24.50) includes all of the *Queen Mary* Passport attractions along with a ticket to your choice of the Glory Days Historical Tour or the Haunted Encounters Tour.

The *Queen Mary* offers a large paid parking lot near the ship's berth. You'll walk from the parking area up to a square with a ticket booth and several shops and a snack bar. Purchase your general-admission ticket to get on board the ship. It's also a good idea to buy any guided tour tickets at this point. Night tours can fill up in advance, so call ahead to reserve a spot.

SCORPION SUBMARINE

Berthed right next to the luxurious *Queen Mary* is a much smaller and more lethal boat, the **Scorpion Submarine** (877/342-0752, www.queenmary.com, 10am-5pm daily, adults $14, children $12). This Russian sub helped the Soviet Union spy on the United States for more than 20 years during the Cold War. Admission includes the opportunity to explore the innards of the undersea vessel by squeezing through the tiny spaces, mimicking how the Soviet submariners lived and worked during the sub's secret mission.

AQUARIUM OF THE PACIFIC

The **Aquarium of the Pacific** (100 Aquarium Way, 562/590-3100, www.aquariumofpacific.org, 9am-6pm daily, adults $29, seniors $26, children $15) hosts animals and plant life native to the Pacific Ocean, from the local residents of SoCal's sea up to the northern Pacific and down to the tropics. While the big modern building isn't much to look at from the outside, it's what's inside that's beautiful—sea stars, urchins, and rays in the touch-friendly tanks, and a Shark Lagoon where you can pet a few of the more than 150 sharks that live here.

Entertainment and Events

NIGHTLIFE
Bars and Clubs

Hit **The Rainbow Bar & Grill** (9015 W. Sunset Blvd., 310/278-4232, www.rainbowbarandgrill.com, 11am-2am daily) to see an amazing myriad of rock-and-roll memorabilia and get a taste of music history. A group of musicians known as the "Hollywood Vampires," which included Alice Cooper, Keith Moon, John Lennon, Ringo Starr, Harry Nilsson, and Micky Dolenz, congregated here in the 1970s. Today, rockers still drop in after playing shows in the neighborhood.

Featured in films like *L.A. Confidential,* the historic **Formosa Café** (7156 Santa Monica Blvd., 323/850-9050, 4pm-2am Mon.-Fri., 6pm-2am Sat.-Sun.) is a West Hollywood landmark that has changed little since 1925.

Side Trip to Pasadena

Once a resort-like haven for the very wealthy, Pasadena is now a charming upper-middle-class town. You can still see fabulous examples of the craftsman architecture and visit one of the best-known and most-attended parades in the U.S.

THE HUNTINGTON

Some of the most beautiful botanical gardens in the world grow at The Huntington (1151 Oxford Rd., San Marino, 626/405-2100, www.huntington.org; 10:30am-4:30pm Wed.-Mon., Memorial Day-Labor Day; noon-4:30pm Wed.-Fri. and Mon., 10:30am-4:30pm Sat.-Sun., Labor Day-Memorial Day; adults $23-25, seniors and students $19-21, children free), which also includes an amazing library filled with rare and ancient books and manuscripts. Admission to the center includes a docent-led garden tour. During your visit, make reservations for a scrumptious buffet-style high tea at the Rose Garden Tea Room and Café (tea room reservations 626/683-8131, no reservations needed for café, noon-4:30pm Mon. and Wed.-Fri., 10:45am-4:30pm Sat.-Sun., adults $31, ages 4-8 $15, ages 2-3 $7.50).

THE GAMBLE HOUSE

The Gamble House (4 Westmoreland Pl., 626/793-3334, www.gamblehouse.org, 11:30am-1:30pm Tues., noon-4pm Thurs.-Sun., adults $15, seniors and students $12.50, under age 12 free) was designed and decorated by legendary SoCal architects Greene and Greene in the American craftsman or American arts and crafts style. Admission is by tour only (schedules vary by season), where you'll learn how they created this masterpiece and see how the Gambles lived.

NORTON SIMON MUSEUM

Wealthy industrialist Norton Simon collected thousands of works of art over 30 years that are now housed in the Norton Simon Museum (411 W. Colorado Blvd., 626/449-6840, www.nortonsimon.org, noon-5pm Mon. and Wed.-Thurs., 11am-8pm Fri.-Sun., adults $12, seniors $9, students and children free). The lovely modern building houses large, airy galleries holding beautiful works of the European Renaissance, South and Southeast Asia, and 20th-century sculpture.

ROSE BOWL STADIUM

The Rose Bowl Stadium (1001 Rose Bowl Dr., 626/577-3101, www.rosebowlstadium.com, office 8:30am-5:30pm Mon.-Fri.) is home to the famed granddaddy of the bowl games and to the UCLA college football team, as well as the Rose Parade (New Year's Day). You can visit the Rose Bowl anytime, although you might need a ticket during an event, and you'll definitely need to plan in advance to attend the Rose Bowl game.

Chinese decor embellishes the dimly lit main bar, and two large patios pack in young hipsters.

There are few dive bars that will entertain as well as Jumbo's Clown Room (5153 Hollywood Blvd., 323/666-1187, http://jumbos.com, 4pm-2am daily), which has a blood-red interior, a circus theme, and a low stage where burlesque dancers impress with acrobatic moves.

In the Sunset Tower Hotel, The Tower Bar (8358 Sunset Blvd., 323/654-7100, 6pm-11pm Sun.-Thurs., 6pm-11:30pm Fri.-Sat.) offers a glimpse of old Hollywood with walnut-paneled walls, a fireplace, and dim lighting so that celebrities can keep their cool.

With beautiful ocean views, glittering mosaics, marble floors, and romantic piano music, Casa del Mar Lobby Lounge (1910 Ocean Way, Santa Monica, 310/581-5533, www.hotelcasadelmar.com, 10:30am-midnight Sun.-Thurs., 10:30am-1:30am Fri.-Sat.) is a dramatic real-life sand castle on Santa Monica State Beach and offers perhaps the most elegant cocktail experience in the city.

Also in Santa Monica, **Ye Olde King's Head** (116 Santa Monica Blvd., Santa Monica, 310/451-1402, www.yeoldekingshead.com, 10am-2am daily) is a British pub, restaurant, and gift shop. Crowded on most nights, the pub is home to dart games and a wide range of imbibing patrons visiting from far and near.

While in Venice Beach, skip the loud tourist bars and head to the **Townhouse and the Del Monte Speakeasy** (52 Windward Ave., Venice Beach, 310/392-4040, www.townhousevenice.com, 5pm-2am Mon.-Fri., noon-2am Sat.-Sun.). Upstairs, enjoy the candlelit tables and pool table of the oldest bar in Venice. Downstairs, the speakeasy is a cellar space that hosts jazz bands, DJs, comedians, and burlesque troupes.

The Thirsty Crow (2939 W. Sunset Blvd., 323/661-6007, www.thirstycrowbar.com, 5pm-2am Mon.-Fri., 2pm-2am Sat.-Sun.) is a neighborhood bar in hip Silver Lake. The focus is on whiskey, with 100 different kinds, including more than 60 small-batch bourbons. Stop by for happy hour (5pm-8pm Mon.-Fri., 2pm-8pm Sat.-Sun.) to get a low-priced, finely crafted Manhattan, old-fashioned, or Moscow mule. It's the setting of the Father John Misty song "Nothing Good Ever Happens at the Goddamn Thirsty Crow."

For those in the know, **Karma Lounge** (3954 Beverly Blvd., 213/375-7141, http://karmaloungela.com, 5pm-midnight Tues.-Thurs., 5pm-2am Fri.-Sat.) is a worthy stop for drinks or dancing. Karma frequently hosts DJs spinning everything from industrial to Latin along with burlesque shows.

Dance to world-famous DJs under pulsating lights, falling confetti, or floating bubbles at **Create** (6021 Hollywood Blvd., 323/463-3331, http://sbe.com, 10pm-4am Fri.-Sat.). You may catch Kaskade or Afrojack on the turntables at this weekend-only dance club.

The **Three Clubs Cocktail Lounge** (1123 Vine St., Hollywood, 323/462-6441, www.threeclubs.com, 5pm-2am daily) acts both as a locals' watering hole and a reasonably priced nightclub catering mostly to the collegiate set. Expect to find the dance floor of the rear club crowded and sweaty, with modern dance mixes blaring out over the crush of writhing bodies.

Gay and Lesbian

Akbar (4356 Sunset Blvd., Silver Lake, 323/665-6810, www.akbarsilverlake.com, 4pm-2am daily) pulls in a gay-friendly crowd with its cozy Moroccan-themed decor, neighborhood vibe, and friendly, unpretentious bartenders.

Sleek, glamorous, and candlelit, **The Abbey Food and Bar** (692 N. Robertson Blvd., West Hollywood, 310/590-7440, http://sbe.com, 11am-2am Mon.-Thurs., 10am-2am Fri., 9am-2am Sat.-Sun.) is a popular bar with a great outdoor patio and pillow-strewn private cabanas, all of which are usually jam-packed.

Every Thursday night, **Avalon Hollywood** (1735 Vine St., Hollywood, 323/462-8900, http://avalonhollywood.com, 9:30pm-3am Thurs., 9:30pm-5am Fri., 9:30pm-8am Sat.) hosts **TigerHeat,** which is said to be the West Coast's largest gay event. Lady Gaga, Britney Spears, and Elton John have made appearances in the club, which is a renovated theater where the Beatles performed their first West Coast show.

Live Music

The clubs in the West Hollywood district, particularly those on the Sunset Strip, incubated some of the biggest rock acts of all time long before anybody knew who they were. The **Whisky a Go Go** (8901 Sunset Blvd., West Hollywood, 310/652-4202, www.whiskyagogo.com, cover from $10) has helped to launch the careers of The Doors, Mötley Crüe, and Guns N' Roses. Most nights you'll get a lineup of new bands, sometimes including as many as seven in one evening.

Almost next door to the Whisky you'll find **The Roxy Theatre** (9009 Sunset Blvd., West Hollywood, 310/278-9457, www.theroxy.com, ticket prices vary), which opened in 1973 with

Neil Young performing. Today, you'll find icons like Dave Davies of The Kinks or new acts like the Savages gracing the stage.

It's not on the Strip, but **The Troubadour** (9081 Santa Monica Blvd., West Hollywood, 310/276-1158, www.troubadour.com, ticket prices vary) is just as big and bad as its brethren. Over its more than 50 years, Bob Dylan jammed, totally unknown comic Steve Martin sang, Tom Waits was discovered, Billy Joel opened for somebody else, Metallica headlined for the first time, and countless A-list bands have recorded songs in and even about The Troubadour.

The Theatre at Ace Hotel (929 Broadway, 213/623-3233, www.acehotel.com) has hosted big acts like Coldplay. The restored 1,600-seat movie theater from the 1920s features more than just rock shows; it also puts on lectures, film festivals, and dance productions.

Comedy

L.A.'s live comedy scene is second only to Manhattan's. **The Comedy Store** (8433 Sunset Blvd., West Hollywood, 323/650-6268, www.thecomedystore.com, age 21 and older, $15-20) is owned by 1980s comedian Pauly Shore's mother, Mitzi. With three separate rooms, The Store has a show going on every night of the week; most start at 9pm or later.

Current comedy greats including Will Ferrell, Kristen Wiig, Lisa Kudrow, and Will Forte are alumni of **The Groundlings Theatre and School** (7307 Melrose Ave., 323/934-4747, www.groundlings.com, prices vary). Get tickets to take in some sketch comedy by up-and-coming talents or enroll in the improv comedy school.

For a true grassroots comedy experience, watch comedians in hostess Marissa's backyard every second Saturday of the month at underground favorite **Brew Haha** (4221 Normal Ave., www.brewhahacomedy.com, free).

THE ARTS
Theater

In addition to the Academy Awards, the

Dolby Theatre (6801 Hollywood Blvd., 323/308-6300, www.dolbytheatre.com, box office 10am-5pm Mon.-Sat., 10am-4pm Sun.) hosts various live performances, from ballet to shows from music legends like Bob Dylan. Half-hour **tours** (on the half-hour 10:30am-4pm daily, adults $19, seniors and children $15) include a view of an Oscar statuette.

The **Ahmanson Theatre** (135 N. Grand Ave., 213/628-2772, www.centertheatregroup. org, box office noon-6pm Tues.-Sun. and two hours before performances, ticket prices vary) specializes in big Broadway-style productions. With hundreds of seats (all of them expensive), there's usually enough room to provide entertainment, even for last-minute visitors.

The intimate **Kirk Douglas Theatre** (9820 Washington Blvd., Culver City, 213/628-2772, www.centertheatregroup.org) hosts world premieres and edgy productions like David Mamet's *Race* and Samuel Beckett's *Endgame*.

Well-known television actors, including Jason Alexander and Neil Patrick Harris, frequently act in the productions at the **Geffen Playhouse** (10886 Le Conte Ave., 310/208-5454, http://geffenplayhouse.com, ticket prices vary).

Classical Music

The **Los Angeles Opera** (135 N. Grand Ave., 213/972-8001, www.laopera.org, box office 10am-6pm Tues.-Sat., prices vary) has become one of the largest opera companies in the United States. The dazzling performances are held in the Dorothy Chandler Pavilion at the Music Center of Los Angeles County. Grammy-winning singer Plácido Domingo has been the opera's general director since 2003.

Better known as the LA Phil, the **Los Angeles Philharmonic** (111 S. Grand Ave., 323/850-2000 or 800/745-3000, www.laphil.com, prices vary) performs primarily at the **Walt Disney Concert Hall** (111 S. Grand Ave.). With its art deco band shell set against canyon chaparral, the **Hollywood Bowl** (2301 N. Highland Ave., 323/850-2000 or

800/745-3000, www.hollywoodbowl.com, box office noon-6pm Tues.-Sun.) has long been a romantic setting for outdoor summer concerts by the L.A. Philharmonic and other artists.

The **Los Angeles Doctors Symphony** (310/476-5512, http://ladso.org, prices vary) has been performing regularly since its inception in 1953. They play everything from Mozart to Schubert.

Cinema

Movie premieres are a big deal in L.A. Crowds throng the streets outside of the Chinese Theatre and the Egyptian, where the stars tromp down the red carpets to enjoy the sight of themselves on the big screen. Even the standard AMC and other theater chains get packed on opening nights, so come early or buy tickets online to assure yourself of seats to your favorite star's latest release.

The current favorite movie house for star sightings is the **ArcLight Hollywood Cinema** (6360 W. Sunset Blvd., Hollywood, 323/464-1478, www.arclightcinemas.com). The ArcLight complex offers the best visual and sound technologies, all-reserved seating, and the updated geodesic Cinerama Dome theater. Make reservations in advance (buy tickets online or at the theater) and ask for parking validation for a discount on the adjacent parking structure.

For eclectic films and movie-related events, seek out **The Cinefamily at the Silent Movie Theatre** (611 N. Fairfax Ave., 323/655-2510, www.cinefamily.org). Their screenings unearth eclectic gems, midnight movies, and under-the-radar flicks.

Acclaimed filmmaker and movie enthusiast Quentin Tarantino owns and programs the slate of 35-millimeter films at the **New Beverly Cinema** (7165 Beverly Blvd., 323/938-4038, www.thenewbev.com). The movies screened here reflect Tarantino's sensibilities: spaghetti westerns, horror films, classics, and selections from the filmmaker's personal collection.

FESTIVALS AND EVENTS

The **Pasadena Tournament of Roses Parade** (Pasadena, 626/449-4100, www.tournamentofroses.com, New Year's Day) is one of the nation's most popular New Year's Day events. Watched by millions on TV, the parade of flower-covered floats has been occurring since 1890.

Fiesta Broadway (S. Broadway and W. 1st St., 310/914-0015, http://fiestabroadway.la, Apr.) is the largest Cinco de Mayo celebration in the world. Enjoy the fun, food, music, and culture along with the occasional appearance of a Mexican pop superstar.

Overshadowed by celebrations in San Francisco and San Diego, the **L.A. Pride Festival** (West Hollywood, 323/969-8302, http://lapride.org, June) draws 400,000 celebrants to West Hollywood. There's a multiblock parade along with lots of music and art events. The 2015 entertainment lineup included Wilson Phillips, Tinashe, and Kesha.

Shopping

DOWNTOWN AND VICINITY
Flower District

If you love plants and flowers, don't miss the world-famous **L.A. Flower District** (700 block of Wall St., 213/622-1966, www.laflowerdistrict.com, 8am-noon Mon. and Wed., 6am-11am Tues., 6am-noon Thurs., 8am-2pm Fri., 6am-2pm Sat., admission $1-2). Anyone can come and stroll the narrow aisles of the various markets, and you'll find plenty of premade bouquets with which to impress your sweetie. Just about every kind of cut flower, potted plant, and exotic species can be purchased here.

One caution: While the flower market itself

is safe for visitors, the area to the south is not. Don't wander the neighborhood on foot.

Jewelry District

If you're looking for the bleeding edge of style, you can't do much better than the Los Angeles **Jewelry District** (bounded by 5th St., 8th St., Broadway, and Olive St.). There are more than 3,000 wholesalers, ensuring that even the most avid lover of sparkly stones and glittering gold will get his or her fill. The district's website provides information on vendor ratings and a map to help you get around more easily. Be careful if you're a woman alone, especially after dark, as this isn't the safest part of L.A.

Chung King Road

A mix of modern art galleries and fun, touristy gift shops line the 900 block of **Chung King Road** (http://chungkingroad.wordpress.com/galleries), a one-block stretch of Chinatown. Interior decorators often browse the eclectic selection. It can be quiet during the day, but it comes alive during art-opening evenings.

LOS FELIZ AND SILVER LAKE

Artsy, hip boutiques, cafés, and restaurants line **Sunset Junction** (Sunset Blvd. from Santa Monica Blvd. to Maltman Ave.), a colorful stretch of Sunset Boulevard concentrated around where Sunset meets Santa Monica Boulevard (or, rather, where Santa Monica Boulevard ends). Weekend mornings bring floods of neighborhood locals down from the hills. This strip is also home to the **Silver Lake Certified Farmers Market** (323/661-7771, 2pm-7:30pm Tues., 9am-1pm Sat.).

The fiercely independent **Skylight Books** (1818 N. Vermont Ave., 323/660-1175, www.skylightbooks.com, 10am-10pm daily) in Los Feliz features alternative literature, literary fiction, Los Angeles-themed books, and an extensive film section. It hosts frequent author events and sells signed books.

Hollywood and Highland Center

HOLLYWOOD

The **Hollywood and Highland Center** (6801 Hollywood Blvd., 323/467-6412 or 323/817-0200, www.hollywoodandhighland. com, 10am-10pm Mon.-Sat., 10am-7pm Sun., parking $2-13) flaunts outlandish architecture that's modeled after the set of the 1916 film *Intolerance*. Stroll amid the more than 70 retail stores and 25 eateries that surround the open-air Babylon Court. Save yourself stress and park in the center's lot ($2 for up to two hours with validation).

Encompassing an entire city block and two floors, **Amoeba Music** (6400 Sunset Blvd., 323/245-6400, www.amoeba.com, 10:30am-11pm Mon.-Sat., 11am-10pm Sun.) is the world's largest independent music store. This is the place in L.A. to find that rare record or used CD.

LA BREA, FAIRFAX, AND MIRACLE MILE

The stretch of charming and eclectic shops on **West 3rd Street** (between Fairfax Ave. and

La Cienega Blvd.) encompasses one-of-a-kind clothing boutiques, home stores, and bath-and-body shops. At one end you'll find The Original Farmers Market and The Grove shopping center; at the other, the Beverly Center.

Among the home and clothing stores on West 3rd Street, **Traveler's Bookcase** (8375 W. 3rd St., 323/655-0575, www.travelbooks. com, 11am-7pm Mon., 10am-7pm Tues.-Sat., noon-6pm Sun.) offers an extensive selection of guidebooks and travel-oriented literature.

BEVERLY HILLS AND WEST HOLLYWOOD

The hottest stars and other big spenders come to the three-block stretch of luxury stores at **Rodeo Drive** (www.rodeodrive-bh.com) to purchase the best and most expensive goods the world has to offer. Among the upscale retailers are **Chanel** (400 N. Rodeo Dr., Beverly Hills, 310/278-5500, www.chanel.com, 10am-6pm Mon.-Sat., noon-5pm Sun.), **Tiffany's** (210 N. Rodeo Dr., Beverly Hills, 310/273-8880, www.tiffany.com, 10am-7pm Mon.-Sat., 11am-5pm Sun.), and **Frette** (445 N. Rodeo Dr., Beverly Hills, 310/273-8540, www.frette. com, 10am-6pm Mon.-Sat., noon-5pm Sun.). The Rodeo Drive Walk of Style salutes fashion and entertainment icons with sidewalk plaques.

Melrose Avenue (between San Vicente Blvd. and La Brea Ave.) is really two shopping districts. High-end fashion and design showrooms dominate the western end, near La Cienega Boulevard; head east past Fairfax Avenue for tattoo parlors and used clothing.

For vintage castoffs, check out **Decades** (8214 Melrose Ave., 323/655-1960, www.deca-desinc.com, 11am-6pm Mon.-Sat., noon-5pm Sun.), while **Ron Robinson at Fred Segal** (8118 Melrose Ave., 323/651-1935, www.ron-robinson.com, 10am-7pm Mon.-Sat., noon-6pm Sun.) is a deluxe department store that has everything from the ridiculously trendy to the severely tasteful.

On the strip of Sunset Boulevard famous for nightlife, indie bookstore **Book Soup** (8818 Sunset Blvd., 310/659-3110, www. booksoup.com, 9am-10pm Mon.-Sat., 9am-7pm Sun.) crams every nook and cranny of its space, but the film section is particularly strong.

Sports and Recreation

BEACHES

Southern California has a seemingly endless stretch of public beaches with lots of visitor amenities, such as snack bars, boardwalks, showers, beach toy rental shacks, surf schools, and permanent sports courts. However, you won't always find clean, clear water to swim in, since pollution is a major issue on the L.A. coast, and water temperatures cool off significantly when you dive into the surf.

Leo Carrillo State Park

Just 28 miles north of Santa Monica on the Pacific Coast Highway, **Leo Carrillo State Park** (35000 W. Pacific Coast Hwy., Malibu, 310/457-8143, www.parks.ca.gov, 8am-10pm daily, $12/vehicle) feels like a Central Coast beach even though it's right outside the Los Angeles city limits. Explore the park's natural coastal features, including tide pools and caves. A point break offshore draws surfers when the right swell hits. Dogs are also allowed on a beach at the northern end of the park.

Zuma Beach

Zuma Beach (30000 Pacific Coast Hwy., Malibu, 19 miles north of Santa Monica, surf report 310/457-9701, http://beaches.lacounty. gov, sunrise-sunset daily, parking $3-12.50) is a popular surf and boogie-boarding break, complete with a nice big stretch of clean white sand that fills up fast on summer weekends. Grab a spot on the west side of the Pacific

Coast Highway (Hwy. 1) for free parking, or pay for one of the more than 2,000 spots in the beach parking lot. Zuma has all the amenities you need for a full day out at the beach, from restrooms and showers to a kid-friendly snack bar and a beachside boardwalk.

Malibu Beach

Amid the sea of mansions fronting the beach, **Malibu Lagoon State Beach** (23200 Pacific Coast Hwy., 310/457-8143, www.parks.ca.gov, 8am-sunset daily, $12/vehicle) and its ancillary **Malibu Surfrider Beach** offer public access to the great northern L.A. location. Running alongside the **Malibu Pier** (23000 Pacific Coast Hwy.), this pretty stretch of sugar-like sand offers a wealth of activities as well as pure California relaxation. It's likely to get crowded quickly in the summer, so get here early for a parking spot.

Santa Monica State Beach

Santa Monica State Beach (Pacific Coast Hwy., 310/458-8300, www.smgov.net, parking from $7) lines the water-side edge of town. For 3.5 miles, the fine sand gets raked daily beneath the sun that shines over the beach more than 300 days each year. Enjoy the warm sunshine, take a dip in the endless waves, stroll along the boardwalk, or look for dolphins frolicking in the surf. The best people-watching runs south of the pier area and on toward Venice Beach. For more elbow room, head north of the pier to the less populated end of the beach.

TOP EXPERIENCE

SURFING

The northern section of Los Angeles has some of the region's best surf breaks including County Line, which is on the L.A.-Ventura county line, and Zuma, a series of beach breaks along the beach of the same name. But L.A.'s premier surf spot is Malibu, one of the world's most famous waves. This is where the 1960s surf culture took hold, thanks to legends like Miki Dora, an iconic Malibu-based surfer. The southern section of L.A. County's

coastline offers places to surf, but not with the same quality as the breaks around Malibu.

If you've left your board at home, run to the **Malibu Surf Shack** (22935 Pacific Coast Hwy., 310/456-8508, www.malibusurfshack. com, 10am-6pm daily, surfboards $20/hour, $25-35/day, wetsuits $10-15) to rent a board. It's walking distance to the break.

Learn to Surf LA (641 Westminster Ave., Ste. 5, Venice, 310/663-2479, www.learn-tosurfla.com, $75-120) has lessons on the beach near the Santa Monica Pier (near lifeguard tower no. 18), Manhattan Beach's 45th Street lifeguard tower, and Venice Beach's Navy Street lifeguard tower. Each lesson lasts almost two hours and includes all equipment (you'll get a full wetsuit in addition to a board), shore instruction and practice, and plenty of time in the water. Intermediate and advanced surfers can also find great fun with this school, which has advanced instructors capable of helping you improve your skills.

SPECTATOR SPORTS

In 2016, the St. Louis Rams moved to Los Angeles to become the **Los Angeles Rams.** They play their home games at the **Los Angeles Memorial Coliseum** (3939 S. Figueroa St., 213/747-7111, www.lacoliseum.com).

The **L.A. Kings** (213/742-7100 or 888/546-4752, http://kings.nhl.com, ticket prices vary) are no joke now after winning the Stanley Cup in 2012 and 2014. They play lightning-fast NHL ice hockey in Downtown L.A. at the **Staples Center** (1111 S. Figueroa St., 213/742-7100, www.staplescenter.com).

The **Los Angeles Lakers** (310/426-6031 or 866/381-8924, www.nba.com/lakers, ticket prices vary) play at the **Staples Center** (1111 S. Figueroa St., 213/742-7100, www.staples-center.com), along with the often-overlooked **L.A. Clippers** (213/742-7530, www.nba.com/clippers), who are now rising in stature.

The **Los Angeles Dodgers** (1000 Elysian Park Ave., 866/363-4377, http://losangeles. dodgers.mlb.com, ticket prices vary) play often and well at **Dodger Stadium** (1000 Elysian Park Ave., www.dodgers.com).

Food

DOWNTOWN AND VICINITY

One of Downtown L.A.'s greatest strengths is its ethnic diversity and the great range of cuisine that goes along with it. Getting local recommendations is the best way to find the current hot spots, or choose from among this tiny sampling of what's available.

Gastropub

Worth seeking out, **The Black Sheep** (126 E. 6th St., 213/689-5022, 6pm-midnight Sun. and Tues.-Thurs., 6pm-1am Fri.-Sat., $4-8) has a small menu that focuses on sausages, house-blended beef burgers, creative tater tots, and Asian-influenced pub food like *bánh mì* sliders. Enjoy this new-school pub food with one of the eatery's fine microbrews. This small space has booths and tables lit by candlelight, and an outdoor seating section (expect a constant parade of panhandlers if you sit outside).

Italian

Bestia (2121 7th Pl., 213/514-5724, www.bestiala.com, 5pm-11pm Sun.-Thurs., 5pm-midnight Fri.-Sat., $16-140) is drawing adventurous diners and drinkers to the Arts District for its Italian food and raved-about cocktails. The drink menu includes a white Negroni and an old-fashioned made with salami-infused bourbon. Food ranges from pizza to a whopping 39-ounce rib eye for $140 (though most entrées are closer to $20). The space is appropriately industrial for its location and includes an outdoor patio.

Japanese

For a seriously authentic Japanese cuisine experience, visit ★ **Kagaya** (418 E. 2nd St., 213/617-1016, 6pm-10:30pm Tues.-Sat., 6pm-10pm Sun., $47-128). Even L.A. denizens who've eaten at shabu-shabu places in Japan come back to Kagaya again and again. They make reservations in advance, because the dining room is small and the quality of the food makes it popular even on weeknights. The term *shabu-shabu* refers to paper-thin slices of beef and vegetables that you dip and swish into a pot of boiling *daishi* (broth), then dunk in *ponzu* or other house-made sauces before eating. The shabu-shabu is but one course in the meal you'll get at Kagaya, since all meals include several appetizers (varieties change daily), shabu-shabu with beef and seafood, *udon* noodles, and dessert.

Korean

It's only fitting that a city with such a large Korean population has plenty of good Korean restaurants. One of these is **Chunju Han-il Kwan** (3450 W. 6th St., 213/480-1799, 11am-11pm Mon.-Sat., 11am-10pm Sun., $10-30), a casual restaurant in a strip mall with gas burners on the tables that caters primarily to the Korean expat community. You may not find English menus, but you will find helpful waitstaff who can guide you through the process of ordering. If your server says a dish is spicy, she means it, but that doesn't mean you won't love it anyway. The menu is eclectic: You can get a hot dog, octopus, fish soup, Korean stew (thickened with American cheese), kimchi, and much more.

LOS FELIZ, SILVER LAKE, AND ECHO PARK

American

French fries in origami bags. Toasters on every table. Dishes with names like Bearded Mr. Frenchy and farm-to-table dinners named after sitcoms. Everything plays into the love-it-or-leave-it hip factor at **Fred 62** (1850 N. Vermont Ave., 323/667-0062, www.fred62.com, 24 hours daily, $7-15), where the booths feel like old Chevy backseats and everyone's a garage-band star. The hip eatery hosts many celebrities and was featured in a recent Prince video.

Best Restaurants

★ **Kagaya:** This Japanese restaurant is acclaimed for its thinly sliced shabu-shabu (page 449).

★ **Yuca's:** Not many taquerias win a prestigious James Beard Award; this Los Feliz eatery did (page 450).

★ **The Griddle Café:** Industry insiders meet at this Hollywood restaurant for breakfast creations like red velvet pancakes (page 451).

★ **Neptune's Net:** The crispy shrimp tacos and pitchers of beer at this casual coast-side eatery hit the spot after a long day in the surf (page 452).

Mexican

Not every taco stand wins awards from the James Beard Foundation. ★ **Yuca's** (2056 Hillhurst Ave., 323/662-1214, www.yucasla.com, 11am-6pm Mon.-Sat., $6-12) received the honor in 2005, but that only confirmed what Los Feliz locals have known for decades: This shack serves truly memorable (and cheap) tacos and burritos. Vegetarians beware: Even the beans are made with pork fat. They have also expanded into a Hollywood location (4666 Hollywood Blvd., 323/661-0523, 8am-9pm Mon.-Sat., 10am-4pm Sun.).

Thai

Routinely topping critics' lists of the best Thai restaurants in Los Angeles, elegant **Jitlada** (5233 W. Sunset Blvd., 323/667-9809, www.jitladala.com, 11am-3pm and 5pm-10:30pm Tues.-Sun., $10-30) specializes in the cuisine of southern Thailand, which is rarely seen on U.S. menus. *LA Weekly* food writer Jonathan Gold once proclaimed that Jitlada offered "the spiciest food you can eat in Los Angeles at the moment."

Vegan

Run by a true Renaissance woman—who is a spoken-word poet, filmmaker, and chef—**Sage** (1700 W. Sunset Blvd., 213/989-1718, www.sageveganbistro.com, 11am-11pm Mon.-Fri., 9am-4pm and 5pm-11pm Sat.-Sun., $12-15) keeps Echo Park's hipsters healthy with organic, plant-based cuisine. Order tempura-battered avocado tacos, house-made veggie burgers, flavorful veggie bowls, or butternut squash ravioli at the counter and then wait for your order at a table. Food this healthy means you can justify a scoop of gelato after your meal. There are also locations in Culver City (4130 Sepulveda Blvd., 424/228-5835, 11am-11pm Mon.-Fri., 9am-11pm Sat.-Sun.) and Pasadena (319 S. Arroyo Pkwy., 877/985-5463, 11am-10pm Mon.-Sat., 11am-8pm Sun.).

HOLLYWOOD

For a chance at glimpsing stars of the silver screen, look for upscale California cuisine or perhaps a high-end sushi bar. If all you need is tasty sustenance, you can choose from a range of restaurants.

American

On the casual end of the spectrum, **Pink's Famous Hot Dogs** (709 N. La Brea Ave., 323/931-4223, www.pinkshollywood.com, 9:30am-2am Sun.-Thurs., 9:30am-3am Fri.-Sat., $3.50-7) is hot dog heaven. Frankophiles line up at this roadside stand (lit up like a Las Vegas show club into the wee hours of the morning) for variations on a sausage in a bun that range from the basic chili dog to the more elaborate Martha Stewart Dog. It has been at the same location since 1939.

Brazilian

Need food really, really, *really* late? **Bossa Nova** (7181 W. Sunset Blvd., 323/436-7999, www.bossanovafood.com, 11am-3:30am Sun.-Wed., 11am-4am Thurs.-Sat., $10-20) can hook you up. A big menu of inexpensive entrées can satisfy any appetite from lunch to way past dinnertime. Some of the dishes bear the spicy flavors of the owners' home country of Brazil, but you'll also find a ton of pastas, plenty of salads, and classic Italian-American build-your-own pizzas. Check out the desserts for some South American specialties if you need sweets after a long night out at the clubs.

Breakfast

If you're a flapjack fan, a trip to Hollywood should include a breakfast at ★ **The Griddle Café** (7916 Sunset Blvd., 323/874-0377, www.thegriddlecafe.com, 7am-4pm Mon.-Fri., 8am-4pm Sat.-Sun., $11-30). This hectic, loud breakfast joint serves up creations like a red velvet pancake and a pancake with brown sugar-baked bananas in a buttermilk batter. For those who prefer savory to sweet, the Griddle has delicious breakfast tacos and a Cobb omelet with all the fixings of a Cobb salad except the lettuce. With the Director's Guild of America building next door, The Griddle Café is also a place where you may spot a celebrity.

Gastropub

A playful California take on British pub food, **The Pikey** (7617 Sunset Blvd., 323/850-5400, www.thepikeyla.com, 11:45am-2am Mon.-Fri., 11am-2am Sat.-Sun., $15-32) has a sense of humor. One of the cocktails is named the Divine Brown for the prostitute with whom actor Hugh Grant was caught on this same city block back in 1995. The dinner menu is divided into small plates and large plates. The buttery burger with cheddar and Worcestershire aioli is a highlight. It can get loud and crowded at dinnertime. Happy hour (4pm-7pm daily) offers well cocktails at half price.

Italian

The warm but clamorous dining room at **Pizzeria Mozza** (641 N. Highland Ave., 323/297-0101, www.pizzeriamozza.com, noon-midnight daily, $11-29) has been packed since chef Nancy Silverton, founder of La Brea Bakery, opened the doors in 2006. The wood-fired oven turns out rustic, blistered pizzas with luxurious toppings. Reservations are tough to get, but bar seats are available for walk-ins.

LA BREA, FAIRFAX, AND MIRACLE MILE

California Cuisine

Pairing meat and potatoes with a retro-clubby dining room, **Jar** (8225 Beverly Blvd., 323/655-6566, www.thejar.com, 5:30pm-9:30pm Mon.-Thurs., 5:30pm-11pm Fri.-Sat., 10am-2pm and 5:30pm-10pm Sun., $21-49) puts a Southern California spin on the traditional steak house. Meats and grilled fish are served à la carte with your choice of sauce, and the side orders serve two. You can order a burger for $15 from the bar, or stop in on a Monday night for the featured lobster. Jar is also known for its Sunday brunch.

Deli

Midnight snackers unhinge their jaws on the hulking corned beef sandwiches at **Canter's Deli** (419 N. Fairfax Ave., 323/651-2030, www.cantersdeli.com, 24 hours daily, $12-18), in the heart of the Jewish Fairfax district. Canter's also does burgers, deli melts, triple-decker sandwiches, and hearty dinner entrées. This venerable 24-hour deli boasts its share of star sightings, so watch for noshing rock stars in the wee hours of the morning.

Lunch doesn't get much better than the high-end bounty in the deli cases at **Joan's on Third** (8350 W. 3rd St., 323/655-2285, www.joansonthird.com, 8am-8pm Mon.-Sat., 8am-7pm Sun., $10-15). Mix and match fine sandwiches, roasted vegetables, and artisanal cheeses. There are also sidewalk tables and a breakfast kitchen that serves organic eggs and French toast.

New American

With items including crispy pig head, veal brains, and bone marrow, **Animal** (435 N. Fairfax Ave., 323/782-9225, 6pm-11pm Sun.-Thurs., 6pm-midnight Fri.-Sat., $18-47) is a hot restaurant for foodies. It serves adventurous dishes like a foie gras take on the Hawaiian dish loco moco with a quail egg, Spam, and hamburger. The hamachi tostada is raved about.

BEVERLY HILLS AND WEST HOLLYWOOD

Beverly Hills tends toward high-end eateries serving European and haute California cuisine, while West L.A. boasts a wide array of international restaurants.

Brazilian

There's nothing like a good steak dinner, Brazilian style. At **Fogo de Chão** (133 N. La Cienega Blvd., Beverly Hills, 310/289-7755, www.fogodechao.com, 11:30am-2pm and 5pm-10pm Mon.-Thurs., 11:30am-2pm and 5pm-10:30pm Fri., 4:30pm-10:30pm Sat., 11:30am-2pm and 4pm-9:30pm Sun., lunch $15-34, dinner $25-50), be prepared for an interactive dining experience. The meat is slow roasted, then skewered and cut right onto your plate by ever-moving servers. Use the red-and-green token on your table; if you don't turn it over to the red side occasionally, you will be continuously bombarded with the 15 different kinds of meat the restaurant offers. The fixed-price meal includes endless trips to the salad bar, fresh-cut veggies, and traditional Brazilian side dishes (fried bananas are a starch, not a dessert). The extensive wine list includes plenty of both California and European vintages, plus a wider-than-average selection of ports and dessert wines.

Seafood

With a roof that resembles a giant ray gliding through the sea, **Connie and Ted's** (8171 Santa Monica Blvd., 323/848-2722, www.connieandteds.com, 4pm-10pm Mon.-Tues., 11:30am-11pm Wed.-Sat., 11:30am-10pm Sun., $12-44) brings the fruit of the sea to West Hollywood. The menu is inspired by New England clam shacks, oyster bars, and fish houses and includes a raw bar of oysters and clams. A West Coast influence creeps in on items like the smoked albacore starter, lobster rolls, and a Mexican shrimp dish.

SANTA MONICA, VENICE, AND MALIBU

Caribbean

How can you not love a restaurant called **Cha Cha Chicken** (1906 Ocean Ave., Santa Monica, 310/581-1684, www.chachachicken.com, 11am-10pm Mon.-Fri., 10am-10pm Sat.-Sun., $7-12)? It looks just like it sounds—a slightly decrepit but brightly painted shack only a short walk from the Santa Monica Pier and the Third Street Promenade. The jerk dishes bring a tangy sweetness to the table, while the *ropa vieja* heats up the plate, and the funky enchiladas put a whole new spin on a Mexican classic. Quaff an imported Jamaican soda or a seasonal *agua fresca* with your meal, since Cha Cha Chicken doesn't have a liquor license.

Seafood

Situated on the Malibu coastline adjacent to the County Line surf break, ★ **Neptune's Net** (42505 Pacific Coast Hwy., Malibu, 310/457-3095, www.neptunesnet.com, 10:30am-8pm Mon.-Thurs., 10:30am-9pm Fri., 10am-8:30pm Sat.-Sun., summer; 10:30am-7pm Mon.-Thurs., 10:30am-8pm Fri., 10am-7pm Sat.-Sun., winter; $11-30) catches all kinds of seafood to serve to hungry diners. You'll often find sandy and salt-encrusted local surfers satisfying their enormous appetites after hours out on the waves or bikers downing a beer after a ride on the twisting highway. One of the Net's most satisfying options is the shrimp tacos: crispy fried shrimp on tortillas topped with a pineapple salsa. The large menu includes a seemingly endless variety of other combinations, à la carte options, and side dishes.

Food Trucks

Some of the city's best culinary creations come not from upscale restaurants, but out of food trucks where gourmet chefs can follow their dreams with little overhead. Websites like **Food Truck Maps** (www.foodtruckmaps.com) and **Roaming Hunger** (http://roaminghunger.com) can help you find some roving favorites. Following are some of the best places to grab a bite:

- **Kogi BBQ** (twitter @kogibbq, http://kogibbq.com) serves a hybrid of Mexican and Korean food with items that include kimchi quesadillas and short-rib tacos.

- The most-ordered item at the **Grilled Cheese Truck** (twitter @grlldcheesetruk, www.thegrilledcheesetruck.com) is the cheesy mac and rib, which includes barbecued pork tucked into grilled cheese.

- The **Green Truck** (twitter @GreenTruck, 310/204-0477, http://greentruckonthego.com) rolls around L.A. on veggie-oil fuel serving a menu of healthy organic items for vegans and carnivores alike.

Serious seafood lovers should make time for **The Hungry Cat** (100 W. Channel Rd., Santa Monica, 310/459-3337, http://thehungrycat.com, 5pm-10pm Mon.-Thurs., 5pm-11pm Fri., 11am-3pm and 5:30pm-11pm Sat., 11am-3pm and 5pm-10pm Sun., $11-30). Start with something from the raw bar and move on to a dinner entrée of local white sea bass or a lamb-and-clams dish. Seafood is also the star at weekend brunch, with dishes like soft-shell crab BLT, lobster frittata, and crab-cake Benedict. On Monday, all raw bar oysters are half price. There's a second location in Hollywood (1535 N. Vine St., 323/462-2155, http://thehungrycat.com, noon-10pm Mon.-Wed., noon-11pm Thurs.-Fri., 11am-11pm Sat., 11am-10pm Sun.).

Salt Air (1616 Abbot Kinney Blvd., Venice Beach, 310/396-9333, www.saltairvenice.com, 10am-3pm and 5pm-10pm Sun., 11:30am-2:30pm and 5pm-10pm Mon.-Tues., 11:30am-2:30pm and 5pm-11pm Wed.-Fri., 10am-3pm and 5pm-11pm Sat., $16-36) is a seafood restaurant with a busy bar. Everyone gets a plate of tasty corn fritters stuffed with cheddar cheese and a dollop of molasses butter to start.

The raw bar has oysters from both coasts, while the dinner menu highlights seafood, including slow-cooked cod, grilled trout, and olive oil-poached salmon.

LONG BEACH

Combining elegance, fine Continental-California cuisine, and great ghost stories, **Sir Winston's Restaurant and Lounge** (1126 Queens Hwy., 562/499-1657, www.queenmary.com, 5:30pm-10pm Tues.-Sun., $34-85) floats gently on board the *Queen Mary*. For the most beautiful dining experience, request a window table and make reservations for sunset. Dress in your finest; Sir Winston's requests that diners adhere to its semiformal dress code.

Beachwood BBQ & Brewing (210 E. 3rd St., 562/436-4020, www.beachwoodbbq.com, 11:30am-9:30pm Tues.-Sun., bar 11:30am-midnight Tues.-Sun., $9-28) brings the South to SoCal. This place does things the North Carolina way, with a pulled pork sandwich with a vinegar barbecue-sauce base. Other items include baby back ribs, wild boar meatloaf, and shrimp and grits. All pair well with the 22 craft beers on tap.

Accommodations

DOWNTOWN AND VICINITY

If you want to stay overnight in Downtown L.A., plan to pay for the privilege. Most hostelries are high-rise towers catering more to businesspeople than the leisure set. Once you get into the Jewelry District and farther south toward the Flower Market, the neighborhood goes from high-end to sketchy to downright terrifying. If you need a truly cheap room, avoid these areas and head to the San Fernando Valley instead.

$150-250

With its red-tiled floor, painted furniture, and lushly landscaped poolside bar, the **Figueroa Hotel** (939 S. Figueroa St., 213/627-8971 or 800/421-9092, www.figueroahotel.com, $160-200) is a Spanish-Moroccan oasis in the heart of Downtown. The rooms look like they could have been in the movie *Casablanca,* though they have TVs outfitted with cable stations. There's also a fitness center (5am-11pm daily).

The **O Hotel** (819 S. Flower St., 213/623-9904 or 855/782-9286, www.ohotelgroup.com, $139-400), formerly known as The Orchid Hotel, is an upscale property that takes the modern urban-chic hotel concept and does it L.A.-style. True to its original name, orchids are a major theme of this hotel, and you'll find plants in the common areas. A boutique establishment, the O has only 67 rooms. The nicest suites are spacious with a bedroom, living room, and two baths. You'll find tapas, fish, burgers, and poultry at the on-site restaurant, plus a full bar.

The ★ **Ace Hotel** (929 Broadway, 213/623-3233, www.acehotel.com/losangeles, $200-500) is one of the hippest places to stay in Downtown. Enjoy an evening's entertainment without venturing off the hotel's grounds: The property's 1,600-seat theater hosts the Sundance Next Fest and music performances by acts from Marilyn Manson to Philip Glass and Yo La Tengo. DJs spin poolside at the rooftop bar on the 14th floor, with the Downtown skyline as a backdrop. The modern and minimalist rooms, converted from the former offices of the United Artists film studio, feel like arty studio apartments, with concrete ceilings and exposed concrete floors. Some rooms have private terraces; all have Internet radios. There's a fitness center (24 hours daily) if you need to counteract all the partying.

Over $250

Hipster hotelier André Balazs, of the Chateau Marmont and the Mercer, has transformed the former home of Superior Oil into **The Standard** (550 S. Flower St., 213/892-8080, www.standardhotels.com, $260-1,500), a mecca for the see-and-be-seen crowd. From its upside-down sign to the minimal aesthetic in the rooms, the hotel gives off an ironic-chic vibe. If you're sharing a room, be aware that the shower is only separated from the rest of the room by clear glass. On-site amenities include a gym, a barbershop, and a restaurant open 24-7. The rooftop bar, seen in the 2005 film *Kiss Kiss, Bang Bang,* features spectacular views of the L.A. cityscape.

HOLLYWOOD
Under $150

Reputed to be one of the best hostels in the state, the **USA Hostels—Hollywood** (1624 Schrader Blvd., 323/462-3777 or 800/524-6783 or 323/462-3777, www.usahostels.com, dorm $42-52, private room $125-130) still offers the same great prices you'll find at seedier, more bare-bones hostels. Choose between dorm rooms and private rooms, but even the larger dorm rooms have baths attached, which is a nice convenience that's unusual in the hostel world. The daily all-you-can-make pancake breakfast is included with your room, along

Best Hotels

★ **Ace Hotel:** This Downtown hotel has a lot going for it, including a stunning on-site theater that hosts major entertainment events and a rooftop bar and pool that show off the L.A. skyline (page 454).

★ **Magic Castle Hotel:** Next door to the acclaimed magic club, the Magic Castle Hotel spoils its guests with great customer service, free snacks, and a pool open at all hours (page 455).

★ **Élan Hotel:** Here you'll find comfortable rooms at moderate prices, a rarity at the intersection of ritzy Beverly Hills and glitzy Hollywood (page 456).

★ **Hotel Erwin:** This eclectic hotel is feet from the raucous Venice Boardwalk. Take in the madness from the hotel's rooftop bar (page 458).

★ **The Varden:** You get clean, modern rooms close to Long Beach sights like the *Queen Mary* and the Aquarium of the Pacific (page 458).

★ **Crystal Cove Beach Cottages:** These rustic beachfront cottages are an ideal place to indulge in the SoCal beach lifestyle (page 469).

with all the coffee or tea you can drink. Add that to the $7 barbecue nights on Monday, Wednesday, and Friday, and you've got a great start on seriously diminished food costs for this trip. This smaller hostel goes a long way to foster a sense of community among its visitors, offering a standard array of area walking tours and a beach shuttle, and free comedy nights. There's also free Wi-Fi, plus complimentary Internet kiosks.

$150-250

The ★ **Magic Castle Hotel** (7025 Franklin Ave., 323/851-0800, www.magiccastlehotel. com, $190-370) is named for the world-renowned magic club (7001 Franklin Ave., 323/851-3313, www.magiccastle.com) next door. It boasts the best customer service of any L.A.-area hostelry. Sparkling light rooms with cushy white comforters and spare, clean decor offer a haven of tranquility. A courtyard pool invites lounging day and night. All suites have their own kitchens, and guests enjoy unlimited free snacks (sodas, candy, salted goodies). Enjoy the little luxurious touches, such as high-end coffee, baked goods in the free continental breakfast, plushy robes, and nightly turndown service.

For a nicely priced room in the Hollywood vicinity, stay at the **Hollywood Orchid Suites** (1753 Orchid Ave., 323/874-9678 or 800/537-3052, www.orchidsuites.com, $169-419). The Orchid's location couldn't be better; it's in the Hollywood and Highland Center, right behind the Chinese Theatre, next door to the Dolby Theatre, and around the corner from Hollywood Boulevard and the Walk of Fame. Rooms are actually suites (many with full kitchens), with plenty of space and an eye toward sleeping your large family or several friends all in the same suite. Don't expect luxury, as the furnishings look like last decade's motel stuff, although you'll get a coffee maker, free Wi-Fi, and other better-than-average perks. The pool offers cooling refreshment in the summer, perfect after a long day of stalking Brad or Britney.

The ★ **Hollywood Hotel** (1160 N. Vermont St., 323/315-1800 or 800/800-9733, www.hollywoodhotel.net, $209-309) is in East Hollywood, near the action. Close to Los Feliz and Griffith Park, the 130 rooms surprise with a handful of unexpected amenities including a complimentary hot breakfast with made-to-order omelets, a sauna, an on-site laundry room, and its own comedy club (Thurs.-Sat.) with nationally known comedians. Other pluses include a sunny pool area and a large gated parking lot. Ongoing renovations will include opening a rooftop common area with views of Downtown Los Angeles in the distance.

BEVERLY HILLS AND WEST HOLLYWOOD

West Hollywood, which serves as L.A.'s gay mecca, offers a wider range of accommodations than upscale Beverly Hills, including budget options, chain motels, and unique hotels.

$150-250

Comfortable and quiet, the ★ **Élan Hotel** (8435 Beverly Blvd., 323/658-6663, www.elanhotel.com, $189-259) has a great location where Beverly Hills and West Hollywood meet. The understated rooms are decorated with soothing abstract art. All have mini fridges, coffee makers, flat-screen TVs, and iPod docking stations; many rooms have small balconies or porches for a breath of fresh air.

Wine and cheese is served every evening and a complimentary continental breakfast is offered each morning.

The **Hotel Beverly Terrace** (469 N. Doheny Dr., Beverly Hills, 310/274-8141 or 800/842-6401, www.hotelbeverlyterrace.com, $209-349) is a rare affordable alternative. This spruced-up, retro-cool motor hotel enjoys a great spot on the border of Beverly Hills and West Hollywood. Enjoy one of the 39 recently renovated rooms and lounge in the sun in the garden courtyard or on the rooftop sundeck. In the morning, enjoy a complimentary continental breakfast. The on-site **Trattoria Amici** (310/858-0271) can satisfy your Italian food cravings.

The **Le Montrose Suite Hotel** (900 Hammond St., West Hollywood, 310/855-1115 or 800/776-0666, www.lemontrose.com, $209-399) will give you a taste of the kind of luxury celebrities expect in their accommodations, especially in trendy, gay-friendly West Hollywood. The atmosphere and decor are almost desperately modern, but you'll find lots of plush comfort among the primary colors and plain geometric shapes in your room. Outside your upscale suite, take a dip in the rooftop saltwater swimming pool and whirl-pool, play a set on the tennis courts, or get in

Hollywood Hotel

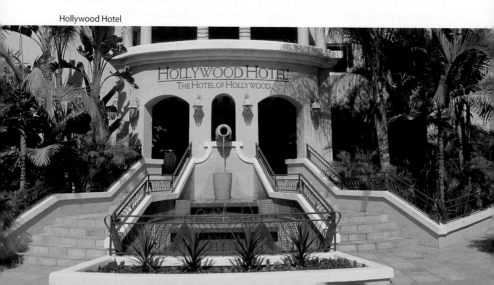

a good workout inside the fitness center. Hotel guests alone can enjoy the gourmet delicacies of the private dining room or order from 24-hour room service.

Over $250

The most famous of all the grand hotels is the **Beverly Wilshire** (9500 Wilshire Blvd., Beverly Hills, 310/275-5200, www.fourseasons.com, $800-5,000). Even the plainest rooms feature exquisite appointments such as 55-inch plasma TVs, elegant linens, and attractive artwork. The presidential suite resembles a European palace, complete with Corinthian columns. With an in-house spa, a dining room, room service, and every other service you could want, folks who can afford it consider a stay at the Beverly Wilshire worth the expense.

With architecture like a French castle, **Chateau Marmont** (8221 Sunset Blvd., West Hollywood, 323/656-1010 or 800/242-8328, www.chateaumarmont.com, $550-5,000) looks out on the city from its perch above the Sunset Strip. It has long attracted the in-crowd, from Garbo to Leo. It's also where writers from F. Scott Fitzgerald to Hunter S. Thompson have holed up to produce work. The design is eccentric and eclectic, from vintage 1940s suites to Bauhaus bungalows. The hotel was front and center in Sofia Coppola's 2010 film *Somewhere*.

SANTA MONICA, VENICE, AND MALIBU

The best place to stay in Los Angeles is down by the beach. It's ironic that you can camp in a park for $25 in exclusive Malibu or pay more than $1,000 for a resort room in "working-class" Santa Monica. But whether you choose either of those or a spot in Venice Beach, you'll get some of the best atmosphere in town.

Under $150

For a bed indoors for cheap, your options near the beach run to youth hostels. The huge **HI-Santa Monica** (1436 2nd St., Santa Monica, 310/393-9913, www.hilosangeles.org, dorm beds $49-65, private rooms $140) offers 260 beds in a building constructed specifically to house the hostel. You'll be right in the thick of downtown Santa Monica in a good neighborhood, within walking distance of the Santa Monica Pier, the Third Street Promenade, the beach, and good restaurants. This ritzy hostel offers tons of amenities for the price, including a computer room, a TV room, a movie room, excursions, wheelchair access, sheets included with the bed price, and even a complimentary continental breakfast every morning. The local public transit system runs right outside the door.

$150-250

The reasonably priced and fantastically fun **Custom Hotel** (8639 Lincoln Blvd., 310/645-0400, www.jdvhotels.com, $179-220) is south of Venice near LAX. The in-room Wi-Fi is free, as are the views of the city. Fear not if you're seeking food and drink and would rather not leave the hotel: Custom Hotel has six social lounges, each with its own concept, including the VIP lounge-inspired LAX Lounge, the Transonic gaming lounge, the Axis Annex art gallery, and the Duty Free vending machine room.

The **Venice Beach Suites & Hotel** (1305 Ocean Front Walk, 310/396-4559 or 888/877-7602, www.venicebeachsuites.com, $209-329) is a surprisingly lovely and affordable little Venice hotel. It sits right on the beach, but it's far enough from the boardwalk to acquire a touch of peace and quiet. Stroll over to Washington Boulevard to grab a meal or a cup of coffee, or just wander out of the lobby and straight onto the beach. Inside, the rooms and suites all have mini kitchens so you can cook for yourself, which is perfect for budget-conscious travelers and folks staying in Venice for several days. The decor is cuter than that of an average motel; you might find exposed brick walls and polished hardwood floors stocked with rattan furniture and appealing accessories.

Over $250

There's probably no hotel in Venice Beach that is a better reflection of the edgy beach town's attitude than ★ **Hotel Erwin** (1697 Pacific Ave., 800/786-7789, www.hotelerwin.com, $280-700). Situated just feet from the Venice Boardwalk and Muscle Beach, Hotel Erwin has graffiti art adorning the outside wall by its entrance and in some of its rooms. The rooms all have balconies and playful decor including lamps resembling the barbells used by the weightlifters at nearby Muscle Beach. Sitting atop the hotel is **High,** a rooftop bar that allows you to take in all the action of the bustling boardwalk while sipping a cocktail. The staff is laid-back, genial, and accommodating. Parking is a nightmare in Venice Beach during the summer, but a stay at the Erwin includes complimentary valet parking, a major plus.

Yes, you really can stay at the **Hotel California** (1670 Ocean Ave., Santa Monica, 310/393-2363 or 866/571-0000, www.hotelca. com/losangeles, $309-369). Appropriately decorated with classic longboards and electric guitars, this midrange hotel sits a short block from the beach and next to the Santa Monica Pier.

LONG BEACH

★ **The Varden** (335 Pacific Ave., 562/432-8950, www.thevardenhotel.com, $139-179) offers the type of tiny, clean, and modern rooms you'd expect to find in Europe. If you don't mind your bathroom being a foot or two from your bed, the sleek little rooms in this hotel, which dates back to 1929, are a great deal. The oldest operating hotel in Long Beach, The Varden is named after an eccentric circus performer named Dolly Varden, who is rumored to have hoarded jewels on the premises. The staff is very friendly and helpful, coffee, ice, and fresh fruit are available to guests 24 hours daily, and it's one block from the restaurants and bars on Pine Street.

Transportation and Services

GETTING THERE
Air

L.A. is one of the most commercial airport-dense metropolitan areas in the country. Wherever you're coming from and whichever part of L.A. you're headed for, you can get there by air. **Los Angeles International Airport** (1 World Way, Los Angeles, 855/463-5252, www.lawa.org), known as LAX, has the most flights to and from the most destinations of any area airport. LAX is also the most crowded of the L.A. airports, with the longest security and check-in lines. If you can find a way around flying into LAX, do so.

One option is to fly into other airports in the area, including **Bob Hope Airport** (BUR, 2627 N. Hollywood Way, Burbank, 818/840-8840, www.burbankairport.com) and the **Long Beach Airport** (LGB, 4100 Donald Douglas Dr., Long Beach, 562/570-2600, www. lgb.org). It may be a slightly longer drive to your final destination, but it can be well worth it. If you must use LAX, arrive a minimum of two hours ahead of your domestic flight time for your flight out, and consider three hours on busy holidays.

Train
Amtrak (800/872-7245, www.amtrak.com) has an active rail hub in Los Angeles. Most trains come in to **Union Station** (800 N. Alameda St., 213/683-6729), which has been owned by the Los Angeles Metropolitan Transportation Authority (MTA, www.metro. net) since 2011. From Union Station, which also acts as a Metro hub, take Metro Rail to various parts of Los Angeles. Against fairly significant odds in the region that invented car culture, Los Angeles has created a functional and useful public transit system.

Side Trip to Catalina Island

You can see Catalina from the shore of Long Beach on a clear day, but for a better view, you've got to get onto the island. The port town of Avalon welcomes visitors with Mediterranean-inspired hotels, restaurants, and shops. But the main draw of Catalina lies outside the walls of its buildings. Catalina beckons hikers, horseback riders, ecotourists, and most of all, water lovers.

The **Catalina Casino Theatre and Ballroom** (1 Casino Way, 310/510-7428, www.visit-catalinaisland.com) is a round, white art deco building, opened in 1929 not for gambling but as a community gathering place. Today, it hosts diverse activities, including the Catalina Island Jazz Festival. Stroll through the serene **Wrigley Memorial and Botanical Garden** (Avalon Canyon Rd., 1.5 miles west of town, 310/510-2897, www.catalinaconservancy.org, 8am-5pm daily, adults $7, seniors and veterans with ID $5, ages 5-12 and students with ID $3) in the hills above Avalon.

Outdoor recreation is the main draw. Swim or snorkel at the **Avalon Underwater Park** (Casino Point). A protected section at the north end of town offers access to a reef with plentiful sea life, including bright orange garibaldi fish. Out at the deeper edge of the park, nearly half a dozen wrecked ships await exploration. For a guided snorkel or scuba tour, visit **Catalina Snorkel & Scuba** (310/510-8558, www.catalinasnorkelscuba.com, tours $49-199). If you need snorkeling gear, hit up **Wet Spot Rentals** (310/510-2229, www.catalinakayaks.com, snorkel gear $10 per hour, $20 per day).

Descanso Beach Ocean Sports/Catalina Island Kayak & Snorkel (310/510-1226, www.kayakcatalinaisland.com, half-day to full-day tours $40-60) offers several kayak tours to different parts of the island. **Jeep Eco-Tours** (310/510-2595, www.catalinaconservancy.org, chartered half-day tour $549 for up to six people, chartered full-day tour $889, nonchartered two-hour tour $70 pp, nonchartered two-hour tour $109 pp) will take you out into the wilderness to see bison, wild horses, and plant species unique to the island.

The best dining option is **The Lobster Trap** (128 Catalina St., 310/510-8585, www.catalinalobstertrap.com, 11am-late daily, $12-30), which serves up its namesake crustacean in various forms, along with other seafood.

GETTING THERE

The **Catalina Express** (800/481-3470, www.catalinaexpress.com, round-trip adults $75, seniors $68, ages 2-11 $59, under age 2 $5, bicycles and surfboards $7) offers multiple ferry trips every day, even in the off-season. During the summer, you can depart from Long Beach, San Pedro, or Dana Point. Bring your bike, your luggage, and your camping gear aboard for the hour-long ride.

GETTING AROUND
Car

Los Angeles is crisscrossed with freeways, providing numerous yet congested access points into the city. From the north and south, I-5 provides the most direct access to Downtown L.A. From I-5, U.S. 101 south leads directly into Hollywood; from here, Santa Monica Boulevard can take you west to Beverly Hills. Connecting from I-5 to I-210 will take you east to Pasadena. The best way to reach Santa Monica, Venice, and Malibu is via Highway 1, also known as the Pacific Coast Highway. I-10 can get

you there from the east, but it will be a long, tedious, and trafficked drive. I-710, which runs north-south, is known as the Long Beach Freeway. Along the coast, the Pacific Coast Highway (Hwy. 1) can get you from one beach town to the next.

PARKING

Parking in Los Angeles can be as much of a bear as driving. And it can cost you quite a lot of money. You will find parking lots and structures included with many hotel rooms, but parking on the street can be difficult or impossible, parking lots in sketchy areas (like the Flower and Jewelry Districts) can be dangerous, and parking structures at popular attractions can be expensive. Beach parking on summer weekends is the worst, but on weekdays and in the off-season you can occasionally find a decent space down near the beach for a reasonable rate.

Public Transit

The **Metro** (www.metro.net, cash fare $1.75, day pass $7) runs both the subway Metro Rail system and a network of buses throughout the L.A. metropolitan area. Pay on board a bus if you have exact change. Otherwise, purchase a ticket or a day pass from the ticket vending machines at all Metro Rail stations.

Some buses run 24 hours. The Metro Rail lines start running as early as 4:30am and don't stop until as late as 1:30am. See the website (www.metro.net) for route maps, timetables, and fare details.

Taxis

Taxis aren't cheap, but they're quick, easy, and numerous. And in some cases, when you add up gas and parking fees, you'll find that the cab ride isn't that much more expensive than driving yourself.

To call a cab, try **Yellow Cab** (424/222-2222, www.layellowcab.com, L.A., LAX, Beverly Hills, Hollywood) or **City Cab** (888/248-9222, www.lacitycab.com, San Fernando Valley, Hollywood, and LAX), which now has a small fleet of green, environmentally friendly vehicles. Or check out www.taxicabsla.org for a complete list of providers and phone numbers.

SERVICES

The **Hollywood and Highland Visitors Center** (6801 Hollywood Blvd., 323/467-6412, 9am-10pm Mon.-Sat., 10am-7pm Sun.) is adjacent to a Metro station and includes a self-serve kiosk where you can purchase discount tickets to area attractions. There are additional self-serve centers at the Los Angeles Convention Center, the Port of Los Angeles (Berth 93), and the California Science Center.

For medical assistance, **USC Medical Center** (1200 N. State St., emergency 911, 323/409-1000, www.ladhs.org) can fix you up no matter what's wrong with you, or visit the emergency room at the **Long Beach Memorial Medical Center** (2801 Atlantic Ave., Long Beach, 562/933-2000, www.memorialcare.org).

Disneyland and Orange County

The lure of Orange County tends to be dominated by the Mouse. But if you just have to get away from the overwhelming cutesy happiness for a while, the Orange County beaches are your best bet.

TOP EXPERIENCE

DISNEYLAND

The "Happiest Place on Earth" lures millions of visitors of all ages each year with promises of fun and fantasy. During high seasons, waves of humanity flow through **Disneyland** (1313 N. Harbor Blvd., Anaheim, 714/781-4623, http://disneyland.disney.go.com;

9am-midnight daily; ticket prices vary; one-day over age 9 $99, ages 3-9 $93; one-day Hopper Ticket for entry to both parks over age 9 $150, ages 3-9 $144), moving slowly from land to land and ride to ride. The park is well set up to handle the often-immense crowds. Despite the undeniable cheese factor, even the most cynical and jaded resident Californians can't quite keep their cantankerous scowls once they're ensconced inside Uncle Walt's dream. It really *is* a happy place.

Orientation

The Disneyland Resort is a massive kingdom that stretches from **Harbor Boulevard** on

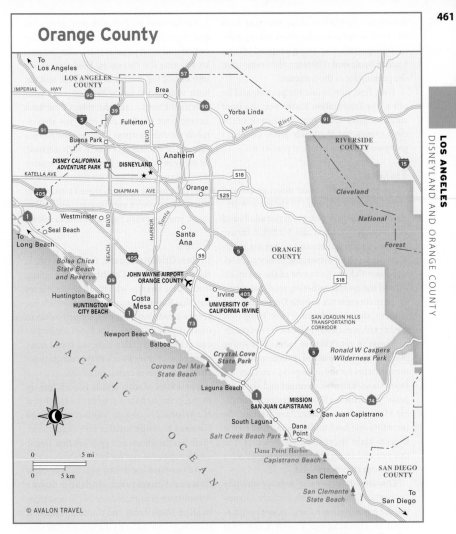

Orange County

To Los Angeles

LOS ANGELES COUNTY

IMPERIAL HWY

Brea

Yorba Linda

Fullerton

Buena Park

Anaheim

DISNEY CALIFORNIA ADVENTURE PARK   DISNEYLAND

KATELLA AVE

CHAPMAN AVE

Orange

Westminster

Seal Beach

To Long Beach

Santa Ana

Bolsa Chica State Beach and Reserve

JOHN WAYNE AIRPORT ORANGE COUNTY

Huntington Beach

HUNTINGTON CITY BEACH

Costa Mesa

Irvine

UNIVERSITY OF CALIFORNIA IRVINE

ORANGE COUNTY

RIVERSIDE COUNTY

Cleveland

National

Forest

SAN JOAQUIN HILLS TRANSPORTATION CORRIDOR

Newport Beach

Balboa

Corona Del Mar State Beach

Crystal Cove State Park

Ronald W Caspers Wilderness Park

Laguna Beach

MISSION SAN JUAN CAPISTRANO

San Juan Capistrano

South Laguna

Dana Point

Salt Creek Beach Park

PACIFIC

OCEAN

Dana Point Harbor

Capistrano Beach

San Clemente

San Clemente State Beach

SAN DIEGO COUNTY

To San Diego

0   5 mi

0   5 km

© AVALON TRAVEL

the east to **Walnut Street** on the west and from **Ball Road** to the north to **Katella Avenue** to the south. It includes two amusement parks, three hotels, and an outdoor shopping and entertainment complex. The Disneyland-affiliated hotels (Disneyland Hotel, Paradise Pier Hotel, and Disney's Grand Californian) all cluster on the western side of the complex, between Walnut Street and **Disneyland Drive (West St.).** The area between Disneyland Drive and Harbor Boulevard is shared by **Disneyland** in the northern section and **Disney California Adventure Park** in the southern section, with **Downtown Disney** between them in the central-west section. There is no admission fee for Downtown Disney. You can reach the amusement park entrances via Downtown Disney (although visitors going to Disneyland or Disney California Adventure Park should park in the paid lots, rather than the Downtown Disney self-park lot, which is only free for the first three hours) or from the walk-in entrance (for those taking public transportation or being dropped off) on Harbor Boulevard. There are also trams from the parking lot to the entrance.

Your first stop inside the park should be one of the information kiosks near the front entrance gates. Get a map, a schedule of the day's events, and the inside scoop on what's going on in the park during your visit.

Tickets

There are as many varied ticket prices and plans as there are themes in the park. A single-day theme park ticket will run adults and kids over age 9 $99, and ages 3-9 $93. A variety of other combinations and passes are available online (http://disneyland.disney.go.com).

To buy tickets, go to one of the many kiosks in the central gathering spot that serves as the main entrance to both Disneyland and Disney California Adventure Park. Bring your credit card, since a day at Disney is not cheap. After you've got tickets in hand (or if you've bought them online ahead of time), proceed to the turnstiles for the main park. You'll see the Disneyland Railroad terminal and the large grassy hill with the flowers planted to resemble Mickey's famous face. Pass through the turnstiles and head under the railroad trestle to get to Main Street and the park center. You can exit and reenter the park on the days for which your tickets are valid.

The already expensive regular one-day Disneyland ticket doesn't include Disney California Adventure Park. If you're interested in checking out Disney California Adventure Park as well as Disneyland, your best bet is to buy a **Park Hopper pass** (additional $51), which lets you move back and forth between the two parks at will for a slight discount. If you're planning to spend several days touring the Houses of Mouse, buy multiday passes in advance online to save a few more bucks per day. It'll help you feel better about the cash you'll spend on junk food, giant silly hats, stuffed animals, and an endless array of Disney apparel.

Fastpasses are free with park admission and might seem like magic after a while. The newest and most popular rides offer Fastpass kiosks near the entrances. Feed your ticket into one of the machines and it will spit out both your ticket and a Fastpass with your specified time to take the ride. Come back during your window and enter the always-much-shorter Fastpass line, designated by a sign at the entrance. If you're with a crowd, be sure you all get your Fastpasses at the same time, so you all get the same time window to ride. It's possible to claim three Fastpasses at a time. Once you've used up your initial allotment, you can visit a Fastpass kiosk to reload.

Rides

In **New Orleans Square,** the favorite ride is the **Pirates of the Caribbean.** Beginning in the dim swamp, which can be seen from the Blue Bayou Restaurant, the ride's classic scenes inside have been revamped to tie in more closely to the movies. Lines for Pirates can get long, so grab a Fastpass if you don't want to wait. Pirates is suitable for younger children as well as teens and adults.

For a taste of truly classic Disney, line up in the graveyard for a tour of the **Haunted Mansion.** The sedate motion makes the Haunted Mansion suitable for younger children, but the ghosts and ghoulies that amuse adults can be intense for kids.

Adventureland sits next to the New Orleans Square area. **Indiana Jones Adventure** is arguably one of the best rides in all of Disneyland, and the details make it stunning. This one isn't the best for tiny tots, but the big kids love it. Everyone might want a Fastpass for the endlessly popular attraction.

In **Frontierland**, take a ride on a Wild West train on the **Big Thunder Mountain Railroad,** an older roller coaster that whisks passengers on a brief but fun thrill ride through a "dangerous, decrepit" mountain's mineshafts.

Fantasyland rides tend to cater to the younger set. For many Disneyphiles, **"it's a small world"** is the ultimate expression of

Uncle Walt's dream, and toddlers adore this ride. Older kids might prefer **Mr. Toad's Wild Ride.** The wacky scenery ranges from a sedate library to the gates of hell. If it's a faster thrill you're seeking, head for the **Matterhorn Bobsleds.** You'll board a sled-style coaster car to plunge down a Swiss mountain on a twisted track that takes you past rivers, glaciers, and the Abominable Snowman.

The best thrill ride of the main park sits inside **Tomorrowland. Space Mountain** is a fast roller coaster that whizzes through the dark. Despite its age, Space Mountain remains one of the more popular rides in the park. Get a Fastpass to avoid long lines.

★ Disney California Adventure Park

Disney California Adventure Park (http:// disneyland.disney.go.com; 8am-10pm daily; ticket prices vary; one-day over age 9 $99, ages 3-9 $93; one-day Hopper Ticket for entry to both parks over age 9 $150, ages 3-9 $144) celebrates much of what makes California special. If Disney is your only stop on this trip but you'd like to get a sense of the state as a whole, this park can give you a little taste.

Disney California Adventure Park is divided into themed areas. You'll find two information booths just inside the main park entrance, one off to the left as you walk through the turnstile and one at the opening to Sunshine Plaza.

RIDES

Celebrating SoCal's famed film industry, **Hollywood Land** holds the ultimate thrill ride inside: **The Twilight Zone Tower of Terror.** Enter the creepy "old hotel," go through the "service area," and take your place inside an elevator straight out of your worst nightmares. This ride aims for teens and adults rather than little kids, and it's not a good one for folks who fear heights or don't do well with free-fall rides.

Less extreme but also fun, **Monsters, Inc. Mike & Sully to the Rescue!** invites guests into the action of the movie of the same name.

You'll help the heroes as they chase the intrepid Boo. This ride jostles you around but is suitable for smaller kids as well as bigger ones.

Get a sample of the world of tiny insects on **It's Tough to Be a Bug!** This big-group, 3-D, multisensory ride offers fun for little kids and adults alike. You'll fly through the air, scuttle through the grass, and get a good idea of what life is like on six little legs.

For the littlest adventurers, **Flik's Fun Fair** offers almost half a dozen rides geared toward toddlers and little children. They can ride pint-size hot-air balloons known as Flik's Flyers, climb aboard a bug-themed train, or run around under a gigantic faucet to cool down after hours of fun.

Paradise Pier mimics the Santa Monica Pier and other waterfront attractions like it, with thrill rides and an old-fashioned midway. **California Screamin'** is a high-tech roller coaster designed after the classic wooden coasters of carnivals past. This extra-long ride includes drops, twists, a full loop, and plenty of time and screaming fun. California Screamin' has a four-foot height requirement and is just as popular with nostalgic adults as with kids. **Toy Story Midway Mania!** magnifies the midway mayhem as passengers of all ages take aim at targets in a 4-D ride inspired by Disney-Pixar's *Toy Story.*

In **Condor Flats, Soarin' Over California** is a combination ride and show that puts you and dozens of other guests on the world's biggest "glider" and sets you off over the hills and valleys of California. Get Disney's version of a wilderness experience at **Grizzly Peak.** Enjoy a white-water raft ride through a landscape inspired by the Sierra Nevada foothills on the **Grizzly River Run.**

Cars Land was inspired by the hit 2006 film *Cars.* Float on larger-than-life tires on the **Luigi's Flying Tires** ride or be serenaded by Mater as you ride in a tractor on **Mater's Junkyard Jamboree.** The **Radiator Springs Racers** finds six-person vehicles passing locations and characters from *Cars* before culminating in a real-life race with a car of other park visitors.

Parades and Shows

Watch your favorite Pixar characters come to life in the **Pixar Play Parade**. Other regular shows are **Disney Junior—Live on Stage!** and **Disney's Aladdin—A Musical Spectacular.** Both of these shows hark back to favorite children's activities and movies. Check your park guide and *Time Guide* for more information about these and other live shows.

Food

DISNEYLAND

One of the few things the Mouse doesn't do too well is haute cuisine. For a truly good or healthy meal, get a hand stamp and go outside the park. But if you're stuck inside and you absolutely need sustenance, you can get it. The best areas of the park to grab a bite are Main Street, New Orleans, and Frontierland, but you can find at least a snack almost anywhere in the park.

For a sit-down restaurant meal inside the park, make reservations in advance for a table at the **Blue Bayou Restaurant** (New Orleans Square, 714/781-3463, $30-50). The best part about this restaurant is its setting in the dimly lit swamp overlooking the Pirates of the Caribbean ride. Appropriately, the Bayou has Cajun-ish cuisine and a reputation for being haunted. You will get large portions, and tasty desserts make a fine finish to your meal. Watch your silverware, though; the alleged ghosts in this restaurant like to mess around with diners' tableware.

If you need to grab a quicker bite, *don't* do it at the French Market restaurant in the New Orleans area. It sells what appears to be day-old (or more) food from the Bayou that has been sitting under heat lamps for a good long time.

DISNEY CALIFORNIA ADVENTURE PARK

If you need a snack break in Disney California Adventure Park, you'll find most of the food clustered in the Golden State area. For a Mexican feast, try **Cocina Cucamonga** Mexican Grill ($15). For more traditional American fare, enjoy the food at the **Pacific Wharf Cafe** ($15) or the **Taste Pilots' Grill** ($15).

Unlike Disneyland proper, in Disney California Adventure Park, responsible adults can quash their thirst with a variety of alcoholic beverages. If you're just dying for a cold beer, get one at **Bayside Brews.** Or, if you love the endless array of high-quality wines produced in the Golden State, head for the **Mendocino Terrace,** where you can learn the basics of wine creation and production. Have a glass and a pseudo-Italian meal at the sit-down **Wine Country Trattoria at the Golden Vine Winery** (714/781-3463, $15-36).

DOWNTOWN DISNEY

Downtown Disney is outside the amusement parks and offers additional dining options. National chains like **House of Blues** (1530 S. Disneyland Dr., Anaheim, 714/778-2583, www.houseofblues.com, 11am-1am daily, $15-30) and **Rainforest Café** (1515 S. Disneyland Dr., Anaheim, 714/772-0413, www.rainforest-cafe.com, 8am-11pm Sun.-Thurs., 8am-midnight Fri.-Sat., $11-18) serve typical menu staples like sandwiches, burgers, pasta, and steak and seafood entrées, with House of Blues putting a Southern spin on these items and adding live-music shows, while kid-friendly Rainforest Café puts on tropical touches like coconut and mango. **ESPN Zone** (1545 Disneyland Dr., Anaheim, 714/300-3776, www.espnzone.com, 11am-11pm Sun.-Thurs., 11am-midnight Fri.-Sat., $11-26) has similar offerings with a "sports bar on steroids" restaurant concept.

There are also more individual restaurants, but even these feel a little like chains. The most distinctive of them, **Ralph Brennan's Jazz Kitchen** (1590 S. Disneyland Dr., Anaheim, 714/776-5200, www.rbjazzkitchen.com, 11am-10pm Sun.-Thurs., 11am-11pm Fri.-Sat., $24-39), is meant to replicate the experience of eating in New Orleans's French Quarter. The Cajun menu hits all the staples, including

Alternatives to the Mouse

UNIVERSAL STUDIOS HOLLYWOOD

The longtime Hollywood-centric alternative to Disneyland is the **Universal Studios Hollywood** (100 Universal City Plaza, Los Angeles, 800/864-8377, www.universalstudios.com, hours vary, adults $85-95, children under 48 inches tall $72, parking $10-15) theme park. Kids adore this park, which puts them right into the action of their favorite movies. Flee the carnivorous dinosaurs of *Jurassic Park,* take a rafting adventure on the pseudo-set of *Waterworld,* or quiver in terror of an ancient curse in *Revenge of the Mummy.* If you're more interested in how the movies are made than the rides made from them, take the **Studio Tour.** You'll get an extreme close-up of the sets of major blockbuster films like *War of the Worlds.* Better yet, be part of the studio audience of TV shows currently taping by getting tickets at the Audiences Unlimited Ticket Booth. If you're a serious movie buff, consider buying a **VIP pass**—you'll get a six-hour tour that takes you onto working sound stages, into the current prop warehouse, and through a variety of working build shops that service movies and programs currently filming.

SIX FLAGS MAGIC MOUNTAIN

Six Flags Magic Mountain (Magic Mountain Parkway, Valencia, 661/255-4100, www.six-flags.com, hours vary, adults $73, children $48) provides good fun for the whole family. Magic Mountain has long been the extreme alternative to the Mouse, offering a wide array of thrill rides. You'll need a strong stomach to deal with the g-forces of the major-league roller coasters and the death-defying drops, including the Lex Luthor: Drop of Doom, where you plummet 400 feet at speeds up to 85 mph. For the younger set, plenty of rides offer a less intense but equally fun amusement-park experience. Both littler and bigger kids enjoy interacting with the classic Warner Bros. characters, especially in Bugs Bunny World, and a kids' show features Bugs Bunny, Donald Duck, and more. Other than that, Magic Mountain has little in the way of staged entertainment—this park is all about the rides. The park is divided into areas, just like most other major theme parks; get a map at the entrance to help you maneuver around and pick your favorite rides.

KNOTT'S BERRY FARM

For a taste of history along with some ultramodern thrill rides and plenty of cooling waterslides, head for **Knott's Berry Farm** (8039 Beach Blvd., Buena Park, 714/220-5200, www.knotts.com, hours vary, adults $38, seniors and children $34, parking $15). From the tall landmark GhostRider wooden coaster to the 30-story vertical-drop ride to the screaming Silver Bullet suspended coaster, Knott's supplies excitement to even the most hard-core ride lover. For the younger crowd, Camp Snoopy offers an array of pint-size rides and attractions, plus Snoopy and all the characters they love from the *Peanuts* comics and TV shows.

In the heat of the summer, many park visitors adjourn from the coasters to **Knott's Soak City** (www.soakcityoc.com, hours vary daily Memorial Day-Labor Day, adults $28-34, seniors and children $24, parking $15-20), a full-size water park with 22 rides, a kid pool and water playground, and plenty of space to enjoy the O.C. sunshine.

Convenient to the parks, **Knott's Berry Farm Resort Hotel** (7675 Crescent Ave., Buena Park, 714/995-1111, www.knotts.com, $155-222) is a high-rise resort with a pool and spa, a fitness center, and several on-site restaurants.

jambalaya, beignets, and various blackened meats and seafood.

The Patina Restaurant Group runs **Catal Restaurant** (1580 Disneyland Dr., Anaheim, 714/774-4442, www.patinagroup. com, 8am-11am and 5pm-10pm daily, $19-41), with Mediterranean fare; **Naples Ristorante** (1550 Disneyland Dr., Anaheim, 714/776-6200, www.patinagroup.com, 8am-10pm daily, $15-46) for Italian food; and **Tortilla**

Jo's (1510 Disneyland Dr., Anaheim, 714/535-5000, www.patinagroup.com, 11am-10pm Sun.-Thurs., 11am-11pm Fri.-Sat., $15-21) for Mexican food.

Finally, **La Brea Bakery** (1556 Disneyland Dr., Anaheim, 714/490-0233, www.labreabakery.com, 8am-9pm Sun.-Thurs., 8am-2pm Fri.-Sat., $10-28) is the Disney outpost of an L.A. favorite. This bakery, founded by Nancy Silverton, supplies numerous markets and restaurants with crusty European-style loaves. The morning scones, sandwiches, and fancy cookies are superb.

Accommodations

The best way to get fully Disney-fied is to stay at one of the park's hotels. Several sit just beside or across the street from the park.

DISNEY HOTELS

For the most iconic Disney resort experience, you must stay at the **Disneyland Hotel** (1150 Magic Way, Anaheim, 714/778-6600, http://disneyland.disney.go.com, $460-1,016). This nearly 1,000-room high-rise monument to brand-specific family entertainment has everything a vacationing Brady-esque bunch could want: themed swimming pools, themed play areas, and even character-themed rooms that allow the kids to fully immerse themselves in the Mouse experience. Adults and families on a budget can also get rooms with either a king or two queen beds and more traditional motel fabrics and appointments. The monorail stops inside the hotel, offering guests the easiest way into the park proper without having to deal with parking or even walking.

It's easy to find the **Paradise Pier Hotel** (1717 S. Disneyland Dr., Anaheim, 714/999-0990, http://disneyland.disney.go.com, $344-952); it's that high-rise thing just outside Disney California Adventure Park. This hotel boasts what passes for affordable lodgings within walking distance of the parks. Rooms are cute, colorful, and clean; many have two doubles or queens to accommodate families or couples traveling together on a tighter

budget. You'll find a (possibly refreshing) lack of Mickeys in the standard guest accommodations at the Paradise, which has the feel of a beach resort motel. After a day of wandering the park, relax by the rooftop pool.

Disney's Grand Californian Hotel and Spa (1600 S. Disneyland Dr., Anaheim, 714/635-2300, http://disneyland.disney.go.com, $547-1,216) is inside Disney California Adventure Park, attempting to mimic the famous Ahwahnee Lodge in Yosemite. While it doesn't quite succeed (much of what makes the Ahwahnee so great is its views), the big-beam construction and soaring common spaces do feel reminiscent of a great luxury lodge. The hotel is surrounded by gardens and has restaurants, a day spa, and shops attached on the ground floor; it can also get you right out into Downtown Disney and thence to the parks proper. Rooms here offer more luxury than the other Disney resorts, with dark woods and faux-craftsman detailing creating an attractive atmosphere. Get anything from a standard room that sleeps two up to spacious family suites with bunk beds that can easily handle six people. As with all Disney resorts, you can purchase tickets and a meal plan along with your hotel room (in fact, if you book via the website, they'll try to force you to do it that way).

OUTSIDE THE PARKS

The massive park complex is ringed with motels, both popular chains and more interesting independents. **The Anabella** (1030 W. Katella Ave., Anaheim, 714/905-1050 or 800/863-4888, www.anabellahotel.com, $170-215) offers a touch of class along with a three-block walk to the parks. The elegant marble-clad lobby seems like it belongs closer to Downtown L.A. than Downtown Disney. A decent restaurant, two pools, a whirlpool tub, and a fitness center are on-site. You can get limited room service at the Anabella, and you can leave your car in the hotel's parking lot to avoid the expense of parking at Disneyland.

Within walking distance is the **Desert**

Palms Hotel & Suites (631 W. Katella Ave., 888/788-0466, www.desertpalmshotel.com, $175-415). The pool and spa provide fun for children and adults alike, and the many amenities make travelers comfortable. Guests with more discretionary income can choose from a number of suites, some designed to delight children and others aimed at couples on a romantic getaway. There are even condo-style accommodations with kitchens.

Away from the Disneyland complex and surrounding area, the accommodations in Orange County run to chain motels with little character or distinctiveness, but the good news is that you can find a decent room for a reasonable price.

The **Hyatt Regency Orange County** (11999 Harbor Blvd., Garden Grove, 714/750-1234, http://orangecounty.hyatt.com, $199-289) in Garden Grove is about 1.5 miles (10 minutes' drive on Harbor Blvd.) south of the park. The family-friendly suites have separate bedrooms with bunk beds and fun decor geared toward younger guests. Enjoy a cocktail in the sun-drenched atrium, or grab a chaise lounge by the pool or take a refreshing dip.

Transportation

The nearest airport to Disneyland, serving all of Orange County, is **John Wayne Airport** (SNA, 18601 Airport Way, Santa Ana, 949/252-5200, www.ocair.com). It's much easier to fly into and out of John Wayne than LAX, though it can be more expensive. John Wayne's terminal has plenty of rental car agencies, as well as many shuttle services that can get you where you need to go—especially to the House of Mouse.

If you have to fly into LAX for scheduling or budget reasons, catch a shuttle straight from the airport to your Disneyland hotel. Among the many companies offering and arranging such transportation, the one with the best name is **MouseSavers** (www.mousesavers.com). Working with various shuttle and van companies, MouseSavers can get you a ride in a van or a bus from LAX or John Wayne to your destination at or near Disneyland.

Disneyland is on Disneyland Drive in Anaheim and is most accessible from I-5 south where it crosses Ball Road (stay in the left three lanes for parking). The parking lot (1313 S. Disneyland Dr.) costs $17 for a car or motorcycle, $22 for an oversize vehicle such as a motor home or tractor without the trailer, and $27 for buses and tractor-trailer rigs.

If you're coming to the park from elsewhere in Southern California, consider leaving the car (avoiding the parking fees) and taking public transit instead. **Anaheim Resort Transit** (ART, 1280 Anaheim Blvd., Anaheim, 714/563-5287, www.rideart.org) can take you to and from the Amtrak station and all around central Anaheim for $4 per day. Buy passes via the website or at conveniently located kiosks.

Services

Each park has information booths near the park entrance. On the website for **Visit Anaheim** (http://visitanaheim.org), you can plan a trip to the area in advance by looking at the upcoming events and suggested itineraries or by downloading the travel guide.

If you need to stow your bags or hit the restroom before plunging into the fray, banks of lockers and restrooms sit in the main entrance area. If mobility is a problem, consider renting a **stroller, wheelchair,** or **scooter.** Ask for directions to the rental counter when you enter the park.

Disneyland offers its own minor medical facilities, which can dispense first aid for scrapes, cuts, and mild heat exhaustion. They can also call an ambulance if something nastier has occurred. The **West Anaheim Medical Center** (3033 W. Orange Ave., Anaheim, 714/827-3000, www.westanaheimmedctr.com) is a full-service hospital with an emergency room.

ORANGE COUNTY BEACHES

The Orange County coast begins at Huntington Beach and stretches south across a collection of sunny, scenic beach towns (Newport Beach, Laguna Beach, and Dana Point) until ending at San Juan Capistrano. The surf here is world-renowned.

Huntington Beach

This Orange County beach town is known for its longtime association with surfing and surf culture, beginning when Hawaiian legend Duke Kahanamoku first rode waves here back in 1922. Surfers still ride the surf on either side of the **Huntington Beach Pier,** a large concrete pier that offers fine views of the beach scene on both sides. Across the Pacific Coast Highway, Huntington Beach's Main Street is full of restaurants, bars, and shops, including lots of surf shops.

BEACHES

Huntington City Beach (Pacific Coast Hwy. from Beach Blvd. to Seapoint St., beach headquarters 103 Pacific Coast Hwy., 714/536-5281, www.huntingtonbeachca.gov, beach 5am-10pm daily, office 8am-5pm Mon.-Fri.) runs the length of the south end of town, petering out toward the oil industry facilities at the north end. This famous beach hosts major sporting events such as the U.S. Open of Surfing and the X Games. But even the average beachgoer can enjoy all sorts of activities on a daily basis, from sunbathing to beach volleyball, surfing to skimboarding. There's a cement walkway for biking, in-line skating, jogging, and walking. Plus, you'll find a dog-friendly section at the north end of the beach where dogs can be let off-leash.

FOOD

The Black Trumpet Bistro (18344 Beach Blvd., 714/842-1122, www.theblacktrumpetbistro.com, 4pm-10pm Tues.-Sat., $12-23) is named for the jazz greats who lend their names to the menu items. Here, Duke is a Cornish game hen, while Louis is a Greek spaghetti dish. Paintings of jazz legends also adorn the walls. The owner wants to represent Mediterranean cuisine from tapas to more substantial entrées. His endeavor has caused The Black Trumpet to be proclaimed one of Huntington Beach's best restaurants by the *OC Weekly.*

For a quick bite to eat, stop off at the **Bodhi Tree Vegetarian Cafe** (501 Main St., Ste. E, 714/969-9500, www.bodhitreehb.com, 11am-10pm Wed.-Mon., $6-10) for vegetarian soups, salads, and sandwiches. **Sugar Shack Café** (213 Main St., 714/536-0355, www.hbsugarshack.com, 6am-2pm Mon.-Tues and Thurs.-Fri., 6am-8pm Wed., 6am-2pm 6am-3pm Sat.-Sun., $7-10) is a great place for breakfast, serving omelets and breakfast burritos.

ACCOMMODATIONS

The 17-room **Sun 'N Sands Motel** (1102 Pacific Coast Hwy., 714/536-2543, www.sunnsands.com, $169-269) is a tiny place where you can expect the standard motel room, but the main attraction is across the treacherous Pacific Coast Highway: long, sweet Huntington Beach. Be careful crossing the highway to get to the sand. Find a traffic light and a crosswalk rather than risking life and limb for the minor convenience of jaywalking.

For something more upscale, book a room at the **Shorebreak Hotel** (500 Pacific Coast Hwy., 714/861-4470, www.jdvhotels.com, $350-890). Some rooms have private balconies looking out over the beach and pier. Everyone can enjoy the hotel's on-site restaurant, fitness center, and courtyard with fire pits.

Newport Beach

Affluent Newport Beach is known for its beaches, harbor, and The Wedge, a notorious bodysurfing and body-boarding wave.

BEACHES

Most of the activity in **Newport Beach** (www.visitnewportbeach.com) centers around Newport Pier (McFadden Pl.) and Main Street on the Balboa Peninsula. This 10-mile stretch of sand is popular for fishing, swimming, surfing, and other ocean activities. On the east end of Balboa Peninsula,

The Wedge is the world's most famous bodysurfing spot. On south swells, the wave jacks up off the adjacent rock jetty and creates monsters up to 30 feet high that break almost right on the beach. Beginners should stay out of the water and enjoy the spectacle from the sand.

FOOD

For something French, colorful **Pescadou Bistro** (3325 Newport Blvd., 949/675-6990, www.pescadoubistro.com, 5:30pm-9pm Tues.-Sun., $21-36) fills the bill. Meanwhile, **Eat Chow** (211 62nd St., 949/423-7080, www. eatchownow.com, 8am-9pm Mon.-Thurs., 8am-10pm Fri., 7am-10pm Sat., 7am-9pm Sun., $9-18) is a local favorite with items like breakfast *carnitas* tacos and shredded redeye burritos.

Expect a line outside **Cappy's Café & Cantina** (5930 W. Coast Hwy., 949/646-4202, 6am-3pm Mon.-Fri., 6am-4pm Sat.-Sun., $10-20), a low-slung building that has served breakfast and lunch since 1957. Cappy's serves expand-your-waistband items including a 20-ounce porterhouse steak and eggs and a knockwurst and eggs dish. Enjoy the fare while mellowing out in a beachy atmosphere with plenty of colorful murals.

ACCOMMODATIONS

South of downtown Newport Beach, the ★ **Crystal Cove Beach Cottages** (35 Crystal Cove, 949/376-6200, www.crystalcovebeachcottages.org, reservations www. reserveamerica.com, dorms $42-83, cabins $162-249) give anyone the opportunity to experience life right on the Southern California sand. Some of the cabins are individual rentals that you can have all to yourself. The dorm cottages offer by-the-room accommodations for solo travelers (linens included; room doors lock). None of the cottages have TVs or any type of digital entertainment. And all the cottages include a common refrigerator and microwave, but no full kitchen, so plan to eat out, perhaps at the adjacent **Beachcomber Cafe** (15 Crystal Cove, 949/376-6900, www.thebeachcombercafe.com, 7am-9:30pm daily, $18-37), where items like breakfast *chilaquiles* and crab-stuffed salmon are served.

Laguna Beach Area

Laguna Beach stands apart from other Orange County beach communities with its long-running arts scene, touted fine-dining restaurants, tidepool-pocked coastline jammed between sandy beaches, and clear

Crystal Cove Beach Cottages

ocean water that beckons snorkelers and divers underwater.

MISSION SAN JUAN CAPISTRANO

Mission San Juan Capistrano (26801 Ortega Hwy., 949/234-1300, www.mission-sjc.com, 9am-5pm daily, adults $9, seniors $8, ages 4-11 $6, under age 3 free), in the lovely little town of San Juan Capistrano, has a beautiful Catholic church and extensive gardens and grounds. In late fall and early spring, monarch butterflies flutter about in the flower gardens and out by the fountain in the courtyard. Inside the original church, artifacts from the early time of the mission tell the story of its rise and fall, as does an audio tour available in the museum.

BEACHES

Heisler Park and **Main Beach Park** (Pacific Coast Hwy., Laguna Beach, www.laguna-beachinfo.com) offer protected waterways, with tide pools and plenty of water-based playground equipment. The two parks are connected, so you can walk from one to the other. If you're into scuba diving, there are several reefs right off the beach. You'll find all the facilities and amenities you need at Heisler and Main Beach Parks, including picnic tables, lawns, and restrooms. Park on the street if you find a spot, but the meters get checked all the time, so feed them well.

Laguna Beach has a lot more undeveloped space than other Orange County communities, and **Crystal Cove State Park** (8471 N. Coast Hwy., 949/494-3539, www.crystalcovestatepark.org, 6am-sunset daily, $15/vehicle) just north of town has 3.2 miles of lightly developed coastline with sandy coves and tidepools. Offshore is the Crystal Cove Underwater Park, which has several snorkeling and diving sites. The park also includes a 2,400-acre inland section with unpaved roads and trails that are open to hikers, bikers, and horseback riders.

At the southern tip of the O.C., Dana Point has a harbor (34551 Puerto Pl., 949/923-2280, www.ocparks.com) that has become a recreation marina that draws locals and visitors from all around. It also has several beaches nearby. One of the prettiest is **Capistrano Beach** (35005 Beach Rd., 949/923-2280 or 949/923-2283, www.ocparks.com, 6am-10pm daily, parking $1-2 per hour). You'll find a metered parking lot adjacent to the beach, plus showers and restrooms available.

Also in Dana Point, **Doheny State Beach** (25300 Dana Point Harbor Dr., 949/496-6172, www.parks.ca.gov, daily 6am-10pm, $15) is popular with surfers and anglers. The northern end of Doheny has a lawn along with volleyball courts, while the southern side has a popular campground with 121 campsites.

Visit **Salt Creek Beach** (33333 S. Pacific Coast Hwy., 949/923-2280, www.ocparks.com, 5am-midnight daily, parking $1 per hour) for a renowned surf break and a great place to spend a day in the sun.

FOOD

★ **Carmelita's Kitchen De Mexico** (217 Broadway, 949/715-7829, www.carmelitaskdm.com, 11am-10pm Mon.-Fri., 9am-10pm Sat., 9am-9pm Sun., $14-28) is a popular local favorite serving upscale Mexican cuisine. The open kitchen puts out terrific entrées including *tampiqueña* (marinated skirt steak) and a seafood trio platter with a lobster enchilada, shrimp taco, and crab relleno. Carmelita's also does some twists on the classic margarita with cilantro-cucumber and strawberry-jalapeño versions.

★ **Watermarc** (448 S. Coast Hwy., 949/376-6272, http://watermarcrestaurant.com, 11am-10pm Mon.-Fri., 8am-11pm Sat., 8am-10pm Sun., small plates $7-14, entrées $24-34), run by executive chef Marc Cohen, focuses on its "grazing plates," from filet mignon potpie to smoked bacon-wrapped dates. The two-story restaurant also has exceptional cocktails. Happy hour (4pm-6pm daily) offers burgers at half price, while all drinks and appetizers are $2 off.

For a casual meal, visit **The Stand** (238 Thalia St., 949/494-8101, 7am-8pm daily,

$7-11), a shack that has lovingly served up vegan food for more than 40 years. Order at the window and dine on the small outdoor porch or take your meal a couple of blocks to the beach.

At **Sapphire Laguna** (1200 S. Coast Hwy., 949/715-9888, www.sapphirellc.com, 11am-10:30pm Mon.-Thurs., 10am-11pm Fri.-Sat., $24-37), chef Azmin Ghahreman knows no national boundaries. His international seasonal cuisine might include a Greek octopus salad, Moroccan couscous, a half *jidori* chicken, or Hawaiian-style steamed mahi-mahi.

South of Nick's (110 N. El Camino Real, San Clemente, 949/481-4545, http://thenickco.com, 11am-10pm Sun.-Thurs., 11am-11pm Fri.-Sat., $10-38) offers a menu with an upscale Mexican twist. The bar keeps up with the kitchen's creativity by serving up regular margaritas as well as coconut and cucumber versions.

Worth the trip inland, **The Ramos House** (31752 Los Rios St., San Juan Capistrano, 949/443-1342, www.ramoshouse.com, 8:30am-3pm daily, $16-20) is in a building that dates back to 1881. The Ramos House is known for its soju Bloody Mary that comes with a Scotch quail egg and a crab claw. It also serves a smoked bacon scramble, a crab hash, and a buttermilk biscuit with apple butter.

ACCOMMODATIONS

Perched on a bluff over Laguna Beach's Main Beach, ★ **The Inn at Laguna Beach** (211 N. Pacific Coast Hwy., 800/544-4479, $289-1,074) is the ideal place to stay for an upscale beach vacation. Half of its rooms face the ocean, and a majority of those have balconies to take in the salt air and sound of the sea. Hit up the inn's beach valet for complimentary beach umbrellas, chairs, and towels. After time on Main Beach, retire to the inn's brick pool deck with its pool and hot tub, or head up to the rooftop terrace and warm up by the fire pit.

The ★ **Laguna Beach House** (475 N. Pacific Coast Hwy., 800/297-0007, www.thelagunabeachhouse.com, $299-559) is a casual, surfing-obsessed motel geared toward wave riders and surf-culture aficionados, with killer decor (including a surfboard shaped by the owner) in each of its 36 rooms and a daily surf report written up on a chalkboard in the lobby. The U-shaped structure surrounds a pool deck with pool, hot tub, and fire pit. Before hitting the waves, enjoy

The Inn at Laguna Beach

a complimentary breakfast parfait and coffee put out in the lobby.

The **Blue Lantern Inn** (34343 Street of the Blue Lantern, Dana Point, 800/950-1236, www.bluelanterninn.com, $200-600) crowns the bluffs over the Dana Point Harbor. This attractive contemporary inn offers beachfront elegance in 29 rooms boasting soothing colors, charming appointments, and lush amenities, including a spa tub in every bath, gas fireplaces, and honest-to-goodness free drinks in the mini fridge; some feature patios or balconies with impressive views of the harbor and the Pacific. The inn also offers complimentary bike usage, a hot breakfast, and an afternoon wine-and-appetizers spread.

Stay in a historic and stunning Spanish colonial villa at the **Beachcomber Inn** (533 Avenida Victoria, San Clemente, 949/492-5457, $270-405). The 10 standard villas and two deluxe villas all come with porches, full kitchens, and full views of the ocean, the beach, and the pier.

Transportation

Huntington Beach is one of the closest beaches to Disneyland, just 16 miles away. From Disneyland, get on Highway 22 west for four miles and then turn onto the Beach Boulevard exit. Take Beach Boulevard (Highway 39) for eight miles to Huntington Beach. From Huntington Beach, Newport Beach is just five miles' drive south on the Pacific Coast Highway.

The drive from Disneyland to Laguna Beach is only 30 minutes without traffic. Just take I-5 south for 13 miles and then get on Highway 133 south for 10 miles. Laguna Beach is an 11-mile drive south of Newport Beach on the Pacific Coast Highway.

San Diego

Sights 478
Entertainment and Events 490
Shopping 497
Sports and Recreation 500
Food 507
Accommodations 517
Transportation and Services . . . 523

Highlights

★ **San Diego Zoo:** There's no topping the city's best kid-friendly attraction, where millions bring their children to view lions, tigers, and pandas (page 479).

★ **Old Town State Historic Park:** This state park preserves the surviving structures that made up the original Mexican pueblo of San Diego (page 483).

★ **Cabrillo National Monument:** Perched on the Point Loma Peninsula, the views from this monument are stunning (page 484).

★ **Sunset Cliffs Natural Park:** These sandstone cliffs face a western sky known to put on a show when the sun drops behind scattered clouds (page 485).

★ **Hotel del Coronado:** It may not be the modern resort it was in 1888, but the Hotel Del is still gorgeous and one of a kind (page 485).

★ **Mission Bay Park:** Mission Bay provides sailing, kayaking, and stand-up paddleboarding along this 4,200-acre waterway (page 486).

★ **Ocean Beach Pier:** A walk out on the OB Pier offers a peak at the local surf lineup (page 501).

S an Diego is a golden-hued playground beckoning thrill seekers, revelers, and soul searchers with its magnificent sunsets, sparkling waters, and promise of the good life.

San Diego offers 80 miles of coastline, but with the resources of a major metropolitan city. For all its leisurely appearance, the city supports thriving industries—a vibrant performing arts scene, an emerging culinary identity, the finest craft brewing, and research institutions that attract some of the world's brightest scientific minds. On the beaches, locals sport board shorts, wetsuits, and bikinis, and the air carries the mingled scents of surf wax, sunscreen, and salt water. On a clear day, sailboats traverse the bay, scuba divers explore underwater canyons, golfers tee up, and bicyclists cruise from beach to beach.

PLANNING YOUR TIME

San Diego makes a perfect destination for a weekend getaway. **July** and **August** are peak season in San Diego, with hot sunny days and large crowds. July consistently provides the year's best weather, but the crowds can be outrageous, especially during the long weekend around the immeasurably popular **Comic Con** (usually the second week of July). Hotel prices go through the roof that week, often triple the standard rate. **September** and **October** are the "locals' summer," with warm, sunshiny days, medium crowds, and a mix of surf conditions.

Previous: Balboa Park; the Gaslamp Quarter. **Above:** surfers on the beach.

San Diego

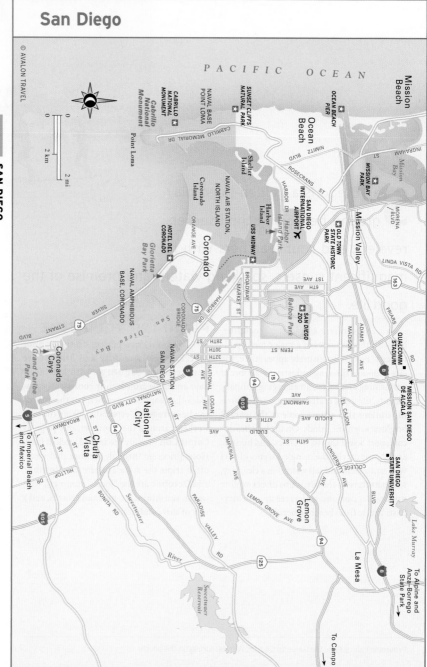

© AVALON TRAVEL

PACIFIC OCEAN

Mission Beach

OCEAN BEACH PIER

Ocean Beach

SUNSET CLIFFS NATURAL PARK

NAVAL BASE POINT LOMA

CABRILLO NATIONAL MONUMENT

Cabrillo National Monument

Point Loma

Shelter Island

Coronado Island

NAVAL AIR STATION, NORTH ISLAND

Coronado

HOTEL DEL CORONADO

Glorietta Bay Park

NAVAL AMPHIBIOUS BASE, CORONADO

CORONADO BRIDGE

Coronado Cays

Grand Caribe Park

San Diego Bay

SILVER STRAND BLVD

NATIONAL CITY BLVD

National City

Chula Vista

To Imperial Beach and Mexico

INGRAHAM ST

MISSION BAY PARK

Mission Bay

MORENA BLVD

Mission Valley

OLD TOWN STATE HISTORIC PARK

LINDA VISTA RD

CABRILLO MEMORIAL DR

NIMITZ BLVD

ROSECRANS ST

HARBOR DR

SAN DIEGO INTERNATIONAL AIRPORT

Harbor Island

Island Park

USS MIDWAY

ORANGE AVE

HARBOR DR

BROADWAY

MARKET ST

1ST AVE
6TH AVE

163

FRIARS RD

ADAMS AVE

MADISON AVE

QUALCOMM STADIUM

MISSION SAN DIEGO DE ALCALA

SAN DIEGO STATE UNIVERSITY

SAN DIEGO ZOO

Balboa Park

FERN ST

28TH ST
30TH ST
32TH ST

NATIONAL AVE

LOGAN AVE

94

15

805

FAIRMONT AVE

EUCLID AVE

47TH ST

EUCLID AVE

54TH ST

IMPERIAL AVE

UNIVERSITY AVE

COLLEGE AVE

Lemon Grove

LEMON GROVE AVE

El Cajon BLVD

Lake Murray

To Alpine and Anza-Borrego State Park

La Mesa

PARADISE VALLEY RD

HILLTOP DR

BONITA RD

Sweetwater River

125

94

To Campo

Sweetwater Reservoir

0   2 km
0   2 mi

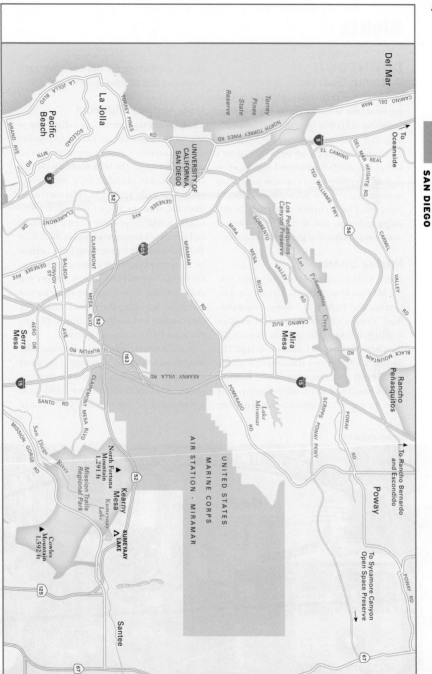

Sights

DOWNTOWN
Gaslamp Quarter

Shops, restaurants, and nightclubs pepper the **Gaslamp Quarter** (along 5th Ave. from Broadway to Harbor Dr.), an area historically attractive to sailors on shore leave. Though it's cleaned up quite a bit since then, there's still plenty of life on weekend nights, when dressed-up young adults carouse from place to place, cruising the sidewalks or riding in pedicabs. The daytime crowds stick to gift shops, galleries, and architectural tours of downtown's oldest and grandest structures.

Marina District

Boats, parks, restaurants, and shops line the **Marina District**'s (N. Harbor Dr. bet. Kettner and Park Blvd.) downtown waterfront. Visitors will find plenty to do, whether strolling, biking, or feasting on views of the San Diego skyline and Coronado Bridge. The **Seaport Village** and Headquarters gather restaurants and shopping, while **Marina Parks** north and south offer grassy respite from the nearby convention center. If nothing else, a stroll along the **harbor bike path** yields excellent viewing opportunities.

USS *Midway* Museum

The museum tag almost does a disservice to this 64-ton historical artifact—a true-to-life aircraft carrier. Commissioned at the end of World War II, the **USS *Midway*** (910 N. Harbor Dr., 619/544-9600, www.midway.org, 10am-5pm daily, adults $20, children $10, seniors $17, students $15, retired military $10) was the world's largest ship when it was built, and served as a temporary home to more than 200,000 sailors before retiring to its current location after nearly half a century in service. Each year, one million visitors explore the close confines experienced by those service members, inspecting their bunks, examining the bulwarks, and comparing them to the relative luxury of the captain's quarters.

Audio tours included with admission offer insights into the inner workings of the sonar and engine rooms. When it gets too claustrophobic, head up to the massive flight deck, where many of the museum's 29 vintage

Gaslamp Quarter

Two Days in San Diego

Base yourself in Little Italy, so that you can be within walking distance of its fantastic restaurant scene and a quick stroll from waterfront attractions like the **Maritime Museum of San Diego** and **USS *Midway* Museum.** Spend the first day at the **San Diego Zoo,** then go next door to **Balboa Park** to enjoy an afternoon of museum-hopping at the San Diego Museum of Art, the San Diego Museum of Man, and the San Diego Air and Space Museum. That evening, drive over the Coronado Bridge to wander the impressive **Hotel del Coronado.**

Spend the next day at the beach. Head north to **Mission Beach** to enjoy some prime people-watching on the Pacific Beach Boardwalk or ride over to **Ocean Beach** for a walk along the lengthy Ocean Beach Pier, a great vantage point for watching surfers. On your way back to downtown, stop at **Old Town State Historic Park** to explore the adobe buildings and browse the many gift shops.

military aircraft have been restored to original condition. To gain an even more dynamic understanding of just how vital a role behemoths like this play in our nation's military defenses, check out one of the ship's flight simulators, where you can experience the vertigo of aerial combat, and discover just how much skill it takes to land planes on an ocean vessel.

Maritime Museum of San Diego

Cruising down Harbor Drive, it's tough to miss the *Star of India,* canvas unfurled from its 127-foot top mast. After all, how many 19th-century merchant sailing vessels do you see on a daily basis? The striking ship is the oldest active clipper of its type, and just one of many boats that make up the **Maritime Museum** (1492 N. Harbor Dr., 619/234-9153, www.sdmaritime.org, 9am-8pm daily, adults $16, ages 3-12 $8, ages 13-17 $13, seniors $13, military $13). Beside it is the HMS *Surprise,* a replica 17th-century British frigate best known for its role in the film *Master and Commander.* Nearby is the *Berkeley,* a steamboat that once served as a ferry in early-20th-century San Francisco. Museum guests board each ship to explore the deck and cabins and stand where the captain once stood.

Perhaps none of these vessels is more intriguing than the pair of Cold War-era submarines. The USS *Dolphin* holds the distinction of diving deeper than any other operational sub, and its compact decks and sailors' quarters aren't for the claustrophobic. More confining still is the B-39 Soviet sub, which cannot be traversed end-to-end walking upright. History is alive within these boats, providing one of San Diego's most memorable museum experiences.

TOP EXPERIENCE

BALBOA PARK
★ San Diego Zoo

With more than 600 species covering 100 acres smack in the middle of Balboa Park, it takes some time to fully explore the "World Famous" **San Diego Zoo** (2920 Zoo Dr., 619/231-1515, www.sandiegozoo.org, 9am-9pm daily July-Aug.; 9am-6pm daily Mar., May-June, and Sept.-Oct.; 9am-7pm daily Apr.; 9am-5pm daily Jan-Feb. and Nov.-early Dec.; 9am-8pm Dec. holidays, $46 adults, $36 ages 3-11, free parking). Popular beasts include some playful polar bears, gorgeous tigers, charming elephants, majestic lions, and no shortage of monkeys, chimps, and gorillas. But the zoo's pride and joy is its family of pandas. Technically on loan from China, the pandas have been actively breeding, and park visitors line up for the chance to see panda cubs doing their adorable thing.

Most of the zoo grounds are built into canyons, which means lots of walking—often up and down hills—which can be especially tiring on sunny days. Fortunately, the zoo operates an aerial tram that offers gondola rides from the lower zoo level to its top, as well as bus tours with a quick overview of the park. Mornings are the best time to visit by far, offering easier parking, cooler weather, and livelier animals, though late hours in summer offer a chance to see the zoo at night. During the winter holidays, special decorative lighting makes evening visits a real treat.

El Prado

Balboa Park houses a number of museums, theaters, and gardens, but the central promenade known as **El Prado** (El Prado between Cabrillo Bridge and Park Ave.) serves as a sight in itself. Locals regularly stroll the 0.5-mile-long Prado just for the pleasure of wandering its fountains, plazas, and ponds, and appreciating the Spanish Revival architecture throughout the park. Others hop on and off a circling tram that shuttles between parking lots and popular attractions. During the park's December Nights events (usually the first weekend in December), thousands arrive to enjoy the park's decorative holiday light show.

Museums and Gardens

There's more to see and do at Balboa Park than can comfortably be accomplished in one day. If you're only going to make one pass through the treasured cultural center of San Diego, here are the best museums and gardens.

The flora inside the **Botanical Building** (1549 El Prado, 619/239-0512, www.balboapark.org, 10am-4pm Fri.-Wed., free) is as lovely as the building itself. Fronted by a reflecting pool populated by ducks and lily pads, the building hosts a tropical oasis of more than 2,000 flowers and fronds, including orchids, ferns, and palms. Tucked between El Prado and the Spreckels Organ Pavilion, the **Japanese Friendship Garden** (2215 Pan American Rd., 619/232-2721, www.niwa.org, 10am-4:30pm daily, adults $6, under age 7 free) features bonsai trees, a koi pond, and

resident panda at the San Diego Zoo

a small exhibition house with culturally relevant artwork.

The **San Diego Museum of Art** (1450 El Prado, 619/232-7931, www.sdmart.org, 10am-5pm Mon.-Tues. and Thurs.-Sat., noon-5pm Sun., adults $12, ages 7-17 $4.50, under age 7 free) doesn't have the most outstanding collection of paintings, but it's always reliable for enchanting visual moments, and the visiting exhibitions tend to be quite good. The **San Diego Museum of Man** (1350 El Prado, 619/239-2001, www.museumofman.org, 10am-5pm Sun.-Wed., 10am-7:30pm Thurs.-Sat., adults $12.50, ages 3-12 $6, under age 3 free) can be thought of as a museum of anthropology, and you may learn a lot about our biological and cultural origins.

A stealth bomber is on display in front of the **San Diego Air and Space Museum** (2001 Pan American Plaza, 619/234-8291, www.sandiegoairandspace.org, 10am-5pm daily, adults $18, ages 3-11 $9, under age 3 free), and inside there is much more. Everybody's going to have fun here. Blow

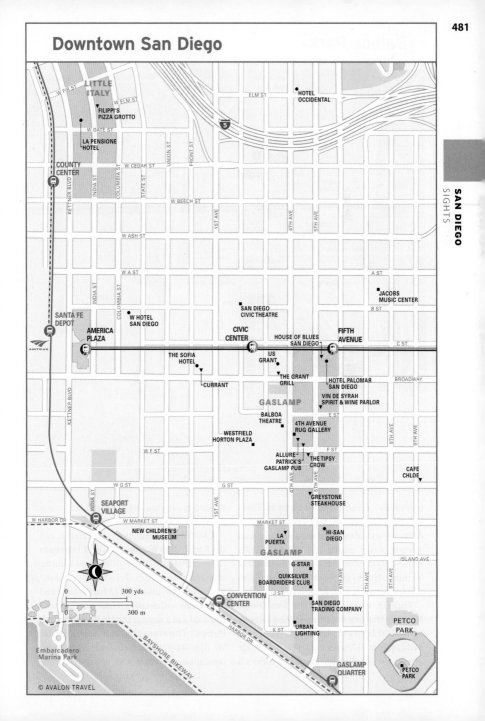

Downtown San Diego

LITTLE ITALY

W FIRST ST
W ELM ST
ELM ST
HOTEL OCCIDENTAL

FILIPPI'S PIZZA GROTTO

W DATE ST

LA PENSIONE HOTEL

W CEDAR ST

COUNTY CENTER

W BEECH ST

W ASH ST

W A ST

JACOBS MUSIC CENTER

A ST

B ST

SAN DIEGO CIVIC THEATRE

SANTA FE DEPOT

W HOTEL SAN DIEGO

AMERICA PLAZA

CIVIC CENTER

HOUSE OF BLUES SAN DIEGO

FIFTH AVENUE

C ST

AMTRAK

THE SOFIA HOTEL

US GRANT

THE GRANT GRILL

HOTEL PALOMAR SAN DIEGO

BROADWAY

CURRANT

VIN DE SYRAH SPIRIT & WINE PARLOR

GASLAMP

E ST

BALBOA THEATRE

4TH AVENUE RUG GALLERY

WESTFIELD HORTON PLAZA

F ST

ALLURE PATRICK'S GASLAMP PUB

THE TIPSY CROW

CAFE CHLOE

W F ST

SEAPORT VILLAGE

W G ST
G ST

GREYSTONE STEAKHOUSE

W HARBOR DR

NEW CHILDREN'S MUSEUM

W MARKET ST
MARKET ST

LA PUERTA

HI-SAN DIEGO

ISLAND AVE

GASLAMP

G-STAR

QUIKSILVER BOARDRIDERS CLUB

J ST

0   300 yds

CONVENTION CENTER

SAN DIEGO TRADING COMPANY

PETCO PARK

0   300 m

K ST

URBAN LIGHTING

HARBOR DR

Embarcadero Marina Park

BAYSHORE BIKEWAY

GASLAMP QUARTER

PETCO PARK

© AVALON TRAVEL

INDIA ST
COLUMBIA ST
STATE ST
UNION ST
FRONT ST
1ST AVE
4TH AVE
5TH AVE
8TH AVE
9TH AVE
6TH AVE
7TH AVE
8TH AVE
KETTNER BLVD

Balboa Park

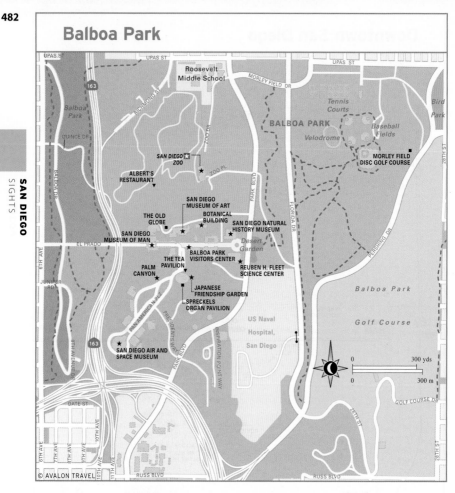

everybody's mind at the **Reuben H. Fleet Science Center** (1875 El Prado, 619/234-8291, www.sandiegoairandspace.org, 10am-4:30pm daily, adults $18, ages 3-11 $9, active-duty military free), where hundreds of learning stations trick you with optical illusions or turn common sense on its ear.

Frankly, some parts of the **San Diego Natural History Museum** (1788 El Prado, 619/232-3821, www.sdnhm.org, 10am-5pm daily, adults $17, ages 3-17 $11, under age 3 free) are kind of ho-hum, but there's a

mastodon skeleton, a 3-D theater, and some pretty engaging temporary exhibits.

Children love miniatures and trains, and the **San Diego Model Railroad Museum** (1649 El Prado, 619/696-0199, www.sdmrm.org, 11am-4pm Tues.-Fri., 11am-5pm Sat.-Sun., adults $8, under age 13 free) is huge and remarkably well detailed. Those with kids also could take in a show at the **Marie Hitchcock Puppet Theater** (2130 Pan American Rd. W., 619/544-9203, www.balboaparkpuppets.com, adults $5, children $5, under age 2 free).

OLD TOWN

★ Old Town State Historic Park

The name San Diego once referred to this small strip of land tucked under a hill next to where the I-5 and I-8 freeways now meet. Most of its residents left more than a century ago, though many of the original buildings remain. The city's oldest standing structures are now historic landmarks preserved within Old Town State Historic Park (4002 Wallace St., 858/220-5422, www.oldtownsandiegoguide. com, 10am-5pm daily, free). A visit here gives a sense of what the original settlement must have been like, a combination of Spanish colony and the American Old West.

Built between the 1820s and the 1850s, most buildings are old family residences, including the homes of Spanish soldiers who came here to fortify the presidio just up the hill. The restored adobe buildings are furnished to their period, each telling a story about daily life here in the early 19th century. Dining tables in the Commercial Kitchen are set with old-fashioned plates and utensils, as if dinner were about to be served.

Strolling around the park, you can bear witness to how the city matured. Later generations of wood and eventually brick buildings reflect the influx of American settlers from the East Coast. The Mason Street Schoolhouse depicts a reconstructed 19th-century classroom complete with desks and chalkboards. The San Diego Union Building features the typesetting tables and a printing press of the city's first newspaper. The Colorado House, site of the Wells Fargo Museum, invites guests inside an old bank vault.

Just off the southeast corner of the park lies Heritage Park Victorian Village (2454 Heritage Park Row, 858/565-3600, www.co.san-diego.ca.us, 9am-5pm daily, free), where seven gorgeous, brightly colored Victorian structures from around the city have been relocated to preserve their historic architecture. These include the Temple Beth Israel, San Diego's first synagogue, which also served as the birthplace of numerous other local congregations of varied faiths.

Many of the old structures in Old Town now house shops and restaurants, turning the park into a mall of sorts. The overall experience retains its historical character, though, with Mexican food and crafts commemorating the decades that San Diego belonged to what was then a Spanish colony. A visit here

Old Town State Historic Park

is a must for anyone keen on gaining a sense of local history.

Junípero Serra Museum

Spain established its first permanent presence in San Diego on Presidio Hill in 1769. The **Junípero Serra Museum** (2727 Presidio Dr., 619/220-5422, www.sandiegohistory.org, 10am-5pm Fri.-Sun., adults $6, ages 6-17 $3, under age 6 free) sits perched on its crest and tells the stories of the settlers who came here, as well as the indigenous Kumeyaay people who lived in communities scattered throughout the region. Named for the Catholic priest who founded the original mission, the Spanish revival building was not part of the original settlement, which fell into ruin more than a century ago. However, it does house relics of the mission, including an 18th-century olive press, and one of the cannons that guarded the walls of the presidio built to protect it.

POINT LOMA
Ocean Beach

Ocean Beach (4800-5000 block of Newport Ave., between Abbott St. and Cliffs Blvd., Ocean Beach, www.oceanbeachsandiego.com) may be called a lot of strange things (and most are true), but the name that sticks

is "OB." Backpackers, teenagers, bikers, surfers, service members, yoga adepts—all types congregate on this stretch of coastal un-real estate, which began its days amid the carnival atmosphere of a beachfront amusement park built in the early 1900s. The park closed 100 years ago, but the vibe remains. Visitors will find ocean-themed souvenirs, bead shops, swimwear boutiques, and plenty of countercultural businesses kept alive by wave after wave of the wild diversity this little beach community with a quirky reputation tends to attract.

The concrete **Ocean Beach Pier** offers a great view of surfers riding wave faces just a few feet below, and is perfect for a scenic stroll. Along the way you'll pass promenading families, the occasional romantic couple on a sunset walk, and a lot of recreational anglers trying their hand at a different kind of catch (usually herring). A café bravely does business in the middle of the pier, which isn't impervious to occasional waves in winter months.

★ Cabrillo National Monument

Named for Juan Rodríguez Cabrillo (the first European explorer to sail into San Diego Bay), **Cabrillo National Monument** (1800 Cabrillo Memorial Dr., Point Loma,

Cabrillo National Monument

Sunset Cliffs Natural Park

survive within the shallow pools of seawater left behind at low tide. Time your visit by consulting a daily tide schedule.

★ Sunset Cliffs Natural Park

Sunset Cliffs (700-1300 block of Sunset Cliffs Blvd., between Adair St. and Ladera St., and extending south of Ladera St., www.sunsetcliffs.info, free) delivers gorgeous, unobstructed Pacific views from the top of eroding sandstone cliffs. On the east side of Sunset Cliffs Boulevard are rows of beautiful homes built to appreciate the scenery. The west side is reserved for public access: a narrow strip of trail winds along the waxing and waning cliffs' edge, overlooking the rocky outcroppings below. More than a mile of walking offers plenty of opportunities to stop and watch the surfers who consider this long stretch of waves their greatest local resource.

At the southern end of the road, the park opens up to a wider embankment of short hiking trails and desert foliage, as well as a large parking lot. The lot fills up on spring and fall evenings, when partly cloudy days culminate in vibrant orange and electric pink sunsets, and onlookers flock to the cliffs hoping to spot the elusive green flash, rumored to appear the moment the sun finally touches below the horizon.

A word of caution: These sandstone cliffs are in a perpetual state of decay, and while many ledges are fenced off for safety, that's not to say the unfenced areas are safe. Lives have been lost and many injuries sustained by people trying to take photos near the cliffs' edge, or navigate the steep trails down to the water.

619/557-5450, www.nps.gov/cabr, 9am-5pm daily, $5) is only a small part of what draws people to the "most southwesterly spot in the contiguous United States." Comprising 144 acres at the tip of the narrow Point Loma Peninsula, the monument centers on a statue of Cabrillo that commands a breathtaking panorama with views of the Pacific Ocean.

At the peninsula's highest point stands the historic **Old Point Loma Lighthouse,** a preserved 19th-century structure that only ceased operation because low clouds and fog too often obscured its signal (it was retired in favor of a newer lighthouse down the hill).

A series of trails crisscross the monument, including the **Bayside Trail** (2.5 miles), a scenic trek overlooking the bay while traversing rare coastal sage scrub habitat on the peninsula's eastern side. It's just a short drive down the hill to the new lighthouse and the 0.5-mile **Coastal Tidepool Trail,** which winds past a series of protected tide pools. These play home to entire ecosystems of starfish, anemones, and other exotic sea life that has evolved to

CORONADO
★ Hotel del Coronado

It's rare that a hotel can be considered a sight in its own right, but then few carry the panache of **Hotel del Coronado** (1500 Orange Ave., 619/435-6611, www.hoteldel.com). Built in 1888, the all-wood Victorian construction of the original building can take your breath away, particularly the grandly furnished lobby and the iconic dome over its historic **Crown**

Room, which hosts a lavish Sunday brunch. Once the world's largest resort, the Del has been a popular destination among Hollywood VIPs for nearly a century. Movie buffs will remember it as the location of Billy Wilder's comedy classic *Some Like It Hot.* Much of the luxury resort is open to the public: sip a drink at the outdoor **Sunset Bar** or enjoy a beachside outdoor ice-skating rink set up between Thanksgiving and New Year's. Of course, the main attraction remains the same after all these years: one of the nation's finest beaches. Rent a cabana for the day and enjoy cocktail service on the sand as you watch sailboats, navy ships, and the occasional breaching whale enhance the panoramic Pacific view.

MISSION BAY AND BEACHES
★ Mission Bay Park

While surfing reigns up and down the coast, Mission Bay is the undeniable epicenter of all other action water sports—from Jet Skis and wakeboard-toting powerboats to sailboats, kite-surfers, and kayaks. This artificial bay is really a network of parks and peninsulas that split the 4,200-acre **Mission Bay Park** (2688 E. Mission Bay Dr., 619/525-8213, www.sandiego.gov, 4am-midnight daily) into a couple

of bays, six or seven small coves, and at least one "basin." For every small waterway filled with rowdy pontoons speeding along, there is a tranquil cove for stand-up paddleboarding or a romantic cruise in a paddleboat. If you prefer to stay on dry land, there are plenty of beaches, picnic areas, and playgrounds, and a scenic bike path that circles the entire bay.

Belmont Park

For 90 years there has been an amusement park on Mission Beach. While the amusements may change, there are still plenty of bells and whistles attempting to lure visitors from the gorgeous beach out front. One of **Belmont Park**'s (3146 Mission Blvd., 858/228-9283, www.belmontpark.com, 11am-9pm Mon.-Thurs., 11am-10pm Fri., 11am-midnight Sat., 11am-11pm Sun., free) biggest attractions is the **Wave House,** an outdoor beachfront restaurant and lounge built around a pair of wave machines. The standing waves are always up at the push of a button; would-be surfers can try it on the beginner-friendly **FlowRider.** The bigger and faster **FlowBarrel** rides are reserved for seasoned pros who stage acrobatic surfing shows on the hour. Belmont Park also features a small roller coaster, bumper cars,

Hotel del Coronado

laser maze, arcade, and carousel. Parking and admission are free, prices for rides and other amusements vary.

SeaWorld

Combine the most popular parts of a zoo, aquarium, and circus and you'll get something a lot like **SeaWorld** (500 Sea World Dr., 800/257-4268, www.seaworldparks.com, 10am-6pm daily, peak summer and winter holidays: 10am-9pm daily, adults $84, ages 3-9 $78). The aquatic mammal theme park features thousands of sea creatures in observable habitats as well as trained performances, none more famous than the orcas. (By 2017, SeaWorld plans to shift from trained killer whale performances to shows focused on simply observing the sea mammals at play.) Plenty of other attractions may be found in the park, including dancing dolphins and a couple of hilarious vaudevillian sea lions.

LA JOLLA
Sunny Jim Cave

One of seven **La Jolla** smugglers caves, Sunny Jim allegedly received its name from L. Frank Baum, author of *The Wizard of Oz*. Apparently the shape of the cave mouth reminded Baum of the original cartoon serial cereal box mascot, Sunny Jim, who first appeared on a box of Force Wheat Flakes in 1903.

There are two ways to see **Sunny Jim Cave** (1100 Coast Blvd., 858/459-0746, www.cavestore.com, 10am-5:30pm daily, adults $5, under age 16 $3): from the ocean or through the Cave Store (which rents snorkeling gear and sells souvenirs). A steep, slippery set of stairs leads into the cave from above and through a tunnel carved by immigrant laborers to smuggle more immigrant laborers and, during Prohibition, booze. Daily kayak tours are also available.

La Jolla Cove

It's a wonder how so many folks flock onto this little stretch of sand just a few steps from La Jolla Village. **La Jolla Cove** (1100 Coast Blvd.) teems with underwater life, making it a popular spot for scuba divers and snorkelers, often seen floating just a few dozen yards off shore. Sea lions lounge on the large rocks sitting on either side of the beach, lolling on top of each other, barking, and catching some sun. Most of the year, waves are small or nonexistent, making for a fun swimmers' beach and snorkeling access. But in the winter, uncommonly large swells may kick up a wave known as the Sleeping Giant,

La Jolla Cove

La Jolla

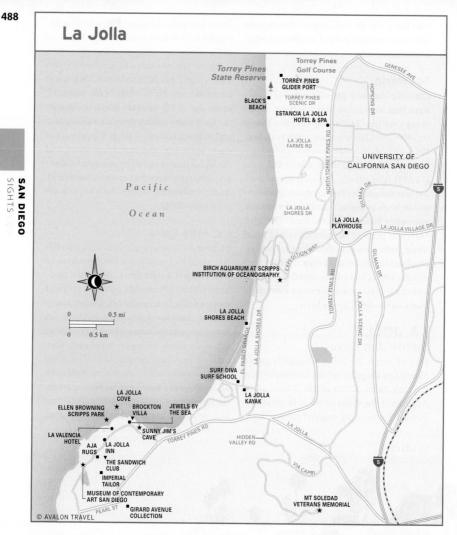

Torrey Pines
Golf Course

GENESEE AVE

Torrey Pines
State Reserve

**TORREY PINES
GLIDER PORT**

HOPKINS DR

TORREY PINES
SCENIC DR

**BLACK'S
BEACH**

**ESTANCIA LA JOLLA
HOTEL & SPA**

LA JOLLA
FARMS RD

NORTH TORREY PINES RD

UNIVERSITY OF
CALIFORNIA SAN DIEGO

GILMAN DR

5

Pacific

Ocean

LA JOLLA
SHORES DR

**LA JOLLA
PLAYHOUSE**

LA JOLLA VILLAGE DR

EXPEDITION WAY

GILMAN DR

**BIRCH AQUARIUM AT SCRIPPS
INSTITUTION OF OCEANOGRAPHY** ★

TORREY PINES RD

LA JOLLA SCENIC DR

0   0.5 mi

0   0.5 km

**LA JOLLA
SHORES BEACH**

LA JOLLA SHORES DR

**SURF DIVA
SURF SCHOOL**

**LA JOLLA
COVE** ★

**LA JOLLA
KAYAK**

**ELLEN BROWNING
SCRIPPS PARK**

**BROCKTON
VILLA**

**JEWELS BY
THE SEA**

EL PASEO GRANDE

LA JOLLA

**LA VALENCIA
HOTEL**

**SUNNY JIM'S
CAVE**

TORREY PINES RD

HIDDEN
VALLEY RD

**AJA
RUGS**

**LA JOLLA
INN**

**THE SANDWICH
CLUB**

VIA CAPRI

**IMPERIAL
TAILOR**

**MUSEUM OF CONTEMPORARY
ART SAN DIEGO**

**MT SOLEDAD
VETERANS MEMORIAL**
★

PEARL ST

**GIRARD AVENUE
COLLECTION**

© AVALON TRAVEL

5

and local big-wave surfers flock to the cove to give onlookers an exhilarating show.

Birch Aquarium

The **Birch Aquarium** (2300 Expedition Way, 858/534-3474, www.aquarium.ucsd.edu, 9am-5pm daily, adults $17, ages 13-17 $14, ages 3-12 $12.50) is overseen by the Scripps Institution of Oceanography and includes plenty of interesting exhibits devoted to local aquatic life—reef ecosystems, kelp forests, lagoons, and

underwater canyons. A great deck features touchable tide pools and boasts a fantastic view of La Jolla below. Jellyfish, anemones, and leopard sharks are always fascinating, but it's tough to imagine another creature as marvelous as the leafy sea dragon.

Museum of Contemporary Art San Diego

The **Museum of Contemporary Art San Diego** (700 Prospect St., 858/454-3541, www.

mcasd.org, 11am-5pm Thurs.-Tues., adults $10, seniors $5, 25 and under free, military families free) rotates several installations and borrowed collections at any given time, from classic paintings to modern conceptual pieces set next to picture windows overlooking a rocky little cove. Though small by museum standards, the rotating exhibits keep the place feeling vital during each visit.

Children's Pool Beach

It may sound like a place for children to swim, but not these days. In 1931 Ellen Brown Scripps commissioned construction of a seawall to create a wave barrier along the beach so that small children could play safely at the water's edge. Over time, the local seal population decided to start bringing their pups here, to the point that bacteria levels in the water became too high for humans. Today, a rope barrier keeps people off **Children's Pool Beach** (850 Coast Blvd.) and the seawall serves as a vantage point to watch the seals belly along and roll around in the sand.

Mount Soledad Veterans Memorial

A 29-foot cross stands atop **Mount Soledad** (6905 La Jolla Scenic Dr. S., 858/459-2314, www.soledadmemorial.com), La Jolla's highest point, which boasts a panoramic view that surveys the entire county on a clear day. It's currently the centerpiece of a Korean War memorial enumerating the names of thousands of veterans who served their country during that conflict. However, ownership of the cross has changed hands several times over the years as legal battles were waged to have it removed from government land. At the moment it remains, and the memorial isn't going anywhere. Bring something to eat, picnic in the grass, and enjoy the beauty of greater San Diego.

NORTH COUNTY

San Diego Zoo Safari Park

Though related to the zoo at Balboa Park,

San Diego Zoo Safari Park (15500 San Pasqual Valley Rd., 760/747-8702, www.sdzsafaripark.org, 9am-7pm daily, hours vary seasonally, adults $46, ages 3-12 $36) does things differently. Here the animals have a lot more space to roam, with the landscape made to more closely resemble the natural habitat of a number of African species, including lions and elephants. Options to see these creatures include riding around in a jeep and getting a close-up look at some pretty majestic animals.

Mission San Luis Rey de Francia

Oceanside's top attraction is the **Mission San Luis Rey de Francia** (4050 Mission Ave., Oceanside, 760/757-3651, www.sanluisrey.org, 9:30am-5pm Mon.-Thurs., 10am-5pm Sat.-Sun., adults $5, seniors and ages 6-18 $4, military free), the 18th of California's 21 Franciscan missions. Founded in 1798 by Fermín Lasuén, it's known as the "King of the Missions."

San Diego Botanic Garden

Don't miss the chance to wander amid the unique and expansive **San Diego Botanic Garden** (230 Quail Gardens Dr., Encinitas, 760/436-3036, www.sdbgarden.org, 9am-5pm daily, adults $14, seniors, students, and military $10, ages 3-12 $8). A stroll through the gardens almost feels like a geography lesson. Plants and flowers range from desert cacti to tropical rain forest plants, plus the nation's largest collection of bamboo.

Carlsbad's Flower Fields

Carlsbad's Flower Fields (5704 Paseo Del Norte, 760/431-0352, www.theflowerfields.com, 9am-6pm daily Mar. 1-May 10, adults $12, seniors $11, ages 3-10 $6) are endlessly beautiful during the spring bloom, with more than 50 acres devoted to the Giant Ranunculus. Check the venue's online calendar to time your visit.

Best Craft Beer Spots

San Diego is crazy for beer and has dozens of small breweries. Beer drinkers come from all over to taste their wares.

- **AleSmith:** In Miramar, next to the Marine Corps Air Station, AleSmith may have the greatest international reputation. The brewery shows off its stellar lineup of flagship beers and some rarely seen special issues.

- **Green Flash:** The brewery doubles as one of the better tasting rooms in town, turning an industrial park drinking patio in Mira Mesa into a hoppy party, sometimes serving the rare beers of brew-buddy Alpine Beer Company.

- **Lost Abbey:** Lost Abbey is a California outpost of brewing that's been handed down by Belgian monks for centuries. As far as West Coast beers go, they've nailed it, with excellent craft beers in an unlikely location—a San Marcos business park.

- **Modern Times:** The latest San Diego beer company to capture the world's imagination, Modern Times tasting rooms boast unique artwork and decor to go along with beers ranging from experimental to flat out delicious.

- **Societe:** Societe is taking the region by storm, with a deep roster of ales ranging from hoppy West Coasters to British and Belgian styles. Located in Kearny Mesa, it's not easy to find, but the beer is worth it.

- **Stone World Bistro & Gardens:** Located in Escondido, this gorgeous brewery sports indoor and outdoor bars, a restaurant, a desert garden, and an illuminating brewery tour. Many Stone beers are served here, as are some of the brewery's favorite craft beers.

- **Stone World Bistro & Gardens Liberty Station:** This location may not have the cachet of its Escondido sibling, but it has plenty of space to serve up a huge variety of beers.

Entertainment and Events

San Diego's Gaslamp is the epicenter for rowdy nightlife in Downtown. Most weeknights—and especially weekends—the bars, clubs, and restaurants bring out large crowds from all over the city. Avoiding Downtown may be the impetus for the growth of North Park's nightlife. The Uptown neighborhood has flourished as a destination for creative and design-savvy types, and it's a hub for craft beer aficionados. Nearby Hillcrest caters to the LGBT community, with gleeful dance clubs and pickup scenes. But when the sun goes down, there's nothing like the beach communities of Ocean Beach's Newport Avenue and Pacific Beach's Garnet Avenue.

NIGHTLIFE
Bars and Clubs

Lounge Six (Solamar Hotel, 616 J St., East Village, 619/531-8744, www.hotelsolamar. com, 11:30am-2:30pm and 3:30pm-11pm Mon.-Thurs., 11:30am-2:30pm and 3:30pm-midnight Fri.-Sat.) entices with an outdoor bar, poolside cocktails, cabanas, and plenty of lounge chairs from which to lord over East Village from above. Umbrellas shade the daylight, while heat lamps warm up the night, providing everything you need to stay comfortably warm while looking cool.

Tipsy Crow (770 5th Ave., Gaslamp, 619/338-9300, www.thetipsycrow.com, 3pm-2am Mon.-Fri., noon-2am Sat.-Sun.) knows it

Side Trip to Julian

An adventurous day trip takes you to this little mountain town east of San Diego that started as a mining town and today is known for its apple pies.

SIGHTS

Eagle Mining Company (2320 C St., 760/765-0036, www.theeaglemining.com, 10am-4pm Mon.-Fri., 10am-5pm Sat.-Sun., adults $5-10) offers a glimpse into Julian's gold rush past with tours into the mile-deep mine, while the history of Julian is on display at the **Julian Pioneer Museum** (2811 Washington St., 760/765-0227, www.julianpioneermuseum.org, 10am-4pm daily, adults $3). Dating to the 1870s, **Julian Pioneer Cemetery** (Farmer Rd. at A St., 760/765-1857, www.juliancemetery.org) is the final resting place of some of those Julian natives.

Julian apple pies and ciders are standout regional treats, and apple picking is a popular late-summer activity. The **Julian Apple Days Festival** (www.julianmerchants.org, early Oct.) celebrates the annual harvest that has kept Julian a happy little mountain town for nearly 150 years.

FOOD

The **Julian Café & Bakery** (2112 Main St., 760/765-2712, www.juliancafe.com, 8am-7:30pm Mon.-Thurs., 8am-8:30pm Fri., 7am-9pm Sat., 7am-8:30pm Sun., $10-15) captures that old-time spirit, with an extensive breakfast menu and apple pies. Just up the street, the **Miner's Diner** (2134 Main St., 760/765-3753, www.minersdinerjulian.com, 10:30am-6pm Mon.-Fri., 8am-6pm Sat., 8am-5pm Sun., $8-15) has more of a 1950s look and feel, with burgers and malts.

For a slice of famous Julian pie, try **Julian Pie Company** (2225 Main St., 760/765-2449, www.julianpie.com, 9am-5pm daily, $8-12) or **Mom's Pies** (2119 Main St., 760/765-2472, www.momspiesjulian.com, 8am-5pm daily, $35 for whole pie). Wash it down with delicious cider from **Julian Cider Mill** (2103 Main St., 760/765-1430, www.juliancidermillinc.com, 9:30am-5pm Mon.-Thurs., 9:30am-5:30pm Fri.-Sun.) or **Julian Hard Cider Co.** (4470 Julian Rd., 760/765-2500, www.julianhardcider.biz, 11am-5pm daily).

Bailey Barbecue (2307 Main St., 760/765-3757, 11:30am-8:30pm daily, $11-25) serves tasty barbecue and doubles as the home of the Julian Beer Company. More Julian craft beer is at **Nickel Beer Co.** (1485 Hollow Glen Rd., 760/765-2337, www.nickelbeerco.com, 3pm-7pm Mon., 2pm-6pm Thurs., 11:30am-6pm Fri., 11:30am-7pm Sat., 11:30am-5pm Sun.).

ACCOMMODATIONS

Julian Gold Rush Hotel (2032 Main St., 760/765-0201, www.julianhotel.com, $150-250) is the "oldest continuously operated hotel in Southern California," though it has been upgraded since 1897. The more modern **Julian Lodge** (2720 C St., 760/765-1420, www.julianlodge.com, $150-250) is just off Main Street. The lodge rooms and cottages at deluxe **Orchard Hill Country Inn** (2502 Washington St., 760/765-1700, www.orchardhill.com, from $250) are country hospitable, right down to the patchwork quilts.

GETTING THERE

Julian is located 60 miles northeast of San Diego, about a 1.5-hour drive. From San Diego, take I-8 east for about 25 miles, then head north on Highway 79 for 25 miles to Julian.

can't please all of the people all of the time, but with three levels and a wide variety of entertainment, it casts an incredibly wide net. The space combines comedy nights, live music, dancing, and chilled lounge vibes, sometimes all on the same night. Expect a mix of people from different walks of life occasionally bonding over drinks at one of the bars.

Float (Hard Rock Hotel, 207 5th Ave., Gaslamp, 619/764-6924, www.hardrockhotelsd.com, 11am-2pm daily) finds any excuse to become a sexy open-air nightclub. During the day, lounge seating and poolside drinks set against the San Diego skyline couldn't feel cooler. Weekend nights and Sunday afternoons in the summer, world-famous DJs turn the club inside out, with beautiful young people dancing four stories above the hustling Gaslamp scene. Look your best to get in; some days it can be difficult.

High-concept decor, incredible-sounding bands and DJs, bottle service, and go-go dancers are what you can look forward to after standing in line at **Fluxx** (207 5th Ave., Gaslamp, 619/764-6924, www.hardrockhotelsd.com, 11am-2am daily). And most likely a lot of moneyed, beautiful people dressed like they know it.

Cheap beer, Jack Daniels, and line dancing: If that's what you look for in a night out, **Moonshine Flats** (344 7th Ave., East Village, 619/255-7625, www.moonshineflats.com, 6pm-1:30am Thurs., 8pm-2am Fri.-Sat.) has it. Jeans are acceptable, but are much better paired with a cowboy hat and a pair of boots. Music takes on a country tone; sometimes the place feels like a large barn with a disco ball.

This close to the border, you'd better believe there's a top-flight Latin music club, and *caliente* doesn't begin to describe it. By the time the late-night line has formed in front of **Sevilla Nightclub** (353 5th Ave., Downtown, 619/807-4481, www.sevillanightclub.com, 8pm-2am Mon.-Thurs., 9:30pm-2am Fri., 10pm-2am Sat., 9:30pm-2am Sun.), you'll wish you had reserved a spot on the guest list.

If given the choice between a well-stocked bar and a well-stocked bar with vintage arcade games, which would you choose? For games, there's only one choice—North Park's **Coin-Op** (3926 30th St., North Park, 619/255-8523, www.coinopsd.com, 4pm-1am Mon.-Fri., 11:30pm-1am Sat.-Sun.). Along with the nostalgic stand-up video game kiosks and pinball machines, there's a legit tap list and cocktails to spare.

Somewhere between hunting lodge and jazz club, the main attraction at **Seven Grand** (3054 University Ave., North Park,

619/269-8820, www.sevengrandbars.com, 5pm-2am Mon.-Sat., 8pm-2am Sun.) is whiskey—bourbon, scotch, rye, and Irish. With hunting trophies on walls of plaid wallpaper, the idea that there's a jazz stage in the back seems incongruous, but crowds keep coming back for both the music and the booze. A deep menu features single malts and single casks along with blends, oak barrel-aged, and reserves. Order a favorite right away, because you're going to be reading that menu for a while before deciding on your second.

The beautifully verdant "living wall" decor of **The Patio on Goldfinch** (4020 Goldfinch St., Mission Hills, 619/501-5090, www.thepatioongoldfinch.com, 8am-midnight daily) attracts diners all day long, but anyone who skips the tequila selection is missing out. Alternate between sips of tequila and the fruity, spicy, house *sangrita* and you'll never want to drink it any other way. The open patio restaurant also offers a lengthy list of barrel-aged cocktails worth delving into.

The upstairs bar of **Eddie V's** (1270 Prospect St., 858/459-5500, www.eddiev.com, 4pm-11pm Sun.-Thurs., 4pm-midnight Fri.-Sat.) offers one of the most scenic drinking venues in town. While nightly jazz performances play, sip drinks overlooking the La Jolla Caves with a view of the shores beyond.

Breweries and Taprooms

Bottlecraft (2252 India St., Little Italy, 619/487-9493, www.bottlecraftbeer.com, noon-10pm Mon.-Thur., noon-midnight Fri.-Sat., 11am-10pm Sun.) serves as both a beer-centric bottle shop and 24-tap tasting room. For the ideal shopping experience, order a glass at the bar and sip while you browse a great variety of San Diego's—and the world's—best bottles and cans.

Billed as a "San Diego brewery tour under one roof," **The Brew Project** (3683 Fifth Ave., Hillcrest, 619/795-7890, www.thebrewproject.com, 11am-midnight Mon.-Thurs., 11am-2am Fri., 9am-2am Sat.-Sun.) serves local beer exclusively. That could mean beer from Alpine 30 miles east or Oceanside 35 miles north. The carefully curated selection allows an exploration of the best of San Diego's craft community, all from a single, comfortable indoor/outdoor location.

One of the newer craft breweries to gather a following over the past couple years, **Modern Times** (1521 30th St., North Park, 619/238-5460, www.moderntimesbeer.com, 3pm-2am Mon.-Fri., 1pm-2am Sat.-Sun.) operates a couple of smartly decorated tasting rooms, including this North Park space, highlighted by a mural of floppy discs and a ceiling made from old lampshades. Style and location win bonus points, but the tasty beer selection is still the best reason to visit.

Amplified Ale Works (4150 Mission Blvd. #208, Pacific Beach, 858/270-5222, www.amplifiedales.com, 11am-11pm Sun.-Wed., 11am-midnight Thurs.-Sat.) doesn't stand out from the street or the beach, but when you find it on the second floor of its PB strip mall, you'll be grateful you did. Drink the house beer, eat some döner, or simply grab some sun with an ocean view on the killer west-facing deck, which alone is reason enough to visit.

Stone World Bistro & Gardens Liberty Station (2816 Historic Decatur Rd., Suite 116, Point Loma, 619/269-2100, www.stone-libertystation.com, 11:30am-10pm Mon.-Sat., 11am-9pm Sun.) reigns as the biggest and most successful craft brewer in town. This 40,000-square-foot organic, farm-to-table restaurant offers 40 taps of Stone special releases, collaborations, and dozens of hand-picked guest beers. Relax on the massive outdoor patio and enjoy a bocce ball game with your beer.

To many, ★ **AleSmith Brewing Company** (9990 Empire St., Miramar, 858/549-9888, www.alesmith.com, noon-9pm Mon.-Fri., 11am-9pm Sat., 11am-6pm Sun.) isn't just the best brewery in San Diego—it ranks among the best on the planet. After nearly two decades, AleSmith moved into this giant facility with the county's largest tasting room—of interest to baseball fans as it houses a Tony Gwynn museum.

An indispensable stop on San Diego's craft beer tour, **Green Flash Brewing Company**'s (6550 Mira Mesa Blvd., Mira Mesa, 858/622-0085, www.greenflashbrew.com, 3pm-9pm Tues.-Thurs., 3pm-10pm Fri., noon-9pm Sat., noon-6pm Sun.) open warehouse space is nice, but its drinking patio is nicer. Though surrounded by industrial parks, the sunny patio is bolstered by the presence of daily food trucks and stellar Green Flash beer, as well as occasional kegs from nearby

Stone World Bistro & Gardens Liberty Station

Festivals and Events

Cinco de Mayo is celebrated in Mexico as a day of national pride, and the **Fiesta Old Town Cinco De Mayo** (Old Town, www.oldtownsandiegoguide.com, May) is the "largest of its kind" three-day festival. You'll find food, music, traditional attire, costumes, shopping, lowriders, and tequila.

From the second week of June through July 4, the **San Diego County Fair** (2260 Jimmy Durante Blvd., Del Mar, 858/755-1161, www.sdfair.com, June) offers food, music, rides, animals, car shows, and one or two beer festivals right beside the **Del Mar Racetrack and Fairgrounds**.

The **Shakespeare Festival** (Balboa Park, 619/234-5623, www.theoldglobe.org, June-Sept.) usually offers two or three productions in the outdoor venue of the Old Globe Theatre complex.

Year after year, **Comic Con** (111 W. Harbor Dr., www.comic-con.org, July) is the biggest event at the Downtown San Diego Convention Center. More than 125,000 people descend on San Diego to attend 600 staged events and 1,500 exhibitor booths. Take note when Comic Con takes place. It sells out far in advance, as do most of the hotels anywhere near Downtown at triple their normal rates.

San Diego's gay, lesbian, bisexual, and transgender community congregates around Hillcrest, its de facto hub, to stage the **San Diego LGBT Pride** (University Ave. from Normal St. to Upas St., 619/297-7683, https://sdpride.org, July, free) parade to Balboa Park and back. Weekend festivities include live music, rallies, and a massive block party.

San Diego's beloved Stone Brewing throws the **Stone Anniversary Celebration and International Beer Festival** (333 S. Twin Oaks Valley Rd., Escondido, www.stonebrewing.com, Aug., $45-85), a massive weekend-long birthday bash. Stone invites 60 or so of its favorite craft-brewing friends from around the country to participate. More than 100 beers are on hand and guests can opt to taste special releases from some of their favorite brewers or discover something new.

Labor Day weekend, San Diego Bay brings another era back to life with the **Festival of Sail** (1492 North Harbor Dr., www.sdmaritime.org, Sept.). A parade of beautiful vintage tall ships sails across the bay, firing cannon salutes and coming to dock.

Federal funds permitting, aviators put on a dazzling show during the **MCAS Miramar Air Show** (Marine Corps Air Station Miramar, Miramar Way, http://miramarairshow.com, Oct., free). The event is held over the airfield at the Marine Corps Air Station Miramar, which is home to some of the world's best jet pilots, including the headliners, the Blue Angels.

The second week of November is when **San Diego Beer Week** (locations vary, www.sdbw.org, Nov.) kicks off. Events are tailored around seasonal and special-release beers that could be the best new ale or stout in town.

Billing itself as the "largest free community festival in San Diego," the annual **Balboa Park December Nights** (Balboa Park, www.balboapark.org, Dec.) draws hundreds of thousands of people to Balboa Park for holiday lights, special performances, and free museum entry (5pm-9pm). The event is usually the first Friday and Saturday evenings of December.

colleagues. Alpine Beer Company Tours ($5) of the brewery are available daily.

Gay and Lesbian

From mimosas to margaritas to shots, **Baja Betty's** (1421 University Ave., Uptown, 619/269-8510, www.bajabettyssd.com, 11am-1am Mon.-Fri., 10am-1am Sat.-Sun.) has the drinks to match every time of day. This popular gathering spot's impeccable Mexican

decor and tequila cocktails make for raucous brunches and happy hours, with build-your-own nacho platters available until the kitchen closes at 11pm, just in case you drank through dinner.

The irreverent "home of the two-finger pour," the **Gossip Grill** (1220 University Ave., Uptown, 619/260-8023, www.thegossipgrill.com, Mon.-Fri. 11am-2am, Sat.-Sun. 10am-2am) is Hillcrest's women's bar boasting cocktail names among the most poetically bawdy in all of Southern California. It's a lounge and patio space where simply ordering a round of drinks sets the tone.

Billing itself as "the first gay brewery in the world," **Hillcrest Brewing Company** (1458 University Ave., Uptown, 619/269-4323, www.hillcrestbrewingcompany.com, 4pm-midnight Mon.-Fri., noon-midnight Sat., 9am-11pm Sun.) serves up suds with names like Banana Hammock scotch ale and an award-winning red ale called Crotch Rocket. Up to 15 guest beers from around San Diego round out the tap list.

Where in San Diego can you find a gender-bending Cher impersonator lip-synching in an outlandish outfit? At **Lips** (3036 El Cajon Blvd., Uptown, 619/295-7900, www.lipssd.com, 7pm-10pm Tues.-Thurs., 6pm-midnight Fri.-Sat., 11am-3pm and 7pm-10pm Sun.), the raunchy and playful drag shows cover any number of celebrity divas, and performers are far from shy about including audience members in their songs. It's a popular spot for bachelorette and birthday parties, with dinner shows most nights as well as a Sunday brunch.

Urban Mo's (308 University Ave., Hillcrest, 619/491-0400, www.urbanmos.com, 9am-1:30am daily) claims to be the "Best Gay Bar in San Diego," if not the world. The only way to find out for sure is to drop in on its burger-loving patio and find out. Chances are you're going to meet people in the process, drink another couple of rounds, and find yourself declaring something the best of somewhere before the night ends.

Live Music

San Diego's indie rock scene has a clear epicenter, and it's **The Casbah** (2501 Kettner Blvd., Little Italy, 619/232-4355, http://casbahmusic.com, 8:30pm-2am daily), which has brought the nation's best burgeoning talent to its intimate club stage for more than a quarter century. Some of the grayer rockers sipping drinks in the courtyard between sets might reminisce about before-they-were-big shows by Nirvana, No Doubt, or Arcade Fire.

Meanwhile, young local and touring bands still know the Little Italy venue to be a vital stop along the way to making it.

Recently remodeled, **Music Box** (1337 India St., Little Italy, 619/795-1337, www.musicboxsd.com, showtimes vary) boasts top-of-the-line sound, VIP balcony seating, and eclectic nightly bookings that range from bluegrass and jazz to local rock and punk. Drink prices are through the roof, but some great music can be expected.

People watch summer shows at **Humphrey's Concerts by the Bay** (2241 Shelter Island Dr., Shelter Island, 619/224-3577, www.humphreysconcerts.com, May-Oct.) from their boats—kayaks, paddleboats, or one of the yachts moored next door to this Shelter Island venue. It's one of the best places in town to catch a music or comedy show. Most simply buy a ticket for a folding seat inside the outdoor amphitheater or reserve one of the hotel rooms connected to the balcony overlooking the stage. These high-end accommodations offer some of the best seats in the house.

Comedy

Friday and Saturday nights offer an opportunity to see some of the top touring comics pass through the **Comedy Store** (916 Pearl St., La Jolla, 858/454-9176, www.lajolla.thecomedystore.com), with the occasional legend popping up. The rest of the week, watch some of the best local comedians fine-tune their craft on the big stage.

THE ARTS

San Diego's well-known image as a sun-drenched surfer's paradise may not merit comparison to major cultural offerings in other cities, but it may surprise you.

The theater scene is not only one of high quality, but it is also one of the most productive in the country, routinely assembling world-class productions and inspiring the curiosity and respect of out-of-towners and locals alike.

While endeavors in other artistic areas

might not have the same prestige, San Diego is a surprisingly intellectual town once the craft beer bottles and surfboards are put away. There are always a number of interesting things brewing under the surface—outdoor cinemas under the stars, the historical and cultural museums of Balboa Park, and an intense gallery scene in La Jolla. It's tough to balance sunshine, coastline, beer, and culture, yet somehow San Diego manages.

Theater

The historic **Balboa Theatre** (868 4th Ave., Gaslamp, 619/570-1100, www.sandiegotheatres.org) sat empty for decades before being faithfully restored and reborn as a state-of-the-art music and comedy venue. Its Southwestern appeal and Gaslamp location provides a great setting for some good shows.

The 3,000-seat **San Diego Civic Theatre** (1100 3rd Ave., Downtown, 619/570-1100, www.sandiegotheatres.org) might bring a Broadway touring company or stage a large production of the San Diego Ballet. If it's playing here, it's worth seeing.

For more than 100 years, the **Spreckels Theatre** (121 Broadway, Suite 600, Gaslamp, 619/235-9500, www.spreckels.net) has seen every manner of cultural performance, ranging from dance companies and rock bands to the Chinese Circus. The beautifully kept space offers terrific lines of sight and acoustics, with plenty of Gaslamp restaurants and bars nearby to make a night of it.

Gathered at the northwest end of El Prado, the **Conrad Prebys Theatre Center** (1363 Old Globe Way, Balboa Park, 619/234-5623, www.theoldglobe.org, ticket prices vary) actually comprises three different theater spaces. Most famous is the **Old Globe Theatre,** which is modeled on Shakespeare's Globe in London and features world-class theatrical talent. The 580-seat venue stages classics as well as new productions year-round. Then there's **Lowell Davies Festival Theatre** for outdoor events, including a summer Shakespeare festival, and the **Sheryl and Harvey White Theatre** in the round.

Spreckels Theatre

With a reputation as an incubator for Broadway productions, **La Jolla Playhouse** (2910 La Jolla Village Dr., La Jolla, 858/550-1010, www.lajollaplayhouse.org) stages original productions with a remarkable success rate. Recent years have seen the world premieres of *Jersey Boys* and *The Who's Tommy.* The group was cofounded by Gregory Peck and manages to stay vital whether producing unknown shows of emerging talents or bringing the very best to local audiences.

Cinema

Hillcrest Cinemas (3965 5th Ave., Hillcrest, 619/298-2904, www.landmarktheatres.com) hosts some of the year's best movies—just not major blockbusters. Indie comedies and intimate dramas are what fill this art deco-inspired Landmark theater, and great conversations can be overheard on the way out. Parking in this neighborhood is tough; validate your ticket for accessible parking in the basement of the building.

Classic movies and cult films are screened

at **Cinema under the Stars** (4040 Goldfinch St., Mission Hills, 619/295-4221, www.topspresents.com, 8pm Thurs.-Sun.), a comfortable outdoor venue that has a retractable roof in case those stars come with a chance of showers. Reserve your zero-gravity recliner or cabana seating online or at the box office after 6pm on show nights.

The **Arclight La Jolla** (4425 La Jolla Village Dr., La Jolla, 858/768-7770, www.arclightcinemas.com) hosts a couple of 3-D auditoriums and even one outfitted with a sophisticated Atmos surround-sound system. A café serves food and drinks in the lobby, where guests may relax until just before showtime (thanks to assigned seating). Select screenings for adults 21 and over permit bringing beer or wine into the theater.

Don't be fooled into thinking the simple three-screen **Village Theatres Coronado** (820 Orange Ave., Coronado, 619/437-6161, www.vintagecinemas.com) isn't state of the art. A recent remodel brought the 65-year-old venue up to spec, with 4K digital projection technology as well as 3-D and surround sound. Come for first-run blockbusters as well as the occasional indie flick.

Galleries

A Wile E. Coyote statue greets you at the entrance to the **Chuck Jones Gallery** (232 5th Ave., Gaslamp, 619/294-9880, www.chuckjones.com, 10am-7pm Mon.-Wed., 10am-8pm Thurs.-Sat., 11am-6pm Sun.), which celebrates *Looney Tunes* creator Chuck Jones as both an artist and inspiration. A Pepé Le Pew charcoal sketch may not be everyone's idea of fine art, but a number of interesting pieces exhibit Jones's fanciful vision, making for the rare art gallery an entire family can enjoy.

Though moved from its original oceanfront location, the **Madison Gallery** (1055 Wall St #100., Suite 130, La Jolla, 858/459-0836, www.madisongalleries.com, 10am-6pm Mon.-Sat., 10am-4pm Sun.), remains among the best 100 galleries in the nation. It hosts the work of up to 15 artists at a time, usually active and well-established names, with a few notable rising talents producing contemporary work across a variety of media.

For more than three decades, emerging and established artists from all over the world have exhibited a wide range of contemporary works at **Quint Gallery** (7547 Girard Ave., La Jolla, 858/454-3409, www.quintgallery.com, 10am-5:30pm Tues.-Sat., free). Exhibitions typically run about six weeks, whether highlighting the work of an individual or curating cohesive group shows.

Shopping

DOWNTOWN
Little Italy

With about 9,000 square feet of space dedicated to estate sales, antiques, and collectibles, **Antiques on Kettner** (2400 Kettner Blvd., Little Italy, 619/234-3332, www.antiquesonkettner.com, 10am-6pm daily) in the Kettner Art & Design District can keep you browsing for hours, whether you're looking for furnishings, decorative art, curios, or cabinets for your curios.

When old and antiquated buildings are torn down or refurbished, the original construction materials have to go somewhere. The good stuff goes to **Architectural Salvage** (2401 Kettner Blvd., Little Italy, 619/696-1313, www.architecturalsalvagesd.com, 11am-5pm Sun.-Mon., 10am-6pm Tues.-Sat.). Stained-glass windows, vintage drawers and cabinet hardware, wooden doors, and iron gates are merely some of the fascinating items you'll uncover. Much of it can't even be categorized, and they're rarely things you'd expect. Homeowners will be thrilled, while dreamers and design enthusiasts will be inspired.

Mexican folk art inspires many of the crafts, jewelry, and decorative wares at **Casa Artelexia** (2400 Kettner Blvd., Suite 102, Little Italy, 619/544-1011, www.artelexia. com, 11am-6pm Tues.-Sat., 11am-4pm Sun.), whether it's Roman Catholic mysticism, *papel picado,* or the skull-heavy styling of Día de los Muertos (Day of the Dead). It's unique, often kitschy, and usually enriching—you won't find the likes of it elsewhere.

The **Kettner Art & Design District** (Kettner Blvd. and India St., between Laurel St. and Hawthorn St., Little Italy) boutiques operate out of the north end of Little Italy. Some shops are temporary, some are well known, and some obscure, but all hold potential. Interior and landscape design buffs should loop through the neighborhood to check out places like **Love and Aesthetics** (621 W. Fir St.). Keep your eyes open—any little door could lead to something amazing.

The city's best farmers market, the **Mercato** (Date St. from Kettner Blvd. to Front St., Little Italy, 8am-2pm Sat.) sells produce, local seafood, and a few craft goods to happy throngs of locals who make a date of it week in and week out. Copious California sunshine helps regional farmers grow year-round, so there's always something in season, and usually more than enough for a great meal. Walk away with some fresh avocados, or order breakfast or lunch to go at any number of booths.

Gaslamp Quarter

Horton Plaza (324 Horton Plaza, Gaslamp, 619/239-8180, www.westfield.com/horton-plaza) opened in 1985 in an effort to revitalize Downtown after rough times through the 1970s. Anchored by Macy's, Nordstrom's, and Jimbo's (a natural grocery store), the colorful open-air mall fills about six square blocks with typical mall stores. There's an eight-screen movie theater, a playhouse and music venue, and an outdoor ice rink that opens in the winter. Kiosk machines validate up to three hours of parking in a vast parking garage, giving you enough time to shop, see a

Horton Plaza

movie, and maybe catch a drink or a meal in the Gaslamp.

OLD TOWN
Old Town State Historic Park

Where else are you going to go to find proper saloon garb? **Johnson House Haberdashery** (2706 Calhoun St., 619/291-5170, 10am-6pm daily) features vintage clothing, custom hats, and unique accessories, whether you're into steampunk or just enjoy the fineries of ye olde times.

While greater San Diego did experience a small and short-lived gold rush, **Miner's Gems & Minerals** (2616 San Diego Ave., 619/688-1178, www.minersgemsandminerals.com, 10am-6pm Sun.-Thurs., 10am-7pm Fri.-Sat.) does not technically match the historical accuracy of Old Town. Nevertheless, it offers a unique and interesting assortment of geodes, old bones, and precious stone jewelry.

Presumably, the residents of 19th-century Old Town wore a lot of leather—at least that's the conceit of **Toler's Leather Depot** (2625

Calhoun St., 619/295-7511, 10am-6pm daily). Plenty of belts, buckles, bolo ties, cowboy hats, and moccasins are on hand to help complete your Western outfit.

San Diego's first cigar store dates back to 1868 and still sells stogies as well as pipes and other tobacco products. **Racine and Laramie Tobacconist** (2737 San Diego Ave., 619/291-7833, www.racineandlaramie. com, 10am-8pm Mon.-Sat., 10:30am-6pm Sun.) also doubles as a museum of sorts, with a few vintage pipes, lighters, and matchbooks on display, making it the rare smoke shop of some interest.

Old Town teems with souvenir and gift shops. Those searching for better offerings might appreciate **Captain Fitch's Mercantile** (2627 San Diego Ave., 619/298-3944, 10am-6pm Mon.-Fri., 10am-8pm Sat.-Sun.), which embraces both the cowboy and sailor sides of the city's history. Vintage compasses, Marshall's stars, and model ships, in addition to quite a few children's books and assorted San Diego-themed trinkets, offer a more interesting variety to choose from.

Old Town and Mission Hills

You can't find nautical antiques just anywhere. **SeaJunk** (1891 San Diego Ave., 800/732-5865, www.seajunk.com, 10am-5pm Mon.-Fri., 11am-5pm Sat.), a Maidhof Brothers shop near the border of Mission Hills and Old Town, sells gorgeous wood stateroom furniture and oil lanterns, plus ridiculously cool items like spyglasses, sextants, portholes, ship's telegraphs, and inclinometers.

Made-in-Mexico planters and wind chimes are the reasons to visit **El Centro Artesano** (2637 San Diego Ave., 619/297-2931, 9:30am-6pm Mon.-Thurs., 9:30am-9pm Fri.-Sun.), a pottery lot that is both colorful and well stocked. It's also a great spot to get acquainted with the *chimenea,* an outdoor fireplace for cool nights.

Just around the corner from Old Town State Historic Park, **Bazaar del Mundo** (4133 Taylor St., 619/296-3161, www.bazaardelmundo.com, 10am-6pm daily) steps up the Mexican cultural experience by offering a better brand of wares in a less-hectic environment. While there's still plenty of kitschy fun, there's also some seriously tasteful and colorful merchandise—from hand-painted textiles and clothing to Native American jewelry and Mata Ortiz pottery. You can accomplish some serious shopping here.

Tucked into the northern corner of Old Town State Historic Park, **Fiesta de Reyes** (2754 Calhoun St., 619/220-5040, www.fiestadereyes.com, 10am-9pm daily) holds three Mexican restaurants and has a small stage for traditional music and dance performances. You'll also find a number of specialty shops devoted to Mexican Talavera tiles, olive oil, silver jewelry, beef jerky, and souvenirs galore. It's clearly designed to please visitors and occasionally succeeds.

Not a lot of independent music stores operate in San Diego anymore, but **M-Theory Music** (915 W. Washington St., 619/220-0485, www.mtheorymusic.com, 10am-8pm Mon.-Sat., 11am-7pm Sun.) is still at it, serving up vinyl and CDs instead of downloads. It also stocks a fair number of local recordings, and the clerks will gladly turn you on to some of the best homegrown music.

LA JOLLA

La Jolla Design District (Girard Ave. between Kline St. and Genter St.) is a top-notch home and design quarter, with antiques, designer interiors, high-end furniture, and architectural boutiques. These shops thrive here for a reason—each ranges from interesting to outstanding, offering an amazing resource for decorators and dreamers.

Decorative-art shoppers will find plenty to browse with a short stroll on the north end of **Prospect Street** (between Herschel Ave. and Cave St.), which might be entirely devoted to artisanal goods were it not for the occasional restaurant. Specialty shops like **Africa and Beyond** (1250 Prospect St., 858/454-9983) and **Arte de Origen** (1264 Prospect St., 858/456-2200) feature African and Central American craft objects, while other shops focus on photography, fine-art prints, or digital creations.

Fashion boutiques come and go, and vary by season or taste. What remains constant is that **Girard Avenue** (between Prospect and Kline Sts.) plays home to a wealth of trendy and designer women's clothing and accessories boutiques. This is a window shopper's dream, with internationally known retailers along the lines of **Ralph Lauren** (7830 Girard Ave., 858/459-0554) and **Kate Spade** (7931 Girard Ave., 858/454-2548), exquisitely curated local boutiques like **Kerut** (7944 Girard Ave., 858/456-0800) and **La Donna** (937 Silverado St., 858/459-3410), and national retailers like **Chico's** (7855 Girard Ave., 858/456-6273) and **White House Black Market** (7925 Girard Ave., 858/459-2565).

Any man who wants his wardrobe to be absolutely on point should step inside the **Ascot Shop** (7750 Girard Ave., 858/454-4222, www.ascotshop.com, 10am-6pm Mon.-Sat.), an independently owned shop that has provided top fashions from this location since 1950. Aside from a turn-of-the-20th-century redesign by the architect of the Coronado Bay Bridge, this upscale destination operates as it has for decades, outfitting men with the finest selection of dress and casual threads in town.

A men's clothing and accessories shop, **Le Chauvinist** (7709 Fay Ave., 858/456-0117, www.lechauvinist.com, 10am-5pm Mon.-Fri., 11am-4pm Sat., 9am-2pm Sun.) offers a mix of new and consignment fashions. Prepared to outfit a guy for a business meeting, a rock concert, or opening day at the Del Mar racetrack, the store's selection ranges from socks and cufflinks to seersucker suits and Panama hats.

Sports and Recreation

BEACHES

Ocean Beach

The 0.5-mile stretch of **Ocean Beach** (west of Abbott St., between Newport Ave. and Voltaire St., 619/221-8899, lifeguards on duty 9am-dusk daily, free) runs from the Ocean Beach Pier in the south to the shallow San Diego River bordering the beach's northern edge. Around the pier are surfers and some saltier souls that earn the place comparisons to L.A.'s Venice Beach. Move north to find a welcoming stretch of sand with beach volleyball courts, restrooms, and areas designated for swimming and bodyboarding. Beach bonfires (within designated fire rings) are popular on summer nights, and there's an off-leash dog beach at the park's northernmost section. Parking lots are at the end of Voltaire Street and Santa Monica Avenue.

Mission Beach

You can cruise about two miles along Mission Beach Boardwalk and still not run out of beach or boardwalk. At its northern point it becomes Pacific Beach (PB), whereas the southern stretch is dominated by Belmont Park. While the huge parking lot in south Mission Beach offers easy access, it also means crowds. Meanwhile, PB to the north usually means rowdy singles. That long stretch in the middle? *That's* **Mission Beach** (Ocean Front Walk, between Pacific Beach Dr. and N. Jetty Rd.), where you finally just settle on an empty spot and enjoy, provided you can find street parking.

Pacific Beach

Pacific Beach (Ocean Front Walk, between Pacific Beach Dr. and Law St.) offers a beach experience with a party atmosphere, with people (mostly young adults, including lots of singles) partying at the edge of the sand. They used to party *on* the sand until a city beach alcohol ban was put into effect, but a number of beachfront bars and restaurants ensure that the good times continue, especially south of Crystal Pier. North of the pier tends to be a little quieter, with swimming, surfing, and beach volleyball just a few of the popular activities. Limited spaces can make street parking hit or miss, especially in the summer.

Coronado Beach

Routinely listed among the best beaches in the United States, **Coronado Beach** (Ocean Blvd. from Hotel del Coronado to North Island Naval Air Station, 619/522-7346, www.coronado.ca.us) is what makes this place a dreamy summer destination. During fall and winter months, the beach is often protected from large surf and fog, so while beaches to the north may be overcast, Coronado should be just about right. Bear in mind, when big waves do hit here, it ceases to be an ideal place for less-experienced swimmers. There are several access points from Ocean Boulevard along the mile-long beach.

La Jolla Shores

One of the most popular beaches in town, **La Jolla Shores** (8200 Camino Del Oro, 619/221-8899, www.sandiego.gov, daily 24 hours) offers nearly 1.5 miles of sand where beach-lovers can swim, surf, bodyboard, play volleyball, scuba dive, and launch small watercraft. A beachside park and playground round out the family friendliness of the place.

It's extremely crowded in summer, when small waves and warm water are the norm.

Torrey Pines State Beach

Sandstone cliffs add a little scenic oomph at **Torrey Pines State Beach** (12600 North Torrey Pines Rd., 858/755-2063, www.parks.ca.gov, 7:15am-sunset daily), between La Jolla and Del Mar. The long, wide stretch of sand offers plenty for swimmers and bodyboarders, as well as for surfers toward the north end. Limited parking is available in a lot beside the beach. If that's full, just loop around to park on Carmel Valley Road. It's just a short walk to the sand via the McGonigle Road underpass.

TOP EXPERIENCE

SURFING
Surf Beaches
★ OCEAN BEACH PIER

The waters adjacent to the **OB Pier** (Newport Ave. and Abbott St., Ocean Beach) are reserved for surfers at all times. Anyone wishing to swim or bodyboard must move north of a yellow checkered flag posted in front of the lifeguard tower. Surfers must respect this delineation, or the lifeguards will let them hear about it. During modest 2-4-foot conditions,

Mission Beach

this can be a decent beginner's beach—but try to sneak any waves away from well-established locals and they will also let you hear about it. Waves typically break left off the pier on any western swell. Newbies are better off trying some fun at the left and right beach break farther down the line. Once these waves begin to surpass the six-foot range, leave it to the pros and watch from the pier for an amazing close-up look.

TOURMALINE SURF PARK

A dedicated surf park in every sense of the word, **Tourmaline**'s (Tourmaline St., west of La Jolla Blvd.) charm begins in the parking lot, where crusty old surfers congregate over longboards and listen to classic rock anthems on the stereo of someone's VW bus. The waves here often favor longboards, but the way waves spread out across the length of the beach make it possible for different levels of surfers to coexist. This is one of the top beaches for beginner surfers to learn, though watch out for rocks on the north end of the beach and floating kelp beds—the ropey seaweed can wrap around your arms, legs, and surfboard leash. Whenever the surf forecast is below four feet, the free parking, lifeguards, restrooms, showers, ease of access, and gentle surf make Tourmaline a great spot to learn.

BLACK'S BEACH

An underwater canyon off the coast lines up some of the best waves in town, and difficult access never prevents surfers from hitting **Black's Beach** (9601 La Jolla Farms Rd.) when the waves are breaking. Getting to the sand from the cliffs above requires a hike, whether down a path from the Torrey Pines Glider Port or walking down a gated, steep, and winding driveway hundreds of yards from La Jolla Farms Road. Between the waves, crowds, and nudists (users consider the beach clothing-optional), it's definitely not for families or beginners.

LA JOLLA SHORES AND SCRIPPS PIER

Most days the smaller waves and shallow water leave conditions hospitable enough for beginners, but when the swell picks up, the breaks at **La Jolla Shores** (8200 Camino del Oro, 619/221-8899, www.sandiego.gov, 24 hours daily) are quick and powerful. More experienced riders opt for slightly larger, better-structured waves farther north at Scripps Pier.

La Jolla Shores

TRESTLES

North of Oceanside, is one of the top surf breaks in the county at **San Onofre State Beach** (Old Hwy. 101 at Basilone Rd., 949/492-4872, www.parks.ca.gov, noon-midnight daily, $15), which is home to **Trestles.** Named for a trestle bridge that surfers used to cross underneath to reach the world-class breaks, Trestles is most easily accessed by a 1.5-mile nature trail that connects the campground to Trestle Beach. While camping has its own merits, people come here to seek the surf, which remains crowded despite the complicated access.

Surf Schools and Equipment

Barneys, kooks, grommets, and beginners of all ages can sign up for group or private surf lessons at **Ocean Beach Surf Lessons** (4940 Newport Ave., Ocean Beach, 858/964-3760, oceanbeachsurflessons.com, hours vary daily, group lessons $55, private $85), including stand-up paddleboard instruction and children's day camps during the summer. Equipment is provided and classes are taught by experienced local surfers, delivering a combination of detailed on-beach instruction and in-water guidance, with the hope of standing you up your first time out.

Local board shapers and riders have made **South Coast Surf Shop** (5023 Newport Ave., 619/223-7017, www.southcoast.com, 10am-7pm daily) an OB surfer hub for 40 years, buying wetsuits, board shorts, bikinis, and surf wax on the reg. Even if you're not a surfer, there's still plenty of gear to help you look the part, as well as surfboard rentals should conditions favor the pier a block away. Women can seek out a better-suited selection at **Wahines** (5037 Newport Ave., 619/223-8808), South Coast's sister shop a few doors down.

Rent surfboards, bikes, kayaks, paddleboards, wetsuits, snorkeling gear, beach umbrellas, and chairs from **Cheap Rentals** (3689 Mission Blvd., Mission Beach, 858/488-9070, www.cheap-rentals.com, 9am-7pm daily). Other items for rent include a GoPro camera to attach to the front of your surfboard to capture the highs and lows of your wave session. The main shop sits on Mission Boulevard, a short walk from the beach or bay.

If you don't learn to surf during your first lesson at **Surfari** (3740 Mission Blvd., 858/337-3287, www.surfarisurfschool.com, 9am-5pm daily), your second is free. Such is the guarantee from this North Mission Beach rental shop and surf school. Lessons head out at 9am, 11am, 1pm, and 3pm; each lasts 1.5 hours plus an extra hour with the board for practice. Class sizes run 3-5 people per instructor, with prices favoring groups signing up together. Stand-up paddleboarding classes and rentals are also available.

La Jolla Water Sports (1551 Grand Ave., Pacific Beach, 619/788-6416, www.lajollawatersports.com, 9am-5pm daily) will take you to look at sharks, dive for lobster, or teach you how to spearfish. Or simply motor along the water's surface with a water scooter, goggles down, watching the underwater life unfold as you explore La Jolla Cove.

Every family member can benefit from the surf lessons, clinics, and camps offered by **Surf Diva** (2160 Avenida de la Playa, 858/454-8273, www.surfdiva.com, 8:30am-7:30pm Mon-Thurs., 8:30am-8pm Fri.-Sun.). Women-only clinics are its specialty, though kids' camps in the summer get boys and girls out in the water and up on their boards. Men may opt for a coed group or private lessons.

BOATING

Mission Bay is a watery playground, and **Adventure Watersports** (1710 W. Mission Bay Dr., Mission Beach, 619/226-8611, www.adventurewatersports.com, 8am-5pm daily) has all the toys and equipment you need to join in the fun. Rent a powerboat and cruise the bay, go wakeboarding or waterskiing, ride Jet Skis, or take it slow with paddleboats, aqua cycles, and stand-up paddleboards. All the gear offers direct access to the south portion of the bay. There's a second location on the north end at **Campland on the Bay** (2211 Pacific Beach Dr., 858/581-9300).

A lot of Mission Bay watersports take a little instruction the first time. **Mission Bay Aquatic Center** (1001 Santa Clara Pl., Mission Beach, 858/488-1000, www.mbaquaticcenter.com, 8am-6pm daily) offers lessons to help you get your sea legs. Windsurfing, wakeboarding, stand-up paddleboarding, kayaking, sailing—just listing all the classes this place offers is enough to wipe you out. It's certainly the kind of coursework that can make for a memorable vacation.

Watersports rentals abound at **Mission Bay Sportscenter** (1010 Santa Clara Pl., 858/488-1004, www.missionbaysportcenter.com, 10am-6pm Mon.-Fri., 9am-7pm Sat-Sun. summer, 10am-5pm daily winter), which covers tow sports, paddle sports, wave and wind sports—basically a little bit of everything. Rentals don't require any instruction or pre-certification, so you can enter your small catamaran on the bay right there and see how well your instincts handle turning a small sail into the wind. If you want to rent a powerboat and add a couple of wakeboards or Jet Skis, this is your spot.

Kayaking

Specializing in bicycle, kayak, and snorkel excursions—with an increasing emphasis on stand-up paddleboards—**Bike & Kayak Tours** (2158 Avenida de la Playa, 858/454-1010, www.bikeandkayaktours.com, 8am-8pm daily) help you make the most of La Jolla outdoors, providing guidance and gear to show you exactly what you came to see.

La Jolla Kayak (2199 Avenida de la Playa, 858/459-1114, www.lajollakayak.com, 8am-6pm daily) offers kayak tours of La Jolla's seven sea caves—*and* a snorkeling tour as part of the kayak tour. It's a nice all-in-one way to explore local coastal life. If you want to get a land-based view from the seat of a bicycle, it offers tours for that, too.

Sailing

San Diego Sailing Tours (1450 Harbor Island Dr., Harbor Island, 619/786-0173, www.sandiegosailingtours.com, 9am-7pm daily) offers shared sailing packages to individuals and small groups, taking up to six people at a time for 2-4-hour tours of San Diego Bay. You can help work the boat, or sit back and enjoy complimentary drinks and snacks. Reasonable private packages are also available.

Most summer weekends, the Maritime Museum's 1848 cutter replica *The Californian* sets out on a four-hour **Ocean Adventure Sail** (1492 N. Harbor Dr., 619/234-9153, www.sdmaritime.org, 11:30am-4pm Sat.-Sun., adults $60, under age 13 $48). The tall ship boasts 7,000 square feet of canvas sails as well as four deck guns—it had to be fast to chase down smugglers and tax evaders. Passengers may man the helm, haul some line, and finish the voyage with a cannon salute, the type of sailing adventure few get to embark upon.

Learning to sail doesn't happen in an afternoon, but San Diego's protected bays offer a perfect environment to get started. **Seaforth Boater Education** (1715 Strand Way, 888/834-2628, www.seaforthboatrental.com, 9am-sunset Mon.-Fri., 8am-sunset Sat.-Sun.) will teach you how to skipper a 22-foot sloop in moderate conditions. Return for more advanced classes later, or to its other locations in Harbor Island (955 Harbor Island Dr., Suite 130) and Mission Bay (1641 Quivira Rd.).

If you're an experienced boater who didn't bring your sailboat or yacht with you, talk to **Seaforth Boat Rentals** (333 West Harbor Dr., Gate 1, 888/834-2628, www.seaforthboatrental.com, 10am-5:30pm Mon.-Fri., 9am-5:30pm Sat.-Sun.), which charters and rents both. Larger boats head out from its Downtown, Harbor Island (955 Harbor Island Dr., Suite 130), and Coronado (1715 Strand Way) locations. For smaller craft, look to Mission Bay (1641 Quivira Rd.).

Want to sleep on a yacht? You can—and that's only one of the choices offered by **California Cruisin'** (1450 Harbor Island Dr., Harbor Island, 619/296-8000, www.californiacruisin.com, 8:30am-5:30pm daily), a charter boat service that includes private dinner cruises, sailing charters, and houseboat rentals on San Diego Bay.

SNORKELING AND SCUBA

Two underwater canyons, a couple of reefs, and a kelp forest are some of the highlights of **La Jolla Underwater Park** (2000 block of Avenida de la Playa, 619/221-8824, www.sandiegocoastlife.com), San Diego's deepest water park, which spans the equivalent of 6,000 acres off the coast between La Jolla Cove and La Jolla Shores. Plentiful marine life may be seen for those willing to snorkel or scuba—look for several nonthreatening species of shark, dolphins, sea lions, starfish, anemones, and hundreds of colorful fish and flora. Several shops offer kayak and snorkeling tours, or rent your own to access the south end of the shores.

Snorkel & Scuba (1133-1188 Coast Blvd., 858/539-0054, www.snorkelsandiegoscuba.com, tours 9am, noon, 3pm, 6pm, and sunset daily) offers regular dives for scuba-certified clients (including night dives), as well as guided tours below the surface of La Jolla. Newbies can sign up for the beginner's tour or select options from a snorkeling menu.

FISHING

Heading out into deep waters to troll for big fish is what **Seaforth Sportfishing** (1717 Quivira Rd., 619/224-3383, www.seaforthlanding.com, 5am-6pm daily) is all about. Guides take you as far as coastal Mexican waters on half-day or overnight trips in search of active spots. Choose from large boats with dozens of people or smaller private charters.

The simplest way to fish in San Diego is at the end of a pier, where you don't need a license or a boat. As you head toward the end of **OB Pier** (5091 Niagara Ave., Ocean Beach), the bites get fewer, but the fish get bigger—anything from mackerel and halibut to white sea bass and the rare yellowtail. Bait and tackle (and tacos) are available in a café set in the middle of the pier.

With regularly scheduled half-day trips,

long-range excursions, and charters, **Point Loma Sportfishing** (1403 Scott St., Point Loma, 619/223-1627, www.pointlomasportfishing.com, from 6am daily, from $45) offers a chance to hit the open sea and chase down some yellowtail. In addition to a small fleet of fishing boats, the shop sells equipment rentals, fishing licenses, and secures permits for trips to the well-populated waters off Mexico. Earn your dinner by bringing home a fresh catch.

WHALE-WATCHING

San Diego's ocean is teeming with life, and it's ironic that the largest creatures out there may be the toughest to spot. **San Diego Whale Watch** (1717 Quivira Rd., 619/839-0128, www.sdwhalewatch.com, 10am-1pm and 1:30pm-4:30pm Fri.-Tues., 10am-1pm Wed.-Thurs.) offers three-hour whale-watching tours that help seek them out, hopefully on days they're willing to breach. The boat departs from this bayside facility. Snacks and drinks are available during the tour and there are some activities for kids. Bring a jacket, as it's usually cooler out on the ocean than it is on land.

Once you hear about **Adventure R.I.B. Rides** (1380 Harbor Island Dr., Harbor Island, 619/808-2822, www.adventureribrides.com, 8am-6pm daily), you'll think this whale-watching trip is a lot cooler. Rigid inflatable boats (R.I.B.) were built for navy SEAL missions. A maximum of six passengers per trip head out in search of whales and dolphins, moving fast enough to find and follow. This badass outfit also conducts scuba charters and offers "Adventure Picnics."

GOLF

It's certainly not the best-known city golf course, but the 18 holes at **Balboa Park City Golf Course** (2600 Golf Course Dr., 619/239-1660, www.balboagc.com, 7am-4pm daily) deserve better notice, if only for the view. One end of the course looks out at the bay and skyline, while another strolls past beautiful Craftsman homes of the North Park and South Park neighborhoods. Warm up on one of the 14 station driving ranges, practice on the putting green, or beef up your technique with instruction from one of the PGA-certified golf pros on staff.

Established in 1932, **Presidio Hills Golf Course** (4136 Wallace St., 619/295-9476, www.presidiohillsgolf.com, daily) is the oldest in town, featuring 18 par-3 holes for a cheap, short course central to the city. Pay special attention to the clubhouse, which predates the golf course by more than a century (built in 1820, it would be the oldest residential structure in San Diego were it not part of the golf course). **Mission Bay Golf Course and Practice Center** (2702 N. Mission Bay Dr., 858/581-7880, www.sandiego.gov, 6:30am-10pm daily) has a couple of things going for it: location and lights. Located at the northeast corner of Mission Bay, it's easy to get to whether you're staying in Mission Beach or Pacific Beach. The 18-hole, mostly par-3 course is the only lighted one in town, making it the best bet for a late round on a quick, inexpensive course.

Torrey Pines Golf Course (11480 Torrey Pines Park Rd., 858/581-7171, www.sandiego.gov, 7am-4pm daily), the home of the 2021 U.S. Open, is a city golf course, which means that it's open to the public. But it can be tough to get a tee time on the most famous course in town, particularly for nonresidents. Reservations are accepted up to 90 days out, with short-term allotments available via a lottery system. The reward is playing at one of two world-class William P. Bell-designed 18-hole courses atop bluffs overlooking the Pacific—either the north course or the challenging legendary south course.

SPECTATOR SPORTS

When the home of the **San Diego Padres** opened in 2004, local fans rejoiced. Though the Padres still didn't make the postseason, their fans do love **Petco Park** (100 Park Blvd., 619/795-5000, www.petcoparkevents.com, hours and admission vary), which easily boasts the best beer selection in the Major Leagues. An iconic brick Western Metal Works building backs up the left field fence, while an ingenious **Park at the Park** (open to the public during nongame times) sits behind the center field bullpen, a grassy slope with a partial view into the stadium and a large screen televising any game action hidden from view. Anyone with a ticket can check out this brilliant 7th-inning-stretch territory, which also happens to be served by favorite

Petco Park

local vendors, including Stone Brewing, Green Flash, Hodad's, and Phil's BBQ.

Formerly known as Jack Murphy Stadium, **Qualcomm Stadium** (9449 Friars Rd., Mission Valley, 619/641-3100, www.sandiego. gov/qualcomm) plays home field to both the National Football League's **San Diego Chargers** and the **Aztecs** of San Diego State University. It also comes alive every so often hosting international club soccer matches.

Food

DOWNTOWN
American

Top Chef All Stars winner Richard Blais found a receptive audience when he opened ★ **Juniper and Ivy** (2228 Kettner Blvd., Little Italy, 619/269-9036, www.junipe-randivy.com, 4pm-10pm Sun.-Thurs., 4pm-11pm Fri.-Sat., $20-34). San Diego foodies have enthusiastically embraced his creative approach—liquid nitrogen tricks come into play while crafting the horseradish "pearls" that top oysters with a melon mignonette. A Southern California take on steak tartare comes with Carne Cruda Asada, which incorporates jalapeño, cotija, and plenty of quail eggs. Blais and his team constantly redraft the imaginative menu with dozens of intriguing dishes; there's even a "secret menu" that often features a burger paying tribute to the In-N-Out chain's regional classic.

Popular Little Italy hangout the **Waterfront Bar and Grill** (2044 Kettner Blvd., Little Italy, 619/232-9656, www.water-frontbarandgrill.com, 6am-2am daily, $8-14) opened back in 1933, just as Prohibition ended, making it San Diego's oldest continually operating bar. Best known for its burgers, the place also covers breakfast, serving Mexican brunch, including the classic salsa and egg dishes *chilaquiles* (served over tortilla chips) and huevos rancheros (served with fresh tortillas). The bar opens to a dining patio and serves enough beer to keep it lively and easy to spot from the sidewalk all day long.

California Cuisine

Avocado fries, duck wings, and lamb ribs paired with a tasting flight of six different sangrias make **Café 21** (802 5th Ave., Gaslamp, 619/795-0721, www.cafe-21. com, 8am-11pm Sun.-Thurs., 8am-midnight Fri.-Sat., $15-30) a perfect happy-hour spot. For dinner, the kitchen turns out great dishes featuring a rotating selection of local and sustainable ingredients. Live music sometimes accompanies the grass-fed steak or fresh catch of the day in this stylish restaurant, which boasts a warm brick bar, a colorful dining room, and a bank of large windows looking out onto the lively Gaslamp sidewalk.

Seasonal local cuisine and matching craft cocktails are the hallmark of **Jsix** (616 J St., 619/531-8744, www.jsixrestaurant.com, 7am-10pm Sun.-Fri., 8am-10pm Sat., $18-30), though on pleasant days its most remarkable feature may be the beautiful rooftop lounge just a quick elevator ride away. Service upstairs may not match the promptness and enthusiasm found within the brick and brass dining room, but either way you'll enjoy cleverly conceived meat, fish, and vegetable dishes made by kitchen staff who seem genuinely interested in pleasing customers.

Technically a chain, **Tender Greens** (110 W. Broadway, Gaslamp, 619/795-2353, www. tendergreens.com, 11am-9pm Mon.-Fri., 11:30am-9pm Sat.-Sun., $12-15) breaks the mold by practicing farm-to-table principles. Each restaurant is overseen by a pedigreed executive chef who makes the most out of seasonal ingredients and natural meats, including cured-in-house salami, marinated steak, and buttermilk fried chicken. You won't get fries with that; instead, enjoy assorted grilled vegetables and some of the best salads available Downtown.

Best Restaurants

★ **Juniper and Ivy:** *Top Chef All-Stars's* Richard Blais chose San Diego as the location of his "left coast cookery" (page 507).

★ **Cowboy Star:** This unlikely combination of American steak house and French fine dining experience works across the board (page 509).

★ **Carnita's Snack Shack:** This North Park pork specialist turns out the area's best burger (page 511).

★ **URBN Pizza:** This North Park favorite also features a great tap list and terrific cocktails (page 512).

★ **Whisknladle:** The farm-to-table ethos stands out in a variety of fantastic tasting dishes (page 515).

★ **Puesto:** Puesto's all-sustainable, high-quality ingredients still capture the flavors of the city's beloved hole-in-the-wall taco shop (page 515).

★ **El Pescador Fish Market:** This La Jolla market serves simple fresh fish done right (page 515).

★ **The Marine Room:** The ocean laps against the windows of this elite French-inspired seafood spot (page 516).

Italian

Stuffed deep-dish Chicago pies have a home in San Diego thanks to **Berkeley Pizza** (539 Island Ave., Gaslamp, 619/937-0808, www. berkeleypizza.net, 11am-11pm Sun.-Thurs., 11am-3am Fri.-Sat., $6-12). The pizza is the real deal, thick with toppings and a delicious chunky marinara—a single slice will fill most. Berkeley started as a farmers market booth, then opened a storefront to keep up with the high demand caused by excellent word of mouth. Its small, barebones Gaslamp location may lack ambience, but things look a little better at the North Park location (3934 30th St.).

Northern Italian cuisine is the calling card of **Monello** (750 W. Fir St., Little Italy, 619/501-0030, www.lovemonello.com, 11:30am-close Tues.-Fri., 10am-close Sat.-Sun., $15-25), specifically the street food of the owners' hometown of Milan. This translates to light calzone-like *panzerotti,* fresh-cut prosciutto, flaky *raspa dura* cheese, polenta, and a variety of sauces topping the homemade pasta. Pizza lovers won't go wrong here, and any drink made with the house-made sweet vermouth is sure to be tasty.

The dining room at **Mimmo's Italian Village** (1743 India St., 619/239-3710, www. mimmos.biz, 10am-3pm and 5pm-9pm Mon.-Wed., 10am-3pm and 5pm-10pm Thurs., 10am-3pm and 5pm-11pm Fri., 5pm-11pm Sat., noon-9pm Sun., $15-20) literally resembles a small Italian village, with a traditional Italian menu and dining experience. Feast on pasta, olives, and caprese, then choose from cannoli, tiramisu, or mascarpone for dessert. A sidewalk dining patio proves a popular spot to eat and people-watch.

Mexican

The contemporary fusion cuisine known as Baja Med has garnered a stellar international reputation from its south-of-the-border origins, spearheaded by renowned chef Javier

Plascencia. Naturally, when Plascencia opened ★ **Bracero Cocina de Raiz** (1490 Kettner Blvd, Little Italy, 619/756-7864, www.bracerococina.com, 11:30am-11pm Sun.-Thurs., 11:30am-midnight Fri.-Sat., $20-30), San Diego's foodie class took notice, quickly making it one of the hottest restaurants in town. Share small plates to make the most of the Mediterranean-infused Mexican dishes that range from out-of-this-world tacos to crudo to slow-roasted meats.

A custom red-oak-burning Santa Maria grill and Caja-China-style subterranean roasting oven ensures **Don Chido** (527 5th Ave., Gaslamp, 619/232-8226, www.donchido.com, 11am-midnight Sun.-Mon. and Wed., 11am-2am Tues., 11am-2am Thurs.-Sat., $12-20) serves up succulent, perfectly cooked meat dishes, ranging from a skirt steak carne asada to braised pork *carnitas*. A tortilla station ensures that all the sustainable ingredients show up at your table with warm, handmade corn tortillas.

Excellent tacos are the dominion of **¡Salud!** (2196 Logan Ave., Barrio Logan, 619/255-3856, www.saludsd.com, 10am-9pm Tues.-Thurs., 10am-11pm Fri.-Sat., 9am-5pm Sun., $6-10). The colorful spot dishes up gourmet tacos with classic Barrio flair—walls plastered with murals, car parts, and skate decks. And since it's San Diego, there's craft beer aplenty.

Steak

Combine a Western steak house with sustainable principles and European fine dining standards and you'll have a fair approximation of ★ **Cowboy Star** (640 10th Ave., East Village, 619/450-5880, www.thecowboystar.com, 4pm-10pm Mon., 11:30am-2:30pm and 4pm-10pm Tues.-Thurs., 11:30am-2:30pm and 4pm-10:30pm Fri., 5pm-10:30pm Sat., 5pm-9pm Sun., $30-50). Enjoy prime-grade rib eye or "intensely marbled" *wagyu* beef while comfortably seated in a leather booth beneath a painting of John Wayne. Impeccable service comes from a supremely knowledgeable waitstaff prepared to suggest a wine pairing for the exquisite filet mignon steak tartare (complete with a quail egg). Everything—from the cocktails to the wine list to the long list of hormone- and antibiotic-free meats—is top-shelf, with several selections cured or dry-aged in the restaurant's own butcher shop. The menu varies with the whims of the French-trained chef, though you'll always find seafood and game selections in addition to a variety of

Cowboy Star

steaks. This may well be the future of prime steak houses.

USDA prime steak reigns supreme at **Donovan's Steak & Chop House** (570 K St., Gaslamp, 619/237-9700, www.donovans-steakhouse.com, 4pm-10pm Mon.-Thurs., 4pm-11pm Fri.-Sat., $30-50). It's the sort of restaurant professional athletes might eat at following a game, where bartenders wear tuxedoes and captains of industry drop tips that could singlehandedly change the lives of the waitress. Everything here is top-shelf all the way, from the dark wood paneling to the enormous glass wine vault filled with superb bottles of the good stuff.

Seafood

Mermaids, fish skulls, and brass tables set the tone in the design-savvy raw bar and seafood restaurant **Ironside** (1654 India St., Little Italy, 619/269-3033, www.ironsidefishandoyster.com, 11:30am-2:30pm and 5pm-10pm Mon.-Fri., 10am-10:30pm Sat.-Sun., $14-30). Start with oysters, mussels, clams, or ceviche, then move on to San Diego's best lobster roll or a whole roasted fish. This place knows seafood—cold or cooked—so you could even try the "fries with eyes" while you marvel at mermaid statues and a wall made from barracuda skulls.

Vegan

Rejuvenating fare is the mission at **Café Gratitude** (1980 Kettner Blvd., Little Italy, 619/736-5077, www.cafegratitude.com, 8am-10pm daily, $14-18). From macrobiotic quinoa bowls to sprouted rice soul food combos, it's rich food for the self-affirming and meatless set—always free of animal products, served raw or gluten-free. But it's also just terrific dining in stylish surroundings that carnivores won't mind being dragged to.

BALBOA PARK AND HILLCREST
California Cuisine

Tucked in a courtyard beside the Museum of Art's sculpture garden sits **Panama 66** (1549 El Prado, 619/557-9441, www.panama66. blogspot.com, 11:30am-3pm Mon., 11:30am-10pm Tues.-Thurs., 11:30am-11pm Fri., 11am-11pm Sat., 11am-10pm Sun., $8-14), the latest addition to Balboa Park's dining scene. This locally sourced gastropub features a rotating selection of San Diego's best beers to help wash down tasty sandwiches, salads, and charcuterie plates. Dine at one of the shady tables, or ask for a blanket and picnic among the artwork.

UPTOWN
Breakfast and Brunch

Heaping portions of farm-style breakfasts keep **Hash House a Go Go** (3628 5th Ave., Hillcrest, 619/298-4646, www.hashhouse-agogo.com, 7:30am-2pm Mon., 7:30am-2pm and 5:30pm-9pm Tues.-Thurs., 7:30am-2pm and 5:30pm-10pm Fri., 7:30am-2:30pm and 5:30pm-10pm Sat., 7:30am-2:30pm and 5:30pm-9pm Sun., $10-15) busy during breakfast and brunch, especially on weekends, when locals line up for pancakes, waffles, Benedicts, and meaty hashes. The simple farmhouse interior will do, but for the best experience, hold out for patio seating. Consider splitting a meal or be prepared to walk away with a full belly as well as leftovers.

Pancake lovers will find the wait at **Snooze** (3940 5th Ave., Hillcrest, 619/500-3344, www. snoozeeatery.com, 6:30am-2:30pm Mon.-Fri., 7am-2:30pm Sat.-Sun., $10-15) worth it. The variety of specialty flavors includes sweet potato, strawberry malted, and pineapple upside-down cakes, with a rotating selection of daily specials. Savory eaters will find solace in traditional and experimental egg dishes, including Benedicts with lox, prosciutto, or pulled pork. Be ready to share, because you will want to try everything. Despite a large dining room, wait times can be long.

Coffee and Tea

Fresh-roasted beans make superior coffee, and if you already know this you'll want to check out **Caffé Calabria** (3933 30th St., North Park, 619/291-1759, www.caffecalabria.com,

6am-3pm Mon.-Tues., 6am-11pm Wed.-Fri., 7am-11pm Sat.-Sun., $3-6). A variety of dark-roasted, single-origin beans and blends can be purchased in bulk or brewed into your preferred coffee drink, and they'll taste great, because they were recently roasted on the premises. Inside, TV screens show Italian league soccer or cycling races, or opt for parklet seating outside.

Third-wave coffee grew up in San Diego with **Bird Rock Coffee Roasters** (2295 Kettner Blvd., Little Italy, 619/272-0203, www.birdrockcoffee.com, 6am-6pm Mon.-Fri., 7am-7pm Sat.-Sun., $4-8). The La Jolla-based shop (5627 La Jolla Blvd.) pursues direct trade relationships, meaning its coffee team travels the world seeking out top-quality coffee beans you won't find at other shops in town, or in most cities for that matter.

American

It's no accident you'll come across **Bread & Cie** (350 University Ave., Hillcrest, 619/683-9322, www.breadandcie.com, 7am-7pm Mon.-Fri., 7am-6pm Sat., 8am-6pm Sun., $7-9) baked goods in restaurants and markets all over town. The French-style bakery bakes some of the best bread in San Diego. Stop in for sandwiches, either to dine in or take out for a picnic, and grab some desserts while you're here—you'll have to have one once you see them. The *macarons* in particular deliver a decadently sweet dose of Parisian nostalgia, perfect for nibbling on the restaurant's bistro-style dining patio.

You don't need to dig swine to enjoy ★ **Carnita's Snack Shack** (2632 University Ave., North Park, 619/294-7675, www.carnitassnackshack.com, noon-midnight daily, $8-12), but you'll sure love this street-side casual outdoor eatery if you do. Between the braised pork belly appetizer, pulled pork tacos, and fries served with bacon ketchup, hog heaven becomes a delectable possibility. Other regular menu items include a cheese bread and sliced rib-eye steak sandwich, one of the city's best burgers, and a terrine made from beets, spinach, and goat cheese (in case there's a vegetarian in your group). Local carnivores line up all day for this, even when the über-decadent *poutine* isn't on the menu.

With a cobblestoned exterior and polished interior, **Great Maple** (1451 Washington St., 619/255-2282, www.thegreatmaple.com, 8am-2pm and 5pm-9pm Sun.-Thurs., 8am-2pm and 5pm-10pm Fri.-Sat., $15-25) feels like the contemporary version of a mountain town diner. Hardwood floors, green vinyl booths, and white marble countertops give it a clean look that matches its impeccable menu, which strikes an unusually good balance between meat and vegetable dishes. You may choose between steak tartare and beet tartare, and for every succulent grass-fed burger there's a creatively assembled salad. Nevertheless, keep reading, the list goes on and includes occasional surprises like Maine lobster *poutine*. Also, save room for dessert—the place is known for its pies as well as a decadent take on the maple-bacon doughnut.

With 30 rotating taps, including two nitro, you won't have trouble finding fantastic beer at **Waypoint Public House** (3794 30th St., North Park, 619/255-8778, www.waypoint-public.com, 4pm-1am Mon.-Fri., 10am-1am Sat.-Sun., $10-15), but if you need pointers, the menu always recommends a couple of worthy beer pairings for each dish. The corner restaurant's a lot brighter and airier than the name might suggest, with huge rows of windows open on warm days, which are, of course, most of them. The breezy contemporary decor matches the playful menu, which bounces creatively between comfort food and light California cuisine.

Japanese

Ramen is having a moment, and its best local representation might just be this beer drinker's haven. **Underbelly** (3794 30th St., 619/255-8778, www.godblessunderbelly.com, 4pm-1am Mon.-Fri., 10am-1am Sat.-Sun., $10-16) offers a succulent take on pork marrow tonkotsu, and its soy and mushroom-based broths also do well to flavor perfectly cooked noodles with add-ons such as char-siu pork belly, hoisin short ribs, and charred kimchi. Be prepared to order before you take a seat, and don't forget to explore the yakitori menu. Grab a craft beer to wash it all down while you sit on the incredibly spacious street-side patio, which dazzles even when the fire tables aren't lit.

Mexican

Eating tacos must be done in San Diego, and there are a number of places that serve them, whether authentic Baja street tacos or some traditional local take on fried fish. Then there's **City Tacos** (3028 University Ave., North Park, 619/294-8292, www.cityta-cossd.com, 11am-11pm Mon.-Thurs., 11am-2am Fri.-Sat., noon-10pm Sun., $6-10), which turns tradition on its head for foodies looking to enjoy traditional flavor profiles in creative new ways. The chile relleno taco invokes the classic dish with mild spice and a gloriously melted cheese blend. The mahimahi adobo sears a lovely piece of fish and pairs it with mango salsa. Then there's the Borrego taco—lamb, mushroom, and fried leeks. You won't find the likes of it elsewhere, much to the detriment of elsewhere.

If you're ready to experience homemade Mexican food, **El Comal** (3946 Illinois St., 619/294-8292, www.elcomalsd.com, 10am-3pm and 5pm-9pm Mon.-Wed., 10am-10pm Thurs.-Fri., 9am-10pm Sat., 9am-9pm Sun., $12-15) offers a delicious and down-to-earth experience. *Comal* translates to "griddle," a reference to the restaurant's *antojitos,* traditional small dishes built around the ground hominy dough masa, used to make tamales and the best corn tortillas you'll ever taste. Consequently, any taco on the menu is a go, especially the goat *barbacoa.* To see what else masa can do, try the *mulitas,* gorditas, huaraches, or the green mole enchiladas, if they're available. And if you see a soup you like, just order it—they're all fantastic.

Pizza

Tasty Napolitano pizza and 26 craft beers on tap would probably be enough to keep

Blind Lady Alehouse (3416 Adams Ave., 619/255-2491, www.blindladyalehouse.com, 11:30am-midnight daily, $10-13) popular. But a comfortable wood dining room filled with community tables elevates this to a joy-filled space where families and friends bond over great ales. Whether you order a pie with house-made chorizo and sausage toppings, *moules frites,* or a charcuterie board, it's tough to go wrong, especially if you try one of the beers brewed in-house by Automatic Brewing Co.

The best crust in town hails from the coal-fire ovens of this chic pizza spot—and yes, pizza spots can be chic. A full bar turns out tasty cocktails as well as local craft beer, so the place often fills up with thirsty pretty things, hipsters, and cocktail connoisseurs. But excellent pizza is the root of ★ **URBN Pizza's** (3085 University Ave., 619/255-7300, www.urbnnorthpark.com, noon-10pm Sun.-Mon., noon-midnight Tues.-Thurs., noon-2am Fri.-Sat., $15-20) success, with toppings like sausage-stuffed peppers, fresh clams, and mashed potatoes. Great happy hour specials make a visit worth your while.

OLD TOWN
Mexican

Old Town's historic park has no shortage of "authentic" Mexican restaurants vying for tourist attention. If you're intent on finding the classic Mexican margarita and Latin music patio-dining experience, do as the locals do and head to **Casa Guadalajara** (4105 Taylor St., 619/295-5111, www.casaguadalajara.com, 11am-10pm Mon.-Thurs., 11am-11pm Fri., 11am-10pm Sat.-Sun., $8-12), the best of the bunch. Dishes like *chile colorado* and carne asada *tampiqueña* offer all the flavors you seek, though tacos, enchiladas, and fajitas always prove popular. Sit on the patio, order some chips and guacamole, and savor the experience.

El Agave (2304 San Diego Ave., 619/220-0692, www.elagave.com, 11am-10pm daily, $15-25) creates a "Mexican Gastronomy," crafting a menu of authentic dishes that range from the usual to the exotic, including an appetizer called *tlacoyos cuitlacoche* (a rarely found delicacy of blue masa and corn fungus). For the less adventurous, the menu's safest bets include any of its 10 moles, each a worthy excuse to dine here. The restaurant doubles as a tequila museum, and its walls are lined by more than 2,000 bottles that add a beautiful brightness to the rustic decor.

For 75 years **El Indio** (3695 India St., Mission Hills, 619/299-0333, www.el-indio.com, 8am-9pm daily, $8-12) has been churning out homemade tortillas and tortilla chips. During most of that time, it has also been serving up beloved and authentic Mexican food to a loyal following of locals and visitors. The founder of the family-owned mainstay is said to have invented the term *taquito,* so the little rolled tacos are worth a try. Sit down in the busy casual dining room, the patio, or order to go.

If you like your Mexican food with a side of extreme kitsch, dive into **Lucha Libre** (1810 W. Washington St., 619/296-8226, www.tacos-mackdown.com, 8am-11pm Sun.-Thurs., 8am-2:30am Fri.-Sat., $6-10), a campy masked wrestling-themed taco and burrito shop. Wrestler murals and a mask gallery liven up the bright-pink walls, and old matches and movies usually run on TV screens, playing up the wild vibe. You'll find some pretty authentic San Diego-style Mexican food here, as well as a few modern takes along the lines of a lettuce-wrapped taco and creamy cilantro salsa. It's a kooky way to eat like a local while still living like a traveler. With 24 hours' notice, you can even reserve the Champion's Booth, which must be seen to be believed.

Seafood

The secret got out about Blue Water when the beloved fresh-catch seafood spot was covered on *Diners, Drive-Ins and Dives,* but the line out the door always existed near lunchtime at **Blue Water Seafood Market & Grill** (3667 India St., 619/497-0914, www.bluewaterseafoodsandiego.com, 11am-9pm

Mon.-Thurs., 11am-10pm Fri., 11:30am-10pm Sat., 11:30am-9pm Sun., $12-18). That line moves quickly, though, guiding you past the market counter where you can linger over the different cuts of fish available. Decide which looks best and then order it as a sandwich, salad, taco, or on a plate with your choice of seasoning. The place always seems packed, but tables open up frequently. Grab one on the patio if you can.

POINT LOMA

Asian

The popularity of this gastropub and noodle house led to its recent expansion into a larger location a mere block from the OB Pier. Locals love **OB Noodle House** (4993 Niagara Ave., Ocean Beach, 619/255-9858, www.obnoodlehouse.com, noon-11pm Mon.-Thurs., 11am-11pm Fri.-Sun., $10-16) and seek out their favorite dishes among udon, pho, lo mein, and other pan-Asian noodles, as well as a fine rotation of local craft brews to drink with them. It's never a bad place to be on a warm evening, enjoying a beer on the outdoor patio as the neighborhood's nightlife starts to pick up.

Mexican

With windows overlooking the pier, OB's always-bustling ★ **South Beach Bar & Grille** (5059 Newport Ave., Ocean Beach, 619/226-4577, www.southbeachob.com, 11am-2am daily, $8-12) is the fish taco destination for locals and out-of-town guests. Choices range from traditional Baja battered-and-fried tacos to grilled options, including wahoo, mahi mahi, lobster, and shark. Wash these down with one of the local beers on tap. You're on your own finding an open table amid the constant rush, but once you've claimed your spot, you've earned the right to enjoy it awhile.

Seafood

When do you know the seafood's truly fresh? When you pass a fleet of fishing boats outside the restaurant. **Point Loma Seafood** (2805

Emerson St., Point Loma, 619/223-1109, www.pointlomaseafoods.com, 9am-7pm Mon.-Sat., 10am-7pm Sun., $8-14) has achieved cultlike status over the years, with a glass deli counter displaying your choice of the latest catch. Line up at the counter and choose your fresh catch for fish tacos, seafood salad, sushi, or plates with fries and slaw. The best-known option may be the simplest: a piece of fish on fresh-baked sourdough with tartar sauce—that's it. The freshness of the fish is all the frills this sandwich needs.

CORONADO
American

A local institution, **Coronado Brewing Company** (170 Orange Ave., 619/437-4452, www.coronadobrewingcompany.com, 10:30am-9pm Sun.-Thurs., 10:30am-10pm Fri.-Sat., $10-16) has been serving up pub grub for decades, which goes great with its award-winning beers. Order a tasting flight with appetizers, then settle on a pint to go with your burger, pizza, or taco plate. Aim for lunch or an early dinner to enjoy the shaded dining patio on a sunny day. With the city skyline within view, you can check a few items off your San Diego to-do list all in one place.

MISSION BAY AND BEACHES
Mexican

There's not much to look at within **La Perla Cocina** (745 Emerald St., Pacific Beach, 858/274-3038, 8:30am-9pm Mon.-Sat., 8:30am-8:30pm Sun., $5-8), it's the lamb tacos and one of the city's best California burritos (marinated carne asada, grated cheddar cheese, and french fries) that keeps people coming back. This staple street food proves tasty and filling, but if you want to take it further, try the Oaxacacalifornia burrito—a California burrito wrapped inside a quesadilla.

Why do lines of people keep forming beside the taco truck mural of that hole-in-the-wall in north PB? Because the fish tacos demand it. **Oscar's Mexican Seafood** (703 Turquoise St., Pacific Beach, 858/488-6392, www.oscarsmexicanseafood.com, 8am-9pm Sun.-Thurs., 8am-10pm Fri.-Sat., $5-10) excels at the classic Baja-style battered fish, available for $1 on weekday afternoons. Smoked fish, shrimp, and steak tacos also go great with the house ceviche or fish stew. There's a less charming central Pacific Beach location (746 Emerald St.) and another in Hillcrest (646 University Ave.).

Coronado Brewing Company

Seafood

Line up for grilled fish, sandwiches, or tacos at the counter of **Pacific Beach Fish Shop** (1775 Garnet Ave., Pacific Beach, 858/483-4746, www.thefishshoppb.com, 11am-10pm daily, $8-18), a local's favorite that's easy to spot thanks to a marlin trophy out front. Order your choice of fish based on what looks good that day accompanied by marinades such as blackened lemon-butter or chipotle. Or keep it *crudo* with ceviche, oysters, a shrimp cocktail, or sashimi of the day. Take it to the patio with a draft beer and relish where you are.

LA JOLLA
California Cuisine

Sitting on the 11th floor of the Hotel La Jolla, a panoramic ocean view might be the only decor **Cusp Dining & Drinks** (7955 La Jolla Shores Dr., 858/551-3620, www.cusprestaurant.com, 7am-10:30am and 5pm-9pm Mon.-Thurs., 7am-10:30am and 5pm-10pm Fri, 8am-2pm and 5pm-10pm Sat., 8am-2pm and 5pm-9pm Sun., $18-30) really needs. But inside, a slick contemporary design incorporates organic shapes that contrast the industrial polished steel of its open kitchen. The always-changing menu loosely adopts California and Mediterranean influences, though don't be surprised to find deviations among the pan-seared proteins and house-made pastas. The cocktail list runs even farther afield, with classic drinks and a number of adventurous craft concoctions.

Chef Jason Knibb has earned accolades over the years for the "evolving California cuisine" served at **Nine-Ten** (910 Prospect St., 858/964-5400, www.nine-ten.com, 6:30am-11am, 11:30am-2:30pm, and 3:30pm-9:30pm Mon., 6:30am-11am, 11:30am-2:30pm, and 3:30pm-10pm Tues.-Sat., 6:30am-2:30pm and 3:30pm-9:30pm Sun., $24-36), the Grande Colonial Hotel's restaurant. Appetizers may include squid-ink spaghettini with bay scallops in an *uni* emulsion, while entrée options range from a creatively dressed prime steak dish to succulent seafood prepared *sous vide*.

Local produce dictates the weekly flavor profiles, and the excellently prepared staff can recommend perfect wine pairings all the way through dessert. Reserve a spot on the sidewalk patio for people watching along Prospect Street, or request terrace dining for a partial sunset view of the Pacific.

The covered patio at ★ **Whisknladle** (1044 Wall St., 858/551-7575, www.whisknladle.com, 11:30am-9pm Mon.-Thurs., 11:30am-10pm Fri., 10am-10pm Sat., 10am-9pm Sun., $14-30) is where you'll find one of the best dining (and people-watching) experiences in San Diego. Seasonal dishes are prepared from scratch, usually dependent on which organic produce and sustainably sourced meats and seafood are available fresh. The result is out-of-this-world quality; even a routine charcuterie plate stands out, with exceptional house-cured meats, brined-in-house olives, and house-baked breads. You can't go wrong with any pasta entrée, especially a pork sausage *ragù* over tagliatelle that will make you question every Italian restaurant you've ever visited.

Mexican

It's tough to do better than this of-the-moment Mexican spot. ★ **Puesto** (1044 Wall St., 858/454-1260, www.eatpuesto.com, 11am-9pm Sun.-Thurs., 11am-10pm Fri.-Sat., $13-20) offers a wide variety of taco fillers boasting authentic flavors and made with local and sustainable ingredients. Mix-and-match tacos include lobster, nopale cactus, or filet mignon served in a house-made corn tortilla with crispy melted cheese, avocado, and pistachio jalapeño salsa. Sample some of the great tequila-based cocktails to wash it down, and if you truly enjoy living, order the flan. The pair of small dining rooms open to a bustling sidewalk; for a much larger experience, try the newer Seaport Village location (789 W. Harbor Dr.).

Seafood

Fresh seafood in La Jolla has a long history. ★ **El Pescador Fish Market** (634

Pearl St., 858/456-2526, www.elpescadorfishmarket.com, 10am-8pm daily, $8-14) offers a bounty of fresh-catch seafood, served in sandwiches, burritos, or tacos—all very satisfying. High ceilings and picture windows light up a long glass counter filled with local fish, including yellowtail, sea bass, and Mexican white shrimp. To truly embrace the beauty of this spot, grab the sashimi platter of the day.

★ **The Marine Room** (2000 Spindrift Dr., 866/644-2351, www.marineroom.com, 4pm-9:30pm Sun.-Thurs., 4pm-10pm Fri.-Sat., $35-50) has been a legendary draw since the 1940s, famous for being so close to the ocean that waves splash against the windows during high tide. Diners enjoy a little thrill each time the water splashes only inches away, but ultimately the food lives up to its reputation as well. Globally sourced seafood is supplemented by French gastronomy that includes everything from Maine lobster tail to lamb osso buco.

NORTH COUNTY
Del Mar and Solana Beach

Del Mar's known to have a lot of upscale restaurants, but none do fine dining as well as the five-star, five-diamond **Addison** (5200 Grand Del Mar Way, 858/314-1900, www.addisondelmar.com, 6pm-9pm Tues.-Thurs., 5:30pm-9:30pm Fri.-Sat., $98-125). The refined tastes and disciplined kitchen of renowned chef William Bradley send seasonally designed dishes to a dining room sitting above the 18th green of the exclusive golf course of the Grand Del Mar resort, complete with a Mediterranean-style patio to enjoy the sommelier's best picks.

If you prefer your meals coastal, **Jake's Del Mar** (1660 Coast Blvd., 858/755-2002, www.jakesdelmar.com, 4pm-9pm Mon., 11:30am-9pm Tues.-Thurs., 11:30am-9:30pm Fri.-Sat., 10am-9pm Sun., $20-36) is famous among locals for its Sunday brunch directly overlooking the beach at Del Mar's Powerhouse Park, but it actually has the same view all day long,

serving California cuisine mixed with a few Hawaiian dishes.

Encinitas

Encinitas has become "coffee rich." The old train station building now houses San Diego's original coffee roaster, **Pannikin Coffee & Tea** (510 N. Coast Hwy. 101, 760/436-5824, www.pannikincoffeeandtea.com, 6am-6pm daily, $3-5), with a lovely patio for drinking both. Not far down the road is **Lofty Coffee Company** (90 N. Coast Hwy. 101, Suite 214, 760/230-6747, www.loftycoffeeco.com, 6am-6pm Mon.-Fri., $4-5). The organic specialty coffee roaster's shop manages to feel beachy yet design savvy, with glass, steel, and wood panels housing a space that opens up in the summer, when a Kyoto-drip cold-brew iced coffee proves ideal.

To take advantage of this gorgeous coastline, reserve a patio table at **Pacific Coast Grill** (2526 S. Coast Hwy. 101, Cardiff by the Sea, 760/479-0721, www.pacificcoastgrill.com, 11am-4pm and 4:30pm-9pm Mon.-Thurs., 11am-4pm and 4:30pm-10pm Fri.-Sat., 11am-4pm Sun., $25-45). Set on top of gorgeous Cardiff State Beach, this surf-and-turf restaurant lets you dine about as close to the ocean as you can without getting sand in your lap. In addition to the spectacular view, the kitchen provides a worthy dining experience, with strips of ahi tuna and a fillet you sear yourself on a sizzling hot stone. Follow it up with a fish perfectly cooked *sous vide* while you enjoy the sunset.

Carlsbad and Oceanside

Beer drinkers have plenty to celebrate at the shared tables of **Pizza Port** (571 Carlsbad Village Dr., 760/720-7007, www.pizzaport.com, 11am-10pm Sun.-Thurs., 11am-midnight Fri.-Sat., $10-25). The beachy brewpub chain has won numerous awards over the years and given starts to some of the county's most successful brewers—including several who worked out of this location. Expect doughy pizza meant to soak up lots of excellent suds.

Accommodations

San Diego is a sprawling city, with a mix of neighborhoods and attractions. Hotels spring up mostly around the areas where people visit most—Downtown and the beach neighborhoods—with the exception of Balboa Park and Old Town, which would have to sacrifice charm for lodging. Mission Valley is home to most of the larger chain hotels, with rates more affordable than those downtown, but you'll need a car to see anything other than the I-8 freeway.

DOWNTOWN
Under $150

Classed up by a recent remodel, **Hostelling International San Diego, Downtown** (521 Market St., Gaslamp, 619/525-1531, www.sandiegohostels.org, $40-120) offers 60 dorm beds, 38 private rooms, and a fully equipped shared kitchen, providing clean accommodations at bargain prices. A no-alcohol policy keeps the place quiet, and reading and TV lounges offer a nice respite from exploring the dozens of bars, clubs, and restaurants within a five-block radius.

Clean, independently decorated rooms give **Hotel Vyvant** (505 W. Grape St., Little Italy, 619/230-1600, www.hotelvyvant.com, $140-190) a fair amount of charm. Quick access to the freeway and airport also make it a decent launchpad for exploring the city. The only drawback is the lack of parking, but given the nice rooms at a low rate, it could be the key to a stress-free visit—no getting lost, no designated drivers. Plus, plenty of the city's best restaurants happen to be in the neighborhood.

Porto Vista Hotel (1835 Columbia St., Little Italy, 619/544-0164, www.portovistasd.com, $120-160), an urban boutique hotel with a rooftop deck, offers a variety of options at reasonable rates. The on-site restaurant has a nice view of the harbor, as do some of the rooms. It's located in a great neighborhood with quick trolley and freeway access.

$150-250

Overlooking Petco Park, pet-friendly, LEED-certified **Hotel Indigo** (509 9th Ave., East Village, 619/371-5756, www.hotelinsd.com, $200-260) isn't just an environmentally friendly place to bring your dog and catch a ballgame. It's also centrally located to explore Downtown, or just relax on the rooftop lounge. Prices vary with a range of sleeping and view options, including rooms with a clear view of the Padres at work.

A central Little Italy location gives clean and simple ★ **La Pensione Hotel** (606 W. Date St., Little Italy, 619/236-8000, www.lapensionehotel.com, $150) a leg up, whether or not you opt for a room with a harbor view. A trolley stop is a couple of blocks away, and a short walk gets you to the Midway and Maritime Museums, not to mention all the great restaurants in the neighborhood, starting with a pizza place and café in the shared courtyard. The biggest drawback? Limited daily parking on a first-come basis.

Experience the quaint appeal of San Diego's gorgeous Craftsman homes by renting one of the fully furnished apartments of ★ **Mudville Flats** (747 10th Ave., East Village, 619/232-4045, www.mudvilleflats.com, $180-200), a 1905 boutique hotel. Rooms feature built-in shelves and wood detailing that make Craftsmans so appealing, plus private kitchens and one amenity few of those cottages can claim: air-conditioning.

Old European elegance is on display at the **Westgate Hotel** (1055 2nd Ave., Gaslamp, 619/238-1818, www.westgatehotel.com, $150-180). The lobby features vintage furniture, a curved staircase, and a grand piano. On weekends a high tea comes complete with a harpist. A third-floor roof deck adds an outdoor lounge, a swimming pool, and even a small running track—all benefit from the views of Downtown and the harbor. Good-size comfortable rooms figure nicely into

Best Accommodations

★ **La Pensione:** This Little Italy gem offers good rooms on the cheap within walking distance of the Gaslamp and the trolley (page 517).

★ **Mudville Flats:** Beautiful Craftsman-style rooms with private kitchens make the East Village a satisfying place to return to at night (page 517).

★ **Lafayette:** A stay here allows a little respite from the heavily trafficked tourist areas but is still close to evening entertainment (page 519).

★ **Hotel del Coronado:** A stay at the legendary Hotel Del is like vacationing in another era (page 520).

★ **Tower 23 Hotel:** This boutique hotel on the beach is in a lively area, with a hip restaurant and bar and convenient access to Mission Bay and Mission Beach (page 521).

★ **Lodge at Torrey Pines:** This is hallowed ground—rooms overlook the ocean and you're close to the sights and shopping of La Jolla (page 522).

the continental motif, and many share a private foyer with the room next door, great for groups booking rooms together.

Originally built as two separate hotels during the 1880s, the architecture of beautifully appointed **Horton Grand Hotel** (311 Island Ave., Gaslamp, 619/544-1886, www.hortongrand.com, $200-240) leaves a fine impression. The two buildings connect to form a graceful, shady courtyard. No two rooms are alike, though a number do offer a lovely courtyard balcony.

Over $250

Built by the family of the 18th president and named in his honor, the **U. S. Grant Hotel** (326 Broadway, 619/232-3121, www.usgrant. net, $260-300) opened in 1910 with much pomp. This classic century-old hotel offers a grand entrance: An elegant lobby presents marble floors and silk carpets, with high ceilings furnished with crystal chandeliers. A 2006 restoration renewed glamour to the place, including its 47 luxurious suites. Standard rooms go for reasonable rates, considering the style and location, though pricey parking ($40 per day) can eat into that.

Steps from the Marina, Seaport Village, Convention Center, and USS *Midway* Museum, the dual high-rises of **Manchester Grand Hyatt** (1 Market Pl., 619/232-1234, www.manchestergrand.hyatt.com, $280-330) overlook Downtown. The large rooftop pool and cabanas are a favorite of the celebrities working Comic Con each July, and the luster seems to hold most of the year. Other rooftops feature tennis, basketball and volleyball courts, and a separate lap pool. The business-friendly place has an excellent hotel bar, the penthouse Top of the Hyatt, known for panoramic views and a mostly sophisticated clientele.

BALBOA PARK AND HILLCREST
Under $150

With only nine rooms within the 19th-century **Keating House** (2331 2nd Ave., Banker's Hill, 619/239-8585, www.keatinghouse.com, $120-150), each has its own peculiar charm—and a private bath. The romantic and affordable bed-and-breakfast stands a mere four blocks from the western edge of Balboa Park in a quiet part of Banker's Hill.

Aside from a little gold-leafing, the home's colorfully painted exterior and interiors adhere to its original 1888 palette. A full breakfast is made from scratch each morning, using mostly natural and organic ingredients. Room prices remain constant year-round.

$150-250

North Park has emerged as one of San Diego's hippest neighborhoods, but the ★ **Lafayette** (2223 El Cajon Blvd., North Park, 619/296-2101, www.lafayettehotelsd.com, $200-250) was here long before it was cool. When it first opened 70 years ago, it was a popular destination for celebrities and jet-setters. Amid the recent resurgence, this historic hotel has been redesigned to bring its amenities up to par with its vintage charm. Contemporary decor and comfortable beds make all the bungalows and suites desirable—but especially those sitting poolside. Today, the Lafayette can be quite the scene, hosting pool parties in the summer, with occasional live music events during holiday weekends. Within a few blocks are North Park, Hillcrest, and University Heights restaurants and bars.

OLD TOWN
Under $150

To get into the spirit of Old Town, reserve one of the 10 guest rooms in the **Cosmopolitan Hotel** (2660 Calhoun St., 619/297-1874, www.oldtowncosmopolitan.com, $120-160), a 19th-century hotel located within the historic park. Rooms are outfitted with furnishings from the era, such as claw-foot tubs, with views of San Diego's original city center. Guests should pose for a photograph in the hotel's vintage saloon.

POINT LOMA
Under $150

Backpackers and world travelers are just as woven into the fabric of OB as surfers and Volkswagen buses blasting "Hotel California" from their cassette players. **Ocean Beach International Hostel** (4961 Newport Ave., Ocean Beach, 800/339-7263, www.californiahostel.com, $30-100) is like a "Hostel California," where a constant flow of curious young people gathers, regardless of language, to sleep in bunk beds and embrace the countercultural SoCal beach lifestyle. Adventurers tend to find an engaging temporary home here.

Mixed reviews about the condition of some of the rooms occasionally tarnish this **Ocean Beach Hotel**'s (5080 Newport Ave., Ocean Beach, 619/223-7191, www.obhotel.com, $140-200) reputation, but as far as OB is concerned, that's part of the zeitgeist. Its location cannot be beat—smack on the corner of action-packed Newport Avenue right where it hits the sand. Affordable rooms, sweet ocean views, and close proximity to the lively world of Ocean Beach will keep you living like a local: up late, rowdy, and never wanting to leave the neighborhood.

$150-200

Humphrey's Half Moon Inn (2303 Shelter Island Dr., Shelter Island, 619/224-3411, www.halfmooninn.com, $200-250) offers a unique set of views. In the distance is the San Diego skyline. Look a little closer to admire the San Diego Yacht Club boats moored just outside. But the real views are of the city's best summer concert venue. The intimate outdoor stage sits right on the water and attracts some of the world's most celebrated musicians and comedians. Room packages may be paired with front-and-center seating, and some suites open up to a balcony with the best view in the house. Regardless of whether there's a show scheduled, this is one of the most enjoyable hotels in the city.

Over $250

Believe it or not, there's a hip place to stay in Point Loma that doesn't command a harbor view. **The Pearl** (1410 Rosecrans St., Point Loma, 619/226-6100, www.thepearlsd.com, $260-300) is central to Shelter Island, but makes its mark through stylish decorating at modest rates and the sort of local-friendly hotel scene that makes dinner in the courtyard worth dressing for. In summer, the hotel hosts movie screenings, projecting cult and comedy classics on a blank wall over the swimming pool. It's a surprisingly fun way to watch a movie, and smiling crowds of savvy locals attending couldn't agree more.

CORONADO
Under $150

No two rooms are alike in **Cherokee Lodge** (964 D Ave., 619/437-1967, www.cherokeelodge.com, $120-150), an 1896 "bed and board" just a block off Orange Avenue and a short walk from Coronado Beach. The 12-bedroom property doesn't serve breakfast, instead sending guests a few doors down for a complimentary meal at Panera Bread. There's also no designated parking, though plenty of charm—and some of the more affordable rooms in the area—makes up for it.

The onetime mansion and residence of John Spreckels, one of the wealthiest and most influential men in San Diego history, the **Glorietta Bay Inn** (1630 Glorietta Blvd., 800/283-9383, www.gloriettabayinn.com, $140-200) may not seem so grandiose sitting in the shadow of the Hotel del Coronado across the street. However, opt for one of the 11 mansion rooms and you'll experience a taste of what life may have been like for the real-estate magnate. A spate of modern accommodations offers the same bayside location at more affordable rates, but all guests enjoy the splendor of the mansion's sitting room, where you can take your coffee with a little Old World opulence.

Over $250

Historically one of San Diego's finest resorts, the ★ **Hotel del Coronado** (1500 Orange Ave., 619/435-6611, www.hoteldel.com, $320-500) doesn't come cheap, but it delivers a great number of amenities and charm in addition to its incredible beachfront location. Accommodations fall into a few distinct categories. While most people may gravitate toward the rooms filling the 19th-century halls of the original all-wood Victorian structure,

these may not be the best choice for everyone. Those traveling with families might prefer the poolside **California Cabanas,** which offer more space, easier access, and more modern comfort. The modern architecture of the **Ocean Towers** may seem less appealing, but with the best ocean views and an adults-only pool, couples may prefer this to the main building. The gated **Victorian Village** is an exclusive little neighborhood of high-end villas featuring its own restaurant, parking lot, pools, and jetted tubs. Wherever you stay, you'll have access to the hotel's restaurants and shops, beach rentals, and spa services. The hotel is ideally situated to enjoy Coronado village and Downtown San Diego just across the bay, but many visitors seem content to spend their entire trip within the memorable landscape of the Del's 28 acres, just as many of Hollywood's elite have done during the resort's 125-year history.

MISSION BAY AND BEACHES
Under $150

It's tough to find fault with the moderately priced, pet-friendly **Surfer Beach Hotel** (711 Pacific Beach Dr., Pacific Beach, 858/483-7070, www.surferbeachhotel.com, $140-200), located right on the boardwalk at Pacific Beach. Standard rooms feature king or double beds, some with balconies. Amenities include on-site parking ($15) and a heated pool. Access to the surf is almost immediate, and the nightlife of PB is a just a few minutes' walk.

Over $250

How central to Pacific Beach do you want to be? **Crystal Pier Hotel** (4500 Ocean Blvd., Pacific Beach, 858/483-6983, www.crystalpier.com, $215-525) juts right out from the center of PB, and these historic, moderately appointed guest cottages sit right on top of the pier itself. Cottages feature kitchenettes and decks, with prime views of the surfers and beach life below.

Just a short distance from Belmont Park,

the **Bahia Resort Hotel** (998 W. Mission Bay Dr., Mission Bay, 858/488-0551, www.bahiahotel.com, $310-360) fronts Mission Bay, offering a laid-back bit of beachfront in contrast to the lively boardwalk and amusement park scene. Both the price point and the calm waters of the bay suit families with young children, and the resort offers some mellow activities, including a steamboat ride to the Catamaran, its sister resort across the bay.

Inspired by a trip to Hawaii, the **Catamaran Resort** (3999 Mission Blvd., Pacific Beach, 858/488-1081, www.catamaranresort.com, $310-360) captures a tropical resort atmosphere with leafy plants, colorful birds, and twice-weekly luaus along its bayside beach. Water activities are available on the placid bay, and a short walk across Mission Boulevard takes you to the Pacific side of the peninsula.

A Tempur-Pedic mattress in every room ensures ★ **Tower 23 Hotel** (723 Felspar St., Pacific Beach, 858/270-2323, www.t23hotel.com, $380-420) remains the most comfortable place to sleep in Pacific Beach. Its location fronting the boardwalk gives you plenty to do and see to earn that sleep. Guests may enjoy the view from their balconies or the shared rooftop deck, or step onto the beach from the hotel's well-appointed **JRDN** restaurant and bar. With surf lockers available, and beach and bike rentals on-site, it's a chic home base for a beachy stay in this lively part of town.

LA JOLLA
Under $150

A lot changes if you move a few blocks east of La Jolla Cove—at least the hotel rates do. **La Jolla Village Lodge** (1141 Silverado St., 858/551-2001, www.lajollavillagelodge.com, $131-184) won't win any design awards, it doesn't have a pool, and there are no luxury suites. However, complimentary parking and affordable rates make it feel like a steal this close to the action.

$150-250

Specializing in oceanview suites, **La Jolla Cove Suites** (1155 Coast Blvd., 858/459-2621, www.lajollacove.com, $180-240) offers some reasonable rates, considering the rooftop deck, heated swimming pool, and other amenities. Grab one of the few single rooms without a view for a really good deal, but you might be cranky when you realize what you're missing: a chance for balcony views of Scripps Park and the ocean off La Jolla Cove.

Bahia Resort Hotel

Over $250

The best thing about **La Jolla Shores Hotel** (8110 Camino Del Oro, 858/459-8271, www.ljshoreshotel.com, $350-380) is its location—right on La Jolla Shores, one of the best family beaches in San Diego. Guest rooms come with patios or balconies and an on-site restaurant hosts a Sunday brunch buffet. With a pool, Ping-Pong tables, and plenty of beach activities on hand, there's little chance of getting bored. A courtesy shuttle can whisk you into downtown La Jolla when you're ready to shop or dine.

With a central location in downtown La Jolla, **La Valencia Hotel** (1132 Prospect St., 858/454-0771, www.lavalencia.com, $300-350) overlooks the lovely Scripps seaside park on one side and the many shops, galleries, and restaurants of Prospect Street on the other. The Spanish Colonial beauty was built in 1926, but recent updates ensure its guests experience contemporary comforts, whether from an ocean- or garden-view room. A terraced layout keeps the entire property open to sunlight and ocean air, lending a Mediterranean feel that's tough to improve upon.

Sitting on the 18th hole of the famous Torrey Pines golf course atop cliffs overlooking the Pacific, the beautifully designed arts-and-crafts ★ **Lodge at Torrey Pines** (11480 N. Torrey Pines Rd., 858/453-4420, www.lodgetorreypines.com, $320-360) offers a wealth of amenities, including spa services, access to hiking trails in Torrey Pines Nature Reserve, and a shuttle to La Jolla's nearby village or idyllic shores. It also boasts one of the city's most highly regarded restaurants, **A. R. Valentien,** and a more casual restaurant, **The Grill.** It's rare to encapsulate so much of the San Diego experience in so luxurious a package, though none will appreciate it more than the golfers in your party. One of the hotel's greatest perks is its preferred tee times for guests at the always booked-solid Torrey Pines golf course.

Lodge at Torrey Pines

Transportation and Services

GETTING THERE
Air
Also known as Lindbergh Field, **San Diego International Airport** (SAN, 619/400-2404, www.san.org) is a centrally located urban airport a mere three miles from the city center. While the location makes it a little noisy for those living in neighborhoods under the flight path, it makes getting to and from the airport a quick trip from most parts of the city. The airport is split into two major terminals plus a small commuter terminal, hosting 20 airlines and subsidiaries.

The county-operated **McClellan-Palomar Airport** (CLD, 760/431-4646, www.sandiegocounty.gov) is served by United Express (800/864-8331, www.united.com), which operates a regular daily schedule of commuter flights between Carlsbad and Los Angeles's LAX only. It's a convenient option if you plan to spend a lot of time in North County.

The opening of a pedestrian bridge border crossing in summer 2015 has made **Tijuana International Airport** (TIJ, 52/664-607-8200, www.tijuana-airport.com) a much more convenient option for travelers visiting San Diego from cities without direct flights to San Diego, or those wishing to fly on more affordable airlines, including **Aeroméxico** (800/237-6639, www.aeromexico.com), **Interjet** (866/853-8307, www.interjet.com), **VivaAerobus** (888/935-9848, www.vivaaerobus.com), and **Volaris** (866/988-3527, www.volaris.com).

Train and Bus
Amtrak (800/872-7245, www.amtrak.com) offers daily service to and from San Diego on its *Pacific Surfliner* route, which extends up the coast, connecting to Los Angeles, Santa Barbara, and San Luis Obispo. Trains depart from the Downtown Santa Fe Depot (1050 Kettner Blvd.), with stops in Solana Beach (105 North Cedros Ave.) and Oceanside (235 South Tremont St.).

Some *Surfliner* trains also make stops in Old Town (4005 Taylor St.), Sorrento Valley (11170 Sorrento Valley Rd.), and at two stations in Carlsbad (6511 Avenida Encinas; 2775 State St.). Consult schedules online for these additional stops.

Greyhound Bus Lines (800/752-4841, www.greyhound.com) has its terminal (1313 National Ave., 619/515-1100) in Downtown San Diego's East Village, with the option to stop in Oceanside (205 S. Tremont St., 760/722-1587) or Escondido (700 W. Valley Pkwy., 760/745-6522).

GETTING AROUND
Car
San Diego is a freeway town, but getting around will be a lot less frustrating—and safer—if you know where you're going and how to get there before you hop on the road. GPS navigation services help, but the city is constantly bisected by canyons and waterways, the quickest way to get somewhere is often not a straight line.

I-5 stretches through Downtown San Diego, from the Mexican border north to La Jolla and the North County beach towns. I-5 connects to Highway 163 north through Balboa Park to both I-8 and I-805, to I-805 again farther north in Sorrento Valley, and in Oceanside to Highway 78, which leads east to San Marcos and Escondido. Driving the I-5 north of Del Mar can be a traffic nightmare during rush hour. Avoid traveling south in the morning or north in the afternoon.

Within San Diego, **I-8** offers east-west access to Ocean Beach, Mission Beach, and Mission Valley before connecting to I-805 and I-15 at its eastern points. Note that while I-5 crosses I-8 near Old Town, you cannot merge onto I-8 westbound from I-5 southbound. If you're heading to Mission Beach or Ocean

Beach from the north, exit on Sea World Drive instead.

I-15 provides access to San Diego from the northeast, and runs to Escondido, Riverside County, and eventually into Nevada and Las Vegas. This freeway is the most direct route to inland North County; in light traffic, it can take 30-60 minutes to drive the 30 miles north from Downtown to Escondido. However, I-15 suffers from impacted rush-hour traffic as commuters return home to Miramar, Mira Mesa, Poway, and Rancho Bernardo.

I-805 runs parallel to I-5 a few miles inland, passing through the North Park neighborhood in Uptown and reconnecting with I-5 just before Del Mar at Sorrento Valley. Take heed: Sorrento Valley is widely considered the city's tech hub and has the region's worst traffic during morning and afternoon rush hours (7am-9:30am and 3:30pm-6:30pm Mon.-Fri.).

CAR RENTALS

Most car rental agencies operate near the San Diego International Airport. The closest are **Hertz** (3202 N. Harbor Dr., 619/767-5700), **National** (3280 N. Harbor Dr., 888/826-6890), and **Avis** (3180 N. Harbor Dr., 619/688-5000). All are a short shuttle ride way, so Thrifty and even farther-away Enterprise are accessible enough. From the train station, **Avis** (1670 Kettner Blvd., Suite 1, 619/231-7137) is within short walking distance.

Bus and Trolley

San Diego's public transportation is operated by the **Metropolitan Transit System** (619/557-4555, www.sdmts.com), which includes buses, a trolley system, and the Coaster, a commuter rail line run by the North County Transit District that extends from Downtown San Diego to Oceanside. The **Coaster** (760/966-6500, www.gonctd.com, operating hours and schedules vary, $4-5.50 one-way) is a great way to visit Solana Beach, Encinitas, or Carlsbad. The **trolley** (one-way $2.50, all-day pass $5) operates daily, offering three color-coded routes that make a good option for visiting Downtown (all lines), Old Town

and Mission Valley (Green Line), or south to Tijuana (Blue Line).

While the bus system is extensive and runs countywide, it can be complicated and slow. The uninitiated should plan the trip in advance by visiting the **SDMTS** website (www.sdcommute.com).

The **North County Transit District** (760/966-6500, www.gonctd.com) operates the **Sprinter** (4am-9pm Mon.-Fri., 10am-6pm Sat.-Sun., $2 one-way) rail line from Oceanside to Escondido, a bus system serving mostly suburban areas, and a reservation-based shuttle, **Flex** (855/844-1454, call 30 minutes in advance, $5), which may be a handy option for those looking to get around between Encinitas and Solana Beach.

Taxi

For taxis, try **San Diego Cab** (619/226-8294) or **Yellow Cab** (619/239-8061). For traditional limos and hired cars, contact **Flex Transportation** (619/796-3539, www.flextranspo.com) or **City Captain** (619/800-3515, www.citycaptain.com).

Bicycle

Bike-sharing company **Deco Bikes** (619/297-0433, www.decobike.com) has set up automated kiosks around the city where bicycles may be rented by the half hour, then dropped off at another kiosk elsewhere in the city. Access requires a credit card and internet connection.

SERVICES

For in-person conversations and all the pamphlets you could ask for, stop by one of San Diego's many regional tourism offices: the **San Diego International Visitor Information Center** (1140 N. Harbor Dr., 619/236-1212), Downtown at the Embarcadero; **La Jolla Village Information Center** (1162 Prospect St., La Jolla, 858/454-5718); or the **California Welcome Center** (928 North Coast Hwy., Oceanside, 760/721-1101). Information is also available online at www.sandiego.org.

If an immediately life-threatening situation occurs, call **911** on any phone for emergency help, and an ambulance will respond quickly. If the ill or injured person is mobile enough to travel, you may also drive to the nearest of these emergency rooms: **UCSD Medical Center** (200 W. Arbor Dr., 858/657-7000, Hillcrest, http://health.ucsd.edu); **Scripps Memorial Hospital La Jolla** (9888 Genesee Ave., La Jolla, 858/626-4123, www.scripps.org); or **Sharp Coronado Hospital** (250 Prospect Pl., 619/522-3600, Coronado, www.sharp.com/coronado).

Palm Springs and the Deserts

Palm Springs 530
Joshua Tree. 542
Death Valley. 548

Cosmopolitan Palm Springs is a haven for residents of northern climates who come down each winter to escape the cold.

But beauty can be harsh, and nowhere is this more true than in the California deserts. Just miles away, Joshua Tree National Park sprawls across the desert landscape, featuring the strange shapes of the plant that is its namesake. The seemingly endless Mojave Desert stretches northeast across the state, with hiking trails, preserves, ghost towns, and campgrounds for the hardy traveler.

The southernmost desert is in Anza-Borrego State Park, home to ocotillo fields, palm oases, and profuse spring wildflower blooms, as well as a diverse array of wildlife.

Death Valley's barrenness is legendary. Hugging the Nevada border, this vast forbidding landscape encompasses a wealth of life—a vast variety of plants, animals, birds, and even fish. Spring is the best time to experience this contradiction, when an astonishing bloom of wildflowers brightens the desert landscape.

PLANNING YOUR TIME

Palm Springs makes a relaxing **weekend getaway**. In winter, mild temperatures lure Palm Springs visitors out for easy hikes or day trips to Joshua Tree. Anza-Borrego makes another great weekend destination. If you're a true "desert rat," plan at least a week to tour the major deserts; the distances between the parks can take hours to drive, and you'll want to spend a day or two exploring each.

Previous: Coachella Valley Preserve; Johnson Canyon. **Above:** Joshua Tree National Park.

Look for ★ to find recommended sights, activities, dining, and lodging.

Highlights

★ **Palm Springs Aerial Tramway:** For a stunning view of Palm Springs and the San Jacinto Mountains, nothing beats this exhilarating ride (page 530).

★ **Keys View:** This panoramic view is one of the best in Joshua Tree (page 544).

★ **Oasis of Mara:** Explore Joshua Tree's lush side at this fan palm oasis (page 544).

★ **Badwater Basin:** This dry lake bed is situated at the lowest elevation in the Western Hemisphere (page 548).

★ **Artist's Palette:** Nature is the ultimate artist here, where a combination of minerals paints the badlands in brilliant colors (page 549).

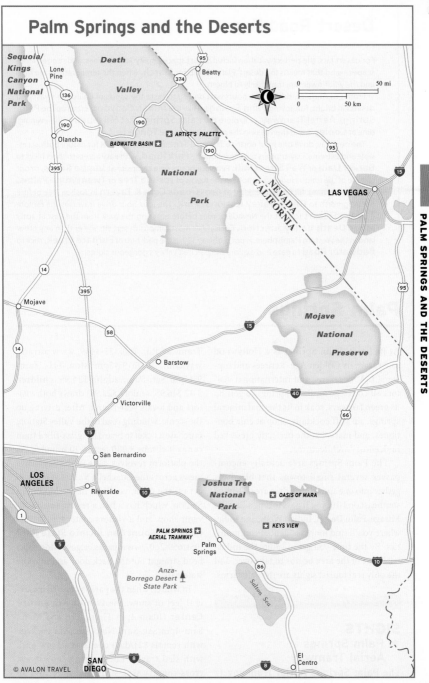

Palm Springs and the Deserts

Sequoia/
Kings
Canyon
National
Park

Lone
Pine

Death

Valley

Beatty

374

95

Olancha

136

190

190

★ ARTIST'S PALETTE

BADWATER BASIN ★

190

395

National

Park

NEVADA

CALIFORNIA

LAS VEGAS

95

0   50 mi

0   50 km

14

395

Mojave

95

58

15

Mojave

National

Preserve

14

O Barstow

40

O Victorville

66

15

O San Bernardino

**LOS
ANGELES**

O Riverside

10

**Joshua Tree
National
Park**

★ OASIS OF MARA

★ KEYS VIEW

1

PALM SPRINGS ★
AERIAL TRAMWAY

Palm
Springs

5

86

_Anza-
Borrego Desert
State Park_

Salton
Sea

10

8

**SAN
DIEGO**

8

El
Centro

© AVALON TRAVEL

Desert Road Trip

For desert rats, the perfect vacation includes vast spaces, spiky Joshua trees, and rugged landscapes—and that means the desert. Plan this trip for **March,** when the temperatures are mild and the wildflowers are most likely to bloom.

From Los Angeles, drive three hours east on I-10 to taste the sands of California's vast arid deserts in bright, fun-loving **Palm Springs.** Hike the **Indian Canyons,** crawl up the **Palm Springs Aerial Tramway,** or explore the **Palm Springs Art Museum.** In the evening, dine at **Copley's** and then soak in the retro-kitsch at the **Tonga Hut.**

The next day, drive one hour north to **Joshua Tree National Park** for nature both accessible and extreme. Day-trippers tend to follow the **Park Road,** with easy access to short hikes to **Barker Dam** or **Wall Street Mill.** Peg your hopes on a campsite at **Jumbo Rocks,** or opt for one of the unique lodging options in the towns of **Joshua Tree** or **Twentynine Palms.**

In the morning, fill up on breakfast at **Crossroads Cafe & Tavern** in Joshua Tree before heading north to **Death Valley National Park.** The four-hour drive traverses the remote **Mojave Desert** to skirt the Nevada border before entering the park from the east at aptly named **Death Valley Junction.** California's most famous desert sits lower than any other land in the Western Hemisphere. From Highway 190 in the park hub of **Furnace Creek,** stick to **Badwater Road** to gaze and explore the parched valley's gorgeous sights.

Palm Springs

At its heart, Palm Springs is a Hollywood town from its Golden Age. Retirees and hipsters, L.A. denizens, and international visitors all converge on Palm Springs to golf on its green fairways, soak in its thermal mineral springs, sip stiff cocktails, shop at chic boutiques, and marvel at the perfectly preserved midcentury architecture.

The Palm Springs area actually encompasses several small towns that bleed together into one sprawling urban area. Driving southeast on I-10, you'll pass through Rancho Mirage, Palm Desert, Indian Wells, and Indio, where you'll find more residential communities. By the time you get to Indio, the industrial part of the area begins to take over, and the only real tourist sights are the date farms.

TOP EXPERIENCE

SIGHTS
★ Palm Springs Aerial Tramway
The **Palm Springs Aerial Tramway** (1 Tramway Rd., 760/325-1449, www.pstramway.com, 10am-9:45pm Mon.-Fri., 8am-9:45pm Sat.-Sun., adults $24.95, children 3-12 $16.95, seniors $22.95) draws both visitors and locals year-round. After driving up the scenic, winding road to the Valley Station, purchase a ticket to board the glass-filled tram car as it climbs 8,000 feet in 10 minutes. As the platform revolves, take in the expansive views across the Coachella Valley. When you get off the tram, you'll be in the Mountain Station, which has a bar, a restaurant, a souvenir shop, and a visitors center for the surrounding **Mount San Jacinto State Park** (951/659-2607, www.parks.ca.gov). Most folks head straight out the back door and into the state park.

In winter, when the park is covered by several feet of snow, the **Winter Adventure Center** (10am-4pm Thurs.-Fri. and Mon., 8am-4pm Sat.-Sun. Nov.-Apr., ski package with rentals $21/day) opens as a snow park with sled tracks. Locals bring snowshoes, cross-country skis, sleds, and snow toys up on the tram (all of these are allowed in the car) for a fun few hours in the snow. In the summer, when the snow is gone, those same locals take picnic supplies and walking sticks up to the mountain for a cool day's hiking and nature loving.

Palm Springs Art Museum

The **Palm Springs Art Museum** (101 Museum Dr., 760/322-4800, www.ps-museum.org, 10am-5pm Tues.-Wed. and Fri.-Sat., noon-8pm Thurs., adults $12.50, seniors $10.50, students $5) shows off the finest modern art in a variety of media. The museum's central permanent collection is a mix of Western and Native American fine art and crafts. From local artists and craftspeople as well as those from around the Western states, these pieces evoke the sense of space and beauty found in Palm Springs and beyond. Other permanent exhibits include an ever-changing array of modern glass sculpture. The Palm Springs Art Museum also hosts an endless parade of traveling shows and special exhibitions.

Palm Springs Air Museum

Clear desert skies and vintage World War II aircraft come together at the superb **Palm Springs Air Museum** (745 N. Gene Autry Trail, 760/778-6262, http://palmspringsairmuseum.org, 10am-5pm daily, adults $16, youth and seniors $14, children 6-12 $9, 5 and under free). Three immaculate and climate-controlled hangers (a bonus on hot afternoons) showcase more than 40 flyable planes from World War II and the Korean and Vietnam Wars. The friendly and knowledgeable docents (many of whom flew similar planes during their time of service) encourage visitors to touch and explore the exhibits, and even to climb into some of the cockpits. The Youth Exploration Center features additional interactive displays and the flight simulator will thrill anyone's inner child. If you hear the wild blue yonder call, purchase a ticket to fly in the WWII C-47 Skytrain ($195 for 20 minutes), one of the planes used in the D-Day invasion of Normandy.

Moorten Botanical Garden

Visitors who've come to the desert to learn and view the variety of desert wildlife will love the **Moorten Botanical Garden** (1701 S. Palm Canyon Dr., 760/327-6555, http://moortenbotanicalgarden.com, 10am-4pm Thurs.-Tues fall, winter, and spring; 9am-1pm

view from the Palm Springs Aerial Tramway

Palm Springs and the Coachella Valley

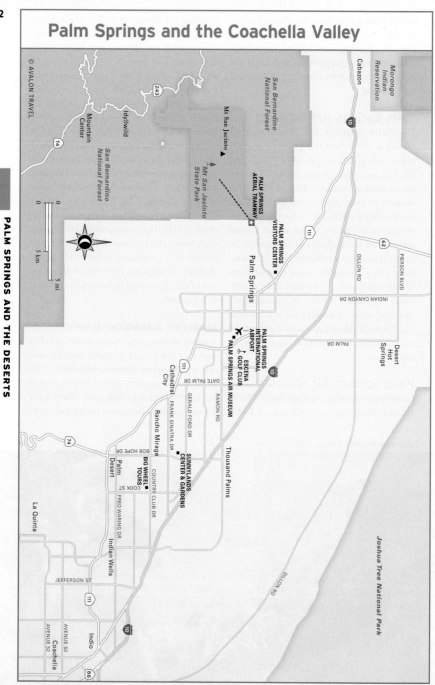

© AVALON TRAVEL

Thurs.-Tues. summer; adults $5, children $2). This charming garden specializes in cacti and succulents, growing more than 3,000 varieties of desert plants from all over the world. Wander the outdoor gardens, then head inside to the Cacterium, a greenhouse in which the more delicate specimens thrive.

The Living Desert

At **The Living Desert** (47900 Portola Ave., Palm Desert, 760/346-5694, www.living-desert.org, 9am-5pm daily Oct.-May, 8am-1:30pm daily June-Sept., adults $19.95, seniors $17.95, children $9.95), you can visit botanical gardens as well as the furry, scaly, feathered, and bald animals that inhabit the world's great deserts. The Living Desert focuses primarily on the desert habitats of Africa and the western United States. Some of the African natives, such as the gazelles and sand cats, are endangered species; others, like the meerkats, are stars of the small screen. The Discovery Center offers educational opportunities and interactive exhibits, while the WaTuTu Village focuses on the lives of human natives of desert regions.

Amenities include two restaurants, two gift shops, and restrooms. The paved paths are wheelchair- and stroller-accessible. In addition, a number of shaded spots have water misters that cool off guests during the heat of summer.

ENTERTAINMENT AND EVENTS
Bars and Clubs

For an evening of old-school Hollywood glamour, order a martini at **Melvyn's** (200 W Ramon Rd., 760/325-2323, www.inglesideinn.com, 6pm-2am daily), where Frank Sinatra, Bob Hope, and Lucille Ball were regulars. Much of the history is preserved in the black-and-white photos on the walls, solidifying its place among Hollywood elites.

Retro-cool becomes retro-kitsch at **Bootlegger Tiki** (1101 N Palm Canyon Dr., 760/318-4154, www.bootleggertiki.com, 4pm-2am daily), in the original home of "Don the Beachcomber." Red vinyl booths and blow-fish lights set the stage for exotic drinks that flame, smoke, or are drunk out of a skull-shaped glass.

The **Tonga Hut** (254 N. Palm Canyon Dr., 760/322-4449, www.tongahut.com/tonga-hut-palm-springs.html, 5pm-10pm Wed., 5pm-midnight Thurs., 4pm-2am Fri., noon-2am Sat., noon-10pm Sun.) has its own Tiki pedigree. An offshoot of the first Hollywood Tiki

Moorten Botanical Garden

Coachella Valley Date Farms

In the south part of the urban region, groves of dates provide most of the U.S. crop of the sweet Middle Eastern staple fruit. The **Oasis Date Farm** (59-111 Grapefruit Blvd., Thermal, 800/827-8017, http://oasisdategardens.com, 9am-5pm daily) in the thriving metropolis of Thermal has a good-sized storefront and a demonstration "arbor" of date palms where visitors can walk around. In the store, you can learn about the many different varieties of dates (interestingly, most dates originally came from Iraq) and taste almost all of them. You can buy whole dates, mixed boxes, and date candies. Over at the ice-cream counter, the one thing you simply must try is the date shake—a super-sweet regional specialty that's perfect on both hot summer and mild winter days. Out in the orchard, you'll see how dates cluster and grow as you enjoy a few minutes in the shade of the thickly fronded palm trees.

Another famous date orchard that's open to the public is the **Shields Date Garden** (80-225 Hwy. 111, Indio, 800/414-2555, www.shieldsdategarden.com, 9am-5pm daily) in Indio. The café serves breakfast and lunch, and the oasis-like garden is a pleasant walk adorned with unique sculptures of biblical scenes.

bar that opened in 1958, the Tonga Hut has all the requisite cocktail umbrellas and Tiki totems. To feel really in the know, look for the secret doorway through the old-fashioned phone booth.

For the latest definition of cool, step into hipster **BAR** (340 N Palm Canyon Dr., 760/537-7337, www.barwastaken.com, 5pm-midnight Sun.-Thurs., 5pm-2am Fri.-Sat.). Inside the darkly lit bar, DJs spin tunes while bartenders pour a dizzying array of whiskey. As with any good hipster institution, BAR's food menu has star status, particularly its bacon-wrapped dates and pizza.

Gay and Lesbian

Even in gala Palm Springs, **Toucan's Tiki Lounge** (2100 N. Palm Canyon Dr., 760/416-7584, www.toucanstikilounge.com) draws notice. A locals' favorite, this Tiki-themed nightspot has go-go dancers, a tiny dance floor that gets crowded on weekends, and a drag show every Sunday night. Bring a friend or four to make the most of a night out at Toucan's Live Shows.

To dance the night away, join the crowd at **Hunters Nightclub** (302 E. Arenas Rd., 760/323-0700, http://hunterspalmsprings. com, 10am-2am daily), which also hosts weekly events such as karaoke and trivia

contests. Fur Fridays keep the party from getting old.

Alibi Azul (369 N. Palm Canyon Dr., 760/325-5533, www.alibiazul.com, 4pm-close daily) brings the party uptown. At 4pm, the doors open for happy hour; after that, it's anyone's guess. Pool, drag shows, bingo, karaoke, cabaret variety acts, and DJs–Alibi Azul has something for everyone.

The queen of the nightclubs is **Copa** (244 E. Amado Rd., 760/866-0021, http://copapalmsprings.com, 6pm-11:30pm daily). The U-shaped bar may be where the action is, but the stage is the big draw. Everyone from local musicians to drag show queens strut their stuff. After the show, the tables are cleared away and DJs get the floor pumping.

Channeling its history as a Rat Pack hangout, the **Purple Room** (1900 E. Palm Canyon Dr., 760/322-4422, www.purpleroompalmsprings.com, 4pm-close Tues.-Sun.) bills itself as a supper club with local acts filling the bill during the week, while bigger names take the stage on the weekends. Expect plenty of Judy Garland and Joan Rivers tributes.

Festivals and Events

Modernism Week (www.modernismweek. com, Feb.) is the ideal time to explore the city's midcentury chic. The event features architectural walking tours, visits to iconic homes, a film and lecture series, vintage fashion and travel trailer exhibitions, and a special expedition to Sunnylands, the wonderland known as the "Camp David of the West." Even if you're not a midcentury nut, the city puts on its prettiest face for the event.

A perennial favorite for music lovers is the **Coachella Valley Music Festival** (Empire Polo Field, 81-800 Ave. 51, Indio, 888/833-1031, www.coachella.com, 3-day pass $459), where concertgoers immerse themselves in live music from sunup to sundown. The festival runs two long weekends each spring (usually Apr.), and includes art installations and plenty of pop-up restaurants. The fun rarely stops after the music ends, so many choose to camp at the festival. Check the website for music lineups, gate-opening hours, and current ticket prices.

Palm Springs holds many gay- and lesbian-themed events each year. The annual **Greater Palm Springs Pride Parade** (www.pspride.org, Nov.) is plenty of fun, as is the **Dinah Shore Weekend** (http://thedinah.com, Apr.), held especially for women. But, break out your best whites for the annual **White Party** (277 Avenida Caballeros, www.jeffreysanker.com, Apr.), a weeklong event of pool parties, after-hours clubs, and plenty of happening nights. The Saturday night White Party hosts up to 20,000 white-clad men intent on dancing the night away to fabulous, top-end DJs. Drag and dance shows light up the stage throughout the evening, while side lounges offer spots to kick back and relax. The White Party typically runs 9pm-5am, with an after-party for the seriously dedicated.

SHOPPING
Uptown Design District
Part of the fun of Palm Springs is browsing the stylish boutique wares, and the **Uptown Design District** (N. Palm Canyon Dr. between El Alameda and Alejo Rd.) is the hippest place to go. **Trina Turk** (891 N Palm Canyon Dr., 760/416-2856, www.trinaturk.com, 10am-6pm Mon.-Sat., 11am-5pm Sun.) is

considered the godmother of the district, with chic women's clothing and home furnishings. Next door, men can find some threads at **Wil Stiles** (875 N. Palm Canyon Dr., 760/327-9764, www.wilstiles.com, 10am-5pm Mon.-Sat., noon-5pm Sun.), which is equally hip and bold. To take a piece of midcentury with you, visit **Just Modern** (901 N. Palm Canyon Dr., 760/322-5600, www.justmoderndecor.com, 10am-5pm Sun.-Fri., 10am-6pm Sat.), where bold colors, simple lines, and plenty of kitsch inform its wide array of home decor.

In this growing swath of upmarket real estate, you'll also find countless design studios, galleries, and delectable eats. **VillageFest** (http://villagefest.org, 7pm-10pm Thurs.) transforms the Uptown area into an open-air market, with vendors, street food, and artists.

El Paseo Shopping District
Big retail names can be found at **El Paseo** (El Paseo bet. Lupine and Larkspur Lns., Palm Desert, http://palmsprings.com/el-paseo). You'll find Saks Fifth Avenue, Brooks Brothers, and Burberry, plus nearly 300 shops, galleries, salons, and restaurants on both sides of the legendary shopping street. El Paseo also hosts a number of festivals each year, and weekly Art Walks during the winter high season.

SPORTS AND RECREATION
Hiking
The **Indian Canyons** (38500 South Palm Canyon Dr., 760/323-6018, www.palm-springs.com, 8am-5pm daily Oct.-June, 8am-5pm Fri.-Sun. July-Sept., adults $9, children $5), the home of the ancestors of the Agua Caliente Cahuilla Native Americans, are open to excellent hiking. The most popular is **Palm Canyon,** an aptly named 15-mile-long oasis of color, water, and beauty. A paved footpath makes it easy to explore the palms, wildflowers, and creek that feeds the canyon. A ranger-led one-mile hike ($3) offers a chance to learn more about the canyon.

A beautiful and well-traveled spot,

Tahquitz Canyon (500 W. Mesquite Rd., 760/416-7044, www.tahquitzcanyon.com, 7:30am-5pm daily Oct.-June, 7:30am-5pm Fri.-Sun, July-Sept., adults $12.50, children $6) holds a waterfall that cascades 60 feet down into a pool. The fall is seasonal, so come in spring to see the show. Operated by the Cahuilla tribe, Tahquitz Canyon has its own visitors center, complete with an interpretive exhibit, short educational film, an observation deck, and some archaeological artifacts.

Located at the top of the Aerial Tramway, **Mount San Jacinto State Park** (25905 Hwy. 243, 951/659-2607, www.parks.ca.gov, daily 8am-4pm) offers 14,000 acres of hiking, camping, and winter snow play only 10 minutes from Palm Springs. The gondola ride climbs 2.5 miles to the Mountain Station at 6,000 feet. A short walk from the tram station is the Long Valley ranger station, with a picnic area and restrooms, an adventure center, nature trails, and the Desert View Trail (2 miles, easy) overlooking Palm Springs and the Coachella Valley. To reach the **Desert View Trail,** follow the park's nature trail to where it joins Desert View.

Indian Canyons

Golf

Palm Springs' golf courses are integral to the town's oasis allure. **Indian Canyons Golf Resort** (1097 Murray Canyon Dr., 760/833-8700, www.indiancanyonsgolf.com, $45-125) was the first 18-hole course here, opening in 1961. Rat Pack regulars and two U.S. presidents (Ford and Reagan) have played here. The course is divided into the North and South courses. The North is a long par-72 course and is highlighted by the copper Disney fountain that shoots water 100 feet in the air. The shorter South Course is considered the "women's favorite," studded with graceful palms and four ponds.

The equally beautiful **Tahquitz Creek Golf Resort** (1885 Golf Club Dr., 760/328-1005, www.tahquitzgolfresort.com, $26-80) offers two courses each designed by William F. Bell. **Mesquite** (2700 E. Mesquite Ave., 800/727-8331, www.palmsprings.com/golf/mesquite.html, $22-55) is where Bob Hope used to bring his friends. This 18-hole, par-72 course has a slightly more casual dress code.

Spas

Just as lush fairways and chic style are a part of the Palm Springs DNA, personal pampering is a key part of the desert experience. Begin your treatment at the sleek **Estrella Spa** (415 S. Belardo Rd., 877/760-0846, www.avalon-palmsprings.com, $105-195) with a dip in the spa's three pools, followed by reflexology, deep tissue, or Swedish massage. At the **Feel Good Spa at Ace Hotel & Swim Club** (701 E. Palm Canyon Dr., 760/866-6188, www.acehotel.com), indulgence comes au naturel. Seaweed body wraps, hot rock massages, healing energy, and vibrations are some items on the crunchy spa menu.

Cheekiness doesn't come cheap at the ultra-stylish **Spa at the Parker Palm Springs** (4200 E. Palm Canyon Dr., 760/321-4606, www.theparkerpalmsprings.com/spa, $195-440). Choose from a multitude of massages, facials, waxing, and mani-pedis, or dive in for one of the overindulgent packages. Popular with the jet-set crowd, the spa exudes an over-the-top British colonial decadence.

To dip your toes into some actual springs, book a massage at **Two Bunch Palms** (67425 Two Bunch Palms Trail, Desert Hot Springs, 760/329-8791, www.twobunchpalms.com, $90-135) for access to this true oasis sitting above the Desert Hot Springs Aquifer. The pools are surrounded by lush vegetation and you're apt to see a surprising variety of wildlife. If the soothing waters, Watsu Massage, and mud bath don't heal what ails you, book an appointment with the resident shaman.

FOOD
Breakfast and Cafés
In the chic Uptown Design District, the only place to start your day is the hip ★ **Ernest Coffee** (1101 N. Palm Canyon Dr., 760/318-4154, www.ernestcoffee.com, 6am-7pm daily). The Stumptown coffee, dripped or pulled, will wake anyone up, and the assortment of bagels, doughnuts, and pastries helps soak up that extra espresso shot while lounging on the outdoor patio. Wine and light snacks in the afternoon make this a 21-and-over coffee shop (seriously). At 4pm, watch out as part of the space transforms into the Bootlegger Tiki Bar.

Deciding what to order at breakfast-favorite **Cheeky's** (622 N. Palm Canyon Dr. 760/327-7595, www.cheekysps.com, 8am-2pm Thurs.-Mon., $6-16) is no small task. House-made pastries twirled in sugar, bacon flights, paleo granola, strawberry waffles, and custard cheesy eggs fill the menu, but the indoor/outdoor patio is the perfect place, over coffee or a specialty morning cocktail, to make that decision. Lunch is a bit more straightforward, with salads, burgers, and sandwiches.

You know what you're going to get at **Elmer's Pancake House** (1030 E. Palm Canyon Dr., 760/327-8419, www.eatatelmers.com, 6am-9pm daily, $6-20). Crepes, omelets, Benedicts, and a variety of pancakes are served in the morning. Lunch and dinner is your standard American fare in this small chain diner.

In the Smoke Tree Village Shopping Center, **Native Foods** (1775 E. Palm Canyon Dr., Ste. F, 760/416-0070, www.nativefoods.com, 11am-9pm daily, $10) is a vegan restaurant offering a large menu of salads, sandwiches, soups, and delicious desserts. You'll find tasty seitan, faux meats and tempeh, as well as bean dishes, veggie pizzas, and Middle Eastern-inspired cuisine.

American
Tyler's Burgers (149 S. Indian Canyon Dr., 760/325-2990, www.tylersburgers.com, 11am-4pm Mon.-Sat., $7-10, cash only) is the "it" spot for burgers and milkshakes. This laid-back burger joint serves fantastic potato salad and coleslaw to go alongside its paper-wrapped hot sandwiches. Inside the charming eatery, you'll find plenty of bar seating. You can also take your food outside and snag a wood table on the covered patio.

Asian
Friday evening happy hour at **Wang's in the Desert** (424 S. Indian Canyon Dr., 760/325-9264, www.wangsinthedesert.com, 5pm-9pm Mon.-Thurs., 5pm-10pm Fri.-Sat., 3pm-9pm Sun., $16-25) tends to draw a big and mostly gay crowd, but if you're looking for great Chinese food, you'll find it here too. Wang's puts its own stamp on the cuisine with unique appetizers and entrées. Make reservations a couple of days in advance; Wang's gets crowded with locals at dinnertime, especially on weekends.

California Cuisine
In the Uptown Design District, the superbly modern **Trio** (707 N. Palm Canyon Dr., 760/864-8746, www.triopalmsprings.com, 11am-10pm Mon.-Thurs., 11am-11pm Fri., 10am-11pm Sat., 10am-10pm Sun., $16-28) has an upscale feel without astronomical prices. For dinner, order the burger, opt for the three-course prix fixe (served 11am-6pm daily, $20), or try the pot roast, roast chicken, ribs, or mac

'n' cheese. The cocktail menu is where Trio really struts its stuff, while the lunch menu offers the best variety.

From the highly epicurean menu, it is clear that **Workshop Kitchen and Bar** (800 N. Palm Canyon Dr., 760/459-3451, www.work-shoppalmsprings.com, dinner 5pm-11pm Sun.-Thurs. and 5pm-midnight Fri.-Sat., brunch 10am-2:30pm Sun., $26-38) has perfected its craft, but the severe space is a far cry from any workshop. High-backed booths stretch to the ceiling and line both sides of a dining room cast in unadorned concrete, which gives this James Beard award-winning design a church-like atmosphere. The relaxed back patio is ideal for Sunday brunch.

Whether you are an early bird or a night owl, vegan or paleo, desiring comfort food or something exotic, **Lulu's** (200 S. Palm Canyon Dr., 760/327-5858, www.lulupalm-springs.com, 8am-10pm Sun.-Thurs., 8am-1am Fri.-Sat., $12-30) has something for you. The indoor-outdoor space is as expansive as the menu.

Italian

If pizza means deep dish, **Giuseppes Pizza & Pasta** (Smoke Tree Village Shopping Center, 1775 E. Palm Canyon Dr., 760/537-1890, www. giuseppesps.com, 11am-9pm Sun.-Thurs., 11am-9:30pm Fri.-Sat., $15-30) is the place. Order house-made, Italian comfort food such as thin-crust pizza, pasta dishes, salads, big meaty platters, and appetizers. Wine, beer, and a full bar help wash it all down.

At the polished **Appetito Cal-Italian Deli** (1700 S. Camino Real #2, 760/327-1929, www. appetitodeli.com, 11am-10pm Sun.-Thurs., 11am-11pm Fri.-Sat., $10-20), located next to the Ace Hotel, grab a premade gourmet lunch to take on your adventure or a pizzette to share over a bottle of wine on the spacious back patio.

Seafood

Don't expect Chinese food at ★ **Shanghai Red's** (235 S. Indian Canyon Dr., 760/322-9293, www.fishermans.com, 5pm-10pm Mon.-Thurs., 5pm-11:30pm Fri., 11am-4pm and 5pm-11:30pm Sat., 11am-4pm and 5pm-10pm Sun., $5-35). Instead you'll find the Anthony Bourdain-acclaimed fish tacos, as well as a whole menu of American-style sea-food. Hidden behind the Fisherman's Market, this small seafood joint has a full bar, live music, outdoor seating, and a cultivated divvy atmosphere.

Fine Dining

On the former estate of Cary Grant, **Copley's on Palm Canyon** (621 N. Palm Canyon Dr., 760/327-9555, www.copleyspalmsprings.com, 5:30pm-close daily Oct.-May, call for summer hours, $22-40) offers fine dining with an eye toward global and tropical flavors. The elegant dining room and the outdoor patio make the most of its 1940 location.

For a meal in a beautifully lit, tree-covered patio, there's no better place than **Spencer's** (701 W. Baristo Rd., 760/327-3446, www. spencersrestaurant.com, 8am-2:30pm and 5pm-10pm daily, $15-38). A Palm Springs institution, the restaurant is elegant without being stuffy or exclusive. Breakfast, lunch, and dinner menus are expansive and have something for everyone.

ACCOMMODATIONS
$100-150

Pools, palms, and 1960s Tiki kitsch come to-gether at the fun-loving **Caliente Tropics** (411 E. Palm Canyon Dr., 760/327-1391, www. calientetropics.com, $50-160). The rooms are a grade above standard hotel accommoda-tions, but the convenient location plus ame-nities like a spa, restaurant and bar, and a pool with private cabanas make it a great bargain.

$150-250

Once a resident hotel in Palm Springs's hey-day, the ★ **Orbit In** (562 W. Arenas Rd., 760/323-3585 or 877/996-7248, www.orbitin. com, $170-270) has maintained its midcen-tury roots. Facing the rectangular saltwater pool and bar, each of the nine studio rooms is sparely decorated to enhance the modern vibe. Expect French-press coffee and a complimentary continental breakfast in the morning and a gratis poolside cocktail hour in the evening.

Channeling a more distant past is the **Hotel California** (424 E. Palm Canyon Dr., 800/642-7079, www.palmspringshotelcalifornia.com, $159-240). The Mission-style inn centers around a courtyard and pool lush with banana trees and birds of paradise. Tile work, wrought iron, and bubbling fountains complete the Californio atmosphere.

Bright colors splash against the arid backdrop of the San Jacinto Mountains at **The Saguaro** (1800 E. Palm Canyon Dr., 760/323-4441, www.thesaguaro.com/palm-springs, $200-300). The pool party vibe might not be for everyone (particularly on Coachella weekends), but for some the outdoor fun—enhanced by yoga, a spa, and the poolside bar—is ideal.

The **Del Marcos Hotel** (225 W. Baristo Rd., 760/325-6902, www.delmarcoshotel.com, $150-210) is a small boutique hotel that has won awards for its dedication to preserving its midcentury modern design. The guest room decor screams late 1940s and early 1950s, complete with prints of Hollywood idols of the time. With only 16 rooms, the Del Marcos feels more like an inn; it's convenient to the shops and restaurants of Palm Canyon Drive.

Over $250

The hipster hangout is definitely **Ace Hotel & Swim Club** (701 E. Palm Canyon Dr., 760/325-9900, www.acehotel.com/palm-springs, $250-460), complete with art, bingo, a dog park, and Stumptown coffee. Artisanal cocktails are served in the bar, where DJs spin nightly and a stuffed grizzly hovers above the whiskey selection. The economy rooms have a vaguely teenager-room feel, while larger suites grow up with sleek fireplaces and cool sitting areas. True to its name there is a large pool and hot tub, both open for night swimming.

The **Movie Colony Hotel** (726 N. Indian Canyon Dr., 888/953-5700, www.moviecolonyhotel.com, $260-339) takes its price tag seriously and kicks its midcentury style up a notch. Designed in 1935 by Albert Frey, the compound is vintage-meets-modern luxury. Rooms tend toward simple elegance in white and neutral colors, while the poolside bar and fire pit lets you know you've arrived.

Colony Palms Hotel (572 N. Indian Canyon Dr., 760/969-1800 or 800/557-2187, www.colonypalmshotel.com, $259-499) has a storied history that includes names like Ronald Reagan, Jack Dempsey, Seabiscuit, and Al Wertheimer, a notorious member of the Purple Gang. Rich Moroccan flourishes of carved wood, red accents, and bold patterns retain the Hollywood allure, as do the oversized pool and spa. The on-site restaurant, the Purple Palm, serves additional helpings of glamour, along with oysters, duck, and Bavette steak.

Bold patterns and bright colors can be found at the **Riviera Palm Springs** (1600 N. Indian Canyon Dr., 760/327-8311, www.rivierapalmsprings.com, $200-300). This large and stylish hotel has nearly 400 rooms and 73 suites, plus two pools, a spa, a restaurant and two lounges, and caters somewhat to business travelers and conferences.

At **Parker Palm Springs** (4200 E. Palm Canyon Dr., 760/770-5000, www.parkerpalmsprings.com, $259-1,575), you can sleep in the modest two-bedroom home of Gene Autry, but don't expect any wagon wheel coffee tables. High style is taken very seriously (although not without a sense of humor) at this chic compound. Expect plenty of modern flourishes and a variety of accommodations, plus croquet, tennis courts, two outdoor pools (one saltwater, one kid friendly), an indoor warm pool, spa, and swank dining options.

Gay and Lesbian Resorts

Whisking your partner away for a luxurious long weekend? Book a suite at **The Hacienda at Warm Sands** (586 Warm Sands Dr., 800/359-2007, www.thehacienda.com, $229-329). At this small resort you'll have plenty of privacy with large suites, secluded patios, and enough in-room amenities that you'll never have to leave. For extra pampering, massages are available in the garden. Both pools are clothing optional and a continental breakfast is included.

INNdulge (601 Grenfall Rd., 760/327-1408, http://inndulge.com, $195-225) wants you to do just that. Outdoor misters, a saltwater pool, and an oversized hot tub surrounded by 24 stylish rooms create this party-like retreat. Suites include kitchens.

To make the most of the desert's mid-century style, stay at the clothing-optional **Century Palm Springs** (598 Grenfall Rd., 800/475-5188, www.centurypalmsprings. com, $199-249). Built in 1955 as an apartment building, the nine-room resort had a complete makeover and is now deliciously decorated in bold colors and modern lines. Rooms boast Egyptian sheets, refrigerators, and bathrobes and open out to the pool.

At the **East Canyon Hotel and Spa** (288 E. Camino Monte Vista, 877/324-6835, www. eastcanyonps.com, $169-239), expect a low-key, grown-up elegance. Rooms and suites with an almost Eastern simplicity circle the pool, and a full spa offers massages, body wraps, and facials.

For the ladies, the **Queen of Hearts** (435 E. Avenida Olancha, 760/322-5793, www. queenofheartsps.com, $120-160) is one of the oldest lesbian resorts in Palm Springs. The nine rooms include designer appointments, queen beds, full kitchens, and comfortable bathrooms. Amenities include a sparkling courtyard pool and an outdoor above-ground whirlpool tub.

A tight collection of suites and cozy villas, **Casitas Laquita** (450 E. Palm Canyon Dr., 760/416-9999, www.casitaslaquita.com, $165-250) is like a small, well-appointed Mexican village. White stucco and red-tile roofs and narrow paths lined with palms and cacti provide the perfect retreat. Many accommodations have full kitchens, fireplaces, private patios, and hot tubs, but the central pool and courtyard is open to all.

Camping

Mount San Jacinto State Park (25905 Hwy. 243, 800/444-7275, www.reserveamerica.com, $20-45) is home to a few primitive and backpacking campgrounds not far from the upper tramway terminal (backcountry permits are required). Those who want the comfort of car camping can pick from two developed campgrounds several miles apart near the town of Idyllwild. The closest, appropriately named Idyllwild, has the most amenities, including showers; the other is Stone Creek, which borders the San Bernardino National Forest.

TRANSPORTATION AND SERVICES

The **Palm Springs International Airport** (3400 E. Tahquitz Canyon Way, 760/318-3800, www.palmspringsairport.com) offers flights with most major carriers and a few minor airlines.

The **SunLine Transit Agency** (800/347-8628, www.sunline.org, $1-6) runs a number of bus lines throughout the Palm Springs region, from Desert Hot Springs down through Palm Springs proper, into Indio and all the way down to Coachella and Thermal. A route map is available online.

From Los Angeles, I-10 is the most direct route east, running through Palm Springs and down through Indio, then out east past the South Entrance of Joshua Tree. Palm Canyon Drive is the main drag through downtown Palm Springs. Plan at least two hours for the drive from L.A. (more in rush hour traffic).

Perhaps the most striking visitors center in the state, the **Palm Springs Visitors Center** (2901 N. Palm Canyon Dr., 760/778-8418, www.visitpalmsprings.com, 9am-5pm daily) is worth a stop even if just to ogle the Albert Frey building. Once a gas station and conveniently located at the base of the tramway, the visitors center now offers everything you need to enjoy the area, including real opinions on local attractions and restaurants, and the lowdown on the best events and parties while in town.

Anza-Borrego Desert State Park

Located south of Palm Springs (and east of San Diego) is the largest state park in California. Yet it receives fewer visitors, but has more services, than its more famous neighbors to the north. **Anza-Borrego Desert State Park** (760/767-5311, www.parks.ca.gov) encompasses 600,000 acres of desert wilderness surrounding the town of Borrego Springs. The park features miles of hiking trails and slot canyons, developed and primitive campgrounds, and a popular off-road area for OHV enthusiasts. Bighorn sheep dot the canyon walls, hidden waterfalls and palm oases nestle out of sight, and an epic wildflower show erupts every spring.

SIGHTS

First-time visitors should start at the underground **Visitors Center** (200 Palm Canyon Dr., 760/767-4205, www.parks.ca.gov, 9am-5pm daily Oct.-May, 9am-5pm Sat.-Sun. only June-Sept.) for maps, road conditions, trail updates, and park information. An interpretive desert garden surrounds the center, where you'll learn the names of many regional plants and animals. From the visitors center, walk (or drive) to the trailhead for the **Borrego Palm Canyon**, where an easy three-mile loop trail leads to a surprising and lovely desert palm oasis.

From the visitors center, follow Palm Canyon Drive east through the small town of Borrego Springs, stopping to explore the **Galleta Meadows** (Borrego Springs Rd., www.galletame-adows.com, free). Scattered about the valley floor, saber-toothed tigers chase rearing elephants while a 350-foot serpent snakes across the road. These enormous metallic sculptures are the work of artist Ricardo Breceda and are easily accessible via park roads. Pick up a map at the visitors center.

As the road heads east, it becomes the Borrego Salton Seaway (S-22). In 10 miles, the turn for **Font's Point** offers a dramatic perspective of the Borrego Badlands. From the overlook, the geologic formation of the desert lies below—the view is truly stunning. Access is via four miles of sandy road; it's usually passable by standard vehicles, but check at the visitors center.

CAMPING AND FOOD

Campgrounds (800/444-7275, www.reserveamerica.com, $25) include **Borrego Palm Canyon**, a large campground with more than 100 sites, plus showers and restrooms, and **Tamarisk Grove** (S-3 and Hwy. 78), with 27 RV sites, showers, and toilets

The town of Borrego Springs has several dining options. A favorite for breakfast, **Red Ocotillo** (721 Ave. Sureste, 760/767-7400, www.thepalmsatindianhead.com, 7am-8:30pm daily, $10-20) sits tucked away off Christmas Circle. Lunch and dinner items run to classic American entrées.

Hidden away in The Mall, **Carmelitas Mexican Grill** (575 Palm Canyon Dr., 760/767-5666, 10am-9pm daily, $10-20) serves fresh, authentic Mexican cuisine in a friendly and relaxed setting.

Carlee's (660 Palm Canyon Dr., 760/767-3262, www.carleesplace.com, 11am-10pm Sun.-Thurs., 11am-midnight Fri.-Sat., $10-25) is a Borrego mainstay, serving beer and burgers for decades.

GETTING THERE

The drive to Anza-Borrego State Park takes about 1.5 hours from Palm Springs. Take I-10 south for 6.5 miles to Highway 86 (around Indio). Continue south on Highway 86 for about 50 miles. At the intersection with S-22 (Borrego-Salton Seaway), turn right and continue 28 long desert miles to the town of Borrego Springs. If you need gas, the Highway 86 intersection is the last place to get it.

Joshua Tree

Joshua Tree National Park (760/367-5500, www.nps.gov/jotr, $20), and its namesake "trees," lies just east of Palm Springs and offers easy access from the Los Angeles area. The northern half of the park sits in the high-altitude Mojave Desert. But as the park's lands stretch south, they also dip down into the lower-set Colorado Desert. While many visitors stick exclusively to the north end of the park, it's worth the time to drive the main park road south to check out a really different desert region.

SIGHTS

Black Rock Canyon

In the northwest corner of the park, just south of the town of Yucca Valley, **Black Rock Canyon** (Joshua Ln., Hwys. 62 and 247) makes a great introduction to the park. The **Black Rock Nature Center** (9800 Black Rock Canyon Rd., 8am-4pm Sun.-Thurs., noon-8pm Fri.), a developed **campground,** and hiking trails are all surrounded by the park's famed Joshua trees. First-time visitors often walk the **Hi-View Nature Trail** (1.3 miles), a lovely interpretive stroll that describes the regional plants. Black Rock Canyon also includes a trailhead for a 35-mile stretch of the California Riding and Hiking Trail and several other longer hiking trails. Check in at the ranger station for a wilderness permit if you plan to go backpacking in the area.

Hidden Valley

In the center of Joshua Tree, the **Hidden Valley** (Park Blvd., 10 miles south of West Entrance) offers hikes, a **campground,** and a rare view of a tiny desert valley. Park in the day lot and follow the nature trail (1 mile) onto and through big tan boulders. You'll scramble up, getting a great up-close view of the surprising granite mineral content of the pale boulders on either side of you. Emerge from the rocky trail into a small, rocky, meadowlike area, which includes small signs describing the natural features.

Keys Ranch

William and Frances Keys were among the rugged settlers of the Mojave Desert. They ranched on the sparse desert grasses and raised five children on this patch of ranch that would become part of Joshua Tree. Today, the only way to get a look at **Keys Ranch** (Keys Ranch Rd., reservations 760/367-5522, www.nps.gov/jotr, 10am and 2pm Wed. and Fri.-Sun. Oct.-May, adults and students $10, children 6-11 $5, under 6 free) is to take a docent-guided tour of the buildings and land. Visitors will see the weathered pine buildings that housed the original ranch house, the schoolhouse that educated the few local children, the local general store, and a workshop. The orchard and landscaping have been replanted and revived. A collection of mining and farm equipment sits in the dry desert air, and relics like the old well dot the property here. Advanced reservations are recommended, but you may also purchase tickets a day in advance at the Joshua Tree and Oasis Visitor Centers.

Cap Rock and Skull Rock

Among the wonders of Joshua Tree are fabulous boulder formations scattered about the landscape. Driving south on Park Boulevard through Hidden Valley, you'll pass **Cap Rock** (0.4 mile) and its interesting geology. A small picnic area sports a good spot to watch rock climbers scramble, as does a short interpretive loop trail.

Continuing east on Park Boulevard, look for one of the jumble of giant stones that provide shade at the aptly named Jumbo Rocks campground. From the campground, a short 1.5-mile interpretive trail leads to **Skull Rock,** with its spooky hollow eyes.

Joshua Tree and the Yucca Valley

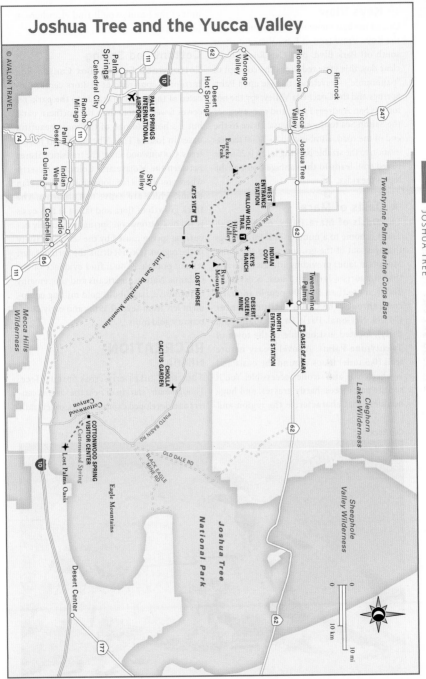

© AVALON TRAVEL

★ Keys View

One of the best views in all of Joshua Tree is the **Keys View** (end of Keys View Rd., bear south off Park Blvd. past Cap Rock). On a clear day, this view redefines the concept of "panoramic"—travelers will gaze upon Palm Springs and the Coachella Valley, spy the notorious San Andreas Fault, and may even see the Salton Sea to the southeast. Drive to the end of the road, climbing up to 5,000 feet elevation to the sizable parking lot. A 0.25-mile paved trail leads to the vantage point at the top of the ridge.

★ Oasis of Mara

The **Oasis of Mara** (Hwy. 62 and Utah Trail) is home to a number of small springs that well out of the ground along the Pinto Mountain fault, providing life-giving water that supports a large and lush ecosystem. Today, more than 140,000 people annually come through the **Oasis Visitors Center** (74485 National Park Dr., 8:30am-5pm daily), located just outside of the town of Twentynine Palms. A lovely, easy nature trail (0.5 mile) loops around the oasis and is wheelchair and stroller accessible. You'll see the palm trees, hardy grasses, and huge boulders that characterize the region and hint at the beauty you'll find elsewhere in Joshua Tree.

Cottonwood Spring

Cottonwood Spring (Box Canyon Rd., turn onto spur road at visitors center), located at the South Entrance to the park, receives fewer visitors than the northern park, but it's home to one of the most beautiful oases in Joshua Tree. The catch? No Joshua trees. Cottonwood sits at the transitional area between the Mojave and Colorado Deserts, where you'll see a fabulous grove of desert fan palms, which are native to California. The thick growth of flora and fauna at this oasis is fed by Cottonwood Spring, a naturally occurring spring caused by the seismic activity in the region. (Do not drink the spring water; it's not potable.) You'll find evidence of the Cahuilla Native Americans and the remains of primitive, hand-built gold milling equipment left from several 19th- and early 20th-century gold mills.

RECREATION
Hiking

Numerous hikes crisscross Joshua Tree. Though many start in or near the visitors centers and developed campgrounds, other trails

Cap Rock

begin off the paved and unpaved roads of the park. Before beginning your hike, load up on water (up to two gallons per person), pick up a trail map at the visitors center, and pack food or light snacks. Joshua Tree National Park is a harsh and unforgiving desert; even a short hike can have dire consequences for the unprepared. Talk to park rangers about safety, weather, and trail conditions before you head out.

A number of trails start at the **Black Rock Canyon** campground. To reach the summit of **Eureka Peak** (10 miles round-trip, 4-5 hours), take the California Riding and Hiking Trail to the Eureka Peak Trail. You'll ascend 1,500 feet on this trek up to some of the most beautiful views in the park. Another option is the **Panorama Loop** (7.4 miles round-trip, 4-5 hours), also off the Black Rock Canyon Trail. Be sure to bring your camera!

In the Hidden Valley area at the center of the park, the easy trail to **Barker Dam** (1.3 miles, 30 min.) provides a quick scenic loop to a small pond amid boulders and Joshua trees. From the same trailhead, you can also hike to the ruins of the **Wall Street Mill** (3 miles round-trip, 1.5 hours). Follow Park Boulevard south to climb **Ryan Mountain** (3 miles round-trip, 1.5 hours), a popular trek to a view-strewn peak. Follow Pinto Basin Road to the southern section of the park, where you can hop on the easy interpretive trail to the **Cholla Cactus Garden** (0.25 mile). Near the Cottonwood Spring Visitor Center is the long, rewarding hike to the **Lost Palms Oasis** (7.2 miles round-trip, 4-5 hours), home to the largest grove of fan palms in Joshua Tree. The climb up **Mastodon Peak** (3 miles round-trip, difficult) takes you above 3,000 feet, for views of Eagle Mountain and the Salton Sea. Check out the Mastodon Mind and the Winona Mill along the way.

Rock Climbing

Joshua Tree is one of the finest places to rock climb. The good climbing regions are almost all found in the northern Mojave area, which is filled with granite canyons and fantastical boulder formations. Strict rules govern climbing at Joshua Tree, and all climbers are responsible for knowing the rules before they begin. Check the park website (www.nps.gov/jotr) or visit the ranger station to pick up a copy of climbing rules and the Fixed Anchor Checklist. The website also offers topographical maps of the major climbing areas.

More than a dozen climbing spots surround the **Indian Cove Campground**. A tangle of paved roads service the area, while a large parking lot provides easy access to the boulders and cliff faces. Test your skills against Dos Equis Wall or Apparition Rock to the west, or Upper and Lower Dodge City to the south of the central camping area.

The climbing areas associated with the **Hidden Valley** are more spread out, but there are more of them and they range into the wilderness part of the park. Near the parking lot and campground, you'll find The Real Hidden Valley Area, Cyclops, Echo Cove, and a number of others. Northeast, you can hike or drive a dirt road out to Willow Hole to climb the Fortress, Super Dome, or Valley of Kings.

Between the **Sheep Pass** and **Ryan Campgrounds**, several parking lots make it easy to stage climbs at Cap Rock, Hall of Horrors, and Love Nest. Other good places to stage climbs include the rough roads of the Geology Tour, the Queens Valley, and Split Rock.

The small towns surrounding the border of Joshua Tree National Park support a number of climbing outfitters. **Joshua Tree Rock Climbing School** (800/890-4745, www.joshuatreerockclimbing.com, $175/one-day session) is prominent among these outfits. You can also stop by **Climbers Coffee** (8am-10am Sat.-Sun., mid-Oct.-Apr.) at the Hidden Valley Campground to meet the climbing ranger and other climbers for advice and updates on the best routes and any closures over a cup of tea, coffee, or cocoa.

FOOD

There's no food inside Joshua Tree National Park. Picnickers and campers must pack in everything they intend to eat. The only visitors centers that maintain snack bars reside just outside the park boundaries. You can also drive into Twentynine Palms or Joshua Tree for a meal.

Joshua Tree

The Western-themed **Crossroads Cafe & Tavern** (61715 29 Palms Hwy., 760/366-5414, www.crossroadscafejt.com, 7am-9pm Mon.-Sat., 7am-8pm Sun., $6-13) is a popular spot for breakfast, with an array of egg dishes. Tacos, burgers, hot sandwiches, and salads fit the bill for lunch and dinner. Kids (and parents) will love the kids' menu and the variety of dessert offerings.

Do you crave ethnic, but the kids will only eat pizza? You're in luck! **Sam's Pizza** (61380 29 Palms Hwy., 760/366-9511, www.samspizza.com, 11am-9pm Mon.-Sat., 3pm-8pm Sun., $5-20) serves great pies and hot sandwiches in addition to serious Indian food. Pick from a range of curries plus tikka masala, vegetable biryani, and crispy samosas, or even combine East and West for a surprisingly tasty curry pizza.

To grab a coffee, snack, or lunch before exploring the park, the **Joshua Tree Park Rock Café** (6554 Park Blvd., http://jtparkrockcafe.com, 760/366-8200, 8am-4pm Mon.-Fri., 8am-5pm Sat.-Sun., $10-20) is a convenient spot right next to the Joshua Tree Visitors Center, near the West Entrance to the park. There is a reasonable selection of salads and sandwiches, plus boxed lunches.

Twentynine Palms

Decent and inexpensive Mexican cuisine is served at **Castaneda Mexican Food** (73680 Sun Valley Dr., 760/361-0202, 24 hours daily, $5-10). Grab a burrito, a couple of tacos, or even a combo plate here, and top it off with an offering from the open salsa bar.

The restaurant at the **29 Palms Inn** (73950 Inn Ave., 760/367-3505, www.29palmsinn.com, 11am-2pm and 5pm-9pm Mon.-Sat., 9am-2pm and 5pm-9pm Sun., $10-30) serves lunch and dinner daily with a view of the pool.

Dinner entrées rely on steak and pasta, with fresh ingredients from the on-site organic garden.

ACCOMMODATIONS

Most of the lodging adjacent to Joshua Tree lies in the towns of Joshua Tree or Twentynine Palms. If you're looking for luxury accommodations, stay in Palm Springs instead. Inside the park, your choices are developed, primitive, and backcountry campgrounds.

Joshua Tree

At the edge of the park, the colorful ★ **Spin and Margie's Desert Hide-A-Way** (64491 29 Palms Hwy., 760/774-0850, www.deserthideaway.com, $145-185) is a lovely reprieve after a day exploring the desert. Each of the four suites has a kitchen plus a sitting room. While the stand-alone cabin is smaller, the charm and privacy make up for it. The quirky and bright decor channels the 1950s heyday of highways like Route 66.

The lovely **Joshua Tree Inn** (61259 29 Palms Hwy., 760/366-1188, www.joshuatreeinn.com, $89-159) is a 1950s hacienda-style inn with 11 rooms conveniently located near the park's West Entrance. All rooms have refrigerators and microwaves. You'll also find a koi pond, a Zen garden, and a pool.

For an adventurous stay that embraces the region's artistic roots, book a uniquely themed trailer at the **Hicksville Trailer Palace** (Joshua Tree, 310/584-1086, www.hicksville.com, $75-275). Choose from the Fifi, the Integratron, or the Cramps-themed Lux, among others. Amenities include a fire pit, saltwater pool (seasonal), Ping-Pong table, hot tub, and the best jukebox you'll ever rock out to.

Twentynine Palms

U2 fans should stay at the **Harmony Hotel** (71161 29 Palms Hwy., 760/367-3351, www.harmonymotel.com, $75-95), where the band stayed while recording their album of the same name. The small, casual motel only has eight rooms, some with kitchenettes and all with outdoor patios. The hot tub and pool overlook the Mojave wilderness.

The **29 Palms Inn** (73950 Inn Ave. 760/367-3505, www.29palmsinn.com, $115-195) offers a collection of pet-friendly, eclectic adobe bungalows and cabins nestled amid lush grounds and gardens within walking distance of the Oasis of Mara. Amenities include a restaurant, a heated pool, yoga classes, and free Wi-Fi.

There is nothing rough in **Roughley Manor** (74744 Joe Davis Dr., 760/367-3238, www.roughleymanor.com, $150-185). In fact, the genteel, stone-clad B&B feels slightly out of place with its floral Victorian furnishings and gourmet breakfast, but the estate was once a homestead dating back to 1925. Some guest rooms are pet friendly and many suites feature kitchenettes and dining areas. A shared pool is located in the main courtyard.

CAMPING

Many of the outdoors-loving visitors to Joshua Tree prefer to sleep out under the brilliantly glittering stars. The developed campgrounds observe quiet hours, generator-use restrictions, and no showers. In fact, only a few campgrounds offer any water.

Black Rock Campground (Black Rock Canyon, open year-round, reservations Oct.-May 877/444-6777 or www.recreation.gov, $20) is one of the biggest and most developed campgrounds in Joshua Tree. With 100 sites, running potable water, and full bathroom facilities, Black Rock offers a semblance of comfort in the harsh desert. Some spots take RVs, and the site has a dump station. Black Rock is also one of two park facilities where equestrians can camp with their horses.

The other horse-friendly campground is **Ryan** (Park Blvd. south of Hidden Valley, first-come, first-served, $15), which has more primitive facilities and fewer sites. Expect pit toilets and no available drinking water. Each site has a grate for cooking and campfires, and a picnic table.

Two other popular campgrounds, **Hidden Valley** (Park Blvd. south of West Entrance, first-come, first-served, $15) and **Jumbo Rocks** (Park Blvd. east of Geology Tour Rd., first-come, first-served, $15), sit near the center of the most traveled areas of the park. Both are primitive, with pit toilets and no water, but Jumbo Rocks has more than 100 sites in great locations. At Hidden Valley, RVs must be 25 feet or less.

Indian Cove (Indian Cove Rd. south of North Entrance, reservations 877/444-6777 or www.recreation.gov, Sept.-May, $20) offers more than 100 campsites along the northern park boundary in a location convenient to the small towns just north of Joshua Tree. While there's no water on-site, it's easy to come by at Joshua Tree and Twentynine Palms. The Indian Cove area offers a 0.5-mile nature trail.

In the south of the park, **Cottonwood** (Hwy. 195 at the Cottonwood Visitors Center, first-come, first-served, $20) offers water and flush toilets, as well as a dump station for RVs. The nearby visitors center offers a few basic supplies and some lovely hikes.

TRANSPORTATION AND SERVICES

The nearest major airport is **Palm Springs International Airport** (3400 E. Tahquitz Canyon Way, Palm Springs, 760/318-3800, www.palmspringsca.gov).

To explore Joshua Tree National Park, you will need a car. To get there from Palm Springs, take I-10 heading west to Twentynine Palms Highway (Hwy. 62). From Highway 62, you can access Black Rock Canyon, the Joshua Tree Visitors Center, or the Oasis of Mara. To get to the South Entrance, take I-10 east and turn north (left) onto Box Canyon Road, which takes you right up to the Cottonwood Spring Visitor Center.

Parking inside Joshua Tree usually isn't too difficult, as ample parking lots are provided for the major attractions. On holiday weekends, come early for the best spots and least-crowded hikes.

Mojave National Preserve

The **Mojave National Preserve** (btw. I-15 and I-40, 760/928-2572, www.nps.gov/moja, free) can be an easy day trip from Palm Springs (3 hours), Joshua Tree (2 hours), or even Death Valley (3 hours) and offers a less-crowded way to explore California's vast Mojave region. If you've only got one day, the best (and easiest) introduction is the **Mojave Scenic Drive** from the northern edge of the park along the smooth, well-kept pavement of I-15.

From the town of Baker, turn south off I-15 onto **Kelbaker Road** for the 35-mile drive to Kelso. You'll traverse an alien landscape composed of volcanic activity, part of the Cinder Cones National Natural Landmark. Stop in Kelso to explore the Spanish Revival facade of the **Kelso Depot Visitor Center** (Kelbaker Rd., 760/252-6108, 9am-5pm daily), which once held the railroad depot that supported the many desert mining camps. Park rangers are on hand with advice on yearly road conditions.

Climbing back into your car, turn onto **Kelso-Cima Road.** The road follows the Union Pacific rail line along the edge of the Providence Mountains to the town of Cima, where you'll find snacks and drinks (but no gas). Cima also serves as a convenient fork; if you're in a hurry to get back to I-15, stay left on Cima Road. The right fork, **Morning Star Mine Road,** offers a more interesting route, including a turnoff to the abandoned mine that gives the road its name. From the mine, turn left onto Ivanpah Road and continue to Nipton Road to return to the freeway.

This drive takes about 90 minutes without stops, but consider hiking the many desert trails or spending the night at one of the two **campgrounds** (first-come, first-served, $12).

Death Valley

For a valley famed for its uncompromising climate, **Death Valley National Park** (760/786-3200, www.nps.gov/deva, $20) teems with life. Desert plants, including funky pickleweed and more common creosote, wildflowers, and even desert-dwelling fish and snails live here in profusion. Plan at least a weekend to take in the main sights.

TOP EXPERIENCE

SIGHTS

In the town of Furnace Creek are two tiny museums that give guests a deeper understanding of both the natural and human history of Death Valley. The **Borax Museum** (760/786-2345, 10am-6pm Mon.-Fri., 9am-9pm Sat.-Sun., free) at Furnace Creek Ranch focuses on the mining history of the area, with a tiny interior gallery/bookshop filled with mineral samples, books and documents, and smaller mining tools. The bulk of the museum sits outdoors, displaying an array of desiccated large mining and support equipment. You'll see hand-built mining machines, carriages and wagons, a steam locomotive, and more.

Just a few yards north of the ranch sits the **Furnace Creek Visitors Center and Museum** (Hwy. 190 at the gas station, 760/786-3200, 8am-5pm daily year-round). The interpretive museum here tells the story of Death Valley's long, slow formation and erosion. This is also a good spot to talk to rangers about the various rugged roads in the park.

★ Badwater Basin

At 281 feet *below* sea level, **Badwater Basin** (Hwy. 178, 18 miles south of Furnace Creek, turn off I-190 onto Hwy. 178 at Furnace Creek Inn) holds the title of the lowest elevation in the Western Hemisphere. Visitors love to take photos beside the elevation sign on the boardwalks that protect the tiny salt pond here.

Keep to the boardwalk as you gaze into the water of the temporary lake that seems impossible in the blinding heat of the salt flats of this long-dried-out lake bed. You can walk off the boardwalk and out onto the salt flats; just follow the obvious path. Ahead of you, the western mountain range might boast a coating of snow during the winter months, and the view up the valley is astonishing on a clear day.

Potable water is available at the restrooms adjacent to the parking lot. Expect to find plenty of other cars in that parking lot, as Badwater is one of the most popular spots to visit in Death Valley, but it is best to avoid it during the summer months.

★ Artist's Palette

The **Artist's Palette** (Artists Dr., turn off Hwy. 178 about 7 miles south of Furnace Creek) almost looks like some sort of trick—but all those brilliant colors splashed together in one spot is really a random conglomeration of different minerals. Along the Artist's Palette cutoff, swaths of color spill down the mountains for miles through the narrow canyon.

The one-way road through Artist's Palette splits off from Highway 178 and runs for about five miles (entrance at the south side); the road is paved and drivable by regular cars. Keep driving until you see the Artist's Palette sign and turn right into the drive for the parking lot. Walk a few steps up a tiny rise and you'll see the Palette right in front of you in all its pastel glory. You'll also see a number of other tourists at all times of day. No restrooms or water are available.

Devil's Golf Course

One of the eeriest formations is the **Devil's Golf Course** (Hwy. 178, about 11 miles south of Furnace Creek), part of a low salt flat that was the bottom of a long-vanished lake. Acre upon acre of the chewed-up ground is covered with delicate crystalline salt formations. Be very careful when walking out onto the Devil's Golf Course; the ruts, holes, and crevices can be knee-deep, and the rocks and crystals are razor-sharp.

The road in to Devil's Golf Course is dirt and can get rough, but it's passable by passenger car. The slower you drive, the better condition the road will stay in. There's a parking lot in the Devil's Golf Course and a couple of plaques describing the formation and geology of the area. However, there are no restrooms or water.

the Borax Museum

Death Valley National Park

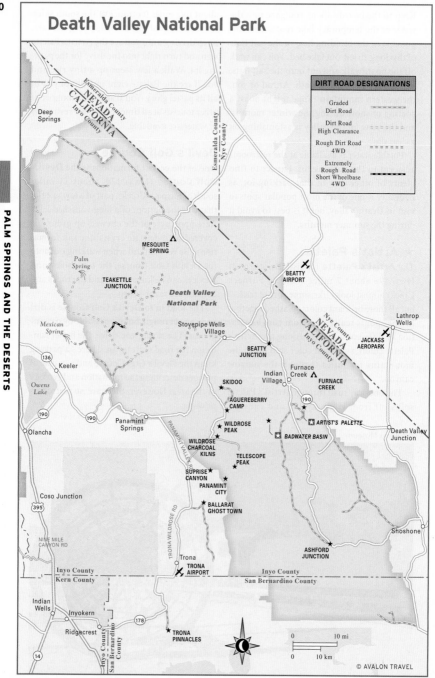

DIRT ROAD DESIGNATIONS

Graded Dirt Road

Dirt Road High Clearance

Rough Dirt Road 4WD

Extremely Rough Road Short Wheelbase 4WD

Deep Springs

Esmeralda County
NEVADA
CALIFORNIA
Inyo County

Esmeralda County
Nye County

Palm Spring

MESQUITE SPRING

TEAKETTLE JUNCTION

Death Valley National Park

BEATTY AIRPORT

Nye County
NEVADA
CALIFORNIA
Inyo County

Lathrop Wells

JACKASS AEROPARK

Mexican Spring

Stovepipe Wells Village

BEATTY JUNCTION

136

Keeler

Owens Lake

190

190

Panamint Springs

SKIDOO

AGUEREBERRY CAMP

Indian Village

Furnace Creek

FURNACE CREEK

190

Olancha

PANAMINT VALLEY

WILDROSE PEAK

WILDROSE CHARCOAL KILNS

TELESCOPE PEAK

ARTIST'S PALETTE

BADWATER BASIN

Death Valley Junction

Coso Junction

395

SUPRISE CANYON

PANAMINT CITY

BALLARAT GHOST TOWN

Shoshone

NINE MILE CANYON RD

TRONA WILDROSE RD

ASHFORD JUNCTION

Trona

TRONA AIRPORT

Inyo County
Kern County

Inyo County
San Bernardino County

Indian Wells

Inyokern

178

TRONA PINNACLES

Ridgecrest

14

Inyo County
San Bernardino County

0   10 mi

0   10 km

© AVALON TRAVEL

Zabriskie Point

A stunning view of Badwater Basin awaits at **Zabriskie Point,** an easily accessible viewpoint off Highway 190, east of Furnace Creek. Follow the short trail from the parking area to gaze at the backdrop of badlands and canyons; the setting is particularly atmospheric at sunrise and sunset.

Dante's View

One of the many glorious views can be accessed by car at **Dante's View** (end of Dante's View Rd., turn off Hwy. 190 about 10 miles southeast of Furnace Creek). From more than a mile up, you can look out over what feels like the whole valley—right down into the salt flats of Badwater, up to Furnace Creek, and beyond. Right next door you can wave at the thematically named Coffin Peak to the south of Dante's. As the main views spread out to the west, Dante's Peak is a great place to watch the sun set over Death Valley.

Salt Creek

The Death Valley pupfish is a species of fish that lives in only one spot on the globe—here at **Salt Creek** (Hwy. 190, about 15 miles north of Furnace Creek, turnoff on west side of the highway). Salt Creek runs year-round from a small spring; its terminus is the hard ground where a miniature delta spreads out then dries up. To protect the delicate ecosystem in and around the heavily salinated creek, the Park Service has built a boardwalk that lets visitors see the plants, algae, and pupfish without treading on and in the delicate landscape here. The boardwalk runs from the parking lot up to the area where the pupfish spawn early in the wintertime. As spring comes, the pupfish swim downstream, making viewing easy even for visitors who don't want to take a hike.

The drive from the highway is about two miles on a dirt road that's passable in a passenger car. Pit toilets sit in the parking lot area. The boardwalk trail is wheelchair accessible.

Ubehebe Crater

In the north end of the valley, a recent (in geologic time) volcano left behind **Ubehebe Crater** (8 miles west of Scotty's Castle, from Hwy. 190 take left fork at the Grapevine). A quick walk up from the parking lot takes you right to the edge of the crater, which consists of razor-sharp black volcanic rock that is on the opposite inner face of the crater, fading into a bright salmon pink and even a stark white. The view over the edge of the crater back down the valley is worth coming up here

the Devil's Golf Course

for. You can climb up from the parking area along the crater's rim to Little Hebe crater, a smaller crater created by the same volcano about 2,000 years ago.

Get to Ubehebe Crater by taking the other fork at the intersection that takes you to Scotty's Castle. The road is easily traversable by passenger car; there's a parking lot but no restroom or water here.

Scotty's Castle

Note that due to flood damage, Scotty's Castle and the road to access it remained closed at time of publication and will not likely reopen to the public until 2019.

Scotty's Castle (Hwy. 267 in Grapevine Canyon) is a Spanish-style home, the only private mansion ever built in Death Valley. Contrary to popular legend, it never was the home of infamous huckster Death Valley Scotty—he actually lived in a rough cabin on the property. The mansion was built and furnished by Albert Johnson and his wife, a wealthy couple from Chicago who initially invested in Scotty's oft-lauded but never-seen gold mine. The Johnsons and Scotty often entertained at the castle, and movie stars and presidents came to stay in the guest rooms

here. The only way to see the main house is with a tour (877/444-6777, www.recreation.gov, adults $15, children 6-15 $7.50, children under 6 free).

Amargosa Opera House

Outside the park proper, in the town of Amargosa Valley, Nevada, you'll find the **Amargosa Opera House** (Death Valley Junction, 760/852-4441, www.amargosa-opera-house.com, 7pm Fri.-Sat., 2pm Sun., Nov.-May, $20). This lovely small theater is the pride and joy of Marta Beckett, a dancer from New York City who found her "home" in an abandoned theater in Death Valley Junction. She and her husband repaired and renovated the theater, creating an intimate space where Marta could perform for an appreciative, if small, audience. That was in 1968. In the early 1970s, Marta was inspired to paint murals of people on the walls and ceiling of her theater—a permanent audience for her ballets, which lasted until she retired in 2012. Visitors still pack the house for the weekend performances of Marta's original ballets.

The opera house is also a hotel ($70-80), with small, simple rooms featuring king, queen, or double beds.

colorful Ubehebe Crater

4WD Road Trips

The Racetrack

Many of Death Valley's off-the-beaten-track sights and trails can only be accessed by high-clearance and four-wheel-drive vehicles.

- **The Racetrack** (27 miles from Ubehebe Crater): This 27-mile drive on an incredibly rough road leads to a patch of desert where rocks mark deep grooves along the barren lake bed.

- **Eureka Dunes** (10 miles south of Big Pine Rd.): In the north end of the valley, these striking sand dunes rise 700 feet above the valley floor. The drive lasts about 40 miles or so on a long unpaved road running north from the Y-intersection to Scotty's Castle, then on a 4WD-only track about 10 miles to the dunes.

- **Titus Canyon** (from Hwy. 374 to Hwy. 190): This one-way 4WD track begins near the town of Beatty, Nevada, and runs 26 miles west to intersect with Highway 190 near Stovepipe Wells. Along the way, you'll see Native American petroglyphs, the ghost town of Leadfield, colorful mineral deposits, and skinny "narrows," where the walls soar overhead and almost black out the sun.

- **Aguereberry Point** (off Emigrant Canyon Rd.): In the Panamint Springs area, this drive passes the ghost town of Harrisburg to climb to Aguereberry Point, providing more beautiful valley vistas to enjoy.

HIKING

The best time to hike the floor of Death Valley is in winter or spring, when temperatures are cool to moderate. But if you're interested in hiking the Panamint Mountains, the best time to explore the ridges is in the summer, when the snow has melted.

For a fun, moderate walk, park on the side of Highway 190 and wander out to the **Mesquite Flat Sand Dunes** (2-4 miles round-trip) near Stovepipe Wells. From the roadside parking area, head straight toward the cluster of dunes—there's no trail. The dunes may look like they're only a few yards away, but it's about a mile to the edge of the first dune. Hundreds of pockmarked footprints bear witness to other visitors' climbs. If you climb as far as you can up the tallest dune, the round-trip is four miles.

Mosaic Canyon (1-4 miles round-trip,

moderate) offers a variable-length hike with beautiful rock formations that resemble mosaics. Check out the canyon walls on the first 0.5 mile of the walk for the best mosaics. If you want more, continue a couple of miles farther into the canyon. This hike starts at the Mosaic Canyon parking lot, a couple of miles past Stovepipe Wells Village off Highway 190.

The drive out to the **Natural Bridge** (Hwy. 190, 1-2 miles south of Devil's Golf Course) isn't long or aggressive, but the road condition makes high-clearance or 4WD vehicles preferable. Once you park, you've got a 0.5-mile walk in to see the magnificent stone arch stretching across yet another beautiful desert canyon.

Located off Badwater Road, the hike through Golden Canyon (1 mile, easy) leads to **Red Cathedral**, a dry rockfall dyed in hues of red. The narrow canyon continues to either Gower Gulch or Zabriskie Point, where a trail map will come in handy.

For a scenic summer walk, **Dante's Ridge** (1-8 miles, moderate to strenuous) offers soaring vistas and cool temperatures even in July. A short 0.5-mile climb from the Dante's View parking lot leads to the first peak in the chain.

Horseback Riding

At **Furnace Creek Stables** (Hwy. 190, 760/614-1018, www.furnacecreekstables.net), you can take a horseback ride out into the desert October-May. One- or two-hour tours ($60, $75, respectively) are available, as are the Sunset rides ($75). Call to make a reservation.

Golf

If you're just burning to play a round, book a tee time at the **Furnace Creek Ranch Golf Course** (Hwy. 190, 760/786-2345, www.furnacecreekresort.com, greens fee $30-75). It's not the shining green you'll find at most golf courses, as limited water can be spared to irrigate greens and fairways. This 18-hole, par 70 course is 214 feet below sea level and is part of the Furnace Creek Ranch complex near the center of Death Valley. You'll find restaurants

and a general store at the ranch. Check the website for golf and lodging packages.

FOOD

Meal planning is essential as quick, spur-of-the-moment options are limited. Either bring a stocked cooler, stay near one of the three resort areas, or plan excursions around where you plan to eat lunch or dinner. If you do plan to feed yourself, stock up on staples outside the park. The Furnace Creek area has the most dining options.

The **49er Café** (Hwy. 190 at Furnace Creek Ranch, 760/786-2345, breakfast 6am-10:30am, lunch 11:30am-3pm, dinner 4pm-10pm daily, $8-15) serves traditional breakfasts, filling lunches, and hearty dinners in a casual, diner-style setting. The **Wrangler Steakhouse** (Hwy. 190 at Furnace Creek Ranch, 760/786-2345, breakfast 6am-10am, lunch 11am-2pm, dinner 5pm-9pm daily, $25-35) offers breakfast and lunch buffets, and a steakhouse dinner menu loaded with meaty choices. If you're looking to wet your whistle, amble over to the **Corkscrew Saloon** (Furnace Creek Ranch, Hwy. 190, 760/786-2345, noon-midnight daily), a cowboy-styled bar with a wood floor and dim lighting.

Limited groceries are available at the **Furnace Creek Ranch General Store** (Hwy. 190 at Furnace Creek Ranch, 760/786-3385, www.furnacecreekresort.com, 7am-10pm daily).

For high-end dining, make reservations at the **Furnace Creek Inn Dining Room** (Hwy. 190 at Furnace Creek Ranch, 760/786-3385, www.furnacecreekresort.com, breakfast 7am-10:30am, lunch noon-2pm, dinner 5pm-9pm Mon.-Sat., brunch 10am-2pm, dinner 5pm-9pm Sun., Oct.-May, $18-35), which offers large portions of delectable California cuisine. Reservations are recommended for dinner, especially on weekend evenings, and a dress code may be required.

In Stovepipe Wells Village, your meal option is the **Toll Road Restaurant** (Hwy. 190, Stovepipe Wells, 760/786-2387, www.death-valleyhotels.com, 7am-10am and 5:30pm-9pm daily), serving American food that fits the rustic decor. Prepare to wait for a table on weekends in high season. Lunch is served next door at **Badwater Saloon** (11:30am-9pm daily). The bar also serves more than 20 beers on tap, decent wine, and plenty of spirits, in addition to bar snacks (5pm-9pm daily). The small **Stovepipe Wells General Store** (7am-10pm daily) sells water, soft drinks, and limited food items.

The **Panamint Springs Resort** (40440 Hwy. 190, 775/482-7680, www.panamintsprings.com, 7am-9pm daily, $12-30) serves pizza and a variety of Angus burgers to diners year-round. Take a seat out on the large patio and enjoy a glass of beer before lunch or dinner—the restaurant offers more than 100 varieties from around the world.

ACCOMMODATIONS

If you prefer to stay on the west side of Death Valley (a good idea for at least one night if you're driving in from the California side), book a room or a camping spot at the tiny **Panamint Springs Resort** (40440 Hwy. 190, 775/482-7680, www.panamintsprings.com, $79-170). This rustic lodge-style motel is the only independently owned lodging in Death Valley, and has a temperature generally 10-15 degrees lower than other areas in the park. You'll also find a bar, restaurant, gas station, and general store on site.

The motel at **Stovepipe Wells** (51880 Hwy. 190, 760/786-2387, www.deathvalleyhotels.com, $120-210) offers basic rooms and amenities at reasonable prices. Choose from ground-floor rooms with one or two beds; all are only a few steps from the restaurant and saloon, the swimming pool, and across the street from the general store. From the motel, you'll have easy access to Mosaic Canyon, the local dunes, and Salt Creek.

The biggest resort complex in the park, **The Ranch at Furnace Creek** (Hwy. 190, 800/236-7916 or 760/786-2345, www.furnacecreekresort.com, $259-309) acts as the hub of Death Valley. It's on the same property as two restaurants, a tavern, a general store, a museum, a gas station, a golf course, an airstrip, and the main park visitors center. With a wide lawn, a playground, and a mineral spring-fed swimming pool, this is a great place for a desert vacation. The guest accommodations are deliberately casual; choose from standard, deluxe, or cabin-style accommodations, all in a chain-motel styling. Some rooms have tiny patios or balconies overlooking the lawns and pools.

The lone high-end resort is ★ **The Inn at Furnace Creek** (Hwy. 190. at Hwy. 178, 800/236-7916 or 760/786-2345, www.furnacecreekresort.com, $499-587, mid-Oct.-mid-May only), a beautiful property constructed in the 20th century by the Pacific Borax Company. The castle-like stone and tile building is a lovely palm oasis, and you'll find a mineral pool fed by a hot spring with poolside food service, a fine dining room, spa services, and more. Some rooms are on the small side and not all overlook the valley.

CAMPING

Folks quickly fill the campgrounds that dot the park. During high season (winter), the popular central campgrounds fill up fast. You can make **reservations** for Furnace Creek Campground for camping October-April. The remaining park campgrounds are first-come, first-served, though some private campgrounds accept reservations. Camping June-September is not recommended, and many campgrounds are closed May-September.

RV campers love to hang out in Death Valley. Accordingly, several RV campgrounds offer dump stations and hookups. Both on the same side as the ranch and across the road, **Furnace Creek Campground** (136 sites, Hwy. 190 at Furnace Creek, 877/444-6777, www.recreation.gov, reservations Oct.-Apr., $18; first-come, first-served Apr.-Oct., $12) offers both RV spaces and tent sites, in addition to drinking water, flush toilets, and a dump station. Neighboring full-service **Furnace Creek Resort** (800/365-2267, www.furnacecreekresort.com, year-round, $38) operates two private campgrounds. Campers gain access to the facilities at the ranch, including the swimming pool, golf course, restaurants, and store, plus running water, flush toilets, and RV hookups. The downside is it is largely a stretch of barren asphalt with no shade whatsoever.

Located near Furnace Creek Ranch are **Texas Springs** (92 sites, Oct.-Apr., $14) and **Sunset** (270 sites, Oct.-Apr., $12). Both feature drinking water, flush toilets, and RV dump stations. Of the two, Texas Springs has the nicest amenities, which include picnic tables and fire rings.

The **Stovepipe Wells Campground** (190 sites, Oct.-May, $12) is geared largely to tent camping. You'll find drinking water and flush toilets, while also enjoying the proximity to the motel at Stovepipe Wells, plus pool and shower access ($12). The motel at **Stovepipe Wells** (Hwy. 190, 760/786-2387, www.death-valleyhotels.com, Oct.-Apr., $34) is also a popular RV park with hookups.

Mesquite Spring (30 sites, off Hwy. 190, south of Scotty's Castle, year-round, $12) offers both tent and RV sites that are first-come, first-served, with self-registration. The campground has potable water, flush toilets, and an RV dump station. If you're specifically looking for a more isolated and rugged experience, this might be the place for you.

Panamint Springs (40440 Hwy. 190, 775/482-7680, www.panamintsprings.com, $10-65) offers 37 RV spaces, 26 tent sites, and 7 tent cabins. You'll find water, showers, and toilets throughout the campground. Some RV spots have full hookups with 50-amp electricity.

For a less-crowded camping experience, head to the Panamint Mountains. You'll pass tent-only **Emigrant** (10 sites, Hwy. 190 at Emigrant Canyon Rd., year-round, free), which sits halfway between Panamint Springs and Stovepipe Wells. You'll get a spot to pitch your tent, access to potable water, and flush toilets, but no fire rings. Turning left onto Wildrose Canyon Road, **Wildrose** (23 sites, year-round, free) has a lower elevation and a few more in-season amenities, including potable water (Nov.-Apr.) and pit toilets. **Thorndike** (6 sites, Wildrose Canyon Rd., Mar.-Nov., free) is a primitive campground, with pit toilets, picnic tables, and fire pits, but no water. Access may require a four-wheel-drive vehicle. At the end of Wildrose Canyon Road sits **Mahogany Flat** (10 sites, Mar.-Nov., free), at 8,200 feet, requiring four-wheel drive to reach it. Amenities are limited to tables, fire pits, and pit toilets; there is no drinking water.

TRANSPORTATION AND SERVICES

The closest major airport to Death Valley is the **Las Vegas International Airport** (5757 Wayne Newton Blvd., Las Vegas, 702/261-5211, www.mccarran.com). From Vegas, it's a 2-3-hour drive to Furnace Creek. **Los Angeles International Airport** (LAX, 1 World Way, Los Angeles, 855/463-5252, www.lawa.org) offers access from the west, but it's a longer drive (five hours without traffic) to reach Furnace Creek.

The main road through Death Valley is **Highway 190,** which runs north-south until midway through the park, where it passes through Stovepipe Wells. Numerous paved, unpaved, and four-wheel-drive roads branch off from Highway 190 throughout the park, accessing the main attractions and trailheads.

To enter the park from the west, access Highway 190 from **U.S. 395** near the town of Lone Pine. From the south, Highway 178 leads north from Ridgecrest to Highway 190 at Panamint Springs in about 50 miles. To enter through the park's east side, take I-15 east to Baker, then turn north on **Highway 127** to Death Valley Junction. Highway 190 intersects here, and you can follow the road west to Furnace Creek.

Fill up on **gas** before entering the park, as services are limited. Gas is available *only* at the resort areas of Panamint Springs, Stovepipe Wells, and Furnace Creek and prices reflect this.

Las Vegas

Sights 560

Casinos 565

Entertainment 582

Food 583

Accommodations 586

Transportation and Services . . . 588

Look for ★ to find recommended
sights, activities, dining, and lodging.

Highlights

★ **Fremont Street Experience:** The six-minute light shows are a four-block-long, 12-million-diode, 550,000-watt burst of sensory overload (page 560).

★ **The Mob Museum:** Explore a time when wiseguys ran the town, meting out their own brand of justice (page 560).

★ **Gondola Rides:** The Venetian's waterway meanders along the Strip, with gondoliers providing the soundtrack (page 561).

★ **Secret Garden and Dolphin Habitat:** Tigers, lions, and leopards play impromptu games while the bottlenose dolphins never resist the spotlight (page 561).

★ **High Roller:** The world's largest observation wheel overwhelms the senses with driving music, videos, and unmatched views of the Strip (page 563).

★ **Las Vegas Springs Preserve:** These natural springs display the area's geological, anthropological, and cultural history (page 563).

★ **Atomic Testing Museum:** This museum traces the military, political, and cultural significance of the atom bomb (page 564).

★ **Caesars Palace:** Caesars Palace carries on

the Roman Empire's regality and decadence with over-the-top excess (page 569).

Las Vegas seduces the senses, indulges the appetite, and sparks the imagination.

An oasis of flashing marquees, feathered showgirls, chiming slot machines, and endless buffets, the city is a monument to fantasy.

Each megaresort offers more to do than many small cities. Under one roof you can indulge in a five-star dinner, attend spectacular productions, dance until dawn with the beautiful people, and browse in designer boutiques. The buffet, a fitting metaphor for this city with an abundance of everything, still rules in the hearts of many locals and visitors, but an influx of celebrity chefs is turning the town into a gastronome's paradise. Similarly, cutting-edge performers such as Blue Man Group and Cirque du Soleil have taken up residence.

So pack your stilettos, string bikini, money clip, and favorite hangover remedy, and join the 35 million others who trek to Sin City every year. No one back home has to know you've succumbed to the city's siren song. After all, "What happens in Vegas . . . ."

ORIENTATION

Las Vegas Boulevard South is **The Strip**, a four-mile stretch between Tropicana and Sahara Avenues. This is what most folks think of as "Vegas." The **Lower Strip** (from the "Welcome to Fabulous Las Vegas" sign to Harmon Ave.) is made for budget-conscious families with plenty of kid-friendly attractions. Along the **Center Strip** (from Harmon Ave. to Spring Mountain Rd.), the casinos are packed tight and the sidewalks become masses of humanity on weekend nights. The **Upper Strip** (from Spring Mountain Rd. to the Stratosphere) has opulent casinos aside friendly standbys. The compact **Downtown** casino district (Fremont St. between Main St. and S Las Vegas Blvd.) is north of The Strip.

Previous: the High Roller observation wheel at Linq; the Bellagio Conservatory. **Above:** Las Vegas welcome sign.

Two Days in Las Vegas

DAY 1

Pick a hotel based on your taste and budget. We suggest **The Linq,** close to the High Roller observation wheel, fine dining, hip watering holes, and rocking live music venues.

Get your gambling fix for a few hours before heading across the street for brunch at The Mirage's **Cravings Buffet.** It operates on a familiar theory, with separate stations highlighting different cuisines. After the gorge-fest, you'll be ready for a nap, and you'll need it. This is Vegas; no early nights for you!

Couples should start the evening off with a romantic dinner at Paris's **Mon Ami Gabi.** For a more modest meal, the eponymous offering at The Palazzo's **B&B Burger & Beer** hits the spot. If you only have time for one show, make it *LOVE* at The Mirage. The show is a loose biography of the Beatles' creative journey, told by tumblers, roller skaters, clowns, and the characters from John, Paul, George, and Ringo's songs—Eleanor Rigby, Lucy in the Sky, and Sgt. Pepper.

DAY 2

Celebrate the kitsch and class of vintage Vegas. Head downtown to stock up on Elvis sideburns and Sammy Davis Jr. sunglasses before loading up on eggs Benedict and 1970s flair at the **Peppermill Restaurant & Fireside Lounge.** While it's daylight, make your way to the **Neon Museum and Boneyard,** the final resting place of some of Las Vegas's iconic signage. And while you're in the neighborhood, witness the rise and fall of the Mafia in Las Vegas at **The Mob Museum.**

Back at the hotel, change into your glad rags and beat it over to the Tuscany's Copa Room. Order up a neat bourbon and watch Sinatra try to make it through a rendition of "Luck Be a Lady" while Dino and Sammy heckle and cut up from the wings in *The Rat Pack Is Back.* Then get out there and gamble into the wee hours! For a chance to rub elbows with celebrities, head over to **XS** at The Wynn. Expect celebrity DJs, a major party, and steep prices.

Sights

DOWNTOWN
★ Fremont Street Experience

The **Fremont Street Experience** (Fremont St. between N. Main St. and N. 4th St., 702/678-5777) is downtown's answer to the Strip's erupting volcanoes and fantastic dancing fountains. The former "Glitter Gulch" is now a pedestrian-friendly enclave highlighted by a four-block-long canopy festooned with 12 million light-emitting diodes 90 feet in the air.

Neon Museum and Boneyard

Book a one-hour guided tour of the **Neon Museum and Boneyard** (770 Las Vegas Blvd. N., 702/387-6366; 9am-4pm and 7:30pm-9pm daily; adults $18-25; students,

seniors, and veterans $12-22) and take a trip to Las Vegas's more recent past. The boneyard displays 200 old neon signs that were used to advertise casinos, restaurants, bars, and even a flower shop. The **visitors center** (9:30am-8pm daily) is housed in the relocated scallop-shaped lobby of the historic La Concha Motel. You can skip the boneyard and take a free self-guided tour of nine restored signs displayed as public art. Note that the neighborhood can be sketchy.

★ The Mob Museum

The **National Museum of Organized Crime and Law Enforcement** (300 Stewart Ave., 702/229-2734, http://themobmuseum.

org; 10am-7pm daily; adults $20; seniors, military, and teachers $18; age 11-17 $14, under age 11 free)—aka The Mob Museum—celebrates Las Vegas's Mafia past and the cops and agents who finally ran the mob out of town. The museum is located inside the city's downtown post office and courthouse, appropriately the site of the 1951 Kefauver Hearing investigating organized crime.

CENTER STRIP
Madame Tussauds Las Vegas

Madame Tussauds Las Vegas (3377 Las Vegas Blvd. S., 702/862-7800, www.madametussauds.com/lasvegas, 10am-8pm Sun.-Thurs., 10am-9pm Fri.-Sat., adults $30, children 4-12 $20, under age 4 free) encourages guests to get up close and "personal" with the world leaders, sports heroes, and screen stars immortalized in wax. Photo ops and interactive activities abound.

★ Gondola Rides

The half-mile **indoor gondolas** (3355 Las Vegas Blvd. S., 702/607-3982, 10am-11pm Sun.-Thurs., 10am-midnight Fri.-Sat., $21) skirt the Grand Canal Shoppes inside The Venetian hotel under the mall's painted-sky ceiling fresco; **outdoor gondolas** (11am-10pm daily, weather permitting, $19) skim The Venetian's 31,000-square-foot lagoon for 12 minutes, giving riders a unique perspective on the Las Vegas Strip. Plying the waters at regular intervals, the realistic-looking gondolas seat four, but couples who don't want to share a boat can pay double.

★ Secret Garden and Dolphin Habitat

Legendary Las Vegas magicians Siegfried and Roy, who have dedicated much of their lives to preserving big cats, opened the **Secret Garden** (The Mirage, 3400 Las Vegas Blvd. S., 702/791-7188, 11am-5:30pm daily, adults $22, children 4-12 $12) in 1990. In addition to the milky-furred tigers, the garden is home to blue-eyed, black-striped white tigers as well as panthers, lions, and leopards. Although caretakers don't "perform" with the animals, if your visit is well timed, you could see the cats playing, wrestling, and even swimming in their pristine waterfall-fed pools.

Visit the Atlantic bottlenoses at the **Dolphin Habitat** right next door, also in the middle of The Mirage's palm trees and jungle foliage. An underwater viewing area provides an unusual perspective into the dolphins' world. Feeding times are a hoot.

Fremont Street Experience

The Strip

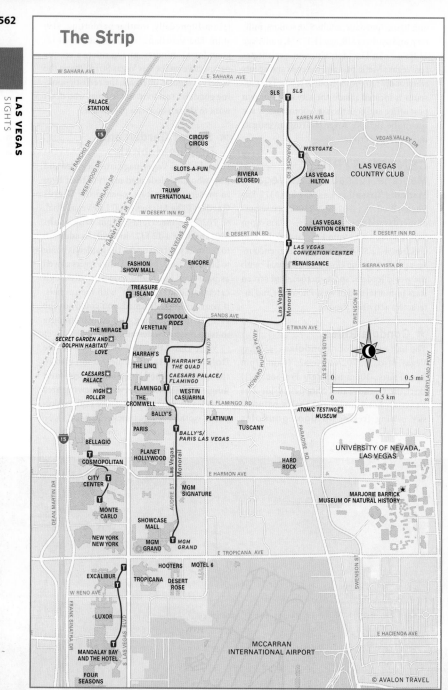

★ High Roller

Taller than even the London Eye, the 550-foot **High Roller** (The Linq, 3545 Las Vegas Blvd. S., 702/777-2782 or 866/574-3851, noon-2am daily, $27-37) is the highest observation wheel in the world. Two thousand LED lights dance in intricate choreography among the ride's spokes and pods. The dazzling view from 50 stories up is unparalleled. Ride at night for a perfect panorama of the famous Strip skyline. Forty passengers fit in each of the High Roller's 28 compartments, lessening wait time for the half-hour ride circuit. During **"happy half hour"** (4pm-7pm $37; 10pm-1am $47) passengers can board special bar cars and enjoy unlimited cocktails during the ride. Book online to save $7 on admission.

LOWER STRIP
Shark Reef

Shark Reef (Mandalay Bay, 3950 Las Vegas Blvd. S., 702/632-4555, 10am-8pm Sun.-Thurs., 10am-10pm Fri.-Sat., adults $20, children 5-12 $14) is home to 2,000 animals—almost all predators. Transparent walkthrough tubes and a sinking-ship observation deck allow terrific views, bringing visitors nearly face-to-face with some of the most fearsome creatures in the world. In addition to 15 species of sharks, guests can view a sand tiger shark, whose mouth is so crammed with razor-sharp teeth that it doesn't fully close. You'll also find golden crocodiles, moray eels, piranhas, giant octopuses, the venomous lionfish, stingrays, jellyfish, water monitors, and the fresh-from-your-nightmares eight-foot-long Komodo dragon.

OFF THE STRIP
★ Las Vegas Springs Preserve

The **Las Vegas Springs Preserve** (333 S. Valley View Blvd., 702/822-7700, 10am-6pm daily, adults $19, students and seniors $17, children 5-17 $11, free under age 5) is where Las Vegas began, at least from a Eurocentric viewpoint. More than 100 years ago, the first nonnatives in the Las Vegas Valley—Mormon missionaries from Salt Lake City—stumbled on this clear artesian spring. Of course, the native Paiute and Pueblo people knew about the springs and exploited them millennia before the Mormons arrived. You can see examples of their tools, pottery, and houses at the site, now a 180-acre monument to environmental stewardship, historic preservation, and geographic discovery. The preserve

gondola rides at The Venetian

is home to lizards, rabbits, foxes, scorpions, bats, and more.

Nevada State Museum

Visitors can spend hours studying Mojave and Spring Mountains ecology, southern Nevada history, and local art at the **Nevada State Museum** (309 S. Valley View Blvd., 702/486-5205, 10am-6pm Thurs.-Mon., $19, included in admission to the Springs Preserve). Permanent exhibits on the 13,000-square-foot floor describe southern Nevada's role in warfare, mining, and atomic weaponry and include skeletons of a Columbian mammoth, which roamed the Nevada deserts 20,000 years ago, and the ichthyosaur, a whale-like remnant of the Triassic Period.

★ Atomic Testing Museum

Kids might not think it's da bomb, but if you were part of the "duck and cover" generation, the **Atomic Testing Museum** (755 E. Flamingo Rd., 702/794-5161, 10am-5pm Mon.-Sat., noon-5pm Sun., adults $22) provides plenty to spark your memories of the Cold War. The museum presents atomic history without bias, walking a fine line between appreciation of the work of nuclear scientists, politicians, and the military and the catastrophic consequences their activities and decisions could have wrought. The museum's best permanent feature is a short video in the Ground Zero Theatre, a multimedia simulation of an actual atomic explosion. The theater, a replica of an observation bunker, is rigged for motion, sound, and rushing air.

Your ticket includes admission to the Area 51 exhibit. Built in consultation with former workers at the top-secret Groom Lake facility, the exhibit invites you to take the tour and decide for yourself whether alien autopsies, futuristic aircraft, and other *X-Files*-style activities are part of Area 51's mission.

The Mirage's Dolphin Habitat

Casinos

UPPER STRIP
Stratosphere Casino, Hotel, and Tower

Restaurants: Top of the World, McCalls, Nunzio's Pizzeria, Fellini's, Cannery 108, Stratosphere Buffet, Roxy's Diner, 8 Pool Café and Bar, Mookies, Starbucks, McDonald's, El Nopal Mexican Grill
Entertainment: *Pin Up, MJ Live*, Level 107, L.A. Comedy Club
Attractions: Observation Deck, Top of the Tower thrill rides, Roni Josef Spa, Tower Shops
Nightlife: Level 107 Lounge, Radius Wet Lounge, Airbar, McCall's Whiskey Bar, Margarita Bay, CBar, Images

It's altitude with attitude at this 1,149-foot-tall exclamation point on the north end of the Strip. Depending on how nitpicky you want to be, the **Stratosphere Tower** (2000 Las Vegas Blvd. S., 702/380-7777 or 800/998-6937, $69-180 d) is either the largest *building* west of Chicago or the largest *tower* west of St. Louis. Daredevils will delight in the vertigo-inducing thrill rides on the tower's observation deck. The more faint of heart may want to steer clear not only of the rides, but also the resort's double-decker elevators that launch guests to the top of the tower at 1,400 feet per minute.

If the thrill rides on the observation deck aren't your style, get a rush of gambling action on the nearly 100,000-square-foot ground-floor casino, two swimming pools (one has a tops-optional policy), and a dozen bars and restaurants more your speed.

ENTERTAINMENT

One of the better tribute shows in town, *MJ Live* (7pm daily, $74-104) features a rotating roster of three Michael Jackson impersonators backed by a full cast of dancers, a live band, and a dazzling array of lighting effects in the Stratosphere Theater. *Pin Up* (9:30pm Thurs.-Mon., $65-76) is a cheeky (all four cheeks) musical examination of a year in the life of sexy, but not raunchy, vixens. Picture a soft-R-rated video of Neil Sedaka's "Calendar Girl," with 2011 Playboy Playmate of the Year Claire Sinclair turning the pages.

RESTAURANTS

The 360-seat, 360-degree **Top of the World** (702/380-7711 or 800/998-6937, 11am-11pm daily, $50-80) sits on the 106th floor more than 800 feet above the Strip and makes a complete revolution once every 80 minutes. Order the seafood fettuccine or surf-and-turf gnocchi with lobster and beef short rib while enjoying the full Vegas panorama during dinner.

Wall frescoes put you on an Italian thoroughfare as you dine on authentic cuisine at **Fellini's** (702/383-4859, 5pm-11pm Sun.-Thurs., 5pm-midnight Fri.-Sat., $25-45), though the food is more the American idea of classic Italian than authentic. **Roxy's Diner** (24 hours daily, $10-15) is a trip back to the malt shop for comfort food and singing waitstaff.

SLS

Restaurants: Katsuya, Bazaar Meat, Cleo, Ku Noodle, Umami Burger, 800 Degrees, Northside Cafe, The Perq
Nightlife: Foxtail, Sayers Club, Center Bar, Monkey Bar

On the site of the legendary Sahara Casino, **SLS** (2535 Las Vegas Blvd. S., 855/761-7757, $149-249 d) targets the swanky sophisticate market. SLS channels Rat Pack cool through a modern lens, aiming to be a major player in Vegas. Three towers offer standard rooms of 325-435 square feet. All boast 55-inch televisions, soft pastel accents, and 310-thread-count sheets atop BeautyRest mattresses. The all-suite Lux Tower attracts resort visitors with luxurious peekaboo showers and the hotel's signature Saints and Sinners snack box. World Tower rooms take aim at business travelers, with extra seating areas, work desks, and infinity sinks. Story Tower is for the urban crowd, featuring big beds as center points for socialization.

Sayers Club (7pm-11pm Sun.-Wed., 7pm-3am Thurs.-Sat., $11) bills itself as a live-music venue. There's plenty of live indie pop, folk, and psychobilly bands on weekends, but with lots of open space and an industrial-warehouse feel, it's a natural environment for DJs.

Chef José Andrés's Spanish-influenced, meat-centric dishes at **Bazaar Meat** (5:30pm-10pm Sun.-Thurs., 5:30pm-11pm Fri.-Sat., $65-120) are meant to be shared with everyone in your party. The restaurant's decor reinforces that aim with long communal tables, open cooking stations, and a small gaming area.

Wynn Las Vegas/Encore

Restaurants: Andrea's, Botero, Country Club, Lakeside Seafood, Mizumi, Sinatra, SW Steakhouse, Tableau, Wing Lei, Allegro, The Buffet, Drugstore Café, La Cave, Red 8, Society Café, Terrace Pointe Café, Wazuzu, Zoozacrackers

Entertainment: *Showstoppers, Le Rêve,* Michael Monge

Attractions: Lake of Dreams, Wynn Golf Course, Penske Wynn Ferrari

Nightlife: XS, Surrender, Encore Beach Club, Eastside, Encore Lobby Bar, Parasol Down, Parasol Up, Tower Suite Bar, VDKA

★ **Wynn** (3131 Las Vegas Blvd. S., 702/770-7000 or 888/320-9966, $259-500 d) invites fellow multimillionaires to wallow in the good life and the hoi polloi to sample a taste of how the other half lives: Gaze at Wynn's art, one of the best and most valuable private collections in the world, or drool over the horsepower at **Penske Wynn Ferrari,** the dealership Wynn partly owns. Wynn-Encore's formal sophistication belies its location on the site of the old Desert Inn with the unselfconscious swagger Frank, Dino, and Sammy brought to the joint. Both towers boast some of the biggest guest rooms and suites on the Strip, with the usual (although better-quality) amenities and a few extra touches, like remote-controlled drapes, lights, and air-conditioning.

Wynn's guest rooms are appointed in wheat, honey, and other creatively named shades of beige. Encore is more colorful, with the color scheme running toward dark chocolate and cream.

Oscar de la Renta opened his first retail store in the country at the indulgent **Esplanade** (Wynn, 3131 Las Vegas Blvd. S., 702/770-7000, 10am-11pm daily). A cursory look at the tenant stores is enough to convince you that the Esplanade caters to the wealthy, the lucky, and the reckless.

ENTERTAINMENT

From the creative geniuses behind Cirque du Soleil, *Le Rêve* (702/770-9966 or 888/320-7110, 7pm and 9:30pm Fri.-Tues., $114-130) presents an aquatic stream-of-unconsciousness dream in the form of human athleticism and beauty. More than 2,000 guests fill the theater in the round, with seats all within 50 feet; those in the first couple of rows are in the "splash zone." A cast of singers and dancers re-create climactic scenes from a dozen of Broadway's best in *Showstoppers* (702/770-9966, 7:30pm Sat. and Mon.-Thurs., 8pm Fri., $100-150).

RESTAURANTS

The duck hash and eggs and the brown butter apple pancakes in the garden atrium at **Tableau** (702/770-3330, 7am-2:30pm daily, $17-25) make breakfast here the most important meal of the day. At **Wing Lei** (702/770-3388, 5:30pm-9:30pm Sun.-Thurs., 5:30pm-10pm Fri.-Sat., $40-65), French colonialism comes through in Chef Ming Yu's Shanghai style. In addition to the casino's gourmet offerings, don't miss the dim sum at **Red 8 Asian Bistro** (11:30am-midnight Sun.-Thurs., 11:30am-1am Fri.-Sat., $20-30).

CENTER STRIP
The Venetian

Restaurants: AquaKnox, B&B Burger & Beer, B&B Ristorante, Bouchon, Buddy V's, Café Press, Canaletto, Canonita, Canyon Ranch Café, Carlo's Bakery, Casanova, db Brasserie, Delmonico Steakhouse, Grand

Lux Café, Grimaldi's, Lobster ME, Noodle Asia, Otto Enoteca Pizzeria, Prime Burger, Public House, Tao Asian Bistro, Tintoretto Bakery, Trattoria Reggiano, Yardbird, Zeffirino, Food Court (Bella Panini, Café Pan, Chicken Now, Chipotle, Johnny Rockets, Panda Express, Social Life Pizza, Subway, Wasabi Jane)

Entertainment: *Lipshtick*

Attractions: Madame Tussauds Las Vegas, Gondola Rides, Streetmosphere

Nightlife: Tao, Tao Beach, Bellini Bar, Rockhouse, Bourbon Room, V Bar, Oculus

The Venetian (3355 Las Vegas Blvd. S., 702/414-1000 or 866/659-9643, $209-349 d) comes pretty close to capturing the elegance of Venice. An elaborate faux-Renaissance ceiling fresco greets visitors in the hotel lobby, and the sensual treats just keep coming. A life-size streetscape with replicas of the Bridge of Sighs, Doge's Palace, the Grand Canal, and other treasures give the impression that the best of the Queen of the Adriatic has been transplanted in toto. Tranquil rides in authentic gondolas with serenading pilots are perfect for relaxing after a hectic session in the 120,000-square-foot casino. The Venetian spares no expense in the hotel department. Its 4,027 suites are tastefully appointed with Italian (of course) marble, and at 650 square feet, they're big. They include sunken living rooms and luxe Roman tubs.

Canal-side, buskers entertain the guests in the **Streetmosphere** (various times and locations daily, free), and the **Grand Canal Shoppes** (10am-11pm Sun.-Thurs., 10am-midnight Fri.-Sat.) entice strollers, window-shoppers, and serious spenders along winding streetscapes. **Madame Tussauds Las Vegas** (10am-8pm Sun.-Thurs., 10am-9pm Fri.-Sat., adults $30, children 4-12 $20, under age 4 free) invites stargazers for hands-on experiences with their favorite entertainers, superheroes, and athletes. Then you can dance the night away at **Tao** (10pm-5am Thurs.-Sat., lounge 5pm-1am daily).

RESTAURANTS

Tao (702/388-8338, 5pm-midnight Sun.-Wed., 5pm-1am Thurs.-Sat., $30-40) is where pan-Asian dishes like the roasted Thai Buddha chicken and an extensive sake selection are served in decor that is a trip through Asian history. **Canaletto** (702/733-0070, 11am-11pm Sun.-Thurs., 11am-midnight Fri.-Sat., $15-25) focuses on Venetian cuisine. The kitchen staff performs around the grill and rotisserie—a demonstration kitchen—creating sumptuously authentic dishes.

Submerge yourself in the cool, fluid atmosphere at **AquaKnox** (702/414-3772, noon-3pm and 5:30pm-11pm Sun.-Thurs., noon-3pm and 5:30pm-10pm Fri.-Sat., $40-70). The fish soup is the signature entrée, but the crab dishes are the way to go. Fine-dining options abound, but for a change, try the lobster ravioli or traditional pizza and pasta dishes in the bistro setting of **Trattoria Reggiano** (11am-11pm Sun.-Thurs., 11am-midnight Fri.-Sat., $20-30).

The Palazzo

Restaurants: Café Presse, Canyon Ranch Grill, Carnevino, CUT, Dal Toro, Espressamente Illy, I (heart) Burgers, JuiceFarm, Grand Lux Café, Hong Kong Café, LAVO, Legasse's Stadium, Morels, Sushisamba, Table 10

Attractions: Grand Canal Shoppes, Atrium Waterfall

Nightlife: Laguna Champagne Bar, Double Helix, LAVO Lounge, The Label, Salute Lounge, Fusion Latin Mixology Bar, The Lounge at Sushisamba

The lobby at **The Palazzo** (3325 Las Vegas Blvd. S., 702/607-7777 or 866/263-3001, $199-339 d), The Venetian's sister property next door, is bathed in natural light from an 80-foot domed skylight focused on a faux-ice sculpture, bronze columns, and lush landscaping. Half of the 100,000-square-foot casino is smoke-free, part of The Palazzo's efforts in achieving energy efficiency and environmentally friendly design. Accommodations are all suites, with Roman tubs, sunken living rooms, and sumptuous beds that would make it tough to leave the room if not for the lure of the Strip.

LAVO (5pm-midnight daily) pours top-shelf booze amid subdued lighting, first editions, and burnished leather. LAVO recently added the Casino Club, a sort of high-class speakeasy. Waiters deliver premium bottles, appetizers, and even full dinners directly to your personal gaming table.

The Palazzo is a gourmand's dream, with a handful of four-star establishments. **Carnevino** (noon-midnight daily, $45-70) is light and bright, with snootiness kept to a minimum, but that does not mean Chef Mario Batali skimps on quality. He selects the best cuts and refrains from overwhelming them in preparation.

The Mirage

Restaurants: Tom Colicchio's Heritage Steak, Fin, Morimoto, Stack, Portofino, Samba Brazilian Steakhouse, BLT Burger, California Pizza Kitchen, Cravings Buffet, Carnegie Delicatessen, Paradise Café, Pantry, Blizz Frozen Yogurt, The Roasted Bean, Starbucks
Entertainment: The Beatles *LOVE*, Terry Fator Boys II Men, Aces of Comedy
Attractions: Secret Garden and Dolphin Habitat, Aquarium, Mirage Volcano, Atrium
Nightlife: 1 Oak, Revolution Lounge, Rhumbar, High Limit Lounge, Heritage Steak Lounge, Japonais Lounge, The Sports Bar, Dolphin Bar, Bare Pool Lounge, Lobby Bar, Stack Lounge

The Mirage (3400 Las Vegas Blvd. S., 702/791-7111 or 800/627-6667, $129-300 d) greets visitors with exotic bamboo, orchids, banana trees, secluded grottoes, and peaceful lagoons. Dolphins, white tigers, stingrays, sharks, and a volcano provide livelier sights. This Bali Ha'i-themed paradise lets guests bask in the wonders of nature alongside the sophistication and pampering of resort life. The Mirage's guest rooms have tasteful appointments and some of the most comfortable beds in town. The standard 371-square-foot rooms emit a modern and relaxing feel in browns, blacks, and splashes of tangerine, mauve, and ruby.

ENTERTAINMENT

The Mirage commands performances by the world's top headliners, but **The Beatles LOVE** (7pm and 9:30pm Thurs.-Mon., $79-209) packs 'em in every night. It's a celebration of the Fab Four's music, but even more an exploration of classic Beatles tunes come to life. *America's Got Talent* champion **Terry Fator** (7:30pm Mon.-Thurs., $59-149) combines two disparate skills—ventriloquism and impersonation—to channel Elvis, Garth Brooks, Lady Gaga, and others.

1 Oak (10:30am-4am Tues. and Fri.-Sat.) has two separate rooms with bars, DJs, and crowded dance floors. With dark walls and no lighting, 1 Oak makes no excuses for providing a sinful, sexy venue for the beautiful people to congregate.

RESTAURANTS

You may pay for the setting as much as for the food at **Fin** (866/339-4566, 5pm-10pm Thurs.-Mon., $30-50). The metallic-ball curtains evoke a rainstorm in a Chinese garden and set just the right romantic but non-cloying mood. While the prices are not outrageous, the food is not gourmet quality either.

Harrah's

Restaurants: Ruth's Chris Steak House; Flavors, the Buffet; Oyster Bar; Ice Pan; Toby Keith's I Love This Bar & Grill; Fulton Street Food Hall; Starbucks
Entertainment: *Million Dollar Quartet, Menopause the Musical,* The Improv Comedy Club, Mac King Comedy Magic Show, Big Elvis, *X Country*
Nightlife: Carnaval Court, Numb Bar, Piano Bar, Signature Bar

Seemingly unwilling to engage in the one-upmanship of its neighbors, ★ **Harrah's** (3475 Las Vegas Blvd. S., 800/214-9110, $55-165 d) has been content instead to carve out a niche as a middle-of-the-action, middle-of-the-road, middle-of-the-price-scale option.

ENTERTAINMENT

Carnaval Court, outside on the Strip's sidewalk, capitalizes on the street-party atmosphere with live bands and juggling bartenders. Just inside, Vegas icon **Big Elvis** (2pm, 3:30pm, and 5pm Mon., Wed., and Fri., free) performs in the **Piano Bar,** which invites aspiring singers to the karaoke stage Monday through Wednesday evenings, and dueling twin sister keyboardists take over each night at 9pm.

Don't miss *Million Dollar Quartet* (5:30pm and 8pm Mon. and Thurs.; 7pm Tues., Fri., and Sun.; 6:30pm Wed.; $71-97), which re-creates the serendipitous star convergence-jam session with Elvis, Carl Perkins, Jerry Lee Lewis, and Johnny Cash. Even 60 years later (and with actors portraying the icons) the magic is still palpable. It's even kid-friendly!

The **Mac King Comedy Magic Show** (1pm and 3pm Tues.-Sat., $32-42) fills the bill for talent and affordability. With a plaid suit, good manners, and a silly grin, he cuts a nerdy figure, but his tricks and banter are skewed enough to make even the most jaded teenager laugh.

RESTAURANTS

The country superstar lends his name and unapologetic patriotism to **Toby Keith's I Love This Bar & Grill** (11:30am-2am Sun.-Thurs., 11:30am-3am Fri.-Sat., $15-25). Try the fried bologna sandwich.

★ Caesars Palace

Restaurants: Bacchanal Buffet, Rao's, Nobu, Gordon Ramsay Pub and Grill, Old Homestead Steakhouse, Payard Patisserie & Bistro, Serendipity 3, Mesa Grill, Beijing Noodle No. 9, Restaurant Guy Savoy, Searsucker Las Vegas, Café Americano, Sushi Roku, Forum Food Court (Smashburger, Phillips Seafood Express, Earl of Sandwich, Graeter's, Tiger Wok & Ramen, Difara Pizza, La Gloria)

Entertainment: *Absinthe*, Matt Goss

Attractions: *Fall of Atlantis* and *Festival Fountain Show*, aquarium, Appian Way Shops, Forum Shops

Nightlife: Omnia, Fizz, Cleopatra's Barge, Seahorse Lounge, Numb Bar & Frozen Cocktails, Lobby Bar, Spanish Steps, Vista Cocktail Lounge

Caesars Palace (3570 Las Vegas Blvd. S., 866/227-5938, $175-300 d) has incorporated all the ancient empire's decadence and overindulgence while adding a few thousand slot machines. Like the empire, it continues to expand, now boasting 3,348 guest rooms in six towers and 140,000 square feet of gaming space accented with marble, fountains, gilding, and royal reds. Wander the grounds searching for reproductions of some of the world's most famous statuary. The casino is so big that the website includes a "slot finder" application so gamblers can navigate to their favorite machines. Most newer guest rooms are done in tan, wood, and marble. Ask for a south-facing room in the Augustus and Octavius towers to get commanding

Million Dollar Quartet

vistas of both the Bellagio fountains and the Strip.

ENTERTAINMENT

Cleopatra's Barge (5pm-3am daily), a floating lounge, attracts the full spectrum of the 21-and-over crowd for late-night bacchanalia. Carmine and gold accents only add to the decadence. A live band and the Dirty Virgins dancers back **Matt Goss** (9:30pm Tues. and Fri.-Sat., $75-144) and his original compositions and interpretations of the Great American Songbook.

All roads lead to the **Forum Shops** (10am-11pm Sun.-Thurs., 10am-midnight Fri.-Sat.), a collection of famous designer stores, specialty boutiques, and restaurants. You'll also find the *Fall of Atlantis* and *Festival Fountain Show* (hourly 10am-11pm Sun.-Thurs., 10am-midnight Fri.-Sat., free), a multisensory, multimedia depiction of the gods' wrath.

RESTAURANTS

The decor at **Payard Patisserie & Bistro** (702/731-7292 or 866/462-5982, 6:30am-2:30pm Sun.-Thurs., 24 hours Fri.-Sat., $18-30, pastry counter 7am-10pm Sun.-Thurs., 24 hours Fri.-Sat.) evokes the delightful French pastries for which François Payard is famous.

Indeed, the bakery takes up most of the restaurant, but the restaurant stands on its own, with the quiches and panini taking best in show.

Within **Sushi Roku** (702/733-7373, 7am-2:30pm and 5:30pm-10:30pm daily, $30-50) is a veritable Zen garden, bamboo, and shadowy table alcoves. Outside are unparalleled views up and down the Strip.

If you (or your wallet) tire of Caesars's high-on-the-hog dining, nosh on British pub food at **Gordon Ramsay Pub and Grill** (11am-11pm Sun.-Thurs., 11am-midnight Fri.-Sat., $25-40). When in doubt, you can never go wrong with the fish-and-chips.

The Linq

Restaurants: Guy Fieri's Vegas Kitchen and Bar, Chayo Mexican Kitchen & Tequila Bar, Hash House a Go Go

Entertainment: *Divas Las Vegas,* Mat Franco

Attractions: Auto Collection, O'Shea's

Nightlife: Yes, 3535, Fat Tuesday, Catalyst, TAG Lounge and Bar

At **The Linq** (3535 Las Vegas Blvd. S., 800/634-6441, $89-210 d), rooms are sleek, stylish, and smallish, at 245-350 square feet. Pewter and chrome accented with eggplant, orange, or aqua murals evoke vintage Vegas.

the Forum Shops at Caesars Palace

Other amenities include marble countertops, 47-inch flat-screen TVs, and iPod docks. But the hotel is really just a way to stay close to all the Gen X-focused boutiques, bars, and restaurants in the adjacent outdoor promenade. The high point of this pedestrian-friendly plaza is the **High Roller,** the highest observation wheel in the world, but there's plenty more to warrant a stop.

ENTERTAINMENT

Veteran female impersonator Frank Marino has been headlining on the Strip for 25 years, and he still looks good—with or without eye shadow and falsies. Marino stars as emcee Joan Rivers, leading fellow impersonators who lip-synch their way through cheeky renditions of tunes by Lady Gaga, Katy Perry, Cher, Madonna, and others in *Divas Las Vegas* (702/777-2782 or 866/574-3851, 9:30pm Sat.-Thurs., $65-94).

Vegas icon and locals' favorite **O'Shea's** (24 hours daily) brings back the kegger party, with all its lowbrow frivolity. Cheap drafts, heated beer pong challenges, and Lucky the Leprechaun keep the festivities raging well into the wee hours.

America's Got Talent winner **Mat Franco** (7pm Thurs.-Tues., additional matinee 4pm Sat., $46-90) combines jaw-dropping production illusions with how'd-he-do-that close-up tricks. His easygoing banter and anything-to-please attitude ensure it's never the same show twice.

RESTAURANTS

Don't let the presentation turn you off—the shrimp cocktail served at **Haute Doggery** (702/430-4435, 10am-midnight Sun.-Thurs., 10am-2am Fri.-Sat., $1) is heaven. **Brooklyn Bowl** (5pm-late daily, $15-30) has you covered on "eat, drink, and be merry," combining dozens of beer taps with delectable noshes and live entertainment. The cuisine at **Guy Fieri's Kitchen and Bar** (8am-midnight Sun.-Thurs., 8am-2am Fri.-Sat., $20-35) is gourmet bar food, with sashimi tacos and truffled french fries.

Flamingo

Restaurants: Center Cut Steakhouse, Paradise Garden Buffet, Jimmy Buffett's Margaritaville, Carlos'n Charlie's, Beach Club Bar & Grill, Club Cappuccino, Food Court

Entertainment: Donny and Marie, *Legends in Concert, X Burlesque, X Comedy – Uncensored Fun,* Jeff Civillico: *Comedy in Action*

Attractions: Wildlife Habitat

Nightlife: It's 5 O'Clock Somewhere Bar, Garden Bar, Bugsy's Bar

Named for Virginia Hill, the long-legged girlfriend of Benjamin "don't call me Bugsy" Siegel, the **Flamingo** (3555 Las Vegas Blvd. S., 702/733-3111 or 800/732-2111, $80-150 d) has at turns embraced and shunned its gangster ties, which stretch back to the 1960s. Today, its art deco architecture and pink-and-orange neon beckon pedestrians and conjure images of aging Mafiosi lounging by the pool. Siegel's penthouse suite, behind the current hotel, has been replaced by the **Flamingo Wildlife Habitat** (8am-dusk daily, free), where ibis, pelicans, turtles, koi fish, and, of course, Chilean flamingos luxuriate amid riparian plants and meandering streams. The Flamingo transformed many of its guest rooms into Fab Rooms in 2012, but the older Go Rooms are actually more modern, dressed in swanky mahogany and white with bold swatches of hot pink. The rooms are only 350 square feet, but boast high-end entertainment systems. Suite options are just as colorful and include 32-inch TVs, vintage art prints, padded leather headboards, and all the other Vegas-sational accouterments.

ENTERTAINMENT

The best of the celebrity impersonator shows, *Legends in Concert* (702/777-7776 or 866/983-4279, 7:30pm and 9:30pm Mon., 9:30pm Tues., 4pm and 9:30pm Wed.-Thurs. and Sat., 7:30pm Sun., $55-98) brings out the "stars"—from Sinatra and Elvis to Madonna and Michael Jackson—in rapid-fire succession. A Vegas fixture for 25 years, *Legends* is truly legendary.

A little bit country, a little bit rock and roll,

Donny and Marie Osmond (702/733-3333, 7:30pm Tues.-Sat., $117-135) manage a bit of hip-hop and soul as well, as they hurl affectionate put-downs at each other between musical numbers.

RESTAURANTS

Guests can search for their lost shaker of salt in paradise at **Jimmy Buffett's Margaritaville** (11am-2am Sun.-Thurs., 11am-3am Fri.-Sat., $20-30) while people-watching on the Strip and noshing on jambalaya and cheeseburgers.

Rio

Restaurants: Royal India Bistro, Hash House a Go Go, Village Seafood Buffet, Martorano's, VooDoo Steakhouse, Búzio's Seafood Restaurant, KJ Dim Sum & Seafood, Wine Cellar & Tasting Room, All-American Bar & Grille, BK Whopper Bar, Pho Da Nang Vietnamese Kitchen, Sports Deli, Carnival World Buffet

Entertainment: Penn & Teller, Chippendales, The Eddie Griffin Experience, *X Rocks*

Attractions: VooDoo Zip Line, Masquerade Village

Nightlife: VooDoo Rooftop Nightclub & Lounge, Masquerade Bar, IBar, Flirt Lounge

With three towers and 2,500 suites, terrific buffets, beautiful people-magnet bars, and steamy shows, the **Rio** (3700 W. Flamingo Rd., 866/746-7671, $89-180 d) keeps the party going. Dancers and other performers may materialize at your slot machine to take your mind off your losses. All of the Rio's guest rooms are suites—a sofa and coffee table replace the uncomfortable easy chair found in most standard guest rooms. A dressing area separate from the bathroom makes night-on-the-town preparations easy. Rio suites measure about 600 square feet. The hotel's center-Strip location and room-tall windows make for exciting views.

ENTERTAINMENT

While topless dancers and hard rock are the premise of every strip club in town, the focus at *X Rocks* (10pm Thurs.-Sun., $62-95, 18 and over) is on the choreography and props, rather than the flesh (yeah, right!). Comedian John Bizarre yuks it up between routines.

Chippendales (702/777-2782, 8:30pm and 10:30pm daily, $50-73) delivers a little gender equity: dancers in tight jeans and rippled abs bump and grind with their female admirers.

Oddball comedy magicians **Penn & Teller** (866/983-4279, 9pm Sat.-Wed., $91-104) reveal the preparation and sleight-of-hand involved in performing tricks. The hitch is that even when forewarned, observers still often can't catch on.

Everyone hangs out at Sin City Sundays at **VooDoo Lounge** (8pm-2am Sun.-Thurs., 8pm-3am Fri.-Sat.), 51 stories up. If that's not enough physical perfection for you, **Flirt Lounge** (6:30pm-midnight Sun.-Tues. and Thurs., 6:30pm-1am Fri.-Sat.) and its easy-on-the-eyes waiters keep the Rio's Ultimate Girls Night Out churning.

RESTAURANTS

The best buffet for under $85 in Las Vegas is, without a doubt, the **Village Seafood Buffet** (702/777-7943, 3:30pm-9:30pm daily, adults $49, children 4-10 $25). Garlic butter lobster tails are the main attraction, but other seafood preparations include grilled scallops, shrimp, mussels, and calamari with assorted vegetables and sauces; snow crab legs; oysters on the half shell; peel-and-eat shrimp; and steamed clams. There's even hand-carved prime rib, ham, chicken, and pasta for the nonfan of seafood.

Getting to **VooDoo Steakhouse** (702/777-7923, 5pm-11pm daily, $40-60) requires a mini thrill ride to the top of the Rio tower in the glass elevator. Set across two floors, the VooDoo double-decker provides a great view of the Strip, though the N'awlins creole and Cajun food and drinks are expensive and tame.

Búzio's (5pm-10pm daily, $25-45) has great crab-shack appetizers and buttery lobster and steak entrées.

LOWER STRIP
The Palms

Restaurants: N9NE Steakhouse, Lao Sze Chuan, Nove Italiano, Alizé, 24 Seven Café, Bistro Buffet, Café 6,

Hooters, The Eatery
Entertainment: The Lounge, Brendan Theater
Nightlife: Ghostbar, Social

The expression "party like a rock star" could have been invented for **The Palms** (4321 W. Flamingo Rd., 866/942-7770, $110-175 d). Penthouse views, uninhibited pool parties, lavish theme suites, and starring roles in MTV's *The Real World: Las Vegas* and Bravo's *Celebrity Poker Showdown* have brought notoriety and stars to the clubs, concert venue, and recording studio.

The Fantasy Tower houses the fantasy suites, while the original Ivory Tower offers large guest rooms. They're sleek, with geometric shapes and a designer mural, but their best features are the feathery beds and luxurious comforters that make it easy to roll over and go back to sleep, even if you're not nursing a hangover. The newest tower, Palms Place, is part of the Las Vegas "condotel" trend. Its 599 studios and one-bedrooms, restaurant, spa, and pool offer opportunities to recuperate from the partying.

ENTERTAINMENT

The 2,500-seat **Pearl Concert Theater** regularly hosts rock concerts. **Ghostbar** (8pm-late daily), 55 floors atop the Ivory Tower, treats partiers to vistas of the Strip and night sky. Eclectic entertainers play **The Lounge** (24 hours daily): comedy tonight, heavy metal cover bands tomorrow, and funky soul next week.

RESTAURANTS

Sleek furnishings of chrome highlighted by rich colored lighting add accompaniment, but ★ **N9NE** (702/933-9900, 5:30pm-10pm Sun.-Thurs., 5:30pm-11pm Fri.-Sat., $50-80) never loses focus on its raison d'être: flawlessly prepared steak and seafood and impeccable service.

Andre Rochat's **Alizé** (702/951-7000, 5:30pm-10pm daily, $45-70) is the quintessential French restaurant: authentic fare, a cognac cellar, snooty clientele, sophisticated decor, and top-of-the-world views.

Bellagio

Restaurants: Jasmine, Le Cirque, Michael Mina, Picasso, Prime Steakhouse, Fix, Lago, Todd English's Olives, Noodles, Yellowtail, Harvest by Roy Ellamar, Circo, Sensi, The Buffet, Café Bellagio, Pool Café, Café Gelato, Palio, Snacks, Jean Philippe Patisserie
Entertainment: Cirque du Soleil's O
Attractions: The Fountains at Bellagio, The Conservatory, Bellagio Gallery of Fine Art, public art
Nightlife: The Bank, Hyde, Lily Bar & Lounge, Petrossian Bar, Baccarat Bar, Pool Bar, Sports Bar Lounge

With nearly 4,000 guest rooms and suites, ★ **Bellagio** (3600 Las Vegas Blvd. S., 702/693-7111 or 888/987-6667, $200-320 d) boasts a population larger than the village perched on Lake Como from which it borrows its name. And to keep pace with its Italian namesake, Bellagio created an 8.5-acre lake between the hotel and Las Vegas Boulevard. The view of the lake and its **Fountains at Bellagio** (3pm-midnight Mon.-Fri., noon-midnight Sat.-Sun.) are free, as is the aromatic fantasy that is **Bellagio Conservatory** (24 hours daily). And the **Bellagio Gallery of Fine Art** (10am-8pm daily, $14-19) would be a bargain at twice the price—you can spend an edifying day at one of the world's priciest resorts (including a cocktail and lunch) for less than $50. Even if you don't spring for gallery admission, art demands your attention throughout the hotel and casino. The glass flower petals in Dale Chihuly's *Fiori di Como* sculpture bloom from the lobby ceiling, foreshadowing the opulent experiences to come. Masatoshi Izumi's *A Gift from the Earth,* four massive basalt sculptures representing wind, fire, water, and earth, dominates the hotel's main entrance. The display of artistry continues but the bargains end at **Via Bellagio** (10am-midnight daily), the resort's shopping district, including heavyweight retailers Armani, Prada, Chanel, Tiffany, and their ilk.

Bellagio's tower rooms are the epitome of luxury, with Italian marble, oversize bathtubs, remote-controlled drapes, Egyptian-cotton sheets, and 510 square feet in which to spread out. The sage-plum and indigo-silver color schemes are refreshing changes from the goes-with-everything beige and the camouflages-all-stains paisley often found on the Strip.

ENTERTAINMENT

The Vegas Cirque du Soleil **O** (702/693-7722 or 888/488-7111, 7:30pm and 10pm Wed.-Sun., $132-210) involves a $90 million set, 80 artists, and a 1.5-million-gallon pool of water. The production involves both terrestrial and aquatic feats of human artistry, athleticism, and comedy.

RESTAURANTS

Befitting Bellagio's world-class status, intriguing and expensive restaurants abound. **Michael Mina's** (5pm-10pm Mon.-Sat., $50-80) restrained decor adds to the simple elegance of the cuisine, which is mostly American beef and seafood with European and Asian influences. With limited seating in its Picasso-canvased dining room and a small dining time window, **Picasso** (702/693-7223, 6pm-9:30pm Wed.-Mon., $113-123) has a couple of prix fixe menus. It's seriously expensive, and if you include Kobe beef, lobster, wine pairings, and a cheese course, you and a mate could easily leave several pounds heavier and $500 lighter.

Traditional Asian dishes are the specialty at **Noodles** (11am-2am daily, $15-20), if you're in search of something more affordable. Chinese art in a Hong Kong bistro setting makes **Jasmine** (5:30pm-10pm daily, $30-60) one of the most visually striking Chinese restaurants in town.

Paris Las Vegas

Restaurants: Burger Brasserie, Mon Ami Gabi, Martorano's, Hexx, Gordon Ramsay Steak, Eiffel Tower Restaurant, Café Belle Madeleine, La Creperie, JJ's Boulangerie, Le Café Ile St. Louis, Le Village Buffet, Yong Kang Street
Entertainment: *Jersey Boys,* Anthony Cools
Attractions: Eiffel Tower
Nightlife: Napoleon's Lounge, Le Cabaret, Le Central, Le Bar du Sport, Gustav's, Chateau Nightclub & Rooftop

Designers used Gustav Eiffel's original drawings to ensure that the half-size tower that anchors **Paris Las Vegas** (3655 Las Vegas Blvd. S., 877/242-6753, $120-250 d) conformed—down to the last cosmetic rivet—to the original. That attention to detail prevails throughout this property, which works hard to evoke the City of Light, from large-scale reproductions of the Arc de Triomphe, Champs Élysées, and Louvre to more than half a dozen French restaurants. The cobblestone lanes and brass streetlights of **Le Boulevard** (8am-2am daily) invite shoppers into quaint shops and "sidewalk" patisseries. The casino offers its own attractions, not the least of which is the view of the Eiffel Tower's base jutting through the ceiling.

Standard guest rooms in the 33-story tower are decorated in a rich earth-tone palette and have marble baths. There's nothing Left Bank bohemian about them, however. The guest rooms exude little flair and little personality, but the simple, quality furnishings make Paris a moderately priced option in the middle of a top-dollar neighborhood. Book a Red Room if modern decor is important to you.

ENTERTAINMENT

The rise of Frankie Valli and the Four Seasons from street-corner doo-woppers to superstars gets the full Broadway treatment in *Jersey Boys* (7pm Tues.-Sun., $60-150), the true story of the falsetto-warbling Valli and his bandmates. The **Paris Theatre** hosts headliners. **Anthony Cools—The Uncensored Hypnotist** (9pm Tues. and Thurs.-Sun., $49-82) cajoles his mesmerized subjects through very adult simulations.

RESTAURANTS

Paris's **Eiffel Tower Restaurant** (702/948-6937, 11:30am-3pm and 4:30pm-10:30pm Mon.-Thurs., 11:30am-3pm and 4:30pm-11pm Fri., 11am-3pm and 4:30pm-11pm Sat., 11am-3pm and 4:30pm-10:30pm Sun., $35-75) hovers 100 feet above the Strip. Order the soufflé, have a glass of wine, and bask in the romantic piano strains as the culinary staff performs delicate French culinary feats.

The steaks and seafood at ★ **Mon Ami Gabi** (702/944-4224, 7am-11pm Sun.-Thurs., 7am-midnight Fri.-Sat., $35-50) are comparable to those at any fine Strip establishment—at about half the price. You'll be wishing you had packed your beret when you order a beignet and cappuccino at **Le Café Ile St. Louis** (6am-11pm daily, $15-25). While the look and feel is a French sidewalk café, the menu tends toward American.

The Cosmopolitan

Restaurants: Beauty & Exxex, Blue Ribbon Sushi Bar & Grill, China Poblano, D.O.C.G., Estiatorio Milos, Holsteins, Jaleo, Overlook Grill, Rose. Rabbit. Lie., Scarpetta, Secret Pizza, STK, The Henry, Va Bene Caffè, Wicked Spoon

Attractions: Lucky Cat, public art

Nightlife: Rose. Rabbit. Lie., The Chandelier, Vesper Bar, Book & Stage, Bond, Queue Bark, The Neapolitan, Marquee Nightclub & Day Club

Modern art, marble bath floors, and big soaking tubs in 460-square-foot rooms evoke urban penthouse living at ★ **The Cosmopolitan** (3708 Las Vegas Blvd. S., 702/698-7000, $280-440 d). Because it's too cool to host production shows, the resort's entertainment schedule mixes DJs of the moment with the most laid-back headliners. **The Chelsea** hosts mixed martial arts cards regularly. That nouveau riche attitude carries through to the restaurant and nightlife offerings. **Vesper Bar** (24 hours daily), named for James Bond's favorite martini, prides itself on serving hipster versions of classic (and sometimes forgotten) cocktails. Possibly the best day club in town, **Marquee** (11am-6pm) brings in the beautiful people with DJs and sweet bungalow lofts on the roof. When darkness falls, the day club becomes an extension of the pulsating Marquee nightclub.

RESTAURANTS

With lines snaking out its unmarked entrance, in a dark alleyway decorated with record covers, **Secret Pizza** (11am-5am Fri.-Mon., 11am-4am Tues.-Thurs., slices $5-6) is not so secret anymore. Located next to Blue Ribbon Sushi on The Cosmopolitan's third floor, it's a great place to get a quick, greasy slice.

Equal parts supper club, nightclub, and jazz club, ★ **Rose. Rabbit. Lie.** (702/698-7000, 6pm-midnight Wed.-Thurs., 6pm-1am Fri.-Sat., $80-130) is equal parts supper club, nightclub, and jazz club. Throughout the evening bluesy, jazzy torch singers, magicians, tap and hip-hop dancers, and a rocking, if a touch loud, sound system keep the joint jumping. If you go for dinner, order 5-6 small plates per couple.

Aria

Restaurants: Aria Café, Bardot, BarMasa, Blossom, the Buffet, Carbone, Five50, Herringbone, Javier's, Jean Georges Steakhouse, Jean Philippe Patisserie, Julian Serrano, Lemongrass, Pressed Juicery, The Roasted Bean, Sage, Starbucks, Tetsu

Entertainment: Cirque du Soleil's *Zarkana*

Attractions: Public art, Crystals

Nightlife: Alibi, Baccarat Lounge, High Limit Lounge, Lift Bar, Lobby Bar, Pool Bar, Sports Bar

All glass and steel, ultramodern ★ **Aria** (3730 Las Vegas Blvd. S., 702/590-7757, $210-500) would look more at home in Manhattan than Las Vegas. Touch pads control the drapes, the lighting, and the climate in Aria's blueberry- or grape-paletted guest rooms—one touch transforms the room into sleep mode. A traditional hotel casino, Aria shares the City Center umbrella with **Vdara**, a Euro-chic boutique hotel with no gaming. Guests are invited to browse an extensive public art collection, with works by Maya Lin, Jenny Holzer, and Richard Long, among others. **Crystals**, a 500,000-square-foot mall, lets you splurge among hanging gardens.

RESTAURANTS

Lighting and decor suggesting screens and lanterns set the stage for a journey into the depths of Chinese cuisine at **Blossom** (877/230-2742, 5:30pm-10:30pm daily, $50-80). Much of the menu is exotic, bold, and playful, but there are plenty of selections tempered toward Western palates. Culinary genius Masa Takayama guarantees that the bluefin at **BarMasa** (5pm-11pm daily, $25-40) goes from the Sea of Japan to your spicy tuna roll in less than 24 hours.

Hard Rock

Restaurants: 35 Steaks+Martinis, Culinary Dropout, Fu Asian Kitchen, Mr. Lucky's, Nobu, Pink Taco, Juice Bar, Fuel Café, Pizza Forte
Entertainment: The Joint, Vinyl, Soundwaves
Nightlife: Rehab Pool Party, The Ainsworth, Center Bar, Sidebet Draft Bar, Luxe Bar, Midway Bar

Young stars and the media-savvy 20-somethings who idolize them contribute to the frat party and spring break mojo at the **Hard Rock** (4455 Paradise Rd., 800/473-7625, $170-320 d) and the spring-break atmosphere poolside. While the casino is shaped like an LP, if your music collection dates back to wax records, this probably isn't the place for you. The gaming tables and machines are located in the "record label," and the shops and restaurants are in the "grooves." Contemporary and classic rockers regularly grace the stage at **The Joint** and party with their fans at **Rehab Pool Parties** (11am-dusk Fri.-Sat.).

Several rounds of expansion have brought the resort's room count to a Vegas-respectable 1,500. Guest rooms are decorated in mint, cinnamon, or gray, and include stocked minibars, Bose CD sound systems, and plasma TVs, as befitting wannabe rock stars.

RESTAURANTS

★ **Culinary Dropout** (702/522-8100, www.culinarydropout.com, 11am-11pm Mon.-Thurs., 11am-midnight Fri., 10am-midnight Sat., 10am-11pm Sun., $15-30) takes comfort food seriously, with home-style favorites like fried chicken and grilled cheese sliders. The provocatively named **Pink Taco** (11am-10pm Sun.-Thurs., 11am-midnight Fri.-Sat., $15-25) dishes up Mexican and Caribbean specialties.

New York New York

Restaurants: Tom's Urban, Nine Fine Irishmen, Shake Shack, Gallagher's Steakhouse, Il Fornaio, Chin Chin Café & Sushi, Gonzalez y Gonzalez, America, 48th and Crepe, Nathan's Hot Dogs, New York Pizzeria, Broadway Burger Bar, Quick Bites, Village Street Eateries
Entertainment: Cirque du Soleil's *Zumanity*, Brooklyn Bridge buskers, dueling pianos
Attractions: Hershey's Chocolate World, Big Apple Coaster & Arcade
Nightlife: Coyote Ugly, The Bar at Times Square, Center Bar, Pour 24, Big Chill, High Limit Bar, Lobby Bar, Chocolate Bar

From the city skyline outside (the skyscrapers contain the resort's hotel rooms) to laundry hanging between crowded faux brownstones indoors, **New York New York** (3790 Las Vegas Blvd. S., 866/815-4365, $130-230 d) will have even grizzled Gothamites feeling like they've come home again. Window air-conditioners in the Greenwich Village apartments evoke the city's gritty heat. New York New York's 2,023 guest rooms are standard size, 350-400 square feet. The roller coaster zooms around the towers, so you might want to ask for a room out of earshot.

ENTERTAINMENT

Cirque du Soleil seems to have succumbed to the titillation craze with the strange melding of sexuality, athleticism, and comedy that is **Zumanity** (866/983-4279, 7pm and 9:30pm Tues.-Sat., $88-127). The cabaret-style show makes no pretense of story line, but instead takes audience members through a succession of sexual and topless fantasies.

The **Big Apple Coaster** (11am-11pm Sun.-Thurs., 10:30am-midnight Fri.-Sat., $14) winds its way around the resort, an experience almost as hair-raising as a New York City cab ride, which the coaster cars are painted to resemble. **Big Apple Arcade** (8am-midnight daily) has games of skill and luck, motion simulators, and rides.

Dueling pianists keep **The Bar at Times Square** (1pm-2:30am Mon.-Thurs., 11am-2:30am Fri.-Sun.) rocking into the wee hours, and the sexy bar staff at **Coyote Ugly** (6pm-2am Sun.-Thurs., 6pm-3am Fri.-Sat.) defy its name.

RESTAURANTS

The original **Gallagher's Steakhouse** (702/740-6450, 4pm-11pm Sun.-Thurs., 4pm-midnight Fri.-Sat., $60-75) has been an institution in New York City since 1927. You'll know why the longevity is deserved after sampling the restaurant's famed dry-aged beef and notable seafood selection.

MGM Grand

Restaurants: Joel Robuchon Restaurant, L'Atelier de Joël Robuchon, Tom Colicchio's Craftsteak, Hecho en Vegas, Shibuya, Fiamma, Michael Mina Pub 1842, Emeril's New Orleans Fish House, Wolfgang Puck Bar & Grill, Grand Wok and Sushi Bar, Crush, Hakkasan, Avenue Café, Stage Deli, Corner Cakes, Food Court, MGM Grand Buffet, Tap Sports Bar, Starbucks, Centrifuge, Blizz Frozen Yogurt & Dessert, Cabana Grill, Project Pie

Entertainment: Cirque du Soleil's *Kà*, David Copperfield, Jabbawockeez, Brad Garrett's Comedy Club

Attractions: CSI: The Experience, CBS Television City Research Center

Nightlife: Centrifuge, Rouge, Lobby Bar, Wet Republic Ultra Pool, Hakkasan Night Club, Whiskey Down, West Wing Bar

Gamblers enter **MGM Grand** (3799 Las Vegas Blvd. S., 888/646-1203, $130-250 d) through portals guarded by MGM's mascot, the 45-foot-tall king of the jungle. The uninitiated may feel like a gazelle on the savanna, swallowed by the 171,000-square-foot casino floor, the largest in Las Vegas. But the watering hole, MGM's 6.5-acre pool complex, is relatively predator-free. MGM capitalizes on the movie studio's greatest hits. Even the hotel's emerald facade evokes the magical city in *The Wizard of Oz*.

Standard guest rooms in the Grand Tower are filled with the quality furnishings you'd expect in Las Vegas's upscale hotels. The West Tower guest rooms are smaller, at 350 square feet, but exude the swinging style of an upscale Hollywood studio apartment crammed with a CD and DVD player and other high-tech gizmos; the 450-square-foot rooms in the Grand Tower are more traditional.

ENTERTAINMENT

Cirque du Soleil's *Kà* (702/531-3826 or 866/983-4279, 7pm and 9:30pm Sat.-Wed., $77-150) explores the yin and yang of life through the story of twins on a journey to meet their shared fate. Martial arts, acrobatics, puppetry, plenty of flashy pyrotechnics, and lavish sets and costumes bring cinematic drama to the variety-show acts. **David Copperfield** (866/740-7711; 7pm and 9:30pm Sun.-Fri.; 4pm, 7pm, and 9:30pm Sat.; $121) also plays long-term gigs here.

Boob tube fans can volunteer for studies at the **CBS Television City Research Center** (10am-8:30pm daily, free), where they can screen pilots for shows under consideration by the network and its competitors. And if your favorite show happens to revolve around solving crimes, don some rubber gloves and search for clues at **CSI: The Experience** (9am-8pm daily, ages 12 and up $31.50, not recommended for children under 12). Three crime scenes keep the experience fresh.

RESTAURANTS

MGM Grand houses enough top restaurants for a week of gourmet dinners. If you only have the time (or budget) to try one, make it **Shibuya** (5:30pm-10pm Sun.-Thurs., 5:30pm-10:30pm Fri.-Sat., $75-120). The sushi and sashimi will draw the eye, but you'll do yourself a disservice if you don't order the pork belly.

The quality of Tom Colicchio's **Craftsteak** (702/891-7318, 5pm-10pm Sun.-Thurs., 5pm-10:30pm Fri.-Sat., $50-75) is evident in the full flavor of the excellently seasoned steaks and chops.

Tropicana

Restaurants: Bacio Italian Cuisine, Biscayne, Beach Café, South Beach Food Court

Attractions: Xposed!

Entertainment: Rich Little, *Raiding the Rock Vault*, *Illusions* starring Jan Rouven, Laugh Factory

Nightlife: Tropicana Lounge, Lucky's Sports Bar, Coconut Grove Bar

When it opened in 1959, the **Tropicana** (801

Las Vegas Blvd. S., 888/381-8767, $140-200 d) was the most luxurious, most expensive resort on the Strip. It has survived several boom-and-bust cycles since then, and its decor reflects the willy-nilly expansion and refurbishment efforts through the years. Today, the rooms have bright, airy South Beach themes with plantation shutters and light wood, 42-inch plasma TVs, and iPod docks. The beach chic atmosphere includes a two-acre pool complex with reclining deck chairs and swim-up blackjack. On summer Saturdays (noon-7pm) the pool deck hosts **Xposed!,** a gay pool party with sand volleyball, go-go dancers, and trendy DJs.

The time-capsule premise is a bit tired, but the music in *Raiding the Rock Vault* (8pm Wed.-Mon., $59-99) is a rollicking nostalgic look at the rock era, from the British Invasion and free love through disco and Vietnam protests to '80s hair bands and the rise of commercialism.

Luxor

Restaurants: Tender Steak & Seafood, Rice & Company, Public House, T&T Tacos & Tequila, More Buffet, Pyramid Café, Backstage Deli, Food Court, Blizz, Burger Bar, Ri Ra Irish Pub, Slice of Vegas, Hussong's Cantina

Entertainment: Criss Angel: *Believe*, Carrot Top, Blue Man Group, *Fantasy*

Attractions: *Bodies...the Exhibition*, *Titanic* artifacts

Nightlife: LAX, Centra, Aurora, Flight, High Bar, PlayBar

Other than its pyramid shape and name, not much remains of the Egyptian theme at the **Luxor** (3900 Las Vegas Blvd. S., 877/386-4658, $89-220 d). In its place are upscale and decidedly post-pharaoh nightclubs, restaurants, and shops. What remain are the 120,000-square-foot casino and 4,400 guest rooms in the pyramid and twin 22-story towers. You can also see the largest atrium in the world, an intense light beam that is visible from space, and inclinators—elevators that move along the building's oblique angles.

Staying in the pyramid makes for interesting room features, such as a slanted exterior wall. Stay on higher floors for panoramic views of the atrium below. Tower rooms are newer and more traditional in their shape, decor, and amenities.

ENTERTAINMENT

Although they are tastefully and respectfully presented, the dissected humans at *Bodies... the Exhibition* (10am-10pm daily, adults $32, seniors $30, children 4-12 $24, under age 4 free) still have the creepy factor. That uneasiness quickly gives way to wonder and interest as visitors examine 13 full-body specimens, carefully preserved to reveal bone structure and muscular, circulatory, respiratory, and other systems. Luxor also hosts the 300 less surreal but just as poignant artifacts and re-productions commemorating the 1912 sinking of the *Titanic* (10am-10pm daily, adults $32, seniors $30, children 4-12 $24, under age 4 free). The 15-ton rusting hunk of the ship's hull is the biggest artifact on display, but it is the passengers' personal effects (a pipe, luggage, an unopened bottle of champagne) and re-created first-class and third-class cabins that provide some of the most heartbreaking discoveries.

Bald, blue, and silent (save for homemade PVC musical instruments), **Blue Man Group** (7pm and 9:30pm daily, $86-149) continues to wow audiences with its thought-provoking, quirkily hilarious gags and percussion performances.

There is a story line in Criss Angel's *Believe* (702/262-4400 or 866/983-4279, 7pm and 9:30pm Wed.-Sat., 7pm Sun., $65-142), but it's really just a framework for the magician's mind-freaking illusions and engaging personality. The **Atrium Showroom** (702/262-4400 or 800/557-7428) is home to *Fantasy* (10:30pm daily, $42-65), a typical jiggle-and-tease topless review with some singing and comedy thrown in, and comedian and prop jockey **Carrot Top** (8pm Wed.-Mon., $60-71).

Old-school touches such as chandeliers and red leather sofas contrast the young and flat-bellied guests at **LAX** (5pm-late Wed. and Fri.-Sat.).

Mandalay Bay

Restaurants: Aureole, Border Grill, Burger Bar, Charlie Palmer Steak, Citizens Kitchen & Bar, Crossroads at House of Blues, Fleur, Kumi, Lupo, RM Seafood, Rivea, Stripsteak, Bayside Buffet, Beach Bar & Grill, House of Blues Foundation Room, Hussong's Cantina, Mizuya, Noodle Shop, Raffles Café, Red Square, Ri Ra Irish Pub, RX Boiler Room, Sea Breeze Ice Cream and Juices, Slice of Vegas, Sports Book Grill, Veranda, Yogurt In, Starbucks

Entertainment: *Michael Jackson ONE*

Attractions: Shark Reef

Nightlife: Light, Daylight Beach Club, Bikini Bar, Evening Call, Eyecandy Sound Lounge, Fat Tuesday, House of Blues Foundation Room, Minus 5 Ice Lounge, Orchid Lounge, Press, Skyfall Lounge, Verandah Lounge, 1923 Bourbon Bar

★ **Mandalay Bay** (3950 Las Vegas Blvd. S., 877/632-7800, $150-300 d) has one of the largest casino floors in the world at 135,000 square feet. Wander into Mandalay's beach environment, an 11-acre paradise comprising three pools, a lazy river, and a 1.6-million-gallon wave pool complete with a real beach made of five million pounds of sand. There's also a tops-optional sunbathing pool deck. The beach hosts a concert series during summer.

Standard guest rooms are chic and roomy (550 square feet), with warm fabrics and plush bedding. Get a north-facing room and put the floor-to-ceiling windows to use gazing the full length of the Strip. The guest rooms are big, but nothing special visually, yet the baths are fit for royalty, with huge tubs, glass-walled showers, and king's-and-queen's commodes. To go upscale, check out the Delano boutique hotel; for very upscale, book at the Four Seasons—both are part of the same complex.

ENTERTAINMENT

When you're ready to check out the rest of the property, don't miss **House of Blues** (hours vary by event), with live blues, rock, and acoustic sets as well as DJs spinning dance tunes.

Mandalay Place (10am-11pm daily), on the sky bridge between Mandalay Bay and Luxor, is smaller and less hectic than other casino malls. Unusual shops such as The Guinness Store, where fans can pick up merchandise celebrating their favorite Irish stout, share space with eateries and high-concept bars like **Minus 5** (11am-2am Sun.-Thurs., 11am-3am Fri.-Sat.), where barflies

Mandalay Bay's Daylight Beach Club

don parkas before entering the below-freezing (23°F) establishment. The glasses aren't just frosted; they're fashioned completely out of ice.

An urban hip-hop worldview and the King of Pop's unmatched talent guide the vignettes in *Michael Jackson ONE* (7pm and 9:30pm Fri.-Tues., $69-160). Michael's musical innovation and the Cirque du Soleil trademark aerial and acrobatic acts pay homage to the human spirit.

Sheathed in Indian artifacts and crafts, the **Foundation Room** (5pm-late daily) is just as dark and mysterious as the subcontinent, with private rooms, a dining room, and several bars catering to various musical tastes.

RESTAURANTS

Rick Moonen is to be commended for his advocacy of sustainable seafood harvesting, and ★ **RM Seafood** (702/632-9300, 11:30am-11pm daily, $40-70) practices what he preaches. You can almost hear the tide-rigging whirr and the mahogany creak in the yacht-club restaurant setting.

Vegas pays tribute to Paris, Rome, New York, and Venice, so why not Moscow? Round up your comrades for caviar and vodka as well as continental favorites at **Red Square** (5pm-10pm Sun.-Thurs., 5pm-11pm Fri.-Sat., $35-50). Look for the headless Lenin statue at the entrance.

DOWNTOWN
Binion's

Restaurants: Top of Binion's Steakhouse, Binion's Deli, Binion's Café, Benny's Smokin BBQ & Brews, Cowgirl Up Cantina, Whiskey Licker

Binion's (128 Fremont St., 702/382-1600) attracts players with occasional $1 blackjack tables and a poker room frequented by grizzled veterans. While Binion's and the rest of Las Vegas have been overtaken by Strip megaresorts, the little den on Fremont Street still retains the flavor of Old Vegas. The hotel at Binion's closed in 2009, but the casino and restaurants remain open, including the **Top of Binion's Steakhouse** (5pm-10pm daily, $30-55), famous for its Fremont Street views and aged Black Angus.

Golden Nugget

Restaurants: Vic & Anthony's, Chart House, Grotto, Lillie's Asian Cuisine, Red Sushi, Cadillac Mexican Kitchen & Tequila Bar, Buffet, The Grille, Claim Jumper, Starbucks
Entertainment: Gordie Brown
Attractions: Hand of Faith, Shark Tank
Nightlife: Rush Lounge, Gold Diggers, H2O Bar at the Tank, Claude's Bar, Ice Bar, Bar 46, Cadillac Tequila Bar

Considered by many to be the only Strip-worthy resort downtown, the ★ **Golden Nugget** (129 E. Fremont St., 800/634-3454, $89-179) has been a fixture for nearly 70 years, beckoning diners and gamblers with gold leaf and a massive gold nugget. Landry's, the restaurant chain and new Nugget owner, has embarked on an ambitious campaign to maintain the hotel's opulence, investing $300 million for casino expansion, more restaurants, and a new 500-room hotel tower. When checking in, pause to have your picture taken with the **Hand of Faith,** a 62-pound gold nugget. Rooms are appointed in dark wood and warm autumn hues.

ENTERTAINMENT

If you don't feel like swimming with the sharks in the poker room, you can get up close and personal with their finned namesakes at the **Golden Nugget Pool** (9am-6pm daily, free), an outdoor pool with a three-story waterslide that takes riders through the hotel's huge aquarium, home to sharks, rays, and other exotic marine life. Bathers can also swim up to the aquarium for a face-to-face with the aquatic predators, or schedule a **guided tour** (1:30pm Wed., $30). Waterfalls and lush landscaping help make this one of the world's best hotel pools.

Gold Diggers nightclub (9pm-late Wed.-Sun.) plays hip-hop, pop, and classic rock for the dancing pleasure of guests and go-go girls. A terrific song stylist in his own right, **Gordie Brown** (855/397-1191, 7:30pm Tues.-Thurs. and Sat.-Sun., $38-76) uses his targets'

Grand Canyon Tours from Vegas

Nearly a dozen tour companies relay visitors from Vegas to and through the Grand Canyon via a variety of conveyances—buses, airplanes, helicopters, off-road vehicles, and rafts. Coupons and discounts for online reservations and off-season bookings are plentiful; it is not uncommon to book tours at less than half the rack rates listed here.

GRAND CANYON TOURS

Grand Canyon Tours (702/655-6060 or 800/222-6966, www.grandcanyontours.com) packs plenty of sightseeing into its bus tours ($80-200), which can include the Grand Canyon Railway or Hualapai Ranch. Helicopter tours ($275-408) cut down the commute, leaving more time at the canyon, and allow an earlier return. Choppers skim over Hoover Dam, Lake Mead, the Black Mountains, and the Strip during the 1.5-hour flight. Stops can include the Grand Canyon Skywalk, Grand Canyon West Ranch, and the canyon floor.

LOOK TOURS

Look Tours (4285 N. Rancho Dr., 702/749-5715 or 888/796-4345, www.looktours.com) also offers bus tours (6am-10pm daily, $80-115) and an overnight trip via fixed-wing aircraft ($160-309). Do-it-yourselfers can rent an SUV from Look (7am, 8am, or 9am daily, $170 pp, 2-person minimum) for a leisurely 24-hour exploration of the West Rim.

MAVERICK HELICOPTER TOURS

Maverick Helicopter Tours (6075 Las Vegas Blvd. S., 702/261-0007 or 888/261-4414, and 1410 Jet Stream Dr., Ste. 100, Henderson, 702/405-4300 or 888/261-4414, www.maverickhelicopter.com) shuttles its customers to the canyon via spacious, quiet Eco-Star helicopters (7am-4:30pm daily, $619) and partners with Pink Jeep Tours for a guided road tour to the West Rim followed by a slow descent to the bottom of the canyon (6am-5pm daily, $395).

SWEETOURS

SweeTours (6363 S. Pecos Rd., Ste. 106, 702/456-9200 or 877/997-9338, http://sweetours.com) offers several packages ($169-385), which include options for travel by bus, SUV, helicopter, and boat.

peccadilloes as fodder for his song parodies, poking serious fun with a surgeon's precision.

RESTAURANTS

The food at **The Buffet** (702/385-7111, 7am-10pm daily, breakfast $13, lunch $15, dinner $21, weekend brunch $19, Fri.-Sun. seafood dinner $27) leaves nothing to be desired, with extras like an omelet station, calzone, Greek salad, and a delicate fine banana cake putting it a cut above the ordinary buffet, especially for downtown. Decidedly uncave-like with bright lights and an earthen-tile floor, **The Grotto** (702/386-8341, 11:30am-10:30pm Sun.-Thurs., 11:30am-11:30pm Fri.-Sat., $15-30) offers top-quality northern Italian-influenced sandwiches and pizza with a view of the Golden Nugget's shark tank.

Entertainment

SHOWS

Production shows are classic Las Vegas-style diversions. The big shows are fairly reliable, and you can count on them being around for a while. Lounge acts change often enough to make them hangouts for locals. Most acts are listed in the free entertainment magazines and the *Las Vegas Review-Journal*'s helpful website, but unless you're familiar with the performers, it's the luck of the draw: They list only the entertainer's name, venue, and showtimes.

Cirque du Soleil production *Mystère* (TI, 3300 Las Vegas Blvd. S., 702/894-7722 or 800/392-1999, 7pm and 9:30pm Sat.-Wed., $76-149) plays on performance archetypes, including classical Greek theater, Kabuki, athletic prowess, and surrealism.

Pop superstar **Britney Spears** (Planet Hollywood, 3667 Las Vegas Blvd. S., 866/919-7472, 9pm Wed. and Fri.-Sat., $77-344) shows off her patented dance moves and choreography incorporating fly systems, fire, mirrors, and barely-there costumes.

Feuding future in-laws, a drunken priest, a libidinous nun, and a whole flock of black sheep can't keep Tony and Tina from finding wedded bliss in *Tony 'n Tina's Wedding* (Bally's, 3645 Las Vegas Blvd. S., 702/777-2782 or 866/983-4279, 5:30pm Mon., Wed., and Fri.-Sat., $138-163). Diners play the role of wedding guests and sit among the actors, where you learn where the family skeletons are hidden and the bodies are buried.

Pound on the table with your goblet and let loose a hearty "huzzah!" to cheer your king to victory over the other nations' regents at the *Tournament of Kings* (Excalibur, 3580 Las Vegas Blvd. S., 702/597-7600 or 866/983-4279, 6pm Mon. and Fri., 6pm and 8:30pm Wed.-Thurs. and Sat.-Sun., $76), an equestrian theater where heroes participate in jousts, sword fights, riding contests, and lusty-maid flirting at this festival hosted by King Arthur and Merlin.

Relive the golden era when Frank, Dean, Sammy, and Joey ruled the Strip with *The Rat Pack Is Back* (Tuscany, 255 E. Flamingo Rd., 702/947-5981, 7:30pm Mon.-Sat., $60-66). Watch Sinatra try to make it through "Luck Be a Lady" amid the others' sophomoric antics.

All Shook Up (Planet Hollywood, 3667 Las Vegas Blvd. S., 866/932-1818, 6pm daily, $60-70) is the only all-Elvis impersonator show on the Strip. Both rotating impressionists bear a strong resemblance to the King, capturing not only his voice, but also his mannerisms, as they recount Elvis's hits from rock 'n' roll pioneer to movie idol.

COMEDY

Comedy in Las Vegas has undergone a shift in recent years: Carrot Top (at the Luxor) is about the only long-term funnyman left. However, A-list funny females have a new stage, *Lipshtick* (The Venetian, 3355 Las Vegas Blvd. S., 866/641-7469, 10pm Fri., 7:30pm Sat., $54-118), which hosts the likes of Lisa Lampanelli, Joy Behar, Wendy Williams, and Roseanne Barr. The other biggies—Daniel Tosh, Jay Leno, and Ron White, among others—still make regular appearances in the major showrooms on big Vegas weekends at venues such as **Aces of Comedy** (3400 Las Vegas Blvd. S., 702/791-7111, 10pm Fri., 8pm Sat., $55-100) at The Mirage.

The journeymen and up-and-coming have half a dozen places to land gigs when they're in town. Among the best clubs are **The Improv** (3475 Las Vegas Blvd. S., 800/214-9110, 8:30pm Sun. and Tues.-Thurs., 8:30pm and 10:30pm Fri.-Sat., $39-55) at Harrah's, **Brad Garrett's Comedy Club** (3799 Las Vegas Blvd. S., 866/740-7711, 8pm daily, $43-65, plus $20 when Garrett performs) at the MGM Grand, **L.A. Comedy Club** (Stratosphere, 2000 Las Vegas Blvd. S., 702/380-7777 or 800/998-6937,

8pm Sun.-Thurs., 8pm and 10pm Fri.-Sat., $30-50), and the **Laugh Factory** (Tropicana, 801 Las Vegas Blvd. S., 702/739-2222, 8:30pm and 10:30pm daily, $35-55).

MAGIC ACTS

The best smaller-scale shows include *Illusions* starring Jan Rouven (Tropicana, 3801 Las Vegas Blvd. S., 800/829-9034, 6pm Wed.-Mon., $76-124), with its death-defying illusions involving knives and water chambers; the kid-friendly **Nathan Burton Comedy Magic** (Planet Hollywood, 3663 Las Vegas Blvd. S., 702/866-0703 or 866/932-1818, 4pm Tues., Thurs., and Sat.-Sun., $20-60); and the budget-conscious **Laughternoon** (The D, 301 Fremont St., 702/388-2400, 4pm daily, $25), where Adam London turns his unhealthy obsession with duckies into comedy sleight-of-hand.

Food

Buffets are still a big part of the Las Vegas vacation aura, but when the town's swank and swagger came back in the 1990s, it brought sophisticated dining with it. Most major hotels have 24-hour coffee shops, a steak house, and a buffet along with a couple of international restaurants. See the *Casinos* section for information on casino dining.

UPPER STRIP

It's all about hen fruit at ★ **The Egg & I** (4533 W. Sahara Ave., 702/364-9686, 6am-3pm daily, $10-20). It serves other breakfast fare as well, of course—the banana muffins and stuffed French toast are notable—but if you don't order an omelet, you're just being stubborn. Enjoy the huge portions, fair prices, and on-top-of-it service.

The retro-deco gaudiness of the neon decor and bachelor pad-esque sunken fire pit may not do wonders for a Vegas-sized headache, but the tostada omelet at the **Peppermill Restaurant & Fireside Lounge** (2985 Las Vegas Blvd. S., 702/735-7635, 24 hours daily, $12-20) will give it what-for. For a little less zest, try the French toast ambrosia.

The pink accents at **Pamplemousse** (400 E. Sahara Ave., 702/733-2066, 5pm-10pm daily, $35-56) hint at the name's meaning (grapefruit) and set the stage for cuisine so fresh that the menu changes daily. Specialties include leg and breast of duck in cranberry-raspberry sauce and a terrific escargot appetizer with butter, shallots, and red wine sauce. Save room for chocolate soufflé.

The perfectly cooked steaks and attentive service that once attracted Frank Sinatra, Nat "King" Cole, Natalie Wood, and Elvis are still trademarks at **Golden Steer** (308 W. Sahara Ave., 702/384-4470, 4:30pm-10:30pm daily, $35-50). A gold-rush motif and 1960s swankiness still abide here, along with classics like crab cakes, big hunks of beef, and Caesar salad prepared tableside.

CENTER STRIP

The offerings at **The Buffet at TI** (TI, 3300 Las Vegas Blvd. S., 702/894-7355, 7am-10pm Mon.-Fri., breakfast $22, lunch $24, dinner $28, weekend brunch $27, weekend seafood dinner $32) are mostly standard—barbecue ribs, pizza, Chinese—but the ingredients are fresh, and the few nontraditional buffet selections (especially the sushi and made-to-order pasta) make the higher-than-average price worthwhile.

You can almost picture Old Blue Eyes himself between shows, twirling linguini and holding court at **Sinatra** (Encore, 3131 Las Vegas Blvd. S., 702/770-5320 or 888/352-3463, 5:30pm-10:30pm daily, $40-70). The Chairman's voice wafts through the speakers, and his iconic photos and awards decorate the walls while you tuck into classic Italian food tinged with Chef Theo Schoenegger's special touches.

Best Restaurants

★ **N9NE:** You *have* to get the steak, but make sure others in your party order the gnocchi and the lobster ravioli, so you can sneak bites from their plates (page 573).

★ **Mon Ami Gabi:** Order the baked gruyére and a baguette and channel your inner Hemingway for a traditional French bistro experience (page 575).

★ **Rose. Rabbit. Lie.:** Order six or eight small plates per couple, and let the sultry torch singers and rousing dancers play on as you nosh the night away (page 575).

★ **Culinary Dropout:** This creative gastropub takes its comfort food very seriously. The soft-pretzel fondue appetizer will have you dreaming of melted cheese (page 576).

★ **RM Seafood:** Soft lines and brushed metal accents evoke a glittering sea while the menu reflects Chef Rich Moonen's advocacy of sustainable fishing practices (page 580).

★ **The Egg & I:** You can order something other than eggs—but given the name, why would you (page 583)?

★ **Le Thai:** The best of Las Vegas's impressive roster of Thai restaurants, Le Thai boasts playful interpretations of traditional Thai cuisine in a trendy yet unpretentious atmosphere (page 585).

Likewise, the "Old Vegas" vibe is thick at **Piero's** (355 Convention Center Dr., 702/369-2305, 5pm-10pm daily, $30-50). The decor, colorful owner Freddie Glusman, and low-key sophistication give the place a vaguely speakeasy feel.

LOWER STRIP

Lighting and decor suggesting screens and lanterns set the stage for a journey into the depths of Chinese cuisine at **Blossom** (Aria, 3735 Las Vegas Blvd. S., 877/230-2742, 5:30pm-10:30pm daily, $50-80). Much of the menu is exotic, bold, and playful, but there are plenty of selections tempered toward Western palates.

The **Veranda** (Four Seasons, 3960 Las Vegas Blvd. S., 702/632-5000, 6:30am-10pm Mon.-Fri., 7am-10pm Sat.-Sun., $30-45) transforms itself from a light, airy, indoor-outdoor breakfast and lunch nook into a late dinner spot oozing with Mediterranean ambience and a check total worthy of a Four Seasons restaurant.

If you think "Las Vegas buffet" means a call to the trough of cheap prices and get-what-you-pay-for food quality, Bally's would like to invite you and your credit card to the **Sterling Brunch** (3645 Las Vegas Blvd. S., 702/967-7258, 9:30am-1:30pm Sun., $90). That's right, $90 for one meal, per person, and you have to fetch your own vittles. But the verdict is almost unanimous: It's worth it, especially if you load up on the grilled lobster, filet mignon, caviar, sushi, Perrier-Jouet champagne, and other high-dollar offerings.

On the other hand, for the price of that one brunch at Bally's, you can eat for two days at the **Roundtable Buffet** (Excalibur, 3580 Las Vegas Blvd. S., 7am-10pm daily, breakfast $18, lunch $19, dinner $24-27, children 5-11 get $7 off). The Excalibur started the trend of the all-day-long buffet, and the hotel sells all-day wristbands for $36-40. The **French Market Buffet** (The Orleans, 4500 W. Tropicana Ave., 702/365-7111, 8am-9pm daily, breakfast $10, lunch $12, dinner $19-26, Sun. brunch $22, age 16 and under get $5 off, children under 43 inches are free) has a similar all-day deal for $28 (Fri.-Sun. $31).

Andre's (Monte Carlo, 3770 Las Vegas Blvd. S., 702/798-7151, 5:30pm-10pm Tues.-Sun., $40-65) has an up-to-date yet old-country feel, with smoky glass, silver furnishings, and teal-and-cream accents. The menu combines favorites from around the world with French sensibilities to create unique "French fusion" fare, such as lamb with eggplant or a peppercorn and cognac cream sauce for the delectable fillet of beef.

DOWNTOWN

A perfect little eatery for the budding Bohemia of East Fremont Street, ★ **Le Thai** (523 E. Fremont St., 702/778-0888, 11am-11pm Mon.-Thurs., 11am-midnight Fri.-Sat., 4pm-10pm Sun., $10-25) attracts a diverse clientele ranging from ex-yuppies to body-art lovers. Most come for the three-color curry, and you should too. Choose your spice level wisely; Le Thai does not mess around.

Assuming you're not a food snob, the **Garden Court Buffet** (Main Street Station, 200 N. Main St., 702/387-1896 or 800/713-8933, 7am-9pm Mon.-Thurs., 7am-10am Fri.-Sun., breakfast $8, lunch $9, dinner $12-14, Fri. seafood $23-26) will satisfy your taste buds and your bank account. The fare is mostly standard, with some specialties designed to appeal to the casino's Asian and Pacific Islander target market. At **The Buffet** (Golden Nugget, 129 E. Fremont St., 702/385-7111, 7am-10pm daily, breakfast $13, lunch $15, dinner $21, weekend brunch $19, Fri.-Sun. seafood dinner $27), the food leaves

nothing to be desired, with extras like an omelet station, calzone, Greek salad, and a delicate fine banana cake putting it a cut above the ordinary buffet, especially for downtown.

Hugo's Cellar (Four Queens, 202 E. Fremont St., 702/385-4011, 5pm-10pm daily, $40-65) delivers romance from the moment each woman in your party receives her red rose until the last complimentary chocolate-covered strawberry is devoured. It is pricey, but the inclusion of sides, a mini dessert, and salad—prepared tableside with your choice of ingredients—helps ease the sticker shock. Sorbet is served between courses.

The prime rib gets raves, but the seafood and the prices are the draw at **Second Street Grill** (Fremont, 200 Fremont St., 702/385-3232, 5pm-10pm Thurs. and Sun.-Mon., 5pm-11pm Fri.-Sat., $15-25). The grill bills itself as "American contemporary with Pacific Rim influence," and the menu reflects this Eastern inspiration with steaks and chops—but do yourself a favor and order the crab legs with lemon ginger butter.

Steaks and seafood get equal billing on the menu at **Triple George** (201 N. 3rd St., 702/384-2761, 11am-10pm Mon.-Fri., 4pm-10pm Sat.-Sun., $25-55), but again, the charbroiled salmon and the martinis are what brings the suave crowd back for more.

The Golden Gate's **Du-Par's** (1 Fremont St., 702/366-9378, 24 hours daily, $4) began serving a San Francisco-style shrimp cocktail in 1955, and more than 30 million have been served since. In fact, it's the oldest meal deal in Las Vegas—appropriate for the oldest hotel in Las Vegas.

Accommodations

Las Vegas boasts more than 100 hotels and 200 motels. Most accommodations either sell out or nearly sell out every weekend of the year. Long weekends and holidays, especially New Year's Eve, Valentine's Day, Memorial Day, Fourth of July, Labor Day, and Thanksgiving, are sold out weeks in advance. Special events such as concerts, title fights, the Super Bowl, the Final Four, NASCAR Weekend, and the National Finals Rodeo are sold out months in advance. Reservations are made for the biggest conventions (Consumer Electronics, Men's Apparel, and so on) a year ahead of time.

If you're just coming for the weekend, most of the major hotels don't even let you check in on a Saturday night. You can stay Friday and Saturday, but not Saturday alone. It may be easier to find a room Sunday-Thursday, when there aren't any large conventions or sporting events. Almost all the room packages and deep discounts are only available on these days.

Casinos offer both the most opulent hotel accommodations in town and the widest variety of options. See the *Casinos* section for information on these rooms.

CENTER STRIP

With a name like **Trump** (2000 Fashion Show Dr., 702/892-0000, $120-220), you know that no whim will go unfulfilled. Standard rooms open onto an Italian marble entryway leading to floor-to-ceiling windows with the requisite magnificent views. In-room amenities include dual sinks with Italian marble countertops, as well as 32-inch flat-screen TVs and luxury appliances. Feather comforters and Italian linens make for heavenly restfulness. **DJT** (6:30am-10pm daily, $30-45) is a classy steakhouse, but the food is more style than substance. The hip **H2(EAU)** (11am-5pm daily, depending on the weather, $15-20) poolside, however, dishes up some tasty chicken Katsu sliders. **The Spa at**

Trump offers unique packages such as the Las Vegas Oxygenating Facial, to give your pores a breath of fresh air.

Platinum (211 E. Flamingo Rd., 702/365-5000 or 877/211-9211, $113-194) treats both guests and the environment with kid gloves. The resort uses the latest technology to reduce its carbon footprint through such measures as low-energy lighting throughout, ecofriendly room thermostats, and motion sensors to turn lights off when restrooms are unoccupied. Suites are an expansive 950 square feet of muted designer furnishings and accents, and they include all modern conveniences, such as high-speed Internet, high-fidelity sound systems, full kitchens, and oversize tubs. **Kil@ watt** (6am-2pm daily, $10-15), with sleek silver decor accented with dark woods, is a feast for the eyes and the palate for breakfast and lunch.

LOWER STRIP

Feel like royalty at the ★ **Mandarin Oriental Las Vegas** (3752 Las Vegas Blvd. S., 702/590-8888, www.mandarinoriental.com/lasvegas, $295-399), which looks down on the bright lights of the Strip from a peaceful remove. A master control panel in each of the modern rooms sets the atmosphere to your liking, controlling the lights, temperature, window curtains, and more. Once everything is set, sink into a warm bath and watch TV on the flat screen embedded in the bath mirror. Another impressive feature is the valet closet, which allows hotel staff to deliver items to your room without entering your unit. The **Mandarin Bar** (888/881-9367, 4pm-1am Mon.-Thurs., 4pm-2am Fri.-Sat., 4pm-11pm Sun.) on the 23rd floor offers stunning views of the city skyline and several signature martinis. And it's all environmentally friendly, or at least LEED-certified.

Offering sophisticated accommodations and amenities without the hubbub of a rowdy

Best Hotels

★ **Wynn:** No castles, no pyramids. Opting for class over kitsch, substance over splash, the Wynn is a worthy heir to "Old Vegas" joints (page 566).

★ **Harrah's:** It may seem middle-of-the-road, but its location puts it in the middle of the action (page 568).

★ **Bellagio:** All the romance of Italy manifests through dancing fountains, lazy gondola rides, intimate bistros, and—in case the spirit moves you—a wedding chapel (page 573).

★ **The Cosmopolitan:** Part Museum of Modern Art, part *Cabaret* Kit Kat Klub, this center-Strip resort blends visual overload with sensuous swank (page 575).

★ **Aria:** The centerpiece of City Center makes no concessions to old-school Sin City, choosing an urban feel accentuated by marble, steel, glass, and silk (page 575).

★ **Mandalay Bay:** Let the conscientious staff and serene elegance of this end-of-the-Strip hotel take you away from Vegas's pounding hip-hop and clanging slot machines (page 579).

★ **Golden Nugget:** A Strip-style resort in the otherwise staid downtown district, the Nugget features a waterslide surrounded by a shark-filled aquarium (page 580).

★ **Mandarin Oriental:** Splurge for environmentally friendly luxury at this LEED-certified hotel (page 586).

---

casino, the **Renaissance** (3400 Paradise Rd., 702/784-5700, $129-179) has big, bright, airy standard guest rooms that come complete with triple-sheeted, 300-thread-count Egyptian cotton beds with down comforters and duvets, walk-in showers, full tubs, 42-inch flat-panel TVs, a business center, and high-speed Internet. Onyx- and burgundy-clad **Envy Steakhouse** (6:30am-11am and 5pm-10pm Mon.-Sat., $35-60) has a few poultry and seafood entrées, but the Angus beef gets top billing.

Every guest room is a suite at the **Signature** (145 E. Harmon Ave., 702/797-6000 or 877/612-2121, $140-320) at MGM Grand. Even the junior suite is a roomy 550 square feet and includes a standard king bed, kitchenette, and spa tub. Most of the 1,728 smoke-free guest rooms in the gleaming 40-story tower include private balconies with Strip views, and guests have access to the complimentary 24-hour fitness center,

three outdoor pools, a business center, and free wireless Internet throughout the hotel. A gourmet deli and acclaimed room service satisfy noshing needs, and **The Lounge** provides a quiet, intimate spot in soothing blue hues for discussing business or pleasure over drinks.

Although it includes a full-service casino and is just steps from the Strip, the draw of the **Tuscany** (255 E. Flamingo Rd., 702/893-8933 or 877/887-2264, $90-180) is the relaxed atmosphere, from its restaurants and lounges to its lagoon pool. The sprawling 27-acre site with footpaths and impeccable landscaping belies its proximity to the rush-rush of the Strip one block west. Although there is a semiformal restaurant, **Tuscany Gardens** (5pm-10pm daily, $18-35), the casual **Cantina** (11am-9:30pm Mon.-Thurs., 11am-midnight Fri., 10am-midnight Sat., 10am-9:30pm Sun., $10-20) and **Marilyn's Café** (24 hours daily, $8-15)

Side Trip to Hoover Dam

The 1,400-mile Colorado River has been carving and gouging great canyons and valleys with red sediment-laden waters for 10 million years. For 10,000 years Native Americans, the Spanish, and Mormon settlers coexisted with the fitful river, rebuilding after spring floods and withstanding the droughts that often reduced the mighty waterway to a muddy trickle in fall. But the 1905 flood convinced the Bureau of Reclamation to "reclaim" the West, primarily by building dams and canals. The most ambitious of these was Hoover Dam: 40 million cubic yards of reinforced concrete, turbines, and transmission lines.

Hoover Dam remains an engineering marvel, attracting millions of visitors each year. It makes an interesting half-day escape from the glitter of Las Vegas, only 30 miles to the north. The one-hour **Dam Tour** (every 30 minutes, 9:30am-3:30pm daily, ages 8 and over, $30) offers a guided exploration of its power plant and walkways, along with admission to the visitors center. The two-hour **Power Plant Tour** (adults $15; seniors, children, and military $12; uniformed military and under age 4 free) focuses on the dam's construction and engineering through multimedia presentations, exhibits, a docent talk, and a power plant tour.

GETTING THERE

The bypass bridge diverts traffic away from Hoover Dam, saving time and headaches for both drivers and dam visitors. Still, the **35-mile drive** from central Las Vegas to a parking lot at the dam will take **45 minutes** or more. From the Strip, **I-15 South** connects with I-215 southeast of the airport, and **I-215 East** takes drivers to US 93 in Henderson. Remember that US 93 shares the roadway with US 95 and I-515 till well past Henderson. Going south on **US 93**, exit at **NV-172** to the dam. Note that this route is closed on the Arizona side; drivers continuing on to the **Grand Canyon** must retrace **NV-172** to **US 93** and cross the bypass bridge. A **parking garage** ($10) is convenient to the visitors center and dam tours, but free parking is available at turnouts on both sides of the dam for those willing to walk.

---

are more in keeping with the resort's métier. The 50,000-square-foot casino has all the games you expect in Las Vegas, and there's entertainment Tuesday-Saturday in the **Piazza Lounge.** All suites, the Tuscany's guest rooms boast more than 650 square feet and come with galley kitchens, coffeemakers, 25-inch TVs, and mini fridges.

Transportation and Services

CAR

Downtown Las Vegas crowds around the junction of I-15, US 95, and US 93. I-15 runs from Los Angeles (272 miles, 4-5 hours' drive) to Salt Lake City (419 miles, 6-8 hours).

Car Rental

When you call around to rent, ask what the *total* price of your car is going to be. With sales tax, use tax, airport fees, and other miscellaneous charges, you can pay as much as 60 percent over and above the quoted rate.

Typical shoulder-season weekly rates run from about $170 total for economy and compact cars to $280 for vans and $500 for luxury sedans, but prices increase by one-third or more during major conventions and holiday periods. Parking is free in casino surface lots and garages.

Most of the large car-rental companies have desks at the **McCarran Rent-A-Car Center** (702/261-6001). Dedicated McCarran shuttles leave the main terminal from outside exit doors 10 and 11 about every five minutes bound for the Rent-A-Car Center. International airlines and a few domestic flights arrive at Terminal 3. Here, the shuttle picks up outside doors 51 through 58. Taxicabs are also available at the center. Companies represented at the center include **Advantage** (800/777-9377), **Alamo** (800/462-5266), **Avis** (800/331-1212), **Budget** (800/922-2899), **Dollar** (800/800-4000), **Enterprise** (800/736-7222), **E-Z** (800/277-5171), **Firefly** (888/296-9135), **Hertz** (800/654-3131), **National** (800/227-7368), **Payless** (800/729-5377), **Thrifty** (800/367-2277), and **Zipcar** (866/494-7227). Others will pick up customers at the center.

MONORAIL

The **Las Vegas Monorail** (702/699-8200, 7am-midnight Mon., 7am-2am Tues.-Thurs., 7am-3am Fri.-Sun., $5, 24-hour pass $12)

stops at the SLS, Westgate, Convention Center, Harrah's/The Linq, Flamingo/Caesars Palace, Bally's/Paris, and MGM Grand. More than 30 major resorts are within easy reach along the Strip without a car or taxi. Tickets are available at vending machines at each station as well as at station properties.

TAXI

Except for peak periods, taxis are numerous and quite readily available, and drivers are good sources of scuttlebutt (not always accurate) and entertainment (not always wholesome). Of course, Las Vegas operates at peak loads most of the time, so if you're not in a taxi zone right in front of one of the busiest hotels, it might be tough to get one. The 16 companies plying the streets of Las Vegas charge $3.45 for the flag drop and $2.68 per mile. Waiting time is $0.54 per minute.

Background

The Landscape 591

Plants and Animals 593

History 597

The Landscape

GEOGRAPHY

California's geographic profile is as diverse as its population. At nearly 159,000 square miles, California is the third-largest state in the United States, stretching 770 miles from the Oregon state line to its southern border with Mexico. Inside its borders is just about every geographical feature imaginable, from alpine lakes to parched deserts to active volcanoes and sun-swept Pacific beaches. The state is trisected vertically by mountain ranges, with valleys in between, and terminates west at the coast of the Pacific Ocean. Many rivers flow west as the ocean wears away at the land, creating coves, waterfalls, and immense bays.

To the east, the Sierra Nevada mountain range looms above all other geography, with craggy snowcapped peaks, alpine lakes and meadows, and gold-producing foothills. The northern mountains—Shasta and Lassen—are the southern tip of the Cascade Range that stretches far into the Pacific Northwest. This youthful volcanic chain is part of the Pacific Ring of Fire, contributing to recent eruptions by Mount Lassen and Mount St. Helens. Though it's been a while since Shasta's fires last burbled to the surface, the mountain is classed as dormant, not extinct; if it ever blows again, the effects on the whole of the American West will be staggering.

At the foot of the Sierras sits a giant fertile valley that is the produce capital of the state, and much of the West. Maps and books refer to it as the San Joaquin Valley, but Californians usually call it the Central Valley, and much of the state's massive agricultural industry resides here.

To the south, deserts rule the landscape. California boasts two distinct desert regions: the northern and higher-elevation Mojave Desert as well as the southern and lower-elevation Colorado Desert, which encompasses Anza-Borrego State Park and the southern half of Joshua Tree National Monument.

The coastal region is bounded by a mountain range, famed in the north for forests filled with enormous coast redwood trees. The northern coastline winds along soaring craggy cliffs overlooking rocky beaches and coves, while the southern coastline tends toward the broad, sandy beaches for which California is famous.

Earthquakes and Faults

So much of California's geography is thanks to the dynamic geology below its surface. Three tectonic plates meet in the Golden State and these collisions have compressed, folded, jammed, and pushed up the Earth's crust, making California's diverse assemblage of mountain ranges as well as some of its other geologic oddities like hot springs, volcanoes, geysers, and lava tubes. As the plates pass each other they frequently catch, storing energy and causing tension to build. When the plates jolt past one another, they release this energy in the form of an earthquake.

The most famous plate-on-plate collision is the San Andreas Fault, an infamous strike-slip fault (when two tectonic plates move horizontally). The North American Plate moves southward while the Pacific Plate moves northward; this fault line runs along the north coast near San Francisco and east of Los Angeles before branching off into Mexico and the Pacific Ocean. It was along this fault that California's two largest and most devastating earthquakes took place: the 1906 San Francisco earthquake, which had a magnitude of 7.7-8.3, and the 1989

BACKGROUND
THE LANDSCAPE

Previous: Yosemite Valley; Channel Islands National Park.

Loma Prieta earthquake, at magnitude 6.9. The San Andreas Fault is not the only fault in California; earthquakes along numerous faults happen daily, up to 10,000-37,000 times each year. Most register less than magnitude 3 and go unnoticed by Californians used to the shake, rattle, and roll. California's stringent building codes, developed in the wake of deadly and destructive earthquakes, have brought older buildings, overpasses, bridges, and other structures up to strict standards.

CLIMATE

Vast in size and varied in geography, California also has a vastly diverse climate, from boiling heat in the deserts to subarctic temperatures at mountain summits.

Along the North Coast, the weather stays fairly constant: chilly, windy, and foggy. Summer days rarely reach 80°F, and winter rainstorms can pound the area. San Francisco shares this cool and foggy climate, with temperatures in the 50s and 60s well into summer. Farther south, the temperature may rise 20-30 degrees and the fog often makes way for sun. The Central Coast has somewhat warmer temperatures than the Bay Area, but you can still expect average cool temperatures and plenty of fog in the summer, with chilly winds and some rain in the winter.

North of San Francisco, the Wine Country is graced with milder weather and warm summers, perfect for growing grapes. Inland Sacramento and the Central Valley can be very hot. Daily temperatures in summer can peak well over 100°F and often worsen air quality, causing Spare the Air alerts. Winters in the Central Valley are cool and usually clear, though the nearby Sierra Nevada foothills often receive snow in the winter, and roads can become impassable.

Expect harsh weather if you head to Yosemite, Lake Tahoe, Mount Shasta, Mount Lassen, or the Eastern Sierra in the winter. Snowfall in a 24-hour period can be measured in feet, forcing road closures and power outages that wreak havoc on travel plans.

But activities such as skiing, snowboarding, sledding, snowshoeing, and snow camping abound. The short, hot summers draw campers, hikers, and mountain bikers.

From the Los Angeles Basin south to San Diego and up the coast to Santa Barbara, temperatures are mild year-round. Expect fog on the beaches in summer, cool days in winter, and hotter temperatures in the inland valleys (including at Disneyland). For the best summer beach weather in the state, head for San Diego.

The central and eastern deserts in the southern end of the state experience typical desert climates. That means mild, comfortable winters perfect for hiking and outdoor sports, but with nighttime temperatures in the 30s and 40s. The deserts' dangerously hot summers can easily reach 110-120°F.

ENVIRONMENTAL ISSUES

Californians face several major environmental issues. Los Angeles is rightly famous for its smog, though the San Francisco Bay Area is rapidly catching up in this unattractive race. If you're sensitive to airborne pollution, take special precautions on days that local air quality officials designate "Spare the Air." These are days (usually in summer) when pollution levels are especially high. Stay indoors; when going out, use public transportation.

The state battles drought, so water for crops, farms, and human consumption is in short supply. Conservation measures include limiting development and urban sprawl, restricting water usage, and designating set periods for personal and recreational use, such as watering lawns. Going hand in hand with the drought is the proliferation of wildfires. In 2015, more than 300,000 acres burned in California. Wildfires are often caused by human carelessness, so exercise extreme caution during the parched summer and fall months.

Water pollution is another issue. Most tap water is safe to drink, but swimming in California's plentiful bays, lakes, and rivers, as well as the Pacific Ocean, requires more caution. Pollution may cause *E. coli* outbreaks at beaches, affecting wildlife and beachgoers alike. There are major restrictions on fishing across the state; check the regulations with the Department of Fish and Game (916/445-0411, www.dfg.ca.gov) for any lake or river before planning a trip.

Plants and Animals

PLANTS

Redwoods

A visit to Northern California's famous redwoods should be on every traveler's list. The coast redwood (*Sequoia sempervirens*) grows along the North Coast as far south as Big Sur. Coast redwoods are characterized by their towering height, flaky red bark, and moist understory. Among the tallest trees on earth, they are also some of the oldest, with certain individual trees being almost 2,000 years old. Coast redwoods occupy a narrow strip of coastal California, growing less than 50 miles inland to collect moisture from the ocean and fog. Their tannin-rich bark is crucial to their ability to survive wildfires and regenerate afterward. The best places to marvel at the giants are within the Redwood National and State Parks, Muir Woods, and Big Basin State Park.

The giant sequoia (*Sequoiadendron giganteum*) grows farther inland in a 260-mile belt at 2,700-8,900 feet elevation in the Sierra Nevada mountain range. Giant sequoias are the largest trees by volume on earth; they can grow to heights of 280 feet, with a diameter up to 26 feet, and can live for thousands of years. Giant sequoias share the ruddy bark of their coastal cousins, as well as its fire-resistant qualities. The best places to see giant sequoias up close are at Sequoia and Kings Canyon National Parks, Calaveras Big Trees State Park, and the Mariposa Grove at Yosemite National Park.

Oaks

Northern California is home to many native oaks. The most common are the valley oak, black oak, live oak, and coastal live oak. The deciduous valley oak (*Quercus lobata*) commonly grows on slopes, valleys, and wooded foothills in the Central Valley. The black oak, also deciduous, grows throughout the foothills of the Coast Range and Sierra Nevada; it is unfortunately one of the victims of sudden oak death. The live oak habitat is in the Central Valley, and the coastal live oak occupies the Coast Range. The acorns of all these oaks were an important food supply for California's Native American population and continue to be an important food source for wildlife.

Joshua Trees

One famous California tree isn't a tree at all. The desert-dwelling Joshua tree (*Yucca brevifolia*) is actually a member of the yucca family. You can't miss a Joshua tree—from a distance, it almost resembles an honest-to-goodness deciduous tree. But when you get up close, the scaly "bark" starts to look strange and the "leaves" even odder—spiky and big. Larger Joshua trees can get up to 15 feet tall, with dozens of leafy "branches" at their tops. While the best place to see forests of Joshua trees is, of course, in Joshua Tree National Monument, Joshua trees thrive in the Mojave Desert ecosystem—they're all over the Mojave Preserve and can even be found alongside the desert's highways.

Wildflowers

California's state flower is the California poppy (*Eschscholzia californica*). The pretty little perennial grows just about everywhere, even on the sides of the busiest highways. The flowers of most California poppies are bright orange, but they also appear occasionally in white, cream, and an even deeper red-orange.

ANIMALS
Mountain Lions

Mountain lions (*Felis concolor*) are an example of powerful and potentially deadly beauty. Their solitary territorial hunting habits make them elusive, but human contact has increased as more homes are built in mountain lion habitat throughout California. Many parks in or near mountain lion territory post signs with warnings and advice: Do not run if you come across a mountain lion; instead make noise and raise and wave your arms so that you look bigger. The California Fish and Game Department (www.dfg.ca.gov) offers a downloadable brochure on encounters and other tips.

Black Bears

Don't take the name black bear (*Ursus americanus*) too literally. The black bear can actually have brown and even cinnamon-colored fur, sometimes with a white patch on the chest. The black bear is pretty common throughout North America, including in the forests and mountains of California. Although the black bear can appear cuddly from a distance,

distance is exactly what should separate bears and humans—at least 25 feet or more

Coyote

Coyotes (*Canis latrans*), wild canines related to wolves, are everywhere in California—even suburbs and city parks, and especially on trails. Coyotes have a storied place in the tall tales and native legends of the West, often portrayed as a wily and shrewd beast with a shrill "yip-yip-yip" howl that's downright spooky. Like black bears, coyotes usually won't hurt humans; these resourceful critters mostly hunt small mammals and reptiles or even medium-sized livestock like pigs and sheep. Coyotes don't have the fearsome reputation of wolves, but, nonetheless, be careful and don't feed them; though incidents are uncommon, coyotes have been known to attack humans.

Tule Elk

Tule elk (*Cervus elaphus nannodes*, also known as wapiti, California elk, or dwarf elk) are the smallest elk in North America and once thrived in the Central Valley, but were nearly hunted to extinction to feed Gold Rush settlers. There are now almost 3,000 tule elk in approximately 20 free-range and

a California poppy

protected herds in several grassland habitats in the Central Valley and Point Reyes National Seashore. Usually pale gray, brown, or tan, with thick chestnut-brown necks, the male bull can grow antlers that stretch five feet or more. In the fall, the bull gives a low bellow followed by a distinctive far-carrying whistle or bugle, and the female whistles in spring.

Whales

The massive, majestic gray whale (*Eschrichtius robustus*) was once endangered, but its numbers have rebounded with international protection. The gray whale measures about 40 feet long and has mottled shades of gray with black fins; its habitat is inshore ocean waters, so there is a chance to get a glimpse of them from headlands up and down the coast. Gray whales generally migrate south along the coast November-January, and closer to shore February-June, when they migrate northward. Mendocino County is a perfect place to watch the water for a glimpse of whales breaching.

Perhaps a more recognizable behemoth is the humpback whale (*Megaptera novaeangliae*). At 45-55 feet long, the humpback is the only large whale to breach regularly, then roll and crash back into the water, providing one of the best shows in nature. Humpbacks generally stay a little farther from shore, so it may be necessary to take a whale-watching cruise to catch a glimpse of them, but their 20-foot spouts can help landlubbers spot them from shore. Look for humpbacks April-early December off the coast near Big Sur, particularly at Julia Pfeiffer Burns State Park.

The blue whale (*Balaenoptera musculus*) is the largest animal on earth. At 70-90 feet long, the blue whale even exceeds dinosaurs in size. With a blue-gray top and a yellowish bottom, the blue whale has a heart the size of a small car, along with two blowholes, but alas does not breach. They can be seen June-November off the Northern California coast, but especially at Monterey and north of Point Reyes.

California Sea Lions

Watching a beach full of California sea lions (*Zalophus californianus*) sunning themselves and noisily honking away can be a pleasure. Sea lions are migratory, so they come and go at will, especially in the fall, when they head to the Channel Islands for breeding. If you have a serious hankering to see California sea lions, try Pier 39 near Fisherman's Wharf or on the coast at Seal Rocks, both in San Francisco.

a black bear in Sequoia National Park

Sea Otters

Much higher on the cuteness scale is the sea otter (*Enhydra lutris*), which can be spotted just off shore in shallow kelp beds. Once near extinction, the endearing playful sea otter has survived; now there are more than 2,000 in California waters. It can be a bit mesmerizing to witness a sea otter roll on its back in the water and use a rock to break open mollusks for lunch. Sea otter habitat runs mainly from Monterey Bay to Big Sur, but they have also been spotted in the waters farther north, near Mendocino.

Birds

California has a wide range of habitat with accessible food and water that makes it perfect for hundreds of bird species to nest, raise their young, or just stop over and rest during long migrations. Nearly 600 species have been spotted in California, so it may be just the place for a bird-watcher's vacation.

Among the most regal of California's bird species are raptors. The red-tailed hawk (*Buteo jamaicensis*) is found throughout California and is frequently sighted perched in trees along the North Coast highway, in the Central Valley, and even in urban areas such as San Francisco. The red-tailed hawk features a light underbelly with a dark band and a distinctive red tail that gives the bird its name.

Reptiles

Several varieties of rattlesnakes are indigenous to the state. The Pacific Northwest rattler makes its home in Northern California, while more than half a dozen different rattlesnake varieties live in Southern California, including the western diamondback and the Mojave rattlesnake.

If you spot California's most infamous native reptile, keep your distance. All rattlesnakes are venomous, though death by snakebite is extremely rare in California. Most parks with known rattlesnake populations post signs alerting hikers to their presence; hikers should stay on marked trails and avoid tromping off into meadows or brush.

sea lions at Pier 39 in San Francisco

Pay attention when hiking, especially when negotiating rocks and woodpiles, and never put a foot or a hand down in a spot you can't see first.

Butterflies

California's vast population of wildflowers attracts an array of gorgeous butterflies. The monarch butterfly (*Danaus plexippus*) is emblematic of the state. These large orange-and-black butterflies have a migratory pattern that's reminiscent of birds. Starting in August, they begin migrating south to cluster in groves of eucalyptus trees. As they crowd together and close up their wings to hibernate, their dull outer wing color camouflages them as clumps of dried leaves, thus protecting them from predators. In spring, the butterflies begin to wake up, fluttering lazily in the groves for a while before flying north to seek out milkweed on which to lay their eggs. Pacific Grove, Santa Cruz, and Cambria are great places to visit these California "butterfly trees."

History

THE FIRST RESIDENTS

The diverse ecology of California allowed Native Americans to adapt to the land in various ways. Communities settled from the border of present-day Oregon south through the mountain ranges and valleys, along the coast, into the Sierra Nevada, and in the arid lands that stretch into Mexico. These groups include the Maidu, Miwok, Yurok, and Pomo. More than 100 Native American languages were spoken in California, and each language had several dialects, all of which were identified with geographic areas. There are about two dozen distinct Native American groups in the Del Norte-Humboldt-Mendocino area alone.

THE MISSION PERIOD

In the mid-1700s, Spain pushed for colonization of Alta California, rushing to occupy North America before the British beat them to it. The effort was overly ambitious and underfunded, but missionaries started to sweep into present-day California, altering the world of California's indigenous people forever.

The priest Junípero Serra is credited with influencing the early development of California—and not necessarily for the better. A Franciscan monk, Serra played a prominent role in bringing Christianity and European diseases to Native American people from San Diego north to Sonoma County. The Franciscan order built a string of missions; each was intended to act as a self-sufficient parish that grew its own food, maintained its own buildings, and took care of its own people. Spanish soldiers housed in the nearby presidios (royal forts) used subjugation to control indigenous people, pulling them from their villages and lands to the missions, as they helped carry out the overall goal of finding wealth in the New World. The monks also created a road between the missions—El Camino Real—with the idea that a pilgrim could travel the length of El Camino Real and find a bed at the next mission after only one day's journey. Today, El Camino Real remains a vital part of the state, and much of the original path still exists; just look for the mission bells mounted on curved poles posted along the sides of much of U.S. 101 and the business corridor, El Camino Real, through the San Francisco Peninsula.

THE GOLD RUSH

James Marshall was a carpenter employed by John Sutter to build a sawmill in Coloma, near Placerville. Marshall made a glittery discovery on January 24, 1848, in a nearby stream—gold. Soon news spread to Sacramento and San Francisco that chunks of gold were on the riverbeds for the taking, and the Gold Rush was on. Thousands of people streamed into Northern California seeking gold. The most productive region was a swath of land nearly 200 miles long, roughly from El Dorado south to Mariposa, known as the Mother Lode or Gold Country. Mining towns such as Sonora, Volcano, Placerville, Sutter's Creek, and Nevada City swelled to huge proportions, only to shrink back into obscurity as the mines eventually closed one by one. Today Highway 49 winds from one historical Gold Rush town to the next, and gold mining has mostly given way to tourism.

The Gold Rush also drew immigrants from China. Most were forced to pass through the wretched immigration facilities on Angel Island in the middle of San Francisco Bay before being allowed onto the mainland; others were summarily shipped back to China. San Francisco's Chinatown became a hub for the immigrants, a place where their language was spoken and their culture understood. Thousands headed east, becoming low-level laborers in the industry surrounding the mines or workers on the railroads continuously being built to connect Gold Country to the rest of the nation.

The dramatic population boom caused by the Gold Rush ensured that California would be on the fast track to admission into the United States, bypassing the territorial phase. California became a state in 1850—it had gone from a Mexican province to the 31st U.S. state in a little more than four years.

THE GREAT DEPRESSION

The stock market crash of 1929 and the Great Depression transformed the nation and California. California was seen as the last hope from economic agony and drew people from all over the country hoping for a better future. Settling primarily in the Central Valley, these Midwest transplants preserved their ways and retained identities separate from other Californians. The Midwest migrant plight was captured in John Steinbeck's 1939 novel *The Grapes of Wrath*.

Despite the challenges, Californians did continue to build and move forward. The San Francisco-Oakland Bay Bridge was completed in 1936 and the Golden Gate Bridge in 1937, connecting the land around San Francisco Bay and putting people to work. The 1939 Golden Gate International Exposition on Treasure Island in San Francisco Bay helped show the Great Depression the door. In Southern California, the need for escape fueled the growing movie industry. During the 1930s, Hollywood began its golden age, producing such classics as *Citizen Kane*, *The Wizard of Oz*, *Gone with the Wind*, and *Mr. Smith Goes to Washington*.

WORLD WAR II

During World War II, San Francisco became the point of debarkation for the Pacific Theater, and overnight both Northern and Southern California became lead producers of military armaments, ranking California third in the nation. This industrial boom produced a second massive wave of immigration, altering the cultural landscape a second time in less than 100 years. Often, new workers fresh from other parts of the country moved into homes vacated by the 110,000 Japanese Americans who, under Executive Order 9066 in 1942, were forced to relocation camps located in desolate areas such as Manzanar, in the dry basin of the eastern Sierra, and Tule Lake, in the remote northeast corner of the state.

Carmel Mission

THE 1960S

A generation later, the culture was going to shift again. Few places in the country felt the impact of the radical changes of the 1960s more than California. It's arguable that the peace and free-love movements began here, probably on the campus of the indomitable University of California, Berkeley, which was the home of the Black Panthers, anti-Vietnam War sit-ins, and numerous protests for many progressive causes.

If Berkeley was the de facto home of 1960s political movements, then San Francisco was the base of its social and cultural phenomena. Free concerts in Golden Gate Park and the growing fame of the hippie community taking over a neighborhood called Haight-Ashbury drew young people from across the country. Many found themselves living on Haight Street for months and experimenting with the mind-altering chemicals emblematic of the era. The music scene became the stuff of legend.

CONTEMPORARY TIMES

In many ways the individualism and ground-breaking spirit of the 1960s helped to fuel California's next boom: the tech industry. Beginning in the halls of Stanford and the garages of what became known as the Silicon Valley, the electronics industry innovated personal computers, video games, and networking systems, transforming the way we live in so many ways. Tech giants such as Hewlett-Packard, Facebook, Google, and Apple call the Bay Area home, and the effects of this boom can be felt in the skyrocketing cost of living.

Throughout California's booms and busts, its main constant and number one industry is agriculture. The lush fields that drew Steinbeck's migrants still supply much of the world with crops of almost all kinds, from grapefruit to grass-fed beef. Along the fertile Central Valley you'll find everything from rice to corn to tomatoes to cotton. Elsewhere, orchards of nut and fruit trees, fields of sweet strawberries and spiky artichokes, and vineyards producing world-class wine fill the landscape. As the push toward local and sustainable agriculture grows, most communities host weekly farmers markets in the summertime, many lasting year-round, making it possible to enjoy the abundance of each region.

California, from the ground beneath its feet to the cloud computing it creates, is nothing if not diverse and dynamic. In addition to progressive and radical political ideas, you will find plenty of conservative swaths throughout the state, making for an entertaining political system. Catholics, Protestants, Jews, Muslims, Buddhists, and even Wiccan religions and Scientologists all call the state home, as do speakers of Chinese, Cantonese, Korean, Vietnamese, and Japanese. In both Los Angeles and the Bay Area, tightly knit Asian and Hispanic communities sometimes feature little-to-no signs or menus in English, and few proprietors speak standard English. Throughout the state, this multilingualism and multiculturalism results in a colorful blend of cultures and attitudes. Exploring the culture of California means exploring the backgrounds of those who live here, so be prepared to learn more about the world even as you learn more about the state.

Essentials

Transportation.................. 601

Visas and Officialdom.......... 605

Travel Tips..................... 605

Health and Safety.............. 608

Internet Resources............. 610

Transportation

GETTING THERE AND AROUND
Air
SAN FRANCISCO BAY AREA

San Francisco's major airport is **San Francisco International Airport** (SFO, U.S. 101, Millbrae, 800/435-9736, www.flysfo.com), located approximately 13 miles south of the city. Plan to arrive at the airport up to three hours before your flight leaves. Airport lines, especially on weekends and holidays, are notoriously long, and planes can be grounded due to fog.

To avoid the SFO crowds, consider booking a flight into one of the Bay Area's less-crowded airports. **Oakland International Airport** (OAK, 1 Airport Dr., Oakland, 510/563-3300, www.flyoakland.com) serves the East Bay, with access to San Francisco via the Bay Bridge and BART, the regional commuter train. **Mineta San Jose International Airport** (SJC, Airport Blvd., San Jose, 408/392-3600, www.flysanjose.com) is south of San Francisco in the heart of Silicon Valley. These airports are quite a bit smaller than SFO, but service is brisk from many U.S. destinations.

Sacramento International Airport (SMF, Airport Blvd., Sacramento, 916/929-5411, www.sacramento.aero) is a good launching point for trips in the Central Valley, Gold Country, or the Sierra Nevada and Lake Tahoe areas.

Several public and private transportation options can get you into San Francisco. **Bay Area Rapid Transit** (BART, www.bart.gov) connects directly with SFO's international terminal, providing a simple and relatively fast (under 1 hour) and inexpensive ($8.65) trip to downtown San Francisco. The BART station is an easy walk or a free shuttle ride from any point in the airport. **Caltrain** (www.caltrain.com, $3-13) is a good option if you are staying farther south on the peninsula. San Jose is also serviced by Caltrain via the free **Valley Transit Authority Airport Flyer** (VTA, www.vta.org), and BART runs a connector shuttle from Oakland, making both airports accessible by public transit.

Shuttle vans congregate outside the baggage claim areas of both the domestic and international terminals. Advance reservations guarantee a seat, but aren't required. **Quake City Shuttle** (415/255-4899, www.quakecityshuttle.com) services SFO, SJC, and OAK airports, while **SuperShuttle** (800/258-3826, www.supershuttle.com) can be found at all Bay Area airports and Sacramento. Rates typically range $17-35 per person. For **taxis,** the average fare to downtown San Francisco is around $40.

LOS ANGELES AREA

The greater Los Angeles area is thick with airports. **Los Angeles International Airport** (LAX, 1 World Way, 310/646-5252, www.lawa.org) is located about 10 miles south of the city of Santa Monica. International travelers are likely to find their flight coming into this endlessly crowded hub. If flying home from LAX, plan plenty of time to get through security and the check-in lines (up to three hours for a domestic flight on a holiday weekend).

To miss the major crowds, consider flying into one of the many suburban airports. Just 20 miles north of downtown Los Angeles is **Bob Hope Airport** (BUR, 2627 N. Hollywood Way, Burbank, 818/840-8840, http://bobhopeairport.com). **John Wayne Airport** (SNA, 18601 Airport Way, Santa

---

Previous: San Francisco cable car; Highway 1.

Ana, 949/252-5200, www.ocair.com) serves Disneyland perfectly, and **Long Beach Airport** (LGB, 4100 Donald Douglas Dr., 562/570-2600, www.lgb.org) is convenient to the beaches. **Ontario Airport** (ONT, 1923 E. Avion Dr., Ontario, 909/937-2700, www.lawa. org) is farther out, but a good option for travelers dividing their time between Los Angeles, Palm Springs, and the deserts.

From LAX, free shuttle buses provide service to **Metro Rail** (323/466-3876, www. metro.net), accessible at the Green Line Aviation Station. Metro Rail trains connect Long Beach, Hollywood, North Hollywood, Downtown Los Angeles, and Pasadena. Passengers should wait under the blue "LAX Shuttle Airline Connection" signs outside the lower-level terminals and board the "G" shuttle. Passengers may also take the "C" shuttle to the **Metro Bus Center** (323/466-3876, www. metro.net), which connects to city buses that serve the entire L.A. area. Information about bus service is provided via telephones on the Information Display Board inside each terminal.

Shuttle services are also available if you want to share a ride. **Prime Time Shuttle** (800/733-8267, www.primetimeshuttle. com) and **SuperShuttle** (800/258-3826, www.su-pershuttle.com) are authorized to serve the entire Los Angeles area from LAX. These vans can be found on the lower arrivals deck in front of each terminal, under the orange "Shared Ride Vans" signs. Average fares for two people are about $32 to Downtown Los Angeles, $34 to West Hollywood, and $30 to Santa Monica.

Taxis can be found on the lower arrivals level islands in front of each terminal, below the yellow Taxi signs. Only licensed taxis are allowed into the airport; they have standard rates of about $40 to downtown and $30 to West Los Angeles.

SAN DIEGO
San Diego International Airport (SAN, 619/400-2404, www.san.org) is a centrally located urban airport a mere three miles from the city center. While the location makes it a little noisy for those living in neighborhoods under the flight path, it makes getting to and from the airport a quick trip from most parts of the city. The airport is split into two major terminals plus a small commuter terminal, hosting 20 airlines and subsidiaries.

Train
Several long-distance **Amtrak** (www.am-trak.com) trains rumble through California daily. Eight train routes serve the region: The *California Zephyr* runs from Chicago and Denver to Emeryville; the *Southwest Chief* runs from Chicago to Los Angeles; the *Capitol Corridor* serves Auburn, Sacramento, Emeryville, Oakland, and San Jose, and is a popular route with local commuters; the *Coast Starlight* travels down the West Coast from Seattle and Portland as far as Los Angeles; the *Pacific Surfliner* will get you to the Central Coast from Southern California; the *San Joaquin* connects the southern Central Valley to the Bay Area; and the famed *Sunset Limited* runs from Jacksonville, Florida, to New Orleans, El Paso, and then Los Angeles.

Bus
Greyhound (800/231-2222, www.grey-hound.com, rates vary) has several stations in California. The San Francisco (200 Folsom St., 415/495-1569) and Los Angeles (1716 E. 7th St., 213/629-8401) stations are hubs for Greyhound bus lines, but there are also stations all along the coast from Crescent City to San Diego. Greyhound routes generally follow the major highways. **Megabus** (http://us.megabus.com) provides another inexpensive option, with stops in San Francisco, San Jose, and Los Angeles.

Car
The main transportation artery in California is **I-5**, which runs north-south from Oregon through Sacramento and ending at the Mexican border.

Highway 1, also known as the Pacific Coast Highway, follows the North Coast from

Winter Driving

It can snow in the California mountains anytime between November and April; if you plan on crossing any high passes, make sure to carry tire chains in your vehicle. In winter, the mountain passes on I-5 near Mount Shasta and on I-80 to Tahoe and over the Sierra Nevada can be hazardous and may require chains, snow tires, or both. Close to Tahoe, many roadside chain installers set up in pullouts along the side of I-80 and will install tire chains for a hefty fee. Chains can also be rented at certain automotive stores and service stations.

Road closures elsewhere in the state can be common in winter. Highway 1 along the coast can shut down because of flooding or landslides. I-5 through the Central Valley can either close or be subject to hazardous driving conditions resulting from tule fog, which can reduce visibility to only a few feet. Some highways avoid these problems altogether by closing for part of the year. Highway 120, which runs over Tioga Pass and connects Yosemite Valley with the Eastern Sierra, is generally closed October-April.

The **California Department of Transportation** (Caltrans, 800/427-7623, http://dot. ca.gov) has a very user-friendly website to check current road conditions before your trip. In an emergency, **dial 911** from any phone. The American Automobile Association, better known as **AAA** (800/222-4357, www.aaa.com, membership fees apply), also offers roadside assistance.

Leggett to San Luis Obispo on the Central Coast and points south. Running parallel and intertwining with Highway 1 for much of its length, **U.S. 101** stretches north-south from Oregon to Mexico, crossing over the Golden Gate Bridge (toll, $7) in San Francisco. These alternate routes are longer but prettier than I-5.

The main east-west conduit in Northern California is **I-80,** which begins as part of the Bay Bridge (toll, $6) in San Francisco and runs east through Sacramento to Tahoe and over the Sierras into Nevada. I-80 can close because of heavy winter snows. In Southern California, **I-10** and **I-15** allow access from Los Angeles and San Diego.

Highway 120 from San Francisco southeast to Yosemite National Park is one of California's best mountain drives. In summer or fall, Highway 120 climbs east across the park and over Tioga Pass to connect with **U.S. 395** in the Eastern Sierra. Desert highways **I-95** and **I-40** connect California with neighboring states Nevada and Arizona, respectively.

Highway speeds in California are generally 55 mph, unless otherwise posted. Larger freeways, such as I-5, may have posted speed limits of 65-70 mph. California law requires that all drivers carry liability insurance for their vehicles.

CAR AND RV RENTAL

Most car rental companies are located at each of the major California airports. To reserve a car in advance, contact **Budget** (800/527-0700, www.budget.com), **Dollar** (800/800-4000, www.dollar.com), **Enterprise** (800/261-7331, www.enterprise.com), or **Hertz** (800/654-3131, www.hertz.com).

To rent a car, drivers in California must be at least 21 years of age and have a valid driver's license. California law also requires that all vehicles carry liability insurance. You can purchase insurance with your rental car, but it generally costs an additional $10 per day, which can add up quickly. Most private auto insurance will also cover rental cars. Before buying rental insurance, check your car insurance policy to see if rental-car coverage is included.

The average cost of a rental car is $50 per day or $250 per week; however, rates vary greatly based on the time of year and distance traveled. Weekend and summer rentals cost significantly more. Generally, it is more expensive to rent from car rental agencies at an airport. To avoid excessive rates, first plan travel to areas where a car is not required, then rent a car from an agency branch in town to explore more rural areas. Rental agencies occasionally allow vehicle drop-off at a different location from where it was picked up for an additional fee.

If you rent an RV, you won't have to worry about camping or lodging options, and many facilities, particularly farther north, accommodate RVs. However, RVs are difficult to maneuver and park, limiting your access to metropolitan areas. They are also expensive, in terms of both gas and the rental rates. Rates during the summer average $1,300 per week and $570 for three days, the standard minimum rental.

Cruise America (800/671-8042, www.cruiseamerica.com) has branches in San Mateo (just south of San Francisco), San Jose, San Luis Obispo, Los Angeles, and Costa Mesa. **El Monte RV** (800/337-2214, www.elmonterv.com) operates out of San Francisco, San Jose, Santa Cruz, Paso Robles, Los Angeles, and Newport Beach. **Jucy Rentals** (800/650-4180, www. jucy-rentals.com) rents minivans with pop-up tops. These colorful vehicles are smaller and easier to manage than large RVs, but still come equipped with a fridge, a gas cooker, a sink, a DVD player, and two double beds. Rental locations are in San Francisco, Los Angeles, and Las Vegas.

PARKING

Parking is at a premium in big cities. Most hotels within San Francisco, Los Angeles, and Las Vegas will charge guests $50 or more per night for parking. Remove any valuables from your vehicle for the evening, as some hotel valets just park your car in an adjacent public parking deck. Many attractions charge visitors an admission fee and a parking fee. For instance, Disneyland charges a $17 parking fee.

Parking is strictly regulated at the national parks. At Yosemite, park entrance fees include entry and parking for up to seven days. Visitors are encouraged to park their cars and use the extensive network of free shuttles to get around the park.

INTERNATIONAL DRIVERS

If you are visiting the United States from another country, you need a valid driver's license issued from your home country. California does not require an International Driving Permit; however. if your license is not written in English, a car rental agency may. If you plan on renting a car during your stay, secure an International Driving Permit from your home country before coming to the United States. It can't be obtained once you're here. You must also bring your government-issued driving permit.

Visitors from outside the United States should check the driving rules of the states they will visit at www.usa.gov/Topics/Motor-Vehicles.shtml. Among the most important rules is that traffic runs on the right side of the road in the United States. Note that both California and Nevada have bans on using hand-held cell phones (this includes texting) while driving. If you get caught, expect to pay a hefty fine.

Visas and Officialdom

PASSPORTS AND VISAS

If visiting from another country, you must have a valid passport and a visa to enter the United States. In most other countries, the local U.S. embassy should be able to provide a tourist visa. The average fee for a visa is US$160. While a visa may be processed as quickly as 24 hours on request, plan at least a couple of weeks, as there can be unexpected delays, particularly during the busy summer season (June-Aug.). However, before doing so, check with the U.S. Department of Homeland Security (www.cbp.gov) to see if you qualify for the Visa Waiver Program. Passport holders of certain countries can apply online with the Electronic System for Travel Authorization at least 72 hours before traveling. Have a return plane or cruise ticket to your country of origin dated less than 90 days from your date of entry. Holders of Canadian passports don't need visas or visa waivers.

EMBASSIES

If you should lose your passport or find yourself in some other trouble while visiting California, contact your country's offices for assistance. To find an embassy, check online at www.state.gov/s/cpr/rls/dpl/32122.htm, which lists the websites for all foreign embassies in the United States. A representative will be able to direct you to the nearest embassy or consulate.

CUSTOMS

Before you enter the United States from another country by sea or by air, you'll be required to fill out a customs form. Check with the U.S. embassy in your country or the Customs and Border Protection website (www.cbp.gov) for an updated list of items you must declare.

Also, pack documentation describing your need for any narcotic medications you've brought with you. Failure to produce documentation for narcotics on request can result in severe penalties in the United States.

If you're driving into California along I-5 or another major highway, prepare to stop at Agricultural Inspection Stations a few miles inside the state line. You don't need to present a passport, a visa, or even a driver's license; instead, you must be prepared to present all your fruits and vegetables. California's largest economic sector is agriculture, and a number of the major crops grown here are sensitive to pests and diseases. If you've got produce, especially homegrown or from a farm stand, it could be infected by a known problem pest or disease. Expect it to be confiscated on the spot.

Travel Tips

TOURIST INFORMATION

When visiting California, you might be tempted to stop in at one of several **Golden State Welcome Centers** (www.visitcwc.com) scattered throughout the state. If you're in an area that doesn't have its own visitors center, the State Welcome Center might be a useful place to pick up maps and brochures. Otherwise, stick with local, regional, and national park visitors centers, which tend to be staffed by volunteers or rangers who have a real passion for their locale.

If you are looking for maps, almost all gas stations and drugstores sell maps both of the place you're in and of the whole state. **AAA** (https://calstate.aaa.com) is the auto club for California, and it offers free maps to auto club members.

Many local and regional visitors centers also offer maps, but you'll need to pay a few dollars for the bigger and better ones. If all you need is a wine-tasting map in a known wine region, however, you can probably get one for free along with a few tasting coupons at the nearest regional visitors center. Basic national park maps come with your admission payment. State park maps can be free or cost a few dollars at the visitors centers.

The state's **California Travel and Tourism Commission** (916/444-4429, http://gocalif.ca.gov) also provides helpful and free tips, information, and downloadable maps and guides.

California is in the Pacific time zone (PST and PDT) and observes daylight saving time March-November.

Money

California businesses use the U.S. dollar ($). Most businesses also accept the major credit cards Visa, MasterCard, Discover, and American Express. ATM and debit cards work at many stores and restaurants, and ATMs are available throughout the region. In more remote areas, such as Gold Country and the North Coast, some businesses may only accept cash, so don't depend entirely on your plastic.

You can change currency at any international airport in the state. Currency exchange points also crop up in downtown San Francisco and at some of the major business hotels in urban areas.

California is not a particularly expensive place to travel, but keeping an eye on your budget is still important. San Francisco and the Wine Country are the priciest regions for visitors, especially with the amount of high-quality food and luxury accommodations. Advance reservations for hotels and marquee restaurants in these areas are recommended.

Banks

Traveling with a huge amount of cash is not recommended, which may make frequent trips to the bank necessary. Fortunately, most destinations have at least one major bank.

Usually Bank of America or Wells Fargo can be found on the main drags through towns. Banking hours tend to be 8am-5pm Monday-Friday, 9am-noon Saturday. Never count on a bank being open on Sunday or federal holidays. If you need cash when the banks are closed, there is generally a 24-hour ATM available. Furthermore, many cash-only businesses have an ATM on-site for those who don't have enough cash in their wallets. The unfortunate downside to this convenience is a fee of $2-4 per transaction. This also applies to ATMs at banks at which you don't have an account.

Tax

Sales tax in California varies by city and county, but the average rate is around 8.5 percent. All goods are taxable, with the exception of food not eaten on the premises. For example, your bill at a restaurant will include tax, but your bill at a grocery store will not. The hotel tax is another unexpected added expense to traveling in California. Most cities have enacted a tax on hotel rooms largely to make up for budget shortfalls. As you would expect, these taxes are higher in areas more popular with visitors. In Wine Country you can expect to add an additional 12-14 percent onto your hotel bill, while in San Francisco the tax tops 15 percent. Some areas, like Eureka, have a lower hotel tax of 10 percent.

Tipping

Tipping is expected and appreciated, and a 15-20 percent tip for restaurants is about the norm. When ordering in bars, tip the bartender or waitstaff $1 per drink. For taxis, plan to tip 15-20 percent of the fare, or simply round the cost up to the nearest dollar. Cafés and coffee shops often have tip jars out. There is no consensus on what is appropriate when purchasing a $3 beverage. Often $0.50 is enough, depending on the quality and service.

Tipping is also expected in hotels and B&Bs. Often you'll find an envelope on the desk for the housekeeping staff. Depending on the type of accommodations, $1-5 per night is the standard rate.

Communications and Media

Cell phone reception is good except in places far from any large town. Likewise, you can find Internet access just about anywhere. The bigger cities are well wired, but even in small towns you can log on either at a library or in a café with a computer in the back. Be prepared to pay a per-minute usage fee or purchase a drink. The desert regions have limited or non-existent cell phone reception.

The main newspapers in California are the *San Francisco Chronicle* (www.sfchronicle. com) and the *Los Angeles Times* (www.lat-imes.com). Each major city also has a free weekly newspaper that has comprehensive arts and events coverage. As for radio, there are some news stations on the FM dial, and in most regions you can count on finding a **National Public Radio** (NPR, www.npr.org) affiliate. While they will all offer some NPR news coverage, some will be more geared toward music and local concerns.

Because of the area's size both geographically and in terms of population, you will have to contend with multiple telephone area codes even within the same city. The 800 or 866 area codes are toll-free numbers. Any time you are dialing out of the area, you must dial a 1 plus the area code followed by the seven-digit number.

Conduct and Customs

The legal drinking age in California is 21. Expect to have your ID checked if you look under age 30, especially in bars and clubs, but also in restaurants and wineries. Most California bars and clubs close at 2am; you'll find the occasional after-hours nightspot in San Francisco and Los Angeles.

Smoking has been banned in many places throughout California. Don't expect to find a smoking section in any restaurant or an ashtray in any bar. Smoking is illegal in all bars and clubs, but your new favorite watering hole might have an outdoor patio where smokers can huddle. Taking the ban one step further, many hotels, motels, and inns throughout California are strictly nonsmoking, and you'll be subject to fees of hundreds of dollars if your room smells of smoke when you leave.

There's no smoking in any public building, and even some of the state parks don't allow cigarettes. There's often good reason for this; the fire danger in California is extreme in the summer, and one carelessly thrown butt can cause a genuine catastrophe.

ACCESS FOR TRAVELERS WITH DISABILITIES

Most California attractions, hotels, and restaurants are accessible for travelers with disabilities. State law requires that public transportation accommodate the special needs of travelers with disabilities and that public spaces and businesses have adequate restroom facilities and equal access. This includes national parks and historical structures, many of which have been retrofitted with ramps and wider doors. Most parks have one or two trails that are accessible to wheelchairs, and most campgrounds designate specific campsites that meet the Americans with Disabilities Act standards. The state of California also provides a free telephone TDD-to-voice relay service; just dial 711.

If you are traveling with a disability, there are many resources to help you plan your trip. **Access Northern California** (http://accessnca.org) is a nonprofit organization that offers general travel tips, including recommendations on accommodations, parks and trails, transportation, and travel equipment. The organization also produces **A Wheelchair Rider's Guide to the California Coast** (www.wheeling-calscoast.org) which includes information about Southern California. For that region, **Accessible San Diego** (http://access-sand-iego.org) is another great resource. In Los Angeles and San Francisco, **Wheelchair Getaways** (800/642-2042, www.wheel-chairgetaways.com, $95-110 per day) rents wheelchair-accessible vans and offers pickup and drop-off service from major airports ($100-300). Likewise, **Avis Access** (888/879-4273, www.avis.com) rents cars, scooters, and other products to make traveling with a disability easier.

SENIOR TRAVELERS

Throughout the state you'll find senior discounts nearly every place you go, including restaurants, golf courses, major attractions, and even some hotels, though the minimum age can range 50-65. Just ask, and be prepared to produce ID if you look young or are requesting a senior discount. You can often get additional discounts on rental cars, hotels, and tour packages as a member of **AARP** (888/687-2277, www.aarp.org). If you're not a member, its website can also offer helpful travel tips and advice. **Elderhostel** (800/454-5768, www.roadscholar.org) is another great resource for senior travelers. Dedicated to providing educational opportunities for older travelers, Elderhostel provides package trips to beautiful and interesting destinations. Called "Educational Adventures," these trips are generally 3-9 days long and emphasize history, natural history, art, music, or a combination thereof.

GAY AND LESBIAN TRAVELERS

The Golden State is a golden place for gay travel—especially in the bigger cities and even in some of the smaller towns around the state. As with much of the country, the farther you venture into rural and agricultural regions, the less likely you are to experience the liberal acceptance the state is known for. The **International Gay and Lesbian Travel Association** (www.iglta.org) has a directory of gay- and lesbian-friendly tour operators, accommodations, and destinations.

San Francisco has the biggest and arguably best **Gay Pride Festival** (www.sfpride.org) in the nation, usually held on Market Street on the last weekend in June. Year-round, the **Castro District** offers fun of all kinds, from theater to clubs to shopping, mostly targeted at gay men but with a few places sprinkled in for lesbians. **Santa Cruz** on the Central Coast is a quirky town specially known for its lesbian-friendly culture. In Los Angeles, **West Hollywood** has its own upscale gay culture, where clubs are havens of the see-and-be-seen crowd. **Palm Springs** and **Guerneville** along the Russian River in Northern California are also major gay destinations despite their small size.

Health and Safety

MEDICAL SERVICES

For an emergency anywhere in California, dial 911. Inside hotels and resorts, check your emergency number as soon as you get to your guest room. In urban and suburban areas, full-service hospitals and medical centers abound, but in more remote regions, help can be more than an hour away.

WILDERNESS SAFETY

Follow all rules and guidelines for backcountry expeditions; obtain wilderness permits and self-register at trailheads. This lets rangers know roughly where you plan to be and when to expect you back. National and state park visitors centers can advise in more detail on any health or wilderness alerts in the area. It is also recommended to let someone outside your party know your route and expected date of return.

Extreme Temperatures

Despite California's relatively mild climate, heat exhaustion and heat stroke can affect anyone during the hot summer months, particularly during a long strenuous hike in the sun. Common symptoms include nausea, lightheadedness, headache, or muscle cramps. Dehydration and loss of electrolytes are the common causes of heat exhaustion. If you or anyone in your group develops these symptoms, get out of the sun immediately, stop all physical activity, and drink plenty of water. Heat exhaustion can be severe, and if untreated can lead to heat stroke, in which the body's core temperature reaches 105°F. Fainting, seizures, confusion, and rapid heartbeat and breathing can indicate the situation has moved beyond heat exhaustion. If you suspect this, call 911 immediately.

Similar precautions hold true for hypothermia, which is caused by prolonged exposure to cold water or weather. For many, this can happen on a hike or backpacking trip without sufficient rain gear, or by staying too long in the ocean or another cold body of water without a wetsuit. Symptoms include shivering, weak pulse, drowsiness, confusion, slurred speech, or stumbling. To treat hypothermia, immediately remove the wet clothing, cover the person with blankets, and feed him or her hot liquids. If symptoms don't improve, call 911.

Altitude

Altitude sickness is a flu-like illness that can affect anyone who has made a quick transition from low to high elevation. It occurs most commonly above 8,000 feet, but some individuals suffer at lower elevations. Headaches are the most common symptom, followed by nausea, dizziness, fatigue, and even the swelling of hands, feet, and face. Symptoms either go away once the individual has acclimated to the thinner air and lower oxygen levels or they don't, requiring either medical attention or a return to lower elevation. To prevent altitude sickness, avoid any strenuous exercise, including hiking, for the first 24 hours of your stay. Drinking alcohol also exacerbates altitude sickness as it can cause dehydration.

Wildlife

Many places are still wild in California, so it's important to use precautions with regard to wildlife. Black bears are often seen in the mountains foraging for food in the spring,

summer, and fall. Never get between a bear and her cub, and if a bear sees you, identify yourself as human by waving your hands above your head, speaking in a calm voice, and backing away slowly. If a bear charges, do not run. One of the best precautions against an unwanted bear encounter is to keep a clean camp, store all food in airtight bear-proof containers, and strictly follow any guidelines given by the park or rangers.

Mountain lions can be found in the Sierra foothills, the Coast Range, grasslands, and forests. Because of their solitary nature, it is unlikely you will see one. If you see a mountain lion and it sees you, make your body appear as big as possible. And never run, which triggers the cat's hunting instincts. If a mountain lion should attack, fight back.

Rattlesnakes can be found in hot and dry areas from the coast to the Sierra Nevada. When hiking in this type of terrain, keep your eyes on the ground and an ear out for the telltale rattle. Snakes like to warn you to keep away. Should you get bitten, seek immediate medical help.

Mosquitoes can be found throughout the state, particularly in the Central Valley and the Sierra Nevada. At higher elevations they can be worse, prompting many hikers and backpackers to don head nets and apply potent repellents, usually DEET. The high season for mosquitoes is late spring-early summer, at the end of snowmelt, when there is lots of still freshwater in which to multiply.

Ticks live in many of the forests and grasslands throughout the state, except at higher elevations. Tick season generally runs late fall-early summer. If you are hiking through brushy areas, wear pants and long-sleeve shirts. Ticks like to crawl to warm moist places (armpits are a favorite) on their host. If a tick is engorged, it can be difficult to remove. There are two main types of ticks found in California: dog ticks and deer ticks. Dog ticks are larger, brown, and have a gold spot on their backs, while deer ticks are small, tear-shaped, and black. Some deer ticks are known to carry Lyme disease. If you are bitten by a deer tick and the bite leaves a red ring, seek medical attention.

Poison oak is a common shrub that inhabits forests throughout the state. Poison oak has a characteristic three-leaf configuration, with scalloped leaves that are shiny green in the spring and then turn yellow, orange, and red in late summer-fall. In fall the leaves drop, leaving a cluster of innocuous-looking branches. The irritating oil in poison oak is present year-round in both the leaves and branches. Your best protection is to wear long sleeves and long pants when hiking. If your skin comes into contact with poison oak, expect an itchy, irritating rash. Poison oak is also extremely transferable, so avoid touching your eyes, face, or other parts of your body. Calamine lotion and Technu scrub can help; in extreme cases, a doctor can administer cortisone to decrease the inflammation.

Internet Resources

CALIFORNIA

California Department of Transportation
www.dot.ca.gov
The website contains state map and highway information.

Visit California
www.visitcalifornia.com
The official tourism site of the state of California.

REGIONAL SITES

Central Coast Regional Tourism
www.centralcoast-tourism.com
A guide to the Central Coast region, including Santa Cruz and Monterey.

Las Vegas Website
www.lasvegas.com
"The only official website of Las Vegas" has hotel deals, show deals, and a downloadable visitors guide.

Los Angeles Convention
and Visitors Bureau
www.discoverlosangeles.com
It's the official website of the Los Angeles Convention and Visitors Bureau.

NapaValley.com
www.napavalley.com
A Napa Valley tourism website from WineCountry.com.

Nevada Department of Transportation
www.nevadadot.com
Nevada Department of Transportation's website has a map detailing current road conditions.

Sacramento Convention
and Visitors Bureau
www.vistsacramento.org
The official website of the Sacramento Convention and Visitors Bureau.

City of San Diego
www.sandiego.gov
Providing information and access to all city departments, this site's especially useful for researching the Parks and Recreation department, including specific rules, regulations, and amenities for all city beaches, including lifeguard information.

Shasta and Lassen Regional Tourism
www.shastacascade.org
The California Travel and Tourism Information Network includes information and a downloadable visitors guide to Mount Shasta, Shasta Lake, Redding, and Lassen.

Visit California Gold Country
www.calgold.org
The website from the Gold Country Visitors Association, with information about

Grass Valley, Nevada City, Placer County, Sacramento, and Amador Country.

WineCountry
www.winecountry.com
This tourism website offers information on all of California's wine regions, including Napa, Sonoma, Mendocino, Carmel Valley, Paso Robles, Santa Barbara, and Temecula.

PARKS AND OUTDOORS

California Outdoor and Recreational Information
www.caoutdoors.com
This recreation-focused website includes links to maps, local newspapers, festivals, and events as well as a wide variety of recreational activities throughout the state.

California State Parks
www.parks.ca.gov
The official website lists hours, accessibility, activities, camping areas, fees, and more information for all parks in the state system.

Lassen Volcanic National Park
www.nps.gov/lavo
The official website for Lassen Volcanic National Park.

Recreation.gov
www.recreation.gov
Recreation.gov is the reservation website for numerous California campgrounds.

Redwood National Park
www.nps.gov/redw
The official website for all Redwood National and State Parks.

Sequoia and Kings Canyon National Parks
www.nps.gov/seki
The official website for Sequoia and Kings Canyon.

State of California
www.ca.gov/visitplay/greatoutdoors
Outdoor resources for California state and government organizations. Check for information about fishing and hunting licenses, backcountry permits, boating regulations, and more.

Yosemite National Park
www.nps.gov/yose
The National Park Service website for Yosemite National Park.

Index

A

Abbots Lagoon: 95
Agate Beach: 186
Aguereberry Point: 553
Ahmanson Theatre: 444
air travel: 601-602
Alamo Square: 51
Alcatraz: 44-45
Alexander Valley Vineyards: 157
Alibi, The: 27, 186
Alpine Meadows: 246-247
Amador 360 Wine Collective: 278
Amargosa Opera House: 552
American Conservatory Theater: 59
American River: 264, 276
amusement parks: 353-354, 435, 438, 460-467
Anacapa Island: 414
Ancient Bristlecone Pine Forest: 347-348
Anderson Valley: 172-173
Andrew Molera State Park: 383-384
Angel Island State Park: 85-87
Angel's Camp: 283, 285-286
Angel's Camp Museum and Carriage House: 285
Annette Green Perfume Museum: 429
Año Nuevo State Park: 108-109
Ansel Adams Gallery: 297
Anza-Borrego Desert State Park: 541
Apple Hill: 275, 277
Aquarium of the Bay: 45
Aquarium of the Pacific: 441
Aquatic Park: 64
Arcata: 27, 186
Arch Rock (Anacapa Island): 414, 415
Arch Rock (Yosemite): 296
Armstrong Redwoods: 155
Arroyo Burro Beach: 404
Artist's Palette: 549
Ash Mountain: 320
Asian Art Museum: 51
Asilomar State Beach: 367
AT&T Park: 66
Atomic Testing Museum: 564
Auburn: 273-275
Auburn State Recreation Area: 274
Austin Creek State Recreation Area: 155
auto travel: 602-604
Autry National Center of the American West: 431
Avalon Underwater Park: 459
Avenue of the Giants: 27, 180

B

Badwater Basin: 548-549
Baker Beach: 64
Balboa Park: 25, 28, 479-480, 482; map 482
Balboa Theatre: 496
Baldwin Museum: 233
Bale Grist Mill State Historic Park: 134
banks: 606
Bay Area Discovery Museum: 84
Beach Blanket Babylon: 59
beaches: general discussion 27; Central Coast 403-405, 411-415; Lake Tahoe 255; Los Angeles 438-439, 447-448, 467-470; Monterey and Big Sur 357-358, 362, 363, 367, 377, 381, 384-386, 392; North Coast 168, 176, 179, 181, 185, 186; San Diego 484, 486, 487, 489, 500-503; San Francisco 64, 82, 89-90, 94, 95, 105, 106, 108-109; Wine Country 154, 158
Bear Valley: 94-95
beer/breweries: Central Coast 402, 413, 418; Lake Tahoe 239; Los Angeles 453, 464; Monterey and Big Sur 357, 366; North Coast 172, 178; Sacramento and Gold Country 274, 277; San Diego 490-495, 511, 512, 514; San Francisco 73, 88, 100; Wine Country 155; Yosemite, Sequoia, and Kings Canyon 346
Belmont Park: 486-487
Ben Lomond: 362
Benziger Family Winery: 146
Beringer Vineyards: 134
Berkeley: 98-101
Beverly Hills: 436-437
bicycling: general discussion 303; Central Coast 406, 411; Lake Tahoe 236-238; Monterey and Big Sur 356, 369; Sacramento and Gold Country 264, 274; San Diego 486; San Francisco 65-66, 82-83, 95-96; Wine Country 128, 138, 144, 158; Yosemite, Sequoia, and Kings Canyon 300, 345
Big Basin Redwoods State Park: 362-363
Big Oak Flat: 24, 296
Big Stump: 320, 324
Big Sur: 26, 303, 380-391; map 382
Big Sur Coast Highway: 380-381, 383-386
Big Sur Discovery Center: 384
Birch Aquarium: 488
Bishop: 347-349
Bixby Bridge: 381
Black Chasm Caverns: 282

Black Rock Canyon: 542, 545
Black's Beach: 502
Black Sheep Winery: 286
Blue Ox Millworks and Historic Park: 27, 184
Bodega Bay: 166, 168
Bodie State Historic Park: 341-342
Bohart Museum of Entomology: 269
Bolinas: 94
Boreal Mountain Resort: 252
Borrego Palm Canyon: 541
Botanical Building (San Diego): 480
botanical gardens/arboretums: 53, 98, 99, 178,
    399-400, 431, 442, 459, 480, 489, 531, 533
Bothe-Napa State Park: 138
Boulder Creek: 362
Boyden Cave: 326
Bradbury Building: 429
Bray Vineyards: 279
Bridalveil Fall: 297, 300
Brokeoff Mountain: 211
Brutocao Cellars: 172
B. Sattui: 132
Buena Vista Peak: 324
Bumpass Hell: 209-210
bus travel: 602
Butterfly Beach: 404

C

Cable Car Beach: 362
Cable Car Museum: 38
cable cars: 37-38
Cabrillo National Monument: 484-485
Calaveras Big Trees State Park: 289
Calaveras County Fair and Jumping Frog Jubilee:
    285
California Academy of Sciences: 24, 52-53
California Caverns: 283, 285
California Coastal Trail: 82, 87, 94, 189
California cuisine: 68
California Missions Museum: 142
California Science Center: 430
California's First Theater: 364
California State Capitol Building: 261-262
California State Railroad Museum: 262-263
Calistoga: 136-139
Cambria: 391-394; map 393
camping: Central Coast 404-406, 411-412, 415-
    416; Deserts 536, 540-542, 545, 547, 548,
    555-556; Lake Tahoe 243, 249-250, 251, 254,
    255; Monterey and Big Sur 358, 362, 363, 375,
    390; North Coast 168, 170, 172, 174, 179-182,
    187, 188-190; Sacramento and Gold Country
    289; San Francisco 83, 86-88, 92, 95, 97, 109-
    110; Shasta and Lassen 198, 205, 212-213, 218,
    221-223, 225; Wine Country 148, 155, 156;
    Yosemite, Sequoia, and Kings Canyon 304,
305-306, 308, 310, 312-313, 317-319, 325, 328,
    329, 334, 335, 337, 340, 343, 348-349
Cannery Row: 364
canoeing: see kayaking/canoeing
Cape Mendocino Lighthouse: 181
Capistrano Beach: 470
Cap Rock: 542
Carlon Falls: 316-317
Carlsbad: 28, 489
Carmel: 376-380
Carmel Beach: 27, 377
Carmel Mission: 376
Carmel River State Beach: 377
Carmel Valley: 378
Carneros: 140, 142-146
Carpinteria State Beach: 404
Carr Winery: 402
car rental: 603-604
car travel: 602-604
Castello di Amorosa: 136
Castle Crags State Park: 222-223
Catalina Island: 459
Cathedral Lakes: 312
Cathedral of Our Lady of the Angels: 426
caves/caverns: 201-202, 224-225, 282, 283, 285,
    286, 326, 331, 374-375, 415, 487
Cedar Grove: 326-328
Central Coast: 395-421; map 400
Chabot Space and Science Center: 102
Channel Islands: 26, 303, 413-416
Chaos Jumbles: 208-209
Charles M. Schulz Museum: 149
Chateau Julien: 378
Chateau Montelena: 136
Chez Panisse: 68, 100
Children's Fairyland: 102
Children's Pool Beach: 489
Chilnualna Falls: 309
Chinatown (San Francisco): 39
Chuck Jones Gallery: 497
City Hall (San Francisco): 51
Clarke Historical Museum: 184
climate: 592
climbing: 216-217, 222, 223, 300-301, 303, 374-
    375, 545
Cline Cellars: 142
Coit Tower: 44
College Cove: 28, 185
Columbia: 287-289
Columbia Museum: 287
Conrad Prebys Theatre Center: 496
Conservatory of Flowers: 53-54
Cook's Meadow: 301
Cornerstone Sonoma: 144
Coronado: 485-486
Coronado Beach: 501

Cottonwood Spring: 544
Cowell Beach: 357, 358
Cowgirl Creamery: 37, 96
Cowgirl Winery: 378
Crescent City: 28, 190-191
Crescent Meadow: 332, 333
Crissy Field: 50, 65
Crocker Art Museum: 264
Crystal Cave: 331
Crystal Cove State Park: 470
Culinary Institute of America: 68, 134
Curran Theatre: 59
customs: 605

D

Daffodil Hill: 282
Dante's View: 551
date farms: 534
Davies Symphony Hall: 59-60
Davis: 269
Death Valley: 25, 548-556; map 550
Deaver Vineyards: 279
Deetjens: 388
Del Monte Beach: 367
Del Norte Redwoods State Park: 189
Devastated Area: 209
Devil's Golf Course: 549
Devils Postpile National Monument: 343-344
de Young Museum: 24, 52
Diamond Peak: 255
Dipsea Trail: 89, 91
di Rosa Preserve: 143-144
disabilities, travelers with: 607-608
Disney California Adventure Park: 463
Disneyland: 25, 28, 460-466
D. L. Bliss State Park: 233, 237-238
Dodger Stadium: 448
Doheny State Bach: 470
Dolby Theatre: 444
Dolphin Habitat: 561
Domaine Carneros: 142
Domaine Chandon: 127
Don Cecil-Lookout Peak: 327
Donner Memorial State Park: 250-251
Donner Summit: 251
Downtown Art Walk (Los Angeles): 429
Dr. Wilkinson's Hot Springs Resort: 137, 139
Dry Creek Vineyard: 157
Dunes Beach: 106
Dutton Estate: 152

E

Eagle Lake: 336
Eagle Mining Company: 491
East Bay: 98-104

East Beach: 403
Eastern Sierra: 25, 337-349; map 338
East Peak Mount Tamalpais: 91
Eberle Winery: 420
Echo Lake: 211
Ed Z'berg Sugar Pine Point State Park: 244
Egyptian Theater: 434
Ehrman Mansion: 244
El Capitan: 24, 300-301, 303
El Capitan State Beach: 406
Elizabeth Lake: 312
Elk: 173-174
El Portal: 319
El Prado: 480
El Pueblo de Los Angeles Historical Monument: 426
Elverhoj Museum: 407
embassies: 605
Emerald Bay: 233, 237
emergencies: general discussion 608; *see specific place*
Emma Wood State Beach: 411
Empire Mine State Historic Park: 269-270
Encinitas: 28, 489
environmental issues: 592-593
Eric Ros Winery: 146
etiquette: 607
Eureka: 27, 184-186
Eureka Dunes: 553
Exploratorium: 44

F

Fairfax: 435-436
Faria Beach: 412
farmers markets: 39, 68, 219, 269, 416, 436, 446, 498
Fashion Institute of Design and Marketing: 429
fauna: 594-596
Felton: 362
Fern Canyon: 28, 188
Ferndale: 182-184
Ferndale History Museum: 182
Ferrari-Carano: 157
Ferry Building: 37, 38-39
festivals and events: Central Coast 398; Deserts 534-535; Los Angeles 434, 442, 445; Monterey and Big Sur 366; Sacramento and Gold Country 266, 285; San Diego 491, 494; San Francisco 60-61, 106
Fillmore, The: 58
Fish Camp: 319
Fisherman's Wharf (Monterey): 364
Fisherman's Wharf (San Francisco): 45-48; map 46-47
fish/fishing: Central Coast 404, 405; Lake Tahoe 233, 236; Los Angeles 440, 468, 470; Monterey

and Big Sur 359, 368; Sacramento and Gold Country 289; San Diego 505; Shasta and Lassen 195, 212, 217, 222
Fitzgerald Marine Reserve: 104-105
flora: 593-594
Font's Point: 541
food trucks: 68, 71, 453
Foothills Visitor Center: 331, 335
Fort Baker: 83-84
Fort Bragg: 27, 178-179
Fort Humboldt State Historic Park: 184
Fort Point: 50
Fort Ross State Historic Park: 27, 170
Foxen Canyon Road: 402
Fox Theater: 102
Francis Beach: 106
Fremont Street Experience: 560
French Laundry, The: 68, 128
Frog's Leap Winery: 130-131
Furnace Creek: 25, 548

G
Galleta Meadows: 541
Gamble House: 442
Gamlin Cabin: 323
Garberville: 179-180
Garrapata State Park: 381
Gaslamp Quarter: 25, 28, 478, 498
Gatekeeper's Museum: 244
Gaviota Peak: 406
Gaviota State Park: 405-406
gay and lesbian travelers: 608
Gaylor Lakes: 312
Geffen Contemporary at MOCA: 429
Geffen Playhouse: 444
General Grant Grove: 322, 323
General Sherman Tree: 330
geography: 591-592
Gerstle Cove: 170
Getty Center: 28, 437-438
Getty Villa: 440
Geyserville: 160-161
Ghirardelli Square: 48
Giant Forest: 328-334; map 330
Giant Forest Museum: 331
Glacier Point: 306-308
Glen Ellen: 146-148
Gloria Ferrer: 142
Goat Rock Beach: 168
Gold Bluffs Beach: 28, 188, 189
Gold Bug Park: 275
Gold Country Museum: 273
Goldeneye: 172
Golden Gate Bridge: 24, 27, 50, 65-66
Golden Gate Park: 24, 51-55, 64-66; map 54-55
Golden Gate Theatre: 59

Golden State Theatre: 366
Goleta Beach: 404
golf: 102, 373, 378, 505-506, 536, 554
Grace Cathedral: 38
Grand Canyon: 581
Granlibakken: 247
Grant Grove: 320, 322-326; map 322
Grass Valley: 268-269, 271-273
gratuities: 606-607
Gray Butte: 215
Great American Music Hall: 58
Greek Theater: 98-99
Greenwood State Beach: 174
Grgich Hills Winery: 130
Griddle Café: 28, 451
Griffith Park: 431
Groveland: 317-318
Gualala: 171-172
Guerneville: 152-157
Gundlach Bundschu Winery: 140

H
Half Dome: 24, 300, 302-303
Half Moon Bay: 105-108
Half Moon Bay State Beach: 106
HALL Wines: 133-134
Hanna Winery: 148
Hans Christian Andersen Museum: 407
Harbor Cove Beach: 411-412
Healdsburg: 157-160
health and safety: 608-610
Hearst Castle: 26, 391-392
Hearst San Simeon State Park: 392
Heavenly: 233-234
Heavenly Gondola: 231
Heisler Park: 470
Heitz: 133
Heller Estate: 233
Hendy Redwoods State Park: 172-173
Henry Cowell Redwoods State Park: 362
Henry Miller Memorial Library: 385
Heritage Park Victorian Village: 483-484
Hetch Hetchy: 297, 316-317
Hidden Valley: 542
High Roller: 563
hiking: general discussion 303; Central Coast 406, 413-414, 419; Deserts 535-536, 541, 542, 544-545, 553-554; Lake Tahoe 236-238, 247-248; Monterey and Big Sur 356, 362, 374-375, 377, 381, 384-386; North Coast 170, 174-175, 179-182, 187-189; Sacramento and Gold Country 264, 271, 274-275, 283; San Diego 485; San Francisco 65, 82, 86-89, 90-91, 94-95, 99, 105; Shasta and Lassen 210-211, 214-216, 222-225, 226; Wine Country 138, 147, 155; Yosemite, Sequoia, and Kings Canyon 300, 301-303, 307-

309, 311-312, 316-317, 322-324, 327-329, 332-333, 335-337, 341, 342, 345
Hiouchi Information Center: 190
Historic Kennedy Gold Mine: 281
history: 597-599
Hollywood: 431-435; map 432
Hollywood Bowl: 444-445
Hollywood Forever Cemetery: 434
Hollywood Sign: 431
Hollywood Walk of Fame: 25, 28, 431, 433
Hollywood Wax Museum: 433
Hoover Dam: 588
Hop Kiln: 153
horseback riding: 96, 147, 212, 218, 238, 274, 309, 328, 345, 356, 554
hot air ballooning: 125, 138, 149
Hotel del Coronado: 485-486, 520
Hot Rock: 209
Humboldt Lagoons State Park: 185
Humboldt Redwoods State Park: 27, 180, 182
Hunt Cellars: 420
Huntington Beach: 468
Huntington, The: 442
Husch Vineyards: 172

IJ

Indian Canyons: 535
Indian Grinding Rock State Historic Park: 282-283
Indian Springs: 137, 139
Inglenook Winery: 130
Internet resources: 610-611
Iron Horse Vineyards: 154
Ironstone Vineyards: 286
itineraries: 24-28; *see also specific place*
Jack London State Historic Park: 147
Jackson: 281-282
Jade Cove: 386, 387
Jalama Beach County Park: 405
Jamestown: 289-290
Japanese American National Museum: 429
Japanese Friendship Garden: 480
Japanese Tea Garden: 24, 53
Jedediah Smith Redwoods State Park: 190
Jenner: 168-169
Jepson Memorial Grove: 94
John Muir Trail: 303, 329, 345
Joshua Tree National Park: 303, 542-547; map 543
Joyce Vineyards: 378
Julian: 491
Julia Pfeiffer Burns State Park: 385, 386-387
Jumbo Rocks: 547
June Lake: 342-343
Junípero Serra Museum: 484
J Winery: 153

K

Kalyra Winery: 402
kayaking/canoeing: general discussion 303; Central Coast 403-406, 413-415; Lake Tahoe 233, 235, 236; Los Angeles 459; Monterey and Big Sur 358-359, 367-368; North Coast 168, 174, 176, 185; Sacramento and Gold Country 274; San Diego 486, 487, 504; San Francisco 92, 96, 102, 106; Shasta and Lassen 195, 209, 217; Wine Country 154, 158-159
Kehoe Beach: 95
Kelham Beach: 94
Kelly Beach: 106
Kendall-Jackson Wine Center: 148
Kenwood: 146-148
Keys Ranch: 542
Keys View: 544
Kings Canyon Overlook: 323
Kings Canyon Scenic Byway: 326
Kings Canyon Visitor Center: 320, 322
Kirk Douglas Theatre: 444
Kirkwood: 234
Knapp's Cabin: 326
Knott's Berry Farm: 465
Kohm Yah-mah-nee Visitors Center: 206, 208
Korbel Cellars: 153
Kruse Rhododendron State Reserve: 170
Kunde Estates: 146

L

La Brea Tar Pits and Museum: 435
Laguna Beach: 469-472
La Jolla: 487-489; map 488
La Jolla Cove: 27, 28, 487-488
La Jolla Playhouse: 496
La Jolla Shores: 501, 502
La Jolla Underwater Park: 505
Lake Merritt: 102
Lake Shasta Caverns: 201-202
Lake Siskiyou: 215
Lake Tahoe: 24, 227-256; maps 230, 232, 245
Lands End: 65
Lassen Peak: 208
Lassen Volcanic National Park: 205-214; map 207
Las Vegas: 557-589; map 562
Las Vegas Springs Preserve: 563-564
Lava Beds National Monument: 224-225
Lawrence Hall of Science: 98
Laws Railroad Museum and Historic Site: 347
L.A. Zoo and Botanical Gardens: 431
Leadbetter Beach: 27, 403-404
Lee Vining: 337, 339-341
Legion of Honor: 54-55
Leland Stanford Mansion: 264
Leo Carrillo State Park: 447

lesbian and gay travelers: 608
Letterman Digital Arts Center: 50
lighthouses: 80, 93-94, 108, 172, 175, 181, 381, 383, 392, 414, 485
Limantour Road: 95
Limekiln State Park: 385
Lincoln Theater: 128
Linq, The: 570-571
Little Baldy: 332
Living Desert, The: 533
Lobero Theater: 402-403
Lodgepole: 328-334; map 330
Lodgepole Village: 329
Lodgepole Visitor Center: 329-330, 331
Lombard Street: 44
Long Beach: 28, 440-441
Loomis Museum: 208
Los Angeles: 422-460; maps 425, 427
Los Angeles County Museum of Art: 28, 436
Los Angeles Doctors Symphony: 445
Los Angeles Memorial Coliseum: 448
Los Angeles Opera: 444
Los Angeles Philharmonic: 444
Lost Coast: 181, 303
LOVE: 568
Lowell Davies Festival Theatre: 496
Lower Yosemite Fall: 301
Luther Burbank Home and Gardens: 149

M

MacCallum House Restaurant: 27, 176-177
Mackerricher State Park: 179
Madame Tussauds Las Vegas: 561
Madison Gallery: 497
Madonna Inn: 416
Main Beach (Santa Cruz): 358
Main Beach Park (Laguna Beach): 470
Majestic Yosemite Hotel: 24, 305
Malakoff Diggins State Historic Park: 271-272
Malibu: 440
Malibu Beach: 448
Malibu Pier: 440, 448
Mammoth Lakes: 343-347
Manzanita Lake: 208
Marie Hitchcock Puppet Theater: 482
Marina State Beach: 367
Marine Mammal Center: 80, 82
Marin Headlands: 80, 82-83
Marin Headlands Visitors Center: 80
Marion Steinbach Indian Basket Museum: 244
Mariposa: 318-319
Mariposa Grove: 308
Maritime Museum of San Diego: 479
Marshall Gold Discovery State Historic Park: 275
Mattole Road: 181
Mavericks Surf Contest: 106

May Lake: 311-312
McAbee Beach: 367
McArthur-Burney Falls Memorial State Park: 223-224
McCloud: 223
McNee Ranch: 105
McWay Falls: 385
media: 607
medical services: 608
Memorial Beach: 158
Mendocino: 27, 174-178; map 175
Mendocino Art Center: 174-175
Mendocino Coast: 171-179; map 167
Mendocino Coast Botanical Gardens: 178
Mendocino Headlands State Park: 27, 176
Mercer Cavern: 286
Mesquite Flat Sand Dunes: 553
Mill Valley: 27, 87-88
Mineral King: 335-337
Miracle Mile: 435-436
Mirror Lake: 300
Mission Bay: 486-487
Mission Bay Park: 486
Mission Beach: 500
Mission Dolores: 51
Mission Dolores Park: 65
Mission San Buenaventura: 411
Mission San Francisco Solano de Sonoma: 142-143
Mission San Juan Bautista: 372
Mission San Juan Capistrano: 470
Mission San Luis Obispo de Tolosa: 416
Mission San Luis Rey de Francia: 489
Mist Falls: 327-328
Mist Trail: 24, 302
Miwok Indian Village (Yosemite): 297
Miwok Village (Indian Grinding Rock): 282
Moaning Cavern: 285
Mob Museum: 560-561
MOCA Pacific Design Center: 429
Modern Times: 490, 493
Mojave National Preserve: 548
Monarch Lakes: 336
money: 606
Mono Lake: 303, 341
Montaña de Oro State Park: 419
Montara State Beach: 105, 106
Monterey: 26, 363-372; map 365
Monterey and Big Sur: 350-394; map 354
Monterey Bay Aquarium: 26, 363-364
Monterey State Beach: 367
Monterey State Historic Park: 364
Monteverde Store Museum: 280
Montevina: 279
Moonstone Beach: 27, 185
Moorten Botanical Garden: 531, 533
Moro Rock: 331-332

Morro Bay: 419
Mosaic Canyon: 553-554
Mosquito Lake: 336
Moss Beach: 104-105
Mountain Theater: 91
Mount Eddy: 216
Mount Hoffman: 311-312
Mount San Jacinto State Park: 530, 536
Mount Shasta: 214-218, 303
Mount Shasta City: 219-222
Mount Soledad Veterans Memorial: 489
Mount Tamalpais State Park: 90-92
Mount Whitney: 303, 329
Mount Wittenberg: 94-95
Mt. Rose: 255
Muir Beach: 24, 89-90
Muir Woods National Monument: 24, 88-89
Mulholland Drive: 435
Mumm: 131
Municipal Winemakers: 402
Murphys: 286-287
Muscle Beach: 439
Musée Mécanique: 48
Museum of Contemporary Art, Los Angeles (MOCA): 429
Museum of Contemporary Art San Diego: 488-489
Museum of Monterey: 364
Mystery Spot: 356

N

Napa: 120-121, 125-126
Napa Valley: 120-139; maps 122-123, 124
Napa Valley Museum: 127-128
Napa Valley Opera House: 121
National Museum or Organized Crime and Law Enforcement: 560-561
National Steinbeck Center: 372, 374
Natural Bridge (Death Valley): 554
Natural Bridges State Park (Santa Cruz): 357
Natural History Museum of Los Angeles County: 430
Navarro River Redwoods State Park: 173
Neon Museum and Boneyard: 560
Neptune's Net: 452
Nevada City: 268-269, 271-273
Nevada Fall: 302
Nevada State Museum: 564
New Brighton State Beach: 358
Newport Beach: 468-469
Newton B. Drury Scenic Parkway: 188
Nike Missile Site: 82
North and West Shores (Lake Tahoe): 244-250; map 245
North Bay: 80-98; map 81
North Beach: 39, 44-49; map 46-47

North Coast: 162-191; map 165
North Dome: 312
Northern Elephant Seal Rookery: 392
Northern Gold Country: 268-278; map 270
Northstar California: 251
North Star Mining Museum: 271
Norton Simon Museum: 442

O

Oakhurst: 319
Oakland: 101-104
Oakland Museum of California: 101
Oakville: 130-132
Oasis of Mara: 544
Ocean Beach (San Diego): 484, 500
Ocean Beach (San Francisco): 64
Ocean Beach Pier: 501-502
Oceanside: 28, 489
Ohlone Bluff: 356
Old Faithful Geyser: 136
Old Globe Theatre: 496
Old Point Loma Lighthouse: 485
Old Sacramento: 262
Old Sacramento Schoolhouse Museum: 262
Old Town San Diego: 483-484
Old Town State Historic Park: 483-484
Olmstead Point: 310, 311
Olvera Street: 426
Orange County: 460-472; map 461
Original Farmers Market: 436
Orpheum Theatre: 59
Orr Hot Springs: 173
O'Shaughnessy Dam: 316
Oxbow Public Market: 121, 125

P

Pacific Beach: 500-501
Pacific Coast Air Museum: 149
Pacific Crest Trail: 248, 303, 345
Pacific Grove Monarch Sanctuary: 364, 366
Pacific Heights: 49-50
Palace of Fine Arts: 49
Palm Canyon: 535
Palm Springs: 25, 530-540; map 532
Palm Springs Aerial Tramway: 530-531
Palm Springs Air Museum: 531
Palm Springs and the Deserts: 526-556; map 529
Palm Springs Art Museum: 531
Panamint Springs: 25, 555
Panoramic Point: 322
Pantoll: 91
Paradise Creek: 335
Paramount Studios: 434-435
parks and gardens: 50, 52-54, 64-65, 99, 405-406, 431, 479-480, 482

Pasadena: 442
Paso Robles: 420
passports/visas: 31, 605
Patriarch Grove: 348
Patrick's Point State Park: 186-187
Patterson's Pub: 27, 177
Pebble Beach: 373
Pelican Inn: 24, 90
Pescadero: 108-110
Pescadero Marsh Natural Preserve: 108
Pescadero State Beach: 108
Petco Park: 506
Petroglyph Point: 226
Pfeiffer Beach: 27, 384-385
Pfeiffer Big Sur State Park: 384
Piedras Blancas Lighthouse: 392
Pierce Brothers Westwood Village Memorial
    Park: 438
Pierce Point Road: 95
Pier 39: 45
Pigeon Point Lighthouse: 108
Pinnacles National Park: 303, 374-375
Pioneer Monument: 250
Pioneer Yosemite History Center: 308
Pismo Beach: 419-421
Placer County Museum: 273
Placerville: 275-278
planning tips: 29-32
plants: 593-594
Plymouth: 278-280
Point Arena: 172-173
Point Arena Lighthouse: 172
Point Bonita Lighthouse: 80
Point Cabrillo Light Station Historic Park: 175
Point Lobos State Natural Reserve: 377-379
Point Loma: 484-485
Point Reyes Historic Lighthouse: 93-94
Point Reyes National Seashore: 93-98, 303
Point Sur Lighthouse: 381, 383
Pope-Baldwin Recreation Area: 233
Pope Mansion: 233
Portalupi: 157-158
Porter Creek Winery: 153
Pothole Dome: 310
Prairie Creek Redwoods State Park: 28, 188
Presidio, The: 49-50, 66
Preston Vineyards: 157
Princeton-by-the-Sea: 105
Puesto: 28, 515

QR
Qualcomm Stadium: 507
Queen Mary: 28, 440-441
Racetrack, The: 553
rafting: 274, 276, 285, 217
Railtown 1897 State Historic Park: 289-290

Rainbow Bar & Grill: 28, 437, 441
Rainbow Falls: 344
Raven Players: 158
Ravenswood Winery: 140
Red Car Winery: 152
Redding: 195, 198-200
Redwood Coast: 179-191
Redwood Mountain Overlook: 323
Redwood Mountain Sequoia Grove: 324
Redwood National Park: 187-188
redwoods: 88, 155, 172-173, 180, 182, 187-190,
    308, 328, 362-363
Redwood State Parks: 187-190, 303
Redwood Trail: 24, 88
Refugio State Beach: 27, 406
Renata's Creperie: 28, 186
Reuben H. Fleet Science Center: 482
Rincon: 404-405
Roaring Camp Railroads: 362
Roaring River Falls: 327
Robert Louis Stevenson Museum: 134
Robert Louis Stevenson State Park: 138
Robert Mondavi Institute for Wine and Food
    Science: 269
Robert Mondavi Winery: 130
Robert Sinskey Vineyards: 127
Rock Springs: 91
Rodeo Beach: 82
Rodin Sculpture Garden: 111
Roederer Estate: 172
Rose Bowl Stadium: 442
Rotta Winery: 420
Roxy Theatre: 437, 443-444
Rubicon Trail: 233, 237
Russian Gulch State Park: 175
Russian River: 154-155, 303
Russian River Valley: 148-161; map 150-151
Russian River Vineyards: 154
Rutherford: 130-132
Ryan Mountain: 545

S
Sacramento: 261-268; map 263
Sacramento and Gold Country: 257-290; maps
    260, 270, 284
safety: 608-610
Salt Air: 28, 453
Salt Creek: 551
Salt Creek Beach: 470
Salt Point State Park: 170
Samuel Oschin Planetarium: 431
San Buenaventura State Beach: 411
San Carlos Beach: 367
Sand Dollar Beach: 385-386
Sand Harbor Beach: 255
San Diego: 25, 28, 473-525; maps 476-477, 481, 482

San Diego Air and Space Museum: 480
San Diego Botanic Garden: 489
San Diego Civic Theatre: 496
San Diego Marina District: 478
San Diego Model Railroad Museum: 482
San Diego Museum of Art: 480
San Diego Museum of Man: 480
San Diego Natural History Museum: 482
San Diego Union Building: 483
San Diego Zoo: 28, 479-480
San Diego Zoo Safari Park: 489
San Francisco: 33-79; maps 40-41, 42-43, 46-47, 54-55
San Francisco Ballet: 60
San Francisco Bay Area: 33-114; map 36
San Francisco Bay Model: 83
San Francisco Botanical Garden: 53
San Francisco Civic Center: 50-51
San Francisco Marina: 49-50
San Francisco Maritime National Historical Park: 48-49
San Francisco Museum of Modern Art (SFMOMA): 39
San Francisco Opera: 60
San Francisco Peninsula: 104-110
San Gregorio General Store: 108
San Gregorio State Beach: 108
San Jose Museum of Art: 111
San Juan Bautista State Historic Park: 372
San Luis Obispo: 26, 416-419; map 417
San Miguel Island: 413
San Simeon: 26, 391-394; map 393
Santa Barbara: 26, 398-411; map 401
Santa Barbara Botanic Gardens: 399-400
Santa Barbara Bowl: 403
Santa Barbara County Courthouse: 400
Santa Barbara Island: 413
Santa Barbara Maritime Museum: 399
Santa Barbara Mission: 398
Santa Barbara Museum of Art: 400
Santa Barbara Museum of Natural History: 399
Santa Barbara Winery: 402
Santa Cruz: 353-362; map 355
Santa Cruz Beach Boardwalk: 27, 353-354
Santa Cruz Island: 413-414
Santa Cruz Mountains: 362-363
Santa Cruz Municipal Wharf: 353
Santa Cruz Surfing Museum: 354
Santa Monica: 28, 438-440; map 439
Santa Monica Pier: 25, 28, 438
Santa Monica State Beach: 27, 448
Santa Rosa: 148-149, 152
Santa Rosa Island: 414-415
Sausalito: 83-85
Scharffenberger Cellars: 172
Scorpion Submarine: 441

Scotty's Castle: 552
Scripps Pier: 502
scuba diving/snorkeling: Central Coast 414, 415; Los Angeles 459; Monterey and Big Sur 367, 378-379, 386-387; North Coast 170; San Diego 487, 505
Seabright Beach: 357-358
Seaport Village: 478
SeaWorld: 487
Sebastopol: 152
Secret Garden: 561
senior travelers: 608
Sentinel Dome: 307
Sequoia and Kings Canyon National Park: 320-327; maps 321, 322
17-Mile Drive: 373
Seymour Marine Discovery Center: 354, 356
Shark Reef: 563
Sharpsteen Museum of Calistoga History: 136-137
Shasta and Lassen: 192-226; map 196-197
Shasta Dam: 202
Shasta Lake: 200-205
Shasta State Historic Park: 195
Sheep Creek Cascade: 327
Shenandoah Valley: 278-283
Sheryl and Harvey White Theatre: 496
Sierra-at-Tahoe: 234
Silicon Valley: 110-114
Silver Lake: 430-431
Sims Flat: 215
Sir Francis Drake Boulevard: 95
Six Flags Magic Mountain: 465
Skull Rock: 542
Skunk Train: 178
Soda Springs: 252
Solvang: 407
Sonoma: 140, 142-146
Sonoma Coast: 166-170; map 167
Sonoma Coast State Park: 166, 168
Sonoma Raceway: 144
Sonoma State Historic Park: 143
Sonoma Valley: 140-148; map 141
Sonora: 287-289
Southern Gold Country: 283-290; map 284
South Shore (Lake Tahoe): 231-243; map 232
South Yuba River State Park: 271
spectator sports: Los Angeles 448; San Diego 506-507; San Francisco 66, 102; Wine Country 144
Spreckels Theatre: 496
Squaw Valley: 246
Stag's Leap Wine Cellars: 127
Stanford University: 110-111
Staples Center: 448
state parks and beaches: Central Coast 405-406, 411-412, 419; Deserts 530, 536, 541;

Lake Tahoe 233, 237-238, 244, 250-251; Los Angeles 447, 448, 470; Monterey and Big Sur 356-358, 362-363, 367, 377, 381, 383-385, 392; North Coast 166, 168, 170-173, 174-176, 179, 180, 182, 185, 186-190; Sacramento and Gold Country 271, 289; San Diego 501, 503; San Francisco 85-87, 90-92, 94, 105, 106, 108-109; Shasta and Lassen 222-224; Wine Country 138

State Street (Santa Barbara): 26, 398
Steamer Lane: 358
Stearns Wharf: 399
Sterling Vineyards: 136
St. Francis Winery: 146-147
St. Helena: 132-136
Stinson Beach: 27, 92-93
Stone World Bistro & Gardens: 490
Stone World Bistro & Gardens Liberty Station: 28, 490, 493
Story Winery: 278
Stow Lake: 65
Strip, The: 561-563, 565-580; map 562
Sugar Bowl: 251-252
Sulphur Works: 210
Summit Lake: 209, 211
Sundial Bridge: 195
Sunny Jim Cave: 487
Sunset Beach: 95
Sunset Cliffs Natural Park: 485
Sunset Strip: 437
Surfers Beach: 106
surfing: Central Coast 404-405; Los Angeles 440, 447, 448, 468, 470; Monterey and Big Sur 358, 367, 386; San Diego 484, 486, 488, 501-503; San Francisco 92, 106
Sutter Creek: 280-281
Sutter's Fort State Historic Park: 263-264

T

Taft Point and the Fissures: 307
Tahoe Donner Ski Area: 252
Tahoe Maritime Museum: 244
Tahoe Rim Trail: 235, 238, 248, 303
Tahquitz Canyon: 536
Tallac Historic Site: 231, 233, 236
taxes: 606
TCL Chinese Theatre: 25, 28, 433-434
Tech Museum of Innovation: 111
Tenaya Lake: 310, 311
Tennessee Valley: 87
Theatre at Ace Hotel: 444
Thomas H. Kuchel Visitor Center: 187
Tiburon: 85-87
Tilden Regional Park: 99
Timber Gap: 336
Tioga Pass: 296, 310-316; map 314-315

tipping: 606-607
Titus Canyon: 553
Tokopah Falls: 332
Tomales Bay State Park: 94
Tor House: 376-377
Torrey Pines State Beach: 501
tourist information: 605-607
Tourmaline Surf Park: 502
Train Town: 143
train travel: 602
transportation: 601-604
Travel Town Railroad: 431
Trentadue: 160
Trestles: 503
Trinidad: 27, 28, 185
Troubadour, The: 444
Truckee-Donner: 250-255; map 251
Tule Lake: 226
Tuolumne Grove of Giant Sequoias: 311
Tuolumne Meadows: 310-316; map 314-315
Twentynine Palms: 546
Twin Lake: 211
Twisted Oak Winery: 286
Ty Warner Sea Center: 399

U

Ubehebe Crater: 551-552
Union Square: 37-39
Union Station (Los Angeles): 426, 429
Universal Studios Hollywood: 435, 465
University of California, Berkeley: 98
University of California, Davis: 269
University of California, Los Angeles: 437
Upper Yosemite Fall: 300
Uptown Theatre: 121
USS *Midway* Museum: 478-479

V

Valley Visitors Center: 297
Van Damme State Park: 174
Venice: 438-440; map 439
Venice Beach (Half Moon Bay): 106
Venice Beach (Los Angeles): 28, 438-439
Venice Boardwalk: 25, 28, 438-439
Venice Canals: 439-440
Ventana Wilderness: 386
Ventura: 411-413
Vernal Fall: 302
Vichy Springs: 173
Vikingsholm Castle: 233
Village at Squaw Valley: 244, 246
Vintner's Collective: 121
Vista Point: 80
Volcano: 282-283

W

Waddell Creek Beach: 363
Walt Disney Concert Hall: 444
Walt Disney Family Museum: 50
War Memorial Opera House: 60
Water Canyon Beach: 415
waterfalls: Monterey and Big Sur 363, 384, 385;
    North Coast 175, 188; Sacramento and Gold
    Country 274; Shasta and Lassen 210, 223-224;
    Yosemite, Sequoia, and Kings Canyon 297,
    300-302, 309, 316-317, 327-328, 332, 335, 344
Wawona: 308-310
weather: 592
Weaverville Joss House State Historic Park: 198-
    199
Wells Fargo History Museum: 262
Wells Fargo Museum: 483
West Beach: 403
West Hollywood: 436-437
Westwood: 437-438
Whalers Cabin Museum: 378
Whiskeytown National Recreation Area: 195, 198
Whisky a Go Go: 437, 443
Wildcat Canyon Regional Park: 99
Wilderotter Vineyard: 279
Wilder Ranch State Park: 356
wildlife/wildlife-watching: general discussion
    594-596; Central Coast 405, 412, 413; Monterey
    and Big Sur 357, 359, 364, 366, 368, 377, 386,
    392; North Coast 166, 168, 188; San Diego 505;
    San Francisco 66, 89, 104-105, 106, 109

Winchester Mystery House: 111-112
Wine Country: 115-161; map 118-119
wine/wineries: Central Coast 402, 420; Monterey
    and Big Sur 378; North Coast 172; Sacramento
    and Gold Country 269, 278-279, 286; Wine
    Country 121, 127, 130-134, 136, 140, 142, 146-148,
    152-154, 157-158, 160-161
winter sports: general discussion 303; Deserts
    530-531; Lake Tahoe 233-235, 246-247, 251-
    253, 255; Shasta and Lassen 217-218; Yosemite,
    Sequoia, and Kings Canyon 307, 342-343,
    344-345
Wolverton: 330
World War II Valor in the Pacific National
    Monument: 226
Wukachi Village: 328-329

XYZ

Yosemite Falls: 24, 300, 301-302
Yosemite Museum: 297
Yosemite National Park: 296-317; maps 294-295,
    298, 314-315
Yosemite, Sequoia, and Kings Canyon: 291-349
Yosemite Theater: 297
Yosemite Valley: 24, 296, 297-306; map 298-299
Yosemite Valley Auditorium: 297
Yountville: 126-130
Zabriskie Point: 551
Zuma Beach: 447-448
Zumwalt Meadow: 327

List of Maps

Front Map
California: 2–3

San Francisco
San Francisco Bay Area: 36
San Francisco: 40–41
Downtown San Francisco: 42–43
North Beach and Fisherman's Wharf: 46–47
Golden Gate Park: 54–55
North Bay: 81

Wine Country
Wine Country: 118–119
Upper Napa Valley: 122–123
Lower Napa Valley: 124
Sonoma Valley: 141
Russian River Valley: 150–151

North Coast
North Coast: 165
Sonoma and Mendocino Coasts: 167
Mendocino: 175

Shasta and Lassen
Shasta and Lassen; : 196–197
Lassen Volcanic National Park: 207

Lake Tahoe
Lake Tahoe: 230
South Shore: 232
North and West Shores: 245
Truckee-Donner: 251

Sacramento and Gold Country
Sacramento and Gold County: 260
Downtown Sacramento: 263
Northern Gold Country: 270
Southern Gold Country: 284

Yosemite, Sequoia, and Kings Canyon
Yosemite National Park: 294–295
Yosemite Valley: 298–299
Tioga Pass and Tuolumne Meadows: 314–315
Sequoia and Kings Canyon: 321
Grant Grove: 322
Giant Forest and Lodgepole: 330
The Eastern Sierra: 338

Monterey and Big Sur
Monterey and Big Sur: 354
Santa Cruz: 355
Monterey Bay: 365
Big Sur: 382
Cambria and SanSimeon: 393

Santa Barbara and the Central Coast
Santa Barbara and the Central Coast: 400
Santa Barbara: 401
San Luis Obispo: 417

Los Angeles
Los Angeles: 425
Downtown Los Angeles: 427
Hollywood: 432
Santa Monica and Venice: 439
Orange County: 461

San Diego
San Diego: 476–477
Downtown San Diego: 481
Balboa Park: 482
La Jolla: 488

Palm Springs and the Deserts
Palm Springs and the Deserts: 529
Palm Springs and the Coachella Valley: 532
Joshua Tree and the Yucca Valley: 543
Death Valley National Park: 550

Las Vegas
The Strip: 562

Photo Credits

Also Available

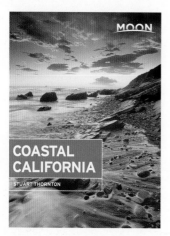

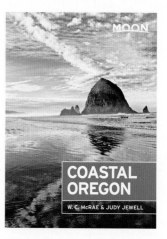

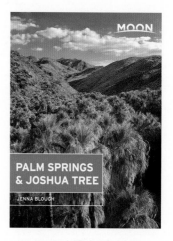

MAP SYMBOLS

▭▭ Expressway	○ City/Town	✈ Airport	⚲ Golf Course
▭ Primary Road	◉ State Capital	✦ Airfield	℗ Parking Area
Secondary Road	⊛ National Capital	▲ Mountain	⛰ Archaeological Site
- - - - Unpaved Road	★ Point of Interest	✛ Unique Natural Feature	⚑ Church
Feature Trail	• Accommodation		⛽ Gas Station
- - - Other Trail	▾ Restaurant/Bar	⟆ Waterfall	Glacier
········· Ferry	■ Other Location	▲ Park	Mangrove
Pedestrian Walkway	Δ Campground	⊓ Trailhead	Reef
▭▭ Stairs		⛷ Skiing Area	Swamp

CONVERSION TABLES

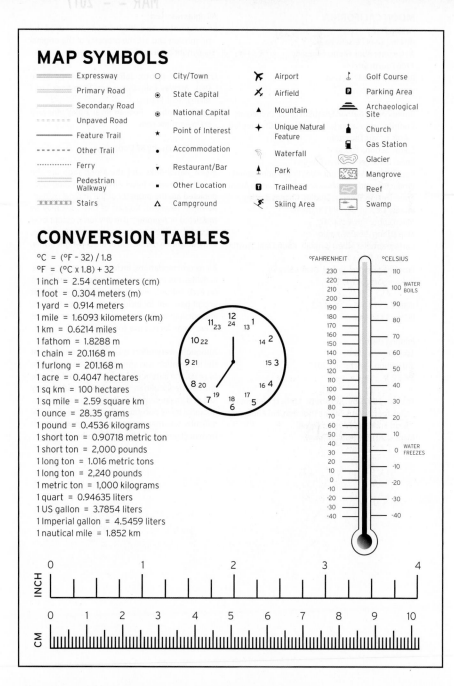

°C = (°F - 32) / 1.8
°F = (°C x 1.8) + 32
1 inch = 2.54 centimeters (cm)
1 foot = 0.304 meters (m)
1 yard = 0.914 meters
1 mile = 1.6093 kilometers (km)
1 km = 0.6214 miles
1 fathom = 1.8288 m
1 chain = 20.1168 m
1 furlong = 201.168 m
1 acre = 0.4047 hectares
1 sq km = 100 hectares
1 sq mile = 2.59 square km
1 ounce = 28.35 grams
1 pound = 0.4536 kilograms
1 short ton = 0.90718 metric ton
1 short ton = 2,000 pounds
1 long ton = 1.016 metric tons
1 long ton = 2,240 pounds
1 metric ton = 1,000 kilograms
1 quart = 0.94635 liters
1 US gallon = 3.7854 liters
1 Imperial gallon = 4.5459 liters
1 nautical mile = 1.852 km

MOON CALIFORNIA

Avalon Travel
An imprint of Perseus Books
A Hachette Book Group company
1700 Fourth Street
Berkeley, CA 94710, USA
www.moon.com

Coordinating Author: Elizabeth Linhart Veneman
Contributing Authors: Ian Anderson, Christopher Arns, Stuart Thornton
Editor: Sabrina Young
Series Manager: Kathryn Ettinger
Copy Editors: Melissa Brandzel, Rosemarie Leenerts
Production and Graphics Coordinator: Darren Alessi
Cover Design: Faceout Studios, Charles Brock
Interior Design: Domini Dragoone
Moon Logo: Tim McGrath
Map Editor: Albert Angulo
Cartographers: Albert Angulo, Karin Dahl, Austin Ehrhardt, Brian Shotwell
Proofreaders: Ann Seifert, Deana Shields
Indexer: Greg Jewett

ISBN-13: 978-1-63121-417-2
ISSN: 1533-354X

Printing History
1st Edition — 2001
3rd Edition — February 2017
5 4 3 2 1

Text © 2017 by Elizabeth Linhart Veneman, Christopher Arns, Stuart Thornton, Ian Anderson, Scott Smith and Avalon Travel.
Maps © 2017 by Avalon Travel.

Front cover photo: Julia Pfeiffer Burns State Park, McWay Falls © Jon Arnold Images Ltd / Alamy Stock Photo
Back cover photo: Russian River Valley vineyard © Dreamstime.com

Printed in China by RR Donnelley